German · English
English · German

J. M. Clark MA, PhD, LLD

*formerly Emeritus Professor of German language and
Literature, University of Glasgow*

Collins
London and Glasgow

General Editor
W. T. McLeod

First published 1953
Latest Reprint 1976

ISBN 0 00 458614 X

© **William Collins Sons & Co. Ltd., 1953**

Contents

Printed in Great Britain by
Collins Clear-Type Press

FOREWORD

THIS is the second volume of a series which at present comprises five bi-lingual dictionaries. The first is the French-English and English-French volume, the third, fourth and fifth are devoted to Italian, Spanish and Latin respectively. Each of these dictionaries has been edited and compiled by a scholar with special qualifications for his task. Immense care has been expended on making the books both comprehensive and reliable.

A pocket dictionary must be planned primarily to meet the requirements of ordinary everyday life. It is the *vademecum* of the traveller, containing such words as he will need for the railway, the customs, the hotel and the shop. It must also make some provision for the reader of German novels, newspapers and business letters. The vocabulary must therefore be of a general and a practical character. All the main branches of human activity must be considered, and above all the vocabulary must be up to date. At least the commonest terms used in aviation, broadcasting, television, motoring, sport, industry and trade must be included, but it is quite impossible to go beyond the bare essentials. For greater detail a larger and more specialised dictionary must be consulted. The chief desideratum is a very high degree of compression. It may happen that one English word has half a dozen German equivalents, and vice versa. It is therefore a case of selecting, if possible, from the six German words four or five that cover the ground of the one English word.

J. M. CLARK.

VORWORT

DER vorliegende Band bildet den zweiten Teil einer Reihe, die vorläufig fünf zweisprachige Wörterbücher umfasst. Der erste Teil ist der französisch-englische und englisch-französische Band; der dritte, vierte und fünfte sind dem Italienischen, Spanischen und Lateinischen gewidmet. Jedes von diesen Wörterbüchern ist von einem Gelehrten bearbeitet worden, der für diese Aufgabe besondere Eignung besitzt. Keine Mühe wurde gescheut, diese Bücher umfassend und zugleich zuverlässig zu machen.

Ein Taschenwörterbuch soll in erster Linie den Anforderungen des täglichen Lebens genügen. Es ist Lehrbuch und Leitfaden des Reisenden und enthält Wörter, die er auf der Eisenbahn, im Zollamt, im Hotel und im Kaufladen braucht. Es soll ferner dem Leser von deutschen Romanen, Zeitungen und Handelsbriefen dienen. Der Wortschatz muss demnach einen allgemeinen und auf das Praktische gerichteten Charakter haben. Sämtliche Hauptgebiete der menschlichen Tätigkeit müssen in ihren modernsten Entwicklungsformen in Betracht gezogen werden. Daher dürfen die geläufigsten Ausdrücke aus Flugwesen, Rundfunk, Fernsehen, Automobilwesen, Sport, Industrie und Handel nicht fehlen. Es ist aber ganz unmöglich, über das Allernotwendigste hinauszugehen : wer weitere Einzelheiten sucht, muss ein grösseres Werk oder ein technisches Wörterbuch zu Rate ziehen. Ein dringendes Erfordernis für ein Taschenwörterbuch ist ferner der höchste Grad von Verdichtung. Es kann vorkommen, dass ein englisches Wort ein halbes Dutzend deutsche Entsprechungen hat, oder umgekehrt. Es handelt sich also darum, aus sechs deutschen Wörtern vier oder fünf zu wählen, die sich mit den wichtigsten Bedeutungen des einen englischen Wortes decken.

J. M. CLARK.

ABBREVIATIONS

a. adjective	*nav.* naval
ad. adverb	*num.* numeral
aut. motoring	*ph.* telephone
av. aviation	*pl.* plural
cj. conjunction	*pn.* pronoun
com. commercial	*vr.* preposition
el. electricity	*rad.* wireless
f. feminine	*rl.* railway
gen. genitive	*sing.* singular
int. interjection	*tec.* technical
ir. irregular	*v.* verb
m. masculine	*vi.* verb intransitive
mil. military	*vr.* verb reflexive
n. noun (after English words)	*vt.* verb transitive
neuter (after German words)*	*w.* weak

* As all German nouns begin with a capital, they are recognizable as such.

PRELIMINARY NOTES

Grammar

1. The Infinitive in German may be used as a neuter noun; thus *schwimmen* means ' to swim,' but *das Schwimmen* is ' the swimming.'

2. Agent Nouns form the feminine by adding *-in*, e.g. *Lehrer* teacher, *Lehrerin* lady teacher; similarly *Entdecker* discoverer, *Entdeckerin* female discoverer. Feminines showing formal differences are listed, e.g. *Mann* man, *Frau* woman.

3. Strong Nouns. Masculines and Neuters normally take *-(e)s* in the Genitive Singular. e.g. *Mann*, *Mannes*; *Kind*, *Kindes*. Feminines remain unchanged in the Singular, e.g. *die Frau* the woman, *der Frau* of the woman. Plurals are listed. Thus, a dash enclosed between brackets after a noun means that the Plural is the same as the Nominative Singular, e.g. *Maler* (—) means that the Singular is *der Maler*, the painter, and the Plural *die Maler*, the painters. *Garten* (*Gärten*) means that the Singular *Garten* corresponds to the Plural *Gärten*, gardens.

4. Weak Nouns. Masculines and Neuters take *-(e)n* in the Genitive Singular. Feminines remain unchanged in the Singular. Thus *der Knabe*, the boy ; *des Knaben*, of the boy. The Plural of Weak Nouns (all genders) ends in *-(e)n*, e.g. *die Knaben* the boys, *die Frauen* the women. All exceptional Genitives are listed.

5. Verbs are regular unless *ir.* (irregular) is added.

Accent

The main stress in a word is indicated by an acute accent placed after the syllable that is emphasized, for instance *geben* is pronounced gay´ben. In German the stress is usually on the stem syllable, which in nouns and adjectives is generally the first. In verbs there is often a prefix before the stem, e.g. *vergeben* (ferr-gay´ben) ; one may compare the English *forgive*, in which the prefix *for-* is unstressed and the stress is on the second syllable. It should be added that in German the stress is a good deal stronger than in English, that is to say there is much more difference between one syllable and another in the amount of stress they take. In other words the waves of speech have a higher crest and a deeper trough in German than in English.

Compounds

The German language contains a large number of compound nouns and verbs, such as *Eisenbahnbrücke* (railway bridge), *Eröffnungsrede* (opening speech), *ausdulden* (*aus*, out of; *dulden* to suffer), to endure to the end. To include all existing compounds would swell this dictionary to double its present size. It has therefore been thought advisable to give only the most important and the commonest of such words. Compounds not given are to be looked up under the component parts, thus *Eisenbahnbrücke* may be looked up under *Eisenbahn* (railway) and *Brücke* (bridge). Similarly, to avoid redundancy, pronunciation is not added for such compounds as *auseinanderbringen* (to separate, bring apart). It should be looked up under *auseinander* and *bringen*.

In order to economize in space, compounds are usually placed under a heading and abbreviated. This is not always possible, or even advisable, because sometimes the accent is not the same in the simple word which forms the heading of the paragraph, and the compound derived from it. Sometimes also a word that appears to be derived from another is from an entirely different root and the similarity is only apparent. In this respect and also in the matter of the strictly alphabetical arrangement of words, absolute consistency has here and there to yield to expediency. In many cases students will be well advised to read the whole paragraph if they are looking up a compound, because many different shades of meaning may be contained in the various derivatives. A good deal of compression had to be carried out and a careful study of a whole section will often bring to light some point that could not be explained in full detail.

PRONUNCIATION

Special care has been given to the subject of pronunciation. A system has been devised by the editor which can be understood by any person of ordinary intelligence who knows English; no previous knowledge of phonetics is required. Whatever advantages can be claimed for a strictly scientific method of reproducing sounds, by means of an international phonetic alphabet or otherwise, the fact remains that for ninety-nine people out of a hundred such a system is absolutely unintelligible. This dictionary is intended for the average man and his every-day requirements, rather than for the exclusive use of philological experts. The latter are welcome to use it if they so desire, but the greatest good of the greatest number is our aim. The task before us is not easy: immense difficulties confront the lexicographer who tries to work out a simple working system of pronunciation. English spelling is notoriously erratic and inconsistent, and hence every sound must be defined most carefully and every effort must be made to avoid ambiguity.

In the first half of this dictionary the German word comes first and is followed by the English equivalent. Immediately after the German word comes the pronunciation. It should be pointed out that no system can give the exact sounds of German in terms of English, because there are slight differences in practically all the sounds in question. No English vowel or consonant (with a few exceptions) corresponds exactly to a German vowel or consonant. All that can be done is to give an approximate rendering of the German sounds that will be understood by German speakers. The student should, therefore, listen carefully to German and obtain the exact sound by imitation. He will then be the better able to apply the information provided by the dictionary.

German Consonants

b   is pronounced as in English, except at the end of a syllable, when it is pronounced **p**, and is here represented by [p]

d   is pronounced as in English, except at the end of a syllable, in which case it is represented by [t]

ch   after **a**, **o**, **au** is pronounced like **ch** in the Scottish *loch* and is represented by [ch]. **ch** after **e**, **i**, **ö**, **ü** or **eu** (**äu**) is represented by [sh]

chs is almost invariably pronounced **x**, represented by [x]

g   is usually pronounced as in English, except at the end of a syllable, when it is pronounced either like **ch** (North Germany) or **k** (South Germany, Austria, Switzerland); it is here represented by [k] except after **i**, where it is represented by [sh]

vii

j	is pronounced and represented by [y]
q	is pronounced and represented by [kv]
r	is rolled, as in Scottish speech, and is normally represented by [rr]
s	at the beginning of a syllable, or between vowels, is represented by [z]. **s** finally, or when doubled is represented by [ss or s]
sch	is represented by [sh]
th	has the same value as **t**, and is represented by [t]
tz	is represented by [ts]
v	is represented by [f] except in foreign words, where it has the value of [v]
w	is represented by [v]
z	is represented by [ts]

Other sounds are pronounced more or less as in English. It should be noted that there are many local variations in German pronunciation, but the best usage is here adopted as the standard. In the German theatre and on the wireless a dialect-free pronunciation is used.

EXAMPLES

p	Rappen [rap'en]. Grab [grahp]. ab [ap].
d	danken [dank'en]. Rad [raht].
ch	after a, o, u, au: Fluch [flōōch]. Bach [bach]. after e, i, ö, ü, eu: Pech [pesh]. ich [ish].
chs	Wachs [vax].
g	finally: Tag [tahk]. *North German* [tach]. after i: Honig [hone'ish].
j	ja [yah].
q	Quelle [kvel'er].
r	hart [harrt].
s	initially or medially: so [zoh]. lesen [lay'zen]. finally: es [ess]. doubled: essen [ess'en].
sch	schon [shown].
th	Themse [tem'zer]
tz	Platz [plats].
v	von [fon]. in foreign words: vag [vahk].
w	wo [voh].
z	zu [tsōō].

German Vowels

Short **a**	is represented by	[a]	as in **man** (Scottish and Northern English pronunciation).
Long **a**	„	„	[ah]	like the sound of a in *father*
Short **e**	„	„	[e]	as in *hen.*
Long **e**	„	„	[ay]	as in *say.*
Long **e** before **r**			[ai]	as in *air.*
Short **i**	„	„	[i]	as in *pin.*
Long **i**	„	„	[ee]	as in *keen.*
Short **o**	„	„	[o]	as in *on.*
Long **o**	„	„	[oh]	like the **o** in *tone* (Scottish and Northern English).
Short **u**	¨	„	[ŏŏ]	as in *foot.*
Long **u**	„	„	[ōō]	as in *soon.*
Short **ä**	„	„	[e]	as in *hen.*
Long **ä**	„	„	[ay]	as in *say.*
ö	„	„	[e(r)]	as in *herb.*
ü	„	„	[ew]	as in *dew.*
ü after **r**	„		[yoo]	like the sound of *you.*
ai, ei	„		[i]	as in *shine,* or **y** as in *sky.*
au	„		[ow]	as in *cow.*
äu, eu	„		[oi]	as in *noise.*

Note: mute **e** is added occasionally, where required to show length, as in (German *ein*), pine (German *Pein*).

Short **a**	**Mann**	[man].
Long **a**	**sagen**	[zah'gen].
Short **e**	**wenn**	[ven].
Long **e**	**sehen**	[zay'en].
Long **e** before **r**	**sehr**	[zairr].
Short **i**	**bin**	[bin].
Long **i**	**wir**	[veerr].
Short **o**	**soll**	[zol].
Long **o**	**Mohn**	[mohn].
Short **u**	**unter**	[oon'terr].
Long **u**	**tun**	[toon].
Short **ä**	**Männer**	[men'err].
Long **ä**	**Räder**	[ray'derr].
ö	**Röhre**	[rer'rer].

> **ü**   **sühnen** [zew'nen].
> **ü** after **r trügen** [tryoo'gen].
> **ai**   **Main** [mine].
> **ei**   **Rhein** [rine].
> **au**   **Frau** [frow].
> **äu**   **Häuser** [hoi'zerr].
> **eu**   **Leute** [loi'ter].

The Sounds of English

The basis of our system of indicating pronunciation is the Oxford English Dictionary, simplified considerably and adapted where necessary to our special purpose, that is to say, for the use of those who speak German, or who approach English from the point of view of German sounds. For them, English consonants and vowels must be expressed in terms of their closest equivalents in German. Particular attention must be paid to cases where the student is apt to go astray. Thus, a vital distinction is that between *s* and *z*, to which English spelling does not always offer a clue: we have *z* in *close* (verb), *rose*, *houses* (twice), *boxes*. In this dictionary we hence use a single *s* for *z*, as in German *so*, *sehr* and for *s* we use double *s* (German *besser*, *Wasser*, *essen*).

It is difficult for German speakers to distinguish between the *o* sounds in *constable* and *connect*. The spelling is no guide here; the same vowel is used to denote two different sounds. Hence we write kAn'stAbl and con-ekt'. It is not so important to make a distinction between the *o*'s in *connect* and *colic*, because the difference in stress itself naturally suggests a difference in pronunciation. Another important distinction is between the vowels in *alter* and *defer*. The latter is practically a lengthened *u*, and is therefore denoted by A, the former is best described in German by *er* (as in *besser*). So we put Ol'ter and di-fAr'.

It will be noticed that in these two words the final *r* is italicised. This is to indicate that it is normally silent (in standard Southern English). But before a word beginning with a vowel, and in the pronunciation of other parts of the English-speaking world, this *r* is sounded. Hence the italics.

The unstressed *e* in words like *gladness*, *badness*, presents a problem. In different parts of Britain the pronunciation is not uniform. The Oxford Dictionary uses a special type of *e*. We use *e* and the absence of stress indicates that it is similar to unstressed German *e*, with a tendency to pass into an i-sound.

English Consonants

ch as in *chin* represented by [tsch]
g as in *George* „ „ [dzh]
j as in *just* „ „ [dzh]
qu as in *queer* „ „ [ku]
sh as in *shut* „ „ [sch]
s at the beginning of a word, as in *some* represented by [ss]
s between vowels or at the end of a word, as in *rosy* and *his* represented by [s]
th as in *think* „ „ [th]
th as in *the* „ „ [dh]
v as in *very* „ „ [w]
w as in *win* „ „ [u]
x as in *vex* „ „ [x]
y as in *yet* „ „ [j]
z as in *zero* „ „ [s]
zh like **s** in *pleasure* „ [zh]
r mute at end of a syllable or before consonant as in *better* represented by [r]

English Vowels

Short **a** as in *man* represented by [æ]
Long **a** as in *father* „ „ [ah]
Short **e** as in *hen* „ „ [e]
Long **e** as in *keen* „ „ [ih]
Short **i** as in *think* „ „ [i]
Long **i** as in *shine* „ „ [ai]
Short **o** as in *on* „ „ [o]
Long **o** as in *tone* „ „ [ou]
aw as in *lawn* „ „ [O]
Short **u** as in *under* „ „ [A]
Short **oo** as in *book* „ „ [u]
Long **oo** as in *shoot* „ „ [uh]
Long **u** as in *use* „ „ [juh]
ai, ay as in *say* „ „ [ei]
ow as in *cow* „ „ [au]
Unstressed vowels, **a, e, o, u,** as in *about, baker, demonstration, corona, uphold* represented by [A]

xl

GERMAN IRREGULAR VERBS

(Compounds to be taken from the simple verbs)

Infinitive	Present Indicative (2nd, 3rd Sing.)	Past Indicative	Past Participle
backen	bäckst, bäckt	buk	gebacken
befehlen	befiehlst, befiehlt	befahl	befohlen
beginnen	beginnst, beginnt	begann	begonnen
beissen	beiss(es)t, beisst	biss	gebissen
bergen	birgst, birgt	barg	geborgen
bersten	birs(tes)t, birst	barst	geborsten
betrügen	betrügst, betrügt	betrog	betrogen
bewegen	bewegst, bewegt	bewog	bewogen
biegen	biegst, biegt	bog	gebogen
bieten	bietest, bietet	bot	geboten
binden	bindest, bindet	band	gebunden
bitten	bittest, bittet	bat	gebeten
blasen	bläs(es)t, bläst	blies	geblasen
bleiben	bleibst, bleibt	blieb	geblieben
braten	brätst, brät	briet	gebraten
brechen	brichst, bricht	brach	gebrochen
brennen	brennst, brennt	brannte	gebrannt
bringen	bringst, bringt	brachte	gebracht
denken	denkst, denkt	dachte	gedacht
dingen	dingst, dingt	dang	gedungen
dreschen	drisch(e)st, drischt	drasch	gedroschen
dringen	dringst, dringt	drang	gedrungen
dürfen	darfst, darf	durfte	gedurft
empfehlen	empfiehlst, empfiehlt	empfahl	empfohlen
erlöschen	erlisch(es)t, erlischt	erlosch	erloschen
essen	iss(es)t, isst	ass	gegessen
fahren	fährst, fährt	fuhr	gefahren
fallen	fällst, fällt	fiel	gefallen
fangen	fängst, fängt	fing	gefangen
fechten	fichtst, ficht	focht	gefochten
fliegen	fliegst, fliegt	flog	geflogen
fliehen	fliehst, flieht	floh	geflohen
fliessen	fliess(es)t, fliesst	floss	geflossen
fressen	friss(es)t, frisst	frass	gefressen

Infinitive	Present Indicative (2nd, 3rd Sing.)	Past Indicative	Past Participle
frieren	frierst, friert	fror	gefroren
gären	gärst, gärt	gor	gegoren
gebären	gebierst, gebiert	gebar	geboren
geben	gibst, gibt	gab	gegeben
gedeihen	gedeihst, gedeiht	gedieh	gediehen
gelingen	———, gelingt	gelang	gelungen
gelten	giltst, gilt	galt	gegolten
genesen	gene(se)st, genest	genas	genesen
geniessen	geniess(es)t, geniesst	genoss	genossen
geraten	gerätst, gerät	geriet	geraten
geschehen	———, geschieht	geschah	geschehen
gewinnen	gewinnst, gewinnt	gewann	gewonnen
giessen	giess(es), giesst	goss	gegossen
gleichen	gleichst, gleicht	glich	geglichen
gleiten	gleit(es)t, gleitet	glitt	geglitten
graben	gräbst, gräbt	grub	gegraben
greifen	greifst, greift	griff	gegriffen
haben	hast, hat	hatte	gehabt
hangen	hängst, hängt	hing	gehangen
hauen	haust, haut	hieb	gehauen
heben	hebst, hebt	hob	gehoben
heissen	heiss(es)t, heisst	hiess	geheissen
helfen	hilfst, hilft	half	geholfen
kennen	kennst, kennt	kannte	gekannt
klimmen	klimmst, klimmt	klomm	geklommen
klingen	klingst, klingt	klang	geklungen
kneifen	kneifst, kneift	kniff	gekniffen
kommen	kommst, kommt	kam	gekommen
können	kannst, kann	konnte	gekonnt
kriechen	kriechst, kriecht	kroch	gekrochen
laden	lädst, lädt	lud	geladen
lassen	läss(es)t, lässt	liess	gelassen
laufen	läufst, läuft	lief	gelaufen
leiden	leidest, leidet	litt	gelitten
leihen	leihst, leiht	lieh	geliehen
lesen	lies(es)t, liest	las	gelesen
liegen	liegst, liegt	lag	gelegen
löschen	lisch(es)t, lischt	losch	geloschen
lügen	lügst, lügt	log	gelogen
meiden	meidest, meidet	mied	gemieden
melken	milkst, milkt	molk	gemolken
messen	miss(es)t, misst	mass	gemessen
misslingen	———, misslingt	misslang	misslungen

Infinitive	Present Indicative (2nd, 3rd Sing.)	Past Indicative	Past Participle
mögen	magst, mag	mochte	gemocht
müssen	musst, muss	musste	gemusst
nehmen	nimmst, nimmt	nahm	genommen
nennen	nennst, nennt	nannte	genannt
pfeifen	pfeifst, pfeift	pfiff	gepfiffen
preisen	preis(es)t, preist	pries	gepriesen
quellen	quillst, quillt	quoll	gequollen
raten	rätst, rät	riet	geraten
reiben	reibst, reibt	rieb	gerieben
reissen	reiss(es)t, reisst	riss	gerissen
reiten	reit(es)t, reitet	ritt	geritten
rennen	rennst, rennt	rannte	gerannt
riechen	riechst, riecht	roch	gerochen
ringen	ringst, ringt	rang	gerungen
rinnen	rinnst, rinnt	rann	geronnen
rufen	rufst, ruft	rief	gerufen
saugen	saugst, saugt	sog	gesogen
schaffen	schaffst, schafft	schuf	geschaffen
schallen	schallst, schallt	scholl	geschollen
scheiden	scheidest, scheidet	schied	geschieden
scheinen	scheinst, scheint	schien	geschienen
schelten	schiltst, schilt	schalt	gescholten
scheren	scherst, schert	schor	geschoren
schieben	schiebst, schiebt	schob	geschoben
schiessen	schiess(es)t, schiesst	schoss	geschossen
schinden	schindest, schindet	schund	geschunden
schlafen	schläfst, schläft	schlief	geschlafen
schlagen	schlägst, schlägt	schlug	geschlagen
schleichen	schleichst, schleicht	schlich	geschlichen
schleifen	schleifst, schleift	schliff	geschliffen
schliessen	schliess(es)t, schliesst	schloss	geschlossen
schlingen	schlingst, schlingt	schlang	geschlungen
schmeissen	schmeiss(es)t, schmeisst	schmiss	geschmissen
schmelzen	schmilzest, schmilzt	schmolz	geschmolzen
schneiden	schneidest, schneidet	schnitt	geschnitten
schrecken	schrickst, schrickt	schrak	geschrocken
schreiben	schreibst, schreibt	schrieb	geschrieben
schreien	schreist, schreit	schrie	geschrie(e)n
schreiten	schreitest, schreitet	schritt	geschritten
schweigen	schweigst, schweigt	schwieg	geschwiegen
schwellen	schwillst, schwillt	schwoll	geschwollen
schwimmen	schwimmst, schwimmt	schwamm	geschwommen
schwinden	schwindest, schwindet	schwand	geschwunden

GERMAN IRREGULAR VERBS

Infinitive	Present Indicative (2nd, 3rd Sing.)	Past Indicative	Past Participle
schwingen	schwingst, schwingt	schwang	geschwungen
schwören	schwörst, schwört	schwur	geschworen
sehen	siehst, sieht	sah	gesehen
sein	bist, ist	war	gewesen
senden	sendest, sendet	sandte	gesandt
sieden	siedest, siedet	sott	gesotten
singen	singst, singt	sang	gesungen
sinken	sinkst, sinkt	sank	gesunken
sinnen	sinnst, sinnt	sann	gesonnen
sitzen	sitz(es)t, sitzt	sass	gesessen
sollen	sollst, soll	sollte	gesollt
speien	speist, speit	spie	gespie(e)n
spinnen	spinnst, spinnt	spann	gesponnen
sprechen	sprichst, spricht	sprach	gesprochen
spriessen	spriess(es)t, spriesst	spross	gesprossen
springen	springst, springt	sprang	gesprungen
stechen	stichst, sticht	stach	gestochen
stehen	stehst, steht	stand	gestanden
stehlen	stiehlst, stiehlt	stahl	gestohlen
steigen	steigst, steigt	stieg	gestiegen
sterben	stirbst, stirbt	starb	gestorben
stinken	stinkst, stinkt	stank	gestunken
stossen	stöss(es)t, stösst	stiess	gestossen
streichen	streichst, streicht	strich	gestrichen
streiten	streitest, streitet	stritt	gestritten
tragen	trägst, trägt	trug	getragen
treffen	triffst, trifft	traf	getroffen
treiben	treibst, treibt	trieb	getrieben
treten	trittst, tritt	trat	getreten
triefen	triefst, trieft	troff	getroffen
trinken	trinkst, trinkt	trank	getrunken
trügen	trügst, trügt	trog	getrogen
tun	tust, tut	tat	getan
verderben	verdirbst, verdirbt	verdarb	verdorben
verdriessen	verdriess(es)t, verdriesst	verdross	verdrossen
vergessen	vergiss(es)t, vergisst	vergass	vergessen
verlieren	verlierst, verliert	verlor	verloren
wachsen	wächs(es)t, wächst	wuchs	gewachsen
wägen	wägst, wägt	wog	gewogen
waschen	wäsch(es)t, wäscht	wusch	gewaschen
weben	webst, webt	wob	gewoben
weichen	weichst, weicht	wich	gewichen
weisen	weis(es)t, weist	wies	gewiesen

xv

Infinitive	Present Indicative (2nd, 3rd Sing.)	Past Indicative	Past Participle
wenden	wendest, wendet	wandte	gewandt
werben	wirbst, wirbt	warb	geworben
werfen	wirfst, wirft	warf	geworfen
wiegen	wiegst, wiegt	wog	gewogen
winden	windest, windet	wand	gewunden
wissen	weisst, weiss	wusste	gewusst
wollen	willst, will	wollte	gewollt
zeihen	zeihst, zeiht	zieh	geziehen
ziehen	ziehst, zieht	zog	gezogen
zwingen	zwingst, zwingt	zwang	gezwungen

GERMAN-ENGLISH DICTIONARY

A

Aal [ahl] *nm.* -e) eel.

Aas [ahs] *n.* (Äser) carrion.

Ab [ap] *ad.* from, off.

Abänder-bar, -lich [ap'en-derr-bahrr] *a.* alterable.

Abändern [ap'en-derrn] *vt.* to alter.

Abänderung [ap'en-der-röong] *nf.* alteration.

Abängstigen [ap'eng-sti-gen] *vr.* to worry, fret.

Abarbeiten [ap'arr-by-ten] *vr.* to wear out, get afloat (*ship*).

Abart [ap'ahrrt] *nf.* variety, degenerate breed.

Abarten [ap'ahrr-ten] *vi.* to degenerate.

Abätzen [ap'et-sen] *vt.* to corrode, cauterize.

Abbalgen [ap'bal-gen] *vt.* to skin, shell.

Abbau [ap'bow] *nm.* demolition, dismantling, staff reduction.

Abbauen [ap'bow-en] *vt.* to pull down (buildings), to work (*mine*), dismantle, discharge (*workers*). [bite off.]

Abbeissen [ap'byce-en] *vt.* to

Abbeizen [ap'bite-sen] *vt.* to remove by caustics, to dress (*skins*). [to recall.]

Abberufen [ap'ber-röö-fen] *vt.*

Abberufung [ap'ber-röö-föong] *nf.* recall, calling away.

Abbestellen [ap'ber-shtel-bahrr] *a* countermandable.

Abbestellen [ap'ber-shtel-en] *vt.* to countermand, annul.

Abbestellung [ap'ber-shtel-öong] *nf.* cancellation, counter-order.

Abbeten [ap'bay-ten] *vt.* to recite mechanically, obtain by prayer.

Abbetteln [ap'bett-eln] *vt.* to obtain by begging.

Abbiegen [ap'bee-gen] *vt.* to turn off, aside.

Abbild [ap'bilt] *n.* portrait, copy.

Abbilden [ap'bil-den] *vt.* to portray, copy.

Abbildung [ap'bil-döong] *nf.* portraying, illustration.

Abbimsen [ap'bim-zen] *vt.* to rub, scrape off with pumice.

Abbinden [ap'bin-den] *vt.* to untie.

Abbitte [ap'bit-te] *nf.* apology.

Abbitten [ap'bit-en] *vt.* to make excuses, ask pardon.

Abblasen [ap'blah-zen] *vt.* to blow off.

Abbleichen [ap'bly-shen] *vi.* to bleach thoroughly.

Abblenden [ap'blen-den] *vt.* to black out, darken, dim (*lights*).

Abblitzen [ap'blit-sen] *vi.* to cease lighting, miss fire.

Abblühen [ap'blyoo-en] *vi.* to wither.

Abbrauchen [ap'brow-chen] *vt.* to use up.

Abbrechen [ap'bresh-en] *vt. & i.* to break off, up, discontinue, interrupt, demolish.

Abbrechung [ap'bres-öong] *nf.* demolition.

Abbremsen [ap'brem-zen] *vi.* to brake; *n.* breaking, running-up (*av.*).

Abbremsplatz [ap'brems-plats] *nm.* tarmac, runway (*av.*).

abb 2 abf

Abbrennen [ap'brenn-en] *vt.i. ir.* to burn off, fire.

Abbringen [ap'bring-en] *vt. ir.* to remove, dissuade from.

Abbröckeln [ap'brer-keln] *vt.i. ir.* to crumble off, away.

Abbruch [ap'brooch] *nm.* (Abbrüche) break, off, diminution; -kommando *n.* demolition squad.

Abbürsten [ap'berr-sten] *vt.* to brush off.

Abbüssen [ap'ba-sen] *vt.* to atone for, serve.

Abdachen [ap'da-en] *vt.* to slant, slope.

Abdämpfen [ap'demp-fen] *vt.* to evaporate, fade down (*rad.*).

Abdämmen [ap'dem-en] *vt.* to dam up.

Abdanken [ap'dang-ken] *vi.* to resign, abdicate; *vt.* to dismiss.

Abdankung [ap'dang-koong] *nf.* notice of retirement, resignation.

Abdecken [ap'deck-en] *vt.* to uncover, skin, clear.

Abdecker [ap'deck-err] *nm.* knacker.

Abdichten [ap'dish-ten] *vt.* to caulk, seal, make watertight.

Abdienen [ap'dee-nen] *vt.* to complete term of service.

Abdingen [ap'ding-en] *vt.i. ir.* to cheapen, beat down, obtain by bargaining.

Abdrängen [ap'dreng en] *vi.* to force away.

Abdrehen [ap'dray-en] *vt.* to wring off, turn, switch off, twist (off).

Abdreschen [ap'dresh-en] *vt.* to thrash out.

Abdringen [ap'dring-en] *vt.i.* to extort from.

Abdringung [ap'dring-oong] *nf.* extortion.

Abdrohen [ap'droh-en] *vt.* to obtain by threats.

Abdrosseln [ap'dross-eln] *vt.* to throttle (down), stall.

Abdruck [ap'drook] *nm.* (Abdrücke) impression, copy, stamp, cast.

Abdrucken [ap'droo-ken] *vt.* to print, impress.

Abdrücken [ap'dryoo-ken] *vt.* to loosen, discharge (*firearms*).

Abdunkeln [ap'doon-keln] *vt.* to darken.

Abdünsten [ap'dewn-sten] *vt.* to evaporate.

Abdünstung [ap'dewn-stoong] *nf.* evaporation.

Abecken [ap'eck-en] *vt.* to remove corners from.

Abend [ah'bend] *nm.* evening.

Abendbrot [ah'bent-broht] *n.* supper.

Abendessen [ah'bent-ess-en] *n.* supper.

Abendgesellschaft [ah'bent-ger-zel-shaft] *nf.* evening party. (the West).

Abendland [ah'bent-lant] *n.* the West.

Abendmahl [ah'bent-mahl] *n.* holy communion.

Abends [ah'bents] *ad.* in the evening.

Abenteuer [ah'ben-toy-err] *n.* adventure.

Abenteurer [ah'ben-toy-rerr] *nm.* adventurer.

Abenteuerlich [ah'ben-toy-err-lish] *a.* adventurous, romantic.

Aber [ah'berr] *conj.* but; *ad.* however.

Aberglaube [ah'berr-glow-ber] (*gen.* Aberglaubens) *nm.* superstition.

Abergläubig [ah'berr-gloy-bish] *a.* superstitious.

Aberkennung [ap'airr-ken-oong] *nf.* deprivation, forfeiture. [again.

Abermals [ap'berr-malss] *ad.*

Abfachen [ap'fach-en] *vt.* to partition, classify.

Abfachung [ap'fach-oong] *nf.* classification.

Abfahren [ap'fahr-ren] *vi.* *a.* to depart; *t.* to cart away.

Abfahrt [ap'fahrrt] *nf.* departure, descent, start, sailing.

Abfall [ap'fall] *nm.* (Abfälle) slope, defection, scrap; *pl.* rubbish, refuse; -produkt *n.* waste product.

Abfallen [ap'fall-en] *vi. ir.* to fall off, away.

Abfällig [ap'fell-isch] *a.* sloping, disapproving, derogatory.

Abfangen [ap'fang-en] *vt.* to catch, intercept, pull out, flatten out (*av.*).

Abfärben [ap'fairr-ben] *vi.* to lose colour.

Abfärbisch [ap'fair-bish] *a.* discolourable.

Abfasern [ap'fah-zerrn] *vt.* to chamfer.

Abfassen [ap'fass-en] *vt.* to compose, weigh out, measure off, write, draft.

Abfassung [ap'fass-ōong] *nf.* composition, writing, wording.

Abfaulen [ap'fow-len] *vi.* to rot off.

Abfedern [ap'fay-derrn] *vt.* to pluck; *vi.* to moult.

Abfegen [ap'fay-gen] *vt.* to sweep off. [off.

Abteilen [ap'file-en] *vt.* to file

Abfeimen [ap'fime-en] *vt.* to skim off.

Abfertigen [ap'fairr-ti-gen] *vt.* to dispatch; kurz – to snub.

Abfertigung [ap'fairr-ti-gōong] *nf.* dispatch, clearance; -schein *nm.* customs declaration. [fire off.

Abfeuern [ap'foy-errn] *vt.* to fire off.

Abfieren [ap'feer-ren] *vi.* to veer, cast off.

Abfinden [ap'fin-den] *vt.* to indemnify; *i.* to come to terms with.

Abfindung [ap'fin-dōong] *nf.* indemnification, composition (*bankruptcy*), allowance (*cash*).

Abflachen [ap'flach-en] *vt.* to flatten.

Abflauen [ap'flow-en] *vi.* to ease off, subside.

Abfliegen [ap'flee-gen] *vi. ir.* to fly off.

Abfliessen [ap'flee-sen] *vi. ir.* to flow off.

Abflug [ap'flōok] *nm.* flight, take off (*av.*), departure (*av.*).

Abflugdeck [ap'flōok-deck] *n.* flight deck (*av.*).

Abfluss [ap'flōos] *nm.* (Abflüsse) flux, drain, outlet, discharge.

Abfordern [ap'forr-dern] *vt.* to demand.

Abforderung [ap'forr-der-rōong] *nf.* demand.

Abformen [ap'forr-men] *vi.* to mould.

Abforsten [ap'forr-sten] *vi.* to deforest, clear.

Abfragen [ap'frah-gen] *vt.* to elicit, question, interrogate, hear (*lesson*).

Abfrieren [ap'free-ren] *vi. ir.* to be frozen off.

Abfuhr [ap'fōorr] *nf.* removal (*goods*).

Abführen [ap'few-ren] *vt.* to lead, carry away, arrest, pay off, discharge (*debts*).

Abführmittel [ap'few-err-mitl] *n.* aperient, purgative.

Abführung [ap'few-rōong] *nf.* removal, taking away, purging.

Abfüllen [ap'few-len] *vt.* to fill out, draw off, tap.

Abfüll-station [ap'fewl-shtat-see-ohn], -stelle *nf.* filling station.

Abfüllwagen [ap'fewl-vah-gen] *nm.* tapping truck.

Abfüttern [ap'fyoo-terrn] *vt.* to feed.

Abgabe [ap'gah-ber] *nf.* delivery, tax, duty (*on goods*), issue, surrender (*equipment*).

Abgabenfrei [ap'gah-ben-fry] *a.* duty free, free from taxation.

Abgabepflichtig [ap'gah-ber-pflish-tish] *a.* taxable.

Abgang [ap'gang] *nm.* (Abgänge) departure, demand,

wastage, casualties (*mil.*), loss (*stocks*).

Abgängig [ap'geng-ish] *a.* saleable, worn-out.

Abgangsrechnung [ap'gangs-resh-noong] *nf.* tare.

Abgangsventil [ap'gangs-ven'teel] *n.* exhaust valve.

Abgas [ap'gahs] *n.* exhaust gas.

Abgeartet [ap'ge-arr-tet] *a.* degenerate, deteriorated.

Abgeben [ap'ge-ben] *vt. ir.* to hand over, give in, deliver, to furnish (*proof*); *r.* to occupy oneself with.

Abgeber [ap'gay-ber] *nm.* seller.

Abgebrannt [ap'ge-brant] *a.* burnt-out.

Abgedroschen [ap'ge-drosh-en] *a.* trivial, commonplace.

Abgefeimt [ap'ge-fimet] *a.* cunning.

Abgegriffen [ap'ge-griff-en] *a.* well thumbed (book).

Abgehen [ap'gay-hen] *vi. ir.* to depart, retire, to sell, to fall (*price*).

Abgemessen [ap'ge-mess-en] *a.* precise.

Abgeneigt [ap'ge-nykt] *a.* averse to, disinclined.

Abgeordnete(r) [ap'ge-ordner-terr] *nm.* representative, deputy, Member of Parliament.

Abgerissen [ap'ge-riss-en] *a.* ragged, torn.

Abgesandte(r) [ap'ge-zanterr] *nm.* delegate, ambassador.

Abgeschmackt [ap'ge-geshmakt] *a.* insipid, in bad taste.

Abgeschmacktheit [ap'ge-shmakt-hite] *nf.* lack of taste.

Abgeschieden [ap'ge-sheed-en] *a.* deceased.

Abgeschliffen [ap'ge-shlif-en] *a.* polished.

Abgeschlossen [ap'ge-shloss-en] *a.* secluded, concluded, settled.

Abgeschmackt [ap'ge-shmakt] *a.* in bad taste, absurd.

Abgesetzt [ap'ge-zetst] *a.* sold, cleared off.

Abgespannt [ap'ge-shpant] *a.* unstrung, tired out, run down.

Abgesperrt [ap'ge-shperrt] *a.* blocked, no entry!

Abgestanden [ap'ge-shtanden] *a.* stale.

Abgestellt [ap'ge-shtelt] *a.* grounded (plane).

Abgestorbenheit [ap'ge-shtorr-ben-hite] *nf.* apathy.   [*a.* shabby.

Abgetragen [ap'ge-trah-gen]

Abgewinnen [ap'ge-vinn-en] *vt.* to win from, acquire, obtain.

Abgewöhnen [ap'ge-ver-nen] *vt.* to wean from; *r.* get rid of, give up.

Abgezogen [ap'ge-tsoh-gen] *a.* remote, bottled.

Abgiessen [ap'ge-geese-en] *vt. ir.* to pour out, decant.

Abgiessung [ap'ge-geese-oong] *nf.* decanting.

Abgleichen [ap'gly-shen] *vt. ir.* to adjust.

Abgleiten [ap'glite-en] *vi. ir.* to glide, slip, slide off.

Abglühen [ap'glÿoo-en] *vt.* to heat thoroughly; *vi.* to lose heat.   [idol.

Abgott [ap'got] *nm.* idol, [Abgötter

Abgötterei [ap'ger-ter-ry] *nf.* idolatry.

Abgöttisch [ap'ger-tish] *a.* idolatrous.

Abgraben [ap'grah-ben] *vt. ir.* to dig off.

Abgrämen [ap'grame-en] *vr.* to pine away.

Abgreifen [ap'grife-en] *vt. ir.* to wear out by handling, measure with compasses.

Abgrenzen [ap'grent-sen] *vt.* to demarcate, fix limits of, limit, define.

Abgrenzung [ap'grent-söong] *nf.* demarcation, limitation, definition.

Abgrund [ap'grŏont] *nm.* (Abgründe) abyss, precipice.

Abgucken [ap'gŏŏ-ken] *vt.* to learn by close observation.

Abguss [ap'gŏŏs] *nm.* (Abgüsse) casting, stem (*pipe*).

Abhaben [ap'hah-ben] *vt. ir.* to have a share in.

Abhacken [ap'hack-en] *vt.* to chop off.

Abhaken [ap'hah-ken] *vt.* to hook off, tick off.

Abhalten [ap'hal-ten] *vt.* to hold off, deter, hold (*meeting*), celebrate.

Abhaltung [ap'hal-tŏŏng] *nf.* hindrance, celebration.

Abhandeln [ap'han-deln] *vt.* to negotiate, discuss, bargain for, beat down (*price*).

Abhanden [ap-han'den] *a.* mislaid, lost.

Abhandlung [ap'hand-lŏŏng] *nf.* transaction, discussion, treatise.

Abhang [ap'hang] *nm.* (Abhänge) slope.

Abhängen [ap'heng-en] *vt.* to take off, down, unhang, hang up (*ph.*); *i.* depend on.

Abhängig [ap'heng-ish] *a.* sloping, dependent.

Abhängigkeit [ap'heng-ish-kite] *nf.* dependence.

Abhärmen [ap'hairr-men] *vr.* to grieve, worry oneself to death.

Abhärten [ap'hairr-ten] *vt.* to harden, temper, toughen, inure.

Abhärtung [ap'hairr-tŏŏng] *nf.* hardening, toughening.

Abhaspeln [ap'has-peln] *vt.* to unwind.

Abhauen [ap'how-en] *vt.* to cut down, off.

Abheben [ap'hay-ben] *vt. ir.* to take off, cut (cards), pull up, rise (*plane*); *r.* contrast with.

Abheften [ap'hef-ten] *vt.* to detach.

Abheilen [ap'hile-en] *vi.* to heal up. [remedy.

Abhelfen [ap'helf-en] *vt. ir.* to

Abhetzen [ap'het-sen] *vt.* to hunt down; *r.* rush about, overtire oneself.

Abhilfe [ap'hil-fer] *nf.* redress, remedy, relief.

Abhobeln [ap'hoh-beln] *vt.* to plane (off), smooth.

Abhold [ap'holt] *a.* averse, ill-disposed.

Abholen [ap'hole-en] *vt.* to fetch away, to call for, meet.

Abholzeit [ap'hole-tsite] *nf.* time of collection (*letters*).

Abholzen [ap'holt-sen] *vt.* to clear (*of timber*), deforest.

Abhorchen [ap'horr-shen] *vt.* to overhear.

Abhören [ap'her-ren] *vt.* to learn by hearing, examine (*witnesses*), tap (*wires*).

Abhub [ap'hŏŏp] *nm.* remains, scum, dross.

Abhungern [ap'hŏŏng-errn] *vt.* to starve. [astray.

Abirren [ap'irr-en] *vi.* to go

Abirrung [ap'irr-ŏŏng] *nf.* deviation.

Abiturient [ab-i-tŏŏ-ri-ent'] *nm.* candidate for school leaving certificate.

Abiturientenprüfung [ab-l-tŏŏ-ri-ent'en-prÿŏ'fŏŏng] *nf.* school leaving examination.

Abiturientenzeugnis [ab-l-tŏŏ-ri-ent'en-tsoig-nis] *n.* higher school certificate.

Abjagen [ap'yah-gen] *vt.* to retrieve.

Abkämpfen [ap'kemp-fen] *vt.* to get by fighting.

Abkanten [ap'kant-en] *vt.* to bevel.

Abkanzeln [ap'kant-seln] *vt.* to scold, blow up.

Abkarten [ap'karr-ten] *vt.* to concert.

Abkauf [ap'kowf] *nm.* (Abkäufe) purchase.

Abkaufen [ap'kow-fen] *vt.* to buy from, buy up.

Abkäufer [ap'koi-ferr] *nm.* purchaser.

Abklären [ap'klairr-en] *vt.* to clarify.

Abklatsch [ap'klach] *nm.* (-e) copy, rough proof (*printing*).

Abklatschen [ap'klach-en] *vt.* to print off, stereotype.

Abklingeln [ap'kling-eln] *vi.* to ring off (*ph.*).

Abklingen [ap'kling-en] *vi. ir.* to die away, fade out (*rad.*).

Abknallen [ap'k-nallen] *vi.* to go off, explode.

Abknöpfen [ap'k-nerp-fen] *vt.* to unbutton.   [*vt.* to undo.

Abknüpfen [ap'k-newp-fen] *vt.*

Abkochen [ap'koch-en] *vt.* to boil down, scald.

Abkommandieren [ap'kom-an-deer-en] *vt.* to detail, detach (*mil.*), second.

Abkomme [ap'kom-er] *m.w.* see Abkömmling.

Abkommen [ap'komm-en] *vi.* to come away, get away, spare (*time*).

Abkommen [ap'komm-en] *n.* arrangement, compact, disuse.

Abkommenschaft [ap'kom-en-shaft] *nf.* descendants, posterity.

Abkömmlich [ap'kerm-lish] *a.* free, disengaged.

Abkömmling [ap'kerm-ling] *nm.* (-e) descendant.

Abkratzen [ap'krats-en] *vt.* to scrape away.

Abkriegen [ap'kree-gen] *vt.* to get one's share.

Abkrümeln [ap'kryoo-meln] *vi.* to crumble away.

Abkühlen [ap'kew-len] *vt.* to cool down, ice.

Abkühler [ap'kew-lerr] *nm.* refrigerator.

Abkühlung [ap'kyoo-loong] *nf.* cooling.

Abkunft [ap'koonft] *nf.* origin, lineage.

Abkuppeln [ap'koo-peln] *vt.* to uncouple, disengage.

Abkürzen [ap'kyoorr-tsen] *vt.* to shorten, reduce, cut.

Abkürzung [ap'kyoorr-tsoong] *nf.* abbreviation.

Abladehafen [ap'lad-der-hah-fen] *nm.* port of shipment.

Abladen [ap'lah-den] *vt.* to unload, disembark (*nav.*), detrain (*mil.*).

Abladung [ap'lah-doong] *nf.* unloading, disembarkation, discharge (*ship*).

Abladungsort [ap'lah-doongs-ort] *nm.* destination (*ship*).   [dump.

Ablage [ap'lah-ger] *nf.* depot.

Ablagern [ap'lah-gerrn] *vi.* to mature; *vt.* to store.

Ablassen [ap'lass-en] *vt. ir.* to leave off, sell; *vi.* to give up.

Ablasten [ap'last-en] *vt.* to unload.

Ablauern [ap'low-errn] *vt.* to lie in wait for.

Ablauf [ap'lowf] *nm.* expiration, maturity (*bill*), drainage, issue, result, launching (*plane, ship*).

Ablaufen [ap'low-fen] *vi.* to expire, become due, end; --lassen to launch.

Ablauschen [ap'low-shen] *vt.* to listen to, learn by listening, pick up (*rad.*).

Ablaut [ap'lowt] *nm.* gradation of vowels.

Abläutern [ap'loy-terrn] *vt.* to clarify, refine.   [cease.

Ableben [ap'lay-ben] *n.* decease.

Ablegen [ap'lay-gen] *vt.* to put down, lay down, take off, give up, pass (*examination*), give (*evidence*).

Ableger [ap'lay-gerr] *nm.* (-) shoot, branch.   [decline.

Ablehnen [ap'lay-nen] *vt.* to

Ableihen [ap'ly-en] *vt. ir.* to borrow from.

Ableisten [ap'lice-ten] *vt.* to complete (period of service).

Ableiten [ap'lite-en] *vt.* to divert, trace to origin.

Ableiter [ap'laite-err] *nm.* (-) conductor.

Ableitung [ap'lite-ōong] *nf.* derivation, leakage, branch-circuit (*el.*).

Ablenken [ap'leng-ken] *vt.* to turn aside, to distract.

Ablenkung [ap'leng-kōong] *nf.* distraction, diversion (*mil. etc.*).

Ablesen [ap'lay-zen] *vt. ir.* to read off.

Ableugnen [ap'loyg-nen] *vt.* to deny.

Ableugnung [ap'loyg-nōong] *nf.* denial.

Abliefern [ap'leef-errn] *vt.* to deliver.

Ablieferung [ap'leef-er-rōong] *nf.* delivery.

Abliegen [ap'lee-gen] *vi. ir.* to be at a distance.

Ablocken [ap'lock-en] *vt.* to entice away.

Ablohnen [ap'lone-en] *vt.* to pay off, dismiss.

Ablösen [ap'ler-zen] *vt.* to detach, relieve, discharge (*debt*).

Ablösung [ap'ler-zōong] *nf.* removal, relief, redemption (*com.*). exhaust.

Abluft [ap'looft] *nf.* air-exhaust.

Abmachen [ap'mach-en] *vt.* to loosen, undo, settle.

Abmachung [ap'mach-ōong] *nf.* arrangement, settlement, payment.

Abmagern [ap'mah-gerrn] *vi.* to grow thin.

Abmahnen [ap'mah-nen] *vt.* to dissuade from.

Abmalen [ap'mah-len] *vt.* to depict, copy.

Abmarsch [ap'marrsh] *nm.* start (*mil.*).

Abmarschbereit [ap'marshber-rite] *a.* ready to start (*mil.*).

Abmatten [ap'matt-en] *vt.* to fatigue.

Abmattung [ap'matt-ōong] *nf.* weariness.

Abmelden [ap'meld-en] *vt.* to give notice to leave.

Abmeldung [ap'mel-dōong] *n* de-registration.

Abmessen [ap'mess-en] *vt. ir.* to measure off, survey.

Abmessung [ap'messōong] *nf.* surveying, gauging (*com.*).

Abmieten [ap'meet-en] *vt.* to rent from.

Abmontieren [ap'mon-teerren] *vt.* dismantle, strip (*tec.*).

Abmühen [ap'myoo-en] *vr.* to toil, exert oneself.

Abmustern [ap'mōo-sterrn] *vt. to* pay off.

Abnahme [ap'nah-mer] *nf.* taking away, sale, decline, decrease, test, amputation, loss, acceptance (*av.*).

Abnehmbar [ap'name-bahrr] *a.* detachable.

Abnehmen [ap'nay-men] *vt. ir.* to take off, buy; *i.* decrease, wane.

Abnehmer [ap'nay-merr] *nm.* purchaser, customer.

Abneigen [ap'ny-gen] *vi.* to turn away, decline, diverge.

Abneigung [ap'ny-gōong] *nf.* aversion, dislike.

Abnötigen [ap'ner-ti-gen] *vt.* to extort.

Abnutzen [ap'nōot-sen] *vt.* wear out.

Abnutzung [ap-nōot-sōong] *nf.* deterioration, wear and tear.

Abonnement [a-bon-er-rmang'] *n* subscription.

Abonnent [a-bo-nent'] *nm.* subscriber.

Abonnieren [a-bo-neer'ren] *vt.* to subscribe. [depute.

Abordnen [ap'ordd-nen] *vt.* to

Abordnung [ap'ordd-nōong] *nf.* deputation.

Abort [ap'orrt] *nm.* lavatory, latrine (*mil.*).

Abpassen [ap'pass-en] *vt.* to fit, time, watch.

Abplacken [ap'plak-en] *vr.* to toil, drudge.

Abplagen [ap'plah-gen] *vr. see* Abplacken

Abplatten [ap'platt-en] *vt.* to flatten.

Abplätten [ap'plett-en] *vt.* to iron (*clothes*).

Abprallen [ap'prall-en] *vi.* to recoil, bounce off, ricochet (*mil.*).

Abpressen [ap'press-en] *vt.* to squeeze, extort from.

Abprotzen [ap'prot-sen] *vt.* to unlimber.

Abputzen [ap'pŏŏt-sen] *vt.* to cleanse, plaster.

Abquälen [ap'kvale-en] *vr.* to toil, worry.

Abraten [ap'rah-ten] *vt. ir.* to dissuade from. [bish.

Abraum [ap'rowm] *nm.* rub-

Abräumen [ap'roy-men] *vt.* to clear away.

Abrechnen [ap'resh-nen] *vt.* to deduct, take off; *vi.* to settle, square.

Abrechnung [ap'resh-nŏŏng] *nf.* deduction, settlement; -stelle *nf.* clearing house.

Abrede [ap'ray-der] *nf.* agreement; in – stellen to deny.

Abreiben [ap'ribe-en] *vt. ir.* to rub off, down, grind (*colours*).

Abreichen [ap'ry-shen] *vt.* to reach down. [ture.

Abreise [ap'rise-er] *nf.* depart-

Abreisen [ap'rise-en] *vi.* to depart, leave, go away.

Abreissen [ap'rice-en] *vt. ir.* to tear down, pull off.

Abreiss–schnur [ap'rice-shnŏŏr] *nf.* rip cord (*av.*).

Abreiten [ap'rite-en] *vt. ir.* to ride away.

Abrichten [ap'rish-ten] *vt.* to drill, coach, train.

Abrichtung [ap'rish-tŏŏng] *nf.* training.

Abriegeln [ap'ree-geln] *vt.* to cut off, block (*mil.*).

Abriegelung [ap'ree-ger-lŏŏng] *nf.* cutting off; -sfeuer *n.* box barrage (*mil.*); -s front *nf.* bolt position.

Abrinden [ap'rin-den] *vt.* to peel.

Abruf [ap'rŏŏf] *nm.* call, recall.

Abrufen [ap-rŏŏf-en] *vt. ir.* to call (off), recall, ring off (*ph.*).

Abrunden [ap'rŏŏn-den] *vt.* to round off.

Abrüsten [ap'ryŏŏ-sten] *vi.* to disarm.

Abrüstung [ap'ryŏŏ-stŏŏng] *nf.* disarmament.

Abrüstwagen [ap'ryŏŏst-vah-gen] *nm.* (–) breakdown lorry.

Abrutschen [ap'rŏŏt-shen] *vt.* to slip off, slide, slip (*av.*).

Absacken [ap'zak-en] *vi.* to stall, pancake (*plane*).

Absage [ap'zah-ger] *nf.* re-vocation, refusal.

Absagen [ap'zah-gen] *vt.* to withdraw from, countermand, refuse; *vi.* renounce.

Absägen [ap'zay-gen] *vt.* to saw off.

Absatz [ap'zats] *nm.* (Absätze) sediment, break, pause (*music*), sale (*goods*).

Absatzgebiet [ap'zats-ge-beet] *n.* (-e) market (*com.*).

Absäugen [ap'zoi-gen] *vt.* to wean.

Abschaffen [ap'shaff-en] *vt.* to abolish, scrap.

Abschaffung [ap'shaf-ŏŏng] *nf.* abolition.

Abschalten [ap'shal-ten] *vt.* to disconnect, cut off (*rad.*).

Abschärfen [ap'shairr-fen] *vt.* to sharpen.

Abschattung [ap'shatt-ŏŏng] *nf.* shading, tint.

Abschätzen [ap'shet-sen] *vt.* to estimate, value.

Abschätzung [ap'shet-sŏŏng] *nf.* valuation, estimate.

Abschätzer [ap'shet-ser] *nm.* valuer, assessor.

Abschäumen [ap'shoy-men] *vt.* to skim.

Abscheiden [ap'shide-en] *vt. ir.* to separate; *i.* to depart.

Abscheren [ap'share-en] *vt.* to shear. [ing, horror.

Abscheu [ap'shoy] *nm.* loath-

Abscheulich [ap-shoy'lish] a. abominable.

Abschicken [ap'shick-en] vt. to send off, forward.

Abschieben [ap'shee-ben] vt. ir. to push off, repatriate, deport.

Abschiebung [ap'shee-boong] nf. deportation, repatriation.

Abschied [ap'sheet] nm. parting, discharge, resignation; – nehmen to take leave.

Abschiessen [ap'shee-sen] vt. ir. to shoot down.

Abschlachten [ap'shlacht-en] vt. to slaughter.

Abschlag [ap'shlahk] nm. (Abschläge) refusal, allowance, reduction; auf – on account.

Abschlagen [ap'shlah-gen] vt. ir. to knock off, refuse, deduct, disconnect, repel.

Abschlägig [ap'shlay-gish] a. negative.

Abschläglich [ap'shlay-klish] a. on account (com.).

Abschlagszahlung [ap'shlahks-tsah-loong] nf. instalment.

Abschleifen [ap'shlife-en] vt. ir. to grind off, polish, sharpen; vr. to acquire breeding.

Abschleppdienst [ap'shlepp-deenst] nm. recovery, towing service (av.).

Abschleppen [ap'shlep-en] vt. to tow off (av.).

Abschleppwagen [ap'shlepp-vah-gen] nm. wrecker, breakdown lorry.

Abschluss [ap'shlōōs] nm. (Abschlüsse) settlement, conclusion, sale (com.).

Abschlussrechnung [ap'shlōōs-resh-nōōng] nf. final account.

Abschmeicheln [ap'shmy-sheln] vt. to coax out of.

Abschmelzen [ap'shmelt-sen] vt. to melt down.

Abschmieren [ap'shmeer-ren] vt. to grease (aut.).

Abschnallen [ap'shnall-en] vt. to unbuckle.

Abschnappen [ap'shnapp-en] vi.t. to stop short, lock.

Abschneiden [ap'shnide-en] vt. ir. to cut off, cut out (pattern), slander.

Abschnellen [ap'shnell-en] vt. to jerk off.

Abschnitt [ap'shnit] nm. section, paragraph, sector (mil.), coupon (ration card, etc.).

Abschnüren [ap'shnyōō-ren] vt. to unlace, mark by a line.

Abschöpfen [ap'sherp-fen] vt. to skim off.

Abschrauben [ap'shrow-ben] vt. to unscrew.

Abschrecken [ap'shreck-en] vt. to frighten, discourage.

Abschreiben [ap'shribe-en] vt. ir. to copy, to write off, deduct (com.).

Abschreibung [ap'shribe-ōōng] nf. copying, depreciation (com.).

Abschreiber [ap'shribe-err] nm. copyist.

Abschrift [ap'shrift] nf. copy.

Abschub [ap'shōōp] nm. removal (material), repatriation (persons).

Abschuften [ap'shōōf-ten] vr. to toil, drudge, slave.

Abschürfen [ap'shyoorr-fen] vt. to scrape, scratch off.

Abschuss [ap'shōōs] nm. discharge (mil.), shooting down (av.). [steep, sheer.

Abschüssig [ap'shyōō-sish] a.

Abschütteln [ap'shyōō-teln] vt. to shake off.

Abschwächen [ap'shvesh-en] vt. to weaken.

Abschweifen [ap'shvife-en] vt. to ramble, digress.

Abschweifung [ap'shvife-ōōng] nf. digression.

Abschwellen [ap'shvel-en] vi. ir. to die down, decrease.

Abschwenken [ap'shvenk-en] vi. to turn aside, wheel.

Abschwören [ap'shver-ren] *vt. ir.* to abjure, deny.

Absegeln [ap'zay-geln] *vi.* to sail away.

Absehbar [ap'zay-bahrr] *a.* within sight; **-e Zeit** the near future.

Absehen [ap'zay-en] *vt.* to foresee, intend, aim at; *vi.* disregard; **abgesehen von** apart from.

Abseihen [ap'zy-en] *vt.* to filter, strain.

Abseits [ap'zites] *ad.* aside.

Absenden [ap'zen-den] *vt. ir.* to send off, dispatch.

Absender [ap'zen-derr] *nm.* sender, consignor (*com.*).

Absendung [ap'zen-dõong] *nf.* forwarding, consignment (*com.*).

Absetzbar [ap'zets-bahrr] *a.* [removable.

Absetzen [ap'zet-sen] *vt.* to remove, set down, sell (*com.*), cashier, degrade (*mil.*), land (*troops*), set up (*type*); *i.* to stop, pause, disengage, retreat (*mil.*).

Absetzung [ap'zet-sõong] *nf.* removal, deposition, setting up (*type*), writing off (*com.*), disengagement, retreat (*mil.*).

Absicht [ap'zisht] *nf.* intention.

Absichtlich [ap'zisht-lish] *a., ad.* intentional(ly).

Absichtslos [ap'zishts-lohs] *a.* unintentional.

Absickern [ap'zick-errn] *vi.* to trickle down.

Absieden [ap'zeed-en] *vt. ir.* to boil, decoct.

Absingen [ap'zing-en] *vt. ir.* to sing by sight, sing to the end.

Absinken [ap'zing-ken] *vi. ir.* to sink down, subside.

Absitzen [ap'zit-sen] *vi. ir.* to dismount; *vt.* to serve a sentence. [absolute(ly).

Absolut [ap-zo-lōōt'] *a. ad.*

Absolutismus [ap-zo-loo-tis'mõõss] *nm.* absolutism.

Absolvieren [ap'zol-veer-en] *vt.* to complete (*schooling*).

Absonderlich [ap'zon-derr-lish] *a.* odd, unusual.

Absondern [ap'zon-derrn] *vt.* to separate off.

Absonderung [ap'zon-der-rõong] *nf.* segregation.

Abspalten [ap'shpal-ten] *vt.* to split off.

Abspannen [ap'shpann-en] *vt.* to unharness, unbend, relax.

Abspannung [ap'shpan-õong] *nf.* exhaustion.

Absparen [ap'shpah-ren] *vr.* to stint oneself, go short, do without.

Abspeisen [ap'shpize-en] *vt.* to put off.

Abspenstig [ap'shpen-stish] *a.* estranged; **– machen** *vt.* to estrange.

Absperren [ap'shperr-en] *vt.* to shut off, confine, close, block, barricade.

Absperrung [ap'shper-rõong] *nf.* blocking, barricading.

Abspielen [ap'shpeel-en] *vt.* to sight-read; *r.* to happen.

Abspitzen [ap'shpit-sen] *vt.* to blunt, sharpen (*pencil*).

Absplittern [ap'shplit-errn] *vt.* to splinter.

Absprechen [ap'shpresh-en] *vt. ir.* to contest, dispute, disallow; **-d** *a., ad.* peremptory, adverse(ly).

Abspringen [ap'shpring-en] *vi. ir.* to jump away from, burst off, bale out (*av.*).

Abspringer [ap'shpring-err] *nm.* parachute jumper (*av.*).

Abspruch [ap'shprōōch] *nm.* (Absprüche) sentence, verdict.

Absprung [ap'shprõong] *nm.* (Absprünge) leaping off, jump, parachute descent, baling out (*av.*); **-hafen** *nm.* advanced landing ground.

Abspülen [ap'shpyoo-len] *vt.* to wash, rinse, flush.

Abstammen [ap shtam-en]

vi. to be derived, descended from; **-ung** *nf.* descent, ancestry.

Abstand [ap'shtant] *nm.* (Abstände (interval, distance, gap, disparity); **-nehmen** *vt.* to renounce; **-swerfen** *n.* pattern bombing (*av.*).

Abstatten [ap'shtat-en] *vt.* to give, render, pay (*visit, etc.*).

Abstäuben [ap'shtoy-ben] *vt.* to dust.

Abstechen [ap'shtesh-en] *vt. ir.* to stab, mark out, engrave; *i.* to contrast. [ramble.

Abstecher [ap'shtesh-err] *nm.*

Abstecken [ap'shtek-en] *vt.* to unfasten, mark out, plot (*course*).

Abstehen [ap'shtay-en] *vi. ir.* to be distant, stand out, refrain from.

Abstehlen [ap'shtay-len] *vt. ir.* to steal from.

Absteigen [ap'shty-gen] *vi. ir.* to dismount, step down, put up at.

Abstell'en [ap'shtell-en] *vt.* to remove from, abolish, switch off (*engine*); **-geleise** *n.* (*rl.*) siding; **-platz** *nm.* parking area (*av.*), aerodrome.

Abstempeln [ap'shtem-peln] *vt.* to stamp.

Absterben [ap'shtairr-ben] *vi. ir.* to die away, rot. [descent.

Abstieg [ap'shteek] *nm.*

Abstich [ap'shtish] *nm.* pattern, tapping, contrast.

Abstimm'en [ap'shtimm-en] *vt.* to tune, to tune in (*rad.*); *i.* to vote; **-knopf** *nm.* tuning knob; **-spule** *nf.* tuning coil (*rad.*); **-ung** *nf.* voting, tuning-in (*rad.*); **-ungs-schärfe** *nf.* accurate tuning-in (*rad.*).

Abstinenzler [ap'sti-nents-lerr] *nm.* (-) teetotaler.

Abstossen [ap'shtoh-sen] *vt. ir.* to thrust away, plane, repel; **-d** *a.* repulsive. [stract.

Abstrakt [ap-strakt'] *a.* ab-

Abstreichen [ap'shtry-shen] *vi. ir.* to scrape off, wipe, cancel.

Abstreifen [ap'shtrife-en] *vi.* to strip off, patrol, picket (*mil.*).

Abstreiten [ap'shtrite-en] *vt. ir.* to gain from, dispute, contest.

Abstrich [ap'shtrish] *nm.* (-e) cut, deduction, down-stroke.

Abströmen [ap'shter-men] *vi.* to flow down.

Abstufen [ap'shtoo-fen] *vi.* to form steps, shade off.

Abstufung [ap'shtoo-foong] *nf.* grading, gradation.

Abstumpfen [ap'shtoomp-fen] *v.t.* to dull.

Absturz [ap'shtoorts] *nm.* (Abstürze) downfall, dive, crash (*av.*).

Abstürzen [ap'shtyoor-tsen] *vt.* to cast down; *vi.* to fall down, dive, crash (*av.*).

Absuchen [ap'zooch-en] *vt.* to scour, search thoroughly.

Absud [apt'zoot] *nm.* decoction.

Abt [apt] *nm.* abbot.

Abtasten [ap'tast-en] *vt.* to probe. [thaw

Abtauen [ap'tow-en] *vi.* to

Abtauschen [ap'tow-shen] *vt.* to exchange.

Abtei [ap-tie'] *nf.* abbey.

Abteil [ap'tile] *n.* compartment; **-en** *vt.* to partition; **-ung** *nf.* classification, section, department.

Abtin [ep'tin] *nf.* abess.

Abtönen [ap'ter-nen] *vt.* to tone (*photo*).

Abtrag [ap'trahk] *nm.* injury.

Abtragen [ap'trah-gen] *vt. ir.* to carry away, discharge (*debt*), wear out (*clothes*).

Abträglich [ap'trive-lich] *a.* harmful.

Abtreiben [ap'trive-en] *vt. ir.* to drive away, overdrive (*horse*), refine (*metal*); *i.* to drift off.

Abtrennen [ap'trenn-en] *vt.* to separate.

Abtreten [ap'tray-ten] *vt. ir.* to tread down, pace out, cede; *i.* retire.

Abtretung [ap'tray-tōong] *nf.* cession, retirement, surrender, assignment.

Abtritt [ap'tritt] *nm.* (-e) withdrawal, exit, lavatory.

Abtrocknen [ap'trock-nen] *vt.* to dry (up).

Abtrumpfen [ap'trōomp-fen] *vt.* to trump, rebuff.

Abtrünnig [ap'tryoo-nish] *a.* rebellious.

Abtun [ap'tōon] *vt. ir.* to take off, end, abolish.

Aburteilen [ap'ōōrt-tile-en] *vt.* to sentence.

Abverdienen [ap'ferr-dee-nen] *vt.* to work off.

Abwägen [ap'vay-gen] *vt. ir.* to weigh, ponder.

Abwälzen [ap'velt-sen] *vt.* to roll down, cast off.

Abwandeln [ap'van-deln] *vt.* to inflect, conjugate, decline.

Abwandlung [ap'vant-lōong] *nf.* variation, inflection, conjugation, declension.

Abwandern [ap'van-derrn] *vi.* to wander off.

Abwarten [ap'vahrr-ten] *vt.* to wait for, await.

Abwartung [ap'vahrr-tōong] *nf.* awaiting.

Abwärts [ap'vairrts] *ad.* downwards, aside.

Abwaschen [ap'vash-en] *vt. ir.* to wash off, wash hands.

Abwasser [ap'vass-err] *n.* sewage water; **-n** *vi.* to take off from the water (*plane*).

Abwässern [ap'vess-errn] *vt.* to drain.

Abwechseln [ap'vex-eln] *vt.* to change, vary; *i.* alternate.

Abwechselnd [ap'vex-elnt] *a., ad.* alternate(ly).

Abweg [ap'vayk] *nm.* (-e) by-path, wrong way.

Abwegig [ap'vay-gish] *a.* devious, wrong.

Abwehr [ap'vairr] *nf.* defence, protection; **-dienst** *nm.* counter-espionage.

Abwehren [ap'vair-ren] *vt.* to ward off.

Abweichen [ap'vy-shen] *vt. ir.* to deviate, stray.

Abweichend [ap'vy-shent] *a.* irregular, dissentient.

Abweisen [ap'vize-en] *vt. ir.* to turn away, repulse.

Abweisung [ap'vize-ōōng] *nf.* refusal.

Abwendbar [ap'vend-bahrr] *a.* avertible.

Abwenden [ap'ven-den] *vt. ir.* to turn aside. [estranged.

Abwendig [ap'ven-dish] *a.*

Abwendung [ap'ven-dōong] *nf.* averting, alienation.

Abwerfen [ap'vairr-fen] *vt. ir.* to throw off, knock down, yield (*profit*), drop (*bombs*).

Abwesend [ap'vay-zent] *a.* absent.

Abwesenheit [ap'vay-zen-hite] *nf.* absence.

Abwickeln [ap'vick-eln] *vt.* to unwind, wind up (*business*); *r.* develop.

Abwicklung [ap'vick-lōong] *nf.* unwinding, winding-up, dispatch (*business*).

Abwinden [ap'vin-den] *vt. ir.* to unwind.

Abwirtschaften [ap'virrt-shaf-ten] *vi.* to ruin.

Abwischen [ap'vish-en] *vt.* to wipe off.

Abwracken [ap'vrak-en] *vt.* to break up (*ships*).

Abwurf [ap'vōōrrf] *nm.* jettisoning, release, dropping (*bombs*); **-behälter** *nm.* slip fuel tank (*av.*).

Abzahlen [ap'tsah-len] *vt.* to pay off, discharge, pay on account.

Abzählen [ap'tsay-len] *vt.* to count (out), subtract.

Abzahlung [ap'tsah-lŏŏng] nf. paying off, instalment, hire purchase.

Abzapfen [ap'tsap-fen] vt. to broach, tap, bleed (of money).

Abzäunen [ap'tsoy-nen] vt. to fence off, in.

Abzehren [ap'tsair-en] vi.t. r. to consume, waste away.

Abzehrung [ap'tsair-rŏŏng] nf. consumption (medical), emaciation.

Abzeichen [ap'tsy-shen] n. token, sign (of office, etc.), insignia.

Abzeichnen [ap'tsych-nen] vt. to draw, sketch, copy; r. contrast, stand out.

Abziehen [ap'tsee-en] vt. ir. to draw off, undress, divert, subtract; i. to move off. [aim.

Abzielen [ap'tsee-len] vi.i. to

Abzug [ap'tsŏŏk] nm. (Abzüge) departure, removal, outlet, deduction (money), proof (printing), trigger (mil.); -sgraben nm, -skanal nm. drain.

Abzüglich [ap'tsyŏŏk-lish] ad. less, minus.

Abzweigen [ap'tsvȳ-gen] vi. to branch off.

Abzweigung [ap'tsvȳ-gŏŏng] nf. branch, off-shoot.

Abzwingen [ap'tsving-en] vt. ir. to force from.

Achse [ax'er] nf. axle; per by road, lorry.

Achsel [axle] nf. shoulder; -höhle [axle'shnŏŏrr] armpit.

Achselschnur [axle'shnŏŏrr] nf. lanyard.

Achselzucken [axle'tsŏŏ-ken] n. shrug of the shoulders.

Acht [acht] nf. attention; - geben, haben, nehmen auf to pay attention to; sich in - nehmen to look out, take care.

Acht [acht] nf. outlawry.

Acht [acht] num. eight; - Tage week (in phrases). [able.

Achtbar [acht'bahrr] a. estim

Achtbarkeit [acht'bahrr-kite] nf. respectability.

Achten [acht'en] vt. to esteem; j. to heed. [ban.

Achten [esh'ten] vt. to outlaw

Achter [acht'err] ad. aft (nav.); -deck n. quarter-deck (nav.); -hütte nf. poop (nav.); -lastig ad. down by the stern (nav.).

Achtlos [acht'lohs] a. careless.

Achtlosigkeit [acht'loh-zish-kite] nf. carelessness. [tive.

Achtsam [acht'zam] a. atten

Achtsamkeit [acht'zam-kite] nf. carefulness.

Achttägig [acht'teh-gish] a. weekly, lasting a week.

Achtung [acht'ŏŏng] nf. attention, consideration, esteem, look out! hullo!

Achtungsverletzung [acht'tŏŏngs-fairr-let-sŏŏng] nf. insubordination (mil.).

Achtungsvoll [acht'tŏŏngs-fol] a, ad. respectful(ly).

Achtungswert [acht'tŏŏngs-vairrt] a. estimable.

Achtzehn [acht'tsehn] num. eighteen. [eighty.

Achtzig [acht'sish] num. eighty.

Achtziger [acht'tsi-gerr] nm. octogenarian.

Ächzen [esh'tsen] vi. to groan.

Acker [ak'err] nm. (Äcker) field, soil.

Acker-bau [a'kerr-bow] nm. agriculture; -gerät n. agricultural implement; -knecht nm (knechte) farm labourer; -land n. (länder) arable land; -schlepper nm. tractor.

Ackern [a'kerrn] vt. to plough.

Addieren [a-dee'ren] vt. to add (up).

Addition [a-dit-si-ohn'] nf. addition; -smaschine nf. adding machine.

Adel [ahdl] nm. nobility.

Adelig [ah'dlish] a. of noble birth.

Ader [ah'derr] nf. vein.

Ädern [eh'derrn] vt. to vein.

Adler [ahd'lerr] *nm.* eagle.

Adjutant [at-yōō-tant'] *m.* adjutant, aide-de-camp (*mil.*).

Adjutantur [at-yōō-tan-tōōrr'] *nf.* staff department (*mil.*).

Admiral [at-mi-rahl'] *nm.* admiral.

Admiralität [at-mi-ra-li-tate'] *nf.* Admiralty.

Adoptieren [ad-op-tee'ren] *vt.* to adopt.

Adoptiv . . . [ad-op-teef'] *a.* adopted; -kind *n.* adopted child; -tochter *nf.* adopted daughter. [addressee.

Adressat [a-dress-aht'] *m.w.*

Adressbuch [a-dress'bōōch] *n.* directory. [dress.

Adresse [a-dress'er] *nf.* ad-

Adressieren [a-dress-ee'ren] *vt.* address.

Advokat [at-vo-kaht'] *m. w.* advocate, lawyer.

Affe [a'fer] *m. w.* ape.

Affektiert [a-fek-teerrt'] *a.* affected.

Affen [e'fen] *vt.* to ape.

After [af'terr] *nm.* anus, buttocks; -könig *nm.* pretender; -miete *nf.* sub-tenancy; -mieter *nm.* sub-tenant.

Agent [a-gent'] *m. w.* agent.

Agentur [a-gen-tōōrr'] *nf.* agency.

Aggregat [a-gre-gaht'] *n.* aggregate, unit, group, gang (*el.*).

Agieren [a-zhee'ren] *vi.* to act.

Agio [ad'jioh] *n.* premium (*com.*).

Agiotage [ad-jio-tah'zher] *nf.* stock-jobbing (*com.*).

Agioteur [ad-jio-ter'] *nm.* stock-jobber (*com.*).

Agiotieren [ad-jio-tee'ren] *vi.* to operate on the stock exchange (*com.*).

Ahn [ahn] *m. w.* ancestor.

Ähneln [ay'neln *vt.* to look like.

Ahnen [ah'nen] *vt.i.* to antici- pate, have a presentiment of.

Ähnlich [ain'lish] *a.* similar.

Ähnlichkeit [ain'lish-kite] *nf.* resemblence.

Ahnung [ah'nōōng] *nf.* antici- pation, presentiment, idea.

Ahnungslos [ah'nōōngs-lohs] *a.* unsuspecting.

Ahnungsvoll [ah'nōōngs-fol] *a.* ominous.

Ahorn [ah'horrn] *nm.* maple.

Akkord [a-korrt'] *nm.* agreed price, contract, arrangement (*com.*); - arbeit *nf.* piece work (*com.*).

Akkordieren [a-korr-dee'ren] *vt.i.* to arrange, contract (*com.*).

Akkumulator [a-kōō-mōō- lah'tohrr] *nm.* accumulator; - enbetrieb *nm.* accumulator drive; - enwagen *nm.* accumu- lator driven car.

Akt [act] *nm.* act, deed, nude study (*art*).

Akte [ac-ter] *nf.* deed (law), document; -nklammer *nf.* paper clip; -nschrank *nm.* filing cabinet; -nständer *nm.* pigeon holes *pl*; -nstück *n.* document; -ntasche *nf.* portfolio. (*com.*).

Aktie [ac'see-er] *nf.* share.

Aktien-bank [ac'see-en-bank] *nf.* joint-stock bank; -gesell- schaft *nf.* joint-stock company; -handel *nm.* stock-jobbing.

Aktionär [ac-see-o-nairr'] *nm.* (-e) shareholder.

Aktiv [ac-teef'] *a.* active, actual, on active service, regular (*mil.*).

Aktiva [ac-tee'vah] *n.pl.* assets

Aktiv-saldo [ac-teef'] *nm.* credit balance (*com.*); -schulden *f.pl.* outstanding debts.

Aktuell [actōō-el'] *a.* topical.

Akzent [ac-tsent'] *nm.* accent, stress.

Akzept [act-sept'] *n.* accept- ance, accepted bill (*com.*).

Akzeptant [ac-tsep-tant'] *m.w.* acceptor (*com.*).

Akzeptieren [ac-tsep-tee'ren] *vt.* accept, honour (*draft*).

Akzise [ac-tseez'er] *nf.* excise.
Akzise-frei *a.* free of duty; -**pflichtig** liable to duty.

Alarm [a-larrm'] *nm.* (-e) alarm, warning; -**bereit** *a.* on the alert, standing by; -**bereit-schaft** *nf.* immediate readiness, alert; -**tauchen** *n.* crash dive (*nav.*); -**zeichen** *n.* alarm signal.

Alaun [a-lown'] *nm.* alum.

Albern [al'berrn] *a.* silly.

Alimente [a-li-men'te] *n.pl.* alimony.

Alkohol [al'coh-hol] *nm.* alcohol; -**frei** *a.* non-alcoholic; -**gegner** *nm.* prohibitionist, tee-totaler; -**verbot** *n.* prohibition.

Alkoholiker [al-coh-hoh'li-kerr] *n.m.* (-) different *n.* drunk-ard.

All [al] *a.* all, every; **alle** *ad.* all gone, exhausted; **Mädchen für alles** maid of all work.

All-bekannt *a.* generally known, notorious; -**jährlich** *a., ad.* annual(ly); -**macht** *nf.* omnipotence; -**täglich** *a.* daily, commonplace.

Allee [a-lay'] *nf.* avenue.

Allein [a-line'] *a., ad.* alone, sole, by oneself; *cj.* but, only; -**handel** *nm.* [Händel] monopoly; -**händler** *nm.* monopolist; -**vertreter** *nm.* sole agent (*com.*); -**verkauf** *nm.* monopoly.

Alleinig [a-line'ish] *a.* sole.

Allemal [a'ler-mahl] *ad.* at all times.

Allenfalls [a'len-fals'] *ad.* at all events, if need be.

Allenthalben [a'lent-hal'ben] *ad.* everywhere.

Aller-best *a.* best of all; -**hand** *a.* of every kind; -**höchst** *a.* supreme; -**seits** *a.* on all sides.

Allerdings [a'lerr-dings'] *ad.* certainly, admittedly, to be sure.

Allerlei [a'lerr-lie'] *a.* of all

Allgemein [al'ger-mine'] *a., ad.* general(ly); -**heit** *nf.* generality; -**kosten** *pl.* overhead expenses, overheads *pl.* (*com.*).

Allianz [a-li-ants'] *nf.* alliance.

Alliierte(r) [a-li-eerr'ter] *nm.* ally.

Allmählich [al-may'lish] *a., ad.* gradual(ly).

Allwellenempfänger [al-ve-len-emp-feng'err] *nm.* all-wave receiver (*rad.*).

Almosen [al'moze-en] *n.* alms.

Alp [alp] *nm.* nightmare; also -**drücken** *n.*

Alpe [al'per] *nf.* Alpine meadow; *pl.* Alps.

Als [alss] *cj.* when, as, than; **nichts als** nothing but.

Also [al'zo] *ad.* thus, therefore, ally.

Alt [alt] *a.* old, second hand (*books, etc.*); **ich bin nicht mehr der Alte** I am not the man I was; **die Alten** the ancients; -**besitzer** *nm.* original owner; -**eisen** *n.* scrap iron; -**material** *n.* cast-off material; -**metall** *n.* scrap(metal); -**modisch** *a.* old-fashioned; -**papier** *n.* waste paper; -**sache** *nf.* cast-off goods.

Alter [al'terr] *n.* (old) age; **im - von** at the age of; -**grenze** *nf.* age limit. [old.

Altern [al'terrn] *vi.* to grow

Altertum [al'terr-tōōm] *n.* antiquity.

Am [am] = **an dem**; **am Sterben** at the point of death.

Amalgam [a-mal-gahm'] *n.* amalgam.

Amboss [am'boss] *nm.* anvil.

Ameise [ah'mize-er] *nf.* ant.

Amme [am'er] *nf.* wet nurse.

Amortisierbar [a-morr-ti-zeerr'bar] *a.* redeemable.

Amortisieren [a-morr-ti-zeerr'ren] *vt.* to redeem, repay, cancel (*bond, etc.*).

Ampel [ampl'] *nf.* hanging lamp, traffic lights.

Ampere [am-pare'] *n.* (-) ampere.

Amphibienpanzerwagen [am-fee'bi-en-pant'serr-vah-gen] *nm.* amphibious tank.

Amphibisch [am-fee'bish] *a.* amphibious.

Amsol [am'zel] *nf.* blackbird.

Amt [amt] *n.* (Ämter) office, administration, public building, exchange (*ph.*).

Amtlich [amt'lish] *a.* official.

Amtmann [amt'man] *nm.* official, steward, bailiff, magistrate.

Amts-charakter [amts] *n.* official capacity; -**führung** *nf.* administration; -**gebühren** *f.pl.* official fees *pl*.; -**stube** *nf.* office; -**zeichen** *n.* dial tone; -**zeit** *f.* tenure of office.

An [an] *pr.* at, in, of, on, to; *ad.* on, up; **von jetzt an** from now on, henceforth; **bergan** uphill.

Analyse [an-a-lÿöö-zer'] *nf.* analysis.

Analysieren [an-a-lÿöö-zeer'en] *vt.* to analyse. [gous.

Analog [an-a-lohk'] *a.* analo-

Analogie [an-a-loh-gee'] *nf.* analogy.

Ananas [ah'na-nass] *nf.* pineapple.

Anarchie [an-arr-shee'] *nf.* anarchy.

Anatom [an-a-tome'] *m.w.* anatomist.

Anatomie [an-a-to-mee'] *nf.* anatomy.

Anbahnen [an'bah-nen] *vt.* to open up, prepare, pave the way for.

Anbändeln [an'ben-deln] *vi.* to flirt.

Anbau [an'bow] *nm.* (Anbauten) cultivation, annexe, (new) wing.

Anbauen [an'bow-en] *vt.* to cultivate, build against, add to, settle (*land*).

Anbefehlen [an'be-fail-en] *vt. ir.* to command.

Anbeginn [an'be-gin] *nm.* beginning.

Anbehalten [an'be-hal-ten] *vt. ir.* to keep on.

Anbei [anby'] *ad.* herewith, enclosed.

Anbeissen [an'bice-en] *vt. ir.* to bite at; *i.* to swallow the bait.

Anbelangen [an'ber-lang-en] *vt.* to concern; **was mich anbelangt** as far as I am concerned. [bark at.

Anbellen [an'bell-en] *vt.* to

Anbequemen [an'ber-kvay-men] *vt. r.* to accommodate.

Anberaumen [an'ber-row-men] *vt.* to appoint, fix (*time*).

Anbeten [an'bay-ten] *vt.* to worship, adore.

Anbeter [an'bay-terr] *nm.* (-) adorer, worshipper.

Anbetracht [an'ber-tracht] *m.* consideration.

Anbetreffen [an'ber-tref-en] *vt. ir.* to concern.

Anbetung [an'bay-töong] *nf.* adoration, worship.

Anbiegen [an'bee-gen] *vt.* to bend towards, enclose (*com.*).

Anbieten [an'bee-ten] *vt. ir.* to offer; *r.* volunteer, offer one's services. [offer.

Anbietung [an'bee-töong] *nf.*

Anbinden [an'bin-den] *vt. ir.* to tie to, up, moor (*ship*); *i.* to have to do with, quarrel with.

Anblasen [an'blah-zen] *vt. ir.* to blow on, in (furnace).

Anblick [an'blik] *nm.* sight, spectacle.

Anblicken [an'blikn] *vt.* to look at.

Anblinzeln [an'blint-seln] *vt.* to wink at.

Anbohren [an'bore-en] *vt.* to broach, tap, bore.

Anbrechen [an'bresh-en] *vt. ir.* to break open, broach, tap, cut into; *i.* dawn.

Anbrennen [an'brenn-en] *vi. ir.* to catch fire; *vt.* set fire to.	**Andrängen** [an'dreng-en] *vt.* to press against.
Anbringen [an'bring-en] *vt. ir.* to bring to, place, dispose of, lodge (*complaint*).	**Andrehen** [an'dray-en] *vt.* to turn on, switch on, start up (*aut.*).
Anbruch [an'brŏŏch] *nm.* (Anbrüche) beginning, starting; — des Tages dawn; — der Nacht nightfall; in — verkaufen to sell in odd lots.	**Andringen** [an'dring-en] *vi. ir.* to press forward.
	Androhen [an'droh-en] *vt.* to threaten with.
Anbrüllen [an'bryŏŏ-len] *vt.* to roar at.	**Androhung** [an'droh-ŏŏng] *nf.* threat.
Andacht [an'dacht] *nf.* devotion, short service, prayers, -svoll *a.* devout.	**Andrücken** [an'dryŏŏ-ken] *vt.* to press against.
Andächtig [an'desh-tish] *a.* devout.	**Aneignen** [an'ig-nen] *vt. r.* to acquire, appropriate.
Andauern [an'dow-errn] *vi. tr.* to last, persist.	**Aneinander** [an'ine-an-derr] *ad.* together.
Andenken [an'deng-ken] *n.* memory, remembrance, keepsake.	**Anekeln** [an'ake-eln] *vt.* to disgust.
Ander [an'derr] *a.* other, different; am — Tage the next day.	**Anempfehlen** [an'emp-fay-len] *vt. ir.* to recommend, advise.
Ändern [en'derrn] *vt.* to alter.	**Anerbieten** [an'airr-bete-en] *n.* offer.
Andrenfalls [an'derrn-falss] *ad.* otherwise.	**Anerkannt** [an'airr-kant] *a.* acknowledged.
Anders [an'derrs] *ad.* otherwise, differently; wer — *pr.* who else.	**Anerkennbar** [an'airr-ken-barr] *a.* recognizable.
Anderseits [an'derr-zites] *ad.* on the other hand.	**Anerkennen** [an'airr-ken-en] *vt. ir.* to acknowledge, appreciate; nicht — to repudiate.
Anders-farbig *a.* of different colour; -gläubig *a.* holding different beliefs; -woher *ad.* from elsewhere; -wohin *ad.* elsewhere.	**Anerkennend** [an'airr-ken-ent] *a.* appreciative.
	Anerkennenswert [an'airr-ken-ŏŏngs-vairrt] *a.* praiseworthy.
Anderthalb [an'derrt-halp] *a.* one and a half.	**Anerkennung** [an'airr-ken-ŏŏng] *nf.* acknowledgment, recognition, appreciation.
Änderung [en'der-rŏŏng] *nf.* alteration.	**Anfachen** [an'fach-en] *vt.* to fan into flame.
Anderweitig [an'derr-vite-ish] *a.* in another place, other.	**Anfädeln** [an'fay-deln] *vt.* to string, begin (*conversation*).
Andeuten [an'doy-ten] *vt.* to indicate, signify, hint at.	**Anfahren** [an'far-ren] *vt. ir.* to convey, put into (*port*), rebuke; *i.* to strike against, drive up.
Andeutung [an'doy-tŏŏng] *nf.* indication, suggestion, hint.	**Anfall** [an'fal] *nm.* (Anfälle) attack, fit, raid.
Andichten [an'dish-ten] *vt.* to attribute to.	**Anfallen** [an'fal-en] *vt. ir.* to attack, invade.
Andrang [an'drang] *nm.* crowd, rush, urgent demand, congestion (*blood*).	**Anfang** [an'fang] *nm.* (Anfänge) beginning, opening.

Anfangen [an'fang-en] *vt. ir. i.* to begin, undertake.

Anfänger [an'feng-err] *nm.* beginner, novice.

Anfänglich [an'feng-lish] *a.* initial, first.

Anfangs [an'fangss] *ad.* at first, at the beginning.

Anfangs-buchstabe *nm.* initial, capital letter; -**gründe** *m pl.* elements *pl.* [handle.

Anfassen [an'fassn] *vt.* to seize.

Anfechten [an'fesh-ten] *vt.* to dispute, trouble, tempt.

Anfechtung [an'fesh-tōōng] *nf.* attack, temptation.

Anfertigen [an'fairr-ti-gen] *vt.* to make, manufacture.

Anfertigung [an'fairr-ti-gōōng] *nf.* making, manufacture.

Anfeuchten [an'foish-ten] *vt.* to moisten, wet.

Anfeuern [an'foy-errn] *vt.* to kindle, heat, encourage.

Anflehen [an'flay-en] *vt.* to implore.

Anflehung [an'flay-ōōng] *nf.* supplication.

Anfliegen [an'flee-gen] *vt. ir.* to fly up to, against, approach; *i.* to land, call (*av.*).

Anflug [an'flōōk] *nm.* (An-flüge) approach (flight), trace, touch (*colour, etc.*).

Anfordern [an'forr-derrn] *vt.* to demand.

Anforderung [an'forr-der-rōōng] *nf.* demand, indent, order, requirements *pl.*

Anfrage [an'frah-ger] *nf.* inquiry.

Anfragen [an'frah-gen] *vt.* to inquire, ask for.

Anfressen [an'fress-en] *vt. ir.* to gnaw, eat into.

Anfreunden [an'froyn-den] *vr.* to make friends with.

Anfügen [an'few-gen] *vt.* to join to, add to, enclose, affix.

Anfühlen [an'few-len] *vr.* to feel.

Anfuhr [an'fōōrr] *nf.* carriage, arrival, imports *pl.*

Anführen [an'few-ren] *vt.* to lead, quote, deceive.

Anführer [an'few-rerr] *nm.* leader, chieftain.

Anführung [an'few-rōōng] *nf.* leadership, quotation, statement; -**zeichen** *n.* quotation marks *pl.* [fill (up).

Anfüllen [an-fyőölen] *vt.* to fill up.

Angabe [an'gah-ber] *nf.* declaration, assignment (*reason*), payment, quotation, (*price*); **nach** – according to statement, as stated.

Angängig [an'geng-ish] *a.* admissible.

Angeben [an'gay-ben] *vt. ir.* to state, assign (*reason*), quote (*price*), inform against; *i.* to deal first (*cards*).

Angeber [an'gay-berr] *nm.* (-) informer.

Angeberei [an'gay-ber-rie'] *nf.* tale-bearing.

Angebinde [an'ger-bin-der] *n.* (-) present.

Angeblich [an'gay-blish] *a.* as stated, alleged, ostensible. [inborn.

Angeboren [an'ger-bor-ren] *a.*

Angebot [an'ger-boht] *n.* (-e) upset price, offer; – **und Nachfrage** supply and demand.

Angedeihen lassen [an'ger-dy-en lass-en] *vt.* to confer, present.

Angegriffen [an'ger-grifn] *a.* fatigued, exhausted.

Angeheitert [an'gay-hite-errt] *a.* tipsy.

Angehen [an'gay-en] *vt. ir.* to approach, solicit, affect, concern; *i.* to begin, be possible, be in order, catch fire.

Angehend [an'gay-ent] *a.* prospective, beginning.

Angehören [an'ger-her-ren] *vi.* to belong.

Angehörig [an'ger-her-rish] *a.* belonging to.

Angehörige(r) [an'ger-hö-rige] *m.w.* relative.

Angel [ang'el] *nf.* hinge, fish-hook; **-haken** *nm.* (-) fish-hook; **-rute** *nf.* fishing rod; **-schnur** *nf.* (schnüre) fishing-line.

[*vi.* to arrive.
Angelangen [an'ger-lang-en]

Angeld [an'gelt] *n.* earnest money, deposit.

Angelegen [an'ger-lay-gen] *a.* important.

Angelegenheit [an'ger-lay-gen-hite] *nf.* affair.

Angelegentlich [an'ger-lay-gent-lish] *a.* urgent, pressing.

Angeln [ang'eln] *vi.* to fish; *n.* angling, fishing.

Angelfischerei [ang'el-fish-er-rie'] *nf.* angling.

Angemessen [an'ger-mess-en] *a.* appropriate.

Angenehm [an'ger-name] *a.* agreeable.

Angenommen [an'ger-nom-en] *a.* supposing, assuming.

Anger [ang-err] *nm.* (-) meadow, paddock.

Angesehen [an'ger-zay-en] *a.* respected, distinguished.

Angesessen [an'ger-zes-en] *a.* settled.

Angesicht [an'ger-zisht] *n.* (-er) countenance.

Angesichts [an'ger-zishts] *prep.* in view of, considering.

Angestammt [an'ger-shtamt] *a.* inherited, hereditary.

Angestellte(r) [an'ger-shtell-te] *m.w.* employee, wage earner.

Angetan [an'ger-tahn] *a.* likely, suitable.

Angewandt [an'ger-vant] *a.* applied (*science*).

Angewöhnen [an'ger-ver-nen] *vt. r.* to accustom.

Angewohnheit [an'ger-vohn-hite] *nf.* habit.

Angiessen [an'geese-en] *vt. ir.* to join by casting; **wie angegossen** a perfect fit.

Angleichen [an'gly-shen] *vt. ir.* to approximate.

Angler [ang'lerr] *nm.* (-) angler.

Angliedern [an'glee-derrn] *vt.* to attach to, to join, affiliate, annex.

Angliederung [an'glee-der-röong] *nf.* joining, annexation.

Anglotzen [an'glot-sen] *vt.* to stare at.

Angreifbar [an'grife-barr] *a.* liable to attack, vulnerable.

Angreifen [an'grife-en] *vt. ir.* to attack, seize, undertake, impair, injure.

Angreifend [an'grife-ent] *a.* fatiguing, tiring, attacking.

Angreifer [an'grife-err] *nm.* (-) aggressor.

Angrenzen [an'grent-sen] *vt.* to border on.

Angrenzend [an'grent-sent] *a.* adjacent.

Angriff [an'grif] *nm.* (-e) attack, aggression; **-sakt** *nm.* act of aggression; **-skrieg** *nm.* aggressive war.

Angst [angst] *nf.* (Ängste) anxiety, dread.

Ängstigen [eng'stig-en] *vt.* to distress.

Ängstlich [eng-stlish] *a.* anxious, timid, scrupulous.

Ängstlichkeit [eng'stlish-kite] *nf.* anxiousness, timidity, scrupulousness.

Anhaben [an'hah-ben] *vt. ir.* to have on.

Anhaften [an'haf-ten] *vi.* to adhere.

Anhaken [an'hah-ken] *vt.i.* to hook on, tick off.

Anhalt [an'halt] *nm.* (-e) prop, support, foothold, check; **-slager** *n.* concentration camp.

Anhalten [an'hal-ten] *vt.i. ir.* to restrain, stop, continue, solicit.

Anhaltend [an'hal-tent] *a.* constant, continuous, steady.

Anhaltspunkt [an'halts-pöönkt] *nm.* (-e) essential fact, clue, guide.

Anhang [an'hang] nm. (Anhänge) appendix, addition, codicil, adherents.

Anhängegerät [an'heng-er-ger-rate] n. (-e) portable set (rad.).

Anhangen [an'hang-en] vi. ir. to hang upon, adhere to.

Anhängen [an'heng-en] vt. to hang up, attach, append, annex, palm off, slander.

Anhänger [an'heng-err] nm. (-er) adherent, trailer.

Anhänge-schloss n. (-schlösser) padlock; -wagen nm. trailer, side-car (aut.).

Anhängig [an'heng-ish] a. pending; - machen to bring (legal action).

Anhänglich [an'heng-lish] a. attached, affectionate.

Anhänglichkeit [an'henglish-kite] nf. attachment.

Anhängsel [an'heng-zel] n. appendage.

Anhauch [an'howch] nm. (-e) touch, tinge.

Anhauchen [an'how-chen] vt. to breathe upon, inspire, scold.

Anhäufen [ah'hoi-fen] vt. to amass. (accumulation.

Anhäufung [an'hoi-fen] nf.

Anheben [an'hay-ben] vt. ir. to begin.

Anheften [an'hef-ten] vt. to fasten, pin, stitch.

Anheimelnd [an'hime-elnt] a. comfortable, cosy.

Anheim'fallen [an-hime'falen] vi. to fall to; -stellen vt. to leave to one's discretion.

Anheischig [an'hy-shish] a. under an obligation.

Anheizen [an'hite-sen] vi. to light a fire.

Anherrschen [an'hairr-shen] vt. to bully. (incite.

Anhetzen [an'het-sen] vt. to

Anhöhe [an'her-er] nf. hill, eminence.

Anhören [an'her-ren] vt. to listen, perceive by listening.

Anilin [an-i-leen'] n. aniline; -farbe nf. aniline dye.

Animieren [an-i-mee'ren] vt. to encourage, urge on.

Anis [a-neece'] nm. anis, aniseed.

Ankämpfen [an'kemp-fen] vi. to struggle against.

Ankauf [an'kowf] nm. (Ankäufe) purchase.

Ankaufen [an'kow-fen] vt. to purchase.

Anker [ang'kerr] nm. (-) anchor, armature (el.); -mine nf. moored mine; -platz nm. (-plätze) berth; -tau n. (-e) cable; -taumine nf. moored mine.

Ankern [ang'kerrn] vt.i. to anchor, moor.

Anketten [an'ketn] vt. to chain to, up.

Anklage [an'clah-ger] nf. accusation, charge (law); -bank nf. (-bänke) dock; -schrift nf. (bill of) indictment.

Anklagen [an'clah-gen] vt. to accuse, charge, denounce.

Ankläger [an'clay-gerr] nm. (-) accuser, plaintiff.

Anklammern [an'clam-errn] vt. to clamp; i.r. to cling to.

Anklang [an'clang] nm. (Anklänge) accord, approval

Ankleben [an'clay-ben] vt.i. to stick on, up, adhere, gum on.

Ankleiden [an'clide-en] vt. to dress.

Anklingeln [an'cling-eln] vt. to ring up, phone.

Anklopfen [an'clop-fen] vt. to knock at.

Anknöpfen [an'cnur-pfen] vt. to button.

Anknüpfen [an'cnew-pfen] vt. to fasten on, tie, begin.

Anknüpfung [an'cnew-pfoong] nf. fastening, beginning; -spunkt nm. (-e) starting point.

Ankommen [an'comm-en] vt. ir. to arrive, depend (on).

Ankömmling [an'kerm-ling] nm. (-e) new-comer.

Ankoppeln [an'cop-eln] vt. to couple (tec.).

Ankopplung [an'cop-lŏŏng] nf. coupling (tec.).

Ankreiden [an'cry-den] vt. to chalk on, mark.

Ankündigen [an'kewn-di-gen] vt. to announce, advertise, notify.

Ankündigung [an'kewn-di-gŏŏng] nf. notification, proclamation, advertisement.

Ankunft [an'kŏŏnft] nf. arrival.

Ankurbeln [an'koorr-beln] vt. to crank up, start (aut.).

Anlage [an'lah-ger] nf. disposition, lay-out, park, plant (com.), investment (com.); pl. gardens, talent.

Anlage-kapital n. (-ien) business capital; -papiere n.pl. investment stocks, shares.

Anlanden [an'lan-den] vi. to land (nav.). [arrive at.

Anlangen [an'lang-en] vi. to

Anlass [an'lass] nm. (Anlässe) occasion, motive.

Anlassen [an'lass-en] vt. ir. to leave on, set going, to temper (tec.); r. to appear.

Anlasser [an'lass-err] nm. (-) self-starter (aut.); resistance (el.).

Anlässlich [an'less-lish] prep. on the occasion of.

Anlasswiderstand [an'lass-vee-derr-shtant] nm. resistance (el.).

Anlauf [an'lowf] nm. (Anläufe) rise, onset, run, take-off (av.).

Anlaufen [an'low-fen] vi. ir. to run against, start, rise; t. to call at (nav.).

Anläuten [an'loy-ten] vt. to ring up.

Anlegen [an'lay-gen] vt. to put on, against, aim at, construct, invest (com.); i. to lie alongside.

Anlege-stelle nf. -platz nm. landing place.

Anlegung [an'lay-gŏŏng] nf. construction, fixing, planning, investment (com.).

Anlehen [an'lay-en] n. loan.

Anlehnen [an'lay-nen] vt. to lean against, leave ajar.

Anleihe [an'ly-er] nf. loan; -papier n. loan.

Anleiten [an'lite-en] vt. to direct, instruct, train.

Anleitung [an'lite-ŏŏng] nf. direction, instruction, guide (book).

Anliegen [an'lee-gen] vi. to lie beside (ship), fit well, be adjacent to; n. request, entreaty.

Anlernen [an'lairr-nen] vt. to teach, instruct, train.

Anlocken [an'lock-en] vt. to decoy, entice.

Anlockung [an'lok-ŏŏng] nf. enticement. [solder on.

Anlöten [an'lur-ten] vt. to

Anlügen [an'lyoo-gen] vt. to lie to, impose upon.

Anmachen [an'mach-en] vt. to attach, add to, kindle.

Anmarsch [an'mahrsh] nm. (Anmärsche) advance (mil.).

Anmassen [an'mah-sen] vr. to arrogate, presume.

Anmassend [an'mah-sent] a. arrogant.

Anmassung [an'mah-sŏŏng] nf. presumption, insolence.

Anmelden [an'mel-den] vi. to announce, apply, report, declare (customs).

Anmeldung [an'mel-dŏŏng] nf. announcement, application, reporting. [to note.

Anmerken [an'mairr-ken] vt.

Anmerkung [an'mairr-kŏŏng] nf. note, remark.

Anmessen [an'mess-en] vt. ir. to measure, fit.

Anmustern [an'mŏŏs-terrn] vt. to enrol; i. sign on.

Anmut [an'mŏŏt] nf. grace, charm.

Anmutig [an'mōō-tish] a. graceful, charming.

Annähen [an'nay-en] vt. to sew on.

Annähern [an'nay-errn] vi. to approximate.

Annähernd [an'nay-errnt] a. approximate.

Annahme [an'nah-mer] nf. acceptance, assumption.

Annehmbar [an'name-barr] a. acceptable, admissible.

Annehmen [an'name-en] vt. ir. to accept, receive, suppose, assume, adopt (child); r. to take charge of.

Annehmlichkeit [an'name-lish-kite] nf. amenity, pleasantness.

Annektieren [a-nek-tee'ren] vt. to annex.

Annexion [a-nek-si-ohn'] nf. annexation.

Annonce [a-nong'tser] nf. advertisement.

Annoncieren [a-nong-tseer'en] vt. to advertise.

Annullieren [a-nōō-leer'en] vt. to cancel.

Annullierung [a-nōō-leer'roong] nf. cancellation.

Anode [a-noh'der] nf. anode, plate; -nbatterie nf. high tension battery; -nspannung nf. anode voltage.

Anonym [a-non-eem'] a. anonymous.

Anordnen [an'orrd-nen] vt. to arrange, regulate.

Anordnung [an'orrd-nōōng] nf. arrangement, regulation.

Anpacken [an'pack-en] vt. to grasp.

Anpassen [an'pass-en] vt. to fit on, adapt; vr. to conform.

Anpassung [an'pass-ōōng] nf. adaption, adjustment.

Anpassungsfähig a. adaptable; -keit nf. adaptability.

Anpeilen [an'pile-en] vi. to take a bearing (nav., av.).

Anpflanzen [an'pflant-sen] vt. to plant, cultivate.

Anpflanzung [an'pflant-sōōng] nf. plantation.

Anpochen [an'poch-en] vt. to knock (at). [shock.

Anprall [an'prall] nm. collision,

Anprallen [an'prall-en] vi. to strike against.

Anpreisen [an'prize-en] vt. to praise, boost.

Anprobe [an'probe-er] nf. trying-on, fitting.

Anprobieren [an'pro-bee-ren] vt. to try on.

Anraten [an'rah-ten] vt. ir. to advise.

Anrauchen [an'rowch-en] vt. to begin to smoke, light, smoke in (pipe).

Anrechnen [an'resh-nen] vt. to charge, impute, value.

Anrechnung [an'resh-nōōng] nf. charge, debit (com.).

Anrecht [an'resht] n. right.

Anrede [an'ray-der] nf. address.

Anreden [an'ray-den] vt. to accost, address.

Anregen [an'ray-gen] vt. to stir up, stimulate, set going, inspire.

Anregend [an'ray-gent] a. stimulating, suggestive.

Anregung [an'ray-gōōng] nf. stimulation, suggestion, inspiration.

Anreihen [an'ry-en] vt. to string; i. to rank, queue.

Anreissen [an'rice-en] vt. ir. to tear off, sketch.

Anreiten [an'rite-en] vi. ir. to break in (horse).

Anreiz [an'rights] nm. (-ungen) incentive, provocation.

Anreizen [an'right-sen] vt. to provoke, spur on, incite.

Anrennen [an'ren-en] vt. ir. to run against, charge.

Anrichte [an'rish-ter] nf. dresser, sideboard.

Anrichten [an'rish-ten] vt. to cause, prepare (food), serve (meal), sight (gun).

Anrollen [an'roll-en] vi. to roll against, taxi (plane).

Anrüchig [an'ryoo-shish] a. notorious.

Anrücken [an'ryoo-ken] vi. to move forward, approach, advance (mil.).

Anruf [an'roof] nm. appeal, call (ph.).

Anrufen [an'roo-fen] vt. ir. to hail, invoke, appeal to, ring up, phone, call (rad.).

Anrühren [an'ryoo-ren] vt. to touch, mix (food).

Ans = an das.

Ansage [an'sah-ger] nf. announcement (rad.).

Ansagen [an'sah-gen] vt. to announce, call (cards).

Ansager [an'zah-gerr] nm. announcer (rad.).

Ansammeln [an'zam-eln] vi. to collect.

Ansammlung [an'zam-oong] nf. accumulation, crowd, collection, concentration (troops).   [resident.

Ansässig [an'zess-ish] a.

Ansatz [an'zats] nm (Ansätze) deposit, start, tendency, charge, mouthpiece, valuation, attachment (tec.).   [tion (tec.).

Ansaug [an'zowk] nm. induc-

Anschaffen [an'shaf-en] vt. to procure, provide, purchase.

Anschaffung [an'shaf-oong] nf. acquisition, provision, purchase, supply.

Anschalten [an'shal-ten] vt. switch on, plug in.

Anschauen [an'show-en] vt. to look at, regard.

Anschaulich [an'show-lish] a. evident, intuitive.

Anschauung [an'show-oong] nf. contemplation, point of view, opinion, intuition.

Anschein [an'shine] nm. appearance; allem – nach to all appearance.

Anscheinend [an'shine-ent] a, ad. apparent(ly).

Anschicken [an'shick-en] vr. to prepare for, set about.

Anschiessen [an'shee-sen] vt. ir. to wound; i. to rush along, shoot first.

Anschirren [an'shi-ren] vt. to harness.

Anschlag [an'shlahk] nm. (Anschläge) estimate, design, poster, attempted murder; -zettel nm. poster, placard.

Anschlagen [an'shlah-gen] vt. ir. to strike against, estimate, nail up, stick up; i. strike, take effect, bark, strike up.

Anschleppen [an'shlep-en] vt. to drag along.

Anschliessen [an'shlee-sen] vt. ir. to join, fasten, chain, add, affiliate, connect (el.), enclose; i. fit; r. join, agree.

Anschluss [an'shlös] nm. (Anschlüsse) addition, junction, connection (rl, el.), supply (water, etc.), union (with Germany), contact (mil.); -linie nf. branch-line; -gleis n. siding.

Anschmelzen [an'shmelt-sen] vt. ir. to solder; i. melt.

Anschmieden [an'shmeed-en] vt. to weld together, fetter.

Anschmiegen [an'shmee-gen] vt. to join closely; r. fit well, nestle to.

Anschmieren [an'shmee-ren] vt. to daub, cheat.

Anschnallen [an'shnall-en] vt. to buckle on.

Anschneiden [an'shnide-en] vt. ir. to carve, broach (subject).

Anschnitt [an'shnit] nm. (-e) first cut, retail (com.).

Anschove [an-shoh'ver] nf. anchovy.

Anschrauben [an'shrow-ben] vt. to screw on.

Anschreiben [an'shribe-en] vt. ir. to write on, note, charge to, debit (com.).

Anschreien [an'shry-en] vt. ir. to shout at.

Anschrift [an'shrift] nf. address.

Anschuldigen [an'shōōl-di-gen] vt. to accuse.

Anschuldigung [an'shōōl-di-gōōng] nf. accusation.

Anschüren [an'shyōō-ren] vt. to stir up.

Anschwärmen [an'shvairr-men] vt. to idolize.

Anschwärzen [an'shvairr-tsen] vt. to blacken, defame, run down.

Anschwärzung [an'shvairr-tsōōng] nf. defamation, slander.

Anschwellen [an'shvell-en] vi. ir. to swell (up).

Anschwindeln [an'shvin-deln] vt. to swindle, defraud.

Ansehen [an'zay-en] vt. ir. to look at, respect, consider; - für take for.

Ansehen [an'zay-en] n. esteem, reputation, appearance, authority.

Ansehnlich [an'zane-lish] a. fine, considerable.

Ansetzen [an'zet-sen] vt. to apply, put on, add to, charge, fix; t. to try, begin.

Ansicht [an'zisht] nf. sight, view, opinion, inspection; zur - on approval; -skarte nf. picture post-card; -ssendung nf. consignment on approval (com.).

Ansiedeln [an'zeed-eln] vt. to settle, colonize.

Ansiedler [an'zeed-lerr] nm. (-) settler.

Ansiedlung [an'zeed-lōōng] nf. settlement.

Ansinnen [an'zinn-en] n. demand.

Anspannen [an'shpan-en] vt. to yoke, harness, strain, stretch.

Anspannung [an'shpan-ōōng] nf. stretching, strain, exertion.

Anspielen [an'shpeel-en] vt.

to play first, lead, allude to, hint at.

Anspielung [an'shpeel-ōōng] nf. allusion, reference, hint.

Anspinnen [an'shpin-en] vt. ir. to plot; i. begin, originate.

Anspitzen [an'shpit-sen] vt. to point, sharpen.

Ansporn [an'shporrn] nm. stimulus, inducement.

Anspornen [an'shporr-nen] vt. to spur on.

Ansprechen [an'shpresh-en] vt. ir. to address, interest.

Ansprengen [an'shpreng-en] vi. to gallop up.

Anspringen [an'shpring-en] vi. ir. to come running along, start (aut.).

Anspruch [an'shprōōch] nm. (Ansprüche) claim, pretension.

Anspruchs-los a. unassuming; -voll a. pretentious, fussy.

Anspucken [an'shpōōk-en] vt. to spit at.

Anspulen [an'shpōōl-en] vt. [reel, wind.

Anspülen [an'shpew-len] vt. to wash up (from the sea).

Anstacheln [an'shtach-eln] vt. to goad.

Anstalt [an'shtalt] nf. institution, preparation, establishment, arrangements.

Anstand [an'shtand] nm. (Anstände) pause, objection, demeanour, decency, decorum.

Anständig [an'shten-dish] a. proper, decent.

Anständigkeit [an'shten-dish-kite] nf. propriety decency.

Anstandslos [an'shtants-lohs] ad. without hesitation.

Anstapeln [an'shtah-peln] vt. to stack up.

Anstarren [an'shtarr-en] vt. to stare at. [stead of.

Anstatt [an'shtat] prep. in-

Anstaunen [an'shtow-nen] vt. to gaze at in astonishment.

Anstechen [an'shtesh-en] vt. ir. to prick, broach.

Ansteckdose [an'shtek-doh-zer] *nf.* wall plug, socket (*el.*).

Anstecken [an'shtek-en] *vt.* to stick on, fasten on, infect, light. [*a.* infectious.

Ansteckend [an'shtek-ent]

Ansteckung [an'shtek-ōong] *nf.* infection.

Anstehen [an'shtay-en] *vi. ir.* to fit, hesitate, stand in a queue.

Ansteigen [an'shti-gen] *vt. ir.* to ascend, rise, increase.

Anstell'en [an'shtell-en] *vt.* to do, cause, appoint, engage, start (*engine*); *r.* act, pretend; **-ig** *a.* handy, skilful; **-ung** *nf.* appointment, engagement, post.

Ansteuern [an'shtoy-errn] *vi.* to make, head for.

Anstich [an'shtish] *nm.* broaching. [ascent.

Anstieg [an'shteek] *nm.* (-e)

Anstift'en [an'shtif-ten] *vt.* to cause, incite, instigate; **-er** *nm.* instigator, author; **-ung** *nf.* instigation.

Anstimmen [an'shtim-en] *vt.* to strike up (*song*).

Anstoss [an'shtohs] *nm.* (An-stösse) shock, impulse, impediment, kick-off (*football*), offence; **-druckschalter** *nm.* flush-pressure switch (*el.*).

Anstossen [an'shtoh-sen] *vt. ir.* to knock, strike against; *i.* to bump against, clink glasses, adjoin, give offence.

Anstössig [an'shter-sich] *a., ad.* offensive(ly), indecent(ly); **-keit** *nf.* offensiveness, indecency.

Anstrahlen [an'shtrah-len] *vt.* to flood-light, shine upon, smile at. [to strive for.

Anstreben [an'shtray-ben] *vt.*

Anstreichen [an'shtrich-en] *vt. ir.* to paint or to underline; weiss- to white-wash.

Anstreicher [an'shtrish-err] *nm.* (-) house-painter.

Anstreng'en [an'shtreng-en] *vt.* to strain, exert, bring (*action*); **-end** *a.* trying, tiring; **-ung** strain, exertion.

Anstrich [an'shtrish] *nm.* (-e) coat of paint, varnish, shade, air, appearance.

Anstricken [an'shtrick-en] *vt.* to knit on to; Strümpfe - to foot stockings.

Anströmen [an'shtrer-men] *vi.* to flow, flock towards.

Anstückeln [an'shtew-keln] *vt.* to piece (together), patch.

Ansturm [an'shtōorm] *nm.* (Anstürme) onset, rush, attack.

Anstürmen [an'shtewr-men] *vt.* to charge, storm.

Ansuchen [an'zōōch-en] *vt.* to apply for, request; *n.* application, petition.

Antasten [an'tast-en] *vt.* to touch, injure, infringe.

Anteil [an'tile] *nm.* (-e) share, dividend, interest, sympathy; **-haber** *nm.* (-) shareholder, partner (*com.*); **-nahme** *nf.* sympathy; **-schein** *nm.* (-e) share certificate, scrip (*com.*).

Antelephonieren [an'tel-e-fo-neer-ren] *vt.* to ring up.

Antenne [an'ten'er] *nf.* aerial; **-nkondensator** *nm.* aerial inductor; **-nkopplung** *nf.* aerial coupling condenser (*rad.*); **-nleitung** *nf.* aerial lead (*rad.*); **-nmast** *nm.* aerial mast (*rad.*).

Anthrazit [an-tra-tseet'] *n.* anthracite.

Antik [an-teek'] *a.* antique; **-e** *nf.* antique, antiquity.

Antiklopfmittel [an'ti-klopf-mitl] *n.* (-) anti-knock fuel.

Antimon [an-tim-ohn'] *n.* antimony.

Antiquar [an-ti-kvahr'] *nm.* second-hand bookseller, antiquary; **-isch** *a.* second-hand.

Antisemiti'sch [an-ti-ze-mee'tish] *a.* anti-Semitic; **-smus** *nm.* anti-Semitism.

Antiseptisch [an'ti-zep'tish] a. antiseptic.

Antlitz [ant'lits] n. (-e) countenance, face.

Antrag [an'trahk] nm. (Anträge) proposal, offer, motion (Parliament); -en vt. ir. to offer, propose.

Antreffen [an'treff-en] vt. ir. to meet, come across.

Antreiben [an'tribe-en] vt. ir. to drive on, urge on; i. drift, float ashore.

Antreten [an'tray-ten] vt. ir. to take over, start, begin, set out (journey); i. fall in (mil.).

Antrieb [an'treep] nm. (-e) impulse, inducement, rotation, power (el.); aus eigenem – spontaneously; -welle nf. propeller shaft, driving shaft (aut.).

Antritt [an'trit] nm. (-e) beginning, entrance (on), first step.

Antun [an'tōōn] vt. ir. to put on, inflict, do (injury).

Antwort [ant'vorrt] nf. answer, reply; -schein nm. reply coupon; -welle nf. answering wave (rad.).

Antworten [ant'vorr-ten] vi. to answer.

Anvertrauen [an'furr-trow-en] vt. to entrust to.

Anverwandt [an'furr-vant] a. related, allied, cognate.

Anwachsen [an'vax-en] vi. ir. to increase, to grow, swell, take root (plants).

Anwalt [an'valt] nm. (-e) solicitor, lawyer, defender.

Anwandeln [an'van-deln] vt. to seize, attack, come over; -lung nf. fit, attack, impulse.

Anwärmen [an'varr-men] vt. to warm (slightly).

Anwärter [an'vairr-terr] nm. (-) candidate, cadet, trainee (mil. etc.).

Anwartschaft [an'varrt-shaft] nf. reversion.

Anwehen [an'vay-en] vt. to blow upon, come over.

Anweisbar [an'vice-barr] a. assignable.

Anweise'n [an'vize-en] vt. ir. to assign, designate, direct, instruct, remit, transfer (money); -schein nm. assignment form; -ung nf. instruction, order, direction, remittance, draft, cheque (com.), money-order.

Anwendbar [an'vent-barr] a. applicable, available, practicable, adapted; -keit nf. applicability, suitability.

Anwend'en [an'ven-den] vt. ir. to use, employ, adopt; -ung nf. application, use.

Anwerb'en [an'vairr-ben] vt. ir. to recruit, raise (troops); -ung nf. enlistment.

Anwerfen [an'vairr-fen] vt. ir. to throw on, at, start (aut.).

Anwesen'd [an'vay-zent] a. present; -heit nf. presence.

Anwidern [an'vee-derrn] vt. to disgust.

Anwinken [an'ving-ken] vt. to beckon to.

Anwuchs [an'vōōx] nm. (Anwüchse) increase.

Anwurf [an'voorrf] nm. (Anwürfe) rough-cast.

Anwurzeln [an'vōorr-tseln] vi. r. to take root.

Anzahl [ant'sahl] nf. number; -en vt. to pay on account; -ung nf. instalment, payment on account. [broach.

Anzapfen [ant'sap-fen] vt. to

Anzeichen [ant'si-shen] n. sign, indication.

Anzeichnen [ant'sish-nen] vt. to mark.

Anzeige [ant'si-ger] nf. intimation, announcement, advertisement, denunciation; -annahme nf. advertising office; -tarif nm. advertising rates; -vorrichtung nf. indicator, detector.

Anzeig'en [ant'sigen] vt. to announce, intimate, advertise, denounce, complain about; -er *nm.* indicator, marker, denouncer, advertiser.

Anzetteln [ant'set-ein] *vt.* to conspire, instigate.

Anziehen [ant'see-en] *vt. ir.* to put on, pull, tighten, attract, interest; *r.* dress; *i.* rise (prices); **~d** *a.* attractive.

Anziehung [ant'see-ōōng] *nf.* attraction; **~skraft** *nf.* power of attraction.

Anzug [ant'sōōk] *nm.* (Anzüge) suit of clothes, costume; im ~ approaching.

Anzüglich [ant'sȳōk-lish] *a.* sarcastic, personal, suggestive; **~keit** *nf.* offensiveness, insult.

Anzünden [ant'sȳōōn-den] *vt.* to light, kindle; **~er** *nm.* (~) lighter.

Anzweifeln [ant'svife-eln] *vt.* to cast doubt on. [stylish.

Apart [a-parrt'] *a.* unusual,

Apfel [ap'fel] *n.m.* (Äpfel) apple; **~sine** *nf.* orange; **~wein** *nm.* cider.

Apostel [a-pos'tel] *nm.* (~) apostle; **~geschichte** *nf.* Acts of the Apostles. [(~e) apostrophe.

Apostroph [a-po-strohf'] *nm.*

Apotheke [a-po-tay'ker] *nf.* pharmacy, chemist's shop, dispensary.

Apotheker [a-po-tay'kerr] *nm.* (~) pharmacist, chemist, druggist; **~waren** *nf.* drugs.

Apparat [a-pa-raht'] *nm.* (~e) apparatus, camera, telephone; am ~ bleiben to hold the line (ph.).

Appell [a-pel'] *nm.* (~e) roll-call, parade, appeal; **~ation** (~) appeal (law); **~ieren** *vt.* to appeal (law).

Appetit [a-pet-eet'] *nm.* appetite; **~lich** *a.* tempting, dainty.

Appretieren [a-prai-teer'ren] *vt.* to finish (com.); **~ur** *nf.* finish, glaze (com.).

Approbieren [a-pro-beer'ren] *vt.* to approve.

Aprikose [a-pri-koh'zer] *nf.* apricot.

April [a-pril'] *nm.* April.

Aquarell [a-kva-rel'] *n.* (~e) water-colour.

Aquatinta [a-kva-tin'ter] *nm.* aquatint engraving.

Äquator [ay-kvah'torr] *nm.* equator.

Arbeit [arr'bite] *nf.* work, task, labour; **~en** *vt. i. r.* to work.

Arbeiter [arr'bite-err] *nm.* (~) worker, workman; **~austand** *nm.* strike; **~mangel** *nm.* labour shortage; **~stand** *nm.* working class.

Arbeit-geber *nm.* employer; **~nehmer** *nm.* employee, wage earner; **~sam** *a.* industrious.

Arbeits-amt *n.* labour exchange; **~anzug** *nm.* dungarees *pl.* overalls *pl.*; **~dienst** *nm.* (compulsory) labour service; **~einsatz** *nm.* direction of workers, (supply of) manpower; **~fähig** *a.* fit for work, able-bodied; **~gemeinschaft** *nf.* study group; **~kräfte** *f.pl.* workers *pl.* labour; **~los** *a.* out of work; **~losigkeit** *nf.* unemployment; **~ministerium** *n.* ministry of labour; **~nachweis** *nm.* labour exchange; **~scheu** *a.* work-shy; **~sperre** *nf.* lock-out; **~trupp** *nm.* fatigue party; **~unfähig** *a.* unfit for work; **~zeug** *n.* tools, working clothes.

Arasche [arr'sher] *nf.* ark.

Architekt [arr'shi-tect'] *m.w.* (~) architect; **~ur** *nf.* architecture.

Archiv [arr-sheef'] *n.* (~e) archives, records; **~ar** *nm.* (~e) keeper of archives.

Arg [arrk] *a.* bad, severe, dreadful; *n.* deceit, malice.

Ärger [airr'gerr] *nm.* vexation worry; **~lich** *a.* vexatious, annoying, vexed, angry; **~n** *vt. r.* to vex, worry, annoy; **~nis** *n.* (~se) vexation, scandal.

Arglist [arrk'list] *nf.* cunning, malice; **~ig** *a.* cunning, deceitful.

Arglos [arrk'lohs] a. unsuspecting, innocent; **-igkeit** nf. guilelessness.

Argwohn [arrk'vone] nm. suspicion.

Argwöhn'en [arrk'ver-nen] vt. to suspect; **-isch** a. suspicious.

Aristokrat [a-ris-to-kraht'] mw. aristocrat; **-ie** nf. aristocracy; **-isch** a. aristocratic.

Arithmetisch [a-rit-may'-tish] a. arithmetical.

Arktisch [arrk'tish] a. arctic.

Arm [arrm] a. poor.

Arm [arrm] nm. (-e) arm, branch; **-band** n. bracelet; **-banduhr** nf. wrist-watch; **-binde** nf. armlet, sling; **-schiene** nf. splint; **-spiegel** nm. arm badge.

Armatur [arr-ma-toor'] nf. armature (el.); **-enbrett** n. dashboard (aut.), instrument panel (av.).

Armee [arr-may'] nf. army; **-befehl** nm. army orders; **-briefstelle** nf. army post-office; **-korps** n. army corps; **-oberkommando** n. army high command; **-schwester** nf. army nurse.

Ärmel [airr'mel] nm. (-) sleeve.

Armen-haus [arr'men] n. alms-house, poorhouse, workhouse; **-pflege** nf. poor relief.

Armier'en [arr-meer'ren] vt. to arm, equip; **-t** a. armed, reinforced. [wretched.

Ärmlich [airrm'lish] a. needy.

Armselig [arrm-zay'lish] a. miserable, **-keit** nf. wretchedness.

Armut [arr'moot] nf. poverty.

Arrest [a-rest'] nm. (-e) arrest, seizure, detention, confinement; **-ant** prisoner, arrested person; **-lokal** n. lock-up.

Art [arrt] nf. manner, way, species, kind, category, (good) manners.

Arten [arr'ten] vt.i. to take after, be of a certain disposition.

Artfremd [arrt'fremt] a. alien.

Artig [arr-tish] a. well behaved, good, kind; ad. graciously; **-keit** nf. good behaviour, politeness, compliment.

Artikel [arr-teekl'] nm. (-) article.

Artillerie [arr-til-er-ree'] nf. artillery; **-flugzeug** n. spotting aircraft; **vorbereitung** nf. artillery preparation.

Artillerist [arr-til-er-rist'] m.w. artilleryman, gunner.

Artischocke [arr-ti-shock'er] nf. artichoke.

Arznei [arrts-ny'] nf. medicine; **-kunde** nf. pharmacy; **-mittel** n. medicine, drug; **-pflanze** nf. (medicinal) herb.

Arzt [arrtst] nm. (Ärzte) doctor, physician. [doctor.

Ärztin [airrts'tin] nf. lady

Ärztlich [airrtst'lish] a. medical.

As [ass] n. A flat.

As [ass] n. (Asse) ace.

Asbest [ass-best'] nm. asbestos.

Asche [ash'er] nf. ashes, cinder; **-nbahn** nf. cinder-track; **-nbecher** nm. ash-tray; **-rmittwoch** nm. Ash Wednesday. [aseptic.

Aseptisch [ah'zep-tish] a.

Asphalt [ass-falt'] nm. asphalt; **-ieren** vt. to asphalt; **-strasse** nf. asphalt road.

Aspirin [a-spi-reen'] n. aspirin. [assistant.

Assistent [ass-iss-tent'] m.w.

Assortieren [ass-orr-teer'ren] vt. to assort.

Ast [ast] nm. (Äste) bough; **-verhau** n. abatis (mil.); **-werk** n. branches.

Asthma [ast'mah] n. asthma.

Astronom [ass-tro-nome'] m.w. astronomer; **-ie** nf. astronomy.

Asyl [a-zeel'] n. asylum, sanctuary.

Atelier [a-tel-yai'] *n.* studio.

Atem [ah'tem] *nm.* breath; -anlage *nf.* oxygen equipment (*av.*); -holen *n.* respiration; -los *a.* breathless, out of breath; -pause *nf.* breathing space; -zug *nm.* breath.

Äther [ay'terr] *nm.* ether.

Athlet [at-lait'] *m.w.* athlete; -ik *nf.* athletics. [atlas.

Atlas [at'las] *nm.* (Atlanten)

Atlas [at'las] *nm.* satin.

Atmen [aht'men] *vt.i.* to breathe.

Atmosphär'e [at-mo-sfair'er] *nf.* atmosphere; -isch *a.* atmospheric.

Atmung [aht'mŏong] *nf.* respiration.

Atom [a-tohm'] *n.* (-e) atom; -bombe *nf.* atom(ic) bomb; -energie *nf.* atomic energy; -spaltung *nf.* splitting of the atom.

Attentat [a-ten-taht'] *n.* (-e) attempt on a person's life.

Attest [a-test'] *n.* (-e) certificate.

Attrappe [a-trap'er] *nf.* dummy, trap.

Ätzbar [ets'bahrr] *a.* corrosive.

Ätzen [et'sen] *vt.* to corrode, etch.

Ätz-kalk *nm.* quicklime; -kunst *nf.* etching; -mittel *n.* caustic. [whoever.

Auch *cj.* *ad.* also, even; wer —

Audienz [ow-dee-ents'] *nf.* audience.

Audionröhre [ow-dee-ohn'rer-rer'] *nf.* detector valve (*rad.*).

Auditorium [ow-di-toh'ri-ŏŏm] *n.* (Auditorien) lecture room.

Aue [ow'er] *nf.* meadow.

Auf [owf] *pr.* on, in, at, to; *ad.* up; *inter* up!

Aufarbeiten [owf'arr-bite-en] *vt.* to work upon, use up, clear off, renovate.

Aufatmen [owf'aht-men] *vi.*

to draw a deep breath, breathe freely (again).

Aufbahren [owf'bah-ren] *vt.* to lay out (*corpse*).

Aufbau [owf'bow] *nm.* (Aufbauten) building, construction, superstructure (*tec.*).

Aufbauen [owf'bow-en] *vt.* to erect, build (up).

Aufbäumen [owf'boy-men] *vr.* to rear, revolt, rebel.

Aufbauschen [owf'bow-shen] *vt.* to exaggerate, puff up.

Aufbehalten [owf'ber-hal-ten] *vt. ir.* to keep on, open.

Aufbersten [owf'bairr-sten] *vi.* to burst open.

Aufbessern [owf'bess-ern] *vt.* to mend, increase.

Aufbewahren [owf'ber-vah-ren] *vt.* to store up, keep, preserve.

Aufbewahrung [owf'ber-vah-rŏŏng] *nf.* storage, preservation, (safe) keeping.

Aufbieten [owf'bee-ten] *vt. ir.* to summon, proclaim, exert, raise (*troops*).

Aufbinden [owf'bin-den] *vt. ir.* to tie on, up, untie, impose upon.

Aufblähen [owf'blay-en] *vt.* to puff up; *vr.* boast.

Aufblasen [owf'blah-zen] *vt. ir.* to inflate, blow up.

Aufbleiben [owf'blibe-en] *vi. ir.* to remain open, up.

Aufblicken [owf'blick-en] *vi.* to look up.

Aufblühen [owf'blyŏŏ-en] *vi.* to blossom, blossom out, flourish.

Aufbrauchen [owf'browch-en] *vt.* to use up.

Aufbrausen [owf'brow-zen] *vt.* to flare up, rage, effervesce; -d *a.* effervescent, hot-tempered.

Aufbrechen [owf'bresh-en] *vt. ir.* to break open, up, prize open; *i.* burst open, start, set out. [*vt.i.* to burn up.

Aufbrennen [owf'bren-

Aufbringen [owf'bring-en] *vt. ir.* to bring up, procure, irritate, raise (*funds*), capture (*ship*).

Aufbruch [owf'brooch] *nm.* (Aufbrüche) departure.

Aufbügeln [owf'bew-geln] *vt.* to iron.

Aufbürden [owf'byoorr-den] *vt.* to burden.

Aufbürsten [owf'byoorr-sten] *vt.* to brush up.

Aufdämmen [owf'dem-en] *vt.* to dam up.

Aufdämmern [owf'dem-errn] *vi.* to dawn upon.

Aufdecken [owf'dek-en] *vt.* to spread, uncover, disclose.

Aufdecker [owf'dek-err] *nm.* (-) detector.

Aufdrängen [owf'dreng-en] *vt.* to press open, force upon; *r.* to intrude.

Aufdrehen [owf'dray-en] *vt.* to turn on, switch on, unscrew.

Aufdringen [owf'dring-en] *vi.r. ir.* to press upon, intrude.

Aufdringlich [owf'dring-lish] *a.* importunate, officious; **-keit** *nf.* importunity.

Aufdruck [owf'drook] *nm.* (im)print, stamp, surcharge (on *stamp*); **-en** *vt.* to imprint.

Aufdrücken [owf'dryook-en] *vt.* to press open, impress, press on.

Aufeinander [owf'ine-an-derr] *ad.* after each other, successively; **-folge** *nf.* succession, series; **-folgen** *vi.* follow (in order); **-folgend** *a.* consecutive.

Aufenthalt [owf'ent-halt] *nm.* (-e) stay, delay, stop, haunt; **-los** *a.* non-stop.

Auferlegen [owf'airr-lay-gen] *vt.* to impose upon.

Auferstehen [owf'airr-shtay-en] *vi. ir.* to rise from the dead; **-ung** *nf.* resurrection.

Auferwecken [owf'airr-veck-en] *vt.* to rise from the dead; **-ung** *nf.* raising from the dead.

Auferziehen [owf'air-tsee-en] *vt. ir.* to bring up.

Aufessen [owf'ess-en] *vt. ir.* to eat up, consume.

Auffahren [owf'fah-ren] *vi. ir.* to rise, start (up), get angry, run aground (*nav.*); *vt.* to drive up, bring up, park (*mil.*); **-d** *a.* hot tempered.

Auffahrt [owf'fahrrt] *nf.* ascent, drive.

Auffallen [owf'fall-en] *vi. ir.* to strike, fall upon; **-d** *a.* striking.

Auffang'en [owf'fang-en] *vt. ir.* to catch up, intercept (*rad., etc.*), round up (*mil.*); **-stelle** *nf.* reception centre. [to dye.

Auffärben [owf'fairr-ben] *vt. ir.*

Auffass'en [owf'fass-en] *vt.* to pick up, understand; **-ung** *nf.* comprehension grasp.

Auffindbar [owf'fint-bahrr] *a.* to be found.

Auffinden [owf'fin-den] *vt. ir.* to find out, trace.

Auffischen [owf'fish-en] *vt.* to fish out.

Aufflackern [owf'flack-errn] *vi.* to flare up.

Aufflammen [owf'flamm-en] *vi.* to flame up.

Auffliegen [owf'flee-gen] *vi. ir.* to fly open, up, explode.

Aufflug [owf'flook] *nm.* (Aufflüge) soaring, ascent.

Aufforder'n [owf'forr-dern] *vt.* to summon, challenge, ask; **-ung** *nf.* summons, invitation.

Aufforsten [owf'forr-sten] *v.* to afforest, plant trees.

Auffressen [owf'fress-en] *vt. ir.* to devour.

Auffrischen [owf'frish-en] *vt.* to freshen up, brush up.

Aufführ'en [owf'few-ren] *vt.* to perform, erect, specify, produce, quote; *r.* behave; **-ung** *nf.* performance, erection, specification, behaviour.

Auffüllen [owf'few-len] *vt.* to fill up, refill.

Aufgabe [owf'gah-ber] nf. task, giving up, exercise, problem, registration (luggage), posting (mail).

Aufgang [owf'gang] nm. (Aufgänge) rise, ascent.

Aufgeben [owf'gay-ben] vt. to give up, resign, give (order), register (luggage), post (mail), set (task).

Aufgebot [owf'ger-boht] n. (-e) notice, calling up (troops), publication (banns).

Aufgedunsen [owf'ger-döön-zen] a. puffed up, bloated.

Aufgehen [owf'gay-en] vi. ir. to rise, open, be spent, absorbed in, be consumed.

Aufgeklärt [owf'ger-klairrt] a. enlightened.

Aufgeld [owf'gelt] n. deposit, premium, agio (com.).

Aufgelegt [owf'ger-laikt] a. disposed.

Aufgeräumt [owf'ger-roimt] a. in good spirits.

Aufgeweckt [owf'ger-vekt] a. intelligent, bright.

Aufgiessen [owf'gee-sen] vt. ir. to pour on, infuse.

Aufgraben [owf'grah-ben] vt. ir. to dig up, trench.

Aufgreifen [owf'grife-en] vt. ir. to take up, snatch.

Aufgürten [owf'györ-ten] vt. to gird (on), tuck up.

Aufguss [owf'gööss] nm. (Aufgüsse) pouring on, infusion.

Aufhaben [owf'hah-ben] vt. ir. to have on, have to do.

Aufhacken [owf'hack-en] vt. to hew up, hack up.

Aufhaken [owf'hah-ken] vt. to hook up, unhook.

Aufhalsen [owf'hal-zen] vt. to saddle with.

Aufhalten [owf'hal-ten] vt. ir. to check, stop, detain, hold open, keep open; r. to stop, reside, stay, scold.

Aufhängen [owf'heng-en] vt. ir. to hang up.

Aufhaspeln [owf'hasp-eln] vt. to wind up, off.

Aufhäufen [owf'hoi-fen] vt. to heap up.

Aufheb'en [owf'hay-ben] vt. ir. to raise, lift, store up, keep, annul, cancel, abolish; -ens n. fuss; -ung nf. raising, lifting, suppression, abolition, repeal (law).

Aufheften [owf'hef-ten] vt. to pin up, unstitch.

Aufheitern [owf'hite-errn] vt. r. to brighten, cheer up.

Aufhelfen [owf'hel-fen] vt. ir. r. to help (up).

Aufhell'en [owf'hell-en] vt. to clear up, elucidate; -ung nf. elucidation.

Aufhetzen [owf'het-sen] vt. to incite, stir up, egg on.

Aufhissen [owf'hiss-en] vt. to hoist.

Aufholen [owf'hole-en] vt. to draw, haul up.

Aufhorchen [owf'horr-shen] vt. to listen (attentively).

Aufhören [owf'her-ren] vi. to stop, cease. [start, rouse.

Aufjagen [owf'yah-gen] vt. to

Aufjauchzen [owf'yowch-tsen] vi. to shout with joy.

Aufkauf [owf'kowf] nm. (Aufkäufe) purchase, buying up; -en vt. to buy up.

Aufkäufer [owf'kow-ferr] nm. (-) speculative buyer.

Aufkeimen [owf'kime-en] vi. to sprout, bud.

Aufklappen [owf'klap-en] vt. to open, turn up.

Aufkläre'n [owf'klairr-en] vt. r. to clear up, enlighten, explain, correct, to reconnoitre, scout (mil.); -r nm. scout, spotter (mil. av.); -ung nf. clearing up, enlightenment, scouting, reconnaissance (mil. av.). [to stick on.

Aufkleben [owf'klay-ben] vt.

Aufklinken [owf'kling-ken] vt. to unlatch.

Aufklopfen [owf'klop-fen] vt. to knock open, on.

Aufknöpfen [owf'knerp-fen] vt. to unbutton.

Aufknüpfen [owf'knewp-fen] vt. to tie, hang up.

Aufkommen [owf'kom-en] vi. ir. to rise, recover, prosper, come into use, make oneself responsible for.

Aufkrempen [owf'krem-pen] vt. to turn up.

Aufkündigen [owf'kewn-di-gen] vt. to give notice, recall, retract, renounce.

Auflachen [owf'lach-en] vi. to burst out laughing.

Aufladen [owf'lah-den] vt. ir. to load; -er nm. (-) packer, porter, supercharger (aut., etc.); -ung nf. loading, load, charge.

Auflage [owf'lah-ger] nf. edition, circulation (newspaper) tax, duty, impression, copy.

Auflager [owf'lah-gerr] n. (-) support, end-bearings (tec.); -n vt. to store (com.), superimpose (tec.); -ung nf. storage.

Auflassen [owf'lass-en] vt. ir. to leave open. [to lie in wait.

Auflauern [owf'low-ern] vi.

Auflauf [owf'lowf] nm. (Aufläufe) riot, pudding.

Auflaufen [owf'low-fen] vi. ir. to run up, rise, run aground.

Aufleben [owf'lay-ben] vi. to revive.

Auflegen [owf'lay-gen] vt. to issue, publish, impose; -ung nf. issuing, imposition.

Auflehnen [owf'lay-nen] vr. to lean against, rise against; -ung nf. insurrection.

Auflesen [owf'lay-zen] vt. ir. to pick up, glean.

Aufleuchten [owf'loish-ten] vi. to flash up.

Aufliegen [owf'lee-gen] vi. ir. to lie on, be on show (com.).

Auflockern [owf'lock-errn] vt. to loosen.

Auflodern [owf'loh-derrn] vi. to blaze up.

Auflösbar [owf'lerss-bahrr] a. soluble; -keit nf. solubility.

Auflösen [owf'ler-zen] vt. r. to loosen, solve, dissolve, decompose, disband (mil.); -ung nf. solution, dissolution, breaking up.

Aufmachen [owf'mahch-en] vt. to open, undo; r. rise, set out.

Aufmarsch [owf'marrsh] nm. (Aufmärsche) concentration, deployment (artillery); -flugplatz nm. base aerodrome; -ieren vi. to march up, form up, deploy (artillery).

Aufmerken [owf'mairr-ken] vt. to note down; i. attend.

Aufmerksam [owf'mairrk-zam] a. attentive; — machen vt. to point out to; -keit nf. attention, attentiveness.

Aufmontieren [owf'mon-tee-ren] vt. to assemble (tec.).

Aufmuntern [owf'mŏon-terrn] vt. to arouse, encourage; -ung encouragement.

Aufnähen [owf'nay-en] vt. to sew on, hem.

Aufnahme [owf'nah-mer] nf. taking up, admission, reception, record, map, photograph; -fähig a. eligible, receptive; -prüfung nf. entrance test, examination; -raum nm. studio (rad.); -streifen nm. teleprinter tape; -wagen nm. recording van (rad.).

Aufnehmen [owf'nay-men] vt. ir. to take up, in, receive, pick up, admit, draw up (will, etc.), record, photograph, survey; -er nm. (-) monitor (rad.).

Aufnötigen [owf'ner-ti-gen]

Aufopfern [owf'op-ferrn] vt.r.

Aufopferung [owf'op-fer-rŏong] nf. sacrifice, devotion.

Aufpacken [owf'pak-en] vt. to pack up, burden with.

Aufpassen [owf'pass-en] vt. to pay attention, watch, waylay; **aufgepasst!** attention, look out !

Aufpasser [owf'pass-err] nm. (-) spy, monitor, spotter.

Aufpflanzen [owf'pflant-sen] vt. to fix (bayonet).

Aufplatzen [owf'plats-en] vi. to burst open.

Aufpolstern [owf'pol-sterrn] vt. to upholster.

Aufprägen [owf'pray-gen] vt. to stamp, imprint.

Aufprallen [owf'prall-en] vi. to strike, hit (av.).

Aufprobieren [owf'pro-beer-ren] vt. to try on.

Aufprotzen [owf'prots-en] vt. to limber up (mil.).

Aufpumpen [owf'pŏŏm-pen] vt. to inflate, pump up. [finery.

Aufputz [owf'pŏŏts] nm.

Aufputzen [owf'pŏŏt-sen] vt. to dress up, adorn, clean up.

Aufquellen [owf'kvell-en] vi. to spring, bubble up.

Aufraffen [owf'raff-en] vt. to snatch up; r. rouse oneself.

Aufrauen [owf'row-en] vi. to roughen, to nap (cloth), to card (wool).

Aufräumen [owf'roy-men] vt. to clear away, tidy up, clear, mop up (mil.).

Aufräumung [owf'roy-mŏŏng] nf. salvage, clearing, mopping up (mil.).

Aufrechnen [owf'resh-nen] vt. to reckon (up), specify, charge to account.

Aufrecht [owf'resht] a. upright; -erhalten vt. ir. to maintain, preserve, keep; -erhaltung nf. maintenance, preservation.

Aufregen [owf'ray-gen] vt. to stir up, excite; r. to be excited.

Aufregung [owf'ray-gŏŏng] nf. excitement.

Aufreiben [owf'ribe-en] vt. ir. to rub open, exhaust, destroy

(mil.); r. to wear oneself out, worry.

Aufreissen [owf'rice-en] vt. ir. to tear open, up, to open wide.

Aufreizen [owf'rights-en] vt. to incite, stir up.

Aufrichten [owf'rish-ten] vt. to erect, lift up, establish, console; r. to rise.

Aufrichtig [owf'rish-tish] a. candid, honest, sincere.

Aufrichtigkeit [owf'rish-tish-kite] nf sincerity.

Aufriegeln [owf'ree-geln] vt. to unbolt.

Aufriss [owf'riss] nm. (-e) elevation, design, draft, vertical section. [slit open.

Aufritzen [owf'rit-sen] vt. to

Aufrücken [owf'ryŏŏ-ken] vt. to move up, be promoted.

Aufruf [owf'rŏŏf] nm. (-e) appeal, call, summons.

Aufrufen [owf'rŏŏ-fen] vt. ir. to call up, recall, call out.

Aufruhr [owf'rŏŏrr] nm. uproar, revolt, riot.

Aufrühren [owf'ryŏŏ-ren] vt. to stir up, incite to rebellion, mutiny, revive.

Aufrührer [owf'ryŏŏ-rerr] nm. mutineer.

Aufrührerisch [owf'ryŏŏ-rer-rish] a. mutinous, inflammatory.

Aufrüsten [owf'ryŏŏ-sten] vt.i. to rearm, arm.

Aufrüstung [owf'ryŏŏ-stŏŏng] nf. rearmament.

Aufrütteln [owf'ryŏŏ-teln] v. r. to shake up.

Aufs = auf das.

Aufsagen [owf'zah-gen] vt. to recite, renounce, give up.

Aufsammeln [owf'zamm-eln] vt. to gather up.

Aufsässig [owf'zess-ish] a. rebellious, refractory.

Aufsatz [owf'zats] nm. (Aufsätze) head-piece, top, paper, essay, gun sight (mil.).

Aufsaugen [owf'zow-gen] vt. to suck up.

Aufschauen [owf'show-en] vi. to look up, glance up.

Aufschaufeln [owf'show-feln] vt. to shovel up.

Aufschäumen [owf'shoy-men] vi. to foam up.

Aufscheuchen [owf'shoy-shen] vt. to scare, frighten.

Aufscheuern [owf'shoy-errn] vt. to scrub, wash, scour.

Aufschichten [owf'shish-ten] vt. to pile up.

Aufschieben [owf'shee-ben] vt. ir. to push open, put off, postpone.

Aufschiessen [owf'shee-sen] vt. ir. to shoot up; i. jump up.

Aufschirren [owf'shir-ren] vt. to harness.

Aufschlag [owf'shlahk] nm. (Aufschläge) cuff, facings, lapel, rise (price); service (games), impact, crash (av.); -zünder nm. percussion fuse.

Aufschlagen [owf'shlah-gen] vt. ir. to turn up, put up, look up, consult (book); pitch (mil.); i. hit, rise (price), land, pancake (av.).

Aufschleppe [owf'shlepp-er] nf. slipway (av.).

Aufschleudern [owf'shloy-derrn] vt. to throw up, cast up.

Aufschliessen [owf'shlee-sen] vt. ir. to open up, unlock, clear up.

Aufschlitzen [owf'shlit-sen] vt. to rip open.

Aufschluss [owf'shlōoss] nm. (Aufschlüsse) unlocking, explanation, information.

Aufschnappen [owf'shnap-en] vt. to snap up, pick up; i. fly open.

Aufschneiden [owf'shnide-en] vt. ir. to cut open, up; i. to brag.

Aufschneider [owf'shnide-err] nm. (-) boaster, bounder.

Aufschneiderei [owf'shnide-er-ry] nf. boasting.

Aufschnellen [owf'shnell-en] vt. to jerk up; i. fly up, open with a jerk.

Aufschnitt [owf'shnit] nm. (-e) slit, incision; kalter - (slice of) cold meat.

Aufschnüren [owf'shnew-ren] vt. to unlace.

Aufschrauben [owf'shrow-ben] vt. to screw on, unscrew.

Aufschrecken [owf'shreck-en] vt. to startle; i. ir. to start up, be startled.

Aufschrei [owf'shry] nm. (-e) outcry, shriek.

Aufschreiben [owf'shribe-en] vt. ir. to write down, charge (com.).

Aufschreien [owf'shry-en] vi. ir. to cry out, scream.

Aufschrift [owf'shrift] nf. address (letters, etc.), inscription, ticket, label.

Aufschub [owf'shōop] nm. postponement, respite.

Aufschürzen [owf'shyoorr-tsen] vt. to tuck, furl, loop up.

Aufschütteln [owf'shyoot-eln] vt. to shake up.

Aufschütten [owf'shyoo-ten] vt. to put, pour on, heap up.

Aufschwatzen [owf'shvat-sen] vt. to persuade by talking, talk into.

Aufschwemmen [owf'shvemm-en] vt. to wash up.

Aufschwingen [owf'shving-en] vt. ir. to soar up, rise, forge ahead.

Aufschwung [owf'shvoong] nm. rise, elevation, prosperity, impetus, flight.

Aufsehen [owf'zay-en] vi. to look up.

Aufsehen [owf-zay-en] n. sensation, notice, stir; -erregend a. sensational.

Aufseher [owf'zay-err] nm. (-) overseer, attendant, inspector, keeper.

Aufsein [owf'zine] vi. ir. to be up, open.

Aufsetzen [owf'zet-sen] vt. to

put on, set on, add, draw up (*document*); *r.* sit upright.

Aufsicht [owf'zisht] *nf.* inspection, control, charge, care; -habende(r) *nm.* supervisor, commanding officer; -sbeamte(r) *nm.* inspector, superintendent; -srat *nm.* board of directors, governors.

Aufsitzen [owf'zit-sen] *vi. ir.* to sit on, mount, to be aground, stranded (*ship*).

Aufspalten [owf'shpal-ten] *vt.* to split open.

Aufspannen [owf'shpann-en] *vt.* to stretch, unfold, put up (*umbrella*), string (*violin*), hoist, to make, set (*sail*).

Aufspeichern [owf'shpy-shern] *vt.* to store up.

Aufsperren [owf'shperr-en] *vt.* to unlock, open wide (*mouth, etc.*).

Aufspielen [owf'shpee-len] *vt.i.* to strike up (*music*); *r.* to put on side, pose (*as*).

Aufspiessen [owf'shpee-sen] *vt. ir.* to spear, pierce, impale.

Aufsprengen [owf'shpreng-en] *vt.* to burst open, explode, blast.

Aufspriessen [owf'shpree-sen] *vt. ir.* to sprout.

Aufspringen [owf'shpring-en] *vi. ir.* to spring up, fly open, crack, chap (*hands*).

Aufspritzen [owf'shprit-sen] *vi.* to squirt, spout up.

Aufsprudeln [owf'shprōō-deln] *vi.* to bubble up.

Aufsprung [owf'shprŏong] *nm.* (Aufsprünge) bound, bursting open.   [to spool.

Aufspulen [owf'shpōō-len] *vt.*

Aufspüren [owf'shpy̆ōōr-en] *vt.* to track down, smell out, trace, discover.

Aufstacheln [owf'shtach-eln] *vt.* to goad on.

Aufstand [owf'shtand] *nm.* (Aufstände) commotion, insurrection, rebellion.

Aufständisch [owf'shten-dish] *a.* riotous insurgent, rebellious.   [*vt.* to pile up.

Aufstapeln [owf'shtah-peln]

Aufstechen [owf'shtesh-en] *vt. ir.* to prick open, puncture, lance.

Aufstecken [owf'shteck-en] *vt.* to stick on, affix, pin up, give up.

Aufstehen [owf'shtay-en] *vi. ir.* to rise, get up, rebel, stand open.

Aufsteigen [owf'shty-gen] *vi. ir.* to ascend, climb, rise up, take off (*av.*).

Aufstellen [owf'shtell-en] *vt.* to set up, put up, exhibit, lay down, adduce, set (*trap*), nominate (*candidate*), draw up (*troops*), state (*rule*), make (*record*), park (*aut.*).

Aufstellung [owf'shtell-ŏŏng] *nf.* formation, disposition, exhibition, nomination, statement, list, parking (*aut.*).

Aufstemmen [owf'shtemm-en] *vt.* to lean upon, force open.

Aufstieg [owf'shteek] *nm.* ascent.

Aufstöbern [owf'shter-bern] *vt.* to rummage out, hunt up.

Aufstöhnen [owf'shter-nen] *vi.* to groan out.

Aufstören [owf'shter-ren] *vt.* to rouse up, disturb.

Aufstossen [owf'shtoh-sen] *vt. ir.* to push open, hit, bump against; *i.* belch, run aground (*nav.*).

Aufstreben [owf'shtray-ben] *vi.* to aspire, struggle up.

Aufstreichen [owf'shtry-shen] *vt. ir.* to spread.

Aufstreifen [owf'shtrife-en] *vt.* to tuck up.   [to strew, scatter.

Aufstreuen [owf'shtroy-en] *vt.*

Aufstrich [owf'shtrish] *nm.* (-e) spread, up-stroke.

Aufstülpen [owf'shtewl-pen] *vt.* to turn up, put on (*hat*), invert (*bottle, etc.*).

Aufstützen [owf'shtewt-sen] vt. to support, prop up; r. lean on.

Aufsuchen [owf'zōōch-en] vt. to seek out, search for, visit.

Auftakeln [owf'tah-keln] vt. to rig (out).

Auftakt [owf'takt] nm. upward beat, unstressed syllable, beat, prelude.

Auftanken [owf'tang-ken] vi. to fuel (av. etc.).

Auftauchen [owf'towch-en vi. to emerge, appear, break surface (nav.). [thaw.

Auftauen [owf'tow-en] vi. to

Aufteilen [owf'tile-en] vt. to divide up, partition.

Aufteilung [owf'tile-ōōng] nf. division, partition.

Auftischen [owf'tish-en] vt. to serve (up).

Auftrag [owf'trahk] nm. (Aufträge) order, commission, mission; im — von by order of; Ihrem — gemäss in accordance with your instructions; -geber nm. purchaser, customer, principal (com.).

Auftragen [owf'trah-gen] vt. ir. to serve (up), put on (paint), send (greetings), wear out (clothes), order (persons).

Auftreiben [owf'tribe-en] vt. ir. to raise, hunt out, secure, get, swell up.

Auftrennen [owf'trenn-en] vt. to undo, unpick.

Auftreten [owf'tray-ten] vt. ir. to kick open; i. come forward, appear, come on the scene.

Auftreten [owf'tray-ten] n. appearance, behaviour, occurrence.

Auftrieb [owf'treep] nm. buoyancy, stimulus, lift.

Auftritt [owf'trit] nm. (-e) scene. [open.

Auftun [owf'tōōn] vt. ir. to

Auftürmen [owf'työōr-men] vt.r. to heap up, tower up.

Aufwachen [owf'vach-en] vt. to wake up. [ir. to grow up.

Aufwachsen [owf'vax-en] vi.

Aufwägen [owf'vay-gen] vt. ir. to counterbalance.

Aufwallen [owf'vall-en] vi. to boil (up), effervesce.

Aufwallung [owf'vall-ōōng] nf. boiling up, effervescence, outburst of emotion.

Aufwand [owf'vant] nm. (Aufwände) expense, expenditure, display; -steuer nf. purchase tax.

Aufwärmen [owf'vairr-men] vt. to warm up, rake up.

Aufwartefrau [owf'varr-ter-frow] nf. charwoman, cleaner.

Aufwarten [owf'varr-ten] vi. to wait on, attend to.

Aufwärter [owf'vairr-terr] nm. (-) attendant, waiter, steward; -in nf. stewardess.

Aufwärts [owf'vairrts] ad. upwards. [nf. call.

Aufwartung [owf'varr-tōōng]

Aufwaschen [owf'vash-en] vt. ir. to wash up. [to waken.

Aufwecken [owf'veck-en] vt.

Aufweichen [owf'vish-en] vt. to soften, soak.

Aufweinen [owf'vine-en] vi. to weep loudly.

Aufweisen [owf'vize-en] vt. ir. to show, exhibit.

Aufwenden [owf'ven-den] vt. ir. to expend, spend, devote (care).

Aufwerfen [owf'vairr-fen] vt. ir. to throw open, up, raise (question).

Aufwerten [owf'vairr-ten] vt. to revalue, raise in value.

Aufwertung [owf'vairr-tōōng] nf. revaluation, revalorization, raising in value.

Aufwickeln [owf'vick-eln] vt. to roll, wind up, unwind.

Aufwiegeln [owf'vee-geln] vt. to stir up, incite; -ung nf. instigation, stirring up (to revolt).

Aufwiegler[owf′vee-gler]*nm.* (-) agitator, hothead.

Aufwieglerisch [owf′vee-gler-rish] *a.* seditious, rebellious.

Aufwiegan [owf′vee-gen] *vt.* to counterbalance.

Aufwind [owf′vint] *nm.* (-e) up-wind, up-current.

Aufwinden [owf′vin-den] *vt. ir.* to wind up, hoist (up).

Aufwirbeln [owf′virr-beln] *vt.* to whirl up.

Aufwischen [owf′vish-en] *vt.* to wipe up, away.

Aufwuchern [owf′vōōch-errn] *vi.* to grow abundantly.

Aufwühlen [owf′vew-len] *vt.* to turn up, root up, agitate.

Aufzählen [owf′tsay-len] *vt.* to count, enumerate.

Aufzehren [owf′tsai-ren] *vt.* to consume, waste.

Aufzeichnen [owf′tsîsh-nen] *vt.* to sketch, note down.

Aufzeichnung [owf′tsîsh-nŏŏng] *nf.* note, list, record.

Aufzeigen [owf′tsi-gen] *vt.* to display, show.

Aufziehen [owf′tsee-en] *vt. ir.* to draw up, wind up, raise, open, undo, bring up, rear, cultivate, tease, pull one's leg; to approach, draw near, appear, march up (*mil.*).

Aufzug [owf′tsŏŏk] *nm.* (Aufzüge) procession, parade, dress, act (play), lift, elevator, hoist.

Aufzwingen [owf′tsving-en] *vt. ir.* to force upon.

Augapfel [owk′apfl] *nm.* (Augäpfel) eye-ball, apple of the eye.

Auge [ow-ger] *n.* (gen. -s; *pl.* -n) eye, bud, pip (*cards.*).

Augen-arzt [ow-gen] *nm.* oculist, eye specialist; **-blick** *nm.* moment; **-blicklich** *a.* momentary, present; *ad.* immediately, instantly; **-braue** *nf.* eye-brow; **-fällig** *a.* evident; **-glas** *n.* eye-glass; **-heilkunde** *nf.* opthalmology; **-höhle** *nf.* eye-

socket; **-lid** *n.* eyelid; **-merk** *n.* attention; **-schein** *nm.* appearance, inspection; **-schein-lich** *a.* obvious, apparent; **-stern** *nm.* pupil of the eye, pet, favourite; **-wimper** *nf.* eyelash; **-zeuge** *nm.* eye-witness.

Äugeln [oy-geln] *vi.* to ogle, make eyes. [ust.

August [ow-gŏŏst] *nm.* Aug-ust.

Auktion [owk-see-ohn′] *nf.* auction.

Auktionator [owk-see-o-nah′torr] *nm.* auctioneer. [ity.

Aula [ow′lah] *nf.* hall (*univers-*

Aus [owss] *pr.* out of, from, of; *ad.* out, past, over, finished.

Ausarbeiten [owss′arr-bite-en] *vt.* to work out, complete, hollow out.

Ausarbeitung [owss′arr-biteŏŏng] *nf.* working out, improvement, elaboration.

Ausarten [owss′arr-ten] *vi.* to degenerate. [al degeneration.

Ausartung [owss′arr-tŏŏng] *nf.* degeneration.

Ausatmen [owss′aht-men] *vi.* to breathe out. [*vt.* to dredge.

Ausbaggern [owss′ba-gerrn] *vt.* to dredge.

Ausbau [owss′bow] *nm.* extension development, consolidation, completion, dismantling.

Ausbauen [owss′bow-en] *vt.* to extend, develop, enlarge, finish, exhaust (*mine*).

Ausbauchen [owss′bowch-en] *vi.* to be puffed out.

Ausbauchung [owss′bowch-ŏŏng] *nf.* bulge.

Ausbedingen [owss′ber-dingen] *vt. ir.* to stipulate.

Ausbeissen [owss′bice-en] *vt. ir.* to bite out.

Ausbesserer [owss′bess-err-err] *nm.* (-) repairer.

Ausbessern [owss′bess-errn] *vt.* to mend, repair, refit, correct.

Ausbesserung [owss′bess-err-ŏŏng] *nf.* repairing, mending; **-anstalt** *nf.* repair shop.

Ausbeute [owss'boy-ter] nf. yield, produce, profit.

Ausbeuten [owss'boy-ten] vt. to exploit, profit by, work (mine), sweat (men).

Ausbeuter [owss'boy-terr] nm. (-) exploiter; -tum n. exploitation, sweating, slave-driving.

Ausbeutung [owss'boy-toong] nf. exploitation.

Ausbiegen [owss'bee-gen] vt. ir. to bend out; i. to make way.

Ausbieten [owss'bee-ten] vt. ir. to offer for sale, advertise.

Ausbilden [owss'bil-den] vt. to shape, develop, cultivate, educate, train (troops).

Ausbildung [owss'bil-doong] nf. development, cultivation, education, training.

Ausbitten [owss'bit-en] vt. ir. to request, insist

Ausblasen [owss'blah-zen] vt. ir. to blow out.

Ausbleiben [owss'blibe-en] vi. ir. to stay away, out, be absent, wanting.

Ausbleiben [owss'blibe-en] n. absence, failure (to appear, etc.), default.

Ausblick [owss'blick] nm. (-e) prospect, outlook, view.

Ausblühen [owss'blew-en] vi. to cease to bloom.

Ausbluten [owss'bloo-ten] vi. to bleed (to death).

Ausblutungsschlacht [owss'bloo-toongs-schlacht] nf. battle of attrition.

Ausbohren [owss'bor-ren] vt. to bore (out), drill. [to buoy.

Ausbojen [owss'boh-yen] vt.

Ausbooten [owss'boh-ten] vt. to disembark, land.

Ausbrechen [owss'bresh-en] vi. ir. to break out, be sick, vomit, escape, burst out.

Ausbreiten [owss'brite-en] vt. ir. to spread (out), propagate, stretch out; r. to spread, enlarge on.

Ausbreitung [owss'brite-oong] nf. spread, extension, propagation.

Ausbrennen [owss'brenn-en] vt. ir. to burn out, scorch, bake; r. to stop burning.

Ausbringen [owss'bring-en] vt. ir. to bring out, realize, propose (health).

Ausbruch [owss'brooch] nm. (Ausbrüche) outbreak, eruption, escape.

Ausbrüten [owss'bryoo-ten] vt. to hatch, plot.

Ausbrütung [owss'bryoo-toong] nf. incubation, hatching.

Ausbuchtung [owss'booch-toong] nf. salient.

Ausbund [owss'boont] nm. (Ausbünde) paragon, model, prodigy, embodiment.

Ausbürgern [owss'bewrr-gerrn] vt. to denationalize, deprive of citizenship.

Ausbürsten [owss'bewrr-sten] vt. to brush.

Ausdauer [owss'dow-err] nf. perseverance, endurance.

Ausdauern [owss'dow-errn] vi. to hold out, endure.

Ausdehnen [owss'day-nen] vt. r. to extend, expand, stretch.

Ausdehnung [owss'day-noong] nf. extension, stretching, expansion, extent.

Ausdenken [owss'deng-ken] vt. ir. to think out, imagine.

Ausdeuten [owss'doy-ten] vt. to interpret.

Ausdienen [owss'dee-nen] vi. to serve one's time, complete term of service.

Ausdorren [owss'dor-ren] vi. to dry up, be parched.

Ausdörren [owss'der-ren] vt. to dry up, parch.

Ausdrehen [owss'dray-en] vt. to turn off, switch off, turn out (light).

Ausdruck [owss'drook] nm. Ausdrücke); expression, phrase, term.

Ausdruckslos [owss'drōōx-lohs] a. expressionless, blank.

Ausdrucksvoll [owss'drōōx-foll] a. expressive.

Ausdrücken [owss'dryōōk-en] vt. to express, squeeze out, press out.

Ausdrücklich [owss'dryōōk-lish] a. express, explicit.

Ausdünsten [owss'dewn-sten] vi.t. to evaporate, perspire, sweat.

Ausdünstung [owss'dewn-stōōng] nf. evaporation, exhalation, perspiration.

Auseinander [owss'ine-an-derr] ad. apart, asunder, from each other; -bringen vt. ir. to separate; -fahren vi. ir. to rush apart, scatter; -gehen vi. to separate, break up, disperse; -halten vt. ir. to distinguish; -legen vt. to take to pieces, explain; -nehmen vt. to take to pieces, dismantle; -setzen vt. to set forth, explain; r. to come to terms, settle; -setzung nf. explanation, argument, discussion, settlement.

Auserlesen [owss'airr-lay-zen] a. chosen, select.

Ausersehen [owss'airr-zay-en] vt. ir. tochoose, mark out, doom.

Auserwählen [owss'airr-vay-len] vt. to select.

Aussessen [owss'ess-en] vt. ir. to eat up, have to pay for.

Ausfädeln [owss'fay-deln] vt. to unthread, unravel.

Ausfahren [owss'fah-ren] vi. ir. to drive out, put out to sea; t. to take for a drive, drive.

Ausfahrt [owss'fahrrt] nf. drive, excursion, sailing, way out, gateway.

Ausfall [owss'fall] nm. (Ausfälle) deficiency, deficit, loss, lunge, sortie, attack (mil.), result, casualties, wastage, breakdown, failure (engine).

Ausfallen [owss'fall-en] vi. ir. to fall out, result, turn out, be wanting, sally out, lunge, attack (mil.), fail, conk out (aut. etc.).

Ausfallstrasse [owss'fall-shtrah-ser] nf. arterial road.

Ausfasern [owss'fah-zerrn] vt. to unravel.

Ausfechten [owss'fesh-ten] vt. ir. to fight out.

Ausfegen [owss'fay-gen] vt. to sweep out.

Ausfeilen [owss'file-en] vt. to file out, perfect.

Ausfertigen [owss'fairr-ti-gen] vt. to execute, draw up (deed), issue, make out (bill); doppelt – to duplicate.

Ausfertigung [owss'fairr-ti-gōōng] nf. execution (deed), drawing up, making out (bill), copy, issue.

Ausfinden [owss'fin-den] vt. ir. to discover.

Ausfindig machen [owss'fin-dish mach-en] vt. to find out.

Ausflaggen [owss'fla-gen] vt. to put out flags.   [to patch.

Ausflicken [owss'flick-en] vt.

Ausfliegen [owss'flee-gen] vt. ir. to fly out, make an excursion, go for a trip.

Ausfliessen [owss'flee-sen] vi. ir. to flow out, arise from.

Ausflucht [owss'flucht] nf. (Ausflüchte) evasion, pretext, excuse.

Ausflug [owss'flōōk] nm. (Ausflüge) excursion, outing.

Ausflügler [owss'flyoo-glerr] nm. (–) excursionist, tripper.

Ausfluss [owss'flōōss] nm. (Ausflüsse) outlet, mouth (river), discharge, result.

Ausfolgen [owss'fol-gen] vt. to hand over, deliver.

Ausforschen [owss'forr-shen] vt. to search for, investigate, explore.

Ausforschung [owss'forr-shōōng] nf. investigation, exploration.

Ausfragen [owss'frah-gen] vt. to interrogate, sound, question.

Ausfressen [owss'fres-en] vt. ir. to eat up, corrode.

Ausfuhr [owss'foorr] nf. exportation, exports; -handel nm. export trade; -zoll nm. export duty.

Ausführbar [owss'fewrr-barr] a. feasible, practicable, exportable.

Ausführbarkeit [owss'fewrr-barr-kite] nf. feasibility.

Ausführen [owss'few-ren] vt. to carry out, execute, perform, detail, explain, export.

Ausführer [owss'few-rerr] nm. (-) exporter.

Ausführlich [owss'fewrr-lish] a. detailed, full; ad. in detail, in full.

Ausführlichkeit [owss'fewrr-lish-kite] nf. completeness, full detail.

Ausführung [owss'few-rōong] nf. execution, performance, completion, explanation, development, statement, exportation. [fill out, up, pad.

Ausfüllen [owss'few-len] vt. to

Ausfüllung [owss'few-lōong] nf. filling up, ballast.

Ausfüttern [owss'few-terrn] vt. to fatten, line, stuff.

Ausgabe [owss'gah-ber] nf. expenditure, outlay, delivery (mail), issue, edition.

Ausgang [owss'gang] nm. (Ausgänge) going out, way out, exit, issue, close, day out, free time; -spunkt nm. starting-point.

Ausgeben [owss'gay-ben] vt. ir. to spend, issue, give out, distribute, deal (cards); r. spend everything, pass off for.

Ausgeber [owss'gay-berr] nm. (-) disburser, issuer, drawer.

Ausgebot [owss'ger-bōrt] n. (-e) putting up for sale, offer.

Ausgebombt [owss'ger-bompt] a. bombed out.

Ausgebrannt [owss'ger-brant] a. burn out, gutted.

Ausgeburt [owss'ger-bōort] nf. offspring, product.

Ausgedient [owss'ger-deent] a. discharged (at end of term of service).

Ausgehanzug [owss'gay-ant-sōok] nm. (-züge) outdoor suit.

Ausgehverbot [owss'gay-ferr-boht] n curfew.

Ausgeglichen [owss'ger-glish-en] a. (well) balanced.

Ausgehen [owss'gay-en] vi. ir. to go out, get off, fail, run out, come to an end, proceed, fade; von etwas - to start from something; - auf aim at; leer - to get nothing; schlecht - to turn out badly.

Ausgelassen [owss'ger-lass-en] a. boisterous, wild, high spirited.

Ausgelassenheit [owss'ger-lass-en-hite] nf. boisterousness, high spirits, exuberance.

Ausgelernt [owss'ger-lerrnt] a. experienced, trained.

Ausgemacht [owss'ger-macht] a. settled, undoubted, certain.

Ausgenommen [owss'ger-nomm-en] pr. except.

Ausgerechnet [owss'ger-resh-net] ad. just, precisely, exactly.

Ausgeschlossen [owss'ger-shloss-en] a. excluded, impossible, out of the question, locked out.

Ausgeschnitten [owss'ger-shnitt-en] a. cut out, low-necked (dress).

Ausgesprochen [owss'ger-shproch-en] a. pronounced, decided.

Ausgestalten [owss'ger-shtal-ten] vt. to shape, work out, form.

Ausgestaltung [owss'ger-shtal-tōong] nf. shaping, elaboration, arrangement.

Ausgesucht [owss'ger-zoocht] a. choice, select(ed), super-fine

Ausgewiesene(r) [owss'ger-vee-ze-ner] nm. deportee, deported person.

Ausgezeichnet [owss'gert-sish-net] a. excellent, distinguished. [abundant.

Ausgiebig [owss'gee-bish] a.

Ausgiessen [owss'gee-sen] vt. ir. to pour out.

Ausgiessung [owss'gee-sŏŏng] nf. pouring out, outpouring.

Ausgleich [owss'glish] nm. (-e) compromise, settlement, agreement, arrangement.

Ausgleich'en [owss'gli-shen] vt. ir. to equalize, balance, compensate, settle, balance (account); -getriebe n. differential (tec.).

Ausgleichung [owss'gli-shŏŏng] nf. adjustment, settlement, compensation, balancing. [ir. to slip.

Ausgleiten [owss'glite-en] vi.

Ausglühen [owss'glew-en] vt. to anneal (tec.).

Ausgraben [owss'grah-ben] vt. ir. to dig out, up, exhume, unearth.

Ausgrabung [owss'grah-bŏŏng] nf. digging up, excavation.

Ausgreifen [owss'grife-en] vi. ir. to step out (horse).

Ausgreifend [owss'grife-ent] a. far-reaching (change, etc.).

Ausguck [owss'gŏŏk] nm. look-out (nav.), periscope.

Ausgucken [owss'gŏŏ-ken] vt. to keep a look-out.

Ausguss [owss'gŏŏs] nm. (Ausgüsse) sink, spout, gutter, mouth (pipe).

Aushacken [owss'hack-en] vt. to hack out.

Aushaken [owss'hah-ken] vt. to unhook.

Aushalten [owss'hal-ten] vt. ir. to bear, endure, stand; i. persevere, hold out.

Aushändigen [owss'hen-di-gen] vt. to hand out, over, deliver.

Aushändigung [owss'hen-di-gŏŏng] nf. handing out, delivery.

Aushang [owss'hang] nm. notice display, placard, poster.

Aushänge-bogen nm. final proof sheet; -schild n. sign board, shop sign.

Aushängen [owss'heng-en] vt.i. ir. to hang out, to be on show, exhibit.

Ausharren [owss'har-ren] vi. to hold out, persist, persevere.

Aushauchen [owss'howch-en] vt. to breathe out.

Aushauen [owss'how-en] vt.ir. to hew out, cut out, thin (forest).

Ausheben [owss'hay-ben] vt. ir. to lift out, pull out, dislocate, levy, enlist (mil.).

Aushebung [owss'hay-bŏŏng] nf. conscription, levying, draft(ing) (mil.).

Aushecken [owss'heck-en] vt. to concoct, think out, plan.

Ausheilen [owss'hile-en] vi. to heal up.

Aushelfen [owss'hel-fen] vt. ir. to help out, assist.

Aushilfe [owss'hil-fer] nf. help, assistance, (temporary) aid; zur = as a makeshift, temporarily; -stellung nf. temporary post.

Aushilfsweise [owss'hilfs-vize-er] ad. temporarily, as a stop-gap.

Aushöhlen [owss'her-len] vt. to hollow out, excavate, groove (tec.).

Aushöhlung [owss'her-lŏŏng] nf. hollowing out, excavation.

Ausholen [owss'hole-en] vt.i. to reach out, lunge, raise (to strike), take a running start, sound (person).

Aushorchen [owss'horsh-en] vt. to sound (persons).

Aushülsen [owss'hewl-zen] vt. to shell.

Aushungern [owss'hoong-errn] *vt.* to starve out.

Ausjagen [owss'yah-gen] *vt.* to drive out, [weed out.

Ausjäten [owss'yay-ten] *vt.* to

Auskämmen [owss'kemm-en] *vt.* to comb out.

Auskämpfen [owss'kemp-fen] *vt.* to fight out.

Auskauf [owss'cowf] *nm* (**Auskäufe**) buying up.

Auskaufen [owss'cow-fen] *vt.* to buy out, up, outbid.

Auskehlen [owss'kay-len] *vt.* to flute, chamfer.

Auskehren [owss'kay-ren] *vt.* to sweep out.

Auskennen [owss'kenn-en] *vt. r.* to know thoroughly, about.

Auskernen [owss'kare-nen] *vt.* to stone (*fruit*).

Ausklagen [owss'klah-gen] *vt.* to sue (for debt); *r.* pour out one's troubles.

Ausklang [owss'klang] *nm.* (**Ausklänge**) end.

Auskleiden [owss'clide-en] *vt.r.* to undress, line, decorate.

Ausklingen [owss'cling-en] *vi. ir.* to die away (*music, etc.*).

Ausklopfen [owss'clop-fen] *vt.* to beat.

Ausklopfer [owss'clop-ferr] *nm.* (**-**) carpet-beater.

Ausklügeln [owss'clew-geln] *vt.* to puzzle out, work out.

Ausknipsen [owss'k-nip-sen] *vt.* to switch out, off.

Auskochen [owss'koch-en] *vt.* to boil thoroughly, extract (by boiling).

Auskommen [owss'komm-en] *vi. ir.* to come, go, get out, manage, have enough, get on well with someone.

Auskommen [owss'komm-en] *n.* subsistence, livelihood.

Auskosten [owss'kost-en] *vt.* to taste, enjoy (to the full).

Auskramen [owss'krah-men] *vt.* to show, display, turn out (*drawer*).

Auskratzen [owss'krat-sen] *vt.* to scratch out, erase.

Auskriechen [owss'kree-shen] *vi.* to creep, crawl out.

Auskühlen [owss'kew-len] *vt.* to cool thoroughly.

Auskundschaften [owss'koönt-shaf-ten] *vt.* to explore, spy out.

Auskunft [owss'koönft] *nf.* (**Auskünfte**) information, details, particulars.

Auskunftei [owss'koönf-tie'] *nf.* information bureau, inquiry office.

Auskunft-bureau *n.* inquiry office; **-erteilung** *nf.* giving of information; **-mittel** *n.* device, expedient.

Auskuppeln [owss'koö-peln] *vt.* to disconnect, ungear (*tec.*).

Auslachen [owss'lach-en] *vt.* to laugh out.

Ausladebahnhof [owss'lah-der-bahn'hofe] *nm.* (**-höfe**) detraining station (*mil.*).

Ausladen [owss'lah-den] *vt. ir.* to unload, detrain (*mil.*), deplane (*av.*); *i.* to stick out, project.

Auslader [owss'lah-derr] *nm.* (**-**) unloader, docker.

Ausladung [owss'lah-doöng] *nf.* unloading.

Auslage [owss'lah-ger] *nf.* outlay, expense, (window) display, shop window, shop front.

Ausland [owss'lant] *n.* foreign countries; **im-, ins-** abroad; **-sendung** *nf.* foreign broadcast.

Ausländer [owss'len-derr] *nm.* (**-**) foreigner, alien.

Ausländisch [owss'len-dish] *a.* foreign.

Auslangen [owss'lang-en] *vi.* to suffice.

Auslassen [owss'lass-en] *vt. ir.* to miss out, omit, leave out, let out, melt; *r.* speak one's mind, express oneself.

Auslassung [owss'lass-oöng]

nf. omission, remarks; **-zeichen** *n.* apostrophe.

Auslauf [owss'lowf] *nm.* (Ausläufe) outflow, outlet, hen-run, finish, landing run (*av.*).

Auslaufen [owss'low-fen] *vi. ir.* to run out, start off, end, leak, put out to sea (*nav.*).

Ausläufer [owss'loy-ferr] *nm.* (-) errand boy, spur (*mountain*), runner (*plant*).

Ausleben [owss'lay-ben] *vr.* to live one's life to the full.

Ausleeren [owss'lair-ren] *vt.* to empty.

Ausleerung [owss'lair-rŏŏng] *nf.* draining, evacuation.

Auslegen [owss'lay-gen] *vt.* to lay out, spend, display, explain, interpret, inlay.

Ausleger [owss'lay-gerr] *nm.* (-) outrigger.

Auslegung [owss'lay-gŏŏng] *nf.* explanation, interpretation, veneering, inlaid floor.

Ausleihen [owss'lie-en] *vt. ir.* to lend out, hire; *r.* borrow.

Ausleiher [owss'lie-er] *nm.* (-) lender.

Auslernen [owss'lairr-nen] *vi.* to learn thoroughly, serve one's apprenticeship.

Auslese [owss'lay-zer] *nf.* selection, fine grapes, choice wine.

Auslesen [owss'lay-zen] *vt. ir.* to select, read to the end.

Ausliefern [owss'lee-ferrn] *vt.* to deliver (up), hand over, extradite (*law*).

Auslieferung [owss'lee-ferrŏŏng] *nf.* delivery, surrender, extradition. [to pay off.

Auslohnen [owss'loh-nen] *vt.*

Auslöschen [owss'ler-shen] *vt.* to extinguish, obliterate, wipe out.

Auslosen [owss'loh-zen] *vt.* to draw lots for, redeem, allot.

Auslösen [owss'ler-zen] *vt.* to loosen, redeem, ransom, uncouple (*tec.*), cause, produce.

Auslöser [owss'ler-zerr] *nm.* (-) release (*camera*).

Auslösung [owss'ler-zŏŏng] *nf.* redemption, release.

Auslug [owss'look] *nm.* lookout (*nav.*).

Ausmachen [owss'mach-en] *vt.* to finish, settle, arrange, agree to, constitute, make; nichts – not to matter.

Ausmalen [owss'mah-len] *vt.* to paint, describe, amplify.

Ausmarsch [owss'mahrrsh] *nm.* (-märsche) departure (*mil.*).

Ausmarschieren [owss'mahrr-sheer-ren] *vi.* to march off, set off.

Ausmass [owss'mahss] *n.* measurement, scale, proportion.

Ausmauern [owss'mow-errn] *vt.* to wall up, line, face.

Ausmeisseln [owss'mice-eln] *vt.* to carve (out), chisel.

Ausmergeln [owss'merr-geln] *vt.* to emaciate, impoverish.

Ausmerzen [owss'mairt-sen] *vt.* to reject, eliminate, expunge

Ausmerzung [owss'mairtsŏŏng] *nf.* rejection, abolition, elimination.

Ausmessen [owss'mess-en] *vt. ir.* to measure, sell retail (*com.*), survey.

Ausmessung [owss'mess-ŏŏng] *nf.* measurement, gauging, surveying.

Ausmitteln [owss'mitt-eln] *vt.* to find out.

Ausmöblieren [owss'merbleer-en] *vt.* to furnish.

Ausmünden [owss'mewn-den] *vi.* to flow into.

Ausmustern [owss'mŏŏsterrn] *vt.* to reject, dismiss, sort out, comb out.

Ausmusterung [owss'mŏŏster-rŏŏng] *nf.* sort out, release, rejection (of unfit) (*mil.*).

Ausnahme [owss'nah-mer] *nf.*

exception; **-fall** nm. exceptional case; **-zustand** nm. state of emergency.

Ausnahms-los ad. without exception, invariably; **-weise** ad. exceptionally, by way of exception, for once.

Ausnehmen [owss'nay-men] vt. ir. to take out, except, gut (fish); r. look, appear; **-d** a. exceptional(ly), exceedingly.

Ausnützen [owss'newt-sen] vt. to turn to account, use, utilize, profit by, exploit.

Auspacken [owss'pack-en] vt. to unpack.

Auspeitschen [owss'pite-shen] vt. to flog.

Auspfänden [owss'pfen-den] vt. to distrain.

Auspflanzen [owss'pflant-sen] vt. to bed out. [to iron.

Ausplätten [owss'plett-en] vt. ir. to rub out.

Ausplaudern [owss'plow-derrn] vt. to let out (secrets).

Ausplündern [owss'plüyon-derrn] vt. to plunder, loot.

Auspolstern [owss'pol-sterrn] vt. to pad, line, upholster.

Ausprägen [owss'pray-gen] vt. to stamp, coin.

Auspressen [owss'press-en] vt. to squeeze out, extort.

Ausprobieren [owss'pro-beer-ren] vt. to test, to sample, try out.

Auspuff [owss'pŏŏf] nm. (Auspüffe) exhaust (tec.), escape; **-klappe** nf. exhaust valve; **-rohr** n. exhaust (pipe); **-topf** nm. silencer (aut.).

Auspumpen [owss'pŏŏm-pen] vt. to pump out.

Auspusten [owss'pŏŏs-ten] vt. to blow out, extinguish.

Ausputz [owss'pŏŏts] nm. ornament.

Ausputzen [owss'pŏŏt-sen] vt. to clean, adorn, decorate; r. to dress up.

Ausquartieren [owss'kvahrr-teer-ren] vt. to billet out.

Ausradieren [owss'ra-deer-ren] vt. to erase, rub out.

Ausrangieren [owss'rong-zheer-ren] vt. to scrap, discard.

Ausräuchern [owss'roy-sherrn] vt. to smoke out, fumigate.

Ausraufen [owss'row-fen] vt. to tear out (hair).

Ausräumen [owss'roy-men] vt. to clear out, away, empty.

Ausrechnen [owss'resh-nen] vt. to calculate.

Ausrechnung [owss'resh-noong] nf. calculation, reckoning. [excuse.

Ausrede [owss'ray-der] nf.

Ausreden [owss'ray-den] vt. to have one's say; t. dissuade from; r. excuse oneself.

Ausreiben [owss'ribe-en] vt. ir. to rub out.

Ausreichen [owss'ri-shen] vi. to suffice; **-d** a. sufficient.

Ausreise [owss'ri-zer] nf. departure, sailing.

Ausreissen [owss'rice-en] vt. ir. to tear, pull out, draw; i. to split, tear make off, desert.

Ausreisser [owss'rice-err] nm. (-) deserter.

Ausreiten [owss'rite-en] vi. ir. to ride out.

Ausrenken [owss'reng-ken] vt. to dislocate.

Ausrichten [owss'rish-ten] vt to carry out, perform, deliver, see to, execute, dress ranks (mil.).

Ausrichtung [owss'rish-tŏŏng] nf. performance, alignment.

Ausringen [owss'ring-en] vt.i. to wring out, cease to suffer.

Ausritt [owss'rit] nm. (-e) ride.

Ausroden [owss'rode-en] vt. to clear (land).

Ausrotten [owss'rot-en] vt. to stamp out, exterminate.

Ausrottung [owss'rot-ŏŏng] nf. extermination.

Ausrücken [owss'ryŏŏ -en]

put out of gear, disengage; i. march out, leave, move off.

Ausruf [owss'roof] nm. (Ausrüfe) cry, exclamation, proclamation.

Ausrufen [owss'roof-en] vt.i. ir. to cry out, exclaim, proclaim.

Ausrufer [owss'roof-err] nm. (-) crier.

Ausrufung [owss'roof-öong] nf. exclamation, cry, proclamation; -szeichen n. exclamation.

Ausruhen [owss'roo-en] vi. to mark.   [rest.

Ausrüsten [owss'ryöo-sten] vt. to equip, arm, furnish, provide, fit out.

Ausrüstung [owss'ryöo-stöong] nf. equipment, fitting out, armament, outfit.

Ausrutschen [owss'root-shen] vi. to slip, skid.

Aussaat [ows'zaht] nf. sowing seed-corn.   (sow.

Aussähen [owss'zay-en] vt. to

Aussage [owss'zah-ger] nf. declaration, assertion, deposition, (prisoner's) statement (mil.).

Aussagen [owss'zah-gen] vt. to declare, assert, give evidence.

Aussatz [owss'zats] nm. leprosy, sheep-scab.

Aussaugen [owss'zow-gen] vt. to suck out, exhaust, bleed.

Aussauger [owss'zow-gerr] nm. (-) parasite, sponger, blood-sucker.

Ausschälen [owss'shale-en] vt. to shell.

Ausschalten [owss'shal-ten] vt. to cut out, switch off, eliminate.

Ausschank [owss'shank] nm. (Ausschänke) retail licence, public house, bar.

Ausscharren [owss'shar-ren] vt. to dig up, unearth.

Ausschau [owss'show] nf. look-out, watch.

Ausschauen [owss'show-en] vi. to be on the look out, look out (for), look, appear.

Ausschaufeln [owss'show-feln] vt. to shovel, scoop out.

Ausscheiden [owss'shide-en] vt. ir. to separate, secrete; i. withdraw, retire.

Ausscheidung [owss'shide-öong] nf. separation, secretion, withdrawal.

Ausschelten [owss'shel-ten] vt. ir. to scold.

Ausschenken [owss'sheng-ken] vt. to pour out, retail (liquor).   (vt. to send out.

Ausschicken [owss'shick-en] vt. ir. to shoot out, throw out, reject, impose (type), discharge (ballast).

Ausschiffen [owss'shif-en] vt. to disembark, discharge, land; i. put out to sea.

Ausschiffung [owss'shif-öong] nf. disembarkation.

Ausschimpfen [owss'shimp-fen] vt. to abuse, scold.

Ausschirren [owss'shir-ren] vt. to unharness.

Ausschlachten [owss'shlach-ten] vt. to cut up, exploit.

Ausschlafen [owss'shlah-fen] vi.r. to have one's sleep out; i. sleep off.

Ausschlag [owss'shlahk] nm. (Ausschläge) result, issue, rash (skin), lock (aut.), deflection (needle); -winkel nm. angle of deflection.

Ausschlagen [owss'shlah-gen] vt. ir. to drive out, knock out, decline, refuse, reject; i. lash out, kick, sprout, turn, deflect, turn out, result.

Ausschlaggebend [owss'-shlahk-gay-bent] a. decisive.

Ausschliessen [owss'shlee-sen] vt. ir. to shut out, lock out, exclude, disqualify.

Ausschliesslich [owss'shlees-lish] a, ad. exclusive(ly).

Ausschluss [owss'shlŏŏss] *nm.* exclusion, lock-out, disqualification.

Ausschmücken [owss'shmew-ken] *vt.* to decorate, embellish.

Ausschnauben [owss'shnow-ben] *vr.* to blow one's nose.

Ausschneiden [owss'shnide-en] *vt. ir.* to cut out, cut low (*dress*).

Ausschnitt [owss'shnit] *nm.* (-e) cut(ting out) section, low neck, retail trade, newspaper cutting.

Ausschöpfen [owss'sher-pfen] *vt.* to empty, drain.

Ausschreiben [owss'shribe-en] *vt. ir.* to write out (in full), copy, plagiarize, publish, announce, proclaim, advertise, throw open to competition.

Ausschreien [owss'shry-en] *vt. ir.* to cry out.

Ausschreiten [owss'shrite-en] *vt. ir.* to step out, overstep.

Ausschreitung [owss'shrite-ŏŏng] *nf.* excess, transgression.

Ausschuss [owss'shŏŏss] *nm.* (Ausschüsse) committee, board, refuse, rubbish, choice articles (*com.*); -sitzung *nf.* committee meeting, board meeting; -ware *nf.* rubbish, rejected goods (*com.*). [eln] *vt.* to shake out.

Ausschütteln [owss'shŏŏt-teln] *vt.* to shake out.

Ausschütten [owss'shŏŏt-ten] *vt.* to pour out, pay, shake (*with laughter*).

Ausschwärmen [owss'shvairr-men] *vi.* to swarm out, extend (*mil.*).

Ausschweben [owss'shvay-ben] *vi.* to flatten out (*av.*).

Ausschweifen [owss'shvife-en] *vi.* to lead an immoral life, to go to excess, be a rake.

Ausschweifend [owss'shvife-ent] *a.* dissipated, debauched.

Ausschweifung [owss'shvife-ŏŏng] *nf.* dissipation, immorality.

Ausschwemmen [owss' shvem-en] *vt.* to scour, wash out.

Ausschwitzen [owss'shvit-sen] *vi.* to exude, sweat out.

Aussehen [owss'zay-en] *vi. ir.* to look, appear.

Aussehen [owss'zay-en] *n.* appearance.

Aussen [ow'sen] *ad.* outside, outwards; -bezirk *nm.* outskirt; -bordmotor *nm.* outboard motor; -böschung *nf.* counterscarp (*mil.*), outside slope; -handel *nm.* foreign trade; -haut *nf.* outside planking, sheathing (*av.*); -minister *nm.* foreign minister; -politik *nf.* foreign policy; -posten *nm.* advanced post (*mil.*); -seite *nf.* outside; -seiter *nm.* outsider; -stände *m. pl.* outstanding debts, arrears (*com.*); -welt *nf.* outside world.

Aussenden [owss'zen-den] *vt. ir.* to send out, emit.

Aussendung [owss'zen-dŏŏng] *nf.* transmission (*rad.*).

Ausser [owss-err] *pr.* out of, besides; *cj.* except, but, unless; — Betrieb out of action; — Dienst retired; — Kraft setzen to cancel, annul; — Kurs obsolete, out of circulation; — wenn unless.

Ausser-dem *ad.* besides, in addition; -dienstlich *a.* unofficial; -ehelich *a.* illegitimate; -gerichtlich *a.* extra-judicial; -gewöhnlich *a.* unusual; -halb *pr.* outside; -ordentlich *a.* extraordinary; -stande *ad.* not in a position, unable.

Äusser [oy'serr] *a.* outer, external; -lich *a.* ad. external.

Äussern [oy'serrn] *vt.* to utter, express, manifest.

Äusserst [oy'serrst] *a.* utmost; *ad.* extremely, most.

Äusserung [oy'ser-rŏŏng] *nf.* utterance, remark, saying.

Aussetzen [owss'zet-sen] *vt.*

to put out, set out, expose, suspend, stop, break down (tec.), land, lower (boat), offer (reward), bequeath, find fault.

Aussicht [owss'zisht] nf. prospect, view, chance; -slos a. hopeless, unpromising; -spunkt nm. view-point; -sreich a. promising, hopeful.

Aussieben [owss'zee-ben] vt. to filter (rad.).

Aussöhnen [owss'zer-nen] vt. to conciliate, reconcile.

Aussöhnung [owss'zer-nōong] nf. reconciliation.

Aussondern [owss'zon-dern] vt. to separate, select.

Aussonderung [owss'zon-der-rōong] nf. elimination.

Ausspähen [owss'shpai-en] vi. to spy out, reconnoitre, scout.

Ausspannen [owss'shpan-en] vt. to stretch out, unharness; i. relax.

Ausspannung [owss'shpan-ōong] nf. unharnessing, relaxation, rest.

Aussparen [owss'shpahr-ren] vt. to by-pass (mil.).

Ausspeien [owss'shpy-en] vi. to spit out.

Aussperren [owss'shper-ren] vt. to shut out, lock out, space out (type).

Ausspielen [owss'shpee-len] vt.i. to play out, lead (card), play off.

Ausspinnen [owss'shpin-en] vt. ir. to spin out, devise.

Ausspionieren [owss'shpee-o-neer-ren] vt. to spy out.

Aussprache [owss'shprach-er] nf. pronunciation, (frank) discussion.

Aussprechen [owss'shpre-shen] vt. ir. to pronounce, express; r. speak one's mind.

Aussprengen [owss'shpreng-en] vt. to noise abroad.

Ausspringen [owss'shpring-en] vi. ir. to project.

Ausspritzen [owss'shprit-sen] vt. to squirt out; i. spout out.

Ausspruch [owss'shprōōch] nm. (Aussprüche) saying, remark, decision, judgment, finding (jury). [vt. to spit out.

Ausspucken [owss'shpook-en]

Ausspülen [owss'shpōōl-en] vt. to wash (away), rinse.

Ausspüren [owss'shpyōōr-ren] vt. to track, trace out.

Ausstaffieren [owss'shtaf-eer-ren] vt. to equip, furnish, dress up, trim.

Ausstand [owss'shtant] nm. (Austände) strike, delay, arrears (com.); -sunterstützung nf. strike pay.

Ausständig [owss'shten-dish] a. on strike, outstanding (debts).

Ausstatten [owss'shtat-en] vt. to provide with, equip, settle on, give dowry to, endow.

Ausstattung [owss'shtat-ōong] nf. outfit, dowry, trousseau, endowment.

Ausstechen [owss'shtesh-en] vt. ir. to put out, dig out, cut out, outshine, put in the shade, engrave.

Ausstecken [owss'shtek-en] vt. to hang out, put out, display.

Ausstehen [owss'shtay-en] vt. ir. to stand, endure; i. to be outstanding, missing, be on strike.

Aussteigen [owss'shti-gen] vi. ir. to get out, alight, bale out (av.).

Aussteinen [owss'shtine-en] vt. to stone (fruit).

Ausstellen [owss'shtel-en] vt. to exhibit, expose, display, post (sentry), make out (receipt, bill), issue (policy, etc.), find fault with, criticize.

Aussteller [owss'shtel-err] nm (-) exhibitor, drawer (bill).

Ausstellung [owss'shtel-ōong] nf. exhibition, drawing up, making out, censure.

Aussterben [owss'shterr-ben] *vi. ir.* to die out.

Aussteuer [owss'shtoy-err] *nf.* dowry, trousseau; **-versicherung** *nf.* endowment insurance.

Aussteuern [owss'shtoy-errn] to endow, provide with a portion.

Ausstich [owss'shtish] *nm.* choicest wine, finest brand.

Ausstopfen [owss'shtop-fen] *vt.* to stuff.

Ausstossen [owss'shtoh-sen] *vt. ir.* to thrust out, expel, utter (*cry*).

Ausstossrohr [owss'shtoce-rohr] *n.* torpedo tube (*nav.*).

Ausstrahlen [owss'shtrah-len] *vt.* to radiate.

Ausstrahlung [owss'shtrah-lŏong] *nf.* radiation.

Ausstrecken [owss'shtreck-en] *vt.* to stretch out.

Ausstreichen [owss'shtry-shen] *vt. ir.* to strike out, cancel, smooth out.

Ausstreuen [owss'shtroy-en] *vt.* to scatter, spread.

Ausströmen [owss'shtrer-men] *vt.i.* to pour out, escape.

Aussuchen [owss'zōōch-en] *vt.* to search out, select, pick out.

Austausch [owss'towsh] *nm.* barter, exchange.

Austauschen [owss'tow-shen] *vt.* to barter, exchange.

Austeilen [owss'tile-en] *vt.* to distribute, apportion.

Austeilung [owss'tile-ŏong] *nf.* distribution, apportioning.

Auster [ow'sterr] *nf.* oyster.

Austiefen [owss'teef-en] *vt.* to deepen, dredge.

Austilgen [owss'til-gen] *vt.* to eradicate, exterminate, wipe out.

Austoben [owss'tobe-en] *vt.* to calm down; *r.* sow one's wild oats.

Austrag [owss'trahk] *nm.* decision, settlement.

Austragen [owss'trah-gen] *vt.*

ir. to carry out, deliver (*letters*), wear out, decide (*quarrel*), spread (*gossip*).

Austräger [owss'tray-gerr] *nm.* (-) carrier, postman, errand boy.

Austreiben [owss'tribe-en] *vt. ir.* to drive out, expel.

Austreibung [owss'tribe-ōong] *nf.* expulsion.

Austreten [owss'tray-ten] *vi. ir.* to go out, retire, overflow; *t.* tread out, trample, wear out.

Austrinken [owss'tring-ken] *vt. ir.* to drink off, drain.

Austritt [owss'trit] *nm.* (Austritte) going out, overflow, withdrawal, retirement.

Austrocknen [owss'trok-nen] *vt.i.* to dry up, dessicate, season (*wood*). [put out.

Austun [owss'tōōn] *vt. ir.* to

Ausüben [owss'yōō-ben] *vt.* to practice, exert, carry out, execute, commit.

Ausübung [owss'yōō-bōong] *nf.* practice, exercise.

Ausverkauf [owss'ferr-cowf] *nm.* clearance sale, selling off.

Ausverkaufen [owss'ferr-cow-fen] *vt.* to sell out.

Auswachsen [owss'vax-en] *vi. ir.* to sprout, grow up.

Auswägen [owss'vay-gen] *vt. ir.* to weigh out.

Auswahl [owss'vahl] *nf.* selection, choice; reiche — large assortment. [to select.

Auswählen [owss'vay-len] *vt.* to select, choose.

Auswanderer [owss'van-derr-err] *nm.* (-) emigrant.

Auswandern [owss'van-derrn] *vi.* to emigrate.

Auswanderung [owss'van-der-rōong] *nf.* emigration; **-messer** *nm.* range corrector.

Auswärtig [owss'vairr-tish]*a.* foreign.

Auswärts [owss'vairrts] *ad.* outwards, abroad, outside.

Auswaschen [owss'vash-en] *vt. ir.* to wash out.

Auswechseln [owss'vex-eln] *vt.* to change, substitute.

Ausweg [owss'vaig] *nm.* (-e) way out, expedient.

Ausweichen [owss'vi-shen] *vt.i. ir.* to make way for, yield, avoid, shunt (*rl.*).

Ausweichend [owss'vi-shent] *a.* evasive.

Ausweich-hafen *nm.* alternative aerodrome (*av.*); **-manöver** *n.* avoiding action (*av.*); **-stelle** *nf.* siding (*rl.*); **-welle** *nf.* alternative wave (*rad.*); **-ziel** *n.* alternative target (*av.*).

Ausweiden [owss'vide-en] *vt.* to eviscerate.

Ausweis [owss'vice] *nm.* (-e) identity card, passport, statement, voucher.

Ausweisen [owss'vize-en] *vt. ir.* to expel, banish; *r.* prove one's identity.

Ausweis-karte *nf.* **-papiere** *n.pl.* identity papers.

Ausweisung [owss'vize-ŏong] *nf.* expulsion, banishment.

Ausweiten [owss'vite-en] *vt.* to stretch, widen.

Auswendig [owss'ven-dish] *a.* outward, external; **- lernen** to learn by heart.

Auswerfen [owss'vairr-fen] *vt. ir.* to throw out, cast up, fix (*salary*), cast (*anchor*).

Auswerten [owss'vairr-ten] *vt.* to make use of, exploit, sift, analyse, compute.

Auswertung [owss'vairr-tŏong] *nf.* analysis, plotting.

Auswetzen [owss'vet-sen] *vt.* to atone for, avenge, wipe out (*injury*).

Auswickeln [owss'vick-eln] *vt.* to unwrap, unroll.

Auswiegen [owss'vee-gen] *vt. ir.* to weigh out, retail.

Auswirken [owss'virr-ken] *vt.* to obtain, get, effect.

Auswischen [owss'vish-en] *vt.* to wipe out, blot (*page*).

Auswuchs [owss'vŏox] *nm.*

(Auswüchse) excrescence, deformity.

Auswurf [owss'vŏorf] *nm.* (Auswürfe) refuse, scum, dregs, expectoration.

Auszacken [owss'tsack-en] *vt.* to indent, scallop.

Auszahlen [owss'tsah-len] *vt.* to pay down, out, pay in full.

Auszahler [owss'tsah-lerr] *nm.* (-) cashier.

Auszahlung [owss'tsah-lŏong] *nf.* disbursement, payment; **-sliste** *nf.* pay sheet.

Auszählen [owss'tsay-len] *vt.* to count out.

Auszehren [owss'tsairr-en] *vt.* to consume; *r.* waste away.

Auszehrung [owss'tsairr-ŏong] *nf.* consumption.

Auszeichnen [owss'tsish-nen] *vt.* to mark out, treat with distinction, ticket, label (*com.*); *r.* distinguish oneself.

Auszeichnung [owss'tsish-nŏong] *nf.* distinction, prize, labelling, marking (*com.*).

Ausziehen [owss'tsee-en] *vt. ir.* to pull out, extract, take off (*clothes*), extract (*dyes*), make (*bill*); *r.* undress; *i.* march off, leave, remove.

Auszug [owss'tsŏok] *nm.* (Auszüge) removal, departure, extract, abstract, statement (*of account*).

Auto [ow'toh] *n.* motor-car; **-bahn** *nf.* trunk road, arterial road; **-bus** *nm.* motor-bus; **-brille** *nf.* goggles; **-droschke** *nf.* taxi-cab; **-heber** *nm.* jack; **-hupe** *nf.* motor horn, hooter; **-mobilist** *nm.* motorist; **-schlepp** *nm.* towing cars, catapulting planes; **-schlosser** *nm.* motor mechanic; **-schuppen** *nm.* garage.

Auto-biographie *nf.* autobiography; **-gramm** *n.* autograph; **-krat** *nm.* autocrat; **-kratie** *nf.* autocracy; **-mat** *nm.* automatic machine;

-matisch a. automatic; **-nom** a. autonomous, self-governing.

Autor [ow'torr] (g. -s; pl. -en) author.

Autorisieren [ow-tor-ri-zeer'ren] vt. to authorize.

Autorität [ow-tor-ri-tate'] nf. authority.

Autostop [ow'toh-shtop] nm. hitch-hiking; **- machen** to hitch-hike.

Avis [a-veess'] nm. information, advice (com.).

Avisieren [a-vee-zeer'ren] vt. to inform (com.).

Axt [akst] nf. axe.

Azetylen [at-say-tew-lain'] n. acetylene.

B

Bach [bach] nm. (**Bäche**) brook, stream. [nf. forecastle.

Back [back] ad. abaft (nav.).

Backbord [back'borrt] n. port (nav.); **-motor** nm. port engine.

Backe [back'er] nf. cheek; **-nbart** nm. whiskers.

Backen [back'en] vt. ir. to bake, dry (fruit), burn (bricks).

Backfisch [back'fish] nm. (-e) fish for frying, flapper.

Back-obst n. dried fruit; **-ofen** nm. oven; **-pfanne** nf. frying pan; **-pflaume** nf. prune; **-pulver** n. baking powder; **-stein** nm. brick; **-teig** nm. dough; **-werk** n. bakery.

Bäcker [beck'err] nm. (-) baker. [bakery.

Bäckerei [beck-er-ri'] nf.

Bad [baht] n. (**Bäder**) bath, watering place, spa, health resort.

Bade-anstalt nf. baths, swimming pool; **-anzug** nm. bathing costume; **-gast** nm. visitor at spa; **-hose** nf. bathing drawers; **-kappe** nf. bathing cap; **-kur** nf. course of treatment; **-mantel** nm. bath-

gown; **-meister** nm. baths attendant; **-ort** nm. bathing place; **-strand** nm. bathing beach; **-tuch** n. bath-towel; **-vorleger** nm. bath-mat, cork; **-wanne** nf. bath, bath-tub; **-zelle** nf. bathing box; **-zimmer** n. bathroom.

Baden [bah'den] vi. to bathe, have a bath; t. bath.

Badende(r) [bah'den-derr] nm. bather. [luggage.

Bagage [ba-gah'zher] nf.

Bagger [ba'gerr] nm. (-) dredger, excavator, bulldozer; **-schute** nf. hopper. [dredge.

Baggern [ba'gerrn] vt. to dredge.

Bähen [bey'en] vt. to foment.

Bahn [bahn] nf. railway track, course, road, way, orbit (planet), width (cloth), face (tool); **-brechend** a. pioneering, original; **-brecher** nm. pioneer, inventive genius; **-gleis** n. railway track.

Bahnen [bah-nen] vt. to pave, prepare the way.

Bahnhof [bahn'hohf] nm. (-höfe) station; **-soffizier** nm. railway transport officer (mil.); **-sschutz** nm. railway guard; **-svorsteher** nm. station master; **-swache** nf. station military guard; **-swirtschaft** nf. railway restaurant.

Bahn-knoten nm. junction; **-körper** nm. permanent way (rl.); **-netz** n. railway system; **-post** nf. travelling post-office; **-steig** nm. platform; **-strecke** nf. section of line (rl.); **-übergang** nm. railway crossing, bridge, level crossing; **-wärter** nm. signalman. [bier.

Bahre [bah'rer] nf. stretcher.

Bai [bie] nf. bay.

Baisse [beh'ser] nf. slump, fall in prices (com.). [bayonet.

Bajonett [ba'jo-net'] n. (-e)

Bake [bah'ker] nf. beacon.

Bakelite [bah-ker-lete'er] nf. bakelite.

Bakterie [bak'tai-ri-er] *nf.*
bacterium.

Balance [ba-long'ser] *nf.*
balance, equilibrium.

Balancieren [ba-long-seer'-
ren] *vi.* to balance.

Bald [balt] *ad.* soon, almost;
bald . . . , bald . . . sometimes
. . . sometimes . . . ; - dieses,
-jenes first this, then that;
Baldig [bal'dish] *a.* early,
speedy.

Baldmöglichst [balt'mer-
glish-st] *ad.* as soon as possible.

Bälde [bel'der] *nf.* a short
time.

Baldrian [bal'dri-ahn] *nm.*
[valerian.

Balg [bal-k] *nm.* (Bälge) skin,
bellows (*organ*).

Balgen [bal'gen] *vi.* to fight,
wrestle, romp.

Balken [bal'ken] *nm.* (-) beam,
rafter, girder, boom; -gesims
n. cornice; -sperre *nf.* barricade.

Balkon [bal-kohn'] *nm.*
balcony.

Ball [bal] *nm.* (Bälle) ball;
-spiel *n.* ball game.

Ball [bal] *nm.* (Bälle) dance,
ball; -kleid *n.* evening dress.

Ballade [ba-lah'der] *nf.* ballad.

Ballast [ba-last'] *nm.* ballast.

Ballen [ba'len] *nm.* bale,
bundle, (-) package.

Ballen [ba'len] *vt.* to clench,
pack in bales (*com.*); *i.* to
conglomerate.

Ballett [ba-lett'] *n.* (-e) ballet.

Ballon [ba-long'] *nm.* (-s)
balloon; -sperre *nf.* balloon
barrage; -wart *nm.* balloon
operator.

Ballung [ba'lŏong] *nf.* conglomeration, concentration
(*gas*), massing (*troops*).

Balsam [bal'zahm] *nm.* balsam, (-e) balm.

Balsamieren [bal-za-meer'-
ren] *vt.* to embalm.

Bambus [bam'bŏŏss] *nm.* (-se)
bamboo; -rohr *n.* bamboo cane.

Banal [ba-nahl'] *a.* commonplace.   [banana.

Banane [ba-nah'ner] *nf.*

Band [bant] *n.* volume (Bände);
(Bänder) ribbon, tape, hoop
(*cask*), ligament; (Bande) tie,
bond; -breite *nf.* band-width
(*rad.*).   [bandage.

Bandage [ban-dah'zher] *nf.*

Bandagieren [ban-da-zheer'-
ren] *vt.* to bandage.

Bande [ban'der] *nf.* band,
gang; -nkrieg *nm.* guerilla
warfare; -nmitglied *n.* gangster.

Band-mass *n.* tape measure;
-schleife *nf.* knot of ribbons;
-waren *f.pl.* haberdashery.

Bändigen [ben'dig-en] *vt.* to
tame, restrain, control.

Bandit [ban-deet'] *nm.* bandit.

Bange [bang'er] *a.* afraid,
anxious.   [afraid.

Bangen [bang'en] *vi.r.* to be

Bangemacher [bang'er-
mach-err] *nm.* (-) alarmist,
defeatist.

Bank [bank] *nf.* (Bänke) bench,
seat, sandbank.

Bank [bank] *nf.* (Banken) bank
(*com.*); -aktie *nf.* bank share;
-anweisung *nf.* cheque;
-beamte(r) *nm.* bank clerk;
-bruch *nm.* bankruptcy; -buch
n. pass book; -direktor *nm.*
bank manager; -diskonto *nm.*
banker's discount, bank rate;
-fach *n.* banking business, bank
safe; -konto *n.* bank account;
-note *nf.* bank note; -satz *nm.*
bank rate; -vorstand *nm.* bank
manager; -wechsel *nm.* bank
draft; -wesen *n.* banking;
-zettelbuch *n.* cheque book.

Bank(e)rott [bank-rot'] *nm.*
bankruptcy; *a.* bankrupt.

Bankett [bank-et'] *n.* (-e)
banquet.

Bankier [bank-ee-ay'] *nm.* (-s)
banker.

Bann [ban] *nm.* ban, excommunication, spell; -kreis *nm.*
sphere of influence; -meile *nf.*

boundary; **-ware** nf. contraband.

Bannen [ban'en] vt. to banish.

Banner [ban'err] nm. (-) banner, standard.

Bar [bahrr] a. bare, destitute, sheer (nonsense), ready (money); **-e Münze** face value; **-zahlen** to pay cash; **-fuss** a. barefoot; **-geld** n. ready money, cash; **-häuptig** a. bareheaded; **-kauf** nm. cash purchase; **-schaft** nf. ready money; **-zahlung** nf. cash payment.

Bär [bahrr] nf. (-s) bar.

Bär [bahrr] nm. bear.

Baracke [ba-rack'er] nf. barrack, hut; **-nlager** n. camp, group of huts, hutment.

Barbar [barr-barr'] m.w. barbarian.

Barbarei [barr-ba-ry'] nf. barbarity, barbarism.

Barbarisch [barr-bah'rish] a. barbarous, barbaric.

Barbier [barr-beerr'] nm. (-e) barber.

Barchent [barr'shent] nm. (-e) fustian. [launch.

Barkasse [barr-kass'er] nf.

Barke [barr'ker] nf. barque.

Bärme [bairr'mer] nf. yeast.

Barmherzig [barrm'hairrt-sish] a. merciful.

Barmherzigkeit [barrm-hairrt'sich-kite] nf. mercy, compassion.

Barometer [ba-ro-may'terr] n. barometer; **-stand** nm. height of barometer.

Baron [ba-rohn'] nm. (-e) baron. [baroness.

Baronin [ba-roh'nin] nf.

Barre [ba'rer] nf. bar, ingot, sandbank.

Barren [ba'ren] nm. (-) parallel bars.

Barriere [ba-ri-air'rer] nf. barrier, gate. [perch.

Barsch [barrsh] nm. (-e)

Barsch [barrsh] a. rough, rude.

Bart [barrt] nm. (Bärte) beard.

Bärtig [bairr'tish] a. bearded.

Base [bah'zer] nf. female cousin.

Base [bah'zer] nf. base.

Basieren [ba-zeer'ren] vt. to base; i. to be based.

Basis [bah'zis] nf. basis.

Bass [bass] nm. (Bässe) bass; **-stimme** nf. bass voice.

Bassin [bass-ang']n. (-s) basin, dock, reservoir. [singer.

Bassist [bass'ist] m.w. bass

Bast [bast] nm. bast.

Bastard [bass'tart] nm. (-e) bastard.

Basteln [bass'teln] vt. to rig up, potter about, go in for a hobby.

Bastler [basst'lerr] nm. (-) amateur, dabbler, fan, handyman.

Bataillon [ba-tal-yohn'] n. (-e) battalion; **-sstab** nm. battalion staff.

Batist [ba-tist'] nm. cambric.

Batterie [ba-ter-ree'] nf. battery, cell; **-chef** nm. battery commander (mil.).

Bau [bow] nm. (Bauten) building, working, cultivation, frame, working (mine); **-amt** n. works office, board of works; **-art** nf. architectural style; **-bagger** nm. excavator; **-bataillon** n. construction, works battalion; **-fällig** a. dilapidated; **-funker** nm. construction mechanic (av.); **-genossenschaft** nf. building society; **-gerüst** n. scaffolding; **-gruppe** nf. construction unit; **-herr** nm. builder, contractor; **-hof** nm. timber yard, stores depot (mil.); **-holz** n. timber, lumber; **-ingenieur** nm. civil engineer; **-kasten** nm. box of bricks; **-kunst** nf. architecture; **-meister** nm. master builder, architect; **-muster** n. type (of aircraft); **-reihe** nf. series of aircraft; **-riss** nm. architect's plan; **-sparkasse** nf. building society; -stab *nm.* construction staff (*av.*); -stein *nm.* building stone, freestone; -stelle *nf.* site; -techniker *nm.* architect; -teile *m.pl.* pre-fabricated parts (*houses*); -tischler *nm.* cabinet maker; -truppe *nf.* wks personnel, construction unit.

Bauch [bowch] *nm.* (Bäuche) stomach, belly; -grimmen *n.*, -kneifen *n.* colic; -redner *nm.* ventriloquist.

Bauen [bow'en] *vt.* to build, cultivate, grow (*corn*), work (*mine*); *i.* depend upon.

Bauer [bow'err] *nm.* (*gen.* -s, -n; *pl.* -n) farmer, peasant, pawn (*chess*).

Bauer [bow'err] *n.* (-) bird cage.

Bäuerin [boy'er-rin] *nf.* country-woman, farmer's wife.

Bäuerisch [boy'er-rish] *a.* rustic, boorish.

Bauern-bursche *nm.* peasant lad, country lad; -fänger *nm.* cheat, rogue; -gut *n.* farm; -hof *nm.* farm, farmyard; -schaft *nf.* peasantry, rural community; -tracht *nf.* peasant costume; -volk *n.* peasantry, country people.

Baum [bowm] *nm.* (Bäume) tree, beam, boom (*nav.*); -garten *nm.* orchard, nursery; -öl *n.* olive oil; -rinde *nf.* bark; -rose *nf.* hollyhock; -schule *nf.* nursery; -schütze *nm.* sniper (*mil.*); -stamm *nm.* tree trunk; -wolle *nf.* cotton; -zucht *nf.* growing of trees, forestry.

Baumeln [bow'meln] *vt.* to dangle.

Bäumen [boy'men] *vr.* to rear.

Bausch [bowsh] *nm.* (Bäusche) bolster, compress; in – und Bogen in bulk.

Bauschen [bow'shen] *vt.r.* to bag out, swell.

Bauschig [bow'shish] *a.* baggy, swollen, puffed out.

Bazillus [bat-sil'õõss] *nm.* (Bazillen) bacillus.

Beabsichtigen [be-ap'zish-ti-gen] *vt.* to intend.

Beachten [be-acht'en] *vt.* to pay attention to, notice, take notice of; -swert *a.* noteworthy.

Beachtung [be-acht'õõng] *nf.* notice, consideration, attention.

Beamte(r) [be-am'terr] *m.w.* official, civil servant, employee (*bank, etc.*).

Beängstigen [be-eng'sti-gen] *vt.* to make anxious, worry, alarm.

Beängstigung [be-eng'sti-gõõng] *nf.* anxiety, alarm.

Beanlagt [be-an'lahkt] *a.* gifted, talented.

Beanspruchen [be-an'shprõõch-en] *vt.* to claim, take up (*time*).

Beanstanden [be-an'shtan-den] *vt.* to object to, contest, complain about.

Beanstandung [be-an'shtan-dõõng] *nf.* objection, complaint.

Beantragen [be-an'trah-gen] *vt.* to propose, move.

Beantworten [be-ant'vorr-ten] *vt.* to answer.

Beantwortung [be-ant'vorr-tõõng] *nf.* answering, reply.

Bearbeiten [be-arr'bite-en] *vt.* to work, work up, cultivate, treat, adapt, revise (*book*).

Bearbeitung [be-arr'bite-õõng] *nf.* treatment, adaptation, revision, elaboration, compilation.

Beaufsichtigen [be-owf'zish-ti-gen] *vt.* to supervise, superintend, control, inspect.

Beaufsichtigung [be-owf-zish-ti-gõõng] *nf.* inspection, supervision, control.

Beauftragen [be-owf'trah-gen] *vt.* to commission, authorize, order.

Beauftragte(r) *m.w.* commissioner, deputy, agent.

Bebauen [be-bow'en] *vt.* to

build on (*land*), cultivate (*soil*), work (*mine*). [quake.

Beben [bay'ben] *vi.* to tremble.

Becher [be'sherr] *nm.* (-) cup, mug; **-glas** *n.* tumbler, beaker.

Becken [beck'en] *n.* basin, cymbal, pelvis. [roof.

Bedachen [Be-dach'en] *vt.* to

Bedacht [be-dacht'] *a.* thoughtful, careful, keen on, intent on; *nm.* consideration, caution, deliberation.

Bedächtig [be-desh'tish] *a.* cautious, prudent, deliberate, slow.

Bedachtsam [be-dacht'zam] *a.* careful, thoughtful.

Bedanken [be-dank'en] *vr.* to thank for, decline.

Bedarf [be-darrf'] *nm.* need, demand, requirements, supply; **-sartikel** *nm.* commodity, necessary, requisite; **-sfall** *nm.* case of need; **-shaltestelle** *nf.* request stop (*tram*).

Bedauerlich [be-dow'err-lish] *a.* regrettable.

Bedauern [be-dow'errn] *vt.* to regret, deplore, be sorry for (*a person*).

Bedauern [be-dow'errn] *n.* regret; **-swert** regrettable, deplorable. [cover.

Bedecken [be-deck'en] *vt.* to

Bedeckt [be-deckt'] *a.* overcast (sky), broken (*ground*).

Be deckung [be-deck'ŏŏng] *nf.* covering, protection.

Bedenken [be-denk'en] *vt.* to think (over), consider, provide; sich eines andern – change one's mind.

Bedenken [be-denk'en] *n.* consideration, scruple, hesitation, doubt.

Bedenklich [be-denk'lish] *a.* doubtful, delicate, suspicious, risky.

Bedenkzeit [be-denk'tsite] *nf.* time for reflection.

Bedeuten [be-doi'ten] *vt.* to mean, signify, be of impor-

tance, point out, inform; **-d** *a.* important, considerable.

Bedeutsam [be-doit'zam] *a.* significant.

Bedeutung [be-doi'tŏŏng] *nf.* meaning, significance, indication, importance; **-slos** *a.* meaningless, unimportant; **-svoll** *a.* momentous, weighty.

Bedienen [be-deen'en] *vt.* to serve, wait upon, work (*tec.*), service, operate (*plane, etc.*); *r.* to make use of, help oneself.

Bediente(r) [be-deen'terr] *m.w.* servant.

Bedienung [be-dee'nŏŏng] *nf.* service attendants, staff (*servants*).

Bedingen [be-ding'en] *vt.* to stipulate, agree upon, involve.

Bedingt [be-dingt'] *a.* conditional, qualified.

Bedingung [be-ding'ŏŏng] *nf.* condition, stipulation, agreement, terms.

Bedingungslos [be-ding'-ŏŏngs-lohs] *a.* unconditional; **-e Kapitulation** unconditional surrender.

Bedrängen [be-dreng'en *vt.* to oppress, distress, harass.

Bedrängnis [be-dreng'nis] *nf.* (-se) oppression, distress, trouble.

Bedrohen [be-droh'en] *vt.* to threaten.

Bedrohlich [be-droh'lish] *a.* threatening, menacing.

Bedrohung [be-droh'ŏŏng] *nf.* threat(ening), menace.

Bedrucken [be-drŏŏk'en] *vt.* to print on. [to oppress.

Bedrücken [be-dryŏŏk'en] *vt.*

Bedünken [be-dyŏŏn'ken] *vt. imp.* to seem, appear.

Bedürfen [be-dyŏŏr'fen] *vt.i. imp. ir.* to need, want, be in need of.

Bedürfnis [be-dyŏŏrf'nis] *n.* necessity, need; **-anstalt** *nf.* public lavatory; **-los** *a.* frugal, unpretentious.

Bedürftig [be-dyöörf'tish] *a.* in need, poor.

Beehren [be-airr'en] *vt.* to honour; **wir — uns** we beg to, have pleasure in.

Beeidig-en [be-i'dig-en] *vt.* to put on oath; **-te Aussage** affidavit.

Beeilen [be-ile'en] *vt. r.* to hurry, hasten.

Beeinflussen [be-ine'flöö-sen] *vt.* to influence.

Beeinflussung [be-ine'flöö-söong] *nf.* influence.

Beeinträchtigen [be-ine'tresh-ti-gen] *vt.* to injure, wrong, infringe upon, prejudice.

Beeinträchtigung [be-ine'tresh-ti-gööng] *nf.* injury, wrong, prejudice, infringement.

Been(d)igen [be-en'den, be-en'di-gen] *vt.* to end, terminate, finish.

Beendigung [be-en'di-gööng] *nf.* end, termination.

Beengen [be-eng'en] *vt.* to cramp, hamper, narrow down, confine.

Beerben [be-airr'ben] *vt.* to be heir to, inherit.   [to bury.

Beerdigen [be-airr'di-gen] *vt.*

Beerdigung [be-airr'di-gööng] *nf.* funeral, burial.

Beere [bai'rer] *nf.* berry.

Beet [bate] *n.* (-e) bed *(garden)*.

Beete [bay'ter] *nf.* beetroot.

Befähigen [be-fay'i-gen] *vt.* to qualify, enable, make fit.

Befähigt [be-fay'isht] *a.* qualified, fit, gifted, able.

Befähigung [be-fay'i-gööng] *nf.* qualification, fitness, aptitude, competence, capacity, talent.

Befahrbar [be-farr'barr] *a.* practicable, navigable.

Befahren [be-farr'en] *vt. ir.* to use *(road, etc.)*, drive over, navigate.

Befallen [be-fal'en] *vt. ir.* to attack, befall.

Befangen [be-fang'en] *a.* shy, embarrassed, self-conscious, perplexed, involved in *(error)*.

Befangenheit [be-fang'en-hite] *nf.* embarrassment, shyness, perplexity, prejudice.

Befassen [be-fass'en] *vr.* to be occupied (with).

Befehden [be-fay'den] *vt.* to make war upon.

Befehl [be-fail'] *nm.* (-e) command, order.

Befehlen [be-fail'en] *vt. ir.* to command, order, brief *(av.)*; *r.* commit oneself; *n.* briefing *(av.)*.

Befehligen [be-fail'i-gen] *vt.* to be in command of, lead.

Befehls-erteilung *nf.* giving of orders; **-form** *nf.* imperative *(mood)*; **-haber** *nm.* commander, commanding officer, admiral *(nav.)*; **-kopf** *nm.* command centre *(mil.)*; **-stand** *nm.* **-stelle** *nf.* command post *(mil.)*, briefing room *(av.)*.

Befestigen [be-fest'i-gen] *vt.* to fasten, fortify *(mil.)*.

Befestigung [be-fest'i-gööng] *nf.* strengthening, fastening, fortification *(mil.)*; **-sanlagen** *f.pl.* **-swerke** *n.pl.* defences *(mil.)*.

Befeuchten [be-foish'ten] *vt.* to damp, moisten.

Befeuerung [be-foi'er-rööng] *nf.* (flare-path) lighting *(av.)*.

Befiedert [be-fee'derrt] *a.* feathered.

Befinden [be-fin'den] *vt. ir.* to find, consider; *r.* feel, be.

Befinden [be-fin'den] *n.* health, view, opinion.

Befindlich [be-fint'lish] *a.* situated, existing.

Beflaggen [be-fla'gen] *vt.* to flag, decorate with flags.

Beflecken [be-fleck'en] *vt.* to pollute, stain.

Befleckung [be-fleck'ööng] *nf.* pollution, stain.

Befleissigen [be-flice'i-gen] *vr.* to take pains, exert oneself.

Befliegen [be-flee'gen] vt. ir. to fly over.

Beflissen [be-fliss'en] a. intent, studious, devoted to, assiduous.

Beflissenheit [be-fliss'en-hite] nf. diligence, perseverance.

Beflügeln [be-flyōō'geln] vt. to wing, speed on.

Befolgen [be-fol'gen] vt. to obey, comply with.

Befolgung [be-fol'gōong] nf. adherence to, compliance with, observation of.

Beförderer [be-fer'der-rerr] nm. (-) promoter.

Befördern [be-fer'derrn] vt. to promote, forward, dispatch, transport.

Beförderung [be-fer'der-rōong] nf. promotion, furtherance, transport, dispatch, forwarding, conveyance.

Befrachten [be-frach'ten] vt. to load, freight, charter (ship).

Befrachtung [be-frach'tōong] nf. loading, chartering, freight, carriage. [question.

Befragen [be-frah'gen] vt. to

Befreien [be-frī'en] vt. to liberate, set free, exempt.

Befreier [be-frī'err] nm. (-) liberator.

Befreiung [be-frī'ōong] nf. liberation, deliverance, exemption; -skrieg nm. war of liberation; -sschein nm. release certificate.

Befremden [be-frem'den] vt. to surprise, impress unfavourably; n. surprise, astonishment.

Befremdlich [be-fremt'lish] a. strange, odd, surprising.

Befreunden [be-froin'den] vt. to befriend; r. to make friends.

Befrieden [be-free'den] vt. to pacify, appease.

Befriedigen [be-free'di-gen] vt. to satisfy; -d satisfactory, gratifying.

Befriedigung [be-free'di-gōong] nf. satisfaction.

Befriedung [be-free'dōong] nf. pacification, appeasement; -spolitik nf. appeasement policy.

Befruchten [be-frŏŏch'ten] vt. to fertilize, stimulate.

Befruchtung [be-frŏŏch'tōong] nf. fertilization.

Befugnis [be-fook'nis] nf. (-se) authorization, powers, right.

Befugt [be-fookt'] a. authorized, entitled, competent.

Befühlen [be-few'len] vt. to touch, feel, handle.

Befund [be-fŏŏnt'] nm. finding, statement, condition, diagnosis; -prüfung nf. inspection.

Befürchten [be-fyŏŏr'shten] vt. to fear, apprehend.

Befürchtung [be-fyŏŏr'shtōong] nf. fear, apprehension.

Befürworten [be-fyŏŏr'vorr-ten] vt. support, speak in favour of, recommend, advocate.

Befürwortung [be-fyŏŏr'vorr-tōong] nf. support, recommendation.

Begabt [be-gahpt'] a. gifted.

Begabung [be-gah'bōong] nf. talents, gifts, ability.

Begaffen [be-gaf'en] vt. to gape at. [pair, mate.

Begatten [be-gat'en] vr. to

Begeben [be-gay'ben] vr. ir. to betake oneself, go, proceed to, happen, take place, renounce; t. negotiate, sell (com.).

Begebenheit [be-gay'ben-hite] nf. event, occurrence, accident.

Begegnen [be-gaik'nen] vi. to meet, come across, happen, treat, face up to; r. cross (letters).

Begegnis [be-gaik'nis] n. (-se) event.

Begegnung [be-gaik'nōong] nf. meeting, interview, reception.

Begehen [be-gay'en] *vt. ir.* to commit, cross, traverse, celebrate.

Begehung [be-gay'ŏŏng] *nf.* commission (*crime*), crossing, traversing, celebration.

Begehr [be-gairr'] *nm.* demand, desire.

Begehren [be-gair'ren] *vt.* to desire, demand, covet; **-t sein** to be in demand (*com.*).

Begehrenswert [be-gair'rensvairt] *a.* desirable.

Begehrlich [be-gairr'lish] *a.* covetous, greedy.

Begehrlichkeit [be-gairr'lishkīte] *nf.* greed, covetousness.

Begeifern [be-gife'errn] *vt.* to slobber on, slander.

Begeistern [be-gi'sterrn] *vt.* to inspire, animate, encourage, fill with enthusiasm.

Begeistert [be-gi'sterrt] *a.* enthusiastic.

Begeisterung [be-gi'sterrŏŏng] *nf.* enthusiasm, inspiration.

Begier(de) [be-geer'der] *nf.* desire, lust.

Begierig [be-geer'rish] *a.* eager, desirous, covetous.

Begiessen [be-gee'sen] *vt. ir.* to sprinkle, water. [ning.

Beginn [be-gin'] *nm.* begin-

Beginnen [be-gin'nen] *vt.i. ir.* to begin; *n.* beginning, undertaking.

Beglaubigen [be-glow'bi-gen] *vt.* to certify.

Beglaubigung [be-glow'bigŏŏng] *nf.* certification, attestation; **-sschreiben** *n.* credentials, letter of credit (*com.*).

Begleichen [be-glī'shen] *vt. ir.* to settle, balance.

Begleichung [be-glī'shŏŏng] *nf.* settlement, balancing.

Begleit-adresse *nf.* declaration form, dispatch note; **-artillerie** *nf.* mechanized artillery (*mil.*);**-brief** *nm.* covering letter (*com.*).

Begleiten [be-glīte'en] *vt.* to accompany, escort, convoy (*nav.*).

Begleiter [be-glīte'err] *nm.* (**-**) attendant, companion, accompanist.

Begleit-erscheinung *nf.* attendant circumstance, symptom; **-papiere** *n.pl.* way-bill, permit (*com.*); **-schein** *nm.* way-bill, permit, credit slip (*bank*); **-schiff** *n.* escort vessel; **-schreiben** *n.* covering letter.

Begleitung [be-glīte'ŏŏng] *nf.* accompaniment, escort, company

Beglücken [be-glew'ken] *vt.* to make happy, delight.

Beglückwünschen [be-glewk'viewn-shen] *vt.* to congratulate.

Beglückwünschung [be-glewk'viewn-shŏŏng] *vt.* congratulation, good wishes.

Begnadigen [be-g-nah'di-gen] *vt.* to pardon.

Begnadigung [be-g-nah'digŏŏng] *nf.* pardon, amnesty.

Begnügen [be-g-new'gen] *vr.* to be satisfied, content oneself.

Begraben [be-grah'ben] *vt. ir.* to bury.

Begräbnis [be-graip'nis] *n.* (**-se**) burial, funeral; **-platz** *nm.* burial ground, cemetery.

Begradigung [be-grah'digŏŏng] *nf.* straightening of line (*mil.*).

Begreifen [be-grīfe'en] *vt. ir.* to understand, grasp, comprehend, include, contain.

Begreiflich [be-grīfe'lish] *a.* understandable.

Begrenzen [be-grent'sen] *vt.* to limit, bound, restrict.

Begrenztheit [be-grentst'hite] *nf.* limitation, restriction, narrowness.

Begrenzung [be-grent'sŏŏng] *nf.* restriction, limitation.

Begriff [be-grif'] *nm.* (**-e**) conception, idea; **-sbestimmung**

nf. definition; **-svermögen** *n.* power of comprehension.

Begründen [be-grӱоōn'den] *vt.* to found, form, establish, prove, substantiate, open (*business*).

Begründer [be-grӱоōn'derr] *nm.* (–) founder.

Begründet [be-grӱоōn'det] *a.* well founded.

Begründung [be-grӱоōn'dōōng] *nf.* foundation, formation, confirmation, proof, reason.

Begrüssen [be-grӱоō'sen] *vt.* greet, welcome.

Begrüssung [be-grӱоō'sōōng] *nf.* greeting, welcome.

Begünstigen [be-gune'stigen] *vt.* to favour, patronize, promote, further.

Begünstigung [be-gune'sti-gōōng] *nf.* favouring, encouragement, promotion (*plans*).

Begutachten [be-gōōt'ach-ten] *vt.* to submit an opinion on, report on.

Begutachtung [be-gōōt'ach-tōōng] *nf.* expert opinion, report.

Begütert [be-gӱоō'terrt] *a.* wealthy, well-to-do.

Begütigen [be-gӱоō'ti-gen] *vt.* to placate, appease, quieten down.

Behaart [be-hahrrt'] *a.* hairy.

Behäbig [be-hay'bish] *a.* comfortable, portly, stout.

Behaften [be-haf'ten] *vt.* to render liable.

Behaftet [be-haf'tet] *a.* burdened, affected with, liable to.

Behagen [be-hah'gen] *vi.* to please; *n.* comfort, ease.

Behaglich [be-hah'klish] *a.* comfortable, cosy.

Behaglichkeit [be-hah'klish-kite] *nf.* comfort, cosiness.

Behalten [be-hal'ten] *vt. ir.* to keep, retain, remember.

Behälter [be-hel'terr] *nm.* (–). **Behältnis** [be-helt'nis] *n.* (-se) case, box, receptacle, container, tank, cistern, reservoir.

Behandeln [be-han'deln] *vt.* to treat, deal with, handle, attend (*patient*).

Behandlung [be-hand'lōōng] *nf.* treatment, handling, management, dealing.

Behang [be-hang'] *nm.* (Behänge) hangings, drapery.

Behängen [be-heng'en] *vt.* to drape; *r.* shoulder (*responsibility*).

Beharren [be-harr'en] *vi.* to persevere, persist in, insist on.

Beharrlich [be-harr'lish] *a.* persevering, persistent, tenacious.

Beharrlichkeit [be-harr'lish-kite] *nf.* perseverance, persistence, tenacity.

Beharrungs-vermögen *n.* inertia; **-zustand** *nm.* persistence, resistance (*tec.*).

Behauen [be-how'en] *vt. ir.* to hew, lop.

Behaupten [be-howp'ten] *vt.* to assert, maintain; *r.* to stand fast, be firm, hold one's own.

Behauptung [be-howp'tōōng] *nf.* assertion, affirmation, statement.

Behausung [be-how'zōōng] *nf.* dwelling, home, lodging.

Beheben [be-hay'ben] *vt. ir.* to remove, take away.

Beheimatet [be-hime'ah-tet] *a.* domiciled.

Behelf [be-helf'] *nm.* (-e) expedient, makeshift, excuse; **-sbrücke** *nf.* emergency bridge; **-sheim** *n.* temporary house.

Behelfen [be-hel'fen] *vr. ir.* to manage, do, get on, contrive.

Behelfsmässig [be-helfs'may-sish] *a.* provisional, improvised, temporary, extemporary, auxiliary.

Behelligen [be-hell'i-gen] *vt.* to molest, trouble.

Behelligung [be-hell'i-gŏŏng] *nf.* molestation, bother.

Behende [be-hen'der] *a. ad.* nimble, agile, adroit, smart.

Behendigkeit [be-hen'dish-kite] *nf.* agility, quickness, smartness.

Beherbergen [be-hairr'bairr-gen] *vt.* to lodge, put up, accommodate.

Beherrschen [be-hairr'shen] *vt.* to govern, control, master.

Beherrscher [be-hairr-sherr] *nm.* (-) ruler.

Beherrschung [be-hairr'-shŏŏng] *nf.* control, mastery, command, rule.

Beherzigen [be-hairrt'si-gen] *vt.* to take to heart.

Beherzigung [be-hairrt'si-gŏŏng] *nf.* consideration.

Beherzt [be-hairrtst'] *a.* spirited, brave.

Behilflich [be-hilf'lish] *a.* helpful, useful.

Behindern [be-hin'derrn] *vt.* to prevent, impede, hinder.

Behinderung [be-hin'der-rŏŏng] *nf.* hindrance.

Beholzen [be-holt'sen] *vt.* to stock with trees.

Behörde [be-her'der] *nf.* authority, board, governing body. [official.

Behördlich [be-hert'lish] *a.*

Behuf [be-hŏŏf'] *nm.* use, purpose.

Behufs [be-hŏŏfs'] *pr.* with the intention of, with a view to, for the purpose of.

Behüten [be-hew'ten] *vt.* to guard, preserve.

Behutsam [be-hŏŏt'zam] *a.* cautious, careful.

Behutsamkeit [be-hŏŏt'zam-kite] *nf.* caution, carefulness.

Bei [by] *pr.* by, at, beside, on the occasion of; - alledem for all that; - uns at home, with us; - Zeiten early.

Beibehalten [by'be-hal-ten] *vt. ir.* to keep, retain.

Beibehaltung [by'be-hal-tŏŏng] *nf.* keeping, retention.

Beiblatt [by'blat] *n.* (-blätter) supplement, extra edition (*paper*). [dinghy (*nav.*).

Beiboot [by'boht] *n.* pinnace,

Beibringen [by'bring-en] *vt. ir.* to give, bring forward, adduce, deal, inflict, teach.

Beichte [bish'ter] *nf.* confession.

Beichten [bish'ten] *vi.t.* to confess, go to confession.

Beichtstuhl [bisht'shtŏŏl] *nm.* (-stähle) confessional.

Beide, beides [by'des] *a. pr.* both.

Beiderseitig [by'derr-zite-ish] *a.* mutual, reciprocal.

Beiderseits [by'derr-zites] *ad.* mutually, on both sides.

Beidrehen [by'dray-en] *vi.t.* to bring to, heave to (*nav.*).

Beidrücken [by'dryŏŏ-ken] *vt.* to affix. [ad. together.

Beieinander [by'ine-an-derr]

Beifahrer [by'fah-rerr] *nm.* (-) spare driver (*mil.*).

Beifall [by'fal] *nm.* applause, approval.

Beifällig [by'fell-ish] *a.* approving, favourable.

Beifilm [by'film] *nm.* (-e) supporting film.

Beifolgend [by'fol-gent] *a.* enclosed, annexed (*com.*).

Beifügen [by'few-gen] *vt.* to add, enclose.

Beigabe [by'gah-ber] *nf.* addition, supplement, gift.

Beigeben [by'gay-ben] *vt. ir.* to add to, give.

Beigeordnete(r) [by'ge-orrt-ne-terr] *nm.* assistant, deputy.

Beigeschmack [by'ge-schmak] *nm.* flavour, tinge.

Beigesellen [by'ge-zell-en] *vt.r.* to associate, join.

Beiheft [by'heft] *n.* supplement, extra number.

Beihilfe [by'hil-fer] *nf.* aid; help; staatliche - subsidy.

Beikommen [bỹ'kom-en] *vi. ir.* to get at, approach, equal.

Beil [bile] *n.* (-e) hatchet, chopper, axe.

Beilage [bỹ'lah-ger] *nf.* enclosure, supplement, addition.

Beiläufig [bỹ'loy-fish] *a.* incidental, occasional, casual; *ad.* incidentally, by the way.

Beilegen [bỹ'lay-gen] *vt.* to enclose, add, attribute, ascribe, settle (*quarrel*), confer (*honour*), bring to (*nav.*).

Beileid [bỹ'lite] *n.* condolence, sympathy.

Beiliegen [bỹ'lee-gen] *vi. ir.* to lie with, lie to (*nav.*); **-d** *a.* enclosed, nearly.

Beim = bei dem.

Beimengen [bỹ'meng-en], **beimischen** [bỹ'mish-en] *vt.* to admix, mix with.

Beimessen [bỹ'mess-en] *vt. ir.* to attribute, ascribe.

Bein [bine] *n.* (-e) bone, leg; **-kleid** *n.* trousers, knickers.

Beinahe [bỹ'nah-er] *ad.* almost, nearly.

Beiname [bỹ'nah-mer] *nm.* (*gen.* -ens; *pl.* -en) surname.

Beiordnen [bỹ'orrt-nen] *vt.* to co-ordinate, add.

Beipflichten [bỹ'pflish-ten] *vi.* to assent, agree to.

Beipflichtung [bỹ'pflish-tŏŏng] *nf.* assent, agreement.

Beirat [bỹ'raht] *nm.* (-räte) legal adviser, advisory council.

Beirren [be-irr'en] *vt.* to mislead, confuse. [together.

Beisammen [bỹ-zam'en] *ad.*

Beisatz [bỹ'zats] *nm.* (-sätze) admixture, addition, alloy.

Beischiff [bỹ'shif] *n.* (-e) tender (*nav.*). [habitation.

Beischlaf [bỹ'shlahf] *nm.* co-

Beischliessen [bỹ'shlee-sen] *vt. ir.* to enclose.

Beischluss [bỹ'shlŏŏs] *nm.* (-schlüsse) enclosure.

Beischreiben [bỹ'shribe'en] *vt. ir.* to add in writing.

Beischrift [bỹ'shrift] *nf.* addition, postscript, note.

Beisein [bỹ'zine] *n.* presence.

Beiseite [bỹ'zite-er] *ad.* aside, on one side.

Beisetzen [bỹ'zet-sen] *vt.* to add, bury. [burial.

Beisetzung [bỹ'zet-sŏŏng] *nf.*

Beisitzer [bỹ'zit-serr] *nm.* (-) assessor.

Beispiel [bỹ'shpeel] *n.* (-e) example; *zum* - for example.

Beispiellos [bỹ'shpeel-lohs] *a.* unprecedented, unexampled.

Beispielsweise [bỹ'shpeel-svize-er] *ad.* for instance, example.

Beispringen [bỹ'shpring-en] *vi. ir.* to hasten to help.

Beissen [bice'en] *vt. ir.* to bite; **-d** *a.* biting, caustic, sarcastic. [pliers, nippers.

Beisszange [bice'tsang-er] *nf.*

Beistand [bỹ'shtant] *nm.* support, help.

Beistehen [bỹ'shtay-en] *vi. ir.* to help, assist.

Beisteuer [bỹ'shtoy-err] *nf.* contribution, collection.

Beisteuern [bỹ'shtoy-errn] *vt.* to contribute.

Beistimmen [bỹ'shtim-en] *vi.* to agree with.

Beistimmung [bỹ'shtim-ŏŏng] *nf.* consent, agreement.

Beistrich [bỹ'shrish] *nm.* (-e) comma.

Beitrag [bỹ'trahk] *nm.* (-träge) contribution, subscription, premium (*insurance*).

Beitragen [bỹ'trah-gen] *vt. ir.* to contribute, subscribe, promote, help.

Beitreiben [bỹ'tribe-en] *vt. ir.* to recover, collect, extort, requisition.

Beitreten [bỹ'tray-ten] *vi. ir.* to join, accept, agree, assent to. [assent.

Beitritt [bỹ'trit] *nm.* joining.

Beiwagen [bỹ'vah-gen] *nm.* (-) side-car (*aut.*). extra

carriage; -**kraftrad** n, -**krad** n.
motor-cycle combination.

Beiwerk [by'verrk] n. accessories.

Beiwohnen [by'voh-nen] vi. to attend, be present at, sleep with.   [adjective.

Beiwort [by'vorrt] n. (-e)

Beize [bite'ser] nf. corrosive, caustic, stain (wood).

Beizeiten [bite-site'en] ad. early, betimes.

Beizen [bite'sen] vt. to corrode, cauterize, stain, tan, etch (metal).   [extra duty.

Beizoll [bite'sol] n. (-zölle)

Bejahen [be'yah'en] vt. to answer in the affirmative, agree.

Bejahung [be-yah'oong] nf. affirmative.

Bejahrt [be-yahrrt'] a. aged.

Bejammern [be-yam'errn] vt. to lament, bewail; -**swert** a. deplorable, lamentable.

Bekämpfen [be-kemp'fen] vt. to combat, fight against.

Bekämpfung [be-kemp'foong] nf. fight, struggle against, opposition.

Bekannt [be-kant'] a. (well) known, noted, acquainted.

Bekannte(r) [be-kan'terr] m.w. Bekannte f. acquaintance.

Bekannt-lich a. as is well known, as you know; -**machen** vt. to acquaint, make known, publish, advertise; -**machung** nf. intimation, announcement, notice, publication advertisement; -**schaft** nf. acquaintance.   [convert.

Bekehren [be-kair'ren] vt. to

Bekehrung [be-kair'roong] nf. conversion.

Bekennen [be-ken'en] vt. ir. to confess, acknowledge, profess (faith); **Farbe** - follow suit.

Bekenntnis [be-kent'nis] n. (-se) confession, creed, denomination; -**kirche** nf. Confessional Church; -**schule** nf. denom-

inational school, school with religious instruction.

Beklagen [be-klah'gen] vt. to deplore, lament; r. complain.

Beklagenswert [be-klah'gens-verrt] a. lamentable, pathetic.

Beklagte(r) m.w, Beklagte f. accused, defendant.

Beklatschen [be-klatch'en] vt. to applaud, clap.

Bekleben [be-klay'ben] vt. to paste on; mit Zetteln - label.

Beklecksen [be-klex'en] vt. to blot.

Bekleiden [be-klide'en] vt. to clothe, invest, occupy (post, etc.), cover (tec.), wainscot.

Bekleidung [be-klide'oong] nf. clothing, investiture, lining, facing.   [to oppress.

Beklemmen [be-klem'en] vt.

Beklemmung [be-klem'oong] nf. Beklommenheit [be-klom'en-hite] nf. oppression, uneasiness.

Beklommen [be-klom'en] a. oppressed, anxious.

Beklopfen [be-klop'fen] vt. to tap, knock.   [coal.

Bekohlen [be-koh'len] vt. to

Bekohlung [be-koh'loong] nf. coaling (ship); -**sanlage** nf. coaling elevator, plant.

Bekommen [be-kom'en] vt. ir. to get, obtain, catch (train); i. agree with (food).

Bekömmlich [be-kerm'lish] a. wholesome, digestible, obtainable.   [to board.

Beköstigen [be-ker'sti-gen] vt.

Beköstigung [be-ker'sti-göong] nf. board, keep, maintenance, messing (mil.).

Bekräftigen [be-kref'tigen] vt. to confirm, corroborate.

Bekräftigung [be-kref'ti-göong] nf. corroboration.

Bekreuzen [be-kroyt'sen] vr. to cross oneself.

Bekriegen [be-kree'gen] vt. to make war on.

Bekritteln [be-kri'teln] *vt.* to criticize, censure.

Bekümmern [be-kew'merrn] *vt.* to grieve, trouble; *r.* worry, trouble about, look after.

Bekümmernis [be-kew'merr-nis] *nf.* grief.

Bekunden [be-koon'den] *vt.* to state, show.

Belachen [be-lach'en] *vt.* to laugh at. [load.

Beladen [be-lah'den] *vt. ir.* to

Belag [be-lahk] *nm.* (Beläge) covering, spread, coating, decking, surface (*av.*). [besiege.

Belagern [be-lah'gerrn] *vt.* to

Belagerung [be-lah'ger-roong] *nf.* siege; -szustand *nm.* state of siege.

Belang [be-lang'] *nm.* importance; -los *a.* unimportant.

Belangen [be-lang'en] *vt.* to concern, prosecute.

Belangung [be-lang'oong] *nf.* prosecution, proceedings.

Belassen [be-lass'en] *vt. ir.* to leave in its place.

Belasten [be-last'en] *vt.* to burden, accuse, debit (*com.*).

Belastung [be-last'oong] *nf.* load, burden, charge, debit (-ing), -sgrenze *nf.* breaking strain (*tec.*); -sprobe *nf.* capacity test (*load*); -szeuge *nm.* witness for prosecution.

Belästigen [be-lest'i-gen] *vt.* to annoy, molest.

Belästigung [be-lest'i-goong] *nf.* molestation, importunity.

Belauf [be-lowf'] *nm.* amount.

Belaufen [be-low'fen] *vr.* to amount to. [to overhear.

Belauschen [be-low'shen] *vt.*

Beleben [be-lay'ben] *vt.* to animate, revive.

Belebt [be-laipt'] *a.* brisk, animated, crowded (*street*).

Belebung [be-lay'boong] *nf.* animation, revival, liveliness, -smittel *n.* restorative.

Beleg [be-laik'] *nm.* (-e) voucher, documentary evidence, proof, quotation, example, receipt.

Belegen [be-lay'gen] *vt.* to cover, lay, reserve (*seat*), verify, prove, book, invest (*money*), staff, billet, invest (*troops*), bomb (*mil.*).

Beleg-schaft *nf.* staff, personnel, shift (*mine*) -stück *n.* voucher, record.

Belegung [be-lay'goong] *nf.* quartering, billeting (*mil.*).

Belehren [be-lair'ren] *vt.* to instruct; eines Besseren - to correct, teach better.

Belehrung [be-lair'roong] *nf.* instruction; -skommando *n.* instruction detachment.

Beleibt [be-lipt'] *a.* stout.

Beleibtheit [be-lipt'hite] *nf.* stoutness.

Beleidigen [be-lide'i-gen] *vt.* to insult, offend. [*nf.* insult.

Beleidigung [be-lide'i-goong] *nf.*

Belesen [be-lay'zen] *a.* well-read.

Beleuchten [be-loish'ten] *vt.* to light, illuminate, throw light on, clear up.

Beleuchtung [be-loish'toong] *nf.* lighting, illumination, elucidation.

Beleumdet [be-loim'det] *a.* reputed; gut - in good repute.

Belfern [bel'ferrn] *vi.* to yelp.

Belichten [be-lish'ten] *vt.* to expose.

Belichtung [be-lish'toong] *nf.* exposure; -ungsmesser *nm.* exposure meter.

Belieben [be-lee'ben] *vt.i.* to please, like; *n.* pleasure, convenience, wish.

Beliebig [be-lee'bish] *a.* any you like, as you like.

Beliebt [be-leept'] *a.* favourite, popular; -heit *nf.* popularity.

Bellen [bell'en] *vi.* to bark.

Beloben [be-loh'ben] *vt.* to praise.

Belohnen [be-loh'nen] *vt.* to reward, remunerate.

Belohnung [be-loh'nŏŏng] *nf.* reward, remuneration.

Belügen [be-lyōō'gen] *vt. ir.* to lie, to deceive.

Belustigen [be-lŏŏs'ti-gen] *vt.* to amuse.

Belustigung [be-lŏŏs'ti-gŏŏng] *nf.* amusement.

Bemächtigen [be-mesh'ti-gen] *vr.* to take possession of, seize.

Bemalen [be-mah'len] *vt.* to paint on, over. [man.

Bemannen [be-man'en] *vt. ir.* to

Bemannung [be-man'ŏŏng] *nf.* manning, crew (*nav. av. etc.*).

Bemänteln [be-men'teln] *vt.* to cloak, hide.

Bemeistern [be-mice'tern] *vt.* to master, overcome; *r.* seize.

Bemerkbar [be-mairk'barr] *a.* perceptible, noticeable.

Bemerken [be-mairr'ken] *vt.* to notice, observe, remark; -enswert *a.* noteworthy.

Bemerkung [be-mairr'kŏŏng] *nf.* remark, note.

Bemessen [be-mess'en] *vt. ir.* to measure.

Bemitleiden [be-mit'lide-en] *vt.* to pity.

Bemittelt [be-mit'elt] *a.* well-to-do, wealthy.

Bemühen [be-mew'en] *vt.* to trouble; *r.* take trouble, pains, strive.

Bemühung [be-mew'ŏŏng] *nf.* trouble, pains, effort.

Bemustern [be-mŏŏs'tern] *vt.* to sample (*com.*).

Benachbart [be-nach'barrt] *a.* neighbouring.

Benachrichtigen [be-nach'rish-ti-gen] *vt.* to inform.

Benachrichtigung [be-nach'rish-ti-gŏŏng] *nf.* information, notification.

Benagen [be-nah'gen] *vt.* to gnaw. [fog.

Benebeln [be-nay'beln] *vt.* to

Benehmen [be-nay'men] *vt.*

ir. to take away; *r.* behave; *n.* behaviour. [envy.

Beneiden [be-nide'en] *vt.* to

Beneidenswert [be-nide'en-svertt] *a.* enviable.

Benennen [be-nen'en] *vt. ir.* to name.

Benennung [be-nen'ŏŏng] *nf.* naming, name, denomination, term. [moisten.

Benetzen [be-net'sen] *vt. ir.* to

Bengel [beng'el] *nm.* (-) boy, brat, lad, lout. [to need.

Benötigen [be-ner'ti-gen] *vt.* to

Benutzen [be-nŏŏt'sen] *vt.* to utilize, use.

Benutzung [be-nŏŏt'sŏŏng] *nf.* use, utilization.

Benzin [bent-seen'] *n.* benzine, petrol (*aut.*), gasoline; -behälter *nm.* petrol tank; -motor *nm.* petrol engine; -uhr *nf.* petrol gauge.

Beobachten [be-oh'bach-ten] *vt.* to observe, notice, watch, keep (*rules, etc.*).

Beobachter [be-oh'bach-terr] *nm.* (-) observer, navigator, spotter.

Beobachtung [be-oh'bach-tŏŏng] *nf.* observation, spotting (*av. mil.*); -schlitz *nm.* loophole; -sstand *nm.* observation; -sstelle *nf.* observation post (*mil.*).

Beordern [be-orr'dern] *vt. ir.* to order. [load, pack, charge.

Bepacken [be-pack'en] *vt.* to

Bepackung [be-pack'ŏŏng] *nf.* load, charge (*mil.*).

Bepanzern [be-pant'sern] *vt.* to armour.

Bepanzerung [be-pant'ser-rŏŏng] *nf.* armour-plate.

Bepflanzen [be-pflant'sen] *vt.* to plant.

Beplattung [be-plat'ŏŏng] *nf.* = Bepanzerung.

Bequem [be-kvaim'] *a.* comfortable, easy-going, convenient.

Bequemen [be-kvai'men] *vr.* to put up with, submit to.

Bequemlichkeit [be-kvaim'-lish-kite] nf. convenience, comfort, indolence.

Berappen [be-rap'en] vt. to plaster, rough-cast.

Beraten [be-rah'ten] vt. ir. to advise; r. deliberate, resolve.

Berater [be-rah'terr] nm. (-) adviser.

Beratschlagen [be-raht'-shlah-gen] vi.r. to deliberate, confer.

Beratschlagung [be-raht'-shlah-goong] nf. deliberation, consultation.

Beratung [be-rah'toong] nf. consultation, council; -sstelle nf. advisory board, office.

Berauben [be-row'ben] vt. to rob.

Beraubung [be-row'boong] nf. robbery, robbing.

Berauschen [be-rowsh'en] vt.r. to intoxicate, dope.

Berechenbar [be-resh'en-barr] a. calculable.

Berechnen [be-resh'nen] vt. to calculate, charge (com.).

Berechnung [be-resh'noong] nf. calculation, charge (com.).

Berechtigen [be-resh'ti-gen] vt. to entitle, empower, justify, authorize.

Berechtigung [be-resh'ti-goong] nf. authorization, justification. [persuade.

Bereden [be-rai'den] vt. to [persuade.

Beredsamkeit [be-rait'zam-kite] nf. eloquence.

Beredt [be-rait'] a. eloquent.

Bereich [be-rish'] nm. (-e) scope, sphere, reach, range, area; -skommando n. operational command. [to enrich.

Bereichern [be-rish'errn] vt. to enrich.

Bereifen [be-rife'en] vt. to hoop (cask), put on tyres (aut.).

Bereifung [be-rife'oong] nf. fitting with tyres, tyres.

Bereinigen [be-rine'i-gen] vt. settle (com.).

Bereinigung [be-rine'i-goong] nf. settling, clearance (stocks).

Bereisen [be-rize'en] vt. to travel through, work (com.).

Bereit [be-rite'] a. ready, prepared.

Bereiten [be-rite'en] vt. to prepare, make ready, cause.

Bereit-halten vt. to keep in readiness; -schaft nf. readiness, serviceability, stand-by, stand-to, alert (mil.); -stehen vi. to be prepared, stand-to (mil.); -stellen vt. to prepare, provide, make ready, get ready for action (mil.); -stellung nf. assembly, support line, provision, battle stations (nav.); -willig a. willing, ready; -willigkeit nf. readiness, willingness.

Bereits [be-rites'] ad. already.

Beritten [be-rit'en] a. mounted. [repent, regret.

Bereuen [be-roi'en] vt. [repent, regret.

Berg [bairrk] nm. (-e) mountain, hill; -ab ad. downhill; -an -auf ad. uphill; -bau nm. mining; -bewohner nm. mountaineer; -gipfel nm. mountain top, peak, summit; -ig a. mountainous, hilly; -kamm nm. crest, ridge; -kette nf. mountain chain; -knappe nm. apprentice miner; -mann nm. miner; -rücken nm. ridge; -rutsch nm. landslide; -schule nf. school of mining; -stütze nf. sprag (aut.); -wand nf. precipice, cliff; -werk n. mine.

Bergen [bairr'gen] vt. ir. to shelter, save, conceal, salvage (nav.), recover.

Berge-gruppe nf. protected category; -lohn nm. salvage money, pay.

Bergung [bairr'goong] nf. salvage, rescue; -skommando n. salvage detachment; -szug nm. salvage platoon (mil.).

Bericht [be-risht'] nm. (-e)

report, statement, account; -erstatter nm. reporter, (newspaper) correspondent, informant.

Berichten [be-rish'ten] vt. to report, inform.

Berichtigen [be-rish'ti-gen] vt. to correct, rectify, adjust, pay (debt).

Berichtigung [be-rish'ti-gŏong] nf. correction, rectification, settlement.

Berieseln [be-reeze'eln] vt. to water, irrigate. (mil.).

Beritt [be-rit'] nm. squad

Beritten [be-rit'en] a. mounted; -e Miliz yeomanry.

Bernstein [bairrn'shtine] nm. amber; schwarzer - jet.

Bersten [bairr'sten] vi. ir. to burst, split.

Berüchtigt [be-ryŏŏsh'tisht] a. infamous, notorious.

Berücken [be-ryŏŏ'ken] vt. to ensnare, captivate

Berücksichtigen [be-ryŏŏk'-zish-ti-gen] vt. to consider, bear in mind.

Berücksichtigung [be-ryŏŏk'zish-ti-gŏong] nf. consideration.

Beruf [be-rŏŏf'] nm. (-e) occupation, profession, vocation, calling, trade.

Berufen [be-rŏŏ'fen] vt. ir. to appoint, send for, call; r. refer to, appeal. [potent.

Berufen [be-rŏŏ'fen] a. com-

Beruflich [be-rŏŏf'lish] a. professional.

Berufs-bildung nf. vocational training; -heer n. professional army; -mässig a. professional, vocational; -schule nf. trade, technical school; -soldat nm. professional soldier, regular; -tätig a. employed.

Berufung [be-rŏŏ'fŏong] nf. appointment, call, appeal (law).

Beruhen [be-rŏŏ'en] vi. to rest, depend on.

Beruhigen [be-rŏŏ'i-gen] vt.

to calm, pacify, soothe; r. grow calm, compose oneself.

Beruhigung [be-rŏŏ'i-gŏong] nf. calming, pacification, reassurance. [famous.

Berühmt [be-ryŏŏmt'] a.

Berühmtheit [be-ryŏŏmt'hite] nf. celebrity, fame.

Berühren [be-ryŏŏr'ren] vt. to touch, affect, concern, mention, allude to.

Berührung [be-ryŏŏr'rŏong] nf. contact, touch, connection; -spunkt nm. point of contact.

Besäen [be-zai'en] vt. to sow.

Besagen [be-zah'gen] vt. to say, mean.

Besagt [be-zahkt'] a. before mentioned.

Besan [bay-zahn'] (-e) nm. mizzen (nav.).

Besänftigen [be-zenf'ti-gen] vt. to soothe, calm.

Besänftigung [be-zenf'ti-gŏong] nf. soothing, calming.

Besatz [be-zats'] nm. (Besätze) trimming, edge, piping, facing; -raum nm. fighting compartment (tank).

Besatzung [be-zat'sŏong] nf. garrison, crew, ship's company (nav.), complement; -sbehörden f.pl. occupation authorities; -sheer n. army of occupation.

Beschädigen [be-shade'i-gen] vt. to injure, hurt, damage, disable.

Beschädigte(r) [be-shade'ish-terr] nm. casualty.

Beschädigung [be-shade'i-gŏong] nf. injury, damage, disablement.

Beschaffen [be-shaf'en] vt. to procure, get, supply; a. constituted.

Beschaffenheit [be-shaf'en-hite] nf. constitution, nature, condition, quality.

Beschaffung [be-shaf'ŏong] nf. procuring, supply.

Beschäftigen [be-shef'ti-gen] vt. to employ, occupy.

Beschäftigt [be-shef'tisht] *a.* busy, occupied.

Beschäftigung [be-shef'ti-gŏŏng] *nf.* occupation, employment; **-slos** *a.* unemployed.

Beschämen [be-shame'en] *vt.* to shame; *r.* be ashamed.

Beschämung [be-shame'-ŏŏng] *nf.* shame, confusion.

Beschatten [be-shat'en] *vt.* shade, shadow.

Beschauen [be-show'en] *vt.* to look at, examine, contemplate.

Beschauer [be-show'err] *nm.* (-) inspector, spectator.

Beschaulich [be-show'lish] *a.* contemplative.

Beschauung [be-show'ŏŏng] *nf.* contemplation, examination.

Bescheid [be-shite'] *nm.* (-e) information, directions; **- wissen** to know one's way about.

Bescheiden [be-shide'en] *vt. ir.* to direct, inform, instruct; *r.* restrain oneself, summon, acquiesce in; *a.* modest, moderate, unpretentious, unassuming.

Bescheidenheit [be-shide'en-hite] *nf.* modesty, discretion.

Bescheinen [be-shine'en] *vt. ir.* to shine on, irradiate.

Bescheinigen [be-shine'i-gen] *vt.* to certify, vouch for, acknowledge.

Bescheinigung [be-shine'i-gŏŏng] *nf.* certificate, voucher, receipt.

Beschenken [be-shenk'en] *vt.* to present.

Bescheren [be-shayr'en] *vt.* to give as a present.

Bescherung [be-share'ŏŏng] *nf.* presentation, mess.

Beschicken [be-shick'en] *vt.* to send to, for, exhibit, alloy (metals).

Beschickung [be-shik'ŏŏng] *nf.* sending, conveying, charging.

Beschiessen [be-shee'sen] *vt. ir.* to fire on, shell, bombard, machine-gun.

Beschiessung [be-shee'sŏŏng] *nf.* bombardment, shelling.

Beschiffbar [be-shif'barr] *a.* navigable.

Beschiffen [be-shif'en] *vt.* to sail on, navigate.

Beschiffung [be-shif'ŏŏng] *nf.* sailing, navigation.

Beschimpfen [be-shimp'fen] *vt.* to abuse, insult.

Beschimpfung [be-shimp'-fŏŏng] *nf.* abuse, insult.

Beschirmen [be-sheer'men] *vt.* to shelter, protect, screen.

Beschirmung [be-sheer'-mŏŏng] *nf.* defence, protection.

Beschlag [be-shlahk'] *nm.* (Beschläge) fittings, mounting, ornament, horse-shoe, distraint, embargo; **-nahme** *nf.* confiscation, distraint, sequestration; **-nahmen** *vt.* to seize, confiscate, requisition.

Beschlagen [be-shlah'gen] *vt. ir.* to mount, cover, shoe, fit; *i.* become covered with.

Beschleichen [be-shli'shen] *vt. ir.* to stalk, steal up to, seize.

Beschleunigen [be-shloi'ni-gen] *vt.* to accelerate, speed up.

Beschleuniger [be-shloi'ni-gerr] *nm.* (-) accelerator (aut.).

Beschleunigung [be-shloi'ni-gŏŏng] *nf.* acceleration, haste.

Beschliessen [be-shlee'sen] *vt. ir.* to decide, resolve on, resolve, end, close, terminate.

Beschluss [be-shlŏŏs'] *nm.* (Beschlüsse) resolution, motion, decision, conclusion, close, end; **-fassung** *nf.* decision, motion.

Beschmieren [be-shmeer'en] *vt.* to smear, spread (butter, etc.).

Beschmutzen [be-shmŏŏt'sen] *vt.* to soil, dirty.

Beschneiden [be-shnide'en] *vt. ir.* to cut, prune, trim, circumcise.

Beschneidung [be-shnide'-oong] *nf.* circumcision.

Beschönigen [be-sher'ni-gen] *vt.* to extenuate, gloss over.

Beschönigung [be-sher'ni-goong] *nf.* extenuation, excuse.

Beschottern [be-shot'errn] *vt.* to metal, ballast (rr.).

Beschränken [be-shrenk'en] *vt.* to limit, restrict.

Beschränkt [be-shrenkt'] *a.* confined, narrow; **-heit** *nf.* narrowness.

Beschränkung [be-shrenk'-oong] *nf.* limitation.

Beschreiben [be-shribe'en] *vt. ir.* to describe.

Beschreibung [be-shribe'-oong] *nf.* description.

Beschreiten [be-shrite'en] *vt. ir.* to walk on.   [to letter.

Beschriften [be-shrift'en] *vt.*

Beschriftung [be-shrift'oong] *nf.* lettering, caption (film, etc.).

Beschuhen [be-shoo'en] *vt.* to shoe.   [gen] *vt.* to accuse.

Beschuldigen [be-shool'di-

Beschuldigung [be-shool'di-goong] *nf.* accusation.

Beschuss [be-shooss'] *nm.* artillery fire, shelling (mil.).

Beschützen [be-shyöt'sen] *vt.* to protect.

Beschützer [be-shyöt'serr] *nm.* (-) protector, patron.

Beschützung [be-shyöt'-soong] *nf.* protection.

Beschwatzen [be-shvat'sen] *vt.* to persuade.

Beschwerde [be-shvairr'der] *nf.* complaint, hardship.

Beschweren [be-shvairr'en] *vt.* to overload, weigh down; *r.* complain.

Beschwerlich [be-shvairr'-lish] *a.* troublesome; **-keit** *nf.* nuisance, difficulty.

Beschwichtigen [be-shvish'-ti-gen] *vt.* to appease, pacify.

Beschwichtigung [be-shvish'ti-goong] *nf.* pacification, calming.

Beschwindeln [be-shvin'-deln] *vt.* to cheat.

Beschwören [be-shver'ren] *vt. ir.* to affirm on oath, implore.

Beschwörung [be-shver'-röng] *nf.* imploring.

Beseelen [be-zail'en] *vt.* to inspirit, inspire, animate.

Beseeltheit [be-zailt'hite] *nf.* = Beseelung.

Beseelung [be-zale'öong] *nf.* inspiration, animation.

Besehen [be-zay'en] *vt. ir.* to inspect.   [to remove.

Beseitigen [be-zite'i-gen] *vt.*

Beseitigung [be-zite'i-goong] *nf.* removal, abolition, elimination.

Besen [bay'zen] *nm.* (-) broom; **-stiel** *nm.* broomstick.

Besessen [be-zes'en] *a.* possessed.

Besetzen [be-zet'sen] *vt.* to occupy, trim, fill, set.

Besetzt [be-zetst'] *a.* occupied, engaged, crowded, full; **-es** Gebiet occupied territory.

Besetzung [be-zet'söong] *nf.* occupation, appointment, filling (post), cast (drama).

Besichtigen [be-zish'ti-gen] *vt.* to inspect.

Besichtigung [be-zish'ti-goong] *nf.* inspection.

Besiedeln [be-zee'deln] *vt.* to colonize.

Besiedelung [be-zee'de-löong] *nf.* settlement, colonization.

Besiegeln [be-zee'geln] *vt.* to seal.   [conquer.

Besiegen [be-zee'gen] *vt.* to

Besieger [be-zee'gerr] *nm.* (-) conqueror, victor.

Besiegung [be-zee'göong] *nf.* conquest.

Besingen [be-zing'en] *vt. ir.* to celebrate (in song).

Besinnen [be-zin'en] *vr. ir.* to think of, reflect, remember; sich anders – to change one's mind.

Besinnung [be-zin'öong] *nf.* recollection; zur – kommen to recover consciousness; **-slos** a. unconscious.

Besitz [be-zits] nm. possession, property; **-anzeigend** a. possessive; **-nahme** nf. occupation, seizure; **-urkunde** nf. title-deeds.

Besitzen [be-zit'sen] vt. ir. to possess, own.

Besitzer [be-zit'ser] nm. (-) owner, proprietor.

Besitztum [be-zit'stŏŏm] n. (-tümer) property.

Besitzung [be-zit'sŏŏng] nf. possession, estate, property.

Besoffen [be-zof'en] a. tipsy.

Besohlen [be-zoh'len] vt. to sole.

Besolden [be-zol'den] vt. to pay salary, wages to.

Besoldung [be-zol'dŏŏng] nf. salary, pay.

Besonder [be-zon'derr] a. special, particular, separate, peculiar; **ins -e** in particular.

Besonderheit [be-zon'derr-hite] nf. peculiarity.

Besonders [be-zon'derrs] ad. peculiarly, particularly, specially, separately.

Besonnen [be-zon'en] a. prudent, sensible.

Besonnenheit [be-zon'en-hite] nf. prudence.

Besorgen [be-zorr'gen] vt. to take care of, look after, see to, do, discharge, get, attend to.

Besorgnis [be-zorrk'nis] nf. (-se) anxiety, fear.

Besorgt [be-zorrkt'] a. anxious, solicitous.

Besorgtheit [be-zorrkt'hite] nf. solicitude, anxiety.

Besorgung [be-zorr'gŏŏng] nf. care, management, purchase.

Bespannen [be-shpan'en] vt. to harness to, stretch, string (violin, etc.).

Bespötteln [be-shper'teln] vt. to ridicule, scoff at.

Besprechen [be-shpresh'en]

vt. ir. to discuss, criticize, review (book).

Besprechung [be-shpresh'ŏŏng] nf. discussion, consultation, review.

Bespritzen [be-shprit'sen] vt. to sprinkle, splash.

Besprühen [be-shprŏŏ'en] vt. to spray.

Besser [bess'err] a. better; **-wisser** nm. (-) wiseacre, carping critic.

Bessern [bess'errn] vt. to make better, improve, mend; r. to improve, reform.

Besserung [bess'er-rŏŏng] nf. improvement; **-anstalt** nf. reformatory.

Best [best] a. best; **aufs -e** in the best possible way; **zum -en geben** to contribute (song), entertain (person)- **zum -en von** for the benefit of.

Bestallen [be-shtal'en] vt. to appoint, install.

Bestallung [be-shtal'ŏŏng] nf. appointment, installation.

Bestand [be-shtant'] nm. (Bestände) duration stability, amount, balance, stock; **eiserner - iron rations**; **-aufnahme** nf. stock-taking; **geld** n. cash in hand (com.); **-teil** nm. part, component, ingredient.

Beständig [be-shten'dish] a. constant, continual.

Beständigkeit [be-shten'dish-kite] nf. constancy, continuation, stability.

Bestärken [be-shtairr'ken] vt. to confirm, support, strengthen.

Bestärkung [be-shtairr'kŏŏng] nf. confirmation, corroboration.

Bestätigen [be-shtate'i-gen] vt. to confirm, acknowledge (receipt).

Bestätigung [be-shtate'i-gŏŏng] nf. confirmation, ratification. [bury.

Bestatten [be-shtat'en] vt. to

Bestattung [be-shtat'ŏŏng]
nf. funeral, interment; **stille ~**
private funeral.

Bestäuben [be-shtoi'ben] *vt.*
to cover with dust, spray.

Bestechen [be-shtesh'en] *vt.
ir.* to bribe, stitch (*books, etc.*).

Bestechlich [be-shtesh'lish] *a.*
corruptible; **-keit** *nf.* cor-
ruptibility.

Bestechung [be-shtesh'ŏŏng]
nf. bribery, corruption.

Besteck [be-shtek'] *n.* (**-e**)
knife, fork, spoon, set of instruments, reckoning, position
(*ship*).

Bestecken [be-shtek'en] *vt.* to
plant, stick (*with pins*).

Bestehen [be-shtay'en] *vi. ir.*
to exist, be, last; *t.* stand,
undergo, overcome, pass
(*exam.*); **~ auf** insist on; **~ aus**
consist of; **-de Preise** ruling
prices. [to rob.

Bestehlen [be-shtay'len] *vt. ir.*

Besteigen [be-shtigh'en] *vt. ir.*
to climb, go up, ascend, board
(*ship*), mount (*horse*).

Besteigung [be-shti'gŏŏng]
nf. ascent, accession, mounting.

Bestellen [be-shtel'en] *vt.* to
order, arrange, cultivate,
deliver (*mail*), carry out
(*errand*), send (*message*).

Bestellung [be-shtel'ŏŏng] *nf.*
ordering, delivery, cultivation,
message. [at best.

Bestenfalls [best-en-fals'] *ad.*

Bestens [best'enss] *ad.* best,
very much. [to tax.

Besteuern [be-shtoi'ern] *vt.*

Besteuerung [be-shtoi'er-
rŏŏng] *nf.* taxation.

Bestie [bes'ti-er] *nf.* beast.

Bestimmbar [be-shtim'barr]
a. ascertainable, definable.

Bestimmen [be-shtim'en] *vt.*
to determine, fix, appoint,
define, induce.

Bestimmt [be-shtimt'] *a.*
definite, fixed, certain, bound
for (*ship*); **-heit** *nf.* certainty.

Bestimmung [be-shtim'ŏŏng]
nf. determination, definition,
destiny, destination; **-sort** *nm.*
destination.

Bestrafen [be-shtrah'fen] *vt.*
to punish.

Bestrafung [be-shtrah'fŏŏng]
nf. punishment.

Bestrahlen [be-shtrah'len] *vt.*
to shine on, treat with X-rays.

Bestrahlung [be-shtrah-
lŏŏng] *nf.* radiation.

Bestreben [be-shtray'ben] *vr.*
to strive; *n.* endeavour.

Bestrebung [be-shtray'-
bŏŏng] *nf.* effort, endeavour.

Bestreichen [be-shtri'chen] *vt.
ir.* to cover with, spread, butter
(*bread*), sweep, enfilade, rake
with fire (*mil.*).

Bestreitbar [be-shtrite'barr]
a. disputable.

Bestreiten [be-shtrite'en] *vt.*
to dispute, defray (*expenses*).

Bestreuen [be-shtroi'en] *vt.*
to sprinkle, scatter over.

Bestricken [be-shtrick'en] *vt.*
to entangle, fascinate.

Bestücken [be-shtew'ken] *vt.*
to arm (with guns).

Bestückung [be-shtew'kŏŏng]
nf. armament.

Bestürmen [be-shtewrr'men]
vt. to storm, assault, overwhelm.

Bestürmung [be-shtewrr'-
mŏŏng] *nf.* storming, assault.

Bestürzen [be-shtewrr'tsen]
vt. to startle, dismay.

Bestürzt [be-shtewrrtst'] *a.*
dismayed.

Bestürzung [be-shtewrrt'-
sŏŏng] *nf.* consternation.

Besuch [be-zŏŏch'] *nm.* (**-e**)
visit, call, visitor; **~ haben** to
have visitors.

Besuchen [be-zŏŏch'en] *vt.* to
visit, attend (*school*).

Besucher [be-zŏŏch'err] *nm.*
(**-**) visitor, guest.

Besuchs-karte *nf.* visiting
card; **-zeit** *nf.* visiting hours.

Besudeln [be-zōō'deln] vt. to soil.   [overdue (com.).

Betagt [be-tahkt'] a. aged,

Betasten [be-tast'en] vt. to touch, finger.

Betätigen [be-tai'ti-gen] vt.r. to practise, work.

Betätigung [be-tai'ti-gŏŏng] nf. practice, activity, operation (tec.).

Betäuben [be-toi'ben] vt. to deafen, stun, stupefy, anaesthetize.

Betäubung [be-toi'bŏŏng] nf. deafening, stupefaction, anaesthesia; -smittel n. anaesthetic, dope, narcotic.

Beteiligen [be-tile'i-gen] vt.r. to take part in, join, share in, participate in.

Beteiligung [be-tile'i-gŏŏng] nf. participation, share, interest, attendance.

Beten [bay'ten] vi. to pray.

Beteuern [be-toi'errn] vt. to affirm, protest.

Beteuerung [be-toi'er-roong] nf. assertion, declaration, protest(ation).

Betiteln [be-tee'teln] vt. to entitle.

Beton [bay-tohn'] nm. concrete.

Betonieren [bay-to-neer'en] vt. to concrete.   [stress.

Betonen [be-tone'en] vt. to

Betonung [be-tone'ŏŏng] nf. stress, emphasis.

Betören [be-ter'ren] vt. to fool, delude.

Betracht [be-tracht'] nm. consideration; in - kommen to be concerned; nicht in- kommen to be out of the question.

Betrachten [be-trach'ten] vt. to look at, consider, regard, contemplate.

Beträchtlich [be-tresht'lish] a. considerable.

Betrachtung [be-trach'tŏŏng] nf. consideration, meditation.

Betrag [be-trahk'] nm. (Be-träge) amount.

Betragen [be-trah'gen] vt. ir. to amount to; r. behave; n. behaviour.

Betrauen [be-trow'en] vt. to entrust, authorize.   [ing. re.

Betreffs [be-trefs'] pr. concern-

Betreffen [be-tref'en] vt. ir. to concern, happen to, surprise; was mich betrifft as for me.

Betreffend [be-tref'ent] a. in question.

Betreiben [be-tribe'en] vt. ir. to carry on, manage, direct, work, go in for (study, hobby), cultivate, urge on.

Betreten [be-tray'ten] vt. ir. to tread, enter; a. disconcerted.

Betrieb [be-treep'] nm. (-e) management, working, trade, plant, activity, action; in - sein to be in operation, to be working.

Betriebsam [be-treep'zam] a. industrious.

Betriebs-führer nm. works manager; -funker nm. mechanic, operator (nav, av.); -jahr n. financial year; -kapital n. working capital; -kosten pl. working expenses; -leiter nm. controller, manager; -sicher a. foolproof; -stoff nm. fuel; -störung nf. breakdown; -unklar a. unserviceable (av, etc.).   [to get drunk.

Betrinken [be-trink'en] vr. ir.

Betroffen [be-trof'en] a. amazed, perplexed.   [grieve.

Betrüben [be-trew'ben] vt. to

Betrübnis [be-trew'pnis] nf. (-e) grief, sorrow.

Betrug [be-trōōk'] nm. (Be-trüge) fraud, cheating.

Betrügen [be-trew'gen] vt. ir. to cheat.

Betrüger [be-trew'gerr] nm. (-) cheat, impostor.

Betrügerisch [be-trew'ger-rish] a. deceitful, deceptive.

Bett [bet] n. (gen. -es; pl. -en) bed; -decke nf. counterpane, quilt, blanket; -flasche nf. hot-water-bottle; -lägerig *a.* bed-ridden; -laken *n.* sheet; -schüssel *nf.* bed-pan; -stelle *nf.* bedstead; -tuch *n.* sheet; -überzug *nm.* pillow slip; -zeug *n.* bed-clothes, bedding.

Bettel [bet'el] *nm.* rubbish; -arm *a.* very poor, destitute; -brief *nm.* begging letter.

Bettelei [bet-e-lŷ'] *nf.* begging.

Betteln [bet'eln] *vi.* to beg.

Betten [bet'en] *vt.* to put to bed, make a bed for.

Bettler [bet'ler] *nm.* (-) beggar.

Bettlerin *nf.* beggar.

Bettung [bet'ŏŏng] *nf.* mounting, base.

Beugen [boi'gen] *vt.* to bend, humble, inflect; *r.* to bow, humble oneself.

Beugsam [boik'zam] *a.* flexible, pliable.

Beugung [boi'gŏŏng] *nf.* bend, bending, inflection.

Beule [boi'ler] *nf.* bump, swelling, boss.

Beunruhigen [be-ŏŏn'rŏŏ-i-gen] *vt.* to disturb, alarm.

Beunruhigung [be-ŏŏn'rŏŏ-i-gŏŏng] *nf.* disturbance, alarm.

Beurkunden [be-ŏŏr'kŏŏn-den] *vt.* to authenticate, attest.

Beurkundung [be-ŏŏr'kŏŏn-dŏŏng] *nf.* verification.

Beurlauben [be-ŏŏr'low-ben] *vt.* to give leave (of absence), send on holiday; *r.* to take one's leave.   [on leave.

Beurlaubt [be-ŏŏr'towpt] *a.*

Beurteilen [be-ŏŏr'tile-en] *vt.* to judge, criticize.

Beurteilung [be-ŏŏr'tile-ŏŏng] *nf.* judgment, criticism.

Beute [boi'ter] *nf.* booty, loot.

Beutel [boi'tel] *nm.* (-) bag, purse, pouch.

Beuteln [boi'teln] *vt.* to bolt (*flour*); *r.* to be baggy, pucker, crease.   [to populate.

Bevölkern [be-ferl'kerrn] *vt.*

Bevölkerung [be-ferl'ker-rŏŏng] *nf.* population; -saus-

tausch *nm.* exchange of population.

Bevollmächtigen [be-fol'mesh-ti-gen] *vt.* to authorize.

Bevollmächtigte(r) [be-fol'mesh-tish-ter] *m.w.* deputy, authorized agent, plenipotentiary, proxy, trustee (*com.*).

Bevollmächtigung [be-fol'mesh-ti-gŏŏng] *nf.* authorization, trusteeship, power of attorney.

Bevor [be-forr'] *cj.* before.

Bevormunden [be-forr'mŏŏn-den] *vt.* to act as guardian to, patronize.

Bevormundung [be-forr'mŏŏn-dŏŏng] *nf.* guardianship.

Bevorstehen [be-forr'shtay-en] *vi. ir.* to be imminent, in store; -d *a.* imminent, approaching.   [*vt.* to favour.

Bevorzugen [be-forr'tsŏŏ-gen] *vt.* to favour.

Bevorzugung [be-forr'tsŏŏ-gŏŏng] *nf.* preference, favour.

Bewachen [be-vach'en] *vt.* to watch, guard.

Bewachung [be-vach'ŏŏng] *nf.* watch, guard, escort (*nav.*).

Bewachsen [be-vax'en] *a.* overgrown.   [arm.

Bewaffnen [be-vaf'nen] *vt.* to arm.

Bewaffnung [be-vaf'nŏŏng] *nf.* armament, arms, armour.

Bewahren [be-vahr'ren] *vt.* to preserve.

Bewähren [be-vair'ren] *vr.* to stand the test; *t.* to prove.

Bewahrung [be-vahr'rŏŏng] *nf.* preservation.

Bewährung [be-vair'rŏŏng] *nf.* verification, proof, probation.   [wooded.

Bewaldet [be-val'det] *a.*

Bewältigen [be-vel'ti-gen] *vt.* to overpower, finish, become proficient in, master.

Bewandert [be-van'derrt] *a.* expert, proficient, conversant.

Bewandtnis [be-vant'nis] *nf.* (-e) state of affairs, circumstance.

Bewässern [be-vess'errn] *vt.* to irrigate.

Bewässerung [be-vess'er-roong] *nf.* irrigation.

Bewegen [be-vai'gen] *vt.r.* to move, agitate; *t. ir.* induce.

Beweggrund [be-vaik'groont] *nm.* (-gründe) motive.

Beweglich [be-vaik'lish] *a.* moveable, moving, mobile, quick; -lichkeit *nf.* mobility.

Bewegung [be-vai'goong] *nf.* motion, movement, commotion, emotion, stir, exercise; sich — machen take exercise; -sfreiheit *nf.* freedom of action; -skrieg *nm.* war of movement, mobile warfare; -slehre *nf.* mechanics; -slos *a.* motionless; -sspiel *n.* outdoor game.

Bewehren [be-vair'ren] *vt.* to arm. [mourn.

Beweinen [be-vine'en] *vt.* to

Beweis [be-vice'] *nm.* (-e) proof; -aufnahme *nf.* hearing of evidence; -führung *nf.* reasoning, demonstration; -grund *nm.* argument; -kraft *nf.* conclusiveness, weight; -kräftig *a.* convincing, conclusive; -last *nf.* onus of proof; -mittel *n.* evidence.

Beweisbar [be-vice'barr] *a.* demonstrable.

Beweisen [be-vize'en] *vt. ir.* to prove, demonstrate.

Bewenden [be-ven'den] *vi. ir.* — lassen to acquiesce in, agree with; *n.* end.

Bewerben [be-vairr'ben] *vt.r. ir.* to apply, compete, court (girl).

Bewerber [be-vairr'berr] *nm.* (-) candidate, applicant, suitor.

Bewerbung [be-vairr'boong] *nf.* candidature, application, courtship.

Bewerfen [be-vairr'fen] *vt. ir.* to pelt, plaster (wall).

Bewerkstellig'en [be-vairrk'shtel-i-gen] *vt.* to effect, bring about, accomplish; -ung *nf.*

achievement, accomplishment.

Bewerten [be-vairr'ten] *vt.* to value, price (com.).

Bewilligen [be-vil'i-gen] *vt.* to grant, allow.

Bewilligung [be-vil'i-goong] *nf.* grant, concession.

Bewillkommnen [be-vil'-kom-nen] *vt.* to welcome.

Bewillkommnung [be-vil'-kom-noong] *nf.* welcome.

Bewirken [be-virr'ken] *vt.* to cause, bring about.

Bewirten [be-virr'ten] *vt.* to entertain.

Bewirtschaften [be-virrt'-shaf-ten] *vt.* to manage.

Bewirtschaftung [be-virrt'-shaf-toong] *nf.* state control, rationing.

Bewirtung [be-virr'toong] *nf.* entertainment, hospitality.

Bewohnbar [be-vohn'barr] *a.* inhabitable.

Bewohnen [be-voh'nen] *vt.* to inhabit, live in.

Bewohner [be-voh'nerr] *nm.* (-) inhabitant, resident.

Bewölkt [be-verlkt'] *a.* cloudy, overcast. [nf. cloud.

Bewölkung [be-verl'koong] *nf.* admirer.

Bewunderer [be-voon'der-rerr] *nm.* (-) admirer.

Bewundern [be-voon'derrn] *vt.* to admire; -swert *a.* admirable, wonderful.

Bewunderung [be-voon'der-roong] *nf.* admiration.

Bewurf [be-voorrf'] *nm.* plaster, rough-cast.

Bewusst [be-voost'] *a.* conscious, aware, in question.

Bewusstlos [be-voost'lohs] *a.* unconscious; -igkeit *nf.* unconsciousness.

Bewusstsein [be-voost'zine] *n.* consciousness.

Bezackt [be-tsakt'] *a.* jagged.

Bezahlbar [be-tsahl'barr] *a.* payable.

Bezahlen [be-tsah'len] *vt.* to pay, pay for, settle (bill)

Bezahlung [be-tsah′loong] *nf.* payment. [tame.

Bezähmen [be-tsai′men] *vt.* to

Bezahnt [be-tsahnt′] *a.* toothed.

Bezaubern [be-tsow′bern] *vt.* to churn, enchant.

Bezeichnen [be-tsish′nen] *vt.* to mark, denote

Bezeichnend [be-tsish′nent] *a.* characteristic, typical.

Bezeichnung [be-tsish′noong] *nf.* marking, mark, designation, name, description.

Bezeigen [be-tsy′gen] *vt.* to show, express.

Bezeigung [be-tsy′goong] *nf.* showing, manifestation.

Bezetteln [be-tset′eln] *vt.* to label; testify, declare, certify.

Bezeugen [be-tsoi′gen] *vt.* to

Bezeugung [be-tsoi′goong] *nf.* testimony, attestation.

Bezichtigen [be-tsish′ti-gen] *vt.* to accuse.

Beziehbar [be-tsee′barr] *a.* habitable (*house*), obtainable (*goods*).

Beziehen [be-tsee′en] *vt. ir.* to cover, remove into, enter, move into (position), mount (guard), draw (pension), obtain, get, draw (*com.*); *r.* relate, refer, cloud over (sky).

Bezieher [be-tsee′err] *nm.* (-) customer, subscriber, drawer (*com.*).

Beziehung [be-tsee′oong] *nf.* relation, reference, drawing, entering; -sweise *ad.* or.

Beziffern [be-tsif′errn] *vt.* to number; *r.* amount to.

Bezirk [be-tseerrk′] *nm.* (-e) district, circuit; -sbombe *nf.* -umleger *nm.* block buster (*av.*).

Bezug [be-tsook′] *nm.*) Bezüge covering, casing, ordering (*goods*), supply, income, salary.

Bezüglich [be-tsewk′lish] *a.*, *pr.* relative, concerning.

Bezugnahme [be-tsook′nah-mer] *nf.* reference.

Bezugs−anweisung *nf.* order for delivery; -bedingungen *f.pl.* terms of delivery; -quelle *nf.* source of supply; -spesen *pl.* delivery charges.

Bezwecken [be-tsveck′en] *vt.* to aim at. [to doubt, query.

Bezweifeln [be-tsvi′feln] *vt.*

Bezwingen [be-tsving′en] *vt. ir.* to overcome.

Bezwingung [be-tsving′oong] *nf.* conquest, mastery, subjugation.

Bibel [bee′bel] *nf.* Bible.

Biber [bee′berr] *nm.* (-) beaver.

Bibliograph [bi-bli-o-grahf′] *m.w.* bibliographer.

Bibliographie [bi-bli-o-gra-fee′] *nf.* bibliography.

Bibliothek [bi-bli-o-take′] *nf.* library.

Bibliothekar [bi-bli-o-take-arr′] *nm* (-e) librarian.

Biblisch [bee′blish] *a.* biblical.

Bieder [bee′derr] *a.* trusty, honest; -mann *nm.* honest fellow.

Biegbar [beek′barr] *a.* flexible.

Biegen [bee′gen] *vt. ir.* to bend; *i.* turn.

Biegsam [beek′zam] *a.* supple, yielding. [curve.

Biegung [bee-goong′] *nf.* bend,

Biene [bee′ner] *nf.* bee.

Bienen-korb [bee′nen] *nm.* beehive; -wachs *nm.* beeswax; -zucht *nf.* beekeeping; -züchter *nm.* beekeeper.

Bier [beerr] *n.* beer; -brauer *nm.* brewer; -filz *nm.* beer mat; -garten *nm.* beer garden; halle- *nf.* -haus *n.* public house; -krug *nm.*, -seidel *n.* beer mug; -schenke *nf.* pothouse.

Biese [bee′zer] *nf.* piping (*mil.*).

Biest [beest] *nm.* -e beast.

Bieten [bee′ten] *vt. ir.* to offer, bid.

Bigamie [bi-ga-mee′] *nf.* bigamy.

Bigott [bi-got′] *a.* bigotted.

Bilanz [bi-lants'] *nf.* balance sheet, balance (*com.*).
Bilanzieren [bi-lant-seer'ren] *vt.* to balance.
Bild [bilt] *n.* (**-er**) picture, image, illustration, portrait, idea, lantern slide; **-aufklärung** *nf.* photographic reconnaissance; **-bericht** *nm.* documentary film.
Bilden [bil'den] *vt.* to form, shape, mould, educate, train, constitute; *r.* to arise, educate oneself.
Bilderbuch [bil'derr-bŏŏh] *n.* picture book.
Bildfläche [bilt'fle-sher] *nf.* surface. [television.
Bildfunk [bilt'fŏŏnk] *nm.*
Bild-hauer [bilt-hou'er] *nm.* sculptor; **-hauerei** *nf.* sculpture; **-gerät** *n.* camera; **-karte** *nf.* relief map; **-lich** *a.* figurative, pictorial; **-ner** *nm.* sculptor, artist, educator; **-nis** *n.* portrait, likeness; **-säule** *nf.* statue; **-schön** *a.* lovely; **-schule** *nf.* photographic school (*av.*); **-streifen** *nm.* film strip; **-zug** *nm.* photography plane (*mil.*).
Bildung [bil'dŏŏng] *nf.* formation, culture, education; **-sanstalt** *nf.* educational institution.
Billard [bil-yarrt'] *n.* billiards, billiard table; **-ball** *nm.*, **-kugel** *nf.* billiard ball; **-stock** *nm.* cue.
Billett [bil-yet'] *n.* ticket.
Billig [bil'ish] *a.* cheap, fair, reasonable. [prove.
Billigen [bil'i-gen] *vt.* to approve.
Billigerweise [bil'i-gerr-vize-er] *ad.* fairly, in fairness.
Billigkeit [bil'ish-kite] *nf.* cheapness, fairness, justice.
Billigung [bi'li-gŏŏng] *nf.* approval. [tinkle.
Bimmeln [bim'eln] *vi.* to
Bimsstein [bims'shtine] *nm.* pumice.
Binde [bin'der] *nf.* bandage,

band, tie, sling, towel; **-glied** *n.* connecting link; **-strich** *nm.* hyphen; **-wort** *n.* conjunction.
Binden [bin'den] *vt. ir.* to bind, tie, contain (*troops*).
Bindfaden [bint'fah-den] *nm.* string.
Binnen [bin'en] *pr.* within; **-fischerei** *nf.* freshwater fishing; **-hafen** *nm.* inland harbour, port, inner dock; **-handel** *nm.* home trade; **-schiffahrt** *nf.* inland navigation; **-währung** *nf.* token currency.
Binse [bin'zer] *nf.* rush, reed.
Biograph [bi-o-grahf'] *m.w.* biographer.
Biographie [bi-o-gra-fee'] *nf.* biography. [biology.
Biologie [bi-o-lo-gee'] *nf.*
Birke [birr'ker] *nf.* birch.
Birk-hahn [birrk'hahn] *nm.* black-cock; **-huhn** *n.* moor-hen.
Birnbaum [birrn'bowm] *nm.* (**-bäume**) pear-tree.
Birne [birr'ner] *nf.* pear, bulb, electric lamp.
Bis [bis] *pr.* till, (up) to; *cf.* till.
Bisam [bee'zam] *nm.* musk.
Bischof [bi'shohf] *nm.* (**Bischöfe**) bishop.
Bischöflich [bi'sherf-lish] *a.* episcopal, Anglican.
Bisher [bis-hairr'] *ad.*, Bisherig [bis-hairr'ish] *a.* till now, hitherto.
Biskuit [bis-kveet'] *nm.* (**-e**) rusk, biscuit, cake.
Bismut [bis'mŏŏt] *nm.* bismuth.
Biss [bis] *nm.* (Bisse) bite.
Bisschen [bis'shen] *n.* bit.
Bissen [bis'en] *nm.* (**-**) morsel, tit-bit. [snappish.
Bissig [bis'ish] *a.* biting,
Bistum [bis'tŏŏm] *n.* (Bistümer) bishopric.
Bisweilen [bis-vile'en] *ad.* at times, occasionally.
Bitte [bi'ter] *nf.* request.
Bitten [bi'ten] *vt. ir.* to ask, beg; bitte please.

Bitter [bit'terr] a. bitter.

Bitterkeit [bi'terr-kite] nf. bitterness. [bitter(ly).

Bitterlich [bi'terr-lish] a., ad.

Bittersalz [bi'terr-zalts] n., Epsom salts. [petition.

Bittschrift [bit'shrift] nf.

Bittsteller [bit'shtel-err] nm. (-) petitioner, supplicant.

Biwak [bee'vak] n. (-s) bivouac.

Blachfeld [blach'felt] n. open field, battle-field.

Blähen [blai'en] vt.r. to blow out, swell, inflate.

Blähung [blai'ōong] nf. inflation, flatulence, wind.

Blaken [blah'ken] vi. to smoke (lamp, etc.). [disgrace.

Blamage [bla-mah'zher] nf.

Blamieren [bla-meer'ren] vt.r. to compromise, make a fool of oneself, disgrace oneself.

Blank [blank] a. bright, bare, clean, polished; - ziehen to draw the sword.

Blanko [blang'ko] a. blank, uncovered; -formular n. blank form; -verkauf nm. short sale, uncovered sale; -vollmacht nf. unlimited power, blank letter of attorney.

Bläschen [blaze'shen] n. (-) bubble, pimple.

Blase [blah'zer] nf. bubble, blister, bladder; -balg nm. bellows; -instrument n. wind instrument; -rohr n. blowpipe, pea-shooter. [blow.

Blasen [blah'zen] vt.r. to blow.

Blass [blas] a. pale.

Blässe [ble'ser] nf. paleness.

Blatt [blat] n. (Blätter) leaf, blade, newspaper, art print, sheet (paper); -blei n. sheet lead; -gold n. gold-foil, gold-leaf; -laus nf. greenfly; -metall n. sheet metal; -seite nf. page; -zeichen n. book-mark.

Blatter [bla'terr] nf. blister, pimple; pl. small-pox; -narbe nf. pock-mark.

Blätterig [blet'er-rish] a. leafy.

Blättern [blet'errn] vt. to turn over the leaves (book).

Blätterteig [blet'err-tike] nm. puff-pastry.

Blau [blow] a. blue; -äugig a. blue-eyed; -beere nf. bilberry; -grau a. slate-coloured; -kohl nm., -kraut n. red cabbage; -meise nf. tom-tit; -pause nf. blue-print; -säure nf. prussic acid; -stift nm. blue pencil.

Bläue [bloi'er] nf. blueness, blue (com.).

Bläuen [bloi'en] vt. to blue.

Blech [blesh] nm. (-e) tin, sheet metal; -büchse nf. -dose nf. tin, can; -geschirr n. tin utensils, mess-tin (mil.); -instrument n. brass instrument; -lehre nf. metal gauge; -musik nf. brass band; -schmied nm. tinsmith.

Blei [blȳ] n., -arbeit nf. plumbing; -rohr n. lead pipe; -soldat m.w. tin soldier; -stift nm. pencil; -stiftspitzer nm. pencil sharpener.

Bleiben [blibe'en] vi. ir. to remain, stay; stehen - to stop, stand still.

Bleich [blish] a. faded, pale.

Bleiche [bli'sher] nf. paleness, bleaching, bleaching ground.

Bleichen [bli'shen] vt. to bleach; i. ir. to grow pale, fade. [n. bleach.

Bleichpulver [blish'pool-ferr]

Bleiern [bli'errn] a. leaden.

Bleie [bli'er] nf. bream.

Blende [blen'der] nf. blind, blocked up door, window, shutter, diaphragm, dead light (nav.).

Blenden [blen'den] vt. to blind, dazzle, hoodwink.

Blend-laterne [blen'd-] nf. bull's-eye lantern; -scheibe nf. shutter; -werk n. illusion, delusion.

Blendung [blen'dōong] nf. blinding, deception.

Blick [blik] *nm.* (-e) glance, glimpse, look, gaze, view.

Blicken [bli'ken] *vi.* to look; **sich - lassen** to put in an appearance.

Blind [blint] *a.* blint, dull; **-er Passagier** stowaway.

Blind-abwurf *nm.* random bombing (*av.*); **-darm** *nm.* appendix; **-darmentzündung** *nf.* appendicitis; **-flug** *nm.* blind flight, flying; **-gänger** *nm.* dud, unexploded shell (*mil.*); **-laden** *vi.* to load blank (*mil.*); **-lings** *ad.* blindly; **-schiessen** *vt. ir.* to fire blind (cartridges); **-schleiche** *nf.* blind-worm.

Blinken [bling'ken] *vi.* to glitter, twinkle, signal (*visual*).

Blink-feuer **-zeichen** *n.* revolving light, intermittent signal, visual signal (*nav., etc.*).

Blinzeln [blint'seln] *vi.* to blink, wink.

Blitz [blits] *nm.* (-e) lightning, flash; **-ableiter** *nm.* lightning conductor; **-blank** *a.* bright and shining; **-krieg** *nm.* lightning war; **-licht** *n.* flash-light; **-strahl** *nm.* flash of lightning

Blitzen [blit'sen] *vi.* to lighten, flash.

Block [blok] *nm.* (Blöcke) block, log of wood, pad (paper); **-haus** *n.* blockhouse; **-schrift** *nf.* block letters; **-stelle** *nf.* signal box (*rl.*); **-wagen** *nm.* truck.

Blockade [blo-kah'der] *nf.* blockade; **-brecher** *nm.* **-fahrer** *nm.*, **-renner** *nm.* blockade breaker.

Blockieren [blo-keer'ren] *vt.* (to blockade, block, lock up *capital*). [shy.

Blöde [bler'der] *a.* silly, stupid,

Blödigkeit [bler'dish-kite] *nf.* shyness, silliness.

Blödsichtig [blert'zish-tish] *a.* weak-sighted, short-sighted.

Blödsinn [blert'zin] *nm.* nonsense. [silly, idiotic.

Blödsinnig [blert'zin-ish] *a.*

Blöken [bler'ken] *vi.* to bleat.

Blond [blont] *a.* blond, fair.

Bloss [blohs] *a.* bare, mere; *ad.* only, barely, merely; **-stellen** *vt.* to expose; **-stellung** *nf.* exposure.

Blösse [bler'ser] *nf.* bareness, weakness; **sich eine - geben** to expose oneself, to lay oneself open to attack.

Blühen [blew'en] *vi.* to bloom, flourish.

Blume [bloo'mer] *nf.* flower, bouquet (*wine*).

Blumen-blatt *n.* petal; **-händler** *nm.* florist; **-kohl** *nm.* cauliflower; **-laden** *nm.* flower shop; **-lese** *nf.* selection, anthology; **-scherbe** *nf.* **-topf** *nm.* flower-pot; **-zwiebel** *nf.* bulb.

Bluse [bloo'zer] *nf.* blouse.

Blut [bloot] *n.* blood; **-arm** *a.* extremely poor, anaemic; **-armut** *nf.* anaemia; **-befleckt** *a.* blood-stained; **-buche** *nf.* copper beech; **-druck** *nm.* blood pressure; **-dürstig** *a.* bloodthirsty; **-egel** *nm.* leech; **-fluss** *nm.* haemorrhage; **-gruppe** *nf.* blood group; **-jung** *a.* very young; **-probe** *nf.* blood test; **-sauger** *nm.* bloodsucker; **-schande** *nf.* incest; **-spender** *nm.* blood donor; **-sturz** *nm.* haemorrhage; **-tausch** *nm.* **-übertragung** *nf.* blood transfusion; **-vergiessen** *n.* bloodshed; **-warm** *a.* at blood heat; **-wurst** *nf.* black pudding.

Blüte [blew'ter] *nf.* blossom, prime; **-zeit** *nf.* flowering time, prime.

Blütenstaub [blew'ten-shtowp] *nf.* pollen.

Bluten [bloo'ten] *vi.* to bleed.

Blutig [bloo'tish] *a.* bleeding, bloody.

Bö [ber] *nf.* squall.

Bock [bok] *nm.* (Böcke) buck, ram, trestle, support, box (*coach*), horse (*gymnasium*); **-sprung** *nm.* caper, gambol.

Böckchen [berk'shen] n. (-) kid.

Boden [boh'den] nm. (-) floor, ground, bottom (sea), attic; -beschaffenheit nf. nature of the soil; -geräte n. ground equipment (av.); -kammer nf. attic, garret; -kredit m. credit on landed property; -los a. bottomless, unfathomable; -luke nf. skylight; -mannschaft nf. ground staff (av.); -satz nm. dregs, sediment; -schätze m.pl. mineral wealth; -sicht nf. ground visibility; -ständig a. native, permanently settled; -tür nf. trap-door.

Bodmerei [boht-me-rỹ'] nf. bottomry (com.).

Bogen [boh'gen] nm. (-) bow, curve, arch; -fenster n. bay-window; -gang nm. arcade; -linie nf. curve; -lampe nf. arc-lamp; -schluss nm. keystone.

Bogen [boh'gen] nm. (-) bow; -schütze nm. archer.

Bogen [boh'gen] nm. (-) sheet; -grösse nf. folio (size).

Bohle [boh'ler] nf. plank.

Bohne [boh'ner] nf. bean; grüne – French bean; – weisse – haricot bean. [polish.

Bohnen [boh'nen] vt. to wax.

Bohnenkaffee [boh'nen-ka-fay'] nm. pure coffee.

Bohnerwachs [boh'nerr-vax] n. floor-polish.

Bohren [bor'ren] vt. to bore.

Bohrer [bor'rerr] nm. (-) borer, drill, gimlet.

Bohr-kurbel nf. crank brace; -loch n. bore-hole; -maschine nf. boring machine, drill; -turm nm. derrick.

Bohrung [bor'rŏŏng] nf. bore.

Boi [boy] nm. (-e) baize.

Böig [ber'ish] a. squally.

Boje [boh'yer] nf. buoy.

Böller [ber'lerr] nm. small mortar. [bulwark

Bolwerk [bol'vairrk] n. (-e)

Bolschewist [bol-she-vist'] m.w. Bolshevist.

Bolschewismus [bol-she-vis'-mōōs] nm. Bolshevism.

Bolzen [bolt'sen] nm. (-) bolt, pin, arrow, peg, wedge.

Bombardieren [bom-barr-deer'ren] vt. to bombard.

Bombe [bom'ber] nf. bomb, shell. [bomb.

Bomben [bom'ben] vt. to

Bomben-abwurf nm. dropping of bombs, release, bombing (av.); -angriff nm. bombing raid; -erfolg nm. huge success; -fernrohr n. telescopic bomb sight (av.); -fest a. bomb-proof; -flugzeug n. bomber (plane); -last nf. bomb load (av.); -punktfeuer n. precision bombing (av.); -punktwurf nm. pin-point bombing (av.); -reihe nf. stick of bombs (av.); -reihenabwurf nm. release of sticks of bombs (av.); -schütze nm. airgunner (av.); -sicher a. bomb-proof; -zielvorrichtung nf. bomb-sight.

Bomber [bom'berr] nm. (-) bomber (av.).

Bonbon [bong-bong'] nm, n. (-s) sweets. [boss.

Bonze [bon'tser] nm. big-wig.

Boot [boht] n. (-e) boat, hull, body (glider); -smann nm. boatswain.

Bor [bohrr] n. boron.

Bord [borrt] nm. (-e) edge, rim, board; an – on board; -funkanlage nf. radio installation (nav.); -funker nm. wireless operator (nav.); -funkstelle nf. wireless telegraphy station; -monteur nm. aircraft fitter; -schütze m.w. air-gunner; -verständigungsanlage nf. intercommunication (av.); -wart nm. mechanic (av.).

Bordell [borr-del'] n. (-e) brothel.

Borg [borrk] nm. (-e) credit, borrowing.

Borgen [borr'gen] *vt.* to borrow, lend. [on credit.

Borgweise [borrk'vize-er] *ad.*

Borke [borr'ker] *nf.* bark.

Borniert [borr-neert'] *a.* narrow-minded.

Borsalbe [borr'zal-ber] *nf.* boracic ointment.

Borsäure [borr'zoy-rer] *nf.* boracic acid. [purse.

Börse [ber'zer] *nf.* exchange.

Börsen-bericht [ber'zen] *nm.* market report, official list (stock exchange); **-fähig** *a.* marketable, negotiable; **-geschäft** *n.* stock exchange transaction; **-kurs** *nm.* market rate; **-makler** *nm.* stockbroker; **-spieler** *nm.* speculator; **-vorstand** *nm.* committee of the stock exchange; **-zeit** *nf.* official hours of the stock exchange.

Borste [borr'ster] *nf.* bristle.

Borsten [borr'sten] *vr.* to bristle.

Borstig [borr'stish] *a.* bristly, cross, irritable.

Borte [borr'ter] *nf.* edge, trimming, border. [angry.

Böse [ber'zer] *a.* bad, evil, malicious, ill-natured.

Böschen [ber'shen] *vi.* to slope steeply.

Böschung [ber'shoong] *nf.* slope, escarpment; **-swinkel** *nm.* angle of elevation.

Bösewicht [ber'ze-visht] *nm.* (-e) scoundrel, rogue.

Boshaft [bohs'haft] *a.* malicious, spiteful, wicked.

Boshaftigkeit [bohs'haf-tish-kite] *nf.* malice, wickedness, spite. [ill-nature.

Bosheit [bohs'hite] *nf.* malice.

Böslich [ber'slish] *a,* *ad.* malicious(ly).

Bossieren [bo-seer'ren] *vt.* to emboss. Bösartig.

Böswillig [ber'svil-lish] *a.* see

Botanik [bo-tah'nik] *nf.* botany.

Botaniker [bo-tah'ni-kerr] *nm.* (-) botanist.

Botanisch [bo-tah'nish] *a.* botanical.

Bote [boh'ter] *m.w.* messenger.

Boten-gang *nm.* errand; **-gänger** *nm.* **-läufer** *nm.* messenger; **-junge** *nm.* errand-boy.

Botmässig [boht'mace-ish] *a.* subject.

Botmässigkeit [boht'mace-ish-kite] *nf.* rule, dominion, sway.

Botschaft [boht'shaft] *nf.* message, news, embassy.

Botschafter [boht'shaf-terr] *nm.* (-) ambassador.

Böttcher [bert'sherr] *nm.* (-) cooper; **-lohn** *nm.* cooperage.

Bottich [bot'ish] *nm.* (-e) vat, tub. [tureen.

Bowle [boh'ler] *nf.* claret cup.

Boxen [box'en] *vi.* to box.

Boxer [box'err] *nm.* (-) boxer; **-handschuh** *nm.* boxing-glove.

Brach [brach] *a.* fallow, uncultivated.

Brackgut [brack'goot] *n.* rubbish, refuse. [mast.

Bram [brahm] *nm.* topgallant

Branche [brong'sher] *nf.* branch, line of business.

Brand [brant] *nm.* (Brände) fire, burn, fire-brand, gangrene, mildew, brand (corn); **-bombe** *nf.* incendiary bomb; **-fest** *a.* fire-proof; **-fleck** *nm.* burn; **-geschoss** *n.* incendiary (shell); **-mal** *n.* scar, brand, stigma; **-marken** *v.t.* to brand, stigmatize; **-mauer** *nf.* fire-proof wall; **-salbe** *nf.* ointment for burns; **-schaden** *nm.* damage by fire; **-schauer** *nm.* fire-guard; **-sohle** *nf.* inner sole, welt; **-stifter** *nm.* incendiary; **-stiftung** *nf.* arson; **-wache** *nf.* fire-guards; **-wunde** *nf.* burn, scald.

Branden [bran'den] *vi.* to surge, break (sea).

Brandig [bran'dish] *a.* blighted, blasted, gangrenous.

Brandung [bran'dŏong] *nf.* surf, breakers.

Branntwein [brant'vine] *nm.* (-e) brandy; **-brennerei** *nf.* distillery. [(*ship*).]

Brasse [brass'er] *nf.* brace

Brassen [brass'en] *vt.* to brace, trim (*ship*).

Bratapfel [braht'ap-fel] *nm.* (-äpfel) baked apple.

Braten [brah'ten] *vt. ir.* to roast, grill, fry; *n.* roast, joint; **-brühe** *nf.* gravy; **-fett** *n.* dripping.

Bratfisch [braht'fish] *nm.* (-e) fried fish.

Brat-kartoffel *nf.* fried potato, chips; **-pfanne** *nf.* frying pan; **-rost** *nm.* grill, gridiron; **-spiess** *nm.* spit; **-spill** *n.* windlass.

Bratsche [brat'sher] *nf.* viola.

Brau, Bräu [brow, broi] *n.* (-e) brew.

Brauch [browch] *nm.* (Bräuche) usage, custom.

Brauchbar [browch'barr] *a.* useful, available, serviceable, wearable, capable (persons).

Brauchbarkeit [browch'barr-kite] *nf.* usefulness, availability, capacity.

Brauchen [brow'chen] *vt.* to use, want, need.

Braue [brow'er] *nf.* brow.

Brauen [brow'en] *vt.* to brew.

Brauer [brow'err] *nm.* (-) brewer. [brewery.]

Brauerei [brow-er-ry'] *nf.*

Brauhaus [brow'hows] *n.* (-häuser) brewery, tavern.

Braun [brown] *a.* brown; **-kohle** *nf.* brown coal, lignite; **-stein** *nm.* manganese.

Bräune [broi'ner] *nf.* brownness.

Bräunen [broi'nen] *vt.i.* to be, make brown, burn (*sugar*).

Brause [brow'zer] *nf.* fermentation, shower-bath, spray; **-kopf** *nm.* hothead; **-pulver** *n.* effervescent powder.

Brausen [brow-zen] *vi.* to rage, roar, rush, ferment, effervesce.

Braut [browt] *nf.* (Bräute) fiancée, bride; **-ausstattung** *nf.* trousseau; **-führer** *nm.* best man; **-jungfer** *nf.* bridesmaid; **-geschenk** *n.* wedding present; **-kleid** *n.* wedding dress; **-paar** *n.* engaged couple; **-ring** *nm.* wedding ring; **-schleier** *nm.* bridal veil; **-stand** *nm.* engagement.

Bräutigam [broi'ti-gam] *nm.* (-e) fiancé, bridegroom.

Bräutlich [broit'lish] *a.* bridal.

Brav [brahf] *a.* honest, good, worthy, brave.

Brechbar [bresh'barr] *a.* breakable. [crowbar.]

Brecheisen [bresh'ize-en] *n.*

Brechen [bresh'en] *vt. ir.* to break, refract, crush, pick (*flower*); *r.* vomit, break.

Brechmittel [bresh'mitl] *n.* emetic.

Brechreiz [bresh'rites] *nm.* retching, nausea.

Brechung [bresh'ŏong] *nf.* breaking, refraction, violation.

Brei [bry] *nm.* pap, porridge, pulp, paste.

Breit [brite] *a.* broad, wide; **sich -- machen** to swagger.

Breitbeil [brite'bile] *n.* (-e) axe, chip-axe.

Breite [brite'er] *nf.* breadth, gauge, latitude, verbosity; **-ngrad** *nm.* degree of latitude.

Breiten [brite'en] *vt.* to spread out, broaden, flatten.

Breit-schultrig *a.* broad-shouldered; **-seite** *nf.* broadside (*nav.*); **-spurig** *a.* broad gauge (*rl.*), bumptious.

Bremse [brem'zer] *nf.* gad-fly, horse-fly, cleg.

Bremse [brem'zer] *nf.* brake.

Bremsen [brem'zen] *vi.* to brake, apply brakes.

Brems-hebel *nm.* brake-lever; **-klotz** *nm.* brake-shoe; **-propeller** *nm.* fan brake; **-vor-**

richtung *nf.* braking mechanism; -zylinder *nm.* recoil cylinder.

Brennbar [bren'barr] *a.* combustible.

Brennen [bren'en] *vi. ir.* to burn, bake, roast, distil.

Brenner [bren'err] *nm.* distiller, gas burner.

Brennerei [bren-er-ry'] *nf.* distillery.

Brenn-holz *n.* firewood; -material *n.* fuel; -ofen *nm.* kiln; -punkt *nm.* focus; -spiritus *nm.* methylated spirits; -stoff *nm.* fuel, petrol.

Brenzlig [brents'lish] *a.* smelling of burning, burnt, precarious.

Bresche [bre'sher] *nf.* breach.

Brett [bret] *n.* (-er) board, plank, shelf; schwarzes – notice board.

Brettern [bret'errn] *a.* made of boards.

Bretter-wand *nf.* partition; -zaun *nm.* fence, hoarding.

Brett-mühle *nf.* saw-mill; -spiel *n.* chessboard.

Brezel [bret'sel] *nf.* cracknel.

Brief [brief] *nm.* (-e) letter; -aufgabe *nf.* posting of letters; -beschwerer *nm.* paper weight; -fach *n.* pigeon hole; -karte *nf.* letter-card; -kasten *nm.* letter-box; -schaften *f.pl.* mails, papers; -tasche *nf.* wallet; -taube *nf.* carrier pigeon; -telegramm *n.* night telegraph letter; -träger *nm.* postman; -umschlag *nm.* envelope; -wechsel *nm.* correspondence.

Brieflich [brief'lish] *a.* ad, by letter, postal.

Briefmarke [brief'mahr-ker] *nf.* postage stamp; -nkunde *nf.* philately; -nsammler *nm.* philatelist, stamp collector.

Brigade [bri-gah'der] *nf.* brigade; -kommandeur *nm.* brigadier.

Brigg [brik] *nf.* (-s) brig.

Brikett [bri-ket'] *n.* (-s) briquette.

Brillantine [bril-yan-tee'ner] *nf.* brilliantine. [goggles.

Brille [bri'ler] *nf.* spectacles.

Bringen [bring'en] *vt. ir.* to bring, take, fetch, induce; nach Hause – to see home; um etwas – to deprive of; es mit sich – involve.

Brisanzgeschoss [bri-zants'-ger-shoss] *n.* high explosive shell.

Brise [bree'zer] *nf.* breeze.

Bröckeln [brer'keln] *vt.i.r.* to crumble.

Bröckelig [brer'ke-lish] *a.* [crumb.

Brocken [brock'en] *nm.*

Brodeln [broh'deln] *vi.* to bubble.

Brodem [brode'em] *nm.* steam, vapour.

Brokat [broh-kaht'] *nm.* (-e) brocade.

Brom [brohm] *n.* bromine; -silber *n.* silver bromide.

Brombeere [brom'bair-er] *nf.* blackberry.

Bronchial [bron-shi-ahl'] *a.* bronchial.

Bronze [brong'zer] *nf.* bronze.

Bronzen [brong'zen] *a.* (of) bronze. [crumb.

Brosam [broh'zam] *nm.* (-e)

Brosche [brosh'er] *nf.* brooch.

Broschieren [bro-sheer'ren] *vt.* to sew, stitch.

Broschiert [bro-sheerrt'] *a.* stitched, in paper covers (*book*).

Broschüre [bro-shyoor'rer] *nf.* pamphlet.

Brot [broht] *n.* bread, loaf; -beutel *nm.* haversack; -erwerb *nm.* livelihood; -neid *nm.* professional jealousy; -rinde *nf.* bread crust; -schnitte *nf.* slice of bread. [roll.

Brötchen [brert'shen] *n.*

Brotlos [broht'lohs] *a.* unemployed (person), unprofitable (*task, etc.*).

Bruch [brŏŏch] nm. (Brüche) breakage, breach, rupture, fraction, fold, crease, rubble, crash (av.); **-machen** to crash (av.); **-band** n. truss; **-belastung** nf. breaking load; **-eisen** n. scrap iron; **-frei** a. free from breakages; **-landung** nf. crash landing (av.); **-schaden** nm. damage; **-spannung** nf. breaking strain; **-stück** n. fragment; **-teil** nm. fraction.

Brüchig [bryŏŏ'shish] a. brittle, fragile, cracked, split.

Brücke [bryŏŏ'ker] nf. bridge; **-nbalken** nm. girder; **-nbau** nm. bridge building; **-nkopf** nm. bridge-head, pier-head; **n-waage** nf. weigh-bridge.

Bruder [brŏŏ'derr] nm. (Brüder) brother.

Brüderlich [bryŏŏ'derr-lish] a. brotherly; **-keit** nf. fraternity.

Brudermord [brŏŏ'derr-morrt] nm. fratricide.

Brüderschaft [bryŏŏ'derr-shaft] nf. brotherhood, fellowship.

Brühe [bryŏŏ'er] nf. broth, gravy.

Brühen [bryŏŏ'en] vt. to scald.

Brühwarm [bryŏŏ'varrm] a. scalding hot, fresh.

Brüllen [bryŏŏ'len] vi. to bellow.

Brummbär [brŏŏm'bairr] m.w. grumbler.

Brummen [brŏŏ'men] vi. to growl, mutter, grumble, hum, buzz.

Brummer [brŏŏ'merr] nm. (-) bluebottle.

Brummkreisel [brŏŏm'krize-el] nm. (-) humming-top.

Brünett [bryoo-net'] a. dark, brunette. (animals).

Brunft [brŏŏnft] nf. heat.

Brunnen [brŏŏ'nen] nm. (-) spring, fountain, well; **-kresse** nf. water-cress.

Brunst [brŏŏnst] nf. lust, heat.

Brünstig [bryŏŏn'stish] a. lustful, ardent.

Brust [brŏŏst] nf. (Brüste) breast, chest, shirt front; **-bild** n. half length portrait; **-fell-entzündung** nf. pleurisy; **-fernsprecher** nm. portable telephone; **-kasten** nm. chest; **-warze** nf. nipple; **-wehr** nf. breast-work, parapet.

Brüsten [bryŏŏ'ten] vr. to boast. [parapet.

Brüstung [bryŏŏ'toong] nf.

Brut [brŏŏt] nf. brood; **-apparat** nm. incubator; **-stätte** nf. breeding-place.

Brutal [brŏŏ-tahl'] a. brutal.

Brutalität [brŏŏ-ta-li-teht'] nf. brutality.

Brüten [bryŏŏ'ten] vt.i. to hatch, brood.

Brutto [brŏŏ'to] ad. gross; **-gewicht** n. gross weight; **-summe** nf. gross amount.

Bube [bŏŏ'ber] m.w. boy, lad, rogue, knave (cards).

Bubikopf [bŏŏ'bi-kopf] nm. (-köpfe) bobbed hair, shingle.

Buch [bŏŏch] n. (Bücher) book, quire (paper); **-binder** nm. bookbinder; **-druck** nm. printing (of books); **-drucker** nm. printer; **-druckerei** nf. printing works; **-form** nf. format, size of books; **-führung** nf. bookkeeping; **-halter** nm. bookkeeper; **-handel** nm. booktrade, publishing trade; **-händler** nm. bookseller, publisher; **-handlung** nf. booktrade, bookseller's shop; **-laden** m. book-shop; **-macher** nm. bookmaker; **-umschlag** nm. jacket, paper cover of book; **-wert** nm. book-value, actuarial value (com.). [tree.

Buche [bŏŏ'cher] nf. beech-

Buchen [bŏŏ'chen] vt. to book, enter (com.).

Bücher-brett n. book-shelf; **-ei** nf. library; **-eigenzeichen** n. book-plate; **-freund** nm. book-lover; **-gestell** n. book-shelves, bookcase; **-revisor** nm.

auditor, accountant; **-schrank** *nm.* bookcase; **-stand** *nm.* book-stall; **-stütze** *nf.* book-end; **-verzeichnis** *n.* list, catalogue of books; **-zeichen** *n.* book-plate.

Buchfink [bōōch′fink] *m.w.* chaffinch.

Buchsbaum [bōox′bowm] *nm.* (**-bäume**) box-tree.

Büchse [bewx′er] *nf.* box, tin, rifle.

Büchsen-fleisch *n.* tinned meat, corned beef; **-gemüse** *n.* tinned vegetables; **-macher** *nm.* gunsmith, gun-maker; **-öffner** [bōō′meln] *vi.* to tin-opener.

Buchstabe [bōōch′shtah-ber] *nm.* (*gen.* **-ns**; *pl.* **-n**) letter of alphabet; **grosser = capital.**

Buchstab-ieren *vt.* to spell; **-ierung** *nf.* spelling.

Buchstäblich [bōōch′shtabe-lish] *a.* literal.

Bucht [bōōcht] *nf.* bay, inlet.

Buchung [bōōch′ōōng] *nf.* entry (*com.*). [boss.

Buckel [bōō′kel] *nm.* (**-**) hump.

Buckelig [bōō′ke-lish] *a.* hunch-backed.

Bücken [bew′ken] *vr.* to bend, bow. [bow.

Bückling [bew′kling] *nm.* (**-e**) kipper, red herring.

Bude [bōō′der] *nf.* booth, stall, lodgings. [buffalo.

Büffel [bew′fel] *nm.* (**-**)

Büffett [bew-fet′] *n.* (**-e**) sideboard, dresser, buffet.

Bug [bōōk] *nm.* (**Büge**) bow (*nav.*), nose (*av.*); **-schütze** *m.w.* forward gunner (*av.*); **-spriet** *n.* (**-e**) bowsprit.

Bügel [bew′gel] *nm.* (**-**) bow, hoop, stirrup; **-eisen** *n.* flat-iron.

Bügeln [bew′geln] *vt.* to iron.

Bugsierboot [bōōk-zeer′-boht] *n.* (**-e**) tug.

Bugsieren [bōōk-zeer′ren] *vt.* to tow.

Buhle [bōō′ler] *nm.f.* lover, mistress; **-rei** *nf.* illicit intercourse; **-rin** *nf.* prostitute; **-risch** *a.* lewd, amorous.

Buhne [bōō′ner] *nf.* dike.

Bühne [bew′ner] *nf.* stage; **-nausstattung** *nf.* scenery, stage setting; **-ndichter** *nm.* playwright; **-nstück** *n.* play.

Bulldogge [bōōl′do-ger] *nf.* bull-dog.

Bulle [bōō′ler] *m.w.* bull.

Bummel [bōō′mel] *nm.* (**-**) stroll; **-ei** *nf.* stroll, loafing, negligence, indolence; **-zug** *nm.* slow train.

Bummeln [bōō′meln] *vi.* to saunter, loaf, loiter.

Bummler [bōōm′lerr] *nm.* (**-**). Bummlerin *nf.* dawdler, loafer.

Buna [bōō′nah] *nm.* synthetic rubber.

Bund [bōōnt] *n.* (**Bunde**) bundle, bunch, bobbin, skein, hank (*com.*); *nm.* (**Bünde**) bond, covenant, confederation.

Bündel [bewn′del] *n.* (**-**) bundle, bale, bunch, truss.

Bündeln [bewn′deln] *vt.* to bundle.

Bundes-genosse *m.w.* ally, confederate; **-hauptstadt** *nf.* federal capital; **-staat** *nm.* federal state.

Bündig [bewn′dish] *a.* binding, concise, flush, countersunk (*tec.*).

Bündigkeit [bewn′dish-kite] *nf.* conclusiveness, conciseness.

Bündnis [bewnt′nis] *n.* (**-se**) alliance.

Bunker [bōōn′kerr] *nm.* (**-**) coal bunker, dug-out (*mil.*).

Bundweise [bewnt′vize-er] *ad.* in bundles.

Bunt [bōōnt] *a.* coloured, bright, variegated, mixed, lively; **-druck** *nm.* colour printing; **-stift** *nm.* coloured pencil.

Bürde [byōōr′der] *nf.* burden.

Bureau [bew-roh′] *n.* office.

Burg [bōōrk] *nf.* castle, fort.

Bürg'e [byōŏr'ger] *m.w.* surety, bail; **-schaft** *nf.* bail, surety; **-schaft leisten** to give security, go bail.

Bürgen [byōŏr'gen] *vt.* to go bail, vouch for.

Bürger [byōŏr'ger] *nm.* (-) citizen, townsman, member of middle class; **-krieg** *nm.* civil war; **-kunde** *nf.* sociology, citizenship; **-meister** *nm.* mayor, burgomaster; **-recht** *n.* citizenship, civic freedom; **-schaft** *nf.* citizens; **-sinn** *nm.* civic sense, public spirit; **-stand** *nm.* middle class; **-steig** *nm.* pa'vement; **-tum** *n.* citizens; **-wehr** *nf.* militia, civic guard.

Bürgerlich [byōŏr'ger-lish] *a.* civil, middle class, unpretentious, plain (*cooking*).

Büro [bew-roh'] *n.* (-s) office.

Bürokrat [bew-ro-kraht'] *m.w.* bureaucrat.

Bürokratie [bew-ro-kra-tee'] *nf.* bureaucracy.

Bürokratisch [bew-ro-krah'-tish] *a.* bureaucratic.

Bürokratismus [bew-ro-krat-is'mŏŏs] *nm.* officialism, red tape, bureaucracy.

Bursch(e) [boor'scher] *m.w.* lad, fellow, student, man servant, orderly, batman.

Bürste [byōŏr'ster] *nf.* brush.

Bürsten [byōŏr'sten] *vt.* to brush.

Bürzel [byōŏr'tsel] *nm.* (-) rump, croup.

Busch [bŏŏsh] *nm.* (Büsche) bush, shrub, tuft.

Büschel [bew'shel] *nm.* (-) tuft, sheaf, cluster.

Büschelboden [bew'shel-boh-den] *nm.* (-) hair-sieve.

Buschig [bŏŏ'shish] *a.* bushy, shaggy.

Busen [bŏŏ'zen] *nm.* (-) bosom.

Busse [bŏŏ'zen] *nf.* atonement, repentance, penance, fine.

Büssen [bew'sen] *vi.t.* to do penance, atone for, expiate.

Bussfertig [bŏŏs'fairr-tish] *a.* penitent. [compass.

Bussole [bŏŏ-soh'ler] *nf.* ship's [compass.

Büste [bew'ster] *nf.* bust; **-nhalter** *nm.* brassière. [brill.

Butt [bŏŏt] *nm.* (-e) flounder.

Bütte [bew'ter] *nf.* tub.

Büttel [bew'tel] *nm.* (-) bailiff, beadle, executioner, jailer.

Butter [bŏŏ'terr] *nf.* butter; **-blume** *nf.* buttercup; **-brot** *n.* bread and butter; **-brotpapier** *n.* grease-proof paper; **-fass** *n.* churn; **-kammer** *nf.* dairy; **-schmalz** *n.* melted butter.

Buttern [bŏŏ'terrn] *vt.i.* to churn.

Butzen [bŏŏt'sen] *nm.* (-) core (*fruit, etc.*); **-scheibe** *nf.* bull's-eye pane (*glass*).

C

(See also under **K** and **Z**;
Ch under **Sch**)

Cafe [ka-feh'] *n.* café, coffee house.

Cellist [tsel'ist] *m.w.* cellist.

Cello [tse'loh] *n.* (-s) cello.

Cellospieler [tse'loh-shpee'lerr] *nm.* (-) *see* Cellist.

Chamäleon [ka-meh'le-on] *n.* (-s) chameleon.

Champagner [sham-pan'yerr] *nm.* champagne.

Champignon [sham-peen-jong'] *nm.* (-s) mushroom.

Chaos [kah'os] *n.* chaos.

Chaotisch [ka-oh'tish] *a.* chaotic.

Charakter [ka-rak'terr] *nm.* (-e) character; **-fest** *a.* of firm character; **-stärke** *nf.* strength of character; **-zug** *nm.* (-züge) trait.

Charakterisieren [ka-rak-te-ri-zee'ren] *vt.* to characterize.

Charakteristik [ka-rak-te-ris'tik] *nf.* characterization.

Charakteristisch [ka-rak-te-ris'tish] *a.* characteristic, typical.

Charakterlos [ka-rak'terr-lohs] *a.* without character; **-igkeit** *nf.* lack of principles.

Charge [shahrr'zher] *nf.* rank, officer.

Chargieren [shahrr-zhee'ren] *vi.* to charge. [chassis.

Chassis [sha-see'] *n.* (—)

Chauffeur [sho-ferr'] *nm.* (-e) chauffeur, driver. [to drive.

Chauffieren [sho-fee'ren] *vt.i.*

Chaussee [sho-say'] *nf.* high road; **-wärter** *nm.* roadman.

Chaussieren [sho-see'ren] *vt.* to pave, macadamize.

Chauvinismus [sho-vi-nis'mōos] *nm.* chauvinism, jingoism.

Chauvinist [sho-vi-nist'] *m.w.* chauvinist, jingo.

Chef [shef] *nm.* (-s) head, principal, boss, commander (*mil.*). [chemistry.

Chemie [shay-mee'] *nf.*

Chemikalien [shay-mi-kahl'yen] *pl.* chemicals.

Chemisch [shay-mi-kahl'ish] *a.* chemical. [(—) chemist.

Chemiker [shay'mi-kerr] *nm.*

Chemisch [shay'mish] *a.* chemical.

Chiffre [shi'ferr] *nf.* cipher; **-schlüssel** *nm.* cipher code.

Chiffrieren [shif-ree'ren] *vt.* to code.

Chiffriermaschine [shi-freerr'ma-shee-ner] *nf.* cipher machine.

Chimäre [shi-meh'rer] *nf.* chimera. [chimerical.

Chimärisch [shi-meh'rish] *a.*

Chinin [shi-neen'] *n.* quinine.

Chirurg [shi-rōork'] *m.w.* surgeon. [surgery.

Chirurgie [shi-rōor-gee'] *nf.*

Chirurgisch [shi-roor'gish] *a.* surgical.

Chlor [klohrr] *n.* chlorine; **-kalk** *nm.* bleaching powder; **-wasserstoff** *nm.* hydrochloric acid. [chloride.

Chlorid [kloh-reet'] *n.* (-e)

Chloroform [kloh-ro-forrm'] *n.* chloroform.

Chloroformieren [kloh-ro-forr-mee'ren] *vt.* to chloroform.

Cholera [koh'ler-rah] *nf.* cholera. [choleric.

Cholerisch [koh-leh'rish] *a.*

Chor [kohrr] *nm, n.* (Chöre) choir, chorus; **-gesang** *nm.* (-gesänge) anthem; **-herr** *m.w.* canon; **-istin** *nf.* chorus girl; **-schranke** *nf.* choir screen.

Chorartig [kohrr'ahrr-tish] *a.* choral. [in chorus.

Chorweise [kohrr'vise-er] *ad.*

Choral [koh-rahl'] *m.w.* (Chöräle) hymn, chorale.

Christ [krist] *m.w.* Christian; **-baum** *nm.* (-bäume) Christmas tree. [nf. Christendom.

Christenheit [krist'en-hite]

Christentum [krist'en-tōōm] *n.* Christianity.

Christlich [krist'lish] *a.* Christian. [chrome.

Chrom [krohm] *n.* chromium;

Chromatisch [kroh-mah'tish] *a.* chromatic.

Chronik [kroh'nik] *nf.* chronicle. [chronical.

Chronisch [kroh-nish'] *a.*

Chronologie [kroh-no-lo-gee'] *nf.* chronology.

Chronologisch [kroh-no-lo-gish'] *a.* chronological.

Code [koh'der] *nf.* code; **-wort** *n.* code word. [partment (*rl.*).

Coupé [kuh-pay'] *n.* (-s) com-

Coupon [kuh-pong'] *nm.* (-s) coupon, counterfoil, dividend warrant (*com.*). [ship.

Cour [kuhrr] *nf.* court, court-

Courage [kuh-rah'zher] *nf.* courage.

Courmacher [kuhrr'mah-cherr] *nm.* ladies' man, flirt.

Courtage [kuhrr-tah'zher] *nf.* brokerage. [(female) cousin.

Cousine [kuh-zee'ner] *nf.*

Creme [kray'mer] *nf.* cream.

Cutaway [kut'a-veh] *nm.* (-s) morning coat.

D

Da [dah] *ad.* there, then; *cj.* as; dasein to exist, be present; *n.* existence.

Dabei [da-by'] *ad.* close to, thereby, at the same time; es bleibt – that is settled.

Dach [dach] *n.* (Dächer) roof; -antenne *nf.* roof aerial; -boden *nm.* attic, loft; -decker *nm.* slater, tiler; -fenster *n.* sky-light; -kammer *nf.* garret, attic; -luke *nf.* dormer window, skylight; -pappe *nf.* roofing felt; -rinne *nf.* gutter; -ziegel *nm.* roof tile. [thatch.

Dachen [dach'en] *vt.* to roof.

Dachs [dax] *nm.* (-e) badger; -hund *nm.* dachshund. [ing.

Dachung [dach'ŏŏng] *nf.* roof-

Dackel [dackl] *nm.* (-) *see* Dachshund.

Dadurch [da-dŏŏrch'] *ad.* in that way, because of that; – dass by reason of the fact that.

Dafür [da-fyŏŏr'] *ad.* for that, in return for that, for it.

Dagegen [da-gay'gen] *ad.* on the other hand, against that.

Daheim [da-hime'] *ad.* at home.

Daher [da-hairr'] *ad.* thence.

Daherum [da-he-rŏŏm'] *ad.* round about, thereabouts.

Dahin [da-hin'] *ad.* thither, there; es – bringen to succeed with a thing, bring about.

Dahinstehen [da-hin'shtay-en] *vi. ir.* to be uncertain.

Dahinten [da-hin'ten] *ad.* behind there.

Dahinter [da-hin'terr] *ad.* behind that; -kommen *vi.* to find out.

Damalig [dah'mah-lish] *a.* of that time, then.

Damals [dah'mahlss] *ad.* at that time, then.

Damast [da-mast'] *nm.* (-e) damask. [damask-

Damasten [da-mastn'] *a.*

Dambrott [dahm'bret] *n.* (-er) draughts board.

Dame [dah'mer] *nf.* lady, queen (*cards*); -nbinde *nf.* sanitary towel; -nheld *nm.* lady killer; -nsattel *nm.* side saddle; -nspiel *n.* draughts.

Damhirsch [dam'heerrsh] *nm.* (-e) fallow deer.

Damit [da-mit'] *ad.* with, by that; *cj.* in order that, to.

Dämlich [dame'lish] *a.* silly, stupid.

Damm [dam] *nm.* (Dämme) dam, mole, embankment. [up.

Dämmen [dem'en] *vt.* to dam

Dämmer [dem'err] *nm.* dusk.

Dämmerig [dem'e-rish] *a.* dim, vague.

Dämmern [dem'errn] *vi.* to grow dusk, dawn.

Dämmerung [dem'er-rŏŏng] *nf.* twilight, dawn.

Dämon [day'mon] *nm.* (*gen.* -s; *pl.* -en) demon.

Dämonisch [day-moh'nish] *a.* demoniacal.

Dampf [dampf] *nm.* (Dämpfe) steam, vapour; -boot *n.* steam-boat; -druckmesser *nm.* steam gauge; -esse *nf.* steam funnel; -maschine *nf.* steam engine; -pfeife *nf.* hooter; -schiff *n.* steamship; -schiffahrt *nf.* steam navigation; -turbine *nf.* steam turbine; -walze *nf.* steam roller. [smoke, steam.

Dampfen [damp'fen] *vi.* to

Dämpfen [demp'fen] *vt.* to damp, extinguish, steam.

Dampfer [damp'ferr] *nm.* (-) steamer.

Dämpfer [demp'ferr] *nm.* (-) damper, extinguisher, baffle (*rad.*).

Dämpfungsplatte [demp'fŏŏngs-pla-ter] *nf.* baffle (*tec.*).

Damstein [dahm'shtine] *nm.* (-e) draughtsman (*game*).

Danach [da-nach'] *ad.* after that, afterwards, according to that.

Daneben [da-nay'ben] *ad.* beside (that)

Danieder [da-nee'derr] *ad.* down, low; -liegen *vi. ir.* to be ill, on one's last legs.

Dank [dangk] *nm.* thanks; -wissen to be grateful; -adresse *nf.* vote of thanks.

Dankbar [dangk'bahrr] *a.* grateful, advantageous.

Dankbarkeit [dangk'bahrr-kite] *nf.* gratitude. [thank.

Danken [dang'ken] *vt.* to thank.

Dankenswert [dang'kens-vairrt] *a.* deserving of thanks, kind.

Dann [dan] *ad.* then; - und wann now and then. [on it.

Daran [da-ran'] *ad.* at, on that.

Darauf [da-rowf'] *ad.* upon that, thereupon, on it.

Daraus [da-rowss'] *ad.* hence, from that, out of it.

Darben [dahrr'ben] *vi.* to be in want.

Darbieten [dahrr'bete-en] *vt. ir.* to offer, tender.

Darbringen [dahrr'bring-en] *vt. ir.* to bring, offer.

D(a)rin [da-rin'] *ad.* in (there), in it. [in, inside.

Darinnen [da-rin'en] *ad.* within.

Darlegen [dahrr'lay-gen] *vt.* to expound, demonstrate.

Darlegung [dahrr'lay-gōōng] *nf.* exposition, demonstration.

Darleh(e)n [dahrr'lay-en] *n.* loan.

Darm [dahrm] *nm.* (Därme) bowels, intestines; -bruch *nm.* hernia, rupture; -seite *nf.* catgut.

Darnieder [dahrr-nee'derr] *ad.* down, on the ground; -liegen *vi. ir.* to be ill on the downgrade; *n.* depression, ruin.

Darre [da'rer] *nf.* kiln, drying in a kiln.

Darren [da'ren] *vt.* to dry in a kiln.

Darrofen [dar'roh-fen] *nm.* (-öfen) drying-kiln.

Darstellen [dahrr'shtel-en] *vt.* to represent, exhibit, show.

Darstellung [dahrr'shtel-ōōng] *nf.* representation, exhibition. [prove.

Dartun [dahrr'tōōn] *vt. ir.* to

Darüber [da-ryōō'berr] *ad.* over, above that, besides.

D(a)rum [da'rōōm] *ad.* for that reason, about that, about it.

Darunter [da-rōōn'terr] *ad.* under, beneath that.

Das [dass] *art.* the; *pn.* that.

Dasein [dah'zine] *n.* presence, existence.

Daselbst [dah-zelbst'] *ad.* there, in that place, of that town.

Dass [dass] *cj.* that. [date.

Datieren [da-tee'ren] *vt.* to

Dativ [dah'teef] *nm.* dative.

Dattel [datl] *nf.* date.

Datum [dah'tōōm] *n.* date; Daten *pl.* dates, data.

Daube [dow'ber] *nf.* stave.

Dauer [dow'err] *nf.* duration, permanence; auf die - in the long run; -befehl *nm.* standing order; -beleg *nm.* permanent voucher; -betrieb *nm.* continuous operation; -feuer *n.* sustained fire (*mil.*); -fleisch *n.* preserved meat; -flug *nm.* non-stop flight; -karte *nf.* permanent pass; -lauf *nm.* long-distance run; -marsch *nm.* forced march (*mil.*); -stellung *nf.* permanent post; -strich *nm.* long stroke (morse); -welle *nf.* permanent wave; -wirkung *nf.* permanent effect.

Dauerhaft [dow'err-haft] *a.* lasting, durable.

Dauerhaftigkeit [dow'err-haf-tish-kite] *nf.* durability.

Dauern [dow'errn] *vi.* to last, keep.

Dauern [dow'errn] *vt. imp.* to be sorry for, regret.

Dauernd [dow'errnt] *a.* enduring, lasting.

Daumen [dow'men] *nm.* (-) thumb; **-abdruck** *nm.* thumbprint; **-rad** *n.* cog-wheel; **-welle** *nf.* cam-shaft.

Daune [dow'ner] *nf.* down; **-ndecke** *nf.* eiderdown (quilt).

Davon [da-fon'] *ad.* of it, thereby, away; **-kommen** *vi. ir.* to escape; **-tragen** *vt. ir.* to win, carry off. [of it.

Davor [da-forr'] *ad.* before it.

Dawider [da-vee'derr] *ad.* against it.

Dazu [da-tsoo'] *ad.* to it, for it, besides, in addition; **-kommen** *vi. ir.* to supervene, arrive; **-tun** *vt. ir.* to add.

Dazumal [dah'tsoo-mahl] *ad.* in those days, then.

Dazwischen [da-tsvi'shen] *ad.* between, among (them), between times; **-kunft** *nf.* intervention; **-treten** *vi. ir.* to intervene. [debate.

Debatte [day-ba'ter] *nf.*

Debattieren [day-ba-tee'ren] *vi.t.* to debate.

Debet [day'bet] *n.* debit; **-posten** *nm.* debit item.

Debit [day-bit'] *nm.* sale.

Debitieren [day-bi-tee'ren] *vt.* to debit, charge. [dean.

Dechant [day-shant'] *m.w.*

Dechiffrieren [day-sheef-ree'ren] *vt.* to decipher, decode.

Dechsel [dexl] *nf.* adze.

Deck [dek] *n.* (-e) deck; **-offizier** *nm.* warrant officer (nav.).

Deck'e [dek'er] *nf.* cover, ceiling, coat; **-adresse** *nf.* accommodation address; **-bezeichnung** *nf.* code name; **-blatt** *n.* outside leaf (cigar); **-mantel** *nm.* cloak (pretext); **-name** *nm.* assumed name; **-nbeleuchtung** *nf.* ceiling lighting; **-wort** *n.* code word.

Deckel [dekl] *nm.* (-) lid, cover.

Decken [dekn] *vt.* to cover; *r.* coincide.

Deckung [de'koong] *nf.* covering, coincidence, cover (mil., com.); **-steuer** *n.* covering fire; **-struppen** *f.pl.* covering force.

Dedizieren [day-dit-see'ren] *vt.* to dedicate, present.

Deduzieren [day-doot-see'ren] *vt.* to deduct, infer, deduce.

Defätismus [day-fay-tiss'mooss] *nm.* defeatism.

Defätist [day-fay-tist'] *m.w.* defeatist.

Defekt [day-fekt'] *nm.* (-e) defect; *a.* damaged, defective.

Defensiv [day-fen-zeef'] *a.* defensive. [defensive.

Defensive [day-fen-zee'ver] *nf.*

Defilieren [day-fi-lee'ren] *vi.* to file, march past, parade.

Definieren [day-fi-nee'ren] *vt.* to define. [definite.

Definitiv [day-fi-ni-teef'] *a.*

Defizit [day-fit-seet'] *n.* deficit, shortage.

Deflation [day-flat-si-ohn'] *nf.* deflation.

Defraudant [day-frow-dant'] *m.w.* defrauder.

Defraudieren [day-frow-dee'ren] *vt.* to defraud, embezzle.

Degen [day'gen] *nm.* (-) sword.

Degenerieren [day-ge-ne-ree'ren] *vi.* to degenerate.

Degradieren [day-gra-dee'ren] *vt.* to degrade.

Dehnbar [dane'barr] *a.* expansible, malleable, elastic.

Dehnbarkeit [dane'bahr-kite] *nf.* malleability, expansibility. [expand.

Dehnen [dane'en] *vt.* to stretch.

Dehnung [dane'oong] *nf.* expansion, stretching, lengthening; **-szeichen** *n.* circumflex.

Deich [dish] *nm.* (-e) dike, embankment.

Deichen [dish'en] *vt.* to dike, bank up.

Deichsel [dixl] *nf.* shaft.

Dein [dine] *poss.* thine, your, yours.

Deinerseits [dine´err-zites] *ad.* on your part.

Deinesgleichen [dine-es-gli´shen] *a.* your equal(s), like you.

Deinet-wegen [dine-et-vayi´gen, -willen [vil´en] *ad.* for your sake, on your account.

Deinige (der, diek das) *poss.* yours, thine.

Dekadent [day-ka-dent´] *a.* decadent.

Dekadenz [day-ka-dents´] *nf.* decadence. [dean.

Dekan [dey-kahn´] *nm.* (-e)

Deklamieren [day-kla-mee´ren] *vt.i.* to declaim.

Deklarieren [day-kla-ree´ren] *vt.* to declare.

Deklination [day-kli-nat-syohn´] *nf.* declension.

Deklinieren [day-kli-nee´ren] *vt.* to decline.

Dekokt [day-kokt´] *n.* (-e) decoction.

Dekorateur [day-ko-ra-terr´] *nm.* (-e) decorator, painter.

Dekoration [day-ko-rat-syohn´] *nf.* scenery (*stage*).

Dekorieren [day-ko-ree´ren] *vt.* to decorate.

Dekret [day-krate´] *n.* (-e) decree.

Dekretieren [day-kray-tee´ren] *vt.* to decree.

Delegat [day-lay-ghat´] *m.w.* delegate.

Delegieren [day-lay-gee´ren] *vt.* to delegate.

Delikat [day-li-kaht´] *a.* dlicate, delicious.

Delikatesse [day-li-ka-te´ser] *nf.* dainty, delicacy; -nhändler *nm.* provision merchant, grocer; -nhandlung *nf.* provision store, grocer's shop.

Delphin [del-feen´] *nm.* (-e) dolphin.

Delta [del´ter] *n.* (-s) delta.

Dem [dame] *def. art.* to the; *pn.* to it, to that, to which.

Demagog [day-ma-gohk´] *m.w.* demagogue.

Demagogisch [day-ma-goh´gish] *a.* demagogic.

Demarkation [day-mahr-kat-syohn´] *nf.* demarcation; -slinie *nf.* demarcation line.

Dementieren [day-meo-tee´ren] *vt.* to deny.

Demgemäss [dame´ger-mace] *ad.* accordingly.

Demissionieren [day-mi-syoh-nee´ren] *vi.* to resign.

Demnach [dame´nahch] *ad.* see Demgemäss.

Demnächst [dame´naish-st] *ad.* shortly.

Demobilisieren [day-mo-bi-li-zee´ren] *vt.* to demobilize.

Demobilisation [day-mo-bi-li-zat-syohn] Demobilmachung [day-mo-beel´mach-ōōng] *nf.* demobilization.

Demokrat [day-mo-kraht´] *m.w.* democrat.

Demokratie [day-mo-kra-tee´] *nf.* democracy.

Demokratisch [day-mo-krah´tish] *a.* democratic.

Demolieren [day-mo-lee´ren] *vt.* to demolish.

Demonstration [day-mon-strat-syohn´] *nf.* demonstration.

Demonstrieren [day-mon-stree´ren] *vi.* to demonstrate.

Demungeachtet [dame´öön-ger-ach´tet] *cj.* notwithstanding. [ity.

Demut [day´mōōt] *nf.* humil-

Demütig [day´myōo-tish] *a.* humble; -en *vt.* to humble, humiliate; -ung *nf.* humiliation.

Demzufolge [dame´tsoo-fol-ger] *ad.* accordingly.

Den [dane] *def. art.* the; *pn.* that, which, who.

Denen [day´nen] *pn.* to whom, to which. [of thinking.

Denkart [dengk´ahrrt] *nf.* way

Denk-bar [*a.* thinkable, conceivable; -freiheit *nf.* freedom of thought; -kraft *nf.* power of

thinking; -mal *n.* (-mäler)
monument; -münze *nf.* medal;
-schrift *nf.* memorial, memoir,
memorandum.

Denken [deng'ken] *vt.i. ir.* to
think. [thinker.

Denker [deng'kerr] *nm.* (-)

Denkungsart [deng'koongs-
arrt] *nf.*—Denkart.

Denkwürdig [dengk'vyoorr-
dish] *a.* memorable; -keit *nf.*
memorable occurrence,
memorableness.

Denn [den] *cj.* for; *ad.* then.

Dennoch [den'noch] *cj.* yet,
nevertheless.

Departement [day-parr-te-
mang'] *n.* department.

Depesche [day-pe'sher] *nf.*
telegram, cable; -nformular *n.*
telegram form; -nschlüssel *nm.*
telegram code.

Depeschieren [day-pe-shee'-
ren] *vt.i.* to telegraph, cable.

Deponent [day-po-nent'] *m.w.*
witness, depositor.

Deponieren [day-po-nee'ren]
vt. to deposit (com.), depose
(law.).

Deport [day-porrt'] *nm.* discount, backwardation (com.).

Deportieren [day-porr-tee'-
ren] *vt.* to deport, carry over
(com.).

Depositum [day-poh'zi-tŏŏm]
n, **Depositen** [day-po-zee'ten]
pl. deposit, trust funds.

Depositen-bank *nf.* deposit
bank; -schein *nm.* deposit
receipt; -zins *nm.* interest on
deposits.

Depot [day-poh'] *n.* warehouse,
storehouse, deposit (com.).

Depression [day-pre-syohn']
nf. depression.

Deprimieren [day-pri-mee'-
ren] *vt.* to depress.

Deputierte(r) [day-pŏŏ-teerr'-
terr] *m.w.* deputy, delegate.

Der [dare], **Die** [dee], **Das** [dass]
def. art. the; *pn.* that, which,
who.

Derart [dare'arrt] *ad.* in such
a way.

Derartig [dare'arr-tish] *a.* of
such a kind.

Derb [dairrp] *a.* sturdy, massive, rude, blunt.

Derbheit [dairrb'hite] *nf.*
sturdiness, massiveness, rudeness, bluntness.

Deren [dare'en] *pn.* whose, of
whom, of them.

Dergestalt [dare'ger-shtalt]
ad. in such a way.

Dergleichen [dare-gli'shen]
pn. of that kind, such.

Derivat [day-ri-vaht'] *n.* (-e)
derivative.

Derjenige [dare'yay-ni-ger],
Diejenige, Dasjenige *pn.* he,
she, it, the one (who, that) or
which; those (who); that.

Dermassen [dare'mah-sen]
ad. to such an extent.

Derselbe [dare-zel'ber], **Die-
selbe, Dasselbe** *pn.* the same.

Derzeitig [dare'tsite-ish] *a.* at
the present time, for the time
being.

Des [dess] *def. art.* of the.

Deserteur [day-zairr-ter'] *nm.*
(-e) deserter.

Desertieren [day-zairr-tee'-
ren] *vt.* to desert.

Desgleichen [dess-gli'shen] *a.*
ad. of the same kind, likewise,
ditto. [fore.

Deshalb [dess'halp] *ad.* there-

Desinfektion [day-zin-fek-
syohn'] *nf.* disinfection;
-smittel *n.* disinfectant.

Desinfizieren [day-zin-fi-
tsee'ren] *vt.* to disinfect.

Desinfizierung [day-zin-fi-
tsee'rŏŏng] *nf.* disinfection.

Despot [dess-poht'] *m.w.*
despot. [despotic.

Despotisch [dess-poh'tish] *a.*

Despotismus [dess-po-tiss'-
mŏŏs] *nm.* despotism.

Dessen [dessn] *pn.* whose, of
whom, of which; -ungeachtet
notwithstanding that in spite
of the fact that.

Dessert [day-sairr'] *n.* dessert.

Dessin [day-sang'] *n.* design, pattern.

Destillateur [day-sti-la-ter'] *nm.* (-e) distiller.

Destillation [day-stil-at-syohn'] *nf.* distillation.

Destillier-apparat *nm.* still; -kolben *nm.* retort.

Destillieren [day-sti-lee'ren] *vt.* to distil.

Destillierung [day-sti-lee'-roong] *nf.* distillation.

Desto [dess'toh] *ad.* the, so much; - besser all the better.

Deswegen [dess-vay'gen] *ad.* therefore, hence.

Detail [day-tie'] *n.* (-s) retail, detail; -geschäft *n.* (-e) retail business; -händler *nm.* retailer, retail dealer.

Detaillieren [day-tie-ee'ren] *vt.* to specify, sell retail (*com.*).

Detaillierung [day-tie-ee-roong] *nf.* specification.

Detaillist [day-tie-ist'] *m.w.* retailer, shopkeeper.

Detektor [day-tek'torr] *nm.* (-en) Detektoren [day-tek-tor'-en] *pl.* detector (*tec.*); -apparat *nm.* crystal set (*rad.*).

Deuteln [doy'teln] *vt.* to interpret artfully, twist meaning of, quibble.

Deutelei [doy-ter-lie'] *nf.* quibbling.

Deuten [doy'ten] *vt.* to interpret, explain; to point to.

Deutlich [doit'lish] *a.* distinct, clear.

Deutlichkeit [doit'lish-kite] *nf.* distinctness.

Deutsch [doitsh] *a.* German; das -e German (language); auf - in German.

Deutschfeindlich [doitsh'-find-lish] *a.* Germanophobe, anti-German.

Deutschfreundlich [doitsh'-froint-lish] *a.* Germanophile, pro-German.

Deutschtum [doitsh'toom] *n.*

German heritage, traditions, way of life.

Deutung [doy'toong] *nf.* interpretation.

Devise [day-vee'zer] *nf.* device, foreign bill of exchange (*com.*).

Dezember [day-tsem'berr] *nm.* December.

Dezennium [day-tsen'yoom] *n.* Dezennien [day-tsen-yen] *pl.* decade.

Dezimalbruch [day-tsi-mahl'-brooch] *nm.* (-brüche) decimal (fraction).

Dezimeter [day'tsi-may-terr] *n.* (-) decimeter.

Diagnose [dee-ag-noh'zer] *nf.* diagnosis.

Diagnostizieren [dee-ag-nos-ti-tsee'ren] *vt.* to diagnose.

Diakon [dee-a-kohn'] (*gen.* -s) *pl.* -en) deacon.

Diakonissin [dee-a-ko-ni'sin] *nf.* deaconess, nurse.

Dialekt [dee-a-lekt'] *nm.* (-e) dialect.

Dialektisch [dee-a-lek'tish] *a.* in dialect, dialectal.

Dialog [dee-a-lohk'] *nm.* (-e) dialogue.

Diamant [dee-a-mant'] *m.w.* diamond.

Diamanten [dee-a-man'ten] *a.* diamond.

Diät [dee-ate'] *nf.* diet; -en *pl.* allowance; (*dietetics*).

Diätetik [dee-a-tay'tik] *nf.* dietetics.

Dich [dish] *pn.* thee, you.

Dicht [disht] *a.* close (to), dense, tight.

Dichte [dish'ter] *nf.* = Dichtig-keit.

Dichten [dish'ten] *vt.* to tighten, condense, caulk (*ship*).

Dichten [dish'ten] *vt.* to compose, write.

Dichter [dish'terr] *nm.* (-) poet, writer.

Dichterin [dish'ter-rin] *nf.* poetess, woman writer.

Dichterisch [dish'ter-rish] *a.* poetical.

Dichtheit [disht'hite], **Dichtig-keit** [dish'tish-kite] *nf.* closeness, density, tightness, compactness. [poetry.

Dichtkunst [dicht'koonst] nf. poetry.

Dichtung [dich'toong] nf. tightening, condensation; -sring nm. washer, gasket (tec.).

Dichtung [dich'toong] nf. poetry, fiction.

Dick [dik] a. thick, fat; -bauch nm. paunch, belly; -darm nm. large intestine; -fellig a. thick-skinned; -kopf nm. blockhead; -tuer nm. boaster.

Dicke [di'ker] nf. thickness, fatness.

Dicklich [dik'lish] a. thickish, fairly thick, fat.

Die [dee] def. art. the; pn. that, which, who.

Dieb [deep] nm. (-e) thief.

Dieberei [dee-ber-rie'] nf. theft.

Dieb(e)s-bande nf. gang of thieves; -hehlerei nf. receiving stolen property; -schlüssel nm. skeleton key; -sicher a. burglar proof. [ish.

Diebisch [dee'bish] a. thievish.

Diebstahl [deep'shtahl] nm. theft.

Diele [dee'ler] nf. board, floor, lobby, loft. [floor.

Dielen [dee'len] vt. to board.

Dienen [dee'nen] vt. to serve.

Diener [dee'nerr] nm. (-) servant.

Dienerin [dee'ner-rin] nf. maid-servant.

Dienerschaft [dee'ner-shaft] nf. servants.

Dienlich [deen'lish] a. useful, serviceable.

Dienlichkeit [deen'lish-kite] nf. serviceableness.

Dienst [deenst] nm. (-e) service; -abzeichen n. badge lanyard; -alter n. seniority; -bereich nm. jurisdiction (area); -bezüge m.pl. service pay; -bote m. domestic servant, maid; -enthebung nf. dismissal (mil. etc.); -fähig a.

fit for service; -frei a. off duty, exempt from service; -grad nm. rank; -gradabzeichen n. badge of rank; -kleidung nf. livery; -mädchen n. domestic servant; -mann nm. outporter; -pflicht nf. duty, conscription, liability to service; -pflichtige(r) nm. conscript; -stelle nf. Mitro, headquarters pl; -stunden f.pl. working hours pl; -tuend a. on duty, acting (mil.); -untauglich a. unfit for service; -vorschrift nf. service regulations; -weg nm. official channels pl; -zeit nf. term of service.

Dienstag [deens'tahk] nm. Tuesday.

Dienstbar [deenst'bahrr] a. serviceable.

Dienstlich [deenst'lish] a. official. [oil.

Dieselöl [dee'zel-erl] n. Diesel oil.

Dieser [dee'zerr], **Diese** [dee'zer], **Dies(es)** [dee'zess] a., pn. this, the latter.

Diesjährig [deess'yeh-rish] a. of this year. [on this side.

Diesseits [dees'zites] ad., pr. on this side.

Dietrich [dee'trish] nm. (-e) skeleton key.

Differential , , , [di-fe-rent-syahl'] a. differential; -getriebe n. differential gear (tec.).

Diktaphon [dik-ta-fohn'] n. dictaphone.

Diktat [dik-taht'] n. (-e) dictation; -friede nm. peace treaty imposed by force.

Diktator [dik-tah'torr] nm. (-en) dictator.

Diktatorisch [dik-ta-tor'ish] a. dictatorial.

Diktatur [dik-ta-toorr'] nf. dictatorship. [dictate.

Diktieren [dik-tee'ren] vt. to

Dilettant [di-le-tant'] m.w. dilettante.

Diner [dee-nay'] n. (-s) dinner.

Ding [ding] n. (-e, -er) thing.

Dingen [ding'en] vt. to hire,

engage, charter (*ship*); *i.* to bargain. [concrete.

Dinglich [ding'lish] *a.* real, concrete.

Dinkel [ding'kel] *nm.* spelt.

Diode [dee-oh'der] *nf.* diode (*rad.*).

Diözese [dee-er-tsay'zer] *nf.* diocese.

Diphtherie [dif-ter-ree'] *nf.* diphtheria.

Diplom [di-plohm'] *n.* (-e) diploma, certificate.

Diplomat [di-ploh-maht'] *m.w.* diplomat.

Diplomatisch [di-ploh-mah'tish] *a.* diplomatic.

Dir [deerr] *pn.* to thee, to you.

Direkt [dee-rekt'] *a.* direct, straight.

Direktion [dee-rek-syohn'] *nf.* management, board of directors.

Direktor [dee-rek'torr] *nm.* (-en) director, headmaster; manager managing director, principal.

Direktorium [dee-rek-tore'yoom] *n.* board of directors.

Dirigent [di-ri-gent'] *m.w.* conductor (*music*).

Dirigieren [di-ri-gee'ren] *vt.* to manage, direct, conduct (*music*).

Dirndl [deerrn'dl] *n.* (-n) Bavarian girl; -kleid *n.* Bavarian peasant dress.

Dirne [deerr'ner] *nf.* girl, prostitute. (*voice*).

Diskant [dis-kant'] *nm.* treble

Diskont(o) [dis-kon'toh] *nm.* discount; -satz *nm.* rate of discount.

Diskontieren [dis-kon-tee'ren] *vt.* to discount.

Diskret [dis-krait'] *a.* discreet, reticent.

Diskretion [dis-krayt-syohn'] *nf.* discretion, reticence.

Diskurs [dis-kŏŏrs'] *nm.* (-e) discourse.

Diskutieren [dis-kŏŏ-tee'ren] *vt.i.* to discuss, dispute.

Disponent [dis-poh-nent'] *m.w.* manager.

Disponieren [dis-poh-nee'ren] *vt.i.* to dispose of, arrange.

Disputieren [dis-pŏŏ-tee'ren] *vt.* to dispute, argue.

Distel [distl] *nf.* thistle.

Disziplin [dis-tsi-pleen'] *nf.* discipline.

Disziplinarisch [dis-tsi-plee-nah'rish] *a.* disciplinary.

Divers [dee-vairrs'] *a.* various, sundry (*com.*).

Diversa [dee-vairr'sah] *pl.* sundries *pl.* (*com.*).

Dividende [di-vi-den'der] *nf.* dividend; -nschein *nm.* dividend warrant.

Dividieren [di-vi-dee'ren] *vt.* to divide. [dash.

Divis [di-veess'] *n.* (-e) hyphen,

Döbel [der'bel] *nm.* (-) peg, dowel, pin.

Doch [doch] *cj.* still, after all; *ad.* indeed, however; nicht -- certainly not.

Docht [docht] *nm.* (-e) wick.

Dock [dok] *n.* (-e) dock; -arbeiter *nm.* docker.

Docke [do'ker] *nf.* skein. [up.

Docken [do'ken] *vt.* to wind

Docken [do'ken] *vt.* to dock

Dogge [do'ger] *nf.* bulldog, mastiff.

Dogma [dog'mah] *n.* (*gen.* -s; *pl.* Dogmen) dogma.

Dogmatisch [dog-mah'tish-a.* Dogmatic.

Dohle [doh'ler] *nf.* jackdaw.

Doktor [dok'torr] *nm.* (*gen.* -s: -en) doctor.

Dokument [do-kŏŏ-ment'] *n.* document.

Dolch [dolsh] *nm.* (-e) dagger.

Dollar [do-larr] *nm.* (s) dollar.

Dollbord [dol'borrt] *nm.* gunwale.

Dolle [do'ler] *nf.* thole-pin.

Dolmetschen [dol'metsh-en] *vt.* to interpret.

Dolmetsch(er) [dol'metsh-er] *nm.* (-) interpreter.

Dom [dome] *nm.* (-e) cathedral, minster; -pfaff *m.w.* bullfinch.

Dominieren [do-mi-nee'ren] *vt.* to dominate, tyrannize.

Donner [do'nerr] *nm.* thunder.

Donnern [do'nerrn] *vi.* to thunder.

Donnerstag [do'nerrs-tahk] *nm.* Thursday.

Doppel [dopl] *n.* duplicate; -bereifung *nf.* twin tyres; -decker *nm.* bi-plane (*av.*); -deutig *a.* ambiguous; -ehe *nf.* bigamy; -gänger *nm.* double; -glas *n.* binoculars *pl.*; -gläser *n.pl.* bifocal lenses *pl.*; -heit *nf.* duplicity; -punkt *nm.* colon; -sinn *nm.* ambiguity; -sinnig *a.* ambiguous; -steuerung *nf.* dual control (*av.*); -turm *nm.* twin turret (*nav.*); -zentner *nm.* ton, 100 kilograms.

Doppeln [do'peln] *vt.i.* to double.

Doppelt [do'pelt] *a.* double.

Dorf [dorrf] *n.* (Dörfer) village; -bewohner *nm.* villager; -rand *nm.* outskirts of a village.

Dörfler [derrf'lerr] *nm.* (-) villager.

Dorn [dorrn] *nm.* (*gen.* -s; *pl.* -en) thorn.

Dornbutte [dorrn'boo-ter] *nf.* turbot.

Dornig [dorr'nish] *a.* thorny.

Dorren [do'ren] *vi.* to dry up.

Dörren [der'ren] *vt.* to dry.

Dorsch [dorrsh] *nm.* (-e) cod.

Dort [dorrt] *ad.* there; -her from that place, from there; -hin to that place, there.

Dortig [dorr'tish] *a.* of that place, in that town.

Dose [doh'zer] *nf.* tin, box; -nbarometer *n.* aneroid barometer; -nöffner *nm.* tin opener. [dose.

Dosis [doh'ziss] *nf.* (Dosen)

Dotter [do'terr] *nm.* (-) yolk of egg.

Dozent [doh-tsent'] *m.w.* university lecturer, reader.

Dozieren [doh-tsee'ren] *vt.* to lecture. [kite.

Drache [drach'er] *m.w.* dragon,

Draganker [drak'ang-kerr] *nm.* (-) grapnel.

Dragoner [dra-goh'nerr] *nm.* (-) dragoon.

Draht [draht] *nm.* (Drähte) wire thread, cable; -anschrift *nf.* telegraphic address; -anweisung *nf.* cable transfer; -bericht *nm.* telegram cable; -hindernis *n.* wire entanglement; -lehre *nf.* wire gauge; -leitung *nf.* lead (*el.*); -mass *n.* wire gauge; -netz *n.* wire netting; -puppe *nf.* puppet; -rolle *nf.* wire spool; -rundfunk *nm.* relaying (*rad.*); -schere *nf.* wire cutters; -seilbahn *nf.* cog railway, funicular; -verhau *n.* wire entanglement; -zange *nf.* wire cutters *pl.*, pincers *pl.*, nippers *pl.*; -zieher *nm.* wire puller.

Drahten [drah'ten] *vt.i.* to wire.

Drahtlos [drah't'lohss] *a.* wireless; -e Telegraphie wireless telegraphy.

Drall [dral] *a.* tight, firm, closely twisted, strapping, buxom.

Drall [dral] *nm.* (-e) rifling, twist (*mil.*); -winkel *nm.* angle of rifling (*mil.*).

Drama [drah'mah] *n.* (*gen.* -s; *pl.* Dramen) drama.

Dramatiker [dra-mah'ti-kerr] *nm.* (-) dramatist.

Dramatisch [dra-mah'tish] *a.* dramatic. [on it.

Dran [dran] *ad.* at, on that,

Drang [drang] *nm.* pressure, distress, impulse, intense desire.

Drängen [dreng'en] *vt.i.* to press, urge, be urgent.

Drangsal [drang'zahl] *n.* (-e) misery, oppression.

Drastisch [dra'stish] *a.* drastic.

Drauf [drawf] *ad.* on it, at

random; -gänger *nm.* daredevil, madcap; -geld *n.* earnest money.

Draussen [drow'sen] *ad.* outside, out of doors.

Drechselbank [drex'el-bank] *nf.* lathe.   [turn (*tec.*).

Drechseln [drex'eln] *vt.* to

Drechsler [drex'lerr] *nm.* (-) turner.

Dreck [drek] *nm.* mud, dirt, filth, muck.

Dreckig [dre'kish] *a.* dirty, filthy, foul.

Dreh . . . [dray] *a.* turning; -achse *nf.* axis of rotation; -bagger *nm.* slewing excavator; -bank *nf.* lathe; -bleistift *nm.* propelling pencil; -buch *n.* script, scenario (*film*); -bühne *nf.* revolving stage; -eisen *n.* turning tool, chisel; -flügelflugzeug *n.* helicopter (*av.*); -gestell *n.* pivot mounting; -kondensator *nm.* variable condenser (*rad.*); -kran *nm.* derrick; -kreuz *n.* turnstile; -orgel *nf.* barrel organ; -punkt *nm.* pivot; -scheibe *nf.* turntable; -spule *nf.* rotating coil (*el.*); -stift *nm.* arbor (*tec.*); -strom *nm.* three-phase current (*el.*); -tür *nf.* revolving door; -zahl *nf.* rate of revolution; -zange *nf.* tweezers *pl.*

Drehbar [dray'bahr] *a.* revolving.

Drehen [dray'en] *vt.i.* to turn, revolve, twist.

Dreher [dray'err] *nm.* (-) turner, winch.

Drehung [dray'ŏŏng] *nf.* turning, rotation.

Drei [dry] *num.* three; -bein *n.* tripod; -bund *nm.* Triple Alliance; -eck *n.* triangle; -eckig *a.* triangular; -einigkeit *nf.* trinity; -elektrodenröhre *nf.* triode (*rad.*); -fuss *nm.* tripod; -jährlich *a.* triennial; -monatlich *a.* quarterly; -punktlandung *nf.* three-

point landing (*av.*); -rad *n.* tricycle; -sitzer *nm.* three-seater, trandem.

Dreierlei [dry'err-lie] *a.* of three kinds.

Dreifach [dry'fach] *a. ad.* triple, treble.

Dreifarbig [dry'fahrr-bish] *a.* of three colours.   [times.

Dreimal [dry'mahl] *ad.* three

Drein [drine] *ad.* in; -legen *vr.* meddle; -reden *vi.* interfere.   [thirty.

Dreissig [dry'sish] *num.*

Dreist [drīst] *a.* bold, audacious.

Dreistigkeit [dry'stish-kite] *nf.* boldness, audacity.

Dreizehn [dry'tsain] *num.* thirteen.

Drell [drel] *nm.* (-e) drill (*cloth*), ticking.

Dreschen [dre'shen] *vt. ir.* to thresh.

Dresch-flegel *nm.* flail; -maschine *nf.* threshing machine.

Dressieren [dre-see'ren] *vt.* to train, break in.

Drillbohrer [dril'bor-rerr] *nm.* (-) drill, auger.   [bore.

Drillen [dri'len] *vt.* to drill.

Driller [dri'lerr] *nm.* (-) *see* Drillbohrer.

Drillich [dri'lish] *nm.* ticking, drill (*cloth*).

Drilling [dri'ling] *nm.* triplet, three-barrelled gun (*mil.*); *a.* triple; -turm *nm.* triple turret.

Drin [drin] *ad.* in it.

Dringen [dring'en] *vi. ir.* to press (forward), penetrate; urge, insist.

Dringend [dring'ent], **Dringlich** [dring'lish] *a. ad.* urgent.

Dringlichkeit [dring'lish-kite] *nf.* urgency.

Drinnen [drin'en] *ad.* inside, indoors.

Dritt [drit] *a.* third.

Drittehalb [dri'ter-halp] *num.* two and a half.

Drittel [dritl'] n. (-) third.

Drittens [dri'tenss] ad. thirdly.

Droben [droh'ben] ad. above, up there.

Droge [droh'ger] nf. drug.

Drogerie [droh-ger-ree'] nf. pharmacy, chemist's shop.

Drogist [droh-gist'] m.w. druggist, chemist. [en.

Drohen [droh'en] vt.w to threat-

Drohne [droh'ner] nf. drone.

Dröhnen [drer'nen] vi. to roar, rumble, clatter.

Drohung [droh'oong] nf. threat.

Drollig [dro'lish] a. droll.

Dromedar [dro-me-dahr'] nm. (-) dromedary.

Droschke [drosh'ker] nf. cab; -nchauffeur nm. taxi-driver; -nkutscher nm. cabman.

Drossel [drosl] nf. throttle; throat; -klappe nf. throttle valve; -vene nf. jugular vein.

Drosseln [dross'eln] vt. to throttle, choke.

Drüben [droo'ben] ad. on the other side, over there.

Drüber [droo'berr] ad. over it, above.

Druck [drook] nm. (-e) pressure, print, engraving, oppression, depression (com.); -bogen nm. proof sheet; -fehler nm. misprint; -fertig a. ready for the press; -kattun nm. chintz print; -knopf nm. patent fastener, snap fastener, press stud; -lehre nf. -messer nm. pressure gauge; -luft nf. compressed air; -probe nf. proof; -pumpe nf. pressure pump; -seite nf. printed page, press side (av.); -umlaufschmierung nf. pressure lubrication; -wasserpumpe nf. hydraulic pump.

Drückeberger [droo'ker-bairr-gerr] nm. (-) shirker, slacker, dodger.

Drucken [droo'ken] vt. to press, print.

Drücken [droo'ken] vt. to press, oppress, depress; i. be heavy, oppressive; r. to shirk, slack, dodge.

Drucker [droo'kerr] nm. printer; -farbe nf. printer's ink.

Drücker [droo'kerr] nm. (-) latch, trigger, latch-key.

Druckerei [droo-ker-ry'] nf. printing works, press; -trupp nm. (-s) map printing section (mil.).

Drunten [droon'ten] ad. below, down there.

Drüse [droo'zer] nf. gland.

Dschungel [dshoong'gl] nf. jungle.

Du [doo] pn. thou, you.

Dübel [dyoo'bel] nm. (-) peg, wall plug. [duplicate.

Dublette [doo-blet'er] nf.

Ducken [doo'ken] vt.i. to duck, bow, yield.

Duckmäuser [dook'moy-zerr] nm. (-) sneak, hypocrite.

Dudelsack [doo'del-zak] nm. bagpipes.

Duell [doo-el'] n. (-e) duel.

Duellieren [doo-el-ee'ren] vt. to fight a duel.

Duett [doo-et'] n. (-e) duet.

Duft [dooft] nm. (Düfte) scent, vapour. [be fragrant.

Duften [doof'ten] vi. to smell,

Duftig [doof'tish] a. fragrant scented, vaporous.

Duldbar [doolt'bahr] a. endurable.

Dulder [dool'derr] nm. (-), sufferer.

Dulderin nf. sufferer.

Duldsam [doolt'zam] a. tolerant.

Dulsamkeit [doolt'zam-kite] nf. tolerance.

Duldung [dool'doong] nf. endurance, tolerance.

Dumm [doom] a. dull, silly, stupid, awkward; -dreist a. impudent, foolhardy; -kop nm. blockhead.

Dummheit [doom'hite] nf folly, stupidity.

Dümmling [dyōōm'ling] *nm.* (-e) simpleton.

Dumpf [dōōmpf] *a.* hollow, dull, close, musty.

Dumpfheit [dōōmpf'hite] *nf.* hollowness, dullness, closeness, mustiness. [down.

Düne [dyōō'ner] *nf.* dune.

Dung [dōōng] *nm. see* Dünger.

Düngen [dyōōng'en] *vt.* to manure.

Dünger [dyōōng'err] *nm.* dung, manure.

Dunkel [dōōn'kel] *a.* dark, gloomy, obscure; **-kammer** *nf.* dark room

Dünkel [dyōōn'kel] *nm.* self-conceit.

Dünkelhaft [dyōōn'kel-haft] *a.* conceited.

Dunkelheit [dōōn'kel-hite] *nf.* darkness, obscurity.

Dunkeln [dōōn'keln] *vi.* to grow dark.

Dünken [dyōōn'ken] *vi. imp.* to seem, appear; *r.* fancy.

Dünn [dyōōn] *a.* thin; **-bier** *n.* small beer; **-druckpapier** *n.* India paper; **-gesät** *a.* sparse; **-schlagen** *vt. ir.* to beat out.

Dünne [dyōō'ner], **Dünnheit** [dyōōn'hite] *nf.* thinness.

Dunst [dōōnst] *nm.* (Dünste) vapour, haze; **-kreis** *nm.* atmosphere.

Dunsten [dōōn'sten] *vi.* to rise as vapour.

Dunstig [dōōn'stish] *a.* vaporous, misty.

Dünung [dyōō'nōōng] *nf.* swell, surf.

Duplikat [dōō-pli-kaht'] *n.* (-e) duplicate.

Dur [dōōrr] *n.* major (*music*).

Dural [dōō-rahl'] *n.* duraluminium.

Durch [dōōrch] *pr.* through, by, during; *ad.* through, throughout; **-aus** *ad.* throughout, absolutely; **-aus nicht** not at all, by no means.

Durcharbeiten [dōōrch'ahrr-bite-en] to work through, polish off; *r.* force a way through.

Durchatmen [dōōrch'aht-men] *vt.* to permeate.

Durchbeissen [dōōrch'bice-en] *vt. ir.* to bite through.

Durchbeuteln [dōōrch'boy-teln] *vt.* to bolt (*flour*).

Durchbilden [dōōrch'bil den] *vt.* to develop, educate thoroughly.

Durchblättern [dōōrch-blet'errn] *vt.* to skim (*book*), peruse.

Durchblick [dōōrch'blik] *nm.* (-e) view, vista.

Durchblicken [dōōrch-bli'ken] *vi.* to look through; *t.* to see through.

Durchbohren [dōōrch-boh'ren] *vt.* to bore through, pierce.

Durchbraten [dōōrch'brah-ten] *vt. ir.* to roast well.

Durchbrechen [dōōrch'bresh'en] *vt.i. ir.* to break through, pierce.

Durchbrennen [dōōrch'bre-nen] *vt. ir.* to burn through, run away, fuse (*el.*).

Durchdringen [dōōrch'bring-en] *vt. ir.* to bring through, squander; *r.* make a living.

Durchbruch [dōōrch'brōōch] *nm.* (-brüche) bursting, eruption, cutting (*teeth*), breakthrough, breach (*mil.*); **-sversuch** *nm.* attempted break-through.

Durchdacht [dōōrch-dacht'] *a.* well planned.

Durchdenken [dōōrch'dengken] *vt. ir.* to weigh, reflect upon; *n.* estimate, critical analysis.

Durchdauern [dōōrch-dow'errn] *vt.* to last through.

Durchdrängen [dōōrch'dreng-en] *vt.* force, thrust through.

Durchdringen [dōōrch'dring-en] *vt. ir.* to penetrate, pervades

Durchdringen [dŏŏrch-dring'-en] vt.i. ir. to press through, prevail, permeate.

Durcheilen [dŏŏrch-ile'en] vt.i. to hurry through.

Durcheinander [dŏŏrch'ine-an-derr] ad. in confusion.

Durchfahren [dŏŏrch'fah-ren] vi. ir. to pass through, current.

Durchfahrt [dŏŏrch'fahrt] nf. passage, thoroughfare.

Durchfall [dŏŏrch'fal] nm. failure, diarrhoea.

Durchfallen [dŏŏrch'fa-len] vi. ir. to fall through, fail.

Durchfechten [dŏŏrch'fech-ten] vt.r. to fight out, carry one's point.

Durchfeuchten [dŏŏrch'-foysh-ten] vt. to steep.

Durchfinden [dŏŏrch'fin-den] vr. ir. to find one's way through.

Durchflechten [dŏŏrch'flesh-ten] vt. ir. to interweave, entwine.

Durchfliegen [dŏŏrch-flee'-gen] vt. ir. [dŏŏrch'flee-gen] i. to fly through, skim through, glance over.

Durchfliessen [dŏŏrch'flee-sen] vt. ir. to flow through.

Durchforschen [dŏŏrch-forr'-shen] vt. to investigate.

Durchfressen [dŏŏrch'fre-sen] vt. ir. to eat through, perforate.

Durchfragen [dŏŏrch'frah-gen] vr. to find one's way by asking.

Durchfrieren [dŏŏrch'free-ren] vi. ir. to freeze completely.

Durchfuhr [dŏŏrch'fŏŏrr] nf. transit; -schein nm. transit permit.

Durchführbar [dŏŏrch'fyŏŏr-bahrr] a. feasible, practicable.

Durchführen [dŏŏrch'fyŏŏ-ren] vt. to lead through, carry out, accomplish, conduct (attack).

Durchführung [dŏŏrch'-

fyŏŏ-rŏŏng] nf. execution, performance.

Durchgang [dŏŏrch'gang] nm. (-gänge) passage, thoroughfare; – verboten no thoroughfare.

Durchgängig [dŏŏrch'geng-ish] a. thorough, universal, current.

Durchgangs-handel [dŏŏrch'-] nm. transit trade; -lager n. transit camp (for prisoners of war); -schein nm. transit permit; -wagen nm. corridor carriage (rl.); -zug nm. corridor train.

Durchgehen [dŏŏrch'gay-en] vi. ir. to pass (through), run away; t. go through, look over, wear out.

Durchgehends [dŏŏrch'gay-ents] ad. generally, invariably.

Durchgiessen [dŏŏrch'gee-sen] vt. ir. to filter.

Durchglühen [dŏŏrch-glyŏŏ'-en] vt. to make red-hot, calcine, inspire.

Durchgraben [dŏŏrch'grah-ben] vt. ir. to dig through.

Durchgreifend [dŏŏrch'grife-ent] a. sweeping, thoroughgoing.

Durchgrübeln [dŏŏrch'gryŏŏ-beln] vt. to examine minutely, ponder over.

Durchhalten [dŏŏrch'hal-ten] vt. ir. to bear to the end, endure.

Durchhauen [dŏŏrch'how-en] vt. ir. to hew, hack through.

Durchhelfen [dŏŏrch'hel-fen] vt.r. to help through, succeed.

Durchhitzen [dŏŏrch'hit-sen] vt. to heat thoroughly.

Durchkämpfen [dŏŏrch'kemp-fen] vt.r. to fight through, out.

Durchkommen [dŏŏrch'kom-en] vi.r. to get through, pass.

Durchkosten [dŏŏrch'ko-sten] vt. to taste to the full.

Durchkreuzen [dŏŏrchkroyt'sen] *vt.* to cross, baffle, frustrate.

Durchlass [dŏŏrch'las] *nm.* (-lässe) opening, passage, filter, inlet; -kreis *nm.* acceptor circuit (*rad.*).

Durchlassen [dŏŏrch'lass-en] *vt. ir.* to let through.

Durchlässig [dŏŏrch'less-ish] *a.* permeable.

Durchlassung [dŏŏrch'lass-ŏŏng] *nf.* transmission.

Durchlaucht [dŏŏrch'lowcht] *nf.* Highness.

Durchlaufen [dŏŏrch'low-fen] *vt. ir.* to run through.

Durchleben [dŏŏrch-lay'ben] *vt. ir.* to live through, experience.

Durchlesen [dŏŏrch'lay-sen] *vt. ir.* to read through.

Durchleuchten [dŏŏrch'loysh-ten] *vi.* to shine through; [dŏŏrch-loysh'ten] *t.* to X-ray.

Durchlochen [dŏŏrch'loch-en], **Durchlöchern** [dŏŏrch-ler'shern] *vt.* to perforate, punch.

Durchlöchert [dŏŏrch-ler'sherrt] *a.* perforated, riddled.

Durchlochung [dŏŏrch'loch-ŏŏng] *nf.* perforation, punching, puncture (*aut.*).

Durchlüften [dŏŏrch-lyŏŏf'ten] *vt.* to air, ventilate.

Durchmachen [dŏŏrch'mach-en] *vt.* to go through, endure.

Durchmarsch [dŏŏrch'mahrsh] *nm.* (-märsche) march through.

Durchmarschieren [dŏŏrch'mahr-shee-ren] *vi.* to march through.

Durchmesser [dŏŏrch'mes-serr] *nm.* (-) diameter.

Durchmustern [dŏŏrch'mŏŏstern] *vt.* to review, scrutinize.

Durchmusterung [dŏŏrch'mŏŏ-ster-rŏŏng] *nf.* review, scrutiny.

Durchnässen [dŏŏrch-ness'en] *vt.* to soak, steep.

Durchnehmen [dŏŏrch'nay-men] *vt. ir.* to go over.

Durchpausen [dŏŏrch'pow-zen] *vt.* to trace, make a carbon copy of.

Durchprügeln [dŏŏrch'pryŏŏ-geln] *vt.* to thrash, beat up.

Durchqueren [dŏŏrch-kveh'ren] *vt.* to traverse, cross.

Durchrechnen [dŏŏrch'resh-nen] *vt.* to calculate again, check.

Durchreize [dŏŏrch'rize-er] *nf.* passage through, transit.

Durchreisen [dŏŏrch'rize-en] *vt.* to travel through.

Durchreissen [dŏŏrch'rice-en] *vt. ir.* to rend, tear apart.

Durchrieseln [dŏŏrch'ree-zeln] *vt.* to flow through.

Durchriss [dŏŏrch'riss] *nm.* (-e) rent, breach.

Durchrufen [dŏŏrch'rŏŏ-fen] *vi. ir.* to pass the word down (*mil.*).

Durchs [dŏŏrchs] **= durch das.**

Durchsacken [dŏŏrch'za-ken] *vi.* to stall, pancake (*av.*).

Durchsägen [dŏŏrch'zay-gen] *vt.* to saw through.

Durchsalzen [dŏŏrch'zalt-sen] *vt.* to salt thoroughly.

Durchsättigen [dŏŏrch'zet-i-gen] *vt.* to saturate.

Durchschauen [dŏŏrch'show-en] *vt.* to look, see through.

Durchschauen [dŏŏrch-show'en] *vt.* to penetrate, see through (*pretence, etc.*).

Durchscheinen [dŏŏrch'shine-en] *vi. ir.* to shine through; -d *a.* transparent.

Durchschiessen [dŏŏrch'shee-sen] *vi. ir.* to shoot, pierce, rush through.

Durchschiessen [dŏŏrch-shee'sen] *vt. ir.* to interleave.

Durchschiffen [dŏŏrch-shif'en] *vt.* to navigate, traverse, cross.

Durchschlafen [dŏŏrchshlah-fen] *vt. ir.* to sleep through.

Durchschlag [dŏŏrch'shlahk] *nm.* (-schläge) opening, strainer, punch, carbon copy (*com.*); -skraft *nf.* penetrating power; -spapier *n.* carbon paper.

Durchschlagen [dŏŏrch'shlah-gen] *vt. ir.* to beat through, pierce, filter; *i.* break through, take effect, operate, succeed.

Durchschleichen [dŏŏrch'shly-shen] *vt. ir.* to creep, slink through.

Durchschlüpfen [dŏŏrch'shlyŏŏp-fen] *vt.* to slip through, escape.

Durchschmuggeln [dŏŏrch'shmŏŏg-eln] *vt.* to smuggle (through).

Durchschneiden [dŏŏrch'shnide-en] *vt. ir.* to cut through, intersect, traverse.

Durchschnitt [dŏŏrch'shnit] *nm.* (-e) cutting (through), section, average; -sansicht *nf.* section; -sgeschwindigkeit *nf.* average speed; -smensch *m.w.* average man, man in the street.

Durchschnittlich [dŏŏrch'shnit-lish] *a.* average, mean; *ad.* on an average.

Durchschreiten [dŏŏrch'shry'ten] *vt.* to traverse.

Durchschuss [dŏŏrch'shŏŏss] *nm.* interleaf, woof, spaceline.

Durchschwärmen [dŏŏrch-shvairm'en] *vt.* to spend in dissipation.

Durchschweifen [dŏŏrch-shvife'en] *vt.* to wander through, stroll round.

Durchschwimmen [dŏŏrch-shvim'en] *vt. ir.* to cross (by swimming).

Durchsegeln [dŏŏrch'zay-geln] *vt.* to sail through.

Durchsehen [dŏŏrch'zay-en] *vt. ir.* to look through, revise.

Durchseihen [dŏŏrch-zy'en] *vt.* to strain, filter.

Durchsetzen [dŏŏrch'zet-sen] *vt.* to break through, carry through, accomplish, prevail upon; *r.* succeed.

Durchsetzen [dŏŏrch-zet'sen] *vt.* to mix with, permeate.

Durchsicht [dŏŏrch'zisht] *nf.* revision, perusal, view.

Durchsichtig [dŏŏrch'zish-tish] *a.* transparent.

Durchsichtigkeit [dŏŏrch-zish-tish-kite] *nf.* transparence; -ssucher *nm.* view finder (*camera*).

Durchsickern [dŏŏrch'zi-kerrn] *vi.* to trickle through, leak out. [*vt.* to sift, riddle.

Durchsieben [dŏŏrch'zee-ben]

Durchsitzen [dŏŏrch'zit-sen] *vt. ir.* to sit through.

Durchspielen [dŏŏrch'shpele-en] *vt.* to play through.

Durchspüren [dŏŏrch'shpyŏŏ-ren] *vt.* to search through.

Durchstechen [dŏŏrch'shtesh'en] *vt. ir.* to cut through, puncture, perforate, transfix.

Durchstecherei [dŏŏrch-shte-sher-ry'] *nf.* intrigue.

Durchstich [dŏŏrch'shtish] *nm.* (-e) cut, aperture, cutting, excavation.

Durchstöbern [dŏŏrch-shter'berrn] *vt.* to ransack, search through.

Durchstossen [dŏŏrch-shtoh'sen] *vt. ir.* to thrust through, transfix.

Durchstrahlen [dŏŏrch-shtrah'len] *vt.* to irradiate.

Durchstreichen [dŏŏrch'shtri-shen] *vt. ir.* to strike, cross out, erase, cancel.

Durchstreifen [dŏŏrch-shtrife'en] *vt.* to roam, wander through.

Durchstrich [dŏŏrch'shtrish] *nm.* (-e) erasure, cancellation.

Durchsuchen [dŏŏrch'zŏŏ-chen] *vt.* to search, examine (thoroughly).

Durchsuchung [dŏŏrch'zŏŏ-chŏŏng] *nf.* search, examination.

Durchträumen [dŏŏrch'troy-men] *vt.* to dream through.

Durchtränken [dŏŏrch'treng-ken] *vt.* to drench, saturate.

Durchtreiben [dŏŏrch'tribe-en] *vt. ir.* to drive, force through.

Durchtrieben [dŏŏrch'trebe-en] *a.* sly, cunning.

Durchwachen [dŏŏrch'vach-en] *vt.* to spend in watching, lie awake.

Durchwachsen [dŏŏrch'vax-en] *a.* streaked, marbled.

Durchwandern [dŏŏrch'van-derrn] *vt.* to traverse, wander through.

Durchwässern [dŏŏrch'vess-errn] *vt.* to irrigate.

Durchweben [dŏŏrch'vay-ben] *vt.* to interweave.

Durchweg [dŏŏrch'vaik] *nm.* (-e) thoroughfare.

Durchweg [dŏŏrch'vek'] *ad.* throughout.

Durchwehen [dŏŏrch'vay-en] *vt.* to blow through.

Durchwerfen [dŏŏrch'vairr-fen] *vt. ir.* to throw through, riddle.

Durchwintern [dŏŏrch'vin-terrn] *vt.i.* to winter, hibernate.

Durchwirken [dŏŏrch'virr-ken] *vt.* to interweave.

Durchwühlen [dŏŏrch'vyōō-len] *vt.* to root up, grub, ransack.

Durchwürzen [dŏŏrch-vyōŏrt'sen] *vt.* to season.

Durchzählen [dŏŏrch'tsay-len] *vt.* to count over.

Durchzeichnen [dŏŏrch'tsish-nen] *vt.* to trace.

Durchziehen [dŏŏrch-tsee-en] *vt. ir.* to interlace, soak, traverse.

Durchziehen [dŏŏrch'tsee-en]

vt. ir. to draw through, thread; i. go through.

Durchziehglas [dŏŏrch'tsee-glahs] *n.* (-gläser) slide.

Durchzoll [dŏŏrch'tsol] *nm.* (-zölle) transit duty.

Durchzucken [dŏŏrch-tsŏŏk-en] *vt.* to flash through, convulse. [passage.

Durchzug [dŏŏrch'tsŏŏk] *nm.*

Durchzwängen [dŏŏrch'tsveng-en] *vt.* to squeeze, force through.

Dürfen [dyōŏr'fen] *vi. ir.* to be allowed, need, have occasion to.

Dürftig [dyōŏrf'tish] *a.* needy, paltry.

Dürftigkeit [dyōŏrf'tish-kite] *nf.* poverty, paltriness, unsufficiency.

Dürr [dyŏŏrr] *a.* arid, lean.

Dürre [dyŏŏ'rer] *nf.* aridity, leanness, drought.

Durst [dŏŏrst] *nm.* thirst.

Dursten [dŏŏr'sten] *vi.* to be thirsty. [Dursten.

Dürsten [dyōŏr'sten] *vi. see*

Durstig [dŏŏr'stish] *a.* thirsty.

Dusche [dŏŏ'sher] *nf.* shower bath.

Düse [dyōŏ'zer] *nf.* jet, nozzle; -nbohrung *nf.* jet; -nflugzeug *n.* jet-propelled aircraft, jetplane; -njäger *nm.* jet-propelled fighter; -nantrieb *nm.* jet propulsion.

Dusel [dŏŏ'zel] *nm.* dizziness, stupor, luck.

Duselig [dŏŏ'zer-lish] *a.* drowsy, dizzy.

Duseln [dŏŏ'zeln] *vi.* to be drowsy. [gloomy.

Düster [dyōŏ'sterr] *a.* dark,

Düsterkeit [dyōŏ'sterr-kite] *nf.* gloom, gloominess.

Dutzend [dŏŏt'sent] *n.* (-e) dozen; -mensch *m.w.* ordinary person; -weise *ad.* by the dozen.

Duzen [dŏŏt'sen] *vt.* to thou, be on intimate terms with.

Dwars [dvahrrs] *ad.* athwart.

Dynamik [dyŏō-nah'mik] *nf.* dynamics, volume range (*rad.*).

Dynamisch [dyŏō-nah'mish] *a.* dynamic.

Dynamit [dyŏō-na-meet'] *n.* dynamite.

Dynamo [dyŏō'na-moh] *nm.* (-s) dynamo. [dynasty.

Dynastie [dyŏō-nas-tee'] *nf.*

E

Ebbe [eb'er] *nf.* ebb.

Ebben [eb'en] *vi.* to ebb, go out (tide).

Eben [abe'en] *a.* even, level, smooth; *ad.* just, precisely, evenly; **-bild** *n.* image; **-bürtig** *a.* of equal rank; **-erdig** *a.* ground-floor; **-mass** *n.* proportion, symmetry; **-mässig** *a.* proportionate, symmetrical; **-sooft** *ad.* just as often; **-soviel** *ad.* just as much; **-soweit** *ad.* just as far. [plane.

Ebene [abe'e-ner] *nf.* plain,

Ebenfalls [abe'en-falss] *ad.* likewise.

Ebenheit [abe'en-hite] *nf.* evenness, plainness, smoothness. [ebony.

Ebenholz [abe'en-holts] *n.*

Eber [abe'err] *nm.* (-) boar; **-esche** *nf.* mountain ash; **-fleisch** *n.* brawn.

Ebnen [abe'nen] *vt.* to level, even.

Echo [esh'oh] *n.* (-s) echo.

Echt [esht] *a.* genuine, pure, real.

Echtheit [esht'hite] *nf.* genuineness.

Eck [ek] *n.* (-e) corner, angle; **-ball** *nm.* corner kick; **-brett** *n.* corner shelf, bracket; **-hölzer** *n.pl.* squared timber; **-stein** *nm.* corner stone, diamond (*card*); **-stütze** *nf.* stay, buttress; **-zahn** *nm.* eye-tooth.

Ecke [ek'er] *nf.* corner, angle.

Eckig [ek'ish] *a.* angular.

Eckigkeit [ek'ish-kite] *nf.* angularity.

Edel [ade'el] *a.* noble; **-fichte** *nf.* silver pine; **-frau** *nf.* noblewoman; **-kastanie** *nf.* sweet chestnut; **-mann** *nm.* (-leute) nobleman; **-metall** *n.* rare metal; **-mut** *nm.* magnanimity, generosity; **-stein** *nm.* precious stone.

Edikt [ade-ikt'] *n.* (-e) edict.

Edul [ade'ōōl] *ad.* counterclockwise.

Efeu [ay'foy] *nm.* ivy.

Effekten [ef-ek'ten] *n.pl.* effects, funds, stocks *pl* (*com.*); **-handel** *nm.* stock exchange business; **-händler** *nm.* stock broker, jobber.

Effektiv [ef-ek-teef'] *a.* effective, actual; **-bestand** *nm.* **-stärke** *nf.* effective strength, effectives *pl* (*mil. etc.*); **-hascherei** *nf.* playing to the gallery, showing off, sensationalism.

Egal [ay-gahl'] *a.* all the same, all one.

Egel [ay'gel] *nm.* (-) leech.

Egge [eg'er] *nf.* harrow.

Eggen [eg'en] *vt.* to harrow.

Egoismus [ay-go-iss'mŏōss] *nm.* selfishness, egoism.

Egoist [ay-go-ist'] *m.w.* egoist.

Egoistisch [ay-go-ist'ish] *a.* selfish, egoistic.

Ehe [ay'er] *ad.* sooner, before; *cj.* before.

Ehe [ay'er] *nf.* marriage; **-brecher** *nm.* **-brecherin** *nf.* adulterer; **-bruch** *nm.* adultery; **-frau** *nf.* married woman, wife; **-gemahl** *nm.* husband; **-leute** *pl.* married people; **-mann** *nm.* married man, husband; **-paar** *n.* married couple; **-scheidung** *nf.* divorce; **-schliessung** *nf.* marrying; **-stand** *nm.* married state, wedlock; **-vertrag** *nm.* marriage settlement.

Ehedem [ay-er-dame'] *see* Ehemals.

Ehlich [ay'e-lish] a. matrimonial, legitimate.

Ehemals [ay'e-mahls] ad. formerly.

Eher [ay'err] ad. sooner, formerly, rather.

Ehern [ay'errn] a. brazen.

Ehestens [ay'est-enss] ad. as soon as possible.

Ehrbar [airr'bahrr] a. honourable, respectable.

Ehrbarkeit [airr'bahrr-kite] nf. respectability, honour.

Ehre [airr'er] nf. honour.

Ehren [airr'en] vt. to honour.

Ehrenhaft [airr'en-haft] a. honourable.

Ehren-klage nf. libel action; **-mal** n. cenotaph; **-punkt** nm. point of honour; **-rechte** n.pl. civic rights pl; **-rührig** a. libellous; **-stelle** nf. dignity, honourable post; **-sturm** nm. guard of honour; **-tafel** nf. roll of honour; **-titel** nm. honorary title; **-voll** a. honourable; **-wache** nf. guard of honour; **-wort** n. word of honour, parole (mil.).

Ehrerbietig [airr'err-bete-ish] a. deferential; **-keit** nf. deference, veneration.

Ehr-furcht nf. awe, deep respect; **-gefühl** n. sense of honour; **-geiz** nm. ambition; **-geizig** a. ambitious.

Ehrlich [airr'lish] a. honest, honourable; **-keit** nf. honesty.

Ehrsucht [airr'zöocht] nf ambition.

Ehrvergessen [airr'ferr-gessen] a. base, dishonourable; **-heit** nf. baseness.

Ehrwürden [airr'vyöōr-den] nf. Reverend.

Ehrwürdig [airr'vyöōr-dish] a. venerable; **-keit** nf. venerableness.

Ei [i] n. (**-er**) egg; **-dotter** nm. yolk of egg; **-förmig** a. oval; **-weiss** n. white of egg, albumen.

Ei [i] interj. why ! indeed !

Eibe [ibe'er] nf. yew-tree.

Eich(e) [i'sher] nf. gauge; **-amt** n. gauging office; **-mass** n. standard (weight, measure).

Eiche [i'sher] nf. oak.

Eichel [i'shel] nf. acorn, club (cards).

Eichen [i'shen] vt. to gauge.

Eichhörnchen [ish'hern-shen] n. (**-**) squirrel.

Eichung [i'shoong] nf. gauging, calibration.

Eid [ite] nm. (**-e**) oath; **-bruch** nm. perjury; **-esleistung** nf. affidavit, swearing an oath, attestation.

Eidechse [i'dex-er] nf. lizard.

Eidgenosse [ite'ger-noss-er] m.w. Confederate, Swiss; **-genossenschaft** nf. Confederation, Switzerland; **-genössisch** a. Swiss.

Eidlich [ide'lish] a. (sworn) upon oath.

Eidechse [ide'ex-er] nf. lizard.

Eider [ide'err] nm. (**-**) eider-duck; **-daunen** f.pl. eider-down.

Eier-becher nm. egg-cup; **-kuchen** nm. omelette; **-löffel** nm. egg-spoon; **-schale** nf. egg-shell; **-speise** nf. egg-dish.

Eifer [ife'err] nm. zeal, enthusiasm; **-sucht** nf. jealousy; **-süchtig** a. jealous.

Eifern [ife'errn] vi. to be zealous, compete with, declaim against.

Eifrig [ife'rish] a. zealous, enthusiastic.

Eigen [i'gen] a. own, peculiar, specific; **-art** nf. peculiarity; **-artig** a. peculiar; **-dünkel** nm. self-conceit; **-frequenz** nf. natural frequency (rad.); **-geschwindigkeit** nf. initial velocity, air speed (av.); **-händig** a. with one's own hand, autograph; **-heim** n. self-contained house; **-lob** n. self-praise; **-mächtig** a. arbitrary, unauthorized; **-name** nm.

proper name; **-nutz** nm. self-interest; **-nützig** a. selfish; **-peilung** nf. bearings taken on plane (av.); **-sinn** nm. obstinacy; **-sinnig** a. obstinate; **-versorgung** nf. self-sufficiency; **-wille** nm. self-will, wilfulness.

Eigenheit [I'gen-hite] nf. peculiarity.

Eigens [I'genss] ad. expressly, on purpose.

Eigenschaft [I'gen-shaft] nf. quality, property, attribute.

Eigentlich [I'gent-lish] a. proper, real; ad. really, rightly.

Eigentum [I'gen-tōōm] n. (-tümer) property, belongings; **-srecht** n. ownership.

Eigentümer [I'gen-tyōō-merr] nm., **Eigentümerin** nf. owner, proprietor.

Eigentümlich [I'gen-tyōōm-lish] a. peculiar.

Eigentümlichkeit [I'gen-tyōōm-lish-kite] nf. peculiarity.

Eignen [Ig'nen] vi.r. to be suited for, be qualified for.

Eigner [Ig'nerr] nm. (-) owner.

Eignung [Ig'nŏŏng] nf. aptitude, fitness; **-sprüfung** nf. psychological test.

Eiland [Ile'ant] n. (-e) island.

Eilbote [Ile'boh-ter] m.w. courier, express. [letter.

Eilbrief [Ile'breef] nm. express

Eile [Ile'er] nf. haste.

Eilen [Ile'en] vi.r. to make haste, hurry. [hasty.

Eilfertig [Ile'fairr-tish] a.

Eilfertigkeit [Ile'fairr-tish-kite] nf. hastiness.

Eilgut [Ile'goot] n. goods sent by passenger train.

Eilig [Ile'ish] a. hasty, hurried.

Eilmarsch [Ile'marrsh] nm. (-märsche) forced march.

Eilzug [Ile'tsŏŏk] nm. (-züge) express train. [pail.

Eimer [Ime'err] nm. (-) bucket,

Ein [Ine], **Eine** [Ine'er], **Ein** num. one; ind. art. a. an; **Einer, Eine, Eines** pn. one, some-

one; **unser eine(r)** one of us.

Einakter [Ine'ak-terr] nm. (-) one-act play.

Einander [Ine-an'derr] pn. one another, each other.

Einarbeiten [Ine'arr-bite-en] vr. to work up, familiarize oneself with; **gegenseitiges –** n. co-ordination.

Einarmig [Ine'arr-mish] a. one-armed.

Einäschern [Ine'esh-errn] vt. to reduce to ashes, incinerate, cremate.

Einäscherung [Ine'esh-er-rŏŏng] nf. cremation; **-shalle** nf. crematorium.

Einatmen [Ine'aht-men] vt. to inhale. [eyed.

Einäugig [Ine'oy-gish] a. one-

Einbahnstrasse [Ine'bahn-shtrah-ser] nf. one-way street.

Einbalsamieren [Ine'bal-za-mee-ren] vt. to embalm.

Einband [Ine'bant] nm. (-bände) binding, cover.

Einbändig [Ine'ben-dish] a. in one volume.

Einbau [Ine'bow] nm. fitting, installation; **-motor** nm. built-in engine.

Einbauen [Ine'bow-en] vt. to build in, dig in.

Einbegreifen [Ine'be-grife-en] vt. ir. to include.

Einbegriffen [Ine'be-grif-en] a. included, inclusive.

Einbekommen [Ine'be-kom-en] vt. ir. to get in (cash).

Einberufen [Ine'ber-rŏŏ-fen] vt. ir. to call in, call up, out (mil.), convene.

Einberufung [Ine'ber-rŏŏ-fŏŏng] nf. convocation, calling up, out. [embed.

Einbetten [Ine'bet-en] vt. to

Einbettig [Ine'bet-ish] a. single (room).

Einbiegen [Ine'bee-gen] vt. ir. to turn, bend in. [imagine

Einbilden [Ine'bil-den] vt.r. to

Einbildung [ine'bil-dŏong] *nf.* imagination, conceit; -skraft *nf.* imaginative power, imagination.

Einbinden [ine'bin-den] *vt. ir.* to bind (up).

Einblasen [ine'blah-zen] *vt. ir.* to blow into, prompt, insinuate.

Einbläser [ine'blay-zerr] *nm.* (-) prompter, insinuator.

Einblattdruck [ine'blat-drŏok] *nm.* (-e) broadsheet.

Einblick [ine'blik] *nm.* (-e) glance, insight, eye-piece.

Einbrechen [ine'bresh-en] *vt. ir.* to break open, into; *i.* set in, (night) burgle.

Einbrecher [ine'bresh-err] *nm.* (-) burglar.

Einbrennen [ine'bren-en] *vt. ir.* to burn in, brand.

Einbringen [ine'bring-en] *vt. ir.* to bring in, yield, capture.

Einbrocken [ine'brok-en] *vt.* to crumble.

Einbruch [ine'brŏoch] *nm.* inroad, burglary, raid, penetration (*mil.*); - der Nacht *n.* nightfall; -flieger *nm.* intruder pilot; -flug *nm.* intruder operation (*av.*); -sstelle *nf.* point of penetration (*mil.*).

Einbürgern [ine'byoor-gern] *vt.* to naturalize; *r.* settle down.

Einbürgerung [ine'byoorger-rŏong] *nf.* naturalization.

Einbusse [ine'bŏo-ser] *nf.* loss.

Einbüssen [ine'byoo-sen] *vt.* to lose, forfeit.

Eindämmen [ine'dem-en] *vt.* to dam up.

Eindecken [ine'dek-en] *vr.* to lay in stocks.

Eindecker [ine'dek-err] *nm.* (-) monoplane.

Eindeckung [ine'dek-ŏong] *nf.* overhead cover (*mil.*); -sangriff *nm.* saturation raid (*av.*).

Eindeutig [ine'doy-tish] *a.* unequivocal.

Eindeutschen [ine'doyt-shen] *vt.* to put into German, Germanize.

Eindeutschung [ine'doitshŏong] *nf.* Germanisation.

Eindringen [ine'dring-en] *vi. ir.* to invade, penetrate, enter forcibly.

Eindringlich [ine'dring-lish] *a.* forcible, urgent, penetrating.

Eindringling [ine'dring-ling] *nm.* (-e) intruder.

Eindruck [ine'drŏok] *nm.* (-drücke) impression; -skunst *nf.* impressionism; -svoll *a.* impressive.

Eindrücken [ine'dryŏo-ken] *vt.* to press in, impress.

Einebnen [ine'abe-nen] *vt.* to level. [amy.

Einehe [ine'ay-er] *nf.* monog-

Einen [ine'en] *vt.* to unite.

Einengen [ine'eng-en] *vt.* to confine, restrict.

Einerlei [ine-err-lie'] *n.* sameness; *a.* of one sort, all the same.

Einernten [ine'errn-ten] *vt.* to reap, gather in.

Einerseits [ine'err-zites] *ad.* on one hand.

Einexerzieren [ine'ex-errtsee-ren] *vt.* to drill.

Einfach [ine'fach] *a.* simple.

Einfachheit [ine'fach-hite] *nf.* simplicity.

Einfädeln [ine'fade-eln] *vt.* to thread (needle), contrive, work into position (troops).

Einfahren [ine'fah-ren] *vt. ir.* to bring in, knock in, break (horses); *i.* drive in.

Einfahrt [ine'fahrrt] *nf.* entrance, drive, descent (mine).

Einfall [ine'fal] *nm.* (-fälle) invasion, inroad, notion, idea; -(s)winkel *nm.* angle of incidence, of descent (*av.*).

Einfallen [ine'fa-len] *vi. ir.* to fall in, break in, occur (idea).

Einfällig [ine'fel-ish] *a.* ruinous.

Einfalt [ine'falt] *nf.* see **Einfältigkeit**.

Einfältig [ine'fel-tish] *a.* artless, silly, simple-minded.

Einfältigkeit [ine'fel-tish-kite] *nf.* artlessness, silliness.

Einfamilienhaus [ine'fa-mee'lyen-howss] *n.* (-häuser) self-contained house, villa, detached house.

Einfangen [ine'fang-en] *vt. ir.* to shut in, apprehend, catch, seize.

Einfarbig [ine'fahr-bish] *a.* self-coloured, of one colour.

Einfassen [ine'fass-en] *vt.* to set, frame, barrel (*beer*), trim, arm (*magnet*).

Einfassung [ine'fass-ōōng] *nf.* enclosure, framing, barrelling, fence. [grease.

Einfetten [ine'fet-en] *vt.*

Einfeuchten [ine'foish-ten] *vt.* to steep.

Einfinden [ine'fin-den] *vr. ir.* to put in an appearance, turn up.

Einflechten [ine'flesh-ten] *vt. ir.* to interweave, insert.

Einflieger [ine'flee-gerr] *nm.* (-) test pilot (*av.*).

Einfliessen [ine'flee-sen] *vi. ir.* to flow in.

Einflössen [ine'fler-sen] *vt.* to imbue, infuse, instil.

Einflug [ine'flook] *nm.* (-flüge) incursion, air penetration (*av.*).

Einfluss [ine'flooss] *nm.* (-flüsse) influence; -**reich** *a.* influential; -**rohr** *n.* flow-in pipe; -**sphäre** *nf.* sphere of influence.

Einflüstern [ine'flyōō-sterrn] *vt.* to whisper in, insinuate.

Einflüsterung [ine'flyōō-ster-rōōng] *nf.* insinuation.

Einfordern [ine'forr-derrn] *vt.* to call in, demand (*com.*).

Einförmig [ine'ferr-mish] *a.* uniform, monotonous.

Einförmigkeit [ine'ferr-mish-kite] *nf.* uniformity, monotony.

Einfressen [ine'fress-en] *vt. ir.* to eat into.

Einfried(ig)en [ine'free-di-gen] *vt.* to enclose, fence in.

Einfried(ig)ung [ine'free-di-gōōng] *nf.* enclosure.

Einfrieren [ine'free-ren] *vi. ir.* to freeze (in).

Einfügen [ine'fyōō-gen] *vt.* to fit in, dovetail.

Einfuhr [ine'fōōr] *nf.* import; -**artikel** *nm.* (article of) import; -**handel** *nm.* import trade; -**waren** *f.pl.* imports *pl.*; -**zoll** *nm.* import duty, tariff.

Einfuhrbar [ine'fyōō-barr] *a.* importable.

Einführen [ine'fyōō-ren] *vt.* to bring in, introduce, import.

Einführer [ine'fyōō-rerr] *nm.* (-) importer, introducer.

Einführung [ine'fyōō-rōōng] *nf.* introduction, importation; -**sschreiben** *n.* letter of introduction.

Eingabe [ine'gah-ber] *nf.* petition, memorial.

Eingabeln [ine'gah-beln] *vt.* to straddle (with bombs).

Eingang [ine'gang] *nm.* entrance, access, arrival, admission; -**szoll** *nm.* import duty; -**szündung** *nf.* priming charge, detonator charge.

Eingeben [ine'gabe-en] *vt. ir.* to give (in), suggest.

Eingebildet [ine'ge-bil-det] *a.* imaginary, conceited.

Eingeboren [ine'ge-bore-ren] *a.* native, innate.

Eingebung [ine'gay-bōōng] *nf.* giving suggestion.

Eingedenk [ine'ge-denk] *a.* mindful.

Eingefleischt [ine'ge-flisht] *a.* inveterate, incorrigible.

Eingefroren [ine'ge-frore-ren] *a.* frozen; -**e Kredite** frozen credits.

Eingehen [ine'gay-en] *vi. ir.* to go into, enter into, come to an end, decay cease, shrink, look into; i. conclude, come to, make, incur.

Eingehend [ine'gay-ent] a. exhaustive, thorough.

Eing(e)leisig [ine'ge-lize-ish] a. single-track.

Eingemacht [ine'ge-macht] a. preserved; -es n. preserves pl.

Eingemeinden [ine'ge-mine-den] vt. to incorporate.

Eingemeindung [ine'ge-mine-dŏŏng] nf. incorporation.

Eingenommen [ine'ge-nom-en] a. prejudiced, prepossessed, taken up by.

Eingenommenheit [ine'ge-nom-en-hite] nf. prejudice, partiality.

Eingeschlossenheit [ine'ge-shlos-en-hite] nf. seclusion.

Eingeschränkt [ine'ge-shrenkt] a. narrow-minded; -heit nf. narrow-mindedness.

Eingeschrieben [ine'ge-shree-ben] a. registered.

Eingesessen [ine'ge-zess-en] a. resident.

Eingeständnis [ine'ge-shtent-nis] n. (-e) admission, confession.

Eingestehen [ine'ge-shtay-en] vt. ir. to confess.

Eingeweide [ine'ge-vide-er] nf. (-) bowels, intestines pl.

Eingewöhnen [ine'ge-ver-nen] vt. to accustom.

Eingewurzelt [ine'ge-vŏŏrt-selt] a. inveterate.

Eingezogen [ine'ge-tsoh-gen] a. secluded, retracted (wheels).

Eingezogenheit [ine'ge-tsoh-gen-hite] nf. seclusion.

Eingiessen [ine'gee-sen] vt. to pour out, fill in. [rail off.

Eingittern [ine'git-errn] vt. to

Eingitterröhre [ine'gi-ter-rer-rer] nf. single-grid valve (rad.).

Eingraben [ine'grah-ben] vt. ir. to dig in, inter, bury, engrave; r. dig oneself in, entrench.

Eingreifen [ine'grife-en] vi. ir. to catch, take hold, gear together, interfere.

Eingrenzen [ine'grent-sen] vt. to localize (tec.).

Eingriff [ine'grif] nm. (-e) catch(ing), interference, trespass, encroachment.

Einguss [ine'gŏŏs] nm. (-güsse) pouring in, mould, infusion, inlet (tec.).

Einhaken [ine'hah-ken] vt. to hook in, catch, link up (mil.).

Einhalt [ine'halt] nm. check, stop.

Einhalten [ine'hal-ten] vt. to check, restrain, observe; i. stop.

Einhaltung [ine'hal-tŏŏng] nf. observance, observation.

Einhandeln [ine'han-deln] vt. to purchase.

Einhändig [ine'hen-dish] a. single-handed, one-handed.

Einhändigen [ine'hen-di-gen] vt. to hand in, deliver.

Einhändigung [ine'hen-di-gŏŏng] nf. delivery.

Einhängen [ine'heng-en] vt. to hang (up). [fence in.

Einhagen [ine'hay-gen] vt. to

Einhauen [ine'how-en] vt. i. to hew, cut open, cut up.

Einheimisch [ine'hime-ish] a. native.

Einheimsen [ine'hime-zen] vt. to gather in, bring home.

Einheit [ine'hite] nf. unity, unit, standard; -sgericht n. one-course meal; -sgeschütz n. dual purpose gun (mil.); -sgewicht n. power weight ratio; -skleider n.pl. utility clothing; -smunition nf. fixed ammunition; -spreis nm. uniform price; -ssatz nm. unit rate; -swaffe nf. dual purpose weapon.

Einheitlich [ine'hite-lish] a. uniform.

Einheizen [ine'hite-sen] vt.i. to warm, make a fire.

Einhellig [ine'hel-ish] *a., ad.*
unanimous(ly).

Einhüllen [ine'hy⊙ol-en] *vt.*
to wrap up.

Einig [ine'ish] *a.* one, some,
united, agreed; **-e** *pl.* some.

Einigen [ine'i-gen] *vt.* to unite;
r. agree.

Einigermassen [ine'i-gerr-mah-sen] *ad.* to some extent,
fairly.

Einigkeit [ine'ish-kite] *nf.*
union, unity, agreement.

Einigung [ine'i-g⊙ong] *nf.*
agreement.

Einimpfen [ine'imp-fen] *vt.* to
inoculate.

Einimpfung [ine'imp-f⊙ong]
nf. inoculation.

Einjagen [ine'yah-gen] *vt.* to
drive in, instil.

Einjährig [ine'yare-ish] *a.* of,
for one year, one-year old.

Einkalken [ine'kal-ken] *vt.* to
lime.

Einkassieren [ine'kass-ee-ren] *vt.* to collect, cash.

Einkauf [ine'kowf] *nm.*
(**-käufe**) purchase, buying in;
-sgenossenschaft *nf.* co-operative society; **-spreis** *nm.* cost
price.   [purchase.

Einkaufen [ine'kow-fen] *vt.* to

Einkäufer [ine'kow-ferr] *nm.*
(**-**) purchaser, buyer.

Einkehr [ine'care] *nf.* lodging;
- in sich selbst contemplation.

Einkehren [ine'care-en] *vi.* to
put up at, stop for refreshment; **in sich -** to commune
with oneself.

Einkeilen [ine'kile-en] *vt.* to
wedge in.   [to notch.

Einkerben [ine'care-ben] *vt.*

Einkerkern [ine'care-kerrn]
vt. to imprison.

Einkesseln [ine'kess-eln] *vt.*
to encircle (*mil.*).

Einkesselung [ine'kess-e-l⊙ong] *nf.* encirclement (*mil.*).

Einklagen [ine'klah-gen] *vt.*
to sue for debt.

Einklammern [ine'klam-ern] *vt.* to put in brackets.
bracket.

Einklang [ine'klang] *nm.*
accord, harmony.

Einkleben [ine'clay-ben] *vt.*
to paste in.

Einkleiden [ine'klide-en] *vt.*
to clothe, invest with.

Einkleidung [ine'klide-⊙ong]
nf. clothing, investiture.

Einklinken [ine'klink-en] *vt.i.*
to latch.

Einknicken [ine'knik-en] *vt.*
to bend in, buckle (*av., etc.*); *i.*
break down.

Einkochen [ine'coch-en] *vt.*
to boil down, preserve.

Einkommen [ine-kom-en] *vi.
ir.* to come in, forward, arrive,
apply, intervene; *n.* income;
-steuer *nf.* income tax; **-steuererklärung** *nf.* income tax return; **-steuerzuschlag** *nm.* super
tax.

Einkreisempfänger [ine'krice-emp-feng-err] *nm.* (**-**)
single circuit receiver (*rad.*).

Einkreisen [ine'kri-zen] *vt.* to
encircle.

Einkreisung [ine'kri-z⊙ong]
nf. encirclement.

Einkünfte [ine'ky⊙onf-ter]
f.pl. income, revenue.

Einkürzen [ine'ky⊙ort-sen] *vt.*
to shorten.

Einladebahnhof [ine'lah-de-bahn-hohf] *nm.* (**-höfe**) loading
station.

Einladen [ine'lah-den] *vt. ir.*
to invite.   [to load.

Einladen [ine'lah-den] *vt. ir.*

Einladung [ine'lah-d⊙ong] *nf.*
invitation.

Einlage [ine'lah-ger] *nf.* enclosure, laying in, deposit, inlet piece (*tec.*); **-nstoss** *nm.*
inlet joint (*tec.*).

Einlagern [ine'lah-gerrn] *vt.*
to store, billet, embed.

Einlagerung [ine'lah-ger-r⊙ong] *nf.* storage.

Einlass [ine'lass] *nm.* admission, inlet; **-geld** *n.* entrance money; **-karte** *nf.* card of admission, ticket; **-rohr** *n.* inlet pipe; **-ventil** *n.* inlet valve, induction valve.

Einlassen [ine'lass-en] *vt. ir.* to let in, admit; *r.* enter into, get involved in. (*harbour*).

Einlauf [ine'lowf] *nm.* entering

Einlaufen [ine'low-fen] *vi. ir* to arrive, enter (*port*), shrink.

Einläufig [ine'loy-fish] *a.* single-barrelled.

Einlegen [ine'lay-gen] *vt.* to enclose, deposit, inlay.

Einleger [ine'lay-gerr] *nm.* (-) depositor.

Einlegestück [ine'lay-ge-shtyōk] *n.* (-e) inlay.

Einleiten [ine'lite-en] *vt.* to introduce, start, initiate.

Einleitung [ine'lite-ōong] *nf.* introduction.

Einlenken [ine'lenk-en] *vt.* to set (*bone*); *i.* turn into, return to one's subject. (*learn.*)

Einlernen [ine'lare-nen] *vt.* to

Einlesen [ine'lay-zen] *vt. ir.* to collect.

Einleuchten [ine'loish-ten] *vi.* to be clear, evident.

Einleuchtend [ine'loish-tent] *a.* obvious.

Einliefern [ine'lee-ferrn] *vt.* to hand over.

Einliegen [ine'lee-gen] *vi. ir.* to lodge.

Einliegend [ine'lee-gent] *a.* enclosed.

Einlöffeln [ine'lerf-feln] *vt.* to take, give with a spoon.

Einlösbar [ine'lerss-barr] *a.* redeemable.

Einlösen [ine'ler-zen] *vt.* to redeem, pay.

Einlösung [ine'ler-zōong] *nf.* redemption, payment.

Einlullen [ine'lōō-len] *vt.* to lull to sleep.

Einmachen [ine'mach-en] *vt.* to wrap up, preserve.

Einmachzucker [ine'mach-tsōō-kerr] *nm.* preserving sugar.

Einmal [ine'mahl] *ad.* once, sometime; **auf** - all at once.

Einmarsch [ine'mahrrsh] *nm.* (-märsche) entry, marching in.

Einmarschieren [ine'mahr-shee-ren] *vi.* to march in.

Einmauern [ine'mow-errn] *vt.* to wall up, immure.

Einmengen [ine'meng-en] *vr.* to interfere with.

Einmieten [ine'meet-en] *vt.r.* to take lodgings.

Einmummen [ine'mōom-en] *vt.r.* to muffle up.

Einmünden [ine'myōōn-den] *vi.* to run into, join.

Einmündung [ine'myōōn-dōong] *nf.* junction, confluence, river mouth, road junction.

Einmütig [ine'myōō-tish] *a.* unanimous.

Einmütigkeit [ine'myōō-tish-kite] *nf.* unanimity.

Einnähen [ine'nay-en] *vt.* to sew up, embroider.

Einnahme [ine'nah-mer] *nf.* takings, revenue.

Einnebeln [ine'nay-beln] *vt.* to screen, conceal by smoke.

Einnehmen [ine'nay-men] *vt. ir.* to take (in), collect, receive, influence. (*a. charming.*)

Einnehmend [ine'nay-ment]

Einnehmer [ine'nay-merr] *nm.* (-) receiver, collector.

Einnicken [ine'nik-en] *vi.* to fall asleep, nod.

Einnisten [ine'nist-en] *vr.* to snuggle, settle oneself, nest.

Einöde [ine'er-der] *nf.* desert.

Einölen [ine'er-len] *vt.* to oil.

Einordnen [ine'orrd-nen] *vt.* to arrange, fit in, co-ordinate.

Einpacken [ine'pak-en] *vt.i.* to pack (up).

Einpauken [ine'pow-ken] *vt.* to cram.

Einpauker [ine'pow-kerr] *nm.* (-) coach, crammer.

Einpeilen [ine'pile-en] vi. to locate (by direction-finding).

Einpferchen [ine'pfairr-shen] vt. to pen in, coop up.

Einpflanzen [ine'pflant-sen] vt. to implant.

Einpflöcken [ine'pfler-ken] vt. to plug, peg in.

Einpfropfen [ine'pfrop-fen] vt. to cork (up), engraft, stuff in. [to pickle.

Einpökeln [ine'per-keln] vt.

Einprägen [ine'pray-gen] vt. to impress, imprint.

Einpressen [ine'press-en] vt. to (com)press.

Einproben [ine'probe-en] vt. to rehearse.

Einquartieren [ine'kvarr-tee-ren] vt. to quarter, billet.

Einquartierung [ine'kvarr-tee-rŏŏng] nf. quartering, billeting.

Einrahmen [ine'rah-men] vt. to frame.

Einrammen [ine'ram-en] vt. to drive (in).

Einräumen [ine'roy-men] vt. to give up, concede, admit, accommodate.

Einräumung [ine'roy-mŏŏng] nf. concession, accommodating. [to comprise.

Einrechnen [ine'resh-nen] vt.

Einrede [ine'ray-der] nf. objection; keine – ! not a word

Einreden [ine'ray-den] vi. to object, interrupt.

Einreibemittel [ine'ribe-e-mitl] n. embrocation.

Einreiben [ine'ribe-en] vt. ir. to rub in.

Einreichen [ine'rish-en] vt. to deliver, hand over.

Einreihen [ine'rie-en] vt. to put in a row, string, filter in (traffic), enrol, allot to regiments.

Einreihung [ine'rie-ŏŏng] nf. arranging, enrolment (mil.).

Einreise [ine'rize-er] nf. entry; -erlaubnis nf. entry permit.

Einreissen [ine'ricc-en] vt. ir. to rend, pull down; i. tear, spread.

Einreiten [ine'rite-en] vi. ir. ride in; t. to break in, overturn. [set (bone).

Einrenken [ine'renk-en] vt. to

Einrichten [ine'rish-ten] vt. to arrange, adjust, prepare; r. establish oneself.

Einrichtung [ine'rish-tŏŏng] nf. adjustment, arrangement, fittings, installation, apparatus.

Einriegeln [ine'ree-geln] vt. to bolt in.

Einritt [ine'rit] nm. (-e) riding in, entry on horseback.

Einröhrenverstärker [ine'rer-ren-ferr-shtair-kerr] nm. one-stage amplifier (rad.).

Einrosten [ine'rost-en] vi. to grow rusty.

Einrücken [ine'ryŏŏk-en] vi. to enter (in); t. enter, insert (advertisement).

Einrückung [ine'ryŏŏk-ŏŏng] nf. entrance, insertion.

Einrühren [ine'ryŏŏr-en] vt. to mix up, stir in.

Eins [ine-s] nf. one, ace.

Eins [ine-s] ad. at one.

Einsalzen [ine'zalt-sen] vt. to salt, cure.

Einsam [ine'zam] a. lonely, solitary.

Einsamkeit [ine'zam-kite] nf. loneliness, solitude.

Einsammeln [ine'zam-eln] vt. to collect.

Einsammlung [ine'zam-lŏŏng] nf. collecting.

Einsargen [ine'zarr-gen] vt. to put in a coffin.

Einsatz [ine'zats] nm. (-sätze) stake, leaf (table), insertion (clothing), operation (mil.); im – in action (mil.); -abteilung nf. operational detachment, battalion; -flugplatz, -hafen nm. advance, operational aerodrome (av.); -staffel nf. active unit, squadron (av.).

Einsaugen [ine'zow-gen] vt. to absorb.

Einsaugung [ine'zow-gŏŏng] nf. absorption.

Einschachteln [ine'shach-teln] vt. to insert (boxes), put in boxes (com.).

Einschalten [ine'shal-ten] vt. to insert, interpolate, switch on (el.), cut in, plug in (rad.).

Einschalter [ine'shal-terr] nm. (-) switch.

Einschalt-stellung nf. switching-on position; -vorrichtung nf. circuit closing device (el.).

Einschaltung [ine'shal-tŏŏng] nf. insertion, interpolation, switching on, putting in circuit, closing of circuit.

Einschanzen [ine'shant-sen] vt.r. to fortify, intrench.

Einschärfen [ine'share-fen] vt. to impress upon.

Einscharren [ine'shar-ren] vt. to bury; i. burrow.

Einschätzen [ine'shet-sen] vt. to estimate, value.

Einschenken [ine'shenk-en] vt. to pour in.

Einschicken [ine'shik-en] vt. to send in.

Einschieben [ine'shee-ben] vt. ir. to put in, push in, insert.

Einschiebsel [ine'sheep-sel] n. (-) interpolation.

Einschiessen [ine'shee-sen] vt. ir. to pay in, shoot down; r. practice shooting, get the range; n. adjustment fire (mil.).

Einschiffen [ine'shif-en] vi.r. to embark, go on board.

Einschiffung [ine'shif-ŏŏng] nf. embarkation.

Einschirren [ine'shir-ren] vt. to harness.

Einschlafen [ine'shlah-fen] vi. ir. to fall asleep, go to sleep.

Einschläfern [ine'shlafe-errn] vt. to lull to sleep.

Einschläferung [ine'shlafe-

er-rŏŏng] nf. lulling to sleep; -smittel n. narcotic, sleeping draught.

Einschlag [ine'shlahk] nm. (-schläge) striking, impact, weft, wrapper; -emesser n. clasp-knife; -papier n. wrapping paper; -wecker n. single-stroke bell (el.); -winkel nm. angle of impact.

Einschlagen [ine'shlah-gen] vt. ir. to drive in, break up, wrap up, strike, take (way); i. shake hands, strike (lightning), succeed, turn out well.

Einschlägig [ine'shlay-gish] a. relative to, relevant.

Einschleichen [ine'shli-chen] vi.r. ir. to creep, steal, slink in.

Einschleifen [ine'shli-fen] vt. ir. to grind in (valve).

Einschleppen [ine'shlep-pen] vt. to drag in, bring in, import (disease).

Einschliessen [ine'shlee-sen] vt. ir. to lock up, include, comprise, surround, encircle (mil.).

Einschliesslich [ine'shlees-lish] a. inclusive.

Einschlingen [ine'shling-en] vt. ir. Einschlucken [ine'shlŏŏk-en] vt. to swallow greedily, gulp down.

Einschlürfen [ine'shlyŏŏr-fen] vt. to suck in.

Einschluss [ine'shlŏŏs] nm. (-schlüsse) enclosure; mit — including.

Einschmeicheln [ine'shmi-sheln] vr. to ingratiate oneself.

Einschmeichelnd [ine'shmi-shelnt] a. insinuating, ingratiating.

Einschneiden [ine'shnide-en] vt. ir. to cut into, indent, notch; i. cut, bite.

Einschneien [ine'shni-en] vt. to snow up.

Einschnitt [ine'shnit] nm. (-e) cutting, incision, indent, cut.

Einschnüren [ine'shnyŏŏr-ren] vt. to lace, cord.

Einschränken [ine'shrenk-en] *vt.* to limit, narrow, restrict.

Einschränkend [ine'shrenk-ent] *a.* restrictive.

Einschränkung [ine'shrenk-ōong] *nf.* restriction, limitation, qualification.

Einschrecken [ine'shrek-en] *vt.* to frighten, intimidate.

Einschreib-brief [ine'shribe-] *nm.* registered letter; **-gebühr** *nf.* registration fee; **-sendung** *nf.* registered packet.

Einschreiben [ine'shribe-en] *vt. ir.* to register, inscribe.

Einschreibung [ine'shribe-ōong] *nf.* registration, enrolment.

Einschrumpfen [ine'shrŏomp-fen] *vi.* to shrink.

Einschub [ine'shŏop] *nm.* (-schübe) leaf (*table*), insertion.

Einschüchtern [ine'shyŏosh-terrn] *vt.* to intimidate.

Einschüchterung [ine'shyŏosh-ter-roong] *nf.* intimidation.

Einschulen [ine'shŏo-len] *vt.* to school, train.

Einschuss [ine'shŏoss] *nm.* (-schüsse) paid-up capital, woof, weft, fill (*mil.*).

Einschwärzen [ine'shvairt-sen] *vt.* to blacken, ink.

Einschwatzen [ine'shvat-sen] *vt.* to talk into, over.

Einschwenken [ine'shvenk-en] *vi.* to wheel in (*mil.*).

Einschwingzeit [ine'shving-tsite] *nf.* building-up time (*rad.*).

Einsegnen [ine'zaig-nen] *vt.* to consecrate, confirm.

Einsegnung [ine'zaig-nōong] *nf.* confirmation, consecration, ordination.

Einsehen [ine'zay-en] *vt. ir.* to see into, realize; *i.* look into; *n.* understanding, consideration.

Einseifen [ine'zife-en] *vt.* to soap, lather, impose upon, cheat.

Einseitig [ine'zite-ish] *a.* one-sided; **-er Verkehr** one-way traffic.

Einseitigkeit [ine'zite-ish-kite] *nf.* one-sidedness.

Einsenden [ine'zen-den] *vt. ir.* to send in, remit.

Einsender [ine'zen-derr] *nm.* (-) remitter, contributor, sender, correspondent (*press*).

Einsendung [ine'zen-dōong] *nf.* remittance, contribution.

Einsenken [ine'zenk-en] *vt.* to sink in, lower, layer, bury, plant.

Einsenkung [ine'zenk-ōong] *nf.* depression.

Einsetzen [ine'zet-sen] *vt.* to put (in), appoint, install, commit, employ (*mil.*), stake, deposit.

Einsetzung [ine'zet-sōong] *nf.* putting in, appointing, staking, depositing.

Einsicht [ine'zisht] *nf.* insight, judgment, inspection; realm *nf.* approval; **-slos** *a.* injudicious; **-svoll** *a.* judicious.

Einsickern [ine'zik-errn] *vi.* to infiltrate, trickle in.

Einsieden [ine'zee-den] *vt. ir.* to boil down.

Einsiedler [ine'zeed-lerr] *nm.* (-) hermit.   [to seal up.

Einsiegeln [ine'zee-geln] *vt.*

Einsilbig [ine'zil-bish] *a.* monosyllabic, taciturn.

Einsilbigkeit [ine'zil-bish-kite] *nf.* taciturnity.

Einsingen [ine'zing-en] *vt. ir.* to sing to sleep; *r.* to practise singing.   [to sink in.

Einsinken [ine'zink-en] *vi. ir.*

Einsitzer [ine'zit-serr] *nm.* (-) one-seater, single seater.

Einsitzig [ine'zit-sish] *a.* single-seated.

Einspannen [ine'shpan-en] *vt.* to harness, stretch.

Einspänner [ine'shpen-err] *nm.* (-) one-horse carriage, trap.

Einsperren [ine'shper-ren] *vt.* to lock up, put in gaol.

Einspielen [ine'shpeel-en] *vr.* to practise (*music*); *n.* co-ordination.

Einsprache [ine'shprach-er] *nf.* objection, mouthpiece.

Einsprechen [ine'shpresh-en] *vt. ir.* to instil; - auf to tune in (*rad.*)

Einsprengen [ine'shpreng-en] *vt.* to sprinkle, blow up force open.

Einspringen [ine'shpring-en] *vi. ir.* to spring into, help out, step into the breach.

Einspritzen [ine'shprit-sen] *vt.* to inject, syringe.

Einspritz-düse *nf.* feul in-jector (*tec.*); **-motor** *nm.* fuel injection engine.

Einspritzung [ine'shprit-soong] *nf.* injection.

Einspruch [ine'shprooch] *nm.* (-sprüche) protest prohibition, objection; **-strecht** *n.* veto.

Einspulig [ine'shpoo-lish] *a.* single-coil.

Einspurig [ine'shpoo-rish] *a.* single-line (*rl.*).

Einst [inst] *ad.* once, some day, some time.

Einstampfen [ine'shtampf-en] *vt.* to stamp, pulp (*paper*).

Einstand [ine'shtant] *nm.* deuce (*tennis*).

Einstauen [ine'shtow-en] *vt.* to stow.

Einstechen [ine'shtesh-en] *vt. ir.* to puncture, perforate.

Einstecken [ine'shtek-en] *vt.* to stick in, insert, pocket, put into goal, post (*letter*).

Einsteck-album *n.* (-s) photograph album; **-schild** *n.* slip-in label, card, ticket, in-sert label.

Einstehen [ine'shtay-en] *vi. ir.* to answer for, guarantee.

Einsteigen [ine'shty-gen] *vi. ir.* to get in, take one's seat, go on board (*ship*).

Einstellbar [ine'shtel-barr] *a.* adjustable.

Einstellen [ine'shtel-en] *vt.i.* to suspend, discontinue, stop, adjust, assign (*to units*), focus (*camera, etc.*), tune in (*rad.*); *r.* set in.

Einstellung [ine'shtel-oong] *nf.* suspension, cessation, ad-justment, focussing, appoint-ment, attitude, enlistment.

Einstig [ine'stish] *a.* former.

Einstimmen [ine'shtim-en] *vt.i.* to agree with, to join in.

Einstimmig [ine'shtim-ish] *a.* unanimous.

Einstimmigkeit [ine'shtim-ish-kite] *nf.* unanimity.

Einstmalig [inst'mah-lish] *a.* former. [formerly.

Einstmals [inst'mahlss] *ad.*]

Einstöckig [ine'shter-kish] *a.* one-storied.

Einstopien [ine'shtop-fen] *vt.* to fill, stuff, plug.

Einstossen [ine'shtoh-sen] *vt. ir.* to knock in, break.

Einstreichen [ine'shtrish-en] *vt. ir.* to sweep in, rake in.

Einstreuen [ine'shtroy-en] *vt.* to intersperse.

Einströmen [ine'shter-men] *vi.* to flow, pour in.

Einströmung [ine'shter-moong] *nf.* influx.

Einstudieren [ine'shtoo-dee-ren] *vt.* to study, rehearse.

Einstündig [ine'shtyon-dish] *a.* one-hour.

Einstündig [ine'shtyon-dish] *a.* one-hour.

Einstürmen [ine'shtyor-men] *vi.* to rush in, attack.

Einsturz [ine'shtoorts] *nm.* (-stürze) (down)fall, collapse.

Einstürzen [ine'shtyoort-sen] *vi.* to fall in, collapse; *vt.* over-throw.

Einstweilen [inst'vile-en] *ad.* meanwhile, temporarily, for a time.

Einstweilig [inst'vile-ish] *a.* temporary, provisional. [day.

Eintägig [ine'tay-gish] *a.* one-]

Eintänzer [ine'tent-serr] *nm.* (-) dancing partner, gigolo.

Eintauchen [ine'tow-chen] *vt.* to immerse, dip in; *i.* dive.

Eintausch [ine'towsh] *nm.* exchange, barter.

Eintauschen [ine'tow-shen] *vt.* to exchange, barter.

Einteilen [ine'tile-en] *vt.* to divide, distribute.

Einteilung [ine'tile-ŏŏng] *nf.* division, distribution.

Eintönig [ine'ter-nish] *a.* monotonous.

Eintönigkeit [ine'ter-nish-kite] *nf.* monotony.

Eintopfgericht [ine'topf-ger-risht] *n.* (-e) one-course meal.

Eintracht [ine'tracht] *nf.* concord, unity.

Einträchtig [ine'tresh-tish] *a.* harmonious, united.

Eintrag [ine'trahk] *nm.* (-träge) damage, injury, entry (com.).

Eintragen [ine'trah-gen] *vt. ir.* to carry in, bring in, yield, enter (in book).

Einträglich [ine'trake-lish] *a.* profitable.

Einträglichkeit [ine'trake-lish-kite] *nf.* productivity, high yield.

Eintragung [ine'trah-gŏŏng] *nf.* carrying in, entering (com.).

Einträufeln [ine'troy-feln] *vt.* to drop in.

Eintreffen [ine'tref-en] *vi. ir.* to happen, arrive.

Eintreiben [ine'tribe-en] *vt. ir.* to drive in, collect, exact.

Eintreibung [ine'tribe-ŏŏng] *nf.* collection, exaction.

Eintreten [ine'tray-ten] *vi. ir.* to occur, enter, intercede for, join up (mil.); *t.* to kick open.

Eintrichtern [ine'trish-terrn] *vt.* to cram, stuff into one's head.

Eintritt [ine'trit] *nm.* (-e) entrance, commencement; -salter *n.* age of enlistment

(mil.); **-sgeld** *n.* charge for admission; **-skarte** *nf.* admission ticket.

Eintrocknen [ine'trok-nen] *vt.* to dry, recondition (air).

Eintröpfeln [ine'trerp-feln] *vt.* to drop in.

Eintunken [ine'tōōn-ken] *vt.* to dip in.

Einüben [ine'yōō-ben] *vt.* to practise, drill.

Einverleiben [ine'ferr-libe-en] *vt.* to incorporate, annex.

Einverleibung [ine'ferr-libe-ŏŏng] *nf.* incorporation, annexation.

Einvernehmen [ine'ferr-nay-men] *n.* agreement, understanding.

Einverstanden [ine'ferr-shtan-den] *a.* agreeable, in agreement.

Einverständnis [ine'ferr-shtent-niss] *n.* (-e) understanding, agreement.

Einwachsen [ine'vax-en] *vi. ir.* to grow into.

Einwägen [ine'vay-gen] *vt. ir.* to weigh in.

Einwand [ine'vant] *nm.* (-wände) objection, pretext.

Einwanderer [ine'van-der-rerr] *nm.* (-) immigrant

Einwandern [ine'van-derrn] *vi.* to immigrate.

Einwanderung [ine'van-der-rŏŏng] *nf.* immigration.

Einwandfrei [ine'vant-fry] *a.* irreproachable, unimpeachable.

Einwärts [ine'vairrts] *ad.* [inwards.

Einwechseln [ine'vex-eln] *vt.* to change, obtain by exchange.

Einweichen [ine'vi-shen] *vt.* to soften by soaking, steep.

Einweihen [ine'vy-en] *vt.* to initiate, consecrate.

Einweihung [ine'vy-ŏŏng] *nf.* initiation, consecration.

Einweiser [ine'vise-err] *nm.* (-) route-guide.

Einweisung [ine'vise-ŏŏng]

nf. military training; -**silug**
nm. instruction flight, training
flight (*parachutists*).

Einwenden [ine'ven-den] *vt.*
ir. to object, oppose.

Einwendung [ine'ven-döong]
nf. objection.

Einwerfen [ine'vairr-fen] *vt.*
ir. to throw in, smash, object,
interpose.   [wrap up.

Einwickeln [ine'vik-eln] *vt.* to

Einwickelpapier [ine'vikl-
pa-peer'] *n.* (-e) wrapping
paper, brown paper.

Einwiegen [ine'vee-gen] *vt.* to
rock to sleep.

Einwilligen [ine'vil-i-gen] *vi.*
to consent to, agree.

Einwilligung [ine'vi-li-
göong] *nf.* consent.

Einwirken [ine'veer-ken] *vi.*
to influence, act upon.

Einwirkung [ine'veer-köong]
nf. influence.

Einwohnen [ine'voh-nen] *vr.*
to settle down.

Einwohner [ine'voh-ner] *nm.*
(-) inhabitant; -**wehr** *nf.* home
guard.

Einwohnerschaft [ine'voh-
ner-shaft] *nf.* population, inhabitants.

Einwurf [ine'vöorf] *nm.*
(-würfe) objection, slot.

Einwurzeln [ine'vöort-seln]
vi. to take root.

Einzahl [ine'tsahl] *nf.* singular.

Einzahlen [ine'tsah-len] *vt.* to
pay (in, up), deposit.

Einzahlung [ine'tsah-löong]
nf. paying (in, up), deposit.

Einzählen [ine'tsay-len] *vt.* to
count in, include.

Einzähnen [ine'tsay-nen] *vt.*
to indent (*tec.*).

Einzäunen [ine'tsoy-nen] *vt.*
to hedge in.

Einzeichnen [ine'tsīsh-nen]
vt. to draw in, note; *r.* sign
one's name, subscribe.

Einzelheit [ine'tsel-hite] *nf.*
particular.

Einzel-abfederung *nf.* independent wheel suspension;
-**arrest** *nm.* solitary confinement; -**ausbildung** *nf.* individual training; -**fall** *nm.* single
instance, individual case; -**flug**
nm. solo flight (*av.*); -**haft** *nf.*
see -arrest; -**kampf** *nm.* hand-
to-hand fight, dog-fight (*av.*,
etc.); -**last** *nf.* concentrated
load (*tec.*); -**person** *nf.* individual; -**teil** *nm.* component
part; -**wurf** *nm.* dropping
single bombs.

Einzeln [ine-tseln] *a.* single,
detached; *ad.* singly; — angeben to specify. [retractable.

Einziehbar [ine'tsee-barr] *a.*

Einzieh'en [ine'tsee-en] *vt. ir.*
to draw in, take in, collect,
draft, call up, confiscate; *r.*
shrink; *i.* move into, remove;
-**fahrgestell** *n.* retractable
under-carriage (*av.*).

Einziehung [ine'tsee-öong] *nf.*
drawing in, collection, confiscation, drafting, calling to the
colours (*mil.*).   [unique.

Einzig [ine'tsich] *a.* only,

Einzigartig [ine'tsish-arr-
tish] *a.* unique.

Einzug [ine'tsöok] *nm.* (-züge)
entry, removal.

Einzwängen [ine'tsveng-en]
vt. to force in, constrain.

Einzwingen [ine'tsving-en]
vt. ir. to force into, upon.

Eirung [ie'roont] *a.* oval, egg-
shaped; *n.* oval.

Eis [ice] *n.* ice, ice-cream;
-**bahn** *nf.* skating rink; -**bär**
m.w. polar bear; -**berg** *nm.*
iceberg; -**brecher** *nm.* ice-
breaker; -**frei** *a.* clear of ice;
-**kalt** *a.* icy cold; -**maschine** *nf.*
freezing machine; -**pickel** *nm.*
ice-axe; -**scholle** *nf.* ice-floe;
-**schrank** *nm.* refrigerator;
-**sporn** *nm.* crampon.

Eisen [ize'en] *n.* iron; -**abfall**
nm. scrap iron; -**beton** *nm.*
ferro-concrete, reinforced con-

crete; -blech n. sheet-iron; -draht nm. iron wire; -fresser nm. fire-eater; -giesserei nf. iron-foundry; -guss nm. iron casting, cast iron; -haltig a. ferruginous; -hammer nm. forge, ironworks; -handel nm. iron trade, hardware trade; -händler nm. ironmonger; -hütte nf. forge; -platte nf. iron plate; -waren f.pl. ironmongery; -werk n. iron works.

Eisenbahn [ize'en-bahn] nf. railway; -betrieb nm. railway traffic, train service; -fähre nf. train ferry; -knotenpunkt nm. railway junction; -netz n. railway system; -oberbau nm. permanent way; -übergang nm. level crossing; -verbindung nf. railway connection; -verkehr nm. railway traffic; -wagen nm. railway carriage.

Eisern [ize'errn] a. iron.

Eisig [ize'ish] a. icy.

Eitel [ite'el] a. vain.

Eitelkeit [ite'el-kite] nf. vanity.

Eiter [ite'err] nm. pus; -beule nf. abscess.

Eiterig [ite'er-rish] a. purulent, suppurating.   [purate.

Eitern [ite'errn] vi. to suppurate.

Eiweiss [ie'vice] n. white of egg, albumen.   [gust.

Ekel [ake'el] nm. nausea, disgust.

Ekelhaft [ake'el-haft]. Ekelig [ake'e-lish] a. nauseous, disgusting.

Ekeln [ake'eln] vi.r. to loathe, be disgusted at.

Ekstase [ex-tah'zer] nf. ecstasy.   [ecstatic.

Ekstatisch [ex-tah'tish] a. ecstatic.

Elastisch [ay-la'stish] a. elastic.

Elastizität [ay-la-stit-si-tate'] nf. elasticity.   [elephant.

Elefant [ay-ler-fant'] m.w.

Elegant [ay-lay-gant'] a. elegant.   [elegance.

Eleganz [ay-lay-gants'] nf.

Elegie [ay-lay-gee'] nf. elegy.

Elektrifizieren [ay-lek-tri-fit-see'ren] vt. to electrify.

Elektrifizierung [ay-lek-tri-fit-see'rŏong] nf. electrification.

Elektriker [ay-lek'tri-kerr] nm. (-) electrician.

Elektrisch [ay-lek'trish] a. electric; -e n. tram.

Elektrisieren [ay-lek-tri-zee'ren] vt. to electrify.

Elektrizität [ay-lek-tri-si-tate'] nf. electricity; -ssammler m. condenser; -swerk n. electricity works, power plant.

Elektrode [ay-lek-troh'der] nf. electrode; -nspannung nf. electric potential.

Elektro-dynamisch a. electrodynamic; -lyse nf. electrolysis; -lytisch a. electrolytic; -magnet nm. electromagnet; -mechaniker nm. electro-mechanic, electrician; -mobil n. electric motor-car, accumulator driven car, van; -motorisch a. electro-motive; -statisch a. electro-static; -technik nf. electrical engineering; -techniker nm. see -mechaniker.

Elektron [ay-lek'tron] n. (-en) electron; -enausstrahlung nf. emission of electrons; -enröhre nf. thermionic valve.

Element [ay-ler-ment'] n. (-e) element, battery, cell (el.).

Elementar [ay-ler-men-tahr'] a. elementary, elemental.

Elend [ay'lent] n. misery. a. miserable; -sviertel n. slum.

Elf [elf] num. eleven.

Elfe [el'fer] nf. fairy, elf.

Elfenbein [el'fen-bine] n. ivory.

Eliminieren [ay-li-mi-nee'ren] vt. to eliminate.

Elle [el'er] nf. ell, yard; -nwaren f.pl. drapery.

Ellbogen [el'boh-gen] nm. (-) elbow.

Ellipse [el-ip-ser] nf. ellipse.

Elster [el'sterr] *nf.* magpie.
Elterlich [el-terr-lish] *a.* parental.
Eltern [el'terrn] *pl.* parents; -los *a.* orphaned.
Email [ay-my'] *nf.* enamel.
Emaillieren [ay-mal-yee'ren] *vt.* to enamel.
Emanzipieren [ay-mant-si-pee'ren] *vt.* to emancipate.
Emigrant [ay-mi-grant'] *m.v.* emigrant. [issue.
Emission [ay-miss-yohn'] *nf.*
Empfang [emp-fang'] *nm.* (-fänge) reception, receipt; -sanlage *nf.* -sapparat *nm.* receiving set (*rad.*); -anzeige *nf.* acknowledgment of receipt; -sschein *nm.* receipt; -sstelle *nf.* receiving station (*rad.*); -sverstärkung *nf.* reception amplification; -szimmer *n.* drawing room.
Empfangen [emp-fang'en] *vt. ir.* to receive; *i.* conceive.
Empfänger [emp-feng'err] *nm.* (-) receiver, consignee, addressee (*com.*).
Empfänglich [emp-feng'lish] *a.* susceptible, receptive.
Empfänglichkeit [emp-feng'lish-kite] *nf.* receptivity, susceptibility.
Empfängnis [emp-feng'nis] *nf.* (-se) conception.
Empfehlen [emp-fay'len] *vt. ir.* to recommend; *r.* take one's leave.
Empfehlenswert [emp-fay'lens-vairrt] *a.* commendable.
Empfehlung [emp-fay'loong] *nf.* recommendation; -sbrief *nm.* letter of recommendation.
Empfinden [emp-fin'den] *vt. ir.* to feel.
Empfindlich [emp-fint'lish] *a.* sensitive, sore, touchy.
Empfindlichkeit [emp-fint'lish-kite] *nf.* sensitiveness, touchiness.
Empfindsam [emp-fint'sam] *a.* sentimental.

Empfindsamkeit [emp-fint'sam-kite] *nf.* sentimentality.
Empfindung [emp-fin'doong] *nf.* feeling, sentiment.
Empfindungslos [emp-fin'doongs-lohss] *a.* unfeeling, insensitive.
Emphase [em-fah'zer] *nf.* emphasis.
Emphatisch [em-fah'tish] *a.* emphatic.
Empor [em-porr'] *ad.* up, upwards.
Emporarbeiten [em-porr'arr-bite-en] *vr.* to work one's way up.
Empören [em-per'ren] *vt.* to rouse, make indignant, shock; *r.* revolt.
Empörend [em-per'rent] *a.* revolting.
Empörer [em-per'rerr] *nm.* (-) insurgent, rebel.
Empörerisch [em-per'er-rish] *a.* insurgent.
Emporkommen [em-porr'kom-en] *vi. ir.* to rise, succeed.
Emporkömmling [em-porr'kerm-ling] *nm.* (-e) upstart.
Emporkriechen [em-porr'kree-shen] *vi. ir.* to creep up.
Emporziehen [em-porr'tsee-en] *vt. ir.* to raise.
Empörung [em-per'roong] *nf* insurrection, indignation.
Emsig [em'zish] *a.* diligent, busy. [industry.
Emsigkeit [em'zish-kite] *nf.*
Endauswertung [ent'ows-vairr-toong] *nf.* final analysis.
Endbahnhof [ent'bahn-hofe] *nm.* (-höfe) terminus, railhead.
Endchen [ent'shen] *n.* (-) bit.
Ende [en'der] *n.* (*gen.* -s; *pl.* -n) end; am - in the end, finally.
Endig(en) [en'di-gen] *vt.* to terminate; *r.i.* to conclude.
Endergebnis [ent'airr-gabe-nis] *n.* (-se) ultimate result.
Endgeschwindigkeit [ent'ger-shvin-dish-kite] *nf.* final, striking velocity.

Endgültig [ent'gÿōōl-tish] *a.* final, definite.

Endlich [ent'lish] *a.* final, finite; *ad.* finally.

Endlos [ent'lohss] *a.* endless, infinite.

Endpunkt [ent'pŏŏnkt] *nm.* (-punkte) extremity, terminus.

Endspiel [ent'shpeel] *n.* (-e) final (*game*).

Endstation [ent'shtat-syohn'] *nf.* terminus.

Endursache [ent'ōōr-zach-er] *nf.* final cause.

Endurteil [ent'ōōr-tile] *n.* (-e) final judgment.

Endziel [ent'tseel] *n.* (-e) final aim.

Endzweck [ent'tsvek] *nm.* (-e) main purpose.

Energie [ay-nairr-gee'] *nf.* energy; -los *a.* slack, lacking in energy.

Energisch [ay-nairr'gish] *a.* energetic.

Eng [eng] *a.* narrow, strict.

Engbrüstig [eng'brüss-tish] *a.* narrow-chested.

Enge [eng'er] *nf.* narrowness, narrows, defile, straits.

Engel [eng'el] *nm.* (-) angel.

Engelgleich [eng'el-glish] *a.* angelic.

Engen [eng'en] *vt.r.* to narrow, contract.

Englisch [eng'glish] *a.* English; -e Krankheit rickets *pl*; -es Pflaster court-plaster.

Engpass [eng'pass] *nm.* (-pässe) defile, gorge, pass.

Engros [ong-groh'] *a.* wholesale; -geschäft *n.* wholesale business.

Engrossist [ong-groh-sist'] *m.w.* wholesaler (*com.*).

Enkel [eng'kel] *nm.* (-) grandson; -kind *n.* grandchild.

Enkelin [eng'ker-lin] *nf.* granddaughter.

Enorm [ay-norrm'] *a.* enormous.

Entarten [ent-arr'ten] *vi.* to degenerate.

Entartung [ent-arr'tŏŏng] *nf.* degeneration.

Entäussern [ent-oy'serrn] *vr.* to rid oneself, renounce.

Entäusserung [ent-oy'ser-rŏŏng] *nf.* relinquishment, discarding.

Entbehren [ent-bair'ren] *vt.* to do without, miss, dispense with.

Entbehrlich [ent-bair'lish] *a.* superfluous, to spare.

Entbehrlichkeit [ent-bair'-lish-kite] *nf.* superfluousness.

Entbehrung [ent-bair'rŏŏng] *nf.* want, lack.

Entbieten [ent-beet'en] *vt. ir.* to send, offer, notify.

Entbinden [ent-bin'den] *vt. ir.* to exonerate, release, deliver.

Entbindung [ent-bin'dŏŏng] *nf.* release, confinement; -sanstalt *nf.* maternity hospital.

Entblättern [ent-blet'errn] *vt.* to strip of leaves.

Entblöden [ent-bler'den] *vr.* to dare.

Entblössen [ent-bler'sen] *vt.* to denude, uncover, deprive.

Entblössung [ent-bler'sŏŏng] *nf.* denudation, uncovering.

Entbrennen [ent-bren'en] *vi. ir.* to take fire.

Entdecken [ent-dek'en] *vt.* to discover, disclose.

Entdecker [ent-dek'err] *nm.* (-) discoverer.

Entdeckung [ent-dek'ŏŏng] *nf.* discovery.

Ente [en'ter] *nf.* duck, false report, fraud, hoax.

Entehren [ent-air'ren] *vt.* to dishonour, disgrace.

Entehrend [ent-air'rent] *a.* dishonourable, disgraceful.

Entehrung [ent-air'rŏŏng] *nf.* dishonouring, degradation.

Enteignen [ent-ig'nen] *vt.* to expropriate, dispossess.

Enteignung [ent-ig-nŏŏng] *nf.* expropriation.

Enteilen [ent-ile'en] vi. to hurry away.

Enteisen [ent-ize'en] vt. to free from ice.

Enteisung [ent-ize'ōōng] nf. de-icing (av.).

Enterben [ent-airr'ben] vt. to disinherit.

Enterich [en'ter-rish] nm. (-e) drake.

Enter'n [en'terrn] vt. to board (ship); **-haken** nm. grappling iron; **-mannschaft** nf. boarding party (nav.); **-messer** n. cutlass.

Enterung [en'ter-rōōng] nf. boarding.

Entfachen [ent-fach'en] vt. to kindle.

Entfahren [ent-fah'ren] vi. ir. to escape; **–lassen** to let slip.

Entfallen [ent-fal'en] vi. ir. to slip from, fall off.

Entfalten [ent-fal'ten] vt. to unfold, exhibit, develop, deploy (mil.); r. expand, develop.

Entfaltung [ent-fal'tōōng] nf. unfolding, development, deployment (mil.); **-szeit** nf. opening time (parachute).

Entfärben [ent-fairr'ben] vt. to decolour, discolour; r. lose, change colour, fade.

Entfasern [ent-fah'zerrn] vt. to shred, unravel.

Entfernen [ent-fairr'nen] vt. to remove, expel; r. go away, retire, withdraw.

Entfernt [ent-fairrnt'] a. distant.

Entfernung [ent-fairr'nōōng] nf. removal, distance, range (mil.); **-sänderung** nf. range correction (mil.); **-smessgerät** n. **-smesser** m. range finder.

Entfesseln [ent-fess'eln] vt. to unfetter.

Entfestigen [ent-fest'i-gen] vt. to demilitarize, destroy fortifications of.

Entfestigung [ent-fest'i-gōōng] nf. demilitarization.

Entfetten [ent-fet'en] vt. to free from fat.

Entfettung [ent-fet'ōōng] nf. freeing from fat; **-skur** nf. slimming cure.

Entflammen [ent-flam'en] vt. to become inflated; t. kindle, inflame.

Entfleischt [ent-flisht'] a. emaciated.

Entfliehen [ent-flee'en] vi. ir. to run away, flee from.

Entfliessen [ent-flee'sen] vi. ir. to flow from.

Entfremden [ent-frem'den] vt. to estrange.

Entfremdung [ent-frem'dōōng] nf. alienation, estrangement.

Entfritten [ent-frit'en] vt. to decohere (rad.).

Entfritter [ent-frit'err] nm. (-) decoherer (rad.).

Entfrittung [ent-frit'ōōng] nf. decoherence.

Entführen [ent-fyōōr'ren] vt. to carry off, abduct.

Entführung [ent-fyōōr'rōōng] nf. abduction, kidnapping.

Entgasen [ent-gah'zen] vt. to decontaminate.

Entgegen [ent-gay'gen] pr. against, towards; ad. towards; **-arbeiten** vi. to counteract; **-gehen** vi. ir. to go to meet, face; **-gesetzt** a. opposite, opposed; **-halten** vt. ir. to compare, contrast, object; **-kommen** vi. ir. to meet, make concessions; n. obligingness, kindness, concessions; **-laufen** vi. ir. to be opposed, run to meet; **-sehen** vi. ir. to look forward to, await; **-setzen** vt. to oppose, contrast; **-setzung** nf. opposition, antithesis; **-stehen** vi. to oppose, confront; **-stellen** vt. to contrast; **-wirken** vi. to counteract, repel.

Entgegnen [ent-gaig'nen] vi. to retort.

Entgegnung [ent-gaig'nōōng] nf. retort.

Entgehen [ent-gay'en] vi. ir.

to escape from; — lassen to miss.

Entgelt [ent-gelt'] *nm.* compensation, remuneration.

Entgelten [ent-gel'ten] *vt. ir.* to atone, pay for.

Entgeltung [ent-gel'tŏŏng] *nf.* expiation.

Entgiften [ent-gif'ten] *vt.* to disinfect, decontaminate.

Entgleisen [ent-glize'en] *vi.* to run off the rails; — lassen to derail.

Entgleisung [ent-glize'ŏŏng] *nf.* derailment, slip, aberration.

Entgleiten [ent-glite'en] *vi. ir.* to slip from.

Entgräten [ent-gray'ten] *vt.* to bone (*fish*).

Enthaaren [ent-hah'ren] *vt.* to remove hair from.

Enthaarungsmittel [ent-hah'rŏŏngs-mitl] *n.* (—) depilatory.

Enthalten [ent-hal'ten] *vt. ir.* to contain, comprise; *r.* abstain.

Enthaltsam [ent-halt'zam] *a.* abstemious, continent.

Enthaltsamkeit [ent-halt'zam-kite] *nf.* abstemiousness, continence. [*vt.* to behead.

Enthaupten [ent-howp'ten]

Enthauptung [ent-howp'tŏŏng] *nf.* beheading, execution.

Entheben [ent-hay'ben] *vt. ir.* to free, take away relieve of (*post*).

Entheiligen [ent-hile'i-gen] *vt.* to profane.

Entheiligung [ent-hile'i-gŏŏng] *nf.* profanation, desecration.

Enthüllen [ent-hyŏol'en] *vt.* to unveil, disclose.

Enthüllung [ent-hyŏol'ŏŏng] *nf.* unveiling disclosure.

Enthülsen [ent-hyŏol'zen] *vt.* to shell.

Enthusiastisch [en-tŏŏ-zi-as'tish] *a.* enthusiastic.

Entkeimen [ent-kime'en] *vt.* to sterilize.

Entkernen [ent-kairr'nen] *vt.* to stone (*fruit*).

Entkleiden [ent-klide'en] *vt.* to undress, divest.

Entkohlen [ent-kohl'en] *vt.* to decarbonize (*aut.*).

Entkommen [ent-kom'en] *vi. ir.* to get away, escape.

Entkorken [ent-korr'ken] *vt.* to uncork.

Entkräften [ent-kref'ten] *vt.* to enfeeble, exhaust.

Entkräftigung [ent-kref'ti-gŏŏng] *nf.* exhaustion, weakening, refutation.

Entkuppeln [ent-kŏŏ'peln] *vt.* to uncouple, disconnect, disengage, declutch (*aut.*).

Entkuppelung [ent-kŏŏ'perloong] *nf.* uncoupling, disconnection.

Entladen [ent-lah'den] *vt.* to unload, free from, discharge.

Entlader [ent-lah'derr] *nm.* (—) extractor, discharging rod (*el.*), discharger, discharging tongs.

Entlade-strom *nm.* discharging current (*el.*); **-taste** *nf.* discharging key (*el.*); **-stunke** *nm.* disruptive spark (*el.*); **-skurve** *nf.* discharging curve (*el.*); **-srohr** *n.* **-sröhre** *nf.* discharge tube. [along.

Entlang [ent-lang'] *pr. ad.*

Entlarven [ent-larr'fen] *vt.* to unmask.

Entlassen [ent-lass'en] *vt. ir.* to dismiss, release, discharge.

Entlassung [ent-lass'ŏŏng] *nf.* dismissal, discharge, resignation; — aus dem Staatsverband denaturalization; **-zeugnis** *n.* discharge papers (*mil.*).

Entlasten [ent-lass'ten] *vt.* to unload, unburden, credit (*com.*), relieve.

Entlastung [ent-last'ŏŏng]

discharge, relief, crediting (*com.*), diversion (*mil.*); -sangriff *nm.* diversionary attack (*mil.*); -sstrasse *nf.* by-pass (road).

Entlaufen [ent-low'fen] *vi. ir.* to run away, escape.

Entlausen [ent-low'zen] *vt.* to delouse, rid of vermin.

Entledigen [ent-lay'di-gen] *vr.* to rid oneself, get rid of, perform.

Entledigung [ent-lay'di-gōōng] *nf.* discharge, riddance.

Entleeren [ent-lair'ren] *vt.* to empty. [remote.

Entlegen [ent-lay'gen] *a.*

Entlegenheit [ent-lay'genhite] *nf.* remoteness.

Entlehnen [ent-lane'en] *vt.* to borrow.

Entlehnung [ent-lay'nōōng] *nf.* borrowing, loan.

Entleihen [ent-lie'en] *vt. ir.* to borrow.

Entleiher [ent-lie'err] *nm.* (-) borrower.

Entlocken [ent-lock'en] *vt.* to elicit.

Entlohnen [ent-loh'nen] *vt.* to pay (off).

Entlosten [ent-lost'en] *vt.* to decontaminate.

Entmannen [ent-man'en] *vt.* to unman, castrate.

Entmannung [ent-man'ōōng] *nf.* unmanning, castration.

Entmenscht [ent-mensht'] *a.* inhuman, brutish.

Entmilitarisieren [ent-mi-li-ta-ri-zeer'ren] *vt.* to demilitarize.

Entmilitarisierung [ent-mi-li-ta-ri-zeer'rōōng] *nf.* demilitarization.

Entmutigen [ent-mōō'ti-gen] *vt.* to discourage.

Entmutigung [ent-mōō'ti-gōōng] *nf.* discouragement.

Entnahme [ent-nah'mer] *nf.* taking away, withdrawal, purchasing.

Entnationalisieren [ent-natsyo-na-li-zeer'ren] *vt.* to denaturalize, deprive of citizenship.

Entnehmen [ent-nay'men] *vt. ir.* to take away, from, draw upon, conclude from (letter).

Entnerven [ent-nairr'fen] *vt.* to unnerve, weaken.

Entpuppen [ent-pōō'pen] *vr.* to reveal oneself as.

Entraten [ent-rah'ten] *vi. ir.* to do without, dispense with.

Enträtseln [ent-rate'seln] *vt.* to puzzle out, solve.

Entreissen [ent-rice'en] *vt. ir.* to tear away, snatch from.

Entrichten [ent-rish'ten] *vt.* to pay.

Entrichtung [ent-rish'tōōng] *nf.* payment, settlement.

Entringen [ent-ring'en] *vt. ir.* to wrest from.

Entrinnen [ent-rin'en] *vi. ir.* to get away (from), escape.

Entrollen [ent-rol'en] *vt.r.* to unroll; *i.* roll down.

Entrücken [ent-ryōōk'en] *vt.* to carry off, remove.

Entrückt [ent-ryōōkt'] *a.* entranced.

Entrüsten [ent-ryōōs'ten] *vt.* to provoke; *r.* grow indignant.

Entrüstet [ent-ryōōs'tet] *a.* indignant. [*nf.* indignation.

Entrüstung [ent-ryōōs'tōōng] *nf.* indignation.

Entsagen [ent-zah'gen] *vi.* to renounce, relinquish.

Entsagung [ent-zah'gōōng] *nf.* renunciation, abandonment, resignation.

Entsatz [ent-zats'] *nm.* relief; -truppen *f.pl.* relieving troops; -versuch *nm.* attempted relief (*mil.*).

Entschädigen [ent-shade'i-gen] *vt.* to indemnify, compensate.

Entschädigung [ent-shade'i-gōōng] *nf.* compensation, indemnity.

Entschärfen [ent-shairr'fen] *vt.* to render harmless (mine).

Entschärft [ent-shairrft'] *a.* unprimed *(fuze)*, disarmed *(ammunition)*.

Entscheid [ent-shite'] *nm.* (-e) decision.

Entscheiden [ent-shide'en] *vt.r. ir.* to decide, make up one's mind.

Entscheidend [ent-shide'ent] *a.* decisive, casting vote).

Entscheidung [ent-shide'ŏŏng] *nf.* decision, sentence; -spunkt *nm.* crisis; -srunde *nf.* final round; -sschlacht *nf.* decisive battle.

Entschieden [ent-sheed'en] *a.* decided, resolute.

Entschiedenheit [ent-shee'den-hite] *nf.* firmness, decision.

Entschlafen [ent-shlah'fen] *vi. ir.* to fall asleep, die.

Entschlagen [ent-shlah'gen] *vr. ir.* to rid oneself, dismiss.

Entschleiern [ent-shly'errn] *vt.* to unveil.

Entschliessen [ent-shlee'sen] *vr. ir.* to decide, resolve, determine.

Entschliessung [ent-shlee'sŏŏng] *nf.* resolution.

Entschlossen [ent-shloss'en] *a.* determined, resolute.

Entschlossenheit [ent-shloss'en-hite] *nf.* determination.

Entschlummern [ent-shlŏŏm'merrn] *vi.* to fall asleep.

Entschlüpfen [ent-shlyŏŏp'fen] *vi.* to slip away, escape.

Entschluss [ent-shlŏŏss'] *nm.* (Entschlüsse) resolve, resolution, decision.

Entschlüsseln [ent-shlyŏŏ'seln] *vt.* to decode, decipher.

Entschuldbar [ent-shŏŏlt'barr] *a.* excusable.

Entschuldigen [ent-shŏŏl'di-gen] *vt.* to excuse; *r.* to apologize.

Entschuldigung [ent-shŏŏl'di-gŏŏng] *nf.* excuse, apology.

Entschwinden [ent-shvin'den] *vi. ir.* to disappear.

Entsenden [ent-zen'den] *vt. ir.* to send off.

Entsetzen [ent-zet'sen] *vt.* to displace, dismiss, relieve *(mil.)*, frighten; *r.* to be horrified, shocked.

Entsetzlich [ent-zets'lish] *a.* frightful, dreadful.

Entseuchen [ent-zoy'shen] *vt.* to disinfect.

Entsichern [ent-zish'errn] *vt.* to release safety catch.

Entsiegeln [ent-zee'geln] *vt.* to unseal.

Entsinken [ent-zink'en] *vi. ir.* to sink.

Entsinnen [ent-zin'en] *vr.* to remember.

Entspannen [ent-shpan'en] *vt.* to release, uncock; *r.* relax.

Entspannung [ent-shpan'ŏŏng] *nf.* relaxation, rest.

Entspinnen [ent-shpin'en] *vi. ir.* to arise, develop.

Entsprechen [ent-shpresh'en] *vi. ir.* to correspond, answer, comply with.

Entsprechend [ent-shpresh'ent] *a.* corresponding, appropriate.

Entsprechung [ent-shpresh'ŏŏng] *nf.* equivalent.

Entspriessen [ent-shpree'sen] *vi. ir.* to sprout (from), arise.

Entspringen [ent-shpring'en] *vi. ir.* to spring from, escape.

Entstammen [ent-shtam'en] *vi.* to be derived from, descend from.

Entstehen [ent-shtay'en] *vi. ir.* to arise, break out.

Entstehung [ent-shtay'ŏŏng] *nf.* origin, rise.

Entsteigen [ent-shty'gen] *vi. ir.* to emerge.

Entstellen [ent-shtel'en] *vt.* to disfigure, distort.

Entstellung [ent-shtel'ŏŏng] *nf.* distortion, disfigurement.

Entstören [ent-shter'ren] *vt.* to eliminate disturbance *(rad.)*.

Entstörung [ent-shter'röong] nf. elimination of disturbance (rad.).

Entströmen [ent-shtrer'men] ni. to stream from, pour from.

Entstürzen [ent-shtyoort'sen] vi. to burst from.

Entsühnen [ent-zyöo'nen] vt. to expiate, absolve.

Enttäuschen [ent-toy'shen] vt. to disappoint, to disillusion, undeceive.

Enttäuschung [ent-toy'-shöong] nf. disappointment, disillusionment.

Entthronen [ent-troh'nen] vt. to dethrone.

Entthronung [ent-troh'-nöong] nf. dethronement.

Entvölkern [ent-ferl'kerrn] vt. to depopulate.

Entvölkerung [ent-ferl'ker-röong] nf. depopulation.

Entwachsen [ent-vax'en] vt. ir. to outgrow.

Entwaffnen [ent-vaf'nen] vt. to disarm.

Entwaffnung [ent-vaf'nöong] nf. disarmament.

Entwalden [ent-val'den] vt. to deforest.

Entwaldung [ent-val'döong] nf. deforestation, clearing.

Entwarnung [ent-varr'-nöong] nf. all clear (signal).

Entwässern [ent-vess'errn] vt. to drain, distil, dehydrate.

Entwässerung [ent-vess'er-röong] nf. drainage, dehydration. [either.

Entweder [ent-vade'err] cj.

Entweichen [ent-vi'shen] vi. ir. to escape, vanish, evade.

Entweichung [ent-vi'shöong] nf. escape, evasion, disappearance.

Entweihen [ent-vie'en] vt. to desecrate.

Entweihung [ent-vie'öong] nf. desecration.

Entwenden [ent-ven'den] vt. ir. to misappropriate, steal.

Entwendung [ent-ven'döong] nf. misappropriation, theft.

Entwerfen [ent-vairr'fen] vt. ir. to sketch, design, plan, draft.

Entwerfer [ent-vairr'ferr] nm. (–) inventor, projector, designer.

Entwerten [ent-vairr'ten] vt. to devalue, reduce in value, cancel (stamp).

Entwertung [ent-vairr'töong] nf. devaluation, depreciation, cancellation.

Entwesung [ent-vay'zöong] nf. disinfection.

Entwickeln [ent-vik'eln] vt.r. to unfold, develop, evolve, deploy (mil.).

Entwickler [ent-vik'lerr] nm. (–) developer.

Entwicklung [ent-vik'löong] nf. development, evolution, deployment (mil.); -sapparat nm. developer box; -sjahre n.pl. adolescence.

Entwinden [ent-vin'den] vt.r. ir. to wrest from.

Entwirren [ent-vir'ren] vt. to disentangle.

Entwischen [ent-vish'en] vi. to slip away, escape.

Entwöhnen [ent-ver'nen] vt. to wean. [nf. weaning

Entwöhnung [ent-ver'nöong]

Entwürdigen [ent-vyöor'di gen] vt. to degrade.

Entwürdigung [ent-vyöor'-di-göong] nf. degradation.

Entwurf [ent-vöorf'] nm (Entwürfe) sketch, draft, design, outline, project.

Entwurzeln [ent-vöort'seln] vt. to uproot, eradicate.

Entzerrer [ent-tser'rerr] nm. (–) equalizer, distortion corrector, rectifier (rad.).

Entzerrung [ent-tser'röong] nf. equalization, rectification (rad.).

Entziehen [ent-tsee'en] vt. ir. to take away, withdraw; r. shun.

Entziehung [ent-tsee'ŏŏng] nf. removal, withdrawal, deprivation.

Entzifferbar [ent-tsi'ferr-barr] a. decipherable.

Entzifferer [ent-tsi'fer-rerr] nm. (-) decoder, decipherer.

Entziffern [ent-tsi'ferrn] vt. to decode, decipher.

Entzifferung [ent-tsi'fer-rŏŏng] nf. decoding, deciphering; -sdienst nm. decoding service. [to delight.

Entzücken [ent-tsyŏŏk'en] vt.

Entzückung [ent-tsyŏŏk'-ŏŏng] nf. rapture, bliss.

Entzündbar [ent-tsyŏŏnt'-barr] a. inflammable.

Entzündbarkeit [ent-tsyŏŏnt'barr-kite] nf. inflammability.

Entzünden [ent-tsyŏŏn'den] vt. to inflame; r. become inflamed, catch fire.

Entzündlich [ent-tsyŏŏnt'-lish] a. inflammatory.

Entzündung [ent-tsŏŏn'-dŏŏng] nf. inflammation.

Entzwei [ent-tsvie'] ad. asunder, in two; -brechen vt. ir. to break in two.

Entzweien [ent-tsvie'en] vt. to alienate, estrange.

Entzweiung [ent-tsvie'ŏŏng] nf. discord, dissension.

Enzian [ent-syahn'] nm. (-e) gentian.

Epidemie [ay-pi-day-mee'] nf. epidemic.

Epidemisch [ay-pi-day'mish] a. epidemic.

Epigone [ay-pi-gone'e] m.w. decadent.

Epik [ay'pik] nf. epic poetry.

Epiker [ay'pi-kerr] nm. (-) epic poet.

Episode [ay-pi-zode'er] nf. episode.

Epos [ay'poss] n. (Epen) epic.

Eppich [ep'ish] nm. celery.

Er [airr] pn. he.

Erachten [er-rach'ten] vt. to think; n. opinion; meines -s in my opinion.

Erbarmen [er-barr'men] vr. to have pity on; n. pity; -enswert a. pitiable.

Erbärmlich [er-bairm'lish] a. pitiable, wretched.

Erbärmlichkeit [er-bairm'-lish-kite] nf. wretchedness, pitiableness.

Erbarmungs-los a. pitiless, merciless; -voll a. compassionate.

Erbauen [er-bow'en] vt. to erect, build, edify.

Erbauer [er-bow'err] nm. (-) builder. [edifying.

Erbaulich [er-bow'lish] a.

Erbauung [er-bow'ŏŏng] nf. construction, edification.

Erbe [airr'ber] m.w. heir; n. inheritance.

Erbeben [er-babe'en] vi. to tremble.

Erben [airr'ben] vt. to inherit.

Erbeuten [er-boy'ten] vt. to carry off, capture, seize.

Erbfall [airrp'fal] nm. succession (law).

Erbfehler [airrp'fale-err] nm. (-) hereditary defect.

Erbfeind [airrp'fint] nm. (-e) hereditary enemy.

Erbfolge [airrp'fol-ger] nf. hereditary succession.

Erbgut [airrp'gŏŏt] n. (-güter) ancestral estate.

Erbieten [er-beet'en] vr. ir. to volunteer, offer.

Erbin [airr'bin] nf. heiress.

Erbitten [er-bit'en] vt. ir. to ask, entreat, request.

Erbittern [er-bit'errn] vt. to embitter, irritate; r. grow embittered, irritated.

Erbitterung [er-bit'er-rŏŏng] nf. acrimony, exasperation.

Erblassen [er-blas'en] vi. to grow pale. [(-) testator.

Erblasser [airrp'lass-err] nm.

Erblasserin [airrp'lass-er-rin] nf. testatrix.

Erblich [airrp'lish] *a.* hereditary.

Erblicken [er-blik'en] *vt.* to
catch sight of.

Erblinden [er-blin'den] *vi.* to
grow blind.

Erblos [airrp'lohss] *a.* disin-
herited, without heir.

Erbosen [er-boh'zen] *vt.* to
anger; *r.* to grow angry.

Erbötig [er-ber'tish] *a.* willing.

Erbrechen [er-bresh'en] *vt. ir.*
to break (open); *r.* vomit.

Erbrecht [airrp'resht] *n.* right
of succession, hereditary right.

Erbschaft [airrp'shaft] *nf.* inheritance, legacy.

Erbse [airrp'ser] *nf.* pea;
-nsuppe *nf.* pea soup.

Erbstück [airrp'shtyōōk] *n.*
(-e) heirloom.

Erdabwehr [airrt'ap-vairr]
nf. anti-aircraft defences.

Erdarbeiter [airrt'arr-bite-
err] *nm.* (-) navvy.

Erdbeben [airrt'babe-en] *n.*
(-) earthquake.

Erdbeere [airrt'bair-rer] *nf.*
strawberry.

Erdboden [airrt'bode-en] *nm.*
ground, soil.

Erddraht [airrt'draht] *nm.*
(-drähte) ground wire (rad.).

Erde [airr'der] *nf.* earth; auf
-n on earth; zu ebener - on
the ground floor, in the base-
ment.

Erden [airr'den] *vt.* to earth
(el.).

Erdenkbar [er-denk'barr],
Erdenklich [er-denk'lish] *a.*
conceivable.

Erdenken [er-denk'en] *vt. ir.*
to conceive, think of.

Erdfunkstelle [airrt'fōōnk-
shte-ler] ground signal station
(rad.).   [*n.* ground floor.

Erdgeschoss [airrt'ger-shoss]

Erdichten [er-dish'ten] *vt.* to
fabricate, invent.

Erdichtung [er-dish'tōōng]
nf. fabrication.

Erdig [airr'dish] *a.* earthy.

Erdkabel [airrt'kah-bel] *n.*
buried cable.

Erdklemme [airrt'klem-er]
nf. ground terminal (el.).

Erdkreis [airrt'krice] *nm.*
earth, world.

Erdkunde [airrt'kŏŏn-der] *nf.*
geography.

Erdleiter [airrt'lite-err] *nm.*
(-), **Erdleitung** [airrt'lite-ōōng]
nf. earth (rad.), ground wire.

Erdoberfläche [airrt'obe-err-
flesh-er] *nf.* surface of the
earth.   [petroleum.

Erdöl [airrt'erl] *n.* mineral oil,

Erdreisten [er-dri'sten] *vr.* to
presume, dare.

Erdrinde [airrt'rin-der] *nf.*
earth's crust.

Erdrosseln [er-dross'eln] *vt.*
to throttle.

Erdrücken [er-dryōōk'en] *vt.*
to stifle crush.

Erdschluss [airrt'shlōōss] *nm.*
(-schlüsse) earth (connection),
accidentally grounded circuit
(el.).   [(-e) zone, region.

Erdstrich [airrt'shtrish] *nm.*

Erdstrom [airrt'shtrohm] *nm.*
natural current (el.).

Erdulden [er-dōōl'den] *vt.* to
endure, suffer.

Erdung [airr'dŏŏng] *nf.*
grounding (av.), ground, earth
(el.).

Erdverbindung [airrt'ferr-
bin-dōōng] *nf.* earth connection, ground.

Ereifern [er-ife'errn] *vr.* to get
excited.   [happen.

Ereignen [er-ig'nen] *vr.* to

Ereignis [er-ig'nis] *n.* (-se)
event, occurrence.

Ereilen [er-ile'en] *vt.* to overtake.

Erfahren [er-fah'ren] *vt. ir.* to
experience, learn; *a.* experienced.

Erfahrung [er-fah'rŏŏng] *nf.*
experience; -sgemäss *ad.* according to experience.

Erfassen [er-fass'en] *vt.* to grasp, seize, include, register (*mil.*).

Erfassung [er-fass'ōong] *nf.* understanding, inclusion, seizing, registration (*mil.*).

Erfinden [er-fin'den] *vt. ir.* to find out, invent. [inventor.

Erfinder [er-fin'derr] *nm.* (-)

Erfinderisch [er-fin'der-rish] *a.* inventive.

Erfindung [er-fin'dōong] *nf.* invention, -sgabe *nf.* inventive faculty.

Erfolg [er-folk'] *nm.* (-e) success, result; -los *a.* unsuccessful; -reich *a.* successful. [result, ensue.

Erfolgen [er-fol'gen] *vi.* to

Erforderlich [er-for'der-lish] *a.* requisite, necessary.

Erfordern [er-for'dern] *vt.* to require, demand.

Erfordernis [er-for'der-niss] *n.* (-se) requisite, exigency.

Erforschen [er-for'shen] *vt.* to investigate.

Erforscher [er-for'sher] *nm.* (-) investigator.

Erforschung [er-for'shōong] *nf.* investigation.

Ertragen [er-trah'gen] *vt.* to ascertain, learn (by asking).

Erfreuen [er-froy'en] *vr.* to enjoy, rejoice; *t.* delight.

Erfreulich [er-froy'lish] *a.* delightful, gratifying.

Erfrieren [er-free'ren] *vi. ir.* to freeze (to death).

Erfrischen [er-frish'en] *vt.* to refresh.

Erfrischung [er-frish'ōong] *nf.* refreshment.

Erfüllen [er-fyōō'len] *vt.* to fulfil, realize.

Erfüllung [er-fyōō'lōong] *nf.* fulfilment, realization.

Erg [airrk] *n.* (-) erg.

Ergänzen [er-gent'sen] *vt.* to complete, supplement.

Ergänzung [er-gent'sōong] *nf.* completion, supplement;

-sfarben *f.pl.* complementary colours; -sheft *n.* supplement; -wahl *nf.* bye-election.

Ergattern [er-gat'errn] *vt.* to pick up.

Ergeben [er-gabe'en] *vt. ir.* to show, yield; *r.* surrender, submit, abandon, result.

Ergeben [er-gabe'en] *a.* devoted, submissive, addicted.

Ergebenheit [er-gabe'en-hite] *nf.* devotion, submissiveness, addictedness.

Ergebnis [er-gabe'niss] *n.* (-se) result; -los *a.* without result.

Ergebung [er-gabe'ōong] *nf.* capitulation, resignation.

Ergehen [er-gay'en] *vr. ir.* to indulge in, take a walk; *i. imp.* get on, to fare.

Ergiebig [er-gee'bish] *a.* productive.

Ergiebigkeit [er-gee'bish-kite] *nf.* productiveness.

Ergiessen [er-gee'sen] *vt. ir.* to pour forth; *r.* overflow, pour out.

Erglühen [erglyōō'en] *vi.* to (begin to) glow, become incandescent, be enthusiastic about.

Ergötzen [er-gert'sen] *vt.r.* to delight, amuse.

Ergötzlich [er-gerts'lish] *a.* delightful, amusing.

Ergrauen [er-grow'en] *vi.* to turn grey.

Ergreifen [er-grife'en] *vt.. ir.* to seize, apprehend, enter on.

Ergreifend [er-grife'ent] *a.* affecting, moving. [angry.

Ergrimmt [er-grimt'] *a.*

Ergrünen [er-gryōō'nen] *vi.* to grow green.

Erguss [er-gōss'] *nm.* (Ergüsse) effusion, discharge.

Erhaben [er-hah'ben] *a.* exalted, lofty, sublime; -e Arbeit relief.

Erhabenheit [er-hah'ben-hite] *nf.* loftiness, sublimity.

Erhalten [er-hal'ten] vt. ir. to receive, preserve, maintain; gut - in good condition.

Erhalter [er-hal'terr] nm. (-) preserver.

Erhaltung [er-hal'tŏong] nf. receiving, preservation, maintenance. [hang.

Erhängen [er-heng'en] vt. to

Erhärten [er-herr'ten] vt. to harden, confirm, affirm.

Erheben [er-habe'en] vt. ir. to raise (up), collect; r. rise (up), arise.

Erheblich [er-habe'lish] a. considerable, weighty.

Erheblichkeit [er-habe'lish-kite] nf. importance, consequence, relevance (law).

Erhebung [er-habe'ŏong] nf. elevation, collection, rebellion, rising ground.

Erheischen [er-hi'shen] vt. to demand, require.

Erheitern [er-hite'errn] vt.r. to cheer (up), brighten up.

Erhellen [er-hel'en] vt. to light; i. be apparent.

Erheucheln [er-hoy'sheln] vt. to sham.

Erhitzen [er-hits'en] vt. to heat; r. grow heated.

Erhoffen [er-hof'en] vt. to hope for.

Erhöhen [er-her'en] vt. to heighten, raise, enhance.

Erhöhung [er-her'ŏong] nf. raising, rise.

Erholen [er-hole'en] vr. to recover, rest, amuse oneself, recuperate.

Erholung [er-hole'ŏong] nf. recovery, recreation, recuperation, rest; -sheim n. convalescent home. [grant, hear.

Erhören [er-her'ren] vt. to

Erika [ay-ri'kah] nf. heather.

Erinnern [er-in'errn] vt. to remind; r. remember, recollect.

Erinnerung [er-in'er-rŏong] nf. reminiscence, recollection, memory.

Erjagen [er-jah'gen] vt. to catch, gain. [grow cold.

Erkalten [er-kal'ten] vi. to cool; r. to catch cold.

Erkälten [er-kel'ten] vt. to cool; r. to catch cold.

Erkältung [er-kel'tŏong] nf. cold.

Erkämpfen [er-kemp'fen] vt. to win by fighting, conquer.

Erkennbar [er-ken'barr] a. recognizable, perceivable.

Erkennen [er-ken'en] vt. ir. to know, recognize credit (com.).

Erkenntlich [er-kent'lish] a. grateful.

Erkenntlichkeit [er-kent'lish-kite] nf. gratitude, gratuity.

Erkenntnis [er-kent'niss] nf. knowledge, discernment; n. (-se) judgment.

Erkennung [er-ken'ŏong] nf. recognition; -smarke nf. identity disc; -ssignal n. recognition signal (av.); -swort n. password; -szeichen n. markings pl. (av.).

Erker [airr'kerr] nm. (-) a bay-window, alcove; -fenster n. bay-window.

Erklärbar [er-klairr'barr] a. explicable.

Erklären [er-klairr'ren] vt. to explain, declare.

Erklärung [er-klairr'rŏong] nf. explanation, declaration.

Erklecklich [er-klek'lish] a. considerable, adequate.

Erklettern [er-klet'errn], **Erklimmen** [er-klim'en] vt. to climb up scale.

Erklingen [er-kling'en] vi. ir. to resound, ring.

Erklügeln [er-klyŏo'geln] vt. to puzzle out.

Erkranken [er-krank'en] vi. to fall ill.

Erkrankung [er-krank'ŏong] nf. falling ill, illness.

Erkühnen [er-kyŏo'nen] r. to dare, make bold to.

Erkunden [er-kŏon'den] vt. to

ascertain, scout, reconnoitre (*mil.*).

Erkundigen [er-kŏŏn'di-gen] *vr.* to enquire.

Erkundigung [er-kŏŏn'di-gŏŏng] *nf.* enquiry, information.

Erkundung [er-kŏŏn'dŏŏng] *nf.* scouting, exploring, (topographical) reconnaissance (*mil.*); -sflugzeug *n.* reconnaissance plane.

Erkünsteln [er-kyŏŏn'steln] *vt.* to affect.

Erlahmen [er-lah'men] *vi.* to go lame, tire, lose interest, flag.

Erlangen [er-lang'en] *vt.* to attain, obtain.

Erlass [er-lass'] *nm.* (-e) order decree, dispensation, pardon, allowance.

Erlassen [er-lass'en] *vt. ir.* to issue, remit, pardon, dispense from.

Erlassung [er-lass'ŏŏng] *nf.* issue, remission.

Erlauben [er-low'ben] *vt.* to permit; *r.* to take the liberty, venture.

Erlaubnis [er-lowp'niss] *nf.* permission; -schein *nm.* pass, permit.

Erläutern [er-loy'terrn] *vt.* to explain.

Erläuterung [er-loy'ter-rŏŏng] *nf.* explanation, commentary.

Erle [airr'ler] *nf.* alder.

Erleben [er-lade'en] *vt.* to live to see, live through, experience.

Erlebnis [er-labe'niss] *n.* (-se) experience, adventure.

Erledigen [er-lade'i-gen] *vt.* to finish, settle, deal with.

Erledigung [er-lade'i-gŏŏng] *nf.* execution, settlement.

Erlegen [er-lay'gen] *vt.* to kill.

Erleichtern [er-lish'terrn] *vt.* to lighten, relieve.

Erleichterung [er-lish'ter-rŏŏng] *nf.* alleviation, relief, facilities.

Erleiden [er-lide'en] *vt. ir.* to suffer, endure.

Erlernen [er-lairr'nen] *vt. ir.* to learn, acquire.

Erlesen [er-laze'en] *vt. ir.* to select; *a.* choice.

Erleuchten [er-loysh'ten] *vt.* to illuminate, enlighten.

Erleuchtung [er-loysh'tŏŏng] *nf.* illumination, enlightenment.

Erliegen [er-lee'gen] *vi. ir.* to succumb, be conquered.

Erlisten [er-list'en] *vt.* to gain by trickery.

Erlogen [er-loh'gen] *a.* false, ficticious.

Erlös [er-lerss'] *n.* proceeds.

Erlöschen [er-ler'shen] *vi.* to go out, expire.

Erlösen [er-ler'zen] *vt.* to redeem, save. [saviour.

Erlöser [er-ler'zerr] *nm.* (-) salvation, deliverance.

Erlösung [er-ler'zŏŏng] *nf.* salvation, deliverance.

Erlügen [er-lyŏŏ'gen] *vt. ir.* to fabricate.

Ermächtigen [er-mesh'ti-gen] *vt.* to empower, authorize.

Ermächtigung [er-mesh'ti-gŏŏng] *nf.* authorization.

Ermahnen [er-mah'nen] *vt.* to admonish, exhort.

Ermahnung [er-mah'nŏŏng] *nf.* admonition.

Ermangeln [er-mang'eln] *vi.* to be in want of, lack, fail to do.

Ermangelung [er-mang'er-lŏŏng] *nf.* default, lack.

Ermannen [er-man'en] *vr.* to pull oneself together, buck up.

Ermässigen [er-may'si-gen] *vt.* to reduce, moderate.

Ermässigung [er-may'si-gŏŏng] *nf.* reduction, moderation.

Ermatten [er-mat'en] *vt.* to fatigue. [fatigue.

Ermattung [er-mat'ŏŏng] *nf.*

Ermessen [er-mess'en] *vt. ir.* to estimate, judge; *n.* estimation.

Ermitteln [er-mit'eln] vt. to ascertain.

Ermittlung [er-mit'lōong] nf. investigation, finding out.

Ermöglichen [er-mer'glishen] vt. to make possible, enable, manage.

Ermorden [er-morr'den] vt. to murder.   [nf. murder.

Ermordung [er-morr'dōong]

Ermüden [er-myōo'den] vt. to tire (out); i. get tired.

Ermüdend [er-myōo'dent] a. wearisome.

Ermüdung [er-myōo'dōong] nf. fatigue.

Ermuntern [er-mōon'ternn] vt. to rouse, encourage, cheer up.

Ermunterung [er-mōon'terrōong] nf. rousing, encouragement.

Ermutigen [er-mōo'ti-gen] vt. to encourage.

Ermutigung [er-mōo'tigōong] nf. encouragement.

Ernähren [er-nare'en] vt. to nourish, support, feed; r. support oneself, find a living.

Ernährer [er-nare'err] nm. (-) bread-winner.

Ernährung [er-nare'ōong] nf. nourishment, nutrition, feeding, maintenance; -samt n. food office; -skrise nf. food shortage; -slage nf. food situation.

Ernennen [er-nen'en] vt. ir. to appoint, nominate, designate.

Ernennung [er-nen'ōong] nf. appointment, nomination, designation.

Erneuern [er-noy'errn] vt. to renew, restore.

Erneuerung [er-noy'er-rōong] nf. renewal, revival, renovation.

Erniedrigen [er-need'ri-gen] vt. to humiliate, degrade.

Erniedrigung [er-need'rigōong] nf. humiliation, degradation.

Ernst [errnst] nm. earnestness, severity; a. earnest, serious; -fall nm. emergency, case of need.

Ernsthaft [errnst'haft] a. serious, grave.

Ernsthaftigkeit [errnst'haftish-kite] nf. seriousness, gravity.   [serious.

Ernstlich [errnst'lish] a.

Ernte [errn'ter] nf. harvest.

Ernten [errn'ten] vt. to reap, gather in.

Erntezeit [errn'ter-tsite] nf. harvest time.

Ernüchtern [er-nyōosh'ternn] vt. to sober, disenchant, disillusion.

Ernüchterung [er-nyōosh'terōong] nf. disillusionment, sobering down.

Eroberer [er-obe'er-rerr] nm. (-) conqueror.

Erobern [er-obe'errn] vt. to conquer.

Eroberung [er-obe'er-rōong] nf. conquest.

Eröffnen [er-erf'nen] vt.r. to open, found, start.

Eröffnung [er-erf'nōong] nf. opening.   [discuss.

Erörtern [er-err'ternn] vt. to

Erörterung [er-err'ter-rōong] nf. discussion.   [erotic.

Erotisch [ay-rote'ish] a.

Erpicht [er-pisht] a. eager, desirous.

Erpressen [er-press'en] vt. to extort, press out.

Erpresser [er-press'err] nm. (-) blackmailer.

Erpressung [er-press'ōong] nf. blackmail, extortion, ramp; -sversuch nm. (attempted) blackmail.

Erproben [er-probe'en] vt. to test, try, prove.

Erprobung [er-probe'ōong] nf. testing, trying; -stelle nf. experimental station.

Erquicken [er-kvik'en] vt. to revive, refresh.

Erquickung [er-kvik'ŏŏng] nf. refreshment, solace.

Erraten [er-rah'ten] vt. ir. to guess. [excitable.

Erregbar [er-raik'barr] a.

Erregbarkeit [er-raik'barr-kite] nf. excitability.

Erregen [er-raig'en] vt. to excite, provoke.

Erreger [er-raig'err] nm. (-) agent; -strom nm. exciting, induction current (el.).

Erregtheit [er-raikt'hite] nf. agitation, excitability.

Erregung [er-raig'ŏŏng] nf. excitement, provocation.

Erreichbar [er-rish'barr] a. attainable.

Erreichen [er-rish'en] vt. to reach, attain, obtain.

Erreichung [er-rish'ŏŏng] nf. attainment.

Erretten [er-ret'ten] vt. to save, rescue.

Erretter [er-ret'err] nm. (-) saviour, rescuer.

Errettung [er-ret'ŏŏng] nf. deliverance, rescue.

Errichten [er-rish'ten] vt. to set up, establish, erect.

Errichtung [er-rish'tŏŏng] nf. erection, establishment.

Erringen [er-ring'en] vt. ir. to achieve, gain by effort.

Erröten [er-rert'en] vt. to blush.

Errungenschaft [er-rŏŏng'-en-shaft] nf. achievement.

Ersatz [er-zats'] nm. substitute, compensation, amends, drafts, reinforcement (mil.); -bataillon n. drafting battalion; -blei n. refill for propelling pencil; -einheit nf. depot unit (mil.); -füllung nf. refill; -mannschaft nf. replacements, drafts (mil.); -mittel n. substitute, make-shift; -pflichtige(r) nm. person liable for damages; -reifen nm. spare tyre (aut.); -teil nm. spare (part); -wahl nf. election of a substitute, bye-election;

-wert nm. replacement value; -wesen n. recruiting, drafting (mil.).

Ersaufen [er-zow'fen] vi. ir. to be drowned, be drowning.

Ersäufen [er-zoy'fen] vt. to drown. [to create.

Erschaffen [er-shaf'en] vt. ir.

Erschaffer [er-shaf'err] nm. (-) creator.

Erschaffung [er-shaf'ŏŏng] nf. creation.

Erschallen [er-shal'en] vi. ir. to resound.

Erscheinen [er-shine'en] vi. ir. to appear.

Erscheinung [er-shine'ŏŏng] nf. appearance, apparition, phenomenon.

Erschiessen [er-shee'sen] vt. ir. to shoot.

Erschlaffen [er-shlaf'en] vi. to relax, slacken.

Erschlaffung [er-shlaf'ŏŏng] nf. laxness, slacking.

Erschlagen [er-shlah'gen] vt. ir. to strike dead.

Erschleichen [er-shlish'en] vt. to obtain by stealth, fraud.

Erschliessen [er-shlee'sen] vt. ir. to unlock, conclude, infer, open up.

Erschnappen [er-shnap'en] vt. to snap up.

Erschöpfen [er-sherp'fen] vt. to exhaust.

Erschöpfend [er-sherp'fent] a. exhaustive, thorough.

Erschöpftheit [er-sherpft'-hite] nf. state of exhaustion.

Erschöpfung [er-sherp'fŏŏng] nf. exhaustion.

Erschrecken [er-shrek'en] vt. to frighten; i. ir. to be frightened.

Erschrocken [er-shrok'en] a. startled, frightened.

Erschüttern [er-shyŏŏt'errn] vt. to move deeply, agitate, move, shake.

Erschütterung [er-shyŏŏt'er-rŏŏng] nf. agitation, shock;

-dämpfung *nf.* shock absorption *(tec.)*.

Erschweren [er-shvair'ren] *vt.* to make heavier, aggravate.

Erschwingen [er-shving'en] *vt.* to afford.

Erschwinglich [er-shving'lish] *a.* what one can afford.

Ersehen [er-zay'en] *vt. ir.* to perceive, gather.

Ersehnen [er-zane'en] *vt.* to long for.

Ersetzen [er-zet'sen] *vt.* to replace, compensate, restore.

Ersetzung [er-zet'sŏong] *nf.* replacement, compensation.

Ersichtlich [er-zisht'lish] *a.* evident.

Ersinnen [er-zin'en] *vt. ir.* to devise. [save.

Ersparen [er-shpah'ren] *vt.* to

Ersparnis [er-shpahr'nis] *n.* (-se) savings, economies.

Erspriesslich [er-shprees'-lish] *a.* profitable, salutary.

Erspriesslichkeit [er-shpress'lish-kite] *nf.* profitableness, salutariness.

Erst [airrst] *a.* first; *ad.* (at) first, only, not till.

Erstarken [er-shtahr'ken] *vi.* to grow strong(er).

Erstarren [er-shtar'ren] *vi.* to stiffen, grow rigid, solidify.

Erstarrung [er-shtar'rŏong] *nf.* stiffness, numbness.

Erstatten [er-shtat'en] *vt.* to render, restore, replace.

Erstaufführung [airrst'owf-fyŏŏr-rŏong] *nf.* first performance, first night.

Erstaunen [er-shtow'nen] *vt.i.* to astonish, be astonished; *n.* astonishment.

Erstaunlich [er-shtown'lish] *a.* astonishing.

Erstausfertigung [airrst'ows-fairr-ti-gŏong] *nf.* original copy. [*ir.* to stab.

Erstechen [er-shtech'en] *vt.*

Erstehen [er-shtay'en] *vt. ir.* to buy.

Erstehung [er-shtay'ŏong] *nf.* purchase.

Ersteigbar [er-shtik'barr] *a* accessible.

Ersteigen [er-shtī'gen] *vt. ir.* to climb, ascent.

Erstens [airr'stens] *ad.* firstly, in the first place.

Ersterben [er-shtairr'ben] *vi. ir.* to die out.

Ersticken [er-shtik'en] *vt.* to stifle, suffocate.

Erstickung [er-shtik'ŏong] *nf.* suffocation, stifling.

Erstmalig [airrst'mah'lish] *a.* for the first time.

Erstreben [er-shtray'ben] *vt.* to strive for, endeavour.

Erstrecken [er-shtrek'en] *vr.* to extend, stretch.

Erstürmen [er-shtyŏŏr'men] *vt.* to take by storm.

Ersuchen [er-zŏŏ'chen] *vt.* to request.

Ersuchung [er-zŏŏ'chŏong] *nf.* request.

Ertappen [er-tap'en] *vt.* to catch, detect.

Erteilen [er-tile'en] *vt.* to give, bestow, grant.

Ertönen [er-ter'nen] *vi.* to resound, sound.

Ertrag [er-trahk'] *nm.* (Erträge) proceeds, profit, yield.

Ertragen [er-trah'gen] *vt. ir.* to bear, bring forth, suffer.

Erträglich [er-traik'lish] *a.* tolerable, bearable.

Ertränken [er-trenk'en] *vt.* to drown.

Erträumen [er-troy'men] *vt.* to imagine, dream of.

Ertrinken [er-trink'en] *vi.* to be drowned.

Ertrotzen [er-trots'en] *vt.* to extort.

Erübrigen [er-yŏŏb'ri-gen] *vt.* to save, spare; *r.* be unnecessary. [awake.

Erwachen [er-vach'en] *vi.* to

Erwachsen [er-vach'sen] *vi. ir.* to grow (up); der, die -e adult.

Erwägen [er-vay'gen] vt. ir. to weigh, consider.

Erwägung [er-vay'göong] nf. consideration.

Erwählen [er-vale'en] vt. to choose, elect.

Erwähnen [er-vane'en] vt. to mention.

Erwähnung [er-vane'öong] nf. mention.

Erwarmen [er-varr'men] vi. to get warm.

Erwärmen [er-vairr'men] vt. to warm, heat.

Erwärmung [er-vairr'möong] nf. warming.

Erwarten [er-varr'ten] vt. to expect, await.

Erwartung [er-varr'töong] nf. expectation.

Erwecken [er-vek'en] vt. to rouse, awake, excite.

Erweckung [er-vek'öong] nf. awakening, revival.

Erwehren [er-vair'ren] vr. to defend oneself, refrain from, forbear.

Erweichen [er-vi'shen] vt. to soften. [proof.

Erweis [er-vice'] nm. (-e)

Erweisen [er-vize'en] vt. ir. to prove, pay, do; r. prove to be.

Erweislich [er-vice'lish] a. demonstrable, provable.

Erweitern [er-vite'errn] vt. to enlarge, dilate, extend.

Erweiterung [er-vite'er-röong] nf. enlargement, dilation, extension.

Erwerb [er-vairrp'] nm. acquisition, profit, trade, industry earnings, livelihood; -slos a. unemployed; -stätig a. (gainfully) employed; -sunfähig a. unemployable.

Erwerben [er-vairr'ben] vt. ir. to acquire, earn.

Erwidern [er-vee'derrn] vt. to reply, retort, return.

Erwiderung [er-vee'der-röong] nf. reply, return.

Erwirken [er-virr'ken] vt. to procure.

Erwischen [er-vish'en] vt. to catch, get hold of. [desired.

Erwünscht [er-vyöonsht'] a.

Erwürgen [er-vyöor'gen] vt. to strangle.

Erz [airrts] n. (-e) ore; -bild n. bronze statue; -gang nm. lode; -probe nf. assay (tec.).

Erzählen [ert-sale'en] vt. to tell, narrate.

Erzähler [ert-sale'err] nm. (-) narrator, story-teller, novelist.

Erzählung [ert-sale'öong] nf. tale, story.

Erzbischof [airrts'bi-shohf] nm. (-bischöfe) archbishop.

Erzdumm airrts'döom] a. very stupid. [show.

Erzeigen [ert-si'gen] vt. to

Erzeugen [ert-soy'gen] vt. to procreate, produce, breed, generate.

Erzeugnis [ert-soyk'nis] n. (-se) product, produce.

Erzeugung [ert-soy'göong] nf. procreation, production, generation.

Erziehbar [ert-see'barr] a. teachable.

Erziehen [ert-see'en] vt. ir. to bring up, teach, train.

Erziehung [ert-see'öong] nf. bringing up, tuition, training, education; -sheim n. school.

Erzielen [ert-see'len] vt. to achieve, aim at, obtain.

Erzürnen [ert-syöor'nen] vt. to make angry, enrage; r. get angry.

Erzwingen [ert-sving'en] vt. ir. to force, obtain by force.

Es [ess] pn. it.

Esche [esh'er] nf. ash.

Esel [ay'zel] nm. (-) ass, donkey.

Espe [es'per] nf. aspen-tree.

Essbar [es'barr] a. eatable, edible.

Ess-apfel nm. eating apple; -besteck n. spoon, knife and fork; -geschirr *n.* mess-tin; -karte *nf.* coupon for meal; -löffel *nm.* table-spoon; -zimmer *n.* dining-room.

Esse [es'er] *nf.* funnel, chimney, forge.

Essen [es'en] *vt.i. ir.* to eat; *n.* meal, food.

Essenz [es-ents'] *nf.* essence.

Esser [es'err] *nm.* (-) eater.

Essig [es'ish] *nm.* (-e) vinegar; -gurke *nf.* pickled cucumber; -sauer *a.* acetic; -saures Salz acetate.

Ester [es'terr] *nm.* (-) ester.

Estrade [es-trah'der] *nf.* dais, platform.

Estrich [es'trish] *nm.* (-e) unboarded, plaster floor.

Etage [ay-tah'zher] *nf.* floor, storey; -nwohnung *nf.* flat.

Etappe [ay-ta'per] *nf.* lines of communication, base.

Etat [ay-tat'] *n.* (-s) budget, establishment (*mil.*), list.

Etatisieren [ay-ta-ti-zeer'ren] *vt.* to fix (establishment).

Ethik [ay'tik] *nf.* ethics.

Ethisch [ay'tish] *a.* ethical.

Etikette [ay-ti-ket'er] *nf.* label, ticket, etiquette.

Etikettieren [ay-ti-ket-eer'ren] *vt.* to label, ticket.

Etliche [et'lish-er] *pl.* some.

Etui [ate-vee'] *n.* (-s) case, small box.

Etwa [et'vah] *ad.* about, perhaps.

Etwaig [et-vah'ish] *a.* possible.

Etwas [et'vas] *pn.* something, somewhat, anything; *ad.* a little, rather.

Etymologie [ay-ti-mo-lo-gee'] *nf.* etymology.

Euch [oish] *pn.* you, to you.

Euer [oy'err] *poss.* your, yours.

Eule [oi'ler] *nf.* owl.

Eurig [oi'rish] *poss.* yours.

Euter [oi'terr] *n.* (-) udder.

Evakuation [ay-va-kōō-at-syohn'] *nf.* evacuation.

Evakuieren [ay-va-kōō-eer'ren] *vt.* to evacuate.

Evangelium [ay-van-gale'yōōm] *n.* (Evangelien) gospel.

Eventuell [ay-ven-tōō-el'] *a.* possible; *ad.* possibly, perhaps.

Ewig [ay'vish] *a.* ad. eternally.

Ewigkeit [ay'vish-kite] *nf.* eternity.

Exakt [ex-akt'] *a.* exact.

Examen [ex-ah'men] *n.* (Examina) examination.

Examinator [ex-a-mi-nah'torr] *nm.* (-en) examiner.

Examinieren [ex-a-mi-neer'ren] *vt.* to examine.

Exekution [ex-ay-kōōt-syohn'] *nf.* distraint, execution (*law*).

Exempel [ex-em'pel] *n.* (-) example, sum.

Exemplar [ex-em-plarr'] *n.* (-e) copy, model.

Exemplarisch [ex-em-plah'rish] *a.* exemplary.

Exerzieren [ex-errt-see'ren] *vt.* to drill.

Exerzierplatz [ex-errt-seer'plats] *nm.* (-plätze) drillground.

Exil [ex-eel'] *n.* exile.

Existenz [ex-is-tents'] *nf.* existence, livelihood, living; -mindestmass *n.* living wage.

Existieren [ex-is-teer'ren] *vi.* to exist.

Exklusiv [ex-klōō-zeef'] *a.* exclusive.

Exotisch [ex-oh'tish] *a.* exotic.

Expedient [ex-pay-dyent'] *m.w.* sender, forwarding clerk.

Expedieren [ex-pay-deer'ren] *vt.* to dispatch.

Expedition [ex-pay-dit-syohn'] *nf.* forwarding, expedition (*mil.*), office (*newspaper*).

Experiment [ex-per-ri-ment'] *n.* (-e) experiment.

Experimentell [ex-per-ri-men-tel'] *a.* experimental.

Experimentieren [ex-per-ri-men-teer'ren] *vi.* to experiment.

Expertise [ex-perr-tee'zer] *nf.* expert report.

Explodieren [ex-ploh-deer'-ren] *vi.* to explode.

Explosion [ex-ploh-zyohn'] *nf.* explosion; **-smotor** *nm.* internal combustion engine.

Explosiv [ex-ploh-zeef'] *a.* explosive.

Exponent [ex-poh-nent'] *m.w.* co-efficient, exponent.

Exponieren [ex-poh-neer'ren] *vt.* to expose (*photo*).

Export [ex-porrt'] *nm.* (-e) export; **-handel** *nm.* export trade.

Exportieren [ex-porr-teer'ren] *vt.* to export. express.

Express [ex-press'] *a.* (by) express.

Extase [ex-tah'zer] *nf.* ecstasy.

Externat [ex-terr-naht'] *n.* (-e) day-school.

Exterritorial [ex-ter-ri-tor-ryahl'] *a.* ex-territorial.

Extra [ex'tra] *ad.* extra, besides, specially; **-blatt** *n.* special edition; **-stunden** *f.pl.* overtime. [extract.

Extrakt [ex-trakt'] *nm.* (-e)

Extrem [ex-trame'] *a.* extreme; *n.* (-e) extreme.

Exzenter [ex-tsen'terr] *nm.* (-) eccentric (*tec.*).

Exzentrisch [ex-tsen'trish] *a.* eccentric.

F

Fabel [fah'bel] *nf.* fable, plot.

Fabelhaft [fah'bel-haft] *a.* fabulous, marvellous.

Fabeln [fah'beln] *vi.* to tell stories, romance.

Fabrik [fab-reek'] *nf.* factory, **-anlage** *nf.* factory plant; **-arbeiter** *nm,* **-arbeiterin** *nf.* factory worker; **-waren** *f.pl.* manufactured goods; **-zeichen** *n.* trade-mark.

Fabrikant [fab-ri-kant'] *m.w.* manufacturer, industrialist.

Fabrikat [fab-ri-kaht'] *n.* (-e) manufacture.

Fabrikation [fab-ri-kat-syohn'] *nf.* manufacturing, production.

Fabrizieren [fab-rit-seer'ren] *vt.* to manufacture.

Fach [fach] *n.* Fächer compartment, department, line (*study, etc.*), subject, speciality; **-arbeiter** *nm.* skilled worker; **-arzt** *nm.* medical specialist; **-ausdruck** *nm.* technical term; **-berater** *nm.* technical adviser; **-bildung** *nf.* technical education; **-genosse** *m.w.* colleague; **-kraft** *nf. see* **-arbeiter**; **-kundig** *a.* expert, specialist; **-lehrer** *nm.* instructor; **-mann** *nm.* specialist; **-norm** *nf.* technical standard; **-schule** *nf.* college, technical school; **-simpeln** *vi.* to talk shop; **-studien** *n.pl.* technical, specialized studies; **-verständige(r)** *nm.* expert; **-vorgesetzte(r)** *nm.* senior specialist; **-werkbrücke** *nf.* truss bridge.

Fächeln [fesh'eln] *vt.* to fan.

Fächer [fesh'err] *nm.* (-) fan.

Fachlich [fach'lish] *a.* professional, expert.

Fackel [fakl] *nf.* torch; **-zug** *nm.* torchlight procession.

Fackeln [fak'eln] *vi.* to dally, hesitate. [dull.

Fade [fah'der] *a, ad.* insipid,

Fädeln [fade'eln] *vt.* to thread.

Faden [fah'den] *nm.* (Fäden) thread, cord, string; **-nudeln** *pl.* vermicelli; **-scheinig** *a.* threadbare.

Fadheit [faht'hite] *nf.* insipidity. [soon.

Fagott [fa-got'] *n.* (-e) bas-

Fähig [fay'ish] *a.* capable, qualified, able.

Fähigkeit [fay'ish-kite] *nf.* capacity.

Fahl [fahl] *a.* sallow, fawn coloured, pale. [pennon.

Fähnchen [fane'shen] *n.* (-)

Fahnden [fahn'den] vt. to search.

Fahndung [fahn'dŏŏng] nf. search (for criminals); -sliste nf. list of wanted criminals.

Fahne [fah'ner] nf. flag, vane, standard; -nabzug nm. galley proof; -neid nm. attestation, oath (mil.); -nflucht nf. desertion; -njunker nm. cadet; -nstange nf. flagstaff.

Fähnrich [fane'rish] nm. (-e) cadet sergeant, ensign, midshipman.

Fahrbar [farr'barr] a. practicable, navigable, transportable.

Fahr-abteilung nf. horse transport column; -bahn nf. roadway (bridge); -bereitschaft nf. readiness for duty; -bootwagen nm. ferryboat truck; -gast nm. passenger; -gestell n. chassis (aut.), under-carriage (av.); -gleis n. rut; -geld n. fare; -karte nf. ticket; -kartenausgabe nf. ticket-office; -lässig a. negligent; -lässigkeit nf. negligence; -plan nm. timetable; -planmässig a. scheduled (rl.); -preis nm. fare; -preisanzeiger nm. taximeter; -preiszone nf. fare stage; -rad n. cycle; -rinne nf. fairway; -schein nm. ticket; -strasse nf. carriage road; -wasser n. fairway; -zeug n. vehicle, vessel.

Fähre [fare'er] nf. ferry.

Fahren [fah'ren] vi.i. ir. to go, travel, drive, sail. [driver.

Fahrer [fah'rerr] nm. (-)

Fahrstuhl [farr'shtŏŏl] nm. (-stühle) lift; -führer nm. lift attendant.

Fahrt [farrt] nf. journey, course, drive, sail, voyage; -messer nm. air speed indicator (av.); -nachweis nm. workman's ticket.

Fährte [fare'ter] nf. track, scent, trail.

Faktisch [fak'tish] a. actual.

Faktor [fak'torr] nm. (gen. -s; pl. -en) factor, manager (com.).

Faktur(a) [fak-tŏŏ'rah] nf. invoice (com.).

Fakturieren [fak-tŏŏ-reer'-ren] vt. to invoice (com.).

Fakultät [fa-kŏŏl-tate'] nf. faculty.

Fakultativ [fa-kŏŏl-ta-teef'] a. optional.

Falb [falp] a. fawn coloured, light brown.

Falbel [fal'bel] nf. flounce.

Falke [fal'ker] nm.w. falcon.

Fall [fal] nm. (Fälle) fall, case; nötigen -s in case of necessity; auf jeden - in any case; bö nf. air pocket (av.); -grube nf. pitfall; -kurve nf. trajectory; -reep n. gangway; -sucht nf. epilepsy; -tür nf. trap-door.

Falle [fal'er] nf. trap, catch.

Fallen [fal'en] vi. ir. to fall.

Fällen [fel'en] vt. to fell, precipitate, pass (judgment).

Fällig [fel'ish] a. due.

Fälligkeit [fel'ish-kite] nf. maturity.

Falls [falss] ad. in case, if.

Fallschirm [fal'shirrm] nm. (-e) parachute; -jäger, -truppen pl. paratroops; -sattel nm. parachute harness; -schütze nm.w. parachute rifleman; -springer nm. parachute jumper. [precipitation.

Fällung [fel'ŏŏng] nf. felling.

Falsch [falsh] a. false; -es Spiel sharp practice; n. guile, cunning; -münzer nm. coiner.

Fälschen [fel'shen] vt. to falsify, forge, tamper with.

Fälscher [fel'sherr] nm. (-) falsifier, forger.

Falschheit [falsh'hite] nf. falsity, falseness. [falsely.

Fälschlich [felsh'lish] ad.

Fälschung [fel'shŏŏng] nf. falsification, forgery.

Fältchen [felt'shen] n. (-) crease, wrinkle.

Falte [fal'ter] *nf.* fold; -nlos *a.* without folds, unwrinkled.

Fälteln [fel'teln] *vt.* to fold, plait.

Falten [fal'ten] *vt.* to fold, wrinkle, crease.

Falz [falts] *n.* (-e) groove, fold, notch, rabbet.

Falzen [falt'sen] *vt.* to groove, fold, rabbet.

Falzig [falt'sish] *a.* grooved.

Familiär [fa-mi-li-ar'] *a.* familiar.

Familiarität [fa-mi-li-a-ri-tate'] *nf.* familiarity.

Familie [fa-meel'yer] *nf.* family; -ähnlichkeit *nf.* family resemblance; -nbad *n.* mixed bathing; -nkreis *nm.* family circle; -nname *nm.* surname; -nunterhalt *nm,* -nzulage *nf.* family allowance.

Famos [fa-mohss'] *a.* splendid, first-rate.

Fanatiker [fa-nah'ti-kerr] *nm.* (-) fanatic.

Fanatisch [fa-nah'tish] *a.* fanatical.

Fanatismus [fa-na-tiss'mōōss] *nm.* fanaticism.

Fanfare [fan-fah'rer] *nf.* fanfare (*of trumpets*).

Fang [fang] *nm.* (Fänge) fang, catch, snare, claw; -leine *nf.* painter (*boat*).

Fangen [fang'en] *vt. ir.* to catch, capture; *i.* take hold.

Fant [fant] *nm.* (*gen.* -s; *pl.* -en) conceited youth, young ass.

Farbe [farr'ber] *nf.* colour, dye, suit (*cards*); echte – fast colour.

Farb-band *n.* typewriter ribbon; -film *nm.* technicolour film; -stoff *nm.* dye. [dye.

Färben [fare'ben] *vt.* to colour, dye.

Farben-brett *n.* palette; -druck *nm.* colour print; -reich *a.* colourful; -stift *nm.* crayon; -ton *nm.* tinge, tone.

Färber [fare'berr] *nm.* (-) dyer. [works.

Färberei [fare-ber-ry'] *nf.* dye-

Farbig [farr'bish] *a.* coloured, stained. [less.

Farblos [farrp'lohss] *a.* colour-

Färbung [fare'bōōng] *nf.* colouring, shade.

Farce [farr'ser] *nf.* stuffing, force-meat, farce.

Farcieren [farr-see'ren] *vt.* to stuff (*cooking*).

Farn [farrn] *nm.* (-e) fern, bracken; -kraut *n. see* Farn.

Fasan [fa-zahn'] *nm.* (-e) pheasant; -enhund *nm.* setter.

Fasching [fash'ing] *nm.* carnival.

Faschismus [fa-shis'mōōss] *nm.* fascism. [fascist.

Faschist [fa-shist'] *nm. m.w.*

Fase [fah'zer] *nf.* fine thread.

Faseln [fah'zeln] *vi.* to talk nonsense, drivel.

Faser [fah'zerr] *nf.* fibre.

Faserig [fah'zer-rish] *a.* fibrous. [ravel.

Fasern [fah'zerrn] *vt.* to un-

Fass [fass] *n.* (Fässer) vat, barrel, drum (*oil*), container (*butter*); Bier vom – draught beer; -band *n.* hoop; -binder *nm.* cooper.

Fässchen [fess'shen] *n.* (-) small barrel, cask.

Fassen [fass'en] *vt.* to hold, grasp, take; *r.* collect oneself, pull oneself together; *i.* catch.

Fasslich [fass'lish] *a.* intelligible.

Fassung [fass'ōōng] *nf.* comprehension, mounting, composure, coolness.

Fast [fast] *ad.* almost.

Fasten [fas'ten] *vi.* to fast; *n.* fasting; -zeit *nf.* Lent.

Fastnacht [fast'nacht] *nf.* Shrove Tuesday, carnival.

Fatal [fa-tahl'] *a.* fatal, disagreeable, awkward.

Fatalismus [fa-ta-lis'mōōss] *nm.* fatalism.

Fatalist [fa-ta-list'] *m.w.* fatalist.

Faul [fowl] *a.* rotten.

Faulen [fow'len] *vi.* to rot.
Faulenzen [fow'lent-sen] *vi.* to idle.
Faulenzer [fow'lent-serr] *nm.* (-) loafer. [ness.
Faulheit [fowl'hite] *nf.* lazi-
Faulig [fow'lish] *a.* putrid.
Fäulnis [foil'nis] *nf.* decay, putrefaction.
Faust [fowst] *nf.* (Fäuste) fist.
Februar [fay'broo-ahrr] *nm.* February.
Fechten [fesh'ten] *vi. ir.* to fight, fence.
Fechter [fesh'terr] *nm.* (-) fencer, fighter.
Feder [fay'derr] *nf.* feather, pen-nib, spring; **-ball** *nm.* shuttlecock; **-ballspiel** *n.* badminton; **-bett** *n.* featherbed, eiderdown; **-halter** *nm.* pen-holder, pen; **-hof** *nm.* poultry yard; **-kraft** *nf.* elasticity; **-leicht** *a.* light as a feather; **-messer** *n.* pen-knife; **-strich** *nm.* stroke of the pen; **-vieh** *n.* poultry; **-waage** *nf.* spring-balance; **-zeichnung** *nf.* pen and ink drawing.
Federig [fay'der-rish] *a.* feathery.
Federlos [fay'derr-lohss] *a.* unfledged, featherless.
Federn [fay'derrn] *vi.* to moult.
Federung [fay'der-rōōng] *nf.* spring suspension.
Fee [fay] *nf.* fairy.
Feenhaft [fay'en-haft] *a.* fairylike.
Fegefeuer [fay'ger-foi-err] *n.* purgatory. [scour.
Fegen [fay'gen] *vt.* to sweep,
Fegsel [fague'sel] *n.* sweepings.
Fehde [fade'er] *nf.* feud.
Fehl [fail] *nm.* fault.
Fehlbar [fale'barr] *a.* fallible.
Fehlbarkeit [fale'barr-kite] *nf.* fallibility.
Fehl-anzeige *nf.* nil return; **-bestand** *nm.* missing stock; **-betrag** *nm.* deficit; **-bitte** *nf.*

vain request; **-druck** *nm.* misprint; **-gebären** *vi.* to miscarry; **-geburt** *nf.* miscarriage; **-gehen** *vi.* to go astray; **-greifen** *vi. ir.* to blunder; **-griff** *nm.* blunder; **-jahr** *n.* year of bad harvest; **-kauf** *nm.* bad bargain; **-schiessen** *vi. ir.* to miss one's aim; **-schlagen** *vi. ir.* to miss the mark; **-schliessen** *vi. ir.* to draw a wrong conclusion; **-schluss** *nm.* wrong conclusion; **-teil** *nm.* missing part; **-treten** *vi. ir.* to stumble, trip; **-tritt** *nm.* false move; **-zünden** *vi.* to misfire (*aut.*); **-zündung** *nf.* misfire, backfire (*aut.*).
Fehlen [fale'en] *vi.* to fail, be wanting, be wrong; *t.* miss.
Fehler [fale'err] *nm.* (-) mistake, error, defect; **-frei** *a.* flawless, free from error; **-grenze** *nf.* margin of error; **-haft** *a.* defective, incorrect; **-haftigkeit** *nf.* incorrectness, defectiveness.
Feier [fi'err] *nf.* celebration, festival; **-abend** *nm.* evening leisure, cessation of work; **-tag** *nm.* holiday.
Feierlich [fi'er-lish] *a.* solemn.
Feierlichkeit [fi'er-lish-kite] *nf.* solemnity.
Feiern [fi'errn] *vt.* to celebrate; *i.* stop work, make holiday.
Feige [fi'ger] *nf.* fig.
Feige [fi'ger] *a.* cowardly.
Feigheit [fik'hite] *nf.* cowardice. [coward.
Feigling [fik'ling] *nm.* (-e)
Feil [file] *a.* for sale, bribable; **-halten** *vi. ir.* to have on sale.
Feile [file'er] *nf.* file.
Feilen [file'en] *vt.* to file.
Feilspäne [file'shpane-er] *pl.* filings.
Feilschen [file'shen] *vi.* to haggle, bargain. [haggler.
Feilscher [file'sherr] *nm.* (-)
Fein [fine] *a.* fine, refined, acute; **-einstellung** *nf.* accurate tuning; **-fühlend** *a.* sensitive;

-gefühl n. delicacy, tact;
-hörig a. quick of hearing;
-mechaniker nm. instrument,
precision mechanic; -schmeck-
er nm. gourmand; -sinnig a.
delicate.

Feind [fīnt] nm. (-e) enemy;
-einbruch nm. enemy penetration; -einwirkung nf. enemy
action; -flug nm. operational
flight (av.); -gelände n. enemy
country.

Feindlich [fīnt'lish] a. hostile.

Feindschaft [fīnt'shaft] nf.
hostility, enmity. [hostile.

Feindselig [fīnt'zale-ish] a.

Feindseligkeit [fīnt'zale-ish-
kīte] nf. hostility.

Feinheit [fīne'hīte] nf. fineness, refinement, acuteness.

Feist [fīst] a. fat.

Feld [felt] n. (-er) field, square
(board), panel (form); -bau
nm. agriculture; -bett n. camp-
bed; -blume nf. wild flower;
-dienst nm. active service;
-einsatz nm. field operation;
-flasche nf. water bottle (mil.);
-flughafen, -flugplatz nm. advance aerodrome, satellite airfield; -geistliche(r) nm. chaplain, padre; -gendarmerie nf.
provost service; -haubitze nf.
gun howitzer; -herr nm. commander, general; -lazarett n.
field hospital; -marschall nm.
field-marshall; -messer nm.
surveyor; -mütze nf. forage
cap; -postamt n. army post-
office; -posten nm. field sentry;
-wache nf. picket; -webel nm.
sergeant; -zeug n. (field)
stores, ordnance; -zug nm.
campaign.

Felge [fel'ger] nf. felloe, felly,
rim (cycle).

Fell [fel] n. (-e) skin, hide.

Fels, Felsen [fel'zen] nm. (-)
rock; -enhöhle nf. grotto.

Felsenfest [fel'zen-fest] a.
firm as a rock.

Felsig [fel'zish] a. rocky.

Fenster [fen'sterr] n. (-)
window; -brett n. window-sill;
-decorateur nm. window-dres-
ser; -laden nm. shutter; -reiter
nm. insert-label; -sims nm.
window-sill.

Ferien [fare'yen] pl. holidays;
-karte nf. tourist ticket.

Ferkel [fairr'kel] n. young pig.

Fern [fairn] a, ad. far, distant;
-amt n. trunk exchange (ph.);
-anschluss nm. trunk connection (ph.); -bedienung nf. remote control (av, etc.); -bild n.
telephoto; -bildübertragung nf.
television; -drucker nm. teleprinter, ticker (com.); -flug
nm. long distance flight; -funk
nm. long range radio; -gelenkt
a. remote controlled; -geschütz
n. long distance gun; -gespräch
n. trunk call (ph.); -glas n.
telescope; -hörer nm. head-
phones; -kabel n. trunk-cable;
-leitung nf. trunk-line; -lenk-
ung nf. remote control; -meld-
ung nf. tele-communication;
-nachtjäger nm. intruder aircraft; -ortung nf. radio-location, radar; -photographie nf.
tele-photography; -rohr n.
telescope; -rohraufsatz nm.
telescopic sight; -schreib-
maschine nf. teleprinter;
-schreibevermittlung nf. teleprinter exchange; -schriftlich
a. by teleprinter; -sehapparat
nm. television set; -sehen vi.
to televise; -sehempfänger
nm. television receiving set,
viewer; -sicht nf. long distance view, perspective;
-sprecher nm. telephone;
-sprechstelle nf. call office
(ph.); -sprechzelle nf. call-box
(ph.); -spruch nm. telephone
message; -verbindung nf.
trunk line (ph.); -waffe nf.
long-range weapon.

Ferne [fairr'ner] nf. remoteness, distance. [farther, further.

Ferner [fairr'nerr] a, ad.

Fernhalten [fairrn'hal-ten] *vr. ir.* to keep away.

Ferse [fairr'zer] *nf.* heel.

Fertig [fairr'tish] *a.* ready, finished, ready-made; **-erzeugnis** *n.* finished product; **-machen** *vt.* to finish.

Fertigen [fairr'ti-gen] *vi.* to produce.

Fertigkeit [fairr'tish-kite] *vt.* dexterity, proficiency, accomplishment, skill.

Fertigung [fairr'ti-gŏŏng] *nf.* production. [smart.

Fesch [fesh] *a.* fashionable.

Fessel [fess'el] *nf.* fetter; **-ballon** *nm.* captive balloon.

Fesseln [fess'eln] *vt.* to fetter, arrest, pin down (*mil.*).

Fesselung [fess'e-lŏŏng] *nf.* pinning down (*troops*).

Fest [fest] *a.* firm, solid, fixed, fast; **-antenne** *nf.* fixed aerial (*rad.*); **-halten** *vt. ir.* to seize, hold fast, portray; **-land** *n.* continent; **-machen** *vt.* to fasten, fix; **-pflöcken** *vt.* to peg; **-setzen** *vt.* to fix, stipulate; **-setzung** *nf.* stipulation, settling; **-stellen** *vt.* to fix, establish; **-stellung** *nf.* ascertaining, confirmation (of appointment).

Fest [fest] *n.* festival; **-esseb** *n.* banquet; **-tag** *nm.* holiday.

Festigen [fest'i-gen] *vt.* to make firm, confirm, establish, stabilize.

Festigkeit [fest'ish-kite] *nf.* firmness, stability, solidity, structural strength (*tec.*).

Festlich [fest'lish] *a.* festive.

Festlichkeit [fest'lish-kite] *nf.* festivity. [ress.

Festung [fest'ŏŏng] *nf.* fortress.

Fett [fet] *n. a.* fat; **-büchse** *nf.* butter container; **-dicht** *a.* grease-proof; **-spritze** *nf.* grease-gun (*aut.*).

Fettheit [fet'hite] *nf.* fatness, greasiness.

Fettig [fet'ish] *a.* fatty.

Fetzen [fet'sen] *nm.* (-) rag, shred.

Feucht [foisht] *a.* moist, wet.

Feuchtigkeit [foish'tish-kite] *nf.* moisture, dampness.

Feuer [foi'err] *n.* (-) fire; **-bereich** *nm.* zone of fire (*mil.*); **-beständig** *a.* fire-proof; **-fangend** *a.* inflammable; **-fest** *a.* fire-proof; **-löschwesen** *n.* fire-service; **-melder** *nm.* fire-alarm; **-sicher** *a.* fire-resisting; **-sperre** *nf.* barrage (*mil.*); **-stoss** *nm.* burst of fire (*mil.*); **-versicherung** *nf.* fire insurance; **-walze** *nf.* creeping barrage (*mil.*); **-wehr** *nf.* fire brigade; **-werk** *n.* fireworks; **-werker** *nm.* armourer, sergeant artificer (*mil.*); **-zeug** *n.* lighter.

Feuerig [foi'er-rish] *a.* fiery, ardent.

Feuern [foi'errn] *vt.i.* to fire.

Fibel [feebl] *nf.* child's reader, ABC-book.

Fiber [fee'berr] *nf.* fibre.

Fichte [fish'ter] *nf.* spruce, pine.

Fidel [fi-dale'] *a.* jolly.

Fidibus [fee'di-bŏŏs] *nm.* spell, pipe-light.

Fieber [fee'berr] *n.* fever; **-thermometer** *n.* clinical thermometer.

Fieberhaft [fee'berr-haft] *a.* feverish. [feverish.

Fiebern [fee'berrn] *vi.* to be **Fiedel** [feed] *nf.* fiddle.

Fiedel [feedl] *nf.* fiddle.

Fiedler [feed'lerr] *nm.* (-) fiddler.

Figur [fi-gŏŏrr'] *nf.* figure, chess-man. [com.

Filiale [fi-li-ah'ler] *nf.* branch

Film [film] *nm.* (-e) film, screen; **-atelier** *n.* film studio; **-aufnahme** *nf.* shooting (*film*); **-streifen** *nm.* reel; **-vorführgerät** *n.* projector.

Filmen [fil'men] *vt.* to film.

Filtrier'en [fil-treer'ren] *vt.to* filter; **-trichter** *nm.* funnel.

Filtrierung [fil-treer'ōōng] *nf.* filtration.

Filz [filts] *nm. nm.* (-e) felt, miser; -hut *nm.* felt hat; -stiefel *nm.* felt boot.

Filzen [filt'sen] *vt.* to felt.

Filzig [filt'sish] *a.* of felt, miserly.

Finanz [fi-nants'] *nf.* finance; -jahr *n.* fiscal year; -prüfer *nm.* auditor; -wesen *n.* financial affairs.

Finanziell [fi-nant-syell'] *a.* financial.

Finanzieren [fi-nant-seer'ren] *vt.* to finance.

Finden [fin'den] *vt. ir.* to find, think; *r.* be (found), offer.

Finder [fin'derr] *nm.* (-) finder. [ful.

Findig [fin'dish] *a.* resource-

Findigkeit [fin'dish-kite] *nf.* ingenuity, resourcefulness

Findling [fint'ling] *nm.* (-e) foundling.

Finger [fing'err] *nm.* (-) finger; -abdruck *nm.* finger-print; -hut *nm.* thimble, fox-glove; -satz *nm.* fingering; -spitze *nf.* finger-tip; -zeig *nm.* hint. [finger.

Fingern [fing'errn] *vt.* to

Fingieren [fing-geer'ren] *vt.* to feign, forge.

Fink [fink] *m.w.* finch.

Finne [fi'ner] *nf.* fin, pimple.

Finnig [fi'nish] *a.* pimply, blotchy.

Finster [fin'sterr] *a.* dark, gloomy; - blicken to frown.

Finsternis [fin'sterr-niss] *nf.* darkness, gloom.

Finte [fin'ter] *n.* feint, trick.

Firma [firr'mah] *nf.* (Firmen)

Firnis [firr'niss] *nm.* (-se) varnish. [varnish.

Firnissen [firr'niss-en] *vt.* to

First [firrst] *nm.* (-e), Firste *nf.* ridge, top.

Fisch [fish] *nm.* (-e) fish; -bein *n.* whalebone; -brut *nf.* fry;

-gräte *nf.* fishbone; -rogen *nm.* roe; -zug *nm.* draught of fish.

Fischen [fish'en] *vt.i.* to fish.

Fischer [fish'err] *nm.* (-) fisherman; -boot *n.* fishing-boat, -smack.

Fischerei [fish'er-rī] *nf.* fishery, fishing.

Fistel [fi'stel] *nf.* fistula, falsetto.

Fittich [fi'tish] *nm.* (-e) wing, pinion.

Fitze [fit'ser] *nf.* skein.

Fix [fix] *a.* fixed, ready.

Fixieren [fix-eer'ren] *vt.* to fix (photo), stare at.

Fixum [fix'ōōm] *n.* (Fixa) fixed salary.

Flach [flach] *a.* flat, shallow.

Fläche [fle'sher] *nf.* flatness, plane (surface); -nbombardierung *nf.* pattern bombing; -nmass *n.* area; -nmessplan *nm.* plotting board (av.); -nziel *n.* area target.

Flachheit [flach'hite] *nf.* flatness, shallowness.

Flachs [flax] *nm.* flax.

Flächsern [flex'errn] *a.* flaxen.

Flackern [flak'errn] *vi.* to flare, flicker.

Fladen [flah'den] *nm.* (-) flat cake.

Flagge [flag'er] *nf.* flag; -nstock *nm.* flagstaff; -ntuch *n.* bunting.

Flak [flak] *nf.* anti-aircraft gunfire; -jäger *nm.* anti-aircraft ship.

Flamme [flam'er] *nf.* flame; -nbombe *nf.* oil bomb; -nwerfer *nm.* flame thrower.

Flammen [flam'en] *vi.* to flame.

Flanell [fla-nel'] *nm.* (-e) flannel.

Flanke [flang'ker] *nf.* flank; -nbewegung *nf.* turning movement, outflanking (mil.).

Flankieren [flang-keer'ren] *vt.* to flank (mil.).

Flasche [flash'er] *nf.* bottle, flask; -nbier *n.* bottled beer.

Flatterhaft [flat'err-haft] *a.* flighty, inconstant.

Flatterhaftigkeit [flat'err-haft-ish-kite] *nf.* flightiness, fickleness.

Flattermine [flat'err-mee-ner] *nf.* contact mine. [flutter.

Flattern [flat'errn] *vi.* to

Flau [flow] *a.* slack, languid, dull; -macher *nm.* defeatist; -macherei *nf.* defeatism.

Flauheit [flow'hite] *nf.* slackness, dullness.

Flaum [flowm] *nm.* down.

Flaumig [flow'mish] *a.* downy.

Flaus [flowss], **Flausch** [flowsh] *nm.* (-e) pilot-cloth.

Flechse [flex'er] *nf.* tendon.

Flechte [flesh'ter] *nf.* plait, wicker-work, dry scab, lichen.

Flechten [flesh'ten] *vt. ir.* to plait, twine.

Flechtwerk [flesht'vairrk] *n.* wicker-work.

Fleck [flek] *nm,* **Flecken** [flek'en] *nm.* blemish, patch.

Flecken [flek'en] *vt.i.* to stain; -los *a.* spotless.

Fleckig [flek'ish] *a.* spotted.

Fledermaus [flay'derr-mowss] *nf.* (-mäuse) bat.

Flegel [flay'gel] *nm.* (-) flail, lout; -haft *a.* loutish, unmannerly; -jahre *n.pl.* years of immaturity, adolescence.

Flehen [flay'en] *vi.* to implore; -tlich *a.* imploringly.

Fleisch [flish] *n.* flesh, meat; -brühe *nf.* broth, beef tea; -farben *a.* flesh-coloured; -konserve *nf.* potted meat; -pastete *nf.* meat-pie.

Fleischer [fli'sherr] *nm.* (-) butcher.

Fleischig [fli'shish] *a.* fleshy.

Fleischlich [flish'lish] *a.* fleshly. [industry.

Fleiss [fliss] *nm.* diligence,

Fleissig [fli'sish] *a.* diligent, industrious.

Flektieren [flek'teer-ren] *vt.* to inflect.

Flennen [flen'en] *vi.* to cry, blubber.

Fletschen [fletsh'en] *vt.* to show (*teeth*).

Flexion [flek-syohn'] *nf.* inflection.

Flick'en [fli'ken] patch; *vt.* to patch; -arbeit *nf.* patchwork; -schneider *nm.* jobbing tailor; -stube *nf.* repair shop.

Flieder [flee'derr] *nm.* ℥(-) elder, lilac.

Fliege [flee'ger] *nf.* fly; -nschrank *nm.* meat-safe.

Fliegen [flee'gen] *vi. ir.* to fly.

Flieger [flee'gerr] *nm.* (-) flier, aviator, airman, sprinter; -abwehr *nf.* air defence; -alarm *nm.* alert; -angriff *nm.* air raid; -aufnahme *nf.* air photograph; -beschädigte *nm.* air-raid casualty; -beschuss *nm.* anti-aircraft fire; -bombe *nf.* aircraft bomb; -ehe *nf.* co-operation of air-crew; -horst *nm.* air-force station; -hose *nf.* flying trousers; -kammer *nf.* air camera; -karte *nf.* air map; -schaden *nm.* air-raid damage; -schirm *nm.* air umbrella; -schutz *nm.* anti-aircraft fire; -schutzanzug *nm.* flying kit; -schütze *nm.* anti-aircraft gunner; -streitkräfte *f.pl.* air arm; -technisch *a.* aero-technical; -truppe *nf.* air-force troops; -wache *nf.* observer post; -warnung *nf.* air-raid warning.

Fliehen [flee'en] *vi. ir.* to flee.

Fliese [flee'zer] *nf.* paving-stone.

Fliess'en [flee'sen] *vi. ir.* to flow; -end *a.* flowing, fluent; -papier *n.* blotting paper.

Flimmer [flim'err] *nm.* glimmer.

Flimmern [flim'errn] *vi.* to glimmer, glitter.

Flink [flink] *a.* nimble, lively.

Flinkheit [flink'hite] *nf.* nimbleness, liveliness.
Flinte [flin'ter] *nf.* rifle, musket, shot-gun.
Flitter [flit'err] *nm.* (-) spangle, tinsel; **-haft** *a.* showy, tawdry; **-werk** *n.* tawdry finery; **-wochen** *f.pl.* honeymoon.
Flitzen [flit'sen] *vi.* to flit.
Flitzer [flit'serr] *nm.* (-) jeep (*mil.*).
Flocke [flik'er] *nf.* flock, flake.
Flocken [flok'en] *vi.* to fall in flakes; *t.r.* flake.
Flockig [flok'ish] *a.* flaky.
Floh [floh] *nm.* (**Flöhe**) flea.
Flor [florr] *nm.* (**Flöre**) gauze, crape, blossoming time, bloom.
Florieren [flor-eer'ren] *vi.* to flourish.
Floss [flohce] *nm.* (**Flösse**) float, raft; **-sack** *nm.* inflatable rubber dinghy (*av.*).
Flosse [floss'er] *nf.* fin.
Flössen [fler'sen] *vt.* to float.
Flösser [fler'serr] *nm.* (-) raftsman.
Flöte [fler'ter] *nf.* flute.
Flotilla [flo-til'ah] *nf.* flotilla.
Flott [flot] *a.* afloat, gay, smart, quick.
Flotte [flot'er] *nf.* fleet, navy; **-nbegleitboot** *n.* escort vessel; **-nfliegerstreitkräfte** *f.pl.* fleet air-arm.
Flöz, Flötz [flerts] *nm.* (-e) layer, seam. [curse.
Fluch [flōōch] *nm.* (**Flüche**) **Fluchen** [flōōch'en] *vi.* to curse.
Flucht [flōōcht] *nf.* flight, row, range, suite (*rooms*).
Flüchten [flyōōsh'ten] *vi.r.* to flee, escape.
Flüchtig [flyōōsh'tish] *a.* fleeting, volatile, transitory.
Flüchtigkeit [flyōōsh'tish-kite] *nf.* transitoriness, volatility.
Flüchtling [flyōōsht'ling] *nm.* -e) fugitive, refugee.

Flug [flōōk] *nm.* (**Flüge**) flying, flight, covey; **im − airborne** (*av.*); **-abwehr** *nf.* anti-aircraft defence; **-befehl** *nm.* brief (*av.*); **-begeistert** *a.* air-minded; **-bereich** *nm.* range (*av.*); **-bereit** *a.* ready for flight (*av.*); **-betrieb** *nm.* aviation, flying organisation; **-boot** *n.* flying boat; **-deck** *n.* flight deck, landing deck; **-form** *nf.* flying formation; **-gast** *nm.* air passenger; **-gewicht** *n.* weight loaded, flying weight (*av.*); **-hafen** *nm.* airfield; **-kapitän** *nm.* civil air pilot; **-klar** *a.* serviceable for flying (*av.*); **-kraftstoff** *nm.* aviation fuel; **-lehrer** *nm.* flying instructor; **-meldeauswerter** *nf.* plotting; **-meldeauswerter** *nm.* plotter (*av.*); **-platz** *nm.* landing ground; **-post** *nf.* air-mail; **-rakete** *nf.* anti-aircraft rocket; **-sand** *nm.* quicksands; **-schrift** *nf.* pamphlet; **-sicherungsboot** *n.* crash boat (*av.*); **-unklar** *a.* unserviceable for flying (*av.*); **-vorbereitung** *nf.* briefing; **-weite** *nf.* range (*av.*); **-wesen** *n.* aviation.
Flügel [flyoo'gel] *nm.* (-) wing, flap, grand piano.
Flügge [flyoo'ger] *a.* fledged.
Flugs [flōōx] *ad.* speedily.
Flugzeug [flōōk'tsoik] *n.* (-e) aircraft, plane; **-führer** *nm.* pilot (*av.*); **-kapitän** *nm.* civil pilot; **-mutterschiff** *n.* träger *nm.* aircraft carrier.
Flunder [flōōn'derr] *nm.* (-e) flounder. [brag, lie.
Flunkern [flōōn'kerrn] *vi.* to
Fluor [flōō-ore'] *n.* fluorine.
Flur [flōōrr] *nf.* field, *nm.* (-e) entrance-hall, lobby.
Fluss [flōōss] *nm.* (**Flüsse**) river, flow, issue. [liquid.
Flüssig [flyōō'sish] *a.* fluid, **Flüssigkeit** [flyōō'sish-kite] *nf.* liquid, fluidity.
Flüster'n [flyoo'sterrn] *vi.t.* to

whisper; -propaganda nf. whisper campaign.

Flut [floot] nf. flood, tide.

Fluten [floo'ten] vi. to rise, flood.

Fockmast [fok'mast] nm. (gen. -es; pl. -en) foremast.

Fohlen [fole'en] n. colt, foal.

Föhn [fern] nm. hot, south wind, hair-drying machine.

Föhre [fer'rer] nf. pine.

Folge [fol'ger] nf. succession, result, consequence, conclusion; -nschwer a. grave, momentous; -richtig a. consistent, logical.

Folgen [fol'gen] vi. to follow, obey; -dermassen ad. in the following way.

Folgern [fol'gerrn] vt. to infer.

Folgerung [fol'ger-roong] nf. inference, conclusion.

Folglich [folk'lish] ad. consequently.

Folgsam [folk'sam] a. obedient, complaint.

Foliant [fo-lyant'] m.w. folio.

Folie [foh'lyer] nf. foil, leaf, silvering. [rack.

Folter [fol'terr] nf. torture.

Foltern [fol'terrn] vt. to torture.

Fonds [fong] pl. funds, stock (com.), fund; -börse nf. stock-exchange; -makler nm. stock-broker, jobber.

Foppen [fop'en] vt. to fool, teaze.

Förderlich [ferr'derr-lish] a. beneficial, useful.

Fordern [forr'derrn] vt. to demand, exact.

Förder'n [ferr'derrn] vt. to promote, benefit, forward; -band n. endless chain; -korb nm. plt-cage.

Forderung [forr'der-roong] nf. demand, summons.

Förderung [ferr'der-roong] nf. furtherance, forwarding.

Forelle [fo-rel'er] nf. trout.

Forke [forr'ker] nf. pitchfork.

Form [forrm] nf. form, mould, shape, model.

Formalität [forr-ma-li-tate'] nf. formality. [size.

Format [forr-maht'] n. (-e)

Formel [forr'mel] nf. formula.

Formell [forr-mel'] a. formal.

Formen [forr'men] vt. to form, mould.

Formieren [forr-meer'ren] vt. to form.

Förmlich [ferrm'lish] a. formal, downright; ad. formally, regularly.

Förmlichkeit [ferrm'lish-kite] nf. formality.

Formlos [forrm'lohss] a. formless, shapeless.

Formular [forr-moo-lahr'] n. (-) form.

Formulieren [forr-m3o-leer'ren] vt. to formulate.

Forsch [forrsh] a. dashing.

Forschen [forr'shen] vt. to search, investigate.

Forscher [forr'sherr] nm. (-) investigator, explorer.

Forschung [forr'shoong] nf. investigation, exploration, discovery, research; -samt n. research station; -sreise nf. voyage of discovery; -sreisende(r) m.w. explorer.

Forst [forrst] nm. (-e) forest; -arbeiter nm. forestry worker; -wesen n -wirtschaft nf. forestry.

Förster [ferr'sterr] nm. (-) forester.

Fort [forrt] ad. away, off, forward; in einem – continually.

Fortbestehen [forrt'ber-stay-en] vi. ir. to continue, persist.

Fortbewegen [forrt'ber-vay-gen] vr. to move on.

Fortbilden [forrt'bil-den] vr. to continue one's education.

Fortbildung [forrt'bil-doong] nf. vocational training; -sanstalt, -sschule nf. continuation school.

Fortbleiben [forrt'blībe-en] *vi. ir.* to stay away.

Fortdauer [forrt'dow-err] *nf.* continuance, permanence.

Fortdauern [forrt'dow-errn] *vi.* to continue, last; **-d** *a.* permanent, incessant.

Fortfahren [forrt'fah-ren] *ir.* to go on, depart, continue.

Fortführen [forrt'fyoor-ren] *vt.* to continue.

Fortführung [forrt'fyoor-roong] *nf.* continuation.

Fortgang [forrt'gang] *nm.* progress, continuation.

Fortgehen [forrt'gay-en] *vi. ir.* to go away.

Fortkommen [forrt'kom-en] *vi. r.* to get on, away: *n.* progress.

Fortlaufend [forrt'low-fent] *a.* serial, continuous.

Fortpflanzen [forrt'pflantsen] *vt.* to propagate, transmit.

Fortpflanzung [forrt'pflantsoong] *nf.* propagation, transmission.

Fortschaffen [forrt'shaf-en] *vt.* to remove, eliminate.

Fortschaffung [forrt'shaf-oong] *nf.* removal, elimination.

Fortschreiten [forrt'shrite-en] *vi. ir.* to proceed, progress, go forward.

Fortschritt [forrt'shrit] *nm.* (-e) progress; **-lich** *a.* progressive.   [to continue.

Fortsetzen [forrt'zet-sen] *vt.*

Fortsetzung [forrt'zet-soong] *nf.* continuation.

Fortwährend [forrt'vare-ent] to pull away; *i.* leave, remove. *a., ad.* incessantly.

Fortziehen[forrt'tsee-en]*vt.ir.*

Fossil [fo-seel'] *n.* (-ien) fossil.

Fracht [fracht] *nf.* freight, carriage, cargo; **-brief** *nm.* bill of lading; **-frei** *a.* carriage paid; **-gut** *n.* consignment sent by goods train.

Frachten [frach'ten] *vt.* to freight, load.

Frachter [frach'terr] *nm.* (-) freighter, cargo-boat.

Frack [frak] *nm.* (**Fräcke**) dress-coat.

Frage [frah'ger] *nf.* question; **-bogen** *nm.* questionnaire; **-zeichen** *n.* question-mark.

Fragen [frah'gen] *vt.* to ask.

Frag-lich [frak'lich] *a.* questionable, doubtful; **-los** *a.* unquestionable; **-würdig** *a.* questionable.

Fragment [frak-ment'] *n.* (-e) fragment; **-arisch** *a.* fragmentary.

Fraktion [frak-syohn'] *nf.* political party.

Fraktur [frak-toor'] *nf.* fracture, black-letter type, German type.

Frank [frank] *a.* frank, open.

Frank [frank] *nm.* (-en) franc.

Franken [frank] *nm.* (-) franc.

Frankieren [frang-keer'ren] *vt.* to stamp, prepay.

Franko [frang'ko] *ad.* post paid, carriage paid.

Franse [fran'zer] *nf.* fringe.

Franzbranntwein [frants'brant-vine] *nm.* brandy.

Fratze [frat'ser] *nf.* grimace, caricature; **-nhaft** *a.* grotesque, distorted.

Frau [frow] *nf.* woman, wife, Mrs; **-enkleid** *n.* dress, frock; **-enzimmer** *n.* female.

Fräulein [froy'line] *n.* (-) young lady, Miss.   [cheeky.

Frech [fresh] *a.* insolent,

Frechheit [fresh'hite] *nf.* cheek, impudence.

Fregatte [fray-gat'er] *nf.* frigate; **-nkapitän** *nm.* commander (*nav.*).

Frei [fri] *a.* free, disengaged, off-duty, voluntary, frank; das **-e** the open air; **-beuter** *nm.* freebooter; **-bleibend** *a.* subject to being sold (*com.*); **-brief** *nm.* charter; **-geist** *nm.* freethinker; **-hafen** *nm.* free port; **-handel** *nm.* free trade; **-herr** *nm.* baron; **-karte** *nf.* free pass ticket; -laufrad *n.* free wheel; -lichtbühne *nf.* open air theatre; -schar *nf.* irregular troops; -schärler *nm.* guerilla fighter, patriot; -zeit *nf.* spare time, off-duty time.

Freien [fri'en] *vi.* to court.

Freier [fri'err] *nm.* (-) suitor.

Freigeben [fri'gabe-en] *vt. ir.* to decontrol.

Freigebig [fri'gabe-ish] *a.* generous; -keit *nf.* generosity.

Freiheit [fri'hite] *nf.* freedom. -lich *a.* liberal; -strafe *nf.* imprisonment.

Freilassen [fri'lass-en] *vt. ir.* to liberate, emancipate.

Freilassung [fri'lass-öong] *nf.* release.

Freilich [fri'lish] *ad.* certainly, it is true. [ness.

Freimut [fri'mōōt] *nm.* frank-

Freimütig [fri'myōō-tish] *a.* frank, candid.

Freisinnig [fri'si-nish] *a.* liberal.

Freitag [fri'tahk] *nm.* (-e) Friday.

Fremd [fremt] *a.* strange, foreign; -artig *a.* strange; -enbuch *n.* visitors' book; -enverkehr *nm.* tourist traffic; -herrschaft *nf.* foreign rule; -ländisch *a.* foreign; -ling *nm.* stranger, foreigner; -sprache *nf.* foreign language.

Fremde [frem'der] *nf.* foreign country; in der - abroad.

Fremde(r) [frem'derr] *m.w.* foreigner, stranger, visitor.

Frequenz [fray-kvents'] *nf.* frequency (*rad.*).

Fressen [fress'en] *vt. ir.* to eat, devour.

Frettchen [fret'shen] *n.* (-) ferret.

Freud'e [froy'der] *nf.* joy, delight; -enfeuer *n.* bonfire; -los *a.* joyless.

Freudig [froy'dish] *a.* joyful, cheerful.

Freuen [froy'en] *v.imp.* make

glad, pleased; *r.* be glad, rejoice.

Freund [froint] *nm.* (-e) friend.

Freundin [froin'din] *nf.* lady friend, girl friend.

Freundlich [froint'lish] *a.* kind, friendly; -keit *nf.* friendliness, kindliness.

Freundlos [froint'lohss] *a.* friendless.

Freundschaft [froint'shaft] *nf.* friendship; -lich *a.* friendly.

Frevel [fray'fel] *nm.* (-) crime, outrage; -tat *nf.* wicked deed.

Frevelhaft [fray'fel-haft] *a.* wicked, criminal.

Freveln [fray'feln] *vi.* to commit an outrage.

Frevler [frafe'lerr] *nm.* (-) criminal.

Friede [free'der] *nm.* peace; -nspreis *nm.* pre-war price; -nsschluss *nm.* conclusion of peace; -nsspruch *nm.* arbitration award; -nsstifter *nm.* peace-maker; -nsstörer *nm.* disturber of the peace; -nsvertrag *nm.* peace treaty; -nszeit *nf.* peace-time.

Friedfertig [freet'fairr-tish] *a.* peaceable.

Friedhof [freet'hohf] *nm.* (-höfe) cemetery.

Friedlich [freet'lish] *a.* peaceful, peaceable.

Frieren [freer'ren] *vt.imp.i.* to freeze.

Fries [freez] *nm.* (-e) frieze (*cloth*), baize.

Fries [freez] *nm.* (-e) frieze (*building*).

Frisch [frish] *a.* fresh, unused, lively.

Frische [frish'er] *nf.* freshness, liveliness.

Friseur [fri-zerr'] *nm.* (-e) hairdresser.

Frisieren [fri-zeer'ren] *vt.* to dress, cut the hair.

Frist [frist] *nf.* term, respite, space (of time); -los *a.* summary (*dismissal*); -tage *m. pl.* days of grace.

Fristen [fris'ten] vt. to delay, postpone, prolong.

Fritten [frit'ten] vi. to cohere (rad.).

Fritter [frit'err] nm. (-) coherer (rad.).

Frivol [fri-vole'] a. frivolous.

Froh [froh] a. glad, gay; **-locken** vi. to exult, gloat over; **-sinn** nm. cheerfulness.

Fröhlich [frerr'lish] a. joyous, gay; **-keit** nf. cheerfulness, gaiety.

Fromm [from] a. pious, good.

Frömmelei [frer-mer-li'] nf. hypocrisy.

Frömmeln [frer'meln] vi. to play the hypocrite.

Frommen [from'en] vi. to avail, profit.

Frömmigkeit [frer'mish-kite] nf. piety.

Frömmler [frerm'lerr] nm. (-) hypocrite, bigot.

Frondienst [frohn'deenst] nm. compulsory labour.

Fronen [froh'nen] vi. to do forced labour, toil. [in.

Frönen [frer'nen] vi. to indulge

Fronleichnamsfest [frohn-lish'nams-fest] n. Corpus Christi Day.

Front [front] nf. front, face; **-flieger** nm. operational airman; **-kämpfer** nm. fighter in first line.

Frosch [frosh] nm. (Frösche) frog, squib.

Frost [frost] nm. (Fröste) frost, chill; **-beule** nf. chilblain.

Frösteln [frer'steln] vi. to feel chilly, shiver.

Frostig [fros'tish] a. chilly, frosty, frigid.

Frottier'en [frot'eer-ren] vt. to rub; **-tuch** n. Turkish towel.

Frucht [frooсht] nf. (Früchte) fruit, corn; **-bringend** a. fruitful; **-los** a. fruitless; **-mark** n. pulp.

Fruchtbar [frooсht'barr] a. fruitful; **-keit** nf. fruitfulness.

Früh [frooй] a, ad. early; morgen – to-morrow morning; **-jahr** n. spring; **-reif** a. precocious; **-reife** nf. precocity; **-stück** n. breakfast; **-zeitig** a. early, untimely.

Frühe [frooй'er] nf. early time, hour.

Frühling [frooй'ling] nm. (-e) spring.

Fuchs [fooх] nm. (Füchse) fox, fresher, first-year student.

Fuchsig [foox'ish] a. foxy.

Füchsin [fyoox'in] nf. vixen.

Fuchtel [fooсh'tel] nf. rod.

Fuchteln [fooсh'teln] vi. to fidget.

Fuder [foo'derr] n. (-) cartload, measure.

Fuge [foo'ger] nf. joint, seam, fugue.

Fugen [foo'gen] vt.i. to join.

Fügen [fyoo'gen] vt. to fit together, dispose, add; r. submit, adapt oneself; imp. happen.

Füglich [fyook'lish] a, ad. fit(ly).

Fügsam [fyook'zam] a. yielding, submissive.

Fügung [fyoo'goong] nf. joint, arrangement, dispensation.

Fühlbar [fyool'barr] a. tangible, palpable, perceptible.

Fühlen [fyoo'len] vt.i.r. to feel, touch. [feeler.

Fühler [fyoo'lerr] nm. (-)

Fühlung [fyoo'loong] nf. touch.

Fuhr'e [foor'er] nf. cart(load), transport; **-mann** nm. carter, carrier; **-werk** n. vehicle; **-wesen** n. transport service.

Führen [fyoo'ren] vt. to lead, conduct, guide, bear, keep (books), deal in (goods).

Führer [fyoo'rerr] nm. (-) leader, commandant, manager, guide, driver (aut.), pilot (av.); **-boot** n. leader in formation (nav.); **-schein** nm. pilot's licence (av.), driving licence (aut.); -sitz nm. cockpit (av.).

Führung [fyōō'rŏŏng] nf. management, control, high command, conduct(ing), direction.

Fülle [fyōō'ler] nf. abundance, fullness.

Füllen [fyōō'len] vt. to fill (up), stuff.

Füllen [fyōō'len] n. foal, colt, filly.

Füll-feder (-halter nm.) nf. fountain pen; -kelle nf. trowel; -werk n. filling, padding, rubble. [ing.

Füllsel [fyōōl'zel] n. (-) stuff-

Füllung [fyōō'lŏŏng] nf. filling, stuffing, door-panel.

Fund [fŏŏnt] nm. (-e) find; -grube nf. mine.

Fundament [fŏŏn-da-ment'] n. (-e) foundation.

Fundieren [fŏŏn-deer'ren] vt. to lay foundations of.

Fünf [fyŏŏnf] num.,five; -zehn num. fifteen.

Fünfte [fyŏŏnf'ter] num. fifth.

Fünfzig [fyŏŏnft'sish] num. fifty.

Fungieren [fŏŏn-geer'ren] vi. to act, officiate, function.

Funk [fŏŏnk] nm. wireless, radio; -aufklärung f. wireless intelligence; -betrieb nm. wireless operating; -bilder n.pl. documentary talk; -feuer n. beacon; -frequenz nf. radio frequency; -gast nm. listener-in; -gebühr nf. wireless licence; -gerät n. wireless set; -messgerät n. radar set, equipment; -messverfahren n. radar; -netz n. radio network; -ortung nf. radar; -peil . . a. direction finding; -sprechverkehr nm. radio-telephony; -spruch nm. wireless message, radiogram; radio message; -stören n. jamming, interference; -telegramm n. radiogram; -telegraphie nf. radio telegraphy; -turm nm.

wireless mast; -überwachung nf. monitoring; -wart nm. wireless mechanic.

Funkeln [fŏŏn'keln] vi. to sparkle.

Funken [fŏŏn'ken] vt. to radio, broadcast.

Funker [fŏŏn'kerr] nm. (-) wireless operator, signaller.

Funktion [fŏŏnk-syōhn'] nf. function.

Für [fyŏŏrr] pr. for; was — what sort of; -bitte nf. intercession; -sorge nf. care, welfare work; -wort n. pronoun.

Furche [fŏŏrr'sher] nf. furrow, wrinkle. [furrow.

Furchen [fŏŏrr'shen] vt. to

Furcht [fŏŏrsht] nf. fear; -bar a. frightful; -los a. fearless; -sam a. timid.

Fürchten [fyŏŏrsh'ten] vt. to fear; r. be afraid.

Furier [fŏŏ-reerr'] nm. (-e) quarter-master sergeant (mil.).

Furnier [fŏŏr-neer'] n. (-e) veneer. [to inlay.

Furnieren [fŏŏr-neer'en] vt.

Fürst [fyŏŏrst] m.w. prince; -in nf. princess; -entum n. principality; -lich a. princely.

Furt [fŏŏrrt] nf. ford.

Fuss [fŏŏs] nm. (Füsse) foot, footing; -ball nm. football; -bekleidung nf. footgear; -beuge nf. instep; -boden nm. floor(ing); -bremse nf. foot-brake (aut.); -fest a. sure-footed; -gänger nm. pedestrian; -hebel nm. pedal; -tritt nm. kick, footstep.

Fussen [fŏŏ'sen] vi. to be based, rest on.

Futter [fŏŏ'terr] n. (-) case, lining. [feed.

Futter [fŏŏ'terr] n. fodder.

Futteral [fŏŏ-ter-rahl'] n. (-e) case, sheath.

Futtern [fŏŏ'terrn], **Füttern** [fyŏŏ'terrn] vt. to line, case.

Füttern, Futtern vt.i. to feed.

G

Gabe [gah'ber] *nf.* gift.

Gabel [gah'bel] *nf.* fork; -**frühstück** *n.* lunch; -**zacke** *nf.* prong.

Gabeln [gah'beln] *vt.r.* to fork.

Gackern [gak'errn] *vi.* to cackle.

Gaffel [gafl] *nf.* fork, gaff.

Gaffen [gaf'en] *vi.* to gape.

Gagat [ga-gaht'] *nm.* (-e) jet; -**kohle** *nf.* pitch coal.

Gähnen [gane'en] *vi.* to yawn.

Gala [gah'lah] *nf.* pomp, show; -**uniform** *nf.* full-dress uniform.

Galant [ga-lant'] *a.* gallant, courteous; -**eriewaren** *f.pl.* fancy goods.

Galgen [gal'gen] *nm.* (-) gallows; -**frist** *nf.* respite.

Galle [gal'er] *nf.* gall, spleen.

Gallerie [ga-ler-ree'] *nf.* gallery.

Gallert [ga'lerrt] *n.* (-e), **Gallerte** [ga-lairr'ter] *nf.* jelly, gelatine.

Galopp [ga-lop'] *nm.* gallop; -**ieren** *vi.* to gallop.

Galvanis'ch [gal-vah'nish] *a.* galvanic; -**ieren** *vt.* to galvanize.

Gamasche [ga-mash'er] *nf.* gaiter, legging, spat.

Gang [gang] *nm.* (Gänge) walk, gait, errand, course, passage, gear (*tec.*); **im** - at work, in action.

Gangbar [gang'barr] *a.* passable, current, saleable.

Gängelband [geng'el-bant] *n.* leading-strings.

Gängeln [geng'eln] *vt.* to lead by the hand.

Gans [ganss] *nf.* (Gänse) goose.

Gäns'chen [genss'shen] *n.* gosling; -**blümchen** *n.* daisy; -**efüsschen** *n.pl.* inverted commas; -**erich** *nm.* gander.

Ganz [gants] *a.* whole, complete; *ad.* wholly, quite;

-**e** *n.w.* whole, entirety, squad (*mil.*).

Gänzlich [gents'lish] *a, ad.* full(y), entire(ly).

Gar [gahrr] *a.* cooked, done (*food*); *ad.* quite, very; - **nichts** nothing at all; -**küche** *nf.* eating house.

Garantie [ga-ran-tee'] *nf.* guarantee; -**ren** *vt.* to guarantee. [(*of fire*).

Garbe [garr'ber] *nf.* sheaf, cone

Garde [garr'der] *nf.* guard(s); -**robe** *nf.* wardrobe, cloak-room.

Gardine [garr-dee'ner] *nf.* curtain. [ferment.

Gären [gairr'en] *vi. ir.* to

Garn [garrn] *n.* (-e) yarn, thread, snare, net.

Garnele [garr-nale'er] *nf.* shrimp, prawn.

Garnieren [garr-neer'ren] *vt.* to trim, garnish.

Garnison [garr-ni-zohn'] *nf.* garrison.

Garnitur [garr-ni-tōōrr'] *nf.* trimming, mounting.

Garstig [garr'stish] *a.* horrid, filthy.

Garten [garr'ten] *nm.* (Gärten) garden; -**bau** *nm.* horticulture; -**haus** *n.* summer house; -**stadt** *nf.* garden city.

Gärtner [gairrt'nerr] *nm.* (-) gardener; -**n** *vi.* to garden.

Gärung [gairr'rŏŏng] *nf.* fermentation.

Gas [gas] *n.* (-e) gas; -**abwehr** *nf.* anti-gas defence; -**behälter** *nm.* gasometer; -**brenner** *nm.* gas-burner, -**ring** *nm.* gas-burner, -**ring** *nm.*; -**einsatz** *nm.* chemical warfare; -**fusshebel** *nm.* accelerator (*aut.*); -**kocher** *nm.*; -**ofen** *nm.* gas-stove; -**krank** *a.* gassed; -**maske** *nf.* gas-mask; -**uhr** *nf.* gas-meter; -**werk** *n.* gas-works.

Gasse [gas'er] *nf.* lane, alley; -**nbube** *nm.* street urchin; -**nhauer** *nm.* popular song.

Gast [gast] *nm.* (Gäste) guest

fellow; **-frei, -freundlich** _a._ hospitable; **-gerber** _nm._ host; **-haus** _n._ inn; **-hof** _nm._ hotel; **-wirt** _nm._ innkeeper.

Gästebuch [ges'ter-booch] _n._ (-b cher) visitor's book.

Gastlich [gast'lish] _a._ hospitable.

Gastrisch [gast'rish] _a._ gastric.

Gatte [gat'er] _m.w._ **Gattin** _nf._ spouse, mate; **-n** _vt.r._ to match, pair.

Gatter [gat'err] _n._ (-) railing, grating.

Gattung [gat'ŏŏng] _nf._ genus, species, kind.

Gau [gow] _nm._ (-e) province, district; **-leiter** _nm._ governor.

Gaukelei [gow-ker-lie'] _nf._ juggling, illusion.

Gaukeln [gow'keln] _vi._ to juggle.

Gaukler [gow'klerr] _nm._ (-) juggler.

Gaul [gowl] _nm._ (**Gäule**) horse, nag.

Gaumen [gow'men] _nm._ (-) palate.

Gauner [gow'nerr] _nm._ (-) rogue; **-ei** _nf._ swindle; **-n** _vi._ to swindle; **-sprache** _nf._ thieves' slang.

Gaze [gah'zer] _nf._ gauze.

Gebäck [ger-bek'] _n._ (-e) pastry.

Gebärde [ger-bairr'der] _nf._ gesture; **-n** _vr._ to behave.

Gebären [ger-bair-ren] _vt. ir._ to give birth to, bring forth.

Gebäude [ger-boy'der] _n._ (-) building.

Geben [gay'ben] _vt. ir._ to give, render; _r._ yield; **es gibt** there is (are).

Gebein [ger-bine'] _n._ (-e) bones.

Gebell [ger-bel'] _n._ barking.

Geber [gay'berr] _nm._ (-) giver; **-station** _nf._ transmitting station (_rad._).

Gebet [ger-bate'] _n._ (-e) prayer.

Gebiet [ger-beet'] _n._ (-e) province, sphere, territory.

Gebieten [ger-beet'en] _vt. ir._ to command; _i._ rule.

Gebieter [ger-beet'err] _nm.i_(-) master, ruler; **-isch** _a._ imperious.

Gebilde [ger-bil'der] _n._ (-) structure, creation.

Gebildet [ger-bil'det] _a._ cultured, shaped.

Gebinde [ger-bin'der] _n._ cask, container, vessel, skein.

Gebirg'e [ger-beerr'ge] _n._ (-) mountain chain; **-ig** _a._ mountainous; **-sjäger** _pl._ Alpine troops.

Gebiss [ger-bis'] _n._ (-e) teeth, denture, bit; **-kette** _nf._ curb.

Gebläse [ger-blay'zer] _n._ blast(-engine), supercharger (_tec._). [race.

Geblüt [ger-blyŏŏt'] _n._ blood.

Gebot [ger-bote'] _n._ (-e) command(ment), bid.

Gebräu [ger-broy'] _n._ (-e) brewing, mixture.

Gebrauch [ger-browch'] _nm._ (**Gebräuche**) use, usage, custom; **-en** _vt._ to use; **-sanweisung** _nf._ directions for use.

Gebräuchlich [ger-broysh'-lish] _a._ usual, customary.

Gebrechen [ger-bresh'en] _v. imp. vr._ to lack; _n._ infirmity.

Gebrechlich [ger-bresh'lish] _a._ fragile, frail; **-keit** _nf._ frailty, infirmity.

Gebrüder [ger-bryŏŏ'der] _m.pl._ brothers.

Gebrüll [ger-bryŏŏl'] _n._ roaring.

Gebühr [ger-byŏŏrr'] _nf._ due, decency; _pl._ charges, fee; **-en** _vi._ to be dur to; to be fitting; **-lich** _a._ due, becoming; **-nis** _n._ pay, emoluments.

Gebunden [ger-bŏŏn'den] _a._ bound, obliged.

Geburt [ger-bŏŏrrt'] _nf._ birth;

-enziffer nf. birth-rate;
-shelferin nf. midwife; **-sschein** nm. birth certificate.

Gebürtig [ger-byŏŏr'tish] a. born in, native of.

Gebüsch [ger-byŏŏsh'] n. (-e) clump of bushes, copse.

Geck [gek] m.w. fop, fool; **-enhaft** a. foolish, foppish.

Gedächtnis [ger-desht'nis] n. (-se) memory; **-feier** nf. commemoration.

Gedanke [ger-dank'er] nm. (gen. **-ns**; pl. **-n**) thought; **-nfolge** nf. train of thought; **-nlos** a. thoughtless; **-nlosigkeit** nf. thoughtlessness; **-nstrich** nm. dash; **-nvoll** a. thoughtful.

Gedärm [ger-dairrm'] n. (-e) intestines, bowels.

Gedeck [ger-dek'] n. (-e) cover(ing).

Gedeihen [ger-die'en] vi. ir. to thrive, prosper.

Gedeihlich [ger-die'lish] a. prosperous.

Gedenk'en [ger-denk'en] vi.t. ir. to remember, mention, intend; **-buch** n. memorandum book; **-feier** nf. commemoration.

Gedicht [ger-disht'] n. (-e) poem.

Gediegen [ger-dee'gen] a. solid, pure, genuine; **-heit** nf. solidity, purity.

Gedinge [ger-ding'er] n. piece-work. [double.

Gedoppelt [ger-dop'elt] a.

Gedränge [ger-dreng'er] n. crowd(ing), difficulty.

Gedrängt [ger-drengt'] a. tight, close, terse.

Gedruckte(s) [ger-dŏŏk'ter(s)] n.w. printed matter.

Geduld [ger-dŏŏlt'] nf. patience.

Gedulden [ger-dŏŏl'den] vr. to have patience.

Geduldig [ger-dŏŏl'dish] a. patient, forbearing.

Gedunsen [ger-dŏŏn'zen] a. bloated.

Geeignet [ger-ike'net] a. fit, appropriate.

Gefahr [ger-farr'] nf. danger; **-enraum** nm. danger area; **-los** a. without risk, danger.

Gefährden [ger-fairr'den] vt. to risk, endanger.

Gefährlich [ger-fairr'lish] a. dangerous.

Gefährt [ger-fairrt'] n. (-e) vehicle; **-e** m.w., **-in** nf. companion.

Gefälle [ger-fel'er] n. (-) gradient, incline.

Gefallen [ger-fal'en] n. (-) pleasure, liking; nm. favour; vi. ir. to please.

Gefällig [ger-fel'ish] a. pleasing, pleasant; **-keit** nf. pleasantness, favour.

Gefall-sucht nf. coquetishness; **-süchtig** a. coquetish, flirtatious.

Gefangen [ger-fang'en] a. captive, in custody; **-e(r)** m.w. captive, prisoner; **-enlager** n. prisoner of war camp; **-ensammelstelle** nf. prisoner of war camp; **-nahme** nf. capture; **-schaft** nf. captivity.

Gefängnis [ger-feng'nis] n. (-se) prison; **-wärter** nm. warder.

Gefäss [ger-face'] n. (-e) vessel.

Gefecht [ger-fesht'] n. (-e) fight; a. active service . . . ; **-sabschnitt** nm. battle sector; **-sauflkärer** nm. pathfinder aircraft **-sbefehl** nm. battle order; **-sbereitschaft** nf. tactical readiness; **-slandeplatz** nm. tactical landing ground; **-smeldung** nf. operational report; **-sstand** nm. battle headquarters; **-sstärke** nf. battle strength; **-sstation** nf. action stations (nav.); **-streifen** nm. attack, battle sector (mil.); **-stross** nm. battle transport; **-swagen** nm. ammunition and tools wagon; **-sziel** n. objective.

Gefieder [ger-feed'err] n. plumage, feathers; **-t** a. feathered.

Geflecht [ger-flesht] n. (-e) plaiting, wicker-work.

Gefleckt [ger-flekt'] a. spotted, mottled.

Geflissen [ger-fliss'en] a. diligent; **-tlich** a. ad. intentionally.

Geflügel [ger-flyōō'gel] n. poultry, fowls.

Gefolge [ger-fol'ger] n. suite, retinue.

Gefragt [ger-frahkt'] a. in demand (com.).

Gefrässig [ger-fray'sish] a. voracious.

Gefreite(r) [ger-frite'er] m.w. lance corporal, leading seaman, aircraftman, 1st class.

Gefrieren [ger-freer'ren] vi. ir. to freeze; **-punkt** nm. freezing-point.

Gefüge [ger-fyōō'ger] n. structure, texture; **-ig** a. pliant, flexible.

Gefühl [ger-fyōōl'] n. (-e) feeling; **-los** a. unfeeling; **-voll** a. (full of) feeling.

Gegebenenfalls [ger-gabe'-en-en-falss] ad. if so, in case.

Gegen [gay'gen] pr. towards, against, about, in (return for); **-angriff** nm. counter attack; **-beschuldigung** nf. recrimination; **-beweis** nm. counterproof; **-bild** n. counterpart.

Gegend [gay'gent] nf. district, neighbourhood, region.

Gegeneinander [gay'gen-ine-an-derr] ad. against one another.

Gegen-forderung nf. counter-claim; **-gewicht** n. counterpoise; **-gift** n. antidote; **-leistung** nf. equivalent, return (service); **-marsch** nm. countermarch; **-part** nm. adversary; **-partei** nf. opposition; **-rechnung** nf. check, set-off (com.);

-rede nf. contradiction, rejoinder; **-satz** nm. contrary, contrast; **-sätzlich** a. contrary.

Gegenseit'e [gay'gen-zite-er] nf. opposite side, reverse; **-ig** a. mutual, reciprocal; **-igkeit** nf. reciprocity.

Gegen-signal n. answering signal; **-stand** nm. subject, object.

Gegenständlich [gay'gen-shtent-lish] a. objective; **-keit** nf. objectivity.

Gegen-stoss nm. counterthrust; **-teil** n. contrary, opposite.

Gegenüber [gay-gen-yōō'berr] ad. pr. opposite; **-stellung** nf. contrast, antithesis.

Gegen-unterschrift nf. counter-signature; **-vertrauensspiel** n. double crossing; **-wart** nf. present (time), presence; **-wärtig** a. (at) present, current(ly); **-wehr** nf. resistance; **-wert** nm. equivalent; **-wind** nm. head-wind; **-wirkung** nf. reaction; **-zug** nm. counter-move.

Gegner [gake'nerr] nm. (-) opponent, enemy; **-schaft** nf. antagonism, opponents.

Gehalt [ger-halt'] nm. (-e) contents, capacity, worth; n. (Gehälter) pay, salary; **-los** a. worthless, superficial; **-losigkeit** nf. worthlessness, superficiality; **-reich** a. valuable, substantial; **-vorschuss** nm. advance on salary.

Gehässig [ger-hess'ish] a. spiteful, odious; **-keit** nf. spitefulness, malice.

Gehäuse [ger-hoy'zer] n. (-) case, box.

Gehege [ger-hay'ger] n. (-) enclosure, preserve.

Geheim [ger-hime'] a. secret, private; **-bund** nm. secret society, underground movement; **-polizist** m.w. detective; **-schrift** nf. cipher, code.

Geheimnis [ger-hime'nis] n. (-se) secret, mystery; -voll a. mysterious.

Geheiss [ger-hice'] n. command.

Gehen [gay'en] vi. ir. to go, walk.

Geheul [ger-hoil'] n. howling.

Gehilfe [ger-hil'fer] nm. -in nf. assistant, orderly (mil.).

Gehirn [ger-hirrn'] n. (-e) brain(s); -erschütterung nf. concussion.

Gehöft [ger-herft'] n. (-e) farm-stead.

Gehölz [ger-herlts'] n. (-e) wood, grove.

Gehör [ger-herr'] n. hearing, ear; -schützer nm. ear-plug.

Gehorchen [ger-horr'shen] vi. to obey.

Gehören [ger-her'ren] vi. to belong; imp.r. be right, fitting.

Gehörig [ger-her'rish] a. pertinent, fit, decent.

Gehorsam [ger-horr'zam] a. obedient; nm. obedience.

Gehre [gair'rer] nf. gore, wedge, bevel; -n vt. to bevel.

Gehrock [gay'rok] nm. (-röcke) frock-coat.

Gehwerk [gay'vairrk] n. works (watch).

Geier [gie'err] nm. (-e) vulture.

Geifer [gife'err] nm. slaver, venomous; -n vi. to slaver, speak venomously; -tuch n. bib.

Geige [guy'ger] nf. fiddle; -n vi. to fiddle; -r nm. fiddler.

Geil [guile'] a. luxurious, lascivious; -heit nf. luxuriance, lasciviousness.

Geisel [guy'zel] nm. (-) hostage.

Geiss [gice] nf. goat; -blatt n. honeysuckle.

Geissel [gice'el] nf. scourge, whip; -n vt. to scourge.

Geist [gist] nm. (-er) spirit, ghost, mind; -erhaft a. ghostly; -esabwesend a. absent-minded; -esgegenwart nf. presence of

mind; -eskrank a. insane; -esverwandt a. congenial.

Geistig [gist'ish] a. intellectual, spiritual, spirituous; -keit nf. intellectuality, spirituality.

Geistlich [gist'lish] a. spiritual, clerical, ghostly; -e(r) m.w. clergyman; -keit nf. spirituality, clergy.

Geistlos [gist'lohss] a. unintellectual, dull.

Geistreich [gist'rish] a. ingenious, smart, witty.

Geistvoll [gist'fol] a. spirited, ingenious.

Geiz [gits] nm. avarice, miserliness; -en vi. to be miserly; -hals nm. miser.

Geklapper [ger-klap'err] n. clatter(ing).

Geklingel [ger-kling'el] n. tinkling, jingling.

Gekritzel [ger-krit'sel] n. scrawl(ing).

Gekünstelt [ger-kyoon'stelt] a. artificial, affected.

Gelächter [ger-lesh'terr] n. laughter.

Geladen [ger-lah'den] a. loaded, live (wire).

Gelage [ger-lah'ger] n. (-) feast, banquet.

Gelände [ger-len'der] n. tract of land, country, terrain; -aufnahme nf. air photograph, survey; -lauf nm. cross country race; -punkt nm. landmark; -spiel n. scouting, learning to use cover.

Geländer [ger-len'derr] n. (-) railing, trellis.

Gelangen [ger-lang'en] vi. to reach, attain.

Gelassen [ger-lass'en] a. calm, composed; -heit nf. calmness, composure.

Geläufig [ger-loy'fish] a. fluent, familiar; -keit nf. fluency, familiarity.

Gelaunt [ger-lownt'] a. disposed.

Geläute [ger-loy'ter] n. ringing [of bells, chime.

Gelb [gelp] a. yellow; -grün-empfindlich a. chromatic; -lich a. yellowish; -sucht nf. jaundice.

Geld [gelt] n. (-er) money, cash; -anlage nf. investment; -anweisung nf. money-order; -ausleiher nm. money-lender; -bedürftig a. in need of money; -bestand nm. cash in hand; -beutel nm. purse; -büchse nf. money-box; -geschäft n. financial transaction; -markt nm. money-market; -mittel pl. means; -not nf. need of money; -schneider nm. sharper; -schrank nm. safe, strong-box; -sendung nf. cash remittance; -stand nm. condition of the money market; -strafe nf. fine; -vorschuss nm. cash advance; -wechsler nm. money-changer; -wesen n. finance.

Gelee [zher-lay'] nf. jelly.

Gelegen [ger-lay'gen] a. situated, convenient, opportune.

Gelegenheit [ger-lay'gen-hite] nf. opportunity, occasion; -sarbeiter nm. casual worker; -skauf nm. bargain.

Gelegentlich [ger-lay'gent-lish] a. occasional, incidental; ad. occasionally; by the way, at one's convenience.

Gelehrig [ger-lair'rish] a. docile, intelligent; -keit nf. docility, intelligence.

Gelehr-samkeit nf. learning; -ta, learned; -te(r) m.w. scholar.

Geleise [ger-lize'er] n. (-) track; see Gleis.

Geleit [ger-lite'] n. retinue, escort; -zug nm. convoy (nav.), escort (mil.).

Geleiten [ger-lite'en] vt. to escort.

Gelenk [ger-lenk'] n. (-e) joint; -binde nf. anklet; -ig a. supple, pliant; -igkeit nf. suppleness.

Gelernt [ger-lairrnt'] a. skilled.

Geliebte(r) [ger-leep'ter] m.w. Geliebte sweetheart, beloved.

Gelind [ger-lint'] a. mild, gentle; -igkeit nf. mildness, gentleness.

Gelingen [ger-ling'en] vi. ir. to succeed, prosper. [yell.

Gellen [gel'en] vi. to shriek,

Geloben [ger-lobe'en] vi.t. to vow. [vow.

Gelöbnis [ger-lerp'nis] n. (-se)

Gelten [gel'ten] vi. ir. to be worth, valid, at stake, pass for, concern; -d machen make good.

Geltung [gel'toong] nf. value, currency, prestige. [vow.

Gelübde [ger-lüp'der] n. (-)

Gelüst [ger-lüst'] n. (-e) desire, lust; -en vi. imp. to desire.

Gemach [ger-mach'] n. (Gemächer) appartment.

Gemächlich [ger-mesh'lish] a. comfortable, leisurely.

Gemahl [ger-mahl'] nm. (-e) husband; -in nf. wife.

Gemahnen [ger-mah'nen] vt. to remind.

Gemälde [ger-male'der] n. (-) picture, painting.

Gemäss [ger-mace'] a. conformable, proportionate; ad. according to; -igt a. moderate.

Gemein [ger-mine'] a. common, vulgar, low; -e(r) m.w. private (mil.); -gefährlich a. dangerous to society; -gut n. public property; -nutz nm. public good; -platz nm. commonplace; -sinn nm. public spirit; -wesen n. community.

Gemeinde [ger-mine'der] nf. parish, commune, municipality; -küche nf. communal kitchen; -schule nf. board school; -vorstand nm. town council; -vorsteher nm. head of commune, mayor.

Gemeinheit [ger-mine'hite[

nf. commonness, vulgarity, mean act.

Gemeinsam [ger-mine'zam] *a., ad.* corporate, (in) common.

Gemeinschaft [ger-mine'shaft] *nf.* community, intercourse; **-lich** *a.* common, joint; *ad.* in common, jointly.

Gemenge [ger-meng'er] *n.* mixture, scuffle.

Gemessen [ger-mess'en] *a.* precise, sedate.

Gemetzel [ger-met'sel] *n.* slaughter, shambles.

Gemisch [ger-mish'] *n.* mixture.

Gemme [gem'er] *nf.* gem.

Gemse [gem'zer] *nf.* chamois, **-leder** *n.* shammy.

Gemurmel [ger-moor'mel] *n.* murmur(ing).

Gemüse [ger-myoo'zer] *n.* vegetables; **-händler** *nm.* greengrocer.

Gemüt [ger-myoot'] *n.* (-er) disposition, mind, heart; **-sbeschaffenheit** *nf.* character; **-sbewegung** *nf.* emotion; **-smensch** *m.w.* sentimental man.

Gemütlich [ger-myoot'lish] *a.* comfortable, good-natured; **-keit** *nf.* comfortableness, good nature, kindliness.

Genau [ger-now'] *a., ad.* exact(ly), precise(ly), accurate (-ly); **-igkeit** *nf.* exactness, accuracy.

Genehm [ger-name'] *a.* agreeable, acceptable; **-igen** *vt.* to accept, sanction, ratify; **-igung** *nf.* acceptance, sanction, ratification.

Geneigt [ger-nikt'] *a.* inclined, disposed, prone; **-heit** *nf.* inclination.

General [gen-er-rahl'] *nm.* (-e) general; **-arzt** *nm.* medical officer; **-bevollmächtigte(r)** *m.w.* commissioner general; **-feldmarschall** *nm.* field marshal; **-inspektor** *nm.* in-

spector general; **-kommando** *n.* army corps headquarters, general high command; **-leutnant** *nm.* lieutenant general, air-marshal; **-major** major general, air-vice-marshal; **-oberst** *m.w.* colonel general; **-probe** *nf.* dress rehearsal; **-rat** *nm.* board of governors (*bank*); **-stab** *nm.* general staff; **-stabskarte** *nf.* ordnance map.

Generalität [gen-er-ra-li-tate'] *nf.* generals.

Generation [gen-er-rat-syohn'] *nf.* generation.

Generator [gen-er-rah'torr] *nm.* (*gen.* -s; *pl.* -en) dynamo, generator, producer.

Genesen [ger-nay'zen] *vi. ir.* to recover; **-de(r)** *m.w.*, **-de** *f.* convalescent.

Genesung [ger-nay'zoong] *nf.* recovery, convalescence; **-surlaub** *n.* sick leave.

Genial [gay-ni-ahl'] *a.* gifted; **-ität** *nf.* brilliance, genius.

Genick [ger-nik'] *n.* (-e) nape of the neck.

Genie [zhay-nee']*n.* (-s) genius, engineer corps (*mil.*).

Genieren [zhay-neer'ren] *vt.* to embarrass; *r.* feel awkward.

Geniess'bar [ger-neess'barr] *a.* palatable; **-en** *vt. ir.* to enjoy, eat, drink.

Genoss'e [ger-noss'er] *m.w.*, **-in** *f.* companion, comrade, colleague; **-enschaft** *nf.* association, company, co-operative society.

Genug [ger-nook'] *ad.* enough; **-sam** *a.* sufficient; **-tuung** *nf.* satisfaction, reparation.

Genüg'e [ger-nyoo'ger] *nf.* sufficiency, satisfaction; **-en** *vi.* to suffice; **-end** *a.* sufficient; **-sam** *a.* temperate, frugal; **-samkeit** *nf.* contentedness, temperance.

Genuss [ger-nooss'] *nm.* (**Genüsse**) pleasure, profit, (par)taking; -mittel *pl.* luxuries; -reich *a.* enjoyable.

Geograph [gay-o-grahf'] *m.w.* geographer; -ie *nf.* geography.

Geolog [gay-o-lohk'] *m.w.* geologist; -ie *nf.* geology.

Geomet'er [gay-o-mate'err] *nm.* (-) geometrician, surveyor; -rie *nf.* geometry.

Georgine [gay-orr-gee'ner] *nf.* dahlia.

Gepäck [ger-pek'] *n.* (-e) luggage, baggage; -träger *nm.* porter (*rl.*); -tross *nm.* convoy, baggage transport (*mil.*).

Gepflogenheit [ger-pfloh'gen-hite] *nf.* habit.

Geplänkel [ger-plenkl'] *n.* (-) skirmish.

Geplapper [ger-plap'err] *n.* chatter.

Geplauder [ger-plow'derr] *n.* talk, chat(ting).

Gepolter [ger-pol'terr] *n.* din.

Gepräge [ger-pray'ger] *n.* coinage, stamp.

Gepränge [ger-preng'er] *n.* pomp, ostentation.

Gerad'e [ger-rah'der] *a.* even, straight(forward), upright; *ad.* directly, blintly, just; -eaus *ad.* straight on; -ezu *ad.* directly, positively; -heit *nf.* straightness, evenness, rectitude; -sinnig *a.* straightforward.

Gerät [ger-rate'] *n.* (-e) tools, utensils, equipment, device, gear; -schaften *pl.* tools, implements.

Geraten [ger-rah'ten] *vi. ir.* to get into, come upon, turn out, prove, thrive; aneinander -n to fall out; *a.* successful, advisable; -wohl *n.* random.

Geraum [ger-rowm'] *a.* ample.

Geräumig [ger-roy'mish] *a.* roomy, vast.

Geräusch [ger-roysh'] *n.* (-e) noise, sound; -los *a.* soundless; -voll *a.* noisy.

Gerben)gairr'ben] *vt.* to tan.

Gerber [gairr'berr] *nm.* (-) tanner; -ei *nf.* tannery.

Gerecht [ger-resht'] *a.* just, upright, fair; -igkeit *nf.* justice, right, fairness.

Gerede [ger-rade'er] *n.* talk, gossip.

Gereichen [ger-rī'shen] *vi.* to rebound, cause.

Gereiztheit [ger-ritst'hite] *nf.* irritation.

Gereuen [ger-roy'en] *vt. imp.* to be sorry, repent.

Gericht [ger-risht'] *n.* (-e) (court of) justice, bench, dish; -lich *a.* judicial, legal; *ad.* judicially, by, at law; -sbarkeit *nf.* jurisdiction; -skosten *pl.* costs (*law*).

Gering [ger-ring'] *a.* small, petty, limited, inferior; -st *a.* least; -fügig *a.* trivial, mean; -schätzung *nf.* disdain.

Gerinn'e [ger-rin'er] *n.* (-) channel, gutter; -en *vi.* to curdle, congeal; -ung *nf.* coagulation.

Gerippe [ger-rip'er] *n.* (-) skeleton.

Gerissen [ger-ris'en] *a.* wily.

Gern(e) [gairr'ner] *ad.* willingly, gladly.

Geröll'e [ger-rer'ler] *n.* rubble, shingle.

Gerste [gairr'ster] *nf.* barley.

Gerte [gairr'ter] *nf.* switch, rod.

Geruch [ger-rooch'] *nm.* (Gerüche) smell, odour; -los *a.* odourless.

Gerücht [ger-ryöcht'] *n.* (-e) rumour. [deign.

Geruhen [ger-röo'en] *vi.* to

Gerümpel [ger-ryöm'pel] *n.* lumber.

Gerüst [ger-ryöost'] *n.* (-e) scaffold(ing), frame.

Gesamt [ger-zamt'] *a.* whole, all-in, total, complete; -heit *nf.* totality, whole; -last *pl.* useful load; -übersicht *nf.* general survey.

Gesandt'e(r) [ger-zan'terr] *m.w.* ambassador; **-schaft** *nf.* embassy.

Gesang [ger-zang'] *nm.* (Gesänge) song, hymn, canto; **-verein** *nm.* choral society.

Gesäss [ger-zace'] *n.* (-e) seat, bottom.

Geschäft [ger-sheft'] *n.* (-e) business, shop; **-ig** *a.* active, busy, officious; **-lich** *a.* commercial; **-führer** *nm.* manager, acting minister; **-smann** *nm.* business man; **-smässig** *a.* business-like; **-spersonal** *n.* (clerical) staff; **-sreisende(r)** *m.w.* commercial traveller; **-sstelle** *nf.* office, place of business; **-sträger** *nm.* agent, chargé d'affaires; **-sviertel** *n.* shopping quarter; **-swagen** *nm.* delivery van; **-szimmer** *n.* general office, orderly room (mil.); **-szweig** *nm.* branch (of business).

Geschehen [ger-shay'en] *vi. ir.* to happen.

Gescheit [ger-shite'] *a.* clever, shrewd.

Geschenk [ger-shenk'] *n.* (-e) present, gift.

Geschicht'e [ger-shish'ter] *nf.* story, affair, history; **-lich** *a.* historical; **-sschreiber** *nm.* historian.

Geschick [ger-shik'] *n.* aptness, aptitude, fate; **-lichkeit** *nf.* skill, dexterity; **-t** *a.* skilful, capable.

Geschiebe [ger-shebe'er] *n.* rubble, shingle, cobbles.

Geschirr [ger-shirr'] *n.* (-e) utensils, harness, apparatus, gear.

Geschlecht [ger-shlesht'] *n.* (-er) species, sex, gender, family; **-lich** *a.* sexual; **-skrankheit** *nf.* venereal disease; **-sreife** *nf.* puberty.

Geschmack [ger-shmak'] *nm.* (Geschmäcke) taste, flavour; **-los** *a.* tasteless, in bad taste;

-ssache *nf.* matter of taste; **-voll** *a.* tasteful, fashionable.

Geschmeide [ger-shmide'er] *n.* jewels, trinkets.

Geschmeidig [ger-shmide'ish] *a.* supple, yielding, malleable.

Geschmeiss [ger-shmiss'] *n.* scum, dung, vermin.

Geschmiere [ger-shmeer'rer] *n.* smearing, scrawl.

Geschöpf [ger-sherpf'] *n.* (-e) creature.

Geschoss [ger-shoss'] *n.* (-e) missile, projectile, shell (mil.).

Geschräge [ger-shray'ger] *n.* (-) paling, hurdle.

Geschraubt [ger-shrowpt'] *a.* stilted, artificial.

Geschrei [ger-shri'] *n.* (-e) cries, clamour, shouting, fuss.

Geschütz [ger-shyöots'] *n.* (-e) gun, cannon; **-bedienung** *nf.* gun-crew (mil.); **-feuer** *n.* artillery fire, gunfire; **-stand** *nm.* gun emplacement; **-t** *a.* protected, armoured (mil.).

Geschwader [ger-shvah'der] *n.* (-) squadron (nav.), group (av.).

Geschwätz [ger-shvets'] *n.* idle talk, gossip; **-ig** *a.* talkative; **-igkeit** *nf.* talkativeness.

Geschweige [ger-shvi'ger] *ad.* not to mention, let alone.

Geschwind [ger-shvint'] *a.* quick, swift; **-igkeit** *nf.* quickness, velocity, speed, gear (aut. etc.); **-igkeitsanzeiger** *nm.* **-messer** speedometer.

Geschwister [ger-shvis'terr] *pl.* brothers and sisters; **-kind** *n.* nephew, niece, cousin.

Geschworene(r) [ger-shvore'en-err] *m.w.* juror; **-** *jury.* jury.

Geschwulst [ger-shvoolst'] *nf.* (Geschwülste) tumour, swelling.

Geschwür [ger-shvyöorr'] *n.* (-e) ulcer.

Gesell'e [ger-zel'er] *m.w.* companion, fellow, artisan, workman; **-en** *vt.r.* to join, associate;

-ig a. sociable, gregarious; -igkeit nf. sociability.

Gesellschaft [ger-zel'shaft] nf. society, company, party; -er nm, -erin nf. partner, companion; -lich a. social, sociable; -svertrag nm. deed of partnership.

Gesetz [ger-zets'] n. (-e) law; -antrag nm, -vorlage nf. bill; -buch n. (legal) code; -gebend a. legislative; -geber nm. legislator; -gebung nf. legislation; -lich a. lawful, legal, legitimate; -lichkeit nf. lawfulness, legality; -los a. lawless; -mässig a. see gesetzlich.

Gesetzt [ger-zetst'] a. sedate, fixed, set up; - dass if, assuming that.

Gesicht [ger-zisht'] n. (-e) sight, vision, (-er) face; -sfarbe nf. complexion; -skreis nm. horizon; -spunkt nm. point of view. [cornice, moulding.

Gesims [ger-zimss'] n. (-e)

Gesindel [ger-zindl'] n. rabble.

Gesinnt [ger-zint'] a. minded, disposed, sympathizing with.

Gesinnung [ger-zin'ōong] nf. disposition, conviction.

Gesittet [ger-zit'et] a. civilized.

Gespann [ger-shpan'] n. (-e) team (horses).

Gespannt [ger-shpant'] a. (in)tense, strained, anxious; -heit nf. tension.

Gespenst [ger-shpenst'] n. (-er) ghost, spectre; -erhaft a. ghostly.

Gesperre [ger-shper'rer] n. block, catch, fuss.

Gespiele [ger-shpele'er] m.w. Gespielin nf. playmate.

Gespinst [ger-shpinst'] n. (-e) yarn, web, tissue.

Gespött [ger-shpert'] n. mockery, laughing-stock.

Gespräch [ger-shpraish'] n. (-e) conversation, interview; -ig a. talkative; -igkeit nf. talkativeness.

Gestaffelt [ger-shtaf'elt] a. staggered, in formation, in echelon (av.).

Gestalt [ger-shtalt'] nf. shape, form, aspect; -en vt. to shape, form; r. take shape, turn out; -los a. shapeless; -ung nf. formation, state.

Geständig [ger-shten'dish] a. pleading guilty, confessing guilt; -nis n. confession.

Gestänge [ger-shteng'er] n. poles, rods, gear change mechanism, valve gear (tec.).

Gestank [ger-shtank'] n. (Gestänke) stench.

Gestatt'en [ger-shtat'en] vi. to permit; r. venture; -ung nf. permission.

Geste [gest'er] nf. gesture.

Gesteh'en [ger-shtay'en] vt. iv. to confess; -ungskosten pl. cost price, cost of manufacture.

Gestein [ger-shtine'] n. (-e) stone, mineral, rock.

Gestell [ger-shtel'] n. (-e) frame, trestle, shelf, stand; -en vr. to present oneself; -ung nf. enlistment; -ungsbefehl nm. order to report (mil.). [day.

Gestern [gest'errn] ad. yester-

Gestirn [ger-shtirrn'] n. (-e) star, constellation.

Gestöber [ger-shter'berr] n. (-) snow-drift, blizzard.

Gesträuch [ger-shtroish'] n. (-e) shrubs, shrubbery, bush.

Gestrig [gest'rish] a. yesterday's.

Gestrüpp [ger-shtryoop'] n. briers, scrub.

Gestüt [ger-shtyoot'] n. (-e) stud.

Gesuch [ger-zooch'] n. (-e) petition, request; -t a. in demand (com.), far-fetched.

Gesund [ger-zoont'] a. healthy, sound, wholesome; -heit nf. health, wholesomeness; -heitlich a. hygienic.

Getäfel [ger-tafe'el] n. wainscot, panelling.

Getränk [ger-trenk'] *n.* (-e) beverage, drink.

Getrauen [ger-trow'en] *vt.i.r.* venture, dare.

Getreide [ger-tride'er] *n.* corn, grain, cereals, produce; -bau *nm.* agriculture; -börse *nf.* corn exchange.

Getreu [ger-troy'] *a.* trusty, loyal; -lich *ad.* faithfully.

Getriebe [ger-tree'ber] *n.* bustle, machinery, driving-gear, pinion; -kasten *nm.* gearbox, -case.

Getrost [ger-trohst'] *a, ad.* confident(ly).

Getue [ger-too'er] *n.* affectation, fuss.

Gevatter [ger-fat'err] *nm. (gen.* -s; *pl.* -en) godfather, gaffer, crony; -in *nf.* godmother.

Geviert [ger-feerrt'] *n.* (-e) square.

Gewächs [ger-vex'] *n.* (-e) growth, plant; -haus *n.* greenhouse.

Gewagt [ger-vahkt'] *a.* daring, risky.

Gewählt [ger-vailt'] *a.* choice, select.

Gewähr [ger-vare'] *nf.* guarantee, voucher, surety; -schein *nm.* bond, warrant; -smann *nm.* informant, guarantor, authority; -ung *nf.* granting.

Gewähren [ger-vare'en] *vt.* to grant, guarantee; - lassen let alone.

Gewahrsam [ger-varr'zam] *nm.* (-e) safe-keeping, custody.

Gewalt [ger-valt'] *nf.* power, force; -herrscher *nm.* despot; -ig *a.* powerful, tremendous; -marsch *nm.* forced march; -sam *a.* forcible, violent; -samkeit *nf.* violence.

Gewand [ger-vant'] *n.* (Ge-wänder) garment.

Gewandt [ger-vant'] *a.* nimble, skilful; -heit *nf.* dexterity, skill.

Gewärtig [ger-vairr'tish] *a.*

awaiting, expecting; -en *vt.* to expect.

Gewäsch [ger-vesh'] *n.* idle talk, nonsense. [waters.

Gewässer [ger-vess'err] *n.* (-)

Gewebe [ger-vabe'er] *n.* (-) texture, tissue.

Geweckt [ger-vekt'] *a.* lively, intelligent; -heit *nf.* liveliness, intelligence.

Gewehr [ger-vairr'] *n.* (-e) gun, rifle; -kammer *nf.* armoury; -lauf *nm.* rifle barrel; -schütze *m.w.* rifleman; -zielfernrohr *n.* telescopic rifle-sight. [antlers.

Geweih [ger-vie'] *n.* (-e)

Gewerb'e [ger-vairr'ber] *n.* trade, calling, industry; -schule *nf.* technical school; -lich *a.* industrial; -smässig *a.* professional, vocational.

Gewerk [ger-vairrk'] *n.* craft, corporation, guild; -schaft *nf.* trade union; -schaftler *nm.* trade unionist; -schaftsbund *nm.* trades union council.

Gewicht [ger-visht'] *n.* (-e) weight, importance; -ig *a.* weighty.

Gewiegt [ger-veekt'] *a.* experienced, fully versed.

Gewillt [ger-vilt'] *a.* willing, disposed.

Gewimmel [ger-viml'] *n.* swarm, throng.

Gewinde [ger-vin'der] *n.* (-) winding, wreath, hank, thread *(screw)*; -bohrer *nm.* gimlet, screw-tap.

Gewinn [ger-vin'] *nm.* (-e) winnings, gain, profit; -sucht *nf.* love of gain; -ung *nf.* winning, extraction *(coal, etc.).*

Gewinnen [ger-vin'en] *vt. ir.* to win, gain (over); -d *a.* winning, attractive. [maze.

Gewirr [ger-virr'] *n.* tangle,

Gewiss [ger-viss'] *a, ad.* sure(ly), certain(ly); -ermassen *ad.* to some extent; -heit *nf.* certainty.

Gewissen [ger-viss'en] n. conscience; -haft a. conscientious; -haftigkeit nf. conscientiousness; -los a. unscrupulous; -losigkeit nf. unscrupulousness; -sbiss nm. remorse, qualms; -sfreiheit nf. freedom of conscience.

Gewitter [ger-vit'err] n. (-) thunderstorm; -n vi. to break (storm), thunder; -schwül a. sultry.

Gewitz(ig)t [ger-vits'isht] a. shrewd, wise.

Gewogen [ger-voh'gen] a. well disposed.

Gewöhn'en [ger-ver'nen] vt.r. to accustom, train; -lich a. usual, ordinary; -ung nf. getting accustomed to, habit.

Gewohnheit [ger-vone'hite] nf. habit, usage; -srecht n. common law.

Gewohnt [ger-vohnt'] a. accustomed.

Gewölbe [ger-verl'ber] n. (-) vault, cellar.

Gewölk [ger-verlk'] n. (banks of) cloud. [turmoil.]

Gewühl [ger-vyool'] n. bustle,

Gewürm [ger-vyoorm'] n. worms, reptiles, creeping things.

Gewürz [ger-vyoorts'] n. (-e) spice, seasoning; -nelke nf. clove; -ig a. spicy, aromatic.

Gezahnt [gert-sahnt'] a. toothed, notched. [ling.]

Gezänk [gert-senk'] n. quarrel-

Gezeiten [gert-site'en] pl. tides.

Gezeter [gert-say'terr] n. outcries, screaming, noise.

Geziemen [gert-seem'en] vr.i. imp. to be fitting; -d a. proper, seemly.

Geziert [gert-seerrt'] a. affected; -heit nf. affectation.

Gezücht [gert-syoosht'] n. breed, pack.

Gezwitscher [gert-svit'sherr] n. twittering.

Gezwungen [gert-svoong'en] a. forced.

Gicht [gisht] nf. gout; -isch a. gouty.

Giebel [gee'bel] nm. (-) gable; -fenster n. attic window.

Giekbaum [geek'bowm] nm. main-, spanker-boom.

Gier [geerr] nf. avidity, greed; -ig a. greedy.

Gieren [gee'ren] vi. to veer.

Giess'en [geese'en] vt. ir. to pour, mould, found; -bach nm. torrent; -er nm. founder, caster; -erei nf. foundry; -kanne nf. watering can.

Gift [gift] n. (-e) poison; -ig a. poisonous.

Gilde [gil'der] nf. guild. [(com.)]

Gimpe [gim'per] nf. gimping.

Gimpel [gim'pel] nm. (-) bullfinch, blockhead.

Ginster [gin'sterr] nm. broom.

Gipfel [gip'fel] nm. (-) summit, peak, climax, top; -höhe nf. ceiling (av.); -n vi. to culminate.

Gips [gips] nm. plaster of Paris; -en vt. to plaster; -figur nf. plaster figure.

Giraffe [gi-raf'er] nf. giraffe.

Girant [zhi-rant'] m.w. endorser.

Girieren [zhi-reer'ren] vt. to endorse, put into circulation.

Giro [zhee'roh] n. (-s) endorsement; -konto n. current account.

Girren [gir'ren] vi. to coo.

Gischt [gisht] nm. foam, spray.

Giss'en [giss'en] vt. to estimate; -ung nf. dead reckoning (nt.).

Gitarre [gi-tar'rer] nf. guitar.

Gitter [git'err] n. (-) trellis, grating, fence, grid (rad.); -batterie nf. grid battery; -bett n. child's cot; -mast nm. pylon; -n vt. to fence, rail in, trellis.

Glacéhandschuh [gla-say-hant-shoo] nm. (-e) kid-glove.

Glanz [glants] nm. brilliance, lustre, splendour, polish, finish (*tec.*); **-kohle** *nf.* anthracite; **-leder** *n.* patent leather; **-papier** *n.* glazed paper.

Glänzen [glent'sen] *vi.* to gleam, glitter, glisten; **-d** *a.* brilliant, glittering.

Glas [glass] *n.* (Gläser) glass; **-bläser** *nm.* glass-blower; **-er** *nm.* glazier; **-hütte** *nf.* glass factory; **-ieren** *vt.* to glaze, varnish, frost; **-ig** *a.* glassy; **-ur** *nf.* glazing, icing, varnishing.

Gläsern [glay'zerrn] *a.* of glass, glassy.

Glatt [glat] *a.* smooth, slippery, safe (*landing*), polished.

Glätte [glet'er] *nf.* smoothness, slipperiness, polish; **-n** *vt.* to polish, plane.

Glatze [glat'ser] *nf.* bald head.

Glaub'e [glow'ber] *nm.* (*gen.* **-ns**) faith, belief; **-en** *vt.* to believe, trust, think; **-ensbekenntnis** *n.* creed; **-haft** *a.* credible; **-haftigkeit** *nf.* credibility; **-lich** *a.* *see* **-haft**; **-würdig** *a.* credible, trustworthy; **-würdigkeit** *nf.* trustworthiness.

Gläubig [gloy'bikh] *a.* believing, trustful, credulous; **-e(r)** *m.w.* believer; **-er** *nm.* creditor.

Gleich [glīsh] *a.* like, equal, level; *ad.* alike, equally; **-artig** *a.* homogeneous, similar; **-bedeutend** *a.* synonymous, tantamount; **-en** *vi.* to be like, equal; **-falls** *ad.* likewise, the same to you; **-förmig** *a.* uniform; **-förmigkeit** *nf.* uniformity; **-gewicht** *n.* equilibrium, balance; **-gültig** *a.* indifferent, unimportant; **-gültigkeit** *nf.* uniformity; **-klang** *nm.* unison, concord; **-mut** *nm.* equanimity; **-mütig** *a.* even-tempered; **-nis** *n.* parable; **-richter** *nm.* rectifier (*rad.*); **-sam** *ad.* as it were, so to speak; **-strom** *nm.* direct current (*el.*); **-ung** *nf.* equation; **-viel** *ad.* no matter,

all one; **-wohl** *ad.* nevertheless; **-zeitig** *a.* simultaneous, contemporary.

Gleis [glīce] *n.* (**-**) track, rails; **-kette** *nf.* caterpillar track; **-kettenschlepper** *nm.* caterpillar tractor.

Gleisner [glīce'nerr] *nm.* (**-**) hypocrite; **-isch** *n.* hypocritical.

Gleit'en [glīte'en] *vi. ir.* to glide, slide, slip; **-fläche** *nf.* tread (*tyre*); **-flieger** *nm.* glider pilot; **-flug** *nm.* glide, gliding (*av.*); **-flugzeug** *n.* glider; **-schutzreifen** *nm.* non-skid tyre (*aut.*).

Gletscher [glet'sherr] *nm.* (**-**) glacier.

Glied [gleet] *n.* (**-er**) member, limb, link, rank(s); **-erlahm** *a.* paralysed; **-ern** *vt.* to organize, articulate, arrange, form; **-erung** *nf.* organisation, articulation, structure, formation (*mil.*).

Glimm'en [glim'en] *vi.* to glimmer, glow; **-er** *nm.* glimmer; **-ern** *vi.* *see* **Glimmen**; **-spur** *nf.* night-tracer.

Glimpflich [glimpf'lish] *a.* lenient, mild, easy.

Glitschen [glit'shen] *vi.* to glide, slide.

Glitzern [glit'serrn] *vi.* to glitter, twinkle.

Glöckchen [glerk'shen] *n.* (**-**) little bell.

Glocke [glok'er] *nf.* bell; **-ngeläute** *n.* peal of bells; **-nspiel** *n.* chime; **-nstuhl** *nm.* belfry.

Glorie [glore'i-err] *nf.* glory, halo; **-nschein** *nm.* halo.

Glossar [gloss-ahrr'] *n.* (**-e**) glossary.

Glosse [gloss'er] *nf.* gloss.

Glotzäugig [glots'oy-gish] *a.* goggle-eyed.

Glotzen [glot'sen] *vi.* to stare.

Glück [glyōōk] *n.* (good) luck, fortune, happiness, lot; **-sbringer** *nm.* mascot; **-en** *vi.* to prosper; **-lich** *a.* fortunate, happy; **-licherweise** *ad.* fortunately; **-selig** *a.* blissful, happy; **-seligkeit** *nf.* bliss, happiness; **-skind** *n.* lucky person; **-sspiel** *n.* game of chance; **-sstern** *nm.* lucky star; **-wunsch** *nm.* congratulations, best wishes.

Glucken [glŏŏk'en] *vi.* to cluck.

Glüh- [glyŏŏ] **-birne** *nf.* bulb (*el.*); **-en** *vi.* to glow; **-faden** *nm.* filament (*el.*); **-licht** *n.* incandescent light; **-ofen** *nm.* annealing furnace; **-strumpf** *nm.* mantle; **-wurm** *nm.* glow-worm.

Glut [glŏŏt] *nf.* glow, fire.

Glyzerin [glyŏŏ-tser-een'] *n.* glycerine.

Gnade [gnah'der] *nf.* favour, grace, mercy; **-nfrist** *nf.* reprieve, respite; **-nstoss** *nm.* knock-out. [kind.

Gnädig [gnay'dish] *a.* gracious,

Gold [golt] *n.* gold; **-arbeiter, -schmied** *nm.* goldsmith; **-en** *a.* golden; **-grube** *nf.* goldmine; **-lack** *nm.* wallflower; **-regen** *nm.* laburnum; **-schnitt** *nm.* gilt edges; **-währung** *nf.* gold standard.

Golf [golf] *nm.* (**-e**) gulf.

Gondel [gon'del] *nf.* gondola.

Gönn'en [ger'nen] *vt.* to grant, not grudge; **-er** *nm.* patron; **-erhaft** *a.* patronising.

Göpel [ger'pel] *nm.* (**-**) winch, capstan.

Gösch [gersh] *nf.* small flag, jack.

Gosse [goss'er] *nf.* gutter.

Gott [got] *nm.* (**Götter**) god; **-esdienst** *nm.* divine service; **-eshaus** *n.* place of worship; **-heit** *nf.* deity; **-los** *a.* impious, ungodly.

Göttin [ger'tin] *nf.* goddess.

Göttlich [gert'lish] *a.* divine.

Götze [gert'ser] *m.w.* idol; **-ndienst** *nm.* idolatry.

Grab [grahp] *n.* (**Gräber**)

grave; **-legung** *nf.* interment; **-rede** *nf.* funeral oration; **-scheit** *n.* shovel; **-stein** *nm.* tombstone; **-stichel** *nm.* chisel.

Graben [grah'ben] *vt. ir.* to dig, trench; *nm.* (**Gräben**) trench, ditch; **-bagger** *nm.* trench excavator.

Grad [graht] *nm.* (**-e**) degree, grade; **-bogen** *nm.* graduated arc; **-einteilung** *nf.* graduation (*map*); **-feld** *n.* map square; **-netz** *n.* grid (*map*); **-weise** *ad.* gradually.

Graf [grahf] *m.w.* count, earl; **-schaft** *nf.* county.

Gräfin [gray'fin] *nf.* countess.

Gram [grahm] *nm.* sorrow, grief.

Gräm'en [gray'men] *vr.* to grieve; **-lich** *a.* peevish, sulky.

Gramm [gram] *n.* (**-e**) gram(me).

Grammati'k [gram-a'tik] *nf.* grammar; **-sch** *a.* grammatical.

Grammophon [gram-o-fohn'] *n.* gramophone; **-nadel** *nf.* gramophone needle; **-platte** *nf.* record.

Gran [grahn] *n.* (**-e**) grain.

Granatapfel [gra-naht'ap-fel] *nm.* (**-äpfel**) pomegranate.

Granat'e [gra-naht'ter] *nf.* grenade, shell (*mil.*); **-werfer** *nm.* trench mortar.

Granit [gra-neet'] *nm.* (**-e**) granite.

Granulieren [gra-nŏŏ-leer'ren] *vt.* to granulate, grain.

Graphisch [grah'fish] *a.* graphic; **-e Darstellung** plotting. [graphite.

Graphit [gra-feet'] *nm.* (**-e**)

Gras [grass] *n.* (**Gräser**) grass; **-en** *vi.* to graze; **-halm** *nm.* blade of grass; **-ig** *a.* grassy.

Grassieren [gra-seer'ren] *vi.* to rage, be rampant.

Grässlich [gress'lish] *a.* horrible.

Grat [graht] *nm.* (**-e**) edge, ridge.

Gräte [gray'ter] nf. fish-bone.

Gratulation [grat-ōō-lat-syohn'] nf. congratulation.

Gratulieren [grat-ōō-leer'ren] vt. to congratulate.

Grau [grow] a. gray; -en vi. to grow gray, dawn; -haarig a. grey-haired; -lich a. grayish.

Grauen [grow'en] vi.r. imp. to shudder, be afraid of; -haft a. horrible.

Graupe [grow'per] nf. hulled grain, groats; -nsuppe nf. barley soup.

Graupeln [grow'peln] pl. hail.

Graus [growss] nm. terror; -en vr. to shudder; -ig a. grisly.

Grazi'e [graht'si-er] nf. grace; -ös a. graceful.

Greif'bar [grife'barr] a. palpable; -en vt. ir. to catch, seize, grasp; um sich = to spread.

Greinen [grine'en] vi. to whine.

Greis [grice] nm. (-e) old man; -enalter n. old age; -enhaft a. senile; -in nf. old woman.

Grell [grell] a. glaring, harsh.

Grenz'e [grent'ser] nf. boundary, frontier; -aufsicht nf. frontier control; -en vi. to border; -enlos a. boundless; -sperre nf. closing of frontier; -verkehr nm. frontier traffic.

Greuel [groy'el] nm. (-) horror, outrage; -tat nf. atrocity.

Greulich [groy'lish] a. atrocious.

Griess [greece] nm. gravel, grit, groats; -mehl n. semolina.

Gries'gram [greece'grahm] nm. grumbler; -grämig a. surly.

Griff [grif] nm. (-e) grip, handle, trick.

Griffel [grif'el] nm. (-) slate pencil, pistil, style.

Grille [gril'er] nf. whim, cricket; -nhaft a. whimsical.

Grimasse [grim'ass-er] nf. grimace. [a. grim, furious.

Grimm [grim] nm. fury; -ig

Grind [grint] nm. (-e) scurf; -ig a. scabby, scurvy.

Grinsen [grin'zen] vi. to grin.

Grippe [grip'er] nf. influenza.

Grob [grop] a. coarse, gross; -heit nf. coarseness, grossness; -mörtel nm. rough concrete; -schmied nm. blacksmith.

Groll [grol] nm. grudge; -en vi. to bear ill will, grumble; -end a. ad. grudging(ly).

Gros [groh] n. main body (mil.).

Gross [groce] a. great, large, tall; -admiral nm. admiral of the fleet; -artig a. grand, splendid; -aufnahme nf. close-up (film); -eltern pl. grandparents; -handel nm. wholesale trade; -händler nm. -ist m.w. wholesaler; -macht nf. great power; -maul n. braggart; -mut nf. magnanimity; -mütig a. generous; -mutter nf. grandmother; -stadt nf. large town, city; -tuer nm. snob; -vater nm. grandfather; -zügig a. liberal, on a large scale.

Gröss'e [grer'ser] nf. size, greatness, height; -t a. greatest, maximum; -tenteils ad. for the most part, mostly. [tesque.

Grotesk [gro-tesk'] a. gro-

Grotte [grot'er] nf. grotto.

Grube [grōō'ber] nf. pit, mine; -narbeiter nm. miner; -nbau nm. mining; -nholz n. pit-props; -nlampe nf. safety lamp.

Grüb'elei [gryōō-ber-lie'] nf. meditation, brooding; -eln vi. to meditate, brood; -ler nm. brooder; -lerisch a. meditative, brooding.

Gruft [grōōft] nf. (Grüfte) tomb, vault.

Grün [gryōōn] a. green; -kram nm. greens; -lich a. greenish; -span nm. verdigris.

Grund [grōōnt] nm. (Gründe) ground, basis, reason; -ausbildung nf. basic training; -bau nm. foundation; -bedingung nf. fundamental condition;

-besitz nm. -eigentum n. landed property, real estate; -besitzer nm. landed proprietor; -ehrlich a. truly honest; -gehalt n. basic salary; -lage nf. foundation; -los a. groundless; -riss nm. ground-plan, outline; -satz nm. principle; -stein nm. foundation stone; -stück n. plot of land; -ton nm. keynote; -verschieden a. utterly different; -zug nm. characteristic.

Gründ'en [gryōn'den] vt. to found, ground, sound, promote (com.); r. be based; -er nm. founder, promoter; -lich a. thorough, fundamental; -ung nf. foundation, promotion.

Grünen [gryōn'en] vi. to grow green, flourish. (grunt.

Grunzen [groont'sen] vi. to

Grupp'e [grōōp'er] nf. group, squad, section (mil.), (av.); -enkommando n. army group headquarters; -enweise ad. in groups; -ieren vt. to group; -ierung nf. grouping.

Grus [grōōss] nm. dross.

Gruselig [grōō'zer-lish] a. creepy; -n vi. to creep (flesh).

Gruss [grōōss] nm. (Grüsse) greeting, salute.

Grüssen [gryōō'sen] vt. to greet, salute.

Grütze [gryōōt'ser] nf. groats.

Guck'en [gōōk'en] vi. to peep, look; -kasten nm. peep-show; -loch n. loop-hole. [florin.

Gulden [gōōl'den] nm. (-)

Gültig [gyōōl'tish] a. valid, good, current; -keit nf. validity, currency.

Gummi [gōō'mih] n. rubber, gum; -band n. elastic; -eren vt. to gum; -schuh n. galosh, rubber overshoe, gumboot.

Gunst [goonst] nf. favour.

Günst'ig [gyōōn'stish] a. favourable; -ling nm. favourite.

Gurgel [gōōr'gel] nf. throat; -n vi. to gargle.

Gurke [gōōr'ker] nf. cucumber.

Gurt [gōōrt] nm. (-e) girth, belt.

Gürtel [gyōōr'tel] nm. girdle, belt, zone; -n vt.r. to gird; -panzer nm. armour belt (nav.).

Guss [gōōss] nm. (Güsse) gush, downpour, cast(ing); -eisen n. cast-iron; -stein nm. gutter, sink.

Gut [gōōt] nm. (Güter) goods, possession, property; a. good; ad. well; -achten n. (expert) opinion; -dünken n. opinion; -haben n. credit, assets; -heissen vt. to approve; -herzig a. good natured; -mütig a. good humoured; -sbesitzer nm. landowner; -schein nm. coupon; -schreiben vt. to credit; -schrift nf. credit.

Güt'e [gyōō'ter] nf. goodness, kindness; -ig a. kind; -lich a. amicable.

Güter [gyōō'ter], -abfertigung nf. goods office (rl.); -bahnhof nm. goods station; -wagen nm. truck, luggage-van; -zug nm. goods train.

Gymnasium [gim-nah'zyōōm] n. (gen. -s; pl. Gymnasien) grammar school.

H

Haar [hahrr] n. (-e) hair; -bürste nf. hair-brush; -klein a. minute; ad. to a hair; -kurve nf. hairpin bend; -scharf a. very sharp; -scheitel nm. parting; -schneiden n. haircutting; -sträubend a. atrocious, outrageous; -zange nf. tweezers. [hair.

Haaren [hahr'ren] vi. to lose

Haarig [hahr'rish] a. hairy, stunning. [less.

Haarlos [hahrr'lohs] a. hair-

Habe [hah'ber] nf. property, goods.

Haben [hah'ben] *vt.* to have, hold; **gern -** to like; *n.* credit.

Habgier [hap'geerr] *nf.* covetousness, greed; **-ig** *a.* covetous, greedy. [hawk.

Habicht [hah'bisht] *nm.* (-e)

Hack|e [hack'er] *nf.* hoe, mattock; **-en** *vt.* to hack, chop, hoe; **-fleisch** *n.* mincemeat; **-früchte** *pl.* root crops; **-maschine** *nf.* mincing machine.

Häcksel [hex'el] *nm.* chopped straw, chaff.

Hader [hah'derr] *nm.* quarrel, brawl; **-n** *vi.* to quarrel.

Hafen [hah'fen] *nm.* (Häfen) harbour, port; **-arbeiter** *nm.* docker; **-bassin** *n.* wet-dock; **-damm** *nm.* jetty, mole; **-sperre** *nf.* boom; **-stadt** *nf.* port.

Hafer [hah'ferr] *nm.* oats; **-schleim** *nm.* gruel.

Haft [haft] *nf.* custody, arrest; **-befehl** *nm.* warrant (of arrest); **-gläser** *pl.* contact lenses; **-mine** *nf.* adhesive mine; **-pflicht** *nf.* liability.

Haftbar [haft'bahrr] *a.* liable, responsible.

Haften [haf'ten] *vi.* to cling, adhere, answer for.

Haftung [haf'tŏong] *nf.* liability, security.

Hag [hahk] *nm.* (-e) hedge; **-ebutte** *nf.* hip, haw; **-edorn** *nm.* hawthorn.

Hagel [hah'gel] *nm.* hail; **-n** *vi. imp.* to hail. [lean.

Hager [hah'gerr] *a.* haggard.

Häher [hay'err] *nm.* (-) jay.

Hahn [hahn] *nm.* (Hähne) cock, tap; **-enschrei** *nm.* cockcrow.

Hähnchen [hane'shen] *n.* (-) cockerel. [shark.

Hai(fisch [hie'fish] *nm.* (-e)

Hain [hine] *nm.* (-e) grove.

Häkchen [hake'shen] *n.* (-) small hook, crotchet.

Häkel [hake'el], **-arbeit** *nf.* crochet-work; **-haken** *nm.* crochet-hook; **-n** *vi.* to crochet.

Haken [hah'ken] *nm.* (-) hook, drawback; **-kreuz** *n.* swastika.

Hakig [hah'kish] *a.* hooked.

Halb [halp] *a.* half; **-dunkel** *n.* dusk; **-gott** *nm.* demigod; **-heit** *nf.* incompleteness; **-insel** *nf.* peninsula; **-jährlich** *a.* halfyearly; **-ketten . .** *a.* halftracked; **-kreis** *nm.* semi-circle; **-kugel** *nf.* hemisphere; **-laut** *a.* in an undertone; **-mond** *nm.* crescent; **-schuh** *nm.* shoe; **-strumpf** *nm.* sock; **-wegs** *ad.* half-way; **-zeug** *n.*

Halber [hal'berr] *pr.* on account of.

Halbieren [hal-beer'ren] *vt.* to halve.

Halde [hal'der] *nf.* slope, dump.

Hälfte [helf'ter] *nf.* half.

Halfter [half'terr] *nf.* halter; **-n** *vt.* to halter.

Hall [hall] *nm.* (-e) sound; **-en** *vi.* to resound.

Halle [hal'er] *nf.* hall, market, hangar (*av.*); **-nbau** *nm.* hangar construction.

Halm [halm] *nm.* (-e) blade, stalk.

Hals [halss] *nm.* (Hälse) neck, throat; **-ader** *nf.* jugular vein; **-band** *n.* necklace, collar (*dogs*); **-bein** *n.* collar-bone; **-binde** *nf.* tie; **-röhre** *nf.* windpipe; **-starrig** *a.* stiff-necked, obstinate; **-tuch** *n.* muffler; **-weh** *n.* sore throat.

Halt [halt] *nm.* stop, hold, steadiness; **-bar** *a.* tenable, durable; **-barkeit** *nf.* durability, reasonableness; **-estelle** *nf.* tram-stop; **-los** *a.* unsteady, untenable, unprincipled; **-losigkeit** *nf.* unsteadiness, lack of principle.

Halten [hal'ten] *vt. ir.* to hold, keep; *i.* stop, hold out; **an sich -** to restrain oneself; *r.* to hold one's own, last.

Halunke [hal-ŏonk'er] *m.w.* rascal.

Hamen [hah'men] *nm.* (-) net.

Hämisch [hame'ish] *a.* malicious.

Hammel [ham'el] *nm.* (**Hämmel**) wether; **-fleisch** *n.* mutton.

Hammer [ham'err] *nm.* (**Hämmer**) hammer; **-werk** *n.* forge.

Hämmern [hem'errn] *vt.i.* to hammer.

Hamster [ham'sterr] *nm.* (-) hamster; **-ei** *nf.* hoarding; **-er** *nm.* hoarder; **-n** *vi.* to hoard.

Hand [hant] *nf.* (**Hände**) hand; **-arbeiter** *nm.* manual worker; **-bohrer** *nm.* gimlet; **-buch** *n.* hand-book, manual; **-fertigkeit** *nf.* manual skill; **-fest** *a.* sturdy, stout; **-feuerwaffen** *pl.* small arms; **-gelenk** *n.* wrist; **-gemenge** *n.* scuffle, hand to hand fighting; **-gepäck** *n.* light luggage; **-greiflich** *a.* palpable; **-griff** *nm.* grasp, knack; **-haben** *vt.* to handle, manage; **-karren** *nm.* hand-cart; **-kurbel** *nf.* crank; **-langer** *nm.* handyman; **-lich** *a.* handy; **-pflege** *nf.* manicure; **-schlag** *nm.* hand-shake; **-schrift** *nf.* handwriting, manuscript; **-schuh** *nm.* glove; **-streich** *nm.* raid (*mil.*); **-tasche** *nf.* hand-bag; **-tuch** *n.* towel; **-werk** *n.* trade, craft; **-werker** *nm.* artisan.

Hände– [hen'der] **-druck** *nm.* handshake; **-klatschen** *n.* clapping, applause.

Handel [handl] *nm.* (**Händel**) trade, transaction, quarrel.

Handeln [han'deln] *vi.* to trade, act, treat of; *r. imp.* to be a question of.

Handels– [han'dels] **-bilanz** *nf.* balance of trade; **-flotte** *nf.* merchant fleet; **-gärtner** *nm.* market gardener; **-gesetz** *n.* commercial law; **-hochschule** *nf.* commercial college; **-korrespondenz** *nf.* commercial correspondence; **-lage** *nf.* state of trade; **-leute** *pl.* tradespeople; **-reisende(r)** *m.w.* commercial traveller; **-(zer)störer** *nm.* commerce raider (*nav.*).

Händler [hend'lerr] *nm.* (-) trader, dealer.

Handlungs– [hand'lōōngss] **-gehilfe** *m.w.* clerk, shop assistant; **-weise** *nf.* manner of dealing.

Hanf [hanf] *nm.* hemp; **-en** *a.* hempen.

Hänfling [henf'ling] *nm.* (-e) linnet. [tion.

Hang [hang] *nm.* slope, inclina-

Hänge– [heng'er] **-bauch** *nm.* paunch; **-brücke** *nf.* suspension bridge; **-matte** *nf.* hammock.

Hangen [hang'en], **Hängen** [heng'en] *vt.i.* to hang, suspend, depend (on). [tease.

Hänseln [hen'zeln] *vt.* to hoax, tease.

Hantel [hantl] *nf.* dumb-bell.

Hantier [han-teer'ren] *vi.* to work; *t.* handle; **-ung** *nf.* trade, business.

Hapern [hah'pern] *vi. imp.* to be amiss.

Happen [hapn] *nm.* mouthful.

Hären [hare'ren] *a.* made of hair.

Harfe [harr'fer] *nf.* harp.

Harke [harr'ker] *nf.* rake; **-n** *vt.* to rake. [wrong.

Harm [harrm] *nm.* grief.

Härmen [hairr'men] *vt.r.* to grieve.

Harmlos [harrm'lohss] *a.* harmless; **-igkeit** *nf.* harmlessness.

Harmoni'e [harr-mo-nee'] *nf.* harmony; **-sch** *a.* harmonious; **-um** *n.* harmonium.

Harmonika [harr-moh'ni-kah] *nf.* concertina.

Harn [harrn] *nm.* urine; **-en** *vi.* to urinate.

Harnisch [harr'nish] *nm.* (-e) armour, temper.

Harpune [harr-pōō'ner] *nf.* harpoon.

Harren [harr'en] vi. to wait for.

Harsch [harsh] a. harsh, rough.

Hart [harrt] a. hard, rough; -gummi n. vulcanite; -herzig a. hard-hearted; -hörig a. hard of hearing; -näckig a. stubborn; -näckigkeit nf. stubbornness; -zinn n. pewter.

Härte [hairr'te] nf. hardness, harshness, cruelty; -n vt. to harden, temper, vulcanize.

Harz [harts] n. (-e) resin.

Haschen [hash'en] vt. to catch, snatch (at).

Haschieren [hash-eer'ren] vt. to hash.

Hase [hah'zer] m.w. hare; -nfuss nm. coward; -nscharte nf. hare-lip.

Haselnuss [hah'zel-nŏŏss] nf. hazel-nut.

Haspe [has'per] nf. hinge, staple; -l nm. reel, bobbin, winch; -ln vt. to wind up, reel.

Hass [hass] nm. hate; -en vt. to hate; -enswert a. hateful.

Hässlich [hess'lish] a. ugly, odious, vicious; -keit nf. ugliness, odiousness, viciousness.

Hast [hast] nf. haste; -en vi. to hasten; -ig a. hasty.

Hätscheln [het'sheln] vt. to pamper, fondle.

Haube [how'ber] nf. cap, hood, bonnet (aut.), engine cowling (tec.).

Haubitze [how'bit-ser] nf. howitzer.

Hauch [howch] nm. (-e) breath, breeze; -en vi. to breathe, exhale.

Haue [how'er] nf. hoe, pick; -n vt. to hew, cut, strike; -r nm. woodcutter, tusk.

Haufe [how'fer] nm. (gen. -ns pl. -n) heap, crowd, quantity; -nweise a. in heaps, crowds.

Häufen [hoy'fen] vt. to heap up, accumulate.

Häufig [hoy'fish] a. ad.

frequent(ly), abundant(ly); -keit nf. frequency.

Haupt [howpt] n. (Häupter) head, chief; -betrag nm. sum total; -buch n. ledger (com.), main log (nav., etc.); -eingang nm. main entrance; -erzeugnis n. staple commodity; -fach n. principal subject; -leder nf. mainspring; -feldwebel nm. regimental sergeant major; -film nm. feature film; -gefreiter nm. leading aircraftman; -industrie nf. key industry; -inhalt nm. gist, tenor; -landstrasse nf. trunk road; -leidenschaft nf. ruling passion; -mann nm. captain (mil.), flight lieutenant (av.); -postamt n. general post-office; -punkt nm. main point; -quartier n. headquarters; -rolle nf. leading part; -sache nf. main thing; -sächlich a, ad. chief, essential(ly); -satz nm. principal clause; -schalter nm. main switch; -schlacht nf. pitched battle; -schlüssel nm. master-key; -segel n. mainsail; -spass nm. great joke, fun; -stadt nf. capital; -strasse nf. main street; -stütze m.w. mainstay; -verbandplatz nm. advanced dressing station; -verzeichnis n. general catalogue; -wort n. noun.

Häuptling [hoipt'ling] nm. (-e) chief; -s ad. head first.

Haus [howss] n. (Häuser) house, home; -angestellte nf. domestic servant; -arzt nm. family doctor; -frau nf. housewife; -freund nm. family friend; -halt nm. household; -halten vi. ir. to keep house, economise; -haltsplan nm. budget; -haltung nf. housekeeping; -lehrer nm. tutor; -lehrerin nf. governess; -mädchen n. housemaid; -meister nm. caretaker; -mittel n. household remedy; -suchung *nf.* police raid; **-wart** *nm.* caretaker; **-wirt** *nm.* landlord.

Häuschen [hoiss'shen] *n.* (-) cottage.

Hausen [how'zen] *vi.* to live (economically), work havoc.

Hausen [how'zen] *nm.* sturgeon; **-bläschen** *n.* isinglass.

Häuser- [hoy'zerr] **-block** *nm.* block of houses; **-makler** *nm.* house agent.

Hausier'en [how-zeer'ren] *vi.* to hawk, peddle; **-er** *nm.* hawker, pedlar.

Häusler [hoice'lerr] *nm.*, **Häuslerin** *nf.* cottager.

Häuslich [hoice'lish] *a.* domestic, economical; **-keit** *nf.* domesticity.

Hauss'e [hoh'ser] *nf.* rise (in prices), boom; **-ier** *nm.* bull (*com.*).

Haut [howt] *nf.* (Häute) skin, hide, membrane; **-farbe** *nf.* complexion.

Häutchen [hoit'shen] *n.* (-) membrane, cuticle, film.

Häuten [hoy'ten] *vi.* to skin; *r.* cast the skin.

Havarie [ha-va-ree'] *nf.* average (*com.*). [midwife.

Hebamme [hebe'am-err] *nf.*

Hebe- [habe'er] **-baum** *nm.* lever; **-eisen** *n.* crowbar; **-l** *nm.* lever.

Heben [habe'en] *vt. ir.* to raise, lift, levy; *r.* rise, cancel out.

Heber [habe'err] *nm.* siphon.

Hebung [habe'oong] *nf.* raising, promotion, removal.

Hechel [hesh'el] *nf.* hackle; **-n** *vt.* to hackle, heckle.

Hechse [hex'er] *nf.* hock.

Hecht [hesht] *nm.* (-e) pike.

Heck [hek] *n.* (-e) stern; **-schütze** *m.w.* rear gunner (*av.*).

Hecke [hek'er] *nf.* hedge, hatch, brood; **-n** *vt.* to hatch, breed; **-nbinder** *nm.* hedger; **-nrose** *nf.* wild rose; **-nschütze** *m.w.* sniper (*mil.*).

Hede [hay'der] *nf.* tow, oakum.

Heer [hairr] *n.* (-e) army; **-esgerät** *n.* army equipment; **-esführung** *nf.* army high command; **-essprache** *nf.* army slang; **-schau** *nf.* review; **-strasse** *nf.* military road, highway.

Hefe [hay'fer] *nf.* yeast, dregs.

Heft [heft] *n.* (-e) pin, handle, haft, exercise book, number (*journal*); **-en** *vt.* to fasten, sew, stitch; **-pflaster** *n.* sticking plaster.

Heftel [hef'tel] *nm.* (-) clasp.

Heftig [hef'tish] *a.* violent, vehement; **-keit** *nf.* violence, vehemence.

Hege'n [hay'gen] *vt.* to cherish, have, foster, preserve (*game*); **-r** *nm.* gamekeeper; **-zeit** *nf.* close season.

Hehl [hale] *n.* concealment; **-en** *vt.* to conceal; **-er** *nm.* receiver (of stolen goods).

Hehr [hairr] *a.* sublime, lofty.

Heide [haide'er] *nf.* heath, moor; **-lbeere** *nf.* bilberry, wortleberry; **-kraut** *nf.* heather.

Heide [hide'er] *m.w.* **Heidin** *nf.* heathen, pagan, Gentile; **-nmässig** *a.* enormous; **-ntum** *n.* heathendom.

Heidnisch [hide'nish] *a.* heathen.

Heikel [hike'el], **Heiklisch** *a.* ticklish, delicate, awkward.

Heil [hile] *n.* prosperity, salvation; *a.* sound, healed; **-and** *nm.* saviour; **-bar** *a.* curable; **-bringend** *a.* salutary; **-en** *vt.* to heal, cure; **-kraft** *nf.* healing power; **-los** *a.* wicked, disastrous; **-mittel** *n.* remedy; **-sam** *a.* salutary, wholesome; **-sarmee** *nf.* Salvation Army; **-ung** *nf.* cure.

Heilig [hile'ish] *a.* holy, sacred; **-e(r)** *m.w.* *nf.* saint; **-en** *vt.* to hallow, sanction; **-enschein** *nm.* halo; **-haltung** *nf.* observation; **-keit** *nf.* holiness

-sprechen *vt. ir.* canonize; -tum *n.* shrine, sanctuary, relic.

Heim [hime] *n.* (-e) home; *ad.* home(ward); -fall *nm.* reversion; -fällig *a.* revertible; -führerin *nf.* matron; -gang *nm.* going home, decease; -isch *a.* native, home(ly); -kehr *nf.* return home; -lich *a.* secret, private; -lichkeit *nf.* secrecy, privacy; -suchen *vt.* to visit, punish; -suchung *nf.* visitation; -tücke *nf.* malice, perfidy; -tückisch *a.* malicious; -wärts *ad.* homewards; -weh *n.* homesickness.

Heirat [hime'at] *nf.* home, native place, country; -lich *a.* native; -schein *nm.* passport.

Heirat [hie'raht] *nf.* marriage; -en *vt.* to marry; -santrag *nm.* proposal.

Heischen [hie'shen] *vt.* to demand, ask.

Heiser [hie'zerr] *a.* hoarse; -keit *nf.* hoarseness.

Heiss [hice] *a.* hot; -blütig *a.* hot-blooded; -hunger *nm.* ravenous hunger.

Heissen [hice'en] *vi. ir.* to be called, mean; *t.* command, name; *imp.* it says, it is said.

Heiter [hite'err] *a.* cheerful, clear; -keit *nf.* cheerfulness, amusement.

Heiz [hits] -apparat *nm.* heating apparatus, -bar *a.* heated, with heating; -batterie *nf.* low-tension battery; -en *vt.* to heat; -er *nm.* stoker, heater; -körper *nm.* radiator; -raum *nm.* stoke hole, boiler room; -sonne *nf.* electric fire; -ung *nf.* heating; -un sanlage *nf.* heating apparatus, plant.

Held [helt] *m.w.* hero; -enmut *nm.* heroism; -enmütig *a.* heroic; -entat *nf.* deed of valour; -entum *n.* heroism; -in *nf.* heroine.

Helfe'n [hel'fen] *vi. ir.* to help,

assist, avail; -r *nm.* helper; -rin *nf.* female auxiliary (*mil.*); -rshelfer *nm.* accomplice.

Hell [hell] *a.* clear, bright, light; -blau *a.* light blue; -dunkel *n.* gloaming; -hörig *a.* keen of hearing; -sehend *a.* clairvoyant.

Helle [hell'er] *nf.* clearness, brightness. [farthing.

Heller [hell'err] *nm.* (-) [farthing.

Helm [helm] *nm.* (-e) helmet, helm, rudder, steeple.

Hemd [hemt] *n.* (*gen.* -es; *pl.* -en) shirt, blouse, chemise, vest; -bluse *nf.* blouse, shirt; -knknopf *nm.* stud; -hose *nf.* combinations, cami-knickers.

Hemm'en [hem'en] *vt.* to stop, curb, check, hinder; -nis *n.* check, drag; -ung *a.* stop(page), check, restraint.

Hengst [hengst] *nm.* (-e) stallion, steed.

Henkel [henk'el] *nm.* (-) handle; -korn *nm.* basket with handles; -krug *nm.* jug.

Henke'n [henk'en] *vt.* to hang; -r *nm.* hangman.

Henne [hen'er] *nf.* hen.

Her [hairr] *ad.* here, ago.

Herab [her-rap'] *ad.* downward(s); -drücken *vt.* to force down, depress; -lassen *vt.* to let down; *r.* condescend; -lassung *nf.* condescension; -sehen *vt. ir.* to look down (on); -setzen *vt.* to lower, disparage, reduce, degrade; -setzung *nf.* reduction, degradation; -steigen *vi. ir.* to descend, dismount; -würdigen *vt.* to demote, degrade; -würdigung *nf.* debasement, degradation.

Heran [her-an'] *ad.* onward(s), on here; -bilden *vt.* to train; -kommen *vi. ir.* to approach, come near; -nahen *vi. ir.* to draw near; -rücken *vi.* to advance, draw near; -wachsen *vi. ir.* to grow up; -ziehen *vi. ir.* to approach.

Herauf [her-rowf'] *ad.* up-ward(s), up here; -**beschwören** *vt.* to conjure up, evoke; -**ziehen** *vt. ir.* to draw, pull up; i. gather, approach.

Heraus [her-rowss'] *ad.* from out, outside; -**arbeiten** *vr.* to extricate oneself; -**bekommen** *vt. ir.* to get back, make out, find out; -**bringen** *vt. ir.* to bring out, make out, elicit, release *(film)*; -**finden** *vt. ir.* to find out; -**fordern** *vt.* to challenge; -**forderung** *nf.* provocation, challenge; -**gabe** *nf.* issue, publication, editing; -**geben** *vt. ir.* to give out, up, give change, edit, publish; -**geber** *nm.* editor, publisher; -**kommen** *vi. ir.* to come out, result, appear; -**nehmen** *vt. ir.* to take out; *r.* presume; -**reissen** *vt. ir.* to tear out, extract; -**rücken** *vt.* to pay up, hand over, speak out; -**stellen** *vt. ir.* to expose; *r.* turn out; -**streichen** *vt. ir.* to praise; -**treten** *vi. ir.* to step out, stick out; -**ziehen** *vt. ir.* to pull out, extract.

Herb [hairp] *a.* bitter, acid, harsh, austere; -**heit** *nf.* acidity, harshness, bitterness, austerity.

Herbei [hairr-by'] *ad.* here, this way, near; -**führen** *vr.* to bring about; -**lassen** *vr.* to condescend; -**schaffen** *vt. ir.* to procure; -**ziehen** *vt. ir.* to draw near.

Herberge [hairr'bairr-ger] *nf.* shelter, lodging, inn; -**n** *vt. ir.* to shelter, lodge.

Herbst [hairrpst] *nm.* (-e) autumn; -**lich** *a.* autumnal.

Herd [hairrt] *nm.* (-e) hearth, seat.

Herde [hairr'der] *nf.* herd; -**nweise** *ad.* in herds.

Herein [her-rine'] *ad.* in (here), here; - ! come in !; -**bitten** *vt. ir.* to invite in; -**brechen** *vi. ir.* to set in; -**dürfen** *vi.*

ir. to have permission to enter; -**fall** *nm.* disappointment, sell; -**fallen** *vi. ir.* to be caught, taken in; -**lassen** *vt. ir.* to admit.

Her-gang *nm.* course of events, circumstances; -**geben** *vt. ir.* to give up, hand over; -**gebracht** *a.* established, traditional; -**gehen** *vi. ir.* to go on.

Hering [hairr'ring] *nm.* (-e) herring.

Her-kommen *vi. ir.* to come from, on, here; *n.* custom; -**kömmlich** *a.* traditional; -**kunft** *nf.* origin, descent; -**leiten** *vt. r.* to derive, deduce; -**leitung** *nf.* derivation, deduction; -**machen** *vr.* to set upon.

Hermelin [hairr-mel-een'] *nm.* ermine.

Hermetisch [hairr-mate'ish] *a.* hermetical.

Her-nach *ad.* afterwards; -**nehmen** *vt. ir.* to take, deduce.

Heroisch [hay-roh'ish] *a.* heroic.   [herald.

Herold [hay'rolt] *nm.* (-e)

Herr [hairr] *m.w.* master, sir, lord, Mr.; -**enhaus** *n.* mansion; -**enlos** *a.* ownerless; -**in** *nf.* lady, mistress; -**isch** *a.* masterful, domineering; -**lich** *a.* grand, glorious; -**lichkeit** *nf.* grandeur, splendour, magnificence; -**schaft** *nf.* power, rule, estate, master and mistress.

Herrsch'en [hairr'shen] *vt.* to rule, prevail, be; *er nm.* ruler; -**sucht** *nf.* love of power, ambition; -**süchtig** *a.* ambitious.

Her-rühren *vt.* to proceed, originate; -**sagen** *vt.* to recite; -**schreiben** *vr.* to date from; -**stammen** *vi.* to descend from; -**stammung** *nf.* descent; -**stellen** *vt.* to make, manufacture, repair, restore, reconstruct; -**stellung** *nf.* manufacture, construction.

Herüber [her-ryōō'berr] *ad.* over (here), across.

Herum [her-rōōm'] *ad.* round, about, here and there; **-führen** *vt.* to show round; **-gehen** *vi. ir.* to go round, walk about; **-irren** *vi.* to wander about; **-treiben** *vi.r. ir.* to drift about; **-ziehen** *vi.r. ir.* to wander about, remove.

Herunter [her-rōōn'terr] *ad.* downward(s), down (there); **-holen** *vt.* to fetch, bring, shoot down (*av.*); **-kommen** *vi. ir.* to come down, decline; **-lassen** *vt. ir.* to let down; **-machen** *vt.* to take down, abuse; **-treiben** *vt. ir.* to force down.

Hervor [herr-forr'] *ad.* out, forth; **-brechen** *vi. ir.* to break out, burst forth; **-bringen** *vt. ir.* to produce, utter; **-bringung** *nf.* production; **-gehen** *vi. ir.* to emerge, issue, result; **-heben** *vt. ir.* to accentuate, stress, set off; **-ragen** *vi. ir.* to project, rise above; **-ragend** *a.* prominent, eminent, projecting; **-rufen** *vt. ir.* to cause, arouse, call forth; **-stechend** *a.* conspicuous, prominent; **-stehend** *a.* projecting; **-suchen** *vt.* to seek out; **-treten** *vi. ir.* to come forward, out; **-tun** *vr. ir.* to come forward, out, distinguish oneself.

Herz [hairrts] *n.* (*gen.* **-ens**; *pl.* **-en**) heart; **-chen** *n.* darling; **-eleid** *n.* sorrow; **-en** *vt.* to caress, embrace; **-ensangst** *nf.* anguish, terror; **-ensfreund** *nm.* bosom friend; **-ensgüte** *nf.* kindness of heart; **-enslust** *nf.* heart's desire; **-fehler** *nm.* heart disease; **-grube** *nf.* pit of the stomach; **-haft** *a.* stout-hearted; **-klopfen** *n.* palpitation; **-lich** *a.* hearty, cordial; **-lichkeit** *nf.* cordiality, heartiness; **-los** *a.* heartless; **-losigkeit** *nf.* heartlessness; **-schlag** *nm.* throb, beat of the heart, stroke; **-zerreissend** *a.* heartrending.

Herzog [herr'tsok] *nm.* (Herzöge) duke; **-tum** *n.* duchy.

Hetze [het'ser] *nf.* hunt, haste, rush, pack; **-n** *vt.* to hunt, rush, bait, stir up, incite; **-rei** *nf.* instigation, harassing, rush.

Heu [hoy] *n.* hay; **-boden** *nm.* hay-loft; **-gabel** *nf.* pitchfork; **-miete** *nf.* schober *nm.* hayrick, haystack; **-schrecke** *nf.* locust.

Heuchelei [hoi-sher-lie'] *nf.* hypocrisy; **-eln** *vt.* to pretend; **i.** play the hypocrite; **-ler** *nm.* hypocrite; **-lerisch** *a.* hypocritical. [hay.

Heuen [hoy'en] *vi.* to make

Heuer [hoy'err] *ad.*, Heurig [hoy'rish] *a.* this year's.

Heulen [hoil'en] *vi.* to howl.

Heut'e [hoy'ter] *ad.* to-day; **-ig** *a.* to-day's; **-zutage** *ad.* nowadays.

Hexe [hex'er] *nf.* witch; **-n** *vi.* to practise magic; **-nmeister** *nm.* wizard; **-nschuss** *nm.* lumbago. [thrust.

Hieb [heep] *nm.* (-e) blow, cut,

Hier [here] *ad.* here; **-auf** *ad.* thereupon, after that; **-bei** *ad.* herewith, enclosed; **-durch** *ad.* by this means, through there; **-her** *ad.* this way, here; **-mit** *ad.* herewith; **-zulande** *ad.* in this country.

Hiesig [hee'zish] *a.* of this place, local.

Hilf'e [hil'fer] *nf.* help; **-los** *a.* helpless; **-losigkeit** *nf.* helplessness; **-reich** *a.* helpful; **-skraft** *nf.* assistant, helper; **-skrankenhaus** *n.* auxiliary hospital; **-skreuzer** *nm.* auxiliary cruiser; **-smittel** *n.* remedy, expedient; **-sschiff** *n.* auxiliary vessel; **-swerk** *n.* charity; **-szeitwort** *n.* auxiliary verb.

Himbeere [him'bair-rer] *nf.* raspberry.

Himmel [himl] *nm.* (-) heaven, sky; **-blau** *n.* sky-blue; **-fahrt** *nf.* Ascension; **-reich** *n.*

heaven; -sgegend, -srichtung *nf.* quarter, compass direction; -wärts *ad.* heavenwards.

Himmlisch [him'lish] *a.* heavenly.

Hin [hin] *ad.* there, in that direction, away, gone (by).

Hinab [hin-ap'] *ad.* down (ward); -sehen *vi. ir.* to look down on.

Hinan [hin-an'] *ad.* up (to); -steigen *vi. ir.* to ascend.

Hinauf [hin-owf'] *ad.* up (there); -arbeiten *vr.* to work one's way up; -steigen *vi. ir.* to climb, ascend.

Hinaus [hin-owss'] *ad.* out; -gehen *vi. ir.* to go out, exceed; -laufen *vi. ir.* to come to, amount to; -schieben *vt. ir.* to put off, postpone; -werfen *vt. ir.* to throw out; -wollen *vi. ir.* to want to go out, aim at; -ziehen *vr. t. ir.* to draw out, be long.

Hinblick [hin'blik] *nm.* regard.

Hinbringen [hin'bring-en] *vt. ir.* to spend.

Hinder'lich [hin'derr-lish] *a.* hindering, awkward; -n *vt.* to hinder, prevent; -nis *n.* hindrance, obstacle.

Hindeuten [hin'doy-ten] *vi.* to point, hint at.

Hindurch [hin-dōorsh'] *ad.* through, across, over.

Hinein [hin-ine'] *ad.* in(to); -gehen *vi. ir.* to enter, hold; -lesen *vi. ir.* to read into; -pfuschen *vi.* to meddle with, tamper with; -reden *vi.* to talk nonsense; -ziehen *vt. ir.* to draw in, implicate.

Hin-fahren [hin'fah-ren] *vi.* to go on, pass away; *t.* convey, drive to; -fahrt *nf.* outward journey; -fallen *vi. ir.* to fall down; -fällig *a.* frail, decrepit, untenable; -fracht *nf.* outward freight; -gabe *nf.* devotion, surrender; -geben *vt.r. ir.* to give up, away, sacrifice; -gegen

ad. on the other hand; -gehen *vi. ir.* to go, pass away; -halten *vt. ir.* to hold out, put off.

Hinken [hink'en] *vi. ir.* to limp.

Hin-länglich [hin-leng'lish] *a.* sufficient, adequate; -legen *vt.* to lay down; -nehmen *vt. ir.* to receive, put up with; -reichen *vi.* to be adequate; *t.* stretch out; -reise *nf.* journey out; -reissen *vt. ir.* to carry away, overcome, transport; -richten *vt.* to execute; -richtung *nf.* execution; -sicht *nf.* respect; -sichtlich *pr.* with regard to; -stellen *vt.* to station, represent; -sterben *vi. ir.* to die away; -streben *vi.* to strive towards.

Hintansetz'en [hin-tan'set-sen] *vt.* to postpone, neglect; -ung *nf.* neglect, disregard.

Hinten [hin'ten] *ad.* behind, aft; -über *ad.* upside down.

Hinter [hin'terr] *pr.* behind, after; *a.* rear, back, posterior; -backe *nf.* buttock; -bein *n.* hind leg; -bleiben *vi. ir.* to survive; -bliebene(r) *m.w.* survivor; -bringen *vt. ir.* to inform of, charge with; -deck *n.* quarter-deck; -drein *ad.* afterwards; -einander *ad.* after each other, successively; -gebäude *n.* back premises; -gedanke *nm.* ulterior motive, reservation; -gehen *vt. ir.* to deceive; -grund *nm.* background; -halt *nm.* ambush; -haus *n.* back of the house; -her *ad.* afterwards, after; -hof *nm.* backyard; -lassen *vt. ir.* to bequeath, leave; -lassenschaft *nf.* testator's estate; -legen *vt.* to deposit; -legung *nf.* deposit; -list *nf.* craft, fraud; -listig *a.* cunning, crafty; -rad *n.* back-wheel; -radantrieb *nm.* back-wheel drive *(aut.)*; -rücks *ad.* from behind; -teil *nm.* back part; -treffen *n.* rearguard; -treiben *vt. ir.* to prevent, frustrate; **-treibung** *nf.* prevention, frustration; **-tür** *nf.* back door; **-wärts** *ad.* backwards, abaft.

Hinüber [hin-yoo'berr] *ad.* across, over; **-gehen** *vi. ir.* to go over, cross.

Hinunter [hin-ŏŏn'terr] *ad.* down, downward(s); **-schauen** *vi.* to look down; **-schlucken** *vt.* to swallow, gulp down; **-steigen** *vi. ir.* to descend, dismount.

Hin-weg [hin'vaik] *nm.* outward journey, way out; **-weg** [-vek'] *ad.* away, hence; **-wegsetzen** *vr.* to disregard; **-weis** *nm.* reference, hint, directive; **-weisen** *vi. ir.* to point to, out, refer to; **-werfen** *vt. ir.* to throw down, out, jot down, sketch; **-ziehen** *vt. i. ir.* to draw along, out, attract, drag on; **-zielen** *vi.* to aim at.

Hinzu [hin-tsōō'] *ad.* to, besides; **-fügen, -rechnen** *vt.* to add; **-kommen** *vi. ir.* to supervene; **-tun** *vt. ir.* to put on, add; **-ziehen** *vt. ir.* to include, bring in.

Hirn [hirrn] *n.* (-e) brain(s); **-schale** *nf.* skull.

Hirsch [hirrsh] *nm.* (-e) stag; **-leder** *n.* buckskin.

Hirse [hirr'zer] *nf.* millet.

Hirt [hirrt] *m.w.* herdsman, shepherd; **-enleben** *n.* pastoral life; **-enschreiben** *n.* pastoral letter.

Hissen [hiss'en] *vt.* to hoist.

Histor'iker [his-tor'ri-kerr] *nm.* (-) historian; **-isch** *a.* historical.

Hitz'e [hit'ser] *nf.* heat; **-ig** *a.* hot, hasty; **-knopf** *nm.* hot-headed person; **-köpfig** *a.* fiery, hot-headed.

Hobel [hoe'bel] *nm.* (-) plane; **-n** *vt.* to plane.

Hoch [hohch] *a.* high, tall; *ad.* highly; *n.* toast, cheer; **-achten** *vt.* to respect, esteem; **-achtung**

nf. esteem, respect; **-achtungsvoll** *ad.* yours faithfully; **-amt** *n.* high mass; **-angriff** *nm.* high level bombing attack; **-antenne** *nf.* overhead, outdoor aerial; **-betagt** *a.* very old; **-deutsch** *n.* High German; **-druck** *nm.* high pressure; **-ebene** *nf.* table-land, plateau; **-erfreut** *a.* highly pleased; **-fahrend** *a.* haughty; **-fliegend** *a.* ambitious; **-frequenz** *nf.* high frequency; **-gradig** *a.* intense, extreme; **-herzig** *a.* noble-minded; **-konjunktur** *nf.* boom; **-land** *n.* highlands; **-länder** *nm.* highlander; **-mut** *nm.* pride; **-mütig** *a.* proud, haughty; **-ofen** *nm.* blast furnace; **-schätzung** *nf.* high esteem; **-schule** *nf.* college, university; **-sommer** *nm.* midsummer; **-spannung** *nf.* high tension; **-stapler** *nm.* swindler; **-trabend** *a.* pompous; **-verrat** *nm.* high treason; **-wasser** *n.* high water; **-wertig** *a.* high class, first rate; **-würden** Reverend; **[highly.**

Höchlich [hersh'lish] *av.*

Höchst [herch-st] *a.* highest, extreme; *ad.* highly, extremely; **-geschwindigkeit** *nf.* maximum speed; **-preis** *nm.* maximum, controlled price.

Hochzeit [hoch'tsite] *nf.* wedding.

Hocken [hok'en] *vi.* to crouch.

Höcker [her'kerr] *nm.* (-) hump, knob, hunchback; **-hindernis** *n.* dragons' teeth (*mil.*); **-ig** *a.* humpy, knobby, hunchbacked.

Hode [hoh'der] *nf.* testicle.

Hof [hofe] *nm.* (Höfe) yard, farm, court; **-hund** *nm.* watchdog; **-mann** *nm.* courtier; **-rat** *nm.* privy councillor.

Höfegruppe [her'fer-grōō-per] *nf.* co-operative farm.

Hof'fart [hof'ahrt] *nf.* arrogance; **-ärtig** *a.* arrogant.

Hoff'en [hof'en] *vt.* to hope; -entlich *ad.* it is to be hoped, I hope; -nung *nf.* hope; -nungslos *a.* hopeless; -nungslosigkeit *nf.* hopelessness; -nungsvoll *a.* hopeful.

Höflich [herf'lish] *a.* courteous, polite; -keit *nf.* courtesy, politeness.

Höhe [her'her] *nf.* height, top, hill; -natmer *nm.* oxygen apparatus; -nflug *nm.* high altitude flight (*av.*); -nkurort *nm.* mountain spa; -nmesser *nm.* altimeter; -nrichtung *nf.* elevation (*gun*); -nschreiber *nm.* barograph; -nzug *nm.* mountain chain; -npunkt *nm.* climax.

Hoheit [hoh'hite] *nf.* highness, grandeur; -sabzeichen *n.* national markings (*av.*); -sgebiet *n.* sovereign territory; -sgewässer *n.pl.* territorial waters.

Höher [her'err] *a.* higher.

Hohl [hole] *a.* hollow, empty; -äugig *a.* hollow-eyed; -bäckig *a.* hollow-cheeked; -bohrer *nm.* auger; -heit *nf.* hollowness, emptiness; -raumpanzerung *nf.* spaced armour (*mil.*); -saum *nm.* hemstitch; -schliff *n.* hollow grinding; -weg *nm.* defile, sunken road.

Höhle [her'ler] *nf.* cavity, hole, cave; -ung *nf.* excavation, cavity.

Hohn [hone] *nm.* scorn; -gelächter *n.* scornful laughter; -lachen *vi.* to sneer, jeer; -sprechen *vi. ir.* to defy.

Höhn'en [her'nen] *vt.* to taunt, scoff at; -isch *a.* scornful, taunting.

Höker [her'kerr] *nm.* (-) hawker; -n *vi.* to hawk.

Hold [holt] *a.* gracious, charming, sweet; -selig *a.* most gracious, charming; -seligkeit *nf.* loveliness, charm.

Holen [hole'en] *vt.* to fetch, take; -- lassen to send for.

Höll'e [her'ler] *nf.* hell; -isch *a.* hellish, infernal.

Holper'ig [hol'per-rish] *a.* rough, bumpy; -n *vi.* to jolt.

Holunder [hol-ōōn'derr] *nm.* (-) elder.

Holz [holts] *n.* (Hölzer) wood; -en *vt.* to line with wood; *i.* to cut, gather wood; -gas *n.* producer gas; -hacker *nm.* woodcutter; -hof *nm.* timber yard; -kohle *nf.* charcoal; -masse *nf.* -stoff *nm.* woodpulp; -säger *n.* sawyer; -schnitt *nm.* woodcut; -späne *m.pl.* shavings; -weg *nm.* wrong track.

Hölzern [herlt'serrn] *a.* wooden, dull, pedantic.

Holzig [holt'sish] *a.* woody.

Honig [hoh'nish] *nm.* honey; -wabe *nf.* honeycomb.

Honor'ar [ho-no-rahr'] *n.* (-e) fee; -ieren *vt.* to honour; -ierung *nf.* payment, acceptance (*com.*).

Hopfen [hop'fen] *nm.* (-) hops.

Hör- [herr] -anlage *nf.* listening set; -aufnahme *nf.* reception (*rad.*); -bar *a.* audible.

Horch- [horrsh] -empfänger *nm.* interception receiver (*rad.*); -en *vi.* to listen, overhear; -er *nm.* listener, eavesdropper; -funk *nm.* wireless interception; -gerät *n.* sound detector; -kompanie *nf.* interception company (*mil.*); -meldung *nf.* listening report; -posten *nm.* listening post.

Horde [horr'der] *nf.* horde.

Hör'en [her'ren] *vt.i.* to hear; -er *nm.* hearer, student, earphone, head-phone, receiver, listener (*rad.*); -ensagen *n.* hearsay, broadcasts; -folge *nf.* series of programmes; -frequenz *nf.* audio-frequency; -muschel *nf.* head-piece; -rohr *n.* speaking trumpet, stetho scope; -saal *nm.* lecture room; -weite *nf.* earshot.

Horizont [hor-rit-sont'] *nm.* horizon; -al *a.* horizontal.

Hormon [horr-mone'] *n.* (-e) hormone.

Horn [horrn] *n.* (Hörner) horn; -ig *a.* horny. [hornet.

Hornisse [horr'niss-er] *nf.* (-n)

Horoskop [hor-ro-skope'] *n.* (-e) horoscope.

Horst [horrst] *nm.* (-e) eyrie, aerie, bushes, air-force station (*av.*).

Hort [horrt] *nm.* (-e) hoard, refuge, nursery-school.

Hose [hose'er] *nf.* trousers, knickers; -nträger *nm.* braces.

Hospiz [hos-peets'] *nm.* (-e) hospice, private hotel, hostel.

Hostie [hos'ti-er] *nf.* host.

Hotel [ho-tel'] *n.* (-s) hotel; -ier *nm.* (-s) hotel-keeper.

Hub [hoop] *nm.* (Hübe) stroke, lift.

Hüben [hyōō'ben] *ad.* on this side.

Hübsch [hyōōpsh] *a.* pretty, nice.

Hudeln [hōō'deln] *vi.* to bungle, be untidy.

Huf [hoof] *nm.* (-e) hoof; -eisen *n.* horse-shoe; -schmied *nm.* farrier.

Hüfte [hyōōf'ter] *nf.* hip.

Hügel [hyōō'gel] *nm.* (-) hill; -ig *a.* hilly.

Huhn [hōōn] *n.* (Hühner) hen.

Hühner- [hyōō'nerr] -auge *n.* corn; -zucht *nf.* poultry rearing.

Huld [hōōlt] *nf.* grace, charm, favour; -igen *vi.* to do homage, subscribe to (*opinion*); -igung *nf.* homage; -reich *a.* gracious.

Hülle [hyōō'ler] *nf.* covering, envelope, wrapping, case ; -n *vt.* to cover, wrap.

Hülse [hyōōl'zer] *nf.* husk, shell; -n *vt.* to shell.

Human [hōō-mahn'] *a.* humane; -ität *nf.* humanity.

Hummel [hōō'mel] *nf.* (-) bumble-bee. [lobster.

Hummer [hōō'merr] *nm.* (-)

Humor [hōō-more'] *nm.* humour; -ist *m.w.* -istisch *a.* humorous.

Humpeln [hōōm'peln] *vi.* to hobble. [tankard.

Humpen [hōōm'pen] *nm.* (-)

Hund [hōōnt] *nm.* (-e) dog, hound; -ehütte *nf.* dog-kennel; -ekuchen *nm.* dog-biscuit; -emarke *nf.* dog-licence.

Hundert [hōōn'derrt] *num, n.* (-e) hundred; -jahrfeier *nf.* centenary.

Hündin [hyōōn'din] *nf.* bitch; -sch *a.* canine, fawning, shameless.

Hunger [hōōng'err] *nm.* hunger; -lohn *nm.* starvation wages; -n *vi.* to be hungry, starve; -snot *nf.* famine.

Hungrig [hōōn'grish] *a.* hungry.

Hupe [hōō'per] *nf.* hooter, klaxon (*aut.*); -n *vi.* to hoot, sound one's horn.

Hüpfen [hyōōp'fen] *vi.* to hop, jump.

Hürde [hyōōr'der] *nf.* hurdle, pen.

Hure [hōō'rer] *nf.* whore.

Hurrapatriotismus [hōō-rah'pat-ri-o-tiss-mōōss] *nm.* jingoism, chauvinism.

Hurtig [hōōr'tish] *a, ad.* brisk(ly), quick(ly); -keit *nf.* briskness, quickness.

Husar [hōō-zahr'] *m.w.* hussar.

Huschen [hōō'shen] *vi.* to hurry, scurry away.

Husten [hōōs'ten] *vi.* to cough; -bonbon *nm.* cough-drop.

Hut [hōōt] *nm.* (Hüte) hat; -macher *nm.* hatter; -zucker *nm.* loaf-sugar.

Hut [hōōt] *nf.* guard, care.

Hüte'n [hyōō'ten] *vt.* to guard; *r.* take care; -r *nm.* keeper, guardian.

Hütte [hyōō'ter] *nf.* hut,

cottage, forge; -nwerk n. foundry.

Hutzelig [hŏŏt'ser-lish] a. shrivelled.

Hyäne [hyŏŏ-ane'er] nf. hyena.

Hyazinthe [hyŏŏ-a-tsin'ter] nf. hyacinth.

Hydraulisch [hyŏŏ-drow'lish] a. hydraulic.

Hydrierung [hyŏŏ-dreer'rŏŏng] nf. hydrogenation.

Hygien'e [hyŏŏ-gi-ay'ner] nf. hygiene; **-isch** a. hygienic.

Hymne [hyŏŏm'ner] nf. hymn.

Hypno'se [hyŏŏp-nose'er] nf. hypnosis; **-tisch** a. hypnotic.

Hypothek [hyŏŏ-po-take'] nf. mortgage.

Hypothe'se [hyŏŏ-po-tay'zer] nf. hypothesis; **-tisch** a. hypothetical.

Hysterie [hyŏŏ-ster-ree'] nf. hysteria; **-isch** a. hysterical.

I

Ich [ish] pn. I; n. self.

Ideal [ee-day-ahl'] n. (-e) ideal; **-ist** m.w. idealist; **-istisch** a. idealistic.

Idee [ee-day'] nf. idea.

Identi'fizieren [ee-den-ti-fit-seer'ren] vt. to identify; **-tät** nf. identity; **-sch** a. identical.

Idiomatisch [i-di-o-mah'tish] a. idiomatic.

Idiot [i-di-oht'] m.w. idiot; **-isch** a. idiotic.

Igel [ee-gel'] nm. (-) hedgehog.

Ignor'ant [ig-no-rant'] m.w. ignoramus; **-ieren** vt. to be ignorant of, ignore.

Ihm [eem] pn. to him, to it.

Ihn [een] pn. him, it.

Ihr [eerr] pn. to her, you.

Ihr, Ihre, Ihrs poss. your, her, its, their.

Ihrige (der, die, das) poss. yours, hers, its, theirs.

Illegitim [il-ay-gi-teem'] a. illegitimate.

Illuminieren [il-ŏŏ-mi-neer'ren] vt. to illuminate.

Illusorisch [il-ŏŏ-zore'ish] a. illusory.

Illustrieren [il-ŏŏs-treer'ren] vt. to illustrate.

Iltis [il'tiss] nm. (-e) polecat.

Im = in dem.

Imaginär [i-ma-gi-nare'] a. imaginary.

Imbiss [im'biss] nm. (-e) snack.

Imker [im'kerr] nm. (-) beekeeper, bee-fancier.

Immatrikul'ation [im-a-tri-kŏŏ-lat-si-ohn'] nf. matriculation; **-ieren** vt. to matriculate.

Immer [im'err] ad. always, ever, still; **-fort** ad. continually; **-grün** a. evergreen; **-hin** ad. still, after all; **-während** a. perpetual.

Immobilien [i-moh-beel'yen] pl. immovable goods.

Immun [i-moon'] a. immune; **-ität** nf. immunity.

Imperativ [im-per-ra-teef'] nm. (-) imperative.

Imperfekt [im-porr-fekt'] n. (-) imperfect, past.

Imperiali'smus [im-per-ri-aliss'mŏŏss] nm. imperialism; **-st** m.w. imperialist.

Impf'en [imp'fen] vt. to graft, inoculate; **-stoff** nm. serum; **-ung** nf. inoculation.

Imponieren [im-poh-neer'ren] vt. to impress.

Importieren [im-porr-teer'ren] vt. to import.

Imprägnier'en [im-prayg-neer'ren] vt. to impregnate; **-ung** nf. impregnation.

Improvisieren [im-pro-vizeer'ren] vt. to improvise.

Impulsiv [im-pŏŏl-zeef'] a. impulsive.

In [in] pr. in, into.

Inanspruchnahme [in-an'shprŏŏch-nah'mer] nf. claiming, being busy.

Inbegriff [in'ber-grif'] nm.

(-e) embodiment, personification.

Inbetriebsetzung [in-ber-treep'zet-sŏong] *nf.* starting, opening. [ardour.

Inbrunst [in'brŏonst] *nf.*

Inbrünstig [in-brÿŏn-stish] *a.* ardent.

Indem [in-dame'] *cj.* while, by.

Indes(sen) [in-dess'en] *ad.* meanwhile; *cj.* while.

Indigo [in'di-gŏ'] *nm.* indigo.

Indikativ [in-di-ka-teef'] *nm.* (-e) indicative. [direct.

Indirekt [in-di-rekt'] *a.* in-

Indiskret [in-di-skrate'] *a.* tactless; -ion *nf.* tactlessness.

Individu'alität [in-di-vee-dŏo-á-li-tate'] *nf.* individuality; -ell *a.* individual; -uum *n.* individual.

Indoss'ament [in-doss-a-ment'] *n.* (-e) endorsement; -ieren *vt.* to endorse.

Induktion [in-dŏok-syohn'] *nf.* induction; -strom *nm.* induced current (*el.*).

Industri'e [in-dŏos-tree'] *nf.* industry, manufacture; -ell *a.* industrial; -alisieren *vt.* to industrialize; -eflugplatz *nm.* factory airfield.

Ineinander [in'ine-an'derr] *ad.* in(to) one another, each other.

Inempfangnahme [in-empfang'nah-mer] *nf.* receipt, taking delivery (*com.*).

Infam [in-fahm'] *a.* infamous; -ie *nf.* infamy.

Infanter'ie [in-fan-ter-ree'] *nf.* infantry; -ist *m.w.* infantryman.

Inflation [in-flat-syohn'] *nf.* inflation.

Ingenieur [in-zhen-yerr'] *nm.* (-e) engineer; -wesen *n.* engineering.

Ingrimm [in'grim] *nm.* sullen fury; -ig *a.* furious.

Ingwer [ing'verr] *nm.* ginger.

Inhaber [in'hah-berr] *nm.* holder, owner, occupier, bearer.

Inhalt [in'halt] *nm.* contents, tenor; -leer, -los *a.* empty, meaningless; -reich *a.* weighty, full of meaning, significant; sangabe *nf.* table of contents, declaration, summary; -sverzeichnis *n.* index.

Initiative [in-it-sia-tee'ver] *nf.* initiative. [ing.

Inkasso [in-kass'oh] *n.* cash-

Inklusive [in-klŏo-zee'ver] *ad.* inclusively, included.

Inkonsequ'ent [in-kon-zay-kvent'] *a.* inconsistent; -enz *nf.* inconsistency.

Inkrafttreten [in-kraft'tray-ten] *n.* coming into force.

Inland [in'lant] *n.* inland, home country, interior.

Inländ'er [in'len-derr] *nm.* (-) native; -isch *a.* inland, native.

Inmitten [in-mit'en] *pr.* amid, among.

Inne [in'er] *ad.* within; -haben *vt. ir.* to own, know; -halten *vt. ir.* to observe; *i.* stop; -werden *vi. ir.* to perceive.

Inner [in'err] *a.* interior, internal; -halb *pr.* within, inside; -lich *a.* inward(ly), cordial(ly); -lichkeit *nf.* inwardness, cordiality, depth; -st *a.* inmost.

Innig [in'ish] *a.* intimate, sincere; -keit *nf.* intimacy, sincerity, feeling.

Innung [in'ŏong] *nf.* corporation, guild. [mate.

Insasse [in'zass-er] *m.w.* in-

Insbesondere [ins-ber-zon'der-rer] *ad.* especially. [tion.

Inschrift [in'shrift] *nf.* inscrip-

Insekt [in-zekt'] *n.* (*gen.* -es; *pl.* -en) insect.

Insel [in'zel] *nf.* island.

Inser'at [in-zer-raht'] *n.* (-e) advertisement; -atenbüro *n.* advertising agency; -ent *m.w.* advertiser; -ieren *vt.* to advertise.

Insgeheim [inss-ger-hime'] ad. secretly.

Insgemein [inss-ger-mine'] ad. in common.

Insgesamt [inss-ger-zamt'] ad. all together, totally.

Insignien [in-zig'nien] pl. insignia.

Insofern [in-zoh-fairrn'], **Insoweit** [in-zoh-vite'] ad. in so far as.

Insolvent' [in-zol-vent'] a. insolvent; **-z** nf. insolvency.

Inspizient [in-spit-sient'] m.w. inspector, manager.

Instand'haltung [in-shtant'-hal-toong] nf. upkeep; **-setzen** vt. to repair, enable, condition (tec.).

Instanz [in-shtants'] nf. court; **-enweg** nm. official channels.

Installateur [in-stal-a-terr'] nm. (-e) electrician, plumber.

Instinkt [in-stinkt'] nm. (-e) instinct; **-iv** a. instinctive.

Institut [in-sti-tōōt'] n. (-e) institute, school.

Instrument [in-strōō-ment'] n. (-e) instrument; **-enbrett** n. dash-board.

Inszenieren [ins-tsay-neer'ren] vt. to put on the stage.

Intelligen't [in-tel-i-gent'] a. clever, intelligent; **-z** nf. intelligence, intelligentsia.

Intendant [in-ten-dant'] m.w. superintendent, administrative officer; **-ur** nf. commissariat (mil.).

Intensi'tät [in-ten-si-tate'] nf. intensity; **-v** a. intensive.

Interess'ant [in-ter-ress-ant'] a. interesting; **-e** n. interest; **-ent** m.w. intending purchaser (com.); **-ieren** v.r.t. to interest.

Intern'at [in-terr-naht'] n. (-e) boarding school; **-ieren** vt. to intern; **-ierung** nf. internment; **-ierungslager** n. internment camp.

Interpunktion [in-terr-pōōnk-syohn'] nf. punctuation.

Intim [in-teem'] a. intimate, familiar; **-ität** nf. intimacy.

Inventar [in-ven-tarr'] n. (-e) inventory; **-aufnahme** nf. stock-taking.

Inwendig [in'ven-dish] a. inside, inward.

Inwiefern [in-vee-fairrn'], **Inwieweit** [in-vee-vite'] ad. how far, to what extent.

Inzwischen [int-svi'shen] ad. meanwhile.

Ird'en [irr'den] a. earthen; **-isch** a. earthly, worldly.

Irgend [irr'gent] ad. ever, some, any; **-ein**, **-eine** a. some, any; **-etwas** pn. anything, something; **-jemand** pn. anyone, someone; **-wie** ad. anyhow, somehow.

Ironi'e [ee-roh-nee'] nf. irony, sarcasm; **-sch** a. ironical.

Irre [irr'er] a. astray, wrong, unsettled, deranged; **-n** v.i.r. to go astray, err, be mistaken; **-führen** vt. to mislead; **-nhaus** n. lunatic asylum.

Irrig [irr'ish] a. erroneous.

Irr'lehre nf. heresy; **-licht** n. will-o'-the-wisp; **-tum** nm. error; **-tümlich** a. erroneous.

Isol'ation [ee-zoh-lat-syohn'] nf. isolation, insulation (el.); **-ator** nm. insulator; **-ieren** vt. to isolate, insulate; **-ierung** nf. insulation.

Ist'-bestand nm. actual, ration strength (mil.); **-stärke** nf. **-stand** nm. actual stocks, stocks in hand.

J

Ja [yah] ad. yes, indeed, certainly, of course; **-wohl** ad. yes, indeed; **-wort** n. consent.

Jacht [yacht] nf. yacht.

Jacke [yak'er] nf. jacket.

Jackett [zha-ket'] n. (-e) (short) jacket.

Jagd [yahkt] nf. hunt(ing),

fighting (av.); -bomber nm. fighter bomber; -gruppe nf. pursuit squadron; -kommando n. fighter command, detachment; -raum nm. fighter sector; -sperre nf. fighter screen; -verband n. fighter unit.

Jagen [yah'gen] vi. to hunt, race; t. hunt, drive (off).

Jäger [yai'gerr] nm. (-) hunter, rifleman, fighter aircraft, pursuit plane (av.); -platz nm. fighter aerodrome; -regiment n. rifle regiment.

Jäh [yay] a. sudden, rash, steep, precipitous; ad. suddenly, steeply; -e nf. abruptness, suddenness; -lings ad. abruptly, suddenly; -zorn nm. sudden anger, irascibility; -zornig a. irascible.

Jahr [yahrr] n. (-e) year; -buch n. year-book; -elang ad. for years; -esbericht nm. annual report; -esfeier nf., -estag nm. anniversary; -eszeit nf. season; -gang nm. age-group, vintage; -geld n. annuity; -hundert n. century; -markt nm. fair; -zehnt n. decade.

Jährig [yare'ish] a, **Jährlich** [yare'lish] a. yearly.

Jammer [yam'err] nm. misery, pity; -leben n. wretched life; -n vi. t. to grieve, wail, lament; t. imp. move to pity.

Jämmerlich [yem'err-lish] a. pitiable; -keit nf. wretchedness.

Januar [jan'oo-arr] nm. January. [mine.

Jasmin [jas'meen] nm. jasmine.

Jaspis [yas'pis] nm. jasper.

Jäten [yay'ten] vt. to weed.

Jauchze'n [yowch'tsen] vi. to rejoice, shout (with joy); -r nm. shout of joy.

Jazz [yats] nm. jazz; -kapelle nf. jazz band.

Je [yay] ad. ever, apiece, the; -nachdem according as, as.

Jeder [yay'derr], **Jede**, **Jedes** a. each; pn. each, everybody.

Jedenfalls [yay'den-falss] ad. in any case, at any rate.

Jedermann [jay'derr-man] pn. everyone.

Jederzeit [yay'derr-tsite] ad. at any time.

Jedesmal [yay'dess-mahl] ad. every time, each time. [ever.

Jedoch [yay-doch'] ad. however. [ever.

Jedweder [yay-vay'derr], **Jeglicher** [yay'glish-err] pn. see Jeder. [time.

Jemals [jay'mahlss] ad. at any time.

Jemand [yay'mant] pn. somebody, anybody.

Jener [yay'nerr], **Jene**, **Jenes** a, pn. that (one).

Jenseits [yane'zites] ad, pr. on the other side (of); n. the other world. [actual.

Jetzig [yet'sish] a. present, now.

Jetzt [yetst] ad. now.

Joch [yoch] n. (-e) yoke.

Jockei [jo-ki'] nm. (-e) jockey

Jod [yoht] n. iodine.

Jodeln [yoh'deln] vi. to yodle.

Johannisbeere [yoh-han'iss-bair-rer] nf. red currant.

Johlen [yoh'len] vi. to yell.

Jolle [yol'er] nf. jolly-boat.

Joppe [yop'er] nf. jacket.

Journalismus [zoōr-nal-is'moōs] nm. journalism; -t n.w.v. journalist.

Jubel [yoō'bel] nm. rejoicing; -jahr n. jubilee, celebration; -n vi. to rejoice.

Jubilieren [yoō-bil-eer'ren] vi. see Jubeln.

Juchten [yōōch'ten] n. Russian leather.

Jucken [yōōk'en] vi. to itch.

Jude [yoō'der] m.w.v. Jew.

Jüdin [yoō'din] nf. Jewess; -sch a. Jewish.

Jugend [yoō'gent] nf. youth; -bewegung nf. youth movement; -lich a. youthful; -herberge nf. youth hostel.

Juli [yoō'lee] nm. July.

Jung [yŏŏng] a. young; **-e** boy, lad; **-fer** nf. spinster, girl; **-fernrede** nf. maiden speech; **-fernschaft** nf. virginity; **-frau** nf. virgin, maid; **-fräulich** a. maidenly; **-geselle** m.w. bachelor.

Jüng'er [yŏŏng'err] nm. disciple; a. younger, junior; **-ling** nm. youth; **-st** a. latest; ad. lately, recently.

Juni [yŏŏ'nee] nm. June.

Junker [yŏŏn'kerr] nm. young nobleman, squire, landowner.

Jurist [yŏŏr-ist'] m.w. lawyer; **-isch** a. of, in law. [exactly.

Just [yŏŏst] ad. just (now),

Justiz [yŏŏs-teets'] nf. legal administration.

Jute [yŏŏ'ter] nf. jute.

Juwel [yŏŏ-vale'] n. (gen. **-s**; pl. **-en**) jewel; **-ier** nm. jeweller.

Jux [yŏŏks] nm. (-e) joke, fun; **-en** vi. to play a joke.

K

Kabel kah'bell n. (-) cable; **-bau** nm. cable-laying; **-bericht** nm, **-depesche** nf. cable(gram); **-n** vi.i. to cable.

Kabeljau [kah'bel-yow] nm. (-e) cod.

Kabine [ka-been'er] nf. cabin, cubicle.

Kabinett [kab-i-net'] n. (-e) cabinet, small room.

Kachel [kach'el] nf. Dutch tile; **-ofen** nm. stove with tiles.

Kadaver [ka-dah'verr] nm. (-) carcass, corpse.

Kadett [ka-det'] m.w. cadet; **-enanstalt** nf. military school; **-enschulschiff** n. training ship (nav.).

Käfer [kay'ferr] nm. (-) beetle.

Kaffee [kaf'ay] nm. (-s) coffee; n. cafe.

Käfig [kay'fish] nm. (-e) cage.

Kahl [kahl] a. bald; **-heit** nf. baldness; **-köpfig** a. baldheaded.

Kahm [kahm] nm. mould; **-ig** a. mouldy. [barge.

Kahn [kahn] nm. (**Kähne**) boat, **Kai** [kie, kay] nm. (-e) quay.

Kaiser [kie'zerr] nm. (-) emperor; **-in** nf. empress; **-lich** a. imperial; **-reich, -tum** n. empire.

Kajüte [ka-yŏŏ'ter] nf. cabin.

Kakadu [ka-ka-dŏŏ'] nm. (-s) cockatoo.

Kakao [ka-kow'] nm. cocoa.

Kakerlak [kah'kerr-lak] m.w. cockroach, albino.

Kalb [kalp] n. (**Kälber**) calf; **-en** vi. to calve; **-fleisch** n. veal; **-sleder** n. calf-leather.

Kaldaunen [kal-dow'nen] pl. guts, tripe.

Kalender [ka-len'derr] nm. (-) calendar. [caulk.

Kalfatern [kal-fah'terrn] vt. to

Kali [kah'lee] n. potash.

Kaliber [ka-lee'berr] nm. (-) calibre, bore.

Kalk [kalk] nm. (-e) lime; **-brennerei** nf. lime-kiln; **-licht** n. limelight; **-stein** nm. limestone.

Kalkulieren [kal-kŏŏ-leer'ren] vt. to calculate.

Kalorie [ka-lor-ree'] nf. calory.

Kalt [kalt] a. cold; **-blütig** a. cold-blooded, cool; **-blütigkeit** nf. coolness.

Kälte [kel'ter] nf. cold, coldness; **-fest, -beständig** a. antifreezing; **-schutzbrille** nf. frost goggles (av.).

Kalzium [kalt-syŏŏm'] n. calcium.

Kamel [kam-ale'] n. (-e) camel.

Kamera [ka'mer-rah] nf. (-s) camera.

Kamerad [ka-mer-raht'] m.w. comrade; **-schaft** nf. comradeship. [mile.

Kamille [ka-mil'er] nf. camomile.

Kamin [ka-meen'] nm. (-e) chimney, fireside, fireplace;

-feger nm. chimney-sweep; **-sims** nm. mantelpiece.

Kamm [kam] nm. (Kämme) comb, ridge; **-garn** n. worsted; **-rad** n. cog-wheel.

Kämmen [kem'en] vt. to comb, card.

Kammer [kam'err] nf. (small) bedroom, chamber, board; **-diener** nm. valet; **-frau** nf. chambermaid; **-herr** m.w. chamberlain.

Kämmerer [kem'er-rerr] nm. (-) chamberlain, treasurer.

Kampf [kampf] nm. (Kämpfe) fight, battle, contest, struggle; **-bahn** nf. arena; **-flugzeug** n. (German) bomber, (Allied) fighter; **-handlung** nf. action (mil.).

Kämpfen [kempf'en] vi. to fight, struggle; **-er** nm. fighter, combatant.

Kampfer [kampf'err] nm. camphor. [to camp.

Kampieren [kam-peer'en] vi. **Kanal** [ka-nahl'] nm. (Kanäle) canal, channel, drain; **-isation** nf. drainage, draining; **-isieren** vt. to drain, canalize.

Kanapee [ka-na-pay'] n. (-s) settee, sofa.

Kanarienvogel [ka-nah'ryan-foh'gel] nm. (-vögel) canary.

Kandare [kan-dah'rer] nf. bit, curb.

Kandidat [kan-di-daht'] m.w. candidate. [to candy.

Kandieren [kan-deer'en] vt. **Kandis** [kan'dis] nm. candy.

Kaneel [ka-nail'] nf. cinnamon.

Känguruh [keng'oo-rōō'] n. (-s) kangaroo.

Kaninchen [ka-neen'shen] n. (-) rabbit.

Kanne [kan'er] nf. jug, can, pot, mug; **-ngiesser** nm. tubthumper, low politician.

Kannibale [kan-i-bah'ler] m.w. cannibal.

Kanon [ka-nohn'] nm. (-s)

canon; **-ikus** nm. canon; **-isch** a. canonical.

Kanonade [ka-no-nah'der] nf. bombardment.

Kanone [ka-noh'ner] nf.canon, gun; **-ier** nm. gunner; **-enboot** n. cannon-boat; **-enfutter** n. cannon-fodder; **-enkugel** nf. cannon ball.

Kantate [kan-tah'ter] nf. cantata. [canteen.

Kantine [kan-tee'ner] nf. **Kanton** [kan-tohn'] nm. (-e) canton; **-ieren** vt. to canton; **-ierung** nf. cantonment.

Kantor [kan'torr] nm. (gen. -s; pl. -en) precentor, choirmaster.

Kanzel [kant'sel] nf. pulpit.

Kanzlei [kants-lie'] nf. chancery, government office; **-er** nm. chancellor; **-ist** m.w. clerk in government office.

Kap [kahp] n. (-e) cape.

Kapazität [kap-ats-i-tate'] nf. capacity, authority.

Kapelle [kap-el'er] nf. chapel, band, choir; **-meister** nm. conductor.

Kaper [kah'perr] nf. caper. **Kapern** [kah'pern] vt. to capture; **-schiff** n. privateer.

Kapital [kap-i-tahl'] n. (gen. -s; pl. -ien) capital; **-isieren** vt. to finance, capitalize; **-ist** m.w. capitalist; **-konto** n. stock-account.

Kapitän [kap-i-tane'] nm. (-e) captain (ship).

Kapitel [kap-i'tel] n. (-) chapter.

Kapitulation [kap-i'-tōō-lat-syohn'] nf. capitulation; **-ieren** vi. to capitulate.

Kaplan [kap-lahn'] nm. (Kapläne) chaplain.

Kappe [kap'er] nf. cap, cape, hood, ridge; **-n** vt. to lop, trim, chop off. [box.

Kapsel [kap'sel] nf. capsule.

Kaputt [kap-ōōt'] a. smashed, broken, exhausted, finished.

Kapuze [kap-ōōt'ser] *nf.* hood, cowl. [er.

Karaffe [kar-af'er] *nf.* decanter.

Karat [kar-raht'] *n.* (-e) carat.

Karawane [kar-ra-vah'ner] *nf.* caravan.

Karbid [karr-beet'] *n.* carbide.

Karbolsäure [karr-bohl'zoy-rer] *nf.* carbolic acid.

Karbonsäure [karr-bohn'zoy-rer] *nf.* carbonic acid.

Karbunkel [karr-bōōn'kel] *nm.* (-) carbuncle.

Kardätsche [karr-detch'er] *nf.* card, curry-comb; **-n** *vt.* to card, curry.

Karde [karr'der] *nf.* card (*tec.*).

Kardinal [karr-di-nahl'] *nm.* (Kardinäle) cardinal.

Karfreitag [karr-fry'tahk] *nm.* Good Friday.

Karfunkel [karr-fōōn'kel] *nm.* (-) carbuncle (*stone*).

Karg [karrk] *a.* niggardly, poor; **-en** *vi.* to be miserly; **-heit** *nf.* poverty, parsimony.

Kärglich [kairrk'lish] *a.* poor, scanty. [check.

Karieren [kar-reer'en] *vt.* to

Karikatur [kar-i-ka-toor'] *nf.* caricature.

Karmesin [karr-may-zeen'] *a.* crimson.

Karmin [karr-meen'] *nm.* carmine.

Karneval [karr'ner-val] *nm.* (-s) carnival. [cornice.

Karnies [karr-neece'] *n.* (-e)

Karo [kah'roh] *n.* (-s) square, diamonds (*card*).

Karosse [kar-ros'er] *nf.* coach, carriage; **-rie** *nf.* body (*aut.*).

Karotte [kar-rot'er] *nf.* carrot.

Karpfen [karrp'fen] *nm.* (-) carp.

Karre [kar'rer] *nf.* cart, barrow; **-n** *nm.* (-) cart, dray; *vt.* to cart, transport.

Karriere [kar-ri-air'er] *nf.* career, fortune.

Kärrner [kerr'nerr] *nm.* (-) carter, drayman.

Karst [karrst] *nm.* (-e) mattock.

Kartätsche [karr'tetch-er] *nf.* case, canister shot.

Karte [karr'ter] *nf.* card, map, bill; **-nbrief** *nm.* letter-card; **-nkunde** *nf.* map reading; **-nspiel** *n.* card game; **-nwerk** *n.* atlas. [index.

Kartei [karr-ty'] *nf.* card-

Kartell [karr-tel'] *n.* (-e) cartel, trust (*com.*).

Kartoffel [karr-tof'el] *nf.* potato; **-mus** *n.* mashed potatoes.

Karton [karr-tong'] *nm.* (-s) cardboard, board(s); **-ieren** *vt.* to bind in boards.

Kartusche [kar-tōōsh'er] *nf.* cartridge.

Karussel [kar-rōō-sel'] *n.* (-s) round-about.

Kaschmir [kash'meerr] *nm.* cashmere.

Käse [kay'zer] *nm.* (-) cheese; **-butter** *nf.* curds, cream-cheese; **-kammer** *nf.* dairy; **-n** *vt.* to curdle, turn into cheese; *i.* curdle; **-wasser** *n.* whey.

Kasematte [kah-zer-mat'er] *nf.* casemate.

Kaserne [ka-zairr'ner] *nf.* barracks; **-iert** *a.* quartered in barracks (*mil.*).

Käsig [kay'zish] *a.* cheesy.

Kasino [ka-zee'noh] *n.* (-s) officers' mess, club; **-älteste(r)** *m.w.* mess president.

Kassa [kass'ah], **Kasse** [kass'er] *nf.* cash, till, pay-desk.

Kassation [kass-at-syohn'] *nf.* cashiering.

Kassen—arzt *nm.* panel doctor; **-bestand** *nm.* cash balance; **-dieb** *nm.* embezzler; **-führer** *nm.* treasurer; **-gehilfe** *m.w.* teller; **-prüfung** *nf.* audit; **-wesen** *n.* finance, accounting.

Kasserolle [kass-er-rol'er] *nf.* casserole, pan for stewing.

Kassette [kass-et'er] *nf.* small box, dark-slide, plate-holder film spool; -nkamera *nf.* plate camera.

Kassier'en [kass-eer'ren] *vt.* to cash, annul, cashier; -er *nm.* cashier, treasurer.

Kastanie [kass-tahn'yer] *nf.* chestnut; -nbaum *nm.* chestnut tree.

Kästchen [kest'shen] *n.* (-) small box, casket.

Kaste [kass'ter] *nf.* caste; -ngeist *nm.* snobbery.

Kasten [kast'en] *nm.* (-) box case, chest; -träger *nm.* box girder.   [to castrate.

Kastrieren [kast-reer'ren] *vt.*

Kasus [kah'zōōss] *nm.* (-) case.

Katalog [ka-ta-lohk'] *nm.* (-e) catalogue; -isieren *vt.* to catalogue.

Katarrh [kat-ahrr'] *nm.* catarrh.

Kataster [kat-ast'err] *nm.* (-) land register.

Katastrophe [kat-as-troh'fer] *nf.* catastrophe.

Kategor'ie [kat-e-gor-ree'] *nf.* category, class; -isch *a.* categorical.

Kater [kah'terr] *nm.* (-) tom-cat, sick headache.

Katheder [ka-tay'derr] *nm.* (-) lecture desk.

Kathedrale [ka-tay-drah'ler] *nf.* cathedral.   [cathode.

Kathode [ka-toh'der] *nf.* (-)

Katholik [ka-toh-leek'] *m.w.* Catholic; -isch *a.* Catholic; -izismus *nm.* Catholicism.

Kattun [kat-oon'] *nm.* (-e) cotton, calico.   [kitten.

Kätzchen [kets'shen] *n.* (-)

Katze [kat'ser] *nf.* cat; -njammer *nm.* seediness.

Kauderwelsch [kow'derr-velsh] *n.* jargon, gibberish.

Kauen [kow'en] *vt.* to chew.

Kauern [kow'errn] *vi.* to cower.

Kauf [kowf] *nm.* (**Käufe**) purchase, buying, bargain;

-bar *a.* purchasable; -brief *nm.* bill of sale; -fahrtei *nf.* commercial navigation; -kraft *nf.* purchasing power; -laden *nm.* shop, store; -preis *nm.* cost price.

Kaufen [kow'fen] *vt.* to buy.

Käufer [koy'ferr] *nm.* (-) buyer; -lich *a, ad.* purchasable, by purchase, venal; -lichkeit *nf.* venality.

Kaufmann [kowf'man] *nm.* (-leute) merchant, shopkeeper; -schaft *nf.* business community; -sstand *nm.* commercial class.

Kaufmännisch [kowf'men-ish] *a.* commercial.

Kaum [kowm] *ad.* hardly, scarcely.   [caustic.

Kaustisch [kow'stish] *a.*

Kaution [kowt-syohn'] *nf.* security, bail.

Kautschuk [kowt'shŏŏk] *nm.* india-rubber.

Kauz [kowts] *nm.* (**Käuze**) owl, queer fellow.

Kavalleri'e [ka-val-er-ree'] *nf.* cavalry; -st *m.w.* trooper.

Kaviar [ka'viahr] *nm.* caviare.

Kebsweib [kaips'vipe] *n.* (-er) concubine.

Keck [kek] *a.* daring, bold, forward; -heit *nf.* boldness, forwardness.

Kegel [kay'gel] *nm.* (-) skittle, cone; -bahn *nf.* skittle alley; -förmig *a.* conical; -getriebe *n.* bevel gear.

Kehle [kay'ler] *nf.* throat; -hauch *nm.* aspirate; -kopf *nm.* larynx; -laut *nm.* guttural; -rinne *nf.* gutter.

Kehlen [kay'len] *vt.* to chamfer, hollow.

Kehre [kair'rer] *nf.* turn(ing), bend; -n *vt.i.r.* to turn, reverse, return.

Kehren [kair'ren] *vt.* to sweep.

Kehricht [kair'risht] *nm.* sweepings; -kasten *nm.* dust-bin.

Kehrreim [kair'rime] nm. (-e) refrain.

Keif'en [kife'en] vi. to bark, scold, nag; **-erin** nf. shrew, scold.

Keil [kile] nm. (-e) wedge, arrowhead (mil.); **-en** vt. to wedge, induce, win over, split.

Keim [kime] nm. (-e) bud, germ; **-frei** a. sterile; **-tötend** a. antiseptic, germicide.

Keimen [kime'en] vi. to germinate, bud.

Kein [kine] a. no, not any; **-er, -e, -es** pn. no one, none; **-eswegs** ad. by no means.

Keks [kakes] nm. (-e) biscuit.

Kelch [kelsh] nm. (-e) cup, goblet, chalice.

Kelle [kel'er] nf. ladle, trowel.

Keller [kel'err] nm. (-) cellar; **-meister** nm. butler.

Kellner [kel'nerr] nm. (-) waiter; **-in** nf. waitress, barmaid.

Kelter [kel'terr] nf. wine-press; **-n** vt. to press, tread.

Kenbar [ken'barr] a. recognizable.

Kenn'en [ken'en] vt. ir. to know; **-lernen** to get to know; **-er** nm. connoisseur, good judge; **-karte** nf. identity card; **-lichter** n.pl. navigation lights (av.); **-linie** nf. characteristic curve; **-nummer** nf. identity number; **-tlich** a. distinguishable, discernible; **-tnis** nf. knowledge, information; **-tnisnahme** nf. taking cognizance of, information; **-ung** nf. morse characteristic; **-ungsfeuer** n. flashing beacon (av.); **-zahl** nf. exchange number; **-zeichen** n. mark, characteristic; **-ziffer** nf. reference number.   [size.

Kentern [ken'tern] vt. to capsize.

Kerb'e [kairr'ber] nf. notch, groove; **-en** vt. to notch; **-ig** a. notched; **-tier** n. insect.

Kerbel [kairr'bel] nm. chervil.

Kerker [kairr'kerr] nm. (-)

prison; **-haft** nf. imprisonment; **-meister** nm. gaoler.

Kerl [kairrl] nm. (-e) fellow.

Kern [kairrn] nm. (-e) kernel, pith, pip, bore, grain, root, heart; **-frucht** nf. stone fruit; **-geschoss** n. armour piercing bullet; **-gesund** a. thoroughly healthy; **-munition** nf. armour piercing ammunition; **-physik** nf. nuclear physics; **-schuss** nm. point-blank shot.

Kernhaft [kairrn'haft], **Kernig** [kairrn'ish] a. pithy, robust.

Kerze [kairrt'ser] nf. candle; **-ngerade** a. straight as a die.

Kessel [kes'l] nm. (-) kettle, boiler, pocket, encircled troops (mil.); **-flicker** nm. tinker; **-pauke** nf. kettledrum; **-wagen** nm. tanker (rl.).

Kette [ket'er] nf. chain, three aircraft; **-nbrücke** nf. suspension bridge; **-ngeschäft** n. chain-store; **-nhandel** nm. black marketing; **-nkasten** nm. gear-case; **-nschutzgehäuse** n. gear-case.

Ketten [ketn] vt. to chain.

Ketzer [kets'err] nm. (-) heretic; **-isch** a. heretical.

Keuch'en [koy'shen] vi. to pant, gasp; **-husten** n. whooping cough.

Keule [koy'ler] nf. club, leg (meat).

Keusch [koish] a. chaste; **-heit** nf. chastity.   [giggle.

Kichern [kish'errn] vi. to

Kiebitz [kee'bits] m.w. peewit.

Kiefer [kee'ferr] nm. (-) jaw.

Kiefer [kee'ferr] nf. pine, fir; **-zapfen** nm. fir-cone.

Kiel [keel] nm. (-e) quill.

Kiel [keel] nm. (-e) keel; **-holen** vt. to careen, keelhaul; **-leine** nf. line astern (nav.); **-wasser** n. wake.

Kieme [kee'mer] nf. gill (fish).

Kien [keen] nm. resinous wood; **-ig** a. resinous.   [basket.

Kiepe [kee'per] nf. wicker-

Kies [keece] nm. (-e) gravel; -ig a. gravelly.

Kiesel [kee'zel] nm. (-) pebble, flint; -stein nm. pebble; -stoff nm. silicon.

Kilogramm [ki-lo-gram'] n. (-e) kilogram. two pounds.

Kilometer [ki-lo-mate'err] n. (-) kilometre; -zähler nm. cyclometer.

Kimme [kim'er] nf. notch, edge; -n vt. to notch, edge.

Kimmung [kim'ŏong] nf. mirage.

Kind [kint] n. (-er) child; -chen n. baby; -erei nf. childishness; -erfräulein n. nursery governess; -ermädchen n. nursemaid; -erraub nm. kidnapping; -erspiel n. child's-play; -erstube nf. nursery; -erwagen nm. pram; -esalter n. infancy; -heit nf. childhood; -isch a. childish; -lich a. childlike.

Kinematograph [kee-nay-ma-to-grahf'] m.w. cinematograph; -enleinwand nf. screen; -ie nf. cinema-photography; -isch a. cinema . . .

Kinn [kin] n. (-e) chin; -backen nm. jaw-bone; -kette nf. curb.

Kino [kee'noh] n. (-s) cinema; -besucher nm. cinema goer, film-fan; -programm n. film programme.

Kiosk [kee'osk] nm. (-e) kiosk, summer house.

Kippe'n [kip'en] v.i.t. to topple over, lose one's balance, overturn; -r nm. tipping truck, tipper.

Kirch'e [kirr'sher] nf. church; -gang nm. going to church; -hof nm. churchyard; -lich a. ecclesiastical; -ner nm. sexton, sacristan; -spiel n. parish; -turm nm. church tower, steeple; -weihe nf. dedication of a church, fair.

Kirchen–älteste(r) m.w. churchwarden, elder; -bann nm. excommunication; -buch

n. parish register; -diener nm. see Kirchner; -fest n. church festival; -lied n. hymn; -recht n. canon law; -stuhl nm. pew.

Kirre [kir'rer] a. tame, tractable; -n vt. to bait, decoy, tame.

Kirsch [kirrsh] nm. (-e) cherry, [brandy.

Kirsch'e [kirr'sher] nf. cherry; -baumholz n. cherry-wood; -wasser n. cherry-brandy.

Kissen [kis'en] n. (-) cushion, pillow. [case.

Kiste [kist'er] nf. chest, trunk, case.

Kitsch [kitch] nm. trash; -ig a. trashy.

Kitt [kit] nm. cement, putty; -en vt. to cement, stick.

Kittel [kit'l] nm. (-) smock, blouse, overall.

Kitz [kits] n. (-e), **Kitze** nf. kid, fawn, kitten.

Kitzel [kits'el] nm. tickling, itch; -ig a. ticklish, awkward; -n vt. to tickle.

Klade [klad'er] nf. rough draft, copy; -buch, note-book.

Kladderadatsch [klad-er-ra-datch'] nm. (-e) crash, smash.

Klaffen [klaf'en] vi. to gape.

Kläffe'n [klef'en] vi. to yelp, brawl, slander; -r nm. barking dog, brawler.

Klafter [klaf'terr] nf. fathom, cord (wood).

Klagbar [klahk'barr] a. actionable.

Klage [klah'ger] nf. complaint, action (law); -n vi. to bewail, complain, go to law; -nswert a. lamentable; -schrift nf. writ.

Kläg'er [klay'gerr] nm. (-) plaintiff; -lich a. wretched.

Klamm [klam] nf. ravine, glen; a. numb, short of money.

Klammer [klam'err] nf. clamp, bracket, clip, peg; -n vt. to clamp, fasten; r. cling to.

Klampe [klamp'er] nf. clamp, hasp.

Klang [klang] nm. (Klänge) sound, timbre; -farbe (nf.) tone colour; **-film** nm. sound film; **-voll** a. sonorous.

Klapp'e [klap'er] nf. flap, valve, tally, damper, stop; **-brücke** nf. folding bridge; **-kragen** nm. turn-down collar; **-messer** n. jack-knife; **-n** vi. to clap, flap, work well, suit; **-nsicherung** nf. centrifugal safety device; **-stuhl** nm. folding camp stool; **-tür** nf. trap-door.

Klapper [klap'err] nf. clapper, rattle; **-ig** a. rattling, shaky, broken-down; **-schlange** nf. rattle-snake.

Klappern [klap'errn] vi. to clatter, rattle.

Klaps [klaps] nm. (-e) slap, clap; **-en** vt. to slap.

Klar [klahrr] a. clear, distinct, lucid, ready for sea (nav.), for action (mil.); **-heit** nf. clearness, lucidity; **-legen** vt. to clear up. [explain.

Klären [klair'ren] vt. to clarify.

Klarinette [klar-ri-net'er] nf. clarinet. [clear.

Klarieren [klar-reer'ren] vt. to

Klasse [klass'er] nf. class, form; **-nälteste(r)** m.w. top boy, head of class; **-nkampf** nm. class conflict; **-nlehrer** nm. form master; **-nliste** nf. register; **-nzimmer** n. class-room.

Klassifizier'en [klass-if-it-seer'ren] vt. to classify; **-ung** nf. classification.

Klassik [klass'ik] nf. classical period, classicism; **-er** nm. classic.

Klassisch [klass'ish] a. classical.

Klatsch [klatch] nm. (-e) smack, crack, gossip; **-base** nf. gossip, scandalmonger; **-en** vi. to clash, gossip, talk scandal; **-erei** nf. gossip; **-haft** a. gossiping.

Klauben [klow'ben] vt. to pick.

Klaue [klow'er] nf. claw; **-n** vt. to claw, clutch, pinch.

Klaus'e [klow'zer] nf. cell, hermitage; **-ner** nm. hermit, recluse.

Klausel [klow'zel] nf. clause.

Klaviatur [kla-vi-a-tōōrr'] nf. keyboard.

Klavier [kla-veerr'] n. (-e) piano; **-spieler** nm. pianist.

Kleb'en [klay'ben] vt. to paste, gum, stick; i. stick; **-erig** a. sticky; **-stoff** nm. paste, glue.

Kleckern [klek'errn] vi. to slobber.

Klecks [kleks] nm. (-e) blot, stain; **-en** vt.i. to blot, scrawl, smudge.

Klee [klay] nm. clover, trefoil; **-blatt** n. clover-leaf, trio.

Kleid [klite] n. (-er) garment, dress; pl. clothes; **-en** vt.r. to clothe, dress; i. fit, suit; **-erablage** nf. cloak-room; **-erbügel** nm. coat-hanger; **-erbürste** nf. clothes brush; **-erhändel** nm. second-hand clothing business; **-erpuppe** nf. dummy; **-errock** nm. skirt; **-erschrank** nm. wardrobe; **-erständer** nm. hall stand; **-erstoff** nm. dress material.

Kleidsam [klite'zam] a. becoming; **-keit** nf. fitness.

Kleidung [klite'dõõng] nf. clothing, **-sstück** n. garment.

Kleie [klie'er] nf. bran.

Klein [kline] a. small, little, minor; **-bahn** nf. light railway; **-flugboot** n. amphibious flying boat; **-geld** n. small change; **-gläubig** a. of little faith; **-handel** nm. retail trade; **-händler** nm. retailer; **-holz** n. firewood; **-kinderschule** nf. infant school; **-kraftrad** nm. auto-cycle; **-krieg** nm. guerilla warfare; **-kunstbühne** nf. cabaret; **-laut** a. dejected, quiet; **-mut** nm. despondency; **-mütig** a. faint-hearted; **-städtisch** a. provincial; **-stunterseeboot** n. midget submarine.

Kleinheit [kline'hite] nf. smallness.

Kleinigkeit [kline'ish-kite] nf. trifle, detail.

Kleinlich [kline'lish] a. petty, paltry; **-keit** nf. pettiness, paltriness.

Kleinod [kline'ote] n. (gen. **-s**) pl. **Kleinodien**) gem, treasure, jewel.

Kleister [kli'sterr] nm. paste; **-n** vt. to paste.

Klemme [klem'er] nf. clip, clamp, difficulty, terminal (el.); **-n** to pinch, nip, squeeze; **-r** nm. eye-glasses.

Klempner [klemp'nerr] nm. tinsmith, plumber, metal worker; **-n** vi. to do plumbing.

Kleriker [klair'ri-kerr] nm. (**-**) cleric.

Klerus [klair'ooss] nm. clergy.

Klette [klet'er] nf. bur; **-n** vr. to hang on to; **-nbombe** **-nmine** nf. limpet mine, adhesive mine.

Kletterer [klet'er-rerr] nm. (**-**) climber; **-n** vi. to climb; **-eisen** n. climbing iron, crampon; **-pflanze** nf. creeper.

Klima [klee'mah] n. (gen. **-s** pl. **Klimate**) climate; **-anlage** nf. air-conditioning plant; **-tisch** a. climatic.

Klimmen [klim'en] vi. ir. to climb.

Klimpern [klim'perrn] vi. to tinkle, strum.

Klinge [kling'er] nf. blade, sword.

Klingel [kling'el] nf. handbell; **-beutel** nm. collection bag; **-n** vi. to ring; **-zug** nm. bell-pull.

Klingen [kling'en] vi. ir. to sound, clink.

Klinik [klee'nik] n f. nursing home; **-sch** a. clinical.

Klinke [klink'er] nf. latch, handle, jack (tec.); **-n** vi. to press the latch.

Klinker [klink'err] nm. (**-**) clinker.

Klippe [klip'er] nf. reef, cliff; **-ig** a. rocky. [jangle.

Klirren [klir'ren] vi. to clank,

Klischee [klee-shay'] nf. stereotype plate, block.

Klistier [klist-eerr'] n. (**-e**) enema. [sewer.

Kloake [kloh-ah'ker] nf.

Kloben [klobe'en] nm. (**-**) block, pulley.

Klobig [kloh'bish] a. clumsy, unwieldy, hulking.

Klopfen [klop'fen] vt.i. to knock, beat, tap; **-er** nm. beater.

Klöppel [kler'pel] nm. bobbin, clapper; **-n** vi. to make lace.

Klosett [klo-zet'] n. (**-s**) lavatory, toilet; **-papier** n. toilet-paper.

Kloss [klohss] nm. (Klösse) clod, lump, dumpling.

Kloster [kloh'sterr] nm. (Klöster) monastery, convent; **-bruder** nm. monk; **-frau**, **-schwester** nf. nun.

Klösterlich [kler'sterr-lish] a. monastic, conventual.

Klotz [klots] nm. (Klötze) log, block; **-bremse** nf. blockbrake.

Klub [kloop] nm. (**-s**) club; **-sessel** nm. easy chair.

Kluft [klooft] nf. (Klüfte) cleft, chasm, gap, abyss, gorge.

Klug [klook] a. clever, wise, intelligent, prudent; **-heit** nf. cleverness, sagacity, shrewdness.

Klügelei [klyoo-ger-lie'] nf. hair-splitting; **-n** vi. to split hairs, brood.

Klüglich [klyook'lish] a. prudently, sensibly.

Klumpen [kloom'pen] nm. (**-**) clod, mass, heap, nugget; **-füssig** a. club-footed.

Klümpchen [klyoomp'shen] n. (**-**) clot, blob.

Klunker [kloonk'err] nm. (**-**) tassel, clot, clod.

Kluppe [klŏŏp'er] *nf.* pincers, clamp.

Klüse [klyŏŏ'zer] *nf.* hawse.

Klüver [klyŏŏ'verr] *n.* (-) jib.

Knabbern [k-nab'err] *vt.* to nibble.

Knabe [k-nah'ber] *m.w.* boy; -nhaft *a.* boyish.

Knack [k-nak] *nm.* (-e) crack, snap, crash; -en *vi.* to crack.

Knackern [k-nak'errn] *vi.* to crackle.

Knall [k-nal] *nm.* (-e) report, detonation, cap; -bonbon *nm.* cracker; -büchse *nf.* pop-gun; -geber *nm.* depth-sounding gong (*nav.*); -rot *a.* bright red.

Knallen [k-nal'en] *vi.* to crack, snap, bang, explode, detonate.

Knapp [k-nap] *a.* tight, scarce, concise, mean; -heit *nf.* tightness, scarcity, conciseness.

Knappe [k-nap'er] *m.w.* young miner; -schaft *nf.* mining community.

Knarre [k-nar'er] *nf.* creak; -n *vi.* to rattle, crack.

Knast [k-nast] *nm.* (-e) knot, stump; -er *nm.* old fellow; -ern *vi.* to crackle.

Knaster [k-nast'err] *nm.* (-) cheap tobacco.

Knattern [k-nat'errn] *vi.* to crackle, rattle.

Knäuel [k-noy'el] *nm.* (-) coil, crowd, knot, skein.

Knauf [k-nowf] *nm.* (Knäufe) knob, pommel (*sword*).

Knauser [k-now'zerr] *nm.* (-) miser; -ei *nf.* meanness; -ig *a.* niggardly; -n *vi.* to be mean.

Knebel [k-nay'bel] *nm.* (-) stick, gag; -bart *nm.* waxed moustache; -n *vt.* to gag, fasten; -ung *nf.* gagging, suppression.

Knecht [k-nesht] *nm.* (-e) servant, farm labourer, menial, jack; -en *vt.* to enslave; -isch *a.* servile; -schaft *nf.* servitude.

Kneten [k-nate'en] *vt.* to knead.

Knick [k-nik] *nm.* (-e) crack, break, bend; -en *vt.* to crack, break, snap.

Knicker [k-nik'err] *nm.* miser; -n *vi.* to be miserly.

Knicks [k-nix] *nm.* (-e) curtsey.

Knie [k-nee] *n.* (-e) knee; -fällig *a.* on one's knees; -hosen *f.pl.* breeches, plus-fours; -scheibe *nf.* knee-cap.

Knieen [k-nee'en] *vi.* to kneel.

Kniff [k-nif] *nm.* (-e) pinch, trick, dodge, fold; -en *vt.* to crease, fold.

Knipsen [k-nip'sen] *vt.* to click, to clip, punch (*ticket*), snap (*photo*). [brat.

Knirps [k-nirr'ps] *nm.* (-e)

Knirschen [k-nirr'shen] *vt.* to gnash.

Knistern [k-nist'errn] *vi.* to crackle.

Knittern [k-nit'errn] *vt.* to crumple. [garlic.

Knoblauch [k-nop'lowch] *nm.*

Knöchel [k-ner'shel] *nm.* knuckle, ankle.

Knochen [k-noch'en] *nm.* (-) bone; -ig *a.* bony. [bone.

Knöchern [k-ner'shern] *a.* of

Knödel [k-ner'del] *nm.* (-) dumpling.

Knolle [k-nol'er] *nf.* bulb; -en *nm.* lump, bulb; -ig *a.* knobby.

Knopf [k-nopf] *nm.* (Knöpfe) button, stud; -loch *n.* buttonhole.

Knöpfchen [k-nerp'shen] *n.* (-) small button, stud.

Knöpfen [k-nerp'fen] *vt.* to button.

Knorpel [k-norr'pel] *nm.* (-) cartilage, gristle; -ig *a.* gristly.

Knorren [k-norr'en] *nm.* (-) stump; -ig *a.* gnarled, knotted.

Knospe [k-nos'per] *nf.* bud; -n *vi.* to bud.

Knoten [k-note'en] *nm.* knot, node; *vt.* to knot; -punkt *nm.* junction.

Knuff [k-nŏŏf'] *nm.* (Knüffe) blow, cuff; -en *vt.* to cuff.

Knüpfen [k-nyöÿ'fen] vt. to join, tie.

Knüppel [k-nyöÿ'pel] nm. (-) cudgel, log; **-damm** nm. corduroy road.

Knurren [k-nöör'ren] vi. to snarl, growl.

Knusper'n [k-nöös'perrn] vt. to crunch; **-ig** a. crisp.

Knüttel [k-nit'el] nm. (-) cudgel; **-verse** m.pl. doggerel.

Koalition [ko-a-lit-syohn'] nf. coalition.

Kobalt [koh'balt] nm. cobalt.

Koben [koh'ben] nm. (-) pig-sty.
                                    [basket.
Kober [koh'berr] nm.-

Kobold [koh'bolt] nm. (-) goblin.

Koch [koch] nm. (**Köche**) cook; **-er** nm. cooker; **-geschirr** n. cooking apparatus, mess-tin (mil.); **-salz** n. common salt.

Kochen [koch'en] vt. to cook, boil.
                                    [quiver.
Köcher [ker'sherr] nm. (-)

Köchin [ker'shin] nf. cook.

Köder [ker'derr] nm. (-) bait, lure; **-n** vt. to bait, lure, entice.

Kodifizieren [koh-di-fit-seer'ren] vt. to codify.

Kodizill [koh-dit-sil'] n. (-e) codicil.

Koffer [kof'err] nm. (-) trunk, suit-case; **-grammophon** n. portable gramophone.

Kohl [kole] nm. (-e) cabbage; **-rübe** nf. swede.

Kohle [kole'er] nf. coal, charcoal, carbon; **-narbeiter** nm. collier; **-nbergbau** nm. coal mining; **-ngrube** nf. coal pit, mine; **-nrevier** n. coalfield; **-nstoff** nm. carbon; **-npapier** n. carbon paper.
                                    [coal.
Kohlen [kole'en] vi. to char.

Köhler [ker'lerr] nm. (-) charcoal burner.

Koje [koh'yer] nf. cabin, bunk.

Kokain [ko-ka-een'] n. cocaine.

Kokarde [ko-karr'der] nf. cocade.

Kokett [ko-ket'] a. coquettish, flirtatious; **-ieren** vi. to flirt.

Kokon [ko-kong'] nm. (-s) cocoon.
                                    [nf. coconut.
Kokosnuss [koh'kos-nöôss]

Koks [kohx] nm. (-e) coke.

Kolben [kol'ben] nm. (-) rifle-but, club, flask, piston (tec.); **-maschine** nf. reciprocating engine; **-stange** nf. piston-rod.

Kolik [koh-leek'] nf. colic, gripe.

Kolleg [ko-lake'] n. (**Kollegien**) lecture course; **-e** m.w. colleague; **-ium** n. board, staff.

Kollekt'e [kol-ek'ter] nf. collection; **-iv** a. collective.

Koller [kol'err] nm. (-) jerkin, staggers, frenzy; **-n** vi. to rave, rumble, gobble.

Kolli'dieren [ko-li-deer'ren] vi. to collide, clash; **-sion** nf. clash, collision.

Kolonial [ko-loh-nyahl'] a. colonial; **-waren** f.pl. groceries.

Koloni'e [ko-lo-nee'] nf. colony; **-sieren** vt. to colonize **-st** m.w. colonist.

Kolonne [ko-lon'er] nf. column.

Kolor'ieren [ko-lo-reer'ren] vt. to colour; **-it** n. colouring, tint, shade.

Koloss [ko-loss'] nm. (-e) colossus; **-al** a, ad. colossal, extreme(ly), immense(ly).

Kolumne [kol-öôm'ner] nf. column.

Kombin'ation [kom-bin-at-syohn'] nf. combination, conjecture, cami-knickers, flying kit (av.); **-ieren** vt. to combine.

Kombüse [kom-byöô'zer] nf. galley.

Komet [ko-mate'] m.w. comet.

Komfort [kom-forrt'] nm. luxury, ease.

Komi'k [ko'mik] nf. humour, comedy; **-ker** nm. comedian, comic actor, writer; **-sch** a. comical, strange, funny.

Komma [kom'ah] n. (-s) comma

Kommand'ant [kom-an-dant'] *m.w.* commander, officer commanding, -atur *nf.* area headquarters; -eur *nm.* officer commanding, -ieren *vt.i.* to command, detail; -ierte *pl.* detached personnel (*mil.*); -itgesellschaft *nf.* limited company.

Kommando [ko-man'do] *n.* (-s) command, order, detachment, squad, party; -brücke *nf.* bridge (*nav.*); -stand *nm.* conning tower (*nav.*); -stelle *nf.* headquarters.

Kommen [kom'en] *vi. ir.* to come, approach, happen; -lassen to send for.

Kommentar [kom-en-tarr'] *n.* (-e) commentary.

Kommersbuch [kom-airss'bōōch] *n.* students' song book.

Kommis [kom-ee'] *nm.* (-) clerk.

Kommis [kom-ece'] *a.* army, regulation; -brot *n.* army bread; -stiefel *m.pl.* army boots.

Kommissar [kom-i-sarr'] *nm.* (-e) commissioner, police inspector.

Kommission [ko-mi-syohn'] *nf.* commission, committee; -är *nm.* agent, commissioner.

Kommode [kom-oh'der] *nf.* (chest of) drawers.

Kommodore [ko-mo-dore'er] *m.w.* commodore.

Kommuni'on [kom-ōō-nyohn'] *nf.* communion; -zieren *vi.* to communicate.

Kommunis'mus [kom-ōō-nis'mōōss] *nm.* communism; -t *m.w.* communist; -tisch *a.* communistic.

Komödiant [kom-er-diant'] *m.w.* comedian.

Komödie [kom-er'dier] *nf.* comedy, farce.

Kompanie [kom-pan-ee'] *nf.* company, squadron (*tanks*); -führer *nm.* company com-

mander (*mil.*); -liste *nf.* company list, roster.

Kompagnon [kom-pan-yong'] *nm.* partner.

Komparativ [kom'par-ra-teef] *nm.* (-e) comparative.

Kompass [kom'pass] *nm.* (-e) compass; -häuschen *n.* binnacle; -peilung *nf.* compass bearing.

Kompetent [kom-pet-ent'] *a.* competent.

Komplett [kom-plet'] *a.* complete.

Kompliment [kom-pli-ment'] *n.* (-e) compliment.

Komplizieren [kom-plit-seer-ren] *vt.* to complicate. [plot.

Komplott [kom-plot'] *n.* (-e)

Kompo'nieren [kom-po-neer-ren] *vt.* to compose, set to music; -nist *m.w.* composer; -sition *nf.* composition.

Kompott [kom-pot'] *n.* (-e) preserves, stewed fruit.

Kompress'e [kom-press'er] *nf.* compress; -or *nm.* compressor.

Kompromiss [kom-pro-miss'] *nm.* (-e) compromise.

Kompromittieren [kom-promit-eer-ren] *vt.* to compromise.

Kondens'ation [kon-den-sat-syohn'] *nf.* condensation; -ator *nm.* condenser; -ieren *vt.* to condense.

Konditor [kon-dee'torr] *nm.* (*gen.* -s; *pl.* -en) confectioner; -ei *nf.* cafe, confectioner's shop.

Kondolenz [kon-do-lents'] *nf.* condolence, sympathy.

Konfekt [kon-fekt'] *n.* (-e) confectionery, sweets.

Konfektion [kon-fek-syohn'] *nf.* ready-made clothing; -är *nm.* clothier.

Konferenz [kon-fer-rents'] *nf.* conference, meeting; -ieren *vi.* to confer, assemble.

Konfession [kon-fess-yohn'] *nf.* creed, denomination; -ell *a.*

confessional; -slos a. undenominational.

Konfirm'and [kon-firr-mant'] m.w. candidate for confirmation; -ation nf. confirmation; -ieren vt. to confirm.

Konfiszieren [kon-fiss-tseer'ren] vt. to confiscate.

Konflikt [kon-flikt'] nm. (-e) conflict.

Konfus [kon-fōōss'] a. confused.

Konglomerat [kon-glo-merraht'] n. (-e) conglomerate.

Kongress [kong-gress'] nm. (-e) congress.

Kongruenz [kong-grōō-ents'] nf. agreement, congruence.

König [ker'nish] nm. (-e) king; -in nf. queen; -lich royal, kingly; -reich n. kingdom; -tum n. kingship.

Konisch [kone'ish] a. conical.

Konjektur [kon-yek-tōōr'] nf. conjecture.

Konjugation [kon-yōō-gat-syohn'] nf. conjugation; -ieren vt. to conjugate.

Konjunktiv [kon-yōōnk-teef'] nm. (-e) subjunctive.

Konjunktur [kon-yōōnk-tōōr'] nf. boom, turn of the market, juncture.   [cave

Konkav [kon-kahf'] a. concave.

Konklave [kon-klah'ver] nf. conclave.

Konkordat [kon-korr-daht'] n. (-e) concordat.

Konkret [kon-krait'] a. concrete.

Konkurr'ent [kon-kŏŏr-rent'] m.w. competitor; -enz nf. competition; -enfähig a. competitive; -ieren vi. to compete.

Konkurs [kon-koorss'] nm. insolvency; -verwalter nm. receiver in bankruptcy.

Können [ker'nen] vt. to know, be able to; i. to be able, allowed.

Konsequen't [kon-zek-vent'] a. consistent; -z nf. consistency, conclusion.

Konservati'v [kon-zairr-va-teef'] a. conservative; -smus nm. conservatism.

Konserv'e [kon-zairr'ver] nf. preserve, tinned food; -enbüchse nf. tin; -ieren vt. to preserve; -ierung nf. preservation.

Konsolidieren [kon-zo-li-deer'ren] vt. to consolidate.

Konsonant [kon-zoh-nant'] m.w. consonant.

Konsort'en [kon-zorr'ten] m.pl. accomplices; -ium n. syndicate.

Konstant [kon-stant'] a. constant.

Konstatieren [kon-sta-teer'ren] vt. to verify, confirm, state.

Konstitution [kon-stit-ōōt-syohn'] nf. constitution; -ell a. constitutional.

Konstruieren [kon-strōō-eer'ren] vt. to construct.

Konsul [kon'zŏŏl] nm. (-n) consul; -at n. consulate.

Konsultieren [kon-zŏŏl-teer'ren] vt. to consult.

Konsum [kon-zōōm'] nm. consumption; -ent m.w. consumer; -ieren vt. to consume; -verein nm. co-operative society.

Kontakt [kon-takt'] nm. (-e) contact; -los a. non-contact (mine); -schlüssel nm. ignition key (aut.); -schnur nf. flex.

Konteradmiral [kon'terr-ad-mir-rahl'] nm. (-e) rear-admiral.

Konterbande [kon'terr-ban-der] nf. contraband.

Kontinent [kon-ti-nent'] n. (-e) continent.

Kontingent [kon-ting-gent'] n. (-e) quota.

Kontinuität [kon-ti-nōō-i-tate'] nf. continuity.

Konto [kon'toh] n. (Konten) account; -auszug nm. statement of account; -buch n. account book, pass book (*bank*); -korrent *n.* current account.

Kontor [kon-torr'] *n.* (-e) office, counting-house; -ist *m.w.* clerk, office worker.

Kontrabass [kon'tra-bass] *nm.* (-bässe) double bass.

Kontrahent [kon-tra-hent'] *m.w.* contractor.

Kontrakt [kon-trakt'] *nm.* (-e) contract; -bruch *nm.* breach of contract.

Kontrast [kon-trast'] *nm.* (-e) contrast; -ieren *vi.* to contrast.

Kontroll'e [kon-trol'er] *nf.* control, supervision; -ieren *vt.* to control, supervise, check; -liste *nf.* checking list; -schein *nm.* counterfoil.

Konvention [kon-ven-tsyohn'] *nf.* convention; -ell *a.* conventional.

Konversation [kon-verr-zat-syohn'] *nf.* conversation; -slexikon *n.* encyclopedia.

Konzentration [kon-tsen-trat-syohn'] *nf.* concentration; -slager *n.* concentration camp.

Konzentrier'en [kon-tsen-treer'ren] *vt.r.* to concentrate; -ung *nf.* concentration.

Konzept [kon-tsept'] *n.* (-e) rough draft.

Konzern [kon-tsairrn'] *nm.* (-e) combine. [concert.

Konzert [kon-tsairrt'] *n.* (-e)

Konzession [kon-tsess-yohn'] *nf.* licence; -ieren *vt.* to license.

Konzipieren [kon-tsi-peer'ren] *vt.* to draft.

Köper [ker'perr] *nm.* (-) twill.

Kopf [kopf] *nm.* (Köpfe) head; -arbeit *nf.* brain work; -haube *nf.* helmet (*av.*); -haut *nf.* scalp; -hörer *nm.* head-phone; -kissen *n.* pillow; -leiste *nf.* heading; -salat *nm.* garden lettuce; -schmerz *nm.* headache; -schützer *nm.* balaclava helmet; -station *nf.* terminus; -tuch *n.* shawl, scarf; -über *ad.* head over heels; -weh *n.* head-

ache; -zerbrechen *n.* pondering, worry.

Köpfen [kerp'fen] *vt.* to behead, lop.

Kopie [ko-pee'] *nf.* copy; -ren *vt.* to copy.

Koppel [kop'el] *nf.* leash, brace, enclosure, belt; -balken *nm.* tie-beam; -n *vt.* to couple, leash; -navigation *nf.* navigation by dead reckoning (*av.*); -ung *nf.* coupling.

Koralle [ko-ral'er] *nf.* coral; -nriff *n.* coral reef.

Korb [korrp] *nm.* (Körbe) basket; -flasche *nf.* demijohn; -stuhl *nm.* basket-work chair, wicker chair. [string.

Kordel [korr'del] *nf.* cord,

Korinthe [ko-rin'ter] *nf.* currant.

Kork [korrk] *nm.* (-e) cork; -stopsel *nm.* cork; -zieher *nm.* corkscrew.

Korken [korr'ken] *vt.* to cork.

Korn [korrn] *n.* (Körner) corn, grain, sight (*gun*); -blume *nf.* cornflower; -boden *nm.*, -kammer *nf.* granary.

Körnchen [kern'shen] *n.* grain, granule.

Körnen [ker'nen] *vt.* to grain, granulate. [cornet.

Kornett [korr-net'] *n.* (-e)

Körper [ker'perr] *nm.* (-) body, bulk, substance; -bau *nm.* build; -beschaffenheit *nf.* physique; -grösse *nf.* stature; -kraft *nf.* physical strength; -lich *a.* physical, bodily; -mass *n.* cubic measure; -schaft *nf.* corporation; -strafe *nf.* corporal punishment; -übung *nf.* physical exercise.

Korporalschaft [korr-por-rahl'shaft] *nf.* squad.

Korps [korr] *n.* (-) corps, students' club.

Korrekt [ko-rekt'] *a.* correct; -heit *nf.* correctness; -or *nm.* proof-reader; -ur *nf.* proof, correction.

Korresponden't [kor-res-pon-dent'] *m.w.* -**tin** *nf.* correspondent; -**z** *nf.* correspondence.

Korrespondieren [kor-res-pon-deer'ren] *vi.* to correspond.

Korridor [kor'ri-dohr'] *nm.* (-e) corridor.

Korrigieren [kor-ri-geer'ren] *vt.* to correct.

Korrumpieren [kor-rŏŏm-peer'ren] *vt.* to corrupt.

Korsett [korr-zet'] *n.* (-e) corset.

Korvette [korr-vet'er] *nf.* corvette, escort vessel; -**nkapitän** *nm.* lieutenant-commander.

Kose'n [koh'zen] *vt.* to caress; *i.* to make love; -**name** *nm.* pet name; -**wort** *nf.* term of endearment. [cosmic.]

Kosmisch [koss'mish] *a.*

Kost [kost] *nf.* food, board; -**gänger** *nm.* boarder; -**geld** *n.* board.

Kostbar [kost'barr] *a.* costly, expensive; -**keit** *nf.* valuable, preciousness.

Kosten [kost'en] *pl.* costs; *vt.* to cost; -**anschlag** *nm.* estimate; -**los** *a.* free of charge; -**preis** *nm.* cost price; -**rechnung** *nf.* costs account.

Kosten [kost'en] *vt.* to taste.

Köstlich [kerst'lish] *a.* precious, delicious, delightful.

Kostspielig [kost'shpeel-ish] *a.* expensive.

Kostum [kos-tyōōm'] *n.* (-e) costume, dress; -**ieren** *vt.* to dress.

Kot [kote] *nm.* mud, filth, dung; -**blech** *n.* flügel *nm.* mudguard, wing (*aut*); -**ig** *a.* muddy; -**schützer** *nm.* mudguard (*cycle*).

Kotelett [ko-ter-let'] *n.* (-e) cutlet, chop.

Köter [ker'terr] *nm.* (-) cur.

Krabbe [krab'er] *nf.* crab; -**ln** *vi.* to crawl, sprawl.

Krach [krach] *nm.* (-e) crash, noise, quarrel, row; -**en** *vi.* to crack, crash.

Krächzen [kresh'tsen] *vi.* to croak.

Kraft [kraft] *nf.* (Kräfte) strength, power, force, worker; *pr.* by virtue of; -**anlage** *nf.* power station; -**brücke** *nf.* fuelling bridge; -**fahrer** *nm.* motor driver; -**fahrtruppen** *f.pl.* mechanised troops, motor transport personnel; -**fahrzeug** *n.* motor vehicle; -**probe** *nf.* trial of strength; -**rad** *n.* motor cycle; -**voll** *a.* vigorous; -**wagen** *nm.* motor vehicle, car; -**werk** *n.* power station, generating station.

Kräftig [kref'tish] *a.* strong, forcible; -**en** *vt.* to strengthen; -**ung** *nf.* strengthening.

Kraftlos [kraft'lohss] *a.* impotent, feeble, invalid; -**erklärung** *nf.* annulment.

Kragen [krah'gen] *nm.* (-) collar; -**binde** *nf.* tie; -**spiegel** *nm.* collar patch, tab.

Krähe [kray'er] *nf.* crow; *vi.* to crow.

Krakeel [kra-kale'] *nm.* quarrel, brawl.

Kralle [kral'er] *nf.* claw, talon; -**n** *vt.i.* to claw, clutch.

Kram [krahm] *nm.* (Kräme) trade, smallware, stuff, rubbish; -**en** *vi.* to rummage; -**laden** *nm.* small shop.

Krämer [kray'merr] *nm.* (-) tradesman, shopkeeper.

Krampe [kramp'er] *nf.* cramp, staple.

Krampf [krampf] *nm.* (Krämpfe) cramp, spasm, fit; -**ader** *nf.* varicose vein; -**en** *vt.* to clench; -**haft** *a.* spasmodic, convulsive.

Kran [krahn] *nm.* (Kräne) crane; -**balken** *nm.* jib, cathead.

Kranich [krah'nish] *nm.* (-e) crane (*bird*).

Krank [krank] *a.* ill, sick;

-enauto *n*, -enkraftwagen *nm*. motor ambulance; -enhaus *n*. hospital; -enliste *nf*. sick-list; -enpfleger *nm*. nursing orderly; -enstuhl *nm*. invalid chair; -enträger *nf*. stretcher; entrager *nm*. stretcher-bearer; enversicherung *nf*. health insurance; -enwagen *nm*. ambulance; -enwärter *nm*. orderly *hospital*).

Kranken [krank'en] *vi*. to be ill.

Kranke'nkasse [krank'en-kass-er] *nf*. health insurance, sick-fund; -narzt *nm*. panel doctor.

Kranke(r) [krank'err] *m.w,* Kranke *f*. invalid, patient.

Krankhaft [krank'haft] *a*. diseased, morbid; -igkeit *nf*. diseased state.

Krankheit [krank'hite] *nf*. illness, disease.

Kränklich [krenk'lish] *a*. sickly.

Kranz [krants] *nm*. (**Kränze**) wreath, garland.

Kränzchen [krents'shen] *n*. (-) small wreath, ladies' party.

Kränzen [krent'sen] *vt*. to crown. [fritter.

Krapfen [krap'fen] *nm*. (-)

Krapp [krap] *nm*. madder.

Krass [kras] *a*. gross, crass.

Krater [krah'terr] *nm*. (-) crater.

Kratz'bürste [krats'byôôrster] *nf*. scrubbing brush; -eisen *n*. scraper.

Krätze [kret'ser] *nf*. itch, scab.

Kratz'en [krat'tser] *vt*. to scratch; -er *nm*. scraper.

Kraus [krowss] *a*. crisp, curly; -e *n*. frill, ruffle; -kopf *nm*. curly head.

Kräuseln [kroy'zeln] *vt*. to curl, frill, ruffle.

Kraut [krowt] *n*. (**Kräuter**) herb, plant. [row, uproar.

Krawall [kra-val'] *nm*. (-e)

Krawatte [kra-vat'er] *nf*. tie.

Kreatur [kray-a-tôôr'] *nf*. creature.

Krebs [krayps] *nm*. (-e) crab, crayfish, cancer.

Kredenz [kray-dents'] *nf*. sideboard.

Kredit [kre-deet'] *nm*. (-e) credit; -brief *nm*. letter of credit; -fähig *a*. solvent; -ieren *vt*. to credit.

Kreid'e [kry'der] *nf*. chalk; -ig *a*. chalky.

Kreis [krice] *nm*. (-e) circle, sphere, district; -ausschnitt *nm*. sector; -förmig *a*. circular; -lauf *nm*. revolution, round, circulation, circuit (*el.*); -messer *nm*. cyclometer; -stadt *nf*. county town; -tag *nm*. county council.

Kreischen [krie'shen] *vi*. to shriek, screech.

Kreisel [krize'el] *nm*. (-) top; -kompass *nm*. gyro compass; -pumpe *nf*. centrifugal pump.

Kreisen [krize'en] *vi*. to circulate, revolve.

Krem [krame] *nf*. cream.

Kremat'ion [krem-at-syohn'] *nf*. cremation; -orium *n*. crematorium.

Krempe [krem'per] *nf*. brim; -l *nm*. rubbish.

Kreosot [kray-o-zoht'] *n*. creosote.

Krepieren [krep-eer'ren] *vi*. to die, burst (*shell*).

Krepp [krep] *nm*. (-s) crape; -sohle *nf*. crêpe-sole.

Kresse [kress'er] *nf*. cress.

Kreuz [kroits] *nm*. (-e) cross, small of the back, clubs (*card*); -band *n*. wrapper; -en *vt.r.* to cross; -i. cruise (*nav.*); -fahrer *nm*. crusader; -fahrt *nf*. crusade, cruise; -gang *nm*. cloisters; -igen *vt*. to crucify; -igung *nf*. crucifixion; -ung *nf*. crossing, junction, cross (*breed*); -weg *nm*. cross-roads; -worträtsel *n*. crossword puzzle; -zug *nm*. crusade.

Kreuzer [kroy'tserr] *nm.* (-) cruiser; **-krieg** *nm.* ocean raiding; **-verband** *n.* cruiser squadron.

Kribbel'n [krib'eln] *vi.* to crawl, swarm, itch, irritate; **-ig** *a.* irritable.

Kriech'en [kree'shen] *vi. ir.* to creep, cringe, fawn; **-er** *nm.* obsequious person; **-stossschwimmen** *n.* crawl-stroke; **-tier** *n.* reptile.

Krieg [kreek] *nm.* (-e) war; **-en** *vt.* to get; *i.* to wage war; **-er** *nm.* warrior; **-erisch** *a.* warlike; **-führung** *nf.* conduct of war; **-sbeorderung** *nf.* call-up; **-sberichter(statter)** *nm.* war correspondent; **-sbeschädigt** *a.* disabled; **-sbrauchbar** *a.* fit for active service; **-sdienst** *nm.* active service; **-sdienstverweigerer** *nm.* conscientious objector; **-seinsatz** *nm.* war effort; **-sfuss** *nm.* war-footing; **-sgefangene(r)** *m.w.* prisoner of war; **-sgegner** *nm.* pacifist; **-sgegnerschaft** *nf.* pacifism; **-sgericht** *n.* court-martial; **-sgewinner** *nm.* war profiteer; **-sgliederung** *nf.* battle-order; **-shetzer** *nm.* warmonger; **-skur** *nf.* sanatorium treatment (*mil.*); **-slazarett** *n.* base hospital; **-sneurose** *nf.* shell shock; **-srecht** *n.* martial law; **-sschiff** *n.* warship; **-sschuld** *nf.* war guilt; **-sspiel** *n.* tactical exercise; **-switschaft** *nf.* war economy; **-sziel** *n.* war aim.

Kriminal [kri-mi-nahl'] *a.* criminal; **-beamte** *m.w.* **-polizist** *m.w.* detective; **-roman** *nm.* detective story.

Kriminell [kri-mi-nell'] *a.* criminal.

Krippe [krip'er] *nf.* manger, crib, crèche.

Krise [kree'zer] *nf.* crisis.

Kristall [kris-tal'] *nm.* (-e) crystal.

Kriti'k [kri-teek'] *nf.* criticism;

-ker *nm.* critic; **-klos** *a.* uncritical; **-sch** *a.* critical; **-sieren** *vt.* to criticize.

Kritteln [krit'eln] *vi.* to find fault, carp.

Kritzeln [krits'eln] *vt.i.* to scribble, scrawl.

Krokodil [kro-ko-deel'] *n.* (-e) crocodile.

Krokus [kroh'kooss] *nm.* (-se) crocus.

Kron'e [kroh'ner] *nf.* crown, top; **-leuchter** *nm.* chandelier; **-prinz** *m.w.* crown prince.

Krön'en [krer'nen] *vt.* to crown; **-ung** *nf.* coronation.

Kropf [kropf] *nm.* (Kröpfe) goitre, crop.

Kröte [krer'ter] *nf.* toad.

Krücke [kryoo'ker] *nf.* crutch, crook.

Krug [krook] *nm.* (Krüge) jug, mug, tavern.

Kruke [kroo'ker] *nf.* stone jar.

Krume [kroo'mer] *nf.* crumb.

Krümeln [kryoo'meln] *vi.* to crumble.

Krumm [kroom] *a.* crooked, curved; **-beinig** *a.* bandy-legged; **-nasig** *a.* hook-nosed.

Krümm'en [kryoo'men] *vt.r.* to curve, crook, bend, wind; **-ung** *nf.* bend, curve, winding.

Kruppe [kroop'er] *nf.* crupper.

Krüppel [kryoo'pel] *nm.* (-) cripple; **-haft, -ig** *a.* crippled.

Kruste [kroos'ter] *nf.* crust, scurf.

Kruzifix [kroo-tsi-fix'] *n.* (-e) crucifix. [pail.

Kübel [kyoo'bel] *nm.* (-) tub,

Kubikmass [koo-beek'mahss] *n.* cubic measure.

Küche [kyoo'sher] *nf.* kitchen, cooking; **-nherd** *nm.* range.

Kuchen [koo'chen] *nm.* (-) cake; **-bäcker** *nm.* pastry-cook.

Küchlein [kyoosh'line] *n.* (-) chicken. [cuckoo.

Kuckuck [koo'kook] *nm.* (-e)

Kufe [koo'fer] *nf.* vat, runner (*sledge*), skid (*wheel*).

Küfer [kyoo'ferr] *nm.* (-) cooper.

Kugel [koo-gel] *nf.* ball, bullet, globe; **-fest, -sicher** *a.* bullet-proof; **-lager** *n.* ball-bearings; **-n** *vt.* to roll, bowl.

Kuh [koo] *nf.* (**Kühe**) cow; **-blume** *nf.* marsh marigold; **-stall** *nm.* cowshed.

Kühl [kyool] *a.* cool; **-anlage** *nf.* refrigerator, refrigerating plant; **-e** *nf.* coolness; **-en** *vt.i.* to cool, anneal (*tec.*); **-er** *nm.* radiator (*aut.*); **-erhaube** *nf.* bonnet (*aut.*); **-mantel** *nm.* air-jacket; **-raum** *nm.* cold-storage chamber; **-ung** *nf.* cooling; **-wagen** *nm.* refrigerator lorry.

Kühn [kyoon] *a.* bold, daring; **-heit** *nf.* boldness.

Küken [kyoo'ken] *n.* (-) chicken.

Kuli [koo'lee] *nm.* (-s) coolie.

Kulisse [koo-liss'er] *nf.* scene, wing (*theatre*).   [cult.

Kult [koolt] *nm.* (-e) worship;

Kultivieren [kool-ti-veer'ren] *vt.* to cultivate.

Kultur [kool-toorr'] *nf.* culture, civilization; **-ell** *a.* cultural; **-film** *nm.* documentary film.

Kümmel [kü'mel] *nm.* (-) caraway seed.

Kummer [koo'merr] *nm.* grief, sorrow, trouble; **-voll** *a.* sorrowful.

Kümmer'lich [kyoo'merr-lish] *a.* poor, miserable, paltry; *ad.* barely; **-n** *vt.r.* to grieve, worry, mind.

Kum(me)t [koo'met] *n.* (-e) horse-collar.

Kumpan [koom-pahn'] *nm.* (-e) companion.

Kund [koont] *a.* known; **-geben, -machen** *vt.* to make known, inform; **-gebung** *nf.* demonstration; **-machung** *nf.* notification; **-schaft** *nf.* customers (*com.*).

Künd'bar [kyoont'barr] *a.*

redeemable, recallable; **-en** *vt.* to announce.

Kunde [koon'der] *m.w.* **Kündin** [kyoon'din] *nf.* customer.

Kündig'en [kyoon'di-gen] *vt.* to give notice; **-ung** *nf.* notice.

Kundig [koon'dish] *a.* expert, experienced.

Künftig [kyoonf'tish] *a.* future; *ad.* in future.

Kunst [koonst] *nf.* (**Künste**) art, skill; **-benzin** *n.* synthetic petrol; **-butter** *nf.* margarine; **-dünger** *nm.* artificial manure; **-flug** *nm.* stunt (*av.*); **-gewerbe** *n.* arts and crafts; **-glaser** *nm.* art glazier; **-griff** *nm.* trick, dexterity; **-händler** *nm.* art dealer; **-harz** *n.* plastics; **-mittel** *n.* artistic device; **-reich** *a.* artistic, skilful; **-sammler** *nm.* art collector; **-seide** *nf.* artificial silk; **-sinn** *nm.* artistic taste; **-stück** *n.* trick, stunt; **-tischler** *nm.* cabinet maker; **-voll** *a.* ingenious, artistic; **-werk** *n.* work of art.

Künst'elei [kyoon-ster-lie'] *nf.* artificiality, affectation; **-eln** *vi.* to elaborate; **-ler** *nm.* artist; **-lerisch** *a.* artistic; **-lich** *a.* artificial.

Kunterbunt [koon'terr-boont] *a.* topsy-turvy, higgledy-piggledy.

Küpe [kyoo'per] *nf.* vat.

Kupfer [koop'ferr] *n.* copper; **-geld** *n.* coppers; **-n** *a.* copper; **-schmied** *nm.* copper-smith; **-stich** *nm.* copperplate-engraving.

Kuppe [koo'per] *nf.* top (*hill*), head (*nail*).   [dome.

Kuppel [koopl] *nf.* cupola,

Kuppel'n [koo'peln] *vt.* to join, couple; *i.* procure; **-ung** *nf.* joint, coupling, clutch (*aut.*).

Kuppler [koop'lerr] *nm.* (-) match-maker, pimp.

Kur [koorr] *nf.* cure, treatment; **-haus** *n.* **-heim** *n.*

sanatorium, spa hotel, spa room; **-ort** nm. health resort; **-pfuscher** nm. quack.

Kurat'el [kŏŏ-ra-tel'] nf. guardianship; **-or** nm. guardian, trustee.

Kurbel [kŏŏr'bel] nf. crank, winch, starting handle (aut.); **-gehäuse** n. crank-case; **-kasten** nm. film camera; **-welle** nf. crank-shaft.

Kürbis [kŭr'bis] nm. (-se) pumpkin, gourd.

Kurfürst [kŏŏr'fyŏŏrst] m.w. elector.

Kurier [kŏŏr-reer'] nm. courier, dispatch rider; **-dienst** nm. courier service; **-offizier** nm. communications officer.

Kurieren [kŏŏr-reer'ren] vt. to cure.

Kurios [kŏŏr-yohss'] a. singular, odd; **-ität** nf. curiosity.

Kurs [kŏŏrrs] nm. (-e) course, rate, exchange, currency, track (radar); **-buch** nm. time-table; **-koppler** nm. automatic navigator (av.); **-makler** nm. stockbroker; **-steuerung** nf. automatic piloting, navigation (av.); **-zettel** nm. stockexchange list.

Kürschner [kŭrrsh'nerr] nm. (-) furrier.

Kursieren [kŏŏr-seer'ren] vi. to circulate.

Kursiv [kŏŏrr-seef'] nf. italics.

Kursus [kŏŏrr'zŏŏss] nm. (Kurse) course.

Kurve [kŏŏr'ver] nf. curve, bend; **-nbild** n. graph.

Kurz [kŏŏrrts] a. short; **-erhand** ad. briefly; **-gefasst** a. concise; **-lebig** a. short-lived; **-schrift** nf. shorthand; **-sichtig** a. short-sighted; **-um** ad. in short; **-weil** nf. pastime; **-weilig** a. amusing.

Kurzwelle [kŏŏrrts'vel·er] nf. short wave (rad.); **-nempfänger** nm. short-wave receiver;

-nsender nm. short-wave transmitter.

Kürz'e [kyŏŏrrt'ser] nf. shortness, brevity; **-en** vt. to cut short, reduce; **-lich** ad. lately.

Kuschen [kŏŏ'shen] vi. to lie down, crouch.

Kusine [kŏŏ-zee'ner] nf. cousin.

Kuss [kŏŏss] nm. (Küsse) kiss.

Küssen [kyŏŏ'sen] vt. to kiss.

Küste [kyŏŏ'ster] nf. coast, shore; **-nfahrer** nm., **-nfahrzeug** n. coaster; **-nsicherung** nf. coastal defence; **-nstrich** nm. coast-line; **-nvorfeld** n. coastal approaches; **-nwache** nf. coastguard station; **-nwacht** nf. coastal patrol; **-nwehr** nf. coastal defence.

Küster [kyŏŏ'sterr] nm. (-) sexton, verger.

Kutsche [kŏŏt'sher] nf. coach, carriage; **-r** nm. coachman.

Kutte [kŏŏ'ter] nf. cowl.

Kutter [kŏŏ'terr] nm. (-) cutter.

Kuvert [kŏŏ-vairr'] n. (-s) envelope, cover.

Kux [kŏŏx] nm. (-e) share in a mine (com.).

L

Lab [lahp] n. rennet.

Labbern [lab'errn] vt.i. to lap.

Lab·en [lah'ben] vt. to comfort, refresh; **-sal** n. (-e) comfort, solace; **-ung** nf. refreshment, comfort.

Laboratorium [la-bo-ra-tor'ryŏŏm] n. (Laboratorien) laboratory.

Lache [lach'er] nf. pool, puddle.

Lach'e [lach'er] nf. laughter; **-en** vi. to laugh; **-gas** n. laughing gas; **-haft** a. laughable; **-taube** nf. ring-dove.

Läch'eln [lesh'eln] vi. to smile; n. smile; **-erlich** a. ridiculous,

laughable; **-erlichkeit** nf. absurdity.

Lachs [lax] nm. (-e) salmon; **-farben** a. salmon-pink; **-schinken** nm. smoked ham.

Lack [lak] nm. (-e) lacquer, varnish; **-ieren** vt. to lacquer, varnish; **-leder** n. patent leather.

Lackmus [lak'mŏŏs] nm. [litmus.

Lade [lah'der] nf. box, chest.

Lade-baum nm. boom, derrick; **-fähigkeit** nf. capacity, tonnage; **-linie** nf. load-line; **-maschine** nf. battery charger (el.); **-raum** nm. hold (ship); **-schein** nm. bill of lading; **-stelle** nf. loading point, charging station (el.).

Laden [lah'den] vt. ir. to load.

Laden [lah'den] vt. ir. to invite, summon.

Laden [lah'den] nm. (Läden) shop, shutter; **-besitzer** nm. shopkeeper; **-hüter** nm. white elephant, unsaleable goods; **-mädchen** n. shop assistant; **-preis** nm. retail price; **-schluss** nm. closing time; **-tisch** nm. counter.

Ladung [lah'dŏŏng] nf. cargo, loading, load; **-sverzeichnis** n. ship's manifest; **-swerfer** nm. spigot mortar (mil.).

Ladung [lah'dŏŏng] nf. invitation, summons, (explosive) charge.

Lafette [laf-et'er] nf. gun-carriage, gun-mounting.

Laffe [laf'er] m.w. fop.

Lage [lah'ger] nf. position, situation, site, state, layer; **-bericht** nm. situation report (mil.); **-karte** nf. situation map (mil.); **-plan** nm. plan of a site; **-weise** ad. in layers.

Lager [lah'ger] n. (-) camp, warehouse, bed, lair, bearing (tec.); **-arbeiter** nm. storehand; **-bestand** nm. stocks in store; **-geld** n. storage (charges); **-haus** n. warehouse,

store; **-hütte** nf. barrack; **-metall** n. antifriction metal; **-schuppen** nm. store-shed; **-stätte** nf. resting place, bed; **-verwalter** nm. store-keeper; **-wart** nm. store-man.

Lager'n [lah'gerrn] vi. to be stored, camp, lie down; t. store, lay down; **-ung** nf. storage, storing, camping.

Lagune [la-gōō'ner] nf. lagoon.

Lahm [lahm] a. lame, paralysed; **-en** vi. to be lame, limp; **-legen** vt. to paralyse.

Lähm'en [lame'en] vt. to lame, paralyse; **-ung** nf. lameness, paralysis.

Laib [lïpe] nm. (-e) loaf.

Laich [lïsh] nm. (-e) spawn; **-en** vi. to spawn.

Laie [ly'er] m.w. layman; **-nhaft** a. amateurish.

Lakai [la-kïe'] m.w. footman, lackey.

Lake [lah'ker] nf. brine, pickle.

Laken [lah'ken] n. (-) sheet, shroud.

Lakritze [lak-rit'ser] nf. liquorice. [mer.

Lallen [lal'en] vi. to lisp, stam-

Lamelle [la-mel'er] nf. commutator, lamina (el.); **-nkupplung** nf. plate-clutch (aut.).

Lamentieren [la-men-teer'ren] vi. to lament.

Lamm [lam] n. (Lämmer) lamb; **-en** vi. to lamb; **-fell** n. lambskin; **-wolle** nf. lamb's wool.

Lampe [lam'per] nf. lamp, bulb (el.); **-nfieber** n. stage-fright; **-nschirm** nm. lamp-shade.

Lampion [lam-pi-ong'] nm. (-s) Chinese lantern.

Lancieren [lan-tseer'ren] vt. to launch, set in motion, start.

Land [lant] n. (Länder) land, country, soil; **-adel** nm. gentry; **-arbeiter** nm. farm, agricultural labourer; **-bau** nm. agriculture; **-besitz** nm. property; **-besitzer** nm. landowner; **-einwärts** ad. up-country; **-erziehungsheim** n. boarding school; **-gut** n. estate; **-haus** n. country house; **-karte** nf. map; **-kreis** nm. county, rural district; **-läufig** a. customary; **-messer** nm. surveyor; **-partie** nf. picnic; **-spitze** nf. cape, headland; **-stadt** nf. country town; **-steuer** nf. land-tax; **-strasse** nf. highroad; **-streicher** nm. tramp; **-strich** nm. region; **-sturm** nm. reservists (over 45); **-tag** nm. diet; **-verschickung, -verschiebung** nf. evacuation; **-wasserpanzer** nm. amphibious tank (mil.); **-wehr** nf. territorial reserve; **-wirt** nm. landed proprietor, farmer; **-wirtschaft** nf. agriculture.

Lande'n [lan'den] vi. to land; **-bahn** [lan'den] nf. runway (av.); **-streifen** nm. landing strip.

Länderei [len-der-ry'] nf. estates. [waltz.

Ländler [lent'lerr] nm. slow

Ländlich [lent'lish] a. rural.

Landes-aufnahme nf. topography, ordnance survey; **-farben** f.pl. national colours; **-gesetz** n. statute, law; **-herr** m.w. sovereign; **-tracht** nf. national costume; **-üblich** a. customary; **-verrat** nm. high treason; **-verweisung** nf. banishment; **-währung** nf. standard currency.

Landsmann [lants'man] nm., **Landsmännin** nf. (Landsleute) compatriot, fellow-countryman, countrywoman.

Landschaft [lant'shaft] nf. landscape, province; **-lich** a. landscape, scenic, provincial.

Landung [lan'dŏŏng] nf. landing, disembarkation; **-sboot** n. landing craft; **-sbrücke** nf. jetty, pier; **-sfunkstelle** nf. wireless homing station; **-sstelle** nf. landing place.

Lang [lang] a. long, tall;

-atmig a. long-winded; **-holz** n. timber; **-lebig** a. long-lived; **-mut** nm. long-suffering, patience; **-mütig** a. forbearing; **-sichtig** a. long-sighted; **-streckenflug** nm. long-distance flight; **-tau** n. drag-rope; **-weile** nf. boredom; **-weilig** a. tedious, boring; **-wellensender** nm. long-distance transmitter (rad.); **-wierig** a. lengthy, long-drawn out.

Lange [lang'er] ad. long, for a long time.

Länge [leng'er] nf. length, size, longitude; **-nmass** n. linear measure.

Langen [lang'en] vi. to do, suffice, reach for.

Länger [leng'err] a. longer, taller. [ish.

Länglich [leng'lish] a. long-

Längs [lengss] pr. along.

Langsam [lang'zam] a., ad. slow(ly); **-keit** nf. slowness.

Längst [lengst] a., ad. longest, long ago for a long time.

Lanze [lant'ser] nf. lance.

Lanzette [lant-set'er] nf. lancet. [trifle.

Lappalie [lap-ahl'yer] nf.

Lappen [lap'en] nm. (-) cloth, shred, rag, lobe, patch.

Läppern [lep'errn] vi. to lap; **-schulden** f.pl. petty debts.

Läppisch [lep'ish] a. foolish.

Lärche [lairr'sher] nf. larch.

Lärm [lairm] nm. noise, alarm; **-en** vi. to be noisy, make a noise.

Larve [larr'fer] nf. mask, larva.

Lasch [lash] a. limp.

Lasche [lash'er] nf. gore, gusset, groove, fish-plate (rl.).

Lassen [lass'en] vt.i. ir. to let, leave, allow, cause, have done; n. conduct.

Lässig [less'ish] a. slack, idle, negligent; **-keit** nf. laziness, slackness.

Lässlich [less'lish] a. indulgent, pardonable.

Last [last] *nf.* load, burden, charge, cargo; -auto *n.* motor lorry; -dampfer *nm.* cargoboat; -enfrei *a.* tax free; -ensegler *nm.* freight-carrying glider; -enträger *nm.* bomb carrier (*av.*); -flugzeug *n.* freight-carrying plane; -igkeit *nf.* tonnage; -kahn *nm.* barge; -kraftwagen *nm.* lorry, truck, van; -pferd *n.* pack-horse; -segelflugzeug *n. see* Lastensegler; -schrift *nf.* debiting, debit item; -tier *n.* beast of burden; -träger *nm.* porter.

Lasten [last'en] *vi.* to weigh on.

Laster [last'err] *n.* (-) vice; -haft *a.* vicious, immoral; -haftigkeit *nf.* wickedness.

Läster|er [lest'er-rerr] *nm.* (-) slanderer; -lich *a.* slanderous, scandalous; -n *vt.i.* to slander, revile; -ung *nf.* slander, blasphemy.

Lästig [lest'ish] *a.* troublesome, tiresome.

Latein [lat-ine'] *n.* Latin; -isch *a.* Latin.

Laternbild [lat-airrn'bilt] *n.* lantern-slide.

Laterne [la-tairr'ner] *nf.* lantern; -npfahl *nm.* lamp-post.

Latrine [lat-ree'ner] *nf.* latrine.

Latsch|e [lat'sher] *nf.* slipper; -en *vi.* to slouch, shuffle; -ig *a.* slouching, slovenly. [pine.

Latsche [lat'sher] *nf.* dwarf

Latte [lat'err] *nf.* lath; -nzaun *nm.* fence.

Lattich [lat'ish] *nm.* (-e) lettuce. [electuary.

Latwerge [lat-vairr'ger] *nf.*

Latz [lats] *nm.* (Lätze) bib, flap, pinafore; -schürze *nf.* pinafore.

Lätzchen [lets'shen] *n.* (-) *see* Latz.

Lau[warm] [low'varrm] *a.* lukewarm.

Lauheit [low'hite] *nf.* lukewarmness, tepidness.

Laub [lowp] *n.* foliage; -säge *nf.* fret-saw.

Laube [low'ber] *nf.* arbour, summer-house; -ngang *nm.* arcade.

Lauch [lowch] *nm.* (-e) leek.

Lauer [low'err] *nf.* ambush, look-out; -n *vi.* to lie in wait for, lurk, watch; -stellung *nf.* silent position (*artillery*).

Lauf [lowf] *nm.* (Läufe) course, path, barrel (*gun*), race, way; -bahn *nf.* career, course; -band *n.* tread (*tyre*), conveyor (*tec.*); -brücke *nf.* flying deck (*av.*); -bursche *nm.* errand-boy; -getriebe *n.* mechanism; -graben *nm.* approach trench; -krippe *nf.* nursery school; -kundschaft *nf.* passing customers; -mantel *nm.* barrel casing; -masche *nf.* ladder (*stocking*); -rad *n.* rotor (*jetplane*); -schritt *nm.* run, (the) double; -steg *nm.* footbridge; -zettel *nm.* clearance chit, circular.

Laufen [low'fen] *vi. ir.* to run, move, flow, pass by; -d *a.* running, current, routine (*duties*); -des Band conveyor belt, assembly line (*tec.*).

Läufer [loy'ferr] *nm.* (-) runner, stair-carpet, line (*music*), bishop (*chess*), half-back (*football*).

Lauge [low'ger] *nf.* lye; -n *vt.* to soak in lye; -nartig *a.* alkaline.

Laun|e [low'ner] *nf.* whim, humour, caprice, temper; -enhaft *a.* capricious, changeable; -enhaftigkeit *nf.* capriciousness; -ig *a.* humorous; -isch *a.* ill-humoured, capricious.

Laus [lowss] *nf.* (Läuse) louse; -bube *m.w.* rascal, imp; -en *vt.* to delouse.

Lausch|en [low'shen] *vi.* to eavesdrop, listen to, listen-in, intercept (*rad.*); -er *nm.* listener; -ig *a.* snug.

Laut [lowt] *a., ad.* loud(ly), aloud; *pr.* according to; *nm.* (-e) sound; **-schrift** *nf.* phonetic alphabet; **-verstärker** *nm.* volume amplifier (*rad.*).

Laute [low'ter] *nf.* lute; **-nschläger** *nm.* lute-player.

Lauten [low'ten] *vi.* to run, read, say, sound.

Läute'n [loy'ten] *vt.i.* to ring, sound; **-werk** *n.* bells.

Lauter [low'terr] *a.* clear, pure, genuine, nothing but, only; **-keit** *nf.* purity, honesty, integrity.

Läuter'n [loy'terrn] *vt.* to purify, refine; **-ung** *nf.* purification, refining.

Lautsprecher [lowt'shpresherr] *nm.* (-) loud-speaker (*rad.*); **-wagen** *nm.* loud-speaker van.

Lautstärke [lowt'shtairr'ker] *nf.* volume range (*rad.*); **-regler** *nm.* volume control.

Lavendel [la-ven'del] *nm.* (-) lavender.

Lavieren [la-veer'ren] *vi.* to tack (*nav.*).

Lawine [la-vee'ner] *nf.* avalanche.

Lax [lax] *a.* lax; **-ieren** *vi.* to take an aperient; *t.* purge.

Lazarett [lat-sar-ret'] *n.* (-e) hospital; **-zug** *nm.* hospital train.

Leber'hoch [lay-ber-hohch'] *n.* cheer, toast; **-mann** *nm.* man about town, rake; **-wesen** *n.* living being; **-wohl** *n.* farewell, good-bye. [life.

Leben [lay'ben] *vi.* to live; *n.*

Lebendig [le-ben'dish] *a.* living, alive, quick; **-keit** *nf.* liveliness.

Lebens-alter *n.* age; **-art** *nf.* way of life, manners; **-beschreibung** *nf.* biography; **-fähig** *a.* vital, capable of living; **-frage** *nf.* vital question; **-gefährlich** *a.* dangerous to life; **-grösse** *nf.* life-size; **-haltung** *nf.* standard of living;

-kosten *pl.* cost of living; **-lauf** *nm.* details of career; **-lage** *nf.* position in life; **-lustig** *a.* merry; **-mittel** *n.pl.* food; **-mittelkarte** *nf.* ration card; **-müde** *a.* tired of life; **-raum** *nm.* living space; **-stellung** *nf.* life-post; **-unterhalt** *nm.* livelihood; **-wandel** *nm.* conduct of life; **-weise** *nf.* manner of life; **-zeichen** *n.* sign of life; **-zeit** *nf.* lifetime, age.

Leber [lay'berr] *nf.* liver; **-tran** *nm.* cod-liver oil; **-wurst** *nf.* liver-sausage.

Lebhaft [lape'haft] *a.* lively, brisk, vivacious; **-igkeit** *nf.* liveliness, briskness, vivacity.

Lebkuchen [lape'koo-chen] *nm.* (-) gingerbread.

Leb-los [lape'los] *a.* lifeless, dull; **-tag** *nm.*, **-zeiten** *f.pl.* lifetime.

Lechzen [lesh'tsen] *vi.* to be parched, long for.

Leck [leck] *a.* leaky, leaking; *n.* leak; **-en** *vi.* to leak.

Lecken [leck'en] *vt.* to lick.

Lecker [leck'err] *a.* delicious, tasty, dainty; **-bissen** *nm.* dainty, titbit; **-maul** *n.* sweet tooth.

Leder [lade'err] *n.* (-) leather; **-handschuh** *nm.* leather gauntlet; **-n** *a.* leather, pedantic, dull.

Ledig [lay'dish] *a.* unmarried, vacant, free; **-lich** *ad.* merely, solely, only.

Lee [lay] *nf.* lee.

Leer [lairr] *a.* empty, unoccupied, vacant, idle (*words*); **-e** *nf.* emptiness, vacuum; **-gebinde** *n.* empty container; **-gewicht** *n.* dead weight, net tare, weight empty; **-gut** *n.* empties (*com.*); **-lauf** *nm.* running idle.

Leer'en [lairr'en] *vt.* to empty, evacuate; **-ung** *nf.* emptying, evacuation, clearing.

Legat [leg-aht'] *a.* (-e) legacy.

Legat [leg-aht'] *m.w.* legate.

Legen [lay'gen] vt. to lay, put, place, deposit; r. lie down, subside.

Legende [leg-en'der] nf. legend; -haft a. legendary.

Legier'en [leg-eer'ren] vt. to alloy; -ung nf. alloy, composition (tec.).

Legitim [leg-i-teem'] a. legitimate; -ation nf. legitimation, proof of identity; -ations-papiere n.pl. identity papers; -ieren vt. to legitimize; r. prove one's identity; -ität nf. legitimacy.

Lehm [lame] nm. loam, clay; -ig a. loamy.

Lehn'e [lane'er] nf. support, arm, back (chair); -en vt.r. to lean, rest; -stuhl nm. armchair.

Lehr'anstalt [lairr'an-shtalt] nf. school, educational establishment; -bataillon n. demonstration battalion; -brief nm. indentures; -buch n. textbook; -film nm. instructional film; -gang nm. course of instruction; -gehilfe m.w. apprentice assistant; -geld n. premium; -haft a. fond of teaching; -jahre n.pl. apprenticeship; -ling nm. apprentice; -plan nm. curriculum; -reich a. instructive; -satz nm. doctrine, proposition; -stab nm. training staff (mil.); -truppen f.pl. demonstration unit (mil.); -zeit nf. apprenticeship.

Lehre [lairr'er] nf. teaching, doctrine, apprenticeship, gauge (tec.); -n vt. to teach; -r nm. (-) teacher, schoolmaster.

Leib [lipe] nm. (-er) body; -binde nf. belt, sash, abdominal belt; -chen n. bodice, vest; -esbeschaffenheit nf. constitution; -esstrafe nf. corporal punishment; -esübung nf. physical exercise; -haftig a. bodily, real, incarnate; -lich a.

bodily, material, real; -riemen nm. belt (av.); -wäsche nf. underware; -weh n. stomachache. [corn.

Leichdorn [lish'dorrn] nm.

Leiche [li'sher] nf. corpse; -nbeschauer nm. coroner; -nbesorger nm. undertaker; -nfrau nf. layer-out; -ngebühr nf. burial fee; -nhemd n. shroud; -nschau nf. inquest, post-mortem; -nträger nm. bearer; -nverbrennung nf. cremation; -nwagen nm. hearse.

Leichnam [lish'nam] m.w. corpse, dead body.

Leicht [lisht] a. light, mild, mobile (mil.), easy; -athletik nf. athletics; -blütig a. sanguine; -fertig a. thoughtless, frivolous; -fertigkeit nf. thoughtlessness, frivolousness; -füssig a. nimble; -gläubig a. credulous; -gläubigkeit nf. credulity; -hin ad. lightly; -igkeit nf. lightness, easiness, ease; -kranke m.pl. minor sick cases (mil.); -lebig a. easygoing; -sinn nm. levity, indiscretion; -sinnig a. thoughtless, frivolous.

Leichter [lish'terr] nm. (-) lighter, tender (nav.).

Leid [lite] n. harm, pain, grief, sorrow; a. (in set phrases) sorry; -tragende(r) m.w. mourner; -wesen n. sorrow.

Leiden [lide'en] vt. ir. to suffer, permit; i. suffer; n. suffering, pain, illness.

Leidenschaft [lide'en-shaft] nf. passion; -lich a. passionate; -slos a. dispassionate.

Leider [lide'err] ad. unfortunately, worse luck!

Leidig [lide'ish] a. miserable, tiresome; -lich a. tolerable; ad. tolerably.

Leier [lie'err] nf. lyre, old story; -kasten nm. barrelorgan; -mann nm. organgrinder.

Leihbibliothek [lie'bib-lio-take] *nf.* lending library.

Leihen [lie'en] *vt. ir.* to lend, borrow.

Leih-haus *n.* pawn-shop; **-pakt** *nm.* lease-lend; **-schein** *nm.* pawn ticket, borrowing slip.

Leim [lime] *nm.* (-e) size, glue; **-en** *vt.* to glue, size; **-farbe** *nf.* distemper; **-ig** *a.* glutinous; **-stoff** *nm.* gluten.

Lein [line] *nm.* (-e) flax; **-e** *nf.* line, cord, leash; **-en** *n.* linen; *a.* linen; **-enband** *n.* cloth binding; **-kuchen** *nm.* oil-cake; **-öl** *n.* linseed oil; **-pfad** *nm.* tow-path; **-tuch** *n.* sheet, linen cloth; **-wand** *nf.* linen (cloth), screen, canvas.

Leise [lize'er] *a., ad.* soft(ly), gentle, gently, low.

Leiste [lie'ster] *nf.* edge, ledge, fillet, groin.

Leisten [lie'sten] *vt.* to perform, achieve, make, do. **Leistung** [lie'stoong] *nf.* performance, achievement; **-sab-zeichen** *n.* proficiency badge; **-sbelastung** *nf.* efficiency load; **-sfähig** *a.* efficient, able, productive; **-sfähigkeit** *nf.* efficiency, power; **-swerte** *m.pl.* piece rates; **-szulage** *nf.* efficiency pay.

Leisten [lie'sten] *nm.* (-) shoemaker's last.

Leit'artikel [lite'arr-tee-kel] *nm.* (-) leading article; **-faden** *nm.* manual, guide; **-fähigkeit** *nf.* conductivity; **-funkstelle** *nf.* wireless control station; **-horst** *nm.* main air-force station; **-kompanie** *nf.* control company; **-offizier** *nm.* control officer; **-schaufel** *nf.* nozzle (*tec.*); **-schiene** *nf.* live wire; **-stand** *nm.* control post (*mil.*); **-stelle** *nf.* forwarding centre, control station; **-stern** *nm.* guiding star, pole-star.

Leite'n [lite'en] *vt.* to lead,

direct, manage, route (*mail*); **-r** *nm.* leader, head, guide, manager.

Leiter [lite'err] *nf.* ladder.

Leitung [lute'öong] *nf.* guidance, conduct, transmission, management, lead, cable, landline (*el.*); **-sdraht** *nm.* wire; **-sende** *n.* terminal (*el.*); **-srohr** *n.* main, conduit; **-sschnur** *nf.* flex; **-szahl** *nf.* consignment number.

Lektion [lek-syohn'] *nf.* (reading) lesson.

Lektor [lek'torr] *nm.* (*gen.* -s; *pl.* -en), **Lektorin** [lek'torin] *nf.* lecturer, reader. [reading.

Lektüre [lek-tyoor'rer] *nf.*

Lende [len'der] *nf.* loin(s); **-nbraten** *nm.* roast sirloin; **-nstück** *n.* fillet, loin.

Lenkbar [lenk'barr] *a.* dirigible, navigable, tractable.

Lenk'en [lenk'en] *vt.* to steer, turn, direct, cast (*attention*); **-er** *nm.* guide, pilot, driver; **-rad** *n.* steering-wheel; **-sam** *a.* easily led, governable, docile; **-säule** *nf.* steering column (*aut.*); **-schlitten** *nm.* bob-sleigh; **-stange** *nf.* handlebar (*cycle*); **-ung** *nf.* driving, steering, directing.

Lenz [lents] *nm.* (-e) spring.

Leopard [lay'o-part] *nm.w.* leopard.

Lerche [lairr'sher] *nf.* lark.

Lern'begierig [lairrn'ber-geer-rish] *a.* eager to learn; **-en** *vt.* to learn; **-zeit** *nf.* apprenticeship.

Lesbar [lace'barr] *a.* readable; **-keit** *nf.* readableness.

Lese [lay'zer] *nf.* gleaning. **Lese-buch** *n.* reading-book, reader; **-halle** *nf.*, **-saal** *nm.* reading-room; **-zeichen** *n.* book-mark.

Lesen [laze'en] *vt. ir.* to read, gather, pick; **-swert** *a.* readable, worth reading.

Leser [laze'err] *nm.* (-) read-

er; -lich *a.* legible; **-lichkeit** *nf.* legibility.

Letten [let'en] *nm.* (-) potter's clay.

Letzen [lets'en] *vt.* to refresh.

Letzt [letst] *a.* last, latest; **-ens** *ad.* lately, lastly; **-ere(r)** *m.w.* the latter; **-hin** *ad.* of late, just now, lately; **-jährig** *a.* last year's.

Leucht'e [loish'ter] *nf.* lamp, light; **-en** *vi.* to light, gleam; **-er** *nm.* candlestick; **-feuer** *n.* beacon, flare; **-geschoss** *n.* star-shell; **-käfer** *nm.* glow-worm; **-kugel** *nf.* Very light; **-munition** *nf.* Very pistol ammunition; **-pfad** *nm.* flare-path; **-rakete** *nf.* rocket; **-schiff** *n.* lightship; **-spur** *nf.* tracer; **-turm** *nm.* lighthouse; **-zifferblatt** *n.* luminous dial.

Leugn'en [loik'nen] *vt.* to deny, disavow; **-ung** *nf.* denial, disavowal.

Leukoplast [loi'ko-plast] *n.* (-e) adhesive tape.

Leumund [loy'mŏŏnt] *nm.* reputation.

Leute [loy'ter] *pl.* people.

Leutnant [loit'nant] *nm.* (-s) second lieutenant (*mil.*), sub-lieutenant (*nav.*), pilot officer (*av.*).

Leutselig [loit'zale-ish] *a.* affable; **-keit** *nf.* affability.

Levkoje [lef-koh'yer] *nf.* stock (*flower*).

Lexikon [lex'i-kon] *n.* (Lexika) dictionary.

Libelle [li-bel'er] *nf.* dragon fly, spirit-level.

Liberal [li-ber-rahl'] *a.* liberal; **-ismus** *nm.* liberalism.

Licht [lisht] *n.* (-er) light, (-e) candle; *a.* light, bright; **-bild** *n.* photograph, lantern-slide; **-bogen** *nm.* arc-lamp; **-bogenschweissung** *nf.* arc-welding; **-echt** *a.* fast to light; **-empfindlich** *a.* sensitive to light; **-erloh** *ad.* blazing; **-kegel** *nm.* search-

light beam, cone; **-mess** *nf.* Candlemass; **-messung** *nf.* flash-ranging (*mil.*); **-reklame** *nf.* sky-signs; **-seite** *nf.* sunny side; **-spielhaus** *n.* cinema; **-voll** *a.* luminous, clear; **-zauber** *nm.* lighting (*av.*); **-zelle** *nf.* photo-electric cell.

Licht'en [lish'ten] *vt.* to clear, weigh (*anchor*); *r.* clear up; **-er** *nm.* lighter (*nav.*); **-ung** *nf.* clearing, glade.

Lid [leet] *n.* (-er) eyelid.

Lieb [leep] *a.* dear, agreeable; **-äugeln** *vi.* to ogle; **-chen** *n.* darling; **-elei** *nf.* flirtation; **-eln** *vi.* to flirt; **-gewinnen** *vt. ir.* to get fond of; **-haben** *vt.* to love; **-haber** *nm.* lover, fancier, amateur; **-haberei** *nf.* hobby, liking; **-kosen** *vt.* to caress; **-kosung** *nf.* caress; **-lich** *a.* lovely; **-ling** *nm.* darling; **-los** *a.* loveless, unkind; **-reiz** *nm.* charm; **-schaft** *nf.* love-affair.

Liebe [lee'ber] *nf.* love; **-diener** *nm.* time-server; **-dienerei** *nf.* servility.

Lieben [lee'ben] *vt.* to love, like; **-swert** *a.* worthy of love, loveable; **-swürdig** *a.* amiable, loveable; **-swürdigkeit** *nf.* amiability, kindness.

Lieber [lee'ber] *a.* dearer; *ad.* rather, preferably.

Liebes'brief [lee'bes-breef] *nm.* (-e) love-letter; **-dienst** *nm.* good turn; **-gabe** *nf.* gift (*parcel*); **-paar** *n.* pair of lovers.

Lied [leet] *n.* (-er) song, hymn; **-chen** *n.* ditty; **-erbuch** *n.* (-) song-book, hymn-book.

Liederlich [lee'derr-lish] *a.* loose, slovenly, immoral; **-keit** *nf.* immorality, slovenliness.

Liefer'ant [lee-fer-rant'] *m.w.* caterer, contractor, purveyor; **-schein** *nm.* receipt, docket; **-wagen** *nm.* delivery van.

Liefern [lee'ferrn] *vt.* to deliver, supply, produce, yield.

Lieferung [lee'fer-rŏŏng] *nf.*

delivery, number (*magazine*); -swagen *nm.* delivery van; -swerk *n.* serial.

Liege'geld [lee'ger-gelt] *n.* demurrage; -platz *nm.* parking point, berth (*nav.*); -stuhl *nm.* deck-chair.

Liegen [lee'gen] *vi. ir.* to lie, be situated; -schaft *nf.* real estate.

Liguster [li-gŏŏ'sterr] *nm.* privet.

Likör [li-kerr'] *nm.* (-e) liqueur.

Lila [li'lah] *a, n.* lilac.

Lilie [leel'yer] *nf.* lily.

Limonade [li-moh-nah'der] *nf.* lemonade.

Limone [li-moh'ner] *nf.* lime-fruit, lemon.

Lind [lint] *a.* gentle, mild; -ern *vt.* to mitigate, alleviate, soothe; -erung *nf.* alleviation.

Linde [lin'der] *nf.* lime-tree, linden.

Lineal [lin-e-ahl'] *n.* (-e) ruler.

Linie [lee'nyer] *nf.* line; -nrichter *nm.* linesman (*football*); -nschiff *n.* battleship; -numschalter *nm.* switch (*el.*).

Liniieren [lee-ni-eer'ren] *vt.* to line.

Link [link] *a.* left; -e *nf.* left side, hand; -isch *a.* clumsy, awkward.

Links [links] *ad.* to, on the left; -aussen *nm.* outside left (*football*); -innen *nm.* inside left; -sozialismus *nm.* left-wing socialism.

Linnen [lin'en] *n.* (-) linen.

Linse [lin'zer] *nf.* lentil, lens.

Lippe [lip'er] *nf.* lip; -nstift *nm.* lipstick.

Liquid'ation [lik-vi-dat-syohn'] *nf.* liquidation; -ieren *vt.* to liquidate.

Lispeln [lis'peln] *vi.* to lisp.

List [list] *nf.* cunning, trick, ruse; -ig *a.* cunning, sly.

Liste [lis'ter] *nf.* list, roster.

Litanei [lit-an-ie'] *nf.* litany.

Liter [lee'terr] *nm.* (-) litre.

Litera'risch [li-ter-rah'rish] *n.* literary; -tur *nf.* literature.

Lithographie [li-to-gra-fee'] *nf.* lithography.

Liturgie [li-tŏŏr-gee'] *nf.* liturgy; -sch *a.* liturgical.

Litze [lit'ser] *nf.* cord, braid, piping, flex (*el.*).

Livree [li-vray'] *nf.* livery.

Lizenziat [li-tsen-tsi-aht'] *m.w.* licentiate. [eulogy.

Lob [lohp] *n.* praise; -rede *nf.*

Loben [lobe'en] *vt.* to praise; -swert *a.* praiseworthy.

Löblich [lerp'lish] *a.* praiseworthy, laudable.

Loch [loch] *n.* (Löcher) hole, puncture (*aut.*); -en *vt.* to perforate, punch; -eisen *n.* punch; -er *nm.* punch, perforator; -karten *f.pl.* perforated cards; -ung *nf.* perforation.

Löche'lchen [ler'shel-shen] *nf.* (-) small hole, eyelet; -rig *a.* full of holes, porous.

Lock'e [lok'err] *nf.* lock, curl; -en *vt.* to curl; -ig *a.* curly.

Lock'en [lok'en] *vt.* to decoy, allure; -mittel *n.* bait; -ung *nf.* enticement.

Locker [lok'err] *a.* loose, lax, frivolous; -n *vt.* to loosen, break up.

Loden [loh'den] *nm.* (-) coarse woollen cloth. [flare up.

Lodern [loh'derrn] *vi.* to blaze,

Löffel [ler'fel] *nm.* (-) spoon; -n *vt.* to sip; -weise *ad.* by spoonfuls.

Log [lok] *n.* (-e) log.

Loge [loh'zher] *nf.* box (*theatre*); masonic lodge.

Logier'en [lo-zheer'ren] *vi.* to lodge, stay; -zimmer *n.* spare room.

Logi'k [loh'gik] *nf.* logic; -sch *a.* logical.

Logis [lo-zhee'] *n.* lodgings.

Lohe [loh'er] *nf.* flame, blaze; -n *vi.* to blaze.

Loh'e [loh'er] *nf.* tan; -en *vt.* to tan; -gerber *nm.* tanner.

Lohn [lone] *nm.* (**Löhne**) reward, pay, wages; -**arbeiter** *nm.* labourer; -**druckerei** *nf.* wage-cutting, sweating; -**empfänger** *nm.* wage-earner; -**minimum** *n.* minimum wage; -**pfändung** *nf.* distraint on pay; -**steuer** *nf.* earned income tax; -**stelle** *nf.* pay-office; -**tag** *nm.* pay-day; -**tüte** *nf.* pay envelope; -**zuschlag** *nm.* bonus.

Lohnen [loh'nen] *vt.i.r.* to reward, pay (for); -**d** *a.* profitable.

Löhn'en [ler'nen] *vt.* to pay; -**ung** *nf.* wages; -**ungsliste** *nf.* pay-list.

Lokal [lo-kahl'] *a.* local; *n.* (-**e**) premises, public house; -**isier-en** *vt.* to localize; -**isierung** *nf.* localization.

Lokomotiv'e [lo-ko-mo-tee'ver] *nf.* locomotive; -**führer** *nm.* engine-driver.

Lorbeer [lore'bairr] *nm.* (-) (*gen.* -**s**; *pl.* -**en**) laurel.

Lore [lore'er] *nf.* lorry.

Los [lohss] *n.* (-**e**) lot, fate, lottery-ticket.

Los [lohss] *a., ad.* loose, free; *ad.* on, forward, off; -**binden** *vt. ir.* to untie; -**brechen** *vt.i. ir.* to break loose; -**fahren** *vi. ir.* to fire; -**fahren** *vi. ir.* to go away, fly at; -**geben** *vt. ir.* to release; -**gehen** *vi. ir.* to come, go off, set out, attack; -**kaufen** *vt. ir.* to redeem, ransom; -**kommen** *vi. ir.* to get loose, away free; -**lassen** *vt. ir.* to let go, loose; -**machen** *vt. ir.* to loosen, disengage; -**reissen** *vt.r. ir.* to tear away, loose; *i.* snap off; -**sagen** *vr.* to renounce; -**sprechen** *vt. ir.* to release, acquit; -**ziehen** *vi. ir.* to set out, run down, revile.

Lösch'en [ler'shen] *vt. ir.* to extinguish, slake, efface, cancel; -**gerät** *n.* fire-extinguisher; -**personal** *n.* fire-fighters; -**papier** *n.* blotting-

paper; -**ung** *nf.* cancellation, extinction.

Lösch'en [ler'shen] *vt.* to unload; -**ung** *nf.* unloading (*cargo*).

Lose [loh'zer] *a.* loose, disconnected, unsteady, dissolute; -**blätterbuch** *n.* loose-leaf book. [lots.

Losen [loh'zen] *vi.* to draw

Lös'en [ler'zen] *vt.* to loosen, detach, solve, dissolve; -**ung** *nf.* loosening (dis)solution, annulment; -**ungsmittel** *n.* solvent.

Löslich [lers'lish] *a.* soluble; -**keit** *nf.* solubility.

Losung [loh'sōong] *nf.* watchword, slogan.

Lot [lote] *n.* (-**e**) lead, solder, plummet; -**en** *vi.* to plumb, sound; -**recht** *a.* perpendicular.

Löt'en [ler'ten] *vt.* to solder; -**kolben** *nm.* soldering iron; -**metall** *n.* solder.

Lotse [lote'ser] *m.w.* pilot; -**n** *vt.* to pilot.

Lotter'bube [lot'err-boo-ber] *m.w.* rascal; -**ig** *a.* slovenly, dissolute. [tery.

Lotterie [lot-er-ree'] *nf.* lottery.

Löwe [ler'ver] *m.w.* lion; -**nanteil** *nm.* lion's share; -**nzahn** *nm.* dandelion.

Löwin [ler'vin] *nf.* lioness.

Loyal [lo-yahl'] *a.* loyal; -**ität** *nf.* loyalty.

Luchs [lŏŏx] *nm.* (-**e**) lynx.

Lücke [lyŏŏ'ker] *nf.* gap, opening, omission; -**nbüsser** *nm.* stop-gap; -**nhaft** *a.* defective, full of gaps.

Luder [loo'derr] *n.* (-) carrion, hag, hussy; -**leben** *n.* immoral life.

Luft [lŏŏft] *nf.* (**Lüfte**) air, breath; -**angriff** *nm.* air-raid; -**aufklärung** *nf.* air reconnaissance; -**aufnahme** *nf.* -**bild** *n.* air-photograph; -**bildgerät** *n.* air-camera; -**blase** *nf.* air-bubble; -**dicht** *a.* air-tight;

-druck *nm.* atmospheric pressure; -drüse *nf.* choke (*aut.*); -erkundung *nf.* air reconnaissance; -fahrt *nf.* aeronautics, aviation; -fahrzeug *n.* aircraft; -gekühlt *a.* air-cooled; -hafen *nm.* air-port; -heizung *nf.* air-conditioning; -herrschaft *nf.* air supremacy; -ig *a.* airy; -kammerreifen *nm.* pneumatic tyre; -kampf *nm.* air-battle; -kampfstoff *nm.* cloud gas; -kissen *n.* air-cushion; -krank *a.* air-sick; -krieg *nm.* war in the air; -kriegsschäden *m.pl.* air-raid damage; -lage *nf.* atmospheric conditions; -landetruppen *f.pl.* air-borne troops; -leerer Raum vacuum; -linie *nf.* bee-line; -loch *n.* air-pocket, air-hole; -markierer *nm.* flare plane; -massen *f.pl.* air currents; -mine *nf.* aircraft mine; -notstandsgebiet *n.* bombed area; -park *nm.* aircraft park; -regulierknopf *nm.* choke (*aut.*); -reinigung *nf.* air-conditioning; -röhre *nf.* windpipe; -schiff *n.* airship; -schiffahrt *nf.* aerial navigation; -schlange *nf.* streamer; -schlauch *nm.* inner tube; -schloss *n.* castle in the air; -schraube *nf.* air-screw; -schutz(dienst) *nm.* air-raid protection; -schutzraum *nm.* air-raid shelter; -schutzwart *nm.* air-raid warden; -segler *nm.* glider; -sicherung *nf.* air-escort; -späher *nm.* spotter; -spiegelung *nf.* mirage; -sperre *nf.* fighter patrol; -sperrgebiet *n.* prohibited area (*av.*); -stoss *nm.* blast of air, gust; -störungen *f.pl.* atmospherics (*rad.*); -stützpunkt *nm.* air-base; -tanken *v.* to refuel in mid-air; -torpedo *nm.* aircraft torpedo; -transport *nm.* air-transport; -tüchtig *a.* air-worthy; -verkehr *nm.* air-traffic; -verkehrslinie *nf.* air-

way. air-line; -vermessung *nf.* aerial survey(ing) *nf.*; -versorgung *nf.* supplying from the air; -waffe *nf.* air-force; -zug *nm.* draught.

Lüftchen [lyōoft'shen] *n.* (-) breeze.

Lüften [lyōof'ten] *vt.* to air, ventilate, disclose; -er *nm.* ventilator; -ung *nf.* ventilation.

Lüge [lyōo'ger] *nf.* lie; -n *vi. ir.* to lie; -nhaft *a.* lying.

Lügner [lyōok'nerr] *nm.* liar; -isch *a.* lying, false.

Luke [lōo'ker] *nf.* dormer-window, hatch.

Lullen [lōo'len] *vt.* to lull.

Lümmel [lyōo'mel] *nm.* (-) lout, ruffian, hooligan; -haft *a.* boorish, ruffianly.

Lump [lōomp] *m.w.* scamp, rascal; -enpack *n.* rabble.

Lump'en [lōom'pen] *nm.* (-) rag, clout; -ehändler *nm.* rag-man; -ig *a.* shabby, ragged.

Lunge [lōong'er] *nf.* lung; -nentzündung *nf.* pneumonia; -nkrank *a.* consumptive.

Lungern [lōong'errn] *vi.* to be idle, hang about.

Lunte [lōon'ter] *nf.* match, fuse. [glass.

Lupe [lōo'per] *nf.* magnifying

Lupine [lōo-pee'ner] *nf.* lupine.

Lust [lōost] *nf.* (Lüste) joy, delight, desire; -barkeit *nf.* amusement; -fahrt *nf.* excursion, outing; -seuche *nf.* venereal disease; -spiel *n.* comedy; -wandeln *vi.* to stroll about.

Lüster [lyōo'sterr] *nm.* (-) chandelier.

Lüstern [lyōo'sterrn] *a.* lustful, desirous; -heit *nf.* lasciviousness.

Lustig [lōo'stish] *a.* merry, cheerful, amusing; -keit *nf.* gaiety, fun, merriment.

Lüstling [lyōost'ling] *nm.* (-e) rake, sensualist.

Luv [lōof] *a.* luff, weather-side.

Luxboje [lŏŏx'boh-yer] nf. flare buoy.
Luxus [lŏŏx'ŏŏss] nm. luxury; -artikel nm. luxury; -ausgabe nf. edition de luxe; -auto n. saloon car; -waren f.pl. luxuries, fancy goods; -zug nm. saloon train.
Lymphe [lŷm'fer] nf. lymph.
Lynchen [lŷn'shen] vt. to lynch.
Lyri'k [lyŏŏr'rik] nf. lyric, poetry; -ker nm. lyric, poet; -sch a. lyrical.
Lyzeum [lyŏŏt-say'ŏŏm] n. (Lyzeen) high school for girls.

M

Maat [maht] nm. (-e) mate, petty officer (nav.).
Mache [mach'er] nf. making, workmanship, show.
Machen [mach'en] vt. to make, do, cause, signify; -schaft nf. machination.
Macher [mach'err] nm. (-) maker; -lohn nm. charge for manufacture.
Macht [macht] nf. (Mächte) might, power; -haber nm. ruler; -politik nf. power politics; -stellung nf. political power; -wort n. word of command.
Mächtig [mesh'tish] a. mighty, powerful, thick.
Machwerk [mach'vairrk] n. inferior work, shoddy.
Mädchen [mate'shen] n. (-) girl; -haft a. girlish; -name nm. maiden name.
Made [mah'der] nf. maggot, mite; -ig a. worm-eaten.
Mädel [made'el] n. (-) see Mädchen.
Magazin [ma-gat-seen'] n. (-e) storehouse, magazine.
Magd [mahkt] nf. (Mägde) maid, servant.
Magen [mah'gen] nm. (-)

stomach; -schmerzen m.pl. stomach-ache.
Mager [mah'gerr] a. lean, thin; -keit nf. leanness, thinness.
Magie [ma-gee'] nf. magic; -ker nm. magician; -sch a. magical.
Magistrat [ma-gis-traht'] nm. (-e) magistrates, town council.
Magnet [mak-nate'] m.w. magnet; -isch a. magnetic; -ische Mine magnetic mine; -isieren vt. to magnetize; -ismus nm. magnetism; -nadel nf. magnetic needle; -zünder nm. magneto (aut.).
Mahagoni [ma-ha-goh'nee] n. (-s) mahogany.
Mahd [maht] nf. mowing.
Mäh'en [may'en] vt. to mow; -er nm. mower, reaper; -maschine nf. reaper, lawn-mower.
Mahl [mahl] n. (-e) meal, -zeit nf. meal.
Mahl'en [mah'len] vt. to mill, grind; -mühle nf. grinding mill; -stein nm. grindstone; -zahn nm. molar.
Mahnbrief [mahn'breef] nm. (-e) dunning letter.
Mähne [may'ner] nf. mane.
Mahn'en [mah'nen] vt. to remind, warn, dun; -er nm. dun; -ung nf. reminder, admonition, warning, application for payment.
Mähre [mair'rer] nf. mare.
Mai [my] nm. May; -glöckchen n. lily of the valley; -käfer nm. cockchafer.
Mais [mice] nm. maize.
Maische [my'sher] nf. mash; -n vt. to mash.
Majestät [ma-yes-tate'] nf. majesty.
Major [ma-yore'] nm. (-e) major (mil.), squadron leader (av.); -ität nf. majority.
Makadamisieren [ma-ka-da-mi-zeer'ren] vt. to macadamize.
Makel [mah'kel] nm. (-) stain,

blemish, defect; **-los** a. spotless, immaculate.

Mäkelei [make-er-lie'] nf. fault-finding, backbiting.

Mäkel'ig [make'er-lish] a. censorious, fastidious; **-n** vi. to find fault.

Makkaroni [ma-ka-roh'ni] pl. maccaroni.

Makler [mah'klerr] nm. (-) broker, jobber; **-gebühr** nf. brokerage.

Mäkler [make'lerr] nm. faultfinder, broker.

Makrele [ma-kray'ler] nf. mackerel. [macaroon.

Makrone [ma-kroh'ner] nf.

Makulatur [ma-kōō-la-tōōr'] nf. waste-paper.

Mal [mahl] n. (-e) mark, sign, start, monument, boundary; time; ad. once, just.

Malen [mah'len] vt. to paint.

Maler [mah'lerr] nm. (-) painter, artist; **-ei** nf. painting; **-isch** a. picturesque.

Malkasten [mahl'kas-ten] nm. (-) paint-box.

Malve [mal'ver] nf. mallow.

Malz [malts] n. (-e) malt; **-bonbon** n. cough-drop; **-en** vt. to malt.

Mälzer [melt'serr] nm. (-) maltster.

Mama [ma-mah'] nf. (-s) mamma. [mammoth.

Mammut [ma'mōōt] nm. (-s)

Mamsell [mam'zel] nf. shopgirl, housekeeper, miss.

Man [man] pn. one, people.

Manch [mansh] a, pn. many a; **-erlei** a. various, sundry; **-mal** ad. sometimes.

Manchester [man'tches-terr] nm. (-) corduroy.

Mandant [man-dant'] m.w. client (law). [mandate.

Mandat [man-daht'] n. (-e)

Mandarine [man-dar-ree'ner] nf. mandarine, tangerine.

Mandel [man'del] nf. almond, tonsil.

Mandoline [man-do-lee'ner] nf. mandoline.

Mangan [mang-gahn'] n. manganese.

Mangel [mang'el] nf. mangle; **-n** vt. to mangle.

Mangel [mang'el] nm. (Mängel) want, lack, need, shortage, defect, fault; **-haft** a. defective, faulty; **-haftigkeit** nf. defectiveness; **-n** vi. impr. to want, lack.

Manie [ma-nee'] nf. mania, enthusiasm.

Manier [ma-neerr'] nf. manner, mannerism, style; **-t** a. affected; **-lich** a. mannerly, good mannered.

Manifest [ma-ni-fest'] n. (-e) manifesto.

Maniküre [ma-ni-kyōōr'rer] nf. manicure; **-n** vt. to manicure.

Manko [mang'ko] n. (-e) deficit, deficiency (com.).

Mann [man] nm. (Männer) man, husband; **-bar** a. marriageable; **-eskraft** nf. virility; **-haft** a. manly; **-haftigkeit** nf. manliness; **-heit** nf. manhood, virility; **-schaft** nf. crew (nav.), team (games), air-crew (av.), other ranks (mil.); **-sleute** pl. menfolk; **-weib** n. virago.

Männchen [men'shen] n. (-) male, little man.

Männlich [men'lish] a. male, masculine.

Mannigfalt [ma'nish-faltish] a. varied, various; **-keit** nf. variety.

Manöver [ma-ner'verr] n. (-) manoeuvres.

Manövrier'en [ma-ner-vreer'ren] vt. to manoeuvre; **-unfähig** a. disabled (ship). [attic.

Mansarde [man-zarr'der] nf.

Manschen [man'shen] vi. to splash about.

Manschette [man-shet'er] nf. cuff; **-nknopf** nm. cuff-link.

Mantel [man'tel] nm. (Mäntel)

mantle, cloak, coat, cover (tyre), case (bomb); -sack nm. valise.

Manufaktur [ma-nōō-fak-tōōr'] nf. manufacture, factory; -waren f.pl. manufactured articles.

Manuskript [ma-nōō-skript'] n. (-e) manuscript.

Mappe [map'e] nf. brief-case, portfolio, file.

Märchen [mairr'shen] n. (-) fairy-tale; -haft a. fabulous.

Marder [marr'derr] nm. (-) marten.

Margarine [marr-ga-ree'ner] nf. margarine.

Marienkäfer [ma-ree'en-kay-ferr] nf. lady-bird.

Marine [ma-ree'ner] nf. navy, marine; -flieger nm. naval airman; -flugzeug n. sea-plane; -flugwesen n. naval aviation; -leitung nf. admiralty; -stosstrupp n. naval landing party; -zahlmeister nm. paymaster (nav.).

Marinieren [ma-ri-neer'en] vt. to pickle.

Marionette [mar-ri-o-net'ter] nf. puppet, marionette; -nspiel n. puppet-show; -ntheater n. marionette theatre.

Mark [marrk] nf. frontier, march; -graf m.w. margrave; -stein nm. boundary stone, landmark.

Mark [marrk] nf. (-) mark (coin).

Mark [marrk] n. marrow; -ig a. pithy.

Markant [marr-kant'] a. striking, well marked.

Marke [marr'ker] nf. (trade) mark, stamp, quality, brand; -nartikel nm. proprietary article.

Marketender [marr-ket-en'derr] nm. (-) canteen man; -ei nf. canteen shop.

Markieren [marr-keer'en] vt. to mark.

Markise [marr-kee'zer] nf. awning, sun-blind.

Markt [marrkt] nm. (Märkte) market; -bude nf. stall; -flecken nm. small market-town; -gängig a. marketable, current; -halle nf. covered market; -platz nm. market-place; -schreier nm. charlatan, showman; -schreierisch a. sensational, showy.

Markten [marrk'ten] vi. to haggle, bargain.

Marmelade [marr-mer-lah'der] nf. jam.

Marmor [marr'more] nm. marble; -bild n. marble statue; -ieren vt. to marble, grain; -n a. marble; -platte nf. marble slab.

Marode [mar-roh'der] a. tired, fagged.

Marod'eur [mar-ro-derr'] nm. (-e) marauder; -ieren vi. to maraud.

Marone [mar-roh'ner] nf. sweet chestnut.

Marotte [mar-rot'er] nf. fancy, whim, hobby. (ship).

Mars [marrss] nm. (-en) top

Marsch [marrsh] nm. (Märsche) march, journey; -befehl nm. marching orders; -bereitschaft nf. readiness to march; -disposition nf. lateral disposition; -decke nf. army blanket; -fahrt nf. journey; -folge nf. order of march; -formation nf. marching formation; -gepäck n. marching kit; -mässig a. in marching order; -tiefe nf. dispersal in depth.

Marsch [marrsh] nf. marsh; -ig a. marshy, boggy.

Marschall [marr'shal] nm. (Marschälle) marshal.

Marschieren [marr-sheer'en] vi. to march.

Marter [marr'terr] nf. torture, agony; -bank nf. rack; -n vt. to torture.

Märtyrer [mairr'tyōōr-rerr]

nm. (-) martyr; -tod nm, -tum n. martyrdom.

März [mairts] nm. (-e) March.

Marzipan [marr-tsi-pahn'] nm. (-e) marzipan.

Masche [mash'er] nf. mesh, stitch; -ndraht nm. wire-netting; -nwerk n. network.

Maschine [ma-shee'ner] nf. machine, engine; -ll a. mechanical; -nbauer nm. mechanical engineer; -ngarn n. twist; -ngefreite(r) nm. stoker (nav.); -ngewehr n. machine gun; -nkanone nf. rapid fire gun; -nmeister nm. master mechanic, engine-driver; -npistole nf. automatic pistol, submachine gun, tommy-gun; -nraum nm. engine-room; -nschaden nm. engine trouble; -nschreiber nf. typist; -nschrift nf. typescript; -ntechniker nm. mechanical engineer.

Maschiner'ie [ma-shee-ner-ree'] nf. machinery; -ist m.w. mechanic, engineer, artificer (nav.).

Maser [mah'zerr] nf. spot, speckle; -ig a. speckled, streaked, grained; -n pl. measles.

Maske [mas'ker] nf. mask; -nanzug nm. fancy dress; -nball nm. fancy dress ball; -rade nf. masquerade.

Maskieren [mas-keer'ren] vt. to mask.

Mass [mahss] n. measure, moderation, degree, extent; -arbeit nf. clothing made to measure; -gabe nf. standard; -gebend a. authoritative; -halten vi. tr. to keep within bounds; -los a. immoderate; -nahme nf, -regel nf. measure, precaution, step; -schneider nm. bespoke tailor; -stab nm. measure, scale; -voll a. moderate, measured.

Mass [mahss] nf. litre; -krug nm. mug, tankard. [massage.

Massage [mass-ah'zher] nf.

Masse [mass'er] nf. mass, bulk, estate, assets; -nabwurf nm, -nartikel nm. staple goods; -nbeschuss nm. concentrated fire; -ngrab n. common grave; -nhaft a. wholesale, enormous; -nherstellung nf. mass production; -nverkauf nm. selling wholesale; -nversammlung nf. mass meeting.

Masseu'r [mass-err'] nm. (-e) masseur; -se nf. masseuse.

Massieren [mass-eer'ren] vt. to massage.

Mässig [may'sish] a. moderate, frugal; -en vt. to restrain, moderate; -keit nf. temperance, moderation.

Massiv [mass-eef'] a. massive, solid.

Massliebchen [mahss'leep-shen] n. (-) daisy.

Mast [mast] nm. (gen. -es; pl. -en) mast, pylon (el.).

Mast [mast] nf. mast, pig food; -kalb n. fatted calf.

Mästen [mest'en] vt. to fatten.

Mastix [mast'ix] nm. mastic, gum, resin.

Material [ma-ter-i-ahl'] n. (gen. -s; pl. -ien) material, stock; -sammelstelle nf. salvage dump; -waren f.pl. groceries.

Materialis'mus [ma-ter-i-al-is'mööss] nm. materialism; -t m.w. materialist; -tisch a. materialistic.

Materie [ma-tair'yer] nf. matter, substance.

Materiell [ma-ter-ri-el'] a. material.

Mathematik [ma-tem-a-teek'] nf. mathematics.

Mathemati'ker [ma-tem-ah'ti-kerr] nm. (-) mathematician; -sch a. mathematical.

Matratze [ma-trat'ser] nf. mattress. [mistress.

Mätresse [mate-ress'er] nf.

Matrikel [mat-ree'kel] nf. register, list, roll.

Matritze [mat-rit'ser] *nf.* matrix.

Matrose [mat-rose'er] *m.w.* sailor; **-ngefreite(r)** *m.w.* leading seaman (*nav.*).

Matsch [match] *nm.* slush; **-ig** *a.* muddy.

Matt [mat] *a.* weary, faint, dim, mat, mate (*chess*); **-glas** *n.* frosted glass; **-heit** *nf.* dimness, dullness; **-herzig** *a.* faint-hearted; **-igkeit** *nf.* faintness, feebleness, weakness; **-scheibe** *nf.* focusing screen, ground glass screen.

Matte [mat'er] *nf.* mat.

Mauer [mow'err] *nf.* wall; **-brecher** *nm.* battering ram; **-schwalbe** *nf.* swift; **-werk** *n.* masonry, stonework, brickwork; **-ziegel** *nm.* brick.

Mauer'n [mow'errn] *vi.* to build, make a wall; **-ung** *nf.* walling, building.

Maul [mowl] *n.* (**Mäuler**) mouth; **-korb** *nm.* muzzle; **-schelle** *nf.* box on the ear; **-sperre** *nf.* lock-jaw.

Maulbeere [mowl'bair-rer] *nf.* mulberry.

Maulesel [mowl'ay-zel] *nm.* (**-**), **Maultier** [mowl'teerr] *n.* (**-e**) mule.

Maulwurf [mowl'vöorrf] *nm.* (**-würfe**) mole; **-sfell** *n.* moleskin; **-shaufen** *nm.* **-shügel** *nm.* mole-hill.

Maurer [mow'rerr] *nm.* (**-**) mason, bricklayer; **-meister** *nm.* master mason.

Maus [mowss] *nf.* (**Mäuse**) mouse; **-efalle** *nf.* mousetrap; **-etot** *a.* stone-dead.

Mausen [mow'zen] *vt.* to steal; *i.* catch mice.

Mäuschenstill [moyss'-shenshtil] *a.* quiet as a mouse.

Mauser [mow'zerr] *nf.* moulting; **-n** *vi.* to moult.

Maximal [max-i-mahl'] *a.* maximum; **-betrag** *nm.* maxi-

mum amount; **-gewicht** *n.* maximum weight.

Maxime [max-ee'mer] *nf.* maxim.

Mechani'k [mesh-ah'nik] *nf.* mechanics, mechanism; **-ker** *nm.* mechanic, engineer; **-sch** *a.* mechanical, automatic.

Mechani'sieren [mesh-a-ni-zeer'ren] *vt.* to mechanize; **-smus** *nm.* mechanism.

Meckern [mek'errn] *vi.* to bleat, grumble.

Medaill'e [med-al'yer] *nf.* medal; **-on** *n.* medallion, locket.

Medikament [med-i-ka-ment'] *n.* (**-e**) medicine.

Meditieren [med-i-teer'ren] *vi.* to meditate.

Medizin [med-it-seen'] *nf.* medicine; **-er** *nm.* medical man, student; **-isch** *a.* medical, medicinal.

Meer [mare] *n.* (**-e**) sea; **-busen** *nm.* bay, gulf; **-enge** *nf.* straits; **-esspiegel** *nm.* sea-level; **-esstrand** *nm.* beach; **-rettich** *nm.* horse-radish; **-schweinchen** *n.* guinea pig. [(**-e**) megaphone.

Megaphon [me-ga-fone'] *n.*

Mehl [male] *n.* (**-e**) flour, meal; **-ig** *a.* floury; **-kloss** *nm.* dumpling; **-speise** *nf.* pudding; **-suppe** *nf.* gruel.

Mehr [mare] *a., ad.* more; **-aufwand** *nm.* **-ausgabe** *nf.* additional expenditure; **-besteuerung** *nf.* additional taxation; **-deutig** *a.* ambiguous; **-einkommensteuer** *nf.* super-tax; **-erzeugung** *nf.* over-production; **-fach** *a.* repeated, manifold; **-heit** *nf.* majority; **-malig** *a.* repeated; **-mals** *ad.* again and again, repeatedly; **-silbig** *a.* polysyllabic; **-stimmig** *a.* for several voices; **-zahl** *nf.* majority, plural; **-zweckflugzeug** *n.* multi-purpose plane.

Mehren [mare'en] *vt.i.* to increase, multiply, grow.

Mehrere [mare'er-rer] *a. pl.*
several.

Meiden [mide'en] *vt. ir.* to
avoid.

Meier [my'err] *nm.* (-) farmer,
bailiff, steward; -ei *nf.,* -hof
nm. farmhouse.

Meile [mile'er] *nf.* mile, league;
-nzeiger *nm.* milestone; -nweit
a. for miles.

Mein [mine] *a.* my, mine;
-erseits *ad.* for my part; -es-
gleichen *pn.* my equals, people
like me; -ethalben, -etwegen
ad. for my sake, for all I care,
as far as I am concerned; -
etwillen *ad.* for my sake.

Meinige [mine'i-ger] (der, die,
das) *poss.* mine.

Meineid [mine'ite] *nm.* (-e)
perjury; -ig *a.* perjured.

Mein'en [mine'en] *vt.i.* to
mean, think, intend; -ung *nf.*
opinion, intention.

Meise [mize'er] *nf.* titmouse.

Meissel [mice'el] *nm.* (-)
chisel; -n *vt.* to chisel.

Meist [mist] *a.* most; -begün-
gungsklausel *nf.* most
favoured nation clause; -ens
ad. mostly, generally; -gebot
n. highest bid.

Meister [mice'terr] *nm.* (-)
master; -haft *a.* masterly;
-schaft *nf.* mastery, champion-
ship; -singer *nm.* master-
singer; -stück, -werk *n.* master-
piece.   [master.

Meistern [mice'terrn] *vt.* to

Melancholie [mel-lan-shol-
lee'] *nf.* melancholy; -sch *a.*
melancholy.

Meld'en [mel'den] *vt.* to announce, report; *r.* apply,
report; -ung *nf.* notice, report,
return, message.

Melde-abwurf *nm.* message
dropping (*av.*); -amt *n.* registration office; -block *n.*
message pad; -gänger *nm.*
messenger, runner; -reiter *nm.*
dispatch rider; -sammelstelle
nf. signal centre; -stelle

reporting centre (*mil.*); -zettel
nm. registration form; -zug
nm. dispatch platoon (*mil.*).

Meliert [may-leert'] *a.* grey.

Melken [mel'ken] *vt.* to milk.

Melkerei [mel-ker-rie'] *nf.*
dairy-farm.

Melodie [me-lo-dee'] *nf.* tune,
melody; -sch *a.* melodious,
tuneful.

Melone [me-loh'ner] *nf.* melon,
bowler hat.

Meltau [male'tow] *nm.* mildew.

Membran [mem-brahn'] *nf.*
membrane, diaphragm.

Memme [mem'er] *nf.* coward.

Memoiren [mem-o-ahr'ren]
n.pl. memoirs

Memorieren [mem-o-reer'ren]
vt. to commit to memory.

Menage [me-nah'zher] *nf.*
household, cruet, set of dishes.

Menagieren [me-na-zheer'en]
vt. to husband.

Menge [meng'er] *nf.* crowd,
quantity, lot.

Mengen [meng'en] *vt.* to mix,
mingle; *r.* meddle with.   [lead.

Mennig [men'ish] *nm.* red

Mensch [mensh] *m.w.* man,
human being; *n.* hussy, wench;
-enalter *n.* generation, age;
-enfeind *nm.* misanthrope;
-enfreundlich *a.* philanthropic-
al; -engedenken *n.* human
memory; -engeschlecht *n.*
human race; -engedenken *n.*
human memory; -enliebe
nf. philanthropy; -enmöglich
a. humanly possible; -enseele
nf. human soul; -enschlag *nm.*
breed, race; -heit *nf.* humanity, mankind; -lich *a.* human,
humane; -lichkeit *n.* humane-
ness, humanity.

Mensur [men-zōōrr'] *nf.*
students' duel, fencing-ground.

Mentalität [men-ta-li-tate']
nf. mentality.   [minuet.

Menuett [men-ŏŏ-et'] *n.* (-e)

Mergel [mairr'gel] *nm.* marl.

Merk'bar [mairrk'barr] *a.*

-lich *a.* noticeable; -blatt *n.* memorandum, leaflet; -mal *n.* sign, characteristic; -zeichen *n.* sign, mark.

Merken [mairr'ken] *vt.* to notice, observe.

Merkwürdig [mairk'vyöorr-dish] *a.* remarkable, strange, curious; -erweise *ad.* strange to say; -keit *nf.* strangeness, curiosity.

Merkur [merr-kōorr'] *nf.* mercury. [sacristan.]

Mesner [mess'nerr] *nm.*

Mess'bar [mess'barr] *a.* measurable; -dienst *nm.* radar service; -flug *nm.* calibration flight (*av.*); -funker *nm.* radar operator; -gerät *n.* surveying equipment; -mann *nm.* radar operator; -stelle *n.* observation post, radar station, site (*av.*); -tisch *nm.* plane table; -tischblatt *n.* ordnance map; -trupp *nm.* surveying section (*mil.*).

Mess'buch [mess'bōoch] *n.* (-bücher) missal; -gewand *n.* chasuble.

Messe [mess'er] *nf.* mass, fair, mess (*mil.*).

Messen [mess'en] *vt. ir.* to measure, survey; *r.* compete with.

Messer [mess'err] *n.* (-) knife; -bänkchen *n.* knife-rest; -schmied *nm.* cutler; -waren *f.pl.* cutlery.

Messing [mess'ing] *n.* brass.

Metall [met-al'] *n.* (-e) metal; -arbeiter *nm.* metal-worker; -en, -isch *a.* metallic.

Meteor [may-tay-ohrr'] *n.* (-e) meteor.

Meter [may'terr] *m.n.* (-) metre; -mass *n.* tape-measure.

Method'e [met-oh'der] *nf.* method; -isch *a.* methodical.

Metri'k [may'trik] *nf.* versification; -sch *a.* metrical.

Metropole [met-ro-poh'ler] *nf.* metropolis.

Metze [met'ser] *nf.* street-walker.

Metzel'ei [met-sel-ei'] *nf.* massacre, butchery; -n *vt.* to massacre.

Metzger [mets'gerr] *nm.* (-) butcher; -ei *nf.* butcher's shop.

Meuchel'mord [moy'shel-morrt] *nm.* assassination, murder; -mörder *nm.* assassin.

Meuch'lerisch [moish'ler-rish], -lings *a. ad.* treacherous(ly).

Meute [moy'ter] *nf.* pack.

Meuter'ei [moy-ter-rie'] *nf.* mutiny; -er *nm.* mutineer; -isch *a.* mutinous; -n *vi.* to mutiny.

Miauen [mi-ow'en] *vi.* to mew.

Mieder [mee'derr] *n.* (-) bodice.

Miene [meen'er] *nf.* mien, air; -nspiel *n.* play of features.

Miesmacher [meess'mach-err] *nm.* (-) alarmist.

Miesmuschel [meess'mōo-shel] *nf.* mussel.

Miete [mee'ter] *nf.* stack.

Miet'e [mee'ter] *nf.* rent(ing), hire; -auto *n.* taxi; -en *vt.* to rent, hire, charter (*ship*); -er *nm.* tenant, lodger; -frei *a.* rent-free; -ling *nm.* mercenary; -vertrag *nm.* lease; -zins *nm.* rent.

Migräne [mee-grane'er] *nf.* migraine. [microbe.]

Mikrobe [mee-kroh'ber] *nf.*

Mikrophon [mee-kro-fone'] *n.* (-e) microphone.

Mikroskop [mee-kro-skope'] *n.* (-e) microscope; -isch *a.* microscopic.

Milbe [mil'ber] *nf.* mite.

Milch [milsh] *nf.* milk, milt, roe; -entrahmer *nm.* separator; -glas *n.* frosted glass; -ig *a.* milky; -säure *nf.* lactic acid; -zucker *nm.* lactose.

Milchen [milsh'en] *vi.* to yield milk.

Mild [milt] *a.* mild, gentle,

kind, charitable; -e nf. mildness, gentleness; -ern vt. to soften, alleviate; -erung f. to alleviation, softening; -tätig a. charitable; -tätigkeit nf. charity.

Milieu [mee-lyer'] n. (-s) background, environment.

Militär [mi-li-tare'] nm. (-s) military man, soldier; n. military, army; -arzt nm. army surgeon; -befehlshaber nm. military commander; -behörde nf. military authorities; -dienst nm. active, military service; -gericht n. military court; -isch a. military; -kapelle, -musik nf. military band; -pflichtig a. liable to military service; -tauglich a. fit for service.

Militarismus [mi-li-tar-riss'moōss] nm. militarism.

Miliz [mi-leets'] nf. militia.

Milliarde [mil-yarr'der] nf. milliard, thousand million.

Million [mil-yohn'] nf. million; -är nm. millionaire.

Milz [milts] nf. spleen; -brand nm. anthrax.

Mimik [mee'mik] nf. mimicry, acting. [mimosa.

Mimose [mee-moh'zer] nf.

Minder [min'derr] a. less, inferior; -betrag nm. deficit; -heit nf. minority; -jährig a. minor; -jährigkeit nf. minority; -wertig a. inferior; -zahl nf. minority.

Minder'n [min'derrn] vt. to diminish, decrease; -ung nf. decrease.

Mindest [min'dest] a. least; -betrag nm. minimum amount; -ens ad. at least; -lohn nm. minimum wage; -mass n. indispensable minimum; -preis nm. minimum price.

Mine [mee'ner] nf. mine; -nfeld n. mine-field; -nhülle nf. canister bomb; -nkarte nf. mine-chart; -nleger nm. mine-layer (tank); -nlegschiff n.

mine-layer (ship); -nräumboot n. minesweeper; -nräumgerät n. paravane; -nsperre nf. minefield; -nsuchboot n. -nsucher nm. mine-sweeper; -nsuchgerät n. mine-sweeping gear; -ntrichter nm. mine crater; -nverseucht a. mined, infested with mines; -nwerfer nm. trench mortar.

Mineral [mi-ner-rahl'] n. (-ien) mineral; -isch a. mineral; -wasser n. mineral water.

Miniatur [mi-ni-a-toörr'] nf. miniature.

Minier'en [mi-neer'nen] vt. to undermine; -er nm. sapper.

Minimalbetrag [mi-ni-mahl'-ber-trahk] nm. minimum amount.

Minister [mi-ni'sterr] nm. (-) minister; -präsident m.w. prime minister; -rat nm. cabinet; -ium n. ministry.

Ministeriell [mi-nis-ter-ri-el'] a. ministerial, cabinet.

Minus [mee'nōōss] ad. minus; n. deficit; -betrag nm. shortage, deficiency.

Minute [mi-nōō'ter] nf. minute; -nzeiger nm. minute hand.

Minze [mint'ser] nf. mint.

Mir [mirr] pr. to me, me.

Mirakel [mi-rah'kel] n. (-) miracle.

Misch'en [mish'en] vt. to mix; -ehe nf. mixed marriage; -ling nm. mongrel, cross; -ung nf. mixture, blend.

Missacht'en [miss-ach'ten] vt. to disregard; -ung nf. disregard.

Missbehagen [miss'ber-hah-gen] n. displeasure, discomfort.

Missbild'en [miss'bil-den] vt. to mis-shape; -ung nf. deformity, disfigurement.

Missbilligen [miss-bil'i-gen] vt. to disapprove.

Missbilligung [miss'bil'i-goong] nf. disapproval.

Missbrauch [miss'browch] nm. (-bräuche) misuse, abuse.

Miss'brauchen [miss-brow'chen] vt. to misuse, abuse; -bräuchlich a. improper, wrong.

Missdeuten [miss-doy'ten] vt. to misinterpret.

Missdeutung [miss'doy-tōong] nf. misinterpretation.

Missen [miss'en] vt. to miss, lack, do without.

Misserfolg [miss'airr-folk] nm. (-e) failure.

Missernte [miss'airrn-ter] nf. bad harvest.

Misse'tat [miss'er-taht] nf. misdeed; -täter nm. malefactor, criminal.

Miss'fallen [miss'fal'en] vi. ir. to displease; -fällig a. displeasing, disparaging.

Missgeburt [miss'ger-bōōrt] nf. abortion, monster.

Missgeschick [miss'ger-shik] n. (-e) misfortune.

Missgestalt [miss'ger-shtalt] nf. see Missgeburt; -et a. misshapen, deformed.

Missglücken [miss-glyōō'ken] vi. to fail, not come off.

Missgönnen [miss-ger'nen] vt. to begrudge.

Missgriff [miss'grif] nm. (-e) mistake, failure.

Missgunst [miss'gōōnst] nf. ill will, envy.

Misshandeln [miss-han'deln] vt. to ill-treat; -lung nf. ill treatment.

Missheirat [miss'hy-raht] nf. ill-assorted match.

Misshellig [miss'hell-ish] a. discordant; -keit nf. variance, disagreement.

Misshören [miss-her'en] vt. to mishear.

Mission [mi-syohn'] nf. mission; -ar nm. (-e) missionary.

Missklang [miss'klang] nm. (-klänge) discord.

Misskredit [miss'kre-deet] nm. discredit.

Misslich [miss'lish] a. awkward, unpleasant, difficult; -keit nf. awkwardness, difficulty, doubtfulness.

Missling'en [miss-ling'en] vi. ir. to fail; n. failure.

Missmut [miss'mōōt] n. bad temper; -ig a. bad tempered.

Missraten [miss-rah'ten] vi. ir. to turn out badly; a. ill bred.

Miss-stimmung [miss'shtim-ōōng] nf. depression, ill humour.

Misstönend [miss'ter-nent] a. discordant.

Misstrau'en [miss'trow-en] vt. mistrust, suspicion; n. distrust; -isch a. distrustful, suspicious.

Missvergnüg'en [miss'fer-gnyōō-gen] n. displeasure; -t a. displeased.

Missverhältnis [miss'fer-helt-nis] n. (-se) disproportion.

Missverständnis [miss'fer-shtent-nis] n. misunderstanding.

Missverstehen [miss'fer-shtay-en] vt. ir. to misunderstand.

Missweisung [miss'vize-ōōng] nf. aberration (compass).

Mist [mist] nm. dung, dirt; -en vt. to manure, clean (stables); -haufen nm. dunghill.

Mistel [mis'tel] nf. mistletoe.

Mit [mit] pr. with, at, by; ad. also, along (with).

Mitarbeite'n [mit'arr-bite-en] vi. to work with, collaborate, co-operate; -r nm. (-) collaborator, fellow-worker.

Mitbesitzer [mit'ber-zit-ser] nm. (-) joint owner.

Mitbewerber [mit'ber-vairr-ber] nm. (-) competitor, rival.

Mitbewohner [mit'ber-vone-er] nm. (-) fellow lodger.

Mitbürger [mit'byōōrr-ger] nm. (-) fellow citizen.

Miteinander [mit'ine-an-derr] ad. together, with one another.

Mitempfinden [mit'emp-fin-den] n. sympathy.

Miterb'e [mit'airr-ber] m.w. coheir; **-in** nf. coheiress.

Mitgeben [mit'gay-ben] vt. ir. to give (as dowry).

Mitgefühl [mit'ger-fyōōl] n. fellow feeling, sympathy.

Mitgehen [mit'gay-en] vi. ir. to go along with.

Mitgift [mit'gift] nf. dowry.

Mitglied [mit'gleet] n. (-er) member.   [assistance.

Mithilfe [mit'hil-fer] nf. help.

Mithin [mit-hin'] ad. there-fore, consequently.

Mithör'en [mit'her-ren] vi. to monitor, tap wires (rad.); **-dienst** nm. monitoring.

Mitkämpfer [mit'kemp-fer] nm. (-) comrade in arms.

Mitkläger [mit'klay-ger] nm. (-) co-plaintiff.

Mitkommen [mit'kom-en] vi. ir. to come along, keep up with.

Mitkriegführ'ende(r) [mit'-kreek-fyōōr-ren-der] m.w. co-belligerent; **-ung** nf. co-belligerency.

Mitläufer [mit'loy-fer] nm. time-server.

Mitleid [mit'lite] n. pity, sympathy; **-ig** a. compassion-ate, sympathetic; **-slos** a. piti-less, unmerciful.

Mitmachen [mit'mach-en] vt. to join in, take part in.

Mitmensch [mit'mensh] m.w. fellow man.

Mitnehmen [mit'name-en] vt. ir. to take with, away, wear out, exhaust.

Mitrechnen [mit'resh-nen] vt. to count in.

Mitreisen [mit'rise-en] vi. to travel with, together.

Mitsamt [mit-zamt'] ad. to-gether with.

Mitschuld [mit'shōōlt] nf. complicity; **-ig** a. implicated in crime; **-ige(r)** m.w. ac-complice.

Mitschüler [mit'shyōō-ler] nm. (-) schoolfellow.

Mitspiele'n [mit'shpee-len] vi. to join in, take part in, accompany; **-r** nm. partner.

Mittäter [mit'tate-er] nm. (-) accomplice.

Mittag [mi'tahk] nm. (-e) mid-day, noon; **-essen** n. lunch, dinner; **-s** ad. at noon; **-spause** nf. lunch, dinner hour.

Mitte [mi'ter] nf. middle, mean.

Mitteil'en [mit'tile-en] vt. to communicate, inform, intim-ate; **-sam** a. communicative; **-ung** nf. communication, in-formation, memorandum, message.

Mittel [mitl] n. (-) means, mean, average, remedy, ex-pedient; **-alter** n. Middle Ages; **-alterlich** a. mediaeval; **-bar** a. indirect; ad. indirectly; **-ernte** nf. medium crop; **-gewicht** n. middle weight; **-grösse** nf. medium size; **-los** a. without means; **-mässig** a. mediocre, middling; **-mässigkeit** nf. mediocrity; **-punkt** nm. centre; **-smann** nm. middleman, go-between; **-stand** nm. middle class; **-stelle** nf. central agency; **-stürmer** nm. centre forward; **-weg** nm. golden mean; **-welle** nf. medium wave (rad.); **-wert** nm. average value, mean.

Mittels [mit'els] pr. by means of.

Mitten [mit'en] ad. in the middle of.

Mitternacht [mit'er-nacht] nf. midnight; **-s** ad. at mid-night.

Mitternächtlich [mit'er-nesht-lish] a. midnight.

Mittler [mit'ler] nm. (-) mediator.

Mittlerweile [mit'ler-vile-er] ad. meanwhile.

Mittschiffs [mit'shifs] ad. amidships.

Mittwoch [mit'voch] *nm.* (-e) Wednesday; **-s** *ad.* on Wednesdays.

Mitunter [mit-ŏŏn'ter] *ad.* occasionally, sometimes.

Mitverschulden [mit'fer-shŏŏl-den] *n.* contributory negligence.

Mitwelt [mit'velt] *nf.* the present age, contemporary world.

Mitwirk'en [mit'virr'ken] *vi.* to co-operate, take part in; **-ung** *nf.* co-operation, help.

Mitwiss'en [mit'viss-en] *n.* knowledge; **-er** *nm.* (-) accessory; **-erschaft** *nf.* complicity.

Mitzählen [mit'tsay-len] *vi.* to be reckoned in, count.

Mixtur [mix-tŏŏrr'] *nf.* mixture.

Möbel [mer'bel] *n.* (-) (piece of) furniture; **-tischler** *nm.* cabinet-maker; **-wagen** *nm.* furniture, removal van.

Mobil [mo-beel'] *a.* mobile, active, mobilized; **-machung** *nf.* mobilization.

Mobiliar [mo-bi-liahrr'] *n.* furniture.

Mobilisation [mo-bil-i-zat-syōn'] *nf.* mobilization.

Mobilisier'en [mo-bil-i-zeerr'] *vt.* to mobilize; **-ung** *nf.* mobilization.

Möbilieren [mer-bleer'ren] *vt.* to furnish.

Mode [moh'der] *nf.* fashion, mode; **-artikel** *m.pl.* fancy goods; **-wort** *n.* fashionable word, slogan; **-zeitung** *nf.* fashion magazine.

Modell [mo-del'] *n.* (-e) model, pattern; **-ieren** *vt.* to model.

Modeln [moh'deln] *vt.* to mould, fashion.

Moder [moh'derr] *nm.* mould, mud; **-geruch** *nm.* mouldy smell; **-ig** *a.* musty, putrid, mouldy; **-n** *vi.* to moulder, decay.

Modern [mo-dairrn'] *a.*

modern, up-to-date, recent, fashionable.

Modifizieren [mo-d-fit-seerren] *vt.* to modify; **-able**.

Modisch [moh'dish] *a.* fashionable.

Modistin [mo-dis'tin] *nf.* milliner.

Modulieren [mo-dŏŏ-leer'en] *vt.* to modulate.

Mögen [mer'gen] *vt.i. ir.* to like, be able, care to.

Möglich [merk'lish] *a.* possible; **-enfalls** *ad.* if possible; **-erweise** *ad.* possibly; **-keit** *nf.* possibility.

Mohn [mone] *nm.* (-e) poppy.

Möhre [mer'rer] *nf.* carrot.

Molch [molsh] *nm.* (-e) salamander.

Mole [moh'ler] *nf.* (harbour) **-mole**.

Molekül [mo-le-kyōōl'] *n.* molecule; *nf.* dairy.

Molke [mol'ker] *nf.* whey; **-rei** *nf.* dairy.

Moll [mol] *n.* minor (key).

Mollig [mo'lish] *a.* cosy, soft.

Molluske [mo-lŏŏs'ker] *nf.* mollusc.

Moment [mo-ment'] *nm.* (-e) moment; *n.* momentum, impetus, element; **-aufnahme** *nf.* snapshot.

Momentan [mo-men-tahn'] *a.* momentary; *ad.* at the moment.

Monarch [mo-narsh'] *m.w.* monarch; **-ie** *nf.* monarchy; **-isch** *a.* monarchical.

Monat [moh'nat] *nm.* (-e) month; **-lich** *a.* monthly; **-sbinde** *nf.* sanitary towel; **-skarte** *nf.* monthly ticket; **-sschrift** *nf.* monthly magazine.

Mönch [mernsh] *m.w.* monk; **-isch** *a.* monastic.

Mond [mohnt] *nm.* (-e) moon; **-finsternis** *nf.* eclipse of the moon; **-hell** *a.* moonlit; **-schein** *nm.* moonlight.

Monokel [mo-nokl'] *n.* (-) monocle.

Monolog [mo-no-lohk'] *nm.* (-e) monologue.

Monopol [mo-no-pohl'] n. (-e) monopoly; **-isieren** vt. to monopolize.

Monoton [mo-no-tohn'] a. monotonous; **-ie** nf. monotony.

Monsun [mon-zuhn'] nm. (-e) monsoon.

Montag [mohn'tahk] nm. (-e) Monday; **-s** ad. on Mondays.

Montage [mon-tah'zher] nf. fitting, erection, assembly (tec.); **-fliessband** n. assembly line; **-halle** nf. assembly shop (tec.).

Montan'industrie [mon-tahn'in-dōō-stree'] nf. mining industry; **-werte** m.pl. mining shares.

Monteur [mon-terr'] nm. (-e) fitter, rigger, mechanic.

Montier'en [mon-teer'ren] vt. to assemble, erect, fit, equip (mil.); **-ung** nf. mounting, fitting, assembling, equipment.

Monument [mo-nōō-ment'] n. (-e) monument.

Moor [more] n. (-e) moor swamp, bog; **-ig** a. marshy; **-torf** nm. peat.

Moos [mohss] n. (-e) moss; **-bedeckt** a. moss-grown; **-ig** a. mossy.

Mops [mopes] nm. (Möpse) pug-dog, blockhead.

Moral [mo-rahl'] nf. morals, morality; **-isch** a. moral; **-isieren** vi. to moralize; **-ist** m.w. moralist; **-ität** nf. morality.

Moräne [mo-ray'ner] nf. [moraine.

Morast [mo-rast'] nm. (Moräste) morass, bog.

Moratorium [mo-ra-tor'ryōōm] n. (Moratorien) moratorium.

Mord [mort] nm. (-e) murder; **-anschlag** nm. attempted murder; **-brenner** nm. incendiary; **-smässig** a. awful, terrible; **-sspektakel** nm. hullabaloo.

Mörder [merr'derr] nm. (-)

murderer; **-in** nf. murdress; **-isch** a. murderous; **-lich** a. fearful, cruel.

Morgen [morr'gen] ad. tomorrow; **-- früh** to-morrow morning; n. following day; nm. (-) morning; **-anzug** nm. morning dress; **-ausgabe** nf. morning edition; **-dämmerung** nf. daybreak, dawn; dusk n. the East; **-ländisch** a. oriental; **-post** nf. first post; **-s** ad. in the morning.

Morphium [morr'fyōōm] n. morphine, morphia; **-einspritzung** nf. morphia injection.

Morsch [morrsh] a. rotten.

Morse'apparat [morr'zer-ap-ar-raht'] nm. (-e) Morse printer; **-n** vi. to transmit a Morse message; **-schrift** nf. Morse code; **-spruch** nm. Morse message.

Mörser [merr'zerr] nm. (-) mortar, heavy howitzer (mil.); **-keule** nf. pestle.

Mörtel nm. (-) mortar, cement plaster.

Moschee [mo-shay'] nf. [mosque.

Moschus [mo'shōōss] nm. musk; **-tier** n. musk-deer.

Moskito [mos-kee'to] nm. (-s) mosquito. [cider.

Most [most] nm. (-e) new wine,

Motiv [mo-teef'] n. (-e) motive, theme.

Motivier'en [mo-ti-veer'ren] vt. to assign reasons for, motivate; **-ung** nf. motivation.

Motor [mo-tore'] nm. (gen. -s; pl. -en) motor, engine; **-boot** n. motor-boat; **-defekt** nm. engine trouble; **-enhaus** n. power house; **-enschlosser** nm. engine fitter, mechanic; **-(fahr)rad** n. motor-cycle; **-tankschiff** n. tanker.

Motorisieren [mo-tor-ri-zeer'ren] vt. to motorize.

Motte [mot'er] nf. moth.

Moussieren [mōō-seer'ren] vi. to sparkle, effervesce.

Möwe [mer'ver] nf. sea-gull.
Mucke [mōō'ker] nf. caprice, whim, idea; **-n** vi. to move, stir, rebel; **-r** nm. hypocrite; **-ertum** n. bigotry.
Mücke [mück'er] nf. midge, gnat; **-nnetz** n. mosquito net; **-nschleier** nm. mosquito veil.
Mucksen [mōōk'sen] vi. to stir, budge.
Müd'e [myōō'der] a. tired; **-igkeit** nf. tiredness, weariness.
Muff [mōōf] nm. musty smell; **-ig** a. musty, mouldy, sulky.
Muff nm. (Müffe) muff.
Muffe [mōō'fer] nf. sleeve, joint, socket.
Muffel [mōō'fel] nf. muffle (tec.); **-ofen** nm. muffle-furnace.
Muffel n. (-) snout, spout, sulky person.
Mühe [myōō'er] nf. trouble, pains; **-los** a. without trouble, easy; **-n** vr. to take pains, trouble, put oneself about; **-voll** a. laborious, difficult.
Muhen [mōō'en] vi. to moo, low.
Mühl'e [myōō'ler] nf. mill; **-graben** nm. mill-race; **-rad** n. mill-wheel; **-stein** nm. mill-stone. [cousin.]
Muhme [mōō'mer] nf. aunt,
Müh'sal [myōō'zahl] n. (-e) toil, hardship, tribulation; **-sam** a. toilsome, troublesome, difficult; **-selig** a. hard, laborious.
Mul [mōōl] ad. clockwise.
Mulatte [mōō-lat'er] m.w, Mulatin nf. mulatto.
Mulde [mōōl'der] nf. trough, hollow, depression.
Müll [mōōl] nm. dust, rubbish; **-abfuhr** nf. rubbish disposal; **-eimer** nm. dust-bin; **-kasten** nm. dust-bin; **-wagen** nm. rubbish cart.
Müller [myōō'lerr] nm. (-) miller.
Mulmig [mōōl'mish] a. rotten.

Multiplizieren [mōōl-ti-plit-seer'ren] vt. to multiply.
Mumie [mōō'mi-er] nf. mummy.
Mummenspiel [mōō'men-shpeel] n. (-e) masquerade.
Mummerei [mōō-mer-ri'] nf. mummery, masquerade.
Mumpitz [mōōm'pits] nm. nonsense, bosh.
Mund [mōōnt] nm. (Münder) mouth, orifice; **-art** nf. dialect; **-faul** a. tongue-tied; **-harmonika** nf. mouth-organ; **-stück** n. mouthpiece, cigarette holder; **-vorrat** nm. provisions; **-wasser** n. mouth-wash, dentifrice; **-werk** n. glib tongue.
Mündel [myōōn'del] nm. (-) ward; **-sicher** a. gilt-edged.
Munden [mōōn'den] vi. to taste good.
Münd'en [myōōn'den] vi. to flow into; **-lich** a. oral; ad. orally; **-ung** nf. mouth, estuary, muzzle (gun).
Mündig [myōōn'dish] a. of age; **-keit** nf. majority.
Munition [mōō-nit-syohn'] nf. ammunition; **-skammer** nf. powder magazine; **-skampfrad** n. ammunition motor-cycle; **-slager** n. ammunition store; **-sstapelplatz** nm. ammunition dump.
Munkeln [mōōn'keln] vi. to mutter, whisper.
Münster [mōōn'sterr] n. (-) minster, cathedral.
Munter [mōōn'terr] a. lively, merry, gay; **-keit** nf. liveliness, gaiety.
Münz'e [myōōnt'ser] nf. coin, mint; **-einheit** nf. monetary standard; **-en** vt. to coin, mint; **-er** nm. coiner; **-fernsprecher** nm. telephone call-box; **-stempel** nm. die.
Mürbe [myōōrr'ber] a. soft, brittle, unnerved, rotten, short (pastry). [child's marble.]
Murmel [mōōrr'mel] nm. (-)
Murmeln [mōōrr'meln] vi. to murmur, mutter.

Murmeltier [moorr'mel-teerr] *n.* (-e) marmot.

Murren [moor'en] *vi.* to grumble, grouse.

Mürrisch [myoor'rish] *a.* morose, sullen.

Mus [mooss] *n.* stewed fruit, jam.

Muschel [moo'shel] *nf.* mussel, shell, telephone receiver.

Muse [moo'zer] *nf.* muse.

Museum [moo-zay'oom] *n.* (Museen) museum, art gallery.

Musik [moo-zeek'] *nf.* music, band; -alisch *a.* musical; -ant *m.w.* (itinerant) musician; -er *nm.* musician.

Musizieren [moo-zit-seer'ren] *vi.* to play.

Muskat [mooss-kaht'] *nm.* (-e) nutmeg.

Muskel [mooss'kel] *nm.* (gen. -s; pl. -n) muscle; -band *n.* ligament; -ig, -stark *a.* muscular.

Musket'e [mooss-kay'ter] *nf.* musket; -ier *nm.* (-e) musketeer.

Musse [moo'ser] *nf.* leisure.

Musselin [moo-ser-leen'] *nm.* (-e) muslin.

Müssen [myoo'sen] *vi. ir.* to have to, to be obliged, must.

Müssig [myoo'sish] *a.* idle; -gang *nm.* idleness; -gänger *nm.* (-) ler.

Muster [mooss'terr] *n.* (-) model, pattern, sample; -gültig, -haft *a.* model, exemplary; -klammer *nf.* paper fastener.

Muster'n [mooss'terrn] *vt.* to inspect, review, examine, figure; -ung *nf.* inspection, review.

Mut [moot] *nm.* courage; -ig *a.* brave; -los *a.* discouraged, despondent; -losigkeit *nf.* despondency.

Mutmass'en [moot'mah-sen] *vt.* to surmise, conjecture, *vt.* suppose; -lich *a.* probable; *ad.*

presumably; -ung *nf.* surmise, conjecture.

Mutter [moo'terr] *nf.* (Mütter) mother; -boden *nm.* native soil; -leib *nm.* womb; -liebe *nf.* motherly love; -mal *n.* birthmark; -schaft *nf.* maternity; -schiff *n.* depot ship (nav.); -sprache *nf.* mother tongue.

Mütterlich [myoo'terr-lish] *a.* motherly.

Mutung [moo'toong] *nf.* mining claim.

Mutwille [moot'vil-er] *nm.* (gen. -ns) mischievousness; -ig *a.* mischievous, playful.

Mütze [myoot'ser] *nf.* cap.

Myrrhe [myoor'rer] *nf.* myrrh.

Myrte [myoor'ter] *nf.* myrtle.

Mysteriös [myooss-ter-ri-erss'] *a.* mysterious.

Mystifizieren [myooss-ti-fit-seer'ren] *vt.* to mystify, puzzle.

Mystik [myooss'tik] *nf.* mysticism; -er *nm.* (-) mystic.

Myth'e [myoo'ter] *nf.* Myth'us [myoo'tooss] *nm.* (Mythen) myth; -isch *a.* mythical.

N

Na! [nah] *interj.* well! Nah!

Nabe [nah'ber] *nf.* hub, boss.

Nabel [nah'bel] *nm.* (-) navel.

Nach [nach] *ad. pr.* after, to, by, for, according to; - und - gradually. [ape

Nachäffen [nach'ef-en] *vt.* to **Nachahm'en** [nach'ah-men] *vt.* to imitate; -enswert *a.* worthy of imitation; -er *nm.* (-) imitator; -ung *nf.* imitation.

Nacharten [nach'arr-ten] *vi.* to take after.

Nachbar [nach'barr] *nm.* (gen. -s; pl. -n) neighbour; -in *nf.* (female) neighbour; -lich *a.* neighbourly; -schaft *nf.* neighbourhood; -staat *nm.* neighbouring state.

Nachbessern [nach'bess-errn] vt. to touch up; -ung nf. touching up, second revision.

Nachbestell'en [nach'ber-shtel-en] vt. to order again; -ung nf. repeat order (com.).

Nachbild'en [nach'bil-den] vt. to copy; -ung nf. imitation, copy.

Nachbleiben [nach'bli-ben] vi. ir. to lag behind, be left over.

Nachdatieren [nach'da-teeren] vt. to post-date.

Nachdem [nach-dame'] ad. afterwards; cj. after, according as.

Nachdenk'en [nach'denk-en] vi. ir. to think over, reflect (on); n. reflection, meditation; -lich a. thoughtful, pensive.

Nachdichtung [nach'dish-toong] nf. free version, translation, imitation.

Nachdruck [nach'drŏŏk] nm. emphasis, force, reprint, reproduction; -en vt. to reprint.

Nachdrück'lich [nach'drŏŏk-lish] a. ad. strong, emphatic.

Nacheichen [nach'i-shen] vt. to recalibrate.

Nacheifer'er [nach'ife-er-rerr] nm. (-) imitator, rival; -n vi. to emulate.

Nacheilen [nach'ile-en] vi. to hasten after.

Nacheinander [nach'ine-anderr] ad. one after the other, successively.

Nachen [nach'en] nm. (-) small boat.

Nachernte [nach'errn-ter] nf. second crop, aftermath.

Nachfahren [nach'fah-ren] vi. ir. to follow, drive, sail after.

Nachfolge [nach'fol-ger] nf. succession; -n vi. to follow, succeed; -r nm. (-) successor.

Nachforderung [nach'forr-der-rŏŏng] nf. additional claim.

Nachforsch'en [nach'forr-shen] vi.t. to inquire, investigate; -ung nf. investigation,

search; -ungsstelle nf. investigation centre.

Nachfrage [nach'frah-ger] nf. inquiry, demand; -n vi. to inquire, demand.

Nachfühlen [nach'fyŏŏ-len] vt. to sympathize with, feel with.

Nachgeben [nach'gay-ben] vi. ir. to give way, yield.

Nachgeboren [nach'ger-boren] a. posthumous.

Nachgebühr [nach'ger-byŏŏrr] nf. excess postage.

Nachgehen [nach'gay-en] vi. ir. to follow, inquire into, be slow (clock).

Nachgerade [nach'ger-rah-der] ad. by degrees, by now, after all.

Nachgeschmack [nach'ger-shmak] nm. aftertaste.

Nachgiebig [nach'gee-bish] a. pliable, submissive, obliging, soft; -keit nf. indulgence, submissiveness, softness.

Nachgrübeln [nach'gryŏŏ-beln] vi. to ponder over, worry about.

Nachhall [nach'hal] nm. echo, resonance; -en vi. to echo, resound.

Nachhaltig [nach hal-tish] a. persistent, lasting, permanent.

Nachhängen [nach'heng-en] vi. to indulge in, give way to.

Nachheizen [nach'hite-sen] vi. to put coal on the fire, stoke up.

Nachhelfen [nach'hel-fen] vi. ir. to assist, help.

Nachher [nach'hairr] ad. afterwards; -ig a. subsequent, later.

Nachholen [nach'hole-en] vt. to catch up with, make up for, take later.

Nachhut [nach'hŏŏt] nf. rear-guard.

Nachjagen [nach'yah-gen] vt. to chase after, pursue.

Nachklang [nach'klang] nm. (-klänge) reminiscence, echo.

Nachkomme [nach'kom-mer] m.w. descendant; -n vi. ir. to

follow, comply with, fulfil, accede to; **-nschaft** *nf.* posterity.

Nachkömmling [nach'kerm-ling] *nm.* (-e) descendant.

Nachkriegszeit [nach'kreeks-tsite] *nf.* post-war period.

Nachkur [nach'koor] *nf.* convalescence.

Nachlass [nach'lass] *nm.* (-lässe) intermission, discount, rebate, estate; **-en** *vi. ir.* to desist, slacken, stop, temper (*tec.*); *t.* leave (behind), reduce (*com.*), slacken, remit.

Nachlässig [nach'less-ish] *a.* negligent, careless, remiss; **-keit** *nf.* negligence, remissness, carelessness.

Nachlaufen [nach'low-fen] *vi. ir.* to run after, chase.

Nachleben [nach'lay-ben] *vi.* to live up to, follow.

Nachlese [nach'lay-zer] *nf.* gleaning(s); **-n** *vt. ir.* to glean.

Nachmachen [nach'mach-en] *vt.* to imitate, counterfeit, copy.

Nachmalen [nach'mah-len] *vi.* to copy, reproduce.

Nachmalig [nach'mah-lish] *a.* subsequent, later; **-s** *ad.* afterwards, subsequently.

Nachmittag [nach'mi-tahk] *nm.* (-e) afternoon; **-s** *ad.* in the afternoon.

Nachnahme [nach'nah-mer] *nf.* payable on delivery; **-betrag** *nm.* fee payable on delivery.

Nachname [nach'nah-mer] *nm.* (*gen.* **-ns**; *pl.* **-n**) surname.

Nachnehmen [nach'nay-men] *vt. ir.* to reimburse oneself, charge forward (*com.*).

Nachporto [nach'por-to] *n.* excess postage, postage due.

Nachprüfen [nach'prÿoo-fen] *vt.* to check, verify.

Nachrechnen [nach'resh-nen] *vt.* to reckon up (again), check, audit (*accounts*).

Nachrede [nach'ray-der] *nf.*

gossip, epilogue; **-n** *vt.* to backbite.

Nachricht [nach'risht] *nf.* news, account, report, information; **-en** *pl.* appears, intelligence (*mil.*); **-enabteilung** *nf.* signals battalion; **-endienst** *nm.* signals service, intelligence; **-eneinheit** *nf.* signals unit; **-enkompanie** *nf.* signals company; **-ensperre** *nf.* black-out of news; **-enstaffel** *nf.* signals section; **-enstelle** *nf.* signals station; **-entruppe** *nf.* corps of signals; **-enwesen** *n.* signals service; **-enzug** *nm.* signals platoon.

Nachrücken [nach'rÿoo-ken] *vi.* to move up, forward, march on.

Nachruf [nach'roof] *nm.* (-e) obituary notice.

Nachrühmen [nach'rÿoo-men] *vt.* to say in praise of.

Nachsagen [nach'zah-gen] *vt.* to repeat, say of.

Nachschicken [nach'shik-en] *vt.* to forward.

Nachschlagen [nach'shlah-gen] *vt. ir.* to look up, consult; *i.* take after; **-werk** *n.* work of reference.

Nachschleppen [nach'shlep-en] *vt.* to drag along, tow.

Nachschreiben [nach'shri-ben] *vt. ir.* to copy, take down; *i.* take notes.

Nachschrift [nach'shrift] *nf.* dictation, copy, notes, postscript.

Nachschub [nach'shoob] *nm.* (-schübe) supplement, reinforcement, supply (*mil.*); **-abwurf** *nm.* supplying from the air; **-flughafen** *nm.* supply airfield (*av.*); **-lager** *n.* supply dump; **-leitstelle** *nf.* supply station (*mil.*).

Nachsehen [nach'zay-en] *vt. ir.* to look after, examine, revise, overlook, excuse, attend to, see to.

Nachsenden [nach'zen-den] *vt. ir.* to send on, forward.

Nachsetzen [nach'zet-sen] *vt.* to put later; *i.* pursue.

Nachsicht [nach'zisht] *nf.* indulgence, leniency; -ig *a.* indulgent, lenient.

Nachsinnen [nach'zin-en] *vi. ir.* to meditate; *n.* contemplation.

Nachsitzen [nach'zit-sen] *vi. ir.* to be kept in.

Nachspeise [nach'shpize-er] *nf.* dessert.

Nachspiel [nach'shpeel] *n.* (-e) sequel, epilogue.

Nachsprechen [nach'shpreshen] *vt. ir.* to repeat.

Nachspüren [nach'shpyöör-ren] *vi.* to track down.

Nächst [naish-st] *a.* next, nearest; *ad, pr.* next to; *cj.* m.w. neighbour; -enliebe *nf.* love of one's fellows; -ens *ad.* shortly; -liegend *a.* nearest, obvious; -treffer *nm.* near miss (*mil.*).

Nachstehen [nach'shtay-en] *vi. ir.* to be inferior to; -d *a.* following.

Nachstell'en [nach'shtel-en] *vi.* to lie in wait for, ambush; *t.* put back; -ung *nf.* pursuit.

Nachstreben [nach'shtray-ben] *vi.* to strive after.

Nachstürzen [nach'shtyöörr-tsen] *vi.* to rush after.

Nachsuchen [nach'zooch-en] *vi.* to search after, apply for.

Nacht [nacht] *nf.* (Nächte) night; -essen *n.* supper; -gleiche *nf.* equinox; -hemd *n.* night-shirt, night-dress; -jagd *nf.* night fighting (*av.*); -lager *n.* night's lodging; -lokal *n.* night-club; -schicht *nf.* night-shift; -sehtauglichkeit *nf.* night vision; -seite *nf.* dark side; -suchgerät *n.* cat's eye (*av.*); -tisch *nm.* bedside table; -topf *nm.* chamber utensil; -visier *n.* night bomb-sight; -wächter *nm.* night watchman; -wandeln

vi. to walk in one's sleep; -zeug *n.* night-clothes.

Nachteil [nach'tile] *nm.* (-e) disadvantage, damage; -ig *a.* disadvantageous.

Nachtigall [nach'ti-gal] *nf.* nightingale. [dessert.

Nachtisch [nach'tish] *nm.* (-e)

Nächtlich [nesht'lish] *a.* nightly. [rear-guard.

Nachtrab [nach'trahp] *nm.*

Nachtrag [nach'trahk] *nm.* (-träge) supplement, postscript; -en *vt. ir.* to add, bear (grudge, etc.).

Nachträg'erisch [nach'tray-ger-rish] *a.* spiteful, resentful; -lich *a, ad.* subsequent(ly), additional(ly).

Nachtrupp [nach'troop] *nm.* rear-guard; -en *f.pl.* covering troops (*mil.*).

Nachts [nachts] *ad.* by night.

Nachtun [nach'töön] *vi. ir.* to copy, equal.

Nachwachsen [nach'vax-en] *vi. ir.* to grow again.

Nachwehen [nach'vay-en] *pl.* after-effects, evil consequences.

Nachweis [nach'vice] *nm.* information, proof, evidence, voucher, schedule, memorandum; -bar *a.* provable, traceable, evident; -en *vt.* to point out, prove; -lich *a.* evident, demonstrable.

Nachwelt [nach'velt] *nf.* posterity.

Nachwirk'en [nach'virr-ken] *vi.* to have after-effects; -ung *nf.* after-effect.

Nachwuchs [nach'vööx] *nm.* fresh crop, rising generation, cadets, aspirants, personnel under training (*mil. etc.*).

Nachzahl'en [nach'tsah-len] *vt.i.* to pay later, in addition; -zahlung *nf.* additional payment, payment after receipt.

Nachzeichn'en [nach'tsish-nen] *vt.* to copy (*drawing*); -ung *nf.* copy, reproduction.

Nachzügler [nach'tsyōok-lerr] nm. (-) straggler.

Nacken [nak'en] nm. (-) nape of the neck.

Nackt [nakt] a. naked, plain, bare; **-heit** nf. nakedness; **-kultur** nf. nudism.

Nadel [nah'del] nf. needle, pin; **-geld** n. pin-money; **-holz** n. conifer; **-kissen** n. pincushion; **-n** vt. to pin; **-öhr** n. eye of a needle; **-stich** nm. pin-prick, stitch.

Nagel [nah'gel] nm. (Nägel) nail; **-bohrer** nm. gimlet; **-bürste** nf. nail-brush; **-feile** nf. nail-file; **-n** vt. to nail; **-neu** a. brand new; **-pflege** af. manicure; **-zieher** n. nail extractor.

Nage'n [nah'gen] vt.i. to gnaw; **-tier** n. rodent.

Nah(e) a, ad. near; **-aufklärung** nf. close reconnaissance; **-aufnahme** nf. close-up; **-egehen** vi. ir. to grieve, pain; **-ekommen** vi. ir. to approach, come near; **-elegen** vt. to suggest; **-eliegen** vi. ir. to be obvious; **-estehen** vi. ir. to be connected with, to be near and dear to; **-etreten** vi. ir. to offend; **-ezu** ad. nearly; **-verkehr** nm. local traffic (rl.).

Nahkampf [nah'kampf] nm. hand-to-hand fighting, close range combat (av.); **-gruppe** nf. close support unit (av.); **-mittel** n.pl. close range weapons.

Nähe [nay'er] nf. nearness, vicinity, neighbourhood.

Nahen [nah'en] vi. to approach, draw near.

Näh'en [nay'en] vt.i. to sew; **-erin** nf. needlewoman; **-garn** n. sewing cotton; **-kasten** nm. work-box; **-korb** nm. work-basket; **-maschine** nf. sewing machine; **-nadel** nf. needle.

Näherei [nay-er-rie'] nf. sewing, needlework.

Näher [nay'err] a. nearer, more closely, more detailed.

Nähere(s) [nay'er-rerss] m.w. details, particulars.

Nähern [nay'errn] vr. to approach; t. bring near.

Nähr'en [nairr'en] vt. to feed, nourish, support, nurse, entertain; r. live on, keep oneself; **-gehalt** nm. nutritive value; **-geld** n. alimony; **-haft** a. nourishing, nutritious; **-präparat** n. patent medicine; **-stand** nm. peasantry; **-stoff** nm. food; **-ung** nf. feeding, nutrition, nourishment; **-wert** nm. nutritional value.

Nahrhaft [nahrr'haft] a. nourishing, nutritious.

Nahrung [nahr'rōong] nf. food, nourishment, support; **-smittel** n.pl. provisions, foodstuffs.

Naht [naht] nf. (Nähte) seam, suture, join; **-los** a. seamless.

Name [nah'mer] nm. (gen. -ns; pl. -n) name; **-nlos** a. nameless; **-ns** ad. by name; **-nsvetter** nm. namesake; **-nszug** nm. signature, autograph; **-ntlich** ad. particularly, especially.

Namhaft [nahm'haft] a. famed, renowned; **-machen** vt. to specify; **-machung** nf. specification.

Nämlich [name'lish] ad. that is to say, naturally; a. the same.

Napf [napf] nm. (Näpfe) bowl, dish, basin.

Narbe [narr'ber] nf. scar, gash; **-en** vt. to grain; **-ig** a. scarred

Narko'se [narr-koh'zer] nf. narcosis, anaesthesia; **-tisch** a. narcotic.

Narr [narr] m.w. **Närrin** nf. fool, buffoon; **-en** vt. to fool; **-enhaus** n. madhouse; **-enpossen** f.pl. tomfoolery, craziness; **-enstreich** nm. mad trick, practical joke; **-heit** nf. folly, craziness, madness.

Narretei [narr-er-ti'] *nf.* fooling, folly.

Närrisch [ner'rish] *a.* foolish, crazy.

Narzisse [narr-tsi'ser] *nf.* narcissus, daffodil.

Naschen [nash'en] *vt.i.* to nibble (sweets), pilfer; **-haft** *a.* sweet-toothed; **-werk** *n.* sweets.

Näscher [nesh'err] *nm.* (-), **-in** *nf.* sweet-tooth.

Nase [nah'zer] *nf.* nose; **-nloch** *n.* nostril; **-nrücken** *nm.* bridge of the nose; **-nrümpfen** *n.* sneering; *vi.* to sneer; **-nstübern** *vt.* to rap on the nose, snub; **-nton** *nm.* nasal twang; **-ntropfen** *vi.* snivel; **-weis** *a.* pert, cheeky.

Näseln [naze'eln] *vi.* to speak through the nose, sniff.

Nasführen [nahss'fyoor-ren] *vt.* to fool, hoax.

Nashorn [nahss'horrn] *n.* (-hörner) rhinoceros.

Nass [nass] *a.* wet; *n.* liquid; **-kalt** *a.* raw.

Nässe [ness'er] *nf.* wet(ness); **-n** *vt.* to wet.

Nation [nat-si-ohn'] *nf.* nation.

National [nat-si-o-nahl'] *a.* national; **-hymne** *nf.* national anthem; **-ökonomie** *nf.* political economy; **-sozialismus** *nm.* national socialism; **-sozialist** *m.w.* national socialist, Nazi.

Nationalisieren [nat-si-ona-li-zeer'ren] *vt.* to nationalize; **-ung** *nf.* nationalization.

Nationalismus [nat-si-o-naliss'mooss] *nm.* nationalism; **-stisch** *a.* nationalistic; **-tät** *nf.* nationality.

Natrium [nah'tri-ŏŏm] *n.* sodium.

Natron [nah'tron] *n.* soda.

Natter [na'terr] *nf.* adder.

Natur [na-tŏŏr'] *nf.* nature, disposition, constitution; **-anlage** *nf.* disposition, temperament; **-butter** *nf.* pure

butter; **-erscheinung** *nf.* phenomenon; **-farben** *a.* (natural) colour; **-forscher** *nm.* scientist; **-gemäss** *a.* natural; **-geschichte** *nf.* natural history; **-gesetz** *n.* law of nature; **-lehre** *nf.* physics; **-spiel** *n.* freak of nature; **-schutzpark** *nm.* national park; **-trieb** *nm.* instinct; **-wissenschaft** *nf.* natural science; **-wissenschaftler** *nm.* scientist.

Naturalien [na-tŏŏ-rah'li-en] *pl.* natural, produce; **-sammlung** *nf.* natural history collection.

Naturalisieren [na-tŏŏr-rali-zeer'ren] *vt.* to naturalize; **-ung** *nf.* naturalization.

Naturalismus [na-tŏŏr-raliss'mooss] *nm.* naturalism; **-t** *m.w.* naturalist; **-tisch** *a.* naturalistic.

Naturalleistung [na-tŏŏr-rahl'lie-stŏŏng] *nf.* payment in kind.

Naturell [na-tŏŏr-rel'] *n.* (-e) disposition.

Natürlich [na-tyŏŏr'lish] *a.* natural; **-erweise** *ad.* naturally, of course; **-keit** *nf.* naturalness.

Nautik [now'tik] *nf.* navigation, nautical matters.

Navigation [na-vi-gat-syohn'] *nf.* navigation, flying (*av.*); **-sgerät** *n.* navigation instruments; **-sraum** *nm.* chart-room (*nav.*). [Hitlerite.

Nazi [nah'tsee] *nm.* (-s) Nazi.

Nebel [nay'bel] *nm.* (-) fog, mist, smoke (*mil.*); **-granate** *nf.* smoke grenade; **-kerze** *nf.* smoke candle; **-n** *vi.* to be misty, foggy; **-schleier** *nm.* smoke screen; **-truppen** *f.pl.* smoke troops, chemical warfare squad; **-walze** *nf.* smoke barrage; **-werfer** *nm.* smoke projector, smoke mortar (*mil.*).

Neben [nay'ben] *pr.* near, next to; **-abdruck** *nm.* spare, extra copy; **-an** *ad.* next door, quite near; -anschluss *nm.* extension (*ph.*), shunt (*el.*); -bei *ad.* besides, by the way, adjoining, -beruf *nm.* side-line; -buhler *nm.* rival; -buhlerei *nf.* rivalry; -einander *ad.* side by side; -einkommen *n.,* -einkünfte *f.pl.* perquisites; -fach *n.* subsidiary subject; -flugpark *nm.* subsidiary air-park; -fluss *nm.* tributary; -gebäude *n.* annexe; -geleise *n.* siding (*rl.*); -geräusch *n.* atmospherics; -geschäft *n.* side-line; besides, incidentally; -produkt *n.* by-product; -sache *nf.* trifle, side issue; -sächlich *a.* incidental, subordinate, unimportant; -stelle *nf.* sub-station, branch office; -strasse *nf.* side-street.

Neblig [nabe'lish] *a.* foggy, misty.   [with.

Nebst [nabe-st] *pr.* (together)

Neck'en [nek'en] *vt.* to tease; -erei *nf.* teasing, chaff; -isch *a.* fond of teasing, queer, comical.

Neffe [nef'er] *m.w.* nephew.

Negativ [nay'ga-teef] *a.* negative; *n.* (-e) negative.

Neger [nay'gerr] *nm.* (-) negro, coloured man; -in *nf.* negress.

Negieren [nay-geer'ren] *vt.* to deny.

Nehmen [nay'men] *vt. ir.* to take, receive, eat.

Nehrung [nair'rŏŏng] *nf.* narrow neck of land, spit.

Neid [nite] *nm.* envy; -en *vt.* to envy; -isch *a.* envious, jealous.

Neig'e [ni'ger] *nf.* decline, slope, dregs; -en *vi.t.r.* to incline, lean, be inclined to come to an end; -ung *nf.* inclination, tendency, liking, affection, gradient, tilt, dip; -ungsehe *n.* love match.

Nein [nine] *ad.* no.

Nelke [nel'ker] *nf.* carnation, pink, clove.

Nenn'en [nen'en] *vt. ir.* to name, call; -enswert *a.* worth mentioning; -er *nm.* (-) denominator; -ung *nf.* naming, entry; -wert *nm.* nominal value, par (*com.*).

Neon [nay'on] *n.* neon; -röhre *nf.* neon tube.

Nerv [nairrf] *nm.* (*gen.* -s; *pl.* -en) nerve; -enerschütterung *nf.* shell-shock; -enkrank *a.* neurotic; -enkrieg *nm.* war of nerves; -enschwäche *nf.* neurasthenia; -ig *a.* nervous, sinewy; -ös *a.* nervous; -osität *nf.* nervousness.

Nerz [nairrts] *nm.* (-e) mink.

Nessel [nessl] *nf.* nettle; -fieber *n.* nettle-rash; -tuch *n.* muslin.   [town.

Nest [nest] *n.* (-e) nest, small

Nesteln [nes'teln] *vt.* to lace.

Nett [net] *a.* neat, nice; -igkeit *nf.* neatness, niceness.

Netto [net'o] *ad.* net; -einnahmen *f.pl.* net receipts; -gewinn *nm.* net profits.

Netz [nets] *n.* (-e) net, network, grid (*rad., el.*); -anschluss *nm.* mains connection; -empfänger *nm.* mains receiving set (*rad.*); -en *vt.* to wet, moisten; -haut *nf.* retina; -hemd *n.* celular shirt; -sperre *nf.* net barrage, boom (*nav.*); -spiel *n.* net-play (*tennis*); -werk *n.* network; -zuleitung *nf.* mains lead (*rad.*).

Neu [noy] *a.* new(ly), recent(ly), modern; -backen *a.* newly baked, new-fangled; -bau *nm.* reconstruction, new construction; -bearbeiten *vt.* revise, recast; -einstellen *vt.* to readjust; -gestaltung *nf.* reorganization; -heit *nf.* newness, novelty; -igkeit *nf.* news; -jahr *n.* New Year; -lich *ad.* recently, the other day, lately; -ling *nm.* (-e) novice; -möblieren *vt.* to refurnish; -reiche(r) *m.w.* new rich (person); -vermählt *a.* newly married; -wert *nm.* purchase price; **-zeit** *nf.* modern age; **-zeitlich** *a.* modern, recent.

Neuer'dings [noy-err-dingss'] *ad.* recently, lately; **-er** *nm.* (-) innovator; **-ung** *nf.* innovation, new departure.

Neugier(de) [noy'geerr-der] *nf.* curiosity; **-ig** *a.* inquisitive, curious.

Neun [noin] *num.* nine; **-zehn** *num.* nineteen; **-zig** *num.* ninety. [neuralgia.

Neuralgie [noy-ral-gee'] *nf.*

Neurasthenie [noy-ras-tay-nee'] *nf.* neurasthenia; **-isch** *a.* neurotic, neurasthenic.

Neurose [noy-roh'zer] *nf.* neurosis.

Neutral [noy-trahl'] *a.* neutral; **-ität** *nf.* neutrality.

Neutrum [noy'trōōm] *n.* (Neutren) neuter.

Newtonsucher [nyōō'ton-zōōch-err] *nm.* (-) view-finder (camera).

Nicht [nisht] *ad.* not, nor, no; **-achtung** *nf.* disregard; **-amtlich** *a.* unofficial; **-anerkennung** *nf.* non-recognition, repudiation; **-angriffspakt** *nm.* non-aggression pact; **-annahme** *nf.* non-acceptance; **-arier** *nm.* (-) non-Aryan, Jew; **-einhaltung** *nf.* non-observation; **-eisenmetall** *n.* non-ferrous metal; **-gewünscht** *a.* undesirable, unwanted; **-kämpfer** *nm.* non-combatant; **-raucher** *nm.* non-smoker; **-rostend** *a.* rustless; **-verbrüderung** *nf.* non-fraternization; **-zieland** *a.* intransitive; **-zutreffend** *a.* not applicable.

Nichte [nish'ter] *nf.* niece.

Nichtig [nish'tish] *a.* null, void, empty, vain; **-keit** *nf.* nullity, futility, invalidity.

Nichts [nishts] *pn.* nothing; *n.* nothingness, nonentity; **-destoweniger** *ad.* nevertheless; **-nutz** *nm.* good-for-nothing; **-nutzig** *a.* worthless, useless;

-sagend *a.* meaningless; **-tun** loafing about, idling; **-würdig** *a.* worthless, base, vile; **-würdigkeit** *nf.* worthlessness, vileness.

Nickel [nikl] *n.* (-) nickel; **-münze** *nf.* nickel coin.

Nick'en [nik'en] *vi.* to nod, doze; **-erchen** *n.* nap.

Nie [nee] *ad.* never.

Nieder [nee'derr] *a.* low, inferior; *ad.* down; **-brennen** *vt. ir.* to burn down; **-deutsch** *a.* Low German; **-drücken** *vt. ir.* to depress; **-fahren** *vi. ir.* to descend, go down; **-frequenz** *nf.* low frequency (*el.*); **-gang** *nm.* decline, setting; **-gehen** *vi. ir.* to decline, set, land (*plane*); **-geschlagen** *a.* depressed; **-geschlagenheit** *nf.* depression, dejection; **-kämpfen** *vt.* to fight down, silence (*fire*); **-kommen** *vi. ir.* to be confined; **-kunft** *nf.* confinement; **-lage** *nf.* warehouse, defeat; **-lassen** *vr.* to settle; **-lassung** *nf.* settlement; **-legen** *vt.* to lay down, resign; **-machen** *vt.* to mow down, kill; **-reissen** *vt. ir.* to pull down; **-schlag** *nm.* precipitate, sediment; **-schlagen** *vt. ir.* to beat down, suppress, dispirit; **-schreiben** *vt. ir.* to write down; **-schrift** *nf.* copy; **-setzen** *vt.* to put down; *r.* sit down; **-spannung** *nf.* low tension (*el.*); **-steigen** *vi. ir.* to descend; **-trächtig** *a.* base, mean; **-trächtigkeit** *nf.* meanness, baseness; **-ung** *nf.* lowland, plain; **-werfen** *vt. ir.* to throw, cast down.

Niedlich [neet'lish] *a.* pretty, neat, dainty, nice; **-keit** *nf.* daintiness, neatness.

Niedrig [nee'drish] *a.* low, lowly, humble, mean, inferior; **-keit** *nf.* lowness, lowliness, humbleness, badness.

Niemals [nee'mahls] *ad.* never.

Niemand [nee'mant] *pn.* nobody, no one; **-sland** *n.* no-man's-land (*mil.*).

Niere [nee'rer] *nf.* kidney; **-nbraten** *nm.* roast loin of veal; **-nentzündung** *nf.* nephritis, Bright's disease; **-fett** *n,* *-talg* *nm.* suet. [drizzle.

Nieseln [nee'zeln] *vi.* to

Niesen [nee'zen] *vi.* to sneeze.

Niessbrauch [neess'browch] *nm.* benefit, usufruct.

Niet [neet] *nm.* (-e) rivet; **-en** *vt.* to rivet; **-er** *nm.* (-) riveter; **-hammer** *nm.* riveting hammer; **-nagel** *nm.* riveting nail.

Niete [nee'ter] *nf.* blank (ticket).

Nihilismus [ni-hi-liss'mōōss] *nm.* nihilism. [nicotine.

Nikotin [ni-ko-teen'] *n.*

Nilpferd [neel'pfairt] *n.* (-e) hippopotamus.

Nimmer [nim'err] *ad.* never; **-mehr** *ad.* nevermore, never again; **-satt** *a.* insatiable; *n.* glutton. [nip.

Nippen [nip'en] *vt.i.* to sip.

Nippel [nipl] *nm.* (-) nipple (*tec.*). [*f.pl.* knick-knacks.

Nippsachen [nip'zach-en]

Nirgend's [nirr'gends] *ad.* nowhere; **-wo** *ad.* nowhere.

Nische [nee'sher] *nf.* niche.

Niss(e) [nis'e] *nf.* nit.

Nisten [nis'ten] *vi.* to nest, build a nest. [nitrate.

Nitrat [ni-traht'] *n.* (-e)

Niveau [ni-voh'] *n.* (-s) standard, level; **-halter** *nm.* level-regulator (*tec.*).

Nivellier'en [ni-ve-leer'ren] *vt.* to level; **-ung** *nf.* levelling; **-waage** *nf.* spirit-level.

Nixe [nix'er] *nf.* water-nymph.

Nobel [no'bel] *a.* generous, noble.

Noch [noch] *ad.* still, yet, in addition, besides; *cj.* nor; **-einmal** once more; **-mal(s)** *ad.* again, once more; **-malig** *a.* repeated, second.

Nock [nok] *n.* (-e) yard-arm.

Nocken [nok'en] *nm.* (-) cam; **-welle** *nf.* cam-shaft (*aut.*).

Nomad'e [no-mah'der] *m.w.* nomad; **-isch** *a.* nomadic.

Nominal [no-mi-nahl'] *a.* nominal, substantival.

Nominativ [no-mi-na-teef'] *nm.* nominative.

Nominell [no-mi-nel'] *a.* nominal, token (*payment*).

Nonne [non'er] *nf.* nun; **-nkloster** *n.* nunnery, convent.

Noppe [nop'er] *nf.* nap, pile (cloth); **-n** *vt.* to nap.

Nord [norrt] *nm.* north; **-isch** *a.* Norse, northern; **-licht** *n.* Northern Lights, aurora; **-pol** *nm.* North Pole; **-polarkreis** *nm.* Arctic Circle; **-wärts** *ad.* northwards.

Nördlich [nert'lish] *a.* northerly, northern. [grumbling.

Nörgelei [nerr-ger-lī'] *nf.*

Nörg'eln [nerr'geln] *vi.* to grumble, grouse, nag; **-ler** *nm.* (-) grumbler, grouser.

Norm [norrm] *nf.* rule, standard.

Normal [norr-mahl'] *a.* normal; **-null** *nf.* sea-level; **-spurbahn** *nf.* standard gauge railway; **-spurweite** *nf.* standard gauge; **-zeit** *nf.* mean time, Greenwich time.

Normen [norr'men], **Normieren** [norr-meer'ren] *vt.* to standardize, regulate.

Not [note] *nf.* (Nöte) need, necessity, distress, trouble; **-anker** *nm.* sheet-anchor; **-ausgang** *nm.* emergency exit; **-bau** *nm.* temporary building; **-behelf** *nm.* expedient, makeshift; **-bremse** *nf.* emergency brake; **-brücke** *nf.* temporary, pontoon bridge; **-durft** *nf.* necessity, urgent need, call of nature; **-dürftig** *a.* scanty, needy; **-dürftigkeit** *nf.* indigence; **-fall** *nm.* case of need, necessity, emergency; **-flagge**

nf. flag of distress; **-gedrungen** *a.* on compulsion, forced; **-geld** *n.* paper money; **-hilfe** *nf.* relief service; **-lage** *nf.* crisis, calamity, distress, emergency; **-landen** *vi.* to make a forced landing; **-landung** *nf.* forced, emergency landing; **-leidend** *a.* distressed, needy, poor; **-leine** *nf.* communication cord (rl.); **-lüge** *nf.* white lie; **-mast** *nm.* jury-mast; **-mittel** *n.* expedient; **-pfennig** *nm.* savings; **-ruf** *nm.* cry of distress; **-schnelltanker** *nm.* bowser (nav.); **-signal** *n.* signal of distress; **-stand** *nm.* state of distress; **-standsarbeiten** *f.pl.* relief works; **-tür** *nf.* emergency exit; **-verband** *nm.* field dressing; **-wehr** *nf.* self-defence; **-zucht** *nf.* rape; **-züchtigen** *vt.* to assault; **-zwang** *nm.* force of circumstances. [notary.

Notar [no-tahr'] *nm.* (-e)

Note [noh'ter] *nf.* note, mark, memorandum, music, bank-note; **-nblatt** *n.* sheet of music, **-npult** *n.* **-nständer** *nm.* music-stand.

Notier'en [noh-teer'ren] *vt.* to note, quote (com.); **-ung** *nf.* quotation.

Nötig [ner'tish] *a.* necessary; **-en** *vt.* to compel, force; **-enfalls** *ad.* in case of need.

Notiz [no-teets'] *nf.* notice, note; **-buch** *n.* note-book.

Notorisch [no-tor'rish] *a.* notorious.

Notwendig [noht'ven-dish] *a.* necessary; **-keit** *nf.* necessity.

Novelle [no-vel'er] *nf.* short story.

November [no-vem'berr] *nm.* (-) November. [novice.

Novize [no-veet'ser] *m.w.*

Nu [noo] *n.* instant.

Nüchtern [nyōōsh'terrn] *a.* sober, prudent, prosaic, insipid; **-heit** *nf.* sobriety, insipidity.

Nudel [nōō'del] *nf.* maccaroni.

Null [nōōl] *a.* null, nil; *n.* nought, nothing, zero; **-ität** *nf.* nullity; **-punkt** *nm.* zero; **-zeit** *nf.* zero hour.

Numerieren [nōō-mer-reer'ren] *vt.* to number, reserve (seat).

Numerisch [nōō-mair'rish] *a.* numerical.

Nummer [nōō'merr] *nf.* number; **-nscheibe** *nf.* telephone dial; **-nschild** *n.* number plate (aut.).

Nun [nōōn] *ad.* now; *cj.* now (that), then; *interj.* well!; **-mehr** *ad.* by now, by this time, now; **-mehrig** *a.* present.

Nur [nōōr] *ad.* only, merely, except, just.

Nuss [nōōs] *nf.* (Nüsse) nut; **-baum** *nm.* walnut-tree; **-knacker** *nm.* (-) nut-cracker; **-kohle** *nf.* nuts (com.); **-schale** *nf.* nut-shell.

Nüster [nyōōs'terr] *nf.* nostril.

Nute [nōō'ter] *nf.* groove, slit, slot, rabbet (tec.).

Nutsche [nōōt'sher] *nf.* suction filter; **-n** *vi.* to suck.

Nutz [nōōts], **Nütze** [nyōōt'ser] *a.* useful; **-anwendung** *nf.* utilization; **-bar** *a.* useful; **-barkeit** *nf.* usefulness; **-barmachung** *nf.* utilization; **-bringend** *a.* profitable; **-en** *nm.* use, profit; **-garten** *nm.* kitchen-garden; **-holz** *n.* timber; **-last** *nf.* pay load, commercial load; **-leistung** *nf.* actual output, effective force; **-los** *a.* useless; **-losigkeit** *nf.* uselessness; **-niessen** *vt.* to derive profit from; **-niessung** *nf.* usufruct (law).

Nützen [nyōōt'sen] *vi.* to be useful, to profit; *t.* make use of, utilize.

Nützlich [nyōōts'lish] *a.* useful; **-keit** *nf.* usefulness; **-keitsprinzip** *n.* utilitarianism.

Nymphe [nyōōm'fer] *nf.* nymph.

O

Oase [o-ah'zer] *nf.* oasis.

Ob [op] *cj.* if, whether; *pr.* on account of, over, above; ob ~ gleich, schon, wohl *see* obgleich, obschon, obwohl.

Obacht [oh'bacht] *nf.* care, heed, attention.

Obdach [op'dach] *n.* shelter, lodging; **-los** *a.* homeless; **-lose(r)** *m.w.* homeless person, casual, tramp, pauper.

O-beine [oh'bine-er] *n.pl.* bow-legs, bandy legs.

Oben [oh'ben] *ad.* above, on the top, upstairs, on high; **-an** *ad.* at the top; **-auf** *ad.* up above, on the top, in form; **-drein** *ad.* over and above, into the bargain; **-erwähnt** *a.* above-mentioned; **-hin** *ad.* cursorily, superficially.

Ober [oh'berr] *a.* upper, superior, higher, senior; **-arm** *nm.* upper arm; **-arzt** *nm.* medical officer, senior physician; **-aufsicht** *nf.* charge, superintendence; **-befehl** *nm.* supreme command; **-befehlshaber** *nm.* commander-in-chief; **-bootsmannsmaat** *nm.* chief petty officer (*nav.*); **-bürgermeister** *nm.* lord mayor; **-deck** *n.* saloon deck, upper deck; **-deckoffizier** *nm.* commissioned officer (*nav.*); **-fähnrich** *nm.* senior cadet sergeant (*mil.*), senior ensign (*nav.*); **-feldwebel** *nm.* company sergeant major (*mil.*); **-fläche** *nf.* surface, area; **-flächlich** *a.* superficial; **-gefreite(r)** *m.w.* senior lance corporal, acting corporal; **-geschoss** *n.* upper story; **-halb** *pr., ad.* above; **-hand** *nf.* upper hand; **-haupt** *n.* head, chief; **-haus** *n.* upper house, House of Lords; **-in** *nf.* matron, Mother Superior; **-ingenieur** *nm.* chief engineer; **-irdisch** *a.*

overhead, above ground; **-kellner** *nm.* head waiter; **-kommando** *n.* supreme command; **-landesgericht** *n.* provincial court of appeal; **-lastig** *a.* top-heavy; **-leitung** *nf.* management, direction, overhead line, wire (*el.*); **-leutnant** *nm.* lieutenant (*mil.*), sub-lieutenant (*nav.*), flying officer (*av.*); **-licht** *n.* skylight; **-meister** *nm.* foreman, police lieutenant; **-quartiermeister** *nm.* chief quarter master; **-schicht** *nf.* upper classes; **-schwester** *nf.* sister (*hospital*); **-stimme** *nf.* soprano, treble; **-strichleistung** *nf.* peak power output; **-wachtmeister** *nm.* company sergeant major.

Oberst [oh'berrst] *a.* highest, supreme, upper, first, topmost, head; *m.w.* colonel, group captain (*av.*); **-leutnant** *nm.* lieutenant colonel, wing commander (*av.*).

Obgenannt [op'ger-nant], **Obgesagt** [op'ger-zahkt] *a.* above-mentioned.

Obgleich [op-glish'] *cj.* although. [though.

Obhut [op'hoot] *nf.* care, protection.

Obig [oh'bish] *a.* above, foregoing.

Objekt [op-yekt'] *n.* (-e) object; **-iv** *a.* objective, detached, impartial; *n.* lens; **-ivität** *nf.* impartiality, objectivity.

Oblate [ob-lah'ter] *nf.* consecrated wafer, host.

Obliegen [op'lee-gen] *vi. ir.* to be incumbent upon, be one's duty; **-heit** *nf.* duty, obligation.

Obligat [ob-li-gaht'] *a.* compulsory, indispensable.

Obligation [ob-li-gat-syohn'] *nf.* obligation, bond (*com.*).

Obligatorisch [ob-li-ga-tor'-rish] *a.* compulsory, obligatory.

Obmann [op'man] *nm.* (-männer) chairman, leader, foreman.

Obo'e [oh-boh'er] *nf.* oboe; -ist *m.w.* oboe player.

Obrigkeit [oh'brish-kite] *nf.* authorities, administration, government; -lich *a.* official, governmental. [though.

Obschon [op-shone'] *cj.* al-

Observatorium [op-zairr-va-tor'ry-ōōm] *n.* (Observatorien) observatory.

Obsiegen [op'zee-gen] *vi.* to triumph over, conquer.

Obst [ohpst] *n.* fruit; -bau *nm.* fruit growing; -garten *nm.* orchard; -händler *nm.* fruiterer, fruit dealer.

Obszön [ops-stsern'] *a.* obscene; -ität *nf.* obscenity.

Obwalten [op'val-ten] *vi.* to exist, prevail.

Ochs(e) [ox'er] *m.w.* ox; -en *vi.* to cram, work hard, swat; -enauge *n.* fried egg; -enhaut *nf.* ox-hide; -enzunge *nf.* ox-tongue.

Ocker [ok'err] *nm.* ochre.

Ode [oh'der] *nf.* ode.

Öde [er'der] *a.* waste, bleak, bare, barren, dull; -n *nf.* desert, waste; -land *n.* uncultivated land; -n *vt.* to bore; *r.* to be bored.

Oder [oh'derr] *cj.* or (else).

Ofen [oh'fen] *nm.* (Öfen) oven, stove; -bank *nf.* chimney corner; -hocker *nm.* stay-at-home; -kachel *nf.* Dutch tile; -klappe *nf.* damper; -rohr *n.* stove-pipe; -setzer *nm.* stove-fitter; -schirm *nm.* fire-screen; -schwärze *nf.* black-lead; -vorsetzer *nm.* fender.

Offen [ofn] *a.* open, frank, blank, vacant (post); -halten *vt. ir.* to keep open, reserve; -heit *nf.* frankness, candour; -herzig *a.* candid, sincere; -herzigkeit *nf.* sincerity, frankness; -kundig *a.* notorious, evident; -sichtlich *a.* evident, obvious; -stehen *vi. ir.* to

stand open, be at liberty to, be unpaid (account).

Offenbar [of'en-barr] *a.* obvious, evident; -en *vt.* to reveal, manifest; -ung *nf.* manifestation, revelation.

Offensiv [of-en-zeef'] *a.* offensive; -e *nf.* offensive.

Öffentlich [er'fent-lish] *a.* public, open; -keit *nf.* publicity, public.

Offerieren [of-er-reer'ren] *vt.* to offer, quote (com.).

Offerte [of-fairr'ter] *nf.* offer, tender, quotation (com.).

Offiziell [of-it-si-el'] *a.* official.

Offizier [of-it-seerr'] *nm.* officer; -sanwärter *nm.* officer cadet; -sbursche *m.w.* batman, orderly; -sheim *n.* officer's mess (mil.); -slager *n.* officer's prisoner of war camp; -smesse *nf.* ward-room (nav.); -snachwuchs *nm.* officer cadets; -spatent *n.* commission.

Offizin [of-it-seen'] *nf.* workshop, printing-office, dispensary, laboratory.

Öffnen [erf'nen] *vt.* to open; -er *nm.* opener; -ung *nf.* opening, hole, gap, aperture, dissection, outlet, mouth.

Oft [oft] *ad.* often; -malig *a.* frequent, repeated; -mals *ad.* often, frequently.

Öfter [erf'terr] *ad.* more often, more frequently; -s *ad.* often, frequently. [uncle.

Oheim [oh'hime] *nm.* (-e

Ohm [ohm] *n.* (-) ohm (el.).

Ohne [oh'ner] *pr.* without, free for; -dies *ad.* without that, besides, all the same; -hin *ad.* in any case, apart from that; -gleichen *a.* unsurpassed, without equal.

Ohnmacht [ohn'macht] *nf.* faint, weakness, impotence; -mächtig *a.* unconscious, in a faint, weak, impotent.

Ohr [ore] *n.* (gen. -es; *p* -enl.)

ear, hearing; **-enarzt** nm. ear specialist; **-enbläserei** nf. scandal; **-enschmalz** n. wax in the ear; **-enschmerz** nm. earache; **-enschützer** nm. ear protector, flap; **-enzerreissend** a. ear-splitting; **-feige** nf. box on the ear; **-gehänge** n. earrings; **-wurm** nm. earwig.

Öhr [err] n. (-e) eye (needle); **-chen** n. (-) eyelet.

Ökonom [er-ko-nome'] m.v. steward, farmer.

Ökonomie [er-ko-no-mee'] nf. economics, agriculture, housekeeping.

ökonomisch [er-ko-noh'mish] a. economical.

Oktav [ok-tahf'] n. (-e) octavo; **-band** n. octavo volume; **-e** nf. octave; **-format** n. octavo (size).

Okulieren [o-kōō-leer'ren] vt. to graft.

Öl [erl] n. (-e) oil; **-baum** nm. olive-tree; **-bild** n. oil-painting; **-farbe** nf. oils, oil paint; **-farbe** nf. oils, oil paint; **-ig** a. oily; **-jacke** nf. oilskin jacket; **-kuchen** n. oil-cake; **-leitung** nf. pipe-line; **-malerei** nf. painting in oils; **-papier** n. oil-paper; **-standsanzeiger** nm. oil-gauge (aut.); **-tuch** n. oilcloth; **-zweig** nm. olive branch.

Öl'en [er'len] vt. to oil, lubricate; **-ung** nf. lubrication.

Olive [o-lee'ver] nf. olive.

Omnibus [om'ni-bōōss] nm. (-se) omnibus, bus.

Ondulieren [on-dōō-leer'ren] vt. to wave.

Onkel [ong'kel] nm. (-) uncle.

Opak [o-pahk'] a. opaque.

Opal [o-pahl'] nm. (-e) opal.

Oper [oh'perr] nf. opera; **-ette** nf. operetta; **-nglas** n. opera glasses; **-nhaus** n. opera-house; **-nsänger** nm. operatic singer.

Operation [o-per-rat-syohn'] nf. operation; **-sbasis** nf. base of operations; **-sgebiet** n.

theatre of operations; **-sziel** n. tactical objective (mil.).

Operative [o-per-ra-teef'] a. operative, tactical.

Operieren [o-per-reer'ren] vt. to operate.

Opfer [op'ferr] n. (-) sacrifice, victim; **-freudig** a. self-sacrificing; **-stock** nm. poor-box; **-tag** nm. flag-day.

Opfer'n [op'ferrn] vt. to sacrifice; **-ung** nf. sacrifice.

Opiat [oh-pi-aht'] n. (-e) opiate.

Opium [oh'pi-ōōm] n. opium.

Opponieren [o-po-neer'ren] vt. to oppose.

Opposition [o-po-zit-syohn'] nf. opposition.

Opportun [o-porr-tuhn'] a. opportune; **-ität** nf. expediency, opportuneness, [choose.

Optieren [op-teer'ren] vt. to

Opti'k [op'tik] nf. optics; **-ker** nm. optician; **-sch** a. optical.

Optimis'mus [op-ti-miss'mōōss] nm. optimism; **-t** m.sv. optimist; **-tisch** a. optimistic.

Orakel [o-rah'kel] n. (-) oracle; **-haft** a. oracular; **-n** vi. to talk in riddles, prophesy; **-spruch** nm. oracle.

Orange [o-rang'zher] nf. orange; **-nblüte** nf. orange blossom; **-nmarmelade** nf. marmalade; **-nschale** nf. orange-peel.

Orchester [orr-kes'terr] n. (-) orchestra; **-begleitung** nf. orchestration.

Orchestrier'en [orr-kes-treer'ren] vt. to orchestrate; **-ung** nf. orchestration, score. [orchid.

Orchidee [orr-shi-day'] nf.

Orden [orr'den] nm. (-) order, decoration; **-sband** n. ribbon (medal, etc.); **-sbruder** nm. monk, friar; **-skleid** n. monastic habit; **-sschwester** nf. nun; **-szeichen** n. badge.

Ordentlich [orr-dent'lish] a. decent, respectable, orderly.

Order [orr'derr] *see* Ordre.
Ordinalzahl [orr-di-nahl'-tsahl] *nf.* ordinal number.
Ordinär [orr-di-nairr'] *a.* ordinary, common, mean, vulgar; -preis *nm.* published, retail price.
Ordinarius [orr-di-nah'ri-ōōss] *nm.* professor.
Ordination [orr-di-natsyohn'] *nf.* ordination, visit (medical); *[vt.* to ordain.
Ordinieren [orr-di-neer'ren] *vt.* to ordain.
Ordn'en [orrd'nen] *vt.* to arrange, regulate, order; -er *nm.* arranger, regulator, organizer, prefect, monitor (school), file (com.).
Ordnung [orrd'nōōng] *nf.* regulation, arrangement, classification, order(ing); -sdienst *nm.* provost service (mil.); -sgemäss *a, ad.* orderly, regular, according to instructions; -sliebe *nf.* tidiness, orderliness; -spolizei *nf.* order police, constabulary; -sstrafe *nf.* fine; -swidrig *a.* contrary to orders, irregular; -szahl *nf.* ordinal number.
Ordonnanz [orr-do-nants'] *nf.* orderly, batman (mil.); -dienst *nm.* orderly duty; -offizier *nm.* assistant adjutant.
Ordre [orr'derr] *nf.* order (com.); -scheck *nm.* cheque payable to order.
Organ [orr-gahn'] *n.* (-e) organ, voice; -isch *a.* organic.
Organis'ator [orr-ga-ni-zah'-torr] *nm.* (gen. -s; pl. -en) organiser; -ieren *vt.* to organize; -ierung *nf.* organization.
Organis'mus [orr-ga-niss'-mōōss] *nm.* organism; -t *m.w.* organist.
Orgel [orr'gel] *nf.* organ; -harmonium *n.* American organ; -n *vi.* to play a barrel-organ; -pfeife *nf.* organ-pipe; -register *n.*, -zug *nm.* organ-stop.

Orgie [orr'gi-er] *nf.* orgy.
Orient [or-ri-ent'] *nm.* orient, east; -alisch *a.* oriental.
Orientier'en [or-ri-en-teer'ren] *vt.* to locate, inform; *r.* find one's way, bearings; -ung *nf.* orientation, information.
Original [or-ri-gi-nahl'] *a.* original; -ei *n.* shell-egg; -ität *nf.* originality.
Originell [or-ri-gi-nel'] *a.* original, peculiar, odd.
Orkan [orr-kahn'] *nm.* (-e) hurricane. *[vestments.*
Ornat [orr-naht'] *nm.* (-e)
Ort [orrt] *nm.* (-e, Örter) spot, place; -sbatterie *nf.* garrison battery; -(s)beschreibung *nf.* topography; -schaft *nf.* village, small town; -sgespräch *n.* local call (ph.); -squartier *n.* local billets (mil.); -ssinn *nm.* sense of locality; -sverbindung *nf.* local call (ph.).
Ort'en [orr'ten] *vi.* to locate (av.); -er *nm.* navigator (av.).
Orthodox [orr-to-dox'] *a.* orthodox; -ie *nf.* orthodoxy.
Orthographie [orr-to-gra-fee'] *nf.* spelling, orthography; -sch *a.* orthographical, as regards spelling.
Orthopädie [orr-to-pay-dee'] *nf.* orthopaedics.
Örtlich [ert'lish] *a.* local, regional; -keit *nf.* locality, place.
Ortung [orr'tōōng] *nf.* orientation, direction-finding, radio-location; -sgerät *n.* direction-finder; -spunkt *nm.* landmark, reference point.
Öse [er'zer] *nf.* eye, loop, ring, eyelet. *[eastwards.*
Ost(en) [ost'(en)] *nm.* east; -wärts *ad.*
Oster'n [oh'sterrn] *pl.* Easter; -abend *nm.* Easter Eve; -ei *n.* Easter egg; -ferien *pl.* Easter holidays; -fest *n.* Easter.
Östlich [erst'lish] *a.* eastern, easterly.
Oszillier'en [os-tsi-leeer'ren]

vi. to oscillate; -ung *nf.* oscillation.

Otter [ot'err] *nm.* (-) otter.

Ouvertüre [ŏŏ-vairr-tyŏŏr'rer] *nf.* overture.

Oval [oh-vahl'] *a.* oval. [head.

Oxhoft [ox'hoft] *n.* (-e) hogs-

Oxyd [ox-yōōt'] *n.* (-e) oxide; -ieren *vt.* to oxidize; -ierung *nf.* oxidization.

Ozean [oh'tsay-ahn] *nm.* (-e) ocean; -dampfer *nm.* liner; -flug *nm.* transoceanic flight; -isch *a.* oceanic.

Ozon [ot-sohn'] *n.* ozone.

P

Paar [pahrr] *n.* (-e) pair, couple; *num.* a few; -en *vi.r.* to pair, mate; -ung *nf.* pairing, mating; -weise *ad.* in pairs, couples.

Pacht [pacht] *nf, m.* (-e) lease, rent; -en *vt.* to lease, rent; -ung *nf.* leasing, leasehold; -vertrag *nm.* lease.

Pächter [pesh'terr] *nm.* (-) farmer, leaseholder, tenant.

Pack [pack] *nm.* (Päcke) packet, bundle, pack, parcel; *n.* mob, rabble; -en *vt.* to pack, grasp, seize, thrill; -er *nm.* packer; -garn *n.* twine, pack-ing thread; -kiste *nf.* packing case (*com.*); -papier *n.* brown paper; -pferd *n.* pack-horse; -träger *nm.* porter; -ung *nf.* packing; -wagen *nm.* luggage van (*rl.*).

Päckchen [peck'shen] *n.* (-) small package, parcel.

Pädagogik [pay-da-goh'gik] *nf.* pedagogy, education; -sch *a.* educational, pedagogical.

Paddeln [pad'eln] *vi.* to paddle; -boot *n.* canoe.

Paff [paf] *nm.* (-e) pop, bang; - sein *vi.* to be amazed, astounded; -en *vt.i.* to puff, pop.

Page [pah'zher] *m.w.* page.

Paginieren [pa-gi-neer'ren] *vt.* to page, number pages of; -ung *nf.* pagination.

Pagode [pa-goh'der] *nf.* pagoda.

Pair [pairr] *nm.* (-s) peer.

Paket [pa-kate'] *n.* (-e) packet, parcel; -annahme *nf.* parcels receiving office (*rl.*); -beför-derung *nf.* parcels delivery; -post *nf.* parcel post.

Pakt [pakt] *nm.* (-e) pact, compact, agreement.

Palast [pa-last'] *nm.* (Paläste) palace; -artig *a.* palatial.

Paletot [pa'ler-toh] *nm.* (-s) greatcoat, overcoat.

Palette [pa-let'er] *nf.* palette; -messer *n.* palette-knife.

Palisade [pa-li-zah'der] *nf.* palisade.

Palisanderholz [pa-li-zan'derr-holts] *n.* rosewood.

Palme [pal'mer] *nf.* palm; -kätzchen *n.* catkin; -sonntag *nm.* Palm Sunday; -woche *nf.* Passion Week.

Pamphlet [pam-flate'] *n.* (-e) scurrilous pamphlet, libellous leaflet.

Paneel [pa-nale'] *n.* (-e) panel, wainscotting; -ieren *vt.* to panel. [banner.

Panier [pa-neerr'] *n.* (-e)

Panik [pah'nik] *nf.* panic; -sch *a.* panic(ky).

Panne [pan'er] *nf.* break-down, puncture (*aut.*).

Pantheismus [pan-tay-iss'mōōss] *nm.* pantheism.

Panther [pan'terr] *nm.* (-) panther.

Pantoffel [pan-tof'el] *nm.* (-) slipper; -held *m.w.* henpecked husband; -regiment *n.* petti-coat government.

Pantomime [pan-to-mee'mer] *nf.* dumb-show, pantomime.

Panzer [pant'serr] *nm.* (-) armour, armour-plate, tank (*mil.*).

Panzerabwehr [pant'serr-ap-vairr] *nf.* anti-tank defence;

-geschütz n. anti-tank gun;
-graben nm. anti-tank ditch.
Panzer-brandgranate nf.
armour-piercing incendiary;
-brechend a. armour-piercing;
-büchse nf. anti-tank rifle;
-deckung nf. armoured shelter;
-division nf. armoured division;
-fahrzeug n. armoured fighting
vehicle; **-falle** nf. tank trap;
-faust nf. mailed fist; **-geschütz**
n. assault gun; **-glas** n. bullet-
proof glass; **-granate** nf.
armour-piercing shell; **-grena-
diere** m.pl. mechanized, lorryborne infantry; **-gruppe** nf.
armoured unit; **-jäger** nm.
anti-tank troops; **-kampfwagen**
nm. tank; **-kopf** nm. armoured
head (shell); **-kraftwagen** nm.
armoured car; **-kreuzer** nm.
battle-cruiser, pocket battleship; **-landeboot** n. tank landing craft; **-mine** nf. anti-tank
mine; **-munition** nf. armour-
piercing ammunition; **-schale**
nf. armoured plate; **-scheibe**
nf. bullet-proof windscreen;
-schiff n. ironclad, armoured
vessel; **-schrank** nm. strong
box; **-schutz** nm. armour
(mil.); **-spähwagen** nm.
armoured scouting car; **-träger**
nm. tank landing craft; **-trans-
portwagen** nm. armoured troop
carrier; **-truppen** f.pl. armoured troops; **-turm** nm. armoured
turret; **-ung** nf. armour (plating); **-wagen** nm. tank, armoured car; **-wagenabbildung** nf.
dummy tank; **-zug** nm.
armoured train.
Panzern [pant'serrn] vt.r. to
armour, arm, protect oneself.
Päonie [pay-oh'ni-er] nf.
peony.
Papagei [pa-pa-gi'] nm. (gen.
-s; pl. **-en**) parrot.
Papier [pa-peerr'] n. (**-e**)
paper; **-e** pl. papers, shares,
securities; **-abfälle** m.pl. waste
paper; **-beschwerer** nm. paper-

weight; **-bogen** nm. sheet of
paper; **-en** a. (of) paper;
-drache nm. kite; **-fabrik** nf.
paper-mill; **-geld** n. paper
money; **-händler** nm. paper
merchant, stationer; **-hand-
lung** nf. stationer's shop; **-korb**
nm. waste-paper basket;
-schlange nf. streamer; **-tüte**
nf. paper-bag; **-waren** f.pl.
stationery; **-warenhändler** nm.
stationer. [popish.]
Papistisch [pa-pis'tish] a.
Papp [pap] nm. (**-e**) paste,
pap; **-band** n. pasteboard,
book bound in boards; **-deckel**
nm. pasteboard; **-einband** n.
binding in boards; **-enstiel** nm.
trifle, mere song; **-schachtel**
nf. cardboard box, bandbox.
Pappel [pap'el] nf. poplar.
Päppeln [pep'eln] vt. to feed
(baby).
Pappen [pap'en] vt. to paste,
stick together.
Pappig [pap'ish] a. pasty,
sticky. [red pepper.]
Paprika [pah'pri-kah] nm. (**-s**)
Papst [pahpst] nm. (Päpste)
pope; **-tum** n. papacy.
Parabel [pa-rah'bel] nf.
parable, parabola.
Parade [pa-rah'der] nf. parade,
review, parry; **-marsch** nm.
march past; **-platz** nm. parade
ground; **-schritt** nm. goose-
step.
Paradieren [pa-ra-deer'ren]
vi. to parade, show off.
Paradies [pa-ra-deess'] n. (**-e**)
paradise; **-isch** a. heavenly.
Paradox [pa-ra-dox'] a.
paradoxical.
Parallel [pa-ra-lale'] a.
parallel; **-e** nf. parallel;
-schaltung nf. parallel connection (el.).
Paralyse [pa-ra-lyöö'zer] nf.
paralysis; **-sieren** vt. to
paralyse; **-tiker** nm. paralytic.
Paranuss [pah'rah-nööss] nf.
Brazil-nut.

Parasit [pa-ra-zeet'] *m.w.* parasite. [prepared.

Parat [pa-raht'] *a.* ready,

Pärchen [pairr'shen] *n.* (-) couple, pair of lovers.

Paranthe'se [pa-ran-tay'zer] *nf.* parenthesis, brackets; -tisch *a.* parenthetical.

Parfüm [parr-fyōōm'] *n.* (-e) perfume; -flasche *nf.* scent-bottle; -ieren *vt.* to scent, perfume.

Pari [pah'ree] *n.* par.

Paria [pah'ri.a] *nm.* (-s) pariah, outcast.

Parieren [pa-reer'ren] *vt.* to parry, rein (*horse*); *i.* obey.

Parieren [pa-reer'ren] *vt.* to wager.

Parität [pa-ri-tate'] *nf.* parity.

Park [parrk] *nm.* (-e) park; -anlage *nf.* park, grounds; -en *vt.* to park; -platz *m.* parking place; -verbot *n.* parking prohibited.

Parkett [parr-ket'] *n.* (-e) parquet (floor), stalls (*theatre*); -boden *nm.* parquet floor; -ieren *vt.* to inlay, parquet; -platz *nm.* orchestra stall.

Parlament [parr-la-ment'] *n.* (-) parliament; -är *nm.* bearer of flag of truce; -arier *nm.* parliamentarian; -arisch *a.* parliamentary; -ieren *vi.* to parley; -smitglied *n.* member of parliament. [parody.

Parodie [pa-ro-dee'] *nf.*

Parole [pa-roh'ler] *nf.* parole, password, countersign.

Partei [parr-ti'] *nf.* party, side, faction; -gänger *nm.* partisan, party man; -genosse *m.* party member, Nazi; -gliederung *nf.* party formation, organization; -isch, -lich *a.* partisan, one-sided, partial, biased; -lichkeit *nf.* partiality, one-sidedness, partisanship; -leitung *nf.* party headquarters; -los *a.* impartial; -losigkeit *nf.* impartiality, neutrality;

-nahme *nf.* partisanship, partiality; -sucht *nf.* faction.

Parterre [parr-tair'rer] *n.* (-s) ground-floor, pit, stalls.

Partie [parr-tee'] *nf.* game, match, set, excursion, trip, outing, part, lot (*com.*).

Partikel [parr-tee'kel] *nf.* particle.

Partikularismus [parr-ti-kōō-lar-riss'mōōss] *nm.* parochialism, separatism.

Partisan [parr-ti-zahn'] *nm.* (-e) partisan, patriot.

Partitur [parr-ti-tōōr'] *nf.* score (*music*).

Partizip [parr-tit-seep'] *n.* (-ien) participle. [allotment.

Parzelle [part-sel'er] *nf.* plot,

Pasche'n [pash'en] *vi.* to smuggle; -r *nm.* (-) smuggler.

Paspel [pas'pel] *nf.* edging, piping.

Pass [pass] *nm.* (Pässe) pass, passport, pace, passage, thoroughfare; -amt *n.* passport office; -bild *n.* passport photograph; -gang *nm.* amble (*horse*); -höhe *nf.* top of pass; -kontrolle *nf.* examination of passports; -stelle *nf.* passport office. [passage.

Passage [pass-ah'zher] *nf.*

Passagier [pass-a-zheer'] *nm.* (-e) passenger; -dampfer *nm.* passenger steamer; -flugzeug *n.* air-liner; -geld *n.* fare; -gut *n.* luggage.

Passant [pass-ant'] *m.w.* passer-by.

Passatwind [pass-aht'vint] *nm.* (-e) trade-wind.

Passen [pass'en] *vi.* to fit, go with, suit, pass (*bridge*); -- auf pay attention to, look out, wait for; *r.* be proper, convenient; *t.* fit (on); -d *a.* fit(ting), suitable, appropriate, convenient.

Passierbar [pass-eerr'barr] *a.* passable.

Passier'en [pass-eer'ren] *vt.* to pass, cross, go through.

sieve; *i.* happen; **-schein** *nm.* pass, permit.

Passion [pass-yohn'] *nf.* passion; *-iert a.* impassioned; **-sspiel** *n.* Passion play.

Passiv [pass'eef] *a.* passive; *n.* (-a) passive; **-a** *pl.* liabilities (*com.*); **-ität** *nf.* passivity, **-seite** *nf.* debit side.

Passkarte [pass'karr-ter] *nf.* passport.

Passlich [pass'lish] *a.* suitable.

Pasta [pass'ta] *nf.* paste.

Pastell [pass-tel'] *n.* (-e) pastel. [pastry.

Pastete [pass-tay'ter] *nf.* pie, **Pasteurisieren** [pass-ter-ri-zeer'ren] *vt.* to pasteurize.

Pastille [pass-til'er] *nf.* pastille, lozenge.

Pastinake [pass-ti-nah'ker] *nf.* parsnip.

Pastor [pass'torr] *nm.* (*gen.* -s; *pl.* **-en**) pastor, minister, clergyman; **-al** *a.* pastoral. *at n.* (-e) pastorate; **-in** *nf.* clergyman's wife.

Pätchen [päht'shen] *n.* (-) godchild.

Pat'e [pah'ter] *m.w.* godfather, **-enkind** *n.* godchild; **-in** *nf.* godmother.

Patent [pa-tent'] *n.* (-e) patent, officier's commission; **-amt** *n.* patent-office; **-anwalt** *nm.* patent-agent; **-ieren** *vt.* to patent; **-inhaber** *nm.* patentee; **-schutz** *nm.* patent laws; **-verschluss** *nm.* patent stopper.

Paternosterwerk [pa'terr-nos-terr-vairrk] *n.* bucketchain, elevator.

Pathetisch [pa-tay'tish] *a.* solemn, lofty, rhetorical.

Patholog [pa-to-lohk'] *m.w.* pathologist; *-isch a.* pathological. [pathology.

Pathologie [pa-to-lo-gee'] *nf.*

Pathos [pah'toss] *n.* pathos, rhetoric.

Patient [pat-si-ent'] *m.w.* **-in** *nf.* patient.

Patriarch [pat-ri-arsh'] *m.w.* patriarch; *-alisch a.* patriarchal.

Patriot [pat-ri-oht'] *m.w.* patriot; *-isch a.* patriotic; **-ismus** *nm.* patriotism.

Patrizier [pat-reet'si-err] *nm.* (-) patrician.

Patron [pat-rohn'] *nm.*(-e) patron, fellow; **-at** (*srechent*) *n.* patronage; **-in** *nf.* patroness.

Patrone [pat-roh'ner] *nf.* cartridge, round (*ammunition*), stencil, model; **-nauswerfer** *nm.* ejector (*machine-gun*); **-ngurt** *nm.* cartridge belt, bandolier; **-nhülse** *nf.* cartridge-case; **-nmunition** *nf.* fixed ammunition; **-ntasche** *nf.* cartridge pouch.

Patrouill'e [pat-rōōl'yer] *nf.* patrol; *-ieren vi.* to patrol.

Patsche [pat'sher] *nf.* slap, mud, mess; *-n vt.i.* to splash, smack, slap. [saucy.

Patzig [pat'sish] *a.* cheeky,

Pauke [pow'ker] *nf.* kettledrum, scolding, lecture ; *-n vt.i.* to beat the kettledrum, beat, swot, cram; **-r** *nm.* (-) kettledrummer, crammer, coach; **-rei** *nf.* cramming, coaching.

Pausbäckig [powss'bek-ish] *a.* chubby-faced.

Pausch- *see* Pauschal-.

Pauschal'(gebühr) [pow-shahl'ger-byoor] *nf.* flat rate; **-kauf** *nm.* purchase in bulk; **-summe** *nf.* lump sum.

Paus'e [pow'zer] *nf.* pause, rest, break, interruption, interval, stop; *-ieren vi.* to make a break, pause.

Paus'e [pow'zer] *nf.* tracing; **-en** *vt.* to trace; **-papier** *n.* tracing paper. [baboon.

Pavian [pa-vi-ahn'] *nm.* (-e)

Pazifis'mus [pat-si-fiss'mōōss] *nm.* pacifism ; **-t** *m.w.* pacifist.

Pech [pesh] *n.* pitch, cobbler's

wax, bad luck; **-blende** *nf.*
pitch-ore; **-draht** *nm.* shoemaker's thread; **-kohl** *nm.*
bituminous coal; **-schwarz** *a.*
pitch-black; **-tanne** *nf.* spruce-
fir; **-vogel** *nm.* unlucky person.
Pedal [ped-ahl'] *n.* (-e) pedal,
treadle; **-achse** *nf.* pedal pin,
spindle (*cycle*); **-rahmen** *nm.*
pedal frame; **-steg** *nm.* pedal
end-plate.
Pedant [ped-ant'] *m.w.* pedant;
-erie *nf.* pedantry; **-isch** *a.*
pedantic. [porter.
Pedell [ped-el'] *nm.* (-e) beadle,
Pegel [pay'gel] *n.* (-) water-
gauge, water-mark; **-n** *vi.* to
take soundings; **-stand** *nm.*
water-level.
Peilen [pile'en] *vt.* to sound,
take bearings of, gauge, locate;
-funk *nm.* direction finding;
-funkgerät *n.* wireless direction
finder; **-lot** *n.* plummet; **-ung**
nf. bearing (*nav.*), direction
finding.
Pein [pine] *nf.* agony, pain;
-igen *vt.* to torture, torment;
-iger *nm.* (-) torturer, tormentor.
Peinlich [pine'lish] *a.* painful,
painstaking, careful, precise;
-keit *nf.* painfulness, scrupulousness.
Peitsche [pite'sher] *nf.* whip,
lash; **-n** *vt.* to whip, lash;
-nreimen *nm.*, **-nschnur** *nf.*
whipcord, thong of a whip.
Pekuniär [pay-koo-ni-airr'] *a.*
pecuniary.
Pelikan [pe-li-kahn'] *nm.* (-e)
pelican. [skin, peel.
Pelle [pel'er] *nf.* skin; **-n** *vt.* to
Pelz [pelts] *nm.* (-e) fur, pelt,
hide, skin; **-händler** *nm.* furrier; **-ig** *a.* furry, **-kragen** *nm.*
fur-collar, tippet; **-mantel** *nm.*
fur-coat; **-stiefel** *nm.* fur-lined
boots; **-ware** *nf.*, **-werk** *n.* furs.
Pendel [pen'del] *nm. n.* (-)
pendulum; **-verkehr** *nm.*
shuttle-traffic.

Pennal [pen-ahl'] *n.* (-e)
pencil-case, secondary school.
Pension [pang-syohn'] *nf.*
pension, superannuation,
boarding house, guest house;
-är *nm.* (-e) boarder, paying
guest, pensioner; **-at** *n.* (-e)
boarding school; **-ieren** *vt.* to
pension (off).
Pensum [pen'zōōm] *n.* lesson,
task, exercise.
Per [perr] *pr.* by, per.
Perennierend [per-ren-eer'-
rent] *a.* perennial.
Perfekt [perr'fekt] *n.* perfect
(*grammar*); *a.* [perr-fekt'] perfect.
Perforieren [perr-for-reer'-
ren] *vt.* to perforate.
Pergament [perr-ga-ment'] *n.*
(-e) parchment.
Periode [per-ri-oh'der] *n.f.*
period, spell; **-isch** *a.* periodic,
recurring (*decimal*).
Peripherie [per-ri-fer-ree'] *nf*
circumference, outskirts.
Perle [perr'ler] *nf.* pearl; **-en**
vi. to sparkle; **-huhn** *n.*
guinea-fowl; **-mutter** *nf.*
mother-of-pearl.
Perpendikel [perr-pen-dee'-
kel] *nm, n.* (-) perpendicular,
plummet-line, pendulum;
-ulär *a.* perpendicular.
Persenning [perr-zen'ing] *nf.*
tarpaulin.
Person [perr-zohn'] *nf.* person;
-enauszug *nm.* lift; **-enschäden**
m.pl. personal injuries; **-en-
verzeichnis** *n.* dramatis
personae; **-enzug** *nm.* passenger train.
Personal [perr-zoh-nahl'] *a,
n.* staff, personnel, employees,
servants; **-angelegenheit** *nf.*
personal affair; **-ien** *pl.* personal particulars, personalia.
Personifizieren [perr-zo-ni-
fit-seer'ren] *vt.* to personify.
Personnel [perr-zo-nel'] *a.*
personal; **-e Rüstung** manning.
Persönlich [perr-zern'lish] *a.*

personal; *ad.* in person; **-keit** *nf.* personality.

Perspektive [parr-spek-tee´ver] *nf.* perspective.

Perücke [per-ryōō´ker] *nf.* wig.

Pervers [perr-vairss´] *a.* perverse; **-ität** *nf.* perversity.

Pessimis´mus [pess-i-miss´ mōōss] *nm.* pessimism; **-t** *m.w.* pessimist; **-tisch** *a.* pessimistic.

Pest [pest] *nf.* plague, epidemic; **-beule** *nf.* plague-spot.

Petersilie [pay-terr-zee´li-er] *nf.* parsley.

Petroleum [pay-roh´li-ŏŏm] *n.* petroleum, paraffin.

Petschaft [pet´shaft] *n.* (-e) seal; **-ring** *nm.* signet-ring.

Petzen [pet´sen] *vt.* to tell tales about, sneak.

Pfad [pfaht] *nm.* (-e) path; **-finder** *nm.* boy-scout; **-finderin** *nf.* girl guide; **-los** *a.* pathless.

Pfaffe [pfaf´er] *m.w.* parson, priest; **-ntum** *n.* clericalism.

Pfaffisch [pfef´ish] *a.* priestridden, parsonical.

Pfahl [pfahl] *nm.* (Pfähle) pile, post, stake, prop; **-bau** *nm.* lake-dwellings; **-brücke** *nf.* pile-bridge; **-werk** *n.* palings; **-zaun** *nm.* stockade.

Pfählen [pfale´en] *vt.* to fence in, enclose.

Pfand [pfant] *n.* (Pfänder) pledge, forfeit; **-brief** *nm.* mortgage bond; **-geschäft** *n.* **-haus** *n.* pawnshop; **-leiher** *nm.* pawnbroker; **-schein** *nm.* pawn-ticket.

Pfänd´bar [pfent´barr] *a.* distrainable; **-en** *vt.* to distrain, seize; **-erspiel** *n.* game of forfeits; **-ung** *nf.* distraint, seizure.

Pfann´e [pfan´er] *nf.* pan; **-kuchen** *nm.* pancake, fritter.

Pfarr´amt [pfarr´amt] *n.* parish; **-e**, **-ei** *nf.* parsonage, vicarage, parish, living; **-er** *nm.* (-) vicar, minister, priest, pastor; **-haus** *n.* vicarage,

manse; **-kirche** *nf.* parish church; **-stelle** *nf.* living, benefice.

Pfau [pfow] *nm.* (gen. -s *pl.* -en) peacock; **-enauge** *n.* peacock butterfly.

Pfeffer [pfef´err] *nm.* pepper; **-büchse** *nf.* pepper caster; **-ig** *a.* peppery; **-kuchen** *nm.* gingerbread; **-n** *vt.* to pepper, season; **-minze** *nf.* peppermint.

Pfeife [pfife´er] *nf.* pipe whistle; **-n** *vi.* to whistle, squeak; **-nspitze** *nf.* mouthpiece; **-r** *nm.* (-) piper, whistler.

Pfeil [pfile] *nm.* (-e) arrow.

Pfeiler [pfile´err] *nm.* (-) pillar, prop, pier.

Pfennig [pfen´ish] *nm.* (-e) pfennig, tenth of a penny.

Pferch [pfairrsh] *nm.* (-e) fold, pen; **-lager** *n.* sheepfold; **-en** *vt.* to fold, pen.

Pferd [pfairrt] *nm.* (-e) horse; **-ausrüstung** *nf.* horse equipment; **-ebremse** *nf.* horse-fly; **-egeschirr** *n.* harness; **-eknecht** *nm.* groom; **-ekraft** *nf.* horsepower; **-erennen** *n.* horse-race; **-estall** *nm.* stable; **-ewagen** *nm.* horse-truck (*vt.*).

Pfiff [pfif] *nm.* (-e) whistle, trick, trice; **-ig** *a.* sly, sharp; **-igkeit** *nf.* slyness.

Pfifferling [pfif´err-ling] *nm.* yellow chanterelle, mushroom, trifle, rap.

Pfingst´en [pfing´sten] *n.* (-) Whitsuntide; **-montag** *nm.* Whit Monday; **-rose** *nf.* peony, peach.

Pfirsich [pfirr´sish] *nm.* (-e) peach.

Pflanze [pflant´ser] *nf.* plant; **-nbeet** *n.* garden bed; **-nbutter** *nf.* margarine, nut butter; **-nfarbe** *nf.* vegetable dye; **-ngarten** *nm.* botanical gardens; **-nhaus** *n.* conservatory; **-nkunde** *nf.* botany; **-nstoff** *nm.* vegetable matter.

Pflanz´en [pflant´sen] *vt.* to plant; **-er** *nm.* (-) planter, colonist; **-garten** *nm,* **-schule** *nf.* nursery (*garden*); **-gärtner** *nm.* nurseryman, nursery gardener; **-ung** *nf.* plantation, settlement.

Pflaster [pflas'terr] *n.* (-) plaster, pavement; **-er** *nm.* paviour; **-n** *vt.* to pave, plaster; **-stein** *nm.* paving stone; **-treterei** *nf.* idling, loafing.

Pflaume [pflow'mer] *nf.* plum.

Pfleg'e [pflay'ger] *nf.* care, nursing, fostering, cultivation; **-ebedürftig** *a.* needing care; **-ekind** *n.* foster-child; **-er** *nm.* (-) guardian, male nurse; **-erin** *nf.* nurse, attendant; **-schaft** *nf.* guardianship.

Pflegen [pflay'gen] *vt.* to care for, nurse, attend to; *i.* be accustomed to.

Pflicht [pflisht] *nf.* duty; **-gefühl** *n.* sense of duty; **-gemäss** *a.* dutiful, incumbent; *ad.* as in duty bound; **-treu** *a.* conscientious; **-vergessen** *a.* disloyal, unfaithful; **-widrig** *a.* undutiful.

Pflock [pflok] *nm.* (Pflöcke)

Pflöcken [pfler'ken] *vt.* to peg.

Pflücken [pflyöö'ken] *vt.* to pluck, gather.

Pflug [pflöök] *nm.* (Pflüge) plough; **-schar** *nf.* ploughshare.

Pflügen [pflyöö'gen] *vt.* to plough.

Pforte [pfor'ter] *nf.* gate.

Pförtner [pfert'nerr] *nm.* (-) porter, doorkeeper, doorman, warder.

Pfosten [pfos'ten] *nm.* (-) post, stake, door-jamb.

Pfote [pfoh'ter] *nf.* paw, scrawl.

Pfriem [pfreem] *nm.* (-e) awl, punch, bodkin; **-en** *vt.* to punch, bore, pierce.

Pfropf [pfropf] *nm.* (Pfröpfe) plug, wad, bung, cork, stopper; **-en** *vt.* to cram, cork, bung, graft (*tree*). [*see* Pfropf.

Pfropfen [prop'fen] *nm.* (-)

(-e) shoot, grafted tree.

Pfründe [pfryön'der] *nf.* living (*church*).

Pfuhl [pfööl] *nm.* (-e) puddle.

Pfühl [pfyööl] *nm, n.* (Pfühle) pillow, bolster.

Pfui [pföö'i] *inter.* fie, shame!

Pfund [pföönt] *n.* (-e) pound; **-stück** *n.* sovereign; **-weise** *ad.* by the pound.

Pfuschen [pföö'shen] *vt.i.* to bungle, scamp, cheat, meddle, butt in; **-er** *nm.* (-) bungler, dabbler, quack; **-erei** *nf.* bungling, muddle, quackery.

Pfütze [pfyöt'ser] *nf.* puddle.

Phänomen [fay-no-mane'] *n.* (-e) phenomenon.

Phantasie [fan-ta-zee'] *nf.* fancy, imagination, ravings; **-ren** *vi.* to indulge in fancies, day-dream, rave.

Phantastisch [fan-tas'tish] *a.* fantastic. [phantom.

Phantom [fan-tome'] *n.* (-e)

Phase [fah'zer] *nf.* phase.

Philanthrop [fi-lan-trope'] *m.w.* philanthropist.

Philist'er [fi-lis'terr] *nm.* (-) Philistine; **-rös** *a.* narrow-minded, middle-class.

Philolog'e [fi-lo-loh'ger] *m.w.* philologist; **-ie** *nf.* philology.

Philosoph [fi-lo-zofe'] *m.w.* philosopher; **-isch** *a.* philosophical.

Philosophie [fi-lo-zo-fee'] *nf.* philosophy.

Phiole [fee-oh'ler] *nf.* phial.

Phlegmatisch [fleg-mah'tish] *a.* phlegmatic, lethargic.

Phonetik [fo-nay'tik] *nf.* phonetics; **-isch** *a.* phonetic.

Phosphor [fos'forr] *nm.* phosphorus.

Phosphoreszieren [fos-forres-tseer'ren] *vi.* to phosphoresce.

Photograph [fo-to-grahf'] *m.w.* photographer; **-ie** *nf.* photography; **-ieren** *vt.* to photograph; -isch a. photographic.

Photo-apparat nm. (-e) camera; **-laden** nm. photographer's shop; **-mappe** nf. photo-album; **-montage** nf. photographic lay-out; **-zelle** nf. photo-electric cell.

Phrase [frah'zer] nf. phrase, empty words, rhetoric.

Physik [fyōō-zeek'] nf. physics; **-alisch** a. physical; **-er** nm. (-) physicist.

Physiolog [fyōō-zee-o-lohk'] m.w. physiologist; **-ie** nf. physiology.

Physisch [fyōō'zish] a. physical.

Pianist [pi-a-nist'] m.w. m.f. pianist. [pianola.

Pianola [pi-a-noh'la] n. (-s)

Pich'eln [pish'eln] vi. to tipple; **-ler** nm. (-) toper, drinker.

Picke [pik'er] nf. pickaxe.

Pickel [pikl] nm. (-) pimple; see also Picke; **-ig** a. pimply.

Pickelflöte [pikl'fler-ter] nf. piccolo.

Pickelhaube [pikl'how-ber] nf. spiked helmet.

Pickelhering [pikl'hair-ring] nm. (-e) pickled herring.

Picken [pik'en] vi. to pick, peck.

Piepen [pee'pen] vi. to chirp.

Pietät [pee-er-tate'] nf. piety, reverence; **-los** a. impious, irreverent.

Pik [peek] nm. (-e) peak, spade (cards), grudge; **-fein** a. fashionable, smart; **-iert** a. offended, hurt.

Pikant [pee-kant'] a. spicy, high-flavoured, suggestive.

Pikkoloflöte [pi'ko-loh-fler'-ter] nf. piccolo.

Pikrinsäure [pi-kreen'zoy-rer] nf. picric acid.

Pilger [pil'gerr] nm. (-) pilgrim; **-fahrt** nf. pilgrimage; **-n** vi. to go on a pilgrimage.

Pille [pil'er] nf. pill.

Pilot'e [pi-loh'ter] m.w. pilot; **-ballon** nm. pilot balloon; **-ieren** vt. to pilot.

Pilz [pilts] nm. (-e) mushroom, fungus, toadstool.

Pimpelig [pim'per-lish] a. flabby, effeminate, sickly.

Pinasse [pi-nas'ser] nf. pinnace. [penguin.

Pinguin [pin-gu-een'] nm. (-e)

Pinie [pee'nyer] nf. stone-pine; **-nnuss** nf. pine-kernel.

Pinne [pin'er] nf. drawing-pin, tack, peg, tiller.

Pinsel [pin'zel] nm. (-) paintbrush, ass, simpleton; **-n** vt.i. to paint, daub.

Pionier [pi-o-neerr'] nm. (gen. -s; pl. -e) pioneer, sapper, engineer.

Pirat [pi-raht'] m.w. pirate; **-entum** n. piracy.

Pirsch [pirrsh] nf. hunting, stalking; **-en** vi. to stalk, hunt.

Pistole [pi-stoh'ler] nf. pistol.

Plack'en [plack'en] vt. to plague, torment; r. toil, drudge; **-erei** nf. drudgery.

Plädieren [play-deer'en] vi. to plead.

Plage [plah'ger] nf. plague, worry, torment; **-geist** nm. plague, nuisance; **-n** vt. to plague, worry, pester; r. to toil, slave.

Plagiat [pla-gi-aht'] n. (-e) plagiarism; or nm. plagiarist.

Plakat [pla-kaht'] n. (-e) placard, poster; **-ankleber** nm. bill-sticker; **-ieren** vt. to stick bills, advertise on hoardings; **-träger** nm. sandwich-man.

Plan [plahn] nm. (Pläne) plan, diagram, map, scheme, design, establishment (mil.); **-feuer** n. barrage fire, directed map fire (mil.); **-gerät** n. plotting equipment; **-los** a. aimless, unplanned, unsystematic; **-mässig** a. according to plan, systematic; **-quadrat** n. map square; **-schiessen** n. shooting by the map (*mil.*); -soll *n.* establishment strength (*mil.*); -stelle *nf.* planning office, centre; -übung *nf.* tewt, tactical exercise without troops.

Plan [plahn] *a.* flat, level; *n.* plain, plane.

Plane [plah'ner] *nf.* tarpaulin, awning; -wagen *nm.* covered cart, waggon.

Planen [plah'nen] *vt.i.* to plan.

Planet [pla-nate'] *m.w.* planet; -getriebe *n.* planet drive (*tank*).

Planier'en [pla-neer'ren] *vt.* to plane, level; -ung *nf.* levelling; -ungsmaschine *nf.* leveller, bulldozer-tractor.

Planke [plang'ker] *nf.* plank.

Plänkelei [pleng-ker-lie'] *nf.* skirmish(ing). [skirmish.

Plänkeln [pleng'keln] *vi.* to

Planschen [plansh'en], **Plantschen** [plant'shen] *vi.* to splash.

Plantage [plan-tah'zher] *nf.* plantation.

Planung [plah'nŏong] *nf.* planning; -samt *n.* planning department.

Plapperei [pla-per-rie'] *nf.* chattering. [*n.* chatterbox.

Plappermaul [pla'perr-mowl]

Plappern [pla'perrn] *vi.* to chatter. [whine.

Plärren [pler'ren] *vi.* to cry,

Plastik [plass'tik] *nf.* sculpture, art. [plasticine.

Plastilin [plass-ti-leen'] *n.*

Plastisch [plass'tish] *a.* plastic; -e Masse plastics.

Platane [pla-tah'ner] *nf.* plane-tree.

Platin [pla-teen'] *n.* platinum.

Plätschern [plet'sherrn] *vi.* to splash, murmur.

Platt [plat] *a.* flat, trite, level, silly; -fuss *nm.* flat foot; -fusseinlage *nf.* instep-support; -heit *nf.* flatness, platitude.

Platte [plat'er] *nf.* plate, tray, flag (*stone*), disc, record (*gramophone*); -nspielapparat *nm.* gramophone.

Plätteisen [plet'ize-en] *n.* iron.

Platten [plat'en] *vt.* to flatten.

Plätten [plet'en] *vt.* to iron.

Plattieren [pla-teer'en] *vt.* to plate.

Platz [plats] *nm.* (Plätze) place, seat, room, square; -anweiser in *nf.* theatre attendant, usherette; -bedarf *nm.* local demand; -befeuerung *nf.* aerodrome lighting; -karte *nf.* reserved seat ticket (*rl.*); -kommandant *nm.* town commander; -kommando *n.* airfield detachment (*av.*); -mangel *nm.* lack of space.

Plätzchen [plets'shen] *n.* (-) spot, little place, biscuit, lozenge.

Platz'en [plat'sen] *vi.* to crack, burst, bang, explode; -munition *nf.* blank ammunition; -patrone *nf.* blank cartridge; -regen *nm.* heavy rain, downpour.

Plauderei [plow-der-rie'] *nf.* chat, conversation, talk (*rad.*).

Plauder'er [plow'der-rerr] *nm.* (-) talker, chatterbox; -haft *a.* talkative, gossipy; -n *vi.* to chat, talk; -ton *nm.* conversational tone.

Plausibel [plow-zeebl'] *a.* plausible.

Plebej'er [ple-bay'yerr] *nm.* (-) plebeian, low-class person; -isch *a.* plebeian.

Plebs [plepss] *nf.* rabble, mob.

Pleuelstange [ploy'el-shtang-er] *nf.* connecting rod.

Plinse [lin'zer] *nf.* fritter, pancake. [pleating.

Plissee [pliss-ay'] *nf.* (-s)

Plomb'e [plom'ber] *nf.* lead seal, tooth stopping, filling; -ieren *vt.* to seal, stop (*teeth*).

Plötzlich [plerts'lish] *a.* sudden; *ad.* suddenly; -keit *nf.* suddenness.

Pluderhosen [plŏŏ'derr-hoezen] *f.pl.* wide trousers, plusfours.

Plump [plŏŏmp] *a.* coarse,

clumsy, shapeless; **-heit** *nf.* coarseness, clumsiness, shapelessness.

Plumpsen [plŏŏmp'sen] *vi.* to plump down, fall, blurt out.

Plunder [plŏŏn'derr] *nm.* rubbish, lumber, junk.

Plünder'er [plyŏŏn'der-rerr] *nm.* (-) plunderer; **-n** *vt.i.* to plunder, sack (*town*); **-ung** *nf.* plundering, sack, pillage.

Plural [plŏŏ'rahl] *nm.* (-e) plural.

Plus [plŏŏss] *n.* (-) plus, amount left over, surplus; **-bestand** *nm.* surplus stock.

Plusquamperfekt [plŏŏss'-kvam-pairr-fekt] *n.* pluperfect.

Plüsch [plyŏŏsh] *nm.* (-e) plush.

Plutonium [plŏŏ-toh'ni-ŏŏm] *n.* plutonium.

Pneuma'tik [p-noy-mah'tik] *nf.* pneumatic tyre; **-sch** *a.* pneumatic.

Pöbel [per'bel] *nm.* mob, rabble; **-haft** *a.* low, vulgar, rowdy; **-haufen** *nm.* mob; **-herrschaft** *nf.* mob rule.

Pochen [poch'en] *vi.* to knock, tap, beat, pound, boast; **-spiel** *n.* poker (*game*); **-werk** *n.* stamping mill.

Pocke [pok'er] *nf.* pock-mark; **-n** *pl.* smallpox; **-nimpfung** *nf.* vaccination; **-nnarbig** *a.* pockmarked.

Poesie [poh-ez-ee'] *nf.* poetry.

Poet [po-ate'] *m.w.* poet; **-isch** *a.* poetic.

Pöhnen [per'nen] *vt.* to paint (*camouflage*).

Pokal [po-kahl'] *nm.* (-e) goblet, cup.

Pökel [per'kel] *nm.* (-) pickle; **-fleisch** *n.* salt meat; **-hering** *nm.* pickled herring; **-n** *vt.* to pickle, salt, preserve.

Pol [pole] *nm.* (-e) pole.

Polar [po-lahr'] *a.* polar; **-kreis** *nm.* arctic circle.

Polem'ik [po-lay'mik] *nf.* polemics; **-isch** *a.* polemical, controversial.

Police [po-lee'ser] *nf.* insurance policy; **-ninhaber** *nm.* policy holder. [man.

Polier [po-leerr'] *nm.* (-) fore-

Polieren [po-leer'ren] *vt.* to polish. [policy.

Politik [po-li-teek'] *nf.* politics.

Politi'ker [po-lee'ti-kerr] *nm.* (-) politician; **-sch** *a.* political.

Politisieren [po-li-ti-zeer'ren] *vi.* to talk politics.

Politur [po-li-toorr'] *nf.* polish.

Polizei [po-lit-sie'] *nf.* police; **-beamte(r)** *m.w.* police officer, constable; **-kommissar** *nm.* police inspector; **-kunder** *nm.* police spy; **-lich** *a.* police; **-ordnung** *nf.* police regulations; **-richter** *nm.* magistrate; **-spitzel** *nm.* police spy, informer; **-streife** *nf.* police raid; **-stunde** *nf.* closing hour; **-truppe** *nf.* constabulary; **-wache** *nf.* police station; **-wachtmeister** *nm.* police sergeant; **-widrig** *a.* illegal, punishable.

Polizist [po-lit-sist'] *m.w.* policeman, constable.

Polster [pol'sterr] *n.* (-) bolster, pillow, padding, pad, stuffing; **-er** *nm.* upholsterer; **-möbel** *n.pl.* upholstered furniture; **-n** *vt.* to upholster, stuff, pad; **-ung** *nf.* upholstery.

Polterabend [pol'terr-ah-bent] *nm.* (-e) party on eve of wedding.

Polter'er [pol'ter-rerr] *nm.* rowdy person, blusterer; **-n** *vi.* to be noisy, bluster; **-geist** *nm.* goblin, noisy ghost.

Polygamie [po-lyŏŏ-ga-mee'] *nf.* polygamy.

Polytechnikum [po-lyŏŏ-tesh'ni-kŏŏm] *n.* technical school, college.

Pomade [po-mah'der] *nf.* pomade.

Pomeranze [po-mer-rant'ser] *nf.* orange.

Pomp [pomp] *nm.* pomp; **-haft**

a. pompous, splendid, magnificent.

Pompelmuse [pom'pel-mōō-zer] *nf.* grape-fruit.

Pontonbrücke [pon-ton'brȳōō-ker] *nf.* pontoon-bridge.

Popanz [po-pantzs'] *nm.* (-e) bugbear, bogey.

Populär [po-pŏō-lairr'] *a.* popular.

Populari'sieren [po-pŏō-lar-ri-zeer'ren] *vt.* to popularize; **-sierung** *nf.* popularization; **-tät** *nf.* popularity.

Pore [por'rer] *nf.* pore.

Porös [por-rerss'] porous.

Porosität [po-ro-zi-tate'] *nf.* porousness.

Porree [por-ray'] *nm.* leek.

Portal [porr-tahl'] *n.* (-e) portal.

Portier [porr-ti-ay'] *nm.* (-s) porter, gate, door-keeper.

Portion [por-syohn'] *nf.* portion, plate(ful), helping, ration.

Porto [porr'tohj'n. (-s) postage; **-frei** *a.* post free, prepaid; **-kasse** *nf.* petty cash; **-zuschlag** *nm.* excess postage.

Porträt [porr-trate'] *n.* (-s) portrait; **-ieren** *vt.* to paint (*portrait*), portray; **-maler** *nm.* portrait painter.

Porzellan [porrt-sel-ahn'] *n.* (-e) china, porcelain; **-aufsatz** *nm.* china service; **-erde** *nf.* china clay, kaolin; **-laden** *nf.* china-shop.

Posamentier [po-zam-en-teerr'] *nm.* (-e) haberdasher; **-waren** *f.pl.* haberdashery.

Posaune [po-zow'ner] *nf.* trombone, trumpet.

Pose [poh'zer] *nf.* quill, pose, attitude; **-ieren** *vi.* to pose.

Position [po-zit-syohn'] *nf.* position (*com.*), station (*av.*); **-slampe** *nf.* recognition light (*av.*).

Positiv [po-zi-teef'] *a.* positive, orthodox, statute (*law*); *n.* print, positive (*photo*).

Positur [po-zi-tōōrr'] *nf.* posture, attitude.

Posse [poss'er] *nf.* farce, fun.

Possen [poss'en] *nm.* (-) trick; **-haft** *a.* farcical; **-reisser** *nm.* (-) buffoon.

Possierlich [po-seerr'lish] *a.* funny, ludicrous.

Possessiv [po-zess-eef'] *a.* possessive; *n.* possessive (*pronoun*).

Post [post] *nf.* post(-office), mail; **-adressbuch** *n.* postal directory; **-amt** *n.* post-office; **-anweisung** *nf.* postal order, money-order; **-auto** *n.* motorbus; **-beamte(r)** *m.w.* post-office official, clerk; **-beförderung** *nf.* postal service; **-bote** *m.w.* postman; **-festkonto** *n.* post-office deposit account; **-karte** *nf.* postcard; **-kasten** *nm.* letter-box; **-lagernd** *a.* poste restante; **-sack** *nm.* mailbag; **-schiff** *n.* mail-boat; **-schliessfach** *n.* post-office box; **-sparkasse** *nf.* post-office savings bank; **-stempel** *nm.* **-zeichen** *n.* post-mark; **-wendend** *a.* by return (of post); **-wertzeichen** *n.* postage stamp.

Postalisch [po-stah'lish] *a* postal, mail.

Postament [pos-ta-ment'] *n.* (-e) pedestal.

Posten [pos'ten] *nm.* (-) post, position, entry, item (*com.*), parcel, sentry, picket (*mil.*); **-kette** *nf.* cordon. [*post*.

Postieren [pos-teer'ren] *vt.* to

Postu'lat [pos-tōō-laht'] *n.* (-e) postulate; **-ieren** *vt.* to postulate.

Potential [po-tents-i-ahl'] *n.* (-e) potential. [power.

Potenz [po-tents'] *nf.* potency

Pottasche [pot-ash'er] *nf.* potash. [to flirt.

Poussieren [pōō-seer'ren] *vi.*

Pracht [pracht] *nf.* splendour, magnificence, luxury; **-ausgabe**

nf. edition de luxe; **-voll** *a.* splendid, magnificent.

Prädikat [pray-di-kaht'] *n.* (-e) title, predicate, mark.

Präfix [pray-fix'] *n.* (-e) prefix.

Präg'en [praig'en] *vt.* to stamp, coin; **-ung** *nf.* stamp, character.

Prägnant' [praig-nant'] *a.* precise, terse, pregnant; **-z** *nf.* conciseness, terseness.

Prahle'n [prah'len] *vi.* to boast, brag; **-rei** *nf.* boasting; **-risch** *a.* boastful.

Prahm [prahm] *nm.* (-e) barge, flat-bottomed boat, punt, lighter.

Prakti'k [prak'tik] *nf.* practice; **-ker** *nm.* (-) practical man; **-sch** *a.* practical, useful, handy, experienced.

Praktikant [prak-ti-kant'] *m.w.* probationer.

Praktizieren [prak-tit-seer'ren] *vt.i.* to practise (*medicine*).

Präjudiz [pray-yōo-dits']*nf.* precedent, prejudice (*law*).

Prälat [pray-laht'] *m.w.* prelate. [chocolate cream.

Praliné [pra-li-nay'] *n.* (-s)

Prall [pral] *a.* tight, taut, rigid, plump; **-en** *vi.* to bounce, rebound, dash, glare (*sun*); **-kraft** *nf.* elasticity; **-schuss** *nm* ricochet.

Prämie [pray'mi-er] *nf.* premium, award, prize; **-nlohnsystem** *n.* (premium) bonus system sliding scale system (*com.*).

Prangen [prang'en] *vi.* to flaunt, be displayed.

Pranger [prang'err] *nm.* (-) pillory. [claw.

Pranke [prank'er] *nf.* paw.

Präpa'rat [pray-par-raht'] *n.* (-e) preparation, medicine; **-ieren** *vt.* to prepare.

Präposition [pray-po-zit-syohn'] *nf.* preposition.

Präsens [pray'zenss] *n.* (Präsentia) present tense.

Präsentierteller [pray-zen-teerr'tel-err] *nm.* (-) tray.

Präsident [pray-zi-dent']*m.w.* president.

Präsidieren [pray-zi-deer'ren] *vi.* to preside, take the chair.

Präsidium [pray-zee'di-ōōm] *n.* presidency, chair(manship).

Prasseln [prass'eln] *vi.* to crackle, rattle, patter.

Prasse'n [prass'en] *vi.* to feast, indulge in dissipation; **-er** *nm.* (-) glutton, prodigal.

Prasserei [prass-er-ri'] *nf.* feasting, dissipation.

Prätendent [pray-ten-dent'] *m.w.* pretender.

Präteritum [pray-tair'ri-tōōm] *n.* past tense. [clutch.

Pratze [prat'ser] *nf.* claw.

Praxis [prax'is] *nf.* practice.

Präzedenzfall [pray-tsay-dents'fal] *nm.* (-fälle) precedent.

Präzis [pray-tseess'] *a.* precise, punctual, accurate.

Präzision [pray-tsee-zjoyn'] *nf.* precision; **-swaage** *nf.* precision balance; **-swerkzeug** *n.* precision tool.

Predige'n [pray'di-gen] *vt.i.* to preach; **-r** *nm.* (-) preacher.

Predigt [pray'disht] *nf.* sermon.

Preis [price] *nm.* (-e) price, prize, praise; **-angabe** *nf.* quotation (*com.*); **-beaufsichtigung** *nf.* price control; **-drückerei** *nf.* price-cutting; **-gabe** *nf.* surrender, sacrifice; **-geben** *vt. ir.* to abandon, sacrifice, expose; **-gebunden** *a.* controlled (*price*); **-lage** *nf.* range of prices; **-liste** *nf.* price-list; **-notierung** *nf.* quotation (*com.*); **-richter** *nm.* judge; **-sturz** *nm.* slump; **-träger** *nm.* prize-winner; **-überwachung** *nf.* price control; **-wert** *a.* cheap.

Preiselbeere [prize'el-bairrer] *nf.* cranberry.

Preisen [prize'en] vt. ir. to praise, glorify.

Prellen [prel'en] vt. to cheat, swindle, bilk, bump.

Prellstein [prel'shtine] nm. (-e) kerb.

Prellstock [prel'shtok] nm. (-stöcke) buffer-stop (rl.).

Press'e [press'er] nf. press; -**freiheit** nf. freedom of the press; -**kohle** nf. briquette; -**luft** nf. compressed air; -**stroh** n. pressed straw.

Pressen [press'en] vt. to press, compress, cram, urge.

Pressieren [press-eer'ren] v.i.t. to (be in a) hurry.

Prickel [prikl] nm. (-) prickle, prick; -**ig** a. prickly; -**n** v.i.t. to prick, sting. [tobacco).

Priem [preem] nm. (-e) plug

Priester [pree'sterr] nm. (-) priest; -**in** nf. priestess; -**schaft** nf. priesthood.

Prima [pree'mah] s. first class, excellent; -**abzug** nm. first proof (printer's); -**anwärter** nm. probationer; -**dienstleistung** nf. probationary period; -**exemplar** n. specimen copy; -**fahrt** nf. trial trip; -**weise** ad. on approval; -**zeit** nf. (time of) probation.

Proben [proh'ben] vt. to try, test, sample, rehearse.

Probieren [proh-beer'ren] vt. to try, attempt, test, taste, sample.

Probier-dame, -mamsell nf. mannequin; -**stein** nm. touchstone. [problem.

Problem [pro-blame'] n. (-e)

Problematisch [pro-blay-mah'tish] a. problematic.

Produkt [pro-dookt'] n. (-e) product, produce; -**enhandel** nm. produce trade; -**ion** nf. production.

Produktiv [pro-dook-teef'] a. productive; -**ität** nf. productivity.

Produzent [pro-doot-sent'] m.w. producer; -**engenossenschaft** nf. co-operative.

Produzieren [pro-doot-seer'ren] vt. to produce.

Professor [pro-fess'orr] nm. (gen. -s; pl. -en) professor; -**ur** nf. professorship.

Profil [pro-feel'] n. (-e) profile; -**dicke** nf. aerofoil section; -**eisen** n. structural iron (av.).

Profilierung [pro-fee-leer'roong] nf. fairing (av.).

Profit [pro-feet'] nm. (-e) profit, yield.

Prisma [priss'mah] n. (Prismen) prism. [bed, bat.

Pritsche [pritch'er] nf. plank

Privat [pri-vaht'] a. private; -**dozent** m.w. university lecturer; -**recht** n. civil law; -**vermögen** n. private means.

Privatisieren [pri-va-tiz-eer'ren] vi. to live on one's means.

Probe [proh'ber] nf. trial, test, sample; -**abzug** nm. proof (printer's); -**anwärter** nm. probationer; -**dienstleistung** nf.

Prinz [prints] m.w. prince; -**gemahl** nm. prince consort.

Prinzessin [print-sess'in] nf. princess. [principle.

Prinzip [print-seep'] n. (-ien)

Prinzipal [print-si-pahl'] nm. (-e) principal, chief, head.

Prinzipiell [print-see-pi-el'] a. ad. on principle.

Priorität [pree-or-ri-tate'] nf. priority; -**saktie** nf. preference share (com.).

Prise [pree'zer] nf. pinch (snuff), prize (nav.); -**ngerichtshof** nm. prize court; -**mannschaft** nf. boarding-party.

Profitieren [pro-fi-teer'ren] vt. to profit, take advantage of.

Prognose [prog-noh'zer] nf. (weather) forecast.

Programm [pro-gram'] n. (-e) programme.

Projekt [pro-yekt'] n. (-e) project, scheme, plan.

Projektion [pro-yek-syohn'] nf. projection; -sapparat nm. projector, epidiascope; -swand nf. cinema screen.

Projizieren [pro-yit-seer'ren] vt. to project.

Proklamieren [pro-kla-meer'ren] vt. to proclaim.

Prokura [pro-koor'rah] nf. proxy.

Prokurist [pro-koor-rist'] m.w. confidential clerk, proxy.

Prolet [pro-late'] m.w. proletarian, low fellow.

Proletariat [pro-le-tar-ri-aht'] n. proletariat.

Proletarier [pro-le-tah'ri-err] nm. (-) proletarian.

Prolog [pro-lohk'] nm. prologue.

Promenade [pro-mer-nah'der] nf. promenade.

Promotion [pro-moht-syohn'] nf. graduation, promotion.

Promovieren [pro-moh-veer'ren] vi. to graduate; t. promote.

Prompt [prompt] a. prompt.

Pronomen [pro-noh'men] n. (Pronomina) pronoun.

Propaganda [pro-pa-gan'dah] nf. propaganda.

Propeller [pro-pel'err] nm. (-) propeller; -bö nf. slipstream (av.); -flügel nm. propeller blade; -los a. without propeller, jet-propelled (av.); -welle nf. propeller shaft.

Prophet [pro-fate'] m.w. prophet; -in nf. prophetess; -isch a. prophetic.

Prophezeien [pro-fet-si'en] vi.t. to prophesy; -ung nf. prophecy.

Proportion [pro-porrt-si-ohn'] nf. proportion; -al a. proportional.

Propst [propst] nm. (Pröbste) (provost).

Prosa [proh'zah] nf. prose; -iker nm. (-) prose-writer; -isch a. prosaic.

Prosit [proh'zit] interj. good health.

Prospekt [pro-spekt'] nm. (-e) prospectus.

Prostituier'en [pro-sti-too-eer'ren] vt. to prostitute; -te f.w. prostitute.

Protektion [pro-tek-si-ohn'] nf. protection, patronage.

Protektorat [pro-tek-tor-raht'] n. (-e) protectorate.

Protest [pro-test'] nm. (-e) protest; -ieren vi. to protest.

Protestant [pro-tes-tant'] m.w. Protestant; -isch a. Protestant; -ismus nm. Protestantism.

Protokoll [pro-to-kol'] n. (-e) register, minutes; -führer nm. secretary, recorder, registrar; -ieren vt. to register, minute, take down minutes.

Proton [proh'ton] n. (-en) proton.

Protz [prots] m.w. snob; -en vi. to put on airs, display one's wealth; -entum n. ostentation, snobbery; -ig a. ostentatious, snobbish (mil.).

Protze [prot'ser] nf. limber.

Proviant [pro-vi-ant'] nm. provisions, supplies; -amt n. supply depot, office; -kolonne nf. supply column; -lager n. supply dump; -meister nm. purser.

Provinz [pro-vints'] nf. province; -iell a. provincial; -ialtag [pro-vint-si-ahl'] a. provincial; -landtag nm. provincial council.

Provision [pro-vi-zi-ohn'] nf. commission (com.).

Provisorisch [pro-vi-zor'rish] a. provisional.

Provokation [pro-vo-kat-si-ohn'] nf. provocation.

Provozieren [pro-vo-tseer'ren] vt. to provoke.

Prozedur [pro-tsay-dŏŏrr'] nf. procedure.

Prozent [pro-tsent'] n. (-e) per cent, percentage; **-satz** nm. percentage.

Prozentual [pro-tsent-ŏŏ-ahl'] ad. per cent.

Prozess [proh-tsess'] nm. (-e) law-suit, process, legal proceedings.

Prozessieren [proh-tsess-eer'ren] vi. to bring an action, go to law.

Prozession [proh-tsess-yohn'] nf. procession. [prudery.]

Prüderie [prȳŏŏ-der-ree'] nf.

Prüf|en [prȳŏŏ'fen] vt. to examine, test, inspect, check, go over; **-er** nm. (-) inspector, examiner, checker, tester; **-leitung** nf. testing control; **-meister** nm. inspector, tester; **-motorenwart** nm. engine-tester (av.); **-netzgerät** n. eliminator (rad.); **-stein** nm. touchstone; **-stempel** nm. check stamp; **-ung** nf. examination, investigation, trial, test.

Prügel [prȳŏŏ'gel] nm. (-) cudgel; pl. beating; **-ei** nf. fight; **-knabe** m.w. scapegoat.

Prügeln [prȳŏŏ'geln] vt. to beat, whip, thrash.

Prunk [prŏŏnk] nm. pomp, show; **-en** vi. to show off; **-haft** a. ostentatious; **-voll** a. splendid, magnificent.

Psalm [psalm] nm. (gen. -es; pl. -en) psalm. [psychic.]

Psychisch [psȳŏ'shish] a.

Psychoanalyse [psȳŏ-sho-a-na-lȳŏŏ'zer] nf. psychoanalysis.

Psycholog|e [psȳŏ-sho-loh'ger] m.w. psychologist; **-ie** nf. psychology.

Pubertät [pŏŏ-berr-tate'] nf. puberty.

Publikum [pŏŏb'li-kŏŏm] n. public.

Publizieren [pŏŏb-blit-seer'ren] vt. to publish, publicize.

Publizist [pŏŏb-bli-tsist'] m.w. publicist.

Puddeln [pŏŏ'deln] vt. to puddle (tec.). [pudding.]

Pudding [pŏŏ'ding] nm. (-s)

Pudel [pŏŏ'del] nm. poodle.

Puder [pŏŏ'derr] nm. (-) powder; **-quaste** nf. powder-puff.

Pudern [pŏŏ'derrn] vt. to powder.

Puff [pŏŏf] nm. (Püffe) thump, push, puff, bang, backgammon; **-en** vt. to thump, push; i. pop, go off.

Puffer [pŏŏ'ferr] nm. (-) buffer; **-staat** nm. buffer state.

Puls [pŏŏlss] nm. (-e) pulse; **-ader** nf. artery; **-wärmer** nm. wristlet, mittens.

Pulsieren [pŏŏl-seer'ren] vi. to throb, pulsate.

Pult [pŏŏlt] n. (-e) desk.

Pulver [pŏŏl'ferr] n. (-) powder; **-fass** n. powder-barrel; **-ig** a. powdery; **-n** vt. to grind to powder; **-schnee** nm. powdery snow.

Pulverisieren [pŏŏl-fer-ri-zeer'ren] vt. to pulverize.

Pump|e [pŏŏm'per] nf. pump; **-en** vt. to pump, lend, borrow; **-hose** nf. wide trousers, plus fours.

Punkt [pŏŏnkt] nm. (-e) point, dot, full stop, matter; **-sieg** nm. victory on points; **-ziel** n. pin-point, precision target (av.).

Punktieren [pŏŏnk-teer'ren] vt. to punctuate, point, dot, stipple.

Punktur [pŏŏnk-tŏŏrr'] nf. puncture.

Pünktlich [pȳŏŏnkt'lish] a., ad. punctual(ly), prompt(ly); **-keit** nf. punctuality, promptness. [punch.]

Punsch [pŏŏnsh] nm. (-e)

Punze [pŏŏnt'ser] nf. Punzen

[pŏont'sen] nm. (-) punch; -n *vt.* to punch, emboss. [(*eye*).

Pupille [pŏo-pil'er] nf. pupil

Puppe [pŏo'per] nf. doll, puppet, pupa, chrysalis; -nspiel n. puppet-show.

Pur [pŏorr] a. pure, sheer.

Purgieren [pŏorr-geer'ren] *vt.* to purge.

Purpur [pŏor'pŏorr] nm. purple; -n a. purple.

Purzelbaum [pŏorr'tsel-bowm] nm. (-bäume) somersault.

Purzeln [pŏor'tseln] *vi.* to turn somersaults.

Puste [pŏos'ter] nf. breath, power, means; -n *vi.* to blow.

Pustel [pŏos'tel] nf. pustule.

Pute [pŏo'ter] nf. turkey-hen; -r nm. (-) turkey-cock.

Putsch [pŏotch] nm. (-e) revolt, riot, revolution; -en *vi.* to revolt, riot; -ist m.w.v. rioter, rebel.

Putz [pŏots] nm. dress, finery, trimming, ornament, plaster, rough-cast; -frau nf. charwoman; -laden nm. milliner's shop; -leiste nf. window-frame; -macherin nf. milliner; -sucht nf. love of finery; -wolle nf. cotton waste.

Putzen [pŏot'sen] *vt.* to clean, groom, wipe, polish, roughcast; r. dress oneself up.

Pyjama [pyŏo-jah'mah] nm. (-s) pyjamas. [nf. pyramid.

Pyramide [pyŏo-ra-mee'der]

Q

Quabbelig [kva'ber-lish] a. wobbly, flabby.

Quabbeln [kva'beln] *vi.* to wobble, quake.

Quacksalber [kvak'zal-berr] nm. (-) quack, charlatan, impostor; -n *vi.* to experiment upon. [square stone.

Quader [kvah'derr] nm. (-)

Quadrat [kva-draht'] n. (-e) square. [*vt.* to square.

Quadrieren [kvad-reer'ren] *vt.* to square.

Quaken [kvah'ken] *vi.* to croak, quack.

Quäken [kvay'ken] *vi.* to squeak; -d a. squeaky.

Qual [kvahl] nf. torment, pang, agony; -enreich, -voll a. painful, excruciating, agonizing.

Quälen [kvay'len] *vt.* to torture, worry; r. toil, drudge; -er, -geist nm. tormentor, nuisance.

Qualifizieren [kva-li-fit-seer'ren] *vt.* to qualify. [quality.

Qualität [kva-li-tate'] nf.

Qualle [kva'ler] nf. jelly-fish.

Qualm [kvalm] nm. (-e) thick smoke, vapour; -en *vi.* to smoke, reek.

Quanten'physik [kvan'ten-fyŏo-zeek'] nf. quantum physics; -theorie nf. quantum theory. [quantity.

Quantität [kvan-ti-tate'] nf.

Quantitativ [kvan-ti-ta-teef'] a. quantitative.

Quantum [kvan'tŏom] n. (Quanten) quantity, sum, amount.

Quarantäne [kva-ran-tay'ner] nf. quarantine.

Quark [kvarrk] nm. curds, trash, rubbish.

Quart [kvarrt] n. (-e) quart, quarto (*volume*).

Quartal [kvarr-tahl'] n. (-e) term, quarter.

Quartaner [kvarr-tah'nerr] nm. (-) third-form boy.

Quartier [kvarr-teerr'] n. (-e) quarters, billet (*mil.*); district; -en *vt.* to quarter, billet; -macher nm. billeting officer.

Quarz [kvarrts] nm. (-e) quartz.

Quast [kvast] nm. (-e), **Quaste** nf. tassel, tuft.

Quatsch [kvatch] nm. rot, rubbish; -en *vi.* to talk nonsense.

Quecksilber [kvek'sil-berr] n. quicksilver.

Quelle [kvel'er] nf. spring, source, fountain; **-n** vi. to spring, gush forth, issue, arise; t. soak.

Quer [kvair] a. transverse, oblique, cross; ad. across, obliquely; **-balken** nm. cross-beam; **-feldein** ad. cross country; **-kopf** nm. queer fellow, eccentric; **-pfeife** nf. fife; **-ruder** n. aileron (av.); **-schiff** n. transept; **-schnitt** nm. cross-section; **-strasse** nf. cross-road; **-strich** nm. cross-stroke; **-verbindung** nf. lateral communications.

Quere [kvair'er] nf. transverse direction; **-n** vt. to traverse, cross.

Quetsch'en [kvetch'en] vt. to squeeze, crush, bruise; **-kartoffeln** f.pl. mashed potatoes; **-ung** nf. bruise, contusion.

Quieken [kvee'ken] vi. to squeak, squeal.

Quietschen [kvee'tchen] vi. to scream, squeak. [form.

Quinta [kvin'tah] nf. second form.

Quintessenz [kvint-ess-ents'] nf. quintessence.

Quintett [kvin-tet'] n. (-e) quintet.

Quirl [kvirrl] nm. (-e) whisk; **-en** vi. to twirl, whisk.

Quitt [kvit] a. quits, even; **-ieren** vt. to settle, receipt; **-ung** nf. receipt. [share.

Quote [kvoh'ter] nf. quota.

R

Raa [rah] see Rahe.

Rabatt [ra-bat'] nm. (-e) rebate, discount.

Rabatte [ra-bat'er] nf. flowerbed, border. [(-) rabbi.

Rabbiner [ra-bee'nerr] nm.

Rabe [rah'ber] m.w. raven; **-nmutter** nf. unnatural mother.

Rabiat [ra-bi-aht'] a. rabid.

Rache [rach'er] nf. vengeance, revenge.

Rachen [rach'en] nm. (-) throat, jaws.

Rächen [resh'en] vt. to avenge, revenge; r. take one's revenge.

Rächer [resh'err] nm. (-) avenger. [rickets.

Rachitis [rach-ee'tis] nf. rickets.

Rachsucht [rach'zöocht] nf. desire for revenge, vindictiveness.

Rachsüchtig [rach'zyöoch-tish] a. revengeful.

Racker [rak'err] nm. (-) rogue, scamp, rascal. [drudge.

Rackern [rak'errn] vr. to

Rad [raht] n. (Räder) wheel; **-antrieb** nm. gear-drive; **-bremse** nf. hub-brake; **-dampfer** nm. paddle-steamer; **-ebrechen** vt. murder (language); **-fahren** vi. to cycle; **-fahrer** nm. (-) cyclist; **-fahrerin** nf. lady cyclist; **-fahrweg** nm. cycling track, path; **-felge** nf. felloe; **-fenster** n. rose-window; **-gehäuse** n. paddle-box; **-kasten** nm. wheel-case; **-kranz** nm. wheel-rim; **-ler** nm. (-) cyclist; **-macher** nm. wheel-wright; **-rennbahn** nf. cycling track; **-rennen** n. cycle race; **-sport** nm. cycling; **-stand** nm. wheelbase; **-steuerung** nf. wheel control (av.); **-sturz** nm. camber; **-zahn** nm. cog; **-zugmaschine** nf. wheeled tractor.

Radau [ra-dow'] nm. row.

Radeln [rah'deln] vi. to cycle.

Rädelsführer [ray'delssfyöor'err] nm. (-) ringleader.

Räder'gehäuse [ray'derr-gerhoy-zer] n. (-) clock-frame, paddle-box; **-kasten** nm. gearbox; **-raupenantrieb** nm. convertible drive; **-werk** n. clockwork, gears, wheels.

Radier'en [ra-deer'ren] vt. to rub out, erase, etch; **-gummi**

nm. indiarubber; -**kunst** *nf.*
etching; -**messer** *nm.* penknife;
-**ung** *nf.* etching.

Radieschen [ra-deess'shen] *n.*
(-) radish.   [radical.

Radikal [ra-di-kahl'] *n.*

Radio [rah'di-o] *n.* (-s) radio,
wireless; -**aktiv** *a.* radio-active;
-**anlage** *nf.* wireless installation; -**apparat** *nm.* wireless
set; -**hörer** *nm.* listener(-in);
-**lokalisierung** *nf.* radio-location; -**röhre** *nf.* thermionic
valve; -**telephonie** *nf.* radio-
telephony; -**wesen** *n.* broadcasting.

Radium [rah'di-ōōm] *n.*
radium; -**heilverfahren** *n.* radio
therapy.

Radius [rah'di-ōōss] *nm.*
(Radien) radius.

Raffen [raf'en] *vt.* to snatch,
pick up.   [refined sugar.

Raffinade [raf-i-nah'de] *nf.*

Raffinier'en [raf-i-neer'ren]
vt. to refine; -**t** *a.* refined,
crafty, sly, cunning.

Ragen [rah'gen] *vi.* to project,
tower up.

Rahe [rah'er] *nf.* yard (*ship*).

Rahm [rahm] *nm.* cream; -**en**
vt. to skim; -**ig** *a.* creamy;
-**käse** *nm.* cream cheese.

Rahmen [rah'men] *nm.* (-)
frame(work), border, surroundings; - *vt.* to frame; -**antenne**
nf. loop, frame aerial (*rad.*);
-**rohr** *n.* outer tube (*cycle*);
-**sucher** *nm.* viewfinder (*photo*).

Rain [rine] *nm.* ridge
between fields, balk.

Rakete [ra-kay'ter] *nf.* rocket;
-**nflugzeug** *n.* rocket(-propel-
led) plane; -**nsatz** *nm.* rocket
attachment (*av.*).

Rakett [ra-ket'] *n.* (-s) racket.
Rammbock *nm.* *see* **Ramme.**
Ramme [ram'er] *nf.* **Rammer**
nm. (-) pile-driver; -**n** *vt.* to
drive, ram in, stamp, ram
(*ship*).

Rampe [ram'per] *nf.* platform,

ramp, ascent, drive; -**nlichter**
n.pl. footlights.

Ramponieren [ram-po-neer'-
ren] *vt.* to damage, spoil,
smash.

Ramsch [ramsh] *nm.* (-e) odds
and ends, rubbish, job lot;
-**en** *vt.* to buy in bulk.

Rand [rant] *nm.* (Ränder) edge,
margin, fringe, border, rim,
brink; -**leiste** *nf.* ledge; -**stein**
nm. kerbstone; -**steller** *nm.*
marginal stop.

Rändern [ren'derrn] *vt.* to
mill edge.   [crust.

Ranft [ranft] *nm.* (Ränfte)

Rang [rang] *nm.* (Ränge) rank,
class, order, circle (*theatre*);
-**abzeichen** *n.* badge of rank;
-**älteste(r)** *m.w.* senior officer;
-**erhöhung** *nf.* promotion; -**liste**
nf. army list; -**ordnung** *nf.*
precedence; -**stufe** *nf.* degree,
grade, order; -**unterschied** *nm.*
difference in rank, class.

Range [rang'er] *m.w.* *nf.* tomboy, rogue, scamp.

Rangier'en [rong-zheer'ren] *vt.*
to shunt, switch; *i.* rank, be
classed; -**bahnhof** *nm.* shunting, marshalling yard; -**geleise**
n. siding; -**lokomotive** *nf.*
shunting engine.

Rank [rank] *a.* slender.

Ranke [rank'er] *nf.* shoot,
tendril; -**n** *vi.* to climb;
-**ngewächs** *n.* creeper.

Ränke [renk'er] *nm.pl.* intrigues,
dodges, wire-pulling; -**schmied**
nm. intriguer; -**voll** *a.*
scheming.

Ranunkel [ra-nōōn'kel] *nf.*
buttercup, crowfoot.

Ränzel [rent'sel] *n.* (-) *see*
Ranzen.

Ranzen [rant'sen] *nm.* (-)
satchel, school-bag, wallet,
knapsack.

Ranzig [rant'sish] *a.* rancid.

Rapier [ra-peerr'] *n.* (-e) rapier.

Rappe [rap'er] *m.w.* black
horse.

Rappen [rap'en] *nm.* (-) Swiss centime, very small farthing.

Raps [raps] *nm.* (-e) rape-seed.

Rar [rar] *a.* rare.

Rarität [ra-ri-tate'] *nf.* rarity, curiosity.

Rasant [ra-zant'] *a.* flat, grazing (*mil.*); -z *nf.* flat trajectory.

Rasch [rash] *a.* quick, hasty.

Rascheln [rash'eln] *vi.* to rustle.

Rasen [rah'zen] *nm.* (-) turf, lawn, green (*golf*); -mähmaschine *nf.* lawn-mower; -platz *nm.* lawn.

Rasen [rah'zen] *vi.* to rave, rage; -d *a.* furious, mad.

Raserei [rah-zer-ri'] *nf.* fury, ravings, rage.

Rasier'en [ra-zeer'ren] *vt.* to shave; -apparat *nm.* safetyrazor; -klinge *nf.* razor-blade; -krem *nm.* shaving cream; -messer *n.* razor; -pinsel *nm.* shaving brush; -seife *nf.* shaving soap, stick.

Räsonieren [ray-zo-neer'ren] *vi.* to argue, grumble.

Raspel [ras'pel] *nf.* grater; -feile *nf.* rasp; -n *vt.* to rasp.

Rasse [rass'er] *nf.* race, breed; -hund *nm.* thoroughbred dog; -nhass *nm.* racial hatred; -nkunde *nf.* ethnology.

Rassel [rass'l] *nf.* rattle; -n *vi.* to rattle, clatter.

Rast [rast] *nf.* rest, halt (*mil.*); -en *vi.* to rest; -los *a.* restless, unwearying; -losigkeit *nf.* restlessness.

Raster [rast'err] *nm.* (-) [screen.

Rasur [ra-zoorr'] *nf.* erasure.

Rat [raht] *nm.* (Ratschläge) advice, counsel, means, remedy, expedient, consultation; *pl.* (Räte) council, councillor; -geber *nm.* counsellor, adviser; -haus *n.* town hall; -schluss *nm.* decree, decision, resolution.

Rate [rah'ter] *nf.* instalment;

-nweise *ad.* by instalments; -nzahlungsgeschäft *n.* hire purchase business.

Raten [rah'ten] *vt.i. ir.* to advise, guess.

Ratifizieren [ra-ti-fit-seer'ren] *vt.* to ratify.

Ration [rat-syohn'] *nf.* ration; -ieren *vt.* to ration.

Rätlich [rate'lish] *a.* advisable.

Ratlos [raht'loce] *a.* perplexed, at a loss, irresolute; -igkeit *nf.* perplexity, irresolution.

Ratsam [raht'zam] *a.* advisable, expedient; -keit *nf.* advisability, expediency.

Ratschlag [raht'shlahk] *nm.* (-schläge) (piece of) advice; -en *vi.* to take counsel.

Rätsel [rate'sel] *n.* (-) riddle, puzzle; -haft *a.* puzzling, enigmatic.

Rats'herr [rahts'hairr] *m.w.* councillor; -kammer *nf.*, -saal *nm.* council chamber; -keller *nm.* underground restaurant.

Ratte [rat'er] *nf.* rat; -nfänger *nm.* rat-catcher. [clatter.

Rattern [rat'errn] *vi.* to rattle,

Raub [rowp] *n.* robbery, loot, booty; -anfall *nm.* robbery with violence; -ausgabe *nf.* piratical edition; -bau *nm.* reckless exploitation; -gier *nf.* rapacity; -gierig *a.* rapacious; -tier *n.* beast of prey; -vogel *nm.* bird of prey.

Rauben [row'ben] *vt.i.* to rob, pillage. [robber.

Räuber [roy'berr] *nm.* (-)

Rauch [rowch] *nm.* smoke; -entwickler *nm.* smoke generator; -fahne *nf.* smoke trail; -gerät *n.* smoke apparatus; -giftnehmer *nm.* dope fiend, drug addict; -patrone *nf.* smoke cartridge; -säule *nf.* column of smoke; -schleier *nm.* smoke-screen.

Rauch'en [row'chen] *vt.i.* to smoke; -er *nm.* (-) smoker.

Räuchern [roy'sherrn] *vt.* to

Rau'be [roy'der] *nf.* scab, mange; -ig *a.* mangy.

Rauf'bold [rowf'bolt] *nm.* (-e) bully, hooligan, rowdy; -lust *nf.* rowdiness, hooliganism, pugnacity.

Raufe [row'fer] *nf.* rack.

Raufen [row'fen] *vt.* to pull out; *r.* fight.

Rauferei [row-fer-ri'] *nf.* scuffle, brawl.

Rauh [row] *a.* rough, coarse, raw, harsh, uneven; -bein *n.* blackguard, cad; -haarig *a.* wire-haired; -heit *nf.* roughness, harshness; -reif *nm.* hoar-frost; [en, pile (*tec.*).

Rauhen [row'en] *vt.* to rough

Raum [rowm] *nm.* (Räume) room, space, space, accommodation, hold (*ship*); -bild *n.* stereoscopic picture; -führer *nm.* sector controller (*av.*); -inhalt *nm.* cubic capacity, volume; -mangel *nm.* lack of space; -messbilder *n.pl.* stereoscopic pictures (*av.*); -meter *nm.* cubic metre; -strahlen *m.pl.* omnidirection-al beam (*rad.*).

Räum'boot [roim'boat] *n.* (-e) motor mine-sweeper; -pflug *nm.* bulldozer.

Räumen [roy'men] *vt.* to clear (away), remove, evacuate, leave; -ung *nf.* clearance, removal, cleaning, evacuation.

Räumlich [roim'lish] *a.* spacial, in space, local; -keit *nf.* space, spaciousness, room, premises. sea, offing.

Räumte [roim'ter] *nf.* open

Raunen [row'nen] *vi.* to whisper mysteriously.

Raupe [row'per] *nf.* caterpillar, caterpillar track; -nband *n.* track (*vehicles*); -ngängig *a.* caterpillar-tracked; -nkette *nf.* caterpillar track; -nkrad *n.* motor-cycle tractor; -nrad *n.*

caterpillar wheel; -nschlepper *nm.* caterpillar tractor; -nwalzer *nm.* bulldozer tractor, leveller.

Rausch [rowsh] *nm.* (Räusche) intoxication; -en *vi.* to rush, rustle, murmur, sound; -gift *n.* narcotic, drug.

Räuspern [roy'spern] *vr.* to clear the throat.

Raute [row'ter] *nf.* lozenge, rhomboid, diamond, rue (*herb*); -nförmig *a.* lozenge-shaped.

Reagens [ray-a-genss'] *n.* (Reagentien) reagent.

Reagenz'glas [ray-a-gents' glass] *n.* (-gläser) test-tube; -papier *n.* reagent paper, litmus paper. [to react.

Reagieren [ray-a-geer'ren] *vi.*

Reaktion [ray-ak-syohn'] *nf.* reaction; -santrieb *nm.* jet-propulsion (*av.*); -getrieben *a.* jet-propelled (*av.*).

Reaktionär [ray-ak-syo-nair'] *a.* reactionary.

Real [ray-ahl'] *a.* real, material; -e *n.w.* reality; -gymnasium *n.* modernized classical school; -ien *pl.* exact sciences, real facts, realities; -katalog *nm.* subject catalogue; -lexikon *n.* encyclopaedia; -politik *nf.* realistic politics; -schule *nf.* modern school; -wert *nm.* actual value.

Realist [ray-a-list'] *m.w.* realist; -mus *nm.* realism; -tisch *a.* realistic.

Rebe [ray'ber] *nf.* vine, tendril; -ensaft *nm.* grape-juice; -stock *nm.* vine.

Rebell [re-bel'] *m.w.* rebel; -ion *nf.* rebellion; -isch *a.* rebellious.

Rebhuhn [rape'hoon] *n.* (-hühner) partridge.

Rechen [resh'en] *nm.* (-) rake; *vt.* to rake.

Rechen'fehler [resh'en-fay-lerr] *nm.* (-) miscalculation; -maschine *nf.* calculating machine; -schaft *nf.* reckoning, account; -schieber *nm.* slide-rule; -stelle *nf.* plotting room (*av.*). [count, reckon.

Rechnen [resh'nen] *vt.i.* to

Rechner [resh'nerr] *nm.* (-) calculator.

Rechnung [resh'nŏong] *nf.* calculation, account, sum, bill, memorandum; -sauszug *nm.* statement of account; -sbuch *n.* account book; -sführer *nm.* book-keeper, accountant; -sjahr *n.* financial year; -sprüfer *nm.* auditor; -sprüfung audit(ing).

Recht [resht] *a., ad.* right(ly), aright, correct(ly); *ad.* very; *n.* right, law; -haberisch *a.* dogmatic; -mässig *a.* lawful; -schreibung *nf.* orthography; -zeitig *a.* prompt, timely.

Rechte [resht'er] *nf.* right hand.

Recht'eck [resht'ek] *n.* rectangle; -ig *a.* rectangular.

Rechtfertig'en [resht'fairr-tigen] *vt.* to justify; -ung *nf.* justification.

Rechtglaubig [resht'gloybish] *a.* orthodox; -keit *nf.* orthodoxy.

Rechtschaffen [resht'shaf-en] *a.* upright, honest; -heit *nf.* uprightness.

Rechts [reshts] *ad.* on, to the right; -anwalt *nm.* solicitor, barrister, lawyer; -aussen-stürmer *nm.* outside right; -drehung *nf.* clockwise rotation; -fall *nm.* lawsuit; -frage *nf.* point of law; -grund *nm.* legal argument; -kräftig *a.* valid, legal; -nachfolger *nm.* assign; -pflege *nf.* administration of justice; -spruch *nm.* verdict, sentence; -widrig *a.* illegal; -wissenschaft *nf.* jurisprudence.

Reck [rek] *n.* (-e) horizontal bar.

Recken [rek'en] *vt.* to stretch.

Redakteur [ray-dak-terr'] *nm.* (-e) editor.

Redaktion [ray-dak-syohn'] *nf.* editing, editorial office, staff.

Rede [ray'der] *nf.* speech, talk, conversation, report; -gewandt *a.* fluent, glib; -freiheit *nf.* freedom of speech; -rei *nf.* nonsense, mere talk.

Reden [ray'den] *vi.* to speak, talk; *n.* speech, talking.

Redensart [ray'denss-arrt] *nf.* expression, phrase.

Redigieren [ray-di-geer'ren] *vt.* to edit.

Redlich [rade'lish] *a.* honest; -keit *nf.* honesty.

Redner [rade'nerr] *nm.* (-) speaker, orator; -bühne *nf.* platform; -isch *a.* oratorical.

Redoute [re-dŏo'ter] *nf.* redoute, masquerade, fancy-dress ball.

Redselig [rate'zay-lish] *a.* talkative, loquacious; -keit *nf.* talkativeness.

Reduzieren [ray-dŏot-seer'-ren] *vt.* to reduce.

Reede [ray'der] *nf.* road (stead), anchorage; -r *nm.* (-) ship-owner.

Reederei [ray-der-ri'] *nf.* shipping line, firm, fitting-out (*vessel*).

Reef [rafe] *n.* (-e) carrier (*for bricks*). [-en *vt.* to reef.

Reef [rafe] *n.* (-e) reef (*sail*).

Reell [ray-el'] *a.* honest, fair, straightforward, real; -ität *nf.* respectability (*com.*).

Reep [rape] *n.* (-e) rope.

Refer'at [ref-er-raht'] *n.* (-e) report, lecture, paper (*read*); -ent *m.w.* speaker, lecturer, expert; -enz *nf.* reference.

Referieren [ref-er-reer'ren] *vi.* to report, lecture on.

Reflektant [ray-flek-tant'] *m.w.* intending purchaser, prospective client.

Reflektieren [ray-flek-teer'-

ren] *vi.t.* to reflect, be interested in (*com.*).

Reflexion [ray-flex-yohn'] *nf.* reflection.

Reflexiv [ray-flex-eef'] *a.* reflexive. [reform.

Reform [ray-forrm'] *nf.*

Reformation [ray-forr-mat-syohn'] *nf.* reformation.

Reformator [ray-forr-mah'-torr] *nm.* (*gen.* -s; *pl.* -en) reformer.

Reformatorisch [ray-forr-ma-to'rish] *a.* reformatory, reforming.

Reformieren [ray-forr-meer'ren] *vt.* to reform.

Refrain [ray-frang'] *nm.* (-s) refrain, chorus.

Regal [ray-gahl'] *nm.* (-e) bookshelf, book-stand, filing cabinet. [brisk.

Rege [ray'ger] *a.* lively, active,

Regel [ray'gel] *nf.* rule; -los *a.* irregular, unsystematic; -recht *a., ad.* regular, proper, thorough; -widerstand *nm.* rheostat (*rad.*); -widrig *a.* irregular.

Regelmässig [ray'gel-may-sish] *a., ad.* regular(ly); -keit *nf.* regularity.

Regeln [ray'geln] *vt.* to regulate, arrange, order; -ung *nf.* regulation, setting in order, control. [stir, budge.

Regen [ray'gen] *vt.r.* to move.

Regen [ray'gen] *nm.* rain; -bogen *nm.* rainbow; -decke *nf.* tarpaulin; -dicht *a.* waterproof; -guss *nm.* shower, downpour; -mantel *nm.* waterproof, raincoat; -schirm *nm.* umbrella; -tag *nm.* rainy day; -wurm *nm.* earth-worm; -zeit *nf.* rainy season, rains; -zelt *n.* tilt (*waggon*).

Regent [ray-gent'] *m.w.* -in *nf.* regent; -schaft *nf.* regency.

Regie [ray-zhee'] *nf.* management, state monopoly, production (*stage, rad.*).

Regieren [ray-geer'ren] *vt.i.* to rule, govern.

Regierung [ray-geer'rŏong] *nf.* government, reign; -santritt *nm.* accession to the throne; -sbezirk *nm.* district, administrative area.

Regiment [ray-gi-ment'] *n.* (-er) regiment; -sbefehl *nm.* regimental order; -skommandeur *nm.* regimental commander; -smusik *nf.* regimental band; -sstab *nm.* regimental staff.

Regisseur [ray-zhi-serr'] *nm.* stage manager, producer.

Register [ray-gi'sterr] *n.* (-) register, table of contents, index, organ-stop; -pflicht *nf.* compulsory registration; -tonne *nf.* registered ton.

Registrator [ray-gi-strah'torr] *nm.* (*gen.* -s; *pl.* -en) registrar; -ur *nf.* registry.

Registrieren [ray-gi-streer'ren] *vt.* to register; -kasse *nf.* cash register; -ung *nf.* registration.

Regnen [raig'nen] *vi.* to rain.

Regnerisch [raig'ner-rish] *a.* rainy.

Regress [ray-gress'] *nm.* (-e) recourse, legal remedy.

Regsam [raig'zam] *a.* agile, active; -keit *nf.* agility, liveliness, activity.

Regulär [ray-gŏo-lairr'] *a.* regular.

Regulieren [ray-gŏo-leer'ren] *vt.* to regulate.

Regung [ray'gŏong] *nf.* motion, emotion, impulse, movement; -slos *a.* motionless.

Reh [ray] *n.* (-e) roe, deer; -bock *nm.* roebuck; -braten *nm.* roast venison; -kalb *n.* fawn; -leder *n.* doeskin.

Reibe [ribe'ər] *nf.*, **Reibeisen** [ripe'ize-en] *n.* (-) grater.

Reiben [ribe'en] *vt. ir.* to rub, grate.

Reiberei [ribe-er-ri'] *nf.* friction, irritation.

Reibfläche [ripe'flesh-er] *nf.* rough surface.

Reibung [ribe'ŏong] *nf.* friction, grating; **-slos** *a, ad.* smooth(ly), without friction.

Reich [rish] *a.* rich; **-lich** *a.* plentiful; **-tum** *nm.* (-tümer) wealth, riches, abundance.

Reich [rish] *n.* (-e) empire, kingdom, Germany; **-sange-hörige(r)** *m.w.* **-sbürger** *nm.* German citizen; **-sangestell-te(r)** civil servant; **-sgericht** *n.* supreme court; **-shauptkasse** *nf.* treasury; **-stag** *nm.* parliament.

Reichen [ri'shen] *vt.* to reach, pass, hand; *i.* reach, suffice.

Reichhaltig [rish'hal-tish] *a.* plentiful, ample, copious, abundant; **-keit** *nf.* abundance, comprehensiveness, fullness, richness.

Reichweite [rish'vite-er] *nf.* range, scope, reach.

Reif [rife] *a.* ripe.

Reif [rife] *nm.* hoar-frost.

Reif [rife] *nm.* (-e) ring.

Reife [rife'er] *nf.* ripeness, maturity; **-n** *vi.* to ripen, mature; **-zeugnis** *n.* school leaving certificate.

Reifen [rife'en] *nm.* (-) ring, hoop, tyre; **-schaden** *nm.* puncture.

Reigen [rie'gen] *nm.* dance.

Reihe [rie'er] *nf.* row, series, turn, queue; **-n** *vt.* to set in a row, range, string; **-nabwurf** *nm.* dropping of bombs in sticks (*av.*); **-nfolge** *nf.* succession, sequence; **-nhäuser-bau** *nm.* ribbon development, building; **-nherstellung** *nf.* mass production.

Reiher [rie'err] *nm.* (-) heron.

Reim [rime] *nm.* (-e) rhyme; **-en** *vt.i.* to rhyme; **-los** *a.* rhymeless.

Rein [rine] *a.* clean, pure, fair,

nett (*com.*); *ad.* quite, absolutely; **-gewicht** *n.* nett weight; **-gewinn** *nm.* nett profit; **-machefrau** *nf.* charwoman; **-schrift** *nf.* fair copy.

Reinheit [rine'hite] *nf.* purity, cleanness.

Reinlich [rine'lish] *a.* cleanly, neat, tidy; **-keit** *nf.* cleanliness, neatness, tidiness.

Reinig'en [rine'i-gen] *vt.* to cleanse, purify; **-ung** *nf.* purification, cleansing.

Reis [rice] *n.* (-er) twig, shoot, sucker, scion. [ground rice.

Reis [rice] *nm.* rice; **-mehl** *n.*

Reise [rise'er] *nf.* journey, voyage, tour; **-n** *pl.* travels; **-begleiter** *nm.* (-) travelling companion; **-bett** *n.* camp-bed; **-büro** *n.* tourist agency; **-decke** *nf.* rug; **-fertig** *a.* ready to start; **-flug** *nm.* cruising flight (*av.*); **-flugzeug** *n.* cruising aircraft; **-führer** *nm.* guidebook; **-gefährte(r)** *m.w.* travelling companion, fellow traveller; **-geld** *n.* travelling expenses; **-gepäck** *n.* luggage; **-grammophon** *n.* portable gramophone; **-koffer** *nm.* trunk, suit-case; **-kosten** *pl.* travelling expenses; **-pass** *nm.* passport; **-pläne** *m.pl.* plans for a journey; **-scheck** *nm.* travellers' cheque; **-stipendium** *n.* travelling scholarship; **-tasche** *nf.* travelling bag, case; **-verkehr** *nm.* tourist traffic; **-wetter** *nm.* holiday weather; **-ziel** *n.* destination.

Reisen [rise'en] *vi.* to travel, sail, go; **de(r)** *m.w.* **-de** *f.w.* traveller. [wood.

Reisig [rise'ish] *n.* brush-

Reiss'aus [rice'owss] *n.* flight, escape, running away; **-blei** *n.* blacklead; **-brett** *n.* drawing-board; **-dreieck** *n.* set-square.

Reiss'en [rice'en] *vt. ir.* to tear, pull, draw, sketch, design; *i.* split, rear (along); **-end** *a.*

ad. rapid, ravenous; **-er** *nm.* (-) thriller, popular play.

Reiss-leine *nf.* rip-cord (*av.*); **-nagel** *nm. see* **-zwecke**; **-schiene** *nf.* T-square; **-verschluss** *nm.* zip-fastener; **-zeug** *n.* mathematical instruments; **-zwecke** *nf.* drawing-pin.

Reiten [rite'en] *vi. ir.* to ride.

Reiter [rite'err] *nm.* (-) rider, horseman, trooper; **-korps** *n.* cavalry corps; **-regiment** *n.* cavalry regiment; **-standbild** *n.* equestrian statue; **-zug** *nm.* cavalry platoon.

Reiterei [rite-er-rī'] *nf.* cavalry.

Reit-gerte *nf.* riding whip; **-hose** *nf.* riding breeches; **-knecht** *nm.* groom; **-pferd** *n.* saddle horse, hack; **-schule** *nf.* riding school; **-stiefel** *nm.* riding boot.

Reiz [rites] *nm.* (-e) charm, irritation; **-los** *a.* unattractive, graceless; **-mittel** *n.* stimulus, stimulant, incentive; **-stoff** *nm.* irritant; **-ung** *nf.* irritation.

Reizbar [rites'barr] *a.* irritable, sensitive; **-keit** *nf.* irritability, sensitiveness.

Reizen [rite'sen] *vt.* to charm, irritate, lure, entice.

Reklamation [ray-kla-matsyohn'] *nf.* claim, complaint.

Reklame [ray-klah'mer] *nf.* advertising, propaganda, boosting (*com.*); **-schild** *n.* signboard.

Reklamieren [ray-kla-meer'ren] *vt.* to protest, claim, reclaim.

Rekognoszier'en [ray-kognos-tseer'ren] *vt.* to reconnoitre; **-ung** *nf.* reconnaissance.

Rekonvaleszent [ray-kon-vales-tsent'] *m.w.* convalescent.

Rekord [ray-korrt'] *nm.* (-e) record.

Rekrut [ray-kroot'] *m.w.* recruit; **-ieren** *vt.* to recruit.

Rektor [rek'torr] *nm.* (*gen.* -s;

pl. -en) rector (*university*), vice-chancellor, headmaster; **-at** *n.* vice-chancellorship.

Relativ [ray-la-teef'] *a.* relative.

Relativität [ray-la-ti-vi-tate'] *nf.* relativity.

Religi'on [re-li-gyohn'] *nf.* religion; **-ös** *a.* religious.

Reling [ray'ling] *nf.* rail (*ship*).

Reliquie [ray-leek'vi-er] *nf.* relic.

Remise [ray-mee'zer] *nf.* shed.

Remittieren [ray-mit-teer'ren] *vt.* to remit.

Remontoiruhr [ray-mon-toahr'ōōrr] *nf.* keyless watch.

Renegat [ray-nay-gaht'] *m.w.* renegade.

Rennbahn [ren'bahn] *nf.* race-course, racing track.

Rennboot [ren'bote] *n.* (-e) racing boat.

Renn'en [ren'en] *vi. ir.* to rush, run, race; *n.* running, race; **-er** *nm.* (-) runner, racehorse; **-pferd** *n.* race-horse; **-platz** *nm.* race-course; **-wagen** *nm.* racing car. [reindeer.

Renntier [ren'teerr] *n.* (-e)

Renommier'en [re-no-meer' ren] *vi.* to boast, brag; **-is** *m.w.* boaster, braggart.

Renonce [ray-nong'ser] *nf.* revoking (*cards*).

Renovier'en [ray-noh-veer' ren] *vt.* to renovate, renew; **-ung** *nf.* renovation.

Rentabel [ren-tahbl'] *a.* profitable, paying, lucrative.

Rentabilität [ren-ta-bi-li-tate'] *nf.* profitableness.

Rente [ren'ter] *nf.* rent, annuity, income, interest, pension; **-nbank** *nf.* annuity office; **-nempfänger** *nm.* annuitant.

Rentieren [ren-teer'ren] *vr.* to pay, be profitable.

Reparation [ray-par-ratsyohn'] *nf.* reparation; **-szahlung** *nf.* reparations payment.

Reparatur [ray-par-ra-tōōrr'] *nf.* repairing, repairs; -**bedürftig** *a.* in need of repair; -**werkstatt** *nf.* repair-shop.

Reparieren [ray-par-ree'ren] *vt.* to repair.

Repetier'en [ray-pet-eer'ren] *vt.* to revise, repeat; -**uhr** *nf.* repeating watch.

Reportage [ray-porr-tah'zher] *nf.* eye-witness account, running commentary (*rad.*).

Repräsent'ant [ray-pray-zen-tant'] *m.w.* representative; -**ieren** *vt.* to represent.

Repressalien [ray-press-ahl'yen] *pl.* reprisals.

Reproduktion [ray-pro-dōōk-syohn'] *nf.* reproduction, rendering, performance.

Reproduzieren [ray-pro-dōōt-seer'ren] *vt.* to reproduce.

Reptil [rep-teel'] *n.* (*gen. -s*; *pl.* -**ien**) reptile.

Republik [ray-pōōb-leek'] *nf.* republic.

Republikan'er [ray-pōō-bli-kah'nerr] *nm.* (-) republican; -**isch** *a.* republican.

Requirieren [ray-kvi-reer'ren] *vt.* to requisition.

Reserve [ray-zairr'ver] *nf.* reserve; -**pilot** *m.w.* relief pilot; -**rad** *n.* spare wheel (*aut.*); -**teil** *nm.* spare part.

Reservieren [ray-zairr-veer'ren] *vt.* to reserve.   [reservist.

Reservist [ray-zairr-vist] *m.w.*

Reservoir [ray-zairr-vo-ahrr'] *n.* (-e) reservoir, tank.

Residenz [ray-zi-dents'] *nf.* residence, seat.

Resignation [ray-zig-nat-syohn'] *nf.* resignation.

Resignieren [ray-zig-neer'ren] *vi.* to resign.

Resonanz [ray-zo-nants'] *nf.* resonance; -**boden** *nm.* sounding-board; -**kasten** *nm.* resonance box.

Respekt [ray-spekt'] *nm.* respect; -**los** *a.* irreverent, disrespectful; -**sperson** *nf.* dis-

tinguished person; -**voll** *a.* respectful.

Respektabel [ray-spek-tahbl'] *a.* respectable.

Respektieren [ray-spek-teer'-ren] *vt.* to respect.

Respektive [ray-spek-tee'ver] *ad.* respectively, or, as the case may be.

Rest [rest] *nm.* (-e) rest, remainder, remains; -**auflage** *nf.* remainders (*books*); -**lich** *a.* left over, remaining; -**los** *a.* complete; *ad.* completely, thoroughly.

Restauration [ray-stow-rat-syohn'] *nf.* restaurant, repair(-ing), restoration (*throne*).

Restaurieren [ray-stow-reer'ren] *vt.* to restore, repair.

Resultat [ray-zōōl-taht'] *n.* (-e) result.   [retort.

Retorte [ray-torr'ter] *nf.*

Rette'n [ret'en] *vt.* to save; -**r** *nm.* (-) rescuer, saviour.

Rettig [ret'ish] *nm.* (-e) radish.

Rettung [ret'ōōng] *nf.* rescue, escape; -**sboje** *nf.* rescue-buoy -**sboot** *n.* life-boat; -**sgürtel** *nm.* life-belt; -**sinsel** *nf.* emergency raft, island (*street*); -**slos** *a.* irretrievable; *ad.* irretrievably; -**stau** *n.* life-line.

Retusch'e [ray-tōō'sher] *nf.* retouching; -**ieren** *vt.* to touch.

Reu'e [roy'er] *nf.* repentance, remorse; -**en** *vt.i. imp.* to repent, be sorry; -**geld** *n.* penalty; -**ig** *a.* penitent.

Reuse [roy'zer] *nf.* wicker basket, fish-trap.

Revanch'e [ray-vong'sher] *nf.* revenge, return match; -**ieren** *vr.* to get one's own back, have one's revenge, reciprocate, return the compliment.

Revidieren [ray-vi-deer'ren] *vt.* to revise.

Revier [ray-veerr'] *n.* (-e) district, preserve, police-beat, barrack accommodation (*mil.*),

sick-bay (*hospital*): -dienst *nm.*
light duties (*mil.*): -stunde *nf.*
sick-parade (*mil.*).

Revision [ray-vee-zyohn'] *nf.*
revision, auditing (*com.*),
appeal (*law*).

Revisor [ray-vee-zorr'] *nm.*
(*gen.* -s; *pl.* -en) auditor.

Revolution [ray-vo-lööt-syohn'] *nf.* revolution; -är *a.*
nm. (-e) revolutionary.

Revolver [ray-vol'verr] *nm.*
(-) revolver; -drehbank *nf.*
turret-lathe; -kanone *nf.*
quick-firing gun.

Rezensent [ray-tsen-zent']
m.w. reviewer, critic.

Rezensieren [ray-tsen-zeer'-ren] *vt.* to review, criticize.

Rezension [ray-tsen-zyohn']
nf. review, criticism, critique.

Rezept [ray-tsept'] *n.* (-e)
recipe, prescription.

Rezitieren [ray-tsi-teer'ren]
vt. to recite.   [rhubarb.

Rhabarber [ra-barr'berr] *nm.*

Rheostat [ray-o-stat'] *nm.*
rheostat (*rad.*).

Rhetorisch [ray-torr'ish] *a.*
rhetorical.

Rheumatismus [roy-ma-tiss'-mõõs] *nm.* rheumatism.

Rhinozeros [ree-noh'tser-ross]
n. (-sse) rhinoceros.

Rhythmisch [rÿöot'mish] *a.*
rhythmical; -mus *nm.* (*pl.*
Rhythmen) rhythm.

Richt'antenne [risht'an-ten-er] *nf.* directional aerial (*rad.*);
-balken *nm.* traverse beam;
-blei *n.* plumb-line; -kanonier
nm. gun-layer (*av.*); -linie *nf.*
criterion, guiding principle;
-mass *n.* gauge; -scheit *n.*
ruler, level; -schnur *nf.* plumb-line, rule, guide; -sendung *nf.*
beam transmission (*rad.*); -ung
nf. direction, route, trend,
tendency, course; -waage *nf.*
level.

Richten [rish'ten] *vt.* to adjust,
direct, judge, regulate, prepare,

aim (*gun*); r. apply, address,
be guided by, dress (*mil.*).

Richter [rish'terr] *nm.* (-)
judge; -lich *a.* judicial.

Richtig [rish'tish] *a., ad.*
aright, right(ly), correct(ly);
-keit *nf.* correctness, rightness;
-stellung *nf.* correction, rectification.

Richtstrahl [risht'shtrahl]
nm. beam transmission (*rad.*);
-er *nm.* beam aerial.   [doe.

Ricke [rik'er] *nf.* female roe,

Riech'en [ree'shen] *vt.i. v.r.* to
smell; -fläschchen *n.* smelling
bottle.

Ried [reet] *n.* (-e) marsh, reed.

Riefe [ree'fer] *nf.* chamfer,
fluting; -ln *vt.* to channel,
flute.   [section.

Riege [ree'ger] *nf.* team, squad,

Riegel [reegl] *nm.* (-) bolt, bar;
-n *vt.* to bolt, bar -stellung *nf.*
bolt position (*mil.*).

Riemen [ree'men] *nm.* (-)
strap, belt, sling; -antrieb *nm.*
belt-drive, transmission;
-scheibe *nf.* pulley; -schuh *nm.*
sandal; -zeug *n.* straps, thongs,
harness.

Riemen [ree'men] *nm.* (-) oar;
-boot *n.* rowing-boat. [(*paper*).

Ries [reece] *n.* (-e) ream

Riese [reez'er] *m.w.* giant;
-nerfolg *nm.* best seller (*book*).
great success; -nflugzeug *n.*
giant plane; -nhaft *a.* collossal,
gigantic, huge; -nschlange *nf.*
python, boa constrictor.

Riesel [reezl] *nm.* (-) rippling,
drizzle; -feld *n.* -wiese *nf.*
sewage farm; -n *vi.* to ripple,
drizzle; -regen *nm.* drizzle.

Riesig [ree'zish] *a.* huge, vast,
gigantic.

Riesin [ree'zin] *nf.* giantess.

Riff [rif] *n.* (-e) reef.

Riffeln [rif'eln] *vt.* to ripple
(*flax*), groove, fide.

Rille [ril'er] *nf.* rill, drill,
chamfer, groove.   [remittance.

Rimesse [ri-mess'er] *nf.*

Rind [rint] n. (-er) ox, cow, cattle; -erbraten nm. roast beef; -ertalg nm. beef suet; -fleisch n. beef; -kraftfleisch n. corned beef; -vieh n. cattle, fool, blockhead. [crust.

Rinde [rin'der] nf. rind, bark.

Ring [ring] nm. (-e) ring, coil, combine, cartel (com.); -bahn nf. circular railway; -buch n. loose-leaf book; -förmig a. circular; -geleis n. loop-line; -sendung nf. relay(ing) (rad.); -strasse nf. ring road, perimeter track.

Ringel [ringl] nm. (-) ringlet, curl, ring; -n vt.r. to curl, wreathe, coil.

Ring'en [ring'en] vi. ir. to struggle, wrestle; t. ring; -kampf nm. wrestling match.

Rings [ringss] ad. round; -um(her) ad. round about, all round.

Rinne [rin'er] nf. gutter, drain, sewer, groove. [stream.

Rinnsal [rin'zahl] n. (-e) rill.

Rinnen [rin'en] vi. ir. to run, trickle.

Rinnstein [rin'shtine] nm. (-e) gutter, sewer, sink.

Rippchen [rip'shen] n. (-) small rib, chop, cutlet.

Rippe [rip'er] nf. rib, wing-rib (av.); -n vt. to rib; -nfellentzündung nf. pleurisy.

Rips [ripss] nm. rep (cloth).

Risiko [ree'zi-koh] n. risk.

Riskant [ris-kant'] a. risky, hazardous. [risk.

Riskieren [ris-keer'en] vt. to risk.

Riss [riss] nm. (-e) tear, scratch, gap, chink, break, breach, design, plan.

Rissig [riss'ish] a. torn, cracked. [wrist.

Rist [rist] nm. (-e) instep.

Ritt [rit] nm. (-e) ride; -meister nm. captain (cavalry).

Ritter [rit'err] nm. (-) knight; -gut n. estate; -schlag nm. knighting; -stand nm. knight-

hood; -tum n. chivalry; -zei nf. age of chivalry.

Ritterlich [rit'err-lish] a. chivalrous; -keit nf. chivalry.

Rittlings [rit'lingss] ad. astride. [rite.

Ritus [ree'tōōss] nm. (Riten)

Ritz [rits] nm. (-e), **Ritze** nf. cleft, crack, chink, scratch; -en vt. to scratch, carve, slit.

Rival'e [ree-vah'ler] m.w. rival; -isieren vi. to rival, vie with; -ität nf. rivalry.

Rizinusöl [rit-see'nōōss-erl] n. castor oil. [n. sealskin.

Robbe [rob'er] nf. seal; -nfell

Robber [rob'err] nm. (-) rubber (whist).

Roche [roch'er] m.w. ray (fish).

Roch'e [roch'er] nf. castle, rook (chess); -ieren vi. to castle.

Röcheln [rer'sheln] vi. to rattle (in throat).

Rock [rok] nm. (Röcke) coat, dress, skirt, tunic, uniform; -schoss nm. coat-tail.

Rocken [rok'en] nm. (-) distaff.

Rodel [roh'del] nf. toboggan; -bahn nf. toboggan run; -schlitten nm. toboggan; -sport nm. tobogganning.

Rode'n [roh'den] vt.i. to root up, clear; -maschine nf. bull-dozer. [ing.

Rodung [roh'dōong] nf. clear-

Rogen [roh'gen] nm. (-) roe, spawn.

Roggen [rog'en] nm. rye; -brot n. rye-bread, black bread.

Roh [row] raw, rough, coarse, cruel, crude; -eisen n. pig-iron; -erzeugnisse n.pl. raw products, materials; -gewicht n. gross weight; -leder n. untanned leather; -öl n. crude oil; -stoff nm. raw material; -seide nf. raw silk.

Roheit [roh'hite] nf. rawness, roughness, coarseness.

Rohling [roh'ling] nm. (-e) hooligan, brute.

Rohr [rore] n. (-e) reed, pipe,

cane, tube, gun-barrel, gun, valve; -bruch *nm.* pipe burst; -geflecht *n.* wicker-work; -leger *nm.* plumber; -leitung *nf.* pipe-line; -netz *n.* system of pipes; -schieber *nm.* sleeve-valve; -schlange *nf.* coil; -stock *nm.* cane; -stuhl *nm.* basket chair; -weite *nf.* bore (*mil.*); -zucker *nm.* cane sugar.

Röhre [rer'rer] *nf.* tube, pipe, duct, valve, vacuum tube; -napparat *nm.* valve set (*rad.*); -nniete *nf.* tubular rivet.

Röhricht [rer'risht] *n.* reeds, rushes.

Rokoko [ro-koh'ko] *n.* rococo.

Rollbahn [rol'bahn] *nf.* arterial, trunk road, tarmac, runway, taxying area.

Roll'e [rol'er] *nf.* roll(er), rôle, pulley, caster; -enbesetzung *nf.* cast (theatre); -enlager *n.* roller bearing; -enoffizier *nm.* details officer; -feld *n. see* Rollbahn; -film *nm.* roll-film; -holz *n.* rolling-pin; -laden *nm.* shutter; -material *n.* rolling stock; -schuh *nm.* roller skate; -sperrfeuer *n.* creeping barrage; -stuhl *nm.* wheel-chair; -treppe *nf.* escalator; -verband *n.* roll bandage; -wagen *nm.* truck (*rl.*); -werk *n.* under-carriage.

Rollen [rol'en] *vt.&i.* to roll, mangle, taxi (*plane*); -d *a.* rolling, incessant, in relays (*attack*).

Roller [rol'err] *nm.* (—) surf, heavy sea, scooter.

Roman [ro-mahn'] *nm.* (-e) novel, romance; -haft *a.* fantastic; -schreiber, -schrift-steller *nm.* novelist.

Romantik [ro-man'tik] *nf.* romanticism; -er *nm.* (—) romanticist, romantic poet.

Romantisch [ro-man'tish] *a.* romantic.

Römer [rer'merr] *nm.* (—) wine-glass.

Röntgen [rernt'shen] *vt.* to X-ray; -strahlen *m.pl.* X-rays; -gehilfe *m.w.* radiographer.

Rosa [roh'zah] *a.* pink, rose.

Rose [roh'zer] *nf.* rose; -nkohl *nm.* Brussels sprouts; -nstock *nm.* rose-tree.

Rosig [roh'zish] *a.* rosy.

Rosine [ro-zee'ner] *nf.* raisin, currant.

Ross [ross] *n.* (-e) horse, steed; -arzt *nm.* veterinary surgeon; -händler *nm.* horse-dealer; -kastanie *nf.* horse-chestnut.

Rost [rost] *nm.* (-e) grate, grill, gridiron; -braten *nm.* joint (*meat*).

Rost [rost] *nm.* rust, blight; -frei *a.* stainless (*knife*); -schutz *nm.* anti-rust preparation.

Rosten [ros'ten] *vi.* to rust.

Rösten [rers'ten] *vi.* to roast, toast, grill.

Rostig [ros'tish] *a.* rusty.

Rot [rote] *a.* red; -bäckig *a.* red-cheeked; -blond *a.* auburn; -glühend *a.* red-hot; -haarig *a.* red-haired; -kehlchen *n.* robin; -kohl *nm.* red cabbage; -kreuz *n.* red cross; -wein *nm.* claret, red wine; -stift *nm.* red pencil; -zunge *nf.* lemon sole.

Röte [rer'ter] *nf.* redness, red.

Rötel [rer'tel] *nm.* red ochre; -n *pl.* German measles. [flush.

Röten [rer'ten] *vt.r.* to redden,

Rotieren [ro-teer'ren] *vi.* to rotate, revolve.

Rötlich [rert'lish] *a.* reddish.

Rotor [roh'torr] *nm.* (*gen.* -s) *pl.* -en) armature (*el.*); -flug-zeug *n.* rotor plane.

Rotte [rot'er] *nf.* gang, pack, band, file (*mil.*), group, two aircraft, two ships.

Rotwelsch [rote'velsh] *n.* thieves' slang.

Rotz [rots] *nm.* mucus, glanders.

Rübe [rÿöö'ber] *nf.* rape, carrot, turnip; -nzucker *nm.* beet-sugar.

Rubel [rÿöö'bel] *nm.* (—) rouble.

Rubin [roo-been'] *nm.* (-e) ruby. [ing, column.

Rubrik [roo-breek'] *nf.* head-

Ruchbar [rŏŏch'barr] *a.* notorious.

Ruchlos [rŏŏch'loce] *a.* wicked; **-igkeit** *nf.* infamy, wickedness.

Ruck [rŏŏk] *nm.* (-e) jolt, start, lurch (*ship*); **-weise** *ad.* jerkily, by fits and starts.

Rück'antwort [ryŏŏk'ant-vorrt] *nf.* reply, answer; **-bezüglich** *a.* reflexive; **-blend-en** *vi.* to flash-back.

Rückblick [ryŏŏk'blik] *nm.* (-e) retrospect, survey; **-end** *a.* retrospective.

Rücken [ryŏŏ'ken] *nm.* (-) back, ridge, rear; **-angriff** *nm.* attack in the rear; **-deckung** *nf.* rear cover (*mil.*); **-flug** *nm.* inverted flight (*av.*); **-lehne** *nf.* chair-back; **-mark** *n.* spinal cord; **-schwimmen** *n.* back-stroke. [move, shift.

Rücken [ryŏŏ'ken] *vt.i.* to

Rück-erinnerung [ryŏŏk'err-] *nf.* reminiscence; **-erstattung** *nf.* return, restitution; **-fahrt** *nf.* return journey; **-fall** *nm.* relapse, reversion; **-fällig** *a.* relapsing; **-flug** *nm.* return flight (*av.*); **-forderung** *nf.* counter-claim; **-führung** *nf.* repatriation; **-fracht** *nf.* return cargo; **-gabe** *nf. see* **erstattung** ; **-gang** *nm.* decline, retrogression ; **-gängig** *a.* cancelled, null; **-grat** *n.* spine, backbone; **-halt** *nm.* reserve, support, backing; **-haltlos** *a.* unreserved; **-hut** *nf.* covering force, rear-guard.

Rückkauf [ryŏŏk'kowf] *nm.* (-käufe) redemption, buying back, repurchase; **-srecht** *n.* right of redemption; **-swert** *nm.* surrender value.

Rückkehr [ryŏŏk'kairr] *nf.* return; **-schein** *nm.* return permit.

Rückkoppel'n [ryŏŏk'kop-

eln] *vt.* to couple back (*rad.*); **-ung** *nf.* reaction, coupling, retro-action.

Rück-ladung *nf.* return cargo; **-lage** *nf.* reserve, savings; **-leitung** *nf.* return line (*el.*); **-lings** *ad.* from behind, backward; **-marsch** *nm.* marching home, homeward journey, voyage; **-nahme** *nf.* taking back, re-acceptance; **-porto** *n.* return postage; **-prall** *nm.* recoil; **-reise** *nf.* return journey, home voyage; **-ruf** *nm.* recall; **-schlag** *nm.* relapse, reverse, set-back, recoil; **-schluss** *nm.* conclusion ; **-schreiben** *n.* answer; **-schritt** *nm.* retrogression, relapse, falling-off; **-schrittlich** *a.* retrograde, backward, reactionary; **-seite** *nf.* back, reverse; **-sicht** *nf.* respect, consideration, regard; **-sichtslos** *a.* inconsiderate; **-sichtsvoll** *a.* considerate; **-sitz** *nm.* back-seat; **-spiel** *n.* return match; **-sprache** *nf.* discussion, talk; **-stand** *nm.* arrears; **-ständig** *a.* in arrears, backward, out-of-date; **-stell-taste** *nf.* back-spacer; **-stoss** *nm.* recoil; **-stossantrieb** *nm.* jet-propulsion; **-stossmotor** *nm.* jet-propulsion engine; **-strahler** *nm.* rear reflector (*cycle*); **-strahlung** *nf.* reverberation, reflection; **-tritt** *nm.* resignation, retirement; **-tritt-bremse** *nf.* back-pedalling brake; **-übersetzung** *nf.* re-translation; **-vergütung** *nf.* repayment, refund (*com.*); **-versicherung** *nf.* reinsurance; **-wanderer** *nm.* returning emigrant; **-wärtig** *a.* backward, rear, behind the lines (*mil.*); **-wärts** *ad.* backward(s), back; **-wärtsgang** *nm.* reverse gear (*aut.*); **-weg** *nm.* return journey, way back; **-wirken** *vi.* to react; **-wirkend** *a.* reacting, retroactive; **-wirkung** *nf.*

reaction, feed-back (*rad.*);
-zahlung *nf.* repayment; -zoll
nm. rebate, drawback (*customs*);
-zug *nm.* retreat; -zugsgefecht
n. rearguard action; -zünden
vi. to backfire (*aut.*).

Rucksack [roŏk'zak] *nm.*
(-säcke) knapsack, wallet, pack
(*mil.*), rucksack.

Rüde [ryoō'der] *a.* rude, rough.

Rüde [ryoō'der] *nf.* hound,
male dog, fox, wolf.

Rudel [roō'del] *n.* (-) herd,
flock, pack, U-boat pack.

Ruder [roō'derr] *n.* (-) oar,
rudder; -boot *n.* rowing-boat;
-dolle *nf.* rowlock; -fuss *nm.*
webbed foot; -gänger *nm.*
helmsman, second pilot (*av.*);
-pinne *nf.* helm.

Ruder'er [roō'der-rerr] *nm.* (-)
rower; -n *vt.i.* to row.

Ruf [roōf] *nm.* (-e) call, cry,
shout, summons, reputation;
-en *vt.i.* to call, cry, summon;
-name *nm.* Christian name;
-nummer *nf.* telephone
number; -weite *nf.* earshot;
-zeichen *n.* call-sign (*rad.*).

Rüffel [ryoō'fel] *nm.* (-)
reprimand, scolding; -n *vt.* to
reprimand, blow up.

Rüge [ryoō'ger] *nf.* censure,
reprimand, scolding; -n *vt.* to
reprimand, censure.

Ruhe [roō'er] *nf.* rest, quiet,
peace, silence, calm; -gehalt *n.*
pension, superannuation; -los
a. restless; -pause *nf.* break,
interval for rest; -platz *nm.*
resting place; -punkt *nm.* rest,
pause, resting place; -stand
nm. retirement; -stätte *nf. see*
-platz; -störung *nf.* breach of
the peace; -tag *nm.* day of
rest.

Ruhen [roō'en] *vi.* to rest, be
based on, be still.

Ruhig [roō'ish] *a.* quiet, still,
calm, silent.

Ruhm [roōm] *nm.* fame, glory;
-los *a.* inglorious; -redig *a.*

boastful; -reich *a.* glorious;
-sucht *nf.* thirst for fame.

Rühmen [ryoō'men] *vt.* to
praise, glorify; *r.* boast.

Rühmlich [ryoōm'lish] *a.*
glorious.

Ruhr [roōrr] *nf.* dysentery.

Rührei [ryoōr'ie] *n.* (-er)
scrambled egg.

Rühr'en [ryoō'rren] *vt.* to
touch, move; *r.* stir, be active;
-end *a.* touching, pathetic;
-fass *n.* churn; -selig *a.*
sentimental, emotional.

Rührig [ryoō'rish] *a.* active,
nimble, quick; -keit *nf.* activity, nimbleness, quickness.

Rührung [ryoōr'roong] *nf.*
feeling, emotion, sympathy.

Ruin [roō-een'] *nm.* Ruine *nf.*
ruin; -enhaft *a.* dilapidated,
delapidated.   [to ruin.

Ruinieren [roō-i-neer'ren] *vt.*

Rülps [ryoōlps] *nm.* (-e) belch,
wind; -en *vi.* to belch, break
wind.

Rum [roōm] *nm.* rum.

Rummel [roō'mel] *nm.* (-)
hubbub, uproar, fair, whole
lot, business; -n *vi.* to rumble.

Rumor [roō-morr'] *nm.* (-e)
din, racket; -en *vi.* to be noisy.

Rumpelei [roōm-per-lie'] *nf.*
constant jolting, rumbling.

Rumpel'n [roōm'peln] *vi.* to
rumble, jolt; -kammer *nf.*
lumber-room; -kasten *nm.*
lumber-chest, old piano.

Rumpf [roōmpf] *nm.* (-, Rümpfe)
rump, trunk, torso, fuselage
(*av.*), hull (*nav.*); -holm *nm.*
longeron (*av.*).

Rümpfen [ryoōmp'fen] *vt.* to
turn up (*nose*), sneer.

Rund [roōnt] *a.* round, plain,
about; -blick *nm.* panorama;
-bogen *nm.* Norman, Roman-
esque arch.

Runde [roōn'der] *nf.* circle,
round, beat; -n *vt.* to round
(off), make round.

Rund-fahrt *nf.* circular tour.

trip; -flug nm. circular flight; -frage nf. questionnaire.

Rundfunk [rŏŏnt'fŏŏnk] nm. (-e) radio, broadcasting, wireless; -empfang nm. broadcast reception; -en vt.i. to broadcast, transmit; -gerät n. wireless set; -gesellschaft nf. broadcasting company; -hörer nm. radio listener, listener-in; -programm n. radio programme; -sender nm. wireless transmitter; -sendung nf. broadcast, radio transmission; -stelle nf. broadcasting station; -teilnehmer nm. owner of wireless set; -übertragung nf. rediffusion.

Rund-gang [rŏŏnt'gang] nm. stroll, round (mil.); -gesang nm. song with chorus; -heraus ad. straight out, bluntly, frankly; -herum ad. round about, all round; -lich a. fat, rounded; -reim nm. refrain chorus; -reise nf. circular tour; -reisebillet n. tourist ticket, circular ticket; -schau nf. panorama, review, magazine; -schreiben n. circular (com.); -ung nf. curve, roundness; -weg ad. straight out, plainly, n. circular road, path.

Rune [rŏŏ'ner] nf. rune.

Runge [rŏŏng'er] nf. stanchion, stake, stud-stave; -nwagen nm. heavy truck (rl.).

Runkelrübe [rŏŏn'kel-ryŏŏ'ber] nf. beet-root.

Runzel [rŏŏnt'sel] nf. wrinkle; -ig a. wrinkled; -n vt. to wrinkle, frown.

Rüpel [ryŏŏ'pel] nm. (-) lout; -haft a. loutish; -ei nf. rudeness, bad manners.

Rupfen [rŏŏp'fen] vt. to pluck.

Ruppig [rŏŏ'pish] a. tattered, mean.

Russ [rŏŏss] nm. (-e) soot; -en vi. to smoke, be sooty; -ig a. sooty. [snout.

Rüssel [ryŏŏ'sel] nm. (-) trunk,

Rüst'en [ryŏŏ'sten] vt. to prepare, equip, arm; -kammer nf. arsenal; -zeug n. tools, capacity.

Rüster [ryŏŏ'sterr] nm. (-) rigger.

Rüster [ryŏŏ'sterr] nf. elm.

Rüstig [ryŏŏ'stish] a. vigorous, hale and hearty; -keit nf. vigour, strength.

Rüstung [ryŏŏ'stŏŏng] nf. preparation, equipment, armour, armaments; -sanlage nf. armament, munitions factory; -shandel nm. armaments industry; -skontrolle nf. armaments control; -swerkstatt nf. war factory, munition works; -swesen n. armaments (organisation).

Rute [rŏŏ'ter] nf. rod, switch; -ngänger nm. dowser, water-diviner.

Rutsch [rŏŏtch] nm. (-e) slide, landslide; -bahn nf. chute, slide; -en vi. to slip, slide; -ig a. slippery.

Rütteln [ryŏŏ'teln] vt.i. to shake, jolt.

S

Saal [zahl] nm. (Säle) hall, room; -einrichtung nf. furniture and fittings.

Saat [zaht] nf. sowing, seed, crop; -bestellung nf. sowing; -enstand nm. condition of crops; -feld n. corn-field; -kartoffel nf. seed-potato; -reihe nf. drill.

Sabbat [za'bat] nm. (-e) Sabbath. [slaver.

Sabbern [zab'errn] vi. to

Säbel [zay'bel] nm. (-) sabre, sword; -beinig a. bow-legged; -koppel nf. sword-belt; -rasseln n. sword rattling.

Sabotage [za-bo-tah'zher] nf. sabotage. [to sabotage.

Sabotieren [za-bo-teer'nen] vt.

Saccharin [za-cha-reen'] n. saccharine.

Sach'bearbeiter [zach'be-arr-bite-err] nm. (-) technical adviser, expert; -dienlich a. relevant, appropriate, suitable.

Sach'e [zach'e] nf. thing, matter, cause, fact; -mässig a. appropriate, suitable; ad. suitably, approximately, to the point, -katalog nm. subject catalogue; -kosten pl. cost of material; -kundig a. expert; -lage nf. situation, state of things; -nummer nf. item; -schaden nm. material damage; -walter nm. advocate, counsel; -wörterbuch n. encyclopaedia.

Sachlich [zach'lish] a. matter-of-fact, to the point, objective, impartial, essential; -keit nf. objectivity, impartiality, realism.

Sächlich [zesh'lish] a. neuter.

Sachte [zach'ter] ad. softly, gently.

Sack [zak] nm. (Säcke) sack, bag, purse; -garn n. twine; -gasse nf. blind alley; -leinwand nf. sackcloth, sacking; -pfeife nf. bag-pipes. [pouch.

Säckchen [zek'shen] n. (-)

Säcken [zek] nm. (-) purse.

Sacken [zak'en] vi. to sag, sink; t. to sack, put into bags.

Sadis'mus [za-diss'mõõs] nm. sadism; -tisch a. sadistic.

Säemann [zay'man] nm. (-männer) sower.

Säemaschine [zay'ma-shee-ner] nf. drill-plough.

Säen [zay'en] vt.i. to sow (seed).

Safran [za'frahn] nm. saffron.

Saft [zaft] nm. (Säfte) sap, juice, liquid; -ig a. juicy, spicy; -los a. dry, insipid.

Sage [zah'ger] nf. legend, myth, tale; -nhaft a. legendary.

Säge [zay'ger] nf. saw; -mehl n. sawdust; -werk n. sawmill.

Sagen [zah'gen] vt.i. to say, tell.

Sägen [zay'gen] vt.i. to saw.

Säger [zay'gerr] nm. (-) sawyer.

Sago [zah'go] nm. sago.

Sahne [zah'ner] nf. cream; -n vt. to skim; -nkäse nm. cream cheese; -nkuchen n. cream cake.

Sahnig [zah'nish] a. creamy.

Saison [say-zong'] nm. (-s) season.

Saite [zie'ter] nf. chord, string; -ninstrument n. string instrument.

Sakkoanzug [za'ko-ant-sook] nm. (-züge) lounge-suit.

Sakrament [zak-ra-ment'] n. sacrament.

Sakristan [za-kri-stahn'] nm. (-e) sacristan. [sacristy.

Sakristei [za-kri-stie'] nf.

Säkularfeier [zay-koo-lairr'fie-err] nf. centenary.

Säkulum [zay'koo-lõõm] n. (-) century. [lettuce.

Salat [za-laht'] nm. (-e) salad.

Salbadern [zal-bah'derrn] vi. to drivel, talk nonsense.

Salband [zahl'bant] n. selvedge, edge, border.

Salbe [zal'ber] nf. ointment, salve; -n vt. to anoint.

Salbei [zal-bie'] nf. sage (herb).

Salbung [zal'bõõng] nf. anointing, -svoll a. ad. unctuous(ly).

Saldier'en [zal-deer'ren] vt. to balance, square, settle (com.); -ung nf. settlement, clearing, balancing (com.).

Saldo [zal'do] nm. (Salden) balance; -betrag nm. amount of balance; -vortrag nm. balance forward (com.).

Saline [za-lee'ner] nf. salt-works. [salacine.

Salizin [za-lit-seen'] n.

Salizylsäure [za-lit-syōōl'zoy-rer] nf. salicylic acid.

Salleiste [zahl'lie-ster] nf. selvedge, border, end.

Salm [zalm] nm. (-e) salmon.

Salmiak [zal'mi-ak] *nm.* sal ammoniac; **-geist** *nm.* liquid ammonia.

Salon [sa-long'] *nm.* **(-s)** drawing-room, saloon; **-wagen** *nm.* Pulman car (*rl.*).

Salopp [za-lop'] *a.* slovenly, sloppy.

Salpeter [zal-pay'terr] *nm.* saltpetre, nitre; **-säure** *nf.* nitric acid.

Salut [za-lōōt'] *nm.* **(-e)** salute.

Salutieren [za-lōō-teer'ren] *vt.* to salute.

Salve [zal'ver] *nf.* salvo, volley.

Salz [zalts] *n.* **(-e)** salt; **-fass** *n.* salt-cellar; **-gurke** *nf.* pickled cucumber; **-ig** *a.* salty; **-säure** *nf.* hydrochloric acid (*solution*).

Salzen [zalt'sen] *vt.* to salt, pickle.

Same [zah'mer] *n.*), **Samen** [zah'men] (*gen.* **-ns**; *pl.* **-n**) seed, sperm; **-nhändler** *nm.* seed merchant; **-nkapsel** *nf.* seed-pod; **-nkorn** *n.* grain of seed.

Sämerei'en [zay-mer-rie'en] *pl.* seeds; **-händler** *nm.* seed-merchant.

Sämischleder [zay'mish-lay-derr] *n.* chamois leather.

Sämling [zame'ling] *nm.* **(-e)** seedling.

Sammel'band [zam'el-bant] *nm.* **(-bände)** volume, collected works; **-becken** *n.*, **-brunnen** *nm.* reservoir, sump; **-glas** *n.* specimen tube; **-kompanie** *nf.* salvage company (*mil.*); **-linse** *nf.* convex lens; **-mappe** *nf.* collective noun; **-mappe** *nf.* herbarium; **-platz** *nm.* assembly point, meeting place; **-stelle** *nf.* collecting point, dump, depot.

Sammeln [zam'eln] *vt./i.* to collect, gather; *r.* assemble, pull oneself together.

Sammler [zam'lerr] *nm.* **(-)** collector; **-batterie** *nf.* storage battery; **-wagen** *nm.* accumu-

lator driven car, electric car, electromobile.

Sammlung [zam'lōong] *nf.* collection, concentration.

Samstag [zams'tahk] *nm.* **(-e)** Saturday.

Samt [zamt] *nm.* **(-e)** velvet.

Samt [zamt] *pr.* (along) with, together with.

Sämtlich [zemt'lish] *a.* all, entire, all together; *ad.* in a body.

Sand [zant] *nm.* **(-e)** sand; **-boden** *nm.* sandy soil; **-ig** *a.* sandy; **-kuchen** *nm.* sponge cake; **-sack** *nm.* sandbag.

Sandale [zan-dah'ler] *nf.* sandal; **-nholz** *nm.* sandalwood.

Sandelholz [zan'del-holts] *n.* sandalwood.

Sanft [zanft] *a.* soft, smooth, gentle; **-heit**, **-mut** *nf.* gentleness, softness; **-mütig** *a.* meek, gentle.

Sang [zang] *nm.* (Sänge) song.

Sänger [zeng'err] *nm.* **(-)**, **-in** *nf.* singer, minstrel.

Sanier'en [za-neer'ren] *vt.* to restore (*in value*), reconstruct; **-ung** *nf.* restoration, reconstruction, reorganisation.

Sanitär [za-ni-tairr'] *a.* sanitary, healthy, hygienic.

Sanität [za-ni-tate'] *nf.* health, hygiene; **-er** *nm.* **(-)** medical orderly; **-sassessor** *nm.* captain (R.A.M.C.); **-sbereitschaft** *nf.* ambulance unit; **-sflugplatz** *nm.* ambulance airfield; **-sflugzeug** *n.* ambulance aircraft; **-skasten** *nm.* first-aid box; **-skolonne** *nf.* ambulance column; **-soffizier** *nm.* medical officer; **-spack** *nm.* first-aid kit; **-spersonal** *n.* medical personnel (*mil.*); **-swagen** *nm.* ambulance; **-swesen** *n.* medical services; **-szug** *nm.* medical platoon.

Sanktion [zank-syohn'] *nf.* sanction.

Sanktionieren [zank-syo-neer'ren] *vt.* to sanction.

Saphir [za'feerr] *nm.* **(-e)** sapphire.

Sappe [za'per] nf. sap (mil.).
Sappeur [zap-err'] nm. (-e) sapper.

Sardelle [zar-del'er] nf. [anchovy.
Sardine [zar-dee'ner] nf. sardine, brisling. [-tuch n. pall.

Sarg [zarrk] nm. (Särge) coffin.
Sarkasmus [zar-kass'mōōss] nm. sarcasm. [sarcastic.
Sarkastisch [zar-kas'tish] a. satiric, diabolical. [satellite.
Satanisch [za-tah'nish] a. satanic, diabolical. [satellite.
Satellit [za-te-leet'] m.w. satellite.
Satin [za-teen'] nm. satin.
Satinieren [za-ti-neer'ren] vt. to glaze, satin.
Satir'e [za-teer'rer] nf. satire; **-isch** a. satirical.
Satt [zat] a. full, satiated, satisfied, tired, deep (colour); **-heit** nf. satiety; **-sam** ad. sufficiently.
Sattel [zatl] nm. (Sättel) saddle, ridge; **-fest** a. well-seated, proficient; **-pferd** n. riding horse.
Satteln [zat'eln] vt. to saddle.
Sättig'en [ze'ti-gen] vt.r. to satiate, saturate, satisfy; **-ung** nf. satisfaction, saturation.
Sattler [zat'lerr] nm. (-) saddler, leather-worker.
Sattlerei [zat-ler-ri'] nf. saddlery. [vt. see Sättigen.
Saturieren [za-tōōr-reer'ren] vt.r. to saturate.
Satz [zats] nm. (Sätze) leap, jump, set, sentence, principle, suite (rooms), movement (music), proposition (logic), sediment, rate (com.); **-bau** nm. syntax; **-fehler** nm. misprint; **-lehre** nf. syntax; **-spiegel** nm. type-face.
Satzung [zat'sōōng] nf. rule, statute, constitution; **-smässig** a. statutory, constitutional.
Sau [zow] nf. (Säue) sow, **-bohne** nf. broad bean; **-stall** nm. pigsty.
Sauber [zow'berr] a. clean, tidy, pretty, nice; **-keit** nf. cleanness, tidiness, neatness.

Säuberlich [zoy'berr-lish] a. see Sauber.
Säubern [zoy'berrn] vt. to clean, clear, cleanse, purge, mop up (mil.).
Säuberung [zoy'ber-rōōng] nf. cleaning, cleansing, purging, mopping up (mil.); **-saktion** nf. purge, mopping-up operations (mil.); **-strupp** n. mopping-up party.
Sauce [zoh'ser] nf. sauce, gravy; **-nlöffel** nm. ladle; **-nnapf** nm, **-schüssel** nf. sauce-boat. [acid.
Sauer [zow'err] a. sour, hard, sourish, acid; **-stoff** [zow'err-shtof] nm. oxygen; **-apparat** nm. oxygen apparatus (av.).
Säuerlich [zoy'err-lish] a. sourish, acid.
Säuren [zoy'errn] vt. to turn sour, leaven.
Sauerstoff [zow'err-shtof] nm. oxygen; **-apparat** nm. oxygen apparatus (av.).
Sauerteig [sow'err-tike] nm. leaven, yeast.
Sauf'en [zow'fen] vt.i. ir. to drink too much, tope, booze; **-bold** nm. (-e) drunkard, toper.
Säufer [zoy'ferr] nm. (-) drunkard. [drinking bout.
Saufgelage [zow-fer-ri'] n.
Säug'en [zoy'gen] vt.i. ir. to suck, absorb; **-flasche** nf. infant's bottle; **-heber** nm. siphon; **-klappe** nf. suction-valve; **-kolben** nm. valve-piston; **-propfen** nm. rubber teat; **-rohr** n, **-röhre** nf. suction-, induction-pipe, suction-jet.
Säug'en [zoy'gen] vt. to suckle, feed, nurse; **-amme** nf. wet-nurse; **-etier** n. mammal.
Säugling [zoy'gling] nm. (-e) infant, baby; **-sausstattung** nf. layette, baby's outfit; **-sheim** n. crèche, baby nursery.
Säule [zoy'ler] nf. column, pillar, pile; **-ngang** nf. arcade; **-nknauf** nm. capital.
Saum [zowm] nm. (Säume) seam, hem, fringe, edge, outskirts (town).

Säumen [zoy'men] vt. to hem.

Säumen [zoy'men] vi. to delay, hesitate.

Säumig [zoy'mish] a. slow, dilatory, negligent.

Saum'pfad [zowm'pfaht] nm. (-e) mule-track; -pferd n. pack-horse; -tier n. beast of burden.

Saumselig [zowm'zay-lish] a. slow, negligent; -keit nf. slowness, negligence.

Säure [zoy'rer] nf. acid, sourness; -beständig a. acid-proof; -haltig a. acid containing; -kittel nm. acid-proof overall; -schurz nm. acid-proof apron.

Saus [zowss] nm. rush, riot.

Säuseln [zoy'zeln] vi. to murmur rustle.

Sausen [zow'zen] vi. to rush, bluster, blow, tear along.

Saxophon [za-xo-fone'] n. (-e) saxophone.

Schabe [shah'ber] nf. cockroach, moth, scraper.

Schabeisen [shahp'ize-en] n. (-) grater, scraper.

Schaben [shah'ben] vt. to scrape, grate.

Schabernack [shah'berr-nak] nm. (-e) trick, hoax.

Schäbig [shay'bish] a. shabby, mean; -keit nf. shabbiness, meanness.

Schablone [shab-loh'ner] nf. stencil, pattern; -nmässig a. stereotyped, conventional.

Schablonieren [sha-blo-neer'ren] vt. to stencil.

Schabsel [shahp'sel] n. (-) shavings.

Schach [shach] n. chess, check; -brett n. chess-board; -figur nf. chessman; -förmig a. checquered; -matt a. checkmate; -partie nf. game of chess.

Schacher [shach'err] nm. higgling, bargaining, usury; -er nm. (-) petty dealer, haggler; -n vi. to bargain, barter, trade in a small way.

Schacht [shacht] nm. (Schächte) shaft, pit, mine, gallery, focussing hood (camera).

Schachtel [shach'tel] nf. box.

Schade [shah'der] a. a pity.

Schädel [shay'del] nm. (-) skull.

Schaden [shah'den] nm (Schäden) damage, harm, hurt, loss, disadvantage; vi. to hurt, harm, injure, damage; -freude nf. malicious joy.

Schadenersatz [shah'den-err-sats] nm. compensation, damages; -klage nf. action for damages; -pflichtig a. liable for damages.

Schadhaft [shaht'haft] a. damaged, ruinous.

Schädigen [shay'di-gen] vt. to injure, damage; -ung nf. damage, injury.

Schädlich [shate'lish] a. pernicious, damaging, dangerous; -keit nf. perniciousness.

Schädling [shate'ling] nm. (-e) pest.

Schadlos [shaht'lohss] a. indemnified; -haltung nf. indemnification, compensation.

Schaf [shahf] n. (-e) sheep; -bock nm. ram; -fell n. sheepskin, fleece; -hirt nm. shepherd; -leder n. sheepskin; -schenkel nm. leg of mutton; -schur nf. sheep-shearing; -skopf nm. blockhead, silly fool.

Schäfchen [shafe'shen] n. (-) lamb; -wolken f.pl. fleecy clouds.

Schäfer [shafe'err] nm. shepherd; -in nf. shepherdess; -hund nm. sheep-dog, collie, Alsatian; -stunde nf. lovers' hour.

Schaffen [shaf'en] vt. ir. to create, make, do; -d a. creative.

Schaffen [shaf'en] vt. to make, do, work, obtain, procure, shift; i. be busy.

Schaffer [shaf'err] *nm.* (-) creator, steward, hard worker.

Schaffner [shaf'nerr] *nm.* (-) conductor (tram), guard (train), steward, manager.   [scaffold.

Schafott [shaf-ot'] *n.* (-e)

Schaft [shaft] *nm.* (Schäfte) shaft, shank, handle, stalk, tree-trunk; -leisten *nm.* boot-tree; -stiefel *nm.* wellington.

Schäften [shef'ten] *vt.* to provide with a handle, shaft.

Schakal [shah'kal] *nm.* (-e) jackal.

Schäker [shake'err] *nm.* (-) joker; -n *vi.* to joke, flirt.

Schal [shahl] *a.* flat, insipid; -heit *nf.* insipidity, staleness.

Schal [shahl] *nm.* (-s) scarf, shawl.   [cup, bowl.

Schälchen [shale'shen] *n.* (-)

Schale [shah'ler] *nf.* (-n) peel, shell, skin, rind, cup, dish, basin.

Schäl'en [shale'en] *vt.* to peel, shell; -seife *nf.* kitchen soap.

Schälhengst [shale'hengst] *nm.* (-e) stallion.

Schalk [shalk] *nm.* (-e) rogue; -haft *a.* roguish.

Schall [shal] *nm.* (-e) sound; -boden *nm.* sounding-board; -dämpfer *nm.* silencer, damper; -dämpfung *nf.* sound insulation, silencing; -dicht *a.* sound-proof; -dose *nf.* sound-box, pick-up; -geschwindigkeit *nf.* speed of sound; -lehre *nf.* acoustics; -platte *nf.* gramophone record, disc; -stärke *nf.* volume (rad.); -trichter *nm.* trumpet, megaphone; -wand *nf.* baffle (rad.); -welle *nf.* sound-wave; -zeichen *n.* sound-signal.

Schallen [shal'en] *vi.n.* to sound, resound, echo, ring.

Schallmess'batterie [shal'-mess-ba-ter-ree'] *nf.* sound-ranging battery; -stelle *nf.* sound-ranging station; -ung *nf.* sound ranging.   [shallot.

Schalotte [sha-lot'er] *nf.*

Schalt'anlage [shalt'an-lah-ger] *nf.* sub-station (el.); -anlasser *nm.* starting-switch; -brett *n.* switch-board, dash-board; -dose *nf.* switch-box; -gestänge *n.* gear-change mechanism (aut.); -getriebe *n.* change-gear (tec.), gear-box (aut.); -hebel *nm.* gear-lever (aut.); -jahr *n.* leap year; -klinke *nf.* latch; -schlüssel *nm.* ignition key (aut.); -tafel *nf. see -brett; -vorrichtung *nf.* switch.

Schalten [shal'ten] *vt.* to switch, close circuit (el.), change gear (aut.); *i.* dispose of, rule, control, direct.

Schalter [shal'terr] *nm.* (-) counter, ticket-office, switch, connector, shutter, circuit-breaker (el.); -beamte(r) *m.w.*; -kupplung *nf.* supercharger (el.); -raum *nm.* booking-office; -zelle *nf.* cell (el.).   [shell-fish.

Schaltier [shahl'teerr] *n.* (-e)

Schaltung [shal'toong] *nf.* circuit, connection (el.), gear-change (aut.), disposal, control.

Schalung [shah'loong] *nf.* boarding, planks.

Schälung [shay'loong] *nf.* peeling.

Schaluppe [sha-loo'per] *nf.* (-n) sloop.

Scham [shahm] *nf.* shame, modesty.

Schamhaft [shahm'haft] *a.* bashful; -igkeit *nf.* bashfulness, modesty.

Schamlos [shahm'lohss] *a.* shameless; -igkeit *nf.* shamelessness.   [ashamed.

Schämen [shay'men] *vr.* to be

Schamotte [sha-mot'er] *nf.* fire-clay; -stein *nm.* fire-brick.

Schampu [sham-poo'] *n.* (-s) shampoo; -nieren *vt.* to shampoo.

Schand'e [shan'der] *nf.* shame, disgrace, scandal; -fleck *nm.* stain, blemish; -tat *nf.* deed of shame, crime.

Schänd'en [shen'den] vt. to disgrace, spoil, violated; -er nm. violater; -ung nf. defamation, violation.

Schändlich [shent'lish] a. shameful, vile, disgraceful; -keit nf. infamy, disgrace.

Schank [shank] nm. liquor licence, public house; -bier n. draught beer; -gerechtigkeit nf. licence; -stätte nf. licensed premises; -stube nf. -tisch nm. bar; -wirt nm. publican.

Schanz'e [shant'ser] nf. fortification, field-work, earthworks, redoubt, fort; -arbeit nf. trenching, entrenchment; -pfahl nm. palisade; -zeug n. entrenching tool.

Schanzen [shant'sen] vi. to entrench, dig in. [risk, hazard.

Schanze [shant'ser] nf. chance.

Schar [sharr] nf. troop, band, squad, crowd, host, flock; -enweise ad. in bands, masses; -führer nm. captain, leader.

Scharade [shar-rah'der] nf. charade.

Scharen [shar'ren] v.r.r. to assemble, rally, crowd together.

Scharbe [sharr'ber] nf. cormorant.

Scharf [sharrf] a. sharp, keen, armed, live (shell); -blick nm. sharp-sightedness, penetration; -eckig a. acute-angled; -machen vi. to make mischief; -macher nm. fire-brand, hot-head; -richter nm. executioner; -schiessen n. firing with live ammunition; -schmeckend a. pungent; -schütze m.w. sniper, marksman, sharpshooter.

Scharfsicht [sharrf'zisht] nf. keen vision, perspicacity; -ig a. discerning, sharp-sighted; -igkeit nf. discernment.

Scharfsinn [sharrf'zin] nm. penetration, sagacity; -ig a. shrewd, discerning.

Schärfe [shairr'fer] nf. sharpness, edge, keenness, rigour.

Schärfen [shairr'fen] vt. to sharpen, grind, pare, make live (shell).

Scharlach [sharr'lach] nm. scarlet; -farben a. scarlet; -fieber n. scarlet fever, scarlatina.

Scharmützel [sharr-myōōt'sel] n. (-) skirmish; -n vi. to skirmish.

Scharnier [sharr-neerr'] n. (-e) joint, hinge; -stift nm. joint-pin.

Schärpe [shairr'per] nf. sash, scarf, sling; -nquaste nf. tassel on sash (mil.).

Scharpie [sharr-pee'] nf. lint.

Scharre [sharr'er] nf. scraper, rake. [scrape, rake, scratch.

Scharren [shar'ren] vt.i. to

Schart'e [sharr'ter] nf. notch, loophole; -enstand nm. pill-box (mil.); -ig a. jagged.

Scharteke [shar-tay'ker] nf. worthless old book, trash, lumber.

Scharwenzel [sharr-vent'sel] nm. (-) toady, knave (cards); -n vi. to toady, curry favour.

Schatten [shat'en] nm. (-) shadow, shade; -bild n. phantom; -fabrik nf. shadow factory; -haft a. shadowy; -linie nf. outline; -seite nf. shady side, dark side.

Schattier'en [sha-teer'ren] vt.i. to shade; -ung nf. shade, shading, hatching.

Schatulle [sha-too'ler] nf. cash-box, casket.

Schatz [shats] nm. (Schätze) treasure, sweetheart; -amt n. treasury; -anweisung nf. treasury bond; -kammer nf. treasury; -meister nm. treasurer. [estimable.

Schätzbar [shets'barr] a.

Schätz'en [shets'en] vt. to value, esteem, estimate; -enswert a. estimable, valued; -ung nf. estimate, estimation; -ungsweise ad. approximately.

Schau [show] *nf.* show, parade, review, exhibition; **-bild** *n.* diagram; **-bude** *nf.* booth; **-bühne** *nf.* stage; **-fenster** *n.* shop-window; **-gerüst** *n.* stage, scaffolding; **-kasten** *nm.* showcase, glass case; **-lustige(r)** *m.w.* onlooker, spectator; **-münze** *nf.* medal; **-platz** *nm.* scene; **-spiel** *n.* drama; **-stellung** *nf.* exhibition, ostentation, show.

Schauder [show'derr] *nm.* shudder(ing), horror; **-haft** *a.* horrible; **-n** *vi.* to shudder, shiver; [(at), see, gaze on.

Schauen [show'en] *vt.i.* to look

Schauer [show'err] *nm.* (-) shower, thrill, fit, horror; **-roman** *nm.* penny dreadful, cheap novel; **-tat** *nf.* atrocity.

Schauern [show'errn] *vi.* to shiver, shudder.

Schaufel [show'fel] *nf.* shovel, paddle, turbine-blade, scoop; **-kette** *nf.* paddle tractor; **-panzer** *nm.* bulldozer; **-rad** *n.* paddle-wheel.

Schaufeln [show'feln] *vt.i.* to shovel, rake, scoop.

Schaukel [show'kel] *nf.* swing, see-saw; **-n** *vt.i.* to rock, swing, pitch (*ship*); **-pferd** *n.* rocking-horse; **-stuhl** *nm.* rocking-chair.

Schaum [showm] *nm.* (Schäume) foam, froth, lather; **-blase** *nf.* bubble; **-ig** *a.* frothy, foamy; **-schläger** *nm.* gasbag; **-wein** *nm.* sparkling wine, champagne. [foam, sparkle.

Schäumen [shoy'men] *vi.* to

Schaurig [show'rish] *a.* horrible, gruesome.

Schauspiel [show'shpeel] *n.* (-e) drama, spectacle, sight; **-er** *nm.* (-) actor; **-erin** *nf.* actress; **-ern** *vi.* to act; **-kunst** *nf.* dramatic art.

Scheck [shek] *m.w.* Schecke *nf.* piebald horse; **-ig** *a.* dappled, piebald.

Scheck [shek] *nm.* (-e) cheque; **-buch** *n.* cheque-book; **-formular** *n.* blank cheque; **-inhaber** *nm.* bearer; **-zahlung** *nf.* payment by cheque.

Scheel [shale] *a.* squint-eyed, envious; **-sucht** *nf.* envy, jealousy.

Scheffel [shef'el] *nm.* (-) bushel; **-weise** *ad.* by the bushel.

Scheffeln [shef'eln] *vt.* to heap up; *i.* yield abundantly.

Scheibe [shi'ber] *nf.* slice, plane, disk, practice target (*mil.*); **-ngardine** *nf.* casement curtain; **-nhonig** *nm.* honey in the comb; **-nkupplung** *nf.* plate clutch (*aut.*); **-nschiessen** *n.* target practice (*mil.*); **-nschlepper** *nm.* target tower (*av.*); **-nstand** *nm.* butts; **-nwischer** *nm.* windscreen wiper (*aut.*).

Scheide [shi'der] *nf.* sheath, boundary; **-brief** *nm.* farewell letter, bill of divorcement; **-gruss** *nm.* farewell; **-kunst** *nf.* analytical chemistry; **-münze** *nf.* small change; **-punkt** *nm.* point of separation; **-wand** *nf.* partition wall; **-weg** *nm.* cross-roads.

Scheiden [shide'en] *vt.* to separate; *r.* part, divorce, leave.

Scheidung [shide'ŏong] *nf.* separation, divorce, analysis, refining (*ore*); **-serkenntnis** *nf.* decree nisi; **-sklage** *nf.* divorce suit.

Schein [shine] *nm.* (-e) light, shine, certificate, semblance, look, (mere) appearance, banknote, licence, pass; **-angriff** *nm.* feint attack; **-anlage** *nf.* dummy position (*mil.*); **-bar** *a.* apparent, seeming, ostensible; **-bild** *n.* illusion; **-ehe** *nf.* mock marriage; **-gefecht** *n.* sham fight; **-gericht** *n.* mock trial; **-geschäft** *n.* fictitious transaction; **-grund** *nm.* pretence, fictitious reason; **-heilig** a. sanctimonious; **-tod** nm. trance; **-verkauf** nm. pro forma sale; **-wechsel** m. accommodation bill; **-werfer** nm. searchlight, reflector, projector, spot-light, headlight (aut.).

Scheinen [shine'en] vi.t. ir. to shine, seem.

Scheit [shite] n. (-er. -e) log.

Scheitel [shite'el] nm. (-) top, parting (hair), summit; vine nf. vertical line; **-n** vt. to part (hair); **-punkt** nm. zenith; **-recht** a. vertical.

Scheitern [shite'errn] vi. to be wrecked, fail.   [shellac.

Schellack [shel'ak] nm.

Schelle [shel'er] nf. small bell; **-n** vi.t. to ring.   [haddock.

Schellfisch [shel'fish] nm. (-e)

Schelm [shelm] nm. (-e) rogue; **-enstreich** nm. trick, practical joke; **-isch** a. roguish.

Schelte [shel'ter] nf. rebuke, scolding; **-n** vt. ir. to scold, blame; **-wort** n. term of abuse.

Schema [shay'mah] n. (-ta) scheme, model, diagram, arrangement.   [a. systematic.

Schematisch [shay-mah'tish]

Schemel [shame'el] nm. (-) stool, footstool.

Schemen [shame'en] nm. (-) shadow, phantom.

Schenk'e [shen'ker] nf. inn, public-house; **-mädchen** n. barmaid; **-stube** nf. bar; **-wirt** nm. publican.

Schenkel [shen'kel] nm. (-) thigh, haunch, shank.

Schenken [shen'ken] vt. to present, give, pour out, sell, remit, forgive.   [donor.

Schenker [shen'kerr] nm. (-)

Schenkung [shen'koong] nf. donation; **-surkunde** nf. deed of gift.

Scherbe [shairr'ber] nf. broken piece, fragment, potsherd.

Scher'e [shairr'rer] nf. scissors,

shears; **-becken** n. shaving basin; **-enfernrohr** n. stereotelescope, scissors telescope; **-enschleifer** nm. knife-grinder; **-enmesser** n. razor.

Scheren [shair'ren] vt. to shear, cut, mow, shave, cheat, sheer (ship); r. bother about, clear off.

Schererei [shair-rer-ry'] nf. bother, fuss, trouble.

Scherflein [shairrf'line] n. (-) mite, bit.

Scherz [shairrts] nm. (-e) joke, jest, fun; **-haft** a. joking, jocular; **-weise** ad. in jest, for fun; **-wort** n. joke.

Scherzen [shairrt'sen] vi. to joke, jest.

Scheu [shoy] a. shy; nf. shyness; **-klappe** nf. blinker.

Scheuche [shoy'sher] nf. scarecrow.   [scare.

Scheuchen [shoy'shen] vt. to

Scheuen [shoy'en] vt.i.r. to shun, be frightened or, fight shy of.

Scheuer [shoy'err] nf. barn.

Scheuern [shoy'errn] vt. to scour, scrub, clean; **-bürste** nf. scrubbing brush; **-frau** nf. charwoman; **-lappen** n. dishcloth, mop; **-leiste** nf. skirtingboard; **-papier** n. emery paper.

Scheune [shoy'ner] nf. barn.

Scheusal [shoy'zahl] n. (-e) monster.

Scheusslich [shoy'slish] a. abominable, horrible, ugly; **-keit** nf. atrocity, horror.

Schicht [shisht] nf. layer, stratum, thick, spell; **-en** vt. to arrange (in layers), distribute.

Schicken [shik'en] vt. to send; r. happen, be becoming, be resigned to.

Schicklich [shik'lish] a. becoming, proper; **-keit** nf. propriety, fitness.

Schicksal [shik'zahl] n. (-e) fate, fortune; **-sschlag** nm. great misfortune, blow;

-swechsel *nm.* change of fortune.

Schickung [shik´ŏong] *nf.* dispensation.

Schiebe´dach [shee´ber-dach] *n.* (-dächer) sliding roof, sunshine roof (*aut.*); -tür *nf.* sliding door.

Schieben [shee´ben] *vt. ir.* to push, shove; *i.* profiteer; *n.* pushing, deflection (*by wind*).

Schieber [shee´berr] *nm.* (-) slide, slide-rule, profiteer; -motor *nm.* sleeve-valve motor; -traktor *nm.* bulldozer.

Schiebkarren [sheep´kar-ren] *nm.* (-) wheelbarrow.

Schiebung [shee´bŏong] *nf.* profiteering, jobbery, graft.

Schiedlich [sheet´lish] *a.* peaceable, by arbitration.

Schieds´gericht [sheets´ger-risht] *n.* (-e) arbitration court; -richter *nm.* referee, umpire, arbitrator; -richtern *vi.* to arbitrate; -spruch *nm.* (arbitration) award.

Schief [sheef] *a.* slanting, oblique, sloping, crooked, wrong; *ad.* askew, awry, askance; -heit *nf.* crookedness, wrongness.   [incline.

Schiefe [shee´fer] *nf.* slope.

Schiefer [shee´ferr] *nm.* slate, splinter; -bruch *nm.* slatequarry; -dach *nm.* slate-roof; -decker *nm.* slater; -stift *nm.* slate pencil; -tafel *nf.* (child's) slate.

Schiefern [shee´fern] *vi.* to flake, splinter.   [squint.

Schielen [shee´len] *vi.* to squint.

Schienbein [sheen´bine] *n.* (-e) shin-bone.

Schiene [shee´ner] *nf.* rail, splint; -n *vt.* to put in splints, put tyres on (*wheel*).

Schienen-leger *nm.* (-) plate-layer (*rl.*); -strang *nm.* rails, track (*rl.*); -weg *nm.* permanent way; -weite *nf.* gauge.

Schier [sheerr] *a.* sheer, clear, pure; *ad.* nearly, almost.

Schierling [sheerr´ling] *nm.* (-e) hemlock.

Schiessbaumwolle [sheess´bowm-vol-er] *nf.* gun-cotton.

Schiessbude [sheess´bŏō-der] *nf.* shooting-gallery.

Schiessen [shee´sen] *vt.i. ir.* to shoot, score (*football*); *i.* dart, shoot, rush, spring, tear.

Schiess´-platz *nm.* artillery range, firing range; -pulver *n.* gunpowder; -scharte *nf.* embrasure, loophole; -stand *nm.* rifle-range; -vorschrift *nf.* gunnery, musketry manual.

Schiff [shif] *n.* (-e) ship, vessel, shuttle, nave (*church*); -bar *a.* navigable; -bau *nm.* shipbuilding; -bruch *nm.* shipwreck; -brüchig *a.* shipwrecked; -brücke *nf.* pontoonbridge; -geleit *n.* convoy; -sjunge *m.w.* cabin-boy; -sküche *nf.* galley; -smakler *nm.* ship-broker; -smannschaft *nf.* crew; -sspur *nf.* wake; -sraum *nm.* hold; -swerft *nf.* dockyard, wharf.

Schiffchen [shif´shen] *n.* (-) small boat, shuttle.

Schiffen [shif´en] *vi.* to sail, navigate; *t.* ship, transport.

Schiffer [shif´err] *nm.* (-) sailor, mariner, seaman, skipper; -klavier *n.* accordion.

Schiffahrt [shif´farrt] *nf.* navigation, shipping; -slinie *nf.* steamship line; -sweg *nm.* route.

Schikane [shi-kah´ner] *nf.* annoyance, vexation, worry.

Schikanieren [shi-ka-neer´ren] *vt.* to annoy, worry, bother.

Schild [shilt] *nm.* (-e) shield, coat-of-arms; *n.* (-er) signboard, name-plate, peak (*cap*); -bürger *nm.* duffer, blockhead; -drüse *nf.* thyroid gland; -erhaus *n.* sentry-box; -ermaler *nm.* sign-painter; **-knappe** *m.w.* squire; **-kröte** *nf.* tortoise, turtle; **-lager** *n.* trunnion bearing; **-patt** *n.* tortoiseshell; **-wache** *nf.* sentry; **-zapfen** *nm.* trunnion.

Schildern [shil'dern] *vt.* to describe, portray, depict; **-ung** *nf.* description, portrayal.

Schilf [shilf] *n.* (-e) reed, sedge, **-rohr** *n.* rushes, reeds.

Schiller [shil'err] *nm.* lustre, shine; **-n** *vi.* to change colour, glitter; **-nd** *a.* iridescent.

Schilling [shi'ling] *nm.* shilling.

Schimmel [shim'el] *nm.* mould, white horse; **-ig** *a.* mouldy; **-n** *vi.* to go mouldy.

Schimmer [shim'err] *nm.* (-) glimmer, glitter; **-n** *vi.* to gleam, glitter, shine.

Schimpanse [shim-pan'zer] *m.w.* chimpanzee.

Schimpf [shimpf] *nm.* (-e) insult, disgrace; **-en** *v.i.t.* to abuse, scold, grumble, grouse; **-lich** *a.* disgraceful; **-wort** *n.* term of abuse.

Schindel [shin'del] *nf.* shingle; **-n** *vt.* to roof with wooden tiles, shingles.

Schinden [shin'den] *vt. ir.* to flay, grind down, sweat, exploit; **r.** drudge, toil, slave; **-mähre** *nf.* old hack.

Schinder [shin'derr] *nm.* (-) knacker, exploiter.

Schinderei [shin-der-ri'] *nf.* sweating, grind, drudgery.

Schinken [shink'en] *nm.* (-) ham; **-brötchen** *n.* ham sandwich.

Schinn [shin] *nm.* (-e) scurf, dandruff.

Schippe [ship'er] *nf.* shovel.

Schirm [shirrm] *nm.* (-e) umbrella, protection, screen, shade, peak (cap); **-antenne** *nf.* umbrella aerial; **-eindecker** *nm.* parasol monoplane; **-futteral** *n.* umbrella-case;

-gitter *n.* screen-grid (rad.); **-herr** *m.w.* patron, protector; **-lafette** *nf.* gun-carriage with shield; **-mütze** *nf.* peaked cap; **-ständer** *nm.* umbrella-case.

Schirmen [shirr'men] *vt.* to protect, screen. [harness.

Schirren [shirr'en] *vt.* to

Schisma [shiss'mah] *n.* (Schismen, Schismata) schism.

Schlacht [shlacht] *nf.* battle; **-bank** *nf.* slaughter-house, abattoir; **-beil** *n.* pole-axe; **-feld** *n.* battle-field; **-flotte** *nf.* battle-fleet; **-flugzeug** *n.* fighter plane; **-geschwader** *n.* battle squadron (nav.); **-gruppe** *nf.* ground attack unit (av.); **-kreuzer** *nm.* battle-cruiser; **-reif** *a.* fat; **-reihe** *nf.* line of battle; **-ruf** *nm.* battle-cry, war-cry; **-schiff** *n.* battleship; **-vieh** *n.* fattened stock.

Schlachten [shlach'ten] *vt.* to slaughter.

Schlächter [shlesh'terr] *nm.* (-) butcher.

Schlächterei [shlesh-ter-ri'] *nf.* butcher's shop.

Schlacke [shlak'er] *nf.* slag, dross, scum; **-nfrei** *a.* free from slag.

Schlaf [shlahf] *nm.* sleep; **-anzug** *nm.* pyjamas; **-decke** *nf.* blanket; **-krankheit** *nf.* sleeping sickness; **-lied** *n.* lullaby; **-losigkeit** *nf.* sleeplessness, insomnia; **-mittel** *n.* narcotic; **-rock** *nm.* dressing gown; **-saal** *nm.* dormitory; **-sack** *nm.* sleeping-bag; **-sucht** *nf.* sleepiness; **-trunk** *nm.* sleeping-draught; **-trunken** *a.* drowsy, half asleep; **-wagen** *nm.* sleeping-car (rl.); **-wandeln** *vi.* to walk in one's sleep; **-zimmer** *n.* bedroom.

Schläfchen [shlafe'shen] *n.* (-) nap, doze.

Schläfe [shlafe'er] *nf.* temple.

Schlafen [shlah'fen] *vi. ir.* to

sleep; **-enszeit** *nf.* bed-time; **-gehen** *n.* going to bed.
Schläfer [shlafe'err] *nm.* sleeper; **-n** *vi.* to feel sleepy, be drowsy.
Schlaff [shlaf] *a.* slack, loose, flabby, limp, lax; **-heit** *nf.* slackness, flabbiness, limpness, laxity.
Schläfrig [shlafe'rish] *a.* sleepy; **-keit** *nf.* sleepiness, drowsiness.
Schlag [shlahk] *nm.* (Schläge) blow, stroke, fit, beat, clap, kind, shock, song (*birds*); door; **-ader** *nf.* artery; **-anfall** *nm.* stroke, fit; **-artig** *a.* sudden, violent, without warning; **-ball** *nm.* rounders, ball; **-baum** *nm.* turnpike; **-bolzen** *nm.* firing pin, striker (*mil.*); **-feder** *nf.* firing pin spring (*mil.*); **-fluss** *nm.* apoplexy; **-instrument** *n.* percussion instrument; **-kraft** *nf.* striking power, force; **-obers** *n.*, **-sahne** *nf.* whipped cream; **-seite** *nf.* list (*ship*); **-uhr** *nf.* striking clock; **-wort** *n.* slogan, catch-word; **-zeile** *nf.* headline.
Schlagen [shlah'gen] *vt.v.* to beat, strike, knock, hit, fell, build (*bridge*), defeat, coin; *r.* fight, strike, clap, sing.
Schlager [shlah'gerr] *nm.* (-) great success, popular song.
Schläger [shlay'gerr] *nm.* (-) beater, fighter, hitter, kicker (*horse*), rapier, tennis racket, bat, golf-club.
Schlägerei [shlay-ger-ri'] *nf.* scuffle, fight.
Schlagfertig [shlahk'fairr-tish] *a.* quick-witted; **-keit** *nf.* striking power, complete preparedness, quickness.
Schlamm [shlam] *nm.* mud, slime; **-ig** *a.* slimy, muddy; **-netz** *n.* drag-net.
Schlämm'en [shlem'en] *vt.* to wash, whitewash, clean; **-kreide** *nf.* whiting.

Schlamp'e [shlam'per] *nf.* slattern, slut; **-ig** *a.* slovenly, messy.
Schlamperei [shlam-per-ri'] *nf.* untidiness, slovenliness, disorder.
Schlange [shlang'er] *nf.* snake, serpent, queue; **-stehen** *vi.* to (form a) queue; **-nlinie** *nf.* spiral curve, wavy line; **-npfad**, **-weg** *nm.* winding path, road.
Schlängeln [shleng'eln] *vi.r.* to meander, twist, wind.
Schlank [shlank] *a.* slim, slender; **-heit** *nf.* slenderness, **-weg** *nf.* flatly.
Schlapp [shlap] *a.* slack, flabby; **-heit** *nf.* slackness; **-hut** *nm.* slouch hat; **-macher** *nm.* slacker, coward.
Schlappe [shlap'er] *nf.* rebuff, check, reverse, defeat.
Schlaraffen'land [shla-raf'en-lant] *n.* land of milk and honey; **-leben** *n.* life of luxury.
Schlau [shlow] *a.* sly, cunning; **-kopf** *nm.* artful dodger, old fox.
Schlauch [shlowch] *nm.* (Schläuche) inner tube (*cycle*), hose, tube, leather bottle, skin, crib (*school*); **-binder** *nm.* connecting hose; **-boot** *n.* inflatable rubber dinghy (*av.*); **-on** *vt.* to fill from a hose, tube, *etc.*; **-ventil** *n.* tyre-valve (*aut. etc.*).
Schläue [shloy'er] *nf.* see **Schlauheit**.
Schlauheit [shlow'hite] *nf.* slyness, cunning.
Schlecht [shlesht] *a.* bad, wicked, poor, ill; **-erdings** *ad.* utterly; **-hin** *ad.* simply; **-igkeit** *nf.* badness, wickedness.
Schlecken [shlek'en] *vt.i.* to lick, be sweet-toothed.
Schlegel [shlay'gel] *nm.* (-) drumstick, mallet, club, hammer.
Schleh'e [shlay'er] *nf.* sloe; **-dorn** *nm.* blackthorn.
Schlei(e) [shli'er] *nf.* tench.

Schleich'en [shli'shen] vi. ir. to creep, slink, skulk; -en a. furtive, slow, crawling; -er nm. sneak, intriguer; -fahrt nf. silent approach (av.); -handel nm. black market; -weg nm. secret path, underhand means.

Schleier [shli'err] nm. (-) veil, (smoke) screen (mil.); -flor nm. crepe; -n vt. to veil, screen.

Schleif'e [shlife'er] nf. loop, noose, bow, looping (av.); -anzug nm. overall; -antenne nf. loop aerial; -dorn n. arbor (tec.); -en vt.ir. to drag, pull, slide, glide, slur, pull down; -kontakt nm. sliding contact (el.).

Schleif'en [shlife'en] vt. ir. to grind, polish; -er nm. (-) grinder, polisher; -lack nm. enamel; -stein nm. grindstone.

Schleim [shlime] nm. (-e) slime, mucus; -ig a. slimy, mucous.

Schleissen [shlice'en] vi.ir. to wear out, slink, split, tear.

Schlemme'n [shlem'en] vi. to guzzle; -r nm. (-) glutton, gourmand.

Schlemmerei [shlem-er-ri'] nf. gluttony, feasting.

Schlendern [shlen'derrn] vi. to saunter.

Schlendrian [shlen'dri-ahn] nm. old-fashioned methods, mere routine.

Schlenkern [shlenk'errn] vt.i. to toss away, fling, swing, shamble along, slouch.

Schlepp'e [shlep'er] nf. train (dress); -antenne nf. trailing aerial (av.); -dampfer nm. tug; -gebühr nf. towage; -netz n. drag-net; -scheibe nf. towed target; -tau n. hawser, tow-line, guide-rope; -zug nm. chain of barges.

Schleppen [shlep'en] vt.r. to drag, haul, tow, carry, trail; -nd a. dragging, trailing, slow, shuffling; -r nm. (-) tug.

Schleuder [shloy'derr] nf.

sling, separator, centrifugal machine, catapult; -flug nm. catapult flight; -preis nm. absurdly low price; -start nm. catapult take-off (av.); -ware nf. goods sold dirt-cheap.

Schleuder'n [shloy'derrn] vt.i. to sling, hurl, catapult, sell too cheap, undercut, skid; -er nm. (-) slinger, undercutter.

Schleunig [shloy'nish] a, ad. quick(ly), prompt(ly); -st ad. as soon as possible.

Schleuse [shloy'zerr] nf. sluice; -ntor a. lock-gate; -nwärter nm. lock-keeper.

Schlich [shlish] nm. (-e) dodge, trick.

Schlicht [shlisht] a. simple, plain, unassuming; -heit nf. plainness, simplicity.

Schlichten [shlish'ten] vt. to make level, smooth, even, adjust, arbitrate, settle; -er nm. (-) arbitrator; -ung nf. settlement, arbitration, arrangement, conciliation.

Schlick [shlik] nm. mud.

Schliess'e [shlee'ser] nf. fastening, clasp, catch; -fach n. safe, post-office box; -feder nf. safety grip spring; -rahmen nm. chase (printing).

Schliessen [shlee'sen] vt.r. to close, shut, lock, stop, finish; i. infer, conclude, judge.

Schliesslich [shlees'lish] a, ad. final(ly), after all.

Schliff [shlif] nm. polish, manners, discipline, rigorous training (mil.).

Schlimm [shlim] a. bad; -er a, ad. worse; -st a. worst; -stenfalls ad. at the worst.

Schling'e [shling'er] nf. sling, noose, snare, knot; -gewächs n. creeper.

Schlingel [shling'el] nm. (-) rascal.

Schlips [shlips] nm. (-e) tie.

Schlingen [shling'en] vt. ir. to wind, tie, twist.

Schlingen [shling'en] *vt.* i. to devour, swallow (up).

Schlinger'n [shling'errn] *vi.* to roll (*ship*); **-anlage** *nf.* stabilizer (*nav.*).

Schlitten [shlit'en] *nm.* (-) sledge, sleigh; **-bahn** *nf.* slide, run for tobogganing; **-fahren** *n.* to toboggan, coast; **-fahrer** *nm.* sledger, coaster, tobogganer; **-sport** *nm.* sledging, tobogganing. [slide.

Schlittern [shlit'errn] *vi.* to slide.

Schlittschuh [shlit'shoo] *nm.* (-e) skate; **- laufen** *vi.* to skate; **-bahn** *nf.* skating rink; **-läufer** *nm.* skater.

Schlitz [shlits] *nm.* (-e) slit, slot, rift, split; **-äugig** *a.* almond-eyed. [rip, slash.

Schlitzen [shlit'sen] *vt.* to slit,

Schlohweiss [shloh'vice] *a.* snow-white.

Schloss [shloss] *n.* (-. Schlösser) lock, fastening, clasp, castle; **-hof** *nm.* castle-yard; **-kurbel** *nf.* crank-handle; **-platte** *nf.* breech-plate (*mil.*). [stone.

Schlosse [shloh'se] *nf.* hail-

Schlosser [shloss'err] *nm.* (-) locksmith, mechanic, fitter; **- n** *vi.* to forge, hammer.

Schlosserei [shloss-er-rī'] *nf.* locksmith's workshop.

Schlot [shlote] *nm.* (-e) flue, chimney, funnel.

Schlotterig [shlot'er-rish] *a.* wobbly, shaky.

Schlottern [shlot'errn] *vi.* to wobble, tremble, shake.

Schlucht [shlŏocht] *nf.* gorge, ravine. [to sob.

Schluchzen [shlŏoch'tsen] *vi.*

Schluck [shlŏok] *nm.* (-e) drop, draught; **-en** *vt.&i.* to swallow, gulp down; *nm.* hiccup; **-er** *nm.* (-) poor devil.

Schlummer [shlŏo'merr] *nm.* slumber; **-lied** *n.* lullaby.

Schlummern [shlŏo'merrn] *vi.* to slumber.

Schlumpe [shlŏom'per] *nf.*

slattern, slut; **-ig** *a.* slatternly.

Schlund [shlŏont] *nm.* (Schlünde) throat, gullet, gulf.

Schlüpfe'n [shlyŏop'fen] *vi.* to slip; **-r** *nm.* knickers.

Schlupf·jacke [shlŏopf'jak-er] *nf.* cardigan, **-loch** *n.* loophole, hiding-place; **-winkel** *nm.* hiding-place.

Schlüpfrig [shlyŏop'frish] *a.* slippery, indecent; **-keit** *nf.* slipperiness, indecency.

Schlürfen [shlyŏor'fen] *vt.* to sip; *i.* shuffle (*feet*).

Schluss [shlŏos] *nm.* (Schlüsse) close, end, closing, conclusion, inference; **-abfertigung** *nf.* final clearance; **-folgerung** *nf.* conclusion; **-formel** *nf.* closing phrase; **-laterne** *nf.*, **-licht** *n.* tail-light, rear-light; **-stein** *nm.* keystone; **-wort** *n.* last word.

Schlüssel [shlyŏo'sel] *nm.* (-) key, spanner, wrench, code; **-bein** *n.* collar-bone; **-bund** *n.* bunch of keys; **-loch** *n.* key-hole; **-ring** *nm.* key-ring, split ring; **-stellung** *nf.* key position; **-wort** *n.* code-word.

Schlüsseln [shlyŏo'seln] *vt.* to code, encode, encipher.

Schlüssig [shlyŏo'sish] *a.* decided, resolved.

Schmach [shmach] *nf.* disgrace, insult, dishonour; **-voll** *a.* disgraceful, dishonourable.

Schmachten [shmach'ten] *vi.* to languish, long for.

Schmächtig [shmesh'tish] *a.* slender, wasted, slim; **-keit** *nf.* slenderness, poor health.

Schmackhaft [shmak'haft] *a.* tasty, appetizing, **-igkeit** *nf.* tastiness.

Schmäh'en [shmay'en] *vt.* to abuse, insult, revile; **-lich** *a.* ignominious, disgraceful; **-schrift** *nf.* libel; **-ung** *nf.* abuse, insulting, slander.

Schmal [shmahl] *a.* narrow, scanty, slight, poor; **-film-kamera** *nf.* miniature cine-

Schmälen [shmäle'en] *vt.* to belittle, diminish, detract from, run down, disparage.

Schmalz [shmalts] *n.* dripping, cooking fat, lard; **-en** *vt.* to cook with dripping or lard; **-ig** *a.* greasy.

Schmarotze'n [shmar-rot'sen] *vi.* to sponge; **-r** *nm.* (-) parasite, sponger, toady.

Schmarre [shmar'rer] *nf.* scar.

Schmatzen [shmat'sen] *vi.* to smack (the lips), kiss.

Schmauchen [shmowch'en] *v.i.t.* to smoke.

Schmaus [shmowss] *nm.* (Schmäuse) banquet, feast.

Schmausen [shmow'zen] *vi.* to feast. [*nf.* feasting.

Schmauserei [shmow-zer-ri']

Schmecken [shmek'en] *v.t.i.* to taste, relish, taste good.

Schmeichelei [shmi-shel-i'] *nf.* flattery.

Schmeich-elhaft *a.* flattering; **-eln** *vi.* to flatter, coax, caress; **-ler** *nm.* (-) flatterer; **-lerisch** *a.* flattering, coaxing.

Schmeissen [shmi'ssen] *vt. ir.* to throw, chuck, drop.

Schmeissfliege [shmice'fleeger] *nf.* bluebottle.

Schmelz [shmelts] *nm.* enamel, finish, mellowness (*voice*); **-bar** *a.* fusible; **-e** *nf.* smelting, composition, foundry; **-en** *vt.* to smelt, melt; *i. ir.* to melt; **-end** *a.* touching, sweet, melting; **-hütte** *nf.* foundry; **-punkt** *nm.* melting-point; **-siche-rung** *nf.* fuse (*el.*); **-tiegel** *nm.* crucible; **-topf** *nm.* melting pot.

Schmelzung [shmelt'soong] *nf.* melting, smelting; **-snum-mer** *nf.* foundry number (*gun*).

Schmer [shmare] *n.* grease; **-bauch** *nm.* paunch, belly.

Schmerz [shmairts] *nm.* (*gen.* -es; *pl.* -en) pain, sorrow, grief; **-en** *vt.* to pain, hurt; **-ensgeld** *n.* compensation; **-haft, -lich, -voll** *a.* painful; **-los** *a.* painless; **-stillend** *a.* soothing.

Schmetterling [shmet'err-ling] *nm.* (-e) butterfly.

Schmettern [shmet'errn] *vt.* to dash, smash; *i.* to crash, blare, peal, resound.

Schmied [shmeet] *nm.* (-e) blacksmith, forger (metal).

Schmiede [shmee'der] *nf.* smithy, forge; **-eisen** *n.* wrought iron; **-esse** *nf.* forge; **-hammer** *nm.* sledge-hammer; **-ware** *nf.* hardware.

Schmieden [shmee'den] *vt.* to forge, plan, concoct, plot, scheme.

Schmiege [shmee'ger] *nf.* bevel, slant; **-n** *vt.* to bend, bevel; *r.* nestle, snuggle, cling to, cuddle.

Schmiegsam [shmeek'zam] *a.* pliant, supple, submissive; **-keit** *nf.* submissiveness, flexibility.

Schmier'e [shmee'rer] *nf.* grease; **-apparat** *nm.* lubricator; **-büchse** *nf.* oil-can, gear-box (*aut.*); **-fett** *n.* grease; **-fink** *nm.v.* dirty brute; **-geld** *n.* bribe, palm-oil; **-ig** *a.* greasy, oily, dirty; **-käse** *nm.* soft cheese; **-mittel** *n.* lubricant; **-öl** *n.* lubricating oil; **-seife** *nf.* soft soap; **-stoffbehälter** *nm.* sump; **-ung** *nf.* lubrication.

Schmiere'n [shmee'ren] *vt.* to smear, oil, grease, lubricate, scribble, bribe; **-r** *nm.* (-) scribbler, dauber, giver of bribes.

Schmiererei [shmeer-rer-ri'] *nf.* greasy mess, daubing, scribble, dirty work.

Schmink'e [shmink'er] *nf.* make-up, paint; **-en** *vi.* to make-up, paint (*face*); **-mittel** *n.* cosmetic.

Schmirgel [shmirr'gel] *nm.* emery; -papier *n.* emery-paper; -rad *n.* emery-wheel.

Schmiss [shmiss] *nm.* (-e) blow, cut, scar, verve.

Schmöker [shmer'kerr] *nm.* (-) dirty old book; -n *ti.* to read old books.

Schmollen [shmol'en] *vi.* to sulk, pout; -d *a.* sulky.

Schmollis [shmol'iss] *n.* good health, fraternization, brotherhood.

Schmor'en [shmorr'en] *vt.* to stew; -braten *nm.* stewed steak; -pfanne *nf.* stew-pot.

Schmuck [shmŏŏk] *nm.* (-e) ornaments, decoration, jewellery; -händler *nm.* jeweller; -los *a.* unadorned, plain; -losigkeit *nf.* simplicity; -sachen *f.pl.* jewels, jewellery.

Schmücken [shmyŏŏ'ken] *vt.* to decorate, adorn, ornament, trim.

Schmugg'el [shmŏŏ'gel] *nm.* smuggling; -eln *vt.i.* to smuggle; -ler *nm.* smuggler.

Schmunzeln [shmŏŏnt'seln] *vi.* to grin, smirk, simper.

Schmutz [shmŏŏts] *nm.* filth, dirt; -ärmel *m.pl.* sleeve protectors; -blech *n.* mudguard; -bogen *nm.* waste sheet (*paper*); -fink *m.w.* low, dirty fellow; -fleck *nm.* stain; -kittel *nm.* overall; -konkurrenz *nf.* unfair, cut-throat competition; -loch *n.* man-hole; -papier *n.* waste paper; -titel *nm.* half-title.

Schmutzen [shmŏŏt'sen] *vt.* to soil; *i.* get dirty.

Schmutzig [shmŏŏt'sish] *a.* dirty, filthy, foul, mean; -keit *nf.* dirtiness.

Schnabel [shnah'bel] *nm.* (Schnäbel) bill, beak, nozzle, spout. [bill and coo.

Schnäbeln [shnay'beln] *vi.* to

Schnack [shnak] *nm.* gossip, chatter; -en *vi.* to chatter.

Schnake [shnah'ker] *nf.* gnat, midge.

Schnalle [shnal'er] *nf.* buckle, clasp, latch; -n *vt.* to buckle, strap; -nschuh *nm.* buckled shoe.

Schnalzen [shnalt'sen] *vi.* to click (*tongue*), snap (*fingers*).

Schnappen [shnap'en] *vi.* to snap, catch, gasp.

Schnapp'schloss [shnap'shloss] *n.* (-schlösser) springlock; -schuss *nm.* snapshot.

Schnaps [shnaps] *nm.* (Schnäpse) gin, spirits; -bruder *nm.* drunkard. [snore.

Schnarchen [shnarr'shen] *vi.*

Schnarren [shnar'ren] *vi.* to rattle, grate, rasp.

Schnattern [shnat'errn] *vi.* to cackle, chatter.

Schnauben [shnow'ben] *vi.* to snort, puff, gasp; *r.* blow one's nose. [puff, pant.

Schnaufen [shnow'fen] *vi.* to

Schnauzbart [shnowts'barrt] *nm.* (-bärte) moustache.

Schnauze [shnowt'ser] *nf.* snout, muzzle, nozzle, jaw; -n *vi.* to shout at, bark.

Schnecke [shnek'er] *nf.* snail, worm gear (*tec.*); -nantrieb *nm.* worm drive; -ngang *nm.* snail's pace; -ngehäuse *n.* worm-gear housing; -ntriebe *n.* worm gearing; -nhaus *n.* snail's-shell; -nverband *nm.* spiral bandage; -nwelle *nf.* worm shaft.

Schnee [shnay] *nm.* snow; -ball *nm.* snowball; -flocke *nf.* snowflake; -gestöber *n.* snowstorm; -glöckchen *n.* snowdrop; -huhn *n.* ptarmigan; -kette *nf.* non-skid chain (*aut.*); -kufe *nf.* landing skid, ski (*av.*); -reifen *nm.* roundel (*ski*); -schuh *nm.* snow-shoe, ski; -wehe *nf.* snowdrift; -weiss *a.* snow-white.

Schneid [shnite] *nm.* dash, pluck; -ig *a.* energetic, plucky, smart.

Schneide [shnide'er] *nf.* edge blade; **-werkzeug** *n.* cutting tool.

Schneiden [shnide'en] *vt. ir.* to cut, carve; *r.* intersect; *-d a.* cutting, biting, sharp.

Schneider [shnide'err] *nm.* (-) tailor; **-in** *nf.* tailoress, dressmaker; **-meister** *nm.* master tailor; **-puppe** *nf.* tailor's dummy.

Schneidern [shnide'errn] *vt.i.* to cut, make, do tailoring.

Schneien [shni'en] *vi.* to snow.

Schneise [shni'zer] *nf.* vista, lane (*av., etc.*).

Schnell [shnel] *a, ad.* quick(ly), fast; **-boot** *n.* motor torpedoboat; **-brücke** *nf.* assault bridge; **-feuergeschütz** *n.* quick-firing gun; **-funk** *n.* high-speed wireless; **-gang** *nm.* high speed; **-hefter** *nm.* rapid file; **-igkeit** *nf.* quickness, velocity, speed; **-kraft** *nf.* elasticity; **-presse** *nf.* high speed printing machine; **-sichtkartei** *nf.* quick reference card system; **-zug** *nm.* express train.

Schnellen [shnel'en] *vi.t.* to let fly, jerk, snap, spring.

Schnepfe [shnep'fer] *nf.* snipe.

Schneppe [shnep'er] *nf.* nozzle, spout, peak (*cap.*).

Schneuzen [shnoits'en] *vr.* to blow one's nose.

Schnickschnack [shnik'shnak] *nm.* tittle-tattle, idle talk.   [dress up.

Schniegeln [shnee'geln] *vr.* to

Schnippeln [shnip'eln] *vt.* to snip, cut up.

Schnippisch [shnip'ish] *a.* flippant, saucy, pert, cheeky.

Schnitt [shnit] *nm.* (-e) cut(ting), slice, section, crop, edge (*book*), style, fashion; **-blumen** *f.pl.* cut flowers; **-bohne** *nf.* French bean; **-fläche** *nf.* section; **-handel** *nm.* drapery trade; **-lauch** *nm.*

chive; **-muster** *n.* pattern; **-warenhändler** *nm.* haberdasher.   [(-) small slice.

Schnittchen [shnit'shen] *n.*

Schnitte [shnit'e] *nf.* slice.

Schnitter [shnit'err] *nm.* (-), **-in** *nf.* reaper, mower.

Schnittig [shnit'ish] *a.* smart, racy, stream-lined.

Schnitzarbeit [shnits'arbite] *nf.* wood-carving.

Schnitzel [shnit'sel] *n.* (-) chip, shavings, parings, cutlet; **-jagd** *nf.* paper-chase; *-n vt.i.* to cut, chip.   [cut, carve.

Schnitzen [shnit'sen] *vt.* to

Schnitzer [shnit'serr] *nm.* (-) cutter, carver, blunder.

Schnitzerei [shnit-ser-ri'] *nf.* carving, carved woodwork.

Schnoddrig [shno'der-rish] *a.* cheeky, impudent.

Schnöde [shner'der] *a.* base, insolent, mean; **-igkeit** *nf.* baseness, insolence.

Schnorchel [shnorr'shel] *nm.* (-) snort (*submarine*).

Schnörkel [shner'kel] *nm.* flourish, scroll; **-haft** *a.* ornate, over-ornamented, capricious, eccentric.

Schnorren [shnor'ren] *vi.* to beg, cadge; *-r nm.* (-) beggar.

Schnüffeln [shnü'feln] *vi.* to sniff, snuffle.   [(-) spy.

Schnüffler [shnü'df'lerr] *nm.*

Schnullen [shnōō'len] *vi.* to suck; *-r nm.* (-) rubber teat, dummy.

Schnupfen [shnōōp'fen] *nm.* (-) cold in the head.

Schnupfen [shnōōp'fen] *vt.i.* to take snuff; **-fieber** *nm.* feverish cold, flu; **-tabak** *nm.* snuff; **-tuch** *n.* handkerchief.

Schnuppe [shnōō'per] *nf.* shooting star, a matter of indifference; *-rn vi.* to sniff out, smell out.

Schnur [shnōōr] *nf.* (Schnüre) string, cord, lanyard, flex (*el.*);

-besatz nm. braid trimming;
-gerade a. straight as a die;
-scheibe nf. grooved pulley;
-stracks ad. at once, directly,
diametrically.

Schnüren [shnȳȫr'ren] vt. to
lace, cord, tie, fasten.

Schnür-leib nm. corset;
-schuh nm. laced shoe; **-senkel**
nm. boot-lace; **-stiefel** nm.
laced boot.

Schnurrbart [shnȫrr'barrt]
nm. moustache.

Schnurr'e [shnȫr'rer] nf.
humming-top, joke, amusing
story; **-en** vi. to hum, purr;
-ig a. funny, queer.

Schober [shoh'berr] nm. (-)
rick, stack; **-hof** nm. stack-
yard; **-n** vt. to stack.

Schock [shok] nm. (-e) shock.

Schock [shok] n. (-) sixty,
threescore.   [vt. to shock.

Schockieren [sho-keer'ren]

Schöffe [sher'fer] m.w. jury-
man; **-ngericht** n. magistrates'
court.

Schokolade [sho-ko-lah'der]
nf. chocolate.

Scholl'e [shol'er] nf. clod,
lump, ice-flow; **-ig** a. lumpy.

Scholle [shol'er] nf. plaice.

Schon [shohn] ad. already, as
early as, as yet, even, indeed,
certainly.

Schön [shern] a. beautiful,
handsome, fair, fine; **-färberei**
nf. embellishment, heighten-
ing, idealizing.

Schoner [shoh'nerr] nm. (-)
antimacassar.   [schooner.

Schoner [shoh'nerr] nm. (-)

Schöngeist [shern'gīst] nm.
(-er) cultured person, aesthete;
-ig a. cultured, aesthetic.

Schönheit [shern'hīte] nf.
beauty; **-smittel** n. cosmetic;
-spflege nf. beauty treatment.

Schonen [shoh'nen] vt. to
save, spare, take care of; **-d** a.
considerate, tactful.

Schonung [shoh'nōōng] nf.

forbearance, consideration,
leniency, indulgence; **-slos** a.
unsparing, harsh.

Schonzeit [shohn'tsīte] nf.
close season.

Schopf [shopf] nm. (Schöpfe)
crown of head, tuft, forelock.

Schöpfeimer [sherpf'īme-err]
nm. (-) bucket.

Schöpfen [sherp'fen] vt. to
draw, scoop, ladle out, obtain.

Schöpfer [sherp'ferr] nm. (-)
creator; **-isch** a. creative.

Schöpf-kelle nf. ladle; **-löffel**
nm. skimmer, scoop.

Schöpfung [sherp'fōōng] nf.
creation.   [pint.

Schoppen [shop'en] nm. (-)

Schöps [sherpss] nm. (-e)
wether, fool; **-enfleisch** n.
mutton.

Schorf [shorrf] nm. scurf; **-ig**
a. scurfy, scabby, scrofulous.

Schornstein [shorrn'shtine]
nm. (-e) chimney, funnel, flue;
-feger nm. chimney-sweep;
-kappe nf. chimney-pot.

Schoss [shoss] nm. (-e) shoot,
sprig, sprout.

Schoss [shohss] nm. (Schösse)
bosom, lap, coat-tail, womb;
-hund nm. pet dog, lapdog.

Schössling [sherss'ling] nm.
(-e) shoot, sprig, sucker.

Schote [shoh'ter] nf. pod,
husk; **-n** pl. green peas.

Schote [shoh'ter] nf. sheet
(sail).

Schott [shot] n. bulkhead,
partition.

Schotter [shot'err] nm. (-)
road-metal, ballast; **-n** vt. to
macadamize; **-strasse** nf.
metalled road.

Schraffier'en [shraf-feer'-
ren] vt. to hatch; **-ung** nf.
hatching.

Schraffur [shra-fōōrr'] nf.
hatching.

Schräg [shrake] a. oblique,
sloping, slanting; **-laufend** a.
diagonal; **-schnitt** nm. diagonal
section; **-über** ad. across.

Schräge [shray'ger] *nf.* slope, slant, bevel.

Schragen [shrah'gen] *nm.* (-) trestle, frame, couch, chair-bed, stand, bread rack, board.

Schräg'en [shray'gen] *vt.* to bevel; -**ung** *nf.* bevel, slope, slant.

Schramm'e [shram'er] *nf.* scratch; -**en** *vt.* to scratch, scar, graze; -**ig** *a.* scarred, bruised, scratched.

Schrank [shrank] *nm.* (Schränke) cupboard, wardrobe; -**fach** *n.* safe, drawer, pigeon-hole; -**koffer** *nm.* wardrobe trunk.

Schranke [shrank'er] *nf.* bar, barrier, limit, restriction, level-crossing (*rl.*), toll-bar; -**nlos** *a.* boundless, unrestrained.

Schränk'en [shrenk'en] *vt.* to cross, fold; -**ung** *nf.* offset.

Schranze [shrant'ser] *m.w.,nf.* toady, yes-man, courtier.

Schrape [shrah'per] *nf.* see Schrapper.

Schrapnell [shrap'nel] *n.* shrapnel, case-shot; -**granate** *nf.* shrapnel shell.

Schrapp'en [shrap'en] *vt.* to scrape; -**er** *nm.* (-) scraper; -**eisen** *n.* scrap-iron.

Schraube [shrow'ber] *nf.* screw; -**ndampfer** *nm.* screw steamer; -**nfeder** *nf.* coil spring; -**nflugzeug** *n.* autogiro, helicopter; -**ngewinde** *n.* thread of screw; -**nmutter** *nf.* nut; -**nschlüssel** *nm.* spanner; -**nstrahl** *nm.* slipstream; -**nwelle** *nf.* propeller shaft (*nav.*); -**nzieher** *nm.* screw-driver, spanner; -**nzug** *nm.* propeller thrust (*av.*).

Schraubstock [shrowp'shtok] *nm.* vice (*tec.*).

Schrauben [shrow'ben] *vt.* to screw, twist, tease, cheat.

Schreber'garten [shray'berr-garr-ten] *nm.* (-gärten) allot-ment garden; -**gärtner** *nm.* smallholder.

Schreck(en) [shrek'en] *nm.* (-) terror, fright, fear; -**bild** *n.* terrible image, vision; -**ens-botschaft** *nf.* terrible news; -**ensherrschaft** *nf.* reign of terror; -**haft** *a.* timid, fearful; -**ladung** *nf.* booby trap; -**schuss** *nm.* shot fired in the air.

Schrecken [shrek'en] *vt.* to frighten, terrify.

Schrecklich [shrek'lish] *a.* frightful, dreadful; -**keit** *nf.* frightfulness.

Schrei [shri] *nm.* (-e) cry, scream, shout.

Schreib'arbeit [shripe'arr-bite] *nf.* clerical work; -**bedarf** *nm.* writing materials; -**block** *nm.* writing pad.

Schreiben [shribe'en] *vt.i. ir.* to write, spell; *n.* letter, com-munication.

Schreiber [shribe'err] *nm.* (-) clerk, scribe, secretary, writer.

Schreiberei [shri-ber-ri'] *nf.* writing, scribbling.

Schreib-feder *nf.* nib, pen; -**fehler** *nm.* clerical error; -**funk** *nm.* broadcast at dictation speed; -**gebrauch** *nm.* usual spelling; -**kästchen** *n.* pen-case; -**krampf** *nm.* writer's cramp; -**mappe** *nf.* portfolio, blotter, writing-case; -**maschine** *nf.* typewriter; -**papier** *n.* note-paper; -**pult** *n.* writing desk; -**stube** *nf.* orderly room, office; -**tisch** *nm.* writing table, desk; -**unterlage** *nf.* blotting pad; -**weise** *nf.* style; -**zeug** *n.* pen and ink, writing materials.

Schreibwaren [shripe'vahr-en] *f.pl.* stationery; -**händler** *nm.* stationer; -**handlung** *nf.* stationer's shop.

Schreibung [shribe'ŏong] *nf.* spelling, orthography, script.

Schreien [shri'en] *vi.* to shriek, scream, cry, screech; -**d** *a.* flagrant, glaring.

Schreier [shri'err] *nm.* (-) shouter, cry-baby.

Schrein [shrine] *nm.* (-e) chest, shrine, cupboard.

Schreiner [shrine'err] *nm.* (-) joiner, carpenter, cabinet-maker; **-n** *vi.* to work as a joiner.

Schreinerei [shrine-er-ri'] *nf.* joiner's workshop, trade.

Schreiten [shrite'en] *vi. ir.* to stride, proceed.

Schrift [shrift] *nf.* writing, pamphlet, book, work, type, script, scripture; **-band** *n.* scroll; **-bild** *n.* type-face; **-deutsch** *n.* educated German; **-führer** *nm.* secretary; **-leiter** *nm.* editor; **-leitung** *nf.* newspaper office, editorial department; **-lich** *a.* written, in writing; **-setzer** *nm.* compositor; **-sprache** *nf.* literary language; **-stück** *n.* document; **-tum** *n.* literature; **-zeichen** *n.* (printed) character, letter.

Schriftsteller [shrift'shtelerr] *nm.* (-) writer, author; **-in** *nf.* lady writer; **-isch** *a.* literary; **-n** *vi.* to write, be an author.

Schrill [shrill] *a.* shrill; **-en** *vi.* to make a shrill sound.

Schrinden [shrin'den] *vi. ir.* to chap, crack.

Schrippe [shrip'er] *nf.* breakfast roll.

Schritt [shrit] *nm.* (-e) stride, step, pace, walk, walking pace; **-macher** *nm.* pace-maker; **-messer** *nm.* pedometer; **-stein** *nm.* stepping-stone; **-weise** *ad.* step by step; **-zähler** *nm. see* **-messer.**

Schroff [shrof] *a.* steep, rugged, rough, gruff, blunt; **-heit** *nf.* steepness, abruptness, bluntness, ruggedness.

Schröpfen [shrerp'fen] *vt.* to bleed, fleece.

Schrot [shrote] *nm., n.* (-e) (small) shot, groats; **-brot** *n.*

wholemeal bread, brown bread; **-büchse, -flinte** *nf.* shot-gun; **-eisen** *n.* chisel; **-korn, -mehl** *n.* groats; **-lauf** *nm.* smooth barrel; **-leiter** *nf.* drayman's ladder.

Schroten [shrote'en] *vt.* to crush, rough-grind, bruise, roll down (*barrel*), parbuckle.

Schrott [shrot] *nm.* scrap metal; **-haufen** *nm.* scrap heap; **-sammlung** *nf.* collection of scrap, dump.

Schrubben [shroo'ben] *vt.* to scrub; **-r** *nm.* (-) scrubbing-brush.

Schrulle [shroo'ler] *nf.* whim, fad; **-nhaft** *a.* faddy, eccentric.

Schrumpfen [shroomp'fen] *vi.* to shrink, shrivel up; **-ung** *nf.* shrinking, contraction.

Schrund [shroont] *nm.* (Schründe) crevice, crack.

Schub [shoop] *nm.* (Schübe) push, shove, heap, batch; **-fach** *n.* drawer; **-karren** *nm.* wheel-barrow; **-lade** *nf.* drawer; **-stange** *nf.* connection-rod; **-ventil** *n.* sliding-valve.

Schüchtern [shyōōsh'terrn] *a.* shy, bashful; **-heit** *nf.* shyness, self-consciousness.

Schuft [shōōft] *nm.* (-e) scamp, scoundrel; **-en** *vi.* to toil, drudge, slave; **-ig** *a.* mean, vile.

Schuh [shōō] *nm.* (-e) shoe, boot; **-absatz** *nm.* heel; **-anzieher** *nm.* shoe-horn, shoe-lift; **-band** *n.* shoe-lace, boot-lace; **-bürste** *nf.* shoe-brush; **-eisen** *n.* shoe-scraper; **-flicker** *nm.* cobbler; **-knöpfer** *nm.* button-hook; **-macher** *nm.* shoemaker; **-putzer** *nm.* shoe-black; **-riemen** *nm.* shoe-lace; **-spanner** *nm.* boot-tree; **-waren** *f.pl.* footwear; **-wichse** *nf.* boot polish, blacking; **-zwecke** *nf.* tack.

Schularbeit [shōōl'arr-bite] *nf.* school, lesson, homework;

-bank nf. bench, form; -behörde nf. education authority; -beispiel n. test-case; -besuch nm. school attendance; -bube m.w. schoolboy; -diener nm. school porter, caretaker; -direktor nm. headmaster; -direktorin nf. headmistress. **Schuld** [shŏŏlt] nf. debt, fault, guilt; -enfrei a. free from debt; -forderung nf. unpaid debt, claim; -los a. innocent; -ner (-) debtor; -schein nm. promissory note. [owe. **Schulden** [shŏŏl'den] vi. to **Schuldig** [shŏŏl'dish] a. indebted, owing, guilty; -keit nf. obligation, duty. **Schule** [shŏŏ'ler] nf. school. **Schulen** [shŏŏ'len] vt. to school, train, teach. **Schul-ferien** pl. school holidays; -flugzeug n. training plane; -freund nm. schoolfriend; -gebäude n. schoolhouse, building; -geld n. school-fees; -hof nm. playground; -junge, -knabe m.w. schoolboy; -mappe nf. schoolbag; -mässig a. scholastic; -meister nm. schoolmaster; -meisterlich a. pedantic; -pflichtig a. of school age; -schiessen n. practice firing (mil.); -schiff n. training ship (nav.); -schluss nm. breaking-up, end of term; -stube nf. schoolroom; -stunde nf. period, lesson; -tasche nf. satchel; -wesen n. educational matters, system; -zeugnis n. certificate, report; -zwang nm. compulsory education. **Schüler** [shyŏŏ'lerr] nm. (-) scholar, pupil, schoolboy; -in nf. schoolgirl. **Schulter** [shŏŏl'terr] nf. shoulder; -blatt n. shoulderblade; -gurt nm., -klappe nf. shoulder-strap (mil.); -stück n. epaulette. [shoulder. **Schultern** [shŏŏl'terrn] vt. to

Schulung [shŏŏ'lŏŏng] nf. schooling, training, indoctrination; -slager n. training camp. **Schund** [shŏŏnt] nm. trash, garbage, refuse, shoddy; -roman nm. trashy novel. **Schupp'e** [shŏŏ'pe] nf. scale, scurf; -en vi.r. to scale, peel, scrape off; -ig a. scaly. **Schuppen** [shŏŏ'pen] nm. (-) shed, garage, hangar. **Schur** [shŏŏrr] nf. shearing, clip, fleece. **Schür'en** [shyŏŏr'ren] vt. to poke, stir up; -eisen n., -haken nm. poker. **Schürf'en** [shyŏŏrr'fen] vt.i. to open up (mine), prospect, dig, scrape, scratch; -er nm. (-) prospector; -ung nf. scratches, prospecting. **Schurk'e** [shŏŏrr'ker] nm. rogue, villain; -isch a. mean, bad. **Schurkerei** [shŏŏrr-ker-ri'] nf. villainy, low trick. **Schurz** [shŏŏrts] nm. (Schürze) apron; -fell n. leather apron. **Schürze** [shyŏŏrt'ser] nf. apron, pinafore; -n vt. to tuck, tie up, hitch up; -nband n. apron-strings; -njäger nm. ladies' man; -nregiment n. petticoat government. **Schuss** [shŏŏs] nm. (Schüsse) shot, gunshot, shoot, wound; -beobachtung n. spotting; -bereich nm. effective range; -fertig a. ready to fire; -feld n. field of fire; -fest a. bulletproof; -folge nf. rate of fire; -garbe nf. burst of fire; -linie nf. line of fire, aim, sight; -öffnung nf. bullet-hole; -sicher a. bullet-proof, self-sealing (tank); -tafel nf. range table; -waffe nf. firearm; -weite nf. range (of fire), gunshot; -winkel nm. angle of elevation; -zahl nf. number of rounds. **Schüssel** [shyŏŏ'sel] nf. dish basin, bowl; -brett *n.* dresser; -schrank *n.* sideboard; -stürze *nf.* dish-cover; -tuch *n.* dish-cloth.

Schuster [shōō'sterr] *nm.* (-) cobbler; -n *vi.* to cobble; -pech *n.* cobbler's wax.

Schute [shōō'ter] *nf.* barge.

Schutt [shōōt] *nm.* rubbish, scree, rubble; -abladeplatz *nm.* refuse dump; -haufen *nm.* dust-heap; -karren *nm.* rubbish-cart; -kärrner *nm.* dustman.

Schüttel'frost [shyōō'tel-frost] *nm.* shivering fit; -reim *nm.* spoonerism.

Schütteln [shyōō'teln] *vt.r.* to shake, tremble, shiver, jolt.

Schütten [shyōō'ten] *vi.* to pour (down).

Schutz [shōōts] *nm.* protection, cover, shelter, care, defence; -anstrich *nm.* baffle paint; -anzug *nm.* overall; -befohlene(r) *m.w.* charge, ward; -blech *n.* mudguard, wing (*aut.*); -bekleidung *nf.* protective clothing; -brief *nm.* safe-conduct; -brille *nf.* goggles; -bündnis *n.* defensive alliance; -dach *n.* roof, shed; -engel *nm.* guardian angel; -färbung *nf.* protective colouring; -gebiet *n.* protectorate; -haft *nf.* protective custody; -heilige(r) *m.w.* patron saint; -insel *nf.* street island; -los *a.* defenceless; -macht *nf.* protecting power; -mann *nm.* policeman; -mannschaft *n.* police force; -marke *nf.* trademark; -massregel *nf.* precaution, preventative; -mittel *n.* preservative, protection; -polizei *nf.* police; -schild *nm.* protective shield; -truppen *f.pl.* colonial troops; -überzug *nm.* protective covering; -umschlag *nm.* jacket (*book*); -unterstand *nm.* dug-out; -vorrichtung *nf.* safety device; -wache *nf.*

armed escort; -wehr *nf.* bulwark, rampart; -zoll *nm.* protective tarif, duty.

Schütze [shyōōt'ser] *m.w.* marksman, rifleman, shot; -nblende *nf.* infantry shield; -nbrigade *nf.* rifle brigade; -nfest *n.* shooting match; -nfeuer *nm.* rifle fire, independent fire; -ngefecht *n.* skirmish; -ngraben *nm.* trench; -nlinie *nf.* single file, firing line; -nloch *n.* fox-hole, rifle pit; -nregiment *n.* rifle, lorryborne regiment; -nschleier *nm.* infantry screen; -nschiessstand *nm.* rifle range; -nverband *nm.* rifle unit.

Schütze [shyōōt'ser] *nf.* sluice, shuttle.

Schützen [shyōōt'sen] *vt.* to protect, shelter, defend.

Schwabe [shvah'ber] *nf.* cockroach.

Schwach [shvach] *a.* weak, feeble, faint, infirm; -heit *nf.* weakness, frailty; -herzig *a.* faint-hearted; -köpfig *a.* silly, foolish; -sichtig *a.* weak-sighted; -sinn *nm.* imbecility; -sinnig *a.* imbecile; -strom *nm.* low-tension current (*el.*).

Schwäch'e [shvesh'er] *nf.* weakness, frailty; -en *vt.* to weaken, impair, enervate; -ung *nf.* weakening.

Schwächlich [shvesh'lish] *a.* sickly, weakly, delicate; -keit *nf.* delicacy, weakness, infirmity.

Schwächling [shvesh'ling] *nm.* (-e) weakling.

Schwaden [shvah'den] *nm.* (-) vapour, fire-damp (*mine*), smoke-screen (*mil.*), swath (*grass*).

Schwadron [shvad-rone'] *nf.* squadron.

Schwadronieren [shva-dro-neer'ren] *vi.* to swagger, brag.

Schwager [shvah'gerr] *nm.* (-) brother-in-law.

Schwägerin [shvay'ger-rin] nf. sister-in-law.

Schwalbe [shval'ber] nf. swallow; **-nschwanz** nm. swallow-tail, dove-tail (wood).

Schwall [shval] nm. swell, flood, torrent.

Schwamm [shvam] nm. (Schwämme) sponge, mushroom, fungus, growth, dryrot; **-ig** a. spongy, fungoid; **-wachs** n. fungous growth.

Schwan [shvahn] nm. (Schwäne) swan; **-en** vi. imp. to have a presentiment, foreboding; **-engesang** nm. swansong.

Schwang [shvang] nm. swing (-ing), vogue, fashion.

Schwanger [shvang'err] a. pregnant; **-schaft** nf. pregnancy.

Schwängern [shveng'errn] vt. to fecundate, impregnate.

Schwank [shvank] nm. (Schwänke) farce, funny story, prank, practical joke.

Schwank [shvank] a. pliable, unsteady, wavering, tottering; **-en** vi. to sway, reel, totter, rock, fluctuate, hesitate, falter; **-ung** nf. hesitation, fluctuation, unsteadiness.

Schwanz [shvants] nm. (Schwänze) tail, train, trail; **-blech** n. trail-plate (mil.); **-fläche** nf. tail-plane (av.); **-landung** nf. tail-landing (av.); **-lastig** a. tail-heavy (av.); **-los** a. tailless; **-rad** n. tail-wheel (av.); **-riemen** nm. crupper; **-sporn** nm. tail-skid (av.); **-welle** nf. propeller shaft (motor boat).

Schwänze'n [shvent'sen], **Schwänzeln** [shvent'seln] vi. to wag the tail; vt./i. play truant, shirk, dodge; **-r** nm. (-) truant.

Schwäre [shvair'rer] nf. sore, abscess, ulcer; **-n** vi. to fester, suppurate, turn septic.

Schwarm [shvarrm] nm. (Schwärme) swarm, herd, flock,

flight, hero; **-linie** nf. extended order (mil.).

Schwärmen [shvairr'men] vi. to swarm, revel, rave (about), gush, enthuse, be mad on, deploy (mil.).

Schwärmer [shvairr'merr] nm. (-), **-in** nf. reveller, enthusiast, faddist, dreamer, squib, cracker, hawk-moth; **-isch** a. wildly enthusiastic, crazy (about), gushing.

Schwärmerei [shvairr-mer-ri'] nf. wild enthusiasm, fanaticism, hero-worship.

Schwart'e [shvart'ter] nf. hard skin, rind; **-ig** a. thick-skinned.

Schwarz [shvarrts] a. black, dark; n. black spot, colour, bull's eye; **-arbeit** nf. blackleg labour; **-brot** n. blackbread; **-fahren** n. joy-ride; **-gar** a. tanned; **-handel** nm. black market; **-hören** vi. to listen-in without a licence; **-hörer** nm. wireless pirate; **-rock** nm. black-coat, parson; **-platte** nf. disc; **-schlachten** n. illegal slaughtering; **-seher** nm. pessimist.

Schwärze [shvairrt'ser] nf. blackness, blacking, printer's ink; **-en** vt. to blacken, run down, denigrate; **-lich** a. blackish, darkish.

Schwatz'en [shvat'sen], **Schwätzen** [shvet'sen] vi. to chatter; **-base** nf. chatterbox; **-haft** a. talkative.

Schwätzer [shvet'serr] nm. (-) gossip, gasbag.

Schweb'e [shvay'ber] nf. suspense, abeyance; **-ebahn** nf. overhead railway; **-en** vi. to soar, hover, float, hang; **-ung** nf. beat (rad.).

Schwefel [shvay'fel] nm. sulphur; **-blei** n. sulphide of lead; **-hölzchen** n. match; **-ig** a. sulphurous; **-kies** n. pyrites; **-n** vt. to vulcanize;

-säure nf. sulphuric acid; **-ung** nf. vulcanization.

Schweif [shvife] nm. (-e) tail, trail; **-wedeln** n. tail-wagging, toadying.

Schweifen [shvife'en] vi. to roam, ramble, stray.

Schweige'n [shvi'gen] vi. to be silent, stop (speaking); n. silence; **-geld** n. hush-money.

Schweigsam [shvīk'zam] a. silent, secretive; **-keit** nf. silence, taciturnity, reserve.

Schwein [shvīne] n. pig, swine, good luck; **-efleisch** n. pork; **-estall** nm. pigsty; **-hund** nm. dirty fellow, cad; **-isch** a. filthy; **-sleder** n. pigskin.

Schweinerei [shvine-er-ri'] nf. filth, mean trick.

Schweiss [shvice] nm. sweat, perspiration; **-hund** nm. bloodhound; **-ig** a. sweaty.

Schweissen [shvice'en] vi.t. to weld, sweat (tec.), refine; **-naht** nf. weld; **-pulver** n. flux.

Schwelen [shvay'len] vi.t. to smoulder, burn slowly.

Schwelge'n [shvel'gen] vi. to revel, feast, indulge; **-r** nm. (-) glutton; **-risch** a. luxurious, voluptuous.

Schwelgerei [shvel-ge-ri'] nf. feasting, revelry, dissipation.

Schwelle [shvel'er] nf. threshold, sill, door-step, beam, sleeper (rl.).

Schwell'en [shvel'en] vi. ir. to swell; **-ung** nf. swelling, tumour.

Schwemme [shvem'er] nf. horse-pond; **-n** vt. to wash up, water.

Schwengel [shveng'el] nm. (-) pump-handle, clapper, swingle.

Schwenk'bar [shvenk'barr] a. swivel-mounted; **-bereich** nm. field of traverse (mil.); **-en** vt.i. to swing, wave, turn, swivel, wheel; **-lafette** nf.

swivel gun-mounting; **-ung** nf. wheeling, turning; **-vorrichtung** nf. turntable.

Schwer [shvairr] a. heavy, difficult, hard, serious, grave; **-arbeiter** nm. manual worker, labourer; **-blütig** a. melancholy; **-enöter** nm. gay spark, ladies' man; **-fällig** a. clumsy, sluggish; **-gewicht** n. heavy weight, emphasis; **-hörig** a. hard of hearing; **-industrie** nf. heavy industry; **-kraft** nf. gravity; **-mut** nf. melancholy; **-mütig** a. melancholy, sad; **-punkt** nm. centre of gravity, strong point, concentration; **-verbrecher** nm. criminal; **-verletzt** a. disabled; **-verwundet** a. seriously wounded; **-wiegend** a. weighty, important.

Schwere [shvair'rer] nf. weight, heaviness, gravity.

Schwerlich [shvairr'lish] a. with difficulty, hardly.

Schwert [shvairrt] n. (-er) sword, centre-board (ship); **-lilie** nf. iris.

Schwester [shves'terr] nf. sister, nurse; **-lich** a. sisterly.

Schwibbogen [shvip'bohgen] nm. arch(way), flying buttress.

Schwieger'mutter [shveegerr-mŏŏ-terr] nf. mother-in-law; **-sohn** nm. son-in-law; **-tochter** nf. daughter-in-law; **-vater** nm. father-in-law.

Schwiele [shvee'ler] nf. weal, stripe; **-ig** a. marked with weals, stripes.

Schwierig [shveer'rish] a. difficult, hard, complicated; **-keit** nf. difficulty.

Schwimm'anstalt [shvim'an-shtalt] nf. swimming baths; **-dock** n. floating dock; **-er** nm. (-) swimmer, float, pontoon (av.); **-fuss** nm. webbed foot; **-gürtel** nm. amphibian tank; **-weste** nf. life-jacket, Mae West.

Schwimmen [shvim'en] *vi. ir.* to swim, float.

Schwindel [shvin'del] *nm.* giddiness, fraud, swindle, racket, humbug; **-frei** *a.* not causing dizziness; **-haft** *a.* fraudulent, dizzy, giddy; **-n** *vi.* to be giddy, cheat.

Schwinden [shvin'den] *vi. ir.* to decrease, decline, disappear.

Schwindler [shvind'lerr] *nm.* (-) swindler, impostor, scoundrel, cheat.

Schwindsucht [shvint'zōōcht] *nf.* consumption.

Schwindsüchtig [shvint'zyōōch-tish] *a.* consumptive.

Schwinge [shving'er] *nf.* fan, wing, flax-swingle, pilot's wings (*av.*), rocking lever (*tec.*).

Schwingen [shving'en] *v.t.&ir.* to swing, flourish, vibrate, oscillate (*rad.*), swingle (*flax*); **-achse** *nf.* independent axle; **-er** *nm.* (-) oscillator (*rad.*); **-ung** *nf.* vibration, oscillation, cycle (*rad.*). [condition.

Schwips [shvipss] *nm.* tipsy

Schwirren [shvir'ren] *vi.* to whir, buzz, hum. [sweat.

Schwitzen [shvit'sen] *vi.* to

Schwören [shvēr'ren] *vi. ir.* to swear.

Schwül [shvyōōl] *a.* sultry, close; **-e** *nf.* sultriness.

Schwulst [shvōōlst] *nm.* bombast, inflated; **-ig** *a.* pompous, inflated.

Schwund [shvōōnt] *nm.* disappearance, falling off, decline, fading (*rad.*); **-wirkung** *nf.* fading effect (*rad.*).

Schwung [shvōōng] *nm.* (Schwünge) swing, oscillation, bound, impulse, elevation, dash, imagination; **-feder** *nf.* pinion; **-haft** *a.* energetic, lively, brisk; **-kraft** *nf.* energy, centrifugal force; **-rad** *n.* fly-wheel; **-scheibe** *nf.* fly-wheel; **-seil** *n.* slack (rope); **-voll** *a.* stirring, spirited, vigorous.

Schwur [shvōōrr] *nm.* (Schwüre) oath.

Sechs [zex] *num.* six; **-zehn** *num.* sixteen. [sixty.

Sechzig [zesh'tsish] *num.*

See [zay] *nf.* sea; *nm.* (*gen.* -*s*; *pl.* -n) lake; **-abrüstung** *nf.* naval disarmament; **-amt** *n.* admiralty court; **-ausdruck** *nm.* nautical term; **-bad** *n.* seaside resort; **-bataillon** *n.* battalion of marines; **-briefe** *m.pl.* ship's papers; **-dampfer** *nm.* liner; **-fähig** *a.* sea-going; **-fahrer** *nm.* seafaring man; **-fahrt** *nf.* voyage, navigation; **-fest** *a.* seaworthy; **-flieger** *nm.* seaplane pilot; **-fliegerhorst**, **-flughafen** *nm.* seaplane station; **-flugstützpunkt** *nm.* seaplane base; **-flugzeug** *n.* seaplane; **-geltung** *nf.* naval prestige; **-gefecht** *n.* naval action; **-hafen** *nm.* sea-port; **-herrschaft** *nf.* command of the sea; **-hund** *nm.* seal; **-kadett** *m.w.* naval cadet; **-klar** *a.* ready to sail; **-kommando** *n.* naval defence; **-krank** *a.* sea-sick; **-krankheit** *nf.* sea-sickness; **-krieg** *nm.* naval war; **-kriegsleitung** *nf.* naval command; **-macht** *nf.* naval forces, power; **-mann** *nm.* (-leute) sailor; **-mannschaft** *nf.* crew; **-maschinist** *m.w.* engineer (*nav.*); **-meile** *nf.* nautical mile, knot; **-motorleichter** *nm.* motor barge; **-notdienst** *nm.* sea rescue service; **-notgerät** *n.* life-saving equipment; **-räuber** *nm.* pirate; **-räuberei** *nf.* piracy; **-schiffahrt** *nf.* maritime shipping; **-soldat** *m.w.* marine; **-streitkräfte** *f.pl.* naval forces; **-ventil** *n.* sea-cock; **-wärts** *ad.* seawards; **-weg** *nm.* sea route, by sea; **-wurf** *nm.* jetsam; **-zeughaus** *n.* naval arsenal; **-zielröhre** *nf.* periscope; **-zunge** *nf.* sole.

Seele [zay'ler] *nf.* soul, mind

bore (*mil.*), core (*cable*); -nachse *nf.* axis of the bore; -ndurchmesser *nm.* calibre; -nfriede *nm.* peace of mind; -ngrösse *nf.* magnanimity; -nheil *n.* salvation; -nverwandt *a.* congenial; -sorge *nf.* parochial work; -sorger *nm.* clergyman. [mental.

Seelisch [zay'lish] *a.* psychic.

Segel [zay'gel] *n.* (-) sail; -flieger *nm.* glider pilot; -flugwesen *n.* gliding; -flugzeug *n.* glider; -schiff *n.* sailing vessel; -tuch *n.* canvas. [soar.

Segeln [zay'geln] *vi.* to sail.

Segen [zay'gen] *nm.* blessing, grace (*meals*); -sreich *a.* prosperous.

Segler [zay'glerr] *nm.* (-) sailer, yachtsman, sailing boat.

Segn'en [zaig'nen] *vt.* to bless; -ung *nf.* blessing, benediction.

Sehen [zay'en] *vt.i. ir.* to see, look; -swert *a.* worth seeing; -swürdigkeiten *nf.pl.* sights (of a town).

Seher [zay'err] *nm.* (-) seer; -gabe *nf.* second-sight; -isch *a.* prophetic.

Seh-feld *n.* field of vision; -kraft *nf.* eyesight, vision; -rohr *n.* telescope, periscope (*nav.*); -schärfe *nf.* sharpness of vision, focus; -schlitz *nm.* observation slit; -weite *nf.* (range of sight). [string.

Sehne [zay'ner] *nf.* sinew.

Sehn'en [zay'nen] *vr.* to long, yearn; -lich *a.* ardent(ly); -sucht *nf.* longing; -süchtig *a.* ad. (longingly).

Sehnig [zay'nish] *a.* sinewy.

Sehr [zairr] *ad.* very, much.

Seicht [zisht] *a.* shallow, flat, insipid; -igkeit *nf.* shallowness, flatness, superficiality.

Seide [zide'er] *nf.* silk; -n *a.* silk; -nbau *nm.* silk culture; -npapier *n.* tissue-paper; -nraupe *nf.* silk-worm

Seidel [zide'el] *n.* (-) beer-mug.

Seidig [zide'ish] *a.* silky.

Seife [zife'er] *nf.* soap; -n *vt.* to soap; -nflocken *f.pl.* soap-flakes; -nlauge *nf.* soap-suds; -nnapf *nm.* soap-dish; -nschaum *nm.* lather; -nsieder soap-maker, manufacturer; -nsiederei *nf.* soap-works.

Seifig [zife'ish] *a.* soapy.

Seihe [zi'er] *nf.* strainer, filter, lees, dregs; -n *vt.* to filter, strain; -r *nm.* (-) filter, strainer.

Seil [zile] *n.* (-e) rope, cable; -bahn *nf.* cable railway; -tänzer *nm.* tight-rope walker; -trommel *nf.* cable drum; -werk *n.* ropes, rigging; -winde *nf.* windlass, winch; -zug *nm.* tackle.

Seim [zime] *nm.* gum, syrup, honey; -en *vt.* to strain, boil down; -ig *a.* sticky, gummy.

Sein [zine] *vi. ir.* to be, exist; *n.* being.

Sein [zine] *poss.* his, her, its; -erseits *ad.* for his part; -erzeit *ad.* in those days, formerly, duly, some day; -esgleichen *pn.* people such as he, his equals; -ethalben, -etwegen, -etwillen *ad.* for his sake, on his account, as far as he is concerned.

Seinige [zine'i-ger], der, die, das *poss.* his, her, its; his, her duty, share; *n. pl.* his, her people.

Seit [zite] *pr., cj.* since; -dem *ad., cj.* since; -her *ad.* since (then).

Seite [zite'er] *nf.* side, page, flank; -nabstand *nm.* interval, lateral displacement, -nabweichung *nf.* deflection error, drift; -nänderung *nf.* deflection correction; -nangriff *nm.* flank attack; -nansicht *nf.* profile; -nband *n.* side-band (*rad.*); -ndeckung *nf.* flank cover; -nflosse *nf.* vertical fin surface (*av.*); -nflügel *nm.* side-aisle, transept; -ngewehr *n.* bayonet; -nheib *n.* home-thrust; -nleitwerk *n.*, -nruder *n.* rudder (*av.*); -nrutsch *nf.* side-slip; -nschiff *n.* aisle; -nsprung *nm.* caper, prank, escapade; -nstreuung *nf.* lateral dispersion; -nstrasse *nf.* side-road; -nstück *n.* companion piece, counterpart; -nwagen *nm.* side-car; -nzahl *nf.* number of page(s). [part of.

Seitens [zite'enss] *ad.* on the

Seitlich [zite'lish] *a.* side, (col)lateral. [sideways.

Seitwärts [zite'vairrts] *ad.*

Sekret'är [ze-kre-tairr'] *nm.* (-e) secretary, bureau; -ariat *n.* secretary's office; -ärin *nf.* (lady) secretary.

Sekt [zekt] *nm.* (-e) champagne.

Sekte [zek'ter] *nf.* sect.

Sektion [zek-syohn'] *nf.* section, post-mortem, autopsy.

Sekunda [ze-koon'dah] *nf.* fifth form; -wechsel *nm.* second of exchange (*com.*).

Sekundär [ze-koon-dairr'] *a.* secondary; -element *n.* second-ary cell (*rad.*). [second.

Sekunde [ze-koon'der] *nf.*

Selber [zel'berr] = Selbst.

Selbst [zelbst] *pn.* myself, yourself, *etc.*; *n.* self; *ad.* even; -achtung *nf.* self-respect; -anlasser *nm.* self-starter (*aut.*); -anschluss *nm.* auto-matic system (*ph.*); -anschluss-gerät *n.* dial telephone; -be-herrschung *nf.* self-control; -bestimmung *nf.* self-determin-ation; -bewusst *a.* self-confid-ent; -bewusstsein *n.* self-consciousness; -binder *nm.* made-up tie; -biographie *nf.* autobiography; -dichtend *a.* self-sealing (*tank*); -erhaltung *nf.* self-preservation; -erreg-end *a.* self-excited (*rad.*); -fahr . . . *a.* self-propelled

(*mil.*); -fahrer *nm.* owner-driver; -gefällig *a.* smug, self-satisfied; -gefühl *n.* self-respect, confidence; -gemacht, -gezogen *a.* home-made; -genügsam *a.* self-sufficing; -gespräch *n.* monologue; -kostenpreis *nm.* cost price; -lader *nm.* automatic weapon; -los *a.* unselfish; -losigkeit *nf.* unselfishness; -mord *n.m.* suicide; -mörder *nm.* suicide; -mörderisch *a.* suicidal; -redend *a.* obviously; -registrierend *a.* self-recording; -retter *nm.* oxygen apparatus; -steuerung *nf.* automatic control (*av.*); -sucht *nf.* selfish-ness; -süchtig *a.* selfish; -tätig *a.* automatic; -unterbrecher *nm.* automatic circuit-breaker (*el.*); -versorger *nm.* farmer living on his own produce; -verständlich *a.* ad. natural(ly), obvious(ly); -vertrauen *n.* self-confidence; -verwaltung *nf.* autonomy, self-government, home rule; -zucht *nf.* discipline; -zweck *n.* end in itself.

Selbständig [zelp'shten-dish] *a.* independent, autonomous, separate; -keit *nf.* independ-ence. [selfish.

Selbstisch [zelps'tish] *a.*

Selektivität [zay-lek-ti-vi-tate'] *nf.* selectivity (*rad.*).

Selen [zay-lane'] *n.* selenium.

Selig [zay'lish] *a.* blessed, happy, late, deceased; -keit *nf.* bliss. [celery.

Sellerie [zel-er-ree'] *nf.*

Selten [zel'ten] *a.* rare; *ad.* seldom, rarely; -heit *nf.* rarity, scarcity. [err] *n.* soda-water.

Selterwasser [zel'ter-vass-

Seltsam [zelt'zam] *a.* strange, curious; -keit *nf.* strangeness.

Semaphor [ze-ma-forr'] *n.* semaphore.

Semester [ze-mes'terr] *n.* (-) session, half-year, (six-monthly) term

Seminar [ze-mi-narr'] n. (-e) training college, tutorial class.

Semmel [zem'el] nf. roll.

Senat [ze-naht'] nm. (-e) senate, council.

Sende antenne [zen'der-an-ten-er] nf. transmitting, mains aerial; **-bereich** nm. range of transmission; **-folge** nf. programme (rad.); **-leistung** nf. power (rad.); **-raum** nm. studio; **-reihe** nf. series of broadcasts; **-spiel** n. radio play; **-station, -stelle** nf. transmitting station.

Senden [zen'den] vt. ir. to send, transmit, broadcast.

Sender [zen'derr] nm. (-) sender, transmitter (rad.).

Sendung [zen'döong] nf. consignment, shipment, mission, transmission, output (rad.).

Senf [zenf] nm. mustard; **-gas** n. mustard gas; **-pflaster** n. mustard plaster.   [scorch.

Sengen [zeng'en] vt. to singe.

Senk blei [zenk'blī] n. sounding lead; **-brunnen** nm. sunk well; **-fuss** nm. flat foot; **-grube** nf. cesspool; **-kasten** nm. caisson; **-lot** n. sounding lead, plummet; **-niete** nf. flush rivet; **-nietung** nf. countersunk riveting; **-recht** a. vertical.

Senkel [zenk'el] nm. (-) shoelace.

Senken [zenk'en] vt.r. to lower, sink, drop, cast down, give way, settle.

Senkung [zenk'öong] nf. lowering, sinking, depression, hollow (ground).

Sensation [zen-zat-syohn'] nf. sensation, stunt; **-slust** nf. sensationalism.

Sensationell [zen-zat-syo-nel'] a. sensational.

Sense [zen'zer] nf. scythe.

Sensibel [zen-zeebl'] a. sensitive.

Sensibilität [zen-zi-bi-li-tate'] nf. sensitiveness.

Sentenz [zen-tents'] nf. epigram, wise saying; **-enhaft** a. pompous.

Sentimental [zen-ti-men-tahl'] a. sentimental.

Sentimentalität [zen-ti-men-ta-li-tate'] nf. sentimentality.

Separat [ze-pa-raht'] a. separate; **-frieden** nm. separate peace.   [nm. (-) September.

September [zep-tem'berr]

Septisch [zep'tish] a. septic.

Sergeant [zer-zhant'] m.w. sergeant.

Serie [zai'ri-er] nf. series, issue; **-nbau** nm. mass production; **-nflugzeug** n. mass produced aircraft; **-nschaltung** nf. series connection (el.).

Seriös [zer-ri-erss'] a. serious, bona fide.

Serum [zay'room] n. (Seren) serum; **-konserve** nf. plasma.

Service [zairr-veess'] nf. service, set (dinner, etc.).

Servierbrett [zairr-veer'bret] n. (-er) tray.   [to serve.

Servieren [zairr-veer'ren] vt.i.

Serviette [zairr-vi-et'er] nf. table-napkin.

Sessel [zesl] nm. (-) armchair, seat.

Sesshaft [zes'haft] a. resident, settled, sedentary, persistent (gas).

Setz brett [zets'bret] n. (-er) compositor's board; **-ei** nf. fried egg; **-eisen** n. chisel.

Setzen [zet'sen] vt. to set, put, erect, fix, stake, wager, compose, plant; r. sit down, subside, settle; i. leap, cross (river).

Setzer [zet'serr] nm. (-) compositor; **-kasten** nm. letter-case.

Setzerei [zet-ser-rī'] nf. compositor's, case room.

Setzling [zets'ling] nm. (-e) slip, young plant.

Seuche [zoy'sher] *nf.* epidemic; **-ngebiet** *n.* infected area; **-nlazarett** *n.* hospital for infectious diseases.

Seufze'n [zoif'tsen] *vi.* to sigh; **-r** *nm.* (-) sigh.

Sexta [zex'tah] *nf.* lowest form.

Sextant [zex-tant'] *m.w.* sextant.

Sexuell [zex-ōō-el'] *a.* sexual.

Sezier'en [zay-tseer'ren] *vt.* to dissect; **-messer** *n.* scalpel.

Sich [zish] *pn.* himself, herself, itself, oneself, yourself, your-selves, themselves, each other.

Sichel [zish'el] *nf.* sickle, crescent.

Sicher [zish'err] *a.* safe, certain, secure, reliable.

Sicherheit [zish'err-hite] *nf.* safety, security, confidence, certainty; **-sdienst** *nm.* air raid protection; **-gerät** *n.* safety equipment; **-sglas** *n.* safety glass; **-shalber** *ad.* for (the sake of) safety; **-slampe** *nf.* safety lamp; **-sleitung** *nf.* security; **-snadel** *nf.* safety-pin; **-spolizei** *nf.* security police; **-srat** *nm.* Security Council; **-sventil** *n.* safety-valve.

Sicher-lich *ad.* certainly, surely; **-n** *vt.* to secure, cover, protect; **-stellen** *vt.* to secure, safeguard; **-stellung** *nf.* safe-guarding, securing.

Sicherung [zish'err-rōōng] *nf.* safety, security, protection, safeguarding, fuse (*el.*), catch, safety device, covering force (*mil.*); **-sfahrzeug** *n.* escort vessel; **-sflügel** *nm.* safety catch, protective flank (*mil.*); **-skappe** *nf.* cap (grenade); **-slinie** *nf.* switch line (*rl.*); **-sschiff** *n.* coastal defence vessel; **-sschloss** *n.* safety-lock.

Sicht [zisht] *nf.* sight, term (*com.*); **-bar** *a.* visible, evident; **-barkeit** *nf.* visibility; **-bereich** *nm.* range of vision; **-kartei** *nf.* card-index; **-lich** *a.* evident,

obvious; **-schutz** *nm.* camouflage (from air); **-verhältnisse** *n.pl.* visibility; **-vermerk** *n.* visa; **-wechsel** *nm.* sight draft; **-weite** *nf.* see Sichtbereich; **-zeichen** *n.* ground signal (*av.*).

Sichten [zish'ten] *vt.* to sift.

Sickern [zik'errn] *vi.* to trickle, ooze, seep. [them.

Sie [zee] *pn.* she, her, you, they, **Sieb** [zeep] *n.* (-e) sieve, strain-er, riddle; **-en** *vt.* to sift, riddle, screen, strain; **-kette** *nf.* band-pass filter (*rad.*).

Sieben [zee'ben] *num.* seven; **-sachen** *f.pl.* belongings; **-schläfer** *nm.* dormouse, slug-gard; **-te** *a.* seventh.

Sieb-te *a.* seventh; **-zehn** *num.* seventeen; **-zig** *num.* seventy.

Siech [zeesh] *a.* sickly, very ill, invalid; **-en** *vi.* to be in chronic ill health, an invalid; **-tum** *n.* chronic illness.

Siede'heiss [zee'der-hice] *a.* boiling hot; **-punkt** *nm.* boiling point.

Siedeln [zee'deln] *vi.* to colonize, settle.

Siedeln [zee'den] *vt.i. ir.* to boil, simmer.

Siedl'er [zeed'lerr] *nm.* (-) settler; **-ung** *nf.* colony, housing estate; **-ungsgesell-schaft** *nf.* building society.

Sieg [zeek] *nm.* (-e) victory; **-en** *vi.* to win, be victorious; **-er** *nm.* (-) victor, conqueror; **-reich** *a.* victorious, triumph-ant.

Siegel [zee'gel] *n.* (-) seal; **-lack** *nm.* sealing-wax.

Siegeln [zee'geln] *vt.* to seal.

Siel [zeel] *nm. n.* (-e) drain, sluice.

Siele [zee'ler] *nf.* harness.

Siezen [zeet'sen] *vt.* to address in a formal, polite manner, not familiarly.

Signal [zig-nahl'] *n.* (-e) signal; **-apparat** *nm.* signalling apparatus; **-auswerter** *nm.*

signaller; **-buch** n. code of signals; **-geschoss** n. flare projectile; **-hupe** nf. siren; **-leine** nf. communication cord; **-patrone** nf. signal cartridge; **-mast** nm. semaphore, signal mast; **-pfeife** nf. whistle; **-scheibe** nf. signalling disc; **-werfer** nm. flare projector; **-wesen** n. signals, signalling.
Signalisieren [zig-na-li-zeer'ren] vt.i. to signal.
Signatur [zig-na-toorr'] nf. sign, mark, characteristic, press-mark (book).
Silbe [zil'ber] nf. syllable; **-nrätseln** n. charade.
Silber [zil'berr] n. silver; **-bergwerk** n. silver-mine; **-hochzeit** nf. silver wedding; **-münze** nf. silver coin; **-n** a. silver; **-papier** n. silver paper; **-pappel** n. white poplar; **-währung** nf. silver currency.
Silikat [zi-li-kaht'] n. silicate.
Silvesterabend [zil-ves'terr-ah-bent'] nm. New Year's Eve.
Simpel [zim'pel] a. simple, foolish; nm. (-) fool.
Sims [zimss] n. (-e) mantelpiece, ledge, window-sill.
Simulant [zi-moo-lant'] m.w. malingerer.
Simulieren [zi-moo-leer'ren] vi. to malinger, sham illness, simulate.
Sinfon'ie [zin-fo-nee'] nf. symphony; **-isch** a. symphonic; **-ieorchester** n. symphony orchestra.
Sing'en [zing'en] vt.i. ir. to sing; **-leiter** nf. choir conductor; **-spiel** n. musical play, operetta; **-stimme** nf. voice part, singing voice; **-vogel** nm. song-bird.
Sink'en [zink'en] vi. ir. to sink, decline, fall; **-kasten** nm. sink, mud-trap.
Sinn [zin] nm. (-e) sense, mind, meaning; **-bild** n. symbol; **-bildlich** a. symbolic; **-engenuss**

nm. sensual pleasure; **-enwelt** nf. material world; **-esänderung** nf. change of mind, heart; **-esart** nf. character; **-gedicht** n. epigram; **-getreu** a. faithful (to original); **-ig** a. thoughtful, considerate; **-igkeit** nf. thoughtfulness; **-lich** a. sensuous, sensual; **-lichkeit** nf. sensuality; **-los** a. senseless; **-losigkeit** nf. senselessness. [ponder.
Sinnen [zin'en] vi. ir. to reflect, [zin'terr] nm. (-) iron
Sinter [zin'terr] nm. (-) iron dross; **-n** vi. to trickle, ooze.
Sintflut [zint'floot] nf. flood.
Sinus [zee'nōōss] nm. (-) sine, bay.
Sipp'e [zip'er] nf. kindred, clan, tribe; **-schaft** nf. relations, gang, tribe. [syrup.
Sirup [zee'rōōp] nm. (-e)
Sitt'e [zit'er] nf. custom, habit, fashion; **-en** pl. morals; **-ig** a. modest; **-lich** a. moral; **-lichkeit** nf. morality; **-sam** a. modest, virtuous; **-samkeit** nf. modesty, virtue.
Situation [zi-too-at-syohn'] nf. situation, position.
Sitz [zits] nm. (-e) seat, fit; **-gelegenheit** nf. seating accommodation; **-platz** nm. seat; **-ung** nf. meeting, session; **-ungsbericht** nm. report.
Sitzen [zit'sen] vi. ir. to sit, fit, stick.
Skal'a [skah'lah] nf. (Skalen) scale; **-enscheibe** nf. dial (ph.).
Skandal [skan-dahl'] nm. (-e) scandal, uproar, noise; **-ös** a. scandalous.
Skandieren [skan-deer'ren] vt. to scan (verse). [skeleton.
Skelett [ske-let'] n. (-e)
Skepsis [skep'sis] nf. scepticism. [sceptical.
Skeptisch [skep'tish] a.
Ski [skee] nm. (-er) ski; **-fahren, -laufen** vi. ir. to ski.
Skizze [skit'ser] nf. sketch; **-nhaft** a. sketchy. [to sketch.
Skizzieren [skit-seer'ren] vt.i.

Sklav'e [sklav'er] *m.w.* **Sklavin** *nf.* slave; **-erei** *nf.* slavery; **-isch** *a.* slavish.

Skonto [skon'to] *nm, n.* (-s) discount. [scurvy.

Skorbut [skorr-buht'] *nm.*

Skrupel [skroo'pel] *nm.* (-) scruple; **-los** *a.* unscrupulous.

Smaragd [sma-rakt'] *nm.* (-e) emerald.

Smoking [smoke'ing] *nm.* dinner-jacket.

So [zoh] *ad.* so, thus; **-eben** *ad.* just (now); **-fern** *cj.* so far as; **-fort** *ad.* at once; **-fortig** *a.* immediate; **-gar** *ad.* even; **-genannt** *a.* so-called; **-mit**, **-nach** *ad.* thus; **-viel** *cj.* as much as; **-wohl** *cj.* both (and), as well; **-zusagen** *ad.* so to speak.

Socke [zok'er] *nf.* sock; **-en-halter** *nm.* suspender.

Sockel [zokl] *nm.* (-) pedestal, base; **-geschütz** *n.* pivot gun.

Sodawasser [zoh'dah-vass-err] *n.* soda-water.

Sodbrennen [zote'bren-en] *n.* heartburn.

Sofa [zoh-fah] *n.* (-s) sofa.

Sog [zohk] *nm.* (-e) suction, undercurrent, wake.

Sohle [zoh'ler] *nf.* sole (shoe); **-n** *vt.* to sole.

Sohn [zone] *nm.* (Söhne) son.

Solawechsel [zoh'lah-vex-el] *nm.* (-) promissory note (com.).

Solbad [zole'baht] *n.* brine-bath.

Solch [zolsh] *pn, a.* such.

Sold [zolt] *nm.* pay; **-buch** *n.* pay-book.

Soldat [zol-daht'] *m.w.* soldier, private, naval rating; **-enheim** *n.* soldiers' institute, mess; **-enrock** *nm.* tunic, **-ensender** *nm.* forces station (rad.); **-isch** *a.* soldierly. [mercenary.

Söldner [zerld'nerr] *nm.* (-)

Solid [zo-leet'] *a.* solid, sound, steady, reliable; **-ität** *nf.* solidity, soundness, steadiness.

Solist [zo-list'] *m.w.* soloist.

Soll [zol] *n.* (-s) debit(-side), establishment (mil.); **-bestand** *nm.* estimated balance (com.), war establishment, establishment stocks (mil.); **-bruchstelle** *nf.* breaking point (tec.); **-stärke** *nf.* establishment strength.

Sollen [zol'en] *vi. ir.* shall, ought to, to have to, to be supposed to, be said to, mean.

Söller [zer'lerr] *nm.* (-) loft, gallery.

Solo [zoh'lo] *n.* (Soli, Solos) solo.

Sommer [zom'err] *nm.* (-) summer; **-fäden** *nfpl.* gossamer; **-frische** *nf.* summer resort; **-sprosse** *nf.* freckle; **-zeit** *nf.* summer time.

Sonate [zo-nah'ter] *nf.* sonata.

Sond'e [zon'der] *nf.* probe, sound, plummet (nav.); **-ieren** *vt.* to probe, sound.

Sonder'ausweis [zon'derr-ows-vice] *nm.* (-e) special pass; **-bar** *a.* singular, strange; **-bündler** *nm.* separatist; **-dienst** *nm.* specialist service; **-frieden** *nm.* separate peace; **-gleichen** *a.* unique, unrivalled; **-lich** *a, ad.* remarkable, special(ly); **-ling** *nm.* (-e) eccentric; **-meldung** *nf.* special report; **-verband** *nm.* task force (mil.).

Sonder'n [zon'derrn] *vt.* to separate; **-ung** *nf.* separation.

Sonett [zo-net'] *n.* (-e) sonnet.

Sonnabend [zon'ah-bent] *nm.* (-e) Saturday.

Sonne [zon'er] *nf.* sun; **-nbrand** *nm.* sunburn; **-nfleck** *nm.* sunspot; **-nschein** *nm.* sunshine; **-nschirm** *nm.* parasol, sunshade; **-nstich** *nm.* sunstroke; **-nzelt** *n.* awning.

Sonn'en [zon'en] *vi.r.* to sun, bask; **-ig** *a.* sunny.

Sonntag [zon'tahk] *nm.* (-e) Sunday; **-skind** *n.* lucky person; **-sstaat** *nm.* Sunday clothes.

Sonst [zonst] *ad.* else, otherwise, formerly; **-ig** *a.* other, former; **-wohin** [ad.] elsewhere; **-woher** *ad.* from elsewhere. [soprano, treble.

Sopran [zo-prahn'] *nm.* (-e)

Sorg'e [zorr'ger] *nf.* care, trouble, worry; **-en** *vi.* to worry, take care, see to; **-enfrei** *a.* care-free; **-enkind** *n.* delicate child; **-envoll** *a.* careworn; **-falt** *nf.* care(fulness); **-fältig** *a.* careful, painstaking; **-los** *a.* careless, carefree, negligent; **-losigkeit** *nf.* carelessness, negligence; **-sam** =fältig.

Sorte [zorr'ter] *nf.* sort, brand.

Sortieren [zorr-teer'en] *vt.* to (as)sort.

Sortiment [zorr-ti-ment'] *n.* (-e) assortment; **-sbuchhändler** *nm.* retail bookseller.

Souffl'eur [zoo-fïerr'] *nm.* (-e) prompter; **-ieren** *vt.i.* to prompt.

Sozial [zoh-tsi-ahl'] *a.* social; **-demokrat** *m.w.* social democrat; **-demokratie** *nf.* social democracy, socialism; **-isieren** *vt.* to socialize; **-ismus** *nm.* socialism; **-ist** *m.w.* socialist.

Sozius [zoh'tsi-ôôss] *nm.* (-se) comrade; **-sitz** *nm.* pillion seat (*aut.*).

Späh'en [shpay'en] *vi.* to spy, peer, scout, reconnoitre, patrol; **-er** *nm.* (-) scout; **-trupp** *nm.* patrol; **-wagen** *nm.* scouting car, patrol car (*mil.*).

Spalier [shpa-leer'] *n.* (-e) trellis.

Spalt [shpalt] *nm.* (-e), **Spalte** *nf.* chink, crack; **-füssig** *a.* cloven-hoofed; **-holz** *n.* firewood; **-ring** *nm.* split ring.

Spalt'en [shpalt'en] *vt.* to split; **-ung** *nf.* split, rupture, splitting, fission (*atom.*).

Span [shpahn] *nm.* chip, splinter; **Späne** *pl.* shavings.

Spanferkel [shpahn'fairr-kel *n.* (-) sucking-pig.

Spange [shpang'er] *nf.* clasp, buckle, bracelet.

Spann [shpan] *nm.* (-e) instep.

Spann'e [shpan'er] *nf.* span; **-en** *vt.* to stretch, strain, cock, excite, thrill; **-kraft** *nf.* tension, elasticity; **-seil** *n.* guy-rope; **-ung** *nf.* tension, excitement, suspense, voltage (*el.*); **-ungsmesser** *nm.* volt-meter; **-weite** *nf.* wing-span, wing-spread (*av.*).

Spant [shpant] *n.* transverse frame (*av.*). [(*ship*).

Spante [shpan'ter] *nf.* rib

Spar'en [shpah'ren] *vt.* to save, spare; *i.* to be sparing; **-büchse** *nf.* money-box; **-flug** *nm.* economical flight (*av.*); **-geld** *n.* savings; **-kasse** *nf.* savings-bank; **-sam** *a.* thrifty; **-samkeit** *nf.* thrift; **-schaltung** *nf.* simplified transformer (*el.*).

Spargel [shparr'gel] *nm.* asparagus.

Spärlich [shpairr'lish] *a.* scanty, frugal; **-keit** *nf.* scantiness, frugality.

Sparren [shpar'ren] *nm.* (-) spar, rafter, cross-bar.

Sparte [shparr'ter] *nf.* department, subject.

Spass [shpahss] *nm.* (Spässe) joke, fun; **-en** *vi.* to joke, make fun; **-haft** *a.* joking, funny; **-macher** *nm.* joker, funny man; **-verderber** *nm.* spoil-sport.

Spät [shpate] *a., ad.* late; **-estens** *ad.* at the latest; **-zündung** *nf.* retarded ignition (*aut.*).

Spatel [shpah'tel] *nm.* (-) trowel. [spade.

Spaten [shpah'ten] *nm.* (-)

Spatz [shpats] *m.w.* sparrow.

Spazier'en [shpat-seer'en] *vi.* to walk about, take a walk; **-fahrt** *nf.* drive; **-gang** *nm.* walk; **-stock** *nm.* walking

stick; -weg nm. promenade,
drive.　　　　　　　[pecker.
Specht [spesht] nm. (-e) wood-
Speck [shpek] nm. bacon;
-seite nf. flitch.
Spedieren [shpe-dee'ren] vt.
to forward.
Spediteur [shpe-di-terr'] nm.
(-e) forwarding-agent; -ion nf.
forwarding (agency).
Speer [shpairr] nm. (-e) spear.
Speiche [shpī'sher] nf. spoke.
Speichel [shpī'shel] nm.
saliva, spittle; -lecker nm.
toady, yes-man; -n vi. to
slaver; -röhre nf. saliva-
ejector.
Speicher [shpī'sherr] nm. (-)
granary, store-room, reservoir;
-n vt. to store.
Speien [shpī'en] vt. to vomit,
spew (forth).
Speigatt [shpī'gat] n. scupper.
Speise [shpī'zer] nf. food; -eis
n. ice-cream; -fett n. cooking
fat; -haus n. restaurant,
-kammer nf. larder; -karte nf.
bill of fare, menu; -leitung nf.
feeder (rad.); -n vt.i. to feed,
eat, dine; -saal nm. dining-
room; -wagen nm. dining-car.
Spektakel [shpek-tah'kel]
nm. (-) row, fuss.
Spekulant [shpe-kŏŏ-lant']
m.w. speculator; -ation nf.
speculation; -ieren vi. to
speculate.
Spelunke [shpe-lŏŏn'ker] nf.
den, slum, low tavern.
Spelz [shpelts] nm. spelt.
Spende [shpen'der] nf. gift,
alms, donation; -n vt. contribute, give, dispense; -er nm.
(-) donor, giver; -ieren vt. to
treat.　　　　　　　[plumber.
Spengler [shpeng'lerr] nm. (-)
Sperber [shpairr'berr] nm. (-)
sparrow-hawk.
Sperling [shpairr'ling] nm.
(-e) sparrow.
Sperrballon [shperr'ba-
long'] nm. (-e) barrage balloon;

-bestand nm. earmarked
stocks; -brecher nm. blockade
runner; -druck nm. spaced
type; -e nf. closing, blockade,
barrier, ban; -en vt. to close,
bar, ban; cut off, block;
-feuer n. barrage fire; -gebiet n
prohibited area; -guthaben n.
blocked account; -holz n. ply-
wood; -lücke nf. lane (in
mines); -sitz nm. stall (theatre).
Spesen [shpay'zen] pl.
expenses, charges.
Spezerei [shpet-ser-rī'] nf.
spice, grocery.
Spezialarzt [shpet-si-ahl'-
artst] nm. (-ärzte) specialist;
-isieren vt. to specialize; -ität
nf. speciality; -unterseeboot n.
midget submarine.
Speziell [shpet-si-el'] a.
special.
Spezifisch [shpet-see'fish] a,
ad. specific(ally).
Sphäre [sfair'rer] nf. sphere.
Spicken [shpik'en] vt. to lard.
Spiegel [shpee'gel] nm. (-)
mirror, stern (ship), collar-
patch, tab (mil.); -ei n. fried
egg; -glas n. plate-glass; -n
vt.i. to reflect, be reflected;
-ung nf. reflection.
Spiel [shpeel] n. (-e) game,
play(ing), acting, pack (cards),
gambling, working; -ball nm.
plaything; -dose nf. musical
box; -en vi. to play, gamble,
perform, act; -er nm. (-) actor,
gambler; -film nm. feature
film; -gefährte m.w. playmate;
-karte nf. playing card; -platz
nm. playground; -raum nm.
scope; -sache nf. -zeug n. toy.
Spiere [shpee'rer] nf. spar,
boom (ship), rib (av.).
Spiess [shpeess] nm. (-e) spit,
pike, spear; -bürger nm. smug
town-dweller, middle-class
person; -en vt. tr. to impale,
pierce; -geselle m.w. accomplice;
-glanz nm. antimony; -ruten-
laufen n. running the gauntlet.

Spill [shpil] n. (-e) windlass, winch. [spinach.
Spinat [shpi-naht'] nm. (-e)
Spind [shpint] nm. (-e) cupboard, wardrobe.
Spindel [shpin'del] nf. spindle, distaff, axle, pivot, arbor, shaft; -dürr a. very thin.
Spinn'e [shpin'er] nf. spider; -en vt. ir. to spin; -erei n. spinning-(mill); -gewebe n. cobweb; -stoffbezugsschein nm. clothing coupon; -stoffwaren f.pl. textiles.
Spion [shpi-ohn'] nm. (-e) spy; -age nf. espionage; -ieren vi. to spy.
Spiral'e [shpi-rah'ler] nf. spiral; -bohrer nm. auger.
Spirituosen [shpi-ri-too-oh'zen] pl. spirits.
Spiritus [shpee'ri-tooss] nm. (methylated) spirit; -brennerei nf. distillery.
Spital [shpi-tahl'] n. (Spitäler) hospital; [nian dog.
Spitz [shpits] nm. (-e) Pomera-
Spitz [shpits] a. pointed, sharp, acute; -bogen nm. pointed arch; -bube n.m.w. rogue; -e nf. point, peak; pl. lace; -el nm. (-) police spy, informer; -en vt. to point, sharpen; -enbelastung nf. peak load (el.); -enleistung nf. maximum performance; -enlohn nm. maximum wage; -findig a. sharp, (over) subtle; -hacke nf. pickaxe; -ig a. sarcastic, pointed; -marke nf. heading; -name nm. nickname. [splice.
Spleissen [shplice'en] vt.i. ir. to
Splitter [shplit'err] nm. (-) splinter; -bombe nf. fragmentation bomb; -graben nm. slit trench; -nackt a. stark naked; -sicher a. splinter-proof; -wirkung nf. fragmentation effect. [spontaneous.
Spontan [shpon-tahn'] a.
Spore [shpohr'rer] nf. spore.
Sporn [shporrn] nm. (gen. -es.

pl. Sporen) spur; -en vt. to spur; -schuh nm. tail-skid (av.); -streichs ad. post-haste.
Sport [shporrt] nm. sport, games, physical training; -funk nm. sports news (rad.); -hemd n. singlet; -höschen n. rompers; -lehrer nm. -lehrkraft nf. trainer, coach; -trikot nm. zephyr.
Sporteln [shporr'teln] pl. fees.
Spott [shpot] nm. ridicule; -billig a. dirt-cheap; -en vi. to mock, ridicule; -name nm. nickname.
Spött'erei [shper-ter-rie'] nf. chaff, banter; -eln vi. to jeer, sneer at; -er nm. (-) mocker, scoffer; -isch a. mocking, scornful.
Sprach'e [shprach'er] nf. language, speech; -fertigkeit nf. fluency; -gebrauch nm. linguistic usage; -kenner nm. linguist; -kundig a. good at languages; -lich a. linguistic; -los a. speechless; -rohr n. speaking-tube, mouthpiece, transmitter (ph.); -schatz nm. vocabulary.
Sprech'en [shpresh'en] vt.i. ir. to speak, talk; -er nm. (-) spokesman; -film nm. talkie; -stunde nf. consultation hour; -weise nf. diction; -zimmer n. consulting room.
Spreiten = Spreizen.
Spreize [shprite'zer] nf. prop; -n vt. to spread (out), prop (up).
Sprengel [shpreng'el] nm. (-) parish, diocese.
Spreng'en [shpreng'en] vt. to sprinkle, break (up), blast; i. gallop; -falle nf. booby-trap; -geschoss n. high-explosive shell; -kapsel nf. detonator, primer; -kommando n. demolition detachment, bomb-disposal squad; -ladung nf. explosive charge; -mine nf. anti-personnel mine; -stück n.

splinter; -wagen *nm.* watering-cart.

Sprenkel [shprenk'el] *nm.* (-) speckle; -ig *a.* speckled; -n *vt.* to speckle, splash.

Spreu [shproy] *nf.* chaff.

Sprichwort [shprish'vorrt] *n.* (-wörter) *n.* proverb; -wörtlich *a.* proverbial. [to sprout.]

Spriessen [shpree'sen] *vi. ir.*

Springbrunnen [shpring'broo-nen] *nm.* (-) fountain.

Spring'en [shpring'en] *vi. ir.* to jump, spring, burst; *n.* leaping, (parachute) jumping; -er *nm.* (-) jumper, knight (*chess*); -insfeld *n.* reckless youth, tomboy; -kraft *nf.* elasticity. [fuel.]

Sprit [shprit] *nm.* motor spirit,

Spritz'e [shprit'ser] *nf.* syringe, spray, fire-engine; -brett *n.* splash-, dash-board; -en *vt.i.* to spurt, squirt, splash; -enhaus *n.* fire-station; -regen *nm.* drizzle.

Spröd'e [shprer'der] *a.* brittle, coy, shy; -igkeit *nf.* brittleness, shyness, reserve.

Spross [shpross] *nm.* (-e) shoot, offspring, antler; -en *vi.* to sprout, germinate. [bar.]

Sprosse [shpros'er] *nf.* rung,

Sprössling [shprers'ling] *nm.* (-e) shoot, scion.

Sprotte [shprot'er] *nf.* sprat.

Spruch [shprooch] *nm.* (Sprüche) saying, maxim, sentence (*law*).

Sprudel [shproo'del] *nm.* (-) spring, well; -n *vi.* to bubble, gush, well forth.

Sprüh'en [shproo'en] *vt.i.* to sparkle, make sparks, flash; -er *nm.* (-) spray.

Sprung [shproong] *nm.* (Sprünge) leap, crack, split; -brett *n.* diving-board; -feder *nf.* spring; -weise *ad.* by leaps, spasmodically.

Spuck'en [shpoo'ken] *vt.i.* to spit; -napf *nm.* spittoon.

Spuk [shpook] *nm.* ghost; -en *vi.* to haunt.

Spule [shpoo'ler] *nf.* spool, coil (*rad.*); -n *vt.* to wind.

Spül'en [shpyoo'len] *vt.* to wash, rinse; -küche *nf.* scullery. [bung, plug.]

Spund [shpoont] *nm.* (Spünde)

Spur [shpoor] *nf.* trace, clue, track, trail; -los *a, ad.* without a trace; -weite *nf.* gauge.

Spüren [shpyoor'ren] *vt.* to track, trace, feel. [hurry.]

Sputen [shpoo'ten] *vr.* to

Staat [shtaht] *nm.* (*gen.* -es; *pl.* -en) state, dress, finery; -enlos *a.* stateless; -lich *a.* state; -sangehörigkeit *nf.* nationality; -sanwalt *nm.* public prosecutor; -sbeamte(r) *m.w.* official; -sdienst *nm.* civil service; -shaushalt *nm.* budget; -spolizei *nf.* secret police; -sschuld *nf.* national debt.

Stab [shtahp] *nm.* (Stäbe) staff, stick, bar; -reim *nm.* alliteration; -sarzt *nm.* captain (medical); -sfeldwebel *nm.* warrant officer (*nav.*); staff sergeant major; -sgefreiter *m.w.* staff lance-corporal (*mil.*), leading aircraftman (*av.*); -skompanie *nf.* headquarters company; -soffizier *nm.* field officer, senior officer.

Stabil [shta-beel'] *a.* stable; -isieren *vt.* to stabilize.

Stachel [shtach'el] *nm.* (*gen.* -s; *pl.* -n) spike, prickle, sting; -beere *nf.* gooseberry; -draht *nm.* barbed wire; -ig *a.* prickly, stinging; -schwein *n.* porcupine.

Stadion [shtah'di-on], **Stadium** [shtah'di-oöm] *n.* (Stadien) stadium, stage.

Stadt [shtat] *nf.* (Städte) town; -köfferchen *n.* attaché case; -kreis *nm.* county borough; -rat *nm.* town council; -schreiber *nm.* town-clerk; -viertel *n.* quarter.

Städt'chen [shtet'shen] n. (-) small town; -enbau nm. town-planning; -er nm. (-) town-dweller; -isch a. municipal.

Staffel [shtaf'el] nf. rung, step, relay (race), echelon (mil.), squadron (av.); -ei nf. easel; -n vi. to graduate, stagger; -ung nf. graduation, staggering, echelon formation (av.).

Stag [shtahk] nm. (-e) stay (nav.).

Stahl [shtahl] nm. (-e) steel.

Stählen [shtäle'en] vi. to temper, steel. [ing. fecne.

Staket [shta-kate'] n. (-e) railing.

Stalag — Stammlager.

Stall [shtal] nm. (Ställe) stable, kennel, hutch, sty.

Stamm [shtam] nm. (Stämme) stem, trunk, tribe, race; -baum nm. pedigree; -buch n. album; -en vi. to come from, originate; -gast nm. regular customer; -lager n. prisoner of war camp; -mannschaft nf. padre (mil.); -rolle nf. muster roll (mil.); -verwandt a. cognate.

Stamm'eln [shtam'eln] vi. to stammer; -ler nm. (-) stammerer.

Stämmig [shtem'ish] a. sturdy; -keit nf. sturdiness.

Stampf'en [shtamp'fen] v.i.s. to stamp, pound, mash, ram; -kartoffeln pl. mashed potatoes; -er nm. (-) rammer, pestle.

Stand [shtant] nm. (Stände) position, condition, class, rank, state; -bild n. statue; -esamt n. registrar's office; -esbeamte(r) m.w. registrar; -haft a. steadfast; -haftigkeit nf. steadfastness; -halten vi. ir. to stand firm, resist; -ort nm. station, garrison; -punkt nm. standpoint; -quartier n. permanent quarters; -recht n. martial law.

Ständ'chen [shtent'shen] n. (-) serenade; -er nm. (-) stand; -ig a. fixed, permanent.

Stange [shtang'er] nf. pole, bar, stick; -nbohne nf. runner bean.

Stänker [shtenk'err] nm. (-) quarrelsome person; -n vi. to stink, quarrel. [foil.

Stanniol [shtan-i-ohl'] n. tin-foil.

Stanze [shtant'ser] nf. stanza, stamp; -n vt. to stamp.

Stapel [shtah'pel] nm. (-) pile, stocks (ship), dump; -lauf nm. launch.

Star [shtarr] nm. (-e) starling.

Star [shtarr] nm. (-e) cataract (eye).

Stark [shtarrk] a. strong, great, heavy, loud (tone); -leibig a. stout; -strom nm. power current (el.).

Stärk'e [shtairr'ker] nf. strength, violence, stoutness, starch; -en vt. to strengthen, starch; -ung nf. strengthening, refreshment; -ungsmittel n. tonic.

Starr [shtarr] a. stiff, rigid, staring; -heit nf. rigidity, obstinacy; -köpfig a. stubborn; -sinn nm. obstinacy.

Starren [shtar'ren] vi. to stare, be rigid, soar up, be full of.

Start [shtarrt] nm. (-e) start, launching (glider), take-off (plane); -bahn nf. runway; -en vi. to start, take off; -er nm. (-) starter; -klar a. ready to take off.

Station [shtat-syohn'] nf. station, hospital ward; -svorsteher nm. station-master.

Statist [shtat-ist'] m.w. supernumerary; -ik nf. statistics; -iker nm. (-) statistician; -isch a. statistical. [tripod, stand.

Stativ [shta-teef'] n. (-e)

Statt [shtat] pr. instead of; nf. place; -finden vi. ir. to take place; -haft a. admissible; -halter nm. governor, viceroy; -lich a. stately, handsome, imposing.

Stätte [shtet'er] nf. place, site.

Statue [shtah'tŏŏ-er] nf. statue.

Statut [shta-tŏŏt'] n. (gen. -s; pl. -en) regulations, articles.

Staub [shtowp] nm. dust; -faden nm. stamen; -ig a. dusty; -sauger nm. vacuum cleaner; -tuch n. duster. [dust.

Stäuben [shtoy'ben] vt. to dust.

Stau'damm [shtow'dam] nm. dam; -ung nf. damming up, traffic block; -werk n. lock.

Stauchen [shtowch'en] vt. to force, cram, ram, stack.

Staude [shtow'der] nf. shrub.

Stau'en [shtow'en] vt. to stow, dam, trim (coal); r. to be blocked, jam; -er nm. (-) stevedore; -ung nf. congestion, jam, bottle-neck.

Staunen [shtow'nen] vi. to be astonished; n. amazement; -swert a. astonishing.

Staupe [shtow'per] nf. flogging, distemper (dog). [flog.

Stäupen [shtoy'pen] vt. to flog.

Stech'becken [shtesh'bek-en] n. (-) bed-pan; -en vt ir. to pierce, cut, sting, engrave; -er nm. (-) hair-trigger; -palme nf. holly; -schritt goose-step.

Steck'brief [shtek'breef] nm. (-e) warrant of arrest; -dose nf. wall socket; -en vt.i. to stick, insert, put, plant, be (fixed); -enpferd n. hobby; -er nm. (-) wall-plug; -ling nm. cutting, slip; -nadel nf. pin.

Steg [shtake] nm. (-e) path, small bridge; -reif nm. impromptu.

Stehen [shtay'en] vi. ir. to stand, be, suit; - bleiben vi. to remain standing, stop, stall (av.); -d a. standing, fixed, permanent, consolidated (debt).

Stehlen [shtay'len] vt. ir. to steal.

Steif [shtife] a. stiff, formal; -en vt. to stiffen, starch; -heit nf. stiffness, formality.

Steig [shtike] nm. (-e) path; -bügel nm. stirrup; -eisen n. crampon; -höhe nf. ceiling (av.).

Steig'en [shtie'gen] vi. ir. to rise, mount, climb, take-off (av.); -ung nf. incline, gradient, rise.

Steiger'n [shtie'gerrn] vt. to raise, work up, heighten; -ung nf. raising, intensification, comparison (grammar).

Steil [shtile] a. steep; -flug nm. climbing flight (av.); -heit nf. steepness.

Stein [shtine] nm. (-e) stone, jewel (watch); -alt a. ancient; -bruch nm. quarry; -butt nm. turbot; -druck nm. lithography; -ern a. stone; -gut n. pottery; -kohle nf. pit-coal; -metz nm. (-e) stone-mason; -pilz nm. edible mushroom.

Steinig [shtine'ish] a. stony; -en vt. to stone.

Steiss [shtice] nm. (-e) rump.

Stell'bock [shtel'bok] nm. trestle; -dichein n. (-) meeting-place; -macher nm. wheelwright.

Stell'e [shtel'er] nf. place, situation, passage (book); -en vt. to put, place, regulate, engage (enemy); r. pretend, sham; -engesuch n. application for post; -enlos a. out of work; -ung nf. position, situation, line (mil.); -ungsbefehl nm. call-up (mil.); -vertreter nm. substitute; -vertretend a. acting; -werk n. signal-box.

Stelz'bein [shtelts'bine] n. (-e) wooden leg; -e nf. stilt.

Stemm'eisen [shtem'ize-en] n. (-) chisel; -en vt. to stem, resist, prop.

Stempel [shtem'pel] nm. (-) stamp, die; -gebühr nf. stamp-duty; -n vt. to stamp.

Stenge [shteng'er] nf. top-mast. [stalk.

Stengel [shteng'el] nm. (-)

Stenograph [shte-no-grahf'] *m.w.* stenographer; **-ie** *nf.* shorthand; **-ieren** *vt.i.* to write shorthand.

Stenotypistin [shte-no-tyōō-pis'tin] *nf.* shorthand typist.

Stepp'decke [shtep'dek-er] *nf.* quilt; **-en** *vt.* to quilt.

Sterbe'bett [shtairr'ber-bet] *n.* (*gen.* -es; *pl.* -en) death-bed; **-n** *vi. ir.* to die.

Sterblich [shtairr'blish] *a.* mortal, **-keit** *nf.* mortality; **-keitsziffer** *nf.* death-rate.

Stereoskopkamera [shter-re-o-shohp'ka-mair-rah] *nf.* stereo-camera.

Stereotyp [shter-reo-tyōōp'] *a.* stereotype.

Steril [shter-eel'] *a.* sterile; **-isieren** *vt.* to sterilize; **-isier-ung** *nf.* sterilization.

Stern [shtairrn] *nm.* (-e) star; **-bild** *n.* constellation; **-chen** *n.* (-) asterisk; **-kunde** *nf.* astronomy.

Stet [shtate] *a.* steady; **-ig** *a.* constant, continual; **-igkeit** *nf.* constancy; **-s** *ad.* continually, always.

Steuer [shtoy'err] *n.* helm, rudder; **-bord** *n.* starboard; **-gitter** *n.* control grid (*rad.*); **-knüppel** *nm.* control column, joy-stick (*av.*); **-mann** *nm.* helmsman, navigator; **-ung** *nf.* steering, piloting, controls; **-rad** *n.* steering-wheel (*av.*), steering-wheel (*aut.*); **-welle** *nf.* lay-shaft.

Steuer [shtoy'err] *nf.* tax; **-amt** *n.* inland revenue office; **-anschlag** *nm.* assessment; **-ausgleich** *nm.* adjustment of tax; **-einnehmer** *nm.* tax-collector; **-erklärung** *nf.* tax-return; **-jahr** *n.* fiscal year; **-n** *vt.i.* to steer, pilot, check, contribute; **-zahler** *nm.* tax-payer.

Steven [shtay'fen] *nm.* (-) stem (*ship*).

Stibitzen [shtee-bit'sen] *vt.* to pilfer, steal.

Stich [shtish] *nm.* (-e) sting, stab, cut, stitch, gibe, tinge, trick (*cards*), engraving; **-el** *nm.* (-) engraving tool; **-elei** *nf.* sneer, taunt; **-eln** *vt.* to prick, stitch, taunt; **-graben** *nm.* slit trench (*mil.*); **-haltig** *a.* sound, tenable; **-probe** *nf.* random sample; **-wahl** *nf.* final ballot; **-wort** *n.* cue, catchword.

Stick'en [shtik'en] *vt.i.* to suffocate, choke; **-luft** *nf.* stuffy air; **-stoff** *nm.* nitrogen.

Sticke'n [shtik'en] *vt.i.* to embroider; **-rei** *nf.* embroidery (factory).

Stieben [shtee'ben] *vi. ir.* to fly about, spray, disperse (*crowd*).

Stief'bruder [shteef'brōō-derr] *nm.* (-brüder) *etc.*, step-brother, *etc.*; **-mütterchen** *n.* pansy.

Stiefel [shtee'fel] *nm.* (-) boot; **-knecht** *nm.* boot-jack; **-putzer** *nm.* boots, shoe-black; **-wichse** *nf.* boot-polish, blacking.

Stiege [shtee'ger] *nf.* staircase.

Stieglitz [shtee'glitz] *nm.* (-e) goldfinch. [handle.

Stiel [shteel] *nm.* (-e) stalk, [steer.

Stier [shteerr] *a.* staring, fixed; **-en** *vi.* to stare.

Stier [shteerr] *nm.* (-e) bull.

Stift [shtift] *nm.* (-e) peg, tack, crayon, pencil.

Stift [shtift] *n.* (-er) (charitable) foundation; **-en** *vt.* to found, cause; **-er** *nm.* (-), **-erin** *nf.* founder, author(ess); **-ung** *nf.* foundation, institution, abbey, chapter.

Stil [shteel] *nm.* (-e) style.

Still [shtil] *a., ad.* still, quiet, silent, secret; **-e** *nf.* stillness, quietness, silence; **-gestanden** *int.* attention!; **-legen** *vt.* to close down; **-schweigen** *vi.* to be silent; *n.* silence; **-schweigend** *a., ad.* silent(ly), tacit(ly).

-stand *nm.* stoppage, stand-still.

Stillen [shtil'en] *vt.* to stop, allay, quench, satisfy, suckle, nurse.

Stimm'e [shtim'er] *nf.* voice, vote; -en *vt.i.* to tune, pitch, dispose, render, harmonize, agree, be correct; -recht *n.* franchise; -ung *nf.* tone, mood, atmosphere, feeling, disposition, frame of mind. [stink.

Stinken [shtink'en] *vi. ir.* to

Stipendium [shti-pen'di-oom] *n.* (*gen.* -s; *pl.* Stipendien) scholarship, grant.

Stirn [shtirrn] *nf.* forehead, brow, impudence; -runzeln *n.* frown(ing); -wind *nm.* head-wind. [rummage.

Stöbern [shter'berrn] *vi.* to

Stock [shtok] *nm.* (Stöcke) stick, cane, storey; -dumm *a.* quite stupid; -fisch *nm.* dried cod, blockhead; -rose *nf.* holly-hock; -taub *a.* stone-deaf; -werk *n.* storey.

Stock'en [shtok'en] *vi.* to come to a standstill, stop, pause, curdle; -ung *nf.* stand-still, stoppage, congestion.

Stoff [shtof] *nm.* (-e) material, cloth, matter, topic, subject; -gamasche *nf.* canvas gaiter; -handschuh *nm.* fabric glove.

Stöhnen [shter'nen] *vi.* to groan. stolz [shtolts] *a.* proud.

Stoppel [shtop'el] *nf.* stubble: -n *vt.* to glean, patch.

Stopp'en [shtop'en] *vi.* to stop; -uhr *nf.* stop-watch.

Stöpsel [shterp'sel] *nm.* (-) stopper, plug.

Stör [shterr] *nm.* (-e) sturgeon.

Storch [shtorrch] *nm.* (Störche) stork.

Stör'angriff [shterr'an-grif] *nm.* (-e) nuisance-raid (*av.*); -einsatz *nm.* harassing operation; -geräusch *n.* background of noise.

Stör'en [shterr'en] *vt.* to disturb, jam, interfere (*rad.*); -ung *nf.* disturbance, annoyance, intrusion, jamming, atmospherics, interference (*rad.*), break-down; -ungstrupp *nf.* break-down squad, repair squad.

Störr'ig, -isch [shterr'ish] *a.* stubborn, sullen.

Stoss [shtohss] *nm.* (Stösse) knock, thrust, heap, joint, kick; -dämpfer *nm.* shock absorber; -en *vt.i.* to thrust, knock, jostle, take offence at, run across, adjoin; -mine *nf.* contact mine; -zange *nf.* bumper (*aut.*).

Stotter'er [shto'ter-rerr] *nm.* stutterer; -n *vi.* to stutter. [ly.

Stracks [shtrax] *ad.* immediate-

Straf'anstalt [shtrahf'an-shtalt] *nf.* (convict) prison, reformatory; -arbeit *nf.* imposition; -bar *a.* punishable; -barkeit *nf.* culpability.

Straf'e [shtrah'fer] *nf.* punishment, fine; -en *vt.* to punish; -gefangene(r) *m.w.* convict; -gericht *n.* criminal court; -gesetzbuch *n.* penal code; -lager *n.* penal camp; -porto *n.* postage due, surcharge; -predigt *nf.* lecture; -recht *n.* criminal law.

Straff [shtraf] *a.* taut, tight, stretched, straight, upright, stern; -heit *nf.* tightness, strictness.

Sträf'lich [shtrafe'lish] *a.* punishable, criminal; -ling *nm.* convict.

Strahl [shtrahl] *nm.* (*gen.* -s; *pl.* -en) ray, flash, beam (*rad.*), jet (*water*); -antrieb *nm.* jet-propulsion (*av.*); -en *vt.i.* to radiate, beam; -enbündel *n.* cluster of searchlight rays; -er *nm.* (-) jet-propelled aircraft; -motor *nm.* jet-engine; -platz *nm.* airfield for jet-propelled aircraft; -sender *nm.* transmittter; -ung *nf.* radiation; -werfer *nm.* directional aerial.

Strählen [shtray'len] *vt.* to comb (horse). [strand, skein.

Strähne [shtray'ner] *nf.* plait,

Stramm [shtram] *a.* taut, tight, erect, robust; -stehen *vi.* to stand at attention (*mil.*).

Strampeln [shtram'peln] *vi.* to toggle, kick.

Strand [shtrant] *nm.* beach, shore, strand; -anzug *nm.* beach-suit; -en *vi.* to run ashore, beach; -gut *n.* flotsam; -schuh *nm.* sand-shoe.

Strang [shtrang] *nm.* (Stränge) cord, rope, trace, rail.

Strapaz'e [shtra-pat'ser] *nf.* fatigue; -ieren *vt.* to wear out, fatigue.

Strasse [shtrah'ser] *nf.* street, road, straits; -nanzug *nm.* lounge-suit; -nbagger *nm.* bulldozer; -nbahn *nf.* tramway; -nbau *nm.* road construction; -nbeleuchtung *nf.* street-lighting; -nfeger *nm.* scavenger; -nhandel, -nverkauf *nm.* hawking; -nsperre *nf.* road-block.

Strateg'e [shtra-tay'ger] *m.w.* strategist; -isch *a.* strategic.

Strato'meldung [shtrah'tomel-dōong] *nf.* radio-sonde report; -sphäre *nf.* stratosphere.

Sträuben [shtroy'ben] *vi.* to ruffle; *r.* bristle up, resist.

Strauch [shtrowch] *nm.* (Sträucher) bush, shrub.

Straucheln [shtrowch'eln] *vi.* to stumble.

Strauss [shtrowss] *nm.* (Strausse) bunch, bouquet, combat. [ostrich.

Strauss [shtrowss] *nm.* (-e)

Strazze [shtrat'ser] *nf.* daybook (*com.*).

Strebe [shtray'ber] *nf.* strut; -balken *nm.* buttress; -bogen *nm.* flying buttress; -n *vi.* to strive, endeavour, aspire; -r *nm.* (-) thruster, climber.

Strebsam [shtrape'zam] *a.* industrious, pushing; -keit *nf.* industry, ambition.

Streck'e [shtrek'er] *nf.* stretch, tract, distance, section (*rl.*); -en *vt.* to stretch, go slow, lay down (*arms*); -en-arbeiter *nm.* plate-layer; -en-beleuchtung *nf.* route lighting (*av.*).

Streich [shtrīsh] *nm.* (-e) stroke, blow, trick; -hölzchen *n.* match; -instrument *n.* string instrument. [stroke.

Streicheln [shtrī'sheln] *vt.* to

Streichen [shtrī'shen] *vi. i.* to stroke, touch, play, paint, strike out, furl, strike; *i.* ramble, wander, run, make one's way.

Streif'abteilung [shtrīfe'ap-tile-ōong] *nf.* raiding-party; -band *n.* wrapper; -blick *nm.* passing glance; -e *nf.* patrol; -en *vt.i.* to graze, scrape, stroke, touch, roam, wander, patrol; *nm.* (-) stripe, slip, strip, sector (*av.*), band (*rad.*); -enaufklärung *nf.* reconnaissance patrolling; -endienst *nm.* patrolling; -enkraftwagen *nm.* police patrol-car; -posten *nm.* roving sentry; -schuss *nm.* grazing shot; -zug *nm.* raid, expedition.

Streik [shtrike] *nm.* (-e) strike; -en *vi.* to strike; -brecher *nm.* strike-breaker; -kasse *nf.* strike-fund; -posten *nm.* strike-picket.

Streit [shtrite] *nm.* dispute, conflict; -bar *a.* valiant, warlike; -en *vi. ir.* to struggle, dispute; -frage *nf.* matter in dispute; -ig *a.* in dispute, debatable; -igkeit *nf.* dispute, quarrel; -lustig *a.* quarrelsome; -sucht *nf.* pugnacity.

Streng [shtreng] *a.* severe, strict, harsh; -e *nf.* severity, strictness, austerity; -gläubig *a.* orthodox.

Streu [shtroy] *nf.* litter, bed of straw; **-en** *vt.* to strew, spread; **-mine** *nf.* floating mine; **-ung** *nf.* dispersal; **-zucker** *nm.* castor sugar.

Strich [shtrish] *nm.*(-e) stroke, line, dash, region, grain, mind, compass point; **-einteilung** *nf.* calibration; **-punkt** *nm.* semicolon; **-vogel** *nm.* bird of passage.

Stricheln [shtrish'eln] *vt.* to hatch.

Strick [shtrik] *nm.* (-e) rope, cord, snare, rogue; **-arbeit** *nf.* knitting; **-en** *vt.i.* to knit, en-snare; **-erin** *nf.* knitter; **-leiter** *nf.* rope-ladder.

Striegel [shtree'gel] *nm.* (-) curry-comb; **-n** *vt.* to curry, comb.

Strieme [shtree'mer] *nf.* **Striemen** (-) stripe, weal.

Strikt(e) [shtrikt'er] *a. ad.* strict(ly), accurate(ly).

Strippe [shtrip'er] *nf.* band, string, lace, tab, strap.

Strittig [shtrit'ish] *a.* in dispute.

Stroh [shtroh] *n.* straw, thatch; **-dach** *n.* thatched roof; **-halm** *nm.* straw; **-mann** *nm.* dummy, lay figure; **-sack** *nm.* straw mattress; **-witwe** *nf.* grass-widow.

Strolch [shtrolsh] *nm.* (-e) idler, tramp; **-en** *vi.* to tramp, loaf about.

Strom [shtrome] *nm.* (Ströme) stream, current; **-abwärts** *ad.* down-stream; **-aufwärts** *ad.* up-stream; **-kreis** *nm.* circuit; **-linienförmig** *a.* stream-lined; **-messer** *nm.* ammeter; **-richter** *nm.* rectifier, converter (*el.*); **-schiene** *nf.* live rail; **-spannung** *nf.* voltage; **-unterbrecher** *nm.* cut-out; **-wender** *nm.* commutator; **-zuführungszange** *nf.* trolley.

Ström'en [shtrer'men] *vi.* to stream, flow, rush; **-ung** *nf.*

stream, flow, tendency, movement.

Strophe [shtroh'fer] *nf.* verse.

Strotzen [shtrot'sen] *vi.* to abound in, be full of; **-d** *a.* robust.

Strudel [shtroo'del] *nm.* whirlpool, rapids; **-n** *vi.* to eddy, gush, whirl.

Struktur [shtrook-toorr'] *nf.* structure; **-ell** *a. ad.* structural(ly).

Strumpf [shtroompf] *nm.* (Strümpfe) stocking, sock; **-band** *n.* garter; **-händler** *nm.* hosier; **-halter** *nm.* suspender; **-waren** *pl.* hosiery. [stump.

Strunk [shtroonk] *nm.* (-e)

Struppig [shtroo'pish] *a.* shaggy, unkempt.

Stube [shtoo'ber] *nf.* room; **-narrest** *nm.* confinement to quarters; **-ngelehrte(r)** *m.w.* book-worm; **-nhocker** *nm.* stay-at-home; **-nmädchen** *n.* housemaid; **-nrein** *a.* house-trained.

Stuck [shtook] *nm.* stucco.

Stück [shtyook] *n.* (-e) piece, bit, play; **-arbeit** *nf.* piece work; **-chen** *n.* (-) little piece, scrap; **-eln** *vt.* to cut up, mince; **-en** *vt.* to patch; **-gut** *n.* general cargo; **-lohn** *nm.* piece-work wages; **-weise** *ad.* piece-meal; **-werk** *n.* patchwork, bad workmanship.

Student [shtoo-dent'] *m.w.* student; **-in** *nf.* female student; **-isch** *a.* undergraduate.

Studie [shtoo'di-er] *nf.* sketch, study (*art*).

Studier'en [shtoo-deer'ren] *vt.i.* to study; **-lampe** *nf.* reading-lamp; **-stube** *nf.* **-zimmer** *n.* study.

Stufe [shtoo'fer] *nf.* step, degree, stage; **-nfolge** *nf.* succession; **-nleiter** *nf.* scale; **-nweise** *ad.* gradually.

Stuhl [shtool] *nm.* (Stühle)

chair; -bein n. chair-leg; -gang
nm. evacuation (of bowels).

Stuka [shtōō'kah] n. dive-bomber.

Stulp'e [shtōōl'per] nf. boot-top, cuff; -handschuh nm. gauntlet; -stiefel nm. top-boot.

Stülp'en [shtyōōl'pen] vt. to turn up, tilt, invert; -nase nf. snub-nose.

Stumm [shtōōm] a. dumb, silent; -heit nf. dumbness.

Stummel [shtōō'mel] nm. (-) stump.

Stümper [shtyōōm'perr] nm. bungler; -n vi. to bungle.

Stumpf [shtōōmpf] a. blunt, dull; -heit nf. bluntness, indifference, apathy; -nase nf. snub-nose; -sinn nm. dullness, stupidity; -sinnig a. stupid, dull.

Stund'e [shtōōn'der] nf. hour; -en vt. to grant a respite; -enkilometer pl. kilometres per hour; -enlang a. for hours; -enplan n. time-table; -ung nf. delay, respite.   [hourly.

Stündlich [shtyōōnt'lish] a.

Sturm [shtōōrrm] nm. storm, assault, attack; -abteilung nf. assault detachment (mil.); -geschütz n. assault boat; -landeboot n. assault boat; -panzer nm. assault tank; -warnung nf. gale warning; -wind nm. gale, hurricane.

Stürm'en [shtyōōrr'men] vt.i. to storm, rage; -isch a. stormy.

Sturz [shtōōrrts] nm. (Stürze) fall, crash, collapse; -bach nm. torrent; -flug nm. nose-dive; -helm nm. crash-helmet; -kampfflugzeug n. dive-bomber; -see nf. heavy sea; -visier n. bomb sight; -wagen nm. tilt-cart.

Stürzen [shtyōōrrt'sen] vt. to hurl, overturn, upset; r. rush, plunge; i. fall heavily, dash, dive (av.).

Stute [shtōō'ter] nf. mare.

Stütz'balken [shtyōōts'bal-ken] nm. joist; -e nf. prop, joist, household help; -mauer nf. buttress; -punkt nm. strong-point (mil.).

Stutz'en [shtōōt'sen] vt. to clip, dock, cut, trim; i. falter, be taken aback; -er nm. (-) dandy; -ig a. taken aback; -uhr nf. clock.

Subjekt [zōop-yekt'] n. (-e) subject; -iv a. subjective; -ivität nf. subjectivity.

Sublimieren [zōo-bli-meer'ren] vt. to sublimate.

Subskribent [zōop-skri-bent'] m.w. subscriber.

Subskription [zōop-skrip-syohn'] nf. subscription.

Substantiv [zōop'stan-teef'] n. (-e) noun.   [substance.

Substanz [zōop-stants'] nf.

Subtil [zōop-teel'] a. subtle.

Subtrahieren [zōop-tra-heer'-ren] vt. to subtract.

Subvention [zōop-vent-syohn'] nf. subsidy, grant.

Such'e [zōoch'er] nf. search; -en vt. to seek, look for, search, try; -er nm. (-) seeker, view-finder; -stellung nf. radio-location site. [passion, disease.

Sucht [zōocht] nf. mania, -elei nf. slovenly work; -scribble; -elhaft a. dirty, slovenly; -eln vi. to bungle, muddle, work in a slovenly way.

Süd [zōot] nm. (-e) boiling; -en nm. south; -früchte pl. fruit from the south; -lich a. southern; -wärts ad. southward.

Suggerieren [zōog-ger-reer'-ren] vt. to suggest.

Suggestion [zōo-ges-tyohn'] nf. suggestion.

Sühn'e [zyōo'ner] nf. expiation; -en vt. to atone for, expiate; -ung nf. expiation.

Sultan [zōol'tahn] nm. (-e) sultan; -ine nf. sultana.

Sülze [zyöolt'ser] *nf.* brawn, jellied meat; **-n** *vt.* to jelly.

Summarisch [zoo-mah'rish] *a.* summary, concise.

Summe [zoo'mer] *nf.* sum, total. [buzz.

Summen [zoo'men] *vi.* to

Summieren [zoo-meer'ren] *vt. r.* to add up (to).

Sumpf [zoompf] *nm.* (-e) swamp, marsh, sump (*aut.*); **-fieber** *n.* malaria; **-ig** *a.* marshy.

Sund [zoont] *nm.* (-e) sound, straits, channel.

Sünd'e [zyön'der] *nf.* sin; **-enbock** *nm.* scapegoat; **-er** *nm.*, **-erin** *nf.* sinner; **-flut** *nf.* deluge; **-haft**, **-ig** *a.* sinful; **-igen** *vi.* to sin.

Superlativ [zoo'pairr-la-teef] *nm.* (-e) superlative.

Suppe [zoo'per] *nf.* soup.

Surren [zoor'ren] *vi.* to buzz, hum. [(-e) substitute.

Surrogat [zoor-ro-gaht'] *n.*

Süss [zyöoss] *a.* sweet; **-e** *nf.* sweetness; **-en** *vt.* to sweeten; **-holz** *n.* liquorice; **-igkeit** *nf.* sweetness, sweet; **-lich** *a.* sweetish, sickly, sentimental; **-speise** *nf.* pudding, sweet; **-stoff** *nm.* saccharin; **-wasser** *n.* fresh water.

Symbol [zyöom-bohl'] *n.* (-e) symbol; **-isch** *a.* symbolic(al).

Symmetr'ie [zyöo-may-tree'] *nf.* symmetry; **-isch** *a.* symmetrical.

Sympath'ie [zyöom-pa-tee'] *nf.* sympathy; **-isch** *a.* congenial, pleasant; **-isieren** *vi.* to sympathize.

Symphonie [zyöom-fo-nee'] *nf.* symphony.

Symptomatisch [zyöom-to-mah'tish] *a.* symptomatic.

Synagoge [zyöo-na-goh'ger] *nf.* synagogue.

Syndikat [zyöon-di-kaht'] *n.* combine, syndicate.

Synkop'e [zyöon-koh'per] *nf.*

syncope; **-ieren** *vt.* to syncopate. [synod.

Synode [zyöo-noh'der] *nf.*

Synonym [zyöo-no-neem'] *n.* synonym.

Syntax [zyöon'tax] *nf.* syntax.

Synthese [zyöon-tay'zer] *nf.* synthesis. [syphilis.

Syphilis [zyöo'fi-liss] *nf.*

System [zyöo-stame'] *n.* (-e) system; **-atisch** *a.* systematic.

Szen'e [st-say'ner] *nf.* scene, stage; **-erie** *nf.* scenery; **-isch** *a.* scenic.

T

Tabak [ta'bak] *nm.* (-e) tobacco; **-händler** *nm.* tobacconist.

Tabell'arisch [ta-bel-ahr'rish] *a.* tabulated; **-e** *nf.* table, schedule, index.

Tachometer [tach-o-may'terr] *nm.* (-) speedometer (*aut.*).

Tadel [tah'del] *nm.* (-) blame, censure, scolding; **-haft** *a.* faulty, to blame; **-los** *a.* faultless, irreproachable; **-n** *vt.* to blame, censure; **-nswert** *a.* blameworthy; **-sucht** *nf.* fault-finding.

Tadler [tah'dlerr] *nm.* (-), **-in** *nf.* fault-finder.

Tafel [tah'fel] *nf.* board, table, meal, slab, tablet, chart, diagram, index; **-birne** *nf.* dessert pear; **-zeug** *n.* table-linen, silver.

Tafel'chen [tafe'el-shen] *n.* (-) lozenge; **-n** *vt.* to inlay; **-ung** *nf.* panelling, inlaying.

Taffet [taf'et] *nm.*, **Taft** *nm.* (-e) taffeta.

Tag [tahk] *nm.* (-e) day, day-light; **-arbeiter** *nm.* (casual) labourer; **-arbeiterin** *nf.* charwoman; **-ebau** *nm.* outcrop (*coal*); **-ebuch** *n.* diary, day-book, journal, log (*nav.*, *av.*).

-dieb *nm.* idler; **-egeld** *n*. daily allowance; **-elang** *ad.* for days; **-elöhner** *nm.* day-labourer; **-esanbruch** *nm.* dawn; **-esbefehl** *nm.* daily routine order, order of the day (*mil.*); **-esjagd** *nf.* day-fighting (*av.*); **-esjäger** *nm.* day-fighter (*av.*); **-eslicht** *n*. daylight; **-essatz** *nm.* daily rate; **-eszeit** *nf.* time of day; **-täglich** *ad.* daily.

Tagen [tah'gen] *vi.* to dawn, sit, meet.

Täglich [take'lish] *a, ad.* daily.

Tagung [tah'gŏŏng] *nf.* session, meeting.

Taille [tal'yer] *nf.* waist.

Takel [tah'kel] *n.* (-) tackle; **-n** *vt.* to rig.

Takt [takt] *nm.* (-e) time (*music*), tact; **-gefühl** *n*. er *nm.* tact, tactfulness; **-los** *a.* tactless, indiscreet; **-losigkeit** *nf.* tactlessness; **-stock** *nm.* (conductor's) baton; **-voll** *a.* tactful.

Taktik [tak'tik] *nf.* tactics; **-er** *nm.* (-) tactician; **-isch** *a.* tactical.

Tal [tahl] *n.* (**Täler**) valley, dale; **-fahrt** *nf.* descent; **-sohle** *nf.* bottom of valley; **-sperre** *nf.* barrage, dam; **-wärts** *a.* downhill.

Talar [ta-larr'] *nm.* (-e) robe, gown (*university*).

Talent [ta-lent'] *n.* (-e) talent; **-voll** *a.* talented, gifted.

Taler [tah'lerr] *nm.* (-) taler, florin.

Talg [talk] *nm.* tallow, suet, grease; **-licht** *n*. tallow-candle.

Talisman [tah'liss-man] *nm.* (-e) talisman, mascot.

Talje [tal'yer] *nf.* tackle.

Talk [talk] *nm.* talc(um); **-erde** *nf.* talcite, magnesia.

Tambour [tam'bŏŏrr] *nm.* et) drummer, drum.

Tambur [tam'bŏŏrr] *nm.* (-e) tambour-frame; **-ieren** (-e) to embroider on a tambour-frame; **-in** *n*. (-e) tambourine.

Tamponieren [tam-po-neer'ren] *vt.* to plug (*wound*).

Tand [tant] *nm.* trifle, toy, trinket, finery.

Tändelei [ten-der-lie'] *nf.* trifling, dawdling, flirting.

Tändeln [ten'deln] *vi.* to trifle, dawdle, flirt; **-markt** *nm.* second-hand market; **-schürze** *nf.* fancy apron.

Tang [tang] *nm.* (-e) seaweed.

Tank [tank] *nm.* (-s) tank; **-abwehr** *nf.* anti-tank defence; **-anlage** *nf.* fuel tank; **-büchse** *nf.* anti-tank rifle; **-en** *vi.* to fuel, fill up with petrol; **-falle** *nf.* tank-trap; **-lager** *n*. fuel depot; **-meister** *nm.* petrol pump attendant; **-pfeiler** *nm.* tank obstacles, asparagus beds; **-motorschiff** *n*. motor tanker; **-schiff** *n.* tanker; **-stelle** *nf.* petrol pump, service station; **-wagen** *nm.* tank lorry.

Tanne [tan'ner] *nf.* fir; **-nbaum** *nm.* fir-tree; **-nwald** *nm.* fir-wood.

Tante [tan'ter] *nf.* aunt.

Tanz [tants] *nm.* (**Tänze**) dance; **-boden** *nm.* dance-hall; **-en** *vt.i.* to dance; **-stunde** *nf.* dancing-lesson.

Tänzeln [tent'seln] *vi.* to trip along, amble.

Tänzer [tent'serr] *nm.* (-), **-in** *nf.* dancer.

Tapete [ta-pay'ter] *nf.* wall-paper, tapestry.

Tapezier'er [ta-pet-seer'rerr] *nm.* (-) paper-hanger, decorator; **-arbeit** *nf.* upholstery; **-en** *vt.* to paper.

Tapfer [tap'ferr] *a.* brave; **-keit** *nf.* courage, bravery.

Tapisserie [ta-pi-sse-ree'] *nf.* tapestry. [poke, fumble.

Tappen [tap'en] *vi.* to grope,

Täppisch [tep'ish] *a.* clumsy.

Tarif [ta-reef'] *nm.* (-e) tariff, scale of charges, rate, fares; **-lohn** *nm.* standard wages.

Tarn'bezug [tarrn'ber-tsōōk] *nm.* camouflage covering; **-en** *vt.* to camouflage; **-gerät** *n.* camouflage equipment; **-mittel** *n.* camouflage material; **-scheinwerfer** *nm.* screened head-lamp (*aut.*); **-ung** *nf.* camouflaging; **-ungstruppe** *nf.* camouflage troops; **-zahl** *nf.* code number; **-zeichen** *n.* code sign.

Tasche [tash'er] *nf.* pocket, hand-bag; **-nbuch** *n.* pocketbook; **-ndieb** *nm.* pickpocket; **-nfeuerzeug** *n.* cigarette lighter; **-nformat** *n.* pocket-size; **-ngeld** *n.* pocket-money; **-nlampe** *nf.* electric torch; **-nmesser** *nm.* penknife; **-nspieler** *nm.* conjurer; **-ntuch** *n.* handkerchief; **-nuhr** *nf.* watch.

Tasse [tass'er] *nf.* cup, cup and saucer; **-nkopf** *nm.* cup.

Tastatur [tas-ta-tōōrr'] *nf.* keyboard.

Tast'e [tas'ter] *nf.* key (*piano, etc.*); **-en** *vt.* to feel, touch; **-**, grope; **-enfeld** *n.* keyboard; **-sinn** *nm.* sense of touch.

Tatauieren [ta-tow-eer'ren] *vt.i.* to tattoo.

Tat [taht] *nf.* act, deed, action; **-bestand** *nm.* facts of the case; **-bestandaufnahme** *nf.* deposition; **-enlos** *a.* inactive; **-kraft** *nf.* energetic, active; **-sache** *nf.* fact; **-sächlich** *a.* actual, real, effective; *ad.* in fact, as a matter of fact.

Täter [tate'err] *nm.* (-) perpetrator, culprit; **-schaft** *nf.* guilt.

Tätig [tate'ish] *a.* active, employed, busy; **-keit** *nf.* activity, occupation.

Tätigen [tate'i-gen] *vt.* to conclude, carry out (*com.*).

Tätlich [tate'lish] *a.* violent; **-keit** *nf.* assault, violence.

Tätowieren = **Tatauieren.**

Tatze [tat'ser] *nf.* paw.

Tau [tow] *n.* (-e) rope, hawser, cable; **-en** *vt.* to tow; **-werk** *n.* rigging; **-ziehen** *n.* tug-of-war.

Tau [tow] *nm.* dew; **-en** *vi.* to fall (*dew*), melt, thaw; **-perle** *nf.* dew-drop; **-wetter** *n.* thaw.

Taub [towp] *a.* deaf, hollow (*nut*), addled (*egg*); **-heit** *nf.* deafness; **-stumm** *a.* deaf and dumb.

Taube [tow'ber] *nf.* dove, pigeon; **-nschlag** *nm.* dovecot.

Tauch'en [towch'en] *vt.i.* to dip, plunge, dive, submerge (*nav.*); **-boot** *n.* submarine; **-er** *nm.* (-) diver; **-rohr** *n.* immersion tube (*aut.*); **-sieder** *nm.* immersion heater, immerser.

Tauf'e [tow'fer] *nf.* baptism; **-becken** *n.*, **-stein** *nm.* font; **-name** *nm.* Christian name; **-pate** *m.w.* godfather; **-zeuge** *m.w.* sponsor.

Taug'en [tow'gen] *vi.* to be of use, fit, serve; **-enichts** *nm.* (-e) good-for-nothing; **-lich** *a.* suitable, fit; **-lichkeit** *nf.* suitability, fitness. **-fender** (*nav.*).

Taukranz [tow'krants] *nm.* fender (*nav.*).

Taumel [tow'mel] *nm.* staggering, frenzy, passion; **-ig** *a.* reeling, staggering; **-n** *vi.* to stagger, reel, totter.

Tausch [towsh] *nm.* (-e) exchange, barter, transfusion (*blood*); **-en** *vt.* to exchange, barter; **-handel** *nm.* barter.

Täusch'en [toy'shen] *vt.* to deceive, cheat, delude; **-end** *a.* deceptive, delusive, deceiving; **-ung** *nf.* deception, illusion.

Tausend [tow'zent] *num.* thousand; *n.* (-e) thousand; **-künstler** *nm.* conjurer.

Taxameter [tax'a-may-terr] *nm.* (-) taximeter; **-droschke** *nf.* taxicab.

Tax'e [tax'er] *nf.* tax, valuation, rate, charge; **-ieren** *vt.* to assess, estimate.

Taxi [tax'i] *n.* (-s) taxi; **-fahrer** *nm.* taxi-driver.

Taxus [tax'ŏŏss] *nm.* (-) yew.

Techni'k [tesh'nik] *nf.* engineering, technical science, technique, skill; **-ker** *nm.* (-) technician, mechanic, engineer; **-sch** *a.* technical.

Tee [tay] *nm.* (-s) tea; **-löffel** *nm.* tea-spoon; **-maschine** *nf.* tea-urn; **-topf** *nm.* tea-pot.

Teer [tair] *nm.* tar; **-en** *vt.* to tar; **-farbstoffe** *pl.* aniline dyes; **-tuch** *n.* tarpaulin.

Teich [tish] *nm.* (-e) pond.

Teig [tike] *nm.* (-e) dough, paste; **-ig** *a.* doughy; **-ware** *nf.* farinaceous food.

Teil [tile] *nm.* (-e) part, share, component; **-bar** *a.* divisible; **-chen** *n.* atom, particle; **-haber** *nm.* partner, sharer; **-haftig** *a.* sharing in; **-nahme** *nf.* participation, interest, sympathy; **-nehmen** *vi.* to take part (in); **-nehmer** *nm.* participant, member; **-s** *ad.* partly; **-strich** *nm.* graduation mark; **-überholung** *nf.* partial overhaul; **-weise** *ad.* in part.

Teil'en [tile'en] *vt.* to share, divide; **-ung** *nf.* division, graduation, scale. [plexion.

Teint [tang] *nm.* (-s) complexion.

Telefon = Telephon.

Telefunken [te-le-fŏŏn'ken] *pl.* wireless telegraphy.

Telegramm [te-le-gram'] *n.* (-e) telegram, wire, cable; **-adresse** *nf.* telegraphic address; **-formular** *n.* telegram form.

Telegraph'ie [te-le-gra-fee'] *nf.* telegraphy; **-ieren** *vt.i.* to telegraph, wire; **-isch** *a.* telegraphic.

Teleobjektiv [te-le-op-yek-teef'] *n.* (-e) tele-photo lens.

Telepathie [te-le-pa-tee'] *nf.* telepathy.

Telephon [te-le-fohn'] *n.* (-e) telephone; **-anruf** *nm.* telephone call; **-ieren** *vt.i.* to telephone; **-isch** *a.* telephonic; **-ist** *m.w.* **-istin** *nf.* telephonist;

-verbindung *nf.* telephone connection; **-zelle** *nf.* call-box; **-zentrale** *nf.* telephone exchange.

Telephotographie [te-le-fo-to-gra-fee'] *nf.* tele-photography.

Teller [tel'err] *nm.* (-) plate; **-gericht** *n.* one-course meal; **-mine** *nf.* anti-tank mine; **-tuch** *n.* dish-cloth.

Tellur [tel-ŏŏr'] *n.* tellurium.

Tempel [tem'pel] *nm.* (-) temple. [distemper.

Tempera [tem'per-rah] *nf.*

Temperament [tem-per-ra-ment'] *n.* (-e) temper, temperament, mood, character; **-voll** *a.* temperamental, high-spirited.

Temperatur [tem-per-ra-toorr'] *nf.* temperature.

Tempo [tem'poh] *n.* (-s, Tempi) time, measure (*music*).

Tendenz [ten-dents'] *nf.* tendency, trend, inclination; **-roman** *nm.* novel with a purpose.

Tendenziös [ten-dent-si-erss'] *a.* biased, one-sided.

Tender [ten'derr] *nm.* (-) tender, supply vessel; **-lokomotive** *nf.* tank engine.

Tenne [ten'er] *nf.* threshing floor.

Tennis [ten'iss] *n.* tennis; **-platz** *nm.* tennis-court; **-schläger** *nm.* tennis-racket; **-spieler** *nm.* tennis-player; **-spielplatz** *nm.* tennis-court.

Tenor [te-norr'] *nm.* (-e) tenor; **-ist** *m.w.* **-sänger** *nm.* tenor.

Teppich [tep'ish] *nm.* (-e) carpet; **-kehrmaschine** *nf.* carpet-sweeper; **-schoner** *nm.* coarse woollen floor-covering.

Termin [tairr-meen'] *nm.* (-e) term, time; **-geschäft** *n.* business in futures; **-zahlung** *nf.* payment by instalments.

Terminologie [tairr-mi-no-lo-gee'] *nf.* terminology.

Terpentin [tairr-pen-teen'] n. (-e) turpentine.

Terrasse [tair-rass'er] nf. terrace, foreground.

Terrine [tair-ree'ner] nf. tureen.

Territorial [tair-ri-tor-ri-ahl'] a. territorial.

Terror [ter-rorr'] nm. terror, terrorism; **-isieren** vt. to terrorize.

Tertia [tairr'tsi-ah] nf. fourth.

Terz [tairrts] nf. third (music); **-iar** nm. (gen. -s; pl. -e) tertiary.

Testament [tes-ta-ment'] n. (-e) will, testament; **-svollstrecker** nm. executor.

Testat [tes-taht'] n. (-e) certificate; **-ator** nm. testator.

Testieren [tes-teer'ren] vt. to bequeath, testify.

Teuer [toy'err] a. dear, expensive; **-ung** nf. scarcity, high prices; **-ungszulage** nf. cost of living bonus.

Teufel [toy'fel] nm. (-) devil; **-elei** nf. devilry; **-lisch** a. devilish, diabolical.

Text [text] nm. (-e) text, letterpress; **-buch** n. words (opera).

Textil [tex-teel'] a. textile; **-gewerbe** n., **-industrie** nf. textile industry; **-waren** textiles.

Textur [tex-tōōr'] nf. texture.

Theater [tay-ah'terr] n. (-) theatre; **-besucher** nm. playgoer; **-kasse** nf. box-office; **-spiel** n. acting; **-stück** n. play.

Theatralisch [tay-a-trah'lish] a. theatrical.

Thema [tay'mah] n. (Themen, -s) theme, topic, subject.

Theologe [tay-o-loh'ger] nm. theologian; **-ie** nf. theology; **-isch** a. theological.

Theoretiker [tay-o-ray'ti-kerr] nm. (-) theoretician, theorist; **-etisch** a. theoretic(al); **-ie** nf. theory.

Theosophie [tay-o-zo-fee'] nf. theosophy; **-isch** a. theosophical.

Therapeutisch [tair-ra-poy'tish] a. therapeutic.

Therapie [tair-ra-pee'] nf. therapy. [thermic.

Thermisch [tairr'mish] a.

Thermit [tairr-meet'] n. thermite.

Thermo'chemie [tairr-mo-shay-mee'] nf. thermochemistry; **-meter** n. (-) thermometer.

Thermosflasche [tairr'mossflash-er] nf. thermos flask.

Thomas'eisen [toe'mas-ize-en] n. basic iron; **-schlacke** nf. basic slag.

Thron [trone] nm. (-e) throne; **-besteigung** nf. accession; **-erbe** m.w. heir to the throne.

Thunfisch [toon'fish] nm. (-e) tunny. [thyme.

Thymian [tyoo'mi-ahn] nm.

Ticken [tick'en] vi. to tick.

Tief [teef] a. deep, profound; n. depression, rut; **-angriff** nm. low-level attack (av.); **-bau** nm. mining; **-druck** nm. low pressure; **-e** nf. deepness, depth; **-ebene** nf. plain; **-einbruch** nm. penetration in depth (mil.); **-flieger** nm. low-flying aircraft; **-gang** nm. draught (ship); **-gegliedert** a. in depth (defence); **-greifend** a. far-reaching; **-land** n. lowlands; **-lot** n. depth-sounder; **-see** nf. deep sea; **-sinn** nm. pensiveness, melancholy; **-sinnig** a. pensive, melancholy, profound; **-stand** nm. low level.

Tiegel [tee'gel] nm. (-) saucepan, crucible.

Tier [teerr] nm. (-e) animal, beast; **-arzt** nm. veterinary surgeon; **-garten** nm. zoological gardens; **-isch** a. bestial; **-kreis** nm. zodiac; **-kunde** nf. zoology.

Tiger [tee'gerr] nm. (-) tiger; **-in** nf. tigress.

Tilg'en [til'gen] vt. to efface, delete, cancel, extinguish, blot out, pay off; **-ung** nf. cancellation, blotting out, redemption, payment. [tincture.

Tinktur [tink-tōōrr'] nf.

Tinte [tin'ter] nf. ink; **-nfass** n. inkstand; **-nfleck** nm. blot; **-nstift** nm. copying, indelible pencil.

Tipp'en [tip'en] vt.i. to tap, touch, type; **-fräulein** n. typist.

Tisch [tish] nm. (-e) table, meal, board; **-decke** nf. table-cloth; **-rede** nf. after-dinner speech; **-tennis** n. table-tennis; **-tuch** n. table-cloth.

Tischler [tish'lerr] nm. (-) carpenter, joiner, cabinet-maker; **-arbeit** nf. carpentry, joinery, cabinet-making; **-ei** nf. joiner's, cabinet-maker's workshop, see also **-arbeit**; **-n** vi. to do carpentry, etc.

Titel [tee'tel] nm. (-) title; **-bild** n. frontispiece; **-n** vt. to entitle (film); **-rolle** nf. title-role; **-verteidiger** nm. title-holder.

Titulieren [ti-tōō-leer'ren] vt. to give a title to, entitle. [rave.

Toben [toh'ben] vi. to rage, **Tob'sucht** [tohp'zōōcht] nf. madness, raving, **-süchtig** a. raving.

Tochter [toch'terr] nf. (Töchter) daughter.

Tod [tote] nm. death; **-esanzeige** nf. obituary (notice); **-esfall** nm. death; **-eskampf** nm. agony; **-esnachweis** nm. proof of death; **-esstoss** nm. death-blow; **-esstrafe** nf. capital punishment; **-estag** nm. anniversary of death; **-esurteil** n. sentence of death; **-krank** a. seriously ill; **-müde** a. tired to death, worn out; **-sünde** nf. deadly sin. [mortal, fatal.

Tödlich [tert'lish] a. deadly,

Toilette [tva-let'er] nf. dressing-table, toilet, lavatory; **-npapier** n. toilet-paper.

Toleran' [to-ler-rant'] a. tolerant; **-z** nf. tolerance, permissible deviation (tec.).

Toll [tol] a. mad, raving, frantic; **-en** vi. to romp; **-haus** n. mad-house; **-häusler** nm. (-) madman; **-heit** nf. madness, fury, frenzy; **-kühn** a. fool-hardy; **-kühnheit** nf. rashness, foolhardiness.

Tolle [tol'er] nf. tuft, tassel.

Tölp'el [terl'pel] nm. (-) oaf, lout, bumpkin; **-isch** a. clumsy, loutish.

Tomate [to-mah'ter] nf. tomato.

Ton [tone] nm. clay; **-erde** nf. aluminium oxide; **-ig** a. clayey, **-pfeife** nf. clay-pipe; **-waren** pl. pottery, earthenware.

Ton [tone] nm. (Töne) sound, note, tone, tint, music; **-abnehmer** nm. pick-up; **-angebend** a. leading; **-art** nf. musical key; **-dichter** nm. composer; **-fall** nm. intonation; **-film** nm. talkie; **-folge** nf. scale, melody; **-höhe** nf. pitch; **-kunst** nf. music; **-künstler** nm. musician; **-leiter** nf. scale; **-los** a. soundless, unaccented; **-spur** nf. sound-track (film); **-stärke** nf. level of tone (rad.); **-stufe** nf. pitch; **-taube** nf. clay-pigeon; **-welle** nf. sound-wave.

Tonen [tōōn'en] vt. to tone (phot.).

Tönen [ter'nen] vi. to (re)sound.

Tönern [ter'nerrn] a. (of) clay.

Tonne [ton'er] nf. barrel, tun, ton (capacity); **-ngehalt** nm. tonnage (ship). [jar.

Topf [topf] nm. (Töpfe) pot,

Töpfer [terp'ferr] nm. (-) potter; **-gut** n. waren pl. earthenware, pottery; **-scheibe** nf. potter's wheel.

Topp [top] int. all right, agreed.

Topp [top] nm. (-e) mast-head; **-laterne** nf. mast-head light; **-mast** nm. topmast.

Tor [torr] *n.* (-e) gate, goal; -weg *nm.* gateway.

Tor [torr] *m.w.* fool; -heit *nf.* folly.

Torf [torrf] *nm.* (-e) peat; -moor *n.* peat-bog; -stechen *n.* peat-cutting.

Törin [ter'in] *nf.* fool.

Töricht [ter'risht] *a.* foolish.

Tornister [torr-nis'terr] *nm.* (-) knapsack, pack, kitbag; -funkgerät *n.* portable wireless set (*mil.*).

Torpedieren [torr-ped-eer'ren] *vt.* to torpedo.

Torpedo [torr-pay'do] *n.* (-s) torpedo; -fangboot *n.* torpedo recovery boat; -flugzeug *n.* torpedo-bomber; -gürtel *nm.* anti-torpedo belt; -leitanlage *nf.* torpedo setting apparatus; -mechaniker *n.m.* torpedo-loader; -rohr *n.* torpedo-tube; -wand *nf.* anti-torpedo plate; -zelle *n.f.* torpedo-tank.

Torte [torr'ter] *nf.* fancy cake, tart, pie.

Tortur [torr-töör'] *nf.* torture.

Tosen [to'zen] *vi.* to roar.

Tot [tote] *a.* dead; -arbeiten *vr.* to work oneself to death; -macher *nm.* cemetery; -enbett *n.* death-bed; -engräber *nm.* grave-digger; -enhemd *n.* shroud; -enkopf *nm.* death's head; -enmarsch *nm.* funeral march; -enschau *nf.* inquest; -enschein *nm.* death certificate; -geboren *a.* still-born; -lachen *vr.* to roar with laughter; -punkt *nm.* dead centre; -schlag *nm.* manslaughter; -schläger *nm.* killer, life-preserver; -schweigen *vt.* to hush up; -sicher *a.* cocksure, absolutely certain; -stellen *vr.* to pretend to be dead; -stürzen *vr.* to be killed by a fall, crash; -treten *vt. ir.* to trample to death.

Totalisator [to-ta-li-zah'torr] *nm.* (*gen.* -s; *pl.* -en) tote.

Totalität [to-ta-li-tairt'] *a.* totalitarian; -staat *nm.* totalitarian state.

Töt'en [ter'ten] *vt.* to kill; -ung *nf.* killing, murder.

Tour [töörr] *nf.* tour, trip, revolution, turn; -enboot *n.* gig, clinker-built boat; -enrad *n.* cycle; -enwagen *nm.* touring car; -enzahl *nf.* number of revolutions; -enzähler *nm.* tachometer.

Tourist [töör-rist'] *m.w.* tourist; -enverkehr *nm.* tourist traffic.

Trab [trahp] *nm.* trot; -en *vi.* to trot.

Trabant [tra-bant'] *m.w.* satellite; -enstadt *nf.* satellite town.

Tracht [tracht] *nf.* costume, dress, load.

Trachten [tracht'en] *vi.* to strive, aspire, endeavour, conspire, attack.

Trächtig [tresh'tish] *a.* pregnant.

Trag'bahre [trahk'bar-rer] *nf.* stretcher; -balken *nm.* beam; -bar *a.* portable, bearable, wearable; -e *nf.* barrow; -deck *n.* -fläche *nf.* -flügel *nm.* wing (*av.*); -fähigkeit *nf.* tonnage, capacity, productivity; -riemen *nm.* carrying strap; -weite *nf.* range, importance; -werk *n.* supporting surface (*av.*); -zapfen *nm.* trunnion.

Tradition [tra-dit-si-ohn'] *nf.* tradition; -ell *a.* traditional.

Träg'e [tray'ger] *a.* lazy, inert, idle, slow; -heit *nf.* slowness, laziness, inertia, indolence.

Tragen [trah'gen] *vt. ir.* to carry, wear, bear, endure, transport.

Träger [tray'gerr] *nm.* (-) porter, bearer, girder (*tec.*); -flugzeug *n.* carrier-borne aircraft; -gestützt *a.* carrier-borne; -truppe *nf.* carrier-borne detachment (*mil.*).

Tragisch [trah'gish] *a.* tragic.

Tragödie [tra-ger'di-er] *nf.* tragedy.

Trainieren [tray-neer'ren] vt. to train, coach.

Training [tray'ning] n. training; -anzug nm. sports suit, training, athletic costume.

Trajekt [tra-yekt'] n. (-e) train-ferry.

Trakt'at [trak-taht'] nm. (-e) treatise, tract; -ieren vt. to treat.

Traktor [trak'tor] nm. (gen. -s; pl. -en) tractor.

Trällern [trel'errn] vi. to trill, sing, hum.

Trampel'n [tram'peln] vi. to trample, stamp; -faden nm. trip-wire.   [blubber.

Tran [trahn] nm. train oil.

Tranchier'en [tran-sheer'ren] vt. to carve; -besteck n. pair of carvers.

Transchieren = Tranchieren.

Träne [tray'ner] nf. tear; -n vi. to water; -ngas n. tear-gas.

Trank [trank] nm. (Tränke) drink, draught.

Tränke [trenk'er] nf. watering-pond; -n vt. to water, soak.

Transformator [trans-form-mah'torr] nm. (gen. -s; pl. -en) transformer; -anlage nf. transformer plant.   [transitive.

Transitiv [transs'i-teef] a.

Transmission [transs-miss-yohn'] nf. transmission (gear); -sanlage nf. transmission plant; -sriemen nm. driving belt; -swelle nf. connecting shaft.

Transpirieren [transs-pi-reer'ren] vi. to perspire.

Transport [transs-port'] nm. transport, carriage; -band n. conveyor (belt); -ieren vt. to transport, convey; -schiff n. troop-ship, transport.

Trapez [tra-paits'] n. (-e) trapeze.

Trappe [tra'per] nf. bustard.

Trass'ant [trass-ant'] m.w. drawer (com.); -at m.w. drawee; -ieren vt. to draw (bill).

Tratte [trat'er] nf. draft, bill of exchange.

Traube [trow'ber] nf. grape, bunch (of grapes); -nlese nf. vintage; -nmost nm. new wine.

Trau'en [trow'en] v.i.r. to trust, dare, venture; t. unite in marriage, marry; -ring nm. wedding ring; -schein nm. marriage certificate; -ung nf. wedding.

Trauer [trow'err] nf. grief, mourning; -anzeige nf. announcement of death; -fall nm. death, bereavement; -marsch nm. funeral march; -n vi. to mourn; -rand nm. black edge; -spiel n. tragedy; -zug nm. funeral cortège.

Trauf'e [trow'fer] nf. eaves, -rinne nf. gutter.

Träufeln [troy'feln] vt.i. to drop, drip.

Traulich [trow'lish] a. comfortable, intimate, cosy; -keit nf. comfort(ableness), smugness.

Traum [trowm] nm. (Träume) dream; -bild n. vision; -haft a. dreamlike.

Träum'en [troy'men] vt.i. to dream; -er nm. dreamer; -erei nf. dreaming, reverie; -erisch a. dreamy.

Traurig [trow'rish] a. sad, dismal; -keit nf. sadness, sorrow.

Traut [trowt] a. dear, cosy.

Treber [tray'berr] pl. husks, grape-skins.

Treff [tref] n. (-s) club (cards).

Treffen [tref'en] vt. ir. to hit, concern, make, take, catch; r. happen; n. encounter, meeting, engagement (mil.); -d a. pertinent, striking.

Treff'er [tref'err] nm. (-) good shot, (lucky) hit, prize; -punkt nm. meeting-place.

Trefflich [tref'lish] a. excellent; -keit nf. excellence.

Treib'en [tribe'en] vt. ir. to

drive, carry on, go in for, study, produce; *i.* drift, sprout; *n.* doings, activity; **-bake** *nf.* floating beacon; **-haus** *n.* hot-house; **-ladung** *nf.* propellant charge; **-mine** *nf.* floating mine; **-rad** *n.* fly-wheel; **-sand** *nm.* quicksand; **-stoff** *nm.* fuel, petrol.

Treidel'n [tride'eln] *vt.* to tow; **-pfad** *nm.* tow-path.

Trenn'bar [tren'barr] *a.* separable; **-en** *vt.* to divide, separate, dissolve, cut off (*ph.*); **-schärfe** *nf.* selectivity (*rad.*); **-ung** *nf.* separation, dissolution.

Trense [tren'zer] *nf.* snaffle.

Trepp'ab [trep-ap'] *ad.* down-stairs; **-auf** *ad.* upstairs; **-e** *nf.* stair(case); **-enabsatz** *nm.* landing; **-enhaus** *n.* hall, well.

Tresse [tress'er] *nf.* braid.

Tret'en [tray'ten] *vi. ir.* to tread, walk, step; *t.* tread on, kick, tramp too on; **-anlasser** *nm.* starter pedal (*aut.*); **-mine** *nf.* contact mine; **-mühle** *nf.* treadmill.

Treu [troy] *a.* faithful, true, sincere; **-bruch** *nm.* breach of faith; **-brüchig** *a.* disloyal; **-e** *nf.* loyalty, faithfulness; **-händer** *nm.* trustee; **-herzig** *a.* frank, trusting; **-lich** *ad.* faithfully; **-los** *a.* faithless.

Tribüne [tri-byoo'ner] *nf.* gallery, grand-stand, platform.

Tribut [tri-bo͞ot'] *n.* (-e) tribute.

Trichter [trish'terr] *nm.* (-) funnel, bomb-crater.   [trick.

Trick [trik] *nm.* (-s) stunt.

Trieb [treep] *nm.* (-e) impulse, instinct, shoot; **-feder** *nf.* spring; **-kraft** *nf.* momentum; **-rad** *n.* driving-wheel; **-werk** *n.* power unit, mechanism, machinery, engine.

Trief'äugig [treef'oi-gish] *a.* bleary; **-en** *vi.* to drip, trickle.

Trift [trift] *nf.* pasture, floating; **-ig** *a.* cogent, conclusive.

Trikot [tree-koh'] *n.* (-s) stockinet; **-hemd** *n.* sports shirt.

Trillern [tril'errn] *vi.* to trill, warble.   [term.

Trimester [tri-mes'terr] *n.*

Trimm'en [trim'en] *vt.* to trim (*ship*); **-tank** *nm.* trimming tank.

Trink'bar [trink'barr] *a.* drinkable; **-becher** *nm.* mug; **-en** *vi. ir.* to drink; **-er** *nm.* (-) drinker; **-geld** *n.* tip; **-glas** *n.* tumbler; **-spruch** *nm.* toast.

Trippeln [trip'eln] *vi.* to trip (along).   [gonorrhoea.

Tripper [trip'err] *nm.*

Tritt [trit] *nm.* (-e) step, tread, kick, pace; **-brett** *n.* running-board, foot-board, step.

Triumph [tri-o͞omf'] *nm.* triumph; **-bogen** *nm.* triumphant arch; **-ieren** *vi.* to triumph.

Trocken [trok'en] *a.* dry, arid; **-bagger** *nm.* excavator; **-dock** *n.* dry-dock; **-element** *n.* dry cell; **-heit** *nf.* dryness; **-legen** *vt.* to drain; **-milch** *nf.* powdered milk; **-ständer** *nm.* clothes-horse.   [dry.

Trocknen [trok'nen] *vt.* to dry.

Troddel [trod'el] *nf.* tassel.

Trödel [trer'del] *nm.* rubbish, lumber; **-bude** *nf.* old-clothes shop; **-n** *vi.* to deal in second-hand things, dawdle.

Trödler [trerd'lerr] *nm.* (-) second-hand dealer.

Trog [trohk] *nm.* (Tröge) trough.

Trommel [trom'el] *nf.* drum; **-fell** *n.* ear-drum; **-feuer** *n.* intense bombardment; **-n** *vi.* to drum; **-schläger** *nm.* drummer.   [drummer.

Trommler [trom'lerr] *nm.* (-)

Trompete [trom-pay'ter] *nf.* trumpet; **-r** *nm.* (-) trumpeter.

Tropen [troh'pen] *pl.* tropics; **-beständig** *a.* suitable for tropics; **-helm** *nm.* topee, sun helmet; **-hemd** *n.* tropical shirt; -untauglich *a.* unfit for service in tropics.

Tropisch [troh'pish] *a.* tropical.   [fool.

Tropf [tropf] *nm.* (Tröpfe) poor

Tröpfeln [trerp'feln] *vt.i* to drop, trickle.

Tropfen [trop'fen] *nm.* (-) drop: *vt.i. see* Tröpfeln; -weise *ad.* by drops.

Tross [tross] *nm.* (-e) transport (column), baggage, supply lines; -schiff *n.* supply ship.

Trosse [tross'er] *nf.* hawser, cable.

Trost [trohst] *nm.* comfort, consolation; -los *a.* disconsolate; -reich *a.* consoling.

Trösten [trer'sten] *vt.* to comfort, console; -er *nm.* (-) comforter; -lich *a.* comforting; -ung *nf.* comfort, consolation.

Trott [trot] *nm.* trot; -en *vi.* to trot.

Trotz [trots] *nm.* obstinacy, defiance; *pr.* in spite of; -dem *ad.*, *cj.* nevertheless, although; -ig *a.* obstinate, defiant.

Trüb [tryoop] *a.* gloomy, dark, dismal, doleful; -en *vt.* to dim, darken; -heit *nf.* gloom, dimness, muddiness; -sal *nf.* (-e) affliction; -selig *a.* sad; -sinn *nm.* depression; -sinnig *a.* miserable.

Trudel'kurve [troo'del-koörver *nf.* spiral curve; -n *vi.* to spin (*av.*).

Trüffel [tryoo'fel] *nf.* truffle.

Trug [trook] *nm.* delusion, fraud; -bild *n.* phantom; -mine *nf.* booby-trap; -schluss *nm.* false conclusion.

Trüge'n [tryoo'gen] *vt.i. ir.* to deceive, be deceptive; -risch *a.* deceitful, deceptive.

Truhe [troo'er] *nf.* chest, trunk.

Trümmer [tryoo'merr] *pl.* fragments, ruins; -haft *a.* ruinous; -mine *nf.* fragmentation mine.

Trumpf [troompf] *nm.* (Trümpfe) trump; -en *vt.i.* to trump.

Trunk [troonk] *nm.* (Trünke) drink; -en *a.* intoxicated; -enbold *nm.* drunkard; -enheit *nf.* intoxication; -sucht *nf.* alcoholism.

Trupp [troop] *nm.* (-s) troop, section, party; -e *nf.* troop, force, squad, formation, company (*actors*); -enausweis *nm.* identity card (*mil.*); -endienstlich *a.* disciplinary; -endienstweg *nm.* service channels; -enführer *nm.* commander of unit; -engattung *nf.* arm (of service); -engliederung *nf.* order of battle; -enkette *nf.* cordon; -enteil *nm.* unit; -enverband *nm.* formation.

Truthahn [troot'hahn] *nm.* (-hähne) turkey.

Tuberkulose [too-bairr-kooloh'zer] *nf.* tuberculosis.

Tuch [tooch] *n.* (-e, Tücher) cloth, shawl; -fühlung *nf.* close touch; -händler *nm.* draper; -hose *nf.* service trousers; -rock *nm.* tunic (*mil.*).

Tüchtig [tyooch'tish] *a.* able, efficient, capable, sound; -keit *nf.* efficiency, ability, capacity.

Tücke [tyoo'ker] *nf.* malice, spite; -sch *a.* spiteful.

Tugend [too'gent] *nf.* virtue; -haft *a.* virtuous.   [spout.

Tülle [tyoo'ler] *nf.* socket,

Tulpe [tool'per] *nf.* tulip.

Tummeln [too'meln] *vr.* to rush round, hurry, romp, gambol; *t.* exercise.

Tun [toon] *vt.i. ir.* to do, act, pretend; -lich *a.* practicable, feasible.

Tünche [tyoon'sher] *nf.* whitewash, distemper; -n *vt.* to whitewash, distemper.

Tunke [toon'ker] *nf.* sauce, gravy; -n *vt.* to dip.   [tunnel.

Tunnel [too'nel] *nm.* (-)

Tüpfel [tyoop'fel] *nm.* (-) dot,

spot; -n *vt.* to dot, spot, tick off. [dot, dab.

Tupfen [tŏŏp'fen] *vt.* to tap.

Tür [tyŏŏrr] *nf.* door.

Turbine [tŏŏrr-bee'ner] *nf.* turbine. [turquoise.

Türkis [tyŏŏrr-keess] *nm.* (-e)

Turm [tŏŏrm], *nm.* (**Türme**) tower, steeple, castle (*chess*), pylon (*el.*), turret (*tank*), conning tower (*nav.*).

Türm'chen [tyŏŏrm'shen] *n.* (-) turret; -en *vi.* to tower up; *t.* heap up.

Turn'en [tŏŏrr'nen] *vi.* to do gymnastics; -er *nm.* (-) gymnast, athlete; -halle *nf.* gymnasium; -hose *nf.* shorts.

Turnier [tŏŏrr-neerr'] *n.* (-e) tournament.

Turteltaube [tŏŏrr'tel-tow-ber] *nf.* turtle-dove.

Tusch'e [tŏŏ'sher] *nf.* Indian ink; -en *vt.* to paint with Indian ink; -farbe *nf.* water-colour; -kasten *nm.* paint-box; -manier *nf.* aquatint.

Tuscheln [tŏŏ'sheln] *vt.i.* to whisper.

Tüte [tyŏŏ'ter] *nf.* paper-bag.

Tüttelchen [tyŏŏ'tel-shen] *n.* (-) dot, jot, tittle.

Typ [tyŏŏp] *n,* **Typus** [tyŏŏ'pōoss] *nm.* (**Typen**) type.

Typ'e [tyŏŏ'per] *nf.* type (*printing*); -ographie *nf.* typography.

Typisch [tyŏŏ'pish] *a.* typical.

Typhus [tyŏŏ'fōoss] *nm.* typhoid fever.

Tyrann [tyoo-rran'] *m.w.* tyrant; -ei *nf.* tyranny; -isch *a.* tyrannical.

U

Übel [yŏŏ'bel] *a.* bad, wicked, sick; *n.* (-) evil, disease, misfortune; -gelaunt *a.* ill-honoured; -keit *nf.* sickness, nausea, qualms; -nehmen *vt.*

ir. to take amiss; -stand *nm.* evil, abuse; -wollend *a.* malevolent. [practise.

Üben [yŏŏ'ben] *vt.i.* to exercise,

Über [yŏŏ'berr] *pr.* over, above, across, by way of, via, about; *ad.* over; -all *ad.* everywhere.

Überalter't [yŏŏ-berr-al'terrt] *a.* superannuated; -ung *nf.* superannuation.

Überanstreng'en [yŏŏ-berr-an'shtreng-en] *v.r.* to over-exert; -ung *nf.* over-exertion.

Überantworten [yŏŏ'berr-ant'vorr-ten] *vt.* to hand over, deliver.

Überarbeiten [yŏŏ-berr-arr'-bite-en] *vt.* touch up, revise; *r.* overwork.

Überaus [yŏŏberr-owss'] *ad.* exceedingly.

Überbelicht'en [yŏŏ-berr-ber-lish'ten] *vt.* to over-expose; -ung *nf.* over-exposure.

Überbieten [yŏŏ-berr-bee'ten] *vt. ir.* to outbid, surpass.

Überbleib'en [yŏŏ-berr-blī'ben] *vi. ir.* to remain (over); -sel *n.* (-) remainder, remains.

Überblick [yŏŏ'berr-blik] *nm.* (-e) survey, summary; -en *vt.* to survey.

Überbring'en [yŏŏ-berr-bring'en] *vt. ir.* to hand over; -er *nm.* (-) bearer.

Überbrücken [yŏŏ-berr-bryŏŏ'cken] *vt.* to bridge (over).

Überdauern [yŏŏ-berr-dow'-errn] *vt.* to outlast.

Überdecken [yŏŏ-berr-dek'-en] *vt.* to cover.

Überdenken [yŏŏ-berr-denk'-en] *vt. ir.* to think over.

Überdies [yŏŏ-berr-deess'] *ad.* besides.

Überdruck [yŏŏ'berr-drŏŏk] *nm.* (-e) surcharge; -höhenkammer *nf.* pressurized cabin (*av.*).

Überdruss [yŏŏ'berr-drŏŏss] *nm.* weariness, disgust.

Überdrüssig [yōo'berr-drйōo-sish] *a.* tired of, disgusted with. [*nm.* excess of zeal.

Übereifer [yōo'berr-ife-err]

Übereil'en [yōo-berr-ile'en] *vt.r.* to hurry too much, rush over; **-t** *a.* rash, thoughtless; **-ung** *nf.* rashness, thoughtlessness.

Überein'ander [yōo-ber-rine-an'derr] one upon the other; **-kommen** *vi. ir.* to come to terms, agree; **-kunft** *nf.* agreement; **-stimmen** *vi. ir.* to agree, correspond; **-stimmung** *nf.* agreement, harmony.

Überetatsmässig [yōo-berr-ay-tats'may-sish] *a.* surplus to establishment.

Überfahr'en [yōo-berr-fah'ren] *vt. ir.* to pass over, cross, traverse; **-t** *nf.* crossing.

Überfall [yōo'berr-fal] *nm.* (-fälle) assault, invasion, surprise, attack, raid (*av.*, etc.); **-en** *vt. ir.* to surprise, attack; **-kommando** *n.* flying squad.

Überfällig [yōo-berr-fel'ish] *a.* overdue.

Überfliegen [yōo-berr-flee'gen] *vt. ir.* to fly over, outfly.

Überfliessen [yōo-berr-flee'sen] *vt.i.* to flow over, overflow.

Überflügeln [yōo-berr-flyōo'geln] *vt.* to surpass, outflank (*mil.*).

Überfluss [yōo-berr-flōoss] *nm.* (super)abundance, exuberance.

Überflüssig [yōo-berr-flyōo-sish] *a.* superfluous.

Überfluten [yōo-berr-flōo'ten] *vt.* to flood, inundate.

Überfordern [yōo-berr-forr'derrn] *vt.* to overcharge.

Überfremdung [yōo-berr-frem-dōong] *nf.* foreign domination.

Überführen [yōo-berr-fyōor'ren] *vt.* to tranport, ferry, convict, convinces.

Überführung [yōo-berr-fyōor'rōong] *nf.* viaduct, bridge, transport, ferrying, conviction; **-sdienst** *nm.* ferrying service (*av.*); **-sflug** *nm.* ferrying flight (*av.*).

Überfülle [yōo-berr-fyōo-ler] *nf.* excess; **-en** *vt.* to crowd, glut; **-ung** *nf.* overcrowding, glut.

Übergabe [yōo'berr-gah'ber] *nf.* delivery, surrender.

Übergang [yōo'berr-gang] *nm.* (-gänge) passage, transition; **-sgeld** *n.* war bonus; **-sgerät:** *nm.* bridging equipment (*mil.*); **-sregierung** *nf.* caretaker, interim government; **-sstelle** *nf.* crossing place; **-szeit** *nf.* time of transition.

Übergeben [yōo-berr-gay'ben] *vt. ir.* to deliver, give up, surrender; *r.* be sick.

Übergehen [yōo-berr-gay-en] *vi. ir.* to pass, cross, change; (-) [yoo-berr-gay'en] *vt.* to pass (over), run over, revise, omit, transgress.

Übergewicht [yōo'berr-ger-visht] *n.* overweight, preponderance.

Übergiessen [yōo-berr-gee-sen] *vt.* to pour over, wet, spill, bathe, cover.

Überglücklich [yōo'berr-glyōok-lish] *a.* overjoyed.

Übergreifen [yōo'berr-grife-en] *vi. ir.* to overlap, encroach, trespass upon.

Übergriff [yōo'berr-grif] *nm.* (-e) encroachment, trespass.

Überhandschuh [yōo'berr-hant-shōo] *nm.* (-e) gauntlet.

Überhand'nahme [yōo-berr-hant'nah-mer] *nf.* great increase, prevalence; **-nehmen** *vi. ir.* to increase rapidly, spread.

Überhang [yōo'berr-hang] *nm.* projection, ledge, crag, curtain; **-en** *vi. ir.* to overhang.

Überhäufen [yōō-berr-hoy'-fen] *vt.* to overload, overwhelm.

Überhaupt [yōō-berr-howpt'] *ad.* in general, at all.

Überheb'en [yōō-berr-hay'ben] *vt. ir.* to exempt, spare; *r.* to be presumptuous; **-ung** *nf.* presumption, exemption.

Überhitzen [yōō-berr-hit'sen] *vt.* to overheat, superheat (*tec.*).

Überhol'en [yōō-berr-hole'en] *vt.* to overtake, surpass; (−) [yōō'berr-hole-en] *vt.* to haul over, heel over (*nav.*); **-t** *a.* out of date, obsolete.

Überhören [yōō-berr-her'ren] *vt.* to overhear, ignore, miss (hearing), hear (*lesson*).

Überirdisch [yōō-berr-irr-dish] *a.* supernatural, heavenly, unearthly.

Überkippen [yōō'berr-kip-en] *vi.* to tip over, overbalance.

Überkleid [yōō'berr-klite] *n.* (-er) overall.

Überklug [yōō'berr-klōōk] *a.* conceited, too clever.

Überkochen [yōō'berr-koch-en] *vi.* to boil over.

Überkommen [yōō-berr-kom'en] *vt. ir.* to get, receive, be seized with, inherit (*custom*).

Überladen [yōō-berr-lah'den] *vt. ir.* to overload.

Überlager'er [yōō-berr-lah'-ger-rerr] *nm.* (−) heterodyne oscillator (*rad.*); **-n** *vt. ir.* to superimpose, heterodyne (*rad.*); **-ungsempfänger** *nm.* superheterodyne set.

Überland [yōō'berr-lant'] *a.* overland; **-flug** *nm.* cross-country flight; **-leitung** *nf.* overhead wires (*el.*); **-zentrale** *nf.* grid.

Überlassen [yōō-berr-lass'en] *vt. ir.* to leave, abandon, give up.

Überlast'en [yōō-berr-last'en] *vt.* to overload; **-er** *nm.* supercharger (*tec.*).

Überlaufen [yōō'berr-low-fen] *vi. ir.* to run, go over, desert; (−) [yōō-berr-low'fen] *vi. imp.* to be seized with, be overrun with; **-läufer** *nm.* (−) deserter.

Überlaut [yōō'berr-lowt] *a.* (too) noisy.

Überleb'en [yōō'berr-lay'ben] *vt.* to survive; **-ende(r)** *m.w.* survivor; **-t** *a.* out-lived, antiquated.

Überleg'en [yōō-berr-lay'gen] *vr.* to consider; (−) [yōō'berr-lay-gen] *vt.* to cover; **-en** *a.* superior; **-enheit** *nf.* superiority; **-ung** *nf.* reflexion, consideration.

Überleit'en [yōō-berr-lite-en] *vt.* to lead over, transfuse; *nf.* transition, transfusion.

Überlesen [yōō-berr-laze-en] *vt. ir.* to read over.

Überliefer'n [yōō-berr-lee'ferrn] *vt.* to deliver, hand down, transmit; **-ung** *nf.* delivery, surrender, tradition.

Überlisten [yōō-berr-list'en] *vt.* to outwit.

Übermachen [yōō-berr-mach'en] *vt.* to make over, remit; **-ung** *nf.* remittance.

Über'macht [yōō'berr-macht'] *nf.* superiority (*numerical*), supremacy; **-mächtig** *a.* too powerful, supreme.

Übermannen [yōō-berr-man'en] *vt.* to overcome.

Über'mass [yōō'berr-mahss] *n.* excess; **-mässig** *a, ad.* excessive(ly).

Übermensch [yōō'berr-mensh] *m.w.* superman; **-lich** *a.* superhuman.

Übermitt'eln [yōō-berr-mit'eln] *vt.* to convey; **-lung** *nf.* transmission, conveying, forwarding.

Übermorgen [yōō'berr-morr-gen] *ad.* the day after to-morrow.

Übermüd'en [yōō-berr-myōō'-

den] *vt.* to overtire; **-ung** *nf.* fatigue, overstrain.

Über'mut [yōō'berr-mōōt] *nm.* exuberance, high spirits, arrogance, pride; **-mütig** *a.* high-spirited, playful, insolent

Übernacht [yōō-berr-nacht'] *ad.* overnight; **-en** *vi.* to spend the night.

Übernächtig [yōō-berr-nesh'-tish] *a.* tired, sleepy.

Übernahme [yōō'berr-nah-mer] *nf.* acceptance, entrance (upon), undertaking.

Übernatürlich [yōō'berr-na-tyōōrr-lish] *a.* supernatural.

Übernehmen [yōō-berr-nay'-men] *vt. ir.* to take (over), undertake.

Überordnen [yōō-berr-ord'-nen] *vt.* to set over.

Überpolstern [yōō-berr-pol'-sterrn] *vt.* to upholster.

Überproduktion [yōō'berr-pro-dōōk-syohn'] *nf.* over-production.

Überprüfen [yōō-berr-pryōō'-fen] *vt.* to examine carefully; **-er** *nm.* (-) censor; **-ung** *nf.* examination, revision; **-ungs-lehrgang** *nm.* refresher course.

Überragen [yōō-berr-rah'gen] *vi.* to overtop, excel.

Überraschen [yōō-berr-rash'-en] *vt.* to surprise; **-ung** *nf.* surprise.

Überreden [yōō-berr-ray'-den] *vt.* to persuade; **-ung** *nf.* persuasion.

Überreich [yōō'ber-rīsh] *a.* very rich, abounding in; **-lich** *a., ad.* in abundance.

Überreichen [yōō-ber-rī'-shen] *vt.* to hand over, deliver, render; **-ung** *nf.* presentation.

Überreif [yōō'ber-rīfe] *a.* over-ripe.

Überreiten [yōō-ber-rīte'en] *vt.ir.* to overtake, run, ride over.

Überreizen [yōō-ber-rīte'sen] *vi.* to over-excite; **-ung** *nf.* over-excitement.

Überrest [yōō'ber-rest] *nm.* (-e) remains, residue, remnant.

Überrock [yōō'ber-rok] *nm.* (-röcke) overcoat.

Überrumpeln [yōō-berr-rōōm'peln] *vt.* to surprise; **-ung** *nf.* surprise attack (*mil.*).

Übersatt [yōō'ber-zat] *a.* surfeited, sick of; **-sättigen** *vt.* to supersaturate.

Überschätzen [yōō-berr-shet'sen] *vt.* to over-estimate, over-tax; **-ung** *nf.* over-estimation.

Überschauen [yōō-berr-show'en] *vt.* to survey, command (view).

Überschiessen [yōō-berr-shee'sen] *vt. ir.* to overshoot, exceed.

Überschäumen [yōō-berr-shoy'men] *vt.* to foam over, abound.

Überschlafen [yōō-berr-shlah'fen] *vr.* to oversleep.

Überschlag [yōō'ber-shlahk] *nm.* (-schläge) estimate, somersault; **-en** *v.r.* to estimate, tuck up, turn, tumble over, loop the loop (*av.*); **-angriff** *nm.* leap-frog attack.

Überschnappen [yōō-berr-shnap'pen] *vt.* to go mad; **-t** *a.* crazy.

Überschreiben [yōō-berr-shrī'ben] *vt. ir.* to carry over, transfer, address, head.

Überschreien [yōō-berr-shrī'en] *vt. ir.* to shout down.

Überschreiten [yōō-berr-shrī'ten] *vt.* to step over, cross, exceed, transgress, violate; **-ung** *nf.* crossing, violation.

Überschrift [yōō'berr-shrift] *nf.* heading, title.

Überschuh [yōō'berr-shōō] *nm.* (-e) over-shoe, galosh.

Überschuss [yōō'berr-shōōss] *nm.* (-schüsse) surplus; **-schüssig** *a.* surplus, excess.

Überschütten [yōo-berr-shyōo′ten] vt. to spill, overwhelm.

Überschwang [yōo-berr-shvang] nm. exuberance.

Überschwemm′en [yōo-berr-shvemm′en] vt. to overflow, flood; **-ung** nf. inundation, flood, deluge.

Überschwenglich [yōo-berr-shveng′lish] a. gushing, extravagant; **-keit** nf. exuberance, extravagance.

Überschwer [yōo′berr-shvairr] a. heavy (gun).

Übersee [yōo′berr-zay] nf. overseas; **-dampfer** nm. liner; **-isch** a. oversea.

Übersehen [yōo-berr-zay′en] vt. ir. to overlook, survey.

Übersend′en [yōo-berr-zent′den] vt. ir. to send, forward, dispatch; **-er** nm. (-) transmitter, sender; **-ung** nf. dispatch, forwarding.

Übersetz′en [yōo′berr-zet′sen] vi. to cross, ferry over; (-) **′en** [yōo-berr-zet′sen] vt. to translate; **-er** nm. (-) translator; **-ung** nf. translation, gear (cycle).

Übersicht [yōo′berr-zisht] nf. survey, summary; **-lich** a. clear, seen at a glance; **-lichkeit** nf. clarity, lucidity.

Übersied′eln [yōo′berr-zee′deln] vi. to remove; **-lung** nf. removal, migration.

Übersinnlich [yōo-berr-zin′lish] a. transcendental, supersensual.

Überspann′en [yōo-berr-shpan′en] vt. to stretch over, bridge, span, overstrain; **-t** a. overstrung, eccentric; **-theit** nf. eccentricity, queerness.

Überspringen [yōo-berr-shpring′en] vt. ir. to jump over, skip, miss out.

Übersprudeln [yōo-berr-shprōo′deln] vi. to bubble over.

Überstechen [yōo-berr-shtesh′en] vt. ir. to play a higher card, trump.

Überstehen [yōo-berr-shtay′en] vt. ir. to endure, survive.

Übersteigen [yōo-berr-shti′gen] vt. ir. to cross, exceed, surmount, overcome.

Übersteigern [yōo-berr-shti′gern] vt. to outbid.

Überstiefel [yōo′berr-shtee′fel] nm. (-) over-boot.

Überstimmen [yōo-berr-shtim′en] vt. to outvote.

Überströmen [yōo-berr-shtrer′men] vt. to overflow.

Überstunden [yōo′berr-shtoon′den] f.pl. overtime.

Überstürz′en [yōo-berr-shtyōort′sen] vt. to overturn, hurry; r. tumble over, rush; **-ung** nf. haste, rush.

Übertäuben [yōo-berr-toy′ben] vt. to deafen, drown.

Überteuern [yōo-berr-toy′errn] vt. to overcharge.

Übertölpeln [yōo-berr-terl′peln] vt. to cheat.

Übertönen [yōo-berr-ter′nen] vt. to drown.

Übertrag [yōo′berr-trahk′] nm. (-träge) transfer, amount brought forward (com.); **-bar** a. transferable, infectious; **-en** vt. ir. to transfer, transmit, relay (rad.), conduct; **-ung** nf. transmission, transfer(ence), relaying (rad.).

Übertreffen [yōo-berr-treff′en] vt. to surpass.

Übertreib′en [yōo-berr-tri′ben] vt. ir. to exaggerate; **-ung** nf. exaggeration.

Übertret′en [yōo-berr-tray′ten] vt. ir. to transgress, violate; (-) [yōo-berr-tray-ten] i. change over, cross over; **-ung** nf. violation, trespass (-ing).

Übertrieben [yōo-berr-tree′ben] a. exaggerated, excessive.

Übertritt [yōo′berr-trit] nm. (-e) change, going over.

Übertrumpfen [yōō-berr-troomp'fen] vt. to outdo, over-trump.

Übertünchen [yōō-berr-tyōōn'shen] vt. to whitewash.

Übervölkert [yōō-berr-ferl'kerrt] a. over-populated.

Übervoll [yōō'berr-fol] a. over-full.

Übervorteilen [yōō-berr-forr'tile-en] vt. to overreach, defraud.

Überwachen [yōō-berr-vach'en] vt. to superintend, look after, supervise; -ung nf. supervision, control, checking.

Überwachsen [yōō-berr-vax'en] vi. ir. to overgrow.

Überwältig'en [yōō-berr-vel'ti-gen] vt. to overpower; -ung nf. conquering, subjugation.

Überwasser'fahrt [yōō-berr-vass'err-farrt] nf. travelling on surface (nav.); -flug-zeug n. surface vessel.

Überweis'en [yōō-berr-vize'en] vt. ir. to transfer, assign; -ung nf. transfer, remittance.

Überwerfen [yōō-berr-vairf'en] vr. to fall out, quarrel with.

Überwiegen [yōō-berr-vee'gen] vi. ir. to outweigh, predominate; -d a. predominating, overwhelming; ad. chiefly, in the main.

Überwinden [yōō-berr-vin'den] vt. ir. to overcome; -er nm. (-) conqueror; -lich a. surmountable; -ung nf. conquest, control.

Überwintern [yōō-berr-vin'terrn] vi. to hibernate, spend the winter.

Überwölken [yōō-berr-verl'ken] vr. to become cloudy.

Überwurf [yōō'berr-vōōrrf] nm. (-würfe) wrap, shawl.

Überzahl [yōō'berr-sahl'] nf. superiority, superior numbers.

Überzähl'en [yōō-berrt-say'len] vt. to count over; -ig a. surplus, supernumerary, redundant.

Überzeug'en [yōō-berrt-soy'gen] vt. to convince; -ung nf. conviction.

Überzieh'en [yōō-berrt-see-en] vt. ir. to put on, over; (-) [yōō-berrt-see'en] vt. ir. to cover, overlay, overdraw (com.); -er nm. (-) overcoat; -hose nf. over-trousers; -ung nf. overdraft.

Überzuckern [yōō-berrt-sōō'kerrn] vt. to sugar (over).

Überzug [yōō'berrt-sōōk] nm. (-züge) coating, cover, case; -spelzstiefel nm. fur overboot.

Überzwerch [yōō-berrt-svairrsh'] ad. across, athwart.

Üblich [yōōp'lish] a. usual, in use.

Übrig [yōō'brish] a. remaining, left over; -ens ad. after all, besides, incidentally, by the way.

Übung [yōō'bōōng] nf. exercise, practice, training; -sflug-zeug n. training plane.

Ufer [ōō'ferr] nm. (-) shore, bank; -brücke nf. cantilever bridge; -damm nm. embankment.

Uhr [ōōrr] nf. clock, watch, time, o'clock; -feder nf. watchspring; -gehäuse n. watchcase; -kette nf. watch-chain; -macher nm. watchmaker; -werk n. clockwork, works of a watch; -werkzünder nm. time fuse, clock fuse. [owl.

Uhu [ōō'hōō] nm. (-e) great owl.

Ulk [ōōlk] nm. (-e) fooling, lark, fun; -en vi. to joke; -ig a. funny.

Ulme [ōōl'mer] nf. elm.

Um [ōōm] pr. (round) about, at, after, in exchange for, to the extent of, by; ad. about, over; cj. in order to.

Umadressieren [ŏŏm'a-dress-eer'ren] *vt.* to readdress.

Umänder'n [ŏŏm'en-derrn] *vt.* to change; **-ung** *nf.* alteration.

Umarbeiten [ŏŏm'ar-bite-en] *vt.* to recast, revise completely.

Umarm'en [ŏŏm-arr'men] *vt.* to embrace; **-ung** *nf.* embrace.

Umbau [ŏŏm'bow] *nm.* (-e, -ten) rebuilding, structural alterations; **-en** *vt. ir.* to rebuild, reconstruct.

Umbehalten [ŏŏm'ber-hal-ten] *vt. ir.* to keep on.

Umbiegen [ŏŏm'bee-gen] *vt. ir.* to turn down, bend.

Umbild'en [ŏŏm'bil-den] *vt.* to transform; **-ung** *nf.* transformation.

Umbinden [ŏŏm'bin-den] *vt. ir.* to put on. [*vt.* to turn over.

Umblättern [ŏŏm'blet-errn]

Umblicken [ŏŏm'blik-en] *vt.* to look round.

Umbrechen [ŏŏm'bresh-en] *vt. ir.* to break down, up.

Umbringen [ŏŏm'bring-en] *vt. ir.* to kill.

Umbruch [ŏŏm'brŏŏch] *nm.* change-over, revolution.

Umbuchung [ŏŏm'bŏŏch-ŏŏng] *nf.* transfer (*com.*).

Umdrängen [ŏŏm-dreng'en] *vt.* to crowd round.

Umdreh'en [ŏŏm'dray-en] *vt.* to turn (round), wring (neck), revolve; **-ung** *nf.* rotation, revolution (*tec.*).

Umdruck [ŏŏm'drŏŏk] *nm.* (-e) reprint; **-en** *vt. ir.* to reprint.

Umeinander [ŏŏm'ine-an-derr] *ad.* round each other.

Umerziehung [ŏŏm'airrt-see-ŏŏng] *nf.* re-education.

Umfahren [ŏŏm'fah-ren] *vt. ir.* to run over; (-) [ŏŏm-fah'ren] *vt. ir.* to drive, sail round; **-t** *nf.* circular tour.

Umfallen [ŏŏm'fal-en] *vi. ir.* to fall down, over; collapse.

Umfang [ŏŏm'fang] *nm.* bulk, volume, circumference, compass, extent; **-en** *vt. ir.* to encircle, surround, clasp; **-reich** *a.* extensive, voluminous, bulky.

Umfass'en [ŏŏm-fass'en] *vt.* to embrace, clutch, comprise include, outflank (*mil.*); **-end** *a.* extensive, comprehensive; **-ung** *nf.* enclosing, enclosure, outflanking (movement).

Umfliegen [ŏŏm-flee'gen] *vt. ir.* to fly round. [muffled.

Umflort [ŏŏm-florrt'] *a.* dim,

Umform'en [ŏŏm'forr-men] *vt.* to transform, recast, reform; **-er** *nm.* (-) rotary converter (*el.*); **-ergerät** *n.* transformer unit.

Umfrage [ŏŏm'frah-ger] *nf.* general inquiry; **-n** *vi.* to inquire, make inquiries.

Umfried'en [ŏŏm-free'den] *vt.* to fence in; **-ung** *nf.* enclosure.

Umfüllen [ŏŏm'fyŏŏ-len] *vt.* to decant.

Umgang [ŏŏm'gang] *nm.* circuit, intercourse, association; **-ssprache** *nf.* colloquial language, everyday speech.

Umgänglich [ŏŏm'geng-lish] *a.* sociable. [to ensnare.

Umgarnen [ŏŏm-garr'nen] *vt.*

Umgeb'en [ŏŏm-gay'ben] *vt. ir.* to surround; **-ung** *nf.* surroundings, environment, social background.

Umgegend [ŏŏm'gay-gent] *nf.* neighbourhood.

Umgeh'en [ŏŏm'gay-en] *vi. ir.* to go round, associate, haunt, treat; (-) [ŏŏm-gay'en] *t. vt.* outflank, avoid, evade; **-ungsstrecke** *nf.* **-ungsweg** *nm.* by-pass.

Umgekehrt [ŏŏm'ger-kairrt] *a.* reversed, inverted; *ad.* vice versa, the other way about.

Umgestalten [ŏŏm'ger-shtal-ten] *vt.* to transform, alter, reorganize. [*ir.* to dig up.

Umgraben [ŏŏm'grah-ben] *vt.*

Umgrenz'en [ōŏm-grent'sen] vt. to bound, limit, enclose; -ung nf. boundary, limitation.

Umgruppieren [ōŏm-grōŏ-peer-ren] vt. to regroup.

Umhalsen [ōŏm-hal'zen] vt. to embrace.

Umhang [ōŏm'hang] nm. (-hänge) wrap, cape.

Umhängen [ōŏm'heng-en] vt. to put on. [ir. to fell.

Umhauen [ōŏm'how-en] vt.

Umher [ōŏm-hairr'] ad. about, around; -gehen vi. ir. to walk about; -reisen vi. to travel about; -schweifen vi. to roam about; -ziehen vi. ir. to wander from place to place.

Umhüll'en [ōŏm-hyōŏ'len] vt. to wrap up, envelop; -ung nf. covering, wrapping; jacket (book).

Umkehr [ōŏm'kairr] nf. change, return, turning back; -en vi. to turn back, about; reform, turn inside out, upside down, reverse; -ung nf. turning over, reform, inversion.

Umkippen [ōŏm'kip-en] vt.i. to tilt over, upset.

Umklammer'n [ōŏm-klam'errn] vt. to clasp, encircle (troops); -ung nf. pincer movement (mil.). [to turn down.

Umklappen [ōŏm'klap-en] vt.

Umkleiden [ōŏm'klide-en] vr. to change one's clothes.

Umkommen [ōŏm'kom-en] vi. ir. to perish, go bad, spoil.

Umkreis [ōŏm'krice] nm. circuit, radius, neighbourhood; -en vt. to circle round; -ung nf. encirclement.

Umlad'en [ōŏm'lah-den] vt. ir. to reload, tranship; -ung nf. reloading, transhipment.

Umlage [ōŏm'lah-ger] nf. assessment. [to besiege, beset.

Umlagern [ōŏm-lah'derrn] vt.

Umlauf [ōŏm'lowf] nm. circulation, turn; -en vi. ir. to revolve, circulate.

Umlaut [ōŏm'lowt] nm. modification, mutation.

Umlege'n [ōŏm'lay-gen] vt. to put on, shift, turn down, over; -kragen nm. turn-down collar.

Umleit'en [ōŏm'lite-en] vt. to divert; -ung nf. diversion, by-pass, re-routing (av.).

Umlenken [ōŏm'lenk-en] vt. to turn round.

Umlernen [ōŏm'lairr-nen] vt. to re-learn, adjust one's views.

Umliegend [ōŏm'lee-gent] a. surrounding.

Ummauern [ōŏm-mow'errn] vt. to wall in.

Ummodeln [ōŏm'mode-eln] vt. to remodel. [to repack.

Umpacken [ōŏm'pak-en] vt.

Umpflanzen [ōŏm'pflant-sen] vt. to transplant.

Umquartier'en [ōŏm'kvarr-teer'ren] vt. to re-billet, evacuate; -ung nf. billeting, evacuation. [vt. to frame.

Umrahmen [ōŏm-rah'men]

Umrändern [ōŏm-ren'derrn] vt. to border, edge.

Umrechn'en [ōŏm'resh-nen] vt. to change, exchange; -ung nf. exchange.

Umreissen [ōŏm'rice-en] vt. ir. to demolish, pull down; (-) [ōŏm-rice'en] outline, sketch.

Umrichter [ōŏm'rish-terr] nm. (-) frequency changer (rad.). [to surround.

Umringen [ōŏm'ring'en] vt.

Umriss [ōŏm'riss] nm. (-e) outline, sketch.

Umsatteln [ōŏm'zat-eln] vt. to change (occupation).

Umsatz [ōŏm'zats] nm. turn-over, sale (com.).

Umsäumen [ōŏm-zoy'men] vt. to enclose; (-) [ōŏm'zoy-men] to hem.

Umschalt'en [ōŏm'shal-ten] vt. to switch, commute (el.); -bar a. interchangeable; -er nm. (-) switch, commutator shift-key; -hebel nm. gear.

lever (*aut.*); **-tafel** *nf.* switchboard.

Umschau [ŏŏm'show] *nf.* look(ing) round, survey; **-en** *vi.r.* to look round.

Umschicht'en [ŏŏm'shish-ten] *vt.* to regroup; **-ig** *a.* alternately; **-ung** *nf.* regrouping, reorganization, rearrangement.

Umschiffen [ŏŏm-shif'en] *vt.* to sail round, circumnavigate.

Umschlag [ŏŏm'shlahk] *nm.* (-schläge) wrapper, envelope. cover, bandage, hem, transfer, unloading (*com.*), change (*weather*), turn-up (*trousers*); **-en** *vi.ir.* to change, be upset; *t.* knock down, upset, turn up, round; **-ekragen** *nm.* turn-down collar; **-etuch** *n.* shawl; **-papier** *n.* brown paper, wrapping paper.

Umschliessen [ŏŏm-shlee'sen] *vt.ir.* to surround, embrace.

Umschlingen [ŏŏm-shling'en] *vt.* to enclasp, cling to.

Umschmelzung [ŏŏm'shmelt-sŏŏng] *nf.* recasting, reorganization; **-sprozess** *nm.* process of reorganization.

Umschreib'en [ŏŏm-shri'ben] *vt.ir.* to rewrite, copy, transfer; (–) [ŏŏm-shri'ben] paraphrase, express in a roundabout way; **-ung** *nf.* transcription, transfer, paraphrase, circumlocution.

Umschrift [ŏŏm'shrift] *nf.* inscription, transcription.

Umschul'en [ŏŏm-shŏŏ-len] *vt.* to change schools, retrain, educate differently; **-ung** *nf.* retraining, re-education.

Umschütten [ŏŏm-shyŏŏ-ten] *vt.* to spill, pour off.

Umschwärmen [ŏŏm-shvairr'men] *vt.* to swarm round, worship, enthuse about.

Umschweif [ŏŏm'shvife] *nm.*

circumlocution, beating about the bush.

Umschwenken [ŏŏm'shvenk-en] *vi.* to turn round.

Umschwung [ŏŏm'shvŏŏng] *nm.* change, revolution.

Umsehen [ŏŏm'zay-en] *vr.ir.* to look round, about, search for; *n.* instant.

Umseitig [ŏŏm'zite-ish] *ad.* overleaf, on opposite page (*com.*).

Umsetz'bar [ŏŏm'zets-barr] *a.* convertible, negotiable (*com.*), **-en** *vt.* to transpose, convert (*com.*).

Umsicht [ŏŏm'zisht] *nf.* prudence, caution; **-ig** *a.* cautious, prudent.

Umsiedeln [ŏŏm'zee-deln] *vi.* to remove (*house*).

Umsonst [ŏŏm-zonst'] *ad.* for nothing, in vain.

Umspann'en [ŏŏm-shpan-en] *vt.* to change horses, transform (*el.*); (–) [ŏŏm-shpan'en] to comprise, include, enclose; **-er** *nm.* (–) transformer (*el.*).

Umspielen [ŏŏm'shpee-len] *vt.* to dodge (*football, etc.*).

Umspringen [ŏŏm'shpring-en] *vi.ir.* to change, veer, handle (*people*).

Umstand [ŏŏm'shtant] *nm.* (-stände) circumstance, fact; *pl.* particulars, fuss, ceremony; **-skasten** *nm.* fussy person pedant; **-skleid** *n.* maternity dress; **-swort** *n.* adverb.

Umständlich [ŏŏm'shtent-lish] *a., ad.* involved, circumstantial, in detail, fussy; **-keit** *nf.* formality, fuss.

Umstehen [ŏŏm-shtay'en] *vi.ir.* to stand about; **-d** *a.* next (*page*); **-de** *pl.* bystanders.

Umsteige'n [ŏŏm'shti-gen] *vi.ir.* to change (*rl.*); **-fahrkarte** *nf.* transfer (ticket).

Umstell'en [ŏŏm-shtel'en] *vt.* to surround; (–) [ŏŏm'shtel-en] to change round, rearrange, transpose, convert; *r.* adapt oneself; **-ung** *nf.* conversion, adaptation, change.

Umsteuer'n [ŏŏm'shtoy-errn] *vt.* to reverse (*et.*); **-barkeit** *nf.* reversability; **-ung** *nf.* reversing.

Umstimmen [ŏŏm'shtim-en] *vt.* to retune, convert, talk over.

Umstossen [ŏŏm'stoh-sen] *vt. ir.* to overturn, abolish, annul.

Umstricken [ŏŏm'shtrik'en] *vt.* to entangle.

Umstritten [ŏŏm'shtrit'en] *a.* disputed.

Umstülpen [ŏŏm'shtyŏŏl-pen] *vt.* to invert, turn upside down.

Umsturz [ŏŏm'shtŏŏrrts] *nm.* overthrow, revolution.

Umstürz'en [ŏŏm'shtyŏŏrrt-sen] *vt.* to overthrow, overturn; **-ler** *nm.* (-) revolutionary, insurgent; **-lerisch** *a.* revolutionary.

Umtausch [ŏŏm'towsh] *nm.* exchange; **-en** *vt.* to exchange.

Umtriebe [ŏŏm'tree-ber] *m.pl.* machinations, intrigue.

Umtun [ŏŏm'tŏŏn] *vr. ir.* to look for, take trouble.

Umwälz'en [ŏŏm'velt-sen] *vt.* to roll round, subvert, revolutionize; **-ung** *nf.* revolution.

Umwand'eln [ŏŏm-van'deln] *vt.* to wander round; [ŏŏm'van-deln] change, convert (*com.*); **-lung** *nf.* change, conversion.

Umwechseln [ŏŏm'vex-eln] *vt.* to change, exchange.

Umweg [ŏŏm'vake] *nm.* (-e) roundabout way.

Umwelt [ŏŏm'velt] *nf.* environment, background.

Umwenden [ŏŏm'ven-den] *vt.r. ir.* to turn (round).

Umwerben [ŏŏm'vairr'ben] *vt. ir.* to court, seek after.

Umwerfen [ŏŏm'vairr-fen] *vt. ir.* to put on, upset, overthrow, knock down.

Umwert'en [ŏŏm'vairr-ten] *vt.* to revalue; **-er** *nm.* (-) convertor (*tec.*); **-ung** *nf.* revaluation, conversion (*tec.*).

Umwickeln [ŏŏm-vik'eln] *vt.* to wrap up.

Umwohner [ŏŏm'voh-nerr] *m.pl.* (-) neighbours.

Umwölken [ŏŏm-verl'ken] *vt.* to overcast, cloud.

Umzäunen [ŏŏm-tsoy'nen] *vt.* to fence in.

Umziehen [ŏŏm'tsee-en] *vt.r. ir.* to change (*clothes*); *i.* remove. [*vt.* to encircle.

Umzingeln [ŏŏm-tsing'eln]

Umzug [ŏŏm'tsŏŏk] *nm.* (-züge) procession, removal.

Unabänderlich [ŏŏn'ap-enderr-lish] *a.* unchangeable, unalterable.

Unabhängig [ŏŏn'ap-hengish] *a.* independent; **-keit** *nf.* independence.

Unabkömmlich [ŏŏn'ap-kerm-lish] *a.* reserved, indispensable. [*a.* incessant.

Unablässig [ŏŏn'ap-less-ish]

Unabsehbar [ŏŏn'ap-zay-barr] *a.* immeasurable, incalculable.

Unabwendbar [ŏŏn'ap-ventbarr] *a.* inevitable.

Unachtsam [ŏŏn'acht-zam] *a.* careless, inattentive; **-keit** *nf.* carelessness.

Unähnlich [ŏŏn'ane-lish] *a.* unlike; **-keit** *nf.* dissimilarity.

Unanfechtbar [ŏŏn'an-feshtbarr] *a.* indisputable.

Unangemessen [ŏŏn'an-germess-en] *a.* unsuitable.

Unangenehm [ŏŏn'an-gername] *a.* unpleasant.

Unannehm'bar [ŏŏn'an-name-barr] *a.* unacceptable; **-lichkeit** *nf.* bother, trouble.

Unansehnlich [ŏŏn'an-zanelish] *a.* insignificant, poor looking.

Unanständig [ŏŏn'an-shtendish] *nf.* indecent, improper;

-keit *nf.* indecency, impropriety.

Unansteckbarkeit [ŏŏn'an-shtek-barr-kite] *nf.* immunity.

Unanwendbar [ŏŏn'an-vent-barr] *a.* inapplicable.

Unappetitlich [ŏŏn'ap-ay-teet'lish] *a.* uninviting.

Unart [ŏŏn'arrt] *nf.* rudeness, bad manners; **-ig** *a.* badly behaved, ill-mannered, naughty.

Unauffindbar [ŏŏn'owf-fint-barr] *a.* not to be found; **-gefordert** *a.* unasked, without being asked; **-haltsam** *a.* irresistible; **-hörlich** *a.* incessant, constant; **-löslich** *a.* insoluble.

Unaufmerksam [ŏŏn'owf-mairrk-zam] *a.* inattentive; **-keit** *nf.* inattention.

Unaufrichtig [ŏŏn'owf-rish-tish] *a.* insincere; **-keit** *nf.* insincerity.

Unausbleiblich [ŏŏn'owss-blibe-lish] *a.* certain, inevitable; **-führbar** *a.* impracticable; **-gemacht** *a.* unsettled; **-gesetzt** *a.* incessant; **-löschlich** *a.* indelible; **-rottbar** *a.* ineradicable; **-sprechlich** *a.* inexpressible, unspeakable; **-stehlich** *a.* unendurable, intolerable.

Unbändig [ŏŏn'ben-dish] *a.* unruly, excessive.

Unbarmherzig [ŏŏn'barrm-hairrt-sish] *a.* pitiless, unmerciful.

Unbeachtet [ŏŏn'be-ach-tet] *a.* unnoticed, ignored.

Unbeantwortet [ŏŏn'be-ant-vorr-tet] *a.* unanswered.

Unbebaut [ŏŏn'be-bowt] *a.* uncultivated.

Unbedächtig [ŏŏn'be-desh-tish] *a.* indiscreet, inconsiderate.

Unbedenklich [ŏŏn'be-denk-lish] *a., ad.* unhesitating(ly).

Unbedeutend [ŏŏn'be-doy-tent] *a.* insignificant, slight, mean.

Unbedingt [ŏŏn'be-dingt] *a., ad.* unconditional(ly), absolute(ly).

Unbeeinflusst [ŏŏn'be-ine-flŏŏst] *a.* uninfluenced, unbiassed.

Unbefahrbar [ŏŏn'be-farr-barr] *a.* impassible.

Unbefangen [ŏŏn'be-fang-en] *a.* impartial, unprejudiced, naïve, dispassionate; **-heit** *nf.* impartiality.

Unbefleckt [ŏŏn'be-flekt] *a.* immaculate, unsullied.

Unbefriedigt [ŏŏn'be-free-di-gent] *a.* unsatisfactory; **-t** *a.* unsatisfied, dissatisfied.

Unbefugt [ŏŏn'be-fŏŏkt] *a.* unauthorized. [not gifted.

Unbegabt [ŏŏn'be-gahpt] *a.*

Unbegreflich [ŏŏn'be-grife-lish] *a.* inconceivable.

Unbegrenzt [ŏŏn'be-grentst] *a.* unlimited.

Unbegründet [ŏŏn'be-gryŏŏn-det] *a.* unfounded.

Unbehagen [ŏŏn'be-hah-gen] *n.* discomfort; **-lich** *a.* uncomfortable, uneasy.

Unbehauen [ŏŏn'be-how-en] *a.* unhewn. [isht] *a.* unmolested.

Unbehelligt [ŏŏn'be-hel-](

Unbeholfen [ŏŏn'be-hol-fen] *a.* awkward; **-heit** *nf.* awkwardness, clumsiness.

Unbeirrt [ŏŏn'be-irrt] *a.* imperturbable.

Unbekannt [ŏŏn'be-kant] *a.* unknown, unacquainted with.

Unbekümmert [ŏŏn'be-kŏŏrrt] *a.* unconcerned.

Unbelästigt [ŏŏn'be-les-tisht] *a.* unmolested.

Unbelebt [ŏŏn'be-laipt] *a.* lifeless, dull.

Unbeliebt [ŏŏn'be-leept] *a.* unpopular; **-heit** *nf.* unpopularity.

Unbemerkbar [ŏŏn'be-mairrk-barr] *a.* imperceptible.

Unbemittelt [ŏŏn'ber-mit-elt] *a.* without means.

Unbenutzt [ŏŏn'ber-nŏŏtst] *a.* unused, idle.

Unbequem [ŏŏn'ber-kvame] *a.* inconvenient, uncomfortable; **-lichkeit** *nf.* discomfort, inconvenience.

Unberechenbar [ŏŏn'ber-resh-en-barr] *a.* incalculable.

Unberechtigt [ŏŏn'ber-resh'tisht] *a.* unjustified, unauthorized.

Unberufen [ŏŏn'ber-rŏŏ-fen] *a.* uncalled for.

Unberührt [ŏŏn'ber-ryŏŏrt] *a.* untouched, intact.

Unbeschadet [ŏŏn'ber-shah-det] *pr.* without detriment to.

Unbeschädigt [ŏŏn'ber-shade-isht] *a.* undamaged, in good condition.

Unbescheiden [ŏŏn'ber-shide-en] *a.* immodest, presumptuous; **-heit** *nf.* immodesty, presumption.

Unbeschnitten [ŏŏn'ber-shnit-ten] *a.* uncut.

Unbescholten [ŏŏn'ber-shol-ten] *a.* blameless.

Unbeschränkt [ŏŏn'ber-shrenkt] *a.* unlimited, absolute.

Unbeschreiblich [ŏŏn-ber-shribe-lish] *a.* indescribable.

Unbeschrieben [ŏŏn'ber-shree-ben] *a.* blank, not written on.

Unbesehen [ŏŏn'ber-zay-en] *ad.* not examined, without inspection, unhesitatingly.

Unbesetzt [ŏŏn'ber-zetst] *a.* free, vacant, unoccupied.

Unbesiegbar [ŏŏn'ber-zeek-barr] *a.* invincible.

Unbesonnen [ŏŏn'ber-zon-en] *a.* unwise, rash, imprudent.

Unbesorgt [ŏŏn'ber-zorrkt] *a.* unconcerned, untroubled.

Unbestand [ŏŏn'ber-shtant] *nm.* instability.

Unbeständig [ŏŏn'ber-shten-dish] *a.* inconstant, unstable,

unsettled; **-keit** *nf.* instability, changeableness.

Unbestechbar [ŏŏn'ber-shtesh-barr] *a.* incorruptible.

Unbestellbar [ŏŏn'ber-shtel-barr] *a.* undeliverable.

Unbestimmt [ŏŏn'ber-shtimt] *a.* indefinite; **-heit** *nf.* vagueness.

Unbestreitbar [ŏŏn'ber-shtrite'barr] *a, ad.* indisputable, certain(ly).

Unbestritten [ŏŏn'ber-shtrit-en] *a.* undisputed.

Unbeteiligt [ŏŏn'ber-tile-isht] *a.* not concerned, not implicated. [unstressed.

Unbetont [ŏŏn'ber-tohnt] *a.*

Unbeugsam [ŏŏn'boik-zam] *a.* inflexible, stubborn.

Unbewacht [ŏŏn'ber-vacht] *a.* unwatched, unguarded.

Unbewaffnet [ŏŏn'ber-vaf-net] *a.* unarmed.

Unbeweglich [ŏŏn'ber-vake-lish] *a.* immovable.

Unbewohnbar [ŏŏn'ber-vone-barr] *a.* uninhabitable; **-t** *a.* uninhabited.

Unbewusst [ŏŏn'ber-vŏŏst] *a.* unconscious. [unpaid.

Unbezahlt [ŏŏn'bert-sahlt] *a.*

Unbezwinglich [ŏŏn-bert-sving-lish] *a.* invincible.

Unbiegsam [ŏŏn'beek-zam] *a.* unbending.

Unbill [ŏŏn'bil] *nf.* injustice; *pl.* inclemency; **-ig** *a.* unfair.

Unbotmässig [ŏŏn'bote-mace-ish] *a.* insubordinate; **-keit** *nf.* insubordination.

Unbrauchbar [ŏŏn'browch-barr] *a.* useless, inefficient; **-keit** *nf.* uselessness.

Und [ŏŏnt] *cj.* and.

Undank [ŏŏn'dank] *nm.* ingratitude; **-bar** *a.* ungrateful; **-barkeit** *nf.* ingratitude.

Undatiert [ŏŏn'da-teert] *a.* undated.

Undenkbar [ŏŏn'ber-denk'barr] *a.* inconceivable.

Undeutlich [ŏŏn'doit-lish] a. indistinct, obscure.

Undicht [ŏŏn'disht] a. leaky.

Unding [ŏŏn'ding] n. (-e) absurdity.

Unduldsam [ŏŏn'dŏŏlt-zam] a. intolerant; -keit nf. intolerance.

Undurch'dringlich [ŏŏn'dŏŏrch-dring-lish] a. impenetrable; -führbar a. impracticable; -lassig a. waterproof, impermeable; -sichtig a. opaque.

Uneben [ŏŏn'ay-ben] a. uneven; -bürtig a. inferior.

Unecht [ŏŏn'esht] a. not genuine, spurious, artificial.

Unehelich [ŏŏn'ay-err-lish] a. illegitimate; -keit nf. illegitimacy.

Unehr'e [ŏŏn'air-rer] nf. dishonour; -enhaft a. dishonourable; -erbietig a. disrespectful; -lich a. dishonest; -lichkeit nf. dishonesty.

Uneigennützig [ŏŏn'I-gen-yŏŏt-sish] a. unselfish.

Uneigentlich [ŏŏn'I-gent-lish] a. not literal.

Uneinig [ŏŏn'ine-ish] a. disunited; -keit nf. discord, dissension.   [variance.

Uneins [ŏŏn'inss] ad. at variance.

Uneinträglich [ŏŏn'ine-trake-lish] a. unprofitable.

Unempfänglich [ŏŏn'emp-feng-lish] a. unreceptive, not susceptible.

Unempfindlich [ŏŏn'emp-fint-lish] a. insensitive, unfeeling; -keit nf. insensibility.

Unendlich [ŏŏn-ent'lish] a. endless, infinite; -keit nf. infinity.

Unentbehrlich [ŏŏn-ent-bairr'lish] a. indispensable.

Unentgeltlich [ŏŏn'ent-gelt-lish] a. free, gratis.

Unenthaltsam [ŏŏn'ent-halt-zam] a. incontinent.

Unentschieden [ŏŏn'ent-

shee-den] a. undecided, irresolute, drawn (game).

Unentschlossen [ŏŏn'ent-shloss-en] a. irresolute, undecided.   [unflinching.

Unentwegt [ŏŏn'ent-vaikt] a.

Unerachtet [ŏŏn'er-rach-tet] pr. in spite of.

Unerbittlich [ŏŏn-err-bit'lish] a. inexorable.

Unerfahren [ŏŏn-err-fah-ren] a. inexperienced.

Unerfindlich [ŏŏn-err-fint-lish] a. undiscoverable.

Unerfreulich [ŏŏn-err-froy-lish] a. unpleasant.

Unerfüllbar [ŏŏn-err-fŏŏl'barr] a. unrealizable.

Unergiebig [ŏŏn-err-gee-bish] a. unproductive.

Unergründlich [ŏŏn-err-gryŏŏnt-lish] a. unfathomable.

Unerheblich [ŏŏn-err-hape-lish] a. trifling, inconsiderable.

Unerhört [ŏŏn-err-herrt'] a. unheard of.   [unrecognized.

Unerkannt [ŏŏn'err-kant] a.

Unerkennbar [ŏŏn-err-ken'barr] a. unrecognizable.

Unerklärbar [ŏŏn-err-klairr'barr] a. inexplicable.

Unerlässlich [ŏŏn-err-less-lish] a. indispensable.

Unerlaubt [ŏŏn-err-lowpt] a. forbidden, unlawful.

Unermesslich [ŏŏn-err-mess'lish] a. immeasurable, immense.

Unermüdlich [ŏŏn-err-myŏŏt-lish] a. indefatigable.

Unerquicklich [ŏŏn-err-kvik-lish] a. unpleasant, unedifying.

Unerreich'bar [ŏŏn-er-rish'barr] a. unattainable; -t a. unequalled.

Unersättlich [ŏŏn-err-zet'lish] a. insatiable.

Unerschöpflich [ŏŏn-err-sherpf'lish] a. inexhaustible.

Unerschrocken [ŏŏn'err-shrok-en] a. intrepid; -heit nf. fearlessness.

Unerschütterlich [ŏŏn-errshyŏŏ'terr-lish] a. imperturbable.

Unerschwinglich [ŏŏn-err-shving'lish] a. exorbitant.

Unersetzlich [ŏŏn-err-zets'lish] a. irreplaceable, irreparable.

Unerspriesslich [ŏŏn-err-shpreess-lish] a. unprofitable.

Unerträglich [ŏŏn-err-trake-lish] a. intolerable, unbearable.

Unerwartet [ŏŏn-err-varr'tet] a. unexpected.

Unerwünscht [ŏŏn'err-vyŏŏnsht] a. undesirable, unwelcome.

Unerzogen [ŏŏn'errt-soh-gen] a. ill-bred, rude.

Unfähig [ŏŏn'fay-ish] a. incapable, unfit; **-keit** nf. incapacity, unfitness.

Unfall [ŏŏn'fal] nm. (-fälle) accident; **-bereitschaft** nf. emergency first-aid; **-versicherung** nf. accident insurance.

Unfehlbar [ŏŏn-fail'barr] a. infallible, unfailing; **-keit** nf. infallibility.

Unfein [ŏŏn'fine] a. coarse, rude, slangy.

Unfern [ŏŏn'fairn] ad., pr.

Unflat [ŏŏn'flaht] nm. filth.

Unflätig [ŏŏn'flay-tish] a. filthy.

Unfolgsam [ŏŏn'folk-zam] a. disobedient.

Unförmlich [ŏŏn'ferrm-lish] a. shapeless, deformed.

Unfreiwillig [ŏŏn'fri-vil-ish] a. involuntary, against one's will.

Unfreundlich [ŏŏn'froint-lish] a. unfriendly, unkind, harsh; **-keit** nf. unkindness.

Unfriede [ŏŏn'free-der] nm. (gen. -ns) dissension.

Unfruchtbar [ŏŏn'frŏŏcht-barr] a. unfruitful, barren; **-keit** nf. unfruitfulness, barrenness.

Unfug [ŏŏn'fŏŏk] nm. nuisance.

Ungangbar [ŏŏn'gang-barr] a. impassible, unsaleable.

Ungar [ŏŏn'garr] a. underdone, raw. [inhospitable.

Ungastlich [ŏŏn'gast-lish] a.

Ungeachtet [ŏŏn'ge-acht-et] pr. notwithstanding.

Ungeahnt [ŏŏn'ge-ahnt] a. unexpected, undreamt of.

Ungebahnt [ŏŏn'ger-bahnt] a. untrodden.

Ungebärdig [ŏŏn'ger-bairr-dish] a. unruly.

Ungebeten [ŏŏn'ger-bay-ten] a. uninvited.

Ungebildet [ŏŏn'ger-bil-det] a. uneducated, ill-mannered.

Ungebühr [ŏŏn'ger-byŏŏrr] nf. indecency; **-lich** a. improper.

Ungebunden [ŏŏn'ger-bŏŏn-den] a. unbound, unrestrained; **-heit** nf. lack of restraint.

Ungeduld [ŏŏn'ger-dŏŏlt] nf. impatience; **-ig** a. impatient.

Ungeeignet [ŏŏn'ge-ig-net] a. unsuitable.

Ungefähr [ŏŏn'ger-fairr] ad. nearly, about; n. chance.

Ungefährlich [ŏŏn'ger-fairr-lish] a. not dangerous.

Ungefällig [ŏŏn'ger-fel-ish] a. disobliging. [a. indignant.

Ungehalten [ŏŏn'ger-hal-ten]

Ungeheissen [ŏŏn'ger-hice-sen] a. unasked, unbidden, of one's own accord.

Ungeheuer [ŏŏn'ger-hoy-err] a. monstrous, huge; n. monster; **-lich** a. prodigious, monstrous; **-lichkeit** nf. enormity.

Ungehobelt [ŏŏn'ger-hobe-elt] a. unpolished.

Ungehörig [ŏŏn'ger-her-rish] a. unseemly, undue, improper; **-keit** nf. impropriety.

Ungehorsam [ŏŏn'ger-horr-zam] a. disobedient; nm. disobedience, insubordination.

Ungekünstelt [ŏŏn'ger-kyŏŏn-stelt] a. natural, unaffected.

Ungekürzt [ŏŏn'ger-kyŏŏrrtst]
a. unabridged.

Ungeladen [ŏŏn'ger-lah-den]
a. uninvited, uncharged, unloaded (*mil.*).

Ungelegen [ŏŏn'ger-lay-gen]
a. inconvenient; **-heit** *nf.* inconvenience.

Ungelenk [ŏŏn'ger-lenk] *a.*
stiff, clumsy. [unskilled.

Ungelernt [ŏŏn'ger-lairrnt] *a.*

Ungemach [ŏŏn'ger-mach] *n.*
hardship, discomfort.

Ungemein [ŏŏn'ger-mine] *a.*
uncommon, extraordinary; *ad.*
exceedingly, most.

Ungemütlich [ŏŏn'ger-
myŏŏt-lish] *a.* uncomfortable,
disagreeable.

Ungenannt [ŏŏn'ger-nant] *a.*
unnamed, anonymous.

Ungenau [ŏŏn'ger-now] *a.* inaccurate; **-igkeit** *nf.* inaccuracy.

Ungeneigt [ŏŏn'ger-nikt] *a.*
disinclined.

Ungeniert [ŏŏn'zhay-neerrt]
a. free and easy, unceremonious.

Ungenüg'end [ŏŏn'ger-nyŏŏ-
gent] *a.* insufficient, inadequate; **-sam** *a.* insatiable.

Ungeprüft [ŏŏn'ger-prŏŏft]
a. unexamined. [*a.* untidy.

Ungepflegt [ŏŏn'ger-pflaikt]

Ungerade [ŏŏn'ger-rah-der] *a.*
uneven, odd, not straight.

Ungeraten [ŏŏn'ger-rah-ten]
a. spoilt.

Ungerecht [ŏŏn'ger-resht] *a.*
unjust; **-fertigt** *a.* unjustifiable; **-igkeit** *nf.* injustice, unfairness. [absurd.

Ungereimt [ŏŏn'ger-rimt] *a.*

Ungern [ŏŏn'gairrn] *ad.* unwillingly, reluctantly, grudgingly.

Ungesäumt [ŏŏn'ger-zoimt]
a. unhemmed, seamless,
prompt; *ad.* immediately.

Ungeschehen [ŏŏn'ger-shay-
en] *a.* undone.

Ungeschick [ŏŏn'ger-shik] *n.*

(**-e**) misfortune; **-lichkeit** *nf.*
clumsiness; **-t** *a.* awkward,
clumsy.

Ungeschlacht [ŏŏn'ger-
shlacht] *a.* boorish, uncouth.

Ungeschliffen [ŏŏn'ger-shlif-
en] *a.* unpolished, coarse.

Ungeschminkt [ŏŏn'ger-
shinkt] *a.* unvarnished.

Ungeschwächt [ŏŏn'ger-
shvesht] *a.* unimpaired.

Ungesellig [ŏŏn'ger-zel-ish]
a. unsociable.

Ungesetzlich [ŏŏn'ger-zets-
lish] *a.* illegal. [uncivilized.

Ungesittet [ŏŏn'ger-zit-et] *a.*

Ungestört [ŏŏn'ger-shterrt] *a.*
undisturbed.

Ungestraft [ŏŏn'ger-shtrahft]
ad. with impunity.

Ungestüm [ŏŏn'ger-shtyŏŏm]
a. blustering, impetuous; *n.*
violence. [unhealthy.

Ungesund [ŏŏn'ger-zŏŏnt] *a.*

Ungetrübt [ŏŏn'ger-tryŏŏpt]
a. untroubled, clear.

Ungewaschen [ŏŏn'ger-vash-
en] *a.* unwashed.

Ungewiss [ŏŏn'ger-viss] *a.*
uncertain; **-heit** *nf.* uncertainty, suspense.

Ungewitter [ŏŏn'ger-vit-err]
n. (thunder) storm.

Ungewöhnlich [ŏŏn'ger-
vern-lish] *a.* unusual.

Ungewohnt [ŏŏn'ger-vohnt]
a. unaccustomed.

Ungezählt [ŏŏn'ger-sailt] *a.*
innumerable, countless.

Ungeziefer [ŏŏn'ger-see-ferr]
n. (**-**) vermine.

Ungezogen [ŏŏn'gert-soh-
gen] *a.* rude; **-heit** *nf.* rudeness.

Ungezwungen [ŏŏn'gert-
svŏŏng-en] *a.* unconstrained,
natural.

Unglaub'e [ŏŏn'glow-ber] *nm.*
unbelief; **-lich** *a.* incredible;
-würdig *a.* unreliable.

Ungläubig [ŏŏn'gloy-bish] *a.*
unbelieving, incredulous

Ungleich [ŏŏn'glïsh] a. uneven, odd, unequal, unlike; ad. incomparably; -artig a. different; -förmig a. irregular, not uniform; -heit nf. inequality, dissimilarity.

Unglimpf [ŏŏn'glïmpf] nm. harshness, insult; -lich a. harsh, insulting.

Unglück [ŏŏn'glyŏŏk] n. (-s) misfortune, disaster, ill luck, distress; -lich a. unhappy, unlucky; -erweise ad. unfortunately; -selig a. miserable, disastrous; -sfall nm. accident, disaster.

Ungnade [ŏŏn'gnah-der] nf. disgrace, displeasure.

Ungnädig [ŏŏn'gnay-dish] a. ungracious.

Ungültig [ŏŏn'gyŏŏl-tish] a. not valid, not current; -keit nf. nullity.

Un'gunst [ŏŏn'gŏŏnst] nf. disfavour; -günstig a. unfavourable.

Unhaltbar [ŏŏn'halt-barr] a. (untenable.

Unhandlich [ŏŏn'hant-lish] a. clumsy, unwieldy.

Unheil [ŏŏn'hïle] n. mischief, evil, misfortune; -bar a. incurable; -bringend a. unlucky; -stifter nm. mischiefmaker; -voll a. disastrous.

Unheimlich [ŏŏn'hïme-lish] a. weird, uncanny; ad. awfully.

Unhöflich [ŏŏn'herf-lish] a. impolite; -keit nf. impoliteness.

Unhold [ŏŏn'holt] nm. (-e) monster, demon; a. ungracious.

Unhörbar [ŏŏn'herr-barr] a. inaudible.

Uniform [ŏŏ-ni-form'] nf. uniform; -iert a. (in) uniform.

Uninteressant [ŏŏn'in-ter-ress-ant'] a. uninteresting.

Universal [ŏŏ-ni-vairr-zahl'] a. universal, sole.

Universität [ŏŏ-ni-vairr-zi-tate'] nf. university.

Unke [ŏŏn'ker] nf. toad.

Unkennt'lich [ŏŏn'kent-lish] a. unrecognizable; -nis nf. ignorance.

Unklar [ŏŏn'klarr] a. not clear, obscure, dim; -heit nf. obscurity, dimness.

Unklug [ŏŏn'klŏŏk] a. unwise.

Unkörperlich [ŏŏn'kerr'perr-lish] a. incorporeal.

Unkosten [ŏŏn'kos-ten] pl. expense(s); (-kräuter) weed.

Unkraut [ŏŏn'krowt] n.

Unkündbar [ŏŏn'kyŏŏnt-barr] a. unredeemable.

Unkundig [ŏŏn'kŏŏn-dish] a. ignorant of. [recently]

Unlängst [ŏŏn'lengst] ad.

Unlauter [ŏŏn'low-terr] a. unfair, impure. [unbearable.

Unleidlich [ŏŏn'lïte-lish] a.

Unleserlich [ŏŏn'lay-zerr-lish] a. illegible.

Unleugbar [ŏŏn'loik-barr] a. undeniable. [-lich a. insoluble.

Unlös'bar [ŏŏn-lerss'barr] a.

Unlust [ŏŏn'lŏŏst] nf. aversion, dislike; -ig a. disinclined, averse.

Unmanierlich [ŏŏn'ma-neer-lish] a. unmannerly.

Unmännlich [ŏŏn'men-lish] a. unmanly.

Unmass [ŏŏn'mahss] n. immense amount; -e nf. enormous quantity; -geblich a. unwarranted.

Unmässig [ŏŏn'mace-ish] a. immoderate, intemperate.

Unmenge [ŏŏn'meng-er] nf. = Unmasse.

Unmensch [ŏŏn'mensh] m.w. brute; -lich a. inhuman, superhuman, tremendous; -lichkeit nf. inhumanity.

Unmerklich [ŏŏn'mairrk-lish] a. imperceptible.

Unmittelbar [ŏŏn'mit-el-barr] a, ad. immediate(ly), direct(ly).

Unmöbliert [ŏŏn'merb-leerrt] a. unfurnished.

Unmöglich [ŏŏn'merk-lish] a.

impossible; **-keit** *nf.* impossibility.

Unmoralisch [ŏŏn'mo-rah-lish] *a.* immoral.

Unmündig [ŏŏn'myŏŏn-dish] *a.* minor, under age; **-keit** *nf.* minority. [humour.

Unmut [ŏŏn'mŏŏt] *nm.* ill-

Unnachahmlich [ŏŏn'nach-ahm'lish] *a.* inimitable.

Unnachgiebig [ŏŏn'nach-gee-bish] *a.* unyielding, adamant.

Unnahbar [ŏŏn'nah-barr] *a.* unapproachable, inaccessible.

Unnatürlich [ŏŏn'na-tyŏŏr-lish] *a.* unnatural, affected.

Unnötig [ŏŏn'ner-tish] *a.* unnecessary. [less, vain.

Unnütz [ŏŏn'nyŏŏts] *a.* use-

Unordentlich [ŏŏn'orr-dent-lish] *a.* disorderly; **-nung** *nf.* disorder.

Unparteiisch [ŏŏn'parr-ti-ish] *a.* impartial; **-ische(r)** *m.w.* umpire; **-lichkeit** *nf.* impartiality.

Unpassend [ŏŏn'pass-ent] *a.* unsuitable, inopportune.

Unpässlich [ŏŏn'pess-lish] *a.* indisposed; **-keit** *nf.* indisposition.

Unpatriotisch [ŏŏn'pa-tri-oh'tish] *a.* unpatriotic.

Unpersönlich [ŏŏn'perr-zern-lish] *a.* impersonal.

Unpraktisch [ŏŏn'prak-tish] *a.* unpractical.

Unpünktlich [ŏŏn'pyŏŏnkt-lish] *a.* unpunctual.

Unrat [ŏŏn'raht] *nm.* refuse, filth.

Unratsam [ŏŏn'raht-zam] *a.* inadvisable.

Unrecht [ŏŏn'resht] *a., ad.* wrong(ly), unjust(ly); *n.* wrong, injustice; **-mässig** *a.* unlawful, illegal.

Unredlich [ŏŏn'rate-lish] *a.* dishonest; **-keit** *nf.* dishonesty.

Unreel [ŏŏn'ray-el'] *a.* dishonest.

Unregelmässig [ŏŏn'ray-gel-

mace-ish] *a.* irregular; **-keit** *nf.* irregularity.

Unreif [ŏŏn'rife] *a.* unripe, immature; **-e** *nf.* unripeness, immaturity.

Unrein [ŏŏn'rine] *a.* dirty, unclean, untidy, foul; **-lich** *a.* uncleanly; **-lichkeit** *nf.* dirtiness.

Unrichtig [ŏŏn'rish-tish] *a.* wrong, incorrect; **-keit** *nf.* incorrectness.

Unruh [ŏŏn'rŏŏ] *nf.* balance (*watch*); **-e** *nf.* unrest, agitation; **-ig** *a.* restless, fidgety, turbulent.

Unrühmlich [ŏŏn'ryŏŏm-lish] *a.* inglorious.

Uns [ŏŏnss] *pn.* us, ourselves.

Unsachlich [ŏŏn'zach-lish] *a.* not to the point, prejudiced.

Unsäglich [ŏŏn-zake'lish] *a.* unspeakable.

Unsauber [ŏŏn'zow-berr] *a.* unclean, dirty, unfair.

Unschädlich [ŏŏn'shate-lish] *a.* harmless.

Unscheinbar [ŏŏn'shine-barr] *a.* insignificant, unpretentious, homely.

Unschicklich [ŏŏn'shik-lish] *a.* unseemly, improper; **-keit** *nf.* impropriety.

Unschlitt [ŏŏn'shlit] *n.* (-e) tallow.

Unschlüssig [ŏŏn'shlyŏŏ-sish] *a.* irresolute; **-keit** *nf.* irresolution.

Unschuld [ŏŏn'shŏŏlt] *nf.* innocence; **-ig** *a.* innocent.

Unselbständig [ŏŏn'zelb-shten-dish] *a.* dependent.

Unselig [ŏŏn'zay-lish] *a.* fatal, unfortunate.

Unser [ŏŏn'zerr] *poss.* our; **-ige,** der, die, das *poss.* ours.

Unsicher [ŏŏn'zi-sherr] *a.* uncertain, insecure, unsafe; **-heit** *nf.* uncertainty, insecurity.

Unsichtbar [ŏŏn'zisht-barr] *a.* invisible; **-keit** *nf.* invisibility.

Unsinn [ŏŏn'zin] *nm.* nonsense; **-ig** *a.* nonsensical.

Unsitte [ŏŏn'zit-er] *nf.* bad habit; **-lich** *a.* immoral; **-lichkeit** *nf.* immorality.

Unsre = **Unsere.**

Unstatthaft [ŏŏn'shtat-haft] *a.* inadmissible.

Unsterblich [ŏŏn'shtairrp-lish] *a.* immortal; **-keit** *nf.* immortality.

Unstern [ŏŏn'shtairrn] *nm.* unlucky star.

Unstet [ŏŏn'shtate] *a.* unsteady, inconstant.

Unstreitig [ŏŏn'shtrite-ish] *a.* unquestionable.

Unsumme [ŏŏn'zŏŏ-mer] *nf.* immense sum.

Unsympathisch [ŏŏn'zÿŏŏm-pah-tish] *a.* unpleasant.

Untadelhaft [ŏŏn-tah'del-haft] *a.* irreproachable.

Untat [ŏŏn'taht] *nf.* outrage.

Untätig [ŏŏn'tate-ish] *a.* inactive, passive, idle; **-keit** *nf.* inactivity.

Untauglich [ŏŏn'towk-lish] *a.* unfit, useless; **-keit** *nf.* unfitness, incapacity, inefficiency.

Unteilbar [ŏŏn-tile'barr] *a.* indivisible.

Unten [ŏŏn'ten] *ad.* below, underneath, downstairs, at the bottom.

Unter [ŏŏn'terr] *pr.* under(neath) below, among, between, of; *a* under, lower.

Unterabteilung [ŏŏn'terr-ap-tile-ŏŏng] *nf.* subdivision.

Unterarm [ŏŏn'terr-arrm] *nm.* (**-arme**) forearm.

Unterbau [ŏŏn'terr-bow] *nm.* substructure; **-en** *vt.* to lay foundations.

Unterbeinkleider [ŏŏn'terr-bine-klide-err] *pl.* pants, knickers.

Unter-belichten *vt.* to underexpose; **-bett** *n.* feather-bed; **-bewusstsein** *n.* sub-conscious; **-bieten** *vt. ir.* to undercut

---

-bilanz *nf.* adverse balance; **-bleiben** *vi. ir.* to cease, not to occur.

Unterbrechen [ŏŏn-terr-bresh'en] *vt. ir.* to interrupt; **-ung** *nf.* interruption.

Unterbreiten [ŏŏn-terr-brite'en] *vt.* to submit.

Unterbringen [ŏŏn'terr-bring-en] *vt. ir.* to shelter, accommodate, store, sell (*com.*).

Unterdeck [ŏŏn'terr-dek] *n.* lower deck.

Unterdessen [ŏŏn-terr-dess'en] *ad.* meanwhile.

Unterdruck [ŏŏn terr-drŏŏk] *nm.* low pressure; **-drücken** *vt.* to suppress, crush, repress; **-drückung** *nf.* suppression.

Untereinander [ŏŏn'terr-ine-an-derr] *ad.* with each other, among themselves, mutually.

Unterernährung [ŏŏn'terr-err-nair-rŏŏng] *nf.* underfeeding.

Unterfangen [ŏŏn'terr-fang-en] *vt. ir.* to undertake, dare; *n.* undertaking.

Unterfeldwebel [ŏŏn'terr-felt-vay-bel] *nm.* (**-**) lance corporal. [**-tigen**] *vt.* to sign.

Unterfertigen [ŏŏn'terr-fairr-]

Unterführer [ŏŏn'terr-fyŏŏr-rerr] *nm.* (**-**) subordinate commander; **-ung** *nf.* subway.

Untergang [ŏŏn'terr-gang] *nm.* setting, (down)fall.

Untergeben [ŏŏn'terr-gay'ben] *a.* subordinate, subject, inferior.

Untergehen [ŏŏn'terr-gay-en] *vi. ir.* to set, sink, perish.

Untergeschoss [ŏŏn'terr-ger-shoss] *n.* (**-e**) ground-floor; **-gestell** *n.* undercarriage, chassis (*aut.*).

Untergraben [ŏŏn'terr-grah'ben] *vt. ir.* to undermine.

Untergrund [ŏŏn'terr-groont] *nm.* subsoil; **-bahn** *nf.* underground (railway).

Unterhalb [ŏŏn'terr-halp] pr. below.

Unterhalt [ŏŏn'terr-halt] nm. livelihood; **-en** vt. ir. to support, maintain, entertain; r. talk, enjoy oneself; **-end** a. entertaining; **-ung** nf. maintenance, entertainment, amusement, talk.

Unter'handeln [ŏŏn-terr-han'-deln] vi. to negotiate; **-händler** nm. (-) negotiator, agent; **-handlung** nf. negotiation.

Unterhemd [ŏŏn'terr-hemt] n. (gen. -s; pl. -en) vest.

Unterhöhlen [ŏŏn'terr-her'-len] vt. to undermine.

Unter-hosen pl. pants; **-irdisch** a. underground; **-jacke** nf. vest; **-jochen** vt. to subjugate; **-kleider** pl. underclothing.

Unter'kommen [ŏŏn'terr-kom-en] vi. ir. to find shelter, work; n. accommodation, employment; **-kunft** nf. lodging.

Unterlage [ŏŏn'terr-lah-ger] nf. foundation, basis, evidence, blotting-pad.

Unterlass'en [ŏŏn-terr-lass'-en] vt. ir. to fail to do, omit; **-ung** nf. omission.

Unterlaufen [ŏŏn'terr-low'-fen] vi. ir. to be bloodshot; [ŏŏn'terr-low-fen] vi. to occur, crop up.

Unterlegen [ŏŏn'terr-lay-gen] vt. to lay, put under.

Unterleib [ŏŏn'terr-lipe] nm. (-er) abdomen.

Unterliegen [ŏŏn'terr-lee-gen] vi. ir. to succumb, be defeated, admit of (doubt).

Untermauern [ŏŏn'terr-mow'errn] vt. to underpin.

Untermieter [ŏŏn'terr-mee-terr] nm. (-) sub-tenant.

Unternehm'en [ŏŏn-terr-nay'men] vt. ir. to undertake, attempt; n. undertaking; **-ung** nf. enterprise.

Unteroffizier [ŏŏn'terr-of-it-seerr'] nm. (-e) corporal, petty officer; **-anwärter** nm. prospective n.c.o.

Unterordn'en [ŏŏn'terr-orrt-nen] vt. to subordinate; **-ung** nf. subordination. [n. pledge.

Unterpfand [ŏŏn'terr-pfant]

Unterred'en [ŏŏn-terr-ray'den] vr. to converse; **-ung** nf. conversation, interview, talk.

Unterricht [ŏŏn'terr-risht] nm. instruction, teaching; **-en** vt. to instruct, inform; **-soffizier** nm. education officer; **-swesen** n. education.

Unterrock [ŏŏn'ter-rok] nm. (-röcke) petticoat.

Untersagen [ŏŏn'terr-zah-gen] vt. to forbid.

Untersatz [ŏŏn'terr-zats] nm. support, stand, saucer, ironstand.

Unterschätzen [ŏŏn-terr-shet'sen] vt. to underrate, underestimate.

Unterscheid'en [ŏŏn-terr-shide'en] vt. to distinguish; r. differ; **-ung** nf. distinction, differentiation.

Unterschieben [ŏŏn-terr-shee'ben] vt. ir. to substitute, foist on, impute to.

Unterschied [ŏŏn-terr-sheet] nm. (-e) difference, distinction; **-en** a. different, distinct; **-slos** ad. indiscriminately.

Unterschlag'en [ŏŏn-terr-shlah'gen] vt. ir. to embezzle, suppress; **-ung** nf. embezzlement.

Unterschleif [ŏŏn'terr-shlife] nm. fraud, embezzlement.

Unterschlupf [ŏŏn'terr-shloopf] nm. refuge.

Unter'schreiben [ŏŏn-terr-shribe'en] vt. ir. to sign; **-schrift** nf. signature, caption (film).

Unterseeboot [ŏŏn'terr-zay-bote] n. (-e) submarine; **-ab-**

wehr nf. anti-submarine defence; -bunker nm. U-boat pen; -falle nf. decoy ship; -sicherung nf. anti-submarine screen.

Unterseeisch [ŏŏn′terr-zay-ish] a. submarine.

Untersetz′en [ŏŏn-terr-zet′sen] vt. to mix; -t a. thick-set.

Unterstand [ŏŏn′terr-shtant] nm. (-stände) dug-out, deep trench.

Unterstehen [ŏŏn-terr-shtay′en] vi. ir. to be under; r. dare.

Unterstell′en [ŏŏn-terr-shtel′en] vt. to subordinate, insinuate; -t a. subordinate; -ung nf. imputation, subordination, garaging (aut.).

Unterstreichen [ŏŏn-terr-shtrī′shen] vt. ir. to underline.

Unterstufe [ŏŏn′terr-shtōō-fer] nf. lower grade.

Unterstütz′en [ŏŏn-terr-shtyŏŏt′sen] vt. to support; -ung nf. support.

Untersuch′en [ŏŏn-terr-zōōch′en] vt. to examine, investigate, explore; -ung nf. examination, inquiry; -ungshaft nf. imprisonment on remand; -ungsstelle nf. medical examination centre.

Untertan [ŏŏn′terr-tahn] nm. (gen. -s; pl. -en) subject.

Untertänig [ŏŏn′terr-tay-nish] a. subject, submissive; -keit nf. submissiveness, humility. [nf. saucer.

Untertasse [ŏŏn′terr-tass-er]

Untertauchen [ŏŏn′terr-towch-en] vi. to dive, disappear.

Unterteil [ŏŏn′terr-tile] nm. (-e) lower part, bottom.

Untervermieten [ŏŏn′terr-verr-mee-ten] vt. to sub-let.

Unterwärts [ŏŏn′terr-vairrts] ad. downwards.

Unterwäsche [ŏŏn′terr-vesh-er] nf. underwear.

Unterwasser′bombe [ŏŏn-

terr-vass′err-bom-ber] nf. depth-charge; -verhau nm. boom.

Unterwegs [ŏŏn-terr-vaix′] ad. on the way.

Unterweis′en [ŏŏn-terr-vize-en] vt. ir. to instruct; -ung nf. instruction.

Unterwerf′en [ŏŏn-terr-vairr′fen] vt. ir. to subdue, subjugate; r. submit; -ung nf. subjection, submission.

Unterwinden [ŏŏn-terr-vind′en] vr. ir. to venture.

Unterwürfig [ŏŏn-terr-vyŏŏrr′fish] a. obsequious, servile.

Unterzeichn′en [ŏŏn-terrt-sish′nen] vt. to sign; -ete(r) m.w. undersigned; -ung nf. signing. [underwear.

Unterzeug [ŏŏn′terrt-soik] n.

Unterziehen [ŏŏn-terrt-see′en] vt. ir. to subject; r. to undergo, take.

Untief [ŏŏn′teef] a. shallow; -e nf. shoal, shallow(ness).

Untrennbar [ŏŏn-tren′barr] a. inseparable.

Untreu [ŏŏn′troy] a. unfaithful; -e nf. unfaithfulness.

Untröstlich [ŏŏn′trerst-lish] a. inconsolable.

Untrüglich [ŏŏn′tryŏŏk-lish] a. unerring.

Untüchtig [ŏŏn′tyŏŏsh-tish] a. incompetent, unfit.

Untugend [ŏŏn′tōō-gent] nf. vice, failing.

Untunlich [ŏŏn′tōōn-lish] a. impracticable.

Unüber′legt [ŏŏn′yŏŏ-berr-laikt] a. inconsiderate, rash; -sehbar a. immense, incalculable; -steigbar a. insurmountable; -troffen a. unsurpassed; -windlich a. invincible, insurmountable.

Ununˈgänglich [ŏŏn′ŏŏm-geng-lish] a. indispensable, vital; -schränkt a. absolute; -wunden a. candid.

Ununterbrochen [ŏŏn'ŏŏn-terr-broch-en] a. uninterrupted.
Unver'änderlich [ŏŏn-verr-enderr-lish] a. unchangeable; -antwortlich a. irresponsible, inexcusable; -besserlich a. incorrigible; -bindlich a. not binding, unkind; -blümt a, ad. plain(ly); -bürgt a. unwarranted, not confirmed; -daulich a. indigestible; -dient a. undeserved; -dorben a. unspoilt; -drossen a. indefatigable; -einbar a. incompatible; -fälscht a. unadulterated, pure; -fänglich a. simple, harmless; -froren a. impudent; -gesslich a. unforgettable; -gleichlich a. incomparable; -heiratet a. unmarried; -hofft a. unexpected; -hohlen a. unconcealed; -kennbar a. unmistakable; -kürzt a. unabridged; -letzt a. uninjured; -meidlich a. unavoidable; -mindert a. undiminished; -mischt a. unmixed; -mittelt a. sudden; -mögen n. impotence, inability; -mutet a. unexpected; -nehmlich a. inaudible; -nunft nf. unreasonableness; -nünftig a. foolish; -schämt a. impudent; -schuldet a. undeserved, unencumbered; -sehens ad. unawares; -sehrt a. uninjured; -söhnlich a. irreconcilable; -stand nm. folly; -ständig a. unwise; -ständlich a. unintelligible; -versucht a. unattempted; -träglich a. incompatible; -wandt a. steady, fixed; -wüstlich a. indestructible; -zagt a. undaunted; -zeihlich a. unpardonable; -züglich a. immediate.
Unvoll'kommen [ŏŏn'foll-kom-en] a. imperfect; -ständig a. incomplete.
Unvor'bereitet [ŏŏn'forr-berrite-et] a. unprepared; -hergesehen a. unforeseen; -sätzlich a. unintentional; -sichtig

a. careless, imprudent; -teilhaft a. disadvantageous.
Unwählbar [ŏŏn'vale-barr] a. ineligible.
Unwahr [ŏŏn'varr] a. untrue; -haftig a. untruthful; -heit nf. untruth; -scheinlich a. improbable; -scheinlichkeit nf. improbability, unlikelihood.
Unwandelbar [ŏŏn-van-del-barr] a. unchangeable.
Unwegsam [ŏŏn'vake-zam] a. pathless.
Unweib [ŏŏn'vipe] n. hag, virago; -lich a. unwomanly.
Unweigerlich [ŏŏn'vie-gerr-lish] a. unquestioning; ad. without fail.
Unweit [ŏŏn'vite] ad, pr. near, not far off. [worthy.
Unwert [ŏŏn'vairrt] a. un-
Unwesen [ŏŏn'vaze-en] n. mischief, nuisance; -tlich a. unessential, unimportant.
Unwetter [ŏŏn'vet-err] n. storm. [unimportant.
Unwichtig [ŏŏn'vish-tish] a.
Unwider'legbar [ŏŏn'vee-derr-lake-barr] a. irrefutable; -ruflich a. irrevocable; -stehlich a. irresistible.
Unwiederbringlich [ŏŏn'vee-derr-bring-lish] a. irretrievable.
Unwill'e [ŏŏn'vil-er] nm. indignation; -ig a. indignant, reluctant; -kommen a. unwelcome; -kürlich a. involuntary.
Unwirksam [ŏŏn'virrk-zam] a. ineffective, inefficient.
Unwirsch [ŏŏn'virrsh] a. cross, surly. [inhospitable.
Unwirtlich [ŏŏn'virrt-lish] a.
Unwissen'd [ŏŏn'viss-ent] a. ignorant; -heit nf. ignorance; -schaftlich a. unscientific.
Unwohl [ŏŏn'vole] a. unwell, ill; -sein n. indisposition.
Unwürdig [ŏŏn'vyoor-dish] a. unworthy; -keit nf. unworthiness.

Un'zahl [ŏont'sahl] nf. immense number; -zählig a. innumerable.

Unzähmbar [ŏont-sáme'barr] a. untamable. [delicate.

Unzart [ŏont'sarrt] a.

Unze [ŏont'ser] nf. ounce.

Unzeit [ŏont'site] nf. wrong time; -gemäss a. inopportune; -ig a. premature.

Unzer'brechlich [ŏont'serr-bresh-lish] a. unbreakable; -reissbar a. untearable; -störbar a. indestructible; -trennlich a. inseparable.

Unziemlich [ŏont'seem-lish] a. unseemly.

Un'zucht [ŏont'sŏocht] nf. lewdness; -züchtig a. unchaste, lewd.

Unzu'frieden [ŏont-sŏo-free-den] a. dissatisfied; -friedenheit nf. discontent; -gänglich a. inaccessible; -länglich a. inadequate; -lässig a. inadmissible; -rechnungsfähig a. irresponsible; -sammenhängend a. disconnected, incoherent; -verlässig a. unreliable.

Unzweckmässig [ŏont'svek-mace-ish] a. unsuitable.

Unzwei'deutig [ŏont'svi-doy-tish] a. unambiguous; -felhaft a. undoubted.

Üppig [yóo'pish] a. luxuriant, voluptuous; -keit nf. luxuriousness, voluptuousness.

Ur'ahn [ŏorr'ahn] m.w. great-grandfather; -alt a. ancient, very old; -anfänglich a. primeval, original; -aufführung nf. first performance.

Urbar [ŏor'barr] a. arable.

Ur'bedeutung [ŏorr'ber-doy-tŏong] nf. original meaning; -bewohner nm. aboriginal; -bild n. original; -eltern pl. ancestors; -enkel nm. great-grandchild; -form nf. original form; -grossmutter nf. great-grandmother; -grossvater nm. great-grandfather

Urheber [ŏorr'habe-err] nm. (-) author, creator; -schaft nf. authorship.

Urkund'e [ŏorr'kŏon-der] nf. document, deed; -lich a. documentary.

Urlaub [ŏorr'lowp] nm. leave; -er nm. (-) man on leave; -sschein nm. leave pass.

Urmensch [ŏorr'mensh] m.w. primitive man.

Urne [ŏorr'ner] nf. urn.

Ur'plötzlich [ŏorr'plerts-lish] ad. all of a sudden; -quelle nf. fountain-head; -sache nf. cause; -sprung nm. origin, source; -sprünglich a. primary, original; ad. primarily, originally.

Urteil [ŏorr'tile] n. (-e) sentence, judgement, opinion; -en vt.i. to judge; -sspruch nm. sentence, verdict.

Ur'text [ŏorr'text] nm. (-e) original text; -volk n. primitive people; -wald nm. virgin forest; -wüchsig a. rough, blunt, original.

Usupator [ŏo-zŏo-pah'torr] nm. (gen. -s; pl. -en) usurper.

Utopie [ŏo-to-pee'] nf. utopia.

V

Vag [vahk] a. vague.

Vagabund [va-ga-bŏont'] m.w. tramp, vagabond; -entum n. vagrancy, tramping.

Vakant' [va-kant'] a. vacant; -z nf. vacancy, vacant post, vacation.

Vakuum [va'kŏo-ŏom] n. vacuum; -reiniger nm. vacuum cleaner.

Valuta [va-lŏo'tah] nf. (Valuten) rate of exchange, value, currency.

Vanille [va-nil'yer] nf. vanilla.

Variété [va-ri-ay-tay'] n. (-s) music-hall.

Vasall [va-zal'] m.w. vassal.

Vase [vah'zer] *nf.* vase.
Vaselin [va-zer-leen'] *n.* vaseline.
Vater [fah'terr] *nm.* (Vöoter) father; **-haus** *n.* home, parents' house; **-land** *n.* native country; **-ländisch** *a.* national; **-lahds-hebe** *nf.* patriotism; **-schaft** *nf.* paternity; **-sname** *nm.* surname; **-stadt** *nf.* native town.
Väterlich [fay'terr-lish] *a.* fatherly. [*nm.* (-) vegetarian.
Vegetarier [ve-ge-tah'ri-err] *n.*
Velichen [file'shen] *n.* violet.
Velin [ve-leen'] *n.* vellum.
Vene [vay'ner] *nf.* vein.
Venerisch [ve-nair'rish] *a.* venereal.
Ventil [ven-teel'] *n.* (-e) valve; **-ator** *nm.* (gen. -s; pl. -en) ventilator; **-ieren** *vt.* to ventilate.
Verab folgen [fer-ap'fol-gen] *vt.* to deliver, hand over; **-folgung** *nf.* delivery; **-reden** *vt.* to agree, fix; **-redung** *nf.* agreement, engagement, appointment; **-reichen** *vt.* to give; **-scheuen** *vt.* to detest, abhor; **-scheuung** *nf.* abomination, detestation; **-scheuungswert** *a.* detestable; **-schieden** *vt.* to dismiss; *r.* take leave; **-schiedung** *nf.* dismissal.
Verachten [fer-ach'ten] *vt.* to despise; **-ung** *nf.* contempt.
Verächtlich [fer-esht'lish] *a.* contemptuous, contemptible.
Verallgemeinern [fer-al-ger-mine'errn] *vt.* to generalize; **-ung** *nf.* generalization.
Veralten [fer-al'ten] *vi.* to grow old, obsolete; **-et** *a.* obsolete, old.
Veranda [ver-an'dah] *n.* (Veranden) veranda.
Veränderlich [fer-en-derr-lish] *a.* changeable; **-lichkeit** *nf.* changeableness, instability; **-vt.r.** to change, alter; **-ung** *nf.* change, alteration.
Verankern [fer-ank'errn] *vt.* to moor (*nav.*).

Veranlagt [fer-an'lahkt] *a.* gifted, talented; **-ung** *nf.* disposition, talent, aptitude.
Veranlassen [fer-an'lass-en] *vt.* to cause, give rise to, make (someone do something); **-ung** *nf.* cause, inducement, motive, order.
Veranschaulichen [fer-an'-show-lish-en] *vt.* to make clear; **-ung** *nf.* demonstration.
Veranschlagen [fer-an'shlah-gen] *vt.* to estimate.
Veranstalten [fer-an'shtal-ten] *vt.* to prepare, arrange, organize; **-ung** *nf.* organization, entertainment, show, event.
Verantworten [fer-ant'vorr-ten] *vt.* to answer for; **-lich** *a.* responsible; **-lichkeit** *nf.* responsibility; **-ung** *nf.* responsibility; **-ungslos** *a.* irresponsible.
Verarbeiten [fer-arr'bite-en] *vt.* to work up, manufacture, assimilate; **-ung** *nf.* manufacturing, finishing (*com.*).
Verargen [fer-arr'gen] *vt.* to blame, begrudge.
Verärgert [fer-airr'gert] *a.* annoyed. [grow, poor.
Verarmen [fer-arr'men] *vi.* to
Verästeln [fer-est'eln] *vr. tg* branch out.
Verausgaben [fer-owss'gah-ben] *vt.* to spend, issue (*mil.*).
Veräusser lich [fer-oy'serr-lish] *a.* alienable, saleable; **-n** *vt.* to alienate, sell; **-ung** *nf.* alienation, sale. [**-en**) verb.
Verb [vairrp] *n.* (gen. -s pl.
Verband [fer-bant'] *nm.* (-bände) bandage, dressing, association, society, party, unit (*mil.*); **-kasten** *nm.* medicine chest, first aid box; **-päckchen** *n.* field dressing; **-platz** *nf.* dressing station; **-stelle** *nf.* first-aid post, field dressing station; **-stoff** *nm.* bandage, dressing material.
Verbannen [fer-ban'en] *vt.*

to banish; **-te(r)** *m.w.* exile; **-ung** *nf.* exile.

Verbauen [fer-bow'en] *vt.* to wall up, obstruct, build badly.

Verbeissen [fer-bice'en] *vt. ir.* to swallow, stifle; *r.* to stick to.

Verbergen [fer-bairr'gen] *vt. ir.* to hide.

Verbesser'er [fer-bess'er-rerr] *nm.* (-) improver, reformer; **-n** *vt.r.* to correct, reform, improve; **-ung** *nf.* improvement, reform.

Verbeugen [fer-boy'gen] *vr.* to bow; **-ung** *nf.* bow.

Verbiegen [fer-bee'gen] *vt. r.i.* to bend; [to forbid, veto.

Verbieten [fer-bee'ten] *vt. ir.* to bind up, tie, unite, join,

Verbilden [fer-bil'den] *vt.* to spoil, educate wrongly.

Verbilligen [fer-bil'i-gen] *vt.* to cheapen.

Verbinden [fer-bin'den] *vt. ir.* to bind up, tie, unite, join, connect (*ph.*), oblige, bandage; **-lich** *a.* obligatory, obliging; **-lichkeit** *nf.* obligation, civility.

Verbindung [fer-bin'doong] *nf.* union, binding (up), combination, compound, connection, club, contact, liaison (*mil.*); **-sflugwesen** *n.* aircraft carrier service; **-sgraben** *nm.* communication trench; **-skommando** *n.* liaison detachment; **-soffizier** *nm.* liaison officer; **-sstürmer** *nm.* inside forward.

Verbissen [fer-biss'en] *a.* dogged, grim; **-heit** *nf.* doggedness, grimness.

Verbitten [fer-bit'en] *vt. ir.* not to permit, stand.

Verbitter'n [fer-bit'errn] *vt.* to embitter; **-ung** *nf.* bitterness.

Verblassen [fer-blass'en] *vi.* to turn pale, fade.

Verbleib [fer-blipe'] *nm.* whereabouts; **-en** *vi. ir.* to remain.

Verbleichen = Verblassen.

Verbleiung [fer-bli'ōong] *nf.* ethylization.

Verblend'en [fer-blen'den] *vt.* to blind, screen, face; **-ung** *nf.* stupefaction.

Verblüff'en [fer-blyōo'fen] *vt.* to stagger, amaze, disconcert; **-ung** *nf.* stupefaction.

Verblühen [fer-blyōo'en] *vi.* to wither, fade.

Verblümt [fer-blyōomt'] *a.* veiled (*allusion*).

Verbluten [fer-blōo'ten] *vi.* to bleed to death.

Verbohren [fer-bor'ren] *vi.* to be mad on. [to lend.

Verborgen [fer-borr'gen] *vt.* [to lend.

Verborgen [fer-borr'gen] *a.* hidden; **-heit** *nf.* concealment retirement.

Verbot [fer-bote'] *n.* (-e) prohibition; **-en** *a.* forbidden.

Verbrämen [fer-brame'en] *vt.* to trim, edge.

Verbrauch [fer-browch'] *nm.* consumption; **-en** *vt.* to consume, use (up), spend; **-er** (-) consumer; **-sbestand** *nm.* consumable stocks; **-smittel** *pl.* consumption goods; **-ssatz** *nm.* consumption unit; **-ssteuer** *nf.* indirect tax, exercise duty.

Verbrech'en [fer-bresh'en] *n.* (-) crime; *vt.* to commit a crime; **-er** *nm.* (-) criminal; **-erisch** *a.* criminal.

Verbreit'en [fer-brite'en] *vt.* to spread; **-ung** *nf.* spread(ing). propagation.

Verbreitern [fer-brite'errn] *vt.* to broaden.

Verbrenn'bar [fer-bren'barr] *a.* combustible; **-en** *vt. ir.* to burn; **-ung** *nf.* burning, combustion; **-ungsmotor** *nm.* internal combustion engine.

Verbringen [fer-bring'en] *vt. ir.* to spend.

Verbrüder'n [fer-bryōo'derrn] *vr.* to fraternize; **-ung** *nf.* fraternization. [to scald.

Verbrühen [fer-bryōo'en] *vt.*

Verbuchen [fer-bŏŏch'en] *vt.* to book. *vt.* to waste.

Verbummeln [fer-bŏŏ'meln]

Verbunden [fer-bŏŏn'den] *a.* obliged, indebted, connected; -heit *nf.* bond, relationship.

Verbünde'n [fer-byŏŏn'den] *vt.* to ally oneself; -te(r) *m.w.* ally. [*vr.* to guarantee.

Verbürgen [fer-byŏŏrr'gen]

Verchromt [fer-krohmt'] *a.* chromium plated.

Ver'dacht [fer-dacht'] *nm.* suspicion; -dächtig *a.* suspicious, suspect; -dächtigen *vt.* to suspect.

Verdamm'en [fer-dam'en] *vt.* to damn, condemn; -nis *nf.* perdition; -ung *nf.* damnation.

Verdampfen [fer-damp'fen] *vi.* to evaporate. [to owe.

Verdanken [fer-dank'en] *vt.*

Verdau'en [fer-dow'en] *vt.* to digest; -lich *a.* digestible; -ung *nf.* digestion.

Verdeck [fer-dek'] *n.* (-e) deck, top, hood (*aut.*); -en *vt.* to cover (up), cloak.

Verdenken [fer-denk'en] *vt. ir.* to blame, take amiss.

Verderb [fer-dairp'] *nm.* ruin; -en *vt. ir.* to spoil, ruin, corrupt; *i.* spoil, decay, come to grief; *n.* ruin; -er *nm.* (-) destroyer; -lich *a.* pernicious, perishable; -lichkeit *nf.* perniciousness, perishableness; -t *a.* depraved; -theit *nf.* depravity.

Verdeutlichen [fer-doit'lish-en] *vt.* to make clear.

Verdeutschen [fer-doitsch'en] *vt.* to put into German.

Verdichten [fer-dish'ten] *vt.* to condense, consolidate; -er *nm.* (-) condenser, compressor (*tec.*); -ung *nf.* condensation.

Verdicken [fer-dik'en] *vt.* to thicken.

Verdien'en [fer-dee'nen] *vt.* to earn, win, deserve; -st *nm.* gain(s), earnings; *n.* (-e) merit,

deserts; -stlich *a.* deserving, meritorious; -t *a.* deserving, well-earned.

Verdingen [fer-ding'en] *vt.* to hire out, place (*contract*).

Verdolmetschen [fer-dol'-met-shen] *vt.* to interpret.

Verdoppel'n [fer-dop'eln] *vt.* to double; -ung *nf.* doubling.

Verdorben [fer-dorr'ben] *a.* spoilt, damaged, rotten.

Verdräng'en [fer-dreng'en] *vt.* to oust, displace, crowd out, inhibit; -ung *nf.* displacement, repression.

Verdreh'en [fer-dray'en] *vt.* to twist, distort; -t *a.* distorted, crazy; -ung *nf.* distortion, misrepresentation.

Verdreifachen [fer-dri'fach-en] *vt.* to treble.

Verdriess'en [fer-drees'sen] *vt. ir.* to vex; -lich *a.* annoyed, peevish, tiresome; -lichkeit *nf.* peevishness, bad temper.

Verdrossen [fer-dross'en] *a.* vexed, sulky.

Verdrucken [fer-drŏŏ'ken] *vt.* to misprint.

Verdruss [fer-drŏŏss'] *nm.* annoyance, worry.

Verduften [fer-dŏŏf'ten] *vi.* to evaporate, disappear.

Verdummen [fer-dŏŏm'en] *vt.* to make stupid; *i.* grow stupid.

Verdumpfen [fer-dŏŏmp'fen] *vi.* to grow damp, dull.

Verdunke'ln [fer-dŏŏn'keln] *vt.* to darken, obscure, eclipse, black-out; -lung *nf.* darkening, black-out.

Verdünn'en [fer-dyŏŏn'en] *vt.* to dilute, attenuate; -ung *nf.* dilution, attenuation.

Verdunst'en [fer-dŏŏn'sten] *vi.* to evaporate, vaporize; -ung *nf.* evaporation.

Verdursten [fer-dŏŏrr'sten] *vi.* to die of thirst.

Verdutzen *vt.* —Verblüffen.

Veredel'n [fer-ade'eln] *vt.* to ennoble, improve, finish (*com.*);

-ung *nf.* ennobling, refinement, finishing.

Verehr'en [fer-air'ren] *vt.* to honour, venerate, worship, respect, present; -er *nm.* (-) worshipper, admirer; -lich *a.* esteemed; -ung *nf.* worship, respect.

Vereidig'en [fer-ide'l-gen] *vt.* to put on oath; -ung *nf.* swearing in.

Verein [fer-ine'] *nm.* (-e) club, union, association; -bar *a.* compatible; -barkeit *nf.* compatibility; -baren *vt.* to agree upon; -barung *nf.* agreement; -fachen *vt.* to simplify; -heitlichen *vt.* to unify, standardize; -igen *vt.* to unite, join; -igung *nf.* union, association, junction; -samen *vt.r.* to become isolated; -zelt *a.* singly, solitary, stray.

Vereis'en [fer-ize'en] *vi.* to freeze, ice; -ung *nf.* icing up.

Vereitel'n [fer-ite'eln] *vt.* to frustrate; -ung *nf.* frustration.

Vereitern [fer-ite'errn] *vi.* to fester.

Verekeln [fer-ake'eln] *vt.* to disgust with. [to narrow.

Verengern [fer-eng'errn] *vt.*

Vererb'en [fer-airr'ben] *vt.* to bequeath, transmit; *r.* be hereditary; -ung *nf.* heredity, transmission, succession (*law*).

Verewig'en [fer-ave'i-gen] *vt.* to immortalize; -t *a.* late, deceased.

Verfahren [fer-fah'ren] *vi. ir.* to act; *r.* get lost; *n.* procedure, process, system, method; *a.* bungled.

Verfall [fer-fal'] *nm.* decline, decay, maturity (*com.*); -en *vi. ir.* to decay, decline, fall due, fall to, hit upon.

Verfälsch'en [fer-fel'shen] *vt.* to falsify, adulterate; -ung *nf.* adulteration, falsification.

Verfangen [fer-fang'en] *vi. ir.* to take effect; *r.* get caught.

Verfänglich [fer-feng'lish] *a.* artful, awkward, insidious.

Verfärb'en [fer-fairr'ben] *vr.* to change colour.

Verfass'en [fer-fass'en] *vt.* to compose, write; -er *nm.* (-) author, writer; -erin *nf.* authoress; -erschaft *nf.* authorship; -ung *nf.* disposition, constitution, constitution; -ungsgemäss *a.* constitutional; -ungswidrig *a.* unconstitutional. [rot.

Verfaulen [fer-fow'len] *vi.* to

Verfecht'en [fer-fesh'ten] *vt. ir.* to maintain, advocate, defend; -er *nm.* (-) champion, defender.

Verfehl'en [fer-fail'en] *vt.i.* to fail, miss; -t *a.* mistaken, unsuccessful, wrong.

Verfeiner'n [fer-fine'errn] *vt.* to refine, polish; -ung *nf.* refinement, polish.

Verfertig'en [fer-fairr'ti-gen] *vt.* to make, manufacture; -ung *nf.* manufacture. [film.

Verfilmen [fer-fil'men] *vt.* to

Verfilzen [fer-filt'sen] *vt.* to felt.

Verfinster'n [fer-fin'sterrn] *vt.* to darken, eclipse; -ung *nf.* darkening, eclipse.

Verflachen [fer-flach'en] *vt.i.* to grow, make flat.

Verfliegen [fer-flee'gen] *vi. ir.* to fly, pass, get lost (*av.*).

Verfliessen [fer-flee'sen] *vi. ir.* to flow away, on, expire.

Verflossen [fer-floss'en] *a.* last, past. [to curse.

Verfluchen [fer-flooch'en] *vt.*

Verflüchtigen [fer-flyoosh'ti-gen] *vt.r.* to volatilize, evaporate.

Verflüssigen [fer-flyoo'si-gen] *vt.* to become liquid.

Verfolg [fer-folk'] *nm.* pursuance, course; -en *vt.* to persecute, pursue, prosecute; -er *nm.* (-) persecutor; -ung *nf.* pursuit, persecution, prosecution. [to charter, ship.

Verfrachten [fer-frach'ten] *vt.*

Verfrüht [fer-fryoot'] *a.* premature.

Verfüg'bar [fer-fyook'barr] *a.* available; **-en** *vi.* to direct, order, arrange; **- über** have at one's disposal; **-ung** *nf.* disposal, instruction, order.

Verführ'en [fer-fyoor'ren] *vt.* to lead astray, seduce, tempt; **-er** *nm.* (-) tempter, seducer; **-erisch** *a.* seductive; **-ung** *nf.* seduction, temptation.

Vergällen [fer-gel'en] *vt.* to embitter, denature.

Vergangen [fer-gang'en] *a.* past; **-heit** *nf.* past.

Vergänglich [fer-geng'lish] *a.* transitory, fleeting; **-keit** *nf.* transitoriness, impermanence.

Vergas'en [fer-gah'zen] *vt.* to gasify; **-er** *nm.* (-) carburettor (*aut.*).

Vergeb'en [fer-gay'ben] *vt. ir.* to forgive, give away; *r.* compromise oneself; **-ens** *ad.* in vain; **-lich** *a.* (in) vain; **-ung** *nf.* forgiveness, giving.

Vergegenwärtigen [fer-gay'-gen-vairr-ti-gen] *vt.* to represent; *r.* imagine.

Vergehen [fer-gay'en] *vi. ir.* to pass away, elapse, stop, waste away, die.

Vergelt'en [fer-gel'ten] *vt. ir.* to repay, requite, return, pay back; **-ung** *nf.* requital, retaliation, reward; **-ungswaffe** *nf.* rocket bomb, flying bomb, doodle-bug.

Vergess'en [fer-gess'en] *vt. ir.* to forget; **-enheit** *nf.* oblivion; **-lich** *a.* forgetful; **-lichkeit** *nf.* forgetfulness.

Vergeud'en [fer-goy'den] *vt.* to squander, waste; **-er** *nm.* (-) spendthrift; **-ung** *nf.* waste, extravagance.

Vergewaltig'en [fer-ge-val'-ti-gen] *vt.* to force, violate; **-ung** *nf.* violence, assault.

Vergewissern [fer-ger-viss'-errn] *vr.* to make sure.

Vergiessen [fer-gee'sen] *vt. ir.* to shed.

Vergift'en [fer-gift'en] *vt.* to poison; **-ung** *nf.* poisoning.

Vergissmeinnicht [fer-giss'-mine-nisht] *n.* (-e) forget-me-not. [glaze

Verglasen [fer-glah'zen] *vt.* to

Vergleich [fer-glish'] *nm.* (-e) arrangement, comparison; *-e vt. ir.* to compare, adjust, settle; **-ung** *nf.* comparison.

Verglimmen [fer-glim'en], **Verglühen** [fer-glyoo'en] *vi.* to go out, die out.

Vergnüg'en [fer-gnyoo'gen] *vr.* to enjoy oneself; *n.* pleasure, enjoyment; **-t** *a.* pleased, cheerful; **-ung** *nf.* pleasure, amusement; **-ungssüchtig** *a.* pleasure-loving.

Vergolden [fer-gol'den] *vt.* to gild

Vergönnen [fer-ger'nen] *vt.* to permit, not to begrudge.

Vergött'ern [fer-ger'terrn] *vt.* to deify, idolize; **-ung** *nf.* deification, idolizing.

Vergraben [fer-grah'ben] *vt.* to bury. [care-worn.

Vergrämt [fer-graimt'] *a.*

Vergreifen [fer-grife'en] *vt.* to touch by mistake; *r.* violate, steal. [of print.

Vergriffen [fer-grif'en] *a.* out

Vergrösser'n [fer-grer'serrn] *vt.* to enlarge, increase, magnify; **-ung** *nf.* enlargement; **-ungsapparat** *nm.* enlarger; **-ungsglas** *n.* magnifying glass.

Vergünstigung [fer-gyoon'-sti-goong] *nf.* concession, favour.

Vergüt'en [fer-gyoo'ten] *vt.* to compensate, refund; **-ung** *nf.* compensation.

Verhaft'en [fer-ha'ten] *vt.* to arrest; **-et** *a.* connected, dependent; **-ung** *nf.* arrest; **-ungsbefehl** *nm.* warrant of arrest. [die away.

Verhallen [fer-hal'en] *vi.* to

Verhalt'en [fer-hal'ten] vt. to retain, suppress; r. to be, stand, behave, be in proportion to; -ung nf. suppression, concealment; -ungsmassregeln pl. instructions, orders.

Verhältnis [fer-halt'nis] n. (-se) relation, proportion, ratio, love-affair; pl. conditions, state of things; -mässig a, ad. relative(ly), comparative(ly).

Verhand'eln [fer-han'deln] vi. to negotiate; t. discuss, dispose of; -lung nf. negotiation.

Verhäng'en [fer-heng'en] vt. to impose, decree, inflict; -nis n. destiny, fate; -nisvoll a. fatal. [remain.

Verharren [fer-har'ren] vi. to **Verharscht** [fer-harrsht'] a. healed, frozen over.

Verhärt'en [fer-hair'ten] vt. r. to harden; -et a. callous; -ung nf. hardening, hardness.

Verhaspeln [fer-has'peln] vr. to entangle, get tied up.

Verhasst [fer-hast'] a. hateful, odious.

Verhau [fer-how'] n. (-e) abatis, entanglement; -en vt. to thrash; r. make a bad blunder.

Verheer'en [fer-hair'ren] vt. to devastate; -ung nf. devastation. [to conceal.

Verhehlen [fer-haie'en] vt. ir.

Verheimlich'en [fer-hime'lish-en] vt. to keep secret; -ung nf. concealment.

Verheirat'en [fer-hi'rah-ten] vt.r. to marry, get married; -ung nf. marriage.

Verheiss'en [fer-hice'en] vt. ir. to promise; -ung nf. promising. [help towards.

Verhelfen [fer-hel'fen] vt. to

Verherrlichen [fer-hairr'lich-en] vt. to glorify.

Verhexen [fer-hex'en] vt. to bewitch.

Verhinder'n [fer-hin'derrn]

vt. to prevent, hinder; -ung nf. hindrance.

Verhöhn'en [fer-her'nen] vt. to mock, sneer at; -ung nf. scorn, mockery.

Verhör [fer-herr'] n. (-e) hearing, trial, cross-examination; -en vt. to examine, hear, try, interrogate; r. misunderstand.

Verhüll'en [fer-hyōō'len] vt. to wrap up, veil; -ung nf. disguise.

Verhungern [fer-hōong'errn] vi. to starve, die of hunger.

Verhunzen [fer-hōont'sen] vt. to bungle.

Verhüt'en [fer-hyōō'ten] vt. to prevent, avert; -ung nf. prevention.

Verirren [fer-ir'ren] vi. to go astray; -t a. lost, stray.

Verjagen [fer-yah'gen] vt. to drive away, out.

Verjähr't [fer-yairrt'] a. old, prescriptive; -ung nf. prescription (law).

Verjüngen [fer-yōōng'en] vt. to rejuvenate, reduce (scale), taper.

Verkalk'en [fer-kalk'en] vi. to calcify; -ung nf. calcination, calcification.

Verkappen [fer-kap'en] vt.r. to disguise, mask.

Verkauf [fer-kowf'] nm. (-käufe) sale; -en vt. to sell; -spreis nm. sale price.

Verkäuf'er [fer-koy'ferr] nm. (-) seller, salesman, shop assistant, distributor; -erin nf. shop-girl, shop assistant; -lich a. saleable, for sale.

Verkehr [fer-kairr'] nm. traffic, intercourse, trade; -en vi. to associate, deal, ply, run, visit regularly; t. turn over, pervert, transform; -sampel nf. traffic lights; -sboot n. passenger boat; -sengpass nm. bottleneck; -sflughafen nm. civil airfield; -sflugzeug n. passenger plane; -sgraben nm. communi-

Verkenn'en [fer-ken'en] vt. ir. to misjudge, underestimate, not recognize; -ung nf. lack of appreciation, misunderstanding.

Verkett'en [fer-ket'en] vt. to chain (together); -ung nf. chain. [putty, cement.

Verkitten [fer-kit'en] vt. to [to sue, accuse.

Verklagen [fer-klah'gen] vt.

Verklär'en [fer-klair'en] vt. to transfigure; -ung nf. transfiguration.

Verkleben [fer-klay'ben] vt. to glue up, paste over, stick.

Verkleid'en [fer-klíde'en] vt. to disguise, dress up; -ung nf. disguise, wainscoting.

Verkleiner'n [fer-kline'errn] vt. to make smaller, diminish; -ung nf. reduction, diminution; -ungswort n. diminutive.

Verklingen [fer-kling'en] vt. ir. to die away.

Verknöchert [fer-kner'sherrt] a. narrow-minded, senile.

Verknoten [fer-knote'en] vt. to knot.

Verknüpf'en [fer-knyoop'fen] vt. to tie (up), knot, unite, involve; -ung nf. combination, joining. [carbonize.

Verkohlen [fer-kohl'en] vt. to

Verkommen [fer-kom'en] vi. ir. to decay, go to the bad; a. ruined, depraved; -heit nf. depravity. [to cork.

Verkorken [fer-korrk'en] vt. to

Verkörper'n [fer-kerr'perrn] vt. to embody, personify; -ung nf. embodiment, personification.

Verköstigen [fer-ker'sti-gen] vt. to board.

Verkraftung [fer-kraf'tŏong] nf. mechanization (mil.).

Verkriechen [fer-kree'shen] vr. to creep away, into a corner.

Verkrümeln [fer-kryoö'meln] vt.r. to crumble away, disappear.

Verkrümm't [fer-kryoömt']a. crooked; -ung nf. bend, crookedness.

Verkrüppelt [fer-kryoö'pelt] a. crippled. [encrusted.

Verkrustet [fer-kroos'tet] a.

Verkümmern [fer-kyoö'merrn] vi. to waste away, shrink.

Verkündig'en [fer-kyöön'digen] vt. to announce, publish, proclaim; -ung nf. announcement, proclamation.

Verkürz'en [fer-kyöörs'en] vt. to shorten, abbreviate, curtail; -ung nf. shortening, abridging, abbreviation.

Verlad'en [fer-lah'den] vt. ir. to load, embark, ship; -ung nf. embarkation, entraining, loading.

Verlag [fer-lahk'] nm. publication, publishing firm; -buchhandlung nf. publisher's business; -srecht n. copyright.

Verlagerung [fer-lah'gerrŏong] nf. evacuation (stocks).

Verlangen [fer-lang'en] vt. to demand, desire; & long for; n. demand, request, desire.

Verlänger'n [fer-leng'errn] vt. to lengthen, prolong; -ung nf. extension, prolongation.

Verlangsamen [fer-lang'zahmen] vt. to decelerate, slow down. [ability.

Verlass [fer-lass'] nm. depend.

Verlassen [fer-lass'en] vt. ir. to leave (behind), abandon, desert; r. rely, depend; a. forsaken; -heit nf. loneliness.

Verlässlich [fer-less'lish] a. reliable. [borne (mil.).

Verlastet [fer-las'tet] a. lorry-

Verlauf [fer-lowf'] nm. course, expiration, lapse; -en vi. ir. to pass,turn out; r.get lost;a. lost.

Verlautbaren [fer-lowt'bar-ren] *vt.* to notify.

Verlauten [fer-lowt'en] *vi. imp.* to become known, be reported.

Verleb'en [fer-lay'ben] *vt.* to live through, spend; -t *a.* past, worn out.

Verleg'en [fer-lay'gen] *vt.* to remove, mislay, misplace, postpone, obstruct, publish; *a.* perplexed, embarrassed; -en-heit *nf.* embarrassment, dilemma, difficulty, scrape; -er *nm.* (-) publisher; -ung *nf.* removal, postponement.

Verleiden [fer-lide'en] *vt. ir.* to spoil.

Verleih'en [fer-lie'en] *vt. ir.* to lend, confer, bestow; -er *nm.* (-) lender; -ung *nf.* bestowal, lending.

Verleiten [fer-lite'en] *vt.* to mislead, lead astray.

Verlernen [fer-lairn'nen] *vt.* to unlearn, forget.

Verlesen [fer-laze'en] *vt. ir.* to read out, pick, gather; *r.* misread, make a slip.

Verletz'en [fer-let'sen] *vt.* to injure, hurt, violate; -lich *a.* vulnerable, susceptible; -ung *nf.* injury, dereliction (of duty), offence.

Verleugn'en [fer-loik'nen] *vt.* to deny, disown; -ung *nf.* denial.

Verleumd'en [fer-loim'den] *vt.* to slander; -er *nm.* (-) slanderer; -erisch *a.* slanderous; -ung *nf.* slander, libel.

Verlieb'en [fer-lee'ben] *vr.* to fall in love; -t *a.* in love; -theit *nf.* amourousness.

Verlieren [fer-leer'ren] *vt. ir.* to lose; *r.* get lost, disappear.

Verlob'en [fer-lobe'en] *vt.r.* to betroth, get engaged; -te *nf.* fiancé; -te(r) *m.w.* fiancé; -ung *nf.* engagement.

Verlöbnis = **Verlobung**.

Verlock'en [fer-lok'en] *vt.* to entice, tempt; -ung *nf.* enticement, temptation.

Verlogen [fer-loh'gen] *a.* lying, untruthful; -heit *nf.* untruthfulness, lying.

Verlohnen [fer-lone'en] *v.imp.* to be worth. [poached (egg).

Verloren [fer-lor'ren] *a.* lost.

Verlöschen [fer-ler'shen] *vi. ir.* to go out; *t.* to extinguish.

Verlos'en [fer-loze'en] *vt.* to raffle, draw lots for; -ung *nf.* lottery.   [solder.

Verlöten [fer-ler'ten] *vt.* to

Verlottern [fer-lot'errn], **Verlumpen** [fer-loom'pen] *vt.* to squander; *i.* go to ruin, to the bad.

Verlust [fer-lõõst'] *nm.* (-e) loss, waste, leak, casualty (*mil.*); -ig *a.* lost; -liste *nf.* casualty-list.

Vermachen [fer-mach'en] *vt.* to bequeath, leave.

Vermächtnis [fer-mesht'nis] *n.* will, legacy.

Vermahl'en [fer-mah'len] *vt.* to grind (down), mill; -ung *nf.* milling.

Vermähl'en [fer-male'en] *vt.r.* to marry; -ung *nf.* marriage.

Vermahnen [fer-mah'nen] *vt.* to admonish.

Vermehr'en [fer-mair'ren] *vt.r.* to increase, multiply; -ung *nf.* increase.

Vermeid'en [fer-mide'en] *vt. ir.* to avoid, evade; -lich *a.* avoidable.

Vermein'en [fer-mine'en] *vt.* to believe, suppose; -tlich *a.* supposed, pretended.

Vermelden [fer-mel'den] *vt.* to announce.

Vermengen [fer-meng'en] *vt.* to mingle, mix (up).

Vermerk [fer-mairrk'] *n.* note; -en *vt.* to note, remark.

Vermess'en [fer-mess'en] *vt. ir.* to measure, survey; *r.* presume; *a.* presumptuous, bold; -enheit *nf.* boldness, presumption; **-ung** *nf.* survey(ing), measurement, calibration; **-ungsschiff** *n.* survey vessel; **-ungswesen** *n.* surveying.

Vermiet'en [fer-mee'ten] *vt.* to let; **-er** *nm.* (-) landlord; **-ung** *nf.* letting.

Vermindern [fer-min'dernn] *vt.* to lessen, reduce, decrease; **-ung** *nf.* reduction, diminution.

Vermisch'en [fer-mish'en] *vt.* to mix, blend; **-ung** *nf.* mixture.

Vermiss'en [fer-miss'en] *vt.* to miss; **-t** *a.* missing.

Vermitt'eln [fer-mit'eln] *vt.* to mediate, negotiate, obtain, arrange; **-elst** *pr.* by means of; **-ler** *nm.* (-) mediator, go-between; **-lung** *nf.* securing, providing, mediation, negotiation, instrumentality; **-lungsamt** *n,* **-lungsstelle** *nf.* exchange (*ph.*). [*vi.* to mould.

Vermodern [fer-mode'errn]

Vermöge [fer-mer'ger] *pr.* by dint of, by virtue of; **-n** *vt. ir.* to be able, induce; *n.* wealth, property, ability; **-nd** *a.* wealthy; **-nssteuer** *f.* property tax.

Vermummen [ver-mōo'men] *vt.* to disguise, muffle up.

Vermut'en [fer-mōo'ten] *vt.* to suppose, suspect; **-lich** *a.* supposed, presumed; *ad.* probably; **-ung** *nf.* supposition, suspicion.

Vernachlässig'en [fer-nach'less-i-gen] *vt.* to neglect; **-ung** *nf.* neglect. [to nail up.

Vernageln [fer-nah'geln] *vt.*

Vernarben [fer-narr'ben] *vi.* to heal up.

Vernarrt [fer-narrt'] *a.* infatuated; **-heit** *nf.* infatuation. [(-) atomizer.

Vernebler [fer-nay'blerr] *nm.*

Vernehm'en [fer-name'en] *vt. ir.* to perceive, hear, learn,

interrogate (*prisoner*); **-lich** *a.* audible; **-ung** *nf.* interrogation, trial; **-ungsoffizier** *nm.* interrogation officer.

Verneig'en [fer-nī'gen] *vr.* to bow; **-ung** *nf.* bow.

Vernein'en [fer-nine'en] *vt.* to deny, answer in the negative; **-end** *a.* negative; **-ung** *nf.* negation, negative.

Vernicht'en [fer-nīsh'ten] *vt.* to annihilate, destroy, do away with; **-ung** *nf.* destruction, annihilation. [nickel-plated.

Vernickelt [fer-nik'elt] *a.*

Verniet'en [fer-neet'en] *vt.* to rivet; **-ung** *nf.* riveting.

Vernunft [fer-nŏŏnft'] *nf.* reason, sense, understanding; **-gemäss** *a.* reasonable.

Vernünft'eln [fer-nyŏŏnf'teln] *vi.* to split hairs; **-ig** *a.* sensible, rational, reasonable.

Veröd'en [fer-er'den] *vi.* to become desolate, waste; **-ung** *nf.* devastation, desolation.

Veröffentlich'en [fer-er'fentlish-en] *vt.* to publish; **-ung** *nf.* publication.

Verordn'en [fer-orrd'nen] *vt.* to order, prescribe; **-ung** *nf.* order, prescription. [to lease.

Verpachten [fer-pach'ten] *vt.*

Verpack'en [fer-pack'en] *vt.* to pack; **-ung** *nf.* packing.

Verpäppeln [fer-pep'eln] *vt.* to pamper. [miss, fit.

Verpassen [fer-pass'en] *vt.* to

Verpesten [fer-pest'en] *vt.* to infect. [to pledge, pawn.

Verpfänden [fer-pfen'den] *vt.*

Verpflanzung [fer-pflant'sen] *vt.* to transplant.

Verpfleg'en [fer-pflay'gen] *vt.* to feed, cater for, care for; **-ung** *nf.* feeding, catering, subsistence, maintenance, supply, messing (*nav, etc.*); **-ungsamt** *n.* food office; **-ungsstärke** *nf.* ration strength (*mil.*); **-ungsunteroffizier** *nm.* quartermaster sergeant.

Verpflicht'en [fer-pflish'ten] *vr.* to oblige, bind, sign on; **-ung** *nf.* obligation, engagement, duty. [*vt.* to bungle.

Verpfuschen [fer-pfoo'shen]

Verplaudern [fer-plow'derrn] *vr.* to blurt out, talk too much.

Verplempern [fer-plem'perrn] *vt.* to waste.

Verpönt [fer-pernt'] *a.* taboo, forbidden.

Verprassen = Verplempern.

Verproviantieren [fer-provi-an-teer'ren] *vt.* to provision.

Verprügeln [fer-prӰoo'geln] *vt.* to thrash.

Verpuff'en [fer-poo'fen] *vt.* to detonate, explode, be wasted on; **-ungsmotor** *nm.* internal combustion engine.

Verputz [fer-poots'] *nm.* plaster, rough-cast.

Verquick'en [fer-kvi'ken] *vt.* to amalgamate; **-ung** *nf.* amalgamation.

Verquollen [fer-kvol'en] *a.* swollen, warped.

Verrammeln [fer-ram'eln] *vt.* to barricade. [obstinate.

Verrant [fer-rant'] *a.* stubborn,

Verrat [fer-raht'] *nm.* treason, treachery; **-en** *vt. ir.* to betray, divulge.

Verräter [fer-ray'terr] *nm.* (-) traitor; **-ei** *nf.* treachery; **-erin** *nf.* traitress; **-erisch** *a.* treacherous.

Verrauchen [fer-row'chen] *vi.* to go up in smoke.

Verräuchern [fer-roi'sherrn] *vt.* to fill with smoke.

Verrauschen [fer-row'shen] *vi.* to die away, pass.

Verrechn'en [fer-resh'nen] *vt.* to reckon up, charge; *r.* miscalculate; **-ung** *nf.* miscalculation. [spoil by rain.

Verregnen [fer-raig'nen] *vt.* to

Verreisen [fer-rize'en] *vi.* to go away, be away.

Verreissen [fer-rice'en] *vt. ir.* to pull to pieces.

Verrenk'en [fer-renk'en] *vt.* to sprain; **-ung** *nf.* dislocation, sprain.

Verricht'en [fer-rish'ten] *vt.* to do, perform; **-ung** *nf.* performance, accomplishment, execution.

Verriegeln [fer-ree'geln] *vt.* to bolt up, lock, cut off (*mil.*).

Verringer'n [fer-ring'errn] *vt.* to diminish, reduce; **-ung** *nf.* diminution, lessening.

Verrinnen [fer-rin'en] *vi. ir.* to run out, away, elapse.

Verroh'en [fer-roh'en] *vi.* to become brutal; **-ung** *nf.* brutalization.

Verrosten [fer-rost'en] *vi.* to rust. [rot.

Verrotten [fer-rot'en] *vi.* to

Verrucht [fer-rooсht'] *a.* infamous; **-heit** *nf.* infamy.

Verrück'en [fer-rӰoo'ken] *vt. r.* to move, shift; **-t** *a.* crazy, mad; **-theit** *nf.* craziness.

Verruf [fer-roof'] *nm.* ill repute; **-en** *a.* notorious, disreputable.

Vers [fairrss] *nm.* (-e) line, verse; **-bau** *nm.* versification.

Versag'en [fer-zah'gen] *vt.* to refuse; *i.* fail (to act), misfire; **-er** *nm.* (-) failure, dud, misfire; **-ung** *nf.* denial.

Versalzen [fer-zalt'sen] *vt.* to put in too much salt, spoil.

Versamm'eln [fer-zam'eln] *vt.r.* to assemble, meet, gather, collect; **-lung** *nf.* meeting, assembly, rally.

Versand [fer-zant'] *nm.* despatch, transport, export; **-anzeige** *nf.* dispatch-note.

Versanden [fer-zan'den] *vi.* to silt up.

Versatz [fer-zats'] *nm.* pledging; **-amt** *n.* pawnshop.

Versauern [fer-zow'errn] *vi.* to turn sour.

Versäum'en [fer-zoy'men] *vt.* to miss, neglect, fail; **-nis** *nf.* (-se) neglect, omission.

Verschaffen [fer-shaf'en] *vt.* to procure.

Verschal'en [fer-shah'len] *vt.* to board up; *-ung nf.* boarding, casing, revetment.

Verschämt [fer-shaimt'] *a.* bashful, confused; *-heit nf.* bashfulness.

Verschanz'en [fer-shant'sen] *vt.* to entrench; *-ung nf.* entrenchment, fortification.

Verschärf'en [fer-shairr'fen] *vt.* to sharpen, intensify; *-ung nf.* tightening up, intensification.   [to bury.

Verscharren [fer-shar'ren] *vt.*

Verscheiden [fer-shide'en] *vi.* *ir.* to expire.

Verschenken [fer-shenk'en] *vt.* to give away.

Verscherzen [fer-shairrt'sen] *vt.* to forfeit, lose.

Verscheuchen [fer-shoy'shen] *vt.* to frighten away.

Verschick'en [fer-shik'en] *vt.* to send away, forward, deport; *-ung nf.* forwarding, deportation.

Verschieb'en [fer-shee'ben] *vt.* *ir.* to shift, shunt, postpone; *-ebahnhof nm.* marshalling yard; *-ung nf.* displacement, shunting, postponement.

Verschieden [fer-shee'den] *a.* different; *pl.* several; *-artig a.* various, of different kinds; *-heit nf.* difference; *-tlich a,* *ad.* different(ly), repeated(ly).

Verschiessen [fer-shee'sen] *vi.* *ir.* to fade; *t.* use up, fire away, expend (*ammunition*).

Verschiff'en [fer-shif'en] *vt.* to ship; *-ung nf.* shipment, exportation.

Verschimmeln [fer-shim'eln] *vi.* to grow mouldy.

Verschlafen [fer-shlah'fen] *vt.* to miss by sleeping, oversleep, sleep through; *a.* sleepy.

Verschlag [fer-shlahk'] *nm.* (*Verschläge*) partition, shed, crate; *-en vt. ir.* to nail, board

up; *i.* matter; *a.* cunning, lukewarm; *-enheit nf.* cunning.

Verschlammen [fer-shlam'en] *vi.* to silt up.

Verschlechter'n [fer-shlesh'terrn] *vi.r.* to spoil, get worse, deteriorate; *-ung nf.* deterioration.

Verschleier'n [fer-shli'errn] *vt.* to veil, screen, camouflage; *-t a.* hazy, husky; *-ung nf.* masking, concealment.

Verschleiss [fer-shlice'] *nm.* retail trade, wear and tear; *-en vt.* to retail, wear out.

Verschlepp'en [fer-shlep'en] *vt.* to carry away, deport, postpone; *-ung nf.* deportation, putting off.

Verschleuder'n [fer-shloy'derrn] *vt.* to throw away, waste, sell at cut-throat prices; *-ung nf.* squandering, selling dirt cheap.

Verschliessen [fer-shlee'sen] *vt. ir.* to close, lock.

Verschlimmer'n [fer-shlim'errn] *vt.r.* to make worse, get worse, deteriorate, aggravate; *-ung nf.* deterioration.

Verschlingen [fer-shling'en] *vt. ir.* to swallow up, devour, twist.

Verschlossen [fer-shlos'en] *a.* reserved, locked; *-heit nf.* reserve.

Verschlucken [fer-shlŏok'en] *vt.* to swallow; *r.* choke.

Verschluss [fer-shlŏoss'] *nm.* (-*schlüsse*) lock, fastener, seal, shutter (*camera*), breech mechanism (*mil.*).

Verschlüsseln [fer-shlyōō'seln] *vt.* to encode, encipher.

Verschmachten [fer-shmach'ten] *vi.* to languish.

Verschmähen [fer-shmay'en] *vt.* to disdain, scorn.

Verschmelzen [fer-shmelt'sen] *vt.i. ir.* to melt, blend, fuse.   [sen] *vt.* to get over.

Verschmerzen [ferr-shmer'-

Verschmieren [fer-shmeer'-ren] *vt.* to smear.

Verschmitzt [fer-shmitst'] *a.* crafty.

Verschmutzen [fer-shmoot'-sen] *vt.* to soil.

Verschnaufen [fer-shnow'fen] *vr.* to recover one's breath.

Verschneiden [fer-shnide'en] *vt. ir.* to cut off, up, prune, mix.

Verschneit [fer-shnite'] *a.* snowed in, snow-bound.

Verschnüren [fer-shnyoor'-ren] *vt.* to lace, tie.

Verschollen [fer-shol'en] *a.* missing, forgotten.

Verschonen [fer-shoh'nen] *vt.* to spare.

Verschöner'n [fer-sher'nerrn] *vt.* to beautify; **-ung** *nf.* embellishment.

Verschränkt [fer-shrenkt'] *a.* crossed, folded.

Verschreiben [fer-shribe'en] *vt. ir.* to write for, order, prescribe; *r.* make a mistake in writing.

Verschreien [fer-shri'en] *vt. ir.* to decry, run down.

Verschroben [fer-shroh'ben] *a.* complicated, confused, queer.

Verschrotten [fer-shrot'en] *vt.* to metal (road), scrap.

Verschuld'en [fer-shool'den] *vt.* to be guilty of; *n.* fault, guilt; **-ung** *nf.* fault, debt.

Verschütten [fer-shyoot'ten] *vt.* to spill, choke up, bury.

Verschweigen [fer-shvi'gen] *vt. ir.* to keep secret.

Verschwend'en [fer-shven'-den] *vt.* to squander; **-er** *nm.* spendthrift; **-erisch** *a.* wasteful; **-ung** *nf.* extravagance.

Verschwiegen [fer-shvee'gen] *a.* discreet, silent; **-heit** *nf.* secrecy, discretion.

Verschwimmen [fer-shvim'-en] *vi. ir.* to grow hazy, fade away.

Verschwinden [fer-shvin'-den] *vi. ir.* to disappear, fade out (*rad.*); *n.* disappearance.

Verschwommen [fer-shvom'-en] *a.* hazy, vague; **-heit** *nf.* haziness.

Verschwör'en [fer-shvor'ren] *vr.* to plot, conspire; *t.* abjure, forswear; **-er** *nm.* (-) conspirator; **-ung** *nf.* conspiracy.

Versehen [fer-zay'en] *vt.* to supply, provide, perform, fill, keep; *r.* make a mistake; *n.* oversight, blunder; **-tlich** *ad.* by mistake.

Verseht'en [fer-zair'ren] *vt.* to injure; **-te(r)** *m.w.* disabled man (*mil.*); **-tengeld** *n.* disablement pension.

Versend'en [fer-zen'den] *vt. ir.* to forward, dispatch, ship, consign; **-ung** *nf.* dispatch, forwarding. [singe, scorch.

Versengen [fer-zeng'en] *vt.* to

Versenk'en [fer-zenk'en] *vt.* to sink, submerge; *r.* become engrossed in; **-ung** *nf.* sinking.

Versessen [fer-zess'en] *a.* mad on.

Versetz'en [fer-zet'sen] *vt.* to displace, put, transfer, mix, pledge; *i.* reply; *r.* imagine oneself; **-ung** *nf.* transfer, mixing, alloy.

Verseuchen [fer-zoy'shen] *vt.* to contaminate.

Versicher'en [fer-zish'er-rerr] *nm.* (-) insurer; **-n** *vt.* to insure, assure; *r.* make sure of; **-ung** *nf.* insurance, assurance; **-ungsschein** *nm.* policy.

Versiegeln [fer-zee'geln] *vt.* to seal (up). [dry up.

Versiegen [fer-zee'gen] *vi.* to

Versilbern [fer-zil'berrn] *vt.* to plate, turn into money.

Versinken [fer-zink'en] *vi. ir.* to sink (down), founder.

Versinnlichen [fer-zin'lish-en] *vt.* to illustrate, make clear.

Versöhn'en [fer-zer'nen] *vt.* to reconcile, conciliate; **-lich** *a.*

forgiving; -ung *nf.* conciliation.

Versorg'en [fer-zorr'gen] *vt.* to provide, supply, nurse, look after; -er *nm.* (-) support; -ung *nf.* provision, maintenance, care. [to brace.

Verspannen [fer-shpan'en] *vt.*

Verspät'en [fer-shpate'en] *vt.* to delay, retard; *r.* be late; -ung *nf.* delay.

Versperr'en [fer-shper'en] *vt.* to bar, block up, obstruct; -ung *nf.* blocking, barrier.

Verspielen [fer-shpeel'en] *vt.* to lose (by gambling), lose favour.

Verspott'en [fer-shpot'en] *vt.* to ridicule, scoff at; -ung *nf.* ridicule.

Versprech'en [fer-shpresh'en] *vt. ir.* to promise; *r.* make a mistake; *n.* promise; -ung *nf.* promise.

Verspreng'en [fer-shpreng'en] *vt.* to disperse, blow up, explode; -te *pl.* stragglers.

Verstaatlichen [fer-shtaht'-lish-en] *vt.* to nationalize.

Verstand [fer-shtant'] *nm.* sense, reason, understanding, intelligence.

Verständ'ig [fer-shten'dish] *a.* sensible, wise, cautious; -igen *vt.* to inform; *r.* make oneself understood, come to an understanding, -igkeit *nf.* good sense, -igung *nf.* agreement, arrangement, information; -lich *a.* intelligible, clear; -lichkeit *nf.* intelligibility, clearness; -nis *n.* understanding, comprehension, appreciation; -nislos *a.* unappreciative; -nisvoll *a.* sympathetic.

Verstärk'en [fer-shtairr'ken] *vt.* to strengthen, amplify; -er *nm.* (-) amplifier; -erröhre *nf.* amplifying valve; -ung *nf.* strengthening, support, reinforcements, amplification (*rad.*).

Verstatten [fer-shtat'en] *vt.* to allow. [*vt.* to sprain.

Verstauchen [fer-shtowch'en]

Verstauen [fer-shtow'en] *vt.* to stow away.

Versteck [fer-shtek'] *nm.* (-e) hiding(-place); -en *vt.* to hide; -spiel *n.* hide and seek; -t *a.* hidden, sly.

Verstehen [fer-shtay'en] *vt. ir. r.* to understand; *r.* agree, consent to.

Versteifen [fer-shtife'en] *vt.* to stiffen, support; *r.* insist upon.

Versteigen [fer-shti'gen] *vr.* to presume too much, go too far.

Versteiger'n [fer-shti'gerrn] *vt.* to sell by auction; -ung *nf.* auction-sale.

Versteinern [fer-shti'nern] *vt.* to petrify.

Verstell'bar [fer-shtel'barr] *a.* adjustable, variable-pitch (*rad.*); -en *vt.* to shift, change the place of, bar, disguise; *r.* feign, pretend; -ung *nf.* disguise, pretence, dissimulation.

Versteuern [fer-shtoy'errn] *vt.* to pay duty on.

Verstiegen [fer-shtee'gen] *a.* eccentric, pretentious.

Verstimmt [fer-shtimt'] *a.* upset, bad-tempered.

Verstockt [fer-shtokt'] *a.* stubborn, hardened; -heit *nf.* stubbornness. [stealthy.

Verstohlen [fer-shtoh'len] *a.*

Verstopf'en [fer-shtop'fen] *vt.* to stop up, constipate; -ung *nf.* constipation, obstruction.

Verstorben [fer-shtorr'ben] *a.* deceased, late.

Verstört [fer-shterrt'] *a.* wild, disordered, troubled, distracted.

Verstoss [fer-shtohss'] *nm.* (Verstösse) offence, error, mistake; -en *vt. ir.* to reject, repudiate; *v.* offend (against); -ung *nf.* rejection, repudiation.

Verstreichen [fer-shtri'shen] *vi.* to elapse, pass by.

Verstreuen [fer-shtroy'en] vt. to scatter (about).

Verstrick'en [fer-shtrik'en] vt. to entangle, ensnare; -ung nf. snare, entanglement.

Verstümmel'n [fer-shtyöö'meln] vt. to maim, mutilate; -ung nf. mutilation.

Verstummen [fer-shtöö'men] vi. to be (struck) dumb.

Versuch [fer-zööch'] nm. (-e) attempt, experiment, trial; -en vt. to try, tempt, sample; -sballon nm. kite; -sflug nm. trial flight; -sstelle nf. experimental station; -sweise ad. by way of experiment; -ung nf. temptation.

Versündigen [fer-zyöön'digen] vr. to sin. [to sweeten.

Versüssen [fer-zyöö'sen] vt.

Vertag'en [fer-tah'gen] vt.i. to adjourn; -ung nf. adjournment.

Vertändeln [fer-ten'deln] vt. to trifle away, waste.

Vertauschen [fer-tow'shen] vt. to exchange.

Verteidigen [fer-tie'di-gen] vt. to defend; -er nm. defender, advocate; -ung nf. defence, advocacy.

Verteil'en [fer-tile'en] vt. to distribute, divide, assign; -er nm. (-) distributor (aut., etc.), subscriber (ph.); -ung nf. distribution, allotment.

Verteufelt [fer-toy'felt] a, ad. devilish, awful(ly).

Vertief'en [fer-tee'fen] vt. to deepen; r. to be engrossed in, absorbed in; -ung nf. depression, hollow, recess, concentration on. [vertical.

Vertikal [verr-ti-kahl'] a.

Vertilg'en [fer-til'gen] vt. to exterminate, destroy; -ung nf. extermination, annihilation.

Verton'en [fer-tone'en] vt. to set to music; -ung nf. composition.

Vertrag [fer-trahk'] nm.

(Verträge) agreement, treaty, contract; -en vt. ir. to carry off, bear, tolerate; r. agree; -lich a. contractual.

Verträglich [fer-traik'lish] a. compatible, good-natured, conciliatory; -keit nf. compatibility, good-nature, sociability.

Vertrau'en [fer-trow'en] vi. to trust; n. confidence; -ensmann nm. reliable person, confidant, shop steward; -ensselig a. too trustful, confiding; -ensvoll a. trustful; -enswürdig a. trustworthy; -lich a. confidential, familiar; -lichkeit nf. familiarity; -t a. intimate, familiar; -te(r) m.w. confidant, close friend; -theit nf. familiarity, intimacy.

Vertrauern [fer-trow'errn] vt. to mourn away.

Vertreib'en [fer-tribe'en] vt. ir. to expel, dispel, sell (com.); -ung nf. expulsion.

Vertret'en [fer-tray'ten] vt. ir to represent, take the place of, defend; -er nm. (-) representative deputy, advocate; -ung nf. representation.

Vertrieb [fer-treep'] nm. retail sale. [vi. to dry up.

Vertrocknen [fer-trok'nen]

Vertröbeln [fer-trer'deln] vt. to fritter away.

Vertrösten [fer-trer'sten] vt. to console, put off.

Vertun [fer-töön'] vt. ir. to squander. [to hush up.

Vertuschen [fer-töö'shen] vt.

Verübeln [fer-yöö'beln] vt. to take in bad part.

Verüb'en [fer-yöö'ben] vt. to commit; -ung nf. perpetration.

Verun'glimpfen [fer-öön'glimp-fen] vt. to disparage; -glücken vi. to meet with an accident, fail, perish; -reinigen vt. to pollute, soil; -reinigung nf. pollution, making dirty; -stalten vt. to disfigure; -treuen *vt.* to embezzle; **-treuung** *nf.* embezzlement.

Verur'sachen [fer-ŏŏrr'zach-en] *vt.* to cause; **-teilen** *vt.* to condemn; **-teilung** *nf.* condemnation, sentence.

Vervielfältig'en [fer-feel'fel-ti-gen] *vt.* to duplicate, multiply, copy; **-ung** *nf.* duplication, reproduction, copying.

Vervoll'kommnen [fer-fol'kom-nen] *vt.* to perfect; **-kommnung** *nf.* perfection, perfecting; **-ständigen** *vt.* to complete; **-ständigung** *nf.* completion.

Verwachsen [fer-vax'en] *a., vi. ir.* to grow together, heal up, be tied to, up with; *a.* deformed.

Verwahr'en [fer-vah'ren] *vt.* to keep, preserve; **-lost** *a.* neglected, degenerate; **-losung** *nf.* neglect; **-ung** *nf.* custody, (safe)keeping, protest.

Verwaist [fer-vïst'] *a.* orphaned.

Verwalt'en [fer-val'ten] *vt.* to administer, manage, superintend; **-er** *nm.* (-) administrator, manager; **-ung** *nf.* administration, management; **-ungsweg** *nm.* administrative channels.

Verwand'eln [fer-van'deln] *vt.* to convert, change, transform; **-lung** *nf.* change, transformation, conversion.

Verwandt [fer-vant'] *a.* related, allied; **-e(r)** *m.w.* relative, relation; **-schaft** *nf.* relationship, relations.

Verwarnen [fer-varr'nen] *vt.* to admonish, caution.

Verwaschen [fer-vash'en] *vt. ir.* to wash out; *a.* faded, indistinct.

Verwässern [fer-vess'errn] *vt.* to dilute, water down.

Verweben [fer-vay'ben] *vt. ir.* to weave up, into.

Verwechs'eln [fer-vex'eln] *vt.*

to confuse, mistake; **-lung** *nf.* confusion, mixing up.

Verwegen [fer-vay'gen] *a.* daring, bold; **-heit** *nf.* audacity, boldness. [blow away.

Verwehen [fer-vay'en] *vt.* to

Verwehren [fer-vair'ren] *vt.* to forbid, refuse.

Verweichlich'en [fer-vïsh'-lish-en] *vt.* to enervate, coddle; **-t** *a.* effeminate, soft; **-ung** *nf.* enervation, growing flabby.

Verweiger'n [fer-vï'gerrn] *vt.* to refuse; **-ung** *nf.* refusal, denial.

Verweilen [fer-vïle'en] *vi.* to stay, dwell upon, linger.

Verweis [fer-vïce'] *nm.* (-e) reprimand, rebuke; **-en** *vt. ir.* to reprimand, scold, exile; **-ung** *nf.* exile. [fade.

Verwelken [fer-vel'ken] *vi.* to

Verweltlichen [fer-velt'lish-en] *vt.* to secularize.

Verwend'en [fer-ven'den] *vt. ir.* to use, employ, apply, spend; *r.* intercede; **-ung** *nf.* use, application; **-ungstähig** *a.* fit for duty (*mil.*).

Verwerf'en [fer-vairr'fen] *vt. ir.* to throw away, reject; **-lich** *a.* objectionable.

Verwert'en [fer-vairr'ten] *vt.* to realize, turn to account; **-ung** *nf.* use, utilization.

Verwesen [fer-vay'zen] *vi.* to decay; *t.* administer; **-er** *nm.* (-) regent; **-ung** *nf.* decomposition, administration.

Verwick'eln [fer-vik'eln] *vt.* to entangle, involve; **-elt** *a.* complicated; **-lung** *nf.* complication, entanglement.

Verwilder'n [fer-vil'derrn] *vt.* to grow wild; **-ung** *nf.* relapse into barbarism.

Verwind'en [fer-vin'den] *vt.* to get over, twist (*av.*); **-ung** *nf.* torsion; **-ungsklappe** *nf.* aileron (*av.*).

Verwirk'en [fer-virr'ken] *vt.* to incur, forfeit; **-ung** *nf.* loss;

-lichen *vt.* to realize; -lichung *nf.* realization.

Verwirr'en [fer-vir'ren] *vt.* to confuse, tangle; -ung *nf.* confusion, disorder.

Verwischen [fer-vish'en] *vt.* to wipe out, efface.

Verwitter'n [fer-vit'errn] *vi.* to weather, decay; -t *a.* weather-beaten, worn.

Verwitwet [fer-vit'vet] *a.* widowed.

Verwöhn'en [fer-ver'nen] *vt.* to spoil; -ung *nf.* pampering, indulgence.

Verworfen [fer-vorr'fen] *a.* depraved; -heit *nf.* depravity.

Verworren [fer-vor'ren] *a.* complicated, confused.

Verwund'en [fer-vŏŏn'den] *vt.* to wound; -etenabzug *nm.* evacuation of wounded; -etenabzeichen *n.* wound stripe; -ung *nf.* wound.

Verwunder'lich [fer-vŏŏn'derr-lish] *a.* surprising; -n *vr.* to wonder, be surprised; -ung *nf.* astonishment.

Verwünsch'en [fer-vyŏŏn'shen] *vt.* to curse; -ung *nf.* curse.

Verwurzeln [fer-vŏŏrrt'seln] *vi.* to become rooted.

Verwüst'en [fer-vyŏŏ'sten] *vt.* to devastate; -ung *nf.* devastation.

Verzag'en [fert-sah'gen] *vi.* to despond, despair; -t *a.* despondent, faint-hearted; -theit *nf.* despondency, faint-heartedness.

Verzahn'en [fert-sah'nen] *vt.* to cog, notch, tooth, dovetail; -ung *nf.* gear.

Verzapfen [fert-sap'fen] *vt.* to retail (*beer*), mortise (*tec.*).

Verzärtel'n [fert-sairr'teln] *vt.* to coddle; -ung *nf.* pampering.

Verzaubern [fert-sow'bern] *vt.* to enchant.

Verzehr'en [fert-sairr'en] *vt.* to consume, devour; -ung *nf.* consumption.

Verzeich'nen [fert-sish'nen] *vt.* to make a list, enter, book; -nis *n.* list, register, catalogue, index.

Verzeih'en [fert-sie'en] *vt. ir.* to pardon, forgive; -lich *a.* pardonable; -ung *nf.* forgiveness, pardon.

Verzerr'en [fert-ser'ren] *vt.* to distort; -ung *nf.* distortion, grimace, caricature.

Verzetteln [fert-set'eln] *vt.* to waste, catalogue.

Verzicht [fert-sisht'] *nm.* renunciation; -en *vt.* to renounce, give up; -leistung *nf.* renunciation.

Verziehen [fert-see'en] *vt.r. ir.* to distort, twist, warp, disappear,spoil; *i.* remove. beslow.

Verzier'en [fert-seer'ren] *vt.* to ornament, decorate; -ung *nf.* decoration, ornament(ation).

Verzinken [fert-sink'en] *vt.* to galvanize. [tin-plate.

Verzinnen [fert-sin'en] *vt.* to

Verzins'en [fert-sin'zen] *vt.* to pay interest on; -ung *nf.* payment of interest.

Verzöger'n [fert-ser'gerrn] *vt.* to delay; -ung *nf.* delay, timelag. [declare, pay duty.

Verzollen [fert-sol'en] *vt.* to

Verzuckern [fert-sŏŏ'kerrn] *vt.* to sweeten, sugar.

Verzückt [fert-syŏŏkt'] *a.* enraptured.

Verzug [fert-sŏŏk'] *nm.* delay.

Verzweif'eln [fert-svie'feln] *vi.* to despair; -elt *a.* desperate; -lung *nf.* despair.

Verzweig'en [fert-svie'gen] *vr.* to branch out; -ung *nf.* branching.

Verzwickt [fert-svikt'] *a.* awkward, complicated.

Vesper [fes'perr] *nf.* vespers; -brot *n.* tea, supper.

Veterinär [fe-ter-ri-nairr'] *nm.* (-e) veterinary officer.

Vetter [fet'err] *nm.* (*gen.* -s; *pl.* -n) cousin.

Vexier'bild [vex-eerr'bilt] *n.* (-er) picture-puzzle; -en *vt.* to tease, puzzle. [vibrate.

Vibrieren [vi-breer'ren] *vi.* to

Vieh [fee] *n.* cattle; -bestand *nm.* live-stock; -isch *a.* bestial; -züchter *nm.* cattle-, stock-breeder.

Viel [feel] *a, ad.* much; -e *pl.* many; -erlei *a.* of many kinds; -heit *nf.* multiplicity, plurality; -leicht *ad.* perhaps; -mal(s) *ad.* many times; -mehr *(rad.)*; -phasig *a.* multi-phase *(rad.)*; -sagend *a.* significant; -seitig *a.* many-sided; -sprachig *a.* polyglot; -weiberei *nf.* polygamy

Vier [feerr] *num.* four; -eck *n.* (-e) square; -eckig *a.* square; -füssler *nm.* (-) quadruped; -sitzer *nm.* four-seater *(aut.)*.

Viertel [feerr'tel] *n.* (-) quarter; -jährlich *a.* quarterly; -jahrschrift *nf.* quarterly; -note *nf.* crotchet; -stunde *nf.* quarter of an hour.

Vier'tens [feerr'tenss] *ad.* fourthly; -zehn *num.* fourteen; — Tage fortnight; -zig *num.* forty. [curate.

Vikar [vi-karr'] *nm.* (-e)

Vill'a [vi'lah] *nf.* villa; -enkolonie *nf.* garden suburb.

Viol'a [vi-oh'lah] *nf.* viola; -ine *nf.* violin; -inist *m.w.* violinist.

Violett [vi-o-let'] *a.* violet.

Visier [vi-zeerr'] *n.* (-e) gun-sight, bomb sight *(av.)*; -en *vt.* to aim at, endorse, visa *(passport)*.

Visite [vi-zee'ter] *nf.* visit; -nkarte *nf.* visiting-card.

Visum [vee'zōōm] *n.* (Visa) visa.

Vize'admiral [veet-say-at-mi-rahl'] *nm.* (-e) vice-admiral; -luftmarschall *nm.* air vice-marshal.

Vlies [fleece] *n.* (-e) fleece.

Vogel [foh'gel] *nm.* (Vögel) bird; -bauer *n.* bird-cage;

-schau *nf.* bird's-eye view; -scheuche *nf.* scarecrow.

Vogt [fohkt] *nm.* (Vögte) governor, bailiff.

Vokabel [voh-kah'bel] *nf.* word. [vowel

Vokal [voh-kahl'] *nm.* (-e)

Volk [fol-k] *n.* (Völker) people, nation, folk; -reich *a.* populous; -sabstimmung *nf.* plebiscite; -sgenosse *m.w.* fellow-countryman; -sküche *nf.* soup kitchen; -skunde *nf.* folk-lore; -slied *n.* folk-song; -sschule *nf.* elementary school; -stümlich *a.* popular; -stümlichkeit *nf.* popularity; -szählung *nf.* census.

Völker'bund [ferl'kerr-bŏŏnt] *nm.* League of Nations; -familie *nf.* commonwealth of nations; -recht *n.* international law.

Voll [fol] *a.* full; -auf *ad.* in abundance; -beschäftigung full employment; -blut *n.* thoroughbred; -bringen *vt. ir.* to accomplish; -enden *vt.* to finish, complete; -endung *nf.* completion; -ends *ad.* entirely, altogether; -er *a.* full of, fuller; -führen *vt.* to carry out; -führung *nf.* execution; -jährig *a.* of age; -kommen *a.* perfect; -kommenheit *nf.* perfection; -leibig *a.* corpulent; -ständig *a.* complete; -ständigkeit *nf.* completeness; -strecken *vt.* to execute; -streckung *nf.* execution; -treffer *nm.* direct hit *(mil.)*; -zählig *a.* complete; -ziehen *vt. ir.* to execute, accomplish; *r.* happen.

Volontär [vo-lon-tairr'] *nm.* (-e) unpaid, voluntary worker.

Voltmesser [volt'mess-err] *nm.* (-) voltmeter.

Volumen [vo-loo'men] *n.* (Volumina) volume, capacity, size; -regler *nm.* volume control *(rad.)*.

Vom [fom] = von dem.

Von [fon] *pr.* of, from, by;
-einander *ad.* from each other,
apart; -nöten *a, ad.* necessary,
in need of; -statten gehen *vi.
ir.* to go well.

Vor [forr] *pr.* before, in front
of; -ab *ad.* above all, besides;
-abend *nm.* evening before;
-ahnung *nf.* presentiment.

Voran [forr-an'] *ad.* before,
first; -gehen *vi. ir.* to go in
advance, ahead.

Vorarbeit [forr'arr-bite] *nf.*
preliminary, preparatory work.

Voraus [forr-owss'] *ad.* in
advance; -bestellen *vt.* to order
in advance; -bezahlen *vt.* to
prepay; -bezahlung *nf.* pre-
payment; -nehmen *vt. ir.* to
anticipate; -sage *nf.* predic-
tion; -sagen *vt.* to predict;
-setzen *vt.* to assume; -setzung
nf. assumption; -sichtlich *ad.*
probably; -wahl *nf.* preliminary selection.

Vorbau [forr'bow] *nm.* front
building, porch; -en *vt.* to
build in front; *i.* take precautions, prevent.

Vorbedacht [forr'ber-dacht]
nm. forethought, premeditation.

Vorbedeut'en [forr'ber-doy-
ten] *vt.* to forebode; -ung *nf.*
omen, foreboding.

Vorbeding'en [forr'ber-ding-
en] *vt.* to stipulate; -ung *nf.*
stipulation.

Vorbehalt [forr'ber-halt] *nm.*
reservation, proviso; -en *vt. ir.*
to withhold, reserve (*rights*);
-lich *pr.* reserving, save; -los
a, ad. unconditional(ly).

Vorbei [forr-bie'] *ad.* past;
-gehen *vi. ir.* to pass, go past;
-marsch *nm.* march-past.

Vorbereit'en [forr'ber-rite-en]
vt. to prepare; -ung *nf.* preparation.

Vorbestraft [forr'ber-shtrahft']
a. previously convicted.

Vorbeug'en [forr'boy-gen] *vt.*

to prevent, obviate; -ung *nf.*
prevention.

Vorbild [forr'bilt] *n.* (-er)
pattern, original; -en *vt.* to
prepare; -lich *a.* typical,
model, ideal.

Vorbinden [forr'bin-den] *vt.
ir.* to tie on, put on.

Vorbote [forr'boh-ter] *m.w.*
forerunner.

Vorbringen [forr'bring-en] *vt.
ir.* to advance, bring forward,
allege, state.

Vordatieren [forr'da-teer-ren]
vt. to antedate.

Vorder [forr'derr] *a.* fore, foremost; -arm *nm.* forearm;
-grund *nm.* foreground.

Vorderhand [forr-derr-hant']
ad. for the present.

Vordringlich [forr'dring-lish]
a. pushing, impertinent, forward, inquisitive.

Voreilig [forr'ile-ish] *a.* rash,
hasty, precipitate, premature.

Voreingenommen [forr'ine-
ger-nom-en] *a.* biassed; -heit
nf. bias.

Vorenthalt'en [forr'ent-hal-
ten] *vt.* to withhold, detain;
-ung *nf.* keeping back, detention. [of all.

Vorerst [forr-airrst'] *ad.* first

Vorerwähnt [forr'err-vaint]
a. above-mentioned.

Vorfahr [forr'farr] *m.w.*
ancestor. [to drive up.

Vorfahren [forr'fah-ren] *vi. ir.*

Vorfall [forr'fal] *nm.* (Vorfälle)
occurrence, event; -en *vi. ir.*
to occur. [of a festival.

Vorfeier [forr'fie-err] *nf.* eve

Vorfenster [forr'fen-sterr] *n.*
n. (-) outside window.

Vorfertigung [forr'fairr-ti-
goong] *nf.* pre-fabrication.

Vorfinden [forr'fin-den] *vt. ir.*
to find; *r.* be forthcoming.

Vorgabe [forr'gah-ber] *nf.*
points given, start.

Vorgang [forr'gang] *nm.*
(Vorgänge) event, proceeding,

precedence; -gänger *nm.* (-) predecessor.

Vorgeb'en [forr'gay-ben] *vt. ir.* to pretend, profess, assert, claim, give (*start, etc.*); **-lich** *a.* pretended.

Vorgefertigt [forr'ger-fairr-tisht] *a.* pre-fabricated.

Vorgefühl [forr'ger-fyōōl] *n.* (-e) presentiment, anticipation.

Vorgehen [forr'gay-en] *vi. ir.* to precede, proceed, lead the way, jut out, go too fast (*watch*); *n.* procedure, action, advance. (-) **gear.**

Vorgelege [forr'ger-lay-ger] *n.*

Vorgeschicht'e [forr'ger-shish-ter] *nf.* pre-historic times, previous history; **-lich** *a.* pre-historic.

Vorgeschmack [forr'ger-shmahk] *nm.* foretaste.

Vorgesetzte(r) [forr'ger-zets-terr] *m.v.* superior, senior man.

Vorgestern [forr'ges-terrn] *ad.* the day before yesterday.

Vorgreifen [forr'grife-en] *vi. ir.* to anticipate, forestall, encroach upon.

Vorhaben [forr'hah-ben] *vt. ir.* to purpose, intend; *n.* purpose, intention.

Vorhalle [forr'hal-er] *nf.* vestibule, porch.

Vorhalt'en [forr'hal-ten] *vt. ir.* to upbraid with, scold, blame; *i.* endure, last (*out*); **-ung** *nf.* reproach.

Vorhand [forr'hant] *nf.* lead, precedence, refusal.

Vorhanden [forr-han'den] *a., ad.* at hand, existing; **-sein** *n.* existence, presence.

Vorhang [forr'hang] *nm.* (Vorhänge) curtain.

Vorhänge'n [forr'heng-en] *vt.* to hang before, stick out; **-schloss** *n.* padlock.

Vorhemd [forr'hemt] *n.* (*gen.* -es; *pl.* -en) shirt-front.

Vorher [forr-hairr'] *ad.* before(hand); **-bestimmen** *vt.*

to preordain; **-gehen** *vi. ir.* to precede; **-ig** *a.* previous.

Vorherrschen [forr'herr-shen] *vi.* to prevail.

Vorhin [forr-hin'] *ad.* not long ago, just now.

Vorhof [forr'hofe] *nf.* (-höfe) outer court, porch. [guard.

Vorhut [forr'hōōt] *nf.* van-

Vorig [forr'ish] *a.* previous, last. [last year's.

Vorjährig [forr'yair-rish] *a.*

Vorkämpfer [forr'kemp-ferr] *nm.* (-) advocate, champion.

Vorkauf [forr'kowf] *nm.* pre-emption; **-en** *vt.* to forestall, buy for future delivery.

Vorkehrung [forr'kair-rōōng] *nf.* provision, precaution.

Vorkenntnis [forr'kent-nis] *nf.* previous knowledge.

Vorkomm'en [forr'kom-en] *vi.* to occur, come forward, happen, seem; **-nis** *n.* occurrence.

Vorkriegszeit [forr'kreex-tsite] *nf.* pre-war period.

Vorlad'en [forr'lah-den] *vt. ir.* to summon; **-ung** *nf.* summons.

Vorlage [forr'lah-ger] *nf.* pattern, model, source (*text*).

Vorlängst [forr'lengst] *ad.* long ago.

Vorlassen [forr'lass-en] *vt. ir.* to admit.

Vorlauf [forr'lowf] *nm.* start; **-laufen** *vi. ir.* to run in front; **-läufer** *nm.* forerunner; **-läufig** *a.* preliminary, provisional.

Vorlaut [forr'lowt] *a.* conceited, impertinent.

Vorleg'en [forr'lay-gen] *vt.* to put on, before, display, offer, submit; **-emesser** *n.* carving knife; **-er** *nm.* (-) mat; **-eschloss** *n.* padlock.

Vorles'en [forr'lay-zen] *vt. ir.* to read aloud; **-ung** *nf.* reading, lecture. [one.

Vorletzt [forr'letst] *a.* last but

Vorleuchten [forr'loish-ten] *vi.* to be a splendid example.

Vorliebe [forr'lee-ber] *nf.* preference, partiality.

Vorliegen [forr'lee-gen] *vi. ir.* to be (present).

Vorlügen [forr'lyōō-gen] *vt. ir.* to tell lies.

Vormach'en [forr'mach-en] *vt.* to impose upon, show how to do; -t *nf.* leading power, superiority. [formerly.

Vormals [forr'mahls] *ad.*

Vormarsch [forr'marrsh] *nm.* advance.

Vormerk'en [forr'mairr-ken] *vt.* to note, book; -ung *nf.* note, memorandum.

Vormittag [forr'mi-tahk] *nm.* (-e) forenoon, morning; -s *ad.* in the forenoon.

Vormund [forr'mōōnt] *nm.* (-münder) guardian. [before.

Vorn [forrn] *ad.* in front,

Vorname [forr'nah-mer] *nm* (*gen.* -ns; *pl.* -n) first, Christian name.

Vornehm [forr'name] *a.* of high rank, aristocratic, distinguished; -en *vt. ir.* to put on, r. decide; -heit *nf.* distinction; -lich *ad.* chiefly specially; [suburb.

Vorort [forr'orrt] *nm.* (-e)

Vorplatz [forr'plats] *nm.* (-plätze) hall, vestibule, landing.

Vorposten [forr'pos-ten] *nm.* (-) outpost, picket; -boot *n.* patrol vessel.

Vorrang [forr'rang] *nm.* precedence, superiority.

Vorrat [for'raht] *nm.* (-räte) stock, supply, spares (*tec.*); -skammer *nf.* pantry, storeroom. [stock.

Vorrätig [for'rate-ish] *a.* in

Vorrecht [for'resht] *n.* (-e) privilege. [preface.

Vorrede [for'ray-der] *nf.*

Vorrücken [for'ryöö-ken] *vi.* to advance, march on; *t.* move, put, push forward.

Vorrichtung [for'rish-tŏŏng]

nf. contrivance, device, arrangement. [ante-room.

Vorsaal [forr'zahl] *nm.* (-säle)

Vorsagen [forr'zah-gen] *vt.* to recite, prompt, dictate, deceive.

Vorsänger [forr'zeng-err] *nm.* (-) precentor, choir leader.

Vorsatz [forr'zats] *nm.* purpose, plan, project.

Vorsätzlich [forr'zets-lish] *a, ad.* intentional(ly).

Vorschau [forr'show] *nf.* programme parade (*rad.*).

Vorschein [forr'shine] *nm.* appearance.

Vorschieben [forr'shee-ben] *vt. ir.* to plead (as excuse), push forward, advance.

Vorschiessen [forr'shee-sen] *vt. ir.* to advance, lend.

Vorschlag [forr'shlahk] *nm.* (-schläge) proposal, gracenote; -en *vt. ir.* to propose, bring forward.

Vorschlussrunde [forr'- shlŏŏs-rŏŏn-der] *nf.* semi-final.

Vorschneiden [forr'shnie- den] *vt. ir.* to carve.

Vorschreiben [forr'shribe- en] *vt. ir.* to dictate, prescribe.

Vorschreiten [forr'shrite-en] *vi. ir.* to advance.

Vorschrift [forr'shrift] *nf.* instructions, regulations, rules, standing orders; -sgemäss *ad.* according to instructions.

Vorschub [forr'shŏŏp] *nm.* aid, support, first stroke (*games*), feed (*tec.*). [vamp.

Vorschuh [forr'shŏŏ] *nm.* (-e)

Vorschule [forr'shŏŏ-ler] *nf.* preparatory school.

Vorschuss [forr'shŏŏss] *nm.* (-schüsse) advance (cash).

Vorschützen [forr'shyöt- sen] *vt.* to pretend, allege, plead (as excuse).

Vorschweben [forr'shvay- ben] *vi.* to hover, have a vague recollection of.

Vorseh'en [forr'zay-en] *vt. ir.*

to provide for; *r.* take care, be careful; **-ung** *nf.* providence.

Vorsetzen [forr'zet-sen] *vt.* to set before, place before, offer, appoint, prefer, prefix; *r.* decide, intend.

Vorsicht [forr'zisht] *nf.* caution, care; **-ig** *a.* cautious, careful. [prefix.

Vorsilbe [forr'zil-ber] *nf.*

Vorsinflutlich [forr'zin-floot-lish] *a.* antediluvian.

Vorsitz [forr'zits] *nm.* chair (-manship); **-ende(r)** *m.w.* chairman.

Vorsorg'e [forr'zorr-ger] *nf.* care, precaution, provision; **-en** *vi.* to take care; **-lich** *a.* careful.

Vorspeise [forr'shpie-zer] *nf.* hors d'oeuvre, appetizer.

Vorspiegel'n [forr'shpee-geln] *vt.* to deceive, dazzle; **-ung** *nf.* misrepresentation.

Vorspiel [forr'shpeel] *n.* (-e) prelude.

Vorsprechen [forr'shpresh-en] *vt. ir.* to pronounce, recite.

Vorspringen [forr'shpring-en] *vi. ir.* to project, leap forward.

Vorsprung [forr'shproong] *nm.* projection, ledge, start, advantage. [suburb.

Vorstadt [forr'shtat] *nf.*

Vorstand [forr'shtant] *nm.* (-stände) directorate, management, principal.

Vorstechen [forr'shtesh-en] *vi. ir.* to project, stand out.

Vorstecknadel [forr'shtek-nah-del] *nf.* scarf pin.

Vorsteh'en [forr'shtay-en] *vi. ir.* to project, superintend, manage; **-er** *nm.* (-) superintendent, foreman, headmaster, station master.

Vorstell'en [forr'shtel-en] *vt.* to put before, introduce, represent; *r.* imagine; **-ung** *nf.* introduction, representation, performance, conception, idea.

Vorstoss [forr'shtohss] *nm.* (-stösse) advance, projection, piping (*uniform*), braid; **-en** *vi. ir.* to push on, advance, project.

Vorstrecken [forr'shtrek-en] *vt.* to stretch out, lead, advance.

Vorstufe [forr'stoo-fer] *nf.* first step(s).

Vorteil [forr'tile] *nm.* (-e) advantage, profit; **-haft** *a.* advantageous.

Vortrag [forr'trahk] *nm.* (-träge) lecture, delivery, rendering, report, balance forward (*com.*); **-en** *vt. ir.* to deliver, lecture, carry forward; **-skunst** *nf.* elocution; **-sweise** *nf.* delivery.

Vortrefflich [for-tref'lish] *a.* excellent; melt; **-keit** *nf.* excellence.

Vortritt [forr'trit] *nm.* precedence.

Vortruppe [forr'troo-per] *nf.* advance troops.

Vorüber [forr-yoo'berr] *ad.* past; expired; **-gehen** *vi. ir.* to pass (by); **-gehend** *a.* passing, fleeting, transient; **-gehende(r)** *m.w.* passer-by; **-ziehen** *vi. ir.* to pass, go by.

Vorurteil [forr'oorr-tile] *n.* (-e) prejudice; **-sfrei** *a.* unprejudiced.

Vorvergangenheit [forr'-ferr-gang-en-hite] *nf.* pluperfect.

Vorverkauf [forr'ferr-kowf] *nm.* advance sale, booking (in advance).

Vorwahl [forr'vahl] *nf.* preliminary election; **-wähler** *nm.* pre-selector (*el.*).

Vorwand [forr'vant] *nm.* (-wände) pretext, pretence.

Vorwarnung [forr'varr-nöong] *nf.* preliminary warning.

Vorwärts [forr'vairrts] *ad.* forward, onward(s); **-gehen** *vi. ir.* to go ahead; **-kommen** *vi. ir.* to progress.

Vorweg [forr-vek'] *ad.* in advance; **-nehmen** *vt. ir.* to anticipate.

Vorweisen [forr'vize-en] *vt. ir.* to produce, show.

Vorwelt [forr'velt] *nf.* antiquity

Vorwerfen [forr'vairr-fen] *vt. ir.* to reproach with.

Vorwiegen [forr'vee-gen] *vi. ir.* to preponderate; **-d** *a.* preponderant; *ad.* mostly.

Vorwissen [forr'viss-en] *n.* previous knowledge.

Vorwitz [forr'vits] *nm.* curiosity; **-ig** *a.* inquisitive.

Vorwort [forr'vorrt] *n.* (-e) preface.

Vorwurf [forr'voorrf] *nm.* (-würfe) reproach; **-sfrei** *a.* irreproachable; **-svoll** *a.* reproachful.

Vorzeich'en [forrt'sish-en] *n.* (-) omen; **-nen** *vt.* to point out, trace out; **-nung** *nf.* tracing.

Vorzeig'en [forrt'sie-gen] *vt.* to show, display, produce; **-ung** *nf.* showing, display.

Vorzeit [forrt'site] *nf.* antiquity; **-ig** *a.* premature.

Vorziehen [forrt'see-en] *vt. ir.* to prefer, draw, advance.

Vorzug [forrt'sook] *nm.* (-züge) preference, merit, good quality, advantage; **-spreis** *nm.* preferential price; **-sweise** *ad.* by choice, preferably.

Vorzüglich [forrt-syook'lish] *a.* excellent, superior, preferable; **-keit** *nf.* superiority, excellence.

Vorzündung [forrt'syöön-dööng] *nf.* advanced ignition (*aut.*).

Vulgär [vööl-gairr'] *a.* vulgar.

Vulkan [vööl-kahn'] *nm.* (-e) volcano; **-isieren** *vt.* to vulcanize.

W

Waag'e [vah'ger] *nf.* balance, scales, level; **-emeister** *nm.*

inspector of weights and measures; **-recht** *a.* horizontal, **-schale** *nf.* scale(s).

Wabbelig [vab'er-lish] *a.* wobbly.

Wabe [vah'ber] *nf.* honeycomb; **-nhonig** *nm.* honey in the comb.

Wabern [vah'berrn] *vi.* to blaze, flicker.

Wach [vach] *a.* awake, alert; **-boot** *n.* patrol boat; **-e** *nf.* watch, guard, picket; **-ehabend** *a.* on guard, duty; **-en** *vi.* to be awake, watch; **-lokal** *n.* guardroom; **-rufen** *vt. ir.* to rouse, wake; **-traum** *nm.* day-dream.

Wacholder [vach-ol'derr] *nm.* (-) juniper; **-branntwein** *nm.* gin.

Wachs [vax] *nm.* (-e) wax; **-abdruck** *nm.* wax impression; **-bild** *n.* wax figure; **-kerze** *nf.* wax-candle; **-leinwand** *nf.* oilcloth; **-taffet** *nm.* oilskin; **-tuch** *n.* oilcloth.

Wachsam [vach'zahm] *a.* watchful, vigilant, alert; **-keit** *nf.* vigilance.

Wachs'en [vax'en] *vi. ir.* to grow; **-tum** *n.* growth.

Wachsen [vax'en] *vt.* to wax.

Wächsern [vex'errn] *a.* waxen.

Wacht [vacht] *nf.* watch, guard; **-meister** *nm.* sergeant.

Wachtel [vach'tel] *nf.* quail.

Wächter [vesh'terr] *nm.* (-) guard, warder, keeper, attendant; **-in** *nf.* nurse, matron.

Wackel'ig [vak'er-lish] *a.* shaky, rickety, wobbly, tottering; **-n** *vi.* to shake, totter, stagger.

Wacker [vak'err] *a.* valiant, honest, worthy; *ad.* well, bravely, thoroughly.

Wade [vah'der] *nf.* calf (*leg*); **-nbein** *n.* fibula; **-nstrumpf** *nm.* long stocking.

Waffe [vaf'er] *nf.* weapon, firearms; **-nbruder** *nm.* comrade (in arms); **-ndienst** nm. military service; **-nfabrik** nf. arms factory; **-ngattung** nf. arm (of service); **-ngewalt** nf. armed force; **-nkammer** nf. armoury; **-npass** nm. permit to bear arms; **-nrock** nm. tunic; **-nschein** nm. licence for firearms; **-nschmied** nm. armourer; **-nstillstand** nm. armistice, truce; **-nstreckung** nf. capitulation; **-ntragend** a. bearing arms; **-nwart** nm. armourer.

Waffel [vaf'el] nf. waffle.

Wage = Waage.

Wägelchen [vay'gel-shen] n (-) small cart, carriage.

Wag'en [vah'gen] vt. to venture, dare; **-emut** nm. daring; **-estück** n. bold enterprise, hazardous venture; **-halsig** a. foolhardy; **-nis** n. (-se) hazard.

Wagen [vah'gen] nm. (-) cart, carriage, truck, van, car; **-bau** nm. coach-building; **-heber** nm. jack; **-klasse** nf. class (rl.); **-park** nm. parking-place; **-spur** nf. rut; **-wechsel** nm. changing (rl.); [weigh.

Wägen [vay'gen] vt. ir. to [weigh.

Waggon [va-gong'] nm. (-s) = Wagen.

Wagner [vahg'nerr] nm. (-) carriage, coach-builder.

Wahl [vahl] nf. choice, election; **-aufruf** nm. election manifesto; **-ausschreibung** nf. writ; **-berechtigt** a. entitled to vote; **-bezirk** nm. constituency; **-bude** nf. polling booth; **-fach** n. optional subject; **-frei** a. optional; **-kasten** nm. ballotbox; **-recht** n. franchise; **-spruch** nm. motto; **-stimme** nf. vote; **-urne** nf. ballotbox; **-zettel** nm. ballot paper.

Wähl'bar [vale'barr] a. eligible; **-barkeit** nf. eligibility; **-en** vt. to choose, elect, vote, dial (ph.); **-erisch** a. fastidious, particular; **-erschaft** nf. voters; **-scheibe** dial (ph.).

Wahn [vahn] nm. delusion, folly, madness; **-bild** n. vision, delusion; **-sinn** nm. insanity, delirium; **-sinnig** a. insane.

Wähnen [vane'en] vt.i. to think, suppose, believe.

Wahr [vahr] a. true, genuine; **-haft** a. truthful, true; **-haftigkeit** nf. truthfulness; **-heit** nf. truth, fact; **-nehmen** vt. ir. to perceive, observe, notice; **-nehmung** nf. perception; **-sagen** vi. to prophesy, tell fortunes; **-sager** nm. (-), **-sagerin** nf. soothsayer, fortune-teller; **-sagung** nf. prophecy; **-scheinlich** a., ad. probable, probably; **-scheinlichkeit** nf. probability; **-spruch** nm. verdict.

Wahr'en [vah'ren] vt. to care for, preserve, maintain; **-ung** nf. preservation, protection.

Währen [vair'ren] vi. to last; **-d** pr. during; cj. while.

Währung [vair'roong] nf. currency, standard.

Waise [vize'er] nf. orphan; **-nhaus** n. orphanage; **-nkind** n. orphan; **-nknabe** nm. orphan boy.

Wald [valt] nm. Wälder) wood, forest; **-bau** nm. forestry; **-frevel** nm. poaching; **-horn** n. bugle; **-ig** a. wooded; **-ung** nf. woodland; **-wirtschaft** nf. forestry. [copse, grove.

Wäldchen [velt'shen] n. (-)

Wal(fisch) [val] nm. (-e) whale; **-bein** n. whalebone; **-fahrer** nm. whaler; **-fett** n. blubber; **-tran** nm. train-oil.

Walk'en [val'ken] vt. to full, mill; **-erde** nf. fuller's earth.

Wall [val] nm. (Wälle) rampart, dike, embankment, dam; **-graben** nm. moat. [gelding.

Wallach [val'ach] nm. (-e)

Wall'en [val'en] vi. to undulate, boil (up); **-ung** nf. undulation, boiling, agitation.

Wall'en [val'en] *vi.* to wander, go on a pilgrimage; **-fahrer** *nm.* pilgrim; **-fahrt** *nf.* pilgrimage. [walnut.]

Walnuss [val'nŏŏss] *nf.*

Walross [val'ross] *n.* (-e) walrus. [govern, dispose of.]

Walten [val'ten] *vi.* to

Walz'e [valt'ser] *nf.* cylinder, roller, tramping; **-blei** *n.* sheetlead; **-en** *vt.* to roll (out); *r.i.* waltz, tramp; **-endruck** *nm.* cylinder printing; **-er** *nm.* (-) waltz; **-werk** *n.* rolling-mill.

Wälz'en [velt'sen] *vt.* to roll (over), shift; *r.* wallow; **-lager** *n.* anti-friction bearings.

Wamme [vam'er] *nf.* belly.

Wams [vamss] *n.* (Wämser) jacket, doublet.

Wand [vant] *nf.* (Wände) wall, screen, partition, precipice, panel; **-karte** *nf.* map; **-putz** *nm.* plaster; **-schrank** *nm.* cupboard; **-uhr** *nf.* clock; **-verkleidung** *nf.* wall-paper, wainscoting.

Wandel [van'del] *nm.* change, conduct; **-bar** *a.* changeable, variable; **-gang** *nm.* gallery, corridor; **-n** *vi.* to change.

Wander-auftrag *nm.* roving commission; **-bühne** *nf.* travelling theatre; **-er** *nm.* (-) wanderer, rambler, hiker; **-lust** *nf.* love of travelling; **-n** *vi.* to walk, roam, hike; **-nd** *a.* itinerant, wandering; **-schaft** *nf.* travelling; **-ung** *nf.* excursion, outing, migration, wandering, hiking; **-vogel** *nm.* hiker, rambler.

Wandlung [vand'lŏŏng] *nf.* change, transformation.

Wandung =Wand.

Wange [vung'er] *nf.* cheek.

Wankelmut [vank'el-mŏŏt] *nm.* vacillation, hesitation, irresolution; **-mütig** *a.* vacillating, inconstant.

Wanken [vank'en] *vi.* to waver, stagger, flinch.

Wann [van] *ad., cj.* when.

Wanne [van'er] *nf.* tub, bath; **-nbad** *n.* slipper bath.

Wanst [vanst] *nf.* belly.

Want [vant] *nf.* shroud (ship).

Wanze [vant'ser] *nf.* bug.

Wappen [vap'en] *n.* (-) coat of arms, crest; **-kunde** *nf.* heraldry.

Ware [vah'rer] *nf.* ware, goods; **-nbestand** *nm.* stock-in-trade; **-nhaus** *n.* departmental store, warehouse; **-nlager** *n.* stock, store; **-nmarkt** *nm.* produce market; **-nmangel** *nm.* shortage of goods, short supply; **-nprobe** *nf.* sample; **-nrechnung** *nf.* invoice; **-nverzeichnis** *n.* list, inventory.

Warm [varrm] *a.* warm; **-herzig** *a.* warm-hearted; **-wasserbereiter** *nm.* geyser; **-wasserheizung** *nf.* central heating.

Wärm'e [vairr'mer] *nf.* warmth; **-eapparat** *nm.* stove, plate-warmer; **-eeinheit** *nf.* thermal unit, calory; **-egrad** *nm.* degree; **-emesser** *nm.* thermometer; **-en** *vt.* to warm, heat; **-flasche** *nf.* hot-water bottle.

Warn'en [varr'nen] *vt.* to warn; **-ruf** *nm.* cry of warning; **-ung** *nf.* warning.

Wart [varrt] *nm.* (-e) attendant, mechanic (*tec.*). [tower.]

Warte [varr'ter] *nf.* watch-

Wart'en [varr'ten] *vi.* to wait; *t.* look after, mind, nurse; **-efrau** *nf.* waiting nurse; **-esaal** *nm.* waiting-room (*rl.*); **-ezimmer** *n.* waiting-room.

Wärter [vairr'ter] *nm.* (-) attendant, caretaker.

Wartung [varr'tŏŏng] *nf.* servicing.

Warum [va-rŏŏm'] *ad.* why.

Warze [varrt'ser] *nf.* wart, nipple.

Was [vass] *pn.* what; **– für** what sort of.

Wasch-anstalt *nf.* laundry;

-bar *a.* washable; -becken *n.* wash-basin; -echt *a.* fast (*dye*), genuine.

Wasch'en [vash'en] *vt. ir.* to wash; -frau *nf.* washer-woman; -handschuh *nm.* washable glove; -korb *nm.* clothes-basket; -leder *n.* wash-leather; -mittel *n.* lotion; -schüssel *nf.* wash-bowl; -zettel *nm.* laundry list.

Wäsch'e [vesh'er] *nf.* wash(-ing), linen, underclothing; -kammer *nf.*, -eschrank *nm.* linen cupboard; -klammer *nf.* clothes-peg; -erin *nf.* washer-woman.

Wasen [vah'zen] *nm.* sod, turf.

Wasser [vass'err] *n.* water; -behälter *nm.* reservoir, tank, boiler; -bombe *nf.* depth-charge; -dicht *a.* water-tight, -proof; -fahrt *nf.* boating trip, sail; -fall *nm.* waterfall; -fang *nm.* cistern, reservoir; -farbe *nf.* water-colour; -fläche *nf.* surface, sheet of water; -flug-zeug *n.* seaplane; -gang *nm.* aqueduct; -glas *n.* tumbler, water-glass; -guss *nm.* downpour; -hahn *nm.* tap; -heizung *nf.* central heating; -kante *nf.* sea-side; -kraft *nf.* water power; -kresse *nf.* water cress; -landflugzeug *n.* amphibious aircraft, seaplane; -lilie *nf.* water-lily; -not *nf.* water famine; -schaden *nm.* flood damage; -scheide *nf.* watershed; -schutz *nm.* river police, weir; -speier *nm.* gargoyle; -stand *nm.* water level; -strasse *nf.* waterway, channel; -stoff *nm.* hydrogen; -sucht *nf.* dropsy; -uhr *nf.* water-meter; -waage *nf.* level; -zeichen *n.* water-mark; -zement *n.* hydraulic cement.

Wässer'ig [vess'er-rish] *a.* watery, aqueous; -n *vt.* to water, irrigate; -ung *nf.* irrigation, washing, hydration.

Wassern [vass'errn] *vi.* to alight (*seaplane*).

Wat'en [vah'ten] *vi.* to wade; -anzug *nm.* waders. [waddle.

Watscheln [vatch'eln] *vi.* to

Watt [vat] *n.* (-e) mud-flats.

Watt [vat] *n.* (-) watt (*el.*).

Watt'e [vat'e] *nf.* wadding; -ieren *vt.* to wad, pad, quilt.

Webe [vay'ber] *n.* web; -n *vt. ir.* to weave; -r *nm.* (-) weaver; -rei *nf.* weaving, texture, weaving-mill.

Wechsel [vex'el] *nm.* (-) change, bill of exchange, draft; -beziehung *nf.* correlation; -geld *n.* change, exchange; -kurs *nm.* rate of exchange; -getriebe *a.* reversing gear; -händler, -makler *nm.* bill-broker; -n *vt.* to exchange, change, substitute, vary; -strom *nm.* alternating current; -weise *ad.* alternately; -wirtschaft *nf.* rotation (*crops*).

Wechsler [vex'lerr] *nm.* (-) money-changer, broker.

Weck [vek] *nm.* (-e), **Wecken** *nm.* (-) roll.

Wecken [vek'en] *vt.* to awaken, call; -er *nm.* (-) alarm-clock.

Wedel [vay'del] *nm.* duster, fan, frond; -bürste *nf.* whisk; -n *vi.* to wag (*tail*), fawn, fan.

Weder [vay'derr] *cj.* neither.

Weg [vake] *nm.* road, way, route; -ebau *nm.* road construction; -elagerer *nm.* highwayman; -scheide *nf.* cross roads; -weiser *nm.* sign post, guide; -zehrung *nf.* provisions.

Weg [vek] *ad.* away, off; -bleiben *vi. ir.* to stay away; -fallen *vi. ir.* to fall away, come to nothing; -gehen *vi. ir.* to go away, off; -haben *vt. ir.* to have one's share, manage; -jagen *vt.* to chase, drive away; *i.* gallop off; -lass-en *vt. ir.* to omit; -machen *vt.* to take away, out; -nahme *nf.*

capture, confiscation; **-nehmen** *vt. ir.* to take away, carry off, confiscate; **-schaffen** *vt.* to clear away, get rid of; **-streichen** *vt. ir.* to strike out, smooth away; **-treiben** *vt. ir.* to drive away; *i.* drift away; **-tun** *vt. ir.* to put, take away; **-weisen** *vt. ir.* to dismiss, refuse; **-werfen** *vt. ir.* to throw away; **-werfend** *a.* disdainfully.

Wegen [vay'gen] *pr.* on account of, for (the sake of), because of, with regard to.

Wegerich [vay'ger-rish] *nm.* (-e) plantain.

Weh [vay] *n.* pain, woe; *a.* sore, sad; **-en** *pl.* labour pains; **-klage** *nf.* lament; **-klagen** *vi.* to wail; **-mut** *nf.* melancholy; **-mütig** *a.* melancholy.

Wehe [vay'er] *nf.* snow-drift; **-n** *vi.* to blow, wave.

Wehr [vairr] *n.*(-e) weir, dam.

Wehr [vairr] *nf.* defence, bulwark, weapon; **-betreuung** *nf.* maintenance of morale; **-dienst** *nm.* military service; **-los** *a.* unarmed; **-macht** *nf.* armed forces; **-machtsangehörige(r)** *m.w.* service-man; **-machtskarte** ordnance map; **-meldeamt** *n.* recruiting office; **-pflicht** *nf.* compulsory service; **-pflichtig** *a.* liable for military service; **-stand** *nm.* army.

Wehren [vair'ren] *vt.* to restrain, hinder; *r.* defend oneself.

Weib [vipe] *n.* (-er) woman, female, wife; **-isch** *a.* womanish; **-lich** *a.* womanly, feminine; **-lichkeit** *nf.* womanliness.

Weich [vish] *a.* soft; **-heit** *nf.* softness; **-lich** *a.* too soft, effeminate; **-ling** *nm.* weakling.

Weiche [vie'sher] *nf.* groin, flank.

Weiche [vie'sher] *nf.* points (*rl.*); **-nsteller** *nm.* (-) pointsman.

Weichen [vie'shen] *vi. ir.* to yield, give way, fall (*price*).

Weide [vide'er] *nf.* willow; **-ngeflecht** *n.* wickerwork.

Weide [vide'er] *nf.* pasture, grazing; **-n** *vi.* to graze; *r.* feast one's eyes on, gloat on.

Weidlich [vite'lish] *a.* brave; *ad.* very much, thoroughly.

Weiger'n [vie'gerrn] *vr.* to refuse; **-ing** *nf.* refusal.

Weihe [vie'er] *nf.* consecration, initiation, inspiration; **-n** *vt.* to consecrate.

Weiher [vie'err] *nm.* (-) fishpond.

Weihnacht'en [vie'nacht-en] *pl.* Christmas; **-sabend** *nm.* Christmas Eve.

Weihrauch [vie'rowch] *nm.* incense; **-wasser** *n.* holy water.

Weil [vile] *cj.* because.

Weile [vile'er] *nf.* while, short time; **-n** *vi.* to stop, stay.

Wein [vine] *nm.* (-e) wine, vine; **-bau** *nm.* cultivation of vines; **-geist** *nm.* spirits of wine; **-geisthaltig** *a.* spirituous; **-händler** *nm.* wine-merchant; **-lese** *nf.* vintage; **-rebe** *nf.* vine; **-stein** *nm.* tartar; **-stock** *nm.* vine.

Wein'en [vine'en] *vi.* to weep, cry; **-erlich** *a.* tearful.

Weis'e [vize'er] *nf.* wise, prudent; **-heit** *nf.* wisdom; **-lich** *ad.* wisely, prudently.

Weise [vize'er] *nf.* manner, way, tune.

Weisen [vize'en] *vt. ir.* to show, point.

Weiss [vice] *a.* white; **-blech** *n.* tin-plate; **-e** *nf.* whiteness; **-glühend** *a.* incandescent, white-hot; **-kreuz** *n.*, **-ring** *nm.* tear-gas; **-waren** *pl.* linen goods. [wash.

Weissen [vice'en] *vt.* to white

Weisung [vize'oong] *nf.* instruction, directive.

Weit [vite] *a., ad.* wide, broad, far (off); **-aus** *ad.* by far; **-blickend** *a.* far-seeing; **-läufig**

a. distant, diffuse, minute, circumstantial; -reichend *a.* far-reaching; -schweifig *a.* rambling; -sichtig *a.* long-sighted, far-sighted; -verbreitet *a.* widespread.

Weite [vite'er] *nf.* width, space; *n. vt.* to widen, stretch.

Weiter [vite'err] *ad.* further, else; -leiten *vt.* to forward; -leitung *nf.* forwarding, transmission.

Weizen [vite'sen] *nm.* wheat.

Welch [velsh] (-er, -e, -es) *a. pn.* which, what, who, that, some.

Welk [velk] *a.* withered.

Well'e [vel'er] *nf.* wave, shaft, axle; -blech *n.* corrugated iron; -enanzeiger *nm.* wave detector (*rad.*); -enbereich *nm.* waveband; -enbrecher *nm.* breakwater; -enlänge *nf.* wavelength.

Welt [velt] *nf.* world; -all *n.* universe, space; -anschauung *nf.* philosophy of life; -bürgerlich *a.* cosmopolitan; -handel *nm.* international trade, commerce; -karte *nf.* map of the world; -klug *a.* worldly wise; -klugheit *nf.* worldly wisdom; -lich *a.* worldly, secular; -stadt *nf.* metropolis.

Wem [vame] *pn.* to whom.

Wen [vane] *pn.* whom.

Wend'e [ven'der] *nf.* turn, change; -en *vt. ir.* to turn; -epunkt *nm.* turning-point, crisis; -ung *nf.* turning.

Wenig [vane'ish] *a, ad.* little; *pl.* few; -gleich although.

Wenn [ven] *cj.* when(ever), if;

wer [yairr] *pn.* who.

werb'en [verr'ben] *vt. ir.* to court, enlist, make propaganda; -ung *nf.* courtship, enlistment.

werden [verr'den] *vi. ir.* to become, turn out, shall, will; *n.* becoming, genesis, growth.

werfen [verr'fen] *vt. ir.* to throw.

Werft [verrft] *n.* (-e) wharf, shipyard, dockyard; -arbeiter *nm.* docker; -halle repair shop (*nav.*).

Werg [verrk] *n.* tow, oakum.

Werk [verrk] *n.* (-e) work(s), mechanism, factory; -meister *nm.* foreman; -statt *nf.* workshop; -student *m.w.* self-supporting student; -tag. *n.m.* working-day; -tätig *a.* working active; -zeug *n.* tool; -zeug-maschine *nf.* machine-tool.

Wermut [verr'mōōt] *nm.* wormwood, vermouth.

Wert [verrt] *nm.* (-e) worth, value; *a.* worth, dear, worthy; -angabe *nf.* declaration of value; -brief *nm.* registered letter (with money); -los *a.* worthless; -losigkeit *nf.* worthlessness; -papier *n.* security, share; -voll *a.* valuable; -zuwachs *nm.* appreciation (*value*).

werten [verr'ten] *vt.* to value.

Wesen [vay'zen] *n.* being, essence, nature, affairs, fuss, conduct; -haft *a.* real; -los *a.* unreal; -tlich *a.* essential, material, integral.

Wespe [ves'per] *nf.* wasp.

West(en) [vest'en] *nm.* west; -lich *a.* western, westerly; -wärts *ad.* westwards.

wett [vet] *a.* even, equal; -e *nf.* bet, wager; -eifer *nm.* rivalry; -en *vt.i.* to bet, wager; -er *nm.* (-) better, backer; -kampf *nm.* prize-fight, contest; -laufen *vi. ir.* to race; -rennen *vi. ir.* to race; *n.* race, racing; -spiel *n.* match; -streit *nm.* contest.

Wetter [vet'err] *n.* weather, storm; -beratung *nf.* meteorological advice; -bericht *nm.* weather report; -dienst *nm.* meteorological service; -fahne *nf.* weather-vane; -kunde *nf.* meteorology; -mantel *nm.* raincoat; -n *vi.* to be stormy, rage; -schutzkleidung *nf.*

weather-proof clothing; **-warte** nf. meteorological station.

wetz'en [vet'sen] vt. to whet, sharpen; **-stein** nm. whetstone.

Wichse [vix'er] nf. polish; v. nt. to polish, wax. [creature.

Wicht [visht] nm. (-e)

wichtig [vish'tish] a. important, weighty; **-keit** nf. importance.

Wickel [vikl] nm. (-) coil, roll; **-n** vt. to roll (up), wind.

Widder [vid'err] nm. (-) ram.

wider [vee'derr] pr. against.

widerfahren [vee-derr-fah'ren] vi. ir. to happen to.

widerhaarig [vee'derr-hah-rish] a. cross-grained.

Widerhaken [vee'derr-hah-ken] nm. (-) barb, barbed hook.

widerleg'en [vee-derr-lay'gen] vt. to refute; **-ung** nf. refutation.

widerlich [vee'derr-lish] a. repugnant, disgusting; **-keit** repulsiveness.

widerrechtlich [vee-derr-resht'lish] a. unjust, unlawful; **-keit** nf. injustice, illegality.

Widerrede [vee-derr-ray'der] nf. objection, contradiction.

Widerruf [vee'derr-rōōf] nm. revocation, countermanding; **-en** vt. ir. to revoke, recant, countermand.

widersetz'en [vee-derr-zet'sen] vt. to oppose; **-lich** a. refractory.

widerspenstig [vee-derr-shpens'tish] a. refractory, intractable; **-keit** nf. obstinacy, refractoriness.

widerspiegel'n [vee-derr-shpee'geln] vt. to reflect; **-ung** nf. reflection.

Widerspiel [vee'derr-shpeel] n. contrary, reverse.

widersprechen [vee-derr-shpresh'en] vi. ir. to contradict; **-d** a. contradictory.

Widerspruch [vee'derr-shprōōch] nm. (-sprüche) contradiction, opposition.

Widerstand [vee'derr-shtant] nm. opposition, resistance; **-bewegung** nf. underground resistance movement; **-snest** n. pocket of resistance (mil.).

wider'stehen [vee-derr-shtay'en] vi. ir. to resist; **-streben** vi. ir. to resist, struggle against.

Widerstreit [vee-derr-shtrite] nm. conflict, opposition; **-en** vi. to clash, conflict.

widerwärtig [vee'derr-verr-tish] a. disagreeable; **-keit** nf. nuisance, calamity.

Widerwille [vee'derr-vil-er] nm. aversion, antipathy; **-ig** a. unwilling, reluctant.

widm'en [vit'men] vt. to dedicate, devote; **-ung** nf. dedication.

widrig [vee'drish] a. contrary, hostile, repugnant; **-enfalls** a. otherwise, failing which; **-keit** nf. adversity.

wie [vee] ad. how; cj. as, how; **-so** ad. why, how so; **-viel** ad. how much; cj. although.

wieder [vee'derr] ad. again, back; **-anfang** nm. recommencement; **-anknüpfen** vt. to renew; **-aufbau** nm. reconstruction; **-aufnahme** nf. resumption; **-aufnehmen** vt. ir. to resume; **-bekommen** vt. ir. to recover; **-beschaffung** nf. replacement, repurchase; **-bringen** vt. ir. to bring back, restore; **-einrichten** vt. to rearrange, refit; **-erkennen** vt. ir. to recognize; **-erstattung** nf. reimbursement; **-gabe** nf. reproduction; **-geben** vt. ir. to return, reproduce, render; **-geburt** nf. rebirth, regeneration; **-gutmachen** vt. to compensate for; **-herstellen** vt. to restore; r. recover; **-herstellung** nf. recovery, restoration; **-holen** vt. to repeat, revise; **-holung** nf. repetition, revision;

-hören *vt.* to hear again; -instandsetzen *vt.* to recondition; -käuen *vt.* to chew the cud, ruminate; -kehr *nf.* return, repetition; -kehren *vi.* to return; -kunft *nf.* return; -sehen *vt. ir.* to see again; -um *ad.* again; -vereinigen *vt.* to reunite; -vergelten *vt. ir.* to retaliate; -zulassung *nf.* readmission.

Wiege [vee'ger] *nf.* cradle; -n *vt.* to cradle; -ndruck *nm.* early printed book; -nlied *n.* lullaby.

wiegen [vee'gen] *vt.i. ir.* to weigh. [neigh.

wiehern [vee'errn] *vi.* to

Wiese [vee'zer] *nf.* meadow.

Wiesel [vee'zel] *n.* weasel.

wild [vilt] *a.* wild, savage; *n.* game, deer; -braten *nm.* venison; -bret *n.* game; -dieb *nm.* poacher; -ern *vi.* to poach; -fang *nm.* tomboy, wild boy; -fremd *a.* quite strange; -heit *nf.* wildness, ferocity; -nis *nf.* (-se) wilderness; -schwein *n.* wild boar.

Wille [vil'er] *nm.* (*gen.* -ns; *pl.* -n) will, intention; -nlos *a.* weak-minded; -nlosigkeit *nf.* indecision.

will'fahren [vil-fah'ren] *vi.* to grant, accede to; -fährig *a.* obliging, compliant; -kommen *a.* welcome.

Willkür [vil'kyöorr] *nf.* arbitrary action, choice; -lich *a.* arbitrary. [swarm.

wimmeln [vim'eln] *vi.* to

wimmern [vim'errn] *vi.* to whimper.

Wimpel [vim'pel] *nm.* (-) pennon, pennant. [lash.

Wimper [vim'perr] *nf.* eyelash.

Wind [vint] *nm.* (-e) wind; -beutel *nm.* wind-bag, éclair; -fang *nm.* ventilator; -hose *nf.* whirlwind; -hund *nm.* greyhound; -ig *a.* windy, unreliable; -messer *nm.* anemometer;

-mühlenflugzeug *n.* autogiro; -pocken *pl.* chickenpox; -schnittig *a.* streamlined; -schutzscheibe *nf.* windscreen (*aut.*); -stille *nf.* calm.

Winde [vin'der] *nf.* windlass, winch, bindweed.

Windel [vin'del] *nf.* napkin; -n *pl.* swaddling clothes; -weich *a.* soft.

wind'en [vin'den] *vt. ir.* to wind, twist; *r.* writhe, wind, meander, twine; -ung *nf.* winding, bend, coil, turn.

Wink [vink] *nm.* (-e) hint, nod, sign; -en *vi.* to beckon, hint, wave, signal, semaphore; -er *nm.* (-) signaller, trafficator; -zeichen *n.* semaphore.

Winkel [vink'el] *nm.* (-) angle, corner, nook, stripe (*mil.*); -advokat *m.w.* cheapjack lawyer; -messer *nm.* protractor; -zug *nm.* dodge, trick.

winklig [vink'lish] *a.* angular, crooked. [whine.

winseln [vin'zeln] *vi.* to

Winter [vin'terr] *nm.* (-) winter; -frische *nf.* winter resort; -garten *nm.* conservatory; -lich *a.* wintry; -n *vi.* to grow wintry; -sport *nm.* winter sports.

Winzer [vint'serr] *nm.* (-) vine-grower.

winzig [vint'sish] *a.* tiny.

Wipfel [vip'fel] *nm.* (-) treetop.

Wippe [vip'er] *nf.* see-saw; -n *vi.* to balance, rock, flap.

wir [veerr] *pn.* we.

Wirbel [virr'bel] *nm.* (-) whirlpool, crown (*head*), roll, peg; -n *vi.* to whirl, swirl, eddy; -säule *nf.* spine; -wind *nm.* whirlwind.

wirk'en [virr'ken] *vt.i.* to work, effect, act, weave, knot; -end *a.* active, effective; -lich *a.* real; -lichkeit *nf.* reality; -sam *a.* effective, efficacious; -samkeit *nf.* efficacy.

Wirkung [virr'kŏong] nf. action, effect; -sbereich nm. effective range; -skreis nm. sphere of activity; -streifen nm. arc of fire (mil.).

wirr [virr] a. confused, wild; -en pl. disturbances; -ung nf. confusion, error; -warr nm. disorder, chaos.

Wirsingkohl [virr'zing-kole] nm. savoy.

Wirt [virrt] nm. (-e) landlord, host; -in nf. landlady, hostess; -shaus n. public house, inn.

Wirtschaft [virrt'shaft] nf. household, housekeeping, economy, inn, public house; -en vi. to manage, keep house; -er nm. (-) manager; -lich a. economic(al); -skammer nf. chamber of commerce; -sprüfer nm. chartered accountant.

Wisch [vish] nm. (-e) slip, scrap of paper; -en vt. to wipe; -er nm. (-) stump, mop, wiper; -lappen nm. duster, rag.

Wismut [vis'mŏot] nm. bismuth.

wispern [vis'pern] vi. to whisper.

Wissbegier(de) [vis'ber-geerr-der] nf. thirst for knowledge, curiosity; -ig a. inquisitive, keen on learning.

Wissen [vis'en] vt. ir. to know; n. knowledge; -schaft nf. learning, science, knowledge; -schaftlich a. scientific, learned; -swert a. worth knowing; -tlich a. ad. knowing(ly).

wittern [vit'errn] vt. to scent, suspect.

Witterung [vit'er-rŏong] nf. scent, weather; -svorhersage nf. weather forecast.

Witwe [vit'ver] nf. widow; -r nm. (-) widower.

Witz [vits] nm. (-e) joke, wit; -blatt n. comic paper; -eln vi. to joke; -ig a. witty.

wo [voe] ad. where, at, in which, when; -anders ad. elsewhere; -bei ad. in, by which;

-durch ad. by which; -für ad. for which; -gegen ad. in return for which; cj. whereas; -her ad. whence; -hin ad. where (to); -nach ad. after, according to which; -zu ad. to which, for what purpose.

Woche [voch'er] nf. week; -nblatt n. weekly (paper), magazine; -nende n. week-end; -nschau nf. news-reel.

wöchentlich [ver'shent-lish] a. ad. weekly.

Woge [von'ger] nf. wave; -n vi. to surge, heave.

wohl [vole] ad. well, probably, I suppose; n. welfare, health, good; -an inter. well; -auf ad. well; inter. come on; -behagen n. comfort; -behalten a. safe and sound, in good condition; -fahrt nf. welfare; -feil a. cheap; -gefallen nm. pleasure; -gefällig a. pleasant; -geneigt a. well-disposed; -gesittet a. well-mannered; -habend a. wealthy; -klang nm. harmony, euphony; -klingend a. harmonious; -schmeckend a. tasty; -stand nm. prosperity; -tat nf. benefit, blessing; -täter nm. benefactor; -tun vi. ir. to do good; -verdient a. well-deserved; -weislich ad. prudently; -wollen n. good will; - wollend a. benevolent.

wohn'en [vone'en] vi. to live, reside; -haft a. resident; -lich a. comfortable; -ort nm. domicile; -ung nf. house, flat, lodgings; -wagen nm. caravan; -zimmer n. living-room.

wölb'en [verl'ben] vi. to vault, arch; -ung nf. vault, dome.

Wolf [volf] nm. (-e, Wölfe) wolf; -shund nm. Alsatian.

Wölfin [verl'fin] nf. she-wolf.

Wolk'e [vol'ker] nf. cloud; -enkratzer nm. sky-scraper; -ig a. cloudy.

Woll'e [vol'er] nf. wool; -en a.

woollen; -ig *a.* woolly; -jacke *nf.* cardigan.

wollen [vol'en] *vt.i. ir.* to wish, desire, intend, will.

Wol'lust [vol'ŏost] *nf.* voluptuousness, lust; -lüstig *a.* voluptuous, lustful.

womöglich [voe-merk'lish] *ad.* if possible.

Wonne [von'er] *nf.* joy, bliss.

wor [vorr] in compounds, where (cf. wo); -an *ad.* of, on what, at which; -auf *ad.* on which; -aus *ad.* from, out of which; -in *ad.* in what; -über *ad.* over, about which; -unter *ad.* among, below which.

worfeln [vorr'feln] *vt.* to winnow.

Wort [vorrt] *n.* (Wörter, Worte) word; -bruch *nm.* breach of one's word; -brüchig *a.* treacherous; -führer *nm.* spokesman; -karg *a.* taciturn; -laut *nm.* wording; -reich *a.* verbose; -schatz *nm.* vocabulary; -spiel *n.* pun; -wechsel *nm.* dispute.

Wörterbuch [verr'ter-bŏŏch] *n.* (-bücher) dictionary.

wörtlich [verrt'lish] *a.* literal, word for word.

Wrack [vrak] *n.* (-e) wreck.

wringen [vring'en] *vt. ir.* to wring; -maschine *nf.* wringing-machine.

Wucher [vŏŏ'cher] *nm.* usury; -er *nm.* (-) usurer; -gewinn *nm.* excessive profit; -isch *a.* profiteering; -n *vi.* to profiteer, be extortionate, grow luxuriantly.

Wuchs [vŏŏx] *nm.* growth, figure, shape.

Wucht [vŏŏcht] *nf.* weight, force; -ig *a.* weighty.

Wühl'en [vȳŏ'len] *vi.* to burrow, rummage, dig up, stir up, gnaw at, agitate; -arbeit *nf.* agitation, sedition; -er *nm.* (-) agitator.

Wulst [vŏŏlst] *nm.* (Wülste) pad, roll, bead, cover of tyre;

-ig *a.* padded, puffy; -reif *nm.* beaded, flanged tyre.

wund [vŏŏnt] *a.* sore, wounded; -arzt *nm.* surgeon; -e *nf.* wound; -gelaufen *a.* footsore.

Wunder [vŏŏn'derr] *n.* (-) wonder, miracle; -bar *a.* wonderful, marvellous; -ding *n.* marvel; -kind *n.* infant prodigy; -lich *a.* odd, peculiar; -lichkeit *nf.* oddness, peculiarity; -n *vr.* to wonder at; -schön *a.* beautiful; -voll *a.* wonderful.

Wunsch [vŏŏnsh] *nm.* (Wünsche) wish; -träume *pl.* wishful thinking.

wünschen [vȳŏn'shen] *vt.i.* to wish; -swert *a.* desirable.

Würd'e [vȳŏrr'der] *nf.* dignity, honour; -enträger *nm.* dignitary; -evoll *a.* dignified; -ig *a.* worthy, deserving; -igen *vt.* to appreciate, condescend.

Wurf [vŏŏrf] *nm.* Würfe) throw, cast, brood; -geschoss *n.* projectile; -scheibe *nf.* quoit.

Würfel [vȳŏrr'fel] *nm.* (-) die, cube, dice; -inhalt *nm.* cubic contents; -kohle *nf.* small coal, nuts; -spiel *n.* game of dice; -zucker *nm.* lump sugar.

würgen [vȳŏrr'gen] *vt.i.* to choke, throttle.

Wurm [vŏŏrrm] *nm.* (Würmer) worm, grub; -fortsatz *nm.* appendix; -ig *a.* -stichig *a.* worm-eaten.

Wurst [vŏŏrrst] *nf.* (Würste) sausage.

Würz'e [vȳŏrr'ser] *nf.* flavour/ing), condiment, seasoning, spice; -en *vt.* to season, spice; -ig *a.* aromatic, seasoned.

Wurzel [vŏŏrr'tsel] *nf.* root; -n *vi.* to take root.

Wust [vŏŏst] *nm.* rubbish, jumble.

wüst [vȳŏst] *a.* desert, muddled, confused, dissolute; -e *nf.* desert; -ling *nm.* rake.

Wut [vŏŏt] *nf.* rage, fury.

mania, frenzy; **-anfall** nm. fit of madness, rage.

wüten [vyōō'ten] vi. to rage; **-erich** nm. (-e) tyrant.

X

X-beine [ix'bine-er] pl. bow-legs; **-beliebig** a. any, whatever you like; **-mal** ad. any number of times; **-Strahlen** pl. X-rays; **-Uhr** nf. zero-hour (mil.).

Z

Zack'e [tsak'er] nf. scallop, tooth, prong; **-en** vt. to tooth, scallop, indent; **-ig** a. pointed, jagged, notched.

zag'en [tsah'gen] vi. to be timid, afraid; **-haft** a. timid; **-haftigkeit** nf. timidity.

zäh [tsay] a. tough, sticky, stubborn; **-igkeit** nf. toughness, stickiness.

Zahl [tsahl] nf. number, figure; **-bar** a. payable; **-en** vt.i. to pay; **-enmässig** a. numerical; **-er** nm. (-) payer; **-los** a. countless; **-meister** nm. paymaster; **-reich** a. numerous; **-tag** nm. pay-day; **-wort** n. numeral.

zähl'en [tsale'en] vt. to count, reckon; **-er** nm. meter, speedometer; **-ung** nf. counting, census.

Zahlung [tsahl'ōōng] nf. payment; **-seinstellung** nf. suspension of payments; **-sfähig** a. solvent; **-sunfähig** a. insolvent.

zahm [tsahm] a. tame; **-heit** nf. tameness.

zähm'en [tsay'men] vt. to tame; **-ung** nf. taming.

Zahn [tsahn] nm. (**Zähne**) tooth, cog; **-arzt** nm. dentist; **-bürste** nf. toothbrush; **-en** vi. to cut teeth; **-fleisch** n. gum(s); **-pasta** nf. toothpaste; **-rad** n.

cog-wheel; **-radbahn** nf. funicular railway; **-schmerz** nm. toothache; **-stein** nm. tartar; **-stocher** nm. toothpick.

Zain [tsine] nm. (-e) ingot.

Zange [tsang'er] nf. tongs, tweezers, forceps; **-nbewegung** nf. pincer movement (mil.).

Zank [tsank] nm. quarrel; **-apfel** nm. bone of contention; **-en** vi. to quarrel; **-süchtig** a. quarrelsome.   [quarrelsome.

zänkisch [tsenk'ish] a.

Zapfen [tsap'fen] nm. (-) plug, bung, pivot, pin, cone; **-streich** nm. tattoo, curfew.

zapf'en [tsap'fen] vt. to tap; **-stelle** nf. petrol pump.

zappel'n [tsap'eln] vi. to fidget, flounder, struggle; **-ig** a. fidgety.

zart [tsarrt] a. tender, gentle, delicate; **-gefühl** n. delicacy, tact; **-heit** nf. tenderness, delicacy.

zärtlich [tserrt'lish] a. tender, affectionate; **-keit** nf. tenderness; pl. endearments.

Zäsur [tsay-zōōr'] nf. caesura.

Zauber [tsow'berr] n. charm, magic, spell; **-ei** nf. magic; **-er** nm. (-) magician, conjurer; **-haft** a. magical; **-in** nf. witch; **-künstler** nm. conjurer; **-n** vi. to conjure, practice magic; **-spruch** nm. magic spell.

zaudern [tsow'derrn] vi. to hesitate, delay; n. hesitation.

Zaum [tsowm] nm. (**Zäume**) bridle, rein.   [bridle.

zäumen [tsoy'men] vt. to

Zaun [tsown] nm. (**Zäune**) hedge, fence, hoarding; **-könig** nm. wren.

zausen [tsow'zen] vt. to pull about, tousle.

Zech'bruder [tsesh'brŏŏ-derr] nm. (-brüder) boon-companion; **-e** nf. bill, score, mine; **-en** vi. to drink.

Zeder [tsay'derr] nf. cedar.

Zehe [tsay'er] *nf.* toe.

zehn [tsane] *num.* ten; **-te** *a.* tenth; *n.* tithe; **-tel** *n.* tenth part.

zehr'en [tsair'ren] *vi.* to feast, consume, waste away; **-ung** *nf.* expenses, waste, provisions.

Zeich'en [tsīe'shen] *n.* (-) sign, token, signal, call-sign (*rad.*); **-enraum** *nm.* drawing-office; **-stift** *nm.* pencil; **-nen** *vt.* to draw, mark, design, subscribe; **-ner** *nm.* (-) designer, draughtsman, subscriber; **-nung** *nf.* drawing, design, subscription.

Zeige'finger [tsī'ger-fing-err] *nm.* (-) forefinger; **-n** *vt.* to show, point at, out; *r.* appear, emerge; **-r** *nm.* (-) hand (*clock*).

Zeile [tsīle'er] *nf.* line, row.

Zeit [tsīte] *nf.* time, period; **-abschnitt** *nm.* period; **-alter** *n.* age; **-aufnahme** *nf.* time exposure; **-folge** *nf.* chronological order; **-genosse** *m.w.* contemporary; **-ig** *a.* timely, ripe; **-igen** *vt.* to ripen, produce; **-karte** *nf.* season-ticket; **-lebens** *ad.* for life; **-lich** *a.* temporal; **-lupe** *nf.* time-lens, slow motion; **-raum** *nm.* period; **-rechnung** *nf.* era; **-schrift** *nf.* periodical; **-verlust** *nm.* loss of time; **-vertreib** *nm.* pastime; **-weilig** *a.* temporary; **-weise** *ad.* for a time; **-wert** *nm.* present value; **-wort** *n.* verb; **-zeichen** *n.* time-signal (*rad.*); **-zünder** *nm.* time-fuse.

Zeitung [tsīte'ŏong] *nf.* newspaper, news; **-sausschnitt** *nm.* press cutting; **-spapier** *n.* newsprint; **-swesen** *n.* press, journalism.

Zell'e [tsel'er] *nf.* cell, airframe (*av.*); **-enförmig** *a.* cellular; **-stoff** *nm.* cellulose; **-wolle** *nf.* staple fibre.

Zelt [tselt] *n.* (-e) tent; **-bahn** *nf.* tarpaulin, ground-sheet;

-dach *n.* awning; **-leine** *nf.* tent-rope.

Zement [tse-ment'] *nm.* (-e) [cement.

Zensur [tsen-zŏŏr'] *nf.* censorship, marks, report.

Zentimeter [tsen'ti-may-terr] *nm., n.* (-) centimeter.

Zentner [tsent'nerr] *nm.* (-) hundredweight.

Zentral'e [tsen-trah'ler] *nf.* central office, exchange (*ph.*); **-heizung** *nf.* central heating.

Zentrum [tsen'trŏŏm] *n.* centre.

Zephirwolle [tsef'irr-vol-er] *nf.* zephir (*com.*).

Zepter [tsep'terr] *n.* (-) sceptre.

zerbeissen [tserr-bīce'en] *vt. ir.* to crunch (up).

zerbrech'en [tserr-bresh'en] *vt. ir.* to break in pieces; **-lich** *a.* fragile, breakable; **-lichkeit** *nf.* fragility.

zerbröckeln [tserr-brer'keln] *vt.* to crumble to pieces.

zerdrücken [tserr-drÿŏ'ken] *vt.* to crumble, crush.

Zeremonie [tser-re-mo-nee'] *nf.* ceremony.

zerfahren [tserr-fah'ren] *vt. ir.* to burst, drive over, destroy; *a.* heedless, careless; **-heit** *nf.* heedlessness, carelessness.

Zerfall [tserr-fal'] *nm.* decay, decadence, disintegration (*atom*); **-en** *vi. ir.* to fall to pieces, decay, quarrel with, disintegrate.

zerfleischen [tserr-flīe'shen] *vt.* to lacerate.

zerfliessen [tserr-flee'sen] *vi. ir.* to dissolve, melt away.

zergehen [tserr-gay'en] *vi. ir.* to melt, disperse.

zergliedern [tserr-glee'derrn] *vt.* to dissect, analyse; **-ung** *nf.* dissection. [cut up.

zerhauen [tserr-how'en] *vt.* to

Zerknirschung [tserr-knirr'-shŏŏng] *nf.* contrition.

zerleg'bar [tserr-laik'barr] *a.*

sectional; **-en** vt. to separate, divide up, split up, strip, dismantle; **-ung** nf. splitting up, dismantling. [ragged.

zerlumpt [tserr-lōōmpt] a.

zermalmen [tserr-mal'men] vt. to crush.

zermürb'en [tserr-myōōrr'ben] vt. to wear out; **-ungskrieg** nm. war of attrition.

zerplatzen [tserr-plat'sen] vi. to burst.

zerquetschen [tserr-kvet'shen] vt. to crush.

Zerrbild [tserr'bilt] n. (**-er**) caricature, distortion.

zerreiben [tser-ribe'en] vt. ir. to grind down.

zerreissen [tser-rice'en] vt. ir. to tear to pieces; i. break, tear, split.

zerren [tser'ren] vt. to tug.

zerrinnen [tser-rin'en] vi. ir. to melt (away).

Zerrissenheit [tser-riss'en-hite] nf. disunion, tattered state, strife, discord.

zerrüt'ten [tser-ryōō'ten] vt. to disorder, destroy; **-ung** nf. disorder, destruction.

zerschellen [tserr-shel'en] vt. to shatter, smash; i. be shattered.

zerschiessen [tserr-shee'sen] vt. ir. to shoot to pieces.

zerschlagen [tserr-shlah'gen] vt. ir. to knock to pieces; i. fall through.

zerschmettern [tserr-shmet'errn] vt. to smash.

zerschneiden [tserr-shni'den] vt. ir. to cut up.

zersetz'en [tserr-zet'sen] vt. to decompose, dissolve; **-ung** nf. decomposition.

zersplittern [tserr-shplit'errn] vt. to splinter, disperse, split up.

zersprengen [tserr-shpreng'en] vt. to burst (open), blow up, rout.

zerspringen [tserr-shpring'-

en] vi. ir. to burst, split, crack.

zerstampfen [tserr-shtampf'-fen] vt. to crush.

zerstäub'en [tserr-shtoy'ben] vt.i. to turn to dust, atomize, spray; **-er** nm. (**-**) atomizer, spray.

zerstechen [tserr-shtesh'en] vt. ir. to pierce, stab.

zerstör'en [tserr-shter'ren] vt. to destroy; **-er** nm. (**-**) destroyer, long-range fighter (av.); **-ung** nf. destruction; **-ungsangriff** nm. nuisance raid; **-ungszug** nm. demolition squad.

zerstossen [tserr-shtoh'sen] vt. ir. to bruise, pound.

zerstreu'en [tserr-shtroy'en] vt. to disperse, scatter, divert; **-t** a. scattered, absent-minded; **-theit** nf. absent-mindedness; **-ung** nf. dispersion, amusement, distraction.

zerstückeln [tserr-shtyōō'keln] vt. to cut into pieces, parcel out.

zerteil'en [tserr-tile'en] vt. to divide, distribute, separate; **-ung** nf. division, dispersion.

zertreten [tserr-tray'ten] vt. to trample under foot.

zertrümmern [tserr-tryōō'merrn] vt. to wreck, demolish, smash, shatter.

Zerwürfnis [tserr-vyōōrrf'nis] n. (**-se**) dissension, quarrel.

zetern [tsay'terrn] vi. to cry out, shout.

Zettel [tset'el] nm. (**-**) note, slip, bill, label, ticket; **-ankleber** nm. bill-poster; **-kasten** nm. filing-cabinet.

Zeug [tsoik] n. (**-e**) stuff, material, tools, implements, cloth; **-haus** n. arsenal.

Zeug'e [tsoy'ger] m.w, **Zeugin** nf. witness; **-en** vi. to bear witness, testify; **-nis** n. testimony, evidence, certificate, reference, report, proof.

Zeug'en [tsoy'gen] vt. to beget, produce; **-ung** nf. procreation,

Zichorie [tsish-or'yer] *nf.* chicory.

Zicklein [tsik'line] *n.* (-) kid.

Zickzack [tsik'tsak] *nm.* zig-zag.

Ziege [tsee'ger] *nf.* goat; **-nhirt** *nm.* goatherd; **-nleder** *n.* kid.

Ziegel [tsee'gel] *nm.* (-) brick, tile; **-brenner** *nm.* brick-maker; **-decker** *nm.* tiler; **-ei** *nf.* brick-works; **-ofen** *nm.* brick-kiln.

zieh'en [tsee'en] *vt. ir.* to draw, pull, drag; *i.r.* draw, wander, march, move; **es zieht** there is a draught; **-harmonika** *nf.* accordion; **-mutter** *nf.* foster-mother; **-tag** *nm.* removal day; **-ung** *nf.* drawing.

Ziel [tseel] *n.* aim, limit, goal, objective, target (*mil.*); **-anflug** *nm.* bombing run (*av.*); **-band** *n.* tape; **-en** *vi.* to aim; **-fernrohr** *n.* telescopic sight; **-scheibe** *nf.* target, butt.

ziem'en [tsee'men] *vi.r.* to be fitting; **-lich** *a.* pretty, moderate(ly), fairly.

Zier [tseerr] *nf.* **-at** *nm.* (-e) decoration; **-en** *vt.* to adorn, decorate; *r.* to be affected, prim, put on airs; **-erei** *nf.* affectation; **-lich** *a.* elegant, dainty, neat; **-lichkeit** *nf.* elegance, prettiness.

Ziffer [tsif'err] *nf.* figure, number, cipher; **-blatt** *n.* clock-face, dial.

Zigarette [tsi-gar-ret'er] *nf.* cigarette; **-netui** *n.* cigarette-case; **-nkiste** *nf.* cigar-box.

Zigarre [tsi-gar'rer] *nf.* cigar; **-nspitze** *nf.* cigar-holder.

Zigeuner [tsi-goy'nerr] *nm.* (-), **-in** *nf.* gipsy.

Zimbel [tsim'bel] *nf.* cymbal.

Zimmer [tsim'err] *n.* (-) room; **-antenne** *nf.* indoor-aerial (*rad.*); **-decke** *nf.* ceiling; **-flucht** *nf.* suite of rooms; **-mädchen** *n.* chamber-maid; **-mann** *nm.* carpenter; **-n** *vt.* to make, shape in wood.

Zimmet [tsim'et] *nm.* cinnamon.

zimperlich [tsim'perr-lish] *a.* affected, prudish.

Zink [tsink] *n.* zinc; **-salbe** *nf.* zinc ointment.

Zinke [tsink'er] *nf.* tooth, prong, cornet.

Zinn [tsin] *n.* tin, pewter; **-ern** *a.* pewter, tin; **-waren** *pl.* pewter. [*pl.* battlements.

Zinne [tsin'er] *nf.* pinnacle;

Zinnoberrot [tsin-oh'berr-rote] *a.* vermilion.

Zins [tsinss] *nm.* (*gen.* -es; *pl.* -en) interest, rent; **-eszins** *nm.* compound interest; **-fuss** *nm.* rate of interest; **-schein** *nm.* dividend warrant.

Zipfel [tsip'fel] *nm.* (-) tip, corner; **-ig** *a.* peaked.

Zirkel [tsirr'kel] *nm.* (-) circle, compasses. [(-e) circular.

Zirkular [tsirr-koo-larr'] *n.*

Zirkus [tsirr'kōōss] *nm.* (-se) circus.

zirpen [tsirr'pen] *vi.* to chirp.

zisch'eln [tsish'eln] *vi.* to whisper; **-en** *vi.* to hiss, whiz.

Zit'at [tsi-taht'] *n.* (-e) quotation; **-ieren** *vt.* to quote, summon.

Zitron'at [tsi-tro-naht'] *n.* candied lemon peel; **-e** *nf.* lemon; **-enlimonade** *nf.* lemon-squash; **-enwasser** *n.* lemonade. [tremble, shake.

zittern [tsi'terrn] *vi.* to

Zitze [tsit'ser] *nf.* udder.

zivil [tsi-veel'] *a.* civil; moderate (*com.*); **-**, civilians, mufti; **-isation** *nf.* civilization; **-isieren** *vt.* to civilize.

Zobel [tsoh'bel] *nm.* sable.

zögern [tserr'gerrn] *vi.* to hesitate, loiter, delay; *a.* hesitation; **-ung** *nf.* delay.

Zögling [tserr'gling] *nm.* (-e) pupil. [*nm.* yard-stick.

Zoll [tsol] *nm.* (-e) inch; **-stock**

Zoll [tsol] *nm.* (Zölle) custom, toll, due, duty; **-amt** *n.* custom-house; **-beamte(r)** *m.w.* customs official; **-frei** a. free of duty; **-ordnung** nf. customs regulations; **-pflichtig** a. dutiable; **-revision** nf. customs examination. [show.

zollen [tsol'en] vt. to pay,
Zöllner [tsœl'nerr] nm. (-) customs official.

Zone [tsoh'ner] nf. zone.

zoologisch [tsoh-loh'gish] a. zoological.

Zopf [tsopf] nm. (Zöpfe) pigtail, plait, queue, red tape.

Zorn [tsorrn] nm. anger; **-ig** a. angry.

Zote [tsoh'ter] nf. obscenity; **-ig** a. obscene, smutty.

zottig [tsot'ish] a. shaggy. [by.

zu [tsoo] pr. to, at, for, with,

Zubehör [tsoo'ber-herr] n. (-e) fittings, accessories.

Zuber [tsoo'berr] nm. (-) tub.

zubereit'en [tsoo'ber-rite-en] vt. to prepare, cook; **-ung** nf. preparation, cooking, dressing.

zubilligen [tsoo'bil-i-gen] vt. to grant.

zubinden [tsoo'bin-den] vt. ir. to tie up, blindfold.

zubring'en [tsoo'bring-en] vt. ir. to spend, pass, take to; **-erschiff** n. tender.

Zucht [tsŏŏcht] nf. rearing, breed(ing), discipline, drill; **-haus** n. convict prison; **-häusler** nm. convict; **-hengst** nm. stallion; **-los** a. insubordinate, undisciplined; **-losigkeit** nf. insubordination, disorderliness; **-stute** nf. brood-mare.

zücht'en [tsyŏŏsh'ten] vt. to breed, cultivate; **-er** nm. (-) breeder, grower; **-ig** a. modest; **-igen** vt. to chastise; **-igkeit** nf. chastity; **-igung** nf. chastisement.

zuck'en [tsŏŏk'en] vi. to jerk, twitch; **-ung** nf. convulsion.

zücken [tsyŏŏk'en] vt. to draw.

Zucker [tsŏŏkerr] nm. sugar; **-bäcker** nf. confectioner; **-guss**

nm. icing; **-n** vt. to sugar; **-rübe** nf. beetroot; **-siederei** nf. sugar-refinery; **-werk** n. confectionery.

zudecken [tsoo'dek-en] vt. to cover up. [besides.

zu dem [tsoo-dame'] ad.

zudenken [tsoo'denk-en] vt. ir. to intend for.

Zudrang [tsoo'drang] nm. rush to.

zudrängen [tsoo'dreng-en] vr. to throng to, press forward

zudrehen [tsoo'dray-en] vt. to turn off, to.

zudringlich [tsoo'dring-lish] a. forward, pushing, intrusive; **-keit** nf. importunity, forwardness.

zueign'en [tsoo'ig-nen] vt. to dedicate; **-ung** nf. dedication.

zueilen [tsoo'ile-en] vi. to hurry to.

zueinander [tsoo'ine-an-derr] ad. to each other, together.

zuerkennen [tsoo'err-ken-en] vt. ir. to award, sentence.

zuerst [tsoo-airrst'] ad. first. [in, approach.

Zufahrt [tsoo'farrt] nf. driving

Zufall [tsoo'fal] nm. (-fälle) accident, chance, event.

zufallen [tsoo'fal-en] vi. ir. to fall to.

zufällig [tsoo'fel-ish] a., ad. (by) chance, accidental(ly).

zufliessen [tsoo'flee-sen] vi. ir. to flow to, in.

Zuflucht [tsoo'flŏŏcht] nf. refuge, recourse.

Zufluss [tsoo'flŏŏss] nm. tributary, supply (com.).

zufolge [tsoo-fol'ger] ad. owing to, in accordance with.

zufrieden [tsoo-free'den] a. content(ed); **-heit** nf. content, satisfaction; **-stellen** vt. to satisfy.

zufrieren [tsoo'freer-ren] vi. ir. to freeze up, over.

zufügen [tsoo'fyoo-gen] vt. to add to, cause.

Zufuhr [tsoo'foorr] *nf.* importation, supplies.
zuführen [tsoo'fyoo-ren] *vt.* to conduct, convey to, supply.
Zug [tsook] *nm.* (Züge) train, drawing, pulling, draught, dash, stroke, move, march, procession, platoon, section (*mil.*), feature, outline; **-brücke** *nf.* drawbridge; **-führer** *nm.* guard (*rl.*), platoon commander (*mil.*); **-leine** *nf.* tow-rope; **-luft** *nf.* current of air; **-maschine** *nf.* traction-engine, tractor; **-mittel** *n.* attraction; **-weise** *ad.* by platoons.
Zugabe [tsoo'gah-ber] *nf.* extra, addition.
Zugang [tsoo'gang] *nm.* access, approach.
zugänglich [tsoo'geng-lish] *a.* accessible, approachable.
zugeben [tsoo'gay-ben] *vt. ir.* to add, throw in, admit, recognize, permit. [present
zugegen [tsoo'gay'gen] *a.*
zugehen [tsoo'gay-en] *vi. ir.* to shut, go on, be sent on.
zugehör'en [tsoo'ger-her-ren] *vi.* to belong to; **-ig** *a.* belonging to; **-igkeit** *nf.* membership.
zugeknöpft [tsoo'ger-knerpft] *a.* reserved, stand-offish.
Zügel [tsyoo'gel] *nm.* (-) rein(s), curb, bridle; **-los** *a.* unrestrained, licentious; **-losigkeit** *nf.* lack of restraint, licentiousness; **-n** *vt.* to curb, rein in.
zugesellen [tsoo'ger-zel-en] *vr.* to join, associate with.
Zugeständnis [tsoo'ger-shtent-niss] *n.* (-se) concession.
zugestehen [tsoo'ger-shtay-en] *vt. ir.* to concede, admit.
zugetan [tsoo'ger-tahn] *a.* attached to. [attached (*mil.*).
zugeteilt [tsoo'ger-tilt] *a.*
zugig [tsoo'gish] *a.* draughty.
zugreifen [tsoo'grife-en] *vi. i. ir.* to help, take hold, fall to, grasp.

zugrunde [tsoo-groon'der] *ad.* to ruin; **-gehen** *vi. ir.* to be ruined; **-liegen** *vi. ir.* to be based upon.
zugunsten [tsoo-goon'sten] *ad.* in favour of.
zugute [tsoo-goo'ter] *ad.* in good stead; **-** *halten* *vt. ir.* to allow for.
zuhalten [tsoo'hal-ten] *vt. ir.* to keep shut, go towards.
zuhanden [tsoo-han'den] *ad.* at hand.
Zuhilfenahme [tsoo-hil'fer-nah-mer] *nf.* help.
zuhinterst [tsoo-hin'terrst] *ad.* at the very end.
zuhör'en [tsoo'her-ren] *vi.* to listen; **-er** *nm.* (-) listener; **-erschaft** *nf.* audience.
zujubeln [tsoo'yoo-beln] *vi.* to cheer. [to paste up, fasten.
zukleben [tsoo'klay-ben] *vt.*
zuknöpfen [tsoo'knerp-fen] *vt.* to button up.
zukommen [tsoo'kom-en] *vi. ir.* to come up to, fall to (as share), be due to, be fitting for.
zukorken [tsoo'korr-ken] *vt.* to cork (up). [tables.
Zukost [tsoo'kost] *nf.* vegetables.
Zukunft [tsoo'koonft] *nf.* future; **-smusik** *nf.* wishful thinking.
zukünftig [tsoo'kyoonf-tish] *a.* future; *ad.* in future.
Zulage [tsoo'lah-ger] *nf.* increase, bonus, extra pay, allowance.
zulangen [tsoo'lang-en] *vt.* to hand; *i.* suffice, help oneself.
zulänglich [tsoo'leng-lish] *a.* sufficient.
zulass'en [tsoo'lass-en] *vt. ir.* to admit, permit; **-ung** *nf.* admission, permission.
zulässig [tsoo'less-ish] *a.* permissible.
Zulauf [tsoo'lowf] *nm.* rush, crowd; **-en** *vi. ir.* to run, flock to. [add, procure.
zulegen [tsoo'lay-gen] *vt.* to

zuleide [tsōō-lide'er] ad. hurt, harm.

zuleit'en [tsōō'līte-en] vt. to lead to; -ung nf. guidance.

zuletzt [tsōō-letst'] ad. finally, at last.

zuliebe [tsōō-lee'ber] ad. to please. [supply.

Zuluft [tsōō'lōōft] nf. air- **zum** = zu dem.

zumachen [tsōō'mach-en] vt. to shut, fasten; i. hurry.

zumeist [tsōō-mīst'] ad mostly.

zumessen [tsōō'mess-en] vt. ir. to measure out, apportion.

zumindest [tsōō-min'dest] ad. at least.

zumute sein [tsōō-mōō'ter-zine] vi. to feel.

zumut'en [tsōō'mōō-ten] vt. to expect, ask of; -ung nf. unreasonable expectation, demand, impertinence.

zunächst [tsōō-naich-st'] ad. nearest, first of all; pr. close to.

zunähen [tsōō'nay-en] vt. to sew up (together). [increase.

Zunahme [tsōō'nah-mer] nf.

Zuname [tsōō'nah-mer] nm. (gen. -ns; pl. -n) surname.

Zünd'apparat [tsyōōnt'ap-ar-raht] nm. (-e) magneto (aut.); -en vi. to light, catch fire; -er nm. (-) fuse, detonator (mil.); -holz n. match; -kerze nf. sparking-plug (aut.); -schnur nf. fuse; -stoff nm. fuel, combustible matter; -ung nf. priming, ignition.

Zunder [tsōō'nderr] nm. tinder.

zunehmen [tsōō'nay-men] vi. ir. to increase, grow.

zuneig'en [tsōō'nie-gen] vi. to incline, lean; -ung nf. inclination, affection.

Zunft [tsōōnft] nf. guild.

zünftig [tsyōōn'tish] a. skilled, thorough.

Zunge [tsōōng'er] nf. tongue, sole (fish); -nfertig a. glib,

voluble; -nfertigkeit nf. glibness.

züngeln [tsyōōng'eln] vi. to leap up, fork, flare.

zunichte [tsōō-nish'ter] ad. to ruin; - machen vt. to frustrate, destroy. [nod to.

zunicken [tsōō'nik-en] vi. to

zunutze [tsōō-nōōt'ser] ad. useful, profitable.

zuoberst [tsōō-obe'errst] ad. at the top.

zupf'en [tsōōp'fen] vt. to pull, pick, pluck; -geige nf. guitar.

zur = zu der.

zurechn'en [tsōō'resh-nen] vt. to include, ascribe; -ung nf. imputation, attribution; -ungsfähig a. responsible; -ungsfähigkeit nf. responsibility, sound mind.

zurecht [tsōō-resht'] ad. right, in good order; -finden vr. to find one's way about; -machen vt. to prepare; -weisen vt. ir. to direct, reprimand; -weisung nf. reprimand, rebuff.

zureden [tsōō'ray-den] vi. to persuade, urge.

zureichen [tsōō'rish-en] vi. to suffice. [to break in.

zureiten [tsōō'rite-en] vt. to

zurich'ten [tsōō'rish-ten] vt. to prepare, dress; -ung nf. preparation, dressing. [angry.

zürnen [tsyōōrr'nen] vi. to be

zurück [tsōō-ryōōk'] ad. back (-wards), behindhand; -beben vi. to start back, shrink; -behalten vt. ir. to keep back; -berufen vt. ir. to recall; -bezahlen vt. ir. to repay; -bleiben vi.ir. to remain behind, lag, go slow; -bringen vt. ir. to bring, fetch back; -datieren vt. to date back, antedate; -drängen vt. to press back, repress; -erobern vt. to reconquer; -fahren vi. ir. to travel back, recoil, start; -fallen vi. ir. to fall back relapse; -finden vt. i. r. to find the way back;

-fordern vt. to reclaim; -führen vt. to lead back, reduce, trace back; -führung nf. reduction; -gabe nf. restoration; -geben vi. ir. to restore; -gehen vi. ir. to go back, down, come to nothing, fall off, originate in, trace back.

zurückgezogen [tsōō-rück'ger-tsoh-gen] a. retired, lonely; -heit nf. seclusion, retirement.

zurückhalt'en [tsōō-rück'-hal-ten] vt. ir. to hold back, in, detain, restrain, hide; -end a. reserved; -ung nf. reserve, retention.

zurück-kaufen vt. to buy back; -kehren vi. to return; -kommen vi. ir. to come back, alter, be reduced, get into arrears; -kunft nf. return; -lassen vt. ir. to leave behind; -legen vt. to put by, attain, complete; -nahme nf. taking back, withdrawal; -nehmen vt. ir. to take back, cancel; -prallen vi. to rebound; -rufen vt. to call back, recall; -schaffen vt. to send back, repatriate; -schlagen vt. ir. to turn back, repel; -schrecken vt. to frighten; i. shrink from; -setzen vt. to put back, slight, reduce; -setzung nf. slight; -springen vi. ir. to spring back, recede; -stellen vt. to put back; -stossen vt. ir. to repulse; -stossung nf. repulsion; -treten vi. ir. to step back, retire, subside; -weichen vi. ir. to recede, give way; -weisen vt. ir. to send back, repulse, reject, refuse; -werfen vt. to throw back; -zahlen vt. to pay back, reimburse; -ziehen vt. ir. to withdraw, r. retire.

Zuruf [tsōō'rōōf] nm. shout, acclamation.

zurüst'en [tsōō'ryōō-sten] vt. to fit out, equip; -ung nf. fitting out, preparation.

Zusage [tsōō'zah-ger] nf.

promise, consent; -n vt. to promise; i. accept, agree with, please.

zusammen [tsōō-zam'en] ad. together; -arbeit nf. co-operation; -arbeiten vi. to co-operate; -ballen vi. to roll into a ball, mass, clench; -basteln vt. to patch up, improvise; -beissen vt. ir. to set (teeth); -brechen vi. ir. to break down, smash, collapse; -bringen vt. ir. to bring, get together, raise, collect; -bruch nm. collapse; -fahren vi. ir. to travel together, collide, wince, start.

Zusammenfass'en [tsōō-zam'en-fass-en] vt. to summarize, comprise, unite; -end a. comprehensive; -ung nf. summary, digest.

zusammen-finden vr. ir. to meet together; -fliessen vi. ir. to flow together, meet; -fluss nm. confluence, concourse; -fügen vt. to join together, unite; -gehen vi. ir. to go together, suit, match; -gehören vi. to belong together, match; -gesetzt a. compound, composite.

Zusammen'hang nm. (-hänge) coherence, cohesion, continuity, context; -hängen vi. ir. to be connected; -hanglos a. disconnected, incoherent.

zusammen-klappbar a. collapsible; -kommen vi. ir. to assemble, meet; -kunft nf. assembly, assignation, meeting; -laufen vi. ir. to flock, run together, converge; -leben vi. to live together, cohabit; -legbar a. collapsible; -legen vt. to put together, collect, combine, unite, fold; -nehmen vt. ir. to take in, together, summon up; r. pull oneself together; -passen vi. to go well together, match; -raffen vt. to snatch, pluck up; -rücken vt. to move nearer, sit closer; -rufen vt. ir.

to call together, convene;
-schiessen *vt. ir.* to shoot down,
club together; -schlagen *vt. ir.*
to strike together, smash up,
clap, engulf; -schliessen *vt. ir.*
to close up; -schluss *nm.* union,
amalgamation; -schnüren *vt.*
to tie together, up; -schrumpf-
en *vt.* to shrink, shrivel up.

zusammensetz'bar *a.* sectional; -en *vt.* to construct,
compose, join; *r.* be composed
of.; -ung *nf.* composition, construction, compound.

zusammen'sinken *vi. ir.* to
collapse; -stellen *vt.* to join,
associate, assort, compile, compare; -stellung *nf.* combination, list, summary, assortment; -stimmen *vi.* to harmonize, accord; -stimmung *nf.*
harmony, accord; -stoss *nm.*
collision, smash, crash; -stoss-
en *vi.t. ir.* to knock together,
collide; -strömen *vi.* to flow,
flock together; -treffen *vi. ir.*
to meet, coincide; *n.* coincidence; -treten *vi. ir.* to meet;
-wachsen *vi. ir.* to coalesce;
-ziehen *vt.i. ir.* to draw together, contract, concentrate;
-ziehung *nf.* contraction, concentration.

Zusatz [tsōō'zats] *nm.* addition,
appendix, supplement, codicil.

zuschanden [tsōō-shan'den]
ad. to death, ruin.

zuschau'en [tsōō'show-en] *vi.*
to watch, look on; -er *nm.* (-)
spectator.

zuschicken [tsōō'shik'en] *vt.*
to send to, forward.

zuschieben [tsōō'shee-ben]
vt. ir. to push on, put on,
shut, close, pass on.

zuschiessen [tsōō'shee-sen]
vt. i. ir. to dash, rush at, fire at,
supply, advance.

Zuschlag [tsōō'shlahk] *nm.*
(-schläge) extra charge, addition, surcharge, surtax; -en *vt.
ir.* to hit out; *i.* slam, knock

down to; -smaterial *n.* flux
(*tec.*).

zuschliessen [tsōō'shlee-sen]
vt. ir. to lock (up).

zuschmeissen [tsōō'shmie-
sen] *vt. ir.* to slam, bang.

zuschnallen [tsōō'shnal-en]
vt. to buckle.

zuschneid'en [tsōō'shnie-
den] *vt. ir.* to cut up, out; -er
nm. (-) cutter.   [cut, style.

Zuschnitt [tsōō'shnit] *nm.*

zuschrauben [tsōō'shrow-
ben] *vt.* to screw down.

zuschreiben [tsōō'shri-be-
en] *vt. ir.* to assign, ascribe,
attribute, accept (*invitation*),
credit (*com.*).

Zuschrift [tsōō'shrift] *nf.*
communication.

zuschulden [tsōō-shōōl'-
den] *ad.* to blame, guilty.

Zuschuss [tsōō'shōōss] *nm.*
(-schüsse) contribution, extra
allowance, salary increase.

zuschütten [tsōō'shyöö-ten]
vt. to fill up, pour in.

zusehen [tsōō'zay-en] *vt. ir.* to
look on, take care; -ds *ad.*
visibly.

zusenden [tsōō'zen-den] *vt. ir.*
to forward, send on.

zusetzen [tsōō'zet-sen] *vt.* to
add, lose; *i.* importune, wear
out.   [to bar, block.

zusperren [tsōō'shper-ren] *vt.*

zuspitzen [tsōō'shpit-sen] *vt.*
to point, sharpen.

zusprechen [tsōō'shpresh-en]
vt. ir. to award; *i.* encourage,
comfort.

Zuspruch [tsōō'shprōōch] *nm.*
encouragement, custom.

Zustand [tsōō'shtant] *nm.*
state, condition; -e kommen
vi. to come off.

zuständig [tsōō'shten-dish] *a.*
belonging to, competent,
responsible; -keit *nf.* competence.

zustatten [tsōō-shtat'en] *ad.*
useful.

zustimm'en [tsoo'shtim-men] *vi.* to agree to, concur; **-ung** *nf.* consent.

zustopfen [tsoo'shtop-fen] *vt.* to stop up, darn, plug.

zustossen [tsoo'shtoh-sen] *vi. ir.* to happen to.

zustreben [tsoo'shtray-ben] *vi.* to strive after.

zustutzen [tsoo'shtŏŏt-sen] *vt.* to trim, cut.

zutage [tsoo-tah'ger] *ad.* to light.

Zutat [tsoo'taht] *nf.* trimmings, seasoning.

zuteil'en [tsoo'tile-en] *vt.* to assign, award; **-ung** *nf.* allocation, appropriation.

zuteil [tsoo-tile'] *ad.* to one's share; **-en** *vt.* to assign, allot, post (*mil.*).

zutragen [tsoo'trah-gen] *vt. ir.* to bring to; *i.* happen.

Zuträg'erei [tsoo-tray-ger-rie'] *nf.* gossip, scandal; **-lich** *a.* beneficial, wholesome; **-lichkeit** *nf.* wholesomeness.

Zutrau'en [tsoo'trow-en] *vt.* to credit with, confide in; **-lich** *a.* confiding; **-lichkeit** *nf.* confidence.

zutreffen [tsoo'tref-en] *vi. ir.* to come true.

zutreten [tsoo'tray-ten] *vi. ir.* to intervene, supervene.

zutrinken [tsoo'trink-en] *vi. ir.* to drink to, toast.

Zutritt [tsoo'trit] *nm.* access, admittance.

Zutun [tsoo'tōōn] *n.* assistance; *vt. ir.* to add, shut; **-lich** *a.* obliging.

zuverlässig [tsoo'ferr-less-ish] *a.* reliable; **-keit** *nf.* reliability.

Zuversicht [tsoo'ferr-sisht] *nf.* confidence; **-lich** *a.* confident; **-lichkeit** *nf.* confidence.

zuviel [tsoo-feel'] *ad.* too much.

zuvorderst [tsoo-forr'derrst] *[ad.* foremost.

zuvorkommen [tsoo-forr'-

kom-en] *vi. ir.* to anticipate; **-d** *a.* obliging.

zuvortun [tsoo-forr'tōōn] *vi. ir.* to outdo.

Zuwachs [tsoo'vax] *nm.* growth, accretion; **-en** *vi. ir.* to close, heal up, accrue to.

zuwandern [tsoo'van-dernn] *vi.* to immigrate.

zuwarten [tsoo'varr-ten] *vi.* to wait.

zuweilen [tsoo-vile'en] *ad.* at times, now and then.

zuweisen [tsoo'vize-en] *vt. ir.* to attribute, allot.

zuwenden [tsoo'ven-den] *vt. ir.* to turn towards, present, devote to.

zuwider [tsoo-vee'derr] *ad., pr.* contrary to; **-handlung** *nf.* contravention; **-laufen** *vi. ir.* to contravene, run counter to.

zuzeiten [tsoo-tsite'en] *ad.* at times.

zuziehen [tsoo'tsee-en] *vt. ir.* to draw (down upon), call in; *i.* move towards.

Zwang [tsvang] *nm.* compulsion, coercion; **-los** *a.* unconstrained; **-losigkeit** *nf.* informality; **-sarbeit** *nf.* hard labour; **-slage** *nf.* constraint, necessity; **-smassnahme** *nf.* sanctions; **-sverschleppte** *pl.* displaced persons; **-sweise** *ad.* compulsorily.

zwängen [tsveng'en] *vt.* to squeeze, jam.

zwanzig [tsvant'sish] *num.* twenty

zwar [tsvarr] *ad.* certainly, it is true, to be sure, and yet.

Zweck [tsvek] *nm.* (-e) object, purpose, aim; **-los** *a, ad.* aimless(ly); **-mässig** *a.* suitable, appropriate; **-mässigkeit** *nf.* suitableness; **-widrig** *a.* unsuitable.

Zwecke [tsvek'er] *nf.* hobnail.

zwei [tsvie] *num.* two; **-bein** *n.* biped; **-bettig** *a.* double-bedded; **-deutig** *a.* ambiguous;

-deutigkeit *nf.* ambiguity;
-elektrodenröhre *nf.* diode;
-jährlich *a.* biennial; -kampf *nm.* duel; -schneidig *a.* two-edged; -sitzer *nm.* two-seater.

zweierlei [tsvie-err-lie'] *a.* of two kinds.

Zwefel [tsvie'fell] *nm.* (-) doubt; -haft *a.* doubtful; -los *a.* doubtless; -n *vi.* to doubt; -sucht *nf.* scepticism.

Zweifler [tsvife'lerr] *nm.* (-) doubter.

Zweig [tsvike] *nm.* (-e) twig, branch; -bahn *nf.* branch line; -geschäft *n.* branch (*com.*).

Zweiheit [tsvie'hite] *nf.* duality.

zweimal [tsvie'mahl] *ad.* twice.

zweit [tsvite] *a.* second; -best *a.* second best; -kommandierende(r) *m.w.* second in command; -letzt *a.* last but one; -nächst *a.* next but one.

zweitens [tsviet'enss] *ad.* twice.

Zwerchfell [tsvairrsh'fel] *n.* diaphragm.

Zwerg [tsvairrk] *nm.* (-e), -in *nf.* dwarf; -artig *a.* dwarfish; -panzer *nm.* radio controlled tank; pferd *n.* pony.

Zwickel [tsvik'el] *nm.* (-) gusset.

zwixken [tsvik'en] *vt.* to pinch, nip.

Zwieback [tsvee'bak] *nm.* (-e) rusk, biscuit.

Zwiebel [tsvee'bel] *nf.* onion, bulb; -artig *a.* bulbous.

Zwie'gespräch [tsvee'ger-shpraish] *n.* (-e) dialogue; -licht *n.* twilight; -spalt *nm.* dissension; -tracht *nf.* discord; -trachtig *a.* discordant.

Zwillich [tsvil'ish] *nm.* (-) tick(ing).

Zwilling [tsvil'ing] *nm.* (-e) twin.

Zwinge [tsving'er] *nf.* ferrule; -n *vt. ir.* to force, subdue; -nd *a.* coercive, cogent.

zwinkern [tsvink'errn] *vi.* to wink, blink.

Zwirn [tsvirrn] *nm.* (-e) yarn, thread; -en *vt.* to twine, twist.

zwischen [tsvish'en] *pr.* between; -akt *nm.* interval (*theatre*); -deck *n.* steerage, lower deck; -ding *n.* cross; -durch *ad.* across, through, occasionally; -fall *nm.* incident; -gebläse *n.* supercharger; -handel *nm.* middleman's trade; -händler *nm.* middleman, agent; -lager *n.* transit camp; -landung *nf.* intermediate landing; -raum *nm.* space, interval; -spiel *n.* interlude; -staatluch *a.* international; -station *nf.* intermediate station; -stecker *nm.* adapter (*el.*); -wand *nf.* partition; -zeit *nf.* interval, interim.

Zwist [tsvist] *nm.* (-e) dissension, dispute; -ig *a.* at variance.

zwitschern [tsvit'sherrn] *vi.* to twitter.

Zwitter [tsvit'err] *nm.* (-) hybrid, mongrel; -fahrzeug *n.* tractor-lorry; -haft *a.* hybrid.

zwölf [tsverlf] *num.* twelve.

Zyklon [tsyook-lohn'] *nm.* (-e) cyclone.

Zyklus [tsyook'lõõss] *nm.* (Zyklen) cycle, series.

Zylinder [tsyi-lin'derr] *nm.* (-) cylinder, top-hat; -förmig *a.* cylindrical; -kopf *nm.* cylinder head.

zynisch [tsyõõ'nish] *a.* cynical, shameless.

Zypresse [tsyõõ-press'er] *nf.* cypress.

GEOGRAPHICAL NAMES

(Together with the related nouns and adjectives)

Aachen *Aix-la-Chapelle.*
Adria (die) *Adriatic Sea.*
Afrika *Africa*; Afrikaner *nm,* afrikanisch *a. African.*
Albanien *Albania.*
Alpen (die) *the Alps.*
Amerika *America*; Amerikaner *nm,* amerikanisch *a. American.*
Antwerpen *Antwerp.*
Arabien *Arabia*; Araber *nm. Arab*; arabisch *a. Arabic.*
Argentinien *the Argentine*; Argentiner *nm,* argentinisch *a. Argentine.*
Armenien *Armenia*; Armenier *nm,* armenisch *a. Armenian.*
Asien *Asia*; Asiate *m.w,* asiatisch *a. Asiatic.*
Athen *Athens.*
Australien *Australia*; Australier *nm,* australisch *a. Australian.*
Azoren *the Azores.*
Bayern *Bavaria*; Bayer *nm,* bayerisch *a. Bavarian.*
Belgien *Belgium*; Belgier *nm,* belgisch *a. Belgian.*
Birma *Burma*; Birmane *m.w,* birmanisch *a. Burmese.*
Biskaya *Biscay.*
Bodensee *Lake of Constance.*
Bozen *Bolzano.*
Brasilien *Brazil*; Brasilianer *nm,* brasilianisch *a. Brazilian.*
Braunschweig *Brunswick.*
Britannien *Britain*; Brite *m.w. Briton*; britisch *a. British.*
Brüssel *Brussels.*
Bulgarien *Bulgaria*; Bulgare *m.w,* bulgarisch *a. Bulgarian.*
Chile *Chile*; Chilene *m.w,* chilenisch *a. Chilian.*
China *China*; Chinese *m.w,* chinesich *a. Chinese.*
Dänemark *Denmark*; Däne *m.w. Dane*; dänisch *a. Danish.*
Deutschland *Germany*; Deutsche(r) *m.w,* deutsch *a. German.*
Donau (die) *Danube.*
Elsass *Alsace*; Elsässer *nm,* elsässisch *a. Alsatian.*
England *England*; Engländer *nm. Englishman*; englisch *a. English.*
Esthland *Esthonia*; Este *m.w,* estnisch *a. Esthonian.*
Etsch (die) *Adige.*

Europa *Europe*; Europäer *nm*, europäisch *a. European.*
Finnland *Finland*; Finnländer *nm. Finn*; finnisch *a. Finnish.*
Flandern *Flanders*; Flame *m.w. Fleming*; flämisch *a. Flemish.*
Florenz *Florence.*
Frankreich *France*; Franzose *m.w. Frenchman*; Französin *nf.*
    Frenchwoman; französisch *a. French.*
Friesland *Frisia*; Friese *m.w.* friesisch *a. Frisian.*
Gallen, St. *St. Gall.*
Genf *Geneva.*
Genua *Genoa.*
Griechenland *Greece*; Grieche *m.w.* griechisch *a. Greek.*
Grossbritanien *Great Britain.*
Haag *The Hague.*
Helgoland *Heligoland.*
Hessen *Hesse*; Hesse *m.w.* hessisch *a. Hessian.*
Hinterindien *Further India.*
Holland *Holland*; Holländer *nm. Dutchman*; holländisch *a.*
    Dutch.
Indien *India*; Inder *nm*, indisch *a. Indian*; Indianer *nm. North*
    American Indian.
Irland *Ireland*, *Eire*; Irländer *nm. Irishman*; irisch *a. Irish.*
Island *Iceland*; Isländer *nm. Icelander*; isländisch *a. Icelandic.*
Italien *Italy*; Italiener *nm*, italienisch *a. Italian.*
Japan *Japan*; Japaner *nm*, japanisch *a. Japanese.*
Jugoslawien *Yugoslavia.*
Kanada *Canada*; Kanadier *nm*, kanadisch *a. Canadian.*
Kapstadt *Cape Town.*
Kärnten *Carinthia.*
Karpathen *The Carpathians.*
Kleinasien *Asia Minor.*
Köln *Cologne*; Kölnisches Wasser *Eau de Cologne.*
Krim (die) *Crimea.*
Kroatien *Croatia*; Kroate *m.w. Croat*; kroatisch *a. Croatian.*
Lappland *Lapland*; Lappe *m.w.*, lappländisch *a. Lapp.*
Lettland *Latvia*; Lette *m.w.* lettisch *a. Latvian.*
Libanon *Lebanon.*
Libyen *Libya.*
Lissabon *Lisbon.*
Litauen *Lithuania*; Litauer *nm.* litauisch *a. Lithuanian.*
Livland *Livonia*; Livländer *nm*, livländisch *a. Livonian.*
Lothringen *Lorraine.*
Löwen *Louvain.*
Lüttich *Liège.*
Luzern *Lucerne.*
Maas (die) *Meuse.*

Mähren *Moravia.*
Mailand *Milan.*
Mandschurei (die) *Manchuria.*
Mazedonien *Macedonia;* Mazedonier *nm,* mazedonisch *a*
Macedonian.
Mitteleuropa *Central Europe.*
Mittelmeer *Mediterranean.*
Moldau (die) *Moldavia.*
Mongolei (die) *Mongolia;* Mongole *m.w.* Mongol; mongolisch *a.*
Mongolian.
Mosel (die) *Moselle.*
Moskau *Moscow.*
München *Munich.*
Neapel *Naples.*
Neufundland *Newfoundland.*
Neuschottland *Nova Scotia.*
Neuseeland *New Zealand.*
Niederlande (die) *Netherlands;* Niederländer *nm.* Dutchman¡
niederländisch *a. Dutch.*
Niederrhein *Lower Rhine.*
Nil (der) *Nile.*
Nordsee (die) *North Sea.*
Norwegen *Norway;* Norweger *nm,* norwegisch *a. Norwegian.*
Nürnberg *Nuremberg.*
Oberbayern *Upper Bavaria.*
Ostasien *Far East.*
Ostindien *East Indies.*
Ostsee (die) *Baltic Sea.*
Österreich *Austria;* Österreicher *nm,* österreichisch *a. Austrian.*
Palästina *Palestine;* Palästiner *nm,* palästinisch *a. Palestinian.*
Pariser *Parisian.*
Persien *Persia;* Perser *nm,* persisch *a. Persian.*
Pfalz (die) *Palatinate.*
Polen *Poland;* Pole *m.w.* Pole; polnisch *a. Polish.*
Pommern *Pomerania.*
Portugal *Portugal;* Portugiese *m.w* portugiesisch *a. Portuguese.*
Prag *Prague.*
Preussen *Prussia;* Preusse *m.w,* preussisch *a. Prussian.*
Pyrenäen (die) *Pyrenees.*
Rhein (der) *Rhine.*
Rom *Rome;* Römer *nm,* römisch *a. Roman.*
Rumänien *Rumania;* Rumäne *m.w,* rumänisch *a. Rumanian.*
Russland *Russia;* Russe *m.w,* russisch *a. Russian.*
Sachsen *Saxony;* Sachse *m.w,* Sächsin *nf,* sächsisch *a. Saxon.*
Schlesien *Silesia;* Schlesier *nm,* schlesisch *a. Silesian.*

Schottland *Scotland*; Schotte *m.w*, Schottin *nf. Scot*; schottisch
   a. Scottish.

Schwaben *Swabia*; Schwabe *m.w*, schwäbisch *a. Swabian.*

Schwarzwald *Black Forest.*

Schweden *Sweden*; Schwede *m.w*, Schwedin *nf. Swede*;
   schwedisch *a. Swedish.*

Schweiz (die) *Switzerland*; Schweizer *nm*, schweizerisch *a.*
   Swiss.

Serbien *Serbia*; Serbe *m.w*, serbisch *a. Serbian.*

Sibirien *Siberia.*

Siebenbürgen *Transylvania.*

Sizilien *Sicily.*

Slowakei (die) *Slovakia*; Slowake *m.w*, slowakisch *a. Slovak.*

Sowjet *Soviet.*

Spanien *Spain*; Spanier *nm. Spaniard*; spanisch *a. Spanish.*

Steiermark *Styria*; Steiermärker *nm*, steiermärkisch *a. Styrian.*

Stiller Ozean *Pacific Ocean.*

Syrien *Syria*; Syrer *nm*, syrisch *a. Syrian.*

Themse (die) *Thames.*

Thrazien *Thrace.*

Thüringen *Thuringia.*

Tirol *Tyrol*; Tiroler *nm*, tirolisch *a. Tyrolese.*

Tschekoslowakei (die) *Czechoslovakia*; Tscheche *m.w*, tschechisch *a. Czech.*

Türkei (die) *Turkey*; Türke *m.w. Turk*; türkisch *a. Turkish.*

Ungarn *Hungary*; Ungar *nm*, ungarisch *a. Hungarian.*

Venedig *Venice.*

Vereinigte Staaten (die) *United States.*

Vierwaldstättersee (der) *Lake of Lucerne.*

Vlissingen *Flushing.*

Vogesen (die) *Vosges.*

Vorderasien *The Near East.*

Warschau *Warsaw.*

Weichsel (die) *Vistula.*

Westfalen *Westphalia.*

Westindien *West Indies.*

Wien *Vienna*; Wiener *nm*, wienerisch *a. Viennese.*

Zypern *Cyprus.*

ENGLISH-GERMAN DICTIONARY

A, an [ei, æn] a. ein, eine, ein.

Aback [A-bæk'] ad. zurück, rückwärts ; taken – verblüfft.

Abaft [A-bæft'] ad. hinterwarts, nach hinten, achter (nav.).

Abandon [A-bæn'dAn] vt. aufgeben, verlassen, im Stich lassen ; -ed a. verlassen, verworfen ; -ment n. Aufgeben n.

Abase [A-beiss'] vt. demütigen, erniedrigen.

Abash [A-bæsch'] vt. beschämen, verlegen machen.

Abate [A-beit'] vt. vermindern, herabsetzen ; vi. nachlassen ; -ment n. Verminderung f. Ermässigung f.

Abatis [æ'bA-tiss] n. (mil.) Astverhau m.

Abattoir [æ-bæt-uahr'] n. Schlachthaus n.

Abbess [æ'bess] n. Äbtissin f.

Abbey [æ'bi] n. Abtei f.

Abbot [æ'bAt] n. Abt m.

Abbreviat'e [A-brih'wi-eit] vt. abkürzen ; -ion n. Abkürzung f.

Abdicat'e [æb'di-keit] vt. niederlegen ; vi. abdanken ; -ion n. Niederlegung f. Abdankung f.

Abdomen [æb'dou'min] n. Unterleib.

Abdominal [æb-do'mi-nAl] a. den Unterleib betreffend ; - belt n. Leibbinde f.

Abduction [æb-dAk'schan] n. Entführung f.

Aberration [æb-be-rei'schAn] n. Irrgang m ; Irrsinn m. Abweichung f.

Abet [A-bet] vt. helfen, anhet-

zen ; -ter n. Helfer m. ; anhetzer m.

Abeyance [A-bei'Anss] n. in – unentschieden, suspendiert.

Abhor [æb-hOr'] vt. verabscheuen ; -rence n. Verabscheuung f, Abscheu m ; -rent a. Abscheu erregend, unvereinbar.

Abid'e [A-baid'] vi. bleiben ; – by verharren bei ; t. leiden ; -ing a. dauernd.

Ability [A-bi'li-ti] n. Geschicklichkeit f, Fähigkeit f.

Abject [æb'dzhekt] a. -ly ad. unterwürfig, niederträchtig, elend.

Abjure [æb-dzhuhr'] vt. abschwören, verschwören.

Able [eibl] a. **Ably** ad. fähig, tüchtig ; to be – vermögen ; – -bodied a. stark, diensttauglich ; – seaman n. Vollmatrose m.

Abnormal [æb-nOr'mAl] a. regelwidrig, abnorm ; -ity n. Abnormität f, Missbildung f, Regelwidrigkeit f.

Aboard [A-bOrd'] ad. an Bord.

Abode [A-boud'] n. Aufenthalt m, Wohnung f.

Abolish [A-bo'lisch] vt. abschaffen, vernichten.

Abolition [A-bo-li'schAn] n. Abschaffung f, Vernichtung f.

Abominab'le [A-bo'mi-nAbl] a. -ly ad. abscheulich.

Abominat'e [A-bo'mi-neit] vt. verabscheuen ; -ion n. Verabscheuung f, Greuel m.

Aborigin'al [æ-bo-ri'dzhi-nAl] a. eingeboren ; -es n. eingeborene Stämme m. pl.

Abort'ion [A-bOr'schAn] Fehlgebären n, Fehlgeburt f; -ive a. verfrüht.

Abound [A-baund'] vi. im Überfluss vorhanden sein.

About [A-baut'] pr. um, gegen, Über; ad. herum, umher; ungefähr; to be – to im Begriff sein zu; to bring – zustande bringen; to come – vi. geschehen; to speak – vt. sprechen über.

Above [A-bAw'] pr. über; ad. oben, darüber; the – der, die, das Obige; -board a. offen und ehrlich, anständig; -ground über Tag (mining); a. obenerwähnt.

Abrasion [A-brei'zhAn] n. Abschaben n. Hautabschürfung f. [einander.

Abreast [A-brest'] ad. nebeneinander.

Abridge [A-bridzh'] vt. abkürzen; -ment n. Abkürzung f.

Abroad [A-brOd'] ad. draussen, im Auslande; to get – ruchbar werden.

Abrogat'e [æb'ro-geit] vt. aufheben; -ion n. Aufhebung f.

Abrupt [Ab-rApt'] a. -ly ad. abgerissen, jäh, schroff; -ness n. Steilheit f. Eilfertigkeit f, Schroffheit f. [wür n.

Abscess [æb'ssess] n. Geschwür n.

Abscond [æb'skond'] vi. sich heimlich flüchten.

Absence [æb'ssAns] n. Abwesenheit f, Mangel m; leave of – Urlaub m.

Absent [æb'ssAnt'] v. ausbleiben; [æb'ssAnt] a. abwesend.

Absentee [æb-ssAn-tih'] n. der Abwesende; -ism n. Abwesenheit f, Ausbleiben n.

Absent-minded [æb'ssAnt-main'did] a. zerstreut; -ness n. Zerstreutheit f.

Absolute [æb'sso-luht] a. unumschränkt, absolut; -ly ad. gänzlich, durchaus.

Absolve [æb-ssolw'] vt. freisprechen, entbinden.

Absorb [æb-ssOrb'] vt. ein-

saugen, verschlingen, (shock) dämpfen.

Absorption [æb-ssOrp'schAn] n. Absorption f, Versunkensein n.

Abstain [æb-stein'] vi. sich enthalten; -er Nichttrinker m, Abstinent m.

Abstemious [æb-stih'miAss] a. enthaltsam; -ness n. Enthaltsamkeit f.

Abstention [æb-sten'schAn] n. Enthaltung f, Entbehrung f.

Abstinence [æb'sti-nAnss] n. Enthaltsamkeit f, Fasten n.

Abstract [æb-stræckt] vt. herausziehen, absondern; entwenden; [æb'stræckt] a. abstrakt, rein, abgesondert; n. Abriss m, Auszug m.

Abstracted [æb-stræk'tid] a. abgesondert, abstrakt, unaufmerksam; -ly ad. unaufmerksam.

Abstraction [æb-stræks'chAn] n. Abstraktion f, reiner Begriff m. [wickelt, unklar.

Abstruse [æb-struhss'] a. verwickelt.

Absurd [æb-ssArd'] a. -ly ad. albern, ungereimt, lächerlich; -ity n. Albernheit f, Ungereimtheit f, Unsinn m.

Abundan'ce [A-bAn'dAnss] n. Fülle f, Überfluss m; -t a. -tly ad. reichlich.

Abuse [A-bjuhs'] vt. missbrauchen, schimpfen, betrügen; — [A-bjuhss'] n. Missbrauch m, Beschimpfung f.

Abusive [A-bjuh'-siw'] a. -ly ad. schimpfend, beleidigend.

Abut [A-bAt'] vi. anstossen; -ment n. Widerlager n.

Abyss [A-biss'] n. Abgrund m.

Acacia [A-kei'schA] n. Akazie f.

Academy [A-kæ'dA-mi] n. Akademie f, höhere Schule f.

Accede [æck-ssihd'] vi. beistimmen, besteigen (throne).

Accelerat'e [æk-ssel'er-eit] vt. beschleunigen; vi. schneller

---

werden ; -ion *n.* Beschleunigung *f.* ; -or *n.* (aut.) Gasfusshebel *m,* -tritt *m,* Beschleuniger *m.*

Accent [æk-ssent'] *vt.* betonen; [æk-ssent] *n.* Akzent *m,* Aussprache *f.*

Accentuat'e [æk-ssen'tju-eit] *vt.* betonen ; -ion *n.* Betonung *f.*

Accept [æk-ssept'] *vt.* annehmen akzeptieren ; (bill) -able *a.* -ably *ad.* annehmbar, erwünscht; -ance *n.* Annahme *f.* Akzept *n.* (bill) ; -officer Vermusterungsoffizier *m.*

Acceptation [æk-ssep-tei'schAn] *n.* Bedeutung *f,* Sinn *m.*

Accepter [æk-ssep'ter] *n.* Akzeptant *m* ; -circuit Durchlasskreis *m* (rad.).

Access [æk-ssess] *n.* Zutritt *m.* Anfall *m* (illness, etc.) ; — hatch Einsteigluke *f.*

Accessib'le [Ak-sse'ssibl] *a.* zugänglich, -ility *n.* Zugänglichkeit *f.*

Accession [Ak-sse'schAn] *n.* Beitritt *m,* Zuwachs *m.* Besteigung *f* (throne).

Accessor'y [Ak-sse'ssA-ri] *a.* hinzugefügt ; beitragend ; Teilnehmer *m,* Anstifter *m,* Mittäter *m,* (law), -ies *n. pl.* Zusatz *m.*

Accident [æk'ssi-dAnt] *n.* Zufall *m,* Unglücksfall *m.*

Accidental [æk-ssi-den'tAl] *a.* zufällig ; -ly *ad.* zufälligerweise.

Acclaim [A-kleim'] *vt.* zujubeln.

Acclamation [æk-lA-meisch-An] *n.* lauter Beifall *m.*

Acclimatization [A-klai-mA-tai-sei'schAn] *n.* Akklimatisierung *f.*

Acclimatize [A-klai'mAtais] *vt. r.* (sich) akklimatisieren.

Accommodat'e [A-ko'mA-deit] *vt.* anpassen, versorgen,

unterbringen ; -ing *a.* gefällig, entgegenkommend.

Accommodation [A-ko-mA-deischAn] *n.* Anpassung *f.* Versorgung *n.* Wohnung *f.* Unterkunft *f* ; - ladder *n.* Fallreepstreppe *f* (nav.).

Accompan'iment [A-kAm'pA-ni-mAnt] *n.* Begleitung *f.* -ist *n.* Begleiter *m,* Klavierspieler *m* ; -y *vt.* begleiten.

Accomplice [A-kom'pliss] *n.* der, die Mitschuldige.

Accomplish [A-kom'plisch] *vt.* ausführen, erreichen ; -ed *a.* vollendet, durchgebildet ; -ment *n.* Ausführung *f.* Ausbildung *f* ; -ments *n.* feinere Bildung *f.* Fertigkeiten *f. pl.*

Accord [A-kOrd'] *n.* Übereinstimmung *f,* Einklang *m* ; *vt.* bewilligen; *i.* übereinstimmen ; -ance *n.* Übereinstimmung *f* ; in — with gemäss ; -ing *c.j.* je nach dem ; — to *pr.* nach, gemäss ; — to plan plangemäss ; -ingly *ad.* danach, also.

Accordion [A-kOr'di-An] *n.* Ziehharmonika *f* ; -pleated skirt gefälteter Rock.

Accost [A-kost'] *vt.* anreden.

Acount [A-kaunt'] *n.* Rechnung *f.* Bericht *m.* Bedeutung *f.* Grund *m.* on no — auf keinen Fall ; - for *vt.* Rechenschaft ablegen, erklären ; -able *a.* verantwortlich ; -ant *n.* Bücherrevisor *m,* Rechnungsführer *m.* (bank), Kassengehilfe *m* (mil.) ; -book *n.* Kontobuch *n.*

Accredit [A-kre'dit] *vt.* beglaubigen, trauen ; -ed *p.p.* beglaubigt. [Zuwachs *m.*

Accretion [A-krih'schAn] *n.*

Accrue [A-kruh'] *vi.* zuwachsen, erwachsen ; -d interest aufgelaufene Zinsen *m. pl.*

Accumulate [A-kjuh-mju-leit'] *vt.* anhäufen ; *i* sich anhäufen, anwachsen ; -tion *n.*

Anhäufung f; -tive a. anhäufend, anschwellend.

Accumulator [A-kjuh'mjuleiter] n. Anhäufer m, Batterie f (rad.), Sammler m, Akkumulator m (el.); Stromsammler m (el.); -battery n. Heizbatterie f (rad.); -drive n. Akkumulatorenantrieb m (el.); -driven car n. Sammler-, Akkumulatorenwagen m (el.); -lamp n. elektrische Grubenlampe (tec.).

Accura'cy [æ'kju-rA-ssi] n. Genauigkeit f, Richtigkeit f; -te a, -tely ad. genau, richtig.

Accursed [A-kAr'ssid] p.p., a. verflucht n. [Anklage f.

Accusation [æ-kju-sei'schAn] n. Anklage f.

Accuse [A-kjuhs'] vt. anklagen, beschuldigen; -d n. der, die Angeklagte; -r n. Ankläger m, Kläger m.

Accustom [A-kA'stAm] vt. gewöhnen; -ed a. gewöhnt.

Ace [eiss] n. As n, Kampfflieger m (av).

Acetate [æss'i-teit] n. essigsaures Salz; - of lead Bleizucker m.

Acetic [A-ssih'tik] a. essigsauer; -acid Essigsäure f.

Acetylene [A-sse'ti-lin] n. Azetylen n; -generator n. Azetylenentwickler m (tec.); -tube n. Gas-, Azetylenschlauch m. [schmerzen.

Ache [eik] n. Schmerz m; vi. Achieve [A-tschihw'] vt. ausführen, verrichten, erlangen; -ment n. Ausführung f, Tat f.

Achromatic [æ-kro-mæ'tik] a. achromatisch, farblos.

Acid [æ'ssid] a. sauer n. Säure f; -test Feuerprobe f.

Acidity [Assi'di-ti] n. Säure f.

Acid proof [æss'id pruhf'] a. säurebeständig; - apron Säureschurz m; - overall Säurekittel m.

Acknowledge [Ak-no'lidzh] vt. anerkennen, zugeben, anzeigen; -ment n. Anerken-

nung f, Empfangsbestätigung f (letter); -ments pl. Erkenntlichkeit f.

Acme [æc'mi] n. Gipfel m.

Aconite [æ'ko-nait] n. Sturmhut, m, Eisenhütchen n (plant), Akonit n (drug).

Acorn [ei'kOrn] n. Eichel f.

Acoustic [A-kuh'stik] a. akustisch; -funnel Schallbecher m (tec.); -s n. pl. Akustik f.

Acquaint [A-kueint'] vt. bekannt machen; -ance n. Bekanntschaft f, der, die Bekannte.

Acquiesce [æ-kui-ess'] vi. sich fügen, einwilligen; -nce n. Sichfügen n, Einwilligung f; -nt a. fügsam.

Acquire [A-ku-ai'er] vt. erwerben, erlernen.

Acquisition [æ-kui-si'schAn] n. Erwerbung f, Erwerb m.

Acquisitive [A-kui'si-tiv] a. erwerbsüchtig; -ness n. Aneignungslust f.

Acquit [A-kuit'] vt. freisprechen; -tal n. Freisprechung f.

Acre [ei'ker] n. Morgen m.

Acrid [æ'krid] a. Acrimonious; [æ-kri-mou'ni-Ass] a. -ly ad. beissend.

Acrobat [æ'kro-bæt] n. Akrobat m, Luftturner m.

Across [A-kross'] ad. kreuzweis; pr. (quer) durch; come - vt. beggegnen; - the road über die Strasse; - it darüber.

Act [ækt] n. Tat f, Gesetz n, Aufzug m (play); vt. eine Rolle spielen; i. wirken, sich betragen.

Acting [æk'ting] n. Schauspielkunst f; a. wirkend, diensttuend, stellvertretend; - petty officer Oberbootsmaat m; -minister geschäftsführender Minister.

Action [æk'schAn] n. Wirkung f, Handlung f, Prozess m (law); Kampfhandlung f, Treffen n.

(mil.), Anklage f (law); in - im Einsatz; naval - Seegefecht n; - stations pl. Gefechtsstation f; -able a. prozessfähig.

Active [æk'tiv] a. -ly ad. tätig, aktiv, behend; - debts n. pl. Aussenstände m. pl; - service n. Frontdienst m; a. Gefechts . . . ; - unit Ein-satzstaffel f.

Activity [Ak-ti'wi-ti] n. Tätig-keit f, Behendigkeit f.

Actor [æk'ter] n. Schauspieler m, Darsteller m.

Actress [æk'triss] n. Schau-spielerin f, Darstellerin f.

Actual [æk'tju-Al] a. -ly ad. wirklich; - stocks pl. Ist-bestand m; - strength Ist-stärke f. [Wirklichkeit f.]

Actuality [æk-tju-ä'li-ti] n.

Actuary [æk'tju-A-ri] n. Ver-sicherungs-Statistiker m.

Actuate [æk'tju-eit] vt. in Gang bringen, antreiben.

Acumen [æ-kju-men] n.Scharf-sinn m.

Acute [A-kjuht'] a. -ly ad. scharf, scharfsinnig, akut; - accent Akut m; - angle spitzer Winkel; -ness n. Schärfe f, Feinheit f, Scharfsinn m.

Adamant [æ'dA-mænt] a. un-nachgiebig. [bearbeiten.]

Adapt [A-dæpt'] vt. anpassen.

Adaptability [A-dæp't-A-bi'li-ti] n. Anwendbarkeit f, An-passungsfähigkeit f (persons).

Adaptible [A-dæp'tAbl] a. anwendbar.

Adaptation [æ-dAp-tei'schAn] n. Anwendung f, Bear-beitung f (novel, etc.).

Add [æd] vt. hinzufügen, bei-tragen, addieren.

Addendum [A-den'dAm] n. Nachtrag m.

Adder [æ'der] n. Natter f.

Addict [æ'dikt] n. Rauchgift-nehmer m (drugs). Trinker m (drink). [ergeben.]

Addict [A-dikt'] vr. sich

Adding machine [æd'ing mæ-schihn'] n. Addier-, Ad-ditions-maschine f.

Addition [A-di'schAn] n. Hinzufügen n, Anhang m, Ad-dition f, Zusammenzählen n; -al a. hinzugefügt, nachträg-lich; -ally ad. als Nachtrag f; - claim Nachforderung f; - expenses pl. Mehraufwand m; - payment Nachzahlung f; - taxation Mehrbesteuerung f.

Address [A-dress'] n. Anrede f, Adresse f, Anschrift f, Ge-wandtheit f; vt. anreden, adressieren; -ing machine Adressiermaschine f (com.).

Addressee [æd-ress-ih'] n. Empfänger m (com.). Adres-sat m (com.).

Addressograph [A-dress'o-grahf] n. Adressiermaschine f (com.). [führen.]

Adduce [A-djuhss'] vt. an-

Adept [A-dept'] a. erfahren, geschickt; n. der Eingeweihte.

Adequa'cy [æ'di-kuA-ssi] n. Hinlänglichkeit f; -te a. -tely ad. angemessen, hinreichend.

Adhere [Ad-hihr'] vi. ankle-ben, angehören; -nt n. An-hänger m.

Adhesion [Ad-hih'zhAn] n. Ankleben n, Beitritt m. Ad-häsion f Reibung f (tec.).

Adhesive [Ad-hih'siw] a. kle-brig, gummiert (stamps); - bomb n. Klettenbombe f; - mine Haftmine f; - tape n. Leukoplast m.

Adjacent [A-dzei'ssAnt] a. angrenzend; - angle Neben-winkel m.

Adjective [æd'zhik-tiv] n. Adjektiv n, Eigenschaftswort n.

Adjoin [A-dzheun'] vi. an-grenzen; -ing p.p., a. anstos-send, Neben . . .

Adjourn [A-dzhArn'] vt. ver-tagen; i. sich vertagen; -ment n. Vertagung f.

Adjudge [A-dẑhAdẑh'] *vt.* richten, zuerkennen.

Adjudicat'ion [A-dzuh-di-kei'schAn] *n.* Zuerkennung *f*, Urteil *m*; -or *n.* Schiedsrichter *m.* [digen, beschwören.

Adjure [A-dẑhuhr'] *vt.* vereidigen, beschwören.

Adjust [A-dẑhAst'] *vt.* zurecht machen, abmachen, einstellen (*focus*); -able *a.* verschiebbare, regulierbar; -back verstellbare Rückenlehne (*chair*); -spanner verstellbarer Schraubenschlüssel, Rollgabelschlüssel *m*; -ing *a.* einstellend; -handle Einstellkurbel *f* (*tec.*); -mechanism Stellvorrichtung *f* (*tec.*); -nut Stellmutter *f* (*tec.*); -screw Stellschraube *f* (*tec.*); -ment *n.* Zurechtmachung *f.* Schlichtung *f*, Ausgleichung *f.* Trieb *m* (*watch*); -echo Nachhallregelung *f* (*rad.*); -speed Geschwindigkeitseinstellung *f* (*camera*); with vertical – in der Höhe verstellbar (*tec.*); -lever Hebel für die Einstellung *m* (*tec.*); -plate Stelleisen *n* (*tec.*).

Adjutant [æ'dẑhu-tAnt] *n.* Adjutant *m.* assistant – Ordonnanzoffizier *m.*

Administer [Ad-mi'ni-ster] *vt.* verwalten, erteilen; -ration *n.* Verwaltung *f*, Amtsführung *f*; -of justice Rechtspflege *f*; -rative *a.* Verwaltungs . . .; Ministerial . . .; -rator *n.* Verwalter *m.*

Admirab'le [æd'mi-rAbl] *a.* -ly *ad.* bewundernswert, herrlich.

Admiral [æd'mi-rAl] *n.* Admiral *m*; -of the Fleet Grossadmiral *m*; -ty *n.* Marineleitung *f.*

Admiration [æd'mi-rei-schAn] *n.* Bewunderung *f.*

Admire [Ad-mai'er] *vt.* bewundern. [zulässig.

Admissible [Ad-mi'ssibl] *a.*

Admission [Ad-mi'schAn] *n.* Zulassung *f*, Einräumung *f*; ticket of – Einlasskarte *f.*

Admit [Ad-mit'] *vt.* einlassen, zugeben; – of *vt.* gestatten; -tance *n.* Eintritt *m.*

Admixture [Ad-mix'tjer] *n.* Beimischung *f.* [ermahnen.

Admonish [Ad-mo'nisch] *vt.*

Admonition [æd-mo-ni'schAn] *n.* Ermahnung *f.* [*m.*

Ado [A-duh'] *n.* Tun *n.* Lärm

Adolescen'ce [æ-do-le'ssAnss] *n.* Jünglingsalter *n*; -t *a.* heranwachsend; *n.* Jüngling *m.*

Adopt [A-dopt'] *vt.* adoptieren, annehmen; -ed daughter Adoptiertochter *f*; -ion *n.* Adoption *f*, Annahme *f.*

Adorable [A-dO'rAbl] *a.* anbetungswürdig.

Adoration [æ-do-rei'schAn] *n.* Anbetung *f.* [*n.* Anbeter *m.*

Adore [A-dO'] *vt.* anbeten; -r

Adorn [A-dOrn'] *vt.* schmücken; -ment *n.* Schmuck *m.*

Adrift [A-drift'] *a. ad.* umhertreibend.

Adroit [A-dreut'] *a.* -ly *ad.* gewandt; -ness *n.* Gewandtheit *f.* [*n.* Schmeichelei *f.*

Adulation [æ-dju-lei'schAn]

Adult [A-dAlt'] *a.* erwachsen; *n.* der, die Erwachsene.

Adulterate [A-dAl'tA-reit]; *vt.* verfälschen, mischen (*wine*) -ion *n.* Verfälschung *f.*

Adultery [A-dAl'tA-ri] *n.* Ehebruch *m.*

Advance [Ad-wahnss'] *vi.* vorrücken, steigen (*price*); *t.* vorrücken, vorschiessen, befördern; *n.* Vorrücken *n*, Beförderung *f*, Vorschuss *m* (*money*), Aufschlag *m* (*price*); in – im voraus; in – of vor, an der Vorderseite von; – on salary Gehaltsvorschuss *m*; -booking Vorverkauf *m*; -guard Vorhut *f*; -personnel Vorauspersonal *n.*

Advanced [Ad-wahnst'] fortgeschritten, vorgerückt; - aerodrome Feld-, Einsatz-flug platz m; - elements pl. Vo rausabteilung f; - ignition Vorzündung f (auf); - landing ground Gefechtslandeplatz m; - post Aussenposten m.

Advancement [Ad-wahnss mAnt] n. Beförderung f, Aufstieg m (social).

Advantage [Ad-wahn'tidzh] n. Vorteil m, Überlegenheit f.

Advantageous [æd-wAn-tei dzhAss] a. -ly ad. vorteilhaft.

Advent [æd'went] n. Advent m. Ankunft f.

Adventitious [æd-wen-ti'sch Ass] a. zufällige.

Adventur'e [Ad-wen'tscher] n. Abenteuer n; -er n. Aben teuerer m; -ous a. -ly ad. abenteuerlich, verwegen.

Adverb [æd'werb] n. Adverb n, Umstandswort n.

Adversary [æd'wer-ssA-ri] n. Gegner m.

Adverse [æd'werss] a. zu wider, ungünstig; - balance Unterbilanz f (com.).

Adversity [Ad-wAr'si-ti] n. Widerwärtigkeit f.

Advertis'e [æd'wer-tais] vt. anzeigen; -ing agency n. In seratenbüro n; - office Anzei geannahme f; - rates pl. Anzeigetarif m.

Advertisement [æd-wAr'tis mAnt] n. Anzeige f, Reklame f.

Advertiser [æd'wer-tai-ser] n. Anzeiger m, Anzeigeblatt n (paper).

Advice [Ad-waiss] n. Rat m, Bericht m, Avisbrief m (com.).

Advisab'le [Ad-wai'sAbl] a. ratsam; -ility -leness n. Rat samkeit f.

Advise [Ad-wais'] vt. raten, melden, avisieren, mitteilen (com.); -dly ad. mit Bedacht (com.); -r n. Ratgeber m, Berater m.

Advisory [Ad-wai'so-ri] be ratend, Beratungs . . . ;

board Beratungsstelle f; - commission beratender Aus schuss m; - council Beirat m.

Advocacy [æd'wo-kA-ssi] n. Befürwortung f, Verteidi gung f.

Advocate [æd'wo-keit] n. Ad vokat m; vt. verfechten, ein treten für.

Adze [æds] n. Dechse m, Breit beil n.

Aerated [ehr'ei-tid] a. kohlen sauer; - waters pl. Mineralwas ser n.

Aerial [ehr'iAl] a. luftig, Luft . . . ; n. Antenne f (rad.); - inductor Antennenkondensa tor m; - navigation Luft schifffahrt f, Flugwesen n; - railway Drahtseilbahn f; - survey Luftvermessung f; - suspension Antennenaufhän gung f.

Aerodrome [ehr'o-droum] n. Flughafen m -platz m; - light ing Befeuerung des Flug platzes f. [n. Flugmotor m.

Aero-engine [ehr'o-en zhAn]

Aerogram [ehr'o-græm] n. Funkspruch m.

Aeronautic'al [ehr-o-nO'ti kAl] a. fliegertechnisch; - map Fliegerkarte f; -s n. pl. Luftschiffwesen n Luftfahrt f, Flugtechnik f.

Aeroplane [ehr'o-plein] n. Flugzeug n; - engine Flug motor m; - photograph Flug zeugaufnahme f, Luftbild n.

Aero-technical [ehr-o-tek ni-kAl] a. fliegertechnisch.

Aero-towing [ehr'o-tou'ing] n. Schleppflug m (av.).

Aesthete [ihss'thiht] n. Ästhe tiker m.

Aesthetic [iss-the'tik] a. äs thetisch, geschmackvoll; -s n. pl. Ästhetik f.

Afar [A-fahr'] ad. von fern; - off in weiter Ferne.

Affability [æ-fA-bi'li-ti] n. Leutseligkeit f.

Affable [æ'fʌbl] a. ad. leutselig.   [heit f, Sache f.
Affair [A-fehr'] n. Angelegen-
Affect [A-fekt'] vt. wirken auf, affektieren beeinflussen, angreifen; -ation n. Affektiertheit f, Heuchelei f; -ed a. gerührt, geziert, angegriffen -ing a. rührend; -ion n. Zuneigung f, Affekt m; -ionate a. -ly ad. liebevoll.

Affidavit [æ-fi-dei'wit] n. schriftliche Eideserklärung.

Affiliate [A-fi'li-eit] vt. anschliessen, angliedern; -d societies pl. Zweigvereine m. pl.

Affiliation [A-fi-li-ei'schan] n. Angliederung f, Zuschreibung der Vaterschaft f (law).

Affinity [A-fi'ni-ti] n. Verwandtschaft f.

Affirm [A-farm'] vt. behaupten; -ation n. Behauptung f, -ative a. bejahend; answer in the — vt. zusagen, zustimmen.

Affix [A-fix'] vt. anschlagen, aufkleben.

Afflict [A-fikt'] vt. betrüben, quälen, heimsuchen; -ion n. Betrübnis f, Leiden n.

Affluen'ce [æ'flu-Anss] n. Reichtum m; -t a. reich.

Afford [A-fOrd'] vt. bieten, tragen, bestreiten.

Afforest [A-fo'rist] vt. aufforsten; -ation n. Aufforstung f.

Affray [A-frei'] n. Schlägerei f, Streit m.

Affront [A-frʌnt'] n. Beleidigung f; vt. beleidigen.

Afield [A-fihld'] ad. im Felde, in die Weite.   [umlaufend.
Afloat [A-flout'] ad. flott,
Afoot [A-fut'] ad. zu Fuss, im Gange.

Afore-mentioned [A-fOr' men'schAnd] p. p. a. vorhererwähnt, obig.

Aforesaid [A-fOr'ssed] a. vorgenannt.

Afraid [A-freid'] a. fürchtend, bange.

Afresh [A-fresch'] ad. von neuem.

Aft [æft] ad. hinten, nach achtern zu (nav.): -deck n. Achterdeck n.

After [ahf'ter] pr. nach: the day — to-morrow übermorgen; ad. nachher, cj. nachdem; -effects pl. Nachwirkung f, -math n. Nachernte f, Nachwirkung f; -noon n. Nachmittag m; -thought n. nachtraglicher Einfall m; -wards ad. nachher.

Again [A-gehn'] ad. wieder, nochmals, ferner; -st pr. gegen, wider.

Agate [æ'gAt] n. Achat m.

Age [eidzh] n. Alter n, Zeitalter n; to be of — mündig sein; — group Jahrgang m; -limit Altersgrenze f.

Aged [ei'dzh-id] a. alt.

Agency [ei'dzhAnssi] n. Wirkung f, Agentur f.

Agenda [A-dzhen'dA] n. die zu verhandelnden Gegenstände, Tagesordnung f.

Agent [ei'dzhAnt] n. wirkende Kraft f, Agent m, Vertreter m.

Agglomeration [A-glo-mA-rei'schAn] n. Zusammenballung f.

Aggrandize [æ'grAn-dais] vt. vergrössern; -ment n. Erhebung f, Erhöhung f.

Aggravate [æ'grA-weit] vt. erschweren, reizen; -ion n. Erschwerung f, Aufreizung f.

Aggregate [æ'gri-geit] n. Aggregat n, Summe f; in the — im ganzen.

Aggression [A-gre'schAn] n. Angriff m; -ive a. angreifend, streitlustig; -or n. Angreifer m.   [ken.

Aggrieve [A-grihw'] vt. kränken.

Aghast [A-gahst'] a. entsetzt.

Agile [æ'dzhail] a. flink.

Agility [A-dzhi'li-ti] n. Flinkheit f.

Agio [æ'dzhio] n. Agio n. Aufgeld n.

Agitate'e [æ'dzhi-teit] vt. bewegen, aufregen; -ion n. Bewegung f. Aufregung f. Aufruhr m; -or m. Aufwiegler m, Wühler m.

Ago [A'gou'] ad. vor; long – lange her; not long – vor kurzen.

Agony [æ'go-ni] n. heftiger Schmerz m. Seelenangest f.

Agrarian [A-greh'ri-An] a. agrarisch; n. Agrarier m, Landwirt m. Grundbesitzer m.

Agree [A-grih'] vi. übereinstimmen, sich bescheiden, einräumen, sich vertragen, beschliessen (decide), einwilligen (consent); -able a. -ably ad. gemäss, angenehm; -ment n. Übereinstimmung f, Vertrag m, Zustimmung f; naval – Flottenabkommen n. pl.

Agricultur'al [æg-ri-kAlt'schA-rAl] a. landwirtschaftlich; – labourer, Landarbeiter m; – products pl. Feldfrüchte f. pl; -ist n. Bauer m, Landwirt m.

Agriculture [æg'ri-kAltscher] n. Landwirtschaft f.

Aground [A-graund'] ad. gestrandet; run – vi. auflaufen, stranden.

Ague [ei'gju] n. Fieberfrost m.

Ahead [A-hed'] ad. vorwärts, voraus. [n. vt. helfen.

Aid [eid] n. Hilfe f, Hilfsmittel.

Aide-de-camp [eid-dA-kong'] n. Adjutant m.

Aileron [eil'A-ron] n. Querruder n. (av.).

Ailing [ei'ling] a. leidend.

Ailment [eil'ment] n. Leiden n.

Aim [eim] n. Ziel n. Absicht f; – at vi. zielen auf; a. richten; -ing mechanism Zieleinrichtung f; -less a. -lessly ad. zellos.

Air [ehr] n. Luft f. Melodie f, Aussehen n; vt. lüften, wär-

men; suppling from the – Nachschubabwurf m; – arm Fliegerstreitkräfte f. pl; – base Flug-, Luftstützpunkt m; – battle Luftkampf m.

Airborne [ehr'bOrn] a. im Flug; – regiment Sturmregiment n; – tropps Sturmlandtruppen f. pl.

Air camera [ehr'kæ'mA-rA] n. Luftbildgerät n. Fliegerkammer f.

Air-conditioning [ehr'kAndisch'A-ning] n. Luftkühlung f, -heizung f; – plant Klimaanlage f.

Air control [ehr'kon'troul] Luftaufsicht f. [luftgekühlt.

Air-cooled [ehr'kuhld] a.

Aircraft [ehr'krahft] n. Flugzeug n. – bomb Fliegerbombe f; -carrier Flugzeug-mutterschiff n. -träger m; – courier service Verbindungs-flugwesen n; – mine Luftmine f. – radio installation Bordfunkanlage f. – torpedo Lufttorpedo m.

Aircraftman [ehr'krahftmAn] Flieger m; first class – Gefreiter m.

Air-crew [ehr'kruh] n. Mannschaft f. Besatzung f.

Air defence [ehr'di-fenss'] n. Luftabwehr f, Fliegerabw., Flugabwehr f. [Luftsicherung f.

Air escort [ehr'ess-kort] n.

Airfield [ehr'fihld] n. Flughafen m, -platz m; – detachment Platzkommando n. (av.).

Airfoil [ehr'feul] n. Flügelprofil n.

Air force [ehr'fOrss] n. Luftstreitkräfte f. pl., Luftwaffe f; – blue Fliegerblau n; – infantry Luftwaffe zu Fuss f; – station Flierierhorst m; – troops pl. Fliebertruppe f.

Air-frame [ehr'freim] n. Zelle f. (av.).

Air gunner [ehr'gA'ner] n. Bordschütze m. [igkeit f.

Airiness [eh'ri-ness] n. Luft-

Air liner [ehr'lai-ner] *n.* Passagierflugzeug *n.* [Luft-post *f.*
Air mail [ehr'meil] *n.* Flug-,
Airman [ehr'mÅn] *n.* Flieger *m.*
Air map [ehr'mæp] *n.* Fliegerkarte *f.*
Air marshal [ehr'mahr'schÅl] *n.* Generalmajor der Flieger *m.*
Air mechanic [ehr'mi-kæ'nik] *n.* Bordmonteur *m.*
Air-minded [ehr'main'did] *a.* luftbegeistert, flugbegeistert.
Air-park [ehr' pahrk] *n.* Luft-Flug-park *m.*
Air passenger [ehr'pæss'ind-zher] *n.* Fluggast *m.*
Air penetration [ehr'pe-nitrei'schAn] *n.* Einflug *m* (*av.*).
Air photograph [ehr'fou'tograhf] *n.* Luftbild, Fliegeraufnahme *f.*
Air pilot [ehr'pai-lit] *n.* Flugzeugführer *m* (*av.*), Flugkapitän *m* (*civil*). [zeug *n.*
Airplane [ehr'plein] *n.* Flug-
Air pocket [ehr'po-kit] *n.* Luftloch *n.* Fallbö *f.*
Air pump [ehr'pAmp] *n.* Luftpumpe *f.*
Air raid [ehr'reid] *n.* Flieger-Luft-angriff *m*; – casualty Fliegerbeschädigter *m*; – damage Luftkriegsschäden *m, pl*; – precautions *n. pl.* Luftschutzdienst *m*; – shelter Luftschutzkeller *m*, -raum *m*; – warden Luft(schutz)wart *m*; – warning Fliegerwarnung *f.*
Air reconnaissance [ehr'ri-kon'iss-Anss] *n.* Luft-aufklärung *f*, -erkundung *f*; – photo Luftaufnahme *f.*
Air-screw [ehr'skruh] *n.* Luftschraube *f*, Propeller *m.*
Airship [ehr'schip] *n.* Luftschiff *n.*
Air-speed [ehr'spihd] *n.* Luftgeschwindigkeit *f*; – indicator Fahrtmesser *m.*
Air squadron [ehr'skuod-rAn] *n.* Luftstaffel *f.*

Air-tight [ehr'tait] *a.* luftdicht.
Air umbrella [ehr'Am-bre'lA] *n.* Fliegerschirm *m.*
Air vice-marshal [ehr'waiss mahr-schAl] *n.* Generalmajor der Flieger *m.*
Airway [ehr'wei] *n.* Luftverkehrslinie *f.* [lufttüchtig.
Air worthy [ehr'wer-dhi] *a.*
Airy [ehr'i] *a.* luftig.
Aisle [ail] *n.* Seitenschiff *n.*
Ajar [A-dzhahr'] *ad.* angelehnt.
Akin [A-kin'] *a.* verwandt.
Alacrity [A-læ'kri-ti] *n.* Bereitwilligkeit *f.*
Alarm [A-lahrm] *n.* Alarm *m,* Besorgnis *f*; *vt.* erschrecken; -clock Weckuhr *f* – signal Alarm-, Melde-zeichen *n*; -ist *n.* Bangemacher *m,* Miesmacher *m.*
Album [æl'bAm] *n.* Album *n,* Stammbuch *n.* photograph – Bilder-, Photo-mappe *f.*
Albumen [æl-bjuh'men] *n.* Eiweiss *n.*
Alcohol [æl'ko-hol] *n.* Alkohol *m* – Alkohol für Betriebszwecke; -ic *a.* alkoholisch, geistig.
Alder [Ol'der] *n.* Erle *f.*
Alderman [Ol'der-mAn] *n.* Stadtverordneter *m,* Ratsherr *m.* [Bierscheune *f.*
Ale [eil] *n.* Bier *n*; -house *n.*
Alert [A-lert'] *a.* wachsam; *n.* Fliegeralarm *m*; to be on the – auf der Hut sein, in Bereitschaft stehen (*mil.*); -ness *n.* Wachsamkeit *f.* [gebra *f.*
Algebra [æl'dzhib-rA] *n.* Algebra
Alias [ei'li-Ass] *ad.* sonst (genannt); *n.* angenommener Name.
Alibi [æl'i-bai] *n.* Alibi *n.*
Alien [ei'li-An] *a.* ausländisch, fremd; *n.* der, die Fremde.
Alienate [ei'li-An-eit] *vt.* entfremden; -ion *n.* Entfremdung *f,* Veräusserung *f* (*com.*).

Alight [A-lait'] a. brennend.

Alight [A-lait'] vi. absteigen. sich setzen, landen, wässern (seaplane).

Alignment [A-lain'ment] n. Ausrichtung f, Absteckung f.

Alike [A-laik'] a. gleich, ähnlich.

Alimony [æl'i-mA-ni] n. Verpflegungsgelder n. pl.

Alive [A-laiw'] a. lebend, lebhaft; – to bewusst, gewahr.

Alizarin [A-li'zA-rin] n. Krapprot n.

Alkali [æl'kA-lai] n. Laugensalz n, Alkali n; -ne a. laugensalzig, alkalisch.

All [Ol] a. pn. all; – the better um so besser; not at – keineswegs.

Allay [A-lai'] vt. lindern, beruhigen.

All-clear [Ol-klihr'] n. Entwarnung f.

Allied powers [æ'laid pau'ers] n. pl. Allies [æ'lais] pl. Alliierte m. pl.

Alligator [æ'li-gei-ter] n. Alligator m.

All-in [Ol-in'] a. Gesamt . . .; – insurance Gesamtversicherung f.

All-metal [Ol-metl'] a. Ganzmetall. . .

Allocate [æ'lo-keit] vt. zuverteilen, zuteilen (rations); -ion n. Verteilung f, Zuteilung f.

Allot [A-lot'] vt. zuteilen; -ment n. Verteilung f, Parzelle f (land), -garden Schrebergarten m, Kleingarten m; -holder Klein-, Schrebergärtner m.

Allow [A-lau'] vt. zugeben, erlauben; -able a. zulässig; -ance n. Erlaubnis f, bestimmter Teil, Taschengeld n, Nachsicht f, Abzug m (account), Zulage f (mil.).

Alloy [A-leu'] n. Legierung f.

All-round [Ol-raund'] a. vielseitig, allgemein; a. ringsum; – screen Vollgürtel m (nav.).

Allude [A-luhd'] vi. anspielen, hinweisen, andeuten.

Allure [A-luhr'] vt. anlocken; -ment n. Lockung f, Reiz m; -ing a. lockend.

Allusion [A-luh'zhAn] n. Anspielung f, Hinweis m, Andeutung f.

Alluvial [A-luh'wi-Al] a. angeschwemmt.

All-wave receiver [Ol-wäw'riss-ih'wer] n. Allwellenempfänger m.

All-wood [Ol-uud'] a. Ganzholz . . .; - construction Ganzholzbauweise f.

Ally [A-lai'] vt. (sich) verbinden; **Ally** [æ'lai] n. der Verbündete.

Almanac [Ol'mA-næk] n. Kalender m, Jahrweiser m.

Almighty [Ol'mai'ti] a. allmächtig; n. der Allmächtige, Herrgott m. [del f.

Almond [ah'mAnd] n. Mandel

Almost [Ol'moust] ad. fast, beinahe.

Alms [ahms] n. Almosen n; -house n. Armenhaus n.

Aloft [A-loft'] ad. oben, empor.

Alone [A-loun'] a. ad. allein; let – geschweige.

Along [A-long'] ad. längs; all – die ganze Zeit über; pr. entlang, -side n. nebenan, längseits (nav.).

Aloof [A-luhf'] ad. abseits; keep – sich fernhalten.

Aloud [A-laud'] ad. laut.

Alpaca [æl-pæ'kA] n. Alpakastoff m (land).

Alphabet [æl'fA-bet] n. Alphabet n; -ical a. alphabetisch, abcelich.

Alpine [æl'pain] a. alpinisch; -troops pl. Gebirgstruppen f. pl.

Alps [ælpss] n. pl. Alpen.

Already [Ol-re'di] ad. schon.

Also [Ol'ssou] ad. auch, ferner.

Altar [Ol'ter] n. Altar m.

Alter [Ol'ter] vt. ändern; t. sich ändern; -able a. veränderlich; -ation n. Änderung f.

Altercation (Ol'ter-kei'schAn] n. Wortwechsel m.

Alternat'e [Ol'ter-neit] vi. abwechseln; - **-ing** current n. Wechselstrom m (el.).

Alternat'e [Ol-ter'nit] a. abwechselnd; **-ely** ad. wechselweise.

Alternation [Ol-ter-nei'schAn] n. Abwechslung f.

Alternative [Ol-ter'ni-tiw] n. Alternative f, Wahl f; - **aero-drome** Ausweichhafen m; - **position** Wechselstellung f; - **target** Ausweichziel n; - **wave** Ausweichwelle f (rad.), [gleich.

Although [Ol-dhou'] cj. ob-

Altitude [Ol'ti-tjud] n. Höhe f.

Alto [ol'tou] n. Alt m.

Altogether [Ol-tu-ge'dher] ad. zusammen, gänzlich, völlig, durchaus.

Altruis'm [æl'tru-ism] n. Nächstenliebe f; **-tic** a. uneigennützig.

Alum [æl'Am] n. Alaun m (-) works n. pl. Alaunsiederei f.

Aluminium [æl-ju-min'i-Am] n. Aluminium n; - **oxide** Tonerde f, Aluminiumoxyd n.

Always [Ol'ueis] ad. immer, stets.

Amalgam [A-mæl'gAm] n. Quecksilberverbindung f, Amalgam n, Mischung f.

Amalgamate [A-mæl-gA-meit] vt. amalgamieren; i. sich vereinigen, fusionieren (com.).

Amalgamation [A-mæl-gA-mei'schAn] n. Amalgamieren n, Vereinigung f, Fusion f (com.), Zusammenschluss m (com.). [ansammeln.

Amass [Amæss'] vt. anhäufen,

Amateur [æm'A-ter] n. Liebhaber m, Bastler m (rad.), a. Liebhaber -, dilettantisch; - **photographer** Liebhaberphotograph m, **-ish** a. dilettantisch, oberflächlich, stümperhaft.

Amaz'e [A-meis'] vt. erstaunen, bestürzt machen; **-ed** p.p. erstaunt, verblüfft, bestürzt;

-ement n. höchstes Erstaunen; **-ing** a. höchst erstaunlich.

Ambassador [æm-bæss'A-der] n. Botschafter m, Gesandter m.

Amber [æm'ber] n. Bernstein m; - **beads** n. pl. Bernsteinperlen f. pl; - **mouthpiece** n. Bernsteinspitze f.

Ambiguity [æm-bi-gjuh'i-ti] n. Zweideutigkeit f, Doppelsinn m.

Ambiguous [æm-bi'gju-Ass] a. **-ly** ad. zweideutig, doppelsinnig.

Ambition [æm-bi'schAn] n. Ehrgeiz m, Ehrsucht f; **-us** a. ehrgeizig, hochstrebend.

Amble [æmbl] vi. den Pass gehen; n. Passgang m.

Ambulance [æm'bju-lAnss] n. Feldlazarett n; **motor -** - Kranken-auto n, **-wagen** m; - **air-craft** Sanitätsflugzeug n; - **column** Sanitätskolonne f; - **train** Lazarettzug m; - **unit** Sanitätsbereitschaft f.

Ambush [æm'busch] n. Hinterhalt m; vt. aus dem Hinterhalt überfallen.

Ameliorat'e [A-mih'li-A-reit] vt. verbessern; n. Verbesserung f.

Amenable [A-mih'nAbl] a. verantwortlich, zugänglich, leitsam, willfährig.

Amend [A-mend'] vt. verbessern, berichtigen; **-ment** n. Verbesserung f, Zusatz-, Verbesserungs-antrag m; **-s** n. pl. Vergütung f; make **-s** wiedergutmachen, ersetzen, entschädigen.

Amenity [A-mih'ni-ti] n. Annehmlichkeit f, Schönheit f.

Amiability [ei-mi-A-bi'li-ti] n. Liebenswürdigkeit f.

Amiable [ei'mi-Abl] a. liebenswürdig, freundlich.

Amicable [æ'mik-Abl] a. freundschaftlich; - **settlement** gütlicher Vergleich.

Amid, -st [A-mid'] *pr.* inmitten: **-ships** *ad.* mittschiffs (*nav.*).

Amiss [A-miss'] *a. ad.* verkehrt, unrecht; **take** = *vt.* übel nehmen. [schaft *f.*]

Amity [æ'mi-ti] *n.* Freundnehmen.

Ammeter [æ'mi-ter] *n.* Strommesser *m* (*el.*), Amperemeter *n* (*el.*).

Ammonia [A-mou'niA] *n.* Ammoniak *n*; liquid = Salmiakgeist *m*; **-um** *n.* Ammonium *n*; **- chloride** Salmiak *m*.

Ammunition [æm-ju-ni'schAn] *n.* Munition *f.*, Schiessbedarf *m*; **-dump** Munitionsstapelplatz *m*; **- motor cycle** Munitionskampfrad *n*.

Amnesty [æm'niss-ti] *n.* Amnestie *f*, Straferlass *m*.

Among, -st [A-mang'] *pr.* (mitten) unter. [liebt.]

Amorous [æ'mA-rAss] *a.* verliebt.

Amorphous [A-mOr'fAss] *a.* formlos, amorphisch.

Amortisation [A-mOr'ti-sei'schAn] *n.* Amortisation *f.*

Amount [A-maunt'] *n.* Betrag *m*; *vi.* betragen.

Ampere [æm'pihr] *n.* Ampere *f.* **-Amphibian** [æm-fi'bi-An] *n.* Lurch *m*, Wasser-land-flugzeug *n.* (*av.*); **-ous** *a.* amphibisch; **- aircraft** Wasserlandflugzeug *n*; **- flying boat** Wasserland-Kleinflugboot *n*; **- tank** Landwasserpanzer *m*.

Amphitheatre [æm'fi-thi-A-ter] *n.* Amphitheater *n*, zweiter Rang (*seat*).

Ample [æm'pli] *a. ad.* weit, weitläufig.

Amplification [æm-pli-fi-kei'schAn] *n.* Erweiterung *f*; **-ier** *n.* Verstärker *m* (*rad.*); **-ier valve** Verstärkerröhre *f* (*rad.*); **-y** *vt.* erweitern, verstärken (*rad.*).

Amplitude [æm'pli-tjuhd] *n.* Umfang *m*, Grösse *f*, Schwingungsweite *f* (*rad.*).

Amputate [æm'pju-teit] *vt.* amputieren, abschneiden; **-ion** *n.* Amputation *f.*

Amuck [A-mAk'] *ad.* amok; run – *vi.* amoklaufen, blindwütig morden.

Amuse [A-mjuhs'] *vt.* unterhalten, amüsieren, **-ement** *n.* Unterhaltung *f*, Zeitvertreib *m*; **-ing** *a.* amüsant.

Anaemia [A-nih'mi-A] *n.* Blutarmut *f*; **-ic** *a.* blutarm.

Anaesthesia [æn-iss-thih'sj-A] *n.* Betäubung *f*; **-tic** *n.* Betäubungsmittel *n*; **-tization** *n.* Betäubung *f*, Narkose *f.*

Analogous [A-næl'A-gAss] *a.* analog.

Analogy [A-næl'A-dzhi] *n.* Analogie *f*, Ähnlichkeit *f.*

Analyse [A-nA-lais] *vt.* analysieren, zergliedern, auswerten (*information*).

Analysis [An-æl'iss-iss] *n.* Analyse *f*, Auswertung *f.*

Analyst [æn'A-list] *n.* Analytiker *m*, Nahrungsmittelchemiker *m*.

Analytic [A-næl'A-gAss] *a.* analytisch.

Anarchical [A-nahr'ki-kAl] *a.* anarchisch; **-ist** *n.* Anarchist *m*; **-y** *n.* Anarchie *f.*

Anatomical [æn-A-to'mi-kAl] *a.* anatomisch; **-ist** *n.* Anatom *m*; **-y** *n.* Anatomie *f.*

Ancestor [æn'ssess-ter] *n.* Vorfahr *m*; **-ral** *a.* angestammt, altererbt; **-ry** Abstammung *f.*

Anchor [æng'ker] *n.* Anker *m*, *vi.* ankern; **-age** *n.* Ankergrund *m*, Ankergeld *n.*

Anchovy [æn'tscho-wi] *n.* Anchovis *f*, Sardelle *f.* [vormalig

Ancient [ein'schent] *a.* alt.

And [ænd] *cj.* und.

Anecdote [æn' ek-dout] *n.* Anekdote *f.*

Anemometer [æ-ni-mo'mi-ter] *n.* Windmesser *m.*

Anew [A-njuh'] *ad.* von neuem.

Angel [ein'dzhAl] *n.* Engel *m.* **-ic** *a.* engelgleich.

Anger [æng'ger] n. Zorn m; vt. erzürnen. [angeln.
Angle [æng'gl] n. Angel f; vi.
Angle [æng'gl] n. Winkel m; - of descent Einfallwinkel m (av.); - of elevation Schusswinkel m; - of impact Einschlagwinkel m; - of slope Steigungswinkel m.
Angler [æng'gler] n. Angler m.
Angrily [æng'gri-li] ad. Angry a. zornig, böse.
Anguish [æng'guisch] n. Angst f.
Angular [æng'gju-ler] a. winkelig; - deflection Ausschlagwinkel m. [farbstoffe pl
Aniline [æn'i-lihn] n. Anilin-
Animal [æn'i-mAl] n. Tier n; a. animalisch.
Animate [æn'i-meit] vt. beleben; -e [æn'i-mAt] a. lebendig; -ed lebhaft; -ion n. Lebhaftigkeit f. [Unwille m.
Animosity [æn-i-moss'i-ti] n. Anis-
Aniseed [æn'iss-ihd] n. Anis m.
Ankle [æng-kl] n. Fussknöchel m. [blinde f.
Anklet [æng'klit] n. Gelenk-
Annals [æn'Als] n. pl. Annalen pl, Jahrbücher n. pl.
Anneal [A-nihl'] vt. ausglühen, tempern, kühlen; -ing furnace Glühofen m; -ing oven Kühlofen m.
Annex [æn'ex] n. Anhang m, Anbau m, Nebengebäude n.
Annex [An-ex'] vt. anfügen, annektieren, angliedern; -ation n. Anfügung f, Annektierung f, Angliederung f.
Annihilate [A-nai'i-leit] vt. vernichten; -ion n. Vernichtung f.
Anniversary [æ-ni-wer'sA-ri] n. Jahrestag m, Jahrfest n.
Anode [æn'oud] n. Anode f (rad.); - battery Anodenbatterie f; - tension, - voltage Anodenspannung f.
Annotate [æn'o-teit] vt. mit Anmerkungen versehen; -ion n.

Kommentieren n, Anmerkung f.
Announce [A-nauns'] vt. ankündigen, bekanntmachen; -ment n. Ankündigung f, Bekanntmachung f, Ansage m (rad.), -r n. Ansager m (rad.).
Annoy [A-neu'] vt. plagen, ärgern; -ance n. Plage f, Ärger m.
Annual [æn'ju-Al] a. jährlich; n. die einjährige Pflanze; - return Jahresausweis m; - subscription Jahresabonnement n.
Annuitant [An-juh'i-tAnt] n. Rentner m, Rentnerin f.
Annuity [An-juh'i-ti] n. Jahresrente f.
Annul [A-nAl'] vt. ungültig machen; -ment n. Kraftloserklärung f.
Anodyne [æ'no-dain] n. schmerzstillendes Mittel n.
Anoint [A-neunt'] vt. salben.
Anomalous [A-nom'A-lAss] a. unregelmässig; -y n. Unregelmässigkeit f.
Anonymous [A-non'i-mAss] a. namenlos, ungenannt.
Another [A-nA'dher] a. pn. ein ander, noch einer; one - einander; - cup of tea noch eine Tasse Tee.
Answer [ahn'sser] n. Antwort f; vt: beantworten, entsprechen; i. antworten, gelingen; - for Rede stehen für, bürgen für; -ing wave Antwortwelle f (rad.); -able a. verantwortlich.
Ant [ænt] n. Ameise f.
Antagonism [æn-tæ'go-nism] n. Widerstreit m; -st n. Gegner m; -stic a. gegnerisch; -ze vt. zum Feinde machen.
Antarctic [æn-tar'ktik] a. antarktisch; - expedition Südpolarexpedition f.
Antecedent [æn-ti-ssih'dAnt] a. vorhergehend; n. das Vorhergehende. [rückdatieren.
Antedate [æn-ti-deit'] vt. zu-

Antelope [æn-ti-loup] n. Antilope f.

Antenna [æn-te'nA] n. Fühler m (insect), Antenne f (rad.).

Anterior [æn-tih'ri-er] a. vorhergehend.

Anteroom [æn-ti-ruhm] n. Vorzimmer n.

Anthem [æn'thim] n. Wechselgesang m, Hymne f.

Anthology [æn-tho'lo-dzhi] n. Anthologie f, Gedichtsammlung f.

Anthracite [æn'thrA-ssait] n. Antrazit m, Glanzkohle f.

Anthrax [æn'thræx] n. Milzbrand m.

Anthropolog'ist [æn-thropol'o-dzhist] n. Anthropolog m; **-y** n. Anthropologie f.

Anti-aircraft [æn-ti-ehr'krahft] a. Flieger-, Flug-abwehr; **-** Flak . . .; **-** defence Flugabwehr f; **-** defences pl. n. Flugabwehr f; **-** Flugabwehrgeschütz n, Flak f; **-** fire Fliegerbeschuss m, Flak f; **-** gun Flugabwehrgeschütz n, Flak f; **-** gunner Fliegerschütze m.

Antic [æn'tik] n. Posse f.

Anticipate [æn-ti'ssi-peit] vt. vorausgeniessen, zuvorkommen, ahnen; **-ion** f. Zuvorkommen n, Vorgefühl n.

Anti-clockwise [æn-ti-klok'uais] ad. entgegen der Uhr laufend, edul.

Anticyclone [æn-ti-ssai'kloun] n. Antizyklone f.

Antidote [æn'ti-dout] n. Gegenmittel n.

Anti-freezing [æn-ti-frih'sing] a. kalte-fest, -beständig.

Anti-friction [æn-ti-frik'schAn] (Mittel) gegen Reibung; **-** bearings n. pl. Wälzlager n; **-** metal Lagermetall n.

Anti-gas [æn-ti-gæss] a. Gas . . .; **-** defence Gasschutz m.

Anti-knock fuel [æn-ti-nok'fjuh-il] n. Antiklopfmittel n.

Antimony [æn'ti-mA-ni] n. Antimon n.

Antipathy [æn-ti'pA-thi] n. [Antipathie f.]

Anti-personnel mine [æn-ti-per-sou-nel'main] r. Spreng-, Schützenmine f.

Antiquarian [æn-ti-kuehr'iAn], Antiquary [æn-ti'kuA-ri] n. Altertumsforscher m, -kenner m; a. Altertums. . . .

Antiquated [æn-ti-kuei-tid] a. veraltet.

Antique [æn-tihk'] a. alt, antik; **-s** n. pl. alte Kunstgegenstände m. pl.

Antiquit'y [æn-ti'kui-ti] n. Altertum n, Alter n; **-ies** pl. Antiquitäten f. pl.

Anti-rust [æn-ti-rAst'] a. Rostschutz. . . .

Anti-semitic [æn-ti-si-mi'tik] a. antisemitisch.

Antiseptic [æn-ti-ssep'tik] a. antiseptisch, keimtötend.

Anti-submarine [æn-ti-ssAb-mA-rihn'] Unterseeboot . . .; **-** defence U-bootabwehr f; **-** screen U-bootsicherung f.

Anti-tank [æn-ti-tængk'] a. Panzer . . .; **-** defence Panzerabwehr f; **-** ditch Panzerabwehrgraben m; **-** gun Panzerabwehrgeschütz n, -jägerkanone f; **-** mine Tellermine f; **-** troops pl. Panzerjäger m. pl.; **-** rifle Panzerbüchse f.

Antithesis [æn-ti'thi-ssiss] n. Gegensatz m. [weih n.]

Antler [æn't'ler] n. Hirschgeweih n.

Anvil [æn'wil] n. Amboss m; **-** block Unteramboss m.

Anxiety [æng-sai'A-ti] n. Angst f, Besorgnis f.

Anxious [ængh'schAss] a. **-ly** ad. ängstlich.

Any [e'ni] pn. irgend ein, eine, (irgend) welche, jeder; ad. irgend; **-body** n. irgend jemand, jedermann; **-how** ad. irgendwie, jedenfalls; **-one** irgend jemand, jedermann; **-thing** n. irgend etwas; **-thing** but nichts

weniger als; -way *ad.* irgend wie, *cj.* jedenfalls; **-where** *ad.* irgendwo. [schnell.

Apace [A-peiss'] *ad.* zusehends,

Apart [A-part'] *ad.* beiseits, abseits; - **from** abgesehen von.

Apartment [A-part'mAnt] *n.* Zimmer *n,* Wohnung *f.*

Apath'etical [æ-pA-the'ti-kAl] *a.* unempfindlich; -**y** *n.* Unempfindlichkeit *f.* Gleichgültigkeit *f.* [äffen.

Ape [eip] *n.* Affe *m; vt.* nach-

Aperient [A-pih'ri-Ant] *a.* öffnend; *n.* Abführmittel *n.*

Aperture [æ'per'tjur] *n.* Öffnung *f,* Spalt *m.*

Apex [ei'pex] *n.* Spitze *f,* Gipfel-, Scheitel-punkt *m.*

Apiece [A-pihss'] *ad.* für jeden, für jedes Stück.

Apish [ei'pisch] *a.* äffisch.

Apolog'etic [A-po-lo-dzhe'tik] *a.* entschuldigend; -**ise** *vi.* sich entschuldigen, Abbitte tun; -**y** *n.* Entschuldigung *f,* Abbitte *f.* [Schlagfluss *m.*

Apoplexy [æ'po-plex-i] *n.*

Apost'le [A-posl'] *n.* Apostel *m;* -**olic** *a.* apostolisch.

Apostrophe [A-po'stro-fi] *n.* Auslassungszeichen *n.*

Apothecary [A-po'thi-kA-ri] *n.* Apotheker *m.*

Appal [A-pOl'] *vt.* erschrecken; -**ling** *a.* erschreckend.

Apparatus [æ-pA-rei'tAss] *n.* Apparat *m,* Gerät *n;* heating- - Heizungsanlage *f.*

Apparent [A-pæ'rAnt] *a.* -**ly** *ad.* scheinbar.

Apparition [æ-pA-ri'schAn] *n.* Gespenst *n,* Erscheinung *f.*

Appeal [A-pihl'] *vi.* flehen, anrufen, zusagen, appellieren (*law*); *n.* Anrufung *f,* Appellation *f,* Anziehungskraft *f* (*charm*).

Appear [A-pihr'] *vi.* erscheinen, scheinen; -**ance** *n.* Erscheinung *f* Schein *m,* Aussehen *n;* - **of legality** legaler Anstrich.

Appease [A-pihs'] *vt.* stillne; -**ment** *n.* Befriedung *f;* - **policy** Befriedungspolitik *f.*

Append [A-pend'] *vt.* anhängen; -**age** Anhang *m.*

Appendicitis [A-pen-di-ssai'tiss] *n.* Blinddarmentzündung *f.*

Appendix [A-pen'dix] *n.* Anlage *f,* Beilage *f,* Anhang *m,* Blinddarm *m* (*human*).

Appertain [æ-per-tein'] *vi.* zugehören.

Appetite [æ'pi-tait] *n.* Appetit *m;* -**zer** *n.* Vorspeise *f;* -**zing** *a.* appetitlich.

Applaud [A-plOd'] *vt.* preisen.

Applause [A-plOs'] *n.* Beifall *m,* Beifallklatschen *n.*

Apple [æpl] *n.* Apfel *m.*

Appliance [A-plai'Anss] *n.* Anwendung *f,* Mittel *n,* Gerät *n.*

Applica'ble [A-pli-kAbl] *a.* anwendbar; -**tion** *n.* Anwendung *f,* Fleiss *m.* Bewerbung *f.* Anmeldung *f* (*for post*).

Apply [A-plai'] *vi.* anwendbar sein; *t.* anwenden, anlegen; sich wenden, sich bewerben; - **oneself** to sich widmen; -**led** *a.* angewandt.

Appoint [A-peunt'] *vt.* festsetzen, ernennen; -**ment** *n.* Festsetzung *f,* Ernennung *f,* Amt *n,* Verabredung *f.* (*meeting*).

Apposite [æ'po-sit] *a.* treffend.

Appraise [A-preis'] *vt.* taxieren, abschätzen.

Apprecia'ble [A-prih'schi-Abl] *a.* merklich; -**te** *vt.* schätzen; *i.* steigen (*price*); -**tion** *n.* Schätzung *f,* Preissteigerung *f.* Wertzuwachs *m* (*value*).

Apprehen'd [æ-pri-hend'] *vt.* verhaften, begreifen, befürchten; -**sion** *n.* Fassungskraft *f.* Furcht *f,* Verhaftung *f* (*law*) -**sive** *a.* furchtsam.

Apprentice [A-pren'tiss] *n.* Lehrling *m,* Bergknappe *m* (*miner*); *vt.* in die Lehre tun; -**ship** *n.* Lehrjahre *vl.* serve one's – seine Lehrzeit durchmachen.

Approach [A-proutsch'] vt. nähern, anfliegen (av.); i. sich nähern; n. Annäherung f; Zugang m, Anflug m (av.); – flight Anflug m; – trench Lauf-, Verbindungs-graben m (mil.); –able a. zugänglich.

Approbation [æ'pro-bei-schAn] n. Billigung f.

Appropriat'e [A-prou'pri-eit] vt. sich aneignen, bestimmen; [A-prou'pri-At] a. zweckmässig; –eness n. Zweckmässigkeit f; –ion n. Aneignung f, Zuteilung f.

Approv'al [A-pru'wal] n. Billigung f, Genehmigung f; on – zur Ansicht; –e vt. i. billigen, genehmigen.

Approximat'e [A-prox'i-mit] a. annähernd; [A-prox'i-meit] vi. nahe kommen; –ion n. Annäherung f.

Appurtenance [A-pAr'ti-nAnss] n. Zubehör n. (kose f.

Apricot [ei'pri-kot] n. Aprikose f.

April [ei'pril] n. April m.

Apron [ei'prAn] n. Schürze f, Schutzleder n (cart, etc.).

Apropos [æ-pro-pou'] ad. gelegen; – of pr. in Bezug auf.

Apt [æpt] a. geneigt, geschickt; –ly ad. treffend; –itude, –ness n. Geneigtheit f, Begabung f, Eignung f (fitness); –itude, –test n. Eignungsprüfung f.

Aquarium [æk-ueh'ri-Am] n. Aquarium n, Glasbehälter m.

Aquatic [A-kuo'tik] a. im Wasser lebend; – plant Wasserpflanze f; – sports pl. Wassersport m.

Aquatint [æ'kuA-tint] n. Tuschmanier f; – engraving n, Aquatintdruck m.

Aqueduct [æk'ui-dAkt] n. Wasserleitung f.

Arable [æ'rAbl] a. pflugbar.

Arbiter [ahr'bi-ter] n. Schiedsrichter m.

Arbitrary [ahr'bi-trAri] a. willkürlich.

Arbitrat'e [ar'bit-reit] vi. Schiedsrichter sein, schlichten, entscheiden; –ion n. Schiedsspruch m, Entscheidung f; –ion award Friedensspruch m; – court Schiedsgerichtshof m; –or n. Schiedsrichter m, Schlichter m.

Arbor [ahr'ber] n. Spindel f (tec.), Schleifdorn n (tec.).

Arbour [ahr'ber] n. Laube f.

Arc [ahrk] n. Bogen m, Lichtbogen m (el.); – of fire Lichtungsstreifen m (mil.); – welding n. Lichtbogenschweissung f.

Arcade [ahrkeid'] n. Arkade f.

Arch [ahrtsch] n. Bogen m; vt. wölben.

Archaic [ahr-kei'ik] a. altertümlich; –ism n. Archaismus m.

Archbishop [ahrtsch'bi-schAp] n. Erzbischof m.

Archer [ahr'tscher] m. Bogenschütze m. [Urtypus m.

Archetype [ahr'ki-taip] n.

Architect [ahr'ki-tekt] n. Architekt m, Baumeister m, Bautechniker m; –'s plan n. Bauplan m; –ure n. Baukunst f.

Archives [ahr'kaiws] n. Archiv n, Urkundensammlung f.

Arc-lamp [ahrk'læmp] n. Bogenlampe f.

Arctic [ahrk'tik] a. arktisch.

Ardent [ahrd'Ant] a. brennend.

Ardour [ahrd-er] n. Eifer m.

Area [ehr'iA] n. Fläche f, Ausdehnung f, Gebiet n, Bereich m; – headquarters pl. Kommandatur f; – target Flächenziel n (av.). [Kampfbahn f.

Arena [A-rih'nA] n. Arena f.

Argue [ahr'giuh] vt. i. erörtern, deuten; vi. Gründe anführen.

Argument [ahr'giuh-ment] n. Beweisführung f, Wortstreit m, Hauptinhalt m (book); –ative a. streitsüchtig.

Arid [æ'rid] a. dürr. [richtig.

Aright [A-rait'] ad. recht,

Arise [A-rais'] vi. sich erheben, aufstehen, entstehen.
Aristocra'cy [æ-riss-tok'rAssi] n. Aristokratie f.; -t n. Aristokrat m; -tic a. aristokratisch, vornehm.
Arithmetic [A-rith'mi-tik] n. Arithmetik f, Rechenkunst f.
Arm [ahrm] n. Arm m; -stroke n. Seitenschwimmen n.
Arm [arm] n. Waffe f, Wappen n (coat of arms); vt. bewaffnen; i. sich waffnen; -ed forces pl. Wehrmacht f; -ed merchant cruiser Hilfskreuzer m; - of service Truppen-, Waffengattung f (mil., etc.).
Armament [ahr'mA-mAnt] n. Kriegsausrüstung f, Bewaffnung f, Bestückung f (nav.), Bordwaffen f. pl. (av.); -s control Rüstungskontrolle f; -s factory Rüstungsanlage f; -s industry Rüstungs-handel m, -wirtschaft f.
Armature [ahrm'A-tjur] n. Anker m (el.), Läufer m (el.).
Armband [ahrm'band] n. Armbinde f. [Lehnstuhl m.
Arm-chair [ahrm-tschehr'] n.
Armful [ahrm'ful] n. Armvoll m.
Armistice [ahr'miss-tiss] n. Waffenstillstand m. [binde f.
Armlet [ahrm'lit] n. Arm-
Armour [ahr'mer] n. Rüstung f, Panzer m, Panzerschutz m (mil.); - belt Gürtelpanzer m.
Armoured [ahr'merd] a. gepanzert; - car Panzer(kraft)wagen m; - concrete Eisenbeton; - cruiser Panzerkreuzer m; - division Panzerdivision f; - fighting vehicle Panzerfahrzeug n; - head (shell) Panzerkopf m; - plate Panzerschale f, Panzerung f; - shelter Panzerdeckung f; - train Panzerzug m; - transport lorry Mannschaftstransportwagen m; - troop carrier Panzertransportwagen m; - troops pl. Panzer-

truppen f. pl; - turret Panzerturm m; - unit Panzer-gruppe f, -truppe f; - vehicle Panzerwagen m; - vessel Panzerschiff n.
Armourer [ahr'mer-er] n. Waffenmeister m, Feuerwerker m; -s' workshop Waffenmeisterei f.
Armour-piercing [ahr'merpir'ssing] a. panzerbrechend; - ammunition Kern-, Panzermunition f; - bullet (Stahl-)-Kerngeschoss n; - incendiary n. Panzerbrandgranate f; - shell Panzer(spreng)granate f.
Armour-plate [ahr'merpleit'] n. Panzerplatte f.
Armour-plating [ahr'merplei'ting] n. Panzerung f, Panzer m.
Armoury [ahr'mA-ri] n. Rüstkammer f. [höhle f.
Armpit [ahrm'pit] n. Achsel-
Army [ahr'mi] n. Heer n, Armee f; - blanket Marschdecke f; - co-operation plane Aufklärungsflugzeug n; - corps n. Armeekorps n; - group headquarters pl. Gruppenkommando n; - headquarters pl. Generalkommando n; - high command Heeres-führung f -leitung f; - list n. Rangliste nf; - orders pl. Armeebefehl m; - post office Armeebriefstelle f (Heeres-)Feldpostamt n.
Aroma [A-rou'mA] n. Aroma n; -tic a. aromatisch.
Around [A-raund'] ad. rund herum; pr. um, herum.
Arouse [A-raus'] vt. aufwecken.
Arrange [A-reinzh'] vt. ordnen, festsetzen; -ment n. Anordnung f, Verabredung f.
Array [A-reï'] n. Reihe f, Aufstellung f, Schlachtordnung f; vt. aufstellen, ordnen, kleiden.
Arrears [æ-rirs'] n. pl. Rückstände pl; - of pay rückständiger Gehalt.
Arrest [A-rest'] n. Verhaftung

f, Beschlagnahme f (goods); vt. verhaften, aufhalten; -ed person Arrestant m.

Arrival [A-rai'wAl] n. Ankunft f.   [men, gelangen.

Arrive [A-raiw'] vi. ankommen; -te vt. sich annassen.

Arroga'nce [æ'ro-gAnss] n. Anmassung f; -nt a. anmassend; -te vt. sich annassen.

Arrow [æ'rou] n. Pfeil m; -head n. Pfeilspitze f, Keil m (mil.); -root n. Pfeilwurze. f, Pfeilwurzmehl n.

Arsenal [ahr'ssi-nAl] n. Zeughaus n.   [nik m.

Arsenic [ahr'ssi-nik] n. Arsenik n.

Arson [ahr'ssAn] n. Brandstiftung f.

Art [ahrt] n. Kunst f; work of - Kunstwerk n; – school Kunstschule f.

Arterial [ahr-tih'ri-Al] a. Arterien . . .; – road Ausfallstrasse f, Roll -, Autobahn f.

Artery [ahr'tA-ri] n. Arterie f, Pulsader f.   [artesisch.

Artesian [ahr'thsi-An] a.

Artful [ahrt'ful] a. listig.

Artichoke [ahr'ti-tschouk] n. Artischocke f.

Article [ahr'tikl] n. Artikel m, Ware f; vt. in die Lehre geben; – of equipment n, Ausstattungsstück n (mil.).

Articulate [ahr-ti'kjuh-leit] a. artikulieren, zusammenfügen (bones); -ely a. vernehmbar; -ion n. Artikulation f, deutliche Aussprache.

Artifice [ahr'ti-fiss] n. List f.

Artificer [ahr-ti'fi-sser] n. Handwerker m, Maschinist m (nav.), Feuerwerker m, Mechanikergefreiter m; – warrant officer Obermaschinist m.

Artificial [ahr'ti-fi'schAl] a. künstlich; – fertilizer - manure Kunstdünger m; – silk Kunstseide f.

Artillery [ahr-til'A-ri] n. Artillerie f; – spotting aircraft Artillerieflugzeug n.

Artisan [ahr-ti-san'] n. Handwerker m. [-ic a. künstlerisch.

Artist [ahr'tist] n. Künstler m;

Artless [ahrt'less] a. ungekünstelt, arglos.

As [æss] cj. ad. da, indem, so, als; – though als ob.

Asbestos [æs-bess'toss] n. Asbest m.

Ascend [Ass-end'] vi. aufsteigen; t. besteigen; -ant n. Steigen n, Überlegenheit f; -ency n. Einfluss m.

Ascension [Ass-en'schAn] n. Aufsteigen n; – Day Himmelfahrtstag m.

Ascent [Ass-ent'] n. Aufstieg m.

Ascertain [Ass-er-tein'] vt. ermitteln, sich erkundigen, feststellen.   [n. Asket m.

Ascetic [Ass-et'ik] a. asketisch;

Ascribe [Ask-raib'] vt. zuschreiben.   [tisch.

Aseptic [ei-sep'tik] a. asep-

Ash [æsch] n. Esche f (tree).

Ash [æsch] n. Ashes pl. Asche f; -tray Aschbecher m.

Ashamed [A-scheimd'] a. beschämt; to be – sich schämen.

Ashore [A-schohr'] ad. aus Land gestrandet.   [für sich.

Aside [Ass-aid'] ad. bei Seite,

Ask [ahsk] vi. fragen, fordern (price), bitten; to – a question eine Frage stellen.

Askance [Ass-kahnss'] ad. schief, von der Seite.

Asleep [Ass-lihp'] ad. schlafend; to be – schlafen; to fall – einschlafen.   [n. Spargel m.

Asparagus [Ass-pæ'rA-gAss]

Aspect [æss'pekt] n. Ansehen n, Lage f, Seite f.

Aspen [æss'pin] n. Espe f.

Asperity [Ass-pe'ri-ti] n. Rauheit f.

Asphalt [æss'fælt] n. Asphalt m; – road n. Asphaltstrasse f.

Aspirant [æss-pai'rAnt] m. Bewerber m; -s Nachwuchs m (mil.); – officer Oberfähndrich m.

Aspiration [æss-pi-ret'schan] *n.* Emporstreben *n.* [rin *n.*

Aspirin [æs'pi-rihn] *n.* Aspi-

Aspire [æss-pai'er] *vt.* emporstreben.

Ass [æss] *n.* Esel *m.*

Assail [Ass-eil'] *vt.* anfallen.

Assailant [Ass-eil'Ant] *An-* greifer *m.*

Assassin [Ass-æss'in] *n.* Meuchelmörder *m;* -**ate** *vt.* ermorden; -**ation** *n.* Meuchelmord *m.*

Assault [Ass-Olt'] *n.* angreifen; *n.* Angriff *m;* - **boat** Sturm-(lande)boot *n* (*mil.*); - **bridge** Schnellbrücke *f;* - **company** Sturmkompanie *f;* - **detachment** Sturmabteilung *f;* - **gun** Sturmgeschütz *n;* - **party** Sturmtrupp *m* (*mil.*); - **tank** Sturmpanzer *m* [probieren.

Assay [ass-ei'] *n.* Probe *f;* *vt.*

Assemblage [Ass-em'blidzh] Versammlung *f.*

Assemble [Ass-embl'] *vt.* versammeln, montieren (*tec.*); *i.* sich versammeln.

Assembly [Ass-em'bli] *n.* Versammlung *f,* Konferenz *f,* Gesellschaft *f,* Montage *f* (*tec.*); - **line** laufendes Band, Montagefliessband *n,* Serie *f;* - **point** Sammelplatz *m* (*mil.*); - **shop** Montagehalle *f.*

Assent [Ass-ent'] *n.* Zustimmung *f;* *vi.* zustimmen, billigen.

Assert [Ass-ert'] *vt.* behaupten; -**ion** *n.* Behauptung *f;* -**ive** *a.* anmassend.

Assess [Ass-ess'] *vt.* abschätzen, besteuern; -**able** *a.* steuerpflichtig; -**ment** *n.* Abschätzung *f,* Steuer *f;* -**or** *n.* Assessor *m,* Steuerrat *m.*

Assets [Ass'ets] *n. pl.* Aktiva *pl,* Masse *f,* Nachlass *m.*

Assiduity [æss-i-djuh'i-ti] *n.* Emsigkeit.

Assiduous [æss-i'dju-Ass] *a.* emsig, unablässig.

Assign [Ass-ain'] *n.* Rechtsnachfolger *m;* *vt.* anweisen, übertragen; -**ment** *n.* Anweisung *f,* Angabe *f,* Zession *f* Abtretung *f;* -**ment** form Anweiseschein *m.*

Assignation [æss-ig-ne:t' schAn] *n.* Anweisung *f,* Übertragung *f.*

Assignee [æss-i-nih'] *n.* Bevollmächtigter *m,* Konkursverwalter *m.*

Assimilat'e [Ass-i'mi-leit] *vt.* einverleiben; -**ion** *n.* Einverleibung *f.*

Assist [Ass-ist'] *vt.* beistehen, mitwirken; -**ance** *n.* Beistand *m;* -**ant** *n.* Gehilfe *m;* *a.* behilflich; - **secretary** Untersekretär *m.*

Associat'e [Ass-ou'schi-eit] *n.* Gesellschafter *m.* Teilhaber *m* (*com.*); *vt.* zugesellen; *i.* sich gesellen zu; -**ion** *n.* Verbindung *f,* Verband *m,* Verein *m;* - **football** *n.* Fussballspiel *n.*

Assort [Ass-Ort'] *vt.* sortieren; -**ment** *n.* Assortieren *n,* Auswahl *f.* [dern.

Assuage [Ass-neidzh'] *vt.* lin-

Assum'e [Ass-juhm'] *vt.* übernehmen, annehmen; -**ed name** Deckname *m;* -**ing** *a.* anmassend; *cj.* angenommen dass.

Assumption [Ass-ump'sch An] *n.* Voraussetzung *f,* Anmassung *f,* Mariä Himmelfahrt *f.*

Assurance [A-schur'Anss] *n.* Versicherung *f,* Zuversicht *f,* Dreistigkeit *f;* - **company** Versicherungsgesellschaft *f* (*com.*).

Assure [A-schur'] *vt.* versichern; -**d** *a.* gewiss; -**dly** *ad.* sicherlich. [chen *n.*

Asterisk [æss'te-risk] *n.* Stern-

Astern [A-stern'] *ad.* nach hinten, achtern.

Asthma [æss'mA] *n.* Asthma *n.*

Astonish [Ass-to'nisch] *vt.* in Erstaunen setzen; -**ing** *n.* erstaunlich; -**ment** *n.* Erstaunen *n.*

Astound [A-staund'] *vt.* erstaunen; **-ing** erstaunlich.

Astray [aystrei'] *ad.* irre; **to go** — verlorengehen.

Astride [A-straid'] *ad.* rittlings.

Astronom'er [A-stro'nA-mer] *n.* Astronom *m*; **-y** *n.* Astronomie *f*, Sternkunde *f*.

Astute [A-stjunt'] *a.* verschlagen, schlau; **-ness** *n.* Verschlagenheit *f*.

Asunder [Ass-An'der] *ad.* auseinander.

Asylum [Ass-ai'lAm] *n.* Asyl *n*, Irrenhaus *n*.

At [et] *pr.* an, in, zu, auf; **at** all überhaupt; **not at all** gar nicht; **at the baker's** beim Bäcker; **at first** zuerst; **at home** zu Hause; **at last** endlich, zuletzt; **at least** wenigstens; **at most** höchstens; **at ten o'clock** um zehn Uhr; **at a high price** um hohen Preis; **at sea** zur See.

Atheis'm [ei'thih-ism] *n.* Atheismus *m*; **-t** *n.* Gottesleugner *m.*

Athlet'e [æth'liht] *n.* Athlet *m*, Volksturner *m*; **-ic** *a.* athletisch; **-ics** *n. pl.* Leichtathletik *f.*

Athwart [Ath-uOrt'] *pr.* über dwars; *ad.* quer.

Atlas [æt'lAs] *n.* Atlas *m.*

Atmospher'e [æt'mo-sfihr] *n.* Atmosphäre *f*, Luft *f*; **-ic** *a.* atmosphärisch, Luft . . .; **-ics** *pl.* atmosphärische Störungen *f. pl* (rad.).

Atom [æ'tAm] *n.* Atom *n.*

Atomic [A-tom'ik] *a.* atomisch; **-bomb** Atombombe *f*; **- energy** Atom-energie.

Atomizer [æ'tA-mai-ser] *n.* Zerstäuber *m.*

Atone [A-toun] *vi.* büssen, wieder gutmachen; **-ment** *n.* Busse *f*, Sühne *f.*

Atrocious [A-trou'schAss] *a.* grässlich; **-ity** *n.* Grässlichkeit *f.* Greueltat *f.*

Attach [A-tætsch'] *vt.* anbinden, beifügen, fesseln; **to** — **importance to** Wert darauf legen; **-ed** zugeteilt (mil.);

-ment *n.* Fesselung *f*, Anhänglichkeit *f*, Ansatz *m*, Anhängsel *n.*

Attaché case [A-tæ'schi-keiss] Stadtköfferchen *f*, Necessairekoffer *m.* [*n.* Angriff *m.*]

Attack [A-tek'] *vt.* angreifen;

Attain [A-tein'] *vt.* erreichen, *i.* erreichbar; **-ment** Erreichung *f*, Fertigkeit *f.*

Attempt [A-temt'] *vt.* versuchen; *n.* Versuch *m.* ; **-ed bribery** Bestechungsversuch *m.*

Attend [A-tend'] *vt.* begleiten, bedienen, beiwohnen; *i.* achten, merken; **to** — **to** besorgen, nachsehen; **-ance** *n.* Bedienung *f*, Anwesenheit *f*; **-ant** *a.* begleitend; *n.* Aufwärter *m*, Wart *m*, Diener *m*, Wärter *m*, Pflegerin *f.*

Attention [A-ten'schAn] *n.* Aufmerksamkeit *f.* [merksam.]

Attentive [A-ten'tiw] *a.* auf-]

Attenuate [A-ten'juh-eit] *vt.* verdünnen, mildern.

Attest [A-test'] *vt.* bezeugen; **-ation** *n.* Bezeugung *f*, Eidesleistung *f* (mil.).

Attic [æ'tik] *n.* Dachstube *f.*

Attire [A-tai'er] *n.* Kleidung *f*; *vt.* kleiden. [tung *f.*]

Attitude [æ'ti-tjuhd] *n.* Haltung

Attorney [A-ter'ni] *n.* Anwalt *m.*

Attract [A-trækt'] *vt.* anziehen; **-ion** *n.* Anziehung *f*; **-ive** *a.* anziehend; **-iveness** *n.* Reiz *m.*

Attribute [A'tri-bjuht] *n.* Eigenschaft *f*; [A-tri'bjuht] *vt.* beilegen.

Attrition [A-tri'schAn] *n.* Abreiben *n*, Ausblutung *f*; **battle of** — Ausblutungsschlacht *f*; **war of** — Zermürbungskrieg *m.*

Attune [A-tjuhn'] *vt.* (ab-)stimmen.

Auburn [O'bern] *a.* nussbraun.

Auction [Ok'schAn] *n.* Auktion *f*; *vt.* öffentlich versteigern; **-eer** *n.* Versteigerer *m*, Auktionator *m.*

Audacious [O-dei'schAss] *a.*
-ly *ad.* verwegen, frech.

Audacity [O-dæ'ssi-ti] *n.* Verwegenheit *f*, Frechheit *f*.

Audib'ility [O-di-bi'li-ti] *n.*
Hörbarkeit *f*; -le *a.* hörbar.

Audience [O'di-Anss] *n.* Zuhörerschaft *f*, Audienz *f*.

Audio-frequency [O'dio-frih'kuen'ssi] *n.* Nieder-, Ton-frequenz *f* (*rad.*).

Audit [O'dit] *n.* Rechnungsprüfung *f*, Kassenprüfung *f*, Bücherrevision *f*; *vt.* (Rechnungen) prüfen; -**or** *n.* Rechnungs-Revisor *m*, Finanzprüfer *m*, Rendant *m*. [Bohrer.

Auger [O'ger] *n.* grosser

Aught [Ot] *pn.* etwas.

Augment [Og-ment'] *vt.* vermehren, steigern, erhöhen; -**ation** *n.* Vermehrung *f*, Zunahme *f*, Erhöhung *f*, Steigerung *f*. [deutung *f*.

Augury [O'gju-ri] *n.* Vorbe-

August [O'gAst] *n.* August *m*.

August [O-gAst'] *a.* erhaben.

Aunt [ahnt] *n.* Tante *f*.

Aural [O'rAl] *a.* Hör . . . ; -frequency Höraufnahme *f* (*rad.*).

Auspices [O'spi-ssis] *n. pl.* Anzeichen *n*, Vorbedeutung *f*, Leitung *f*, Schutz *m*.

Auspicious [O-spisch'Ass] *a.* günstig, glückverheissend.

Austere [O-stihr'] *a.* streng.

Austerity [O-ste'ri-ti] *n.* Strenge *f*, strenger, herber Lebensstil.

Authentic [O-then'tik] *a.* authentisch, glaubwürdig, echt, verbürgt; -ate *vt.* beglaubigen; -ation *f*. Beglaubigung *f*; -ity *n.* Glaubwürdigkeit *f*, Echtheit *f*.

Author [O'ther] *n.* Stifter *m*, Verfasser *m* (*book*), Schriftsteller *m*; -itative *a.* bevollmächtigt, gebieterisch, massgebend; -ity *n.* Autorität *f*, Einfluss *m*, Gewährsmann *m*, Dienststelle

f (*mil.*); -ities *n. pl.* Behörde *f*; -ization *n.* Bevollmächtigung *f*. Berechtigung *f*; -ize *vt.* bevollmächtigen, genehmigen; -ship *n.* Autorschaft *f*.

Autobiograph'ical [O-toh-bai-o-graef'i-kAl] *a.* autobiographisch; -y *n.* Autobiographie *f*. [wagen *m*.

Autocar [O'toh-kar] *n.* Kraft-

Autocracy [O-tok'rA-ssi] *n.* Selbstherrschaft *f*.

Autocrat [O'tok-ræt] *n.* Selbstherrscher *m*.

Auto-cycle [O'to-ssaikl] *n.* Kleinkraftrad *n*, Motorfahr-rad *n*.

Autogenous smelting [O. to'dzhA-nass ssmel'ting] *n.* Autogenschweissung *f*; -- apparatus *n.* Autogenapparat *m*.

Auto-giro [O'to-dzhai'rou] *n.* Schrauben-, Windmühlen-flug-zeug *n*.

Autograph [O'toh-grahf] *n.* Unterschrift *f*, Namenszug *m*; *a.* eigenhändig geschrieben.

Automatic [O-tom'æ'tik] *a.* automatisch, selbsttätig; -- cannon Maschinenkanone *f*; -- connection Selbstanschluss *m*; -- machine Automat *m*; -- navi-gator Kurskoppler *m* (*av.*); -- pilot Kurssteuerung *f* (*av.*); -- pistol Maschinenpistole *f*; -- telephone Fernsprecher mit Selbstanschluss *m*; -- telephone system Selbstanschluss-, Wahl-betrieb *m*; -- weapon Selbst-lader *m*; -- weighing machine Wiegeautomat *m*.

Automaton [O-tom'mA-tAn] *n.* Automat *m*. [Auto *n*.

Automobile [O-tom-Ou'bil]

Autonom'ous [O-to'no-mAss] *a.* autonom; -ous administra-tion Selbstbewirtschaftung *f*; -y *n.* Selbstregierung *f*.

Autopsy [O'top-si] *n.* Sektion *f*.

Autovac [O'to-wak] *n.* Unter-druckförderer *m* (*aut.*).

Autumn [O'tAm] n. Herbst m; -al a. herbstlich.

Auxiliary [Og-si'll-A-ri] a. helfend, Behilfs.... Hilfs...; n. Verbündeter m, Hilfstruppe f, Hilfszeitwort n; – cruiser Hilfskreuzer m; – engine Hilfsmaschine f (naut.), Hilfsmotor m (tec.); – hospital Hilfskrankenhaus n; – verb Hilfszeitwort n; – vessel Hilfsschiff n.

Avail [A-weil'] vt. nützen; – oneself of benützen; i. von Nutzen sein; -ability n. Gültigkeit f; -able a. verfügbar, gültig.   [Schneesturz m.

Avalanche [æ'vA-lahnsch] n.

Avarice [æ'vA-riss] n. Habsucht f; -ious a. habsüchtig, geizig.

Avenge [A-wenzh'] vt. rächen.

Avenue [æ'wenn-juh] n. Allee f, Zugang n; explore all -s nichts unversucht lassen.

Aver [A-wer'] vt. behaupten.

Average [æ'wer-ridzh] n. Durchschnitt m, Havarie f (com.); a. durchschnittlich; vt. den Durchschnitt nehmen; – crop Mittelernte f; – value Mittelwert m.

Averse [A-werss'] a. abgeneigt; -ion n. Abneigung f.

Avert [A-wert'] vt. abwenden.

Aviation [ei'vi-ei'schAn] n. Flugwesen n, Flugsport m. Fliegerei f.

Aviator [ei'vi-ei-ter] n. Flieger m.

Avid [æ'wid] a. gierig, -ity n. Gier f.

Avoid [A-weud'] vt. meiden; -ing (action) Ausweichsmanöver n (av.); -able a. vermeidlich.

Avow [A-wau'] vt. offen bekennen; -al n. Bekenntnis n.

Await [A-ueit'] vt. erwarten.

Awake [A-neik'] vt. erwecken; i. erwachen; -ning n. Erwachen n, Erweckung f; rude -ning Ernüchterung f.

Award [A-uOrd'] vt. zuerkennen; n. Urteil n, Preis m.

Aware [A-ehr'] a. unterrichtet; to be – of wissen, gewahr werden; -ness n. Gewahrsein n, Bewusstsein n.

Away [A-uei'] ad. weg, abwesend; right – sofort; – from home von Hause; give – vt. verraten, bloss-stellen; go – vi. verreisen (for a time), abfort-reisen (for good); make – with vernichten, abschaffen; run – vi. weglaufen.

Awe [O] n. Ehrfurcht f; vt. Ehrfurcht einflössen.

Aweful [O'full] a. furchtbar, schrecklich.   [Weile.

Awhile [A-huail'] ad. eine

Awkward [Ok'uerd] a. -ly ad. ungeschickt, ungelegen; -ness n. Ungeschicklichkeit f, das Unpassende.   [Nagelort n.

Awl [Ol] n. Ahle f, Pfriem m.

Awning [O'ning] n. Sonnenzelt n, Schutzdach n, Markise f.

Awry [A-rai'] ad. schief; go – vi. schiefgehen.

Axe [æx] n. Axt f, Beil n.

Axiom [æx'i-Am] n. Axiom n, -atic a. einleuchtend, allgemein erkannt.

Axis [æx'iss] n. Achse f.

Axle [æxl] n. Achse f; – -tree Achse f, Welle f.

Azure [æ'zher] a. himmelblau.

B

Babble [bæbl] n. Geschwätz n; vi. schwätzen.   [m.

Baboon [bA-buhn'] n. Pavian

Baby [bei'bi] n. Säugling m, Kindchen n; – grand piano n. Stutzflügel m; – linen n. Kinderzeug n, Windeln f. pl.

Babyhood [bei'bi-hud] n. Kindheit f.

Bachelor [bætsch'i-ler] n. Junggeselle m, Bakkalaureus m (B.A.).

Back [bæk] n. Rücken m, Rückseite f. Seitenspieler m (football); vi. rückwarts gehen; vt. unterstützen, fördern; a. hinter; - **wheel** Hinterrad n; - **wheel drive** Hinterradantrieb m; ad. zurück, wieder.

Backbiting [bæk-bai'ting] n. Verleumden f; a. verleumderisch. [tertür f.]

Backdoor [bæk-dOr'] n. Hinter-

Back-entry [bæk-en'tri] n. (com.) Rückbuchung f.

Backer [bæk'er] n. Helfer, Unterstützer m.

Back-fire [bæk'fair'] vt. (tec.) rückzünden.

Background [bæk'graund] n. Hintergrund m; - **of noise** (rad.) Störgeräusch m.

Backing [bæ'king] n. Unterstützung f, Rückbewegung f.

Backslider [bæk'slai-der] n. Abtrünniger m.

Backsliding [bæk'slai-ding] n. Abtrünnigkeit f, Abfall m.

Backward [bæk'uerd] a. spät, zurückgeblieben, rückständig; -**ness** m. Rückständigkeit f, Trägheit f; -**s** ad. rückwärts.

Backwater [bæk'uO-ter] n. Seitenwasser n, Stockung f.

Backwoods [bæk'uuds] n. pl. Hinter-, Ur-wälder m. pl.

Bacon [bei'kAn] n. Speck m; - **fat** Schweinefett n.

Bacteria [bæk-tih'ri-A] n. Bakterien f, Bazillen m. pl.

Bad [bæd] -**ly** ad. schlecht, böse, stark, schädlich; - **debts** pl. uneintreibbare Schulden f. pl.; - **harvest** Missernte f.

Badge [bædʒ] n. Abzeichen n; - **of rank** Rangabzeichen n.

Badger [bædʒ'er] n. Dachs m; vt. plagen.

Badness [bæd'ness] n. Schlechtigkeit f, Bosheit f. [eiteln.]

Baffle [bæfl] vt. verwirren, ver-

Baffle [bæfl] n (tec.), Dämpfungsplatte f, Schallwand f (rad.); - **board** Schallwand f

(rad.); - **paint** Schutzanstrich m.

Bag [Bæg] n. Beutel m, Tasche f; vt. einstecken; i. bauschen; -**ful** n. Sackvoll m.

Baggage [bæg'idʒ] n. Gepäck n; - **transport** (mil.) Gepäcktross m.

Baggy [bæg'i] a. bauschig; - **breeches** m. pl. Pluderhose f.

Bagpipe(s) [bæg'paip] n. Dudelsack m, Sackpfeife f.

Bail [beil] vt. ausschöpfen; - **out** abspringen (av.).

Bail [beil] n. Bürgschaft f; vt. auf Bürgschaft entlassen; **go** - Bürgschaft leisten.

Bailiff [bei'lif] n. Amtmann m, Gerichtsdiener m. [ködern.]

Bait [beit] n. Köder m; vt.

Baize [beis] n. Boi m.

Bak'e [beik] vt. backen, brennen (bricks, etc.); i. backen; -**ehouse** n. Backstube f, Backhaus n; -**er** n. Bäcker m; -**ery** n. Bäckerei f; -**ing powder** m. Backpulver n. [elit m.]

Bakelite [beik'A-lait] n. Bak-

Balaclava helmet [bæ-lA-klah'vA hel'mit] n. Kopfschützer m.

Balance [bæl'Anss] n. Waage f, Gleichgewicht n, Bilanz f (com.); vt. wägen, aufwiegen, saldieren; **amount of** - Saldobetrag m; **to strike a** - die Bilanz ziehen; - **sheet** m. Bilanz f; - **of power** Gleichgewicht der Kräfte n; - **of trade** Handelsbilanz f.

Balcony [bæl'ko-ni] n. Balkon m, Galerie f.

Bald [bOld] a. ad. kahl; -**headed** kahlköpfig; -**ness** n. Kahlheit f.

Bale [beil] n. Ballen m; vt. emballieren; - **out** vi. abspringen (av.).

Balk [bOk] n. Balken m; vt. hemmen, vereiteln.

Ball [bOl] n. Ball m, Kugel f; - **and socket joint** Kugelgelenk

n (tec.); - cartridge n. scharfe Patrone.

Ballad [bæl'Ad] n. Ballade f.

Ballast [bæl'Ast] n. Ballast m, Steinschotter m; vt. ballasten.

Ball-bearings [bOl-behr'ings] n. Kugellager n (tec.).

Ballet [bæl'i] n. Ballett n.

Balloon [bæl-uhn'] n. Ballon m; - operator n. Ballonwart m; - tyre n. Ballonreifen m.

Ballot [bæl'At] n. geheime Abstimmung f, Losen n; vi. abstimmen; - box Wahlurne f; - paper Wahlzettel m.

Ball-room [bOl'ruhm] n. Tanzzimmer n, Tanzlokal n.

Balm, Balsam [bahm, bOl'sAm] n. Balsam m.

Balmy [bah'mi] a. balsamisch, duftig.

Baluster [bæl'Ass-ter] n. Säulchen n, Baluster f.

Balustrade [bæl-Ass-treid'] n. Brüstlehne f.

Bamboo [bæm-buh'] n. Bambus m; - cane n. Bambusstock m; - chair n. Rohrstuhl m.

Ban [bæn] n. Bann m, amtliches Verbot; vt. verbieten.

Banana [bæn-ah'nA] n. Banane f; -plug n. Bananenstecker m (rad.).

Band [bænd] n. Band n, Bande f, (Musik) Kapelle f; Bandweite f, Streifen m (rad.); vt. festbinden; -pass filter Bandfilter m (rad.).

Bandage [bæn'didzh] n. Verband m; vt. verbinden.

Band-box [bænd'box] n. Hutschachtel f.

Band-conveyer [bænd'kAnwei'er] n. laufendes Band (aut.). [Bandelier f.

Bandsman [bænds'mæn] n. Musiker m.

Bandolier [bæn-do-lih'er] n.

Bandmaster [bænd'mah-ster] n. Musikmeister m.

Bandy-(legged) [bæn'di-legd] a. krummbeinig.

Bane [bein] n. Verderben n; -ful a. verderblich.

Bang [bæng] n. Hieb m, Knall m; vt. schlagen; i. knallen.

Bangle [bæng'gl] n. Armring m, Armreif m.

Banish [bæn'isch] vt. verbannen; -ment n. Verbannung f.

Banister(s) [bæn'iss-ter] n. Geländer n.

Banjo [bæn'dzhoh] n. Negergitarre f, Banjo n.

Bank [bængk] n. Ufer n (river, etc.), Bank f (com.); vi. in die Kurve gehen (av.); vt. aufdämmen, bei einer Bank niederlegen; branch - n. Bankfiliale f; - account n. Bankkonto n; - holiday n. Bankfeiertag m, allgemeiner Feiertag; - of issue n. Notenbank f; - manager n. Bankdirektor m; -note n. Banknote f; - rate n. Bankdiskonto n; - statement n. Bankausweis m.

Banker [bæng'ker] n. Bankier m, Bankbeamter m.

Banking [bæng'king] n. Bankgeschäft n, Bankwesen n; - house Bankgeschäft n.

Bankrupt [bænk'rApt] n. der Zahlungsunfähige; a. bankrott; to become - Bankrott machen; -cy n. Bankrott m.

Banner [bæn'er] n. Banner n, Fahne f.

Banns [bæns] n. Aufgebote pl.

Banquet [bæng'kuit] n. Gastmahl n, Festessen n.

Bantam [bæn'tAm] n. Zwerghuhn n. [f; vt. necken.

Banter [bæn'ter] n. Neckerei

Baptism [bæp'tism] n. Taufe f; - of fire Feuertaufe f.

Baptize [bæp-tais'] vt. taufen.

Bar [bahr] n. Stange f, Riegel m, Taktstrich m (music), Sandbank f (harbour), Gericht n (law), Schenktisch m (inn, etc.); vt. sperren, riegeln; pr. ausser; -red gate Gittertor n; -red window Gitterfenster n.

Barb [bahrb] n. Widerhaken m; vt. mit Widerhaken versehen: -ed wire n. Stacheldraht m; -ed wire entanglement n. Stacheldrahthindernis n; -ed wire fence Stacheldrahtzaun m.

Barbar'ian [bah-bei'ri-An] n. Barbar m; a. barbarisch; -ity n. Grausamkeit f; -ous a. grausam.

Barber [bah'ber] n. Barbier m, Haarschneider m; -'s chair n. Rasierstuhl m.

Bare [behr] a. nackt, bar, vt. entblössen; -faced a. unverschämt, frech; -footed a. barfuss; -ly ad. kaum, knapp; -ness n. Nacktheit f, Dürftigkeit f.

Bargain [bahr'gin] n. Kaufvertrag m, vorteilhafter Kauf m, das billig Gekaufte; vi. verhandeln, feilschen, handeln; into the - obendrein; - sale n. Ausverkauf m.

Barge [bahrdzh] n. Lastkahn m, Schute f, Prahm m; -e n. Bootsknecht m. [[erde f.

Barites [bA-rai'tis] n. Schwer- [abrinden.

Barium [beh'ri-Am] n. Barium n.

Bark [bahrk] n. Rinde f.

Bark [tahrk] n. Dreimaster m, Bark f.

Barley [bahr'li] n. Gerste f, French - n. Graupen f. pl, - water n. Gerstenschleim m.

Barmaid [bahr'meid] n. Kellnerin f.

Barman [bahr'mAn] n. Kellner m, Bier-ausgeber m, zapfer m.

Barn [bahrn] n. Scheune f; -door n. Schneunentor n.

Baro'graph [bæ-ro-grahf] n. Höhenschreiber m, Luftdruckmesser m; -meter n. Barometer n, Wetterglas n; -metric a. Barometer...; -metric pressure Luftdruck m. [Freiherr m.

Baron [Bæ'rAn] n. Baron m.

Baroness [bæ'ro-ness] n. Baronin f, Freiherrin f.

Barrack(s) [bæ'rAx] Kaserne f; - accommodation Revier n.

Barrage [bæ'rahzh] n. Sperre f, Talsperre f, (water), Feuersperre f, Walze f (mil.), Unterwasservorhau m (nav.); - balloon Sperrballon m; - breaker Sperrbrecher m; - fire Feuersperre f, Planfeuer n (mil.); - kite Sperrdrache m; - vessel Sperrboot n.

Barrel [bæ'ril] n. Fass n, Lauf m (gun); - casing Laufwandung f; - organ Drehorgel f.

Barren [bæ'ren] a. unfruchtbar; -ness n. Unfruchtbarkeit f.

Barricade [bæ-ri-keid'] n. Weg-, Balken-sperre f; vt. verrammeln, absperren.

Barrier [bæ-ri-er] n. Schranke f, Hindernis n, [nommen.

Barring [bah'ring] pr. ausgenommen.

Barrister [bæ'riss-ter] n. Rechtsanwalt m. [karren m.

Barrow [bæ'rou] n. Schiebkarren m.

Barter [bah'ter] n. Tausch m; vt. vertauschen.

Bascule-bridge [bæ'skjuhl-bridzh] n. Zugbrücke f.

Base [beiss] a. -ly a. unecht, gemein; - metal n. falsches Metall.

Base [beiss] n. Grundlage f, Basis f, (mil.) Stützpunkt m, Bettung f; - aerodrome n. Aufmarschflugplatz m; - hospital n. Kriegslazarett m; -less a. grundlos; -line n. Seitenlinie f (tennis); -ment n. Erdgeschoss n; -ness n. Gemeinheit f, Niedrigkeit f.

Bashful [bæsch'ful] a. -ly ad. schamhaft; -ness n. Schamhaftigkeit f.

Basic [bei'ssik] a. grundlegend - pay n. Grundgehalt n; - ration card Stammkarte f; - slag n. Thomas-schlacke f; - standard n. Grundnorm f; - training n. Grundausbildung f.

Basin [bei'ssin] n. Becken n,

Schale f, Hafenbecken n (port).

Basis [bei'ssiss] n. Basis f.

Bask [bahsk] vi. sich sonnen.

Basket [bah'skit] n. Korb m; -ball Korbball n; - work Flechtwerk n. [Baserelief n.

Bas-relief [bahss-ri-lihf'] n.

Bass [bæss] n. Barsch m (fish).

Bass [beiss] n. Bass m, Bassgeige f (instrument).

Bass [bæss] n. Bast m, Lindenbast m; - mat n. Bastmatte f.

Bastard [bahss'terd] n. Bastard m; a. unehelich, unecht.

Baste [beisst] vt. mit Fett begiessen.

Bast'e [beisst] vt. lose nähen, anheften; -ing thread n. Heftfaden m, Heftgarn n.

Bat [bæt] n. Fledermaus f.

Bat [bæt] n. Schlagholz n (cricket, etc.). [Stoss m.

Batch [bætsch] n. Schub m.

Bath [bahth] n. Bad n; -s pl. Badeanstalt f; - towel n. Badehandtuch n; -tub n. Badewanne f.

Bath'e [beidh] vt. i. baden; -er n. der Badende; -ing costume Badeanzug m; -ing cap n. Badehaube f, Badekappe f; -ing drawers n. pl. Badehose f; -ing place n. Badeort m.

Bathroom [bahth'ruhm] n. Badezimmer n.

Batman [bæt'mAn] n. Offiziersbursche m Ordonnanz f. (mil.).

Batsman [bætss'mAn] n. Schläger m (cricket).

Baton [bæ'tAn] n. Stab m, Taktstock m.

Battalion [bA-tæl'jAn] n. Bataillon n, Abteilung f; - headquarters pl. Bataillonsstab n; - sergeant - major Hauptfeldwebel m. [m; vt. schlagen.

Batter [bæ'ter] n. Schlagteig

Battery [bæ'tA-ri] n. Batterie f; - commander Batteriechef m; - terminal Polklemme f (el.).

Battle [bætl] n. Schlacht f; -

headquarters n. pl. Gefechtsstand m; - order n. Kriegsgliederung f; - sector Gefechtsstreifen m; - stations n (nav.) Bereitstellung f; - training Gefechtsausbildung f; - transport Gefechtstross m.

Battle-cry [bætl'krai] n. Schlachtruf m.

Battle-cruiser [bætl'kruh'ser] Schlachtkreuzer m, Panzerkreuzer m. [Schlachtfeld n.

Battle-field [bætl'fihld] n.

Battle-fleet [bætl'fliht] n. Schlachtflotte f. [Zinne f.

Battlement [bætl'ment] n.

Battleship [bætl'schip] n. Schlachtschiff n.

Battle-squadron [bætl'skuo'drAn] n. Schlachtgeschwader n.

Bawl [bOl] vt. i. laut schreien.

Bay [bei] n. Bai f; - rum n. Pimentrum m.

Bayonet [beh'on-nett] n. Seitengewehr n; vt. mit dem Bayonett erstechen.

Bay-window [bei'win-dou] n. ausgebautes Fenster.

Bazaar [bæ-sahr'] n. Basar m, Warenhaus n. [wohl befinden.

Be [bih] vi. sein; to be well sich

Beach [bihtsch] n. Strand m; vt. auf den Strand laufen lassen; - boat Strandboot n.

Beacon [bih'kAn] n. Bake f, Leuchtfeuer n, Funkfeuer n (rad.).

Bead [bihd] n. Glasperle f, Korn n (mil.), Reifenwulst m (tyre); vt. mit Perlen bedecken, schmücken; -ed tyre Wulstreif m. [diener m.

Beadle [bihdl] n. Kirchendiener m.

Beak [bihk] n. Schnabel m.

Beaker [bih'ker] n. Becher m.

Beam [bihm] n. Balken m, Strahl m, Strah'enbündel n (av.), grösste Schiffsbreite (nav.); vi. strahlen; - -aerial Richtstrahler m; - -compass Stangenzirkel m (tec.); - - radiation Ausstrahlung *f;* – **-transmission** Richtsendung *f;* – **-transmitter** Strahlensender *m.*

Beam-ends [bihm-ends'] *n.* Balkenköpfe *m. pl* (*nav.*).

Bean [bihn] *n.* Bohne *f;* **broad** – Saubohne *f;* **French** – grüne Bohne; **haricot** – Stangenbohne *f.*

Bear [behr] *n.* Bär *m,* Baissier *m* (*com.*); *vt.* drücken (*com.*).

Bear [behr] *vt.* tragen, gebären, hegen, dulden, aushalten, ausstehen; *i.* tragen, peilen (*nav.*); *refl.* sich benehmen; – **away** *vi.* weg-, davontragen, hinreissen; *vi.* abfahren (*nav.*); – **down on** *vi.* zugehen, zuhalten auf; – **a grudge** Groll hegen; – **investigation** der Prüfung standhalten; – **off** entführen, wegnehmen; – **out** bestätigen; – **right** *vi.* rechts halten; – **up** *vi.* dulden, widerstehen, standhalten; – **upon** *vi.* sich beziehen auf; – **with** nachsichtig sein gegen; – **witness** Zeugnis ablegen; **-able** *a.* erträglich. [trotzen.] **-ed** bärtig.

Beard [bihrd] *n.* Bart *m; vt.*

Bearer [beh'rer] *n.* Träger *m,* Diener *m* (*Indian*), Überbringer *m* (*letter*); – **bond** Inhaberschuldschein *m;* – **cheque** Inhaberscheck *m.*

Bearing [beh'ring] *n.* Tragen *n,* Betragen *n,* Beziehung *f,* Lager *n* (*tec.*), Peilung *f* (*nav.*); **-s** *pl.* Orientierung *f.*

Beast [bihst] *n.* Tier *n,* Vieh *n;* **-ly** *a.* viehisch.

Beat [biht] *n.* Schlag *m,* Schwingung *f,* Schwebung *f* (*rad.*), Revier *m* (*police*), Tempo *n* (*music*); *vt.* schlagen, (aus)klopfen, übertreffen, absuchen, bestreichen (*mil.*); *i.* schlagen; **-ing** *n.* Schlagen *n,* Züchtigung *f.*

Beaut'iful [bjuh'ti-ful] *a.* schön; **-ify** *vt.* schön machen; **-y** *n.* Schönheit *f.*

Beaver [bih'wer] *n.* Biber *m.*

Becalm [bi-kahm'] *vt.* beruhigen, bekalmen (*nav.*); to be becalmed blind liegen. [*pr.* wegen.]

Because [bi-kôs] *cj.* weil; – **of**

Beckon [be'kAn] *vt.* winken.

Becom'e [bi-kAm'] *vi.* werden; *t.* sich schicken, anstehen; **-ing** *a.* **-ingly** *ad.* geziemend.

Bed [bed] *n.* Bett *n;* Beet *n;* Lager *n; vt.* betten, pflanzen.

Bedaub [bi-dôb'] *vt.* beschmieren.

Bedclothes [bed'klouds] *n.* Bettzeug *n.* [schüssel *f.*

Bedding [be'ding] *n.* Bettzeug *n,* Lagerstreu *f.* [schüssel *f.*

Bed-pan [bed'pæn] *n.* Bettschüssel *f.*

Bedridden [bed'ri-dAn] *a.* bettlägerig. [Schlafzimmer *n.*

Bedroom [bed'ruhm] *n.*

Bedside [bed'said] *n.* Seite des Bettes *f;* – **table** *n.* Nachttisch *m.* [Bettdecke *f.*

Bedspread [bed'spred] *n.*

Bedstead [bed'sted] *n.* Bettstelle *f.* [fenszeit *f.*

Bedtime [bed'taim] *n.* Schlafbett

Bee [bih] *n.* Biene *f.*

Beech [bihtsch] *n.* Buche *f;* – **mast** *n.* Buchencker *f.*

Beef [bihf] *n.* Rindfleisch *n;* **-steak** *n.* Rindfleischschnitte *f;* – **tea** klare Fleischbrühe *f.*

Beehive [bih'haiw] *n.* Bienenstock *m.*

Beekeep'er [bih'kih'per] *n.* Imker *m;* **-ing** *n.* Bienenzucht *f.*

Beer [bihr] *n.* Bier *n;* – **cellar** Bierkeller *m;* – **garden** Biergarten *m;* – **glass** Bierglas *n;* – **mug** Bierkrug *m,* Seidel *m.*

Beeswax [bihs'wæx] *n.* Bienenwachs *m.*

Beet, Beetroot [biht'ruht] *n.* Runkelrübe *f,* Zuckerrübe *f;* – **sugar** *n.* Rübenzucker *m.*

Beetle [bihtl] *n.* Käfer *m;* **black** – Küchenschabe *f.*

Befall [bi-fôl'] *vt.* widerfahren, zustossen; *i.* sich ereignen.

Befit [bi-fit'] *vi. vt.* sich geziemen.

Befog [bi-fog'] vt. in Nebel hüllen, verwirren.

Befool [bi-fuhl'] vt. betören.

Before [bi-fohr'] ad. vorn, vorher, eher; cj. bevor, ehe; pr. vor; **-hand** ad. vorher, im voraus.

Befriend [bi-frend'] vt. als Freund behandeln.

Beg [beg] vt. ersuchen, betteln; i. betteln, sich erlauben.

Beget [bi-get'] vt. erzeugen.

Beggar [be'ger] n. Bettler m; vt. zum Bettler machen; **-ly** elend; **-y** n. Bettelstand m.

Begin [bi-gin'] vt. i. anfangen, beginnen, antreten; **-ner** n. Anfänger m; **-ning** n. Anfang m.

Begone [bi-gon'] vi. fort! weg!

Begrudge [bi-grudzh'] vt. missgönnen.

Beguil'e [bi-gail'] vt. bestricken, verkürzen; **-ing** a. verführerisch.

Behalf [bi-hahf'] n. Behuf m; **on** - **of** im Namen von, von seiten.

Behav'e [bi-heiw'] vi. r. sich betragen; **-iour** n. Betragen n, Verhalten n. [en.

Behead [bi-hed'] vt. enthaupt-

Behind [bi-haind'] ad. hinten, zurück; pr. hinter; **-hand** ad. zurück, im Rückstande.

Behold [bi-hould'] vt. (an) sehen.

Behoof [bi-huhf'] n. Behuf m.

Behove [bi-houw'] vi. geziemen, nötig sein.

Being [bih'ing] n. Sein n, Wesen n; **for the time** – für den Augenblick. [prügeln.

Belabour [bi-lei'ber] vt. durch-

Belated [bi-lei'tid] a. verspätet. [rülpsen.

Belch [beltsch] vt. i. ausstossen,

Beleaguer [bi-lih'ger] vt. belagern. [turm m.

Belfry [bel'fri] n. Glocken-

Belie [bi-lai'] vt. belügen.

Belie'f [bi-lihf'] n. Glaube m; **-vable** a. glaublich; **-ve** vt. i.

glauben, vertrauen; **-ver** n. der, die Gläubige.

Belittle [bi-lit'l] vt. herabsetzen.

Bell [bel] n. Glocke f, Klingel f; **-s** pl. Läutewerk n; **-handle** n. Glockenschwengel m.

Bellicose [be'li-kouss] a. kriegerisch.

Belligerent [be-li'dzhA-rAnt] a. kriegführend; n. kriegführender Staat.

Bell-metal [bel'me'tAl] n. Glocken-gut n, -speise f.

Bellow [be'lou] vi. brüllen.

Bellows [be'lous] n. pl. Blasebalg m. [Glöckner m.

Bellringer [bel'ring-er] n. –

Belly [be'li] n. Bauch m.

Belong [bi-long'] vi. gehören; **-ings** n. pl. Habe f, Eigentum n.

Beloved [bi-lA'wid] a. geliebt.

Below [bi-lou'] ad. unten; pr. unter.

Belt [belt] n. Gürtel m, Riemen m, Leibriemen m (av.); **cartridge** - **Patronengurt** m (mil.); **- drive** Riemenantrieb m (tec.).

Bemoan [bi-moun'] vt. betrauern.

Bench [bensch] n. Bank f, Gerichtsbank f, Gericht n.

Bend [bend] vt. beugen; i. sich beugen, sich neigen; n. Biegung f, Krümmung f. [pr. unter.

Beneath [bi-nihth'] ad. unten;

Benediction [be-ni-dik'-schAn] n. Segnung f.

Benefactor [be-ni-fak'ter] n. Wohltäter m.

Benefic'e [be'ni-fiss] n. Pfründe f; **-ence** n. Wohltätigkeit f; **-ent** a. wohltätig; **-ial** vorteilhaft, heilsam; **-iary** n. Empfänger m, Begünstigter m.

Benefit [be'ni-fit] n. Wohltat f, Vorteil m, Benefiz n; vt. nützen; i. Nutzen ziehen; **unemployment** – Arbeitslosenunterstützung f.

Benevolen'ce [bi-ne'wo-lenss] n. Wohlwollen n; **-t** a. wohl-

wollend; -t fund, -t society n.
Krankenkasse f. Unterstützungskasse f.
Benign [bi-nain'] a. mild.
Bent [bent] n Neigung f.
Benumb [bi-nAm'] vt. erstarren [zin n.
Benzine [ben-sihn'] n. Ben
Bequeath [bi-kuihdh'] vt. vermachen; [mächtnis n.
Bequest [bih'kuest] n. Ver
Bereave [bi-rihw'] vt. berauben; -d verwaist; -ment n. schmerzlicher Verlust m, Beraubung f.
Beret [be'ri] n. Barett n. Baskenmütze f
Berry [be'ri] n. Beere f.
Berth [bArth] n. Koje f (in ship), Bett n (in train), Ankergrund m, Anker-, Liege-platz m (nav.).
Beseech [bi-ssihtsch'] vt. dringend erbitten, anflehen.
Beset [bi-set'] vt. besetzen, umringen.
Beside [bi-said'] pr. neben, bei, ausser; -s zudem, überdies. [gern, bedrängen.
Besiege [bi-ssihdzh'] vt. bela
Besmear [bi-ssmihr'] vt. beschmieren. [besudeln
Besmirch [bi-ssmArtsch'] vt.
Besom [bih'zAm] n. Besen m.
Besotted [bi-sso'tid] a. betrunken.
Bespeak [bi-spihk'] vt. bestellen, bitten, anzeigen.
Bespoke tailor [bi-spohk'tei'lor] n. Mass-schneider m.
Besprinkle [bi-sprinkl'] vt. besprengen.
Best [best] a. best; ad. am besten; at the — aufs beste; —-seller n. meistverkauftes Buch, Riesenerfolg m.
Bestial [bes'tiAl] a. tierisch; -ity n. Bestialität f.
Bestir [bi-stAr'] vr. sich regen, anstrengen.
Bestow [bi-stou'] vt. schenken, nawenden; -al n. Schenkung f.

Bestrew [bi-struh'] vt. bestreuen. [wetten.
Bet [bet] n. Wette f.; vt. f.
Betake [bi-teik'] vr. sich begeben.
Bethink [bi-thingk'] vr. sich überlegen, sich erinnern.
Betimes [bi-taims'] ad. beizeiten. [zeichnen, voraussagen.
Betoken [bi'toukn'] vt.
Betray [bi-trei'] vt. verraten; -al n. Verrat m.
Betroth [bi-trouth'] vt. verloben; -al n. Verlobung f.
Better [be'ter] a. besser; ad. besser, mehr; vt (ver)bessern.
Between [bi-tuihn'] ad. dazwischen; pr. zwischen.
Bevel [be'wil] n. schräge Richtung, Winkelpasser m (tec.); vt. abkanten, abschrägen; —gear Kegelgetriebe n; -led saw Kreissäge f; -ling plane n. Schräghobel m. [Getränk n.
Beverage [be'wA-ridzh] n.
Bevy [be'wi] n. Flug m, Schar f.
Bewail [bi-ueil'] vt. beweinen
Beware [bi-uehr'] vi. sich hüten.
Bewilder [bi-uil'der] vt. verwirren; -ment n. Verwirrung f.
Bewitch [bi-witsch'] vt. behexen; -ing a reizend.
Beyond [bi-jond'] ad. darüber hinaus; pr. jenseits, ausser.
Bias [bai'Ass] n. Überhang m, Neigung f; vt. beeinflussen.
Bib [bib] n. Geifertuch n, [a. biblisch.
Bible [baibl] n. Bibel f; -ical
Bibliographer [bib-li-o'grAfer] n. Bücherkenner m; -ical a. bücherkundig; -y n. Bibliographie f, Bücherkunde f.
Bicarbonate of soda [bai'kahr-bo-neit ow sou'dA] n. doppelkohlensaures Natron.
Bicker [bi'ker] vi. zanken, streiten.
Bicycle [bai'ssikl] n. Fahrrad n; to ride a — radfahren; -ist n. Radfahrer m.
Bid [bid] vt. befehlen, bieten

(auction); **-der** n. Bieter m; **-ding** n. Bieten n.

Bide [baid] vt. erwarten.

Bier [bihr] n. Totenbahre f.

Big [big] a. gross.

Bifocal [bai'foukl] a. Doppel . . .; **- lenses** n. pl. Doppelglaser n. pl.

Bigamist [bi'gA-mist] n. Bigamist m; **-y** n. Bigamie f.

Bight [bait] n. Bucht f.

Bigness [big'ness] n. Grösse f.

Bigot [bi'gAt] n. Frömmler m; **-ed** a. frömmelnd; **-ry** n Frömmelei f.

Bile [bail] n. Galle f.

Bilge [bilzh] n. Klimm f, Bilge f; **- pump** Lenz-, Sod-pumpe f.

Bilious [bi'li-Ass] a. gallig, gallsüchtig. [zweisprachig.

Bilingual [bai-ling'guAl] a.

Bill [bil] n. Schnabel m.

Bill [bil] n. Zettel m, Rechnung f *(account)*, Plakat n *(poster)*, Gesetzantrag m, **-vorlage** f *(law)*; **- of entry** n. Zolldeklaration f; **- of exchange** n. Wechsel m; **- of fare** n. Speisekarte f; **- of indictment** n. Anklageschrift f; **- of sale** n. Verkaufsvertrag m, Pfandverschreibung f.

Bill-broker [bil'brou-ker] n. Wechselmakler m.

Billet [bi'lit] n. (Orts-)Quartier n, Unterkunft f; vt. einquartieren, belegen; **-ing form** n. Quartierschein m.

Bill-hook [bil'huk] n. Faschinenmesser n. [Billiard f.

Billiards [bil'jerds] n. pl.

Billion [bil'jAn] n. Billione f, Milliarde f (U.S.A.).

Bill-poster [bil'pou-ster] n. Zettelankleber m.

Bimonthly [bai'mAnth'li] a. zweimonatlich.

Bin [bin] n. Kasten m.

Bind [baind] vt. binden, verbinden; n. Binder m, Garbenbinder m; **-ing** n. Einband m.

Binnacle [bin'Akl] n. Kompasshaus n *(nav.)*.

Binocular [bin-ok'ju-ler] n. Doppelfernglas n, Operngucker m.

Biographer [bai-og'rA-fer] n. Biograph m; **-ical** a. biographisch; **-y** n. Lebensbeschreibung f. [logie f.

Biology [bai-ol'od-zhi] n. Bio-

Biped [bai'ped] n. Zweifüssler m. [decker m (av.)

Biplane [bai'plein] n. Doppel-

Bipod [bai'pod] n. Zweibein n.

Birch [bArtsch] n. Birke f, Rute f; vt. mit der Rute züchtegen.

Bird [bArd] n. Vogel m; **-cage** n. Vogelbauer n; **'s-eye** n. Vogelschau f; **'s-eye view** Vogelperspektive f; **-fancier** n. Vogelhändler m, **-lieb-**haber m.

Birth [bArth] n. Geburt f; **-certificate** n. Geburtsschein m; **-rate** Geburtsziffer f; **-day** n. Geburtstag m; **-day present** m. Geburtstagsgeschenk n; **-right** n. Erbgeburtsrecht n.

Biscuit [biss'kit] n. Keks m, Zwieback m.

Bisect [bai-ssekt'] vt. halbieren; **-ing line** n. Mittellinie f.

Bishop [bi'schAp] n. Bischof m; **-ric** n. Bistum n. [nut m.

Bismuth [biss'mAth] n. Wis-

Bit [bit] n. Gebiss n, Bissen m, Stückchen n; **one's -** das Seinige, seine Pflicht.

Bitch [bitsch] n. Hündin f.

Bite [bait] vi. i. beissen, anbeissen; n. Bissen m, Biss m; **- off** vi. abbeissen; **- someone's** head off jemand ausschelten.

Bitter [bi'ter] a. bitter, erbittert; **-ness** n. Bitterkeit f.

Bitumen [bi'tju-men] n. Bitumen n; **-inized road** Asphaltstrasse f. [n; vi. bewässern.

Bivouac [bi'wuh-ak] n. Biwak f.

Black [blæk] a. schwarz, finster; **-list** n. schwarze Liste

- market n. Schleichhandel m,
Kettenhandel m; - beetle m.
Küchenschabe f; -berry n.
Brombeere f; -bird n. Amsel
f; - -coated worker n. kauf-
männischer Angestellter; - en
vt. schwärzen, anschwärzen;
-guard n. Schuft m; - lead n.
Reissblei n; -leg Streikbrecher
m; -mail n. Erpressung f; - en
erpressen; -smith n. Schmied
m; - -out n. Verdunklung f;
vt. abblenden; (of news) Nach-
richtensperre f

Bladder [blæ'der] n. Blase f.
Blade [bleid] n. Halm m
(grass), Klinge f (knife, etc.),
Schaufel f (turbine, etc.); air-
screw — Schraubenflügel m
(av.); (of oar) Ruderblatt n.
Blamable [blei'mAbl] a.
tadelnswert.
Blame [bleim] n. Tadel m,
Schuld f; vt. tadeln; -less a.
tadellos; -worthy a. tadel-
swert.
Blanch [blænsch] vt. bleichen;
i. erbleichen. [Pudding m.
Blancmange [blA-monzh'] n.
Bland [blænd] a. freundlich,
mild; -ishment n. Schmei-
chelei f.
Blank [blængk] a. blank, leer,
blind (ammunition); n. Blan-
kett n. Lücke f, Nichts m; -
cartridge Platzpatrone f; -
cheque unausgefüllter Scheck.
Blanket [blæn'kit] n. wollene
Decke f; vt. bedecken.
Blare [blehr] vi. schmettern.
Blasphemy [blæss'fi-mi] n.
Gotteslästerung f.
Blast [blæst] n. Windstoss m,
Windsturm m, Sprengladung
f (mil.); vt. verderben, ver-
fluchen, sprengen (mining, etc.);
— furnace Hochofen m; - of air
Luftstoss m.
Blatant [blei'tAnt] a. lärmend.
Blaze [bleis] n. Lichtschein m,
lodernde Flamme f; vi. lodern.
Bleach [blihtsch] n. Bleichpul-

ver n, Chlorkalk m; vt. i.
bleichen; -ing n. Bleichen n;
-ing powder Bleichpulver n.
Bleak [blihk] a. rauh, kalt;
-ness n. Rauhheit f, Kälte f.
Bleat [bliht] vi. blöken.
Bleed [blihd] vt. bluten lassen;
i. bluten; to - to death verbluten.
Blemish [ble'mish] n. Fleck-
en m; vt. verunstalten, beflecken.
Blend [blend] vt. mischen; i.
sich vermischen; n. Mischung
f; -er n. Vermischer m.
Bless [bless] vt. segnen; -ing
n. Segnen n, Segnung f, Tisch-
gebet n.
Blight [blait] n. Meltau m,
Gifthauch m; vt. verderben,
vereiteln.
Blind [blaind] a. blind; vt.
blenden, verblenden; n. Blende,
Rouleau n; - -flying Blindflug
m (av.); -spot n. toter Schusswinkel (tank). Funkstelle f
(rad.); -fold a. mit verbunden-
en Augen; (die Augen ver-
binden); -ly a. blindlings; -ness
n. Blindheit f.
Blink [blingk] n. flüchtiger
Bick m, Blinken n; vt. nicht
sehen wollen, i. blinken; -ers
n. pl. Scheuklappen pl.
Bliss [bliss] n. Seligkeit f; -ful
a. selig.
Blister [bliss'ter] n. Blase f;
vt. i. Blasen ziehen; - gas
ätzender Kampfstoff.
Blithe [blaidh] a. munter.
Blizzard [bli'serd] n. heftiger
Schneesturm n. [dunsen.
Bloated [blou'tid] a. aufge-
Bloater [biouter] n. Bückling m.
Block [blok] n. Block m, Klotz
m, Widerlager m (tec.); vt.
blocken, sperren; traffic - Ver-
kehrsstörung f; -ing battalion
Sperrbataillon n; -ing brake
Klotzbremse f; -ade n. Block-
ade f; vt. sperren, blockieren,

versperren: **-ade breaker. -ade
runner** n. Blockadfahrer m.
Sperrbrecher m (nav.); **-**
buster n. Bezirksbombe f.
unleger m (av.); **-head** n
Dummkopf m.   [a. blond.
Blonde [blond] n. Blondine f.
Blood [blAd] n. Blut n; **-**
donor Blutspender m; **-group**
Blutgruppe f; **- transfusion**
Bluttausch f, **-übertragung** f;
-less a. blutlos; **-shed** n. Blut-
vergiessen n; **-shot** a. blut-
unterlaufen; **-stained** a. blut-
befleckt; **-thirsty** a. blutdürs-
tig; **-y** a. blutig.
Bloom [bluhm] n. Blüte f.
Flaum m; vi. blühen; **-ing** a.
verdammt.   [vi. blühen.
Blossom [blossm] n. Blüte f;
Blot [blot] n. Tintenklecks m,
Fleck m; vt. beflecken, löschen.
Blotch [blotsch] n. Pustel f.
Blott'er [blo'ter] n. Tinten-
löscher m, Schreibunterlage f,
-ing-pad n. Schreibunterlage
f; **-ing-paper** n. Löschpapier n.
Blouse [blaus] n. Bluse f.
Blow [blou] n. Schlag, Hieb m.
Blow [blou] vi. blasen, keuch-
en; t. blasen, aufblasen; **to - up**
in die Luft sprengen; **-pipe** n.
Lotrohr n.   [des Walfisches m.
Blubber [blA'ber] n. Speck m.
Bludgeon [blAd'zhAn] n.
Knüttel m; vt. einschüchtern.
Blue [bluh] n. Blau n, Wasch-
blau n; a. blau; **- pencil** n.
Bleistift m; vt. mit dem Blei-
stift streichen; **-bell** n. wilde
Hyazinthe f; **-book** n. Blaubuch
n; **-bottle** n. Fleischfliege f;
-print n. Blaupause f, Ent-
wurf m.
Bluff [blAf] n. Irreführung f;
a. breit, freimütig; vt. absch-
recken, verblüffen.
Blunder [blAn'der] n. grober
Fehler m; vi. einen groben
Fehler machen; **- about** um-
hertappen.
Blunt [blAnt] a. stumpf,

plump; vt. stumpf machen;
-ness n. Stumpfheit f, Plumpheit f.   [flecken, verwischen.
Blur [blAr] n. Fleck m; vt. be-
Blush [blAsch] n. Schamröte
f; vi. erröten. [n; vi. brausen.
Bluster [blAss'ter] n. Brausen
Boa [bou'A] n. Boa f.
Board [bohrd] n. Brett n, Kost
f, Beköstigung f, Behörde f,
Ausschuss m, Bord m, Auf-
sichtsrat m (com.); **- of govern-**
ors n. Generalrat m (bank); **-**
of works n. Bauamt n; **free on**
frei an Bord f. in Kost nehm-
en, entern (nav.), dielen, mit
Brettern verschlagen; **- in** in
Kost sein; **-ing party** Enter-
mannschaft f (nav.); **-er** n.
Kostgänger m; **-ing-house** n.
Pension f; **-ing-school** n. In-
ternat n.   Landerziehungs-
heim n.
Boast [boust] n. Prahlerei f,
Stolz m; vt. rühmen; i. prah-
len; **-er** n. Prahler m; **-ful** a.
prahlerisch.
Boat [bout] n. Boot n; **-hook**
n. Bootshaken m; **-man** n.
Bootmann m.
Boatswain [bou'ssAn] n.
Bootsmann m. (nav.).
Bobbin [bo'bin] n. Spule f.
Bob-sleigh [bob'slei] n. Bob
m, Mannschaftsschlitten m.
Bode [boud] vt. vorbedeuten.
Bodice [bo'diss] n. Leibchen n.
Bodily [bo'di-li] a. körperlich.
Body [bo'di] n. Körper m, Leib
m, Substanz f, Verband m
(mil.), Rumpf m (av.); **-belt**
Leibbinde f.   [sumpfig.
Bog [bog] n. Sumpf m; **-gy** a.
Bogus [bou'gAss] a. unecht.
Boil [beul] n. Beule f; vt. i.
sieden, kochen; **-ed egg** egg
kochtes Ei; **-er** n. Dampfkes-
sel m; **-er room** n. Kessel-
Heiz-raum m; **-ing-point** Siede-
punkt m.   [ungestüm.
Boisterous [beu'stA-rAss] a.

Bold [bould] -ly a. ad. kühn, frech; -ness n. Kühnheit f, Frechheit f.

Bolshevis'm [bol'schi-wism] n. Bolschewismus m; -t Bolschewist m.

Bolster [boul'ster] n. Polster n.

Bolt [boult] n. Bolzen m, Riegel m; vt. zuriegeln; i. davonstürzen; - position n. Riegelstellung f, Abriegelungsfront f (mil.).

Bomb [bom] n. Bombe f; vt. beschiessen, mit Bomben belegen; stick of -s Bombenreihe f; -ed area Luftnotstandsgebiet n; -ed out ausgebombt; - -aimer n. Bombenschütze m (av.); - -carrier n. Lastenträger m (av.); - -disposal area n. Sprengbezirk n; - disposal squad n. Sprengkommando n; - -load n. Bombenlast f; - -release n. Abwurf m (av.); - -thrower n. Granatwerfer m (mil.).

Bombard [bom-bahrd'] vt. beschiessen, bombardieren; -ment n. Beschiessung f.

Bombardier [bom-bahr-dihr'] n. Unteroffizier der Artillerie m.

Bombast [bom'bæst] n. Schwulst m; -ic a. bombastisch.

Bomber [bo'mer] n. Bomber m (av.); - aircraft n. Kampfflugzeug n (av.); - command n. Bombenkommando n; - formation n. Kampfgeschwader n; - pilot n. Kampfflieger m; - observer n. Bombenbeobachter m; - plane n. Kampfflugzeug n.

Bombing [bom'ing] n. Beschiessen n, Belegen n (av.); - plane n. Bomben-, Kampfflugzeug n (av.); - raid n. Bombenangriff m; - run Zielangriff m (av.).

Bomb-proof [bom'pruhf] a.

Bomb-shell [bom'schel] n. Granate f, grosse Überraschung.

Bomb-sight [bom'ssait] n. Bombenzielgerät n (av.), Visier n, Sturzvisier n (dive-bomber).

Bond [bond] n. Band n, Schuldschein n, Anleihepapier n. Zollverschluss m; vt. unter Zollverschluss legen; -holder n. Obligationsinhaber m; -age n. Knechtschaft f.

Bone [boun] n. Knochen m, Gräte f (fish); vt. ausbeinen; - of contention Zankapfel m.

Bonfire [bon'fair] n. Freudenfeuer n.

Bonnet [bo'nit] n. Haube f, Mütze f, Motorhaube f (aut.).

Bonny [bo'ni] a. hübsch.

Bonus [bou'nĕs] n. Prämie f, Extradividende f; cost of living - Teuerungs-, Lohnzuschlag m.

Bony [bou'ni] a. knöchern.

Booby [buh'bi] n. Tölpel m; - -trap Sprengfalle f (mil.).

Book [buk] n. Buch n; vt. einschreiben, belegen, bestellen (seat), lösen (ticket).

Bookbind'er [buk'bain-der] n. Buchbinder m; -ing n. Buchbinderei f. [erschrank m.

Bookcase [buk'keiss] n. Bücherstütze f.

Book-end [buk'end] n. Bücherstütze f.

Booking-office [bu'king-of'iss] n. Schalter m, Fahrkartenausgabe f (rail.), Vorverkaufstelle f (theatre).

Bookish [buk'isch] a. den Büchern ergeben.

Book-keep'er [buk'kih-per] n. Buchhalter m; -ing n. Buchhaltung f, Rechnungswesen n.

Book-learning [buk'lÄrning] n. Büchergelehrsamkeit f. [Bücherfreund m.

Book-lover [buk'lÄ-wer] n.

Book-plate [buk'pleit] n. Bucheignerzeichen n.

Book-post [buk'poust] n. Drucksachenversand m (av.).

Booklet [buk'lit] n. Broschüre f.

Bookmaker [buk'mei-ker] n. Büchermacher m, Buchmacher m (turf). [Buchhändler m.
Bookseller [buk'sse-ler] n.
Bookshelf [buk'schelf] n. Bücherbrett n.
Bookshop [buk'schop] n. Buchhandlung f.
Book-stall [buk'stOl] n. Bücherstand m, Bahnhofsbuchhandlung f.
Book-trade [buk'treid] n. Buchhandel m.
Bookworm [buk'uArm] n. Bücherwurm m.
Boom [buhm] n. Sperrbaum m, Balken m, Sperre f (nav.); – barrage n. Unterwasserverhau n, Hafensperre f; – defence n. Sperrwacht f; – defence vessel n. Sperrbrecher m. [dröhnen.
Boom [buhm] vi. dumpf
Boom [buhm] n. Hochkonjunktur f, Hausse f (com.); vt. in die Höhe treiben; i. flott gehen. [n. Bumerang m.
Boomerang [buh'mA-ræng]
Boon [buhn] n. Wohltat f.
Boor [buhr] n. Flegel m, Lümmel m; -ish a. grob.
Boost [buhst] vt. in die Höhe treiben, Reklame machen für; verstärken (el.). [dynamo m.
Booster [buh'ster] n.
Boot [buht] n. Stiefel m; – -lace n. Schuhriemen m, Schnürsenkel m; – -black n. Stiefelputzer m; – polish m. Stiefelwichse f; – -tree n. Stiefelspanner m.
Bootee [buh'tih] n. wollener Kinderstiefel m. [bude f.
Booth [buhdh] n. Verkaufs-
Bootlegger [buht'le-ger] n. Alkoholschmuggler m.
Bootlegging [buht'le-ging] n. Alkoholschmuggel m.
Boots [buhtss] n. Hausknecht m.
Booty [buh'tih] n. Beute f.
Boracic [bO'rass'ik] a. Bor

. . .; – acid n. Borsäure f; – ointment Borsalbe f.
Borage [bo'ridzh] n. Gurkenkraut n. [borsaures Natron.
Borax [bO'rax] n. Borax n.
Border [bOr'der] n. Einfassung f, Rand m, Saum m, Grenze f; – on vt. grenzen an; – -line n. Grenze f; – -line case n. Grenzfall m.
Bore [bOr] n. Bohrung f, Nageleisen n, langweiliger Schwatzer m, Rohrweite f, Kaliber n (mil.); vt. bohren, langweilen; – of the gun Rohrseele f; – -dom n. Langweile f; – -hole n. Bohrloch n; – r n. Bohrer m. [Borsäure f.
Boric acid [bO'rik-æ'ssid] n.
Borough [bA'rou] n. Stadt f, Stadtgemeinde f.
Borrow [bo'rou] vt. borgen; -er Borger m, Entleiher m.
Bosom [bu'sAm] n. Busen m.
Boss [boss] n. Buckel m, Anschlag m (tec.).
Boss [boss] n. Chef m, Bonze m, w (political).
Botanical [bo-tæ'ni-kAl] a. botanisch; -ist Botaniker m; -y Botanik f.
Both [bouth] a. pn. beide, beides; cj. – and sowohl – als auch.
Bother [bo'dher] n. Plage f; vi. sich beunruhigen; vt. plagen; – ! verdammt !
Bottle [botl] n. Flasche f; vt auf Flaschen ziehen; -d beer n. Flaschenbier n; to – up vt. unterdrücken; -neck n. Verkehrsengpass m, Flaschenhals m.
Bottom [botm] n. Boden m, Fuss m, Ende n; at – im Grunde; to get to the – of a thing etwas gründlich untersuchen; -less a. bodenlos.
Bough [bau] n. Ast m.
Boulder [boul'der] n. Felsblock m.
Bounce [baunss] vi. auf-

springen; *n.* Aufprall *m*; **– off** ger *pl*; *vt.* spannen, stärken,
vi. abprallen. [verpflichtet. abstützen, versteifen.

Bound [baund] *a.* gebunden. **Bracelet** [breiss'lit] *n.* Arm-

Bound(s) [baunds] *n.* Grenze band *n.*
f; *vt.* begrenzen; **out of –s** **Bracket** [bræ'kit] *n.* Konsole
verboten; **to keep within – s** *f,* Klammer *f*; *vt.* einklammern.
den Anstand wahren. **Bracken** [brækn] *n.* Farn-

Bound [baund] *n.* Sprung *m*; kraut *n.* [dahle *f.*
vi. springen. [Grenze *f.* **Bradawl** [bræd'Ol] *n.* Bind-

Boundary [baun'dA-ri] *n.* **Brag** [bræg] *vi.* prahlen.

Boundless [baund'less] *a.* **Braid** [breid] *n.* Borte *f,*
grenzenlos. [freigebig Flechte *f*; *vt.* flechten.

Bounteous [baun'ti-Ass] *a.* **Brain** [brein] *n.* Gehirn *n*; **–**

Bounty [baun'ti] *n.* Freigebig- **-worker** geistiger Arbeiter;
keit *f,* Geschenk *n,* Prämie *f.* **-(s) trust** Gehirnsyndikat *n*;

Bouquet [bu-kei'] *n.* Blumen- Gehirnskartel *n,* Frage und
strauss *m,* Blume *f* (*wine*). Antwort *f* (*rad.*); **-less** *a.*

Bout [baut] *n.* Kampf *m,* hirnlos.
Gelage *n.* [Schleife *f.* **Braize** [breis] *vt.* schmoren; **-d**

Bow [bou] *n.* Bogen *m.* beef *n.* Schmorbraten *m.*

Bow [bau] *n.* Bug *m* (*ship*). **Brake** [breik] *n.* Bremse *f*; *vi.*

Bow [bau] *n.* Verbeugung *f*; bremsen; **– block** Bremsklotz
vt. biegen, neigen; **i.** sich *m*; **– drum** *n.* Bremstrommel *f*;
bücken, sich verneigen. **– van** *n.* Bremswagen *m* (*rl.*).

Bowels [bau'ils] *n. pl.* Einge- **Bramble** [bræmbl] *n.* Brom-
weide *n.* beere *f.*

Bowl [boul] *n.* Schale *f.* **Bran** [bræn] *n.* Kleie *f.*

Bowl [boul] *n.* Kugel *f*; *vt.* **Branch** [brahnsch] *n.* Ast *m,*
kugeln. Zweig *m* (*business*); **– of ser-**

Bowlegged [bou'legd] *a.* **vice** *n.* Truppengattung *f*; **-**
krummbeinig. **office** *n.* Nebenstelle *f*; **-**

Bowser [bou'ser] *n.* Not- **stores** *n. pl.* Zweiglager *n*; **-**
schnelltanker *m* (*av.*). **of industry** Gewerbe *n*; **to**

Bowsprit [bou'sprit] *n.* Bug- **off** *vi.* abzweigen.
spriet *n.* **Brand** [brænd] *n.* Brand *m,*

Box [box] *vi.* Büchse *f,* Marke *f* (*com.*); *vt.* brand-
Schachtel *f,* Dose *f,* Koffer *m,* marken, bezeichnen; **-new** *a.*
Loge *f* (*theatre*); **– barrage** *n.* nagelneu. [schwingen.
Abriegelungsfeuer *n*; **– girder** **Brandish** [bræn'disch] *vt.*
n. Kastenträger *m* (*tec.*). **Brandy** [bræn'di] *n.* Brannt-

Box [box] *vi.* boxen; **– on the** wein *m.*
ear Ohrfeige *f*; **-ing match** **Brass** [brahss] *n.* Messing *n*;
Faustkampf *m.* **– band** *n.* Blechmusik *f.*

Boy [beu] *n.* Knabe *m,* Junge **Brassard** [bræss'ard] *n.* Arm-
m, Diener *m* (*Afrika, etc.*). binde *f.* [Büstenhalter *m.*

Boycott [beu'kot] *n.* Boycot- **Brassière** [brass'i-ehr] *n.*
tung *f*; *vt.* boycottieren. **Bravado** [brA-wah'do] *n.*

Boyhood [beu'hud] *n.* Prahlerei *f.*
Knabenalter *n.* [haft. **Brave** [breiw] *a.* **-ly** *ad.* tapfer;

Boyish [beu'isch] *a.* knaben- *vt.* trotzen; **-ry** Tapferkeit *f.*

Brace [breiss] *n.* Tragband *n,* **Brawl** [brOl] *n.* lauter Zank *m*;
Strebe *f,* Paar *n*; **-s** Hosenträ- *vi.* zanken.

Brawny [brO'ni] *a.* stämmig.

Brazen [breⁱsn] *a.* ehern, unverschämt.

Breach [brihtsch] *n.* Bruch *m*, Bresche *f* (*mil.*), Durchbruch *m*; − of c⟨on⟩tract Kontraktbruch *m.* [butter Butterbrot *n.*

Bread [bred] *n.* Brot *n*; − and

Breadth [bredth] *n.* Breite *f.*

Break [breⁱk] *n.* Bruch *m*, Unterbrechung *f*, Satz *m* (billiards); *vt.* brechen; − off abbrechen; − open aufbrechen; − surface auftauchen (*nav.*); − through *n.* Durchbruch *m* (*mil.*); *vt.* durchbrechen; − up *vt.* aufbrechen, abwracken (*nav.*); zerspringen; − down zusammenbrechen; − out ausbrechen; − up sich auflösen.

Breakable [breⁱ'kAbl] *a.* zerbrechlich. [Bruch *m.*

Breakage [breⁱ'kidzh] *n.*

Breakdown [breⁱk'daun] *n.* Zusammenbruch *m*, Panne *f* (*aut.*) Betriebsstörung *f* (*rail, factory*); − lorry *n.* Abrüst-, Abschleppwagen *m*; −squad *n.* Störungstrupp *m.*

Breakfast [brek'fahst] *n.* Frühstück *n.*

Breakneck [breⁱk'nek] *a.* halsbrecherisch.

Breakwater [breⁱk'uO-ter] *n.* Wellenbrecher *m.*

Breaking [breⁱking] *n.* Bruch *m*; − point Belastungsgrenze *f* (*tec.*); − strain *n.* Bruchspannung *f.*

Breast [brest] *n.* Brust *f*; −height *n.* Anschlagshöhe *f* (*mil.*)

Breath [breth] *n.* Atem *m*, Hauch *m.*

Breathe [brihdh] *vt. i.* atmen.

Breathless [breth'less] *a.* atemlos.

Breech [brihtsch] *n.* Verschluss-stück *n.* Stoss *m*, Boden *m* (*mil.*)). Hose *f.*

Breeches [brit'schis] *n. pl.*

Breed [brihd] *vt.* erzeugen, aufziehen (cattle); *i.* sich vermehren; *n.* Brut *f*, Zucht *f*; −er *n.* Erzeuger *m*, Züchter *m*; −ing *n.* Erziehung *f*, Zucht *f.*

Breeze [brihs] *n.* Brise *f*, leichterWind.

Breezy [brih'si] *a.* windig.

breviary [brih'wi-A-ri] *n.* Brevier *n.*

Brevity [bre'wi-ti] *n.* Kürze *f.*

Brew [bruh] *n.* Gebräu *n*; *vt. i.* brauen; −er *n.* Brauer *m*; −ery *n.* Brauerei *f.* [Bruyère pfeife *f.*

Briar-pipe [braⁱ'er-paⁱp] *n.*

Bribe [braⁱb] *n.* Gabe zur Bestechung *f*; *vt.* bestechen; −ry *n.* Bestechung *f.*

Brick [brik] *n.* Ziegel *m*, Backstein *m*; − to − up *vt.* muern; −kiln *n.* Ziegelei *f*, Zaieglefonen *m*; −layer *n.* Maurer *m*; −work Mauerwerk *n*; −yard *n.* Ziegelei *f.*

Bride [braⁱd] *n.* Braut *f*, junge Frau; −groom *n.* Bräutigam *n*, junger Ehemann; −maid *n.* Brautjungfer *f.*

Bridge [bridzh] *n.* Brücke *f*, Kommandobrücke *f* (*nav.*). Bridge (cards); *vt.* eine Brücke schlagen über; − equipment Übergangsgerät *n.* (*mil.*); −head *n.* Brückenkopf *n.*

Bridle [braⁱdl] *n.* Zaum *m*, *f.* zäumen; −path Saumpfad *m.*

Brief [brihf] *a.* −ly *ad.* kurz; *vt.* zusammenfassen, unterweisen, befehlen (an.); − case *n.* Mappe *f.*

Briefing [brih'fing] *n.* Flugbefehl *m*, Flugvorbereitung *f* (*av.*); − room Befehlsstelle *f* (*av.*).

Brier [braⁱ'er] *n.* Dornstrauch *m*, wilde Rose, Heidekraut *n.*

Brig [brig] *n.* Brigg *f.*

Brigade [bri-geⁱd'] *n.* Brigade *f*; −ier *n.* Brigadekommandeur *m* (*mil.*), Abteilungskommandeur *m* (*artillery*). [ber *m.*

Brigand [bri'gAnd] *n.* Räu-

Bright [brait] a. -ly ad. hell, heiter; -en vt. hell machen, aufheitern; i. hell werden, sich aufheitern; -ness n. Helle f, Heiterkeit f.

Brillian'cy [bril'jAn-ssi] n. Glanz m; -t a. glänzen; -t é. Edelstein m; -tine n. Brillantine f.

Brim [brim] n. Rand m.

Brimstone [brim'stoun] n. Schwefel m.

Brine [brain] n. Salzwasser n.

Bring [bring] vt. bringen; – about zustande bringen, veranlassen, herbeiführen; – against anstreben (lawsuit); – along mitbringen, -schaffen; – away wegnehmen, -schaffen, -back zurückbringen; – down herunter-holen, -drücken; – forth gebären, erzeugen, hervorbringen; – in einführen, hereinbringen, eintragen, (profit); – off davontragen, erzielen (success); – on herbeiführen; – out herausgeben, verlegen (book); – over herüberbringen, überreden (people); – round herbeiholen, wiederherstellen (sick); – through durchbringen; – together zusammenbringen, -führen; – under unterwerfen, bezwingen; – up auferziehen, heraufholen.

Brink [bringk] n. Rand m.

Briquette [bri-ket'] n. Brikett n.

Brisk [brissk] a. -ly ad. lebhaft; -ness n. Lebhaftigkeit f.

Brisling [briss'ling] n. Sardine f.

Bristl'e [brissl] n. Borste f; vi. sich sträuben; -y borstig.

Brittle [britl] a. spröde; -ness n. Sprödigkeit f.

Broach [broutsch] vt. anzapfen, aufs Tapet bringen.

Broad [brOd] a. breit, grob.

Broadcast [brOd'kahst] n. Rundfunksendung f; vt. rundfunken, senden; – amateur

Rundfunkbastler m (rad.); – at dictation speed Schreibfunk m; – reception Rundfunkempfang m.

Broadcaster [brOd'kahst-er] n. Sender m (rad.), Geber m (tel.).

Broadcasting [brOd'kahsting] a. Radio ..., Rundfunk ...; – corporation Rundfunkgesellschaft f; – station Sendestelle f.

Broaden [brO'dn] vt. breit machen.

Broadside [brOd'ssaid] n. Breitseite f (nav.); [kat m.

Brocade [bro-keid'] n. Brokat m.

Broil [breul] n. Tumult m.

Broker [brou'ker] n. Makler m; -age n. Maklergebühr f.

Bromine [brou'mihn] n. Brom n.

Bronchitis [brong-kai'tiss] n. Luftröhrenentzündung f.

Bronze [brons] n. Bronze f.

Brooch [broutsch] n. Brosche f. [bräuten.

Brood [bruhd] n. Brut f; vi. brüten.

Brook [bruk] n. Bach m.

Brook [bruk] vt. ertragen.

Broom [bruhm] n. Besen m, Ginster m. [brühe f.

Broth [broth] n. Fleischbrühe f.

Brothel [brothl] n. Bordell m.

Brother [brA'dher] n. Bruder m; – -in-law n. Schwager m; -hood n. Bruderschaft f; -ly a. brüderlich. [Stirne f.

Brow [brau] n. Augenbraue f.

Brown [braun] a. braun.

Browse [braus] vi. weiden.

Bruise [bruhs] n. Quetschung f; vt. quetschen.

Brunswick black [brAnss'uik blæk'] n. Ofenschwärze f.

Brunt [brAnt] n. Anprall m, Brennpunkt m.

Brush [brAsch] n. Bürste f, Pinsel m; v. bürsten; to – up auffrischen; -wood n. Gestrüpp n.

Brutal [bruh'tAl] a. brutal, roh; -ity n. Brutalität f.

Brute [bruht] n. Vieh n.

Bubble [bAbl] n. Blase f; vi. aufwallen.

Buck [bAk] n. Bock m.

Bucket [bA'kit] n. Eimer m.

Buckle [bAkl] n. Schnalle f; vt. schnallen.

Bud [bAd] n. Knospe f; vi. knospen, keimen.

Budge [bAdzh] vi. sich rühren.

Budget [bA'-zhit] n. Vorrat m, Bündel n, Haushaltsplan m, Staatshaushalt m; to – for in den Haushaltsplan einstellen.

Buff [bAf] a. ledergelb.

Buffalo [bA'fA-lo] n. Büffel m.

Buffer [bA'fer] n. Puffer m, Hemmvorrichtung f.

Buffet [bA'fit] n. Faustschlag m; vi. to – schlagen, umherwerfen. [-car Speisewagen m.

Buffet [bjuh'fi] n. Büffet n;

Buffoon [bA-fuhn'] n. Possenreisser m; -ery n. Possenreisserei f.

Bug [bAg] n. Wanze f.

Bugbear [bAg'behr] n. Popanz m. [-r n. Hornistm.

Bugle [bjuh'gl] n. Jagdhorn n.

Build [bild] vt. bauen; to – in einbauen; -er n. Baumeister m, -ing n. Bauwesen n, Gebäude n; - -ing material n. Baustoff m; - -ing site n. Bauplatz m, -stelle f; - -ing society n. Baugenossenschaft f, Bausparkasse f; - -ing trade Baugewerbe n; -ing-up time n. Einschwingzeit f (rad.).

Built-in [bilt'in] a. eingebaut; - engine n. Einbaumotor m.

Bulb [bAlb] n. knollen m, Birne f, Lampe f (el.); -ous a. knollig.

Bulk [bAlk] n. Grösse f, Masse f, Hauptteil m; to break – die Ladung zu löschen anfangen; to buy in – im grossen einkaufen; - order Rahmenauftrag m; -head n. Schott n (nav.); -y a. dick.

Bull [bul] n. Stier m, Haussier m (com.); vt. in die Höhe treiben; -dog n. Bulldogge f; -dozer n. Räumpflug m.

Bullet [bu'lit] n. Kugel f; - -proof a. kugelfest, -sicher; - -proof glass n. Panzerglas n; - -proof windscreen n. Panzerscheibe f; - wound Schusswunde f. [in n.

Bulletin [bu'li-tin] n. Bullet-

Bull-fight [bul'fait] n. Stiergefecht n. [pfaff m.

Bullfinch [bul'finsch] n. Dom-

Bullion [bul'jAn] n. ungemünztes Gold n.

Bully [bu'li] n. Raufbold m; vt. einschüchtern.

Bulwark [bul'uArk] n. Bollwerk n, Schutzwand f.

Bump [bAmp] n. Stoss m, Beule f; vt. stossen.

Bumper [bAm'per] n. Stosszange f (aut.). [aufgeblasen.

Bumptious [bAmp'schAss] a.

Bumpy [bAm'pi] a. böig.

Bun [bAn] n. Semmel f.

Bunch [bAnsch] n. Bund n, Bündel n, - of flowers Blumenstrauss m.

Bundle [bAndl] n. Bund n, Bündel n, Aktenstoss m (documents).

Bung [bAng] n. Spund m; vt. zuspunden.

Bungalow [bAng'gA-lou] n. ebenerdiges Gebäude, einstöckiges Haus.

Bungl'e [bAng'gl] n. Pfuscharbeit f, Stümperei f; vt. verpfuschen; i. stümpern; -ing a. stümperhaft. [koje f.

Bunk [bAngk] n. Schlaf-

Bunker [bAng'ker] n. Behälter m, Kohlenbunker m (nav.).

Buoy [beu] n. Boje f, Bake f; vt. flott machen, flott erhalten, ermutigen; -ancy n. Schwimmkraft f, Heiterkeit f, Auftrieb m (av.); -ant a. schwimmend, heiter.

Burden [bʌr'dn] n. Last f., Tonnengehalt m; vt. belasten; -some a. lästig.

Bureau [bjuh'rou] n. Bureau n; -cracy n. Bureaukratie f.

Burglar [bʌr'glər] n. Einbrecher m; -y n. Einbruch m.

Burial [be'ri-Al] n. Begräbnis n. [lesk] n. Posse f.

Burlesque [bər-lesk'] a. burlesk.

Burly [bʌr-li] a. stämmig.

Burn [bʌrn] n. Brandwunde f; vt. verbrennen; i. brennen; -n. Brenner m. [lieren.

Burnish [bʌr'nisch] vt. polieren.

Burrow [bʌ'rou] n. Bau m; vi. sich eingraben. [dium n.

Bursary [bʌr'sA-ri] n. Stipendium n.

Burst [bʌrst] vt. sprengen; i. bersten, platzen; n. Bersten n, Bruch m; - of fire Feuerstoss m, Schussgarbe f; -ing n. Durchbruch m; -ing charge n. Sprengladung f; -ing shell n. Sprenggranate f.

Bury [be'ri] vt. begraben, verschütten (in rubble); -ied cable Erdkabel n. [Omnibus m.

Bus [bʌss] n. Autobus m.

Bush [busch] n. Busch m; -y a. buschig. [fel m.

Bushel [bu'schel] n. Scheffel m.

Busily [bi'si-li] a. geschäftig.

Business [bis'niss] n. Geschäft n, Sache f; - -like a. geschäftsmässig; - man Geschäftsmann m.

Bust [bʌst] n. Büste f.

Bustle [bʌssl] n. Lärm m; vi. sich lärmend regen.

Busy [bi'si] a. beschäftigt, fleissig; -body n. Klatschbase f.

But [bʌt] cj. aber, sondern; - yet aber doch; pr. ausser; ad. nur.

Butcher [bu'tscher] n. Metzger m; vt. metzeln, niedermachen; -y n. Metzelei f.

Butler [bʌt'ler] n. der oberste Diener.

Butt [bʌt] n. Fass n, Butte f.

Butt [bʌt] n. Stoss m; vt. stossen.

Butt [bʌt] n. Holzscheibe f, Zielscheibe f; - -s Schiessstand m.

Butt-end [bət'end] n. dickes Ende, Kolben m (mil.).

Butter [bʌ'ter] n. Butter f; vt. mit Butter bestreichen; -cup n. Butterblume f; -fly n. Schmetterling m; -milk n. Buttermilch f. [teil n.

Buttock [bʌ'tAk] n. Hinter-

Button [bʌ'tAn] n. Knopf m; vt. zuknöpfen; -hole n. Knopfloch n; -hook n. Knöpfer m.

Buttress [bʌt'riss] n. Strebepfeiler m.

Buxom [bʌx'Am] a. drall.

Buy [bai] vt. kaufen; - up aufkaufen; -er n. Käufer m.

Buzz [bʌs] vi. summen.

Buzzer [bʌ'ser] n. Summer m.

By [bai] pr. neben, um, von, durch; ad. vorbei; - and - bald, sogleich; - the dozen dutzendweise; - name dem Namen nach; - oneself allein; - the way beiläufig, nebenbei gesagt, übrigens.

By-election [bai'i-lek-schAn] n. Ersatzwahl f.

Bygone [bai'gon] a. vergangen.

By-law [bai'lo] n. Lokalgesetz n.

By-pass [bai'pahss] n. Umgehungsweg m, Umleitung f; - road Entlastungsstrasse f.

By-product [bai'pro'dAkt] n. Nebenprodukt n. [weg m.

By-road [bai'roud] n. Nebenweg m.

Bystander [bai'stæn-der] n. Zuschauer m. [weg m.

By-way [bai'uei] n. Nebenweg m.

By-word [bai'uArd] n. Sprichwort n, Zielscheibe f des Spottes f.

C

Cab [kæb] n. Droschke f; -man n. Droschkenkutscher m; -

-rank m. Droschkenhalteplatz m.   [Ränke m. pl.

Cabal [kA-bæl'] n. Kabale f.

Cabaret [kæ'bA-reï] n. Kabarett n, Überbrettl n, Tingeltangel n.

Cabbage [kæ'bidzh] n. Kohl m.

Cabin [kæ'bin] n. Hütte f, Kajüte f, Flugzeugkabine f (av.); - -boy n. Schiffsjunge m.

Cabinet [kæ'bi-nit] n. Kabinett n, Schrank n, Ministerium n, Kasten m, Gehäuse n (rad.); - -maker n. Kunsttischler m; - minister = Minister m.

Cable [keïbl] n. Kabel n, Seil n, Tau n, Leitung f, Kabeldepesche f; vt. kabeln, verseilen, drahten; - communication n. Kabelverbindung f; -gram n. Drahtdepesche f, Drahtbericht m; - laying Kabelbau m; - -lorry n. Ballonwindewagen m (av.).

Cackle [kækl] vi. gackern.

Cad [kæd] n. gemeiner Kerl, Schurke m.

Cadaverous [kæ'dæ'wA-rAss] a. leichenartig.

Cadence [keï'dAnss] n. Tonfall m, Kadenz f.

Cadet [kA-det'] n. Kadett m, Anwärter m, Fähnrich m (mil.); -s n. pl. Nachwuchs m (mil.).

Cadre [kA-der'] n. Stammmannschaft f (mil.).

Cage [keïdzh] n. Käfig m, Gehege n (animals), Förderkorb m (mine).

Cairn [kehrn] n. Steinhaufen m, Steinmann m. [schwätzen.

Cajole [kA-dzhoul'] vt. beschwätzen.

Cake [keïk] n. Kuchen m; vi. zusammenbacken; - of soap das Stück Seife.

Calamit'ous [kA-læ'mi-tAss] a. unheilvoll; - y n. Unglück n.

Calcium [kæl'ssi-Am] n. Kalzium n; - carbonate kohlensaures Kalk; - carbide Kalziumkarbid n.

Calculable [kæl'kju-lAbl] a. berechenbar.

Calculat'e [kæl'kju-leit] vt. berechnen; -ing machine n. Rechenmaschine f, -gerät n; -ion n. Berechnung f; -or n. Rechner m, Rechenmaschine f, Rechengerät n.   [Kessel m.

Caldron [kôl'drAn] n. grosser

Calendar [kæl'in-der] n. Kalender m.

Calf [kahf] n. Kalb n, Wade f (leg); - -skin n. Kalbfell n, -leder n.

Calibrat'e [kæ'li-breit] vt. eichen; -ion n. Stricheinteilung f, Eichung f, Vermessung f; -ion flight n. Messflug m (av.).

Calibre [kæ'li-ber] n. Kaliber n, Bohrung f, Wert m (value).

Calico [kæ'li-ko] n. Kaliko m, Kattun m.

Call [kôl] n. Ruf m, Berufung f, kurzer Besuch, Anruf m (ph.); vt. rufen, nennen, wecken, anläuten (ph.), anrufen (rad.); on - auf Abruf; - at vt. anlaufen (nav.); - away vt. abrufen; - out vt. ausrufen; - up vt. ausheben (recruits), einberufen (reservists); vi. rufen, vorsprechen; - box n. Fernsprechstelle f (ph.); -er n. Besucher m; -ing n. Beruf m.

Callipers [kæ'li-pers] n. pl. Taster m, Lochzirkel m.

Call-office [kôl'O-fiss] n. Fernsprechamt n (ph.).

Callous [kæ'lAss] a. hart, unempfindlich; -ness n. Härte f.

Call-sign [kôl'ssaïn] n. Rufzeichen n (rad.).

Call-up [kôl'Ap] n. Einberufung f, Kriegsberderung f, Aushebung f (mil.).

Calm [kahm] a. ruhig; -ly ad. ruhig; n. Stille f, Windstille f; vt. beruhigen; -ness n. Stille f, Gemütsruhe f.

Calory [kæ'lo-ri] n. Kilogrammkalorie f, Wärmeeinheit f.

Calumniat'e [kA-lAm'ni-eit]

vt. verleumden, falsch anschuldigen; -or Verleumder *m.*

Calumny [kæl'Am-ni] *n.* Verleumdung *f.*, falsche Anschuldigung.

Calve [kahw] *vi.* kalben.

Cam [kæm] *n.* Knagge *f (tec.)*, Nocke *f (aut.)*; - level *n.* Verschlusskurbel *f (mil.)*; - shaft *n.* Nockenwelle *f (aut.)*.

Camber [kæm'ber] *n.* Wölbung *f.*, Radsturz *m*; *vt.* wölben, biegen. [Batist *m.*]

Cambric [keim'brik] *n.*

Camel [kæ'mil] *n.* Kameel *n*; - hair Kameelhaar *n.*

Cameo [kæ'mi-o] *n.* Kamee *f.*

Camera [kæ'mi-rA] *n.* Kamera *f*, Apparat *m*, Bildgerät *n*; in - unter Ausschluss der Öffentlichkeit *(law)*; - man *n.* Kameramann *m*, Operateur *m (film)*. [kers] *n. pl.* Hemdhose *f.*]

Cami-knickers [kæ'mi-ni'**]

Camisole [kæm'i-sohl] *n.* Kamisol *n.* [Kamille *f.*]

Camomile [kæm'o-mail] *n.*

Camouflage [kæm'u-flahzh] *n.* Tarnung *f*, Verkleidung *f*, Maske *f*; *vt.* tarnen, verschleiern, verdecken; - equipment *n.* Tarngerät *n (mil.)*; - material *n.* Tarnmittel *n (mil.)*; - net *(for helmet) n.* Stahlhelmtarnnetz *n (mil.)*; -ed battery *n.* Scheinbatterie *f (mil.)*; -ed position *n.* Scheinstellung *f*, verdeckte Stellung *(mil.)*; -ed troops *n. pl.* Tarnungstruppe *f (mil.)*. [Quetschmine *f (mil.)*]

Camouflet [kæm'u-flei] *n.*

Camp [kæmp] *n.* Lager *n*; *vi.* sich lagern, zelten.

Campaign [kæm-pein'] *n.* Feldzug *m*, Kriegsdienst *m*; -er Feldzugsteilnehmer *m*, Soldat *m*; old -er ehemaliger Kriegsteilnehmer, alter Kämpfer.

Camp-bed [kæmp'bed] *n.* Feldbett *n.* [pfer *m.*]

Camphor [kæm'fer] *n.* Kam-

Camping-ground [kæm'ping-graund] *n.* Lagerplatz *m.*

Camp-stool [kæmp'stuhl] *n.* Klappstuhl *m*, Feldstuhl *m.*

Can [kæn] *n.* Kanne *f*, Blecheimer *m*, Dose *f*, Büchse *f*; *vt.* in Büchsen einmachen; -ned goods *n. pl.* Konserven *f. pl.* Konserven *n. pl.*; -ned meat Büchsenfleisch *n.*

Can [kæn] *v.* kann.

Canal [kA-næl'] *n.* Kanal *m.*

Canary [kA-neh'ri] *n.* Kanarienvogel *m.*

Cancel [kæn'sil] *vt.* durchstreichen, widerrufen; a connection Verbindung lösen *(ph.)*; -lation *f.* Widerruf *m.*, Annullierung *f.* [-ous *a.* krebsartig.]

Cancer [kæn'sser] *n.* Krebs *m.*

Candid [kæn'did] *a.* -ly *ad.* aufrichtig.

Candidat'e [kæn'di-deit] *n.* Kandidat *m*, Bewerber *m*; -ure *n.* Bewerbung *f.*

Candle [kændl] *n.* Kerze *f*; - power *n.* Lichtstärke *f*; - wick *n.* Lichtdocht *n*; -mas *n.* Lichtmess *f*, 2nd February; -stick *n.* Leuchter *m.*

Candour [kæn'der] *n.* Offenherzigkeit *f.*

Cand'y [kæn'di] *n.* Zuckerwerk *n*; -ied peel *n.* Zitronat *n*; -ied peel *n.* Zitronat *n.*

Cane [kein] *n.* Rohr *n*; *vt.* prügeln; -sugar *n.* Rohrzucker *m.*

Canine [kæ'nain] *a.* hündisch, Hund.

Canister [kæn'iss-ter] *n.* Blechbüchse *f*, Teebüchse *f*, Einsatz *m (gas-mask)*; - bomb *n.* Minenhülle *f*; - shot *n.* Kartätsche *f.*

Canker [kæng'ker] *n.* Krebs *m*; *vi.* aufgefressen werden.

Cannibal [kæ'ni-bAl] *n.* Menschenfresser *m.*

Cannon [kæ'nAn] *n.* Kanone *f*, Geschütz *n*; -ade *n.* Beschiessung *f*; -ball *n.* Kanonenkugel *f*; - fodder *n.* Kanonenfutter *n*; -shot *n.* Kanonenschuss *m*, Schussweite *f.*

Canny [kæ'ni] *a.* vorsichtig.

Canoe [kA-nuh'] n. Kanu n, Baumkahn m, Paddelboot n; vi. paddeln; -ing Paddeln n.

Canon [kæ'nAn] n. Kanon m, Regel f; -ize vt. heiligsprechen.

Can-opener [kæn'ou-p A-ner] n. Büchsenöffner m.

Canopy [kæ'no-pi] n. Baldachin m, Decke f. [Sprache f.

Cant [kænt] n. heuchlerische

Cant [kænt] vt. stossen, kippen, auf die Seite legen; to - off vt. abschrägen.

Canteen [kæn-tihn'] n. Kantine f, Marketenderei f, Feldflasche f.

Canter [kæn'ter] n. kurzer Galopp; vi. kantern.

Cantilever [kæn'ti-lih-wer] n. Sparrenkopf m (tec.); - bridge n. Auslegerbrücke f; - monoplane freitragender Eindecker (av.). [m, Kreis m.

Canton [kæn'ton] n. Kanton

Canton [kæn'ton] n. Einquartierung f, Quartier n; vt. unterbringen, einquartieren, -ment f. Einquartierung f; Unterbringung f; Ortsunterkunft f.

Canvas [kæn'wass] n. Kanevas m, Leinwand f (art, etc.), Segeltuch n (nav.); - gaiters n. pl. Stoffgamaschen f. pl; - jacket, - tunic n. Drillichrock m.

Canvass [kæn'wass] n. Stimmenwerbung f; vi. werben; -er n. Bewerber m.

Cap [kæp] n. Mütze f, Barett n, Deckel m (tec.); vt. übertreffen, beklappen (fuze), bedecken (cover). [Fähigkeit f.

Capability [kei-pA-bi'li-ti] f.

Capable [kei'pAbl] a. fähig, imstande, tüchtig. [geräumig.

Capacious [kA-pei'schAss] a.

Capacity [kA-pæ'si-ti] n. Gehalt m, Fähigkeit f, Stellung f.

Cape [keip] n. Kragenmantel m, Regenumhang m.

Cape [keip] n. Kap n.

Caper [kei'per] n. Kaper f; - sauce n. Kapernsosse f.

Caper [kei'per] n. Luftsprung m; vi. Luftsprünge machen.

Capital [ka'pi-tAl] n. Kapital n, Hauptstadt f, Anfangsbuchstabe m; a. vorzüglich, Leib und Leben betreffend; - letter n. grosser Anfangsbuchstabe; - punishment n. Todesstrafe f; - ship n. Grosskampfschiff m, Schlachtschiff n; -ism n. Kapitalismus m; -ist n. Kapitalist m; -ize vt. kapitalisieren.

Capitation [kæ-pi-tei'schAn] n. Zahlung nach Köpfen f; - tax n. Kopfsteuer f.

Capitulat'e [ka-pi'tju-leit] vi. kapitulieren; -ion n. Kapitulation f, Übergabe f.

Caprice [kA-prihss'] n. Laune f, Grille f. [launenhaft.

Capricious [kA-pri'schAss] a.

Capsize [kæp-ssais'] vt. umwerfen; i. umfallen, kentern (nav.).

Capstan [kæp'stAn] n. Haspel f, Ankerspill n. [sel f.

Capsule [kæp'sjuhl] n. Kapsel

Captain [kæp'tin] n. Hauptmann m (mil.), Kapitän m (boat), Rittmeister m (cavalry).

Caption [kæp'schAn] n. Beschriftung f, erklärender Text.

Captious [kæp'schAss] a. zänkisch.

Captivate [kæp'ti-weit] vt. fesseln, bezaubern.

Captiv'e [kæp'tiw] a. gefangen; n. der Gefangene m; - balloon n. Fesselballon m; -ity n. Gefangenschaft f.

Captor [kæp'ter] n. Fänger m, Kaper m (nav.).

Capture [kæp'tscher] n. Fangen n, Fang m, Einnahme f (town); vt. fangen, erobern.

Car [kahr] n. Wagen m, Kraftwagen m (aut.), Strassenbahnwagen m (tram); - driver n. Kraftfahrer m; -load n.

Wagenladung *f*; - mechanic *n*. Autoschlosser *m*.

Caramel [kæ'rA-mel] *n*. Karamel *m* (*material*), Karamelle *f* (*sweets*).

Carat [kæ'rAt] *n*. Karat *n*.

Caravan [kæ-rA-wan'] *n*. Karawane *f*, Wohnwagen *m*, motor- - *n*. Wohnmotorwagen *m*.

Caraway [kæ'rA-uei] *n*. Kümmel *m*. [bid *n*.

Carbide [kahr'baid] *n*. Karbid *n*.

Carbine [kahr'bin] *n*. Karabiner *m* (*mil.*); - pistol Kolbenpistole *f*.

Carbon [kahr'bAn] *n*. Kohlenstoff *m*; - copy *n*. Durchschlag *m*, Durchschrift *f*; - paper *n*. Durchdruckpapier *n*, Kohlepapier *n*.

Carbonate [kahr'bo-neit] *n*. kohlensaures Salz; - of soda *n*. Soda *f*.

Carbonic acid [kahr-bo'nik-æ'ssid] *n*. Kohlensäure *f*.

Carbonize [kahr'bo-nais] *vt*. verkohlen. [flasche *f*.

Carboy [kahr'beu] *n*. Korbflasche *f*.

Carbuncle [kahr'bAnkl] *n*. Karfunkel *m*, Blutgeschwür *n*.

Carburettor [kahr-bjA-re'ter] *n*. Vergaser *m* (*aut.*).

Carcass [kahr'kAss] *n*. Kadaver *m*, Leichnam *m*, Gerippe *n* (*ship*).

Card [kahrd] *n*. Karte *f*; pack of -s Spielkarten *f. pl*; visiting - *n*. Besuchs-, Visiten-karte *f*.

Card [kahrd] *n*. Kardätsche *f*; *vt*. kardätschen, krempeln; -ed yarn *n*. Streichgarn *n*.

Cardan [kahr'dAn] *n*. Kardan *n* (*tec.*); - joint *n*. Kardangelenk *n*; - shaft *n*. Kardanwelle *f*.

Cardboard [kahrd'bOrd] *n*. Pappe *f*; - box *n*. Schachtel *f*, Pappkasten *m*.

Cardigan [kahr'di-gAn] *n*. Schlupfjacke *f*, Wolljacke *f*.

Cardinal [kahr'di-nAl] *a*.

hauptsächlich, Haupt . . .; *n*. Kardinal *m*; - numbers *pl*. Kardinalzahlen *pl*.

Card index [kahrd' in-dex] *n*. Kartei *f*; - system *n*. Hollerithsystem *n*, -verfahren *n*.

Care [kehr] *n*. Sorge *f*, Vorsicht *f*, Pflege *f*; *vi*. sorgen, besorgt sein, sich kümmern.

Careen [kA-rihn'] *vt*. kielholen (*nav.*).

Career [kA-rihr] *n*. Laufbahn *f*.

Carefree [kehr'frih] *a*. sorgenlos, heiter.

Careful [kehr'ful] *a*. vorsichtig; -ness *n*. Vorsicht *f*, Sorgfalt *f*.

Careless [kehr'liss] *a*. sorglos, unvorsichtig; -ness *n*. Unvorsichtigkeit Nachlässigkeit *f*.

Caretaker [kehr'tei-ker] *n*. Wächter *m*, Wärter *m*, Hauswart *m*; - official *n*. Kastellan *m* (*mil.*); [ung *f*; *vt*. liebkosen.

Caress [kA-ress'] *n*. Liebkosen *n*; *vt*. liebkosen.

Caret [kæ'ret] *n*. Auslassungszeichen *n*. [abgehärmt.

Careworn [kehr'uOrn] *a*.

Cargo [kahr'go] *n*. Fracht *f*, Schiffsladung *f*; general - Stückgut *n*; - boat *n*. Lastdampfer *m*, Frachtschiff *n*.

Caricature [kæ'ri-kA-tjuhr] *n*. Karikatur *f*, Zerrbild *n*; *vt*. karikieren, übertreiben.

Carmine [kahr'min] *n*. Karmin *n*. [metzel *n*.

Carnage [kahr'nidzh] *n*. Gemetzel *n*.

Carnal [kahr-nAl] *a*. -ly *ad*. fleischlich.

Carnation [kahr-nei'schAn] *n*. Fleischfarbe *f*, Nelke *f*.

Carnival [kahr'ni-wAl] *n*. Karneval *m*, Fasching *m*.

Carnivorous [kahr-ni'wA-rAss] *a*. fleischfressend.

Carol [kæ'rAl] *n*. Jubellied *n*; *vi*. jubeln, singen; Christmas - *n*. *pl*. Weihnachtslieder *n. pl*.

Carouse [kA-raus'] *n*. Trinkgelage *n*; *vi*. zechen. [kritteln.

Carp [kahrp] *vi*. tadeln, be-

Carp [kahrp] n. Karpfen m.
Car park [kahr'pahrk] n. Wagenpark m.
Carpent'er [kahr'pin-ter] n. Zimmermann m; **-'s bench** n. Hobelbank f; **-'s rule** n. Zollstock m; **-y** n. Zimmerhandwerk n.
Carpet [kahr'pit] n. Teppich m; vt. mit Teppichen belegen, ausschelten (persons); **-ing** n. Teppichzeug n, Bedecken mit Teppichen n; **- slipper** n. gestickte Pantoffel; **- sweeper** n. Teppichkehrmaschine f.
Carriage [kæ'ridzh] n. Wagen m, Haltung f, Fahren n, Lafette f (mil.), Fracht f (com.); **- paid** a. frachtfrei, franko.
Carrier [kæ'ri-er] n. Fuhrmann m, Träger m, Spediteur m; **-borne aircraft** n. trägergestütztes Flugzeug, Decklandeflugzeug n; **-borne detachment** n. Trägertruppe f (mil.); **- pigeon** n. Brieftaube f; **- plane** n. Trägerflugzeug n.
Carrion [kæ'ridzh] n. Aas m.
Carrot [kæ'rΛt] n. Mohrrübe f.
Carry [kæ'ri] vt. tragen; **-ing agent** n. Spediteur m; **-ing trade** Transportgeschäft n; **- forward** übertragen; **- on** führen, fortsetzen; **- out** ausführen.
Car-stop [kahr'stop] n. Haltestelle f.
Cart [kahrt] n. Karren m, Wagen m; vt. in einem Karren fahren; **-age** n. Fahren n, Transportkosten pl; **-er** n. Fuhrmann m; **-horse** n. Karrengaul n, Zugpferd n; **-load** n. Wagenladung f, Fuhre f.
Cartel [kahr'tel] n. Kartell n, Ring m.
Cartilage [kahr'ti-lidzh] n. Knorpel m.
Cartography [kahr-to'grΛfi] n. Kartenzeichnen n.
Carton [kahr'tΛn] n. Schachtel f.
Cartoon [kahr-tuhn'] n. Kari-

katur f, Musterzeichnung f (com.).
Cartridge [kahr'tridzh] n. Kartusche f, Patrone f; **- belt** n. Patronengurt m; **- pouch** n. Patronentasche f.
Cartwright [kahrt'rait] n. Stellmacher m, Wagenschmied m.
Carve [kahrw] vt. tranchieren, schnitzen.
Carving [kahr'wing] n. Schnitzwerk n, Bildhauerarbeit f; **- fork** n. Vorlegegabel f; **- knife** n. Vorlegemesser n.
Cascade [kæss-keid'] n. Wasserfall m; **- bombing** n. Massenabwurf m (av.).
Case [keiss] n. Behälter m, Hülle f, Gehäuse n (tec.), Mantel m (bomb). [Umstand m
Case [keiss] n. Fall m, Sache f.
Casemate [keiss'meit] n. Kasematte f.
Casement [keiss'ment] n. Fensterflügel m; **- curtain** n. Scheibengardine f.
Cash [kæsch] n. Geld n, Bargeld n, Kasse f; vt. einkassieren, einwechseln, einlösen; **- allowance** n. Barabfindung f; **- book** n. Kassabuch f; **- box** Geldkasten m, Kasse f; **- in hand** n. Barbestand m; **- purchase** n. Barkauf m; **- register** n. Registrierkasse f, Kontrollkasse f; **- sale** Barverkauf m.
Cashew [ka-schuh'] n. Nierenbaum m, Cachou n (com.).
Cashier [ka-schihr'] n. Kassierer m; vt. absetzen, degradieren (mil.). [Kaschmir m.
Cashmere [kæsch'mihr] n.
Casing [kei'ssing] n. Verkleidung f, Überzug m, Gehäuse n, Futter m.
Cask [kæsk] n. Fass n, Tonne f.
Casket [kah'skit] n. Kästchen n.
Cast [kahst] n. Auswerfen n, Form f, Guss m; vt. auswerfen, giessen; **- iron** n. Gusseisen n.

Castaway [kahst'A-weï] n. Schiffbrüchiger m.

Caste [kahst] n. Kaste f.

Caster [kah'ster] n. Rolle f; – –sugar n. Streuzucker m.

Castigate [kah'sti-geit] vt. bestrafen; -ion n. Züchtigung f.

Casting [kah'sting] n. Giessen n, Guss m, Abguss m; – vote n. ausschlaggebende Stimme.

Castle [kahssl] n. Schloss n.

Cast-off [kast'of] n. weggeworfen, abgelegt; – things n. pl. Altsache f.

Castor [kah'ster] n. Streubüchse f, Laufrolle f.

Castor-oil [kah'ster-eul] n. Rizinusöl n.

Castrate [kæss-treit'] vt. kastrieren, verschneiden.

Casual [kæ'zhu-Al] a. -ly ad. zufällig.

Casualty [kæ'zhu-Al-ti] n. Unglücksfall m, Beschädigter m (mil.), Kranker m (mil.); -ies pl. Ausfall m (mil.), Verluste m. pl; – clearing station n. Feldlazarett n; – list n. Verlustliste f; – record n. Veränderungsbuch n (mil.).

Cat [kæt] n. Katze f.

Catalogue [kæ'tA-log] n. Katalog m, Verzeichnis n.

Catapult [kæ'tA-pAlt] n. Schleuder f, Flugzeugschleuder f (av.); – take-off n. Schleuderstart m (av.).

Cataract [kæ'tA-rækt] n. grosser Wasserfall, Star m (eye).

Catarrh [kA-tahr'] n. Katarrh m, Schnupfen m.

Catastrophe [kA-tæss'tro-fi] n. Katastrophe f.

Catch [kætsch] n. Fang m, Falle f, Haken m, Klinke f; vt. fangen, sich holen, erreichen, i. einander greifen; – cold sich erkälten; -ing a. angreifend.

Catchment area [kætsch'mAnt eh'ri-A] n. Stromgebiet n.

Catchword [kætsch'wArd] n. Stichwort n, Schlagwort n.

Catechism [kæ'ti-kism] n. Katechismus m.

Categor'ical [kæ-ti-go'ri-kAl] a. ausdrücklich, bestimmt; -y n. Kategorie f, Art f.

Cater [kei'ter] vi. Lebensmittel einkaufen, versorgen, verpflegen.

Caterer [kei'tA-rer] n. Lieferant m, Restaurateur m, Marketender m.

Caterpillar [kæ'ter-pi-ler] n. Raupe f; – chain n. Raupenkette f; – drive n. Gleisketten-, Raupen-antrieb m; – track n. Gleiskette f; – tracked a. raupengängig; – tractor n. Gleiskettenschlepper m, Artillerie-raupenschlepper m (mil.); – wheel Raupenrad n. [saite f.

Catgut [kæt'gAt] n. Darmsaite f.

Cathedral [kæ-thih'drAl] n. Dom m. [ode f.

Cathode [kæ'thoud] n. Kathode f. [ode f.

Catholic [kæ'tho-lik] a. katholisch; n. Katholik m; -ism n. Katholizismus m.

Cat's-eye [kæts'ai] n. Nachtsuchgerät n (av.). [zeug n.

Catspaw [kæts'pO] n. Werkzeug n.

Cattle [kætl] n. Vieh n; –breeding n. Viehzucht f.

Cauldron [kOl'drAn] n. grosser Kessel.

Cauliflower [ko'li-flau-er] n. Blumenkohl m.

Caulk [kOk] vt. abdichten, kalfatern (nav.).

Cause [kOs] n. Ursache f, Sache f; vt. verursachen; -less a. grundlos.

Causeway [kOs'uei] n. Damm m, Hochstrasse f, Kunststrasse f.

Caustic [kOss'tik] a. ätzend, beissend; – lime n. Ätzkalk m.

Cauterize [kO'tA-rais] vt. ausbrennen, ätzen.

Caution [kO'schAn] n. Vorsicht f, Warnung f; vt. warnen.

Cautious [kO'schAss] a. behutsam.

Cavalier [kæ-wA-lih'er] n. Ritter m, Reiter m; a. ritterlich, anmassend.

Cavalry [kæ'wAl-ri] n. Kavallerie f, Reiterei f; - captain n. Rittmeister m; - charge n. Attacke f; - corps n. Reitekorps n; - man n. Kavallerist m, Reiter m; - platoon n. Reitezug m (mil.); - school n. Reitschule f.

Cave, **Cavern** [keiw, kæ'wern] n. Höhle f; - in vi. einstürzen, klein beigeben (submit.). [hohl.]

Cavernous [kæ'wer-nAss] a.

Cavil [kæ'wil] vi. kritteln.

Cavity [kæ'wi-ti] n. Höhlung, Vertiefung f.

Caw [kO] vi. krächzen.

Cease [ssihss] vt. i. aufhören, einstellen; -less a. unaufhörlich.

Cedar [ssih'der] n. Zeder f.

Cede [ssihd] vt. abtreten, überlassen.

Ceiling [ssih'ling] n. Zimmerdecke f, Gipfelhöhe f (av.).

Celebrat'e [sse'li-breit] vt. feiern; -ed a. berühmt; -ion n. Feier f.

Celebrity [ssi-le'bri-ti] n. Berühmtheit f, berühmter Mensch. [schwindigkeit f.]

Celerity [ssi-le'ri-ti] n. Geschwindigkeit f.

Celery [sse'lA-ri] n. Sellerie f.

Celestial [sse-less'ti-Al] a. himmlisch.

Celiba'cy [sse'li-bA-ssi] n. Ehelosigkeit f; -te a. ehelos.

Cell [ssel] n. Zelle f, Element n (el.), Batterie f (el.).

Cellar [sse'ler] n. Keller m.

Cellist [tsche'list] n. (Violin-)-Cellist m. [Cello n.]

Cello [tsche'lou] n. (Violin-)-Cello n.

Cellu'lar [sse'liu-lA] a. zellig; - shirt n. Netzhemd n; - tissue n. Zellgewebe n; -loid n. Zelluloid n; -lose n. Zellstoff m.

Cement [ssi-ment'] n. Zement m; vt. zementieren, verkitten.

Cemetery [sse'mi-tA-ri] n. Kirchhof m. [Ehrenmal n.]

Cenotaph [sse'no-tahf] n.

Censor [ssen'sser] n. Zensor m, Tadler m; vt. überprüfen; -ship n. Zensur f; -ious a. tadelsüchtig.

Censure [ssen'scher] n. Tadel m, Verweis m, Zensur f; vt. tadeln. [zählung f.]

Census [ssen'ssAss] n. Volks-

Centenary [ssen-tih'nA-ri] n. Hundertjahrfeier f.

Centigrade [ssen'ti-greid] a. hundertteilig; - thermometer n. Celsius'sches Thermometer.

Centimetre [ssen'ti-mih'ter] n. Zentimeter m.

Central [ssen'trAl] a. zentral; - heating n. Zentral-, Warmwasserheizung f; -ization n. Zentralisation f.

Centre [ssen'ter] n. Mittelpunkt m; vt. konzentrieren; i. sich konzentrieren; - of gravity n. Schwerpunkt m; - forward n. Mittelstürmer m; - half n. Mittelläufer m; - line n. Mittellinie f; - of resistance n. Anklammerungspunkt m (mil.); - pin n. Kompassspinne f (nav.).

Centrifugal [ssen-tri'fju-gAl] a. zentrifugal; - safety device n. Klappsicherung f. [hundert n.]

Century [ssen'tju-ri] n. Jahr-

Cereals [ssih'ri-Als] n. pl. Getreide n, Mehlspeise f.

Ceremo'nial [sse-ri-mou'ni-Al] n. Zerimonial n; a. zeremoniell, förmlich; -ous a. feierlich.

Ceremony [sse'ri-mA-ni] n. Zeremonie f, Feierlichkeit f.

Certain [ssAr'tin] a. -ly ad. gewiss, bestimmt; -ty n. Gewissheit f.

Certificate [ssAr-ti'fi-kit] n. Zeugnis n; school leaving - n. Reifezeugnis n.

Certification [ssAr-ti-fi-kei′schAn] n. Bescheinigung f.

Certify [ssAr′ti-fai] vt. bescheinigen, bezeugen.

Cessation [sse-ssei′schAn] n. Aufhören n, Stillstand m.

Cession [sse′schAn] n. Abtretung f. [trittsgrube f.

Cesspool [ssess′puhl] n. Abtrittsgrube f.

Chafe [tscheif] vt. reiben; i. in Zorn geraten.

Chaff [tschaff] n. Häcksel m, Spreu f; vt. necken, aufziehen.

Chaffer [tscha′fer] vi. schachern, handeln. [druss m.

Chagrin [schA-grihn′] n. Verdruss m.

Chain [tschein] n. Kette f; vt. anketten, fesseln; mountain - n. Bergkette f; - cable n. Ankerkette f; - drive n. Kettenantrieb m; - store n. Kettengeschäft n.

Chair [tschehr] n. Stuhl m, Sitz m, Vorsitz m; -man n. der Vorsitzende, Präsident m.

Chalice [tscha′liss] n. Kelch m.

Chalk [tschok] n. Kreide f; vt. mit Kreide anschreiben, bezeichnen; -s n. pl. Buntstifte m. pl; -y a. kreidig.

Challenge [tscha′linzh] n. Aufforderung f, Herausforderung f, Anrufung f (sentry); vt. herausfordern, auffordern, anrufen.

Chamber [tscheim′ber] n. Kammer f; -maid Kammermädchen n; - of commerce Wirtschaftskammer f; - utensil Nachttopf m; -lain n. Kammerherr m. [tscheim′ber]

Chameleon [kA-mih′li-An] n. Chamäleon n.

Chamfer [tscham′fer] vt. abschrägen. [se f.

Chamois [scha′muo] n. Gemse f.

Champagne [scham-pein′] n. Champagner m, Schaumwein m, Sekt m.

Champion [tscham′pi-An] n. Verfechter m, Meister m; vt. verfechten; -ship n. Verfechtung f, Meisterschaft f.

Chance [tschAnss] n. Zufall m, Gelegenheit f, Möglichkeit f; vt. wagen; i. sich ereignen; a. zufällig.

Chancel [tschahn′ssil] n. Altarplatz m, Chor n.

Chancellor [tschahn′ssi-ler] n. Kanzler m.

Chancery [tschahn′ssA-ri] n. Kanzleigericht n, Kanzlei f.

Chandelier [schæn′dA-lier] n. Kronleuchter m.

Chandler [tschænd′ler] n. Lichtzieher m, Händler m.

Change [tscheinzh] n. Änderung f, Tausch m, Kleingeld n; vt. verändern, tauschen, wechseln; i. sich ändern, umsteigen (train); - course Kurs ändern; - gear einen anderen Gang nehmen, schalten (aut.); - weather Umschlag m.

Changeable [tscheinzh′Abl] a. veränderlich; -ness n. Veränderlichkeit f.

Changeless [tscheinzh′less] a. unveränderlich.

Channel [tscha′nl] n. Kanal m, Weg m, Fahrwasser n (in river, etc.); administrative -s Verwaltungsweg m; official -s pl. Dienstweg m, Instanzenweg m. [vt. besingen.

Chant [tschahnt] n. Gesang m;

Chaos [kei′oss] n. Chaos n, Unordnung f.

Chaotic [kei-o′tik] a. chaotisch, ungeordnet.

Chap [tschæp] n. Riss m, Hautschrunde f; vt. aufspringen.

Chap [tschæp] n. Bursche m, Kerl m. [f, Gotteshaus n

Chapel [tscha′pl] n. Kapelle f.

Chaperon [scha′pA-roun] n. Anstandsdame f.

Chaplain [tschæp′lin] n. Kaplan m; army - Feldgeistlicher m.

Chaplet [tschæp′lit] n. Kranz m. [tel m.

Chapter [tschæp′ter] n. Kapitel m.

Char [tschahr] vt. verkohlen.

Charabanc [schæ'rA-bAng] n. Verkehrs-, Rundfahrt-auto n.

Character [kæ'rAk-ter] n. Charakter m, Art f; -ize vt. charakterisieren, beschreiben.

Characteristic [kæ-rAk-tA-riss'tik] a. eigentümlich, bezeichnend, typisch; n. Merkmal n; - curve n. Kennlinie f; -s pl. Kennung f (morse).

Charade [schA-rahd'] n. Silbenrätsel n.

Charcoal [tschahr'koul] n. Holzkohle f; - pencil n. Reisskohle f.

Charge [tschahrdzh] n. Ladung f, Verwahrung f, Preis m, Beschuldigung f, Angriff m; vt. beladen, laden, anschreiben, beschuldigen, angreifen; i. einen Angriff machen; -able a. verantwortlich, zuzuschreiben; -r n. Offizierspferd n (horse), Patronenrahmen m, Ladestreifen m (mil.); -s n. pl. Unkosten pl.

Charging station [tschahr'dzhing-stei'schAn] n. Ladestelle f (el.). [sam.

Charily [tschæ'ri-li] a. behut-

Charitable [tschæ'ri-tAbl] a. wohltätig, nachsichtig; - organization n. Wohltätigkeitsverein m.

Charity [tschæ'ri-ti] n. Wohltätigkeit f, Hilfswerk n, Liebe f.

Charlatan [schahr'lA-tAn] n. Schwindler m, Marktschreier m, Kurpfuscher m.

Charm [tschahrm] n. Zaubermittel n, Zauber m; vt. bezaubern; -ing a. bezaubernd, entzückend.

Chart [tschahrt] n. Karte f, Seekarte f (nav.), Tafel f; vt. auf einer Karte verzeichnen; --room n. Navigationsraum m (nav.).

Charter [tschahr'ter] n. Urkunde f, Freibrief m, Schiffsmiete f; vt. mieten, befrachten

(ship): - party n. Verpachtungsvertrag m.

Charwoman [tschahr'uumAn] n. Arbeitsfrau f, Putzfrau f, Scheuerfrau f.

Chary [tsche'ri] a. behutsam.

Chase [tscheiss] n. Jagd f; vt. jagen, verfolgen; -r n. Jäger m; submarine -r Unterseebootsjäger m.

Chasm [kæsm] n. Kluft f.

Chassis [schæ'ssi] n. Fahrgestell n, Untergestell n (aut.).

Chaste [tscheist] a. keusch.

Chasten, Chastise [tscheissn, tschæ-stais'] vt. züchtigen.

Chastisement [tschæss'tismAnt] n. Züchtigung f.

Chastity [tschæss'ti-ti] n. Keuschheit f. [vi. plaudern.

Chat [tschæt] n. Geplauder n;

Chattel(s) [tschætls] n. Habe f.

Chatter [tschæ'ter] n. Geschwätz n; vi. plappern; -ing n. Geplapper n.

Chatty [tschæ'ti] a. geschwätzig, gesprächig.

Chauffeur [schou'fer] n. Kraftwagenführer m.

Cheap [tschihp] a. -ly ad. wohlfeil, gering, billig; -en vt. herabsetzen, billiger machen; -jack n. Marktschreier m; -ness n. Wohlfeilheit f, Billigkeit f.

Cheat [tschiht] n. Betrüger m; vt. betrügen; -ing n. Betrugerei f.

Check [tschek] n. Einhalt m: Kontrazettel m, Schach m, (chess), Schlappe f (mil.); vt. einhalten, prüfen, kontrollieren; -ing list n. Kontroll-, Überwachungsliste f; - lever n. Sperrhebel m; - stamp n. Prüfstempel m. [er m.

Checker [tsche'ker] n. Prüfer m.

Checker [tsche'ker] vt. karieren; -ed gewürfelt, kariert, bunt.

Checkmate [tschek-meit'] n. Schachmatt n; vt. matt setzen, schlagen.

Cheek [tschihk] n. Backe f. Wange f, Unverschämtheit f.

Cheer [tschihr] n. Beifallsruf m, Freudenruf m, Bewirtung f, Speise f; vt. laut begrüssen, ermutigen, anspornen; i. Vivat rufen, jauchzen; **-ful** a. munter; **-fulness** n. Munterkeit f; **-ing** a. ermunternd; **-io** int. auf Wiedersehen!; **-less** a. traurig, trostlos; **-y** a. heiter.

Cheese [tschihs] n. Käse m.

Chemical [ke'mikl] a. chemisch; **-warfare** n. Gaskampf m, Gaseinsatz m; **-warfare squad** n. Nebeltruppe f; **-works** n. pl. chemische Fabrik; **-s** n. pl. Chemikalien pl.

Chemise [schA-mihs'] n. Frauenhemd n.

Chemist [ke'mist] n. Chemiker m, Apotheker m, Drogist m; **-'s shop** Apotheke f, Drogerie f; **-ry** n. Chemie f.

Cheque [tschek] n. Scheck m; crossed **-** Verrechnungsscheck m; **-book** n. Scheckbuch n; **-form** n. Scheckformular m.

Chequer [tsche'ker] n. Karomuster n; vt. karieren; **-ed** a. kariert, gewürfelt, bewegt (life); [voll behandeln, hegen.

Cherish [tsche'rissh] vt. liebe-

Cheroot [tsche'ruht] n. Manillazigarre f, Stumpe f.

Cherry [tsche'ri] n. Kirsche f; **-brandy** n. Kirsch m; **-tree** n. Kirschbaum m. [ub m.

Cherub [tsche'rAb] n. Cher-

Chess [tschess] n. Schachspiel n; **-board** n. Schachbrett n; **-man** n. Schachfigur f.

Chest [tschest] n. Kiste f, Brust f.; **-of drawers** n. Kommode f. [fihld] n. Sofa n.

Chesterfield [tsche'ster-

Chestnut [tschess'nAt] n. Kastanie f; **-tree** n. Kastanienbaum m.

Chevron [schew'rAn] n. Winkel m (mil.), Sparren m (device).

Chew [tschuh] vt. kauen; **-the cud** wiederkauen; **-ing gum** n. Kaugummi m; **-ing tobacco** n. **-en pox** n. Windpocken f.

Chick, Chicken [tschi'kin] n. Küchlein n, Hühnchen n; **-en pox** n. Windpocken f.

Chicory [tschi'kA-ri] n. Zichorie f, Wegwarte f.

Chide [tschaid] vt. schelten.

Chief [tschihf] a. **-ly** ad. höchst, hauptsächlich; n. Haupt n, Chef m; **-petty officer** n. Oberbootmann m (nav.); **-quarter master** n. Oberquartiermeister m (mil.); **-of staff** n. Chef des Stabes m (mil.). [Frostbeule f.

Chilblain [tschil'blein] n. Frost-

Child [tschaild] n. Kind n; **-birth** n. Niederkunft f; **-hood** n. Kindheit f; **-ish** a. kindisch; **-less** a. kinderlos; **-like** a. kindlich.

Chill [tschil] n. Erkältung f; a. frostig; vt. durchkälten, mutlos machen; i. a. frostig, kältlich.

Chime [tschaim] n. Glockenspiel n; vt. läuten; i. zusammenstimmen.

Chimera [kai-mih'rA] n. Schreckbild n, Hirngespinst n; **-ical** a. chimärisch, eingebildet.

Chimney [tschim'ni] n. Schornstein m, Kamin m; **-sweep** n. Schornsteinfeger m.

Chimpanzee [tschim'pAn-sih] n. Schimpanse m.

Chin [tschin] n. Kinn n.

China [tschai'nA] n. Porzellan n; **-shop** n. Porzellanladen m; **-ware** n. Porzellan n, feines Steingut. [Ritze f.

Chink [tschingk] n. Spalte f,

Chin-strap [tschin'strap] n. Sturmriemen m.

Chintz [tschints] n. Zitz m.

Chip [tschip] n. Splitter m, Schnitzel n; vt. abbrechen, klein schneiden; i. abbrechen; **-s, -ped potatoes** n. pl. Bratkartoffeln f. pl.

Chiropody [kai-ro'po-di] *n.*
Hand- und Fusspflege *f.*

Chirp [tschArp] *vi.* zirpen.

Chisel [tschi'sl] *n.* Meissel *m,*
Betel *m;* – *vt.* meisseln.

Chit [tschit] *n.* Zettel *m,*
Schein *m.*

Chivalr'ous [schi'wAl-rAss]
ritterlich; – **y** *n.* Ritterlich-
keit *f.* [lauch *m.*

Chive [tschaiw] *n.* Schnitt-

Chlorate [klO'rit] *n.* Chlorat
n; – of potash chlorsaures Kali.

Chloride [klO'raid] *n.* Chlor-
verbindung *f;* – of lime *n.*
Chlorkalk *m;* – of potassium *n.*
Chlorkalium *n.*

Chlorine [klo'rin] *n.* Chlor *n.*

Chloroform [klO'ro-fOrm]
Chloroform *n;* *vt.* chloroformieren, einschläfern.

Chocolate [tscho'ko-lAt] *n.*
Schokolade *f;* – creams *n. pl.*
Pralinés *n. pl.*

Choice [tscheuss] *n.* Wahl *f,*
Auswahl *f;* – *a.* auserlesen.

Choir [kuair] *n.* Sängerchor *m;*
– conductor *n.* Singleiter *m.*

Chok'e [tschouk] *n.* Drossel-
spule *f* (*el.*), Luftdüse *f,* Luft-
regulierknopf *m;* *vt. i.* erstick-
en, abdrosseln (*tec.*); – **ing** gas
n. ersticksender Kampfstoff

Cholera [ko'lA-rA] *n.* Cholera *f.* [nig, hitzig.

Choleric [ko-le'rik] *a.* jähzor-

Choose [tschuhs] *vt.* wählen,
auswählen.

Chop [tschop] *n.* Kotelett *n,*
Fleischschnitte *f;* *vt.* zerhack-
en; – **ped** straw Häcksel *m;*
– **house** *n.* Speisehaus *n.*

Chopper [tschop'er] *n.* Hack-
beil *n.*

Chopstick [tschop'stik] *n.*
Ess-stäbchen *n.*

Chord [kOrd] *n.* Saite *f,* Akkord *m* (*music*), Sehne *f*
(*maths.*). [Kehrreim *m.*

Chorus [kO'rAss] *n.* Chor *m.*

Chosen [tschousn] *a.* auser-
wählt, auserlesen.

Christen [krissn] *vt.* (in der
Taufe) benennen, taufen.

Christian [kriss'tiAn] *a.*
christlich; – **name** *n.* Vorname
m; – ity *n.* Christentum *n.*

Christmas [kriss'mAss] *n.*
Weihnachten *pl;* – **box** *n.* Weih-
nachtsgeschenk *n;* – **card** *n.*
Weihnachtskarte *f;* – **Day** *n.*
Christtag *m,* erster Weih-
nachtstag *m;* – **Eve** *n.* heiliger
Abend; – **tree** *n.* Weihnachts-
baum *m.* [chromatisch.

Chromatic [kro-mæ'tik] *a.*

Chromium [krou'mi-Am]
Chrom *n;* – **plated** *a.* verchromt. [isch, langwierig.

Chronic [kro'nik] *a.* chron-

Chronicle [kro'nikl] *n.* Chronik *f;* *vt.* aufzeichnen.

Chronological [kro-no-lo'
dzhikl] *a.* chronologisch.

Chronology [kro-no'lo-dzhi]
n. Zeitrechnung *f.*

Chronometer [kro-no'mi-ter]
n. Chronometer *m,* Taktmesser *m.*

Chum [tschAm] *n.* Kamerad *m.*

Chunk [tschAngk] *n.* kurzes,
dickes Stück, Masse *f.*

Church [tschArtsch] *n.* Kirche
f; – **yard** *n.* Kirchhof *m.*

Churl [tschArl] *n.* Grobian *m;*
– **ish** *a.* mürrisch. [*n;* *vt.* buttern.

Churn [tschArn] *n.* Butterfass

Cider [ssai'der] *n.* Apfelwein *m.*

Cigar [ssigahr'] *n.* Zigarre *f;*
– **box** *n.* Zigarrenkiste *f;* – **case**
n. Zigarrentasche *f;* – **cutter** *n.*
Zigarrenabschneider *m;* – **merchant** *n.* Zigarrenhändler *m.*

Cigarette [ssi-gA-ret'] *n.* Zigarette *f;* – **case** *n.* Zigaretten-
etui *n;* – **holder** *n.* Zigaretten-
spitze *f;* – **lighter** *n.* Zigaretten-
anzünder *m.*

Cinder [ssin'der] *n.* ausge-
glühte Kohle; – **track** *n.* Asch-
enbahn *f.*

Cine-camera [ssi'ni-kæ'mA-
rA] *n.* Bildkamera *f,* Schmal-
kamera *f* (*miniature*).

Cine-film [ssi'ni-film] n. Kinofilm m.

Cinema, Cinematograph [ssi'ni-mA, ssi-ni-mæ'to-grahf] n. Kinematograph m, Lichtspieltheater n, Kino n; -goer n. Kinobesucher m; - screen n. Bildwand f.

Cine-photography [ssi'nifo-to'grA-fi] n. Kinematographie f.

Cinnamon [ssi'nA-mAn] n. Zimt m.

Cipher [ssai'fer] n. Ziffer f, Null f, Chiffre f; - code Chiffreschlüssel m; - machine n. Chiffriermachine f.

Circle [ssArkl] n. Kreis m; vt. einschliessen, umgeben.

Circuit [ssAr'kit] n. Gerichtsbezirk m (law), Stromkreis m (el.), Kreislauf m (tec.); - breaker n. Abschalter m, Unterbrecher m (el.); - closer n. Einschalter m (el.).

Circuitous [ssAr-kju'i-tAss] a. weitschweifig.

Circular [ssAr'kju-lAr] a. kreisförmig; n. Zirkular n; - railway n. Ringbahn f; - ticket n. Rundreisefahrkarte f; - tour n. Rundreise f.

Circularize [ssAr'kju-lA-rais] vt. durch Rundschreiben benachrichtigen.

Circulat'e [ssAr'kju-leit] vt. in Umlauf bringen; i. im Umlauf sein; -ing system n. Kreislauf m (anat.); -ion n. Umlauf m, Verbreitung f; coins in - im Kurs befindliche Münzen f. pl; out of - ausser Kurs.

Circumference [ssAr-kAm'fA-rAnss] n. Kreisumfang m, Umkreis m.

Circumflex [ssAr'kAm-flex] n. Dehnungszeichen n.

Circumlocution [ssAr-kAm-lo-kju'schAn] n. Umschreibung f.

Circumscribe [ssAr'kAm-skraib] vt. beschränken.

Circumspect [ssAr'kAm-spekt] a. umsichtig.

Circumspection [ssAr'kAm-spek'schAn] n. Vorsicht f.

Circumstan'ce [ssAr'kAm-stænss] n. Umstand m; -tial a. umständlich; -tial evidence n. Indizienbeweis m; -tiate vt. den Beweis erbringen für.

Circumvent [ssAr-kAm-went'] vt. überlisten; -ion n. Überlistung f, Umgehen n.

Circus [ssAr'kAss] n. Zirkus m, Platz m (in London).

Cistern [ssi'stern] n. Wasserbehälter m. [feste f, Burg f.

Citadel [ssi'tAdl] n. Stadt-

Citation [ssai-tei'schAn] n. schriftliche Vorladung, Zitat n.

Cite [ssait] vt. vorladen (law), anführen (quote).

Citizen [ssi'tisn] n. Bürger m; -ship n. Bürgerrecht n, Staatszugehörigkeit f; certificate of -ship n. Ausweis-Pass m, Heimatschein m (Austria).

Citron [ssi'trAn] n. Zitrone f.

City [ssi'ti] n. Stadt f, Altstadt f, Stadtzentrum n; - man n. (Londoner) Geschäftsmann m.

Civic [ssi'wik] a. bürgerlich.

Civil [ssi'wil] a. zivil, höflich; - airfield n. Verkehrsflugzeughafen m; - defence n. Luftschutz m; - servant n. Beamter m, Reichsangestellter m; - service n. Verwaltungsdienst m; - war n. Bürgerkrieg m.

Civilian [ssi-wil'jAn] n. Zivilist m; - population n. Zivilbevölkerung f.

Civility [ssi-wi'li-ti] n. Höflichkeit f.

Civilization [ssi-wi-lai-sei'schAn] n. Zivilisation f, Kultur f. [ieren, verfeinern.

Civilize [ssi'wi-lais] vt. zivilis-

Claim [kleim] n. Anspruch m, Schadensforderung f, Mutung f (mining); vt. in Anspruch nehmen, behaupten, fordern; -ant n. Beanspruchende(r) m.

Clamber [klæm'ber] *vi.* klettern.

Clammy [klæ'mi] *a.* klebrig.

Clamo'ur [klæ'mer] *n.* Geschrei *n.*, Lärm *m.*; *vi.* schreien; -rous *a.* lärmend.

Clamp [klæmp] *n.* Klemme *f.*, Zwinge *f.*, Klammer *f.*, Leiste *f.*, Klampe *f.*; *vt.* mit Klammern befestigen; -ing lever *n.* Klemmhebel *m* (*tec.*); -ing ring *n.* Klemmring *m*; -ing screw *n.* Klemmschraube *f* (*camera*).

Clan [klæn] *n.* Sippe *f.*, Stamm *m.*

Clandestine [klæn-dess'tin] *a.* heimlich.

Clang [klæng] *n.* Klang *m*, Schall *m.*   [*vi.* rasseln.

Clank [klængk] *n.* Gerassel *n*;

Clap [klæp] *n.* Knall *m*, Schlag *m*; *vt.* klatschen, schlagen; *i.* klatschen; -trap *n.* Unsinn *m*, Windbeutelei *f.*

Claret [klæ'rAt] *n.* Rotwein *m.*

Clarification [klæ-ri-fi-kei'schAn] *n.* Abklärung *f.*

Clarify [klæ'ri-fai] *vt.* abklären, aufklären.

Clarionet [klæ-ri-o-net'] *n.* Klarinette *f.*   [heit *f.*

Clarity [klæ'ri-ti] *n.* Klarheit *f.*

Clash [klæsch] *n.* Zusammenstossen *n*; *vi.* zusammenstossen, im Widerstreit stehen.

Clasp [klæsp] *n.* Klammer *f.*, Haspe *f.*, Haken *m*, Schnalle *f.*; *vt.* einhaken, festhalten, zuschnallen.

Class [klahss] *n.* Klasse *f.*; *vt.* in eine bestimmte Klasse setzen; -conscious *a.* klassenbewusst; -room Klassenzimmer *n*

Classic [klæ'ssik] *n.* Klassiker *m*; -al *a.* klassisch.

Classification [klæ-ssi-fi-kei'schAn] *n.* Einteilung *f.*, Klassenordnung *f.*

Classify [klæ'ssi-fai] *vt.* klassifizieren.

Clatter [klæ'ter] *n.* Getrappel *n*; *vi.* klappern, rasseln.

Clause [klOs] *n.* Satz *m.*, Klausel *f.*

Claw [klO] *n.* Klaue *f.*, Kralle *f.*; *vt.* kratzen.

Clay [klei] *n.* Ton *m*, Lehm *m*; - modelling *n.* Kneten mit Ton *n*; - pigeon *n.* Tontaube *f.*, Wurftaube *f*; - pipe Tonpfeife *f.*

Clayey [klei'i] *a.* tonig.

Clean [klihn] *a.* rein, sauber; *vt.* reinigen, putzen; - -shaven *a.* glatt rasiert; -er *n.* Arbeitsfrau *f.*, Scheuerfrau *f.*, Putzfrau *f.*   [Reinlichkeit *f.*

Cleanliness [klen'li-ness] *n.*

Cleanly [klen'li] *a.* reinliche.

Cleanness [klihn'ness] *n.* Sauberkeit *f.*   [*n.* Reiniger *m.*

Cleanse [klens] *vt.* reinigen; - *n.* Reiniger *m.*

Clear [klihr] *a.* -ly *ad.* klar, rein; *vt.* klar machen, lichten, aufräumen; - out *v.* ausräumen; - up *v.* aufklären.

Clearance [klih'rAnss] *n.* Ausräumung *f.*, Ausverkauf *m* (*com.*), Bereinigung *f* (*stocks*), Verzollung *f* (*ship*) Spielraum *m* (*tec.*); - circular *n.* Laufzettel *m*; -list *n.* Abfertigungsliste *f.*; - sale *n.* Ausverkauf *m* (*com.*).

Clearing [klih'ring] *n.* Lichtung *f*; -house *n.* Abrechnungsstelle *f.*   [tung *f.*

Cleavage [klih'widzh] *n.* Spaltung *f.*

Cleave [klihw] *vt* spalten; -r *n.* Fleischerbeil *n*, Beil *n*, Hackmesser *n.*

Cleave [klihw] *vi.* kleben.

Clef [klef] *n.* (Noten-)Schlüssel *m*.   [*f.*, Keilschnitt *m.*

Cleft [kleft] *n.* Spalte *f.*, Kluft *f.*

Clemency [kle'mAn-ssi] *n.* Gnade *f.*, Schonung *f.*

Clench [klensch] *vt.* fest zusammenpressen, ballen (*fist*).

Clergy [klAr'dzhi] *n.* Geistlichkeit *f*; -man *n.* der Geistliche.

Clerical [kle'ri-kAl] *a.* schriftlich, geistlich; - error *n.*

Schreibfehler *m*; – **staff** *n*. Geschäftspersonal *n*. – **work** *n*. Schreib-, Kontorarbeit *f*.

Clerk [klahrk] *n*. Schreiber *m*, Kommis *m*, Bankangestellte(r) *m*, Buchhalter *m*.

Clever [kle'wer] *a*. -ly *ad*. klug, geschickt, geistreich; -ness *n*. Klugheit *f*, Geschicklichkeit *f*.

Click [klik] *n*. Ticken *n*, Klinke *f*, Sperrhebel *m*, Sperrkegel *m* (*tec.*); *vi*. klicken; -**ing press** *n*. Stanzmaschine *f*.

Client [klai'Ant] *n*. Klient *m*, Kunde *m*. [küste.

Cliff [klif] *n*. Klippe *f*, Steil-

Climate [klai'mit] *n*. Klima *n*; -ic *a*. klimatisch; -ic conditions *n*. *pl*. Witterungsverhältnisse *n*. *pl*.

Climax [klai'max] *n*. Klimax *f*.

Climb [klaim] *vt*. erklimmen, besteigen; *i*. klettern; -er *n*. Kletterer *m*, Streber *m*.

Clinch [klinsch] *vt*. verklinken, abschliessen; *n*. Niete *f* (*tec.*), Clinch *m*, Nahkampf *m* (*boxing*).

Cling [kling] *vi*. anhängen, ankleben; -ing *a*. anhänglich.

Clinic [kli'nik] *n*. Klinik *f*; -al *a*. klinisch; -al thermometer *n*. Fieberthermometer *n*.

Clinker [kling'ker] *n*. Klinker *m*, verglaster Backstein; -built *a*. klinkergebaut; – **boat** *n*. Klinkerboot *n*.

Clip [klip] *vt*. scheren, beschneiden; – *n*. Schafschur *f*.

Clip [klip] *n*. Zwicke *f*, Briefhalter *m*, Klammer *f*.

Clipper [kli'per] *n*. Schnellsegler *m* (*nav.*); -s *pl*. Schere *f*, elektrische Haarschneidemaschine *f*.

Clique [klihk] *n*. Clique *f*, Sippschaft *f*.

Cloak [klouk] *n*. Mantel *m*; *vt*. bemänteln; – **room** *n*. Garderobe *f*, Gepäckannahme *f* (*rl.*), Toilette *f*.

Clock [klok] *n*. Uhr *f*; – **face** *n*.

Zifferblatt *n*; -**maker** *n*. Uhrmacher *m*; -**wise** *ad*. mit dem Uhrlauf, mul; -**work** *n*. Uhrwerk *n*. [Scholle *f*.

Clod [klod] *n*. Erdkloss *m*,

Clog [klog] *n*. Holzschuh *m*, Hemmschuh *m* (*tec.*); *vt*. hemmen, verstopfen.

Cloister [kleu'ster] *n*. Kloster *n*, Kreuzgang *m*.

Close [klouss] *n*. Gehäge *n*; *a*. verschlossen, knapp, schwül, gedrängt, dicht, genau; *ad*. geschlossen, knapp, verborgen, dicht; [klouss] *n*. Schluss *m*. *vt*. schliessen, verschliessen, abschliessen; *i*. sich schliessen; -**ing time** *n*. Ladenschluss *m* (*shop*), Polizeistunde *f* (*inn*). -**e combat** *n*. Nahkampf *m* (*av.*, *etc.*); -**e fitting** *a*. eng anschliessend; -**e reconnaissance** *n*. Nahaufnahme *f* (*av.*). -**e support unit** *n*. Nahkampfgruppe *f*.

Closeness [klouss'ness] *n*. Verschlossenheit *f*, Verschwiegenheit *f*, Schwüle, Nähe *f*.

Close range [klouss'reinzh] *n*. Nahkampf *m*; -**weapons** *n*. *pl*. Nahkampfmittel *n*. *pl*. (*mil.*).

Closet [klo'sit] *n*. Kabinett *n*, Abort *m*.

Close-up [klouss'Ap] *n*. Nahaufnahme *f*, Grossaufnahme *f* (*film*).

Closure [klou'zhAr] *n*. Verschliessen *n*, Schluss *m*.

Clot [klot] *n*. Klümpchen *n*; *vi*. gerinnen.

Cloth [kloth] *n*. Tuch *n*.

Clothe [kloudh] *vt*. kleiden, bekleiden.

Clothes [kloudhs] *n*. *pl*. Kleider *pl*; – **brush** *n*. Kleiderbürste *f*; – **peg** *n*. Wäscheklammer *f*; – **prop** *n*. Waschestütze *f*.

Clothier [klou'dhi-er] *n*. Kleiderhändler *m*.

Clothing [klou'dhing] *n*. Kleidung *f*; – **card** *n*. Kleiderkarte *f*.

Cloud [klaud] n. Wolke f; vt. bewölken; – gas n. Luftkampfstoff m; -less a. wolkenlos; -y a. wolkig, bewölkt.

Clove [klouv] n. Gewürznelke f.

Clover [klou'wer] n. Klee m.

Clown [klaun] n. Clown m, Hanswurst m, Grobian m; -ish a. bäuerisch, roh.

Cloy [kleu] vt. übersättigen.

Club [klAb] n. Klub m, küttel m, Klub m, Schläger m (golf), Kreuz n (cards); Indian –, Keule f; – officers' – n. Offiziersheim n, Kasino n; -house n. Klubhaus n, Vereins-, Klub-lokal n.

Cluck [klAk] vi. glucken.

Clue [kluh] n. Leitfaden m, Anhaltspunkt m, Spur f.

Clump [klAmp] n. Klumpen m, Gruppe f (trees).

Clumsiness [klAm'si-ness] n. Plumpheit f, Unbeholfenheit f.

Clumsy [klAm'si] a. **Clumsily** ad. plump, unbeholfen.

Cluster [klA'ster] n. Traube f, Gruppe f, Haufen m; vi. sich sammeln, häufen.

Clutch [klAtsch] n. Griff m, Kupplung f (aut. etc.); vt. greifen; – pedal n. Kupplungstritt m.

Coach [koutsch] n. Kutsche f, Einpauker m, Sportlehrkraft f, Personenwagen m (rl.); – body n. Wagenkasten m; – box n. Bock m; vt. einpauken (study), trainieren (sport); -man n. Kutscher m; -work n. Karosse f, Karosserie f (aut. etc.).

Coagulate [ko-æ'gju-leit] vi. gerinnen; -ion n. Gerinnung f.

Coal [koul] n. Kohle f; vi. Kohlen einnehmen; -field n. Kohlenfeld n, Kohlenrevier n; – merchant n. Kohlenhändler m; --mine n. Kohlenbergwerk n; --mining n. Kohlenbergbau m; -pit n. Kohlengrube f.

Coalesce [ko-A-less'] vi. sich vereinigen.

Coalition [ko-A-lischn'] n. Vereinigung f, Koalition f, Bund m.

Coarse [kOrss] a. grob, roh; -ness n. Grobheit f, Roheit f.

Coast [koust] n. Küste f.

Coastal [kou'stAl] a. Küsten-, –: approaches n. pl. Küstenvorfeld n; – command n. Kommando zur See n; – defence n. Küstenwehr n, -sicherung f; – defence vessel n. Sicherungsschiff n; – patrol n. Küstenwacht f; – vessel n. Küstenfahrzeug n.

Coaster [kou'ster] n. Küstenfahrer m; – hub n. Freilaufnabe f.

Coastguard [koust'gahrd] n. Küstenwächter m; – station n. Küstenwache f.

Coastline [koust'lain] n. Küstenlinie f, Küstenstrich m.

Coat [kout] n. Rock m, Haut f, Überzug m; vt. überstreichen, belegen; – of arms n. Wappen n; -hanger n. Kleiderbügel m; -ing n. Überzug m, Anstrich m.

Coax [koux] vt. beschwatzen, anlocken.

Cob [kob] n. kleines Pferd.

Cobalt [kou'bolt] n. Kobalt m.

Cobble [kobl] n. Kiesel m.

Cobble [kobl] vt. flicken; -r n. Schuhflicker m, Schuhmacher m; -r's thread n. Pechdraht m.

Co-belligeren'cy [kou'be-li'dzhA-rAn-ssi] n. Mitkriegsführung f; –t n. Mitkriegsführende(r) m. [webe n.

Cobweb [kob'ueb] n. Spinnge-

Cochineal [kotsch'i-nihl] n. Koschenille f.

Cock [kok] n. Hahn m; vt. den Hahn spannen; -ed hat n. Dreimaster m, Zweispitz m (nav.). [arde f.

Cockade [ko-keid'] n. Kok-

Cockatoo [ko-kA-tuh'] n. Kakadu m.

Cockchafer [kok'tschei'fer] n. Maikäfer m.

[Maiskolben m.

Cockerel [ko'kA-ril] n. junger Hahn.
Cockle [kokl] n. Herzmuschel f.
Cockpit [kok'pit] n. Führersitz m, Kanzel f (av.).
Cockroach [kok'routsch] n. Küchenschabe f.
Cock-sure [kok'schuhr] a. ganz sicher, anmassend.
Cocktail [kok'teil] n. Cocktail m; - mixer n. Getränkemischer m.
Cocoa [kou'kou] n. Kakao m; - nut n. Kokosnuss f; -nut tree n. Kokospalme f.
Cod [kod] n. Kabeljau m; -liver oil n. Lebertran m.
Coddle [kodl] vt. verweichlichen, verhätscheln.
Code [koud] n. Gesetzbuch n, Depeschenschlüssel m; vt. chiffrieren; commercial - n. Handelsgesetzbuch n; morse - n. Morseschrift f; - name n. Deckname m; - number n. Tarnzahl f; - of signals n. Signalbuch n (nav.); - table n. Tarntafel f; - telegram n. Geheimtelegramm n; - word n. Schlüsselwort n.
Codicil [kou'di-ssil] n. Kodizill n.
Codify [kou'di-fal] vt. kodifizieren.
Coerce [ko-Arss] vt. zwingen; -ion n. Zwang m, Nötigung f; -ive a. zwingend, Zwangs . . .; -ive policy n. Zwangspolitik f.
Coextensive [ko-ex-ten'ssiw] a. von gleicher Ausdehnung.
Coffee [ko'fi] n. Kaffee m; - grinder, - mill n. Kaffeemühle f; -house n. Café n; - -pot n. Kaffeekanne f; - service n. Kaffeeservice n, Kaffeegeschirr n. [Geldkasten m.
Coffer [ko'fer] n. Koffer m.
Coffin [ko'fin] n. Sarg m.
Cog [kog] n. Zahn m, Kamm m; - railway n. Zahnradbahn f; - -wheel n. Zahnrad n.
Cogen'cy [kou'dzhAn-ssi] n. Überzeugungskraft f; -t a.

zwingend, triftig, überzeugend.
Cogitat'e [kod'zhi-teit] vi. nachdenken; -ion n. Überlegen n.
Cognac [kon'jak] n. Kognak m.
Cognate [kog-neit'] a. verwandt. [Kenntnis f.
Cognizance [kog'ni-sAnss] n.
Cohabit [ko-hæ'bit] vi. zusammenwohnen. [menhängen.
Cohere [ko-hihr'] vi. zusam-
Cohe'rence [kou-hih'rAnss] n. Zusammenhang m; -nt a. zusammenhängend, einheitlich; -r n. Fritter m (rad.).
Cohesion [ko-hih'zhAn] n. Zusammenhalt m. [kel m.
Coign [keun] n. Ecke f, Win-
Coil [keul] n. Wickel m, Rolle f, Spule f (rad.); vt. aufspulen, aufschiessen; v. sich winden; - induction - Induktionsrolle f (el.); - ignition n. Batteriezündung f (aut.).
Coin [keun] n. Münze f; vt. münzen, prägen; -age Münzen n, gemünztes Geld.
Coincide [kou-in-ssaid'] vi. übereinstimmen, zusammentreffen.
Coincidence [kou-in'ssidAnss] n. Zufall m, Zusammentreffen n.
Coiner [keu'ner] n. Münzer m.
Coke [kouk] n. Koks m; vt. verkoken.
Cold [kould] n. Kälte f, Erkältung f; a. kalt, zurückhaltend; - -blooded a. kaltblütig; to catch - sich erkälten; - comfort n. schwacher Trost.
Cold storage [kould'stO'ridzh] n. Lagerung f im Kühlraum f; - chamber n. Kühlraum m; - plant n. Kühlanlage f.
Colic [ko'lik] n. Kolik f.
Collaborat'e [ko-læ'bo-reit] vi. mit-, zusammen-arbeiten; -ion n. Mitarbeit f, Einverständnis mit dem Feinde n; -ionist a. verräterisch; n. Ver-

räter *m*; -or *n.* Mitarbeiter *m*, Verräter *m* (*with enemy*).

Collaps'e [ko-lapss'] *n.* Zusammenbruch *m*; *vi.* zusammenbrechen, einstürzen; -ible *a.* zusammenlegdbar; -ible boat *n.* Faltboot *n.*

Collar [ko-ler] *n.* Kragen *m*; -bone *n.* Schlüsselbein *n*; -patch *n.* Kragenspiegel *m* (*mil.*); - stud *n.* Kragenknopf *n.* [tragen, vergleichen.

Collate [ko-leit'] *vt.* zusammen-

Collateral [ko-læ'tA-rAl] *a.* seitlich; - security *n.* Nebensicherheit *f.*

Collation [ko-lei'shAn] *n.* Vergleichung *f,* Zwischenmahlzeit *f.* [*m,* Kollegin *f.*

Colleague [ko'lihg] *n.* Kollege

Collect [ko-lekt'] *vt.* sammeln; *i.* sich sammeln; -ing point *n.* Sammelstelle *f*; -ed *a.* gefasst, gesammelt; -ion *n.* Sammlung *f,* Kollekte *f.*

Collective [ko-lek'tiw] *a.* vereint, gesammelt; - noun *a.* Sammelwort *n*; - security *n.* kollektive Sicherheit.

Collectively [ko-lek'tiw-li] *ad.* insgesamt.

Collector [ko-lek'ter] *n.* Sammler *m*, Einnehmer *m* (*taxes*), Stromabnehmer *m* (*el.*).

College [ko'ledzh] *n.* höhere Bildungsanstalt *f,* Hochschule *f,* Fachschule *f*; commercial - Handelshochschule *f*; technical - technische Hochschule.

Collide [ko-laid'] *vi.* zusammenstossen.

Collier [ko'li-er] *n.* Kohlenarbeiter *m*; -y *n.* Kohlenbergwerk *n.* [sammenstoss *m.*

Collision [ko-li'zhАn] *n.* Zu-

Colloid [kol'eud] *n.* Kolloid *n.*

Colloquial [ko-lou'kui-Al] *a.* Alltags . . ., familiär ; - language, - speech *n.* Umgangssprache *f.*

Collusion [ko-ljuh'zhAn] *n.* heimliches Einverständnis.

Colon [kou'lAn] *n.* Doppelpunkt *m.*

Colonel [kA'rnl] *n.* Oberst *m*; lieutenant - *n.* Oberstleutnant *m.*

Colonial [ko-lou'ni-Al] *a.* Kolonial . . .; *n.* Ansiedler *m*; - office *n.* Kolonialamt *n*; - secretary *n.* Kolonial-minister *m*; - trade *n.* Kolonial-handel *m.*

Colonist [ko'lo-nist] *n.* Ansiedler *m.*

Colonization [ko-lo-nai-sei'shAn] *n.* Besiedlung *f.*

Colon'ize [ko'lo-nais] *vt.* kolonisieren, besiedeln; -y *n.* Kolonie *f,* Ansiedlung *f.*

Colossal [ko-lo'ssAl] *a.* kolossal, ungeheuer.

Colour [kA'ler] *n.* Farbe *f*; *vt.* färben; -s *pl.* Fahne *f,* Flagge *f*; - bar *n.* Rassenschranke *f*; - blind *a.* farbenblind; - photography *n.* Farbenphotographie *f*; - printing *n.* Buntdruck *m*; - sergeant *n.* Fahnenjunker *m.*

Colourable [kA'lA-rAbl] *a.* echt aussehend, vorgeblich, annehmbar.

Colour'ing [kA'lA-ring] *n.* Färbung *f,* Schein *m*; -less *a.* farblos.

Colt [kohlt] *n.* Füllen *n,* Fohlen *n.*

Column [ko'lAm] *n.* Spalte *f* (*page*), Kolonne *f,* Säule *f* (*building*); fifth - fünfte Kolonne; steering - Lenksäule *f* (*aut.*); - of vehicles *n.* Fahrkolonne *f* (*mil.*).

Comb [koum] *n.* Kamm *m,* Heckel *f*; *vt.* kämmen; - out *vt.* auskämmen, ausmustern (*mil.*).

Combat [kom'bæt] *n.* Kampf *m*; *vt.* bekämpfen; -ant *n.* Kämpfer *m*; -ive *a.* streitsüchtig.

Combination [kom-bi-nei'shAn] *n.* Verbindung *f,* Mischung *f*; -s *pl.* Hemdhose *f.*

Combine [kom'bain] n. Ring m, Kartell n, Interessengemeinschaft f (com.), Konzern n.

Combin'e [kom-bain'] vt. verbinden; i. sich verbinden, sich verbünden; -ed operations n. pl. vereinigte Operationen f. pl (mil. etc.).

Combustible [kom-bʌss'tibl] a. brennbar.

Combustion [kom-bʌst'ʃʌn] n. Verbrennung f; internal - engine n. Explosionsmotor m; - chamber n. Verbrennungsraum m.

Come [kʌm] vi. kommen; to - a. künftig; - about sich ereignen; - from herkommen.

Comedian [ko-mih'di-An] n. Komödiant m.

Comedy [ko'mi-di] n. Komödie f, Lustspiel n.

Comeliness [kʌm'li-ness] n. Schönheit f.   [schön.

Comely [kʌm'li] a. anmutig,

Comer [kʌ'mer] n. Kommender m; new - Ankömmling m.

Comet [ko'mit] n. Komet m.

Comfort [kʌm'fΛrt] n. Behaglichkeit f, Trost m; vt. trösten; -able a. behaglich, behäbig; -er n. Tröster m; baby's - n. Nuppel m, Schnuller m, Sauger m; -less a. trostlos.

Comic [ko'mik] a. komisch; - paper n. Witzblatt n; -al a. komisch.   [n. Ankunft f.

Coming [kΛ'ming] a. künftig;

Comma [ko'mΛ] n. Komma n, Bistrich m.

Command [ko-mahnd'] n. Befehl m, Kommando n; - centre n. Befehlstelle f; - post n. Befehlstand m, Leitstand m.

Commandant [kom-Andænt'] n. Befehlshaber m, Führer m.

Commandeer[kom-An-dihr'] vt. zu Militärzwecken aneignen, requirieren.

Commander [ko-mahn'der] n. Befehlshaber m, Truppenführer m; - in chief n. Oberbefehlshaber m.

Commandment [ko-mahnd'ment] n. Gebot n.

Commando [ko-mahn'do] n. Freischar f (S. Africa); Mitglied eines Sturmtrupps n. (Europe).

Commemorat'e [ko-me'moreit] vt. feiern; -ion n. Gedenkfeier f, Andenken n.

Commence [ko-menss'] vt. i. anfangen; -ment n. Anfang m.

Commend [ko-mend'] vt. loben, empfehlen; -able a. löblich.   [schΛn] n. Lob n.

Commendation [ko'men-dei'

Commensura'te [kΛ-men'sju-rΛbl] a. vergleichbar; -te a. verhältnismässig.

Comment [ko'mΛnt] n. Anmerkung f, Erklärung f; vt. erläutern; -ary n. Auslegung f, Beschreibung f; running - n. Hörbericht m (rad.); -ator n. Erläuterer m, Ausleger m; radio - n. Funkberichter m.

Commerce [ko'merss] n. Handel m; -raider n. Handelszerstörer m.

Commercial [ko-mΛr'schΛl] a. kaufmännisch, geschäftlich, Handels . . . . . ; - college n. Handelshochschule f; - hotel n. Gasthof für Handelsreisende m; - law n. Handelsrecht n; - plane n. Verkehrsflugzeug n; - school n. Handelsschule f; - traveller n. Geschäfts-, Handelsreisende(r) m; - vehicle n. Last-auto n, -kraftwagen m.

Commisserat'e [ko-mi'sΛreit] vt. bemitleiden; -ion n. Bedauern n.

Commissar [ko-miss-ahr'] n. Kommissar m, Beauftragte(r) m.

Commissariat [ko-miss-æ'ri-At] n. Kommissariat m, Intendantur f.

Commission [ko-mi'schʌn] *n.* Auftrag *m*, Offizierspatent *n*, Kommission *f*, Begehung *f*; - **-agent** *n.* Kommissionär *m*; *vt.* beordern, beauftragen.

Commissionaire [ko-mischʌ-nehr'] *n.* Dienstmann *m*, Portier *m*, Pförtner *m*.

Commissioner [ko-mi'schoner] *n.* Beauftragter *m*, Bevollmächtigte(r) *m*, Kommissionär *m*; - **-general** *n.* Generalbevollmächtigte(r) *m*.

Commit [ko-mit'] *vt.* begehen, anvertrauen, übergeben; *v.r.* sich bloss-stellen; - **to memory** *vt.* auswendig lernen; - **to prison** *vt.* einsperren, ins Gefängnis stecken.

Commitment [ko-mit'mʌnt] *n.* Verpflichtung *f.*

Committee [ko-mi'ti] *n.* Ausschuss *m*, Vorstand *m*, Kommission *f.*

Commode [ko-moud'] *n.* Nachtschränkchen *n.*

Commodious [ko-mou'di-ʌss] *a.* geräumig.

Commodity [ko-mo'di-ti] *n.* Ware *f.*

Commodore [ko'mo-dohr] *n.* Kommodore *m.*

Common [ko'mʌn] *n.* Gemeindeland *n*; *a.* gewöhnlich, gemein, gemeinschaftlich; - **ground** *n.* gemeinsame Grundlage; - **sense** *n.* gesunder Menschenverstand; - **time** *n.* Vierviertaltakt *m.*

Commoner [ko'mʌ-ner] *n.* Bürgerliche(r) *m*, Nichtadelige(r) *m.*

Commonplace [ko'mʌn-pleiss] *a.* alltäglich *n.* Gemeinplatz *m.*

Commonwealth [ko'mʌn-uelth] *n.* Gemeinwesen *n*, Staatenbund *m*, Staat *m*; **British - ** *n.* britisches Weltreich; - **of nations** *n.* Völkerfamilie *f.*

Commotion [ko-mou'schʌn] *n.* heftige Bewegung *f*, Aufstand *m.*

Communal [kom'ju-nʌl] *a.* Gemeinschaft . . . ; - **kitchen** *n.* Gemeindeküche *f.*

Commune [kom'juhn] *n.* Gemeinde *f*; [ ] sich mitteilen.

Commune [kom-juhn'] *n.* Kommune *f.*

Communicable [ko-mjuh'ni-kʌbl] *a.* mitteilbar.

Communicant [ko'mju'ni-kʌnt] *n.* Abendmahlgast *m*, Kommunikant *m.*

Communicate [ko-mjuh'ni-keit] *vt.* mitteilen.

Communication [ko-mju-ni-kei'schʌn] *n.* Mitteilung *f*, Verbindung *f*; - **cord** *n.* Notbremse *f* (*rl.*); - **trench** *n.* Verbindungsgraben *m* (*mil.*); - **headquarters** *n. pl.* Nachrichtenzentrale *f* (*mil.*); - **s officer** *n.* Kurieroffizier *m.*

Communicative [ko-mjuh'ni-kʌ-tiw] *a.* mitteilsam, gesprächig.

Communion [ko-mjuh'ni-ʌn] *n.* Gemeinschaft *f*, das heilige Abendmahl.

Communism [ko'mju-nism] *n.* Kommunismus *m*; - **t** *n.* Kommunist *m.*

Community [ko-mjuh'ni-ti] *n.* Gemeinschaft *f*; - **singing** *n.* gemeinsames Singen; - **spirit** *n.* Gemeinschaftsgeist *m.*

Commutable [ko-mjuh'tʌbl] *a.* vertauschbar.

Commutator [ko'mju-tei-ter] *n.* Stromwender *m*, Umschalter *m* (*el.*); - **bar** *n.* - **segment** *n.* Lamelle *f* (*el.*).

Commute [ko-mjuht'] *vt.* umändern, mildern (*punishment*).

Compact [kom'pækt] *n.* Vertrag *m*; Übereinkunft *f.*

Compact [kom-pækt'] *a.* fest, dicht, bündig.

Companion [kom-pæ'ni-ʌn] *n.* Gefährte *m*, Gespiele *m*; **-able** *a.* gesellig; **-ship** *n.* Gesellschaft *f*, Kameradschaft *f.*

Company [kAm'pA-ni] *n.* Gesellschaft *f*, Verkehr *m*, Umgang *m*; – commander *n.* Kompanieführer *m* (*mil.*); – promoter *n.* Unternehmer *m*, Gründer *m* (*com.*); – roster *n.* Kompanieliste *f* (*mil.*); – sergeant major *n.* Oberfeldwebel *m* (*mil.*).

Comparable [kom'pA-rAbl] *a.* vergleichbar.

Comparative [kom-pæ'rA-tiw] *a.* verhältnismassig; – Komparativ *m*, [gleichen.

Compare [kom-pehr'] *vt.* vergleichen.

Comparison [kom-pæ'ri-sAn] *n.* Vergleich *m*, Steigerung *f* (*adjectives*, etc.).

Compartment [kom-pahrt'mAnt] *n.* Abteilung *f*, Abteil *f* (*train*).

Compass [kAm'pAss] *n.* Umfang *m*, Bereich *m*, Kompass *m*; *vt.* umgeben, einschliessen; – direction *n.* Himmelsrichtung *f*; – point *n.* Strich.

Compasses [kAm'pAss-is] *n. pl.* Zirkel *m.*

Compassion [kom-pæ'schAn] *n.* Mitleid *n*; –ate *a,* mitleidig.

Compatib'le [kom-pæ'tibl] *a.* verträglich, vereinbar; –ility *n.* Vereinbarkeit *f*, Verträglichkeit *f.*

Compatriot [kom-pæ'tri-At] *n.* Landsmann *m*, Landsmännin.

Compel [kom-pel'] *vt.* nötigen.

Compensat'e [kom'pen-ssert] *vt.* ersetzen; –ion *n.* Ersatz *m*, Lohn *m.*

Compete [kom-piht'] *vi.* konkurrieren, sich bewerben.

Competen'ce [kom'pi-tAnss] *n.* Fähigkeit *f*, Kompetenz *f* (*law*), Auskommen *n* (*income*); –t *a.* –tly *ad.* zulänglich, tüchtig, kompetent.

Competition [kom-pi-ti'schAn] *n.* Konkurrenz *f*, Wettbewerb *m*, Preisausschreiben *n.*

Competitive [kom-pe'ti-tiw] *a.* konkurrenzfähig (*com.*).

Competitor [kom-pe'ti-ter] *n.* Konkurrent *m*, Mitbewerber *m.*

Compilation [kom-pi-lei'schAn] *n.* Bearbeitung *f*, Sammelwerk *n.*

Compile [kom-pail'] *vt.* zusammenstellen, sammeln.

Compiler [kom-pai'ler] *n.* Sammler *m*, Verfasser *m.*

Complacen'cy [kom-pleï'ssen-ssi] *n.* Selbstzufriedenheit *f*, Behagen *n*; –t *a.* selbstzufrieden, behaglich.

Complain [kom-plein'] *vi.* klagen; – about *vi.* beanstanden.

Complaint [kom-pleint'] *n.* Klage *f*, Beschwerde *f*, Krankheit *f.*

Complement [kom'pli-mAnt] *n.* Ergänzung *f*; full – Gesamtzahl *f*; –ary *a.* ergänzend.

Complete [kom-pliht'] *a.* –ly *ad.* vollständig, vollendet; *vt.* vollenden, vervollständigen; – service abdienen, ableisten (*mil.*).

Completeness [kom-pliht'ness] *n.* Vollständigkeit *f*, Vollkommenheit *f.*

Completion [kom-pliih'schAn] *n.* Vollendung *f*, Ergänzung *f.*

Complex [kom'plex] *a.* zusammengesetzt, verwickelt; *n.* Komplex *m*, Gesamtheit *f*; –ity *n.* Verwickelung *f*, Schwierigkeit *f.*

Complexion [kom-plek'schAn] *n.* Gesichtsfarbe *f*, Natur *f*, Art *f.*

Compliance [kom-plaï'Anss] *n.* Einwilligung *f*, Fügsamkeit *f.*

Compliant [kom-plaï'Ant] *a.* nachgiebig, willfährig.

Complicat'e [kom'pli-keit] *vt.* verwickeln; –ion *n.* Verwickelung *f*, Schwierigkeit *f.*

Complicity [kom-pli'ssi-ti] *n.* Mitschuld *f.*

Compliment [kom'pli-mAnt] n. Kompliment n; vt. beglückwünschen; **-ary** a. höflich, schmeichelnd; **-ary ticket** n. Freikarte f. [kommen.

Comply [kom-plai'] vi. nachkommen.

Component [kom-pou'nAnt] a. einen Teil ausmachend, Bestandteil m; **- of unit** n. Teileinheit f (mil.). [betragen.

Comport [kom-pOrt'] v.r. sich betragen.

Comportment [kom-pOrt'mAnt] n. Betragen n.

Compose [kom-pous'] vt. verfassen (book), komponieren (music), setzen (type); r. sich beruhigen; **-ing machine** n. Setzmaschine f; **-ing room** n. Setzerei f. [gefasst.

Composed [kom-pousd'] a.

Composer [kom-pou'ser] n. Verfasser m, Komponist m.

Composite [kom'po-sit] a. zusammengesetzt.

Composition [kom-po-si'-schAn] n. Komposition f, Zusammensetzung f, Legierung f (tec.), Aufsatz m (school).

Compositor [kom-po'si-ter] n. Schriftsetzer m; **-'s error** n. Setzfehler m; **-'s room** n. Setzerei f.

Compost [kom'post] n. Mischdünger m; **- heap** n. Mist-, Laub-haufen m.

Composure [kom-pou'zher] n. Gemütsruhe f, Fassung f.

Compound [kom'paund] n. Gemisch n, Verbindung f, umzäunter Hof (Africa, etc.); **-interest** Zinszeins m.

Compound [kom-paund'] vt. zusammensetzen, tilgen (debt); vi. sich vergleichen.

Comprehen'd [kom-pri-hend'] vt. begreifen, enthalten; **-sible** a. begreiflich; **-sion** n. Fassungskraft f; **-sive** a. umfassend.

Compress [kom'press] n. Kompresse f, Umschlag m.

Compress [kom-press'] vt.

zusammendrücken; **-ed air** n. Druckluft f; **-ible** a. komprimierbar; **-ion** n. Druck m, Zusammendrücken n, Verdichtung f; **-or** n. Verdichter m, Druckluftmaschine f, Kettenstopper m (nav.).

Comprise [kom-prais'] vt. in sich fassen, bestehen aus.

Compromise [kom'pro-mais] n. Übereinkunft f, Kompromiss m, Vergleich m; vi. einen Vergleich machen, entgegenkommen (meet), kompromittieren (reputation).

Comptometer [komp-to'miter] n. Rechenmaschine f.

Compulsion [kom-pAl'schAn] n. Zwang m.

Compulsory [kom-pAl'sso-ri] a. obligatorisch; **- education** n. Schulzwang m; **- sale** n. Zwangsverkauf m; **- service** n. Dienstpflicht f.

Compunction [kom-pAngk'-schAn] n. Gewissensbisse m.

Computation [kom-pju-tei'schAn] n. Berechnung f.

Compute [kom-pjuht'] vt. berechnen, ausrechnen, auswerten.

Comrade [kom'reid] n. Kamerad m; **-ship** n. Kameradschaft f.

Concatention [kon-kæ-ti-nei'-schAn] n. Verkettung f.

Concave [kon'keiw] a. konkav, hohlgeschliffen; **- lens** n. Zerstreuungslinse f.

Conceal [kon-ssih'] vt. verhehlen; **-ment** n. Verhehlung f, Verheimlichung f, Tarnung f (from air). [räumen.

Concede [kon-ssihd'] vt. einräumen.

Conceit [kon-ssiht'] n. Eitelkeit f; **-ed** a. eingebildet, dünkelhaft. [a. denkbar.

Conceivable [kon-ssih'vAbl]

Conceive [kon-ssihw'] vt. sich denken; i. schwanger werden, begreifen, sich vorstellen.

Concentrate [kon'ssen-treit]

vt. konzentrieren; **-d fire** *n.* Massenbeschuss *m* (*mil.*); **-d load** *n.* Einzellast *f.*

Concentration [kon'ssentrei'schAn] *n.* Konzentration *f,* Sättigung *f* (*liquid*), Ballung *f* (*gas*); **-** camp *n.* Anhalte-, Konzentrations-lager *n;* **-** of troops *n.* Ansammlung *f* (*mil.*).

Concept [kon'ssept] *n.* Begriff *m.*

Conception [kon-ssep'schAn] *n.* Vorstellung *f* Begriff *m,* Empfängnis *f.*

Concern [kon-ssArn'] *n.* Angelegenheit *f,* Anteil *m,* Sorge *f,* Geschäft *n,* Unternehmen *n; vt.* betreffen, beunruhigen; **-ed** *a.* bekümmert, interessiert, beteiligt; **-ing** *pr.* betreffs.

Concert [kon'ssert] *n.* Konzert *n,* Einverständnis *n.*

Concert [kon-ssArt'] *vt.* abmachen, verabreden, erdenken.

Concertina [kon-sser-tih'nA] *n.* Hand-, Zieh-harmonika *f.*

Concession [kon-se'schAn] *n.* Zugeständnis *n,* Bewilligung *f,* Konzession *f.*

Conciliat'e [kon-ssi'li-eit] *vt.* versöhnen; **-ion** *n.* Versöhnung *f;* **-ory** *a.* versöhnlich, vermittelnd.

Concise [kon-ssaiss'] *a.* **-ly** *ad.* kurz, bündig; **-ness,** concision [kon-ssi'zhAn] *n.* Kürze *f,* Knappheit *f.*

Conclud'e [kon-kluhd'] *vt.* beschliessen, folgern; *i.* endigen; **-ing** *a.* schliessend, Schluss ..

Conclusion [kon-klu'zhAn] *n.* Schluss *m,* Folgerung *f;* **-** of peace Friedensschluss *m.*

Conclusive [kon-klu'siw] *a.* entscheidend, abschliessend; **-ness** *n.* Überzeugungskraft *f.*

Concoct [kon-kokt'] *vt.* aussinnen, zusammenbrauen; **-ion** *n.* Gebräu *n.*

Concord [kon'kOrd] *n.* Eintracht *f,* Übereinstimmung *f.*

Concordat [kon-kohr'dæt] *n.* Konkordat *n.*

Concourse [kon'kOrs] *n.* Zulauf *m,* Menge *f.*

Concrete [kon'kriht] *a.* konkret, greifbar.

Concrete [kon'kriht] *n.* Beton *m,* Steinmörtel *m;* rough **-** Grobmörtel *m.*

Concur [kon-kAr'] *vi.* übereinstimmen, **-rence** *f.* Übereinstimmung *f,* Zustimmung *f.*

Concussion [kon-kA'schAn] *n.* Erschütterung *f.*

Condemn [kon-dem'] *vt.* verdammen, verurteilen, für untüchtig erklären; **-ation** *n.* Verdammung *f,* Verurteilung *f;* **-atory** *a.* verdammend, verurteilend.

Condensation [kon-den-ssei'schAn] *n.* Verdichtung *f.*

Condense [kon-denss'] *vt.* verdichten, abkürzen; **-d milk** kondensierte Milch; **-r** *n.* Kondensator *m* (*rad.*), Sammler *m* (*el.*), Kühler *m* (*tec.*).

Condescen'd [kon-di-ssend'] *vi.* sich herablassen; **-scion** *n.* Herablassung *f.* [Würze *f.*]

Condiment [kon'di-ment] *n.* Condition [kon-di'schAn] *n.* Lage *f,* Bedingung *f,* Zustand *m; vt.* in Stand setzen, bedingen, reinigen, heizen (*air*); **-al** *a.* bedingt, eingeschränkt; *n.* Bedingungsform *f;* **-ally** *ad.* bedingungsweise.

Condole [kon-doul'] *vi.* mittrauern, mitleiden; **-nce** *n.* Beileid *n;* letter of **-** Beileidsbrief *m.* [zeihen.]

Condone [kon-doun'] *vt.* ver**Conduc'e** [kon-djuhss'] *vi.* beitragen; **-ive** *a.* förderlich, dienlich.

Conduct [kon'dAkt] *n.* Leitung *f,* Führung *f,* Benehmen *n; vt.* leiten, führen; **-** oneself sich benehmen.

Conductivity [kon-dAk-ti'witi] *n.* Leitfähigkeit *f.*

Conductor [kon-dAk'ter] n. Leiter m, Kapellmeister m, Schaffner m.

Conduit [kon'dit] n. Wasserleitung f, Kanal m, Röhre f.

Cone [koun] n. Kegel m; - of fire n. Garbe f (mil.).

Confection [kon-fek'schAn] n. das Eingemachte; -er m. Konditor m, Zuckerbäcker m; -er's shop n. Konditorei f; -ery n. Konditorei f, Zuckerwerk n. Konfitüren f. pl.

Confederacy [kon-fe'dA-rA-ssi] n. Bündnis n; -te a. verbündet; -tion n. Bund m.

Confer [kon-fAr'] vt. erteilen; i. beratschlagen.

Conference [kon'fA-rAnss] n. Beratung f, Konferenz f; -table n. Verhandlungs-, Konferenztisch m.

Confess [kon-fess'] vt. zugestehen, beichten; i. beichten.

Confession [kon-fe'schAn] n. Geständnis n, Beichte f; -al a. Bekenntnis n; ; n. Beichtstuhl m; -al church n. Bekenntniskirche f.

Confessor [kon-fe'sser] n. Bekenner m, Beichtvater m.

Confetti [kon-fe'ti] n. Konfetti f [trauen; vi. vertrauen.

Confide [kon-faid'] vt. anvertrauen.

Confidence [kon-fi-dAnss] n. Vertrauen n, Zuversicht f; -t a. zuversichtlich; -tial a. vertraulich; -tial clerk n. Prokurist m (com.); -tially ad. im Vertrauen.

Confiding [kon-fai'ding] a. vertrauensvoll.

Configuration [kon-fi-gju-rei'schAn] n. Gestaltung f.

Confine [kon-fain'] vt. begrenzen, einschliessen; -ment n. Gefangenschaft f, Haft f, Niederkunft f.

Confirm [kon-fArm'] vt. bestätigen, konfirmieren; -ed a. chronisch, unverbesserlich.

Confirmation [kon-fer-mei-

schAn] n. Bestätigung f, Konfirmation f.

Confirmatory [kon-fAr'mA-tA-ri] a. bestätigend.

Confiscate [kon'fiss-keit] vt. beschlagnahmen; -ion n. Beschlagnahme f.

Conflagration [kon-flæ-grei'schAn] n. Feuersbrunst f.

Conflict [kon'flikt] n. Kampf m, Streit m.

Conflict [kon-flikt'] vi. widerstreiten; -ing pres.p. entgegengesetzt.

Conform [kon-fOrm'] vi. in Übereinstimmung sein, sich richten nach; -able a. entsprechend, gemäss; -ity n. Gleichförmigkeit f. Übereinstimmung f.

Conformation [kon-fOr-mei'schAn] n. Bildung f.

Confound [kon-faund'] vt. verwechseln, verwirren.

Confront [kon-frAnt'] vt. entgegentreten, gegenüberstellen.

Confuse [kon-fjuhs'] vt. verwirren, verwechseln; -ion n. Verwirrung f, Verwechslung f.

Confute [kon-fjuht'] vt. widerlegen.

Congeal [kon-dzhihl'] vi. gefrieren.

Congenial [kon-dzhih'ni-Al] a. gleichartig, zusagend.

Congenital [kon-dzhe'nitl] a. angeboren; [Meeraal m.

Conger-eel [kon-ger-ihl'] n. **Congest** [kon-dzhest'] vt. überfüllen, verstopfen; -ion n. Überfüllung f, Stauung f (traffic).

Conglomeration [kon-glo-mA-rei'schAn] n. Anhäufung f.

Congratulate [kon-græ'tjuleit] vt. gratulieren; -ion n. Glückwunsch m, Beglückwünschung f; -ory a. glückwünschend.

Congregate [kon'gri-geit] vi. sich versammeln; -ion n. Versammlung f, Gemeinde f (church).

Congress [kon'gress] n. Kongress m, Versammlung f.

Conic [ko'nik], **Conical** [ko'nikl] a. kegelförmig; – **spring** n. Kegelfeder f (tec.).

Conifer [ko'ni-fer] n. Nadelholz n; -**ous** a. zapfentragend; -**ous tree** n. Nadelbaum m.

Conjectur'al [kon-dzhek'tjurAl] a. mutmasslich; -**e** n. Mutmassung f; vt. mutmassen.

Conjointly [kon-dzheunt'li] ad. gemeinschaftlich.

Conjugal [kon'dzhu-gAl] a. ehelich.

Conjugat'e [kon'dzhu-geit] vt. konjugieren, beugen; -**ion** n. Konjugation f, Beugung f.

Conjunct'ion [kon-dzhAngk'schAn] n. Verbindung f, Konjunktion f, Bindewort n; -**ure** n. Lage f, Krise f, Wendepunkt m.

Conjure [kAn'zher] vi. vt. beschwören, zaubern; -**r** n. Taschenspieler m, Zauberer m.

Conk out [kongk-aut'] vi. ausfallen (aut, av, etc.).

Connect [ko-nekt'] vt. verknüpfen, verbinden, koppeln (el.), schalten (el.); -**ing rod** n. Pleuel-, Schub-stange f (tec.); -**ing shaft** n. Transmissionswelle f (tec.).

Connection [ko-nek'schAn] n. Verbindung f, Verwandtschaft f, Schaltung f (el.), Anschluss m (rl.).

Connector [ko-nek'ter] n. Zuführung f, Verbindungsklemme f (tec.).

Conning tower [kon'ing-tau'er] n. Kommandostand m (nav.).

Connivance [ko-nai'wAnss] n. Übersehen n, Nachsicht f.

Connive [ko-naw'] vi. im Einverständnis stehen, ein Auge zudrücken.

Connotation [ko-no-tei'schAn] n. Bedeutung f, Sinn m.

Conquer [kong'ker] vt. vic. erobern, besiegen; -**or** n. Eroberer m, Sieger m.

Conquest [kon'kuest] n. Eroberung f, Sieg m, erobertes Gebiet.

Consanguinity [kon-sænggui'ni-ti] n. Blutsverwandtschaft f.

Conscience [kon'schAnss] n. Gewissen n; in all – wahrhaftig.

Conscientious [kon-schi-en'schAss] a. gewissenhaft; – **objector** n. Kriegsdienstverweigerer m.

Conscious [kon'schAss] a. -**ly** ad. bewusst; -**ness** n. Bewusstsein n. [ausheben.

Conscript [kon-skript'] vt.

Conscript [kon'skript] n. Dienstpflichtiger m; -**ion** n. Aushebung f, Dienstpflicht f, allgemeine Wehrpflicht.

Consecrat'e [kon-ssi-kreit] vt. weihen, heiligen; -**ion** n. Weihung f.

Consecutive [kon-sse'kju-tiw] a. aufeinanderfolgend.

Consensus [kon-ssen'ssAss] n. allgemeine Übereinstimmung.

Consent [kon-ssent'] n. Zustimmung f; vi. einwilligen, beistimmen.

Consequence [kon'ssi-kuAnss] n. Folge f, Bedeutung f; in – wegen. [a. darauf folgend.

Consequent [kon'si-kuAnt]

Consequential [kon-ssi-kuen'schAl] a. wichtig, zurückzuführen auf, eingebildet.

Consequently [kon'si-kuAnt-li] ad. folglich.

Conservation [kon-sser-wei'schAn] n. Erhaltung f.

Conservat'ism [kon-ssAr'wAtism] n. Konservatismus m; -**ive** a. konservativ; Konservative(r) m; a. konservativ; -**ory** n. Treibhaus n.

Conserve [kon-ssArw'] vt. erhalten, bewahren; -**s** n. pl. Eingemachtes n, Konserve f.

Consider [kon-ssi′der] *vt.* betrachten, erwägen, berücksichtigen, halten für; -able *a.* bedeutend; -ate *a.* rücksichtsvoll; -ation *n.* Betrachtung *f*, Rücksicht *f*; in – of hinsichtlich. [geben, übersenden.

Consign [kon-ssain′] *vt.* über-

Consignee [kon-ssai-nih′] *n.* Empfänger *m.*

Consignment [kon-ssain′mAnt] *n.* Übersendung *f*, Konsignation *f*, Warensendung *f*; – note *n.* Frachtbrief *m*; – number *n.* Fahrnummer *f*, Leitungszahl *f.*

Consignor [kon-ssai′ner] *n.* Übersender *m*, Verfrachter *m.*

Consist [kon-ssist′] *vi.* bestehen; -ence, -ency *n.* Festigkeit *f*, Übereinstimmung *f*, Konsequenz *f*; -ent *a.* -ly *ad.* fest, gemäss, konsequent.

Consolation [kon-so-lei′schAn] *n.* Trost *m.*

Consolatory [kon-ssou′lA-tA-ri] *a.* tröstlich. [ten.

Console [kon-ssoul′] *vt.* trös-

Consolidat′e [kon-sso′li-(d)eit] *vt.* fest machen, verdichten; -d debt *n.* fundierte Schuld, stehende Schuld; -ion *n.* Festmachen *n*, Verdichtung *f*, Ausbau *m* (mil.).

Consols [kon-ssols′] *n.* konsolidierte Staatspapiere *n. pl.*

Consonant [kon′sso-nAnt] *n.* Konsonant *m*, Mitlaut *m.*

Consort [kon′ssort] *n.* Gemahl *m*, Gemahlin *f.*

Consort [kon-ssort′] *vi.* verkehren, sich gesellen.

Conspicuous [kon-spi′kju-Ass] *a.* -ly *ad.* auffallend, berühmt.

Conspira′cy [kon-spi′rA-ssi] *n.* Verschwörung *f*; -tor *n.* Verschwörer *m.*

Conspire [kon-spair′] *vi.* sich verschwören, sich verbinden.

Constable [kAn′stAbl] *n.* Polizist *m.*

Constabulary [kon-stæ′bju-lA-ri] *n.* Ordnungspolizei *f*, Schutzleute *pl.*

Constan′cy [kon′stAn-ssi] *n.* Beständigkeit *f*, Treue *f*; -t *a.* -tly *ad.* beständig, treu; -t *n.* Konstante *f.*

Constellation [kon-ste-lei′schAn] *n.* Sternbild *n.*

Consternation [kon-ster-nei′schAn] *n.* Bestürzung *f.*

Constipation [kon-sti-pei′schAn] *n.* Verstopfung *f.*

Constituen′cy [kon-sti′tju-en-ssi] *n.* Wahlkreis *m*; -t *a.* wesentlich, verfassungsgebend; *n.* Bestandteil *m*, Wähler *m* (person).

Constitute [kon′sti-tjuht] *vt.* ausmachen, festsetzen, ernennen.

Constitution [kons-sti-tjuh′schAn] *n.* Beschaffenheit *f*, Verfassung *f*; -al *a.* verfassungsgemäss.

Constrain [kon-strein′] *vt.* zwingen; -t *n.* Zwang *m.*

Constrict [kon-strikt′] *vt.* zusammenziehen; -ion *n.* Zusammenziehung *f.*

Construct [kon-strAkt′] *vt.* zusammensetzen, aufbauen.

Construction [kon-strAk′schAn] *n.* Zusammensetzung *f*, Aufbauen *n*, Bau *m*, Konstruktion *f*; – battalion *n.* Baubataillon *f*; – column *n.* Herrichtungskolonne *f*; – mechanic *n.* Baufunker *m* (rad.); – office *n.* Neubauamt *n* (rl.); – of roads *n.* Wegebau *m*; – staff *n.* Baustab *m.*

Constructive [kon-strAk′tiw] *a.* aufbauend, förderlich.

Constructor [kon-strAk′ter] *n.* Erbauer *m.*

Construe [kon-struh′] *vt.* deuten, auslegen.

Consul [kon′ssAl] *n.* Konsul *m*; -general *n.* Generalkonsul *m*; -ar *a.* Konsulats...; -ate *n.* Konsulat *n.*

Consult [kon-sAlt'] *vt.* zu Rate ziehen; **-ing room** *n.* Sprechzimmer *n.*

Consultation [kon-ssAl-tei'schAn] *n.* Beratung *f*, Besprechung *f*.

Consultative [kon-ssAl'tА-tiw] *a.* beratend.

Consumable [kon-sjuh'mAbl] *a.* verzehrbar; **-s** — stocks *n. pl.* Verbrauchsbestand *m* (mil.).

Consume [kon-ssjuhm'] *vt.* verzehren; **-r** *n.* Verzehrer *m*, Abnehmer *m*, Verbraucher *m* (com.).

Consumption [kon-ssAmp'schAn] *n.* Verbrauch *m*, Schwindsucht *f*, Konsum *m*; **unit of** — Verbrauchssatz *m*; **-goods** *n. pl.* Verbrauchsmittel *n. pl.* [tiw] *a.* schwindsüchtig.

Consumptive [kon-ssAmp'-

Contact [kon'tækt] *n.* Berührung *f*, Anschluss *m* (el, mil, etc.); *vt.* sich in Verbindung setzen mit; **- lenses** *n. pl.* Haftgläser *n. pl.* **- mine** *n.* Flatter-Tret-mine *f*.

Contagio'n [kon-tei'dzhAn] *n.* Ansteckung *f*; **-us** *a.* ansteckend.

Contain [kon'tein] *vt.* enthalten, binden, festhalten (enemy); **-er** *n.* Büchse *f* (tin), Fass *n* (wood), Gehäuse *n* (tec.), Gebinde *n* (cask).

Contaminat'e [kon-tæ'mi-neit] *vt.* beflecken, verseuchen; **-ion** *n.* Verseuchung *f*, Vergiftung *f*.

Contango [kon-tæng'gou] *n.* Report *m*, Aufgeld *n* (com.).

Contemplat'e [kon'tem-pleit] *vt.* betrachten, beabsichtigen; **-ion** *n.* Betrachtung *f*, Nachsinnen *n.*

Contemporaneous [kon-tem-po-rei'ni-Ass] *a.* gleichzeitig.

Contemporary [kon-tem'po-rA-ri] *n.* Zeitgenosse *m*, Zeitschrift *f*; *a.* zeitgenössisch.

Contempt [kon-tempt'] *n.* Verachtung *f*; **-ible** *a.* verächtlich; **-uous** *a.* geringschätzig.

Contend [kon-tend'] *vi.* streiten; *t.* bestreiten; **-ing** *a.* widerstreitend.

Content [kon-tent'] *a.* zufrieden; *n.* Zufriedenheit *f*; **-ed** *a.* zufrieden; **-ment** *n.* Zufriedenheit *f*.

Contenti'on [kon-ten'schAn] *n.* Streit *m*, Behauptung *f*; **-ous** *a.* streitsüchtig. [Inhalt *m*.

Contents [kon'tentss] *n. pl.*

Contest [kon'test] *n.* Streit *m*, Wettkampf *m*. [streiten.

Contest [kon-test'] *vt.* bestreiten.

Context [kon'text] *n.* Zusammenhang *m.*

Contiguous [kon-ti'gju-Ass] *a.* angrenzend.

Continence [kon'ti-nAnss] *n.* Enthaltsamkeit *f*.

Continent [kon'ti-nAnt] *n.* Kontinent *m*, Festland *n*; **-al** *a.* kontinental, europäisch, Festland ....

Contingen'cy [kon-tin'zhAn-ssi] *n.* Zufälligkeit *f*, Möglichkeit *f*; **-t** *a.* zufällig, möglich, abhängig; *n.* Kontingent *n* (mil.).

Continua'l [kon-tin'ju-Al] *a.* **-ly** *ad.* fortwährend; **-nce** *n.* Fortdauer *f*; **-tion** *n.* Fortsetzung *f*.

Continue [kon-tin'ju] *vt.* fortsetzen; *i.* verbleiben, fortfahren.

Continuity [kon-ti-njuh'i-ti] *n.* Zusammenhang *m*, Stetigkeit *f*.

Continuous [kon-ti'nju-Ass] *a.* ununterbrochen; **- brake** *n.* durchgehende Bremse (rl.); **- fire** Dauerfeuer *n* (mil.); **- operation** Dauerbetrieb *m* (tec.); **- wave** ungedämpfte Welle (rad.).

Contort [kon-tOrt'] *vt.* verdrehen; **-ion** *n.* Verdrehung *f*, Verzerrung *f*.

Contour [kon'tuhr] *n.* Höhen-, Schicht-linie *f*, Umriss *m.*
Contraband [kon'trA-bænd] *n.* verboten; *n.* Bannware *f*, Schmuggelware *f*.
Contract [kon'trækt] *n.* Kontrakt *m.* Vertrag *m*, Verdingung *f* (*com.*), Akkord *m* (*com.*).
Contract [kon-trækt'] *vt.* zusammenziehen; sich aneignen, machen (*debts*); *i.* sich zusammenziehen; **– a cold** sich eine Erkältung zuziehen; **– out** *vi.* sich durch Vertrag zurückziehen. [*n.* Zusammenziehung *f*.
Contraction [kon-træk'schAn]
Contractor [kon-træk'ter] *n.* Unternehmer *m*, Lieferant *m* (*food*). [*a.* verträglich.
Contractual [kon-træk'tju-Al]
Contradict [kon-trA-dikt'] *vt.* widersprechen; **-ion** *n.* Widerspruch *m*; **-ory** *a.* sich widersprechend.
Contradistinction [kon-trA-di-stingk'schAn] *n.* Unterscheidung *f*, Gegensatz *m.*
Contralto [kon-træl'tou] *n.* tiefe Altstimme *f*, zweite Alt.
Contraption [kon-træp'schAn] *n* Maschine *f*, Einrichtung *f*.
Contrariness [kon-treh'riness] *n.* Widerspenstigkeit *f*, Tücke *f*.
Contrarily [kon-treh'ri-li] *ad.* Contrary [kon-treh'ri] *a.* eigensinnig, widerspenstig, ungünstig (*wind*).
Contrary [kon'trA-ri] *n.* Gegenteil *n*; *a.* entgegengesetzt, widrig; **– to** zuwider.
Contrast [kon'trahst] *n.* Gegensatz *m.*
Contrast [kon-trahst'] *vt.* gegenüberstellen; *i.* einen Gegensatz bilden.
Contravene [kon-trA-wihn'] *vt.* übertreten, zuwiderhandeln.
Contravention [kon-trA-wen'schAn] *n.* Übertretung *f*, Verletzung *f*.
Contribute [kon-tri'bjuht] *vt.* *i.* beitragen, mitwirken.
Contribution [kon-tri-bjuh'schAn] *n.* Beitrag *m*, Mitwirkung *f*, Beihilfe *f*.
Contributor [kon-tri'bju-ter] *n.* der Beitragende, Mitarbeiter *m*; **-y** *a.* beitragend; **– negligence** Mitverschulden *n.*
Contrite [kon'trait] *a.* zerknirscht. [Zerknirschung *f*.
Contrition [kon-tri'schAn] *n.*
Contrivance [kon-trai'wAnss] *n.* Vorrichtung *f*, Kniff *m*, Erfindung *f*.
Contrive [kon-traiw'] *vt.* ersinnen; **– to** *vi.* ermöglichen, fertig bringen, einrichten.
Control [kon-troul'] *n.* Einhalt *m*, Leitung *f*, Gewalt *f*; *vt.* leiten, im Zaume halten; **-led price** Höchstpreis *m*; **-s** *n. pl.* Steuerung *f* (*av.*); **– company** *n.* Leitkompanie *f* (*mil.*); **– grid** *n.* Steuergitter *n* (*av.*); **– office** *n.* Überwachungsstelle *f*; **– officer** *n.* Leitoffizier *m* (*mil.*); **– station** *n.* Leitstelle *f*.
Controller [kon-trou'ler] *n.* Leiter *m.*
Controversial [kon-tro-wAr'schAl] *a.* strittig, streitlustig.
Controversy [kon'tro-wAr-ssi] *n.* Streit *m.*
Contumacious [kon-tju-mei'schAss] *a.* widerspenstig.
Contusion [kon-tjuh'zhAn] *n.* Quetschung *f*.
Conundrum [ko-nAn'drAm] *n.* Rätsel *n.*
Convalescence [kon-wA-less'Anss] *n.* Genesung *f*.
Convalescent [kon-wA-less'Ant] *a.* genesen; **– home** *n.* Erholungsheim *n.*
Convene [kon-wihn'] *vt.* zusammenberufen, vorladen; **-r** *n.* Einberufer *m.*
Convenience [kon-wih'niAnss] *n.* Bequemlichkeit *f*, gelegene Zeit; **public –** Bedürfnisanstalt *f*.

Convenient [kon-wih'ni-Ant]
a. -ly *ad.* bequem, gelegen.
Convent [kon'wAnt] *n.* Kloster *n.*
Convention [kon-wen'schAn]
n. Versammlung *f,* Anstandsregel *f,* Vertrag *m;* -al *a.* herkömmlich, verabredet; – signs *n. pl.* Kartenzeichen *n* (*map*).
Converg'e [kon-wArdzh'] *i.* zusammenlaufen; **-ing fire** Punktfeuer *n* (*mil.*).
Conversant [kon'wer-ssAnt]
a. vertraut, bewandert.
Conversation [kon-wer-ssei'schAn] *n.* Unterredung *f.*
Converse [kon'werss] *a.* Gespräch *n,* Verkehr *m.*
Converse [kon-werss'] *vt.* sich unterhalten, [umgekehrt.
Conversely [kon-wArss'li] *ad.*
Conversion [kon-wAr'schAn]
n. Umsetzung *f,* Bekehrung *f,* Umwertung *f* (*tec.*). [Bekehrte.
Convert [kon'wert] *n.* der, die
Convert [kon-wArt'] *vt.* umändern, umsetzen, bekehren; **-er** *n.* Umwerter *m* (*tec.*); **-ible** *a.* umwechselbar, umsetzbar.
Convex [kon'wex] *a.* konvex; **- lenses** *n.* Sammellinse *f.*
Convey [kon-wei'] *vt.* fortbringen, mitteilen, übertragen (*law*); **-ance** *n.* Überbringung *f,* Spedition *f,* Übertragung *f,* Fuhrwerk *n;* **-or** *n.* Hebemaschine *f,* laufendes Band (*tec.*). [ling *m.*
Convict [kon'wikt] *n.* Sträf-
Convict [kon-wikt'] *vt.* überführen, überzeugen; **-ion** *n.* Überzeugung *f,* Schuldigerklärung *f.* [zeugen.
Convince [kon-winss'] *vt.* über-
Convivial [kon-wi-'wi-Al] *a.* festlich, froh.
Conviviality [kon-wi-wi-æ'li-ti] *n.* Gastlichkeit *f,* Zechen *n.*
Convocation [kon-wo-kei'schAn] Einberufung *f,* Versammlung *f.*
Convoy [kon'weu] *n.* Geleit *n,*

Geleitschiff *n,* Geleitzug *m* (*mil.*), Gepäcktross *m* (*mil.*).
Convoy [kon-weu'] *vt.* begleiten. [schütten.
Convulse [kon-wAlss'] *vt.* er-
Convulsion [kon-wAl'schAn]
n. Zuckung *f,* Krampf *m,* Erschütterung *f.*
Coo [kuh] *vi.* girren.
Cook [kuk] *n.* Koch *m,* Köchin *f; vt. i.* kochen; **-ing range** *n.* Küchenherd *m;* **-er** *n.* Kochapparat *m,* Kochgeschirr *n,* Feldküche *f* (*mil.*); **-ery** *n.* Kochkunst *f.*
Cool [kuhl] *a.* kühl, ruhig, frech; *vt.* abkühlen; *i.* kühl werden; **-ing jacket** Kühlmantel *m* (*tec.*); **-ness** *n.* Kühle *f,* Gleichgültigkeit *f,* Frechheit *f.*
Coolie [ku'li] *n.* Lastträger *m,* Kuli *m.* [*vt.* **- up** einsperren.
Coop [kuhp] *n.* Verschlag *m;*
Cooper [kuh'per] *n.* Küfer *m,* Fassbinder *m;* **-age** *n.* Böttcherei *f.*
Co-operate [ko-o'pA-reit] *vi.* mitwirken; **-ion** *n.* Mitwirkung *f,* Zusammenarbeit *f,* Genossenschaft *f,* Fliegerrehe *f* (*av.*).
Co-operative [ko-o'pA-rA-tiw] *a.* zusammenarbeitend; **- farm** Höfegruppe *f;* **- society** *n.* Einkaufsgenossenschaft *f,* Konsumverein *m;* **- store** Konsumvereinsladen *m.* [wählen.
Co-opt [ko-opt'] *vt.* hinein.
Co-ordinate [ko-Or'di-neit] *vt.* einordnen. [aufnehmen.
Cope [koup] *vi.* sich messen, es
Coping [kou'ping] *n.* Mauerkappe *f.* [reichlich.
Copious [kou'pi-Ass] *a.* -ly *ad.*
Copper [ko'per] *n.* Kupfer *m,* Kessel *m; a.* kupfern; **-s** *pl.* Kupfergeld *n,* Kleingeld *n.*
Copra [ko'prA] *n.* Kopra *f.*
Copse [kopss] *n.* Gehölz *n.*
Copy [ko'pi] *n.* Abschrift *f,* Nachbild *n,* Exemplar *n* (*book*); *vt.* abschreiben, nachahmen; **fair – Reinschrift** *f;* **– book**

Schreibheft n; **-ing ink** n.

Kopiertinte f; **-ing pencil** n.

Kopierstift m; **-ist** n. Abschreiber m; **-right** n. Verlagsrecht n; a. verlagsrechtlich; **-right reserved** Nachdruck verboten.

Coquet(te) [ko-ket'] n. Kokette f; vi. liebäugeln; **-ry** n. Gefallsucht f, Koketterie f; **-tish** a. gefallsüchtig.

Coral [ko'rAl] n. Koralle f; a. korallen.

Cord [kOrd] n. Seil n, Strick m; vt. mit Stricken verbinden.

Cordage [kOr'didzh] n. Seilwerk n, Takelung f (nav.).

Cordial [kOr'di-Al] a. herzlich; n. Magenlikör m; **-ity** n. Herzlichkeit f.

Cordite [kOr'dait] n. Kordit f.

Cordon [kOr'dAn] n. Postenkette f, Gürtel m (mil.); vt. absperren.

Corduroy [kOr'dA-reu] a. Kord m, Manchester m; **- road** Knüppeldamm m; **-trousers** pl. Manchesterhose f.

Core [kOr] n. Kern m; vt. entkernen.

Cork [kOrk] n. Kork m; vt. zukorken; **- sole** Korksohle f; **- screw** n. Korkzieher m.

Corn [kOrn] n. Korn n, Getreide n; vt. pökeln; **-ed beef** n. Büchsenfleisch n; **- exchange** n. Getreidebörse f; **- flour** n. Kornmehl n.

Corn [kOrn] n. Hühnerauge n.

Corner [kOr'ner] n. Winkel m, Ecke f; vt. in die Enge treiben.

Coronation [ko-ro-nei'schAn] n. Krönung. [enbeschauer m.

Coroner [ko'ro-ner] n. Leich-

Corporal [kOr'pA-rAl] n. Korporal m, Unteroffizier m.

Corporal [kOr'pA-rAl] a. körperlich; **- punishment** n. Prügelstrafe f.

Corporate [kOr'pA-rit] a. inkorporiert, gemeinsam.

Corporation [kOr'pA-rei'-

schAn] n. Körperschaft f, Korporation f, Gemeindebehörde f.

Corps [kOr] n. Korps n; **- of signals** n. Nachrichtentruppe f (mil.). [dickleibig.

Corpulent [kOr'pju-lAnt] a.

Correct [ko-rekt'] a. richtig, in Ordnung; vt. berichtigen, zurechtweisen; **-ion** n. Berichtigung f, Zurechtweisung f; **-ive** n. Milderungs-, Heil-mittel n; **-ness** n. Richtigkeit f.

Correlate [ko-ri-leit'] vt. in Wechselbeziehung bringen.

Correspond [ko-riss-pond'] vi. entsprechen, korrespondieren; **-ence** n. Entsprechen n, Briefwechsel m; foreign **-ence** fremdsprachige Korrespondenz; vat n. Korrespondenz f; **-ent** m. **special -ent** Sonderberichterstatter m (press).

Corridor [ko'-ri-dOr] n. Korridor m; **- carriage** n. Durchgangswagen m; **- train** n. Durchgangszug m.

Corroborat'e [ko-ro'bA-reit] vt. bekräftigen; **-ion** n. Bekräftigung f. [ätzen.

Corrode [ko-roud'] vt. wegätzen, [ätzen.

Corrosion [ko-rou'zhAn] n. Ätzen n, Zerfressen n; **damage by -** Rostschaden m.

Corrosive [ko-rou'siw] a. ätzend; **- sublimate** n. Sublimat n.

Corrugated iron [ko'rA-geitid ai'rAn] n. Wellblech n.

Corrupt [ko-rApt'] vt. verderben, bestechen; a. verderbt, bestechlich; **-ible** a. verderblich, käuflich; **-ion** n. Verderbnis f, Bestechung f.

Corset [kOr'ssit] n. Korsett n.

Corvette [kOr-wet'] n. Korvette f, Flottengeleitboot m.

Cosmetic [kos-me'tik] a. kosmetisch; n. Schönheitsmittel n, Kosmetik f.

Cosmic [kos'mik] a. kosmisch.

Cosmopolitan [kos-mo-po'litAn] a. kosmopolitisch.

Cost [kost] *n*. Kosten, *pl*, Preis *m*; *vt. i.* kosten; -**ly** *a*. kostbar; - **price** *n*. Selbstkostenpreis *m*.

Costume [kos'tjuhm] *n*. Kostüm *n*. [Teewärmer *m*.]

Cosy [kou'si] *a*. behaglich; *n*.

Cot [kot] *n*. Bettchen *n*.

Cottage [ko'tidzh] *n*. Hütte *f*, Häuschen *n*; - **piano** *n*. Pianino *n*.

Cotton [kotn] *n*. Baumwolle *f*; *a*. baumwollen; - **mill** *n*. Baumwollspinnerei *f*; - **wool** *n*. Watte *f*.

Couch [kautsch] *n*. Ruhebett *n*; *vt*. niederlegen, abfassen.

Cough [kof] *n*. Husten *n*; *vi*. husten; - **drop** *n*. Hustenbonbon *m*.

Council [kaun'ssil] *n*. Rat *m*; -**lor** *n*. Ratsmitglied *n*, Ratsherr *m*; - **town** - Stadtrat *m*.

Counsel [kaun'ssil] *n*. Rat *m*, Rechtsanwalt *m*, Verteidiger *m* (*law*); -**lor** *n*. Ratgeber *m*.

Count [kaunt] *n*. Graf *m*.

Count [kaunt] *vt*. zählen, schätzen; *i*. rechnen.

Countenance [kaun'ti-nAnss] *n*. Gesicht *n*, Schutz *m*, Fassung *f*; *vt*. begünstigen, zulassen.

Counter [kaun'ter] *ad*. entgegen, zuwider; *vt*. einen Gegenschlag führen.

Counter [kaun'ter] *n*. Ladentisch *m*, Spielmarke *f*, Zähler *m* (*tec.*). [entgegenwirken.]

Counteract [kaun-ter-ækt'] *vt*.

Counter-attack [kaun'ter-A-tæk'] *n*. Gegenangriff *m*, Gegenstoss *m* (*immediate*).

Counter-attraction [kaun'ter-At-ræk'schAn] *n*. entgegengesetzte Anziehung.

Counterbalance [kaun-ter-bæ'lAnss] *vt*. aufwiegen.

Counterblast [kaun'ter-blahst] *n*. Gegenerklärung *f*.

Counterfeit [kaun'ter-fiht] *a*. falsch, erheuchelt; *vi*. verfälschen, erheucheln.

Counterfoil [kaun'ter-feul] *n*, Kontrolschein *m*, Abschnitt *m*. Gegenstück *n*.

Countermand [kaun-ter-mahnd'] *vt*. abbestellen, widerrufen. [der] *n*. Gegenbefehl *m*.

Counter-order [kaun-ter-Or'

Counterpane [kaun-ter-pein] *n*. Steppdecke *f*.

Counterpart [kaun'ter-pahrt] *n*. Doppel *n*, Seiten-, Gegenstück *n*.

Countersign [kaun'ter-ssain] *n*. Parole *f*, Gegenzeichnung *f*; *vt*. gegenzeichnen.

Counterstroke [kaun'ter-strouk], **Counterthrust** [kaun'ter-thrAst] *n*. Gegenstoss *m*.

Countess [kaun'tess] *n*. Gräfin *f*.

Counting-house [kaun'ting-hauss] *n*. Geschäftslokal *n*, Büro *n*. [zählig, zahllos.]

Countless [kaun'tless] *a*. un-

Country [kAn'tri] *n*. Land *n*, Vaterland *n*; - **house** *n*. Landhaus *n*, Villa *f*; - **life** *n*. Landleben *n*; - **man** *n*. Landmann *m* (*farmer*), Landsmann *m* (*compatriot*); - **people** *n*. *pl*. Landleute *pl*.; - **seat** *n*. Landsitz *m*; -**side** *n*. Land *n*, Landschaft *f*; -**woman** *n*. Bauernfrau *f*, Landsmännin *f*.

County [kaun'ti] *n*. Grafschaft *f*, Landkreis *m*; - **borough** *n*. Stadtkreis *m*; - **council** *n*. Kreistag *m*, Grafschaftsrat *m*.

Coupé [kuh'pei] *n*. zweisitziges, geschlossenes Auto.

Couple [kApl] *n*. Paar *n*; *vt*. koppeln.

Coupon [kuh'pon] *n*. Coupon *m*, Gutschein *m*, Abschnitt *m* (*rationing*). [-ous *a*. mutig.]

Courage [kA'ridzh] *n*. Mut *m*;

Courier [ku'ri-er] *n*. Kurier *m*, Eilbote *m*; - **service** *n*. Kurierdienst *m*.

Course [kOrss] *n*. Laufbahn *f*, Fortgang *m*, Lauf *m*, Kurs *m*; **golf** - *n*. Golfplatz *m*; of -

natürlich; – of instruction n.
Lehrgang m.

Court [kOrt] n. Hof m, Gericht n; vt. den Hof machen; – of appeal n. Appelationsgericht n; – plaster n. Englischpflaster n.

Courte'ous [kAr'ti-Ass] a. höflich; -sy n. Höflichkeit f.

Courier [kOr'ti-er] n. Hofmacher m, Liebhaber m. [höflich.

Courtier [kOr'ti-er] n. Hofmann m, Höfling m. [höflich.

Courtly [kOrt'li] a. höfisch.

Courtship [kOrt'schip] n. Freien n, Liebeswerben n.

Courtyard [kOrt'jahrd] n. Hof m. [Cousine f.

Cousin [kAsn] n. Vetter m,

Cove [kouw] n. kleine Bucht.

Covenant [kA'wi-nAnt] n. Vertrag m, Bund m; vt. bedingen.

Cover [kA'wer] n. Decke f, Umschlag m, Deckung f (mil.), Mantel m (tyre); vt. decken; to take – in Deckung gehen (mil.); -ed wagon Planwagen m.

Covering [kA'wer-ing] n. Bedeckung f, Deckmaterial n; – fire n. Deckungsfeuer n (mil.); – force n. Rückhut f; – letter n. Begleit-brief m, -schreiben n; – position n. Aufnahmestellung f (mil.); – troops n. pl. Nachtruppen f. pl. (mil.).

Covertly [kA'wert-li] ad. bedeckt, heimlich.

Covet [kA'wit] vt. begehren, -ous a. begehrlich, gierig; -ousness n. Begierde f.

Cow [kau] n. Kuh f; -boy n. Kuhhirte m, Cowboy m.

Cow [kau] vt. einschüchtern.

Coward [kau'erd] n. Feigling m; -ice n. Feigheit f; -ly a. feig. [mann m (nav.).

Coxswain [koksn] n. Steuermann m.

Coy [keu] a. schüchtern, spröde.

Crab [kræb] n. Krabbe f.

Crack [kræk] n. Krach m, Riss m; vt. zerspalten; i. krachen,

bersten; -ed a. verrückt; -er n. Knallbonbon n, Schwärmer m, Keks m; -le vi. knistern.

Cradle [kreidl] n. Wiege f.

Craft [krahft] n. Handwerk n, List f, Schiff n; -ily ad. -y a. listig; -sman n. Handwerker m.

Cram [kræm] vt. stopfen, vollstopfen, einpauken (examinations).

Cramp [kræmp] n. Krampf m, Klammer f, Zwinge f, Kramme f; vt. einschränken, hemmen.

Cranberry [kræn'be-ri] n. Moosbeere f. [(bird), Kran m.

Crane [krein] n. Kranich m

Crank [krængk] n. Kurbel f, grillenhafter Mensch; – case n. Kurbelgehäuse n; – up vt. ankurbeln.

Cranny [kræ'ni] n. Ritze f.

Crape [kreip] n. Krepp m.

Crash [kræsch] n. Gekrach n, Zusammensturz m, Absturz m (av.); vi. krachen, abstürzen (av.); – boat n. Flugsicherungsboot n; – dive n. Alarmtauchen n; – landing n. Bruchlandung f (av.).

Crass [kræss] a. grob.

Crate [kreit] n. Packkorb m.

Crater [krei'ter] n. Krater m, Minentrichter m (bomb).

Cravat [krA-wæt'] n. Krawatte f, Halsbinde f.

Crav'e [kreiw] vt. erflehen, verlangen; -ing n. Verlangen n, Begierde f.

Crawl [krOl] n. Schleichen n, Kriechstoss-schwimmen n; vi. kriechen; – stroke n. Kriechstoss m. [stift m.).

Crayon [krei'on] n. Farbenstift m.

Craz'e [kreis] n. Verrücktheit f; -y a. hinfällig, verrückt.

Creak [krihk] vi. knarren.

Cream [krihm] n. Rahm m, Sahne f; – separator n. Milchentrahmer m; -ery n. Butterei f. [falten.

Crease [krihss] n. Falte f, zu

Create [kri-eit'] vt. schaffen.

hervorrufen, ernennen; -ion *n.* Schöpfung *f.*, Hervorbringung *f.*; -ive *a.* schaffend, schöpferisch; -or *n.* Schöpfer *m.*

Creature [krih'tscher] *n.* Geschöpf *n.* [Säuglingsheim *n.*

Crèche [kreäsch] *n.* Krippe *f.*

Credence [krih'dAnss] *n.* Glaube *m.*

Credentials [kri-den'schAls] *n. pl.* Beglaubigungsschreiben *n.*

Credib'ility [kre-di-bi'li-ti] *n.* Glaubwürdigkeit *f.*; -le *a.* glaublich.

Credit [kre'dit] *n.* Kredit *m.*, Glaube *m.*, Ehre *f.*, Gutschrift *f.*, Frist *f.*, Ziel *n.*; *vt.* glauben, kreditieren, gutschreiben; -balance *n.* Guthaben *n.*, Kreditsaldo *m.*; -slip *n.* Kreditnote *f.*; -or *n.* Gläubiger *m.*

Credulity [kre-djuh'li-ti] *n.* Leichtgläubigkeit *f.*; -ous *a.* leichtgläubig. [kenntnis *n.*

Creed [krihd] *n.* Glaubensbe-

Creek [krihk] *n.* Windung *f.*, kleine Bucht.

Creel [krihl] *n.* Fischkorb *m.*

Creep [krihp] *vi.* kriechen; -ing barrage Feuerwalze *f* (*mil.*); -er *n.* Kriecher *m.*, Schlingpflanze *f.*

Cremation [kri-mei'schAn] *n.* Feuerbestattung *f.*; -e *vt.* verbrennen; -orium *n.* Einäscherungshalle *f.*

Creosote [krih'o-ssout] *n.* Kreosot *n.*; *vt.* mit Kreosot behandeln. [mond *m.*

Crescent [kre'ssAnt] *n.* Halb-

Cress [kress] *n.* Kresse *f.*

Crest [krest] *n.* Kamm *m.*, Helmschmuck *m.*; -fallen *a.* niedergeschlagen, kleinlaut.

Crevasse [kri-wäss'] *n.* Gletscherspalte *f.*

Crevice [kre'wiss] *n.* Spalt *m.*

Crew [kruh] *n.* Haufe *m.*, Mannschaft *f* (*ship*); air — Besatzung eines Flugzeugs *f.* [bett *n.*

Crib [krib] *n.* Krippe *f.*, Kinder-

Cricket [kri'kit] *n.* Grille *f.*

Cricket [kri'kit] *n.* Kricketspiel *n.*, englisches Schlagballspiel; -er *n.* Kricketspieler *m.*; --field *n.* Kricketspielplatz *m.*; --match *n.* Kricketwettspiel *n.*; --pitch *n.* Kricketspielbahn *f.*

Crier [krai'er] *n.* Ausrufer *m.*

Crime [kraim] *n.* Verbrechen *n.*

Criminal [kri'mi-nAl] *n.* Verbrecher *m.*; *a.* verbrecherisch, strafbar; - law *n.* Strafrecht *n.*

Crimson [krim'sAn] *n.* Karmesin *n.*; *a.* karmesin. [men.

Cringe [krinzh] *vi.* sich krüm-

Crinkle [kringkl] *n.* Falte *f.*, Auszackung *f.*; *vt.* falten, auszacken; *i.* sich kräuseln.

Cripple [kripl] *n.* Krüppel *m.*; *vt.* verkrüppeln, lahmlegen.

Crisis [krai'ssiss] *n.* Krise *f.*, Wendepunkt *m.* [perig. kraus.

Crisp [krisp] *a.* -ly *ad.* knus-

Criterion [krai-tih'ri-An] *n.* Prüfstein *m.*, Norm *f.*

Critic [kri'tik] *n.* Kritiker *m.*; -al *a.* kritisch, bedenklich, gefährlich.

Criticis'e [kri'ti-ssais] *vt.* kritisieren, besprechen, beurteilen; -m *n.* Kritik *f.*, Besprechung *f.*, Rezension *f* (*book*).

Croak [krouk] *vi.* quaken, krächzen. [*f*; *vt. i.* häkeln.

Crochet [krou'schi] *n.* Häkelei

Crockery [kro'kA-ri] *n.* irdenes Geschirr. [Krokodil *n.*

Crocodile [kro'ko-dail] *n.*

Crocus [krou'kAss] *n.* Krokus *m.*, Safran *m.*

Croft [kroft] *n.* kleines Pachtgut; -er *n.* Kleinbauer *m.*

Crony [krou'ni] *n.* alter Freund.

Crook [kruk] *n.* Haken *m.*, Schäferstab *m.*, Schwindler *m.*, Gauner *m.*; *vt.* krümmen; -ed *a.* krumm, schief; -edness *f.* Krümmung *f.*, Krummheit *f.*, Unehrlichkeit *f.*

Crop [krop] *n.* Ernte *f.*, Kropf

m; *vt.* kurz abschneiden, abfressen. [spiel *n*.

Croquet [krou'ki] *n*. Krockettspiel *n*.

Cross [kross] *n*. Kreuz *n*; *a*. widerspenstig, übelgelaunt; *vt.* kreuzen, überschreiten überfahren, durchkreuzen; -country flight *n*. Überlandflug *m*. [Mischrasse *f*.

Cross-breed [kross'brihd] *n*.

Cross-examination [kross'eg-sæ-mi-nei'schAn] *n*. Kreuzverhör *n*. [min] *vt.* verhören.

Cross-examine [kross'eg-sæ'min] *vt.* verhören.

Cross-fire [kross'fai-er] *n*. Kreuzfeuer *n* (*mil.*).

Crossing [kross'ing] *n*. Überfahrt *f*, Kreuzung *f*.

Cross-reference [kross're'fA-rAnss] *n*. gegenseitiger Hinweis.

Cross-roads [kross'rouds] *n*. *pl.* Kreuzweg *m*, Scheideweg *m*.

Cross-section [kross'ssek-schAn] *n*. Querschnitt *m*.

Crosswise [kross'uais] *ad.* kreuzweise.

Crossword [kross'uArd] *n*. Kreuzworträtsel *n*.

Crotchet [kro'tschit] *n*. Viertelnote *f*.

Crotchety [kro'tschi-ti] *a*. launenhaft. [ducken.

Crouch [krautsch] *ḇ.*, sich

Croup [kruhp] *n*. Krupp *m*.

Crow [krou] *n*. Krähe *f*; *vi.* krähen; -'s nest *n*. Krähennest *n*, Ausguck *m* (*nav.*); -bar *n*. Brecheisen *n*.

Crowd [kraud] *n*. Gedränge *n*, Menge *f*; *vt.* anfüllen, drängen.

Crown [kraun] *n*. Krone *f*, Kranz *m*; *vt.* krönen; = octavo *n*. Kleinoktav *n*.

Crucial [kruh'schAl] *a*. entscheidend. [gel *m*.

Crucible [kruh'ssibl] *n*. Tiegel *m*.

Crucifix [kruh'ssi-fix] *n*. Kruzifix *n*; -ion *n*. Kreuzigung *f*.

Crucify [kruh'ssi-fai] *vt.* kreuzigen.

Crud'e [kruhd] *a*. roh; - oil *n*.

Rohöl *n*, Dieselöl *n*; -ness *n*. das Rohe; -ity *n*. Rohheit *f*.

Cruel [kruh'il] *a*. -ly *ad.* grausam; -ty *n*. Grausamkeit *f*.

Cruet [kruh'it] *n*. (Essig) Fläschchen *n*.

Cruis'e [kruhs] *n*. Seereise *f*, Erholungsreise *f*; *vi.* kreuzen (*nav.*); -ing aircraft *n*. Reiseflugzeug *n*; -ing flight *n*. Reiseflug *m*; -ing speed *n*. Reisegeschwindigkeit *f*.

Cruiser [kruh'ser] *n*. Kreuzer *m*; - tank *n*. Kreuzerkampfwagen *n*.

Crumb [krAm] *n*. Krume *f*; - tray *n*. Tafelschippe *f*.

Crumble [krAmbl] *vt.* krümeln; *i.* zerbröckeln.

Crumple [krAmpl] *vt.* zerknittern; - up *n*. einschrumpfen, zusammenbrechen.

Crunch [krAnsch] *vt.* zerknirschen.

Crusade [kru-sseid'] *n*. Kreuzzug *m*; -r *n*. Kreuzfahrer *m*.

Crush [krAsch] *vt.* zerdrücken, unterdrücken; - hat *n*. weicher Hut; -ing mill *n*. Brechmaschine *f*, Stampfgang *m*.

Crust [krAst] *n*. Kruste *f*, Strassendecke *f*; -y *a*. krustig, gränlich, mürrisch.

Crutch [krAtsch] *n*. Krücke *f*.

Crux [krAx] *n*. Schwierigkeit *f*.

Cry [krai] *n*. Schrei *m*, Ausruf *m*, Weinen *n*; *vi.* schreien, ausrufen, weinen; - down verschreien.

Crystal [kristl] *n*. Kristall *n*, Uhrglas *n*; *a*. kristallen; - set *n*. Kristallempfänger *m* (*rad.*); -lize *vt.* umkristallisieren; *i.* sich kristallisieren.

Cub [kAb] *n*. das Junge.

Cube [kjuhb] *n*. Würfel *m*; -root *n*. Kubikwurzel *f*; - sugar *n*. Würfelzucker *n*.

Cubic [kjuh'bik] *a*. würfelförmig, Kubik . . . ; - capacity *n*. Raumgehalt *m*; - metre *n*. Kubikmeter *n*.

Cuckoo [ku'ku] n. Kuckuck m.

Cucumber [kjuh'kAm-ber] n. Gurke f.

Cuddle [kAdl] vt. herzen.

Cudgel [kAd'zhAl] n. Knüttel m.

Cue [kjuh] n. Stichwort n.

Cuff [kAf] n. Schlag m; vt. schlagen; – -links n. pl. doppelte Hemdenknöpfe m. pl.

Culminat'e [kAl'mi-neit] vi. kulminieren, gipfeln; -ion n. Gipfel m, Höhepunkt m.

Culpab'ility [kAl-pA-bi'li-ti] n. Strafbarkeit f; -le a. strafbar. [dige.

Cul prit [kAl'prit] n. der Schul-

Cult [kAlt] n. Kultus m.

Cultivat'e [kAl'ti-weit] vt. bebauen, bilden, pflegen; -ion n. Bebauung f, Bildung f.

Cultural [kAl'tschA-rAl] a. kulturell. [kulturell.

Culture [kAl'tscher] n. Kultur f; -d a. gebildet, kultiviert.

Culvert [kAl'wert] n. Abzugskanal m.

Cumbersome [kAm'ber ssAm] a. schwer zu handhaben.

Cumulative [kjuh'mju-lA-tiw] a. anhäufend, wachsend.

Cumulus [kjuh'mju-lAss] n. Haufenwolke f.

Cunning [kA'ning] a. -ly ad. verschlagen; n. List f, Verschlagenheit f.

Cup [kAp] n. Tasse f; – final n. Schlussstufe f (football).

Cupboard [kA'berd] n. Schrank m. [gierde f.

Cupidity [kjuh-pi'di-ti] n. Begierde f.

Cupola [kjuh'pA-lA] n. Kuppel f, Panzerturm m (mil.).

Cur [kAr] n. Köter m.

Curable [kjuh'rAbl] a. heilbar.

Curate [kjuh'rAt] n. Unterpfarrer m. [end.

Curative [kjuh'rA-tiw] a. heilbar.

Curator [kju-rei'ter] n. Direktor m, Verwalter m.

Curb [kArb] n. Kinnkette f,

Spat m, Zügel m; vt. im Zaume halten.

Curd [kArd] n. Dickmilch f; -le vi. t. gerinnen, gerinnen machen.

Cure [kjuhr] n. Heilmittel n, Kur f; vt. heilen, einpökeln (meat).

Curfew [kAr'fju] n. Zapfenstreich m, Ausgehverbot n.

Curiosity [kju-ri-o'ssi-ti] n. Neugier f, Seltenheit f; – shop n. Antiquitätenladen m.

Curious [kjuh'ri-Ass] a. neugierig, seltsam.

Curl [kArl] n. Ringel m; vt. kräuseln; -ing tongs n. pl. Brenn-, Kräuse-eisen n; -y a. lockig.

Currant [kA'rAnt] n. Korinthe f; black – schwarze Johannisbeere; red – Johannisbeere f.

Currency [kA'rAn-ssi] n. Gangbarkeit f, Umlauf m, Valuta f.

Current [kA'rAnt] a. laufend, umlaufend, marktgängig; n. Strom m, Strömung f; – account laufende Rechnung, Girokonto n; – rate Tageskurs m.

Curriculum [kA-ri'kju-lAm] n. Lehrplan m, Studiengang m.

Curry [kA'ri] n. vt. striegeln, zurichten (leather); – favour vt. sich einschmeicheln.

Curse [kArss] n. Fluch m; vt. verfluchen; i. fluchen.

Cursory [kAr'ssA-ri] a. flüchtig.

Curt [kArt] a. -ly ad. kurz.

Curtail [kAr-teil'] vt. abkürzen, beschränken.

Curtain [kAr'tin] n. Vorhang m; vt. mit Vorhängen versehen; – -raiser n. Einakter m (theatre), Vorspannfilm m.

Curtsey [kArt'ssi] n. Knicks m; vi. knicksen.

Curvature [kAr'wA-tjur] n. (Ver-)Krümmung f.

Curve [kArw] n. Krümmung f,

Bogenlinie f, Kurve f; vt. krümmen.

Cushion [ku'schAn] n. Kissen n, Dampfpolster n (tec.); – tyre n. Vollgummireifen m.

Custard [kA'sterd] n. Eierrahmen m.

Custodian [kA-stou'di-An] n. Hüter m, Kustos m.

Custody [kA'stA-di] n. Hut f, Haft f; take into – verhaften.

Custom [k A'stAm] n. Gebrauch m, Kundschaft f (shop); – house n. Zollamt n; -ary a. gebräuchlich; -er n. Kunde m, Kundin f; queer – er sonderbarer Kauz; -s n. pl. Zoll m; -s examination n. Zollrevision f; -s official n. Zollbeamte(r) m; -s regulations n. pl. Zollordnung f.

Cut [kAt] n. Schnitt m; vt. schneiden, aufschneiden, beschneiden, abschneiden (loss), kürzen (wages), abheben (cards); – away vt. abschneiden; – back vt. wiederholen (film); – down vt. fällen, behauen (trees), ermäßigen (price), vermindern, kürzen (length); – fine f. knapp bemessen; – in vi. sich wieder einreihen (aut.); – off vt. abschneiden, trennen (ph.), abschalten, ausschalten (rad.); – out vt. ausschneiden, zuschneiden (clothes), ausschalten (rad.); – short vt. abbrechen, unterbrechen; – up vt. aufschneiden, zerlegen (food), betrüben (persons). | gewecht.

Cute [kjuht] a. schlau, aufgeweckt.

Cutlass [kAt'lAss] n. Entermesser n (nav.).

Cutler [kAt'ler] n. Messerschmied m; -y n. Messerschmiedewaren f. pl, Stahlwaren f. pl.

Cutter [kA'ter] n. Zuschneider m, Schneidemaschine f, Kutter m (nav.); revenue – Zollwachtschiff n.

Cut-throat [kAt'throut] n. Halsabschneider m; a. mörderisch.

Cutting [kA'ting] n. Durchstich m, Steckling m, Ausschnitt m (newspaper); – edge n. Schneide f.

Cycle [ssaikl] n. Zyklus m, Fahrrad n (bicycle), Schwingung f (rad.); vi. radfahren; – race n. Radrennen n; – racing track n. Radrennbahn f; – tyre n. Radreifen m.

Cycling [ssai'kling] n. Radsport m; – club n. Radfahrverein m; – path, – track n. Radfahrweg m.

Cyclist [ssai'klist] n. Radfahrer m, -fahrerin f, Radler m.

Cyclometer [ssai-klo'mi-ter] n. Kreismesser m.

Cyclone [ssai'kloun] n. Wirbelsturm m, Zyklon m.

Cyclopedia [ssai-klo-pih'di-A] n. Konversationslexikon n.

Cylinder [ssi'lin-der] n. Zylinder m, Walze f; – block n. Zylinderblock m (aut.).

Cylindrical [ssi-lin'dri-kAl] a. zylinderförmig.

Cynic [ssi'nik] n. Zyniker m; -al a. -ally ad. zynisch, frech, schamlos.

Cynicism [ssi'ni-ssism] n. Zynismus m, Schamlosigkeit f.

Cypress [ssai'press] n. Zypresse f.

D

Dabble [dæbl] vi. sich befassen, pfuschen; – r n. Stümper m.

Daffodil [dæ'fo-dil] n. gelbe Narzisse. | [risch.

Daft [dahft] a. verrückt, närrisch.

Dagger [dæ'ger] n. Dolch m.

Dahlia [dei'liA] n. Dahlie f, Georgine f.

Daily [dei'li] a. ad. täglich; n. Tageszeitung f; – consumption n. Tagesverbrauch m; – report n. Tagesbericht m.

n. Tagesbericht m; – travelling allowance n. Tagegeld n.

Daintiness [dein'ti-ness] n. Feinheit f. [n. Leckerbissen.

Dainty [dein'ti] a. lecker, fein;

Dairy [deh'ri] n. Molkerei f, Milchgeschäft m. [chen n.

Daisy [dei's'] n. Gänseblüm-

Dale [deil] n. Tal m.

Dally [dæ'li] vi. tändeln.

Dam [dæm] n. Damm m; vt. dämmen, abdämmen.

Damage [dæ'midzh] n. Schaden m; –s pl. Schadenersatz m; vt. beschädigen.

Damask [dæ'mAsk] n. Damast m; a. damasten.

Dame [deim] n. Frau f, alte vt. [chen n.

Damn [dæm] vt. verdammen, verwünschen; –able a. verdammungswürdig, verdammt; –ation n. Verdammung f.

Damp [dæmp] a. feucht; vt. befeuchten. [Dämpfer m tec.]

Damper [dæm'per] n. (Schall-)

Dampness [dæmp'ness] n. Feuchtigkeit f. [n, Jungfrau f.

Damsel [dæm'sAl] n. Mädchen

Damson [dæm'sAn] n. Damaszener Pflaume.

Dance [dahnss] n. Tanz m, Ball m; vi. tanzen; – band n. Tanzkapelle f; – hall n. Tanzlokal n; – music n. Tanzmusik f.

Dancer [dahn'sser] n. Tänzer m, Tänzerin f.

Dandelion [dæn-di-lai-An] n. Löwenzahn m.

Dandruff [dæn'drAf] n. Schorf auf dem Kopfe m.

Dandy [dæn'di] n. Stutzer m.

Danger [dein'zher] n. Gefahr f; – area – zone n. Gefahrenraum m; –ous a. gefährlich.

Dangle [dæng'gl] vi. baumeln.

Dapper [dæ'per] a. schmuck, modisch.

Dapple [dæpl] a. fleckig, getupft; vt. tüpfeln, sprenkeln; – grey a. apfelgrau.

Dar'e [dehr] vt. wagen, herausfordern; –ing a. kühn; n. Kühnheit f.

Dark [dahrk] a. dunkel; –en vt. verdunkeln, abblenden (ship); –ness n. Finsternis f, Dunkelheit f. [ling m.

Darling [dahr'ling] n. Lieb-

Darn [dahrn] n. Stopffleck m; vt. stopfen; –ing needle n. Stopfnadel f; –ing wool n. Stopfwolle f.

Dart [dahrt] n. plötzliche Bewegung; vi. stürzen, hervorschiessen.

Dash [dæsch] n. Strich m, Anlauf m; vt. schmeissen, bespritzen.

Dashboard [dæsch'bOrd] n. Instrumentenbrett n, Armaturenbrett n (aut.).

Dastardly [dæ'sterd-li] a. heimtückisch, hinterlistig.

Data [dei'tA] n. pl. Angaben f, pl. Unterlage f.

Date [deit] n. Datum n; vt. datieren; out of – a. veraltet; – stamp n. Datumstempel m.

Date [deit] n. Dattel f.

Dative [dei'tiw] n. Dativ m, dritter Fall.

Daub [dOb] vt. beschmieren; – schmieren; –er n. Schmierer m.

Daughter [dO'ter] n. Tochter f.

Daunt [dOnt] vt. entmutigen, erschrecken; –less a. furchtlos, unerschrocken. [(nav.).]

Davit [dei'wit] n. Davit m.

Dawdle [dOdl] vi. Zeit vergeuden. [vi. dämmern.

Dawn [dOn] n. Dämmerung f;

Day [dei] n. Tag m; –book n. Tage-, Verkaufs-buch n; –break n. Tagesanbruch m; –fighter n. Tagesjäger m; –fighting n. Tagesjagd f; –light n. Tageslicht n; –time n. Tag m.

Daze [deis] vt. betäuben.

Dazzle [dæsl] vt. blenden; – painting n. Blendanstrich m.

Deacon [dih'kAn] n. Dekan m.

Dead [ded] a. tot, matt; – calm n. Windstille f; – centre n. toter Punkt (tec.); – weight

n. Eigen-, Leer-gewicht n; -en vt. abstumpfen, dämpfen; -liness n. Tödlichkeit f; -ly a. tödlich; -lock n. vollständige Stockung f; -ness n. Unbelebtheit f, Mattigkeit f, Abgestorbenheit f.

Dead reckoning [ded're'kAning] n. Überschlag m, Gissung f; position by - gegisster Standort m.

Deaf [def] a. taub; -en vt. taub machen; -ness n. Taubheit f.

Deal [dihl] n. Menge f, Abschluss m, Handel m; vt. austeilen; i. handeln, Karten geben; - with vt. behandeln, erledigen, besorgen.

Dealer [dih'ler] n. Händler m, Kartengeber m.

Dealings [dih'lings] n. pl. Verfahren n, Geschäftsverkehr m.

Dean [dihn] n. Dekan m.

Dear [dihr] a. -ly ad. teuer, lieb; -ness n. Teuerheit f.

Dearth [dArth] n. Mangel m.

Death [deth] n. Tod m, -'s head n. Totenkopf m; - rate n. Sterblichkeitsziffer f.

Debar [di-bahr'] vt. ausschliessen, versagen. [rigen.

Debase [di-beiss'] vt. erniedrigen.

Debatable [di-bei'tAbl] a. bestreitbar.

Debate [di-beit'] n. Debatte f, Diskussion f; vt. debattieren, diskutieren; i. debattieren.

Debauch [di-bötsch'] n. Prasserei f; vt. verführen, verderben; -ed a. liederlich; -ery n. Ausschweifung f.

Debenture [di-ben'tscher] n. Obligation f. [Schwäche f.

Debility [di-bi'li-ti] n. Debit [de'bit] n. Debet n; vt. belasten, debitieren.

Debt [det] n. Schuld f; -or n. Schuldner m.

Debus [dih-bAss'] vt. abladen, ausladen (mil.). [zehnt n.

Decade [de'keid] n. Jahr-

Decadence [de'kA-dAnss] n.

Verfall m; -t a. dekadent, entartet.

Decamp [di-kæmp'] vi. sich aus dem Staube machen.

Decant [di-kænt'] vt. abgiessen, umfüllen; -er n. Karaffe f.

Decarbonize [dih-kahr'bonais] vt. entkohlen.

Decay [di-kei'] n. Abnahme f, Verfall m; vi. abnehmen, verfallen, absterben.

Decease [di-ssihss'] n. Hinscheiden n; vi. sterben; -d a. verstorben; n. der Verstorbene.

Deceit [di-ssiht'] n. Täuschung f, Trug m; -ful a. -fully ad. täuschend, trügerisch; -fulness n. Trüglichkeit f, Hinterlist f.

Deceive [di-ssihw'] vt. betrügen, täuschen.

Decelerate [dih-sse'lA-reit] vi. t. verlangsamen; -ion n. Verlangsamung f.

December [di-ssem'ber] n. Dezember m.

Decency [dih'ssAn-ssi] n. Schicklichkeit f, Anständigkeit f.

Decent [dih'ssAnt] a. anständig, annehmbar, genügend.

Deception [di-ssep'schAn] n. Betrug m.

Deceptive [di-ssep'tiw] a. trügerisch, täuschend.

Decide [di-ssaid'] vt. entscheiden; i. sich entscheiden; -d a. -dly ad. entschieden, bestimmt.

Decimal [de'ssiml] n. Dezimalbruch m; a. dezimal.

Decimate [de'ssi-meit] vt. dezimieren.

Decipher [di-ssai'fer] vt. entziffern, dechiffrieren.

Decision [di-ssi'zhAn] n. Entscheidung f, Entschiedenheit f.

Decisive [di-ssai'siw] a. entscheidend, entschieden.

Deck [dek] n. Deck n; vt. schmücken; - -chair n. Liegestuhl m. [deklamieren.

Declaim [di-kleim'] vt. i.

Declamation [de-klA-mei'-schAn] n. Deklamation f.

Declaration [de-klA-rei'-schAn] n. Erklärung f.

Declare [di-klehr'] vt. erklären, behaupten.

Decline [di-klain'] n. Abnahme f, Verfall m; vt. ablehnen, deklinieren; i. zu Ende gehen, sich weigern. [hang m.

Declivity [di-kli'-wi-ti] n. Ab-

Declutch [di'-klAtsch'] vi. entkuppeln (aut.).

Decoct [di-kokt'] vt. abkochen; -ion n. Absud m.

Decode [dih-koud'] vt. entziffern, entschlüsseln; -r n. Entzifferer m.

Decompose [dih-kom-pous'] vi. verwesen; t. zerlegen.

Decontaminate [dih-kon-tæ'-mi-neit] vt. entgiften, entlosten. [freigeben.

Decontrol [dih-kon-troul'] vt.

Decorate [de'ko-reit] vt. zieren, dekorieren; -ion n. Verzierung f, Orden m (mil., etc.); -or m. Verzierer m, Dekorateur m.

Decorous [de'ko-rAss] a. anständig, schicklich, geziemend.

Decoy [di-keu'] n. Lockung f, Köder m, Falle f; vt. locken; -ship n. Unterseebootfalle f (nav.).

Decrease [dih'krihss] n. Abnahme f Verminderung f.

Decrease [di-krihss'] vt. vermindern; i. abnehmen.

Decree [di-krih'] n. Erlass m, Entscheidung f; vt. verordnen, entscheiden. [gelebt.

Decrepit [di-kre'pit] a. abgelebt.

Decry [di-krai'] vt. verrufen.

Dedicatory [de-di-kei'tA-ri] a. widmend, zueignend.

Dedicate [de'di-keit] vt. weihen, widmen; -ion n. Widmung f.

Deduce [di-djuhss'] vt. ableiten, schliessen.

Deduct [di-dAkt'] vt. abzie-

hen; -ion n. Abziehen n, Abzug m.

Deed [dihd] n. Tat f, Urkunde f. [len.

Deem [dihm] vt. halten, urtei-

Deep [dihp] a. -ly ad. tief, eindringlich, stark; -en vt. vertiefen.

Deer [dir] n. Rotwild n, Reh n.

Deface [di-feiss'] vt. entstellen; -ment n. Entstellung f.

Defalcation [dih-fæl-kei'-schAn] n. Unterschlagung f, Veruntreuung f.

Defamation [dih-fA-mei'-schAn] n. Verleumdung f.

Defamatory [di-fæ'mA-tA-ri] a. verleumderisch, ehrenrührig.

Defame [de-feim'] vt. verleumden, verschreien.

Default [di-fOlt'] n. Unterlassung f, Nichterscheinen n; vi. nicht zahlen; -er n. Veruntreuer m.

Defeat [di-fiht'] n. Niederlage f, Vereitelung f; vt. schlagen, vereiteln; -ism n. Defätismus m; -ist m. Defätist m.

Defect [di-fekt'] n. Fehler m; -ive a. fehlerhaft, schadhaft.

Defence [di-fenss'] n. Verteidigung f; - area n. Sicherungsgebiet n (mil.); - in depth n. tiefgegliederte Abwehr (mil.); - measures n. pl. Abwehrmassnahmen f. pl; - regiment n. Sicherungsregiment n (mil.).

Defenceless [di-fenss'less] a. schutzlos.

Defend [di-fend'] vt. verteidigen, schützen; -ant n. der, die Beklagte; -er n. Verteidiger m.

Defensive [di-fen'ssiw] n. Defensive f; a. verteidigend, Schutz . . . .

Defer [di-fAr'] vt. aufschieben; i. sich fügen.

Deference [de'fA-rAnss] n. Rücksichtnahme f, Hochachtung f. [a. ehrerbietig.

Deferential [de-fA-ren'schAl]

Defian'ce [di-fai'Anss] n. Trotz m; **-t** a. trotzig.

Deficien'cy [di-fi'schAn-ssi] n. Mangelhaftigkeit f, Minus n, Mangel m; **-t** a. mangelhaft, ungenügend.

Deficit [de'fi-ssit] n. Defi*it n, Fehlbetrag m.

Defile [di-fail'] n. Engpass m, Hohlweg m; vi. vorbeimarschieren.

Defile [di-fail'] vt. beflecken, schänden; **-ment** n. Befleckung f, Schändung f.

Define [di-fain'] vt. festsetzen, bestimmen.

Definite [de'fi-nit] a. **-ly** ad. bestimmt.

Definition [de-fi-ni'schAn] n. Definition f, Begriffsbestimmung f.

Deflat'e [di-fleit'] vt. entleeren (balloon), herunterbringen (prices); **-ion** n. Deflation f.

Deflect [di-flekt'] vt. ablenken; **-ion** n. Ablenkung f, Ausschlag m (needle), Seitenabweichung f (mil.).

Deform [di-fOrm'] vt. entstellen; **-ity** n. Ungestaltheit f.

Defraud [di-frOd'] vt. betrügen; **-er** n. Betrüger m.

Defray [di-frei'] vt. bestreiten.

Deft [deft] a. **-ly** ad. geschickt, gewandt.

Defunct [di-fAnkt'] a. verstorben.

Defy [di-fai'] vt. herausfordern, Trotz bieten.

Degenerate [di-dzhe'nA-reit] a. entartet.

Degenerat'e [di-dzhe'nA-reit] vt. entarten, ausarten; **-ion** n. Entartung f.

Degradation [de-grA-dei'schAn] n. Degradation f, Herabwürdigung f.

Degrad'e [di-greid'] vt. degradieren, entwürdigen; **-ing** a. entehrend.

Degree [di-grih'] n. Grad m.

De-icing [dih-ai'ssing] n. Enteisung f (av.).

Deity [dih'i-ti] n. Gottheit f.

Deign [dein] vi. geruhen.

Dejected [di-dzhek'tid] a. niedergeschlagen.

Dejection [di-dzhek'schAn] n. Niedergeschlagenheit f.

Delay [di-lei'] vt. verzögern, hinhalten; i. zögern; n. Verzögerung f, Aufschub m; **-ed action** n. Verzögerung f, Zugzeit f.

Delegate [de'li-gAt] n. der, die Beauftragte.

Delegate [de'li-geit] vt. delegieren, überweisen.

Delete [di-liht'] vt. ausstreichen.

Deleterious [de-li-ti'ri-Ass] a. schädlich.

Deliberat'e [di-li'bA-reit] vt. erwägen; i. nachdenken; **-ion** n. Überlegung f.

Deliberate [di-li'bA-rit] a. bedächtig, wohlerwogen.

Delicacy [de'li-kA-ssi] n. Feinheit f, Empfindlichkeit f, Leckerbissen n.

Delicate [de'li-kit] a. fein, zart, schwächlich, bedenklich.

Delicious [di-li'schAss] a. **-ly** ad. köstlich.

Delight [di-lait'] n. Lust f; vt. ergötzen; **to be -ed** sich freuen; **-ful** a. höchst erfreulich.

Delineat'e [di-li'ni-eit] vt. entwerfen, zeichnen, schildern; **-ion** n. Entwurf m, Beschreibung f.

Delinquen'cy [di-ling'kuen-ssi] n. Verbrechen n, Missetat f; **-t** n. Verbrecher m.

Delirious [di-li'ri-Ass] a. irre; **-um** n. Fieberwahnsinn m.

Deliver [di-li'wer] vt. befreien, abgeben, überreichen, liefern (com.); **-ance** n. Befreiung f; **-er** n. Befreier m.

Delivery [di-li'wA-ri] n. Abgabe f, Übergabe f, Lieferung f; **- van** n. Liefer-, Geschäftswagen m.

Dell [del] n. enges Tal.

Delouse [dih-laus'] vt. entlausen.

Delta [del'tA] n. Delta n.

Delude [di-luhd'] vt. betrügen, täuschen.

Deluge [de'ljuhdzh] *n.* Überschwemmung *f.*

Delusion [di-ljuh'zhAn] *n.* Täuschung *f*, Irrtum *m.*

Delusive [di-ljuh'sihv] *a.* trügerisch.

Delve [delw] *vt.* graben.

Demagogue [de'mA-gog] *n.* Demagoge *m.*

Demand [di-mAnd'] *n.* Verlangen *n*, Nachfrage *f*; *vt.* verlangen, fragen, erfordern.

Demarcate [dih'mahr-keit] *vt.* abgrenzen; -ion *n.* Abgrenzung *f*, Demarkation *f*; -ion line *n.* Demarkationslinie *f*, Grenze *f*.

Demean [di-mihn'] *vr.* sich Benehmen *n.*

Demeanour [di-mih'ner] *n.* Benehmen *n.*

Demilitarize [dih-mi'li-tA-rais] *vt.* entmilitarisieren.

Demise [di-mais'] *n.* Tod *m*, Ableben *n.*

Demobilization [dih-mou-bi-lai-sei'schAn] *n.* Demobilmachung *f*, Entlassung *f.*

Demobilize [dih-mou'bi-lais] *vt.* demobilieren, ausser Dienst stellen.

Democracy [di-mo'krA-ssi] *n.* Demokratie *f*; -t *n.* Demokrat *m*; -tic *a.* demokratisch.

Demolish [di-mo'lisch] *vt.* niederreissen, vernichten.

Demolition [dih-mo-li'schAn] *n.* Niederreissen *n*, Abbau *m*; - detachment *n*, -squad *n.* Sprengkommando *n*, Zerstörungstrupp *m*.

Demon [dih'mAn] *n.* Teufel *m.*

Demonstrable [di-mon'strAbl] *a.* nachweisbar.

Demonstrate [de'mAn-streit] *vt.* beweisen.

Demonstration [de-mAn-strei'schAn] *n.* Beweisführung *f*, Demonstration *f*, Kundgebung *f*; - battalion *n.* Lehrbataillon *n*; - unit *n.* Lehrtruppe *f.*

Demonstrative [di-mon'strA-tiw] *a.* temperamentvoll, die Gefühle zeigend.

Demoralize [di-mo'rA-lais] *vt.* demoralisieren.

Demur [di-mAr'] *n.* Aufschub *m*; *vi.* zögern, Anstand nehmen.   [lich.

Demure [di-mjuhr'] *a.* zimper-

Den [den] *n.* Höhle *f*, Lager *n.*

Denationalize [di-næ'schA-nA-lais] *vt.* ausbürgern.

Denaturalize [di-næ'schA-rA-lais] *vt.* entnationalisieren; -ation *n.* Entlassung aus dem Staatsverband *f.*

Denominate [di-no'mi-neit] *vt.* benennen; -ion *n.* Sekte *f*, Bekenntnis *n.*

Denote [di-nout'] *vt.* bedeuten.

Denounce [di-naunss'] *vt.* öffentlich anklagen, anzeigen, kündigen (treaty).

Dense [denss] *a.* -ely *ad.* dicht, dick; -ity *n.* Dichtheit *f.*

Dent [dent] *n.* Höhlung *f*, Beule *f*; *vt.* Höhlungen machen, einbeulen.

Dental [dentl] *a.* Zahn ... ; - surgeon *n.* Zahnarzt *m*; -ifrice *n.* Zahnwasser *n*; -ist *n.* Zahnarzt *m*; -ure *n.* künstliches Gebiss.   [blössen.

Denude [di-njuhd'] *vt.* ent-

Denunciation [di-nAn-ssi-ei'schAn] *n.* Anzeigen *n*, Angeben *n*, öffentliche Anklage, Kündigung *f* (treaty).

Deny [di-nai'] *vt.* verneinen, verweigern, abschlagen.

Depart [di-pahrt'] *vi.* abfahren, absterben.

Department [di-pahrt'mAnt] *n.* Abteilung *f*, Departement *n.*

Departmental [di-pahrt-men'tAl] *a.* Abteilungs ... ; - store *n.* Warenhaus *n.*

Departure [di-pahr'tscher] *n.* Abfahrt *f*, Abweichung *f.*

Depend [di-pend'] *vi.* abhängen, sich verlassen; -able *a.* zuverlässig; -ence *n.* Abhängigkeit *f*; -ent *a.* abhängig.

Depict [di-pîkt'] vt. schildern.

Deplane [dih-plein'] vi. aussteigen (av.); t. abladen (av.).

Deplete [di-plîht'] vt. entleeren.

Deplorable [di-plÔ'rAbl] a. bejammernswert. [mern.

Deplore [di-plÔr'] vt. i. bejammern.

Deploy [di-pleu'] vt. i. entfalten, entwickeln (mil.); -ment n. Entfaltung f. [entvölkern.

Depopulate [di-po'pju-leit'] vt.

Deport [di-pÔrt'] vt. abschieben; -ation n. Abschub m, Ausweisung f; -ee n. der, die Ausgewiesene.

Deportment [di-pÔrt'mAnt] n. Betragen n.

Depose [di-pous'] vt. absetzen.

Deposit [di-po'sit] n. Niederschlag m, Depositum n, Einlage f; vt. niederlegen, einzahlen. [n. eidliche Aussage.

Deposition [dih-po-si'schAn]

Depot [de'pou] n. Niederlage f, Lagerhaus n, Ablage f (mil.); - ship n. Bei. Mutter-schiff n, Kasernenschiff (nav.); - unit n. Ersatzeinheit f (mil.).

Depraved [di-preiwd'] a. moralisch verdorben.

Depravity [di-præ'wi-ti] n. Verderbtheit f.

Deprecate [de'pri-keit] vt. ausdrücklich missbilligen.

Depreciate [di-prîh'schi-eit] vt. herabsetzen; i. (im Werte, Preis) sinken; -ion n. Verringerung f, Entwertung f, Abschreibung f.

Depredation [de-pri-dei'schAn] n. Plündern n.

Depress [di-press'] vt. niederdrücken, niederschlagen; -ion n. Nieder-drückung f, -geschlagenheit f, Flauheit f (trade), Mulde f (hollow).

Deprivation [de-pri-wei'schAn] n. Beraubung f, Verlust m, Aberkennung f (rights).

Deprive [di-praiw'] vt. benehmen, entsetzen.

Depth [depth] n. Tiefe f; -charge n. Wasserbombe f (nav.); - sounding gong n. Knallgeber m (nav.).

Deputation [de-pju-tei'schAn] n. Abordnung f, Abgeordnete m. pl. [nen.

Depute [di-pjuht'] vt. abord-

Deputy [de'pju-ti] n. der Abgeordnete, Stellvertreter m; - assistant a. stellvertretend (mil.). [lassen.

Derail [dih-reil'] vt. entgleisen

Derange [di-reindzh'] vt. in Unordnung bringen; -ment n. Geisteszerrüttung f.

De-registration [dih-re-dzhi-strei'schAn] n. Abmeldung f.

Derelict [de'ri-likt] a. herrenlos; n. treibendes Wrack.

Dereliction [de-ri-lik'schAn] n. (Pflicht-) Verletzung f.

Deri'de [di-raid'] vt. verlachen; -sion f. Verspottung f; -sive a. spöttisch.

Derivation [de-ri-wei'schAn] n. Ableitung f.

Derivative [de-ri'wA-tiw] a. abgeleitet; n. das Abgeleitete, Derivat n.

Derive [di-raiw'] vt. ableiten.

Derogatory [di-ro'gA-tA-ri] a. beeinträchtigend.

Derrick [de'rik] n. drehbarer Schiffskran, Lademast m.

Desalination [dih-sse-li-nei'schAn] n. (Wasser-) Entsalzung f.

Descend [di-ssend'] vi. herabsteigen, fallen, herkommen; -ant n. Nachkomme m.

Descent [di-ssent'] n. Herabsteigen n, Fall m, Herkunft f, Abhang m; parachute - f. Absprung m (av.). [schreiben.

Describe [di-skraib'] vt. be-

Description [di-skrip'schAn] n. Beschreibung f, Art f; -ive a. beschreibend.

Descry [diss-krai'] vt. entdecken, erblicken.

Desecrat'e [de'ssi-kreit] *vt.* entweihen; **-ion** *n.* Entweihung *f.* [Wüste *f.*]

Desert [de'sert] *a.* wüst;

Desert [di-ssArt'] *vt.* verlassen, desertieren; **-er** *n.* Ausreisser *m.*, Überläufer *m.*; **-ion** *n.* Verlassen *n.*, Desertion *f.*, Fahnenflucht *f* (mil.).

Deserve [di-sArw'] *vt.* verdienen; **-edly** *ad.* nach Verdienst; **-ing** *a.* verdient, würdig.

Design [di-sain'] *n.* Entwurf *m.*, Absicht *f.*, Muster *n.*, Bauart *f* (style); **-** *vt.* entwerfen, beabsichtigen; **-edly** *ad.* absichtlich; **-er** *n.* Erfinder *m.*, Musterzeichner *m.*; **-ing** *a.* entwerfend, hinterlistig; *n.* Zeichnen *n.*, Zeichenkunst *f*

Designat'e [de'sig-neit] *vt.* bezeichnen, ernennen; **-ion** *n.* Bezeichnung *f.* [schenswert.]

Desirable [di-saïrAbl] *a.* wünschenswert.

Desir'e [di-saïr'] *n.* Begehren *n.*; *vt.* begehren, wünschen; **-ous** *a.* begierig.

Desist [di-sist'] *vi.* abstehen.

Desk [desk] *n.* Pult *n.*

Desolat'e [de'sso-lit] *a.* einsam, öde; **-ion** *n.* Verödung *f* Elend *n.*

Despair [di-spehr'] *n.* Verzweiflung *f*; *vi.* verzweifeln.

Despatch [di-spætsch'] *n.* Absendung *f.*, Depesche *f.*, Meldung *f*; *vt.* absenden; **-** *rider* *n.* Kraftradmelder *m.*, Meldereiter *m.*, Kurier *m.* [zweifelt.]

Desperate [de'spA-rit] *a.* verzweifelt.

Despicable [de'spi-kAbl] *a.* verächtlich. [ten.]

Despise [di-spaïs'] *vt.* verachten

Despite [di-spaït'] *pr.* trotz.

Despoil [di-speul'] *vt.* plündern.

Despond [di-spond'] *vi.* verzagen; **-ency** *n.* Verzagtheit *f*; **-ent** *a.* mutlos.

Despot [de'spot] *n.* Tyrann *m.*; **-ic** *a.* despotisch; **-ism** *n.* Gewaltherrschaft *f*

Dessert [di-sArt'] *n.* Nachtisch *m.*, Dessert *n.*

Destination [de-sti-nei'schAn] *n.* Bestimmung *f.*, Bestimmungsort *m.*

Destin'e [de'stin] *vt.* bestimmen; **-y** *n.* Schicksal *n.*

Destitute [de'sti-tjuht] *a.* leer, hilflos, mittellos; **-ion** *n.* Not *f.*, Armut *f.*

Destroy [di-streu'] *vt.* zerstören, vertilgen.

Destructible [di-strAk'tibl] [*a.* zerstörbar.

Destruct'ion [di-strAk'schAn] *n.* Zerstörung *f*; **-ive** *a.* zerstörend; **-iveness** *n.* zerstörende Gewalt.

Desultory [de'ssAl-tA-ri] *a.* planlos, sprunghaft, unregelmässig.

Detach [di-tætsch'] *vt.* losmachen, abkommandieren (mil.), trennen, abheften (coupons); **-ed** *house* *n.* freistehendes Haus; **-ed** *personnel* *n.* Kommandierte *m. pl.* (mil.).

Detachable [di-tætsch'Abl] *a.* abtrennbar, abnehmbar, zerlegbar.

Detachment [di-tætsch'mAnt] *n.* Losmachen *n.*, Abteilung *f.*, Gruppe *f.*, Kommando *n.* (mil.).

Detail [dih'teil] *n.* Einzelheit *f*; *vt.* umständlich darstellen, abkommandieren (mil.); **-ed** *a.* umständlich.

Detain [di-tein'] *vt.* zurückhalten, festhalten.

Detect [di-tekt'] *vt.* aufdecken; **-ion** *n.* Aufdeckung *f.*; **-ive** *n.* Detektive *m.*, Kriminalpolizist *m.*; **-ive** *story* *n.* Kriminalroman *m.*; **-or** *n.* Aufdecker *m.*, Anzeigevorrichtung *f* (tec.), Wellenanzeiger *m* (rad.).

Detention [di-ten'schAn] *n.* Zurückhaltung *f.*, Haft *f.*; **-in** *remand* *n.* Untersuchungshaft *f*; **~** *camp* *n.* Internierungslager *n.*

Deter [di-tÁr'] *vt.* abschrek-
ken; **-rent** *n.* Abschreckungs-
mittel *n.*

Deteriorat'e [di-tih'ri-Á-reit]
vi. sich verschlimmern; **-ion** *n.*
Verschlimmerung *f.*

Determinable [di-tÁr'mi-
nÁbl] *a.* bestimmbar.

Determination [di-tÁr-mi-
nei'schÁn] *n.* Entschlossenheit *f.*

Determine [di-tÁr'min] *vt.*
bestimmen; **-d** *a.* entschlossen.

Detest [di-test'] *vt.* verabscheuen; **-able** *a.* abscheulich.

Detestation [dih-tes-tei'
schÁn] *n.* Verabscheuung *f.*

Dethrone [di-throun'] *vt.* entthronen.

Detonat'e [de'tou-neit] *vi.* explodieren lassen; **-ion** *n.* Knall
m.; **-or** *n.* Sprengkapsel *f* Zünder *m* (*mil.*).

Detour [dei-tuhr'] *n.* Umgehungsweg *m*, Abstecher *m.*

Detract [di-trækt'] *vi.* schmälern; **-ion** *n.* Verleumdung *f*;
-or *n.* Verleumder *m.*

Detrain [dih-trein'] *vt.* abladen, ausladen (*mil.*); *i.* aussteigen.

Detriment [de'tri-mÁnt] *n.*
Nachteil *m.*

Detrimental [de-tri-men'tÁl]
a. nachteilig.

Devaluation [dih-wæ-lju-ei'
schÁn] *n.* Entwertung *f.*

Devalue [dih-wæ'ljuh] *vt.* entwerten.

Devastat'e [de'wA-steit] *vt.*
verwüsten; **-ion** *n.* Verwüstung *f.*

Develop [di-we'lÁp] *vt.* entwickeln; *i.* sich entwickeln;
-er *n.* Entwickler *m*; **-ment** *n.*
Entwicklung *f*, Ausbau *m*
(*plans*).   [weichen.

Deviate [dih'wi-eit] *vi.* ab-

Deviation [dih-wi-ei'schÁn] *n.*
Abweichung *f.*

Device [di-waiss'] *n.* Erfindung
f, Gerät *n*, Mittel *n.*

Devil [de'wil] *n.* Teufel *m*; **-ish**
a. teuflisch; **-ry** *n* Teufelei *f.*

Devious [dih'wi-Áss] *a.* abweichend, indirekt.   [erdenken.

Devise [di-wais'] *vt.* erfinden,

Devoid [di-woid'] *a.* bar, ohne.

Devolve [di-wolw'] *vi.* zufallen.

Devot'e [di-wout'] *vt.* widmen,
ergeben; **-ed** *a.* Ergeben-; **-ion**
n. Widmung *f*, Ergebenheit *f*,
Andacht *f.*   [schlingen.

Devour [di-wau'er] *vt.* ver-

Devout [di-waut'] *a.* **-ly** *ad.*
andächtig, innig.

Dew [djuh] *n.* Tau *m.*

Dexterity [dex-te'ri-ti] *n.* Ge-
wandtheit *f.*   [wandt.

Dexterous [dex'trAss] *a.* ge-

Diabolical [dai-A-bo'likl] *a.*
teuflisch.   [schräg.

Diagonal [dai-æ'go-nAl] *a.*

Diagram [dai'A-græm] *n.* Plan
m, Tafel *f*, Schaubild *n*, Riss *m.*

Dial [dai'Al] *n.* Zifferblatt *n*,
Skalenscheibe *f*, Wählscheibe *f*
(*ph.*); **-** **telephone** *n.* Fernsprecher mit Selbstanschluss
m; **- tone** *n.* Amtszeichen *n.*

Dialect [dai'A-lekt] *n.* Mund-
art *f.*   [gespräch *n.*

Dialogue [dai'A-log] *n.* Zwie-

Diameter [dai-æ'mi-ter] *n.*
Durchmesser *m.*   [Diamant *n.*

Diamond [dai'A-mond] *n.*

Diaper [dai'A-per] *n.* geblümte
Leinwand, Binde *f.*

Diaphragm [dai'A-fræm] *n.*
Zwerchfell *n*, Blende *f*, Membran *f* (*ph.*).   [Durchfall *n.*

Diarrhœa [dai-A-rih'A] *n.*

Diary [dai'A-ri] *n.* Tagebuch *n*,
Schreibkalender *m.*

Dice [daiss] *n. pl.* Würfel *m. pl.*

Dicky [di'ki] *n.* Notsitz *m*
(*aut.*).   [Diktaphon *n.*

Dictaphone [dik'tA-foun] *n.*

Dictat'e [dik-teit'] *vt.* vorschreiben, diktieren, eingeben;
-ion *n.* Diktieren *n*, Diktat *n*;
-or *n.* Diktator *m*; **-orial** *a.*
gebieterisch, tyrannisch; **-or-
ship** *n.* Diktatur *f*, Diktat *n.*

Dictionary [dik'schA-nA-ri] n. Wörterbuch n.

Die [dai] vi. sterben. [pel m.

Die [dai] n. Würfel m, Stem-

Diet [dai'At] n. Krankenkost f, Nahrung f.

Differ [di'fer] vi. sich unterscheiden, andrer Meinung sein; -ence n. Unterschied m; -ent a. verschieden.

Differential [di-fA-ren'schAl] a. differential; - gear n. Differential-, Ausgleich-getriebe n.

Difficult [di'fi-kAlt] a. schwer, schwierig; -y n. Schwierigkeit f.

Diffidence [di'fi-dAnss] n. Misstrauen n, gegen sich selbst. [schüchtern.

Diffident [di'fi-dAnt] a.

Diffuse [di-fjuhss'] a. -ly ad. zerstreut, weitschweifig.

Diffuser [di-fjuh'ser] n. Leitvorrichtung f (jet-plane).

Diffusion [di-fjuh'zhAn] n. Verbreitung f.

Dig [dig] vt. i. graben; – in vi. sich eingraben (mil.).

Digest [di-dzhest'] vt. verdauen; -ible a. verdaulich f; -ion n. Verdauung f.

Digest [dai'dzhest] n. Zusammenfassung f, Auszug m.

Dignified [dig'ni-faid] a. würdevoll.

Dignify [dig'ni-fai] vt. erhöhen.

Dignity [dig'ni-tij] n. Würde f.

Digress [dai-gress'] vi. abschweifen; -ion n. Abschweifung f.

Dike [daik] n. Deich m.

Dilapidated [di-læ'pi-dei-tid] a. baufällig.

Dilate [dai-leit'] vt. ausdehnen; i. sich ausdehnen, weitläufig sprechen.

Dilatory [di'lA-tA-rij] a. verzögernd.

Dilemma [di-lem'A] n. Verlegenheit f.

Diligence [di'li-dzhAnss] n. Fleiss m; -t a. fleissig.

Dilute [dai-ljuht'] vt. verdünnen; -ion n. Verdünnung f.

Dim [dim] a. trübe, matt; vt. trüben, verdunkeln, abblenden (lights); - out n. Verdunkelung f.

Dimension [dai-men'schAn] n. Ausdehnung f.

Diminish [di-mi'nisch] vt. vermindern.

Diminution [di-mi-njuh' schAn] n. Verminderung f.

Diminutive [di-mi'nju-tiw] a. winzig.

Dimple [dimpl] n. Grübchen n.

Din [din] n. Getöse n.

Dine [dain] vi. speisen.

Dinghy [ding'i] n. kleines Ruderboot; inflatable – Schlauchboot n, Floss-sack m.

Dining-room [dai'ning-ruhm] n. Speisezimmer n; – car n. Speisewagen m (rl.).

Dinner [di'ner] n. Mittagessen, Abendessen n.

Dingy [din'zhi] a. schmutzig.

Dint [dint] n. Strieme f, Beule f, Kraft f; by – of kraft.

Dip [dip] n. Neigung f, Senkung f; vt. eintauchen; i. sich neigen.

Diploma [di-plou'mA] n. Diplom n; -cy n. Diplomatie f; -tist n. Diplomat m.

Dire [dai'er] a. schrecklich.

Direct [dai-rekt'] a. gerade, direkt; vt. richten, hinweisen, führen; – current n. Gleichstrom m (el.); – hit n. Volltreffer m.

Direction [di-rek'schAn] n. Richtung f, Führung f, Anweisung f; – of workers Arbeitseinsatz m; –finder n. Peilfunkgerät n (rad.), Ortungsgerät n (rad.).

Directional [di-rek'schA-nAl] a. Richt...; – aerial n. Richtantenne f (rad.).

Direction-finding [di-rek'-schAn-fain'ding] n. Peilung f, Peilfunk m (rad.); – operator n.

Peilfunker m; – station n. Peilstelle f. [gleich, direkt.

Directly [di-rekt'li] ad. gerade.

Directive [di-rek'tiw] a. Weisung f, Vorschrift f.

Director [di-rek'ter] n. Direktor m, Leiter m; -ate n. Leitung f, Direktion f, Amt n; -y n. Adressbuch n (ph, etc.).

Dirt [dArt] n. Schmutz m; -y a. schmutzig; vt. beschmutzen.

Disability [di-ssA-bi'li-ti] n. Unfähigkeit f, Untauglichkeit f.

Disable [diss-eibl'] vt. unfähig machen; -d a. (dienst)unfähig, kriegsbeschädigt, manövrierunfähig (ship); -ment n. Dienstunfähigkeit f; -ment pension n. Versehrtengeld n.

Disabuse [diss-A-bjuhs'] v.v. enttäuschen.

Disadvantage [diss-Ad-wahn'tidzh] n. Nachteil m; -ous a. nachteilig.

Disaffected [diss-A-fek'tid] missvergnügt, aufrührerisch.a.

Disagree [diss-A-grih'] vi. uneinig sein, streiten; -able a. unangenehm; -ment n. Verschiedenheit f, Streit m.

Disallow [diss-A-lau'] vt. nicht gelten lassen, streichen.

Disappear [diss-A-pihr'] vi. verschwinden; -ance n. Verschwinden n.

Disappoint [diss-A-peunt'] vt. täuschen; -ment n. Enttäuschung f. [Wohl] m. Missbilligung f.

Disapproval [diss-A-pruh'wel] n. Missbilligung f.

Disapprove [diss-A-pruhw'] vt. i. missbilligen.

Disarm [diss-ahrm'] vt. entwaffnen; i. abrüsten; -ament n. Abrüstung f (voluntary), Entwaffnung f (forced).

Disarrange [diss-A-reindzh'] vt. in Unordnung bringen.

Disaster [di-sah'ster] n. Unglück n.

Disastrous [di-sah'strAss] a. unheilvoll.

Disavow [diss-A-wau'] vt. ab-, ver-leugnen. [lassen.

Disband [diss-bænd'] vt. entlassen.

Disbelief [diss-bi-lihf'] n. Unglaube m. [nicht glauben.

Disbelieve [diss-bi-lihw'] vt. i.

Disburse [diss-bArss'] vt. auszahlen.

Disc [disk] n. (Würfel) Scheibe f.

Discard [diss-kahrd'] vt. ablegen.

Discern [di-sArn'] vt. unterscheiden, erkennen; -ing a. scharfsinnig; -ment n. Einsicht f, Scharfsinn m.

Discharge [diss-tschahrdzh'] n. Ausfluss m, Entrichtung f, Entlassung f; vt. ausladen, entlassen, verrichten, abfeuern.

Disciple [di-ssaipl'] n. Jünger m.

Disciplinary [diss'i-pli-nA-ri] a. disziplinarisch; – code n. Strafordnung f. [Zucht f.

Discipline [diss'i-plin'] n.

Disclaim [diss-kleim'] vt. nicht anerkennen.

Disclos'e [diss-klous'] vt. enthüllen; -ure n. Enthüllung f.

Discolour [diss-kA'ler] vt. die Farbe verändern, verfärben.

Discomfort [diss-kAm'fert] n. Unbehaglichkeit f.

Disconcert [diss-kAn-ssArt'] vt. beunruhigen, verlegen machen.

Disconnect [diss-kA-nekt'] vt. entkuppeln, anstellen, ab-, ausschalten, ausklinken (tec.).

Disconsolate [diss-kon'ssA-lit] a. trostlos.

Discontent [diss-kAn-tent'] n. Unzufriedenheit f; -ed a. unzufrieden.

Discontinue [diss-kAn-ti'nju] vt. unterbrechen; i. nachlassen, aufhören. [tracht f.

Discord [diss'kOrd] n. Zwietracht f.

Discordant [diss-kOr'dAnt] a. misstönend.

Discount [diss'kaunt] n. Abzug m, Diskonto m.

Discount [diss-kaunt'] vt. diskontieren, ausser Betracht lassen. [ti-nAnss'] vt. missbilligen.
Discountenance [diss-kaun'-
Discourage [diss-kA'ridzh] vt. entmutigen, abraten.
Discourse [diss'kOrss] n. Rede f. [reden.
Discourse [diss-kOrss'] vi.
Discourtesy [diss-kAr'ti-ssi] n. Unhöflichkeit f.
Discover [diss-kA'wer] vt. entdecken; -er n. Entdecker m; -y n. Entdeckung f.
Discredit [diss-kre'dit] vt. nicht glauben.
Discreet [diss-kriht'] a. -ly ad. umsichtig, verschwiegen.
Discrepancy [diss-kre'pAnssi] n. Widerspruch m, Abstand m.
Discretion [diss-kre'schAn] n. Klugheit f, Gutdünken f.
Discriminat'e [diss-kri'mineit] vt. unterscheiden; -ion n. Unterscheidung f, Scharfsinn m. [abschweifend.
Discursive [diss-kAr'ssiw] a.
Discuss [diss-kAss'] vt. erörtern, verhandeln; -ion n. Erörterung f.
Disdain [diss-dein'] n. Verachtung f; vt. verachten; -ful a. verächtlich.
Disease [di-sihs'] n. Krankheit f; -d a. krank.
Disembark [diss-em-bahrk'] vt. i. ausschiffen, abladen, ausbooten.
Disenchantment [diss-in-tschahnt'mAnt] n. Entzauberung f.
Disengage [diss-in-geidzh'] vt. befreien; i. sich absetzen (mil.); -d a. unbeschäftigt, frei (seat, etc.).
Disentangle [diss-in-täng'gl] vt. auseinanderwickeln, befreien. [gunst f.
Disfavour [diss-fei'wer] n. Un-
Disfigure [diss-fi'ger] vt. entstellen.

Disgorge [diss-gOrdzh'] vt. auswerfen.
Disgrace [diss-greiss'] n. Ungnade f, Unehre f, Schmach f; vt. in Ungnade bringen, entehren; -ful a. entehrend, unerhört.
Disguise [diss-gais'] n. Verkleidung f; vt. verkleiden, verstellen.
Disgust [diss-gAst'] n. Ekel m; vt. anekeln; -ing a. ekelhaft. [richt n.
Dish [disch] n. Schüssel f, Ge-
Dishearten [diss-hahr'ten] vt. entmutigen.
Dishonest [diss-o'nist] a. -ly ad. unehrlich; -y n. Unehrlichkeit f.
Dishonour [diss-o'ner] n. Unehre f; vt. entehren, nicht honorieren (bill); -able a. entehrend.
Disillusion [diss-i-ljuh'zhAn] vt. enttäuschen; -ment n. Enttäuschung f.
Disinclination [diss-in-klinei'schAn] n. Abneigung f.
Disinclined [diss-in-klaind'] abgeneigt.
Disinfect [diss-in-fekt'] vt. desinfizieren; -ant n. Desinfektionsmittel n. [enterben.
Disinherit [diss-in-he'rit] vt.
Disintegrate [diss-in'ti-greit] vt. i. (sich) auflösen.
Disintegration [diss-in-tigrei'schAn] n. Auflösung f.
Disinter [diss-in-tAr'] vt. ausgraben. [a. uneigennützig.
Disinterested [diss-in'tri-stid]
Disjointed [diss-dzheun'tid] a. unzusammenhängend.
Disk [disk] n. Scheibe f.
Dislike [diss-laik'] n. Abneigung f; vt. nicht mögen.
Dislocate [diss'lo-keit] vt. verrenken.
Dislodge [diss-lodzh'] vt. vertreiben, verdrängen, verjagen.
Dismal [dis'mAl] a. düster, trübselig.

Dismantle [diss-mæntl'] vt. schleifen, abtakeln, abmontieren, zerlegen, auseinander nehmen.

Dismay [dis-mei'] n. Schrecken m; vt. in Schrecken setzen.

Dismember [diss-mem'ber] vt. zergliedern.

Dismiss [diss-miss'] vt. entlassen; -al n. Entlassung f, Dienstenthebung f (mil.).

Dismount [diss-maunt'] vi. absteigen; t. abwerfen, zerlegen (tec.).

Disobedience [diss-o-bih'di-Anss] n. Ungehorsam m; -t a. ungehorsam.

Disobey [diss-o-bei'] vt. ungehorsam sein gegen.

Disobliging [diss-o-blai'dzhing] a. ungefällig.

Disorder [diss-Or'der] n. Unordnung f; vt. in Unordnung bringen; -ly a. unordentlich, gesetzwidrig. [vt. zerrütten.

Disorganize [diss-Or'ga-nais]]

Disown [diss-oun'] vt. nicht anerkennen.

Disparage [diss-pæ'ridzh] vt. schmälern; -ment n. Schmälerung f. [gleichheit f.

Disparity [diss-pæ'ri-ti] n. Un-]

Dispatch [di-spætsch'] n. Absendung f, Depesche f, Meldung f; vt. absenden; - note n. Versandanzeige f; - rider n. Kraftradmelder m, Melderreiter m.

Dispassionate [diss-pæ'schAnit] a. leidenschaftslos, unparteiisch. [en.

Dispel [diss-pel'] vt. zerstreuen.]

Dispensary [diss-pen'ssA-ri] n. Apotheke f.

Dispense [diss-penss'] vt. austeilen, bereiten; - with entbehren.

Dispersal [diss-pAr'ssAl] n. Zerstreuung f, Auslagerung f (goods); lateral n. Marschbreite f (mil.); - in depth n. Marschtiefe f.

Disperse [diss-pArss'] vt. zerstreuen; i. sich zerstreuen; -ed a. versprengt (mil.); -ion n. Zerstreuung f.

Dispirited [diss-pi'ri-tid] a. niedergeschlagen.

Displace [diss-pleiss'] vt. verlegen, absetzen; -d persons n. pl. Zwangsverschleppte m. pl; -ment n. Verlegen n, Absetzung f, (Wasser-) Verdrängung f (ship).

Display [diss-plei'] n. Schaustellung f, Pomp m, Aufwand m; vt. entfalten, ausstellen.

Displease [diss-plihs'] vt. missfallen. [Missfallen n.

Displeasure [diss-ple'zher] n.]

Disport [diss-pOrt'] vt. sich belustigen.

Disposal [diss-pou'sAl] n. Verfügung f, Verkauf m, Beseitigung f.

Dispose [diss-pous'] vt. ordnen, lenken, verfügen; - of verkaufen, verschenken; -d a. geneigt.

Disposition [diss-po-si'schAn] n. Einrichtung f, Verfügung f, Gesinnung f, Veranlagung f.

Dispossess [diss-po-sess'] vt. berauben, enteignen.

Disproportion [diss-pro-pOr'schAn] n. Missverhältnis n; -ate a. unverhältnismässig.

Disputable [diss-pjuh'tAbl] a. bestreitbar.

Dispute [diss-pjuht'] n. Streit m; vt. bestreiten; i. streiten.

Disqualification [diss-kuo'li-fi-kei'schAn] n. Unfähigmachung f, Unfähigkeit f.

Disqualify [diss-kuo'lifai] vt. unfähig machen.

Disquieting [diss-kuai'A-ting] a. beunruhigend.

Disregard [diss-ri-gahrd'] n. Nichtachtung f; vt. nicht achten, nicht beachten.

Disreputable [diss-re'pjutAbl] a. verrufen, ehrwidrig, unanständig.

Disrepute [diss-ri-pjuht'] *n.* Verruf *m.*

Disrespect [diss-ri-spekt'] *n.* Unehrbietigkeit *f*; -ful *a.* unehrbietig. [*n.*Zerreissung *f.*

Disruption [diss-rΛp'schΛn] *n.*

Dissatisfaction [diss-sæ'tiss-fæk'schΛn] *n.* Unzufriedenheit *f.* [*a.* unzufrieden.

Dissatisfied [diss-sæ'tiss-faid]

Dissect [diss-ekt'] *vt.* zerlegen, sezieren. [Deuchelei.

Dissemble [diss-embl'] *v. i.*

Disseminat'e [diss-e'mi-neit] *vt.* ausstreuen; -ion *n.* Ausstreuung *f.* [Zwietracht.

Dissension [diss-en'schΛn] *n.*

Dissent [diss-ent'] *n.* Meinungsverschiedenheit *f*; *vi.* nicht übereinstimmen. [unähnlich.

Dissimilar [diss-si'mi-ler] *a.*

Dissipat'e [diss'i-peit] *vt.* zerstreuen, vergeuden; -ed *a.* ausschweifend; -ion *n.* Zerstreuung *f.*

Dissociate [diss-ssou'schi-eit] *vt.* trennen, *r.* sich lossagen.

Dissolut'e [diss'o-luht] *a.* -ely *ad.* ausschweifend; -ion *n.* Auflösung *f.* [en; *i.* sich auflösen.

Dissolve [di-solw'] *vt.* auflösen.

Dissonance [diss'o-nΛnss] *n.* Missklang *m.* [raten.

Dissuade [diss-ueid'] *vt.* ab-

Distan'ce [diss'tΛnss] *n.* Entfernung *f*; -t *a.* entfernt.

Distaste [diss-teist'] *n.* Abneigung *f*; -ful *a.* widerwärtig.

Distemper [diss-tem'per] *n.* Wasserfarbe *f*, Temperafarbe *f*; *vt.* mit Wasserfarben streichen. [Hundestaupe *f.*

Distemper [diss-tem'per] *n.*

Distend [diss-tend'] *vt.* ausdehnen.

Distil [diss-til'] *vt.* destillieren; -ler *n.* Destillateur *m*, Branntweinbrenner *m*; -lery *n.* Branntweinbrennerei *f.*

Distinct [diss-tinkt'] *a.* -ly *ad.* abgesondert, deutlich, ausdrücklich; -ion *n.* Unterscheid-

ung *f*, Auszeichnung *f*; -ness *n.* Deutlichkeit *f.*

Distinguish [diss-ting'guisch] *vt.* unterscheiden, auszeichnen; -ed *a.* ausgezeichnet.

Distort [diss-tOrt'] *vt.* verzerren, verdrehen; -ion *n.* Verzerrung *f*, Verwirrung *f.*

Distract [diss-trækt'] *vt.* ablenken, verwirren; -ed *a.* verstört, wahnsinnig; -ion *n.* Zerstreuung *f*, Verwirrung *f*, Wahnsinn *m.*

Distrain [diss-trein'] *vt.* in Beschlag nehmen; -t *n.* Beschlagnahme *f*; -t of pay *n.* Lohnpfändung *f.*

Distress [diss-tress'] *n.* Not *f*, Kummer *m*; *vt.* peinigen; -signal *n.* Notsignal *n*; -ing *a.* peinlich, betrübend.

Distribute [diss-tri'bjuht] *vt.* verteilen.

Distribution [diss-tri-bjuh'schΛn] *n.* Verteilung *f.*

Distributively [diss-tri'bjutiw-li] *ad.* im einzelnen.

Distributer [diss-tri'bju-ter] *n.* Austeiler *m*, Verteiler *m* (aut.), Verkäufer *m* (com.).

District [diss'trikt] *n.* Bezirk *m*, Gegend *f.*

Distrust [diss-trΛst'] *n.* Misstrauen *n*; *vt.* misstrauen; -ful *a.* misstrauisch.

Disturb [diss-tΛrb'] *vt.* stören; -ance *n.* Störung *f.*

Disunion [diss-juh'ni-Λn] *n.* Uneinigkeit *f.*

Disunite [diss-ju-nait'] *vt.* trennen; *i.* sich trennen.

Disuse [diss-juhss'] *n.* Nichtgebrauch *m*; -d *a.* ausser Gebrauch.

Ditch [ditsch] *n.* Graben *m.*

Dive [daiw] *vi.* tauchen, stürzen (av.); *n.* Absturz *m* (av.); - bomber *n.* Stuka *m*, Sturzkampfflugzeug *n* (plane), Sturzkampfflieger *m* (man); - bombing attack *n.* Sturzkampfangriff *m.*

Diver [dai'wer] n. Taucher m.

Diverge [dai-wArdzh'] vi. auseinandergehen [verschieden.

Diverse [dai'werss] a. -ly ad.

Diversify [dai-wAr'ssi-fai] vt. verschieden machen, vermannigfaltigen.

Diversion [dai-wAr'schAn] n. Ablenkung f, Zeitvertreib m. Ableitung f.

Diversity [dai-wAr'ssi-ti] n. Verschiedenheit f, Mannigfaltigkeit f [ken, belustigen.

Divert [dai-wArt'] vt. ablen-

Divest [dai-west'] vt. berauben, entkleiden.

Divide [di-waid'] vt. teilen, einteilen, dividieren [dende f.

Dividend [di'wi-dend] n. Dividende f.

Divine [di-wain'] a. -ly ad. göttlich; vt. i. weissagen, mutmassen; -ness n. Göttlichkeit f. [bar.

Divinity [di-wi'ni-ti] n. Gottheit f, Theologie f.

Divisible [di-wi'sibl] a. teilbar.

Division [di-wi'zhAn] n. Teilung f, Abteilung f, Einteilung f, Division f.

Divorce [di-wOrss'] n. Ehescheidung f; vt. scheiden.

Divulge [dai-wAlzh'] vt. bekannt machen, ausplaudern.

Dizziness [di'si-ness] n. Schwindel m.

Dizzy [di'si] a. schwindlich.

Do [duh] vt. tun, machen; i. tun, sich befinden, tauglich sein; - without entbehren.

Docile [dou'ssail] a. lenksam.

Docility [dou-ssi'li-ti] n. Lenksamkeit f.

Dock [dok] n. Dock n, Anklagebank f; vt. docken.

Docker [do'ker] n. Dockarbeiter m.

Docket [do'kit] n. Liefer-, Bestell-schein m, Etikette f (com.); vt. mit Inhaltsvermerk versehen.

Dockyard [dok'jahrd] n. Schiffswerft f. [Arzt m.

Doctor [dok'ter] n. Doktor m,

Doctrine [dok'trin] n. Lehre.

Document [do'kju-mAnt'] n. Urkunde f.

Documentary [do-kju-men'tA-ri] a. urkundlich; - evidence n. Unterlage f, Beleg m; - film n. Lehr-, Kultur-film m; - talk n. Funkbild n (rad.). [ausweichen.

Dodge [dodzh] n. Kniff m; vt.

Dog [dog] n. Hund m; vt. dicht auf dem Fusse folgen.

Dogged [do'gid] a. ausdauernd.

Dogma [dog'mA] n. Dogma n.

Dogmatic [dog-mæ'tik] a. dogmatisch.

Dole [doul] n. Almosen n, Arbeitslosenunterstützung f; -ful a. kummervoll.

Doll [dol] n. Puppe f.

Dollar [do'ler] n. Dollar m.

Domain [do-mein'] n. Gebiet n, Gut n.

Dome [doum] n. Kuppel f.

Domestic [do-mess'tik] a. häuslich; - animal n. Haustier n; - servant n. Hausangestellte(r) m, Dienstmädchen n.

Domicile [do'mi-ssail] n. Wohnort m; -d a. wohnhaft.

Dominant [do'mi-nAnt] a. herrschend.

Dominate [do'mi-neit] vt. beherrschen; -ion n. Herrschaft f [ring] a. herrisch.

Domineering [do-mi-nih'**ring**]

Dominion [do-mi'ni-An] n. Gebiet n, Kolonie f, mit Selbstverwaltung n, Staat m.

Donation [do-nei'schAn] n. Gabe f, Schenkung f.

Donkey [dong'ki] n. Esel m.

Donor [dou'ner] n. Geschenkgeber m.

Doom [duhm] n. Urteil n, Schicksal n; vt. verurteilen.

Door [dOr] n. Tür f; -man n. Pförtner m.

Dormant [dOr'mAnt] a. schlafend, ungebraucht.

Dormitory [dOr'mi-tA-ri] n. Schlafsaal m.

Dose [douss] n. Dosis f.

Dot [dot] n. Punkt m; vt. punktieren.

Dotage [dou'tidʒ] n. Verstandesschwäche f.

Double [dĂbl] n. Doppelgänger m, das Doppelte; a. doppelt; vt. verdoppeln; --barrelled a. doppelläufig; --crossing n. Gegenvertrauensspiel n; --decker n. Oberomnibus m.

Doubt [daut] n. Zweifel m; vi. zweifeln; t. bezweifeln; -ful a. zweifelhaft; -less ad. ohne Zweifel.

Dough [dou] n. Teig m.

Dove [dĂw] n. Taube f.

Dowry [dau'ri] n. Mitgift f.

Down [daun] n. Flaum m.

Down [daun] ad. nieder, unten, herunter, hinunter; pr. herab, hinab; [niedergeschlagen].

Downcast [daun'kahst] a.

Downward [daun'uerd] a. sich senkend, abwärts führend; -s ad. abwärts, nach unten.

Downfall [daun'fŎl] n. Untergang m.

Downhearted [daun-hahr'tid] a. niedergeschlagen, mutlos.

Downright [daun'rait] ad. vollständig; a. vollständig, offen.

Downstairs [daun-stehrs'] ad.

Doze [douss] vi. schlummern.

Dozen [dĂsn] n. Dutzend n.

Drab [dræb] a. (maus)grau, düster.

Draft [drahft] n. Entwurf m, Tratte f (com.). Aufriss m (plan); vt. entwerfen, abfassen, einziehen (mil.); -s n. pl. Ersatzmannschaft f (mil.); -ing n. Wehrersatz m (mil.).

Drag [dræg] vt. schleppen; --rope n. Langtau n (nav.).

Dragon [dræ'gĂn] n. Drache m; -'s teeth n. pl. Höckerhindernis n (mil.).

Dragoon [drĂ-guhn'] n. Dragoner m; vt. zwingen.

Drain [drein] n. Abfluss m,

Abflussgraben m; vt ausleeren, drainieren, abwässern; -age n. Ablaufen n, Entwässerung f.

Drake [dreik] n. Enterich m.

Dram [dræm] n. Schluck m.

Drama [drah'mĂ] n. Drama n.

Dramatic [drA-mæ'tik] a. dramatisch. [Dramatiker m.

Dramatist [dræ'mA-tist] n.

Drape [dreip] vt. behängen.

Draper [drei'per] n. Tuchhändler m, Weisswarenhändler m; -y n. Tuchhandel m, Faltenwurf m.

Drastic [dræ'stik] a. drastisch.

Draught [drahft] n. Zug m, Tiefgang m (ship); - beer n. Bier n vom Fass.

Draughts [drahftss] n. pl. Damenspiel n.

Draughtsman [drahftss'mĂn] n. Zeichner m; -ship n. Zeichenkunst f.

Draw [drŎ] vt. ziehen, abziehen, zeichnen, beziehen (com.); i. ziehen, zeichnen; -off vt. abfüllen; - up vt. ausfertigen (document).

Drawback [drŎ'bæk] n. Übelstand m, Nachteil m, Rückzoll m (com.).

Drawer [drŎ'er] n. Zieher m, Zeichner m, Schublade f.

Drawing [drŎ'ing] n. Ziehen n, Zeichnung f; - room n. Salon m; -s pl. Einnahmen f, pl. [den (game).

Drawn [drŎn] a. unentschie-

Drawl [drŎl] n. schleppende Sprechweise; vi. dehnen.

Dread [dred] n. Furcht f; vt. fürchten; -ful a. furchtbar; -naught n. Schlachtschiff n.

Dream [drihm] n. Traum m; vi. träumen; -er n. Träumer m.

Drear'y [drih'ri] a. öde, langweilig; -iness n. Öde f.

Dredge [dredʒ] vt. ausbaggern, draggen; -r n. Bagger m.

Dregs [dregs] n. pl. Hefe f.

Drench [drensch] vt. durchnässen.

Dress [dress] *n.* Kleid *n.* Kleidung *f*; *vt.* kleiden; *i. r.* sich ankleiden, ausflaggen (*ship*); – suit *n.* Gesellschaftsanzug *m.*

Dressing [dress'ing] *n.* Behandeln *n.* Verband *m*; – case *n.* Toilettenkästchen *n.* Verbandkasten *m.* (*doctor's*); – room *n.* Ankleidezimmer *n.* – station *n.* Verband-stelle *f*, –platz *m.* (*mil.*); – table – Toilettentisch *m.*

Dressmaker [dress'mei-ker] *n.* Schneiderin *f.*

Dressy [dress'i] *a.* modisch.

Dribble [dribl] *vi.* tröpfeln.

Drift [drift] *n.* Trieb *m.* Trift *f.* Wehe *f.* Lauf *m*, Zweck *m*; *vi.* treiben, sich aufhäufen, triftig sein.

Drill [dril] *n.* Exerzieren *n.* Drillich (*cloth*), Bohrspitze *f* (*tec.*); *vt. i.* exerzieren, abrichten, drillen (*tec.*); – ground *n.* Exerzierplatz *m.*

Drink [dringk] *n.* Trunk *m*; *vt. i.* trinken; –able *a.* trinkbar.

Drip [drip] *vi.* tröpfeln.

Driv'e [draiw] *n.* Spazierfahrt *f*, Fahrweg *m*, Antrieb *m* (*tec.*); *vi. i.* treiben, fahren; –ing licence *n.* Führerschein *m*; –ing shaft *n.* Antriebswelle *f.* (*tec.*).

Driver [drai'wer] *n.* Kutscher *m.* Fuhrmann *m*, Führer *m* (*train*), (Kraft-) Fahrer *m* (*aut.*).

Drizzle [drisl] *n.* Sprühregen *m.*

Droll [drofil] *a.* drollig.

Dromedary [drA'mA-dA-ri] *n.* Dromedar *n.*

Drone [droun] *n.* Drohne *f.*

Droop [druhp] *vi.* verwelken, hinsinken.

Drop [drop] *n.* Tropfen *m*; *vt.* tropfen, fallen lassen, abwerfen (*bomb*); *i.* triefen, fallen; –ping of supplies *n.* Nachschubabwurf *m* (*mil.*).

Dropsy [drop'ssi] *n.* Wassersucht *f.*

Dross [dross] *n.* Schlacke *f.*

Drought [draut] *n.* Dürre *f.*

Drove [drouw] *n.* Viehherde *f.* –r *n.* Viehtreiber *m.*

Drown [draun] *vt.* ertränken; *i.* ertrinken.

Drowsy [drau'si] *a.* schläfrig.

Drudge [drAdzh] *n.* Packesel *m.* Arbeitstier *n*; *vi.* sich abplacken; –ry *n.* Plackerei *f.*

Drug [drAg] *n.* Arzneimittel *n*; *vt.* betäuben; –gist *n.* Drogist *m.*

Drum [drAm] *n.* Trommel *f*, Fass *n* (*oil*); –mer *n.* Trommler *m.* [trunken.

Drunk(en) [drAng'kn] *a.* betrunken. [trunkenbold *m.*

Drunkard [drAng'kerd] *n.* Trunkenbold *m.*

Drunkenness [drAng'kAnness] *n.* Trunkenheit *f.*

Dry [drai] *a.* trocken, nüchtern; *vt.* trocknen, austrocknen; – cell *n.* Trockenbatterie *f* (*el.*); – element *n* (*el.*). [einheit *f.*

Dryness [drai'ness] *n.* Trockenheit *f.*

Dual [djuh'Al] *a.* doppelt, Zwei . . . ; –control *n.* Doppelsteuerung *f.* (*av.*); – purpose gun *n.* Einheitsgeschütz *n*; – purpose weapon *n.* Einheitswaffe *f.*

Dubious [djuh'bi-Ass]*a.* zweifelhaft, unsicher. [Entchen *n.*

Duck [dAk] *vt. i.* tauchen, bücken.

Duck dAk] *n.* Ente *f.*; –ling *n.*

Dud [dAd] *n.* Blindgänger *m.* Versager *m* (*mil. etc.*).

Due [djuh] *n.* Gebühr *f*; *a.* gebührend, fällig; *ad.* gerade: – to *pr.* infolge.

Duel [djuh'il] *n.* Zweikampf *m.*

Duet [dju-et'] *n.* Duett *n.*

Dug-out [dAg'aut] *n.* (Schutz) Unterstand *m.*

Duke [djuhk] *n.* Herzog *m.*

Dull [dAl] *a.* stumpf, stumpfsinnig, matt, langweilig, trübe; *vt.* abstumpfen.

Dulness [dAl'ness] *n.* Stumpfsinnigkeit *f.* Mattheit *f.*

Duly [djuh'li] *ad.* gehörig, richtig, pünktlich.

Dumb [dAm] *a.* stumm; – -bell *n.* Hantel *f.*

Dummy [dA'mi] *n.* Scheinkiste *f.*, Strohmann *m.*, Schnelderpuppe *f* (*com.*); *a.* Schein ...; – tank *i.* Panzerkampfwagennachbildung *f.*

Dump [dAmp] *n.* Abfallaufen *m.*, Munitionslager *n* (*mil.*); *vt.* umkippen, abladen. [Kloss *m.*

Dumpling [dAmp'ling] *n.* Kloss *m.*

Dun [dAn] *n.* Mahner *m.*; *vt.* mahnen; -ning letter *n.* Mahnbrief *m.* [kopf *m.*

Dunce [dAnss] *n.* Dummkopf *m.*

Dune [djuhn] *n.* Düne *f.*

Dung [dAng] *n.* Mist *m.*; -heap *n.* Misthaufen *m.*

Dungarees [dAng-gA-rihs'] *n. pl.* Arbeitsanzug *m.*

Dupe [djuhp] *n.* der Betrogene; *vt.* betrügen.

Duplicate [djuh'pli-kAt] *a.* doppelt; *n.* Duplikat *n.*

Duplicat'e [djuh'pli-keit] *vt.* verdoppeln, doppelt ausführen; -or *n.* Kopiermaschine *f.*, Vervielfältigungsapparat *m.*

Duplicity [dju-pli'ssi-ti] *n.* Doppelzüngigkeit *f.*

Durability [dju-rA-bi'li-ti] *n.* Dauerhaftigkeit *f.* [haft.

Durable [djuh'rAbl] *a.* dauer-

Duration [dju-rei'schAn] *n.* Dauer *f.*; – of the war *n.* Kriegsdauer *f.* [rend.

During [djuh'ring] *pr.* während.

Dusk [dAsk] *n.* Dämmerung *f.*

Dust [dAst] *n.* Staub *m.*; *vt.* abstäuben, bestäuben. [lappen *m.*

Duster [dA'ster] *n.* Wischlappen *m.*

Dusty [dA'sti] *a.* staubig.

Dutiable [djuh'ti-Abl] *a.* zollpflichtig. [getreu.

Dutiful [djuh'ti-ful] *a.* pflichtgetreu.

Duty [djuh'ti] *n.* Pflicht *f.*, Dienst *m.*, Zoll *m* (*customs*).

Dwarf [duOrf] *n.* Zwerg *m.*

Dwell [duel] *vi.* wohnen; – on verweilen bei; -ing *n.* Wohnung *f.*; -ing house *n.* Wohnhaus *n.*

Dwindle [duindl] *vi.* hinschwinden.

Dye [dai] *n.* Farbstoff *m.*; *vt.* färben; -ing *n.* Färben *n.*, Färbekunst *f.*; -r *n.* Färber *m.*

Dynamics [dai-næ'miks] *n. pl.* Dynamik *f.*

Dynamite [dai'nA-mait] *n.* Dynamit *m.*

Dynamo [dai'nA-mou] *n.*, Dynamo(maschine) *f.*, Stromerzeuger *m.*, Generator *m* (*el.*), Lichtmaschine *f* (*aut, rl, av, etc.*).

Dynasty [di'nA-sti] *n.* Dynastie *f.* [Ruhr *f.*

Dysentery [di'ssAn-tA-ri] *n.*

Dyspeptic [diss-pep'tik] *a.* magenschwach.

E

Each [ihtsch] *pn.* jeder, jede, jedes; – other einander.

Eager [ih'ger] *a.* -ly *ad.* eifrig.

Eagle [ihgl] *n.* Adler *m.*

Ear [ihr] *n.* Ähre *f* (*corn*).

Ear [ihr] *n.* Ohr *n.*

Earl [Arl] *n.* Graf *m.*

Early [Ar'li] *a. ad.* früh.

Earmark [ihr'mahrk] *vt.* kennzeichnen, bezeichnen; -ed stocks *pl.* Sperrbestand *m.*

Earn [Arn] *vt.* verdienen.

Earnest [Ar'nist] *a.* ernst, ernsthaft, ernstlich; *n.* Ernst *m.*; – money *n.* Handgeld *n.*, Draufgeld *n.*; -ness *n.* Ernsthaftigkeit *f.* [Verdienst *m.*

Earnings [Ar'nings] *n. pl.*

Ear-phone [ihr'foun] *n.* Kopfhörer *m*, Hörer *m*, Hörmuschel *f.* [hörschützer *m.*

Ear-plug [ihr'plAg] *n.* Gehörschützer *m.*

Ear-protector [ihr'prou-tek'ter] *n.* Ohrenschützer *m.*

Ear-ring [ihr'ring] *n.* Ohrring *m.*

Earth [Arth] *n.* Erde *f.*, Boden *m.*, Erddraht *m.*, Leitung *f* (*rad.*). [-ware *n.* Töpferware *f.*

Earthen [Ar'dhen] *a.* irden.

Earthquake [Arth'kueik] *n.* Erdbeben *n.*

Earthly [Arth'li] *a.* irdisch.

Ease [ihs] *n.* Gemächlichkeit *f*, Ruhe *f*, Leichtigkeit *f*; *vt.* erleichtern; **- off** abflauen.

Easel [ih'sel] *n.* Staffelei *f*.

Easily [ih'sili] *ad.* leicht.

Easiness [ih'si-ness] *n.* Leichtigkeit *f*.

East [ihst] *n.* Osten *m*; *a.* ad. östlich.

Easter [ih'ster] *n.* Ostern *pl.*

Eastern [ih'stern] **Easterly** [ih'ster-li] *a.* östlich. [ostwärts.

Eastward(s) [ih'stuerds] *ad.*

Easy [ih'si] *a.* leicht, unbesorgt.

Eat [iht] *vt. i.* essen, fressen.

Eatable [ih'tAbl] *a.* essbar.

Eaves [ihws] *n. pl.* Dachtraufe *f*.

Ebb [eb] *n.* Ebbe *f*; *vi.* ebben.

Ebony [e'bo-ni] *n.* Ebenholz *n.*

Ebullition [e-bA-li'schAn] *n.* Aufwallung *f*, Ausbruch *m.*

Eccentric [ex-en'trik] *a.* exzentrisch, überspannt; *n.* Sonderling *m*, Exzenter *m* (tec.); **-ity** *n.* Überspanntheit *f*.

Echelon [e'schA-lon] *n.* Staffel *f* (av.); **in - (formation)** gestaffelt; *vt.* staffeln.

Echo [E'kou] *n.* Echo *n*; *vi. t.* widerhallen.

Economic [ih-ko-no'mik] *a.* ökonomisch, wirtschaftlich; Handels . . . ; **-al** *a.* wirtschaftlich, billig, sparsam, haushälterisch; **-s** *n. pl.* Volkswirtschaft *f*. [*i.* sparen.

Economize [i-ko'no-mais] *vt.*

Economy [i-ko'no-mi] *n.* Ökonomie *f*, Sparsamkeit *f*; political **- Staatswirtschaft *f*.

Ecstasy [ex'tA-ssi] *n.* Rausch *m.* [wirbeln.

Eddy [e'di] *n.* Wirbel *m*; *vi.*

Edge [edzh] *n.* Schärfe *f*, Rand *m*; *vt.* schärfen, säumen, einfassen; **-d** *a.* gesäumt, scharf.

Edible [e'dibl] *a.* essbar.

Edict [ih'dikt] *n.* Verordnung *f*.

Edification [e-di-fi-kei'schAn] *n.* Erbauung *f*. [Gebäude *n.*

Edifice [e'di-fiss] *n.* Bau *m,*

Edify [e'di-fai] *vt.* erbauen; **-ing** *a.* erbaulich.

Edit [e'dit] *vt.* herausgeben.

Edition [i-di'schAn] *n.* Ausgabe *f*. [geber *m.*

Editor [e'di-ter] *n.* Herausgeber *m.*

Editorial [e-di-tO'ri-Al] *n.* Leitartikel *m*; *a.* redaktionell; **- office** *n.* Schriftleitung *f*.

Educate [e'dju-keit] *vt.* erziehen.

Education [e-dju-kei'schAn] *n.* Erziehung *f*, Bildung *f*; **- authority** *n.* Schulbehörde *f*; **- officer** *n.* Unterrichtsoffizier *m.*

Educational [e-dju-kei'schAnAl] *a.* Erziehungs . . .

Eel [ihl] *n.* Aal *m.*

Efface [i-feiss'] *vt.* auswischen, verwischen.

Effect [i-fekt'] *n.* Wirkung *f*; *vt.* bewirken; **-ive** *a.* wirksam; **-ive range** *n.* Schuss-, Wirkungsbereich *m*; **-s** *n. pl.* Effekten *pl*, Vorräte *m. pl*, Guthaben *n*; **-ual** *a.* wirksam; **-uate** *vt.* bewirken, ausführen.

Effeminate [i-fe'mi-nit] *a.* weichlich.

Effervesce [e-fer-wess'] *vi.* aufbrausen; **-nce** *n.* Aufbrausen *n*; **-nt** *a.* Brause . . .

Efficacious [e-fi-kei'schAss] *a.* wirkungsvoll, wirksam.

Efficacy [e'fi-kA-ssi] *n.* Wirksamkeit *f*.

Efficiency [i-fi'schAn-ssi] *n.* Leistungsfähigkeit *f*, Nutzleistung *f* (tec.); **- pay** *n.* Leistungszulage *f*.

Efficient [i-fi'schAnt] *a.* tüchtig, leistungsfähig. [Bild *n.*

Effigy [e'fi-dzhi] *n.* Abbild *n.*

Effort [e'fert] *n.* Anstrengung *f*; **-less** *a.* ohne Anstrengung.

Effrontery [e-frAn'tA-ri] *n.* Frechheit *f*.

Effusion [i-fjuh'zhAn] *n.* Erguss *m*, Ergiessung *f*.

Effusive [i-fju'siw] a. überschwenglich.
Egg [eg] n. Ei n.; – cup n. Ei-
erbecher m; – shaped a. eier-
förmig.
Ego'ism [e'gou-ism] n. Egoismus m; -ist n. Egoist m, -tism
n. Egoismus m, Selbstsucht f;
-tist n. Egoist m; -tistic a.
selbstsüchtig.
Egregious [i-grih'dzAss] a.
vortrefflich, unerhört.
Egress [ih'gress] n. Ausfluss
m, Ausgang m.
Eiderdown [ai'der-daun] n.
Eiderdaune f; – quilt n. Daun-
endecke f.
Eight [eit] a. num. acht; -een
num. achtzehn; -eenth a. acht-
zehnt; -h a. achte; -y num.
achtzig.
Either [ai'dher] a. pn. einer,
eine, eins von zweien; cj. entweder.
Eject [i-dzhekt'] vt. ausstossen,
vertreiben; -ion n. Vertreibung f. [fältig ausgearbeitet.
Elaborate [i-læ'bo-rit] a. sorg-
Elaborat'e [i-læ'bo-reit] vt.
ausarbeiten; -ion n. Verar-
beitung f.
Elapse [i-læpss'] vi. verlaufen.
Elastic [i-læ'stik] n. Gummi-
band n; a. elastisch.
Elasticity [ih-læ-sti'ssi-ti] n.
Elastizität f. [geblasen.
Elated [i-lei'tid] a. froh, auf-
Elation [i-lei'schAn] n. ge-
hobene Stimmung.
Elbow [el'bou] n. Ellbogen m.
Elder [el'der] a. älter; n. Äl-
teste(r) m.
Elder [el'der] n. Holunder m;
-berry n. Holunderbeere f.
Elderly [el'der-li] a. ältlich.
Eldest [el'dist] a. ältest.
Elect [i-lekt'] vt. erwähnen.
Election [i-lek'schAn] n. Wahl
f; -eering n. Stimmenwerben n.
Elector [i-lek'ter] n. Wähler m.
Electric [i-lek'trik] n. -al a. elek-
trisch; – car n. Elektrowagen

m, Elektromobil n; – lorry n.
Elektroschwerlastwagen m; –
torch n. Taschenlampe f; – van
n. Elektrolieferwagen m.
Electrician [i-lek-tri'schAn]
n. Elektrotechniker m.
Electricity [i-lek-tri'ssi-ti] n.
Elektrizität f.
Electrification [i-lek-tri-fi-
kei'schAn] n. Elektrifizierung f.
Electrify [i-lek'tri-fai] vt. elek-
trisieren.
Electro–mechanic [i-lek'tro-
mi-kæ'nik] n. Elektrotechni-
ker m.
Electro–type [i-lek'tro-taip]
n. galvanplastische Vervielfäl-
tigung f.
Elegance [e'li-gAnss] n. Ele-
ganz f, Anmut f, Feinheit f.
Elegant [e'li-gAnt] a. elegant,
zierlich.
Elegy [e'li-dzhi] n. Elegie f.
Element [e'li-mAnt] n. Ele-
ment n, Bestandteil m.
Elementary [e-li-men'tA-ri]
a. elementar, Anfangs . . .
Elephant [e'li-fAnt] n.
Elefant m. [erheben.
Elevate [e'li-weit] vt. erhöhen.
Elevation [e-li-wei'schAn] n.
Erhöhung f, Erhebung f.
Elevator [e'li-wei-ter] n. Fahr-
stuhl m.
Eleven [i-lewn'] num. elf; -th
a. elfte.
Elicit [i-li'ssit] vt. entlocken.
Eligible [e'li-dzhibl] a. wähl-
bar.
Eliminate [i-li'mi-neit] vt. aus-
stossen, ausscheiden, ausschal-
ten, beseitigen.
Elimination [i-li-mi-nei'-
sch An] n. Aussonderung f, Aus-
scheidung f, Ausschaltung f.
Eliminator [i-li'mi-nei-ter] n.
Prüfnetzgerät n.
Elixir [e'lix-er] n. Heiltrank m.
Ell [el] n. Elle f.
Elm [elm] n. Ulme f.
Elocution [e-lo-kjuh'schAn] n.
Vortrag m, Redekunst f.

Elongate [ih'long-geit] vt. verlängern.

Elope [i-loup'] vi. entlaufen; -ment n. Entlaufen n. (mit dem Geliebten).

Eloquen'ce [e'lo-kuAnss] n. Beredsamkeit f.; -t a. beredt.

Else [elss] ad. sonst; -where ad. anderswo.

Elucidate [i-luh'ssi-deit] vt. aufhellen, aufklären.

Elude [i-ljuhd'] vt. entgehen, ausweichen.

Emaciation [i-mei-schi-ei'schAn] n. Abmagerung f.

Emanate [e'mA-neit] vi. ausfliessen.

Emancipat'e [i-mæn'ssi-peit] vt. freilassen, freimachen; -ion n. Befreiung f.

Embalm [em-bahm'] vt. einbalsamieren.

Embankment [em-bænk'mAnt] n. Damm m.

Embargo [em-bahr'gou] n. Sperre f, Beschlag m.

Embark [em-bahrk'] vt. einschiffen; i. sich einschiffen, sich einlassen; -ation n. Einschiffung f, Verladung f, Verlastung f; -ation staff n. Verladestab m.

Embarrass [im-bæ'rAss] vt. in Verlegenheit setzen; -ed a. verlegen; -ment n. Verlegenheit f.

Embassy [em'bA-ssi] n. Botschaft f.

Embed [im-bed'] vt. einbetten.

Embellish [im-be'lisch] vt. verschönern; -ment n. Verschönerung f.

Ember [em'ber] n. glühende Asche.

Embezzle [im-besl'] vt. unterschlagen; -ment n. Unterschlagung f; -r n. Veruntreuer m.

Embitter [em-bi'ter] vt. verbittern; -ment n. Verbitterung f.

Emblem [em'blAm] n. Sinnbild n.

Emblematic [em-blA-mæ'tik] a. sinnbildlich, typisch.

Embodiment [em-bo'di-mAnt] n. Verkörperung f.

Embody [em-bo'di] vt. verkörpern.

Emboss [em-boss'] vt. bosieren, erhaben ausarbeiten.

Embrace [em-breiss'] n. Umarmung f; vt. umarmen, einschliessen.

Embrocation [em-bro-kei'schAn] n. Einreibemittel n.

Embroider [em-breu'der] vt. sticken, -y n. Stickerei f.

Embroil [im-breul'] vt. in Streit verwickeln.

Embryo [em'bri-ou] n. Embryo m, Keim m.

Embus [im-bAss'] vt. verladen, verlasten (mil.).

Emend [i-mend'] vt. verbessern; -ation n. Verbesserung f, (Text-)Besserung f.

Emerald [e'mA-rAld] n. Smaragd m; a. smaragdfarben.

Emerge [i-mArdzh'] vi. auftauchen.

Emergency [i-mAr'dzhAn-ssi] n. Notfall m, Nothilfe f; state of – Ausnahmezustand m, Notstand m; – brake n. Notbremse f; – first aid n. Unfallbereitschaft f; – grant n. Notstandbeihilfe f; – house n. Behelfsheim n.

Emery [e'mA-ri] n. Schmirgel m.

Emetic [i-me'tik] n. Brechmittel n.

Emigrant [e'mi-grAnt] n. Auswanderer m.

Emigrat'e [e'mi-greit] vi. auswandern; -ion n. Auswanderung f.

Eminen'ce [e'mi-nAnss] n. Höhe f, Auszeichnung f; -t a. -tly ad. hoch, ausgezeichnet.

Emissary [e'miss-A-ri] n. Sendling m, Abgesandte(r) m.

Emission [i-mi'schAn] n. Ausstossen n, Ausgabe f (com.).

Emit [i-mit'] vt. ausströmen.

Emollient [i-mo'li-Ant] a. erweichend; n. erweichendes Mittel.

Emolument [i-mo'lju-mAnt] n. Gehalt n.

Emotion [i-mou'schAn] n. Gemütsbewegung f, Gefühl n; -al a. erregbar. [ser m.

Emperor [em'pA-rer] n. Kaiser m.

Emphasis [em'fA-ssiss] n. Nachdruck m. [betonen.

Emphasize [em'fA-ssais] vt.

Emphatic [em-fæ'tik] a. -ally ad. nachdrücklich. [reich n.

Empire [em'pai-er] n. Kaiser-

Emplane [em-plein'] vt. in Flugzeugen verladen, verlasten (mil.).

Employ [em-pleu'] vt. verwenden, beschäftigen, anstellen; -ee n. Arbeiter m; -er n. Arbeitgeber m; -ment n. Beschäftigung f, Geschäft n; -ment exchange n. Arbeitsnachweis m.

Emporium [em-pO'ri-Am] n. Handelsplatz m, Niederlage f, Warenhaus n. [mächtigen.

Empower [em-pau'er] vt. ermächtigen.

Empress [em-press'] n. Kaiserin f.

Empties [emp'tis] n. pl. Leergut n, leere Verpackung (com.).

Emptiness [emp'ti-ness] n. Leere f.

Empty [empt'ti] a. leer; vt. leeren; - container n. Leergebinde n.

Emulate [e'mju-leit] vt. nacheifern; -ion n. Nacheiferung f.

Emulsion [i-mAl'schAn] n. Emulsion f.

Enable [i-neibl'] vt. befähigen, in den Stand setzen.

Enact [i-nækt'] vt. verordnen; -ment n. Verordnung f, Verfügung f.

Enamel [i-næml'] n. Schmelz m; vt. emaillieren. [verliebt.

Enamoured [in-æ'merd] a.

Encamp [in-kæmp'] vi. sich lagern; -ment n. Lager n.

Enchant [in-tschahnt'] vt. bezaubern; -ment n. Bezauberung f.

Encipher [in-ssai'fer] vt. verschlüsseln.

Encircle [in-ssArkl'] vt. umringen, umzingeln, einkreisen; -d troops n. pl. Kessel m; -ment n. Einkreisung f, Einkesselung f (mil.).

Enclose [in-klous'] vt. einzäunen, einschliessen.

Enclosure [in-klou'zher] n. Einzäunung f, Einlage f (letter).

Encode [in-koud'] vt. verschlüsseln.

Encompass [in-kAm'pAss] vt. umschliessen, umzingeln, erreichen (aim).

Encounter [in-kaun'ter] vt. begegnen; n. Begegnen n, Gefecht n.

Encourage [in-kA'ridzh] vt. ermutigen, fördern; -ment n. Ermutigung f, Förderung f.

Encroach [in-kroutsch'] vi. eingreifen, überschreiten; -ment n. Eingriff m.

Encumb'er [in-kAm'ber] vt. belasten; -rance n. Last f.

End [end] n. Ende n, Schluss m, Spitze f; vt. i. enden, schliessen, beendigen; - bearings n. pl. Auflager n (tec.); -less a. endlos, unendlich, ewig.

Endemic [en-de'mik] a. örtlich beschränkt.

Endanger [in-dein'dzher] vt. gefährden.

Endear [in-di'r] vt. lieb machen; -ment n. Liebkosung f.

Endeavour [en-de'wer] vi. sich bestreben; n. Bestrebung f.

Endorse [in-dorss'] vt. indossieren, bestätigen; -ment n. Indossament n, Bestätigung f, Vermerk n.

Endow [in-dau'] vt. ausstatten, dotieren; -ment n. Ausstattung f, Dotierung f.

Endurable [in-djuh'rAbl] a. erträglich.

Endurance [in-djuh'rAnss] n. Ertragen n, Ausdauer f.

Endur'e [in-djuh'er] *vt. i.* ertragen, aushalten; **-ing** *a.* dauernd.

Enemy [e'ni-mi] *n.* Feind *m*; alien – feindlicher Ausländer; **- action** *n.* Feindeeinwirkung *f*; **- country** *n.* Feindgelände *n*; **- forces** *n. pl.* feindliche Streitkräfte *f. pl*; **- intelligence** *n.* Feinderkundung *f*; **- occupied** *a.* feindbesetzt; **- troops** *n. pl.* feindliche Truppen *f. pl.*

Energetic [e-ner-dzhe'tik] *a.* energisch. [*f*, Tatkraft *f*.]

Energy [e'ner-dzhi] *n.* Energie

Enervat'e [e'ner-weit] *vt.* entnerven, schwächen; **-ion** *n.* Entnervung *f.* [kräften.]

Enfeeble [in-fihbl'] *vt.* entkräften.

Enfilad'e [in-fi-leid'] *vt.* flankieren, bestreichen (*mil.*); **-ing fire** *n.* Schräg-, Flankenfeuer *f. pl.*

Enforce [in-fOrss'] *vt.* erzwingen, durchsetzen; **-ment** *n.* Erzwingung *f*, Durchsetzung *f.*

Enfranchise [in-fran'tschais] *vt.* das Wahlrecht verleihen; **-ment** *n.* Wahlrechterteilung *f.*

Engag'e [in-geidzh'] *vt.* verpflichten, anstellen, dingen, angreifen; **-ment** *n.* Verpflichtung *f*, Gefecht *n*, Verlobung *f*; **-ing** *a.* gewinnend.

Engender [in-dzhen'der] *vt.* erzeugen, hervorursachen.

Engine [en'dzhin] *n.* Maschine *f*, Motor *m*; **- driver** *n.* Lokomotivführer *m*; **- cowling** *n.* Haube *f* (*tec.*); **- fitter** *n.* Motorenschlosser *m*; **- tester** *n.* Prüfmotorenwart *m.*

Engineer [en-dzhi-nih'er] *n.* Ingenieur *m*, Techniker *m*, Pionier *m* (*mil*), Seemaschinist *m* (*nav.*).

Engineering [en-dzhi-nih'ring] *n.* Ingenieurwesen *n*, Technik *f*, Genie(wesen) *n* (*mil.*).

Engrav'e [in-greiw'] *vt.* gravieren, stechen; **-er** *n.* Graveur

m, Bildstecher *m*; **-ing** *n.* Gravieren *n*, Stich *m.*

Engrossing [in-grou'ssing] *a.* fesselnd. [schlingen.]

Engulf [in-gAlf'] *vt.* ver-

Enhance [in-hahnss'] *vt.* erhöhen.

Enjoy [in-dzheu'] *vt.* geniessen, sich erfreuen; **-able** *a.* geniessbar, erfreulich; **-ment** *n.* Genuss *m.*

Enlarge [in-lahrdzh'] *vt.* erweitern, vergrössern (*photo, etc.*); **-ment** *n.* Erweiterung *f*, Vergrösserung *f.*

Enlighten [in-lai'ten] *vt.* aufklären; **-ment** *n.* Aufklärung *f.*

Enlist [in-list'] *vt.* anwerben; *i.* sich anwerben lassen.

Enliven [in-laiwn'] *vt.* beleben.

Enmity [en'mi-ti] *n.* Feindschaft *f.* [veredeln.]

Ennoble [i-noubl'] *vt.* adeln,

Enormity [i-nOr'mi-ti] *n.* Ungeheuerlichkeit *f.*

Enormous [i-nOr'mAss] *a.* ungeheuer. [*a. ad.* genug.]

Enough [i-nAf'] *n.* Genüge *f*;

Enquire [in-kuai'er] *vt.* nachfragen, sich erkundigen.

Enquiry [in-kuai'ri] *n.* Nachfrage *f*, Erkundigung *f.*

Enrage [in-reidzh'] *vt.* aufbringen; **-d** *a.* wütend.

Enrich [in-ritsch'] *vt.* bereichern; **-ment** *n.* Bereicherung *f.*

Enroll [in-roul'] *vt.* einschreiben; **-ment** *n.* Einschreibung *f.*

Ensconce [in-skonss'] *vt.* verstecken.

Enshrine [in-schrain'] *vt.* in einen Schrein einschliessen.

Enshroud [in-schraud'] *vt.* umhüllen.

Ensign [en'ssain'] *n.* Flagge *f*, Feldzeichen *n*, Fähnrich *m.*

Enslave [in-ssleiw'] *vt.* zum Sklaven machen. [stricken.]

Ensnare [in-ssneh'er] *vt.* verstricken.

Ensue [in-ssuh'] *vi.* erfolgen.

Ensure [in-schuh'er] *vt.* sichern.

Entangle [in-tæng'g'l] vt. verwickeln.

Enter [en'ter] vt. hineingehen, eintreten, eintragen (com.).

Enterpris'e [en'ter-prais] n. Unternehmung f.; -ing a. unternehmend.

Entertain [en-ter-tein'] vt. unterhalten, bewirten, eingehen auf (suggestion); -ment n. Unterhaltung f., Bewirtung f.

Enthrone [en-throun'] vt. auf den Thron setzen.

Enthusias'm [in-thuh'si-æsm] n. Begeisterung f.; -tic a. begeistert, eifrig.

Entic'e [in-taiss'] vt. locken; -ement n. Verleiten n, Verlockung f.; -ing a. verführerisch. [tigen.

Entitle [en-taitl'] vt. berechtigen.

Entire [in-tai'er] a. -ly ad. ganz; -ty n. Ganzheit f.

Entrails [en'treils] n. pl. Eingeweide pl.

Entrance [en'trAnss] n. Eingang m, Eintritt m. [zücken.

Entrance [in-trahns'] vt. entzücken.

Entrap [in-træp'] vt. fangen.

Entreat [in-triht'] vt. ersuchen; -y n. Gesuch n.

Entrench [in-trensch'] vt. sich eingraben; i. schanzen, graben; -ing tool n. Schanzzeug n.

Entrust [in-trAst'] vt. anvertrauen.

Entry [en'tri] n. Eintritt m., Eingang m, Posten m (com.).

Entwine [in-tuain'] vt. verflechten. [vt. aufzählen.

Enumerate [i-njuh'mA-reit]

Enunciate [i-nAn'ssi-eit] vt. verkünden, aussprechen, erklären.

Envelop [in-we'lAp] vt. einhüllen; -ment n. Umhüllung f, Umfassung f (mil.).

Envelope [en'wA-loup] n. Briefumschlag m, Hülle f, Haut f (av.).

Enviable [en'wi-Abl] a. beneidenswert.

Envious [en'wi-Ass] a. neidisch. [mAnt] n. Umgebung f.

Environment [in-wai'rAn-

Envoy [en'weu] n. Gesandte(r) m. [neiden.

Envy [en'wi] n. Neid m; vt.

Epaulette [e'po-let] n. Schulterstück n.

Ephemeral [i-fe'mA-rAl] a. kurzlebig, vorübergehend.

Epic [e'pik] n. Epos n; a. episch.

Epidemic [e-pi-de'mik] n. Epidemie f; a. epidemisch.

Epigram [e'pi-græm] n. Sinngedicht n. [sucht f.

Epilepsy [e'pi-lep'ssi] n. Fall-

Episcopal [i-pi'sko-pAl] a. bischöflich. [Sendschreiben n.

Epistle [i-pissl'] n. Epistel f.

Epitaph [e'pi-tahf'] n. Grabschrift f. [wort n.

Epithet [e'pi-thet] n. Beiname n.

Epoch [ih'pok] n. Epoche f.

Equable [e'kuAbl] a. gleichförmig, gleichmütig.

Equal [ih'kuAl] a. -ly ad. gleich. [heit f.

Equality [i-kuo'li-ti] n. Gleich-

Equalize [ih'kuA-lais'] vt. gleichmachen; i. Entzerrer m (rad.).

Equanimity [ih-kuA-ni'mi-ti] n. Gleichmut m. [tor m.

Equator [i-kuei'ter] n. Äqua-

Equilibrium [ih-kui-li'bri-Am] n. Gleichgewicht n.

Equip [i-kuip'] vt. ausrüsten; -ment n. Ausrüstung f, Ausstattung f, Geräte n.

Equitable [e'kui-tabl] a. billig, gerecht.

Equivalent [i-kui'wA-lAnt] n. Äquivalent n, Gegenwert m, Ersatz m; a. gleichwertig.

Equivocal [i-kui'wA-kl] a. zweideutig.

Equivocate [i-kui'wA-keit] vi. zweideutig reden; -ion n. Zweideutigkeit f, Lüge f.

Era [ih'rA] n. Zeitrechnung f.

Eradicate [i-ræ'di-keit] vt. ausrotten.

Erase [i-reiss'] vt. ausreiben, ausradieren.

Erasure [i-rei'zher] n. Rasur f, Streichung f.

Ere [eh'er] cj. bevor, ehe; pn. pr. vor; - now schon früher.

Erect [i-rekt'] a. aufrecht; vt. errichten; -ion n. Errichtung f, Gebäude n. [lin n.

Ermine [Är'min] n. Hermelin n.

Erotic [i-ro'tik] a. erotisch.

Err [Är] vi. sich irren.

Errand [e'rAnd] n. Auftrag m; - -boy n. Laufbursche m.

Erratic [i-rä'tik] a. unregelmässig, ungewöhnlich.

Erroneous [i-rou'ni-Ass] a. irrig, irrtümlich.

Error [e'rer] n. Irrtum m.

Eruption [i-rAp'schAn] n. Ausbruch m, Ausschlag m.

Erysipelas [e-ri-ssi'pA-lAss] n. Rotlauf n.

Escalator [e'skA-lei-ter] n. Rolltreppe f.

Escapade [e-skA-peid'] n. mutwilliger Streich.

Escap'e [i-skeip'] n. Entrinnen n, Entweichen n; vt. entrinnen; i. entrinnen, entweichen; -ism n. Weltflucht f.

Escort [e'skOrt] n. Begleitung f, Geleit n, Geleitzug m (mil.); - vessel n. Flottenbegleitschiff n.

Escort [i-skOrt'] vt. geleiten.

Escutcheon [i-skAt'schAn] n. Wappenschild n.

Especial [i-spe'schAl] a. besonder, vorzüglich; -ly ad. besonders.

Esplanade [ess-plA-neid'] n. Esplanade f.

Espouse [i-spaus'] vt. vermählen, annehmen, verfechten (cause).

Essay [ess'ei] n. kleinere Abhandlung, Aufsatz m, -ist n. Essayist m. [Essenz f.

Essence [ess'Anss] n. Wesen n.

Essential [i-ssen'schAl] a. wesentlich.

Establish [i-stäb'lisch] vt. gründen, festsetzen, etablieren; -ment n. Gründung f, Festsetzung f, Etablissement n, Soll n, Plan m, Stärke f, Etat n, Bestand m (mil.); -ment stocks m. pl. Sollbestand m, -ment strength n. (Soll-) Stärke f, Plansoll n (mil.).

Estate [i-steit'] n. Gut n; -agent n. Häusermakler m.

Esteem [i-stihm'] n. Hochachtung f; vt. achten.

Estimable [e'sti-mAbl] a. achtungswert.

Estimate [e'sti-mAt] vt. Schätzung f, Überschlag m.

Estimate [e'sti-meit] vt. schätzen; -d balance n. Sollbestand m (com.). [n. Schätzung f.

Estimation [e-sti-mei'schAn] n.

Estrange [i-streindsh'] vt. entfremden; -ment n. Entfremdung f. [dung f.

Estuary [e'stju-A-ri] n. Mündung f.

Etch [etsch] vt. radieren; -er n. Radierer m; -ing n. Radierung f.

Eternal [i-tAr'nAl] a. -ly ad. ewig.

Eternity [i-tAr'ni-ti] n. Ewigkeit f.

Ether [ih'ther] n. Äther m.

Ethereal [i-thih'ri-Al] a. ätherisch, himmlisch.

Ethic'al [ethik'l] a. ethisch; -s n. pl. Ethik f.

Ethyl [e'thil] n. Äthyl n; -isation n. Verbleiung f.

Etiquette [e-ti-ket'] n. Etikette f, feiner Brauch, Umgangsformen f. pl.

Etymology [e-ti-mo'lo-dzhi] n. Etymologie f.

Eucalyptus [juh-kA-lip'tAss] n. Eukalyptus m.

Eulogize [juh'lo-dzhais] vt. loben. [rede f.

Eulogy [juh'lo-dzhi] n. Lob-

Evacuat'e [i-wæ'kju-eit] vt. entleeren, räumen, abschieben (deport), abbefördern (wounded); -ion n. Ausleerung f.

Räumung f, Land-verschieb-ung f, -verschickung f (civilians), Umquartierung f (troops) Verlagerung f (stocks).

Evade [i-weid'] vt. ausweichen, umgehen.

Evaporat'e [i-wæ'pA-reit] vt. abdampfen lassen; i. verdampfen; -ion Ausdünstung f, Verdampfung f.

Evasion [i-wei'zhAn] n. Ausflucht f, Umgehung f.

Evasive [i-wei'siw] a. -ly ad. ausweichend.

Even [ihw'An] a. eben, gleichmässig, gerade; ad. sogar, überhaupt; – then selbst dann.

Evening [ihw'ning] n. Abend m.

Event [i-went'] n. Ereignis n; -ful a. ereignisvoll; -ual a. schliesslich; -ually ad. am Ende.

Ever [e'wer] ad. immer, stets; -lasting a. immerwährend.

Every [ew'ri] a. jeder, jede, jedes; -body pn. jedermann; -thing pn. alles; -where ad. überall.

Evict [i-wikt'] vt. entsetzen, vertreiben; -ion n. Vertreibung f.

Eviden'ce [e'wi-dAnss] n. Beweis m, Zeugnis n; -t a. -tly ad. augenscheinlich.

Evil [ih'wil] a. übel, schlecht; n. Übel n, Unheil m.

Evince [i-winss'] vt. erweisen, zeigen; [rufen.

Evoke [i-wouk'] vt. hervor-

Evolution [ih-wo-ljuh'schAn] n. Entwicklung f, Evolution f.

Evolve [i-wolw'] vt. entwickeln; i. sich entwickeln.

Ewe [juh] n. Mutterschaf n.

Ewer [juh'er] n. Waschwasserkanne f.

Exact [ig-sækt'] a. genau, ganz richtig; vt. eintreiben, erpressen; -ing a. anspruchsvoll; -ion n. Eintreibung f; -itude n. Genauigkeit f.

Exaggerat'e [ig-sæ'dzhA-reit] vt. übertreiben; -ion n. Übertreibung f.

Exalt [ig-sOlt'] vt. erhöhen, -ation n. Erhebung f, Begeisterung f.

Examination [ig-sæ-mi-nei'schAn] n. Prüfung f, Untersuchung f, Revision f (customs), Kontrolle f (passport), Verhör n (law).

Examine [ig-sæ'min] vt. prüfen, untersuchen, verhören; -r n. (der) Prüfende. [spiel n.

Example [ig-sahmpl'] n. Bei-

Exasperat'e [ig-sæ'spA-reit] vt. aufreizen; -ion n. Erbitterung f, Entrüstung f.

Excavat'e [ex'kA-weit] vt. ausgraben; -ion n. Ausgrabung f, Durchstich m; -or n. Bagger m; slewing -or Drehbagger m (tec.).

Exceed [ik-ssihd'] vt. überschreiten; -ingly ad. übermässig.

Excel [ik-ssel'] vt. übertreffen; i. sich auszeichnen.

Excellen'ce [ex'A-lAnss] n. Vortrefflichkeit f; -t a. ausgezeichnet, vortrefflich.

Except [ik-ssept'] vt. ausnehmen; pr. ausgenommen; cf. ausser; -ion n. Ausnahme f; -ional a. aussergewöhnlich.

Excerpt [ex'sserpt'] n. Auszug m.

Excess [ik-ssess'] n. Übermass n, Unmässigkeit f; -profits n. pl. Wuchergewinn m; -ive a. übermässig.

Exchange [ix-tscheindzh'] n. Austausch m, Wechsel m, Börse f, Zentrale f, Vermittlungsamt n, -stelle f, Amt n (ph.), Fernsprechstelle f (ph.); vt. tauschen, wechseln; – of population Bevölkerungsaustausch m.

Exchangeable [ix-tschein'dzhAbl] a. austauschbar, auswechselbar.

Exchequer [ix-tsche'ker] n.

Staatsschatz *m*, Schatzamt *n*, Reichsfiskus *m*.   [steuerbar.

Excisable [ek-ssai'sAbl] *a.*

Excise [ek'ssais] *n.* Akzise *f*, Verbrauchssteuer *f*; -man *n.* Steuereinnehmer *m*.

Excitable [ik-ssai'tAbl] *a.* erregbar, reizbar.

Excite [ik-ssait'] *vt.* erregen; -ment *n.* Erregung *f*, Aufregung *f*.   [rufen.

Exclaim [ix-kleim'] *vt.* aus-

Exclamation [ex-klA-mei'schAn] *n.* Ausruf *m*.

Exclude [ix-kluhd'] *vt.* ausschliessen.

Exclusion [ex-kluh'zhAn] *n.* Ausschliessung *f*.

Exclusive [ex-kluh'siw] *a.* -ly *ad.* ausschliesslich, exklusiv; -ness *n.* Ausschliesslichkeit *f*.

Excommunicate [ex-kAmjuh'ni-keit] *vt.* in den Kirchenbann tun.   [Kot *m*.

Excrement [ex'kri-mAnt] *n.*

Excrescence [ex-kre'ssAnss] *n.* Auswuchs *m*.

Excrete [ex-kriht'] *vt.* ausscheiden, absondern.

Excretion [ex-kri'schAn] *n.* Aussonderung *f*.

Excruciating [ex-kruh'schiei-ting] *a.* höchst peinlich, qualvoll.

Exculpate [ex'kAl-peit] *vt.* entschuldigen, rechtfertigen.

Excursion [ix-kAr'schAn] *n.* Ausflug *m*, Abstecher *m*.

Excusable [ix-kjuh'zAbl] *a.* entschuldbar.

Excuse [ix-kjuhs'] *vt.* entschuldigen.

Excuse [ix-kjuhss'] *n.* Entschuldigung *f*, Vorwand *m*, Ausrede *f*.   [scheulich.

Execrable [ex'i-krAbl] *a.* ab-

Execration [ex-i-krei'schAn] *n.* Verwünschung *f*.

Execute [ex'i-kjuht] *vt* ausführen, ausfertigen, hinrichten.

Execution [ex-i-kjuh'schAn] *n.* Ausführung *f*, Ausfertigung

f. Hinrichtung *f*; -er *n.* Scharfrichter *m*.

Executive [ig-sek'ju-tiw] *a.* vollziehend; *n.* vollziehende Gewalt; -ot *n.* Vollstrecker *m*.

Exemplary [ig-sem'plA-ri] *a.* musterhaft.

Exemplify [ig-sem'pli-fai] *vt.* erläutern.

Exempt [ig-sempt'] *a.* befreit; *vt.* befreien; -ion *n.* Befreiung *f*, Freiheit *f*.

Exercise [ex'er-ssais] *n.* Übung *f*; *vt.* üben, ausüben.

Exert [ig-sArt'] *vt.* anwenden, ausüben; *r.* sich anstrengen; -ion *n.* Anstrengung *f*.

Exhale [ex-heil'] *vt.* ausdünsten, aushauchen.

Exhaust [ig-sOst'] *vt.* erschöpfen, entleeren; *n.* Auspuff *m* (*aut.*); - gas *n.* Abgas *n*; -valve *n.* Auspuffklappe *f*, Abgangsventil *n*.

Exhausted [ig-sO'stid] *a.* erschöpft, abgebaut (*mine*), vergriffen (*edition*).

Exhaustion [ig-sOss'tschAn] *n.* Erschöpfung *f*.

Exhaustive [ig-sOss'tiw] *a.* -ly *ad.* erschöpfend.

Exhibit [ig-si'bit] *n.* ausgestellte Sache; *vt.* zeigen, ausstellen.

Exhibition [ex-i-bi'schAn] *n.* Darstellung *f*, Ausstellung *f*.

Exhilarate [ig-si'lA-reit] *vt.* erheitern; -ion *n.* Erheiterung *f*.

Exhort [ig-sOrt'] *vt.* ermahnen; -ation *n.* Ermahnung *f*.

Exhume [ex-juhm'] *vt.* ausgraben.

Exigency [ex'i-dzhAn-ssi] *n.* Bedürfnis *n*, Notfall *m*.

Exile [eg'sail] *n.* Verbannung *f*, der, die Verbannte; *vt.* verbannen.

Exist [ig-sist'] *vi.* dasein, leben; -ing *a.* bestehende, vorhanden; -ence *n.* Dasein *n*, Leben *n*; -ent *a.* *see* existing.

Exit [eg'sit] n. Ausgang m, Abgang m.

Exonerate [ig-so'nA-reit] vt. [freisprechen.

Exorbitan'ce [ig-sOr'bitAnss] n. Übermass n; -t a. masslos, unerhört, übermässig.

Exotic [ex-o'tik] a. exotisch.

Expand [ix-pænd'] vt. ausspannen, ausdehnen; i. sich ausspannen, sich ausdehnen.

Expans'e [ix-pænss'] n. weiter Raum; -ion n. Ausdehnung f; -ive a. ausgedehnt.

Expatiate [ex-pei'sch-eit] vi. sich weitläufig auslassen.

Expatriat'e [ex-pæ'tri-eit] vt. aus dem Vaterlande vertreiben, abschieben; -ion n. Verbannung f, Abschieben n.

Expect [ix-pekt'] vt. erwarten.

Expectation [ex-pek-tei'schAn] n. Erwartung f.

Expectorat'e [ex-pek'tA-reit] vt. spucken, auswerfen; -ion n. Ausspucken n, Auswurf m.

Expedien'ce [ix-pih'di-Anssi] n. Ratsamkeit f; -t a. ratsam; n. Mittel n, Hilfsmittel n.

Expedite [ex'pi-dait] vt. beschleunigen.

Expeditio'n [ex-pi-di'schAn] n. Reise f, Fahrt f, Kriegszug m (mil.), Geschwindigkeit f, Eile f (speed); -us a. -usly ad. schnell. [fortschreiben.

Expel [ix-pel'] vt. wegtreiben.

Expend [ix-pend'] vt. ausgeben, aufwenden.

Expenditure [ix-pen'ditscher] n. Expense [ix-penss'] n. Ausgabe f, Aufwand m.

Expensive [ix-pen'ssiw] a. kostspielig.

Experience [ix-pih'ri-Anss] n. Erfahrung f, Erlebnis n; vt. erfahren, erleben, durchmachen; -d a. erfahren.

Experiment [ix-pe'ri-mAnt] n. Versuch m; vi. experimentieren; -al a. Versuchs . . .; -al centre, - al-station n. Erprobungsstelle f.

Expert [ex'pert] a. erfahren, geschickt; n. Sachverständige(r), Fachmann m.

Expiate [ex'pi-eit] vt. sühnen.

Expiration [ex-pi-rei'schAn] n. Ablauf m, Ausatmung f.

Expire [ix-pai'er] vi. ablaufen, sterben.

Explain [ix-plein'] vt. er-[klären.

Explanation [ex-plA-nei'schAn] n. Erklärung f.

Explanatory [ix-plæ'nA-tA-ri] a. erklärend. [erklärlich.

Explicable [ix'pli-kAbl] a.

Explicit [ix-pli'ssit] a. -ly ad. deutlich, bestimmt, ausdrücklich.

Explode [ix-ploud'] vt. explodieren lassen, versprengen; i. explodieren, platzen.

Exploit [ex'pleut] n. Tat f; vt. ausnutzen; -ation n. Ausnutzung f, Ausbeutung f.

Exploration [ex-plO-rei'schAn] n. Erforschung f.

Explore [ix-plOr'] vt. erforschen; -r n. Forschungsreisende(r) m, Erforscher m.

Explosion [ix-plou'schAn] n. Explosion f, Knall m.

Explosive [ix-plou'ssiw] n. Spreng-, Explosions-stoff m; a. explosiv, Knall . . .; -charge n. Sprengladung f; -shell n. Sprenggranate f.

Exponent [ex-pou'nAnt] n. Ausleger m.

Export [ex'pOrt] n. Ausfuhr f; - duty n. Ausfuhrzoll m; -trade n. Ausfuhrhandel m.

Export [ex-pOrt'] vt. ausführen; -ation n. Ausfuhr f, Export m.

Exporter [ex-pOr'ter] n. Exporthändler m.

Expose [ix-pous'] vt. aussetzen, darlegen, ausstellen, belichten (photo).

Exposition [ex-po-si'schAn] n. Auslegung f.

Expostulat'e [ix-po'stju-leit] vi. ernste Vorhaltungen machen; -ion n. Vorhaltung f, Verweis m.

Exposure [ix-pou'zher] n. Blosslegung f, Ausstellung f, Belichtung f (photo).

Expound [ix-paund'] vt. auslegen, deuten.

Express [ix-press'] n. Eilbote m, Eilzug m (rl.); vt. äussern, ausdrücken; a. express, Eil...; -ion n. Ausdruck m; -ive a. ausdrucksvoll.

Expropriat'e [ex-prou'pri-eit] vt. enteignen; -ion n. Enteignung f. [Vertreibung f.

Expulsion [ix-pAl'schAn] n.

Exquisite [ex'kui-sit] a. -ly ad. fein, sehr empfindlich.

Ex-service man [ex-ssAr'wiss-mæn] n. ausgedienter Soldat, Frontkämpfer m.

Extempor'ary [ix-tem'pA-rA-ri] a. unvorbereitet, behelfsmässig; -e ad. aus dem Stegreif.

Extend'd [ix-tend'] vt. ausdehnen, ausstrecken; i. sich erstrecken; -sion n. Ausdehnung f; telephone – Nebenanschluss m; -sive a. ausgedehnt.

Extent [ix-tent'] n. Ausdehnung f, Grösse f.

Extenuat'e [ex-te'nju-eit] vt. verringern, mildern; -ion n. Milderung f, Beschönigung f.

Exterior [ex-tih'ri-er] a. äusserlich; n. das Äussere.

Exterminat'e [ex-tAr'mineit] vt. vertilgen, ausrotten; -ion n. Vertilgung f, Ausrottung f.

Extinct [ix-tinkt'] a. ausgestorben; -ion n. Ausrottung f.

Extinguish [ix-ting'guisch] vt. auslöschen.

Extol [ix-toul'] vt. preisen.

Extort [ix-tOrt'] vt. erpressen; -ion n. Erpressung f; -ionate a. übermässig.

Extra [ex'trA] a. ausserordentlich, besonder, Extra . . . ; ad.

besonders, ausserdem; – copy n. Nebenabdruck m; – freight n. Extrafracht f.

Extract [ex'trækt] n. Auszug m, Extrakt m.

Extract [ix-trækt'] vt. ausziehen, herleiten, ausscheiden; -ion n. Ausziehen n, Gewinnung f.

Extraneous [ex-trei'ni-Ass] a. unwesentlich, fremd.

Extraordinary [ix-trOr'di-nA-ri] a. ausserordentlich.

Extravagan'ce [ix-træ'wAgAnss] n. Verschwendung f; -t a. -tly ad. verschwenderisch, übermässig.

Extreme [ix-trihm'] a. Extrem n; z. äusserst.

Extremity [ix-tre'mi-ti] n. das Äusserste, äusserste Not.

Extricate [ex'tri-keit] vt. losmachen, herauswinden.

Exuberan'ce [ig-suh'bArAnss] n. Überfluss m, Fülle f; -t a. überschwenglich, überreichlich.

Exult [ig-sAlt'] vt. frohlocken; -ation n. Frohlocken n.

Eye [ai] n. Auge n, Öhr n (needle), Öse f (dress); vt. anschauen, mustern; -ball n. Augapfel m; -brow n. Augenbraue f; -glass n. Kneifer m, Zwicker m; -lash n. Augenwimper f; -let n. Schnürloch n; -lid n. Augenlid n; -sight n. Gesicht n, Sehkraft f; – -witness n. Augenzeuge m.

F

Fable [feibl] n. Fabel f.

Fabric [fæb'rik] n. Fabrikat n, Gewebe n, Stoff m, Gebäude n; – glove n. Stoffhandschuh m; -ate vt. verfertigen, erfinden (lies, etc.); -ation n. Herstellung f, Erdichtung f.

Fabulous [fæ'bju-lAss] a. fabelhaft.

Face [feiss] n. Gesicht n, Oberfläche f, Zifferblatt n (clock); vt. das Gesicht zuwenden, gegenüberliegen, mutig entgegentreten.

Facetious [fA-ssih'schAss] a. -ly ad. witzig, spasshaft.

Facile [fæ'ssil] a. leicht, nachgiebig. [leichtern.

Facilitate [fA-ssi'li-teit] vt. er-

Facility [fA-ssi'li-ti] n. Leichtigkeit f, Gelegenheit f.

Facing [fei'ssing] n. Aufschlag m (clothes), Verkleidung f (stone), genaue Nachbildung.

Facsimile [fæk-ssi'mi-li] n.

Fact [fækt] n. Tatsache f.

Factio'n [fæk'schAn] n. Partei f; -us a. aufrührerisch, ungehorsam.

Factor [fæk'ter] n. Umstand m, Moment n, Agent m, Verkäufer m (com.).

Factory [fæk'tA-ri] n. Fabrik f; - airfield n. Industrieflugplatz m; - guard n. Werkschutz m.

Faculty [fæ'kAl-ti] n. Fähigkeit f, Fakultät f.

Fade [feid] vi. welken, verschiessen, schwinden (rad.); - out vt.i. abklingen lassen (rad.), verschwinden lassen (film).

Fag [fæg] n. sich abmühen; -ged a. erschöpft mürbe.

Fail [feil] vi. fehlen, ermatten, fehlschlagen, stehen bleiben, durchsacken, ausfallen (aut. av.); -ing n. Fehler m; -ure n.

Fehlen n, Abnahme f, Fehlschlagen n, Zahlungseinstellung f (com.).

Faint [feint] a. schwach, blass; vi. ohnmächtig werden; -ness n. Schwäche f.

Fair [feh'er] n. Messe f.

Fair [feh'er] a. schön, blond, rein, billig; -ly ad. billig, erträglich, ziemlich; -ness n. Blondheit f, Billigkeit f, Gerechtigkeit f; -way n. Fahrrinne f, Fahrwasser n.

Fairy [feh'ri] n. Fee f; a. feenhaft; - tale n. Märchen n

Faith [feith] n. Glaube m, Vertrauen n; -ful a. treu, beständig; -fulness n. Treue f, Beständigkeit f; -less a. treulos; -lessness n. Treulosigkeit f.

Fake [feik] n. Schwindel m; vt. fälschen.

Falcon [fOl'kAn] n. Falk m.

Fall [fOl] n. Fall m, Fallen n; vi. fallen; - due fällig werden.

Fallacious [fA-lei'schAss] a. trügerisch.

Fallacy [fæ'lA-ssi] n. Trugschluss m.

Fallible [fæ'libl] a. fehlbar.

Fallow [fæ'lo] a. brach.

False [fOlss] a. falsch.

Falsehood [fOlss'hud] n. Unwahrheit f, Unrichtigkeit f.

Falseness [fOlss'ness] n. Falschheit f.

Falsification [fOl-ssi-fi-kei'schAn] n. (Ver-)Fälschung f.

Falsify [fOl'ssi-fai] vt. verfälschen, widerlegen (prove false). [stocken.

Falter [fOl'ter] vi. schwanken.

Fame [feim] n. Ruhm m.

Familiar [fA-mi'li-Ar] a. vertraut, wohlbekannt.

Familiarity [fA-mi-li-æ'ri-ti] n. Vertraulichkeit f.

Familiarize [fA-mi'liA-rais] vt. r. (sich) bekannt machen.

Family [fæ'mi-li] n. Familie f; - allowance n. Familienunterhalt m. [snot f.

Famine [fæ'min] n. Hungersnot f.

Famish [fæ'misch] vt. aushungern; vi. Hunger leiden.

Famous [fei'mAss] a. berühmt.

Fan [fæn] n. Fächer m; vt. fächeln, anfachen, entfachen.

Fan [fæn] n. Liebhaber m; radio - Funkbastler m.

Fanatic [fA-næ'tik] n. Fanatiker m, Schwärmer m.

Fanatical [fA-næ'tikl] a. -ly ad. fanatisch, leidenschaftlich.

Fanaticism [fA-næ'ti-ssism] n. Fanatismus m.

Fanciful [fæn'ssi-ful] a. phantastisch, wunderlich, eingebildet.

Fancy [fan'ssi] n. Phantasie f, Einbildung f, Einfall m, Grille f, Neigung f; vt. sich einbilden, lieben; – dress ball Maskenball m; – goods pl. Galanteriewaren f.pl.; – price übertrieben hoher Preis; – work feine Handarbeit. [zahn m.

Fang [fæng] n. Gift-, Fang-

Fantastic(al) [fæn-tæ'stik] a. närrisch, wunderlich.

Far [fahr] a. ad. fern, weit; --fetched a. gesucht; – -sighted a. weitsichtig.

Farce [fahrss] n. Posse f, Komödie f.

Farcical [fahr'ssik] a. possenhaft, lächerlich.

Fare [feh'er] n. Fahrgeld n, Speise f; bill of – Speisekarte f; – stage Fahrpreiszone f.

Farewell [feh'er-uel] int. Lebewohl!; n. Lebewohl n.

Farm [fahrm] n. Pachthof m, Bauernhof m, Gut n; vt. bebauen; – -hand, – -labourer Knecht m, Landarbeiter m.

Farmer [fahr'mer] n. Pächter m, Meier m; gentleman – Landwirt m.

Farming [fahr'ming] n. Ackerbau m, Landwirtschaft f.

Farrier [fæ'rier] n. Hufschmied m. [ner, weiter.

Farther [fahr'dher] a. ad. fer-

Farthest [fahr-dhist] a. ad. fernst, weitest.

Fascinate [fæ'ssi-neit] vt. bezaubern.

Fascination [fæ-ssi-nei'schAn] n. Bezauberung f, Reiz m. [ismus m.

Fascism [fæ'schism] n. Fasch-

Fascist [fæ'schist] n. Faschist m.

Fashion [fæ'schAn] n. Mode f, Form f, Sitte f, Art f; vt. modeln, bilden, gestalten.

Fashionable [fæ'schA-nAbl] a. modisch, fein, modern.

Fast [fahst] a. ad. fest, schnell, waschecht (dye); vergnügungssüchtig (girl); – train Schnellzug m.

Fast [fahst] vi. fasten.

Fasten [fahssn] vt. fest machen, befestigen.

Fastening [fahss'ning] n. Befestigung f, Schloss n.

Fastidious [fæ-sti'di-Ass] a. wählerisch. [a. fett, dick.

Fat [fæt] n. Fett n, Schmalz n;

Fatal [fei'tl] a. -ly ad. tötlich.

Fatalism [fei'tA-lism] n. Fatalismus m, Schicksalsglaube m.

Fatalist [fei'tA-list] n. Fatalist m. [fatalistisch.

Fatalistic [fei-tA-li'stik] a.

Fatality [fA-tæ'li-ti] n. Verhängnis n, Unglück n.

Fated [fei'tid] a. vom Schicksal bestimmt. [nisvoll.

Fateful [feit'ful] a. verhäng-

Father [fah'dher] n. Vater m.

Father-in-law [fah'dher-in-lO] n. Schwiegervater m.

Fatherland [fah'dher-lænd] n. Vaterland n, Deutschland n.

Fatherless [fah'dher-less] a. vaterlos. [lich.

Fatherly [fah'dher-li] a. väter-

Fathom [fæ'dhAm] n. Klafter f; vt. sondieren, ergründen.

Fathomless [fæ'dhAm-less] a. bodenlos.

Fatigue [fA-tihg'] n. Ermüdung f, Strapaze f; – party Arbeits-trupp m, -kommando n (mil.).

Fatness [fæt'ness] n. Fettigkeit f, Fettleibigkeit f.

Fatten [fæ'tn] vt. fett machen, mästen.

Fatty [fæ'ti] a. fettig.

Fault [fOlt] n. Fehler m, Schuld f; it is not my – ich bin nicht daran schuld.

Faultless [fOlt'less] a. fehlerfrei.

Faulty [fOl'ti] a. fehlerhaft.

Favour [feiwer] n. Gunst f. Gefallen m; vt. begünstigend, unterstützen. [günstig.

Favourable [fei′wA-rAbl] a. günstig, begünstigend.

Favourite [fei′wA-rit] n. Günstling m, Liebling m, Favorit m (horse).

Fawn [fOn] n. Rehkalb n.

Fawn [fOn] vi. kriechend, schmeicheln. [en n.

Fawning [fO′ning] n. Kriecherei f, Furcht f.

Fear [fih′er] n. Furcht f; vt. fürchten. [bar.

Fearful [fih′er-ful] a. furchtbar.

Fearless [fih′er-less] a. furchtlos.

Feasibility [fih-si-bi′li-ti] n. Ausführbarkeit f.

Feasible [fih′sibl] a. ausführbar.

Feast [fihst] n. Fest n. Gastmahl n; vt. festlich bewirten; i. schmausen. [stück n.

Feat [fiht] n. Tat f. Kunststück.

Feather [fe′dher] n. Feder f.

Feathery [fe′dhA-ri] a. federartig.

Feature [fih′tjer] n. Zug m; vt. darstellen, charakterisieren (film); – film Spielfilm m, Hauptfilm m. [bruar m.

February [fe′bru-A-ri] n. Februar m.

Federal [fe′dA-rAl] a. Bundes . . . ; eidgenössisch; – council – n. Bundesrat m; – union n. Bund m.

Federate [fe′dA-reit] vt. zu einem Staatenbund vereinigen, verbünden.

Federation [fe-dA-rei′schAn] n. Vereinigung f. Staatenbund m.

Fee [fih] n. Honorar n. Gebühr f; vt. honorieren, bezahlen.

Feeble [fihbl] a. schwach.

Feed [fihd] vt. füttern, ernähren, speisen; i. essen, fressen, futtern; n. Futter n.

Feeder [fih′der] n. Zuführungsvorrichtung f (tec.). Speiseleitung f. (el.); Kinderlatz n. (bib);

– -service Zubringerdienst m (tec.). [ing f.

Feeding [fih′ding] n. Fütterung f.

Feel [fihl] vt. fühlen, empfinden; i. (sich) fühlen; n. Gefühl n.

Feeling [fih′ling] n. Gefühl n. Empfindung f. [cheln.

Feign [fein] vi. vorgeben, heucheln.

Feigned [feind] a. verstellt, geheuchelt.

Feint [feint] n. Verstellung f. Finte f. Falle f. Scheinangriff m (mil.). [glückwünschen.

Felicitate [fi-li′ssi-teit] vt. beglückwünschen.

Felicity [fi-li′ssi-ti] n. Glückseligkeit f.

Fell [fel] vt. fällen.

Fellow [fe′lou] n. Genosse m, Bursche m, Mitglied n.

Fellowship [fe′lou-schip] n. Genossenschaft f. Kameradschaft f.

Felon [fe′lAn] n. Verbrecher m.

Felonious [fe-lou′ni-Ass] a. verbrecherisch.

Felony [fe′lA-ni] n. schweres Verbrechen.

Felt [felt] n. Filz m; – boot Filzstiefel m; – hat Filzhut m.

Female [fih′meil] n. Weib n; a. weiblich. [lich.

Feminine [fe′mi-nin] a. weiblich.

Fen [fen] n. Sumpf m.

Fence [fenss] n. Zaun m, Umzäunung f. Einfriedigung f; vi. umzäunen, einfriedigen; i. fechten. [kunst f.

Fencing [fen′ssing] n. Fechtkunst f.

Fender [fen′der] n. Ofen-vorsetzer m. Stossfänger m (aut.), Fender m (nav.).

Fennel [fenl] n. Fenchel m.

Ferment [fAr′mAnt] n. Gärungsstoff m. Gärung f.

Ferment [fer-ment′] vt. gären lassen; i. gären.

Fermentation [fer-men-tei′schAn] n. Gärung f.

Fern [fArn] n. Farnkraut n.

Ferocious [fA-rou′schAss] a. wild, grausam.

Ferocity [fA-ro'ssi-ti] n. Wildheit f, Grimmigkeit f.

Ferret [fe'rit] n. Frettchen; - out vt. ausspüren.

Ferric [fe'rik] a. Eisen ...; - oxide n. Eisenoxyd n.

Ferricyanide [fe'ri-ssai'A-naid] n. rotes Blutlaugensalz.

Ferro-boron [fe'ro-boh'ron] n. Boreisen n.

Ferro-concrete [fe'ro-kon'kriht] n. Eisenbeton m.

Ferrocyanide [fe'ro-ssai'A-naid] n. gelbes Rotlaugensalz.

Ferrous [fe'rAss] a. Eisen ...; - sulphate n. Eisenvitriol n.

Ferrule [fe'rjul] n. Stockzwinge f, Eisenband n.

Ferry [fe'ri] n. Fähre f; railway - Eisenbahnfähre f, (Trajekt-) Schiff n; vt. übersetzen.

Ferry-boat [fe'ri-bout] n. Fahrboot n, Fährschiff n; - truck n. Fahrbootwagen m.

Ferryman [fe'ri-mæn] n. Fährmann m.

Ferrying [fe'ri-ing] n. Übersetzen n, Überführen n; - flight n. Überführungsflug m (av.); - service n. Überführung f (av.).

Fertile [fA'rtail] a. fruchtbar.

Fertility [fer-ti'li-ti] n. Fruchtbarkeit f.

Fertilization [fer-ti-lai-sei'schAn] n. Fruchtbarmachung f.

Fertilize [fA'rti-lais] vt. fruchtbar machen.

Fervency [fA'rwAn-ssi] n. Inbrunst f.

Fervent [fA'rvAnt] a. heiss, heftig, inbrünstig.

Fervid [fA'rwid] a. glühend, eifrig, heiss.

Fervour [fA'rwer] n. Hitze f, Inbrunst f.

Fester [fe'ster] vi. schwären.

Festival [fe'sti-wAl] n. Fest n.

Festive [fe'stiw] a. festlich.

Festivity [fe-sti'wi-ti] n. Festlichkeit f, Fröhlichkeit f.

Festoon [fe-stuhn'] n. Girlande f, Blumengewinde n.

Fetch [fetsch] vt. holen, bringen, einbringen (price).

Fetish [fe'tisch] n. Fetisch m.

Fetter [fe'ter] n. Fessel f; vt. fesseln.

Feud [fjuhd] n. Fehde f.

Fever [fih'wer] n. Fieber n.

Feverish [fih'wA-risch] a. fieberhaft, heiss. [wenige.

Few [fjuh] a. wenig; a - einige

Fiancé [fi-ong'sse] n. Bräutigam m; -e n. Braut f.

Fiasco [fi-æ'sko] n. Misserfolg m, Blamage f. [Faser f.

Fibre [fai'ber] n. Fiber f,

Fibrous [fai'brAss] a. faserig, fiberig. [unbeständig.

Fickle [fikl] a. wankelmütig,

Fickleness [fikl'ness] n. Wankelmut m, Veränderlichkeit f.

Fiction [fik'schAn] n. Erdichtung f, Prosadichtung f.

Fictitious [fik'ti-schAss] a. erdichtet, falsch.

Fiddle [fidl] n. Geige f; vt. i. geigen, fiedeln, tändeln, spielen, Zeit verschwenden.

Fiddler [fid'ler] n. Geiger m.

Fidelity [fai-de'li-ti] n. Treue f; - insurance n. Treu-Kautions-versicherung f.

Fidget [fi'dzhit] vi. unruhig sein. [röse Unruhe.

Fidgets [fi'dzhits] n.pl. nervöse Unruhe.

Fidgety [fi'dzhi-ti] a. nervös, unruhig.

Fiduciary [fi-djuh'schA-ri] a. ungedeckt, vertrauensvoll (com.); n. Treuhänder m (com.).

Field [fihld] n. Feld n, Wiese f, Spielplatz m, Bereich m; - allowance n. Feld-, Kriegszulage f; - artillery n. Feldartillerie f; - day n. Felddienstübung f; - dressing n. Verbandpäckchen n; - glass n. Feldstecher m; - gun n. Feldgeschütz n; - hospital n. Feldlazarett n; - kitchen n. Feldküche f; - marshal n. Feldmarschall m; - operation n. Feldeinsatz m; - piece n.

Feldgeschütz n; - -sentry n.
Feldposten m; - -stores pl.
Feldzeug n; - -telegraph n.
Feldtelegraph m; - -unit n.
Truppeneinheit f; - -works pl.
Schanze f.
Fierce [fihrss] a. wild.
Fierceness [fihrss'ness] n.
Wildheit f.
Fiery [fai'e-ri] a. feurig.
Fife [faif] n. Pfeife f. [zehn.
Fifteen [fif-tihn'] num. fünf-
Fifth [fifth] a. fünft; n. Fünftel n; - column fünfte Kolonne.
Fifty [fif'ti] num. fünfzig; -, - halb und halb.
Fig [fig] n. Feige f.
Fight [fait] n. Gefecht n, Kampf m; vt. bekämpfen, streiten über, schlagen (battle) i. kämpfen, schlagen, fechten, sich schlagen.
Fighter [fai'ter] n. Kämpfer m, Jäger m (av.), Jagdflieger m (av.); - aerodrome n. Jägerplatz m; - aircraft n. Jäger m, Jagdflugzeug n; - -bomber n. Jagdbomber m; - -command n. Jagdkommando n; - -detachment n. Jagdabteilung f; -patrol n. Luftsperre f; - screen n. Jagdsperre f; - sector n. Jagdraum m; - unit n. Jagdverband m.
Fighting [fai'ting] Kämpfen n, Jagd f (av.). [bildlich.
Figurative [fi'gju-rA-tiw] a.
Figure [fi'ger] n. Gestalt f, Form f, Figur f, Ziffer f, Zahl f, Preis m (price); vt. bilden, formen, beziffern, berechnen; i. sich zeigen als.
Filament [fi'lA-mAnt] n. Faden m, Faser f, Draht m, Glüh-Heiz-faden m (tec.).
File [fail] n. Aktenbündel n, Liste f, Reihe f, Ringbuch n, Briefordner m, Sammelmappe f (com.); vt. der Reihe nach ordnen, einheften, einreichen (law).
File [fail] n. Feile f; vt. feilen.

Filial [fi'li-Al] a. kindlich.
Filiation [fi-li-ei'schan] n. Kindschaft f, Adoption f.
Filigree [fi'li-grih] n. Filigran n.
Filing [fai'ling] n. Einordnen n; - -cabinet n. Brief-, Registraturschrank m, Kartei f.
Filings [fai'lings] n. Feilspäne m.pl.
Fill [fil] n. füllen, erfüllen, besetzen (post), plombieren (tooth); i. sich füllen; n. Genüge f; - in vt. eintragen; - up vt. voll machen, auffüllen.
Filler [fi'ler] n. Füller m.
Filling [fi'ling] n. Füllung f, Zahnplombe f; - station n. Tankstelle f (aut.). Abfüllstelle f (av.).
Fillip [fi'lip] n. Schneller m, Anregung f.
Filly [fi'li] n. Stutenfüllen n.
Film [film] n. Häutchen n, Film m, Schleier m, feines Gewebe, Rollfilm m (photo), Bildstreifen m (reel); vt. i. verfilmen, sich filmen, filmen; - actor n. Filmschauspieler m, -erin f; - camera n. Schmalfilmkamera f; - pack n. Filmpack m; - shooting n. Filmaufnahme f; - spool n. Filmspule f; - star n. star n. Star m; - strip n. Filmstreifen m; - studio n. Filmatelier n; -unit n. Filmvorführgerät n.
Filter [fi'ter] n. Filter n, Seiher m; vt. filtrieren; i. durchsickern, -laufen, sich einrichten (aut.); - -paper n. Filtrierpapier n.
Filth [filth] n. Unrat m, Schmutz m.
Filthiness [fi'th-ness] n. Unreinlichkeit f, Unflätigkeit f.
Filthy [fi'thi] a. unrein, schmutzig, unflätig.
Fin [fin] n. Flosse f.
Final [fai'nAl] a. endlich, endgültig, entscheidend, schliesslich; - analysis n. Endaus-

wertung f; - **clearance** n.
Schlussabfertigung f.

Finally [fai'nǎ-li] ad. zuletzt,
schliesslich.

Finance [fai-nænss'] n. Finanz-
wesen n, -wissenschaft f, Geld-
wesen n, Kassenwesen n; vt.
finanzieren, mit Geldmitteln
versehen; *pl.* Finanzen pl.

Financial [fi-næn'schǎl] a. -ly
ad. finanziell, Finanz . . ; Ver-
mögens . . ; - **year** n. Rechnungsjahr n.

Financier [fi-næn'sĕ-er] n.
Finanzmann m, Kapitalist m.

Finch [finsch] n. Fink m.

Find [faind] vt. finden, antreffen, versehen mit, liefern;
n. Fund m.

Finding [fain'ding] n. Aus-
Wahr-spruch m, Entdeckung
f; -s pl. Befund m.   [spitz.

Fine [fain] a. fein, vortrefflich,

Fine [fain] n. Geldstrafe f; vt.
zu einer Geldstrafe verurteilen,
bestrafen.   [heit f.

Fineness [fain'ness] n. Fein-

Finesse [fi-ness'] n. List f,
Impass m (bridge).

Finery [fai'nA-ri] n. Putz m.

Finger [fing'ger] n. Finger m;
vt. betasten; - **print** n. Finger-
abdruck m.

Finish [fi'nisch] n. Schluss m,
Vollendung f, Schliff m, Glanz
m, Appretur f (com.); vt. beendigen, veredeln (tec.); i. aufhören; -**ed product** n. Fertig-
erzeugnis n (com.).

Finishing [fi'ni-sching] n.
Vollenden n, Fertigstellen n,
Verarbeitung f, Veredlung f,
Appretur f (tec.).

Finite [fai'nait] a. endlich.

Fir [fAr] n. Tanne f, Fichte f.

Fire [fai'er] n. Feuer n, Brand
m; vt. anzünden, feuern, schiessen (mil.), zünden (mine); -
alarm n. Feuermeldeapparat
m; - **brigade** n. Feuerwehr f;
- **control** n. Feuerleitung f,
-regelung f (mil.); - **escape** n.

Nottreppe f, Rettungsleiter f.
- **extinguisher** n. Feuerlöscher
m, Löschapparat m; - **fighter**
n. Feuerwehrmann m; - **light-**
er n. Kohlenanzünder m;
- **office** n. Feuerversicherungs-
büro n; - **plug** n. Feuerhahn
m; - **policy** n. Feuerversiche-
rungsschein m; - **resisting** a.
feuersicher; - **service** n. Feuer-
löschwesen n.

Fire-arms [fai'er-ahrms] n.pl.
Feuer-, Schuss-waffen f.pl.

Fire-guard [fai'er-gahrd] n.
Kamin-, Feuergitter n; - -s pl.
Brandwache f.pl.

Fireman [fai'er-mæn] Feuerwehrmann m.

Fire-proof [fai'er-pruhf] a.
feuerfest.

Fire-side [fai'er-ssaid] n.
Kamin m, Herd m, Familien-
kreis m.   [Brennholz n.

Fire-wood [fai'er-uud] n.

Fireworks [fai'er-uuOrks] n.
pl. Feuerwerk n.

Firing [fai'er-ing] n. Feuern n,
Schiessen n, Heizung f, Brennstoff m (coal, etc.).

Firm [fArm] n. Firma f, Ge-
schäftshaus n; a. -ly ad. fest,
standhaft.

Firmament [fAr'mA-mAnt]
n. Himmelsgewölbe n.

Firmness [fArm'ness] n. Festigkeit f.

First [fArst] a. erst; ad. zuerst,
erstens; - **cost** n. Selbstkostenpreis m; - **night** n. Erstaufführung f (play); - **offender** n.
Nichtvorbestrafte(r) m; - **re-**
fusal n. Vorkaufsrecht n.

First-aid [fArst-eid'] n. erste
Hilfe, Sanität f; - **box** n. Verbandkasten m; - **kit** n. Sanit-
ätspack m; - **post** n. Verband-
platz m (mil.).

First-class [fArst'klæss] a.
erstklassig, ausgezeichnet; -
rate a. vortrefflich, erstklassig.

Firstly [fArst'li] ad. erstens.

Fiscal [fiskl] a. fiskal, Finanz . . .; ~ year n. Rechnungsjahr n. [fischen.

Fish [fisch] n. Fisch m; vt.i.

Fish-bone [fisch'bonn] n. Gräte f. [Fischer m.

Fisher(man) [fisch'er-mAn] n.

Fishery [fisch'A-ri] n. Fischfang m, Fischerei(gebiet) f.

Fishing [fisch'ing] n. Fischen n, Fischfang m; ~-boat n. Fischerboot n; ~-rod n. Angelrute f; ~-tackle n. Angelgerät n.

Fishmonger [fisch'mAng-ger] n. Fischhändler m.

Fishplate [fisch'pleit] n. Lasche f (rl.).

Fissure [fisch'er] n. Spalt f.

Fist [fist] n. Faust f.

Fit [fit] a. passend, fähig, tauglich, gesund, wohlauf; vt. anpassen, passen zu, einrichten, sitzen (clothes); i. passen; n. genaues Passen, Sitz m; ~ in vt. einfügen, einrichten; ~ on vt. anprobieren; ~ out vt. ausrüsten; ~ up n. ausstatten, möblieren; ~ for duty verwendungsfähig (mil.); ~ for active service kriegsbrauchbar (mil.).

Fit [fit] n. Anfall m, Laune f.

Fitful [fit'ful] a. launenhaft, unterbrochen.

Fitness [fit'ness] n. Schicklichkeit f, Tauglichkeit f, Gesundheit f.

Fitter [fi'ter] n. Zuschneider m, Motorenschlosser m, Monteur m

Fitting [fi'ting] a. schicklich, passend, tauglich.

Fittings [fi'tings] n.pl. Einrichtung f, Ausstattung f (house), Zubehör n, Armatur f (tec.).

Five [faiw] num. fünf.

Fix [fix] vt. befestigen, festsetzen, anheften, bestimmen, aufpflanzen (bayonet), fixieren (photo); n. Klemme f, Verlegenheit f. [bestimmt.

Fixed [fixt] a. fest, beständig,

Fixing [fix'ing] n. Aufstellen n, Festmachen n, Fixierung f (photo).

Fixity [fix'i-ti] n. Festigkeit f, Feuerbeständigkeit f.

Fixture [fix'tjer] n. Festsetzung f, Verabredung f, Zubehör n, Inventarstück n.

Fizz [fis], **Fizzle** [fisl] vi. zischen, sprühen. [vt. verblüffen.

Flabbergast [flæ'ber-gahst]

Flabbiness [flæ'bi-ness] n. Schlaffheit f.

Flabby [flæ'bi] a. schlaff.

Flag [flæg] n. Flagge f, Fahne f; ~-day n. Opfertag m; ~-lieutenant n. Adjutant m, des Admirals; ~-officer n. höherer Seeoffizier (nav.); ~-ship n. Flaggschiff n (nav.); ~-staff n. ~-stock n. Flaggen-stange f.

Flag [flæg] vi. erschlaffen.

Flag [flæg], **Flagstone** [flæg'stoun] n. Steinplatte f, Fliese f; vt. mit Fliesen pflastern.

Flag [flæg] n. Schwertlilie f.

Flagon [flæ'gAn] n. Bocksbeutel m. [offenkundig.

Flagrant [flei'grAnt] a. -ly ad.

Flail [fleil] n. Dreschflegel m.

Flair [fleh'er] n. Spürsinn m.

Flake [fleik] n. Flocke f.

Flakey [flei'ki] a. flockig.

Flame [fleim] n. Flamme f; vi. flammen; ~-thrower n. Flammenwerfer m (mil.).

Flange [flændzh] n. Flansche f, Wulst m (tec.); ~d tyre n. Wulstreif m (aut.).

Flank [flængk] n. Flanke f, Seite f; vt. angrenzen, flankieren, seitlich decken, in die Flanke fallen, bedrohen (mil.); ~ing march n. Umgehungsmarsch m; ~ing movement n. Seitenbewegung f (mil.).

Flannel [flæ'nl] n. Flanell m, Flanellstoff m.

Flap [flæp] n. Klappe f, Krempe f, Schlag m, Flattern n, Patte f, Rockschoss m (coat); vi. schlagen, klappen.

Flare [fleh'er] n. flackerndes Licht, Leuchtfeuer n, Leuchtpatrone f (mil.), Rakete f (nav.), Luftmarkierer m (av.); vi. flackern, auflodern; – -buoy n. Luxboje f; – -path n. Leuchtpfad m (av.); – -shell n. Leuchtgeschoss n (av.).

Flash [flæsch] n. Aufblitzen n, Blitz m; vi. aufflodern, funkeln, blitzen; -ing beacon Kennungsfeuer n (av.); – -lamp n. Taschenlampe f; – -ranging, -spotting n. Lichtmessen f (mil.). [Blitzlicht n.]

Flash-light [flæsch'lait] n.

Flashy [flæ'schi] a. bunt, geschmacklos.

Flask [flahsk] n. (Feld-) Flasche f.

Flat [flæt] a. platt, flach, eben, (com.); n. Etagewohnung f, Stockwerk n; -fish n. Plattfisch m; – -iron n. Plätteisen n, Bügeleisen n; – -rate n. Pauschalgebühr f (com.).

Flatten [flæ'tn] vt. platt machen, breit schlagen.

Flatter [flæ'ter] vt. schmeicheln.

Flatterer [flæ'tA-rer] n. Schmeichler m.

Flattering [flæ'tA-ring] a. schmeichelhaft.

Flattery [flæ'tA-ri] n. Schmeichelei f.

Flatulence [flæ'tju-lAnss] n. Blähsucht f.

Flaunt [flOnt] vt. prunken mit.

Flavour [flei'wer] n. Geschmack m, Duft m, Würze f; vt. würzen.

Flaw [flO] n. Fehler m, Sprung m, Blase f, Riss m. [frei.]

Flawless [flO'less] a. fehlerfrei.

Flax [flæx] n. Flachs m.

Flaxen [flæx'en] a. flächsern.

Flay [fei] vt. schinden.

Flea [flih] n. Flöh m.

Fleck [flek] n. Fleck m.

Fledged [fledzhd] a. flügge, befiedert.

Flee [flih] vi. fliehen.

Fleece [flihss] n. Fliess n; vt. scheren, prellen.

Fleecy [flih'ssi] a. wollig.

Fleet [fliht] n. Flotte f, Kriegsflotte f; a. schnell; – air arm n. Marineluftwaffe f; Flottengerstreitkräfte f.pl.

Fleeting [flih'ting] a. flüchtig.

Flesh [flesch] n. Fleisch n.

Fleshiness [flesch'i-ness] n. Fleischigkeit f.

Fleshly [flesch'li] a. fleischlich.

Fleshy [flesch'i] a. fleischig.

Flex [flex] n. Litze f, Kontaktschnur f (el.).

Flexibility [flex-i-bi'li-ti] n. Biegsamkeit f.

Flexible [flex'ibl] a. biegsam.

Flick [flik] n. Peitschenschlag m; vi. schnellen; -s pl. Kino n.

Flicker [fli'ker] vi. flackern; n. Flackern n.

Flight [flait] n. Flucht f, Flug m, Fliegen n, Flugstrecke f, Staffel f (av.); – -deck n. Flugdeck n (nav.); – -lieutenant n. Fliegerhauptmann m; – -sergeant n. Oberfeldwebel m (av.).

Flighty [flai'ti] a. leichtsinnig.

Flimsy [flim'si] a. dünn, nichtig. [weichen, -schaudern.]

Flinch [flinsch] vi. zurück-

Fling [fling] vt. werfen, schleudern; n. Wurf m.

Flint [flint] n. Kiesel m.

Flinty [flin'ti] a. kieselig, hart.

Flippancy [fli'pAn-ssi] n. Leichtfertigkeit f.

Flippant [fli'pAnt] a. vorlaut, leichtsinnig.

Flirt [flArt] n. Kokette f, gefallsüchtiges Mädchen, Courmacher m; vi. kokettieren, flirten.

Flirtation [flAr-tei'schAn] n. Flirten n, Kokettieren n.

Flit [flit] vi. huschen, flitzen, flattern.

Flitch [flitsch] n. Speckseite f.

Float [flout] n. Floss n, Flösse f, Schwimmer m, Radschaufel f, flacher Heuwagen; vi. auf dem Wasser treiben, schweben; vt. flott machen, flössen, gründen, ausgeben (com.); -ing beacon Treibbake f; -ing debt schwebende Schuld; -ing dock Schwimmdock n; -ing mine Strewim... Treib-mine f.

Flock [flok] n. Herde f; vi. sich scharen, zusammenströmen; -together vi. sich gesellen.

Flock [flok] n. Flocke f; --mattress n. Wollmatratze f.

Floe [flou] n. Treibeis n. [en.

Flog [flog] vt. peitschen, stäupen

Flood [flAd] n. Flut f, Überschwemmung f; vt. überschwemmen; --gate n. Fluttor n; --light n. Flutlicht n; Scheinwerfer m; --tide n. Flut f.

Floor [flOr] n. Fussboden m, Stockwerk n (storey); ground -Erdgeschoss n, Parterre n; -polish n. Bohnerwachs n.

Flooring [flO'ring] n. Dielung f, Fussbodenbelag m.

Flop [flop] vi. hinplumpsen, versagen; n. Plumps m, Misserfolg m.

Florid [flo'rid] a. hochrot, blühend, reich verziert.

Florin [flo'rin] n. Zweischillingstück, Gulden m.

Florist [flO'rist] n. Blumenhändler m.

Flossy [flo'ssi] a. feinseiden.

Flotilla [flo-ti'lA] n. kleines Geschwader, Flotille f; -leader n. Flotillenführer m (nav.).

Flotsam [flot'ssAm] n. Wrackgut n. [Volant m.

Flounce [flauns] vi. Falbel f.

Flounder [flaun'der] n. Flunder f.

Flounder [flaun'der] vt. zappeln, umhertappen.

Flour [flau'er] n. feines Mehl.

Flourish [flA'risch] n. Schnörkel m; vi. blühen; -ing blühend, gesund.

Flour-mill [flau'er-mil] n. Mahlmühel f.

Flout [flaut] vt. verhöhnen.

Flow [flou] n. Fluss m, Strom m, Strömung f; vi. fliessen.

Flower [flau'er] n. Blume f; vi. blühen; --pot n. Blumentopf m. [reich.

Flowery [flau'A-ri] a. blumen-

Flu [fluh] n. Grippe f.

Fluctuate [flAk'tju-eit] vi. schwanken.

Fluctuation [flAk-tju-ei'schAn] n. Schwanken n.

Flue [fluh] n. Rauchfang m.

Fluff [flAf] n. Staubflocke f, Federflocke f, Flaum m.

Fluffy [flA'fi] a. flaumig.

Fluency [fluh'An-ssi] n. Geläufigkeit f, Sprachfertigkeit f.

Fluent [fluh'Ant] a. fliessend, geläufig. [a. flüssig.

Fluid [fluh'id] n. Flüssigkeit f;

Fluke [fluhk] n. Ankerpflug m (nav.). [Zufall, Dusel m.

Fluke [fluhk] n. glücklicher

Flunkey [flAng'ki] n. Livreebediente(r) m, Speichelleckerm.

Fluorine [fluh'A-rin] n. Fluor n.

Flurry [flA'ri] n. nervöse Aufregung; vt. aufregen, verwirren.

Flush [flAsch] n. plötzliches Erröten, Glut f (of colour); vi. plötzlich erröten; vt. erregen, ausschwemmen, aus-, ab-spülen (drains).

Fluster [flA'ster] n. Verwirrung f; vt. erhitzen.

Flute [fluht] n. Flöte f.

Fluted [fluh'tid] a. gerieft, ausgekehlt.

Flutter [flA'ter] n. Geflatter n; vi. flattern, weben. [fluss m.

Flux [flAx] n. Fluss m, Aus-

Fly [flai] n. Fliege f; vi. fliegen, entfliehen; vt. fliegen lassen, führen (plane), überfliegen (ocean); --paper n. Fliegenpapier n; --wheel n. Schwungrad n (tec.).

Flying [flai'ing] a. fliegend; n. Flug m, Fliegen n, Flugwesen n, Navigation f.

Flying-boat [flai'ing-boht] n. Flugboot n, Wasserlandflugzeug n, Wasser-, See-flugzeug n.

Flying-bomb [flai'ing-bom] n. Vergeltungswaffe 1 f, Dödel m; - -site n. Vergeltungsstelle f.

Flying-conditions [flai'ing-kon-di'schAns] n.pl. Luftlage f (av.); - -deck n. Laufbrücke f (av.); - -formation n. Fluggruppe f, Flugform f; - -instructor n. Fluglehrer m; - kit n. Fliegerschutzanzug m; - machine n. Flugmaschine f, Flugzeug n; - -officer n. Oberleutnant der Flieger m; - organization n. Flugbetrieb m, Flugwesen n; - personnel n. Flugpersonal m; - squad n. Überfallkommando n; - weight n. Fluggewicht n.

Foal [foul] n. Fohlen n, Füllen n.

Foam [foum] n. Schaum m; vi. schäumen.

Fob [fob] n. Uhrtasche f.

Focal [foukl] a. Brennpunkt...; Brenn...; - point n. Brennpunkt m.

Focus [fou'kAss] n. Brennpunkt m; vt. (sight) einstellen; in - scharf eingestellt.

Focusing [fou'kA-ssing] n. Einstellung f; - -screen n. Mattscheibe f.

Fodder [fo'der] n. Futter n.

Foe [fou] n. Feeman [fou'mAn] n. Feind m, Gegner m.

Fog [fog] n. Nebel m.

Foggy [fo'gi] a. nebelig.

Foil [feul] vt. vereiteln; n. Florett n, Stossrapier n.

Foil [feul] n. Folie f, Blech n, Belag m.

Fold [fould] n. Falte f; vt. falten.

Fold [fould] n. Hürde f, Schafstall m.

Foliage [fou'li-idzh] n. Laub n.

Folio [fou'li-ou] n. Folio n, Blatt n, Folioformat n.

Folk [fouk] n. Volk n; - -dance n. Volkstanz m; - -lore n. Volkskunde f; - -song n. Volkslied n.

Follow [fo'lou] vt. i. folgen.

Follower [fo'lou-er] n. Nachfolger m, Anhänger m, Diener m; - -on [sinn m.

Folly [fo'li] n. Torheit f, Unsinn m.

Foment [fo-ment'] vt. bähen, anstiften.

Fomentation [fo-men-tei'schAn] n. Bähung f, Umschlag f, Anstiftung f.

Fond [fond] a. zärtlich, liebevoll; be - of gern haben, lieben, gern essen, etc.

Fondly [fond'li] ad. gern, liebevoll, zärtlich. [liebe f.

Fondness [fond'ness] n. Vorliebe f.

Food [fuhd] n. Speise f, Nahrung f, Futter n (animals); - office n. Ernährungs-, Verpflegungs-amt n; - ration n. Lebensmittelration f; - situation n. Ernährungslage f.

Fool [fuhl] n. Narr m, Närrin f; vt. zum Narren haben.

Foolhardy [fuhl'hahr-di] a. tollkühn.

Foolish [fuh'lisch] a. -ly ad. närrisch, albern. [n. Narrheit f.

Foolishness [fuh'lisch-ness]

Food proof [fuhl'pruhf] a. betriebssicher.

Football [fut'bOl] n. Fussball m; - -player n. Fussballspieler m; - -team n. Fussballmannschaft f.

Foot-board [fut'bOrd] n. Fussbrett n, Trittbrett n (aut.); - -bridge n. Steg m; - -fall n. Tritt m; - -gear n. Fussbekleidung f; - guards n.pl. Garderegiment n; - -hold n. Halt m, Tritt m; - -lights n.pl Rampenlichter n.pl.; - -man n. Lakei m, Bediente(r) m; - -note n. Fussnote f, Anmerkung f; - -path n. Fussweg m; - -print n. Fussspur f; - -race n. Wettlauf m; - -rest n. Fussbänkchen n; **Fussruhe** f, Fuss-raste f, -raster *m* (*motor-cycle*), Fussleiste *f* (*stool*); – -rule *n.* Zollstock *m*; – -soldier *n.* Fuss-soldat *m*; – -sore *a.* marschkrank; -step *n.* Tritt *m*; – -stool *n.* Schemel *m*; – -way *n.* Fuss-pfad *m*, -weg *m*, Gehbahn *f*, Bürgersteig *m*; -wear *n.* Fussbekleidung *f*, Schuhwerk *n.*

Footing [fu'ting] *n.* Fuss *m*, Verhältnis *n.*

For [fOr] *pr.* für; – some time seit einiger Zeit, auf einige Zeit; – good auf immer; *cj.* denn.

Forage [fo'ridzh] *n.* Futter *n.*, Fourage *f*; *vi.* fouragieren; – cap *n.* Feldmütze *f.*

Forbear [fOr-beh'er] *vi.* sich enthalten, ablassen.

Forbearance [fOr-beh'rAnss] *n.* Geduld *f*, Nachsicht *f.*

Forbearing [fOr-beh'ring] *a.* geduldig, nachsichtig.

Forbid [fOr-bid'] *vt.* verbieten.

Forbidding [fOr-bi'ding] *a.* abstossend.

Force [fOrss] *n.* Kraft *f*, Gewalt *f*, Zwang *m*; *vt.* zwingen, aufbrechen (*lock*), erstürmen (*town*), treiben (*plants*, *etc.*); -d landing *n.* Notlandung *f* (*av.*); -d landing at sea *n.* Notwassern *n* (*av.*); -d march *n.* Eil-, Dauer-marsch *m* (*mil.*).

Forces [fOr'ssis] *n.pl.* Truppen *f.pl*; – programme *n.* Soldatensender *m.*

Forceps [fOr'ssepss] *n.pl.* [Zange *f.*]

Forcible [fOr'ssibl] *a.* zwingend, gewaltsam.

Forcing [fOr'ssing] *n.* Nötigen *n*, Treiben *n.*

Ford [fOrd] *n.* Furt *f*; *vt.* durchwaten. [watbar.]

Fordable [fOr'dAbl] *a.* durch-]

Forearm [fOr'ahrm] *n.* Vorderarm *m.*

Forebode [fOr-boud'] *vt.* vorbedeuten, ahnen. [Ahnung *f.*]

Foreboding [fOr-bou'ding] *n.*]

Forecast [fOr'kahst] *n.*

aussage *f*; weather – *n.* Wetterbericht *m*, -vorhersage *f.*

Forecast [fOr-kahst'] *vt.* voraussagen, vorhersagen.

Forecastle [fouksl] *n.* Back *f* (*nav.*), Vorderdeck *n* (*nav.*).

Foreclose [fOr-klous'] *vt.* ausschliessen, abweisen, für verfallen erklären (*mortgage*).

Forefathers [fOr'fah-dhers] *n.pl.* Vorfahren *pl.*

Forefinger [fOr'fing-ger] *n.* Zeigefinger *m.*

Forefront [fOr'frAnt] *n.* vorderste Reihe.

Forego [fOr-gou'] *vt.* aufgeben, verzichten auf.

Foreground [fOr'graund] *n.* Vordergrund *m.*

Forehead [fOr'id] *n.* Stirn *f.*

Foreign [fo'rin] *a.* ausländisch, fremd; – broadcast *n.* Auslandssendung *f.*

Foreigner [fo'ri-ner] *n.* Ausländer *m.*

Foreman [fOr'mAn] *n.* Werkmeister *m*, Obmann *m* (*jury*).

Fore-mentioned [fOr-men'shAnd] *a.* vorher erwähnt.

Foremost [fOr'moust] *a.* vorderst, erst. [mittag *m.*]

Forenoon [fOr-nuhn'] *n.* Vor-]

Fore-part [fOr'pahrt] *n.* Vorderteil *m.* [Vorläufer *m.*]

Forerunner [fOr'rA-ner] *n.*]

Foresee [fOr-ssih'] *vt.* vorhersehen. [aussicht *f.*]

Foresight [fOr'ssait] *n.* Vor-]

Forest [fo'rist] *n.* Wald *m*, Forst *m.*

Forestall [fOr-stOl'] *vt.* vorwegnehmen, zuvorkommen, vorkaufen (*com.*). [ster *m.*]

Forester [fo'ri-ster] *n.* För-]

Forestry [fo'ri-stri] *n.* Forstwissenschaft *f.*

Foretaste [fOr'teist] *n.* Vorgeschmack *m.*

Foretell [fOr-tel'] *vt.* vorhersagen.

Forethought [fOr'thOt] *n.* Vorbedacht *m.*

Forewarn [fOr-uOrn'] vt. vorher warnen.

Forfeit [fOr'fit] vt. verwirken; n. Reugeld n, Pfand n, Busse f.

Forfeiture [fOr'fi-tjer] n. Verwirkung f, Aberkennung f (rights).

Forge [fOrdzh] n. Schmiede f; vt. schmieden, fälschen.

Forger [fOr'dzher] n. Fälscher m, Schmied m (metal).

Forgery [fOr'dzhA-ri] n. Fälschung f.

Forget [fOr-get'] vt. vergessen.

Forgetful [fOr-get'ful] a. vergesslich.

Forgetfulness [fOr-get'fulness] n. Vergesslichkeit f.

Forget-me-not [fOr-get'minot] n. Vergissmeinnicht n.

Forgive [fOr-giw'] vt. verzeihen.   [Verzeihung f.

Forgiveness [fOr-giw'ness] n.

Forgiving [fOr-gi'wing] a. versöhnlich.   [auf.

Forgo [fOr-gou'] vt. verzichten

Foregone [fOr-gon'] a. selbstverständlich (conclusion).

Fork [fOrk] n. Gabel f; vi. sich gabeln.

Forked [fOrkt] a. gabelig.

Forlorn [fer-lOrn'] a. verloren, verlassen, elend.

Form [fOrm] n. Gestalt f, Form f, Klasse f (school), Bank f (bench), Formular n, Schema n; vt. bilden, entwerfen, schliessen (friendship).

Formal [fOr'mAl] a. -ly ad. förmlich, formell.

Formality [fOr-mæ'li-ti] n. Förmlichkeit f, Formalität f.

Formation [fOr-mei'schAn] n. Bildung f, Bilden n, Truppe f, Truppenverband n (mil.), Gliederung f (av.); in echelon – gestaffelt (av.); – commander n. Truppenführer m (mil.).

Former [fOr'mer] a. früher, jener, jene, jenes, der, die, das erstere.   [mals.

Formerly [fOr'mer-li] ad. ehe-

Formidable [fOr'mi-dAbl] a. furchtbar, kolossal.

Formula [fOr'mju-lA] n. Formel f, Rezept n.   [formulieren.

Formulate [fOr'mju-leit] vt.

Fornication [fOr-ni-keit'schAn] n. Unzucht f, Hurerei f.

Forsake [fOr-seik'] vt. verlassen, aufgeben.   [lassen.

Forsaken [fOr-seikn'] a. verlassen.

Forswear [fOr-suehr'] vt. abschwören.

Fort [fOrt] n. Schanze f, Fort n.

Forth [fOrth] ad. fort, vorwärts, hinaus.

Forthcoming [fOrth-kAt'ming] a. bevorstehend.

Forthwith [fOrth-uith'] ad. sofort, ohne weiteres.

Fortieth [fOr'ti-Ath] a. vierzigst; n. Vierzigstel n.

Fortification [fOr-ti-fi-keit'schAn] n. Befestigung f, Werk n; -s pl. Befestigunsanlagen f.pl.   [stigen.

Fortify [fOr'ti-fai] vt. befe-

Fortitude [fOr'ti-tjuhd] n. Geistesstärke f, Mut m.

Fortnight [fOrt'nait] n. vierzehn Tage.   [ung f.

Fortress [fOrt'riss] n. Fest-

Fortunate [fOr'tjA-nit] a. glücklich.

Fortunately [fOr'tjA-nAt-li] ad. glücklicherweise.

Fortune [fOr'tjun] n. Glück n, Geschick n (fate), Vermögen n (property), Reichtum m (wealth).

Forty [fOr'ti] num. vierzig.

Forward [fOr'uerd] a. voreilig, keck; ad. vorwärts; vt. befördern, nachschicken.

Forwarding [fOr'uer-ding] n. Beförderung f, Versand m, Nachsendung f, Weiterleitung f, Übermittlung f; – agent n. Spediteur m; – agency n. Speditionsgeschäft n; – centre n. Leitstelle f.

Forwardness [fOr'uerd-ness] n. Voreiligkeit f, Keckheit f.

Fossil [fo'ssil] n. Fossil n.

Foster [fo'ster] vt. pflegen, hegen, begünstigen; - -brother n. Pflegebruder m; - -father n. Pflegevater m; - -mother n. Pflegemutter f.

Foul [faul] a. unsauber, schmutzig, unehrlich.

Foulness [faul'ness] n. Schmutzigkeit f, Unreinheit f.

Found [faund] vt. gründen, stiften.

Foundation [faun-dei'schAn] n. Gründung f, Grundlage f, Stiftung f. [der m.

Founder [faun'der] n. Grün-

Founder [faun'der] vi. sinken.

Foundling [faund'ling] n. Findling m.

Foundry [faund'ri] n. Giesserei f, Hütte f; - number n. Schmelzungsnummer f (gun).

Fount [faunt] n. Quelle f, Schrift f, Satz m, Guss m.

Fountain [faun'tin] n. Quelle f, Brunnen m; - -pen n. Füllfederhalter m.

Four [fOr] num. vier.

Fourteen [fOr-tihn'] num. vierzehn.

Fourteenth [fOr-tihnth'] num. vierzehnt.

Fourth [fOrth] num. a. viert; n. Viertel n, der, die, das Vierte. [tens.

Fourthly [fOrth'li] ad. vier-

Fowl [faul] n. Huhn n.

Fox [fox] n. Fuchs m.

Foxglove [fox'glAw] n. Fingerhut m.

Fraction [fræk'schAn] n. Bruch m, Bruchstück n.

Fracture [fræk'tjer] n. Knochenbruch m. [brechlich.

Fragile [fræ'dzhail] a. zer-

Fragment [fræg'mAnt] n. Bruchstück n.

Fragmentary [fræg'men-tAri] a. abgebrochen, zerstückt.

Fragmentation [fræg-men-tei'schAn] n. Zersplitterung f; - bomb n. Splitterbombe f.

Fragrance [frei'grAnss] n. Wohlgeruch m. [riechend.

Fragrant [frei'grAnt] a. wohl-

Frail [freil] a. gebrechlich.

Frailness [freil'ness], **Frailty** [freil'ti] n. Gebrechlichkeit f, Schwäche f.

Frame [freim] n. Rahmen m, Einfassung f, Gestell n; vt. einrahmen, einfassen, bilden; - aerial n. Rahmenantenne f (rad.); - house n. hölzernes Haus.

Framework [freim'uerk] n. Rahmen m, Fachwerk n, Gestell n, Bau m.

Franchise [fræn'schais] n. Wahlrecht n. [mütig.

Frank [frængk] a. offen, frei-

Frankness [frængk'ness] n. Offenheit f.

Frantic [fræn'tik] a. rasend.

Fraternal [frA-tAr'nAl] a. brüderlich.

Fraternity [frA-tAr'ni-ti] n. Brüderlichkeit f, Verbindung f (club).

Fraternization [fræ-ter-nai-sei'schAn] n. Verbrüderung f.

Fratricide [fræ'tri-ssaid] n. Brüdermord m.

Fraud [frOd] n. Betrug m.

Fraudulence [frO'dju-lAnss] n. Betrüglichkeit f.

Fraudulent [frO'dju-lAnt] a. betrügerisch. [Kampf m.

Fray [frei] n. Schlägerei f.

Fray [frei] vi. sich ausfasern.

Freak [frihk] n. Grille f, Missbildung f.

Freakish [frih'kisch] a. wunderlich, grillenhaft. [sprosse f.

Freckle [frekl] n. Sommer-

Freckled [frekld] a. sommersprossig.

Free [frih] a. frei, unentgeltlich, kostenlos, unabhängig; trade n. Freihandel m.

Freedom [frih'dAm] n. Freiheit f; - of the press Pressefreiheit f; - of speech Redefreiheit f.

Freehold [frih'hould] n. freier, unbeschränkter Grundbesitz, Grundeigentum n.

Freely [frih'li] ad. frei, offen, bereitwillig, reichlich, freigebig. [Freimaurer n.

Freemason [frih-mei'ssAn] n. Hau-, Quader-stein m.

Freethinker [frih-thing'ker] n. Freigeist m.

Free-wheel [frih-huihl'] n. Freilaufrad n.

Freeze [frihs] vt. gefrieren machen; i. frieren, gefrieren.

Freezer [frih'ser] n. Eismaschine f.

Freezing [frih'sing] a. gefrierend; n. Gefrieren n; -ing mixture n. Kältemischung f; -ing point n. Gefrier-, Null-punkt m.

Freight [freit] n. Fracht f, Ladung f, Mietgeld n; vt. befrachten, mieten (charter); -barge n. Lastkahn m; - car n. Güterwagen m; -carrying aircraft n. Lastflugzeug n; -checker n. Verlaster n; -glider n. Lastsegelflugzeug n.

Freightage [frei'tidzh] n. Frachtgeld n.

Freighter [frei'ter] n. Frachter m Frachtdampfer m, Be-, Ver-frachter m.

Frenzy [fren'si] n. Tobsucht f.

Frequency [frih'kuen-ssi] n. Häufigkeit f, Frequenz f (rad.).

Frequent [frih'kuAnt] a. -ly ad. häufig; vt. häufig besuchen.

Fresh [fresch] a. frisch.

Freshen [fre'schen] vt. erfrischen; i. frisch, stärker werden

Fret [fret] vt. sich ärgern, sich kümmern.

Fretful [fret'ful] a. ärgerlich.

Fretwork [fret'uArk] n. Schnitzwerk n, Laubsägearbeit f.

Friable [frai'Abl] a. zerreibbar, bröckelig.

Friction [frik'schAn] n. Reibung f; -clutch n. Reibungskupplung f (tec.).

Friday [frai'di] n. Freitag m; Good - n. Karfreitag m.

Fried [fraid] a. gebraten; - fish n. Bratfisch m; - potatoes n.pl. Bratkartoffeln f.pl.

Friend [frend] n. Freund m, Freundin f.

Friendless [frend'less] a. freundlos. [Freundlichkeit f.

Friendliness [frend'li-ness] f.

Friendly [frend'li] a. freundlich, freundschaftlich.

Friendship [frend'schip] n. Freundschaft f.

Frieze [frihs] n. Fries m.

Frigate [fri'gAt] n. Fregatte f.

Fright [frait] n. Schrecken m.

Frighten [frai'tn] vt. erschrecken; - away ad. verscheuchen. [schrecklich.

Frightful [frait'ful] a.

Frightfulness [frait'ful-ness] n. Schrecklichkeit f, Greueltaten f.pl.

Frigid [fri'dzhid] a. frostig.

Frigidity [fri-dzhi'di-ti] n. Kälte f. [m; vt. kräuseln.

Frill [fril] n. Krause f, Volant

Fringe [frinzh] n. Franse f, Besatz m; vt. befransen.

Frisk [frisk] vi. umherhüpfen.

Frisky [fri'ski] a. munter, ausgelassen, unruhig (horse).

Fritter [fri'ter] n. kleiner Pfannkuchen, Schnittchen n, Stückchen n; - away vt. verschwenden, verändeln.

Frivolity [fri-wo'li-ti] n. Leichtfertigkeit f.

Frivolous [fri'wA-lAss] a. leichtfertig. [n. Gehrock m.

Frock [frok] n. Kleid n; - coat

Frog [frog] n. Frosch m.

Frolic [fro'lik] n. lustiger Streich.

Frolicsome [fro'lik-ssAm] a. lustig, ausgelassen.

From [from] pr. von, aus, nach (to judge by), wegen (because of).

Frond [frond] n. Wedel m.

Front [frAnt] n. Vorderseite f, Vorhemd (shirt), Front f (mil.).

vt. gegenüberstehen, entgegentreten; – door n. Haustür f; –
–line n. Front f; – sector n.
Frontabschnitt m (mil.).

Frontage [frAn'tidzh] n. Vor-
derfront f.

Frontier [frAn'tjer] n. Grenze
f; – control n. Grenz-aufsicht
f. -kontrolle f; – pass n. Pass-
begleitschein m; – region n.
Grenzgebiet n; – traffic n.
Grenzverkehr m.

Frontispiece [frAn'ti-spihss]
n. Titelbild n.

Frost [frost] n. Frost m; –
–bound a. festgefroren, zuge-
froren; – goggles n.pl. Kälte-
schutzbrille f.pl (av.).

Frosted [fro'stid] a. mattiert,
mit Zuckerguss bedeckt (cake);
– glass n. Eis-, Milch-glas n.

Froth [froth] n. Schaum f; vi.
schäumen.

Frothy [fro'thi] a. schäumig.

Frown [fraun] vi. die Stirne
runzeln, finster blicken; n.
Stirnrunzeln.

Frozen [frou'zn] a. zu-, eingefroren; – credits n.pl. ein-
gefrorene Kredite m.pl; – meat
n. Gefrierfleisch n.

Fructify [frAk'ti-fai] vi.
Früchte tragen.

Frugal [fruh'gl] a. genügsam,
sparsam, mässig.

Frugality [fruh-gæ'li-ti] n.
Genügsamkeit f, Einfachheit f.

Fruit [fruht] n. Frucht f,
Obst n.   [Obsthändler m.

Fruiterer [fruh'tA-rer] n.

Fry [frai] vt. in der Pfanne
braten.   [Bratpfanne f.

Frying-pan [frai'ing-pæn] n.

Fuel [fjuh'il] n. Brennstoff m,
Heizmaterial n, Treibstoff m,
Feuerung f, Kraft-, Betriebsstoff m (av.); vt. auftanken
(av.); i. Brennstoff ergänzen;
tanken, Treibstoff einnehmen
(av.); – oil n. Brennöl n; –
–tank n. Behälter m, Tankanlage f.

Fuelling [fjuh'i-ling] n. Tank-
en n; – bridge n. Kraftbrücke
f; – depot n. Tanklager n; –
installation n. Tankanlage f; –
permit n. Tankausweis m; –
point, – station n. Tankstelle f.

Fugitive [fjuh'dzhi-tiw] a.
flüchtig; n Flüchtling m.

Fulfil [ful-fil'] vt. erfüllen.

Fulfilment [ful-fil'mAnt] n.
Erfüllung f.

Full [ful] a. voll, besetzt, vollständig; – dress uniform n.
Gala(uniform) f; – employment
n. Vollbeschäftigung f; – powers n.pl. unbeschränkte Vollmacht; – stop n. Punkt m,
Stillstand m; – swing voller
Gang.

Full [ful] vt. walken.

Fuller [fu'ler] n. Walker m,
Walkmüller m; – 's earth n.
Walkerde f.

Fulness [ful'ness] n. Fülle f.

Fulsome [ful'sAm] a. widerlich.   [führlich.

Fully [fu'li] ad. völlig, aus-

Fumble [fAmbl] vi. herum-
fühlen, tappen.

Fume [fjuhm] n. Dunst f,
Dampf m, Leidenschaft f; vi.
dampfen, rauchen, toben.

Fumigate [fjuh'mi-geit] vt.
ausräuchern, desinfizieren.

Fumigation [fjuh-mi-geit'-
schAn] n. Räucherung f.

Fun [fAn] n. Spass m.

Function [fAngk'schAn] n.
Funktion f, Wirksamkeit f,
Tätigkeit f, Veranstaltung f.

Functionary [fAngk'schA-
nA-ri] n. Beamte(r) m.

Fund [fAnd] n. Geldmittel n,
Fonds m, Kasse f, (Betriebs-)
Kapital n; vt. fundieren, kapi-
talisieren, anlegen.

Fundamental [fAn-dA-
men'tl'] a. grundlegend,
Grund . . .; -s n.pl. Grund-
lagen f.pl.

Fundamentally [fAn-dA-
men'tA-li] ad. im Grunde.

Funeral [fjuh'nA-rAl] *n.* Begräbnis *n.* [Pilz *m.*
Fungus [fAng'gAss] *n.* (Gift-)
Funnel [fA'nl] *n.* Trichter *m* (*for liquids*), Schornstein *m* (*chimney*). [lig.
Funny [fA'ni] *a.* komisch, drol-
Fur [fAr] *n.* Pelz *m*, Fell *n*; --coat *n.* Pelzrock *m*; --lined *a.* pelzgefüttert; - overboot *n.* Überziehpelzstiefel *m* (*av.*).
Furbish [fAr'bisch] *vt.* putzen.
Furious [fjuh'ri-Ass] *a.* -ly *ad.* wütend. [schlagen (*sail*).
Furl [fArl] *vt.* aufrollen, be-
Furlough [fAr'lou] *n.* Urlaub *m* (*mil.*). [Feuerraum *m.*
Furnace [fAr'niss] *n.* Ofen *m*,
Furnish [fAr'nisch] *vt.* möblieren, einrichten, versehen, liefern, verschaffen; -ed rooms *n.pl.* möblierte Zimmer *n.pl.*
Furnisher [fAr'nisch-er] *n.* Lieferant *m*, Möblierer *m.*
Furnishing [fAr'nisch-ing] *n.* Einrichten, Möblieren *n*, Ausstattung *f.*
Furniture [fAr'ni-tscher] *n.* Möbel *pl*, Zimmereinrichtung *f*, Hausgerät *n.*
Furrier [fA'ri-er] *n.* Kürschner *m.* [*vt.* furchen.
Furrow [fA'rou] *n.* Furche *f*;
Further [fAr'dher] *a.ad.* weiter, ferner; *vt.* fördern.
Furtherance [fAr'dhA-rAnss] *n.* Förderung *f.*
Furthermore [fAr'dher-mOr] *ad.* überdies, ausserdem.
Furthest [fAr'dhist] *a. ad.* weitest, fernst. [verstohlen.
Furtive [fAr'tiw] *a.* -ly *ad.*
Fury [fjuh'ri] *n.* Wut *f.*
Furze [fArs] *n.* Stechginster *m.*
Fuse [fjuhs] *n.* Zünder *m*, Zündschnur *f* (*mining, etc.*).
Fuse [fjuhs] *vt. i.* schmelzen, giessen, verschmelzen; durchbrennen (*el.*): *n.* Sicherung *f.* (*el.*).
Fuselage [fjuh'si-lahzh] *n.* Rumpf *m.* (*av.*).
Fusible [fyuh'sibl] *a.* schmelzbar. [zen *n*, Verschmelzung *f.*
Fusion [fjuh'zhAn] *n.* Schmel-
Fuss [fAss] *n.* Aufhebens *n.*
Fusty [fA'sti] *a.* mussig moderig.
Futile [fjuh'tail] *a.* nutzlos.
Futility [fjuh-til'i-ti] *n.* Nutzlosigkeit *f.*
Future [fjuh'tscher] *n.* Zukunft *f*; *a.* künftig; in the near — in nächster Zukunft.
Futurity [fju-tjuh'ri-ti] *n.* Zukunft *f.*

G

Gabble [gæbl] *vi.* schwatzen.
Gabbler [gæ'bler] *n.* Schwätzer *m.*
Gable [geibl] *n.* Giebel *m.*
Gadget [gæd'zhit] *n.* Zubehörteil *m.* Vorrichtung *f.*
Gaff [gæf] *n.* Fischhaken *m.*
Gag [gæg] *n.* Knebel *m*; *vt.* knebeln.
Gage [geidzh] *n.* Pfand *n.*
Gaiety [gei'A-ti] *n.* Heiterkeit *f*, Lustbarkeit *f.*
Gaily [gei'li] *ad.* heiter, bunt.
Gain [gein] *vt. i.* gewinnen; *n.* Gewinn *m.*
Gainful [gein'ful] *a.* einträglich; — ly employed *a.* erwerbstätg.
Gainings [gei'nings] *n.* Ertrag *m.* Gewinn *m.* [sprechen.
Gainsay [gein-ssei'] *vt.* wider-
Gait [geit] *n.* Gang *m.*
Gaiter [gei'ter] *n.* Gamasche *f.*
Gale [geil] *n.* Sturm *m.* heftiger Wind; — warning *n.* Sturmwarnung *f.*
Gall [gOl] *n.* Galle *f.*
Gall [gOl] *vt.* wundreiben, ärgern. [galant.
Gallant [gæ'lAnt] *a.* tapfer,
Gallantry [gæ'lAn-tri] *n.* Tapferkeit *f*, Galanterie *f.*
Gallery [gæ'lA-ri] *n.* Galerie *f*, Säulen-gang *m*, Minen-gang

m, -stollen *m* (*mil., etc.*), Gang *m*, Korridor *m* (house), Galerie *f* (*theatre*).

Galley [gæ'li] *n.* Galeere *f.* Schiffsküche *f*; Setzschiff *n*; — proof *n.* Fahnenabzug *m.*

Galling [gɔ'ling] *a.* ärgerlich.

Gallipot [gæ'li-lot] *n.* Salbentopf *m.*

Gallop [gæ'lʌp] *vi.* sprengen, galoppieren; *n.* Galopp *m.*

Gallows [gæ'lous] *n. pl.* Galgen *m.*

Galoshes [ga-losch'is] *n. pl.* Gummischuhe *m. pl.*, Galoschen *f. pl.*

Galvanic [gæl-wæ'nik] *a.* galvanisch.

Galvanism [gæl'wA-nism] *n.* Galvanismus *m.*

Galvanize [gæl'wA-nais] *vt.* galvanisieren, elektrisieren, verzinken (*iron*).

Gamble [gæmbl] *vi.* um Geld spielen. [Spieler *m.*]

Gambler [gæm'bler] *n.*

Gambling [gæm'bling] *n.* Spielen um Geld *n.*

Gambol [gæmbl] *n.* Freudensprung *m.*; *vi.* fröhlich hüpfen.

Game [geim] *n.* Spiel *n.*, Wild *n.*, Plan *m.*, Unternehmen *n.*

Gamekeeper [geim'kih-per] *n.* Wildhüter *m.* [ler *m.*]

Gamester [geim'ster] *n.* Spieler

Gammon [gæ'mʌn] *n.* geräucherter Schinken. [*f.*]

Gamut [gæ'mʌt] *n.* Tonleiter

Gander [gan'der] *n.* Gänserich *m.*

Gang [gæng] *n.* Bande *f*, Abteilung *f*, Sortiment *f.*

Gangster [gæng'ster] *n.* Bandenmitglied *n.*, Gangster *m.*

Gangway [gæng'wei] *n.* Fallreep *n.*, Durchgang *m.*

Gantry [gæn'tri] *n.* Fasslager *n.*, Krangerüst *n.*

Gap [gæp] *n.* Öffnung *f*, Lücke *f*, Abstand *m.*

Gape [geip] *vi.* gaffen, gähnen, sich spalten.

Garag'e [gæ'rahzh] *n.* Auto-

schuppen *m*, Halle *f*, Garage *f*; — ing Unterstellung *f* (car).

Garb [gahrb] *n.* Tracht *f*, Kleidung *f.*

Garbage [gahr'bidzh] *n.* Abfall *m*, Schund *m.* [meln.

Garble [gahr'bl] *vt.* verstüm-

Garden [gahr'dn] *n.* Garten *m*; kitchen — Gemüsegarten *m*, nursery — Baumschule *f*; — city *n.* Gartenstadt *f*; — shears *pl.* Heckenschere *f*; — suburb *n.* Villenkolonie *f.*

Gardener [gahr'dner] *n.* Gärtner *m.*

Gardening [gahr'dning] *n.* Gartenarbeit *f.* Gartenbau *m.*

Gargle [gahr-gl] *vi.* gurgeln; *n.* Gurgelwasser *n.*

Gargoyle [gahr'geul] *n.* Wasserspeier *m.*

Garish [geh'risch] *a.* grell.

Garland [gahr'lAnd] *n.* Kranz *m*, Laubgewinde *n.*; *vt.* bekränzen. [lauch *m.*

Garlic [gahr'lik] *n.* Knob-

Garment [gahr'mAnt] *n.* Kleidungsstück *n.*

Garner [gahr'ner] *n.* aufspeichern; *n.* Kornspeicher *m.*

Garnet [gahr'nit] *n.* Granat *m.*

Garnish [gahr'nisch] *vt.* verzieren, garnieren.

Garret [gæ'rit] *n.* Dachstube *f.*

Garrison [gæ'tri-sAn] *n.* Garnison *f*, Besatzung *f*, Standort *m*; *vt.* besetzen mit *or* Garnison versehen; — artillery *n.* Festungsartillerie *f*, schwere Artillerie; — commander *n.* Standortältester *m.*

Garrot [gæ-rot'] *vt.* erdrosseln; *n.* Erdrosselung *f.*

Garrulity [gA-ruh'li-ti] *n.* Geschwätzigkeit *f.*

Garrulous [gæ'ru-lʌss] *a.* geschwätzig.

Garter [gahr'ter] *n.* Strumpfband *n*; Order of the — Hosenbandorden *n.*

Gas [gæss] *n.* Gas *n.*, Kampfstoff *m.* (*mil.*); *vt.* vergasen, mit Gas vergiften ; — bracket n. Gasarm m ; — burner n. Gasbrenner m ; — casualty n. Gasbeschädigte(r) m ; — concentration n. Gasballung f ; — cooker n. Gaskocher m ; — defence n. Gas-abwehr f. -schutz m ; — detector n. Gasanzeiger m — fire n. Gasfeuer n ; — lamp n. Gaslampe f ; — light n. Gaslicht n ; — mantle n. Gasstrumpf m ; — mask n. Gasmaske f — meter n. Gasmesser m. Gasuhr f ; — ring n. Gaskocher m ; — shell n. Gasbrisanzgranate f ; — stove n. Gasofen m ; — works pl. Gaswerk n.

Gaselier [gæ-ssA-lihr'] n. Gaskrone f, Gasleuchter m.

Gaseous [gei'schAss] a. gasförmig, gasig.

Gash [gæsch] n. klaffende Wunde ; vt. ins Fleisch schneiden. [ring m. (tec.).

Gasket [gæ'skit] n. Dichtungs-

Gasoline [gæ'ssA-lihn] n. Gasolin n, Benzin n. Treibstoff m. (aut.). [Gasbehälter m.

Gasometer [gæss-o'mi-ter] n.

Gasp [gæsp] n. Keuchen n. vi. schwer atmen, keuchen.

Gassed [gæst] a. gaskrank.

Gastric [gæ'strik] a. gastrisch, Magen-.

Gate [geit] n. Tor n, Pforte f ; — way Torweg m.

Gather [gæ'dher] vt. sammeln, pflücken, erfahren, schliessen, aufnehmen (dress), zusammenziehen (cloth) ; i. sich sammeln. [Versammlung f.

Gathering [gæ'dhA-ring] n.

Gaudy [gO'di] a., Gaudily ad. prunkhaft, geschmacklos, aufgeputzt, bunt.

Gauge [geidzh] n. Mass n, Lehre f, Spurweite f (rl.) ; vt. abmessen, abschätzen, eichen ; broad — Breitspur f (rl.) ; normal — Normal-, Voll-spur f (rl.).

Gauging [gei'dzhing] n. Eichung f, Ausmessung f.

Gaunt [gOnt] a. hager, dürr.

Gauntlet [gOnt'lit] n. Leder-, Überhandschuh m, Fahrhandschuh m (aut.).

Gauntness [gOnt'ness] n. Hagerkeit f. [m.

Gauze [gOs] n. Gaze f, Schleier

Gay [gei] a. heiter, bunt.

Gaze [geis] n. fester Blick ; vi. unverwandt anblicken.

Gazette [gA-set'] n. Amtsblatt n, Zeitung f ; vt. (zum Offizier) ernennen.

Gazetteer [gæ-se-tihr'] n. geographisches Lexikon.

Gear [gihr] n. Geschirr n, Gerät n, Getriebe n, Geschwindigkeit f, Gang m ; vt. einkuppeln, mit Getriebe versehen (tec.) ; vi. ineinander greifen ; high — hohe Übersetzung (cycle) ; top — Höchstgeschwindigkeit f. (aut.) ; — box n. Kettenkasten m. -getriebekasten m ; — case n. Ketten-kasten m, -schützer m (cycle) ; — lever n. Schalthebel m.

Gelatine [dzhe'1A-tihn] n. Gelatine f, Gallerte f ; — plate Gelatineplatte f.

Gem [dzhem] n. Edelstein m.

Gender [dzhen'der] n. Geschlecht n.

General [dzhe'nA-rAl] n. General m, Feldherr m ; a. allgemein, gemeinschaftlich ; — s pl. Generalität f ; — approval n. ungeteilter Beifall ; — cargo n. Stückgut n ; — election n. allgemeine Wahlen f. pl. ; — high command. Generalkommando n ; — hospital n. allgemeines Krankenhaus, Standortslazarett n (mil.) ; — meeting n. Generalversammlung f (com.) ; — office n. Geschäftszimmer n ; — practitioner n. Arzt m ; — service n. Kommiss ...; —

service car n. Gefechtswagen.
m ; — staff n. Generalstab m
Generalissimo [dzhe-nА-
rА-li'ssi-mo] n. Oberbefehlshaber m.
Generality [dzhe-nА-ræ'li-ti]
n. Allgemeinheit f, grösster
Teil.
Generalization [dzhe-nА-
rА-lai-sei'schАn] n. Verall-
gemeinerung f.
Generalize [dzhe'nА-rА-lais]
vt. verallgemeinern.
Generally [dzhe'nА-rА-li] ad.
im allgemeinen.
Generalship [dzhe'nА-rАl-
schip] n. Feldherrnkunst f.
Generate [dzhe'nА-reit] vt.
zeugen, erzeugen.
Generating [dzhe'nА-rei-
ting] a. Erzeugungs . . ., Kraft
. . . ; — station n. Kraftwerk n.
Generation [dzhe-nА-rei'
schАn] n. Erzeugung f, Generation f, Menschenalter n.
Generator [dzhe'nА-rei-ter]
n. Dampfkessel m, Generator
m, Dynamomaschine f.
Generosity [dzhe-nА-ro'ssi-
ti] n. Freigebigkeit f, Gross-
mut f.
Generous [dzhe'nА-rАss] a.
freigebig, grossmütig, edel.
Genial [dzhih'ni-Аl] a. heiter,
froh, munter, günstig.
Genitive [dzhe'ni-tiw] n.
Genitiv m, Wesfall m.
Genius [dzhih'ni-Аss] n. Genie
n, Begabung f, Anlage f.
Genteel [dzhen-tihl'] a. ele-
gant, fein.
Gentian [dzhen'schАn] n.
Enzian m.
Gentile [dzhen'tail] n. Heide
[m.
Gentility [dzhen-ti'li-ti] n.
hohe Abkunft, Vornehmheit f.
Gentle [dzhentl] a., **Gently**
ad. zart, sanft, zahm, vornehm.
Gentleman [dzhentl'mАn] n.
Herr m, feiner, gebildeter
Mann, Landedelmann m,
Rentier m.

Gentleness [dzhentl'ness] n.
Sanftmut f, Milde f, Zartheit
f.
Gentlewoman [dzhentl'uu-
mАn] n. Dame von Stand f.
Gentry [dzhen'tri] n. (nie-
derer) Adel.
Genuine [dzhe'nju-in] a. echt,
unverfälscht.
Genuineness [dzhe'nju-in-
ness] n. Echtheit f. [tung f.
Genus [dzhih'nАss] n. Gat-
Geographical [dzhih-o-græ'
fikl] a. erdgeschichtlich, geo-
graphisch. [Erdkunde f.
Geography [dzhih-o'grА-fi] n.
Geologist [dzhih-o'lo-dzhist]
n. Geolog m. [Geologie.
Geology [dzhih-o'lo-dzhi] n.
Geometrician [dzhih-o-met-
ri'schАn] n. Geometer.
Geometry [dzhi-o'mАt-ri] n.
Raumlehre f, Geometrie f.
Germ [dzhАrm] n. Keim m.
Germanization [dzhАr-mА-
nai-sei'schАn] n. Eindeut-
schung f.
Germanize [dzhАr'mА-nais]
vt. eindeutschen.
Germanophile [dzhАr-mæ'
no-fail] a. deutschfreundlich.
Germanophobe [dzhАr-
mæ'no-foub] a. deutschfeindlich.
Germinate [dzhАr'mi-neit]
vi. keimen, sprossen.
Germicide [dzhАr'mi-ssaid]
a. keimtötend ; n. keim-
tötendes Mittel.
Gesticulate [dzhe-sti'kju-
leit] vi. Gebärden machen.
Gesticulation [dzhe-sti-
kju-lei'schАn] n. Gebärden
(spiel) n.
Gesture [dzhe'ster] n. Gebärde f, Geste f, freundlicher
Schritt, Entgegenkommen n.
Get [get] vt. bekommen, verdienen, besorgen, gewinnen,
bewegen, überreden, veranlassen; i. ankommen, gelangen werden.

Geyser [gih'ser] n. Geyser m, Warmwasserbereiter m.

Ghastly [gah'stli] a. totenbleich, grässlich. [tel n.

Ghetto [ge'tou] n. Judenvier-

Ghost [goust] n. Gespenst n, Geist m. [geisterhaft.

Ghostly [gou'stli] a. geistlich.

Giant [dzhai'Ant] n. Riese m.

Gibbet [dzhi'bit] n. Galgen m, Kranbalken m (tec.).

Gibe [dzhaib] v. Spott m ; vi. verspotten, höhnen.

Giblets [dzhib'lits] n. pl. Gänseklein n.

Giddiness [gi'di-ness] n. Schwindel m, Unbesonnenheit f, Leichtfertigkeit f.

Giddy [gi'di] a. schwindelig, leichtfertig. [n, Begabung f.

Gift [gift] n. Gabe f, Geschenk

Gifted [gif'tid] a. begabt.

Gigantic [dzhai-gæn'tik] a. riesenhaft.

Gig [gig] n. zweirädriger Wagen ; Ruderboot n (nav.).

Giggle [gigl] vi. kichern ; Gekicher n.

Gild [gild] vt. vergolden.

Gilder [gil'der] n. Vergolder m. [n. Vergoldung f.

Gilding [gil'ding], Gilt [gilt]

Gill [dzhil] n. Viertelpinte f.

Gills [gils] n. pl. Kieme f.

Gilt-edged [gilt-edzhd'] a. mit Goldschnitt, hochfein, mündelsicher (com.).

Gimlet [gim'lit] n. Handbohrer m. [f, Gimpe f.

Gimp [gimp] n. Besatzschnur

Gin [dzhin] n. Wacholderbranntwein m. [Winde f, (tec.).

Gin [dzhin] n. Hebezeug z,

Ginger [dzhin'dzher] n. Ingwer m ; — bread n. Pfefferkuchen m. [sachte.

Gingerly [dzhin'dzher-li] ad.

Gingham [ging'Am] n. gingang m. [m, Zigeunerin f.

Gipsy [dzhip'si] n. Zigeuner

Giraffe [dzhi-rahf'] n. Giraffe f.

Gird [gArd] vt. i. gürten.

Girder [gAr'der] n. Tragbalken m, Träger m (bridge).

Girl [gArl] n. Mädchen n ; — guide n. Pfadfinderin f.

Girlhood [gArl'hud] n. Mädchenjahre n. pl.

Girlish [gAr'liscu] a. mädchenhaft.

Girth [gArth] n. Sattelgurt m Umfang m. [m, Kern m.

Gist [dzhist] n. Hauptinhalt

Give [giw] vt. schenken, geben, abgeben, erteilen ; i. nachgeben, weichen. [m.

Glacier [glæ'ssier] n. Gletscher

Glacis [glæ'ssis] n. Abdachung f, Glacis n. (mil.). [sich freuen.

Glad [glæd] a. froh ; be —

Gladden [glæ'dn] vt. froh machen. [f.

Glade [gleid] n. Waldlichtung

Gladly [glæd'li] ad. gern.

Gladness [glæd'ness] n. Fröhlichkeit f, Freude f.

Gladsome [glæd'sAm] a. freudig.

Glamour [glæ'mer] n. Zauber m, das Romantische.

Glance [glahnss] n. Blick m, Schimmer m ; vi. blicken, glänzen ; vt. — at, flüchtig anblicken; — over, flüchtig überblicken.

Gland [glænd] n. Drüse f.

Glanders [glæn'ders] n. pl Druse f.

Glandular [glæn'dju-ler] a. drüsig.

Glare [gleh'er] n. blendendes Licht, wilder Blick ; vi. hell glänzen ; — at vt. anstarren.

Glaring [gleh'ring] a., —ly ad. blendend, offenkundig, grell.

Glass [glahss] n. Glas n ; — es pl. Brille f ; — case n. Glaskasten m ; — house n. Treibhaus n ; — shade n. Glas-glocke f, -schirm m ; — works n. Glashütte, Glasfabrik f.

Glassy [glah'ssi] a. gläsern.

Glaze [gleis] n. Verglasung f. Politur f; vt. verglasen, polieren.

Glazier [glei'si-er] n. Glaser m.

Gleam [glihm] n. Strahl m; vi. strahlen. [auflesen.

Glean [glihn] vt. nachlesen.

Gleaner [glih'ner] n. Ährenleser m, Sammler m.

Gleaning [glih'ning] n. Ährenlesen n, Nachlese f.

Glee [glih] h. Freude f.

Gleeful [glih'ful] a. fröhlich.

Glen [glen] n. enges Tal.

Glib [glib] a. glatt, zungenfertig. [genfertigkeit f.

Glibness [glib'ness] n. Zun-

Glide [glaid] vi. gleiten, fliessen, niedergehen, abrutschen; Gleitflug machen (av.).

Glider [glai'der] n. Luftsegler m, Segelflugzeug n (av.); heavy — n. Gross-segler m; — pilot n. Segelflieger m. Gleitflieger m.

Gliding [glai'ding] n. Segelflugwesen n, Segelfliegerei f.

Glimmer [gli'mer] n. Glimmer m, Schimmer m; vi. glimmern. [tiger Blick.

Glimpse [glimpss] n. flüchtiger Blick.

Glint [glint] n. Glanz m; vi. glänzen. [glistern.

Glisten [glissn] vi. glänzen,

Glitter [gli'ter] vi. glitzern; n. Geglitzer n, Glanz m.

Gloat [glout] vi. sich weiden.

Globe [gloub] n. Kugel f, Glocke f (lamp); — trotter n. Weltreisende(r) m.

Globular [glou'bju-ler] a. kugelförmig. [heit f.

Gloom [gluhm] n. Dunkel-

Gloomy [gluh'mi] a., Gloomily ad. dunkel, schwermütig, düster.

Glorification [gloh-ri-fi-kei'-schän] n. Verherrlichung f.

Glorified [gloh'ri-faid] a. verherrlicht, verschönert, veredelt.

Glorify [gloh'ri-fai] vt. verherrlichen, verklären. [lich.

Glorious [gloh'ri-Ass] a. herr-

Glory [gloh'ri] n. Herrlichkeit f, Ruhm m, Glanz m; vi. stolz sein, sich freuen.

Gloss [gloss] n. Glosse f, Randbemerkung.

Gloss [gloss] n. Glanz m, Politur f; vt. — over beschönigen, vertuschen.

Glossy [glo'ssi] a. glänzend, glatt, mit Hochglanz (photo).

Glove [glAw] n. Handschuh m.

Glover [glA'wer] n. Handschuhmacher m.

Glow [glou] vi. glühen; n. Glühen, Röte f.

Glowing [glou'ing] a. glühend, eifrig. [Glühwurm m.

Glow-worm [glou'uArm] n.

Glucose [gluh'kouss] n. Traubenzucker m.

Glue [gluh] n. Leim m, Klebstoff m; vt. leimen.

Gluey [gluh'i] a. leimig.

Glue-pot [gluh'pot] n. Leimtopf m.

Glum [glAm] a. mürrisch.

Glut [glAt] n. Überfüllung f Übersättigung f, Überfluss m; vt. sättigen, überfüllen.

Glutinous [gluh'ti-nAss] a. leimartig, leimig.

Glutton [glAtn] n. Schwelger m, Schlemmer m.

Gluttonous [glA'tA-nAss] a. gefrässig. [frässigkeit f.

Gluttony [glA'tA-ni] n. Ge-

Glycerine [gli'ssA-rihn] n. Glyzerin n, Ölsüss n.

Gnarled [nahrld] a. knorrig.

Gnash [nasch] vt. knirschen.

Gnat [nät] n. Mücke f.

Gnaw [nO] vt. nagen.

Go [gou] vi. gehen, abgehen, fahren, werden, laufen, arbeiten; — aboard, an Bord gehen; — abroad, ins Ausland gehen; — ahead, vorwärts gehen; — away, weggehen, verreisen; — back, zurückgehen ; — back on vt. zurückscheuen, nicht halten ; — before vi. vorhergehen ; — between vi. Mittelsmann m ; — by vi. vorbeigehen ; — forward, vorwärts gehen, vorrücken ; fortschreiten ; — in, hineingehen ; — in for vt. treiben ; into vt. eingehen auf ; i. eintreten ; — off vi. weggehen, losgehen (pun) ; — out, ausgehen, in den Ausstand treten (strikers) ; — over, übergehen, prüfen, durchgehen ; — together, zusammengehen ; — up, hinaufgehen, steigen ; — upon vt. sich gründen auf ; — with, begleiten, passen zu ; — without vt. entbehren.

Goad [goud] n. Stachel(stock) m ; vt. anstacheln.

Goal [goul] n. Ziel n. Tor n (football).

Goal-keeper [goul'kih-per] n. Torwächter m.

Goat [gout] n. Ziege f.

Goatherd [gout'herd] n. Ziegenhirt m. [verschlingen.

Gobble [gobl] n. vt. hastig

Goblet [gob'lit] n. Kelch m.

Goblin [gob'lin] n. Kobold m.

God [god] n. Gott m.

God-child [god'tschaild] n. Patenkind n.

Goddess [go'dess] n. Göttin f.

Godfather [god'fah-dher] n. Pate m.

God-fearing [god'fih-ring] a. gottesfürchtig.

Godless [god'less] a. gottlos.

God-like [god'laik] a. göttlich.

Godliness [god'li-ness] n. Gottesfurcht f. Frömmigkeit f.

Godly [god'li] a. fromm.

Godmother [god'mA-dher] n. Patin f.

Godsend [god'ssend] n. Gottesgabe, f. wahrer Segen.

Godson [god'ssAn] n. Patenkind n.

Godspeed [god-spihd'] n. Lebewohl n.

Goggle-eyed [gogl'aid] a. glotzäugig. [brille f.

Goggles [gogls] n. pl. Schutz-

Going [gou'ing] n. Gehen n, Gang m, Abreise f ; a. gehend, im Gange ; —s on n. pl. Treiben n.

Gold [gould] n. Gold n ; — braid n. Gold(-) Tresse f ; — leaf n. Blattgold n ; — mine n. Goldgrube f ; — mounted a. in Gold gefasst ; — rush n. Goldjagd f ; — standard n. Goldwährung f (com.).

Golden [goul'dn] a. golden.

Goldfish [gould'fisch] n. Goldfisch m.

Goldsmith [gould'smith] n. Goldschmied m.

Golf [golf] n. Golfspiel n ; — club n. Golfschläger m, Golfklub m ; — links pl. Golfplatz m. [del f.

Gondola [gon'dA-lA] n. Gon-

Gone [gon] a. fort, tot.

Gong [gong] a. Gong m.

Gonorrhœa [go'nA-ri'A] n. Tripper m.

Good [gud] a. gut, gütig. gültig, passend ; n. Wohl n, das Gute ; —s on n. Waren f; pl. ; — for auf immer ; — breeding n. Wohlerzogenheit f ; — deal, viel ; — Friday n. Karfreitag m ; — many a. viele ; — nature n. Gutmütigkeit f ; — turn n. Gefälligkeit f ; — will n. Wohlwollen n, Zuspruch m, Kundschaft f (com.).

Good-bye [gud-bai'] n. Lebewohl n.

Goodly [gud'li] a. schön, stattlich, angenehm. [f.

Goodness [gud'ness] n. Güte

Goods-office n. Güterabfertigung f ; — station n. Güterbahnhof m ; — train n. Güterzug m ; — truck n. Güterwagen m.

Goose [guhss] n. Gans f; — flesh n. Gänsefleisch n, — quill n. Gänzekiel m; — step n. Stechschritt m, Parademarsch m (mil.).

Gooseberry [gus'bA-ri] n. Stachelbeere f. [Blut.

Gore [gO'er] n. geronnenes

Gore [gO'er] n. Keil m, Zwickel m.

Gorge [gOrdzh] n. Bergschlucht f, Schlund m, Gurgel f; vt. i. r. verschlingen, fressen.

Gorgeous [gOr'dzhAss] a. prächtig.

Gorgeousness [gOr'dzhAssness] n. Pracht f.

Gorget [gOrdzhit] n. Ringkragen; — patch n, -tab n. Kragenspiegel m (mil.).

Gorilla [gA-ri'lA] n. Gorilla m.

Gormandize [gOr'mAn-dais] vi. schlemmen, fressen. [m.

Gorse [gOrss] n. Stechginster

Gory [gO'ri] a. blutig.

Gosling [gos'ling] n. Gänschen n.

Gospel [gosspl] n. Evangelium n, buchstäbliche Wahrheit.

Gossamer [go'ssA-mer] n. Sommerfäden n. pl.

Gossip [go'ssip] n. Geklatsch n; vi. schwatzen.

Gouge [gaudzh] n. Hohl-eisen n, -meissel m.

Gourd [gu'erd] n. Kürbiss m.

Gout [gaut] n. Gicht f.

Gouty [gau'ti] a. gichtisch.

Govern [gA'wern] vt. i. herrschen, regieren, bestimmen.

Governable [gA'wer-nAbl] a. lenksam, folgsam.

Governess [gA'wer-ness] n. Erzieherin f, Kinderfräulein n, Gouvernante f.

Government [gA'wern-mAnt] n. Regierung f, Herrschaft f, Beherrschung f, Leitung f, Verwaltung f; local — Lokalverwaltung f; military — Militärverwaltung f; — grant n. staatliche Unter-

stützung, Subvention f; — loan n. Staatsanleihe f; — official n. Staatsbeamte(r) m; — stocks n. pl. Staatspapiere n. pl.

Governmental [gA-wernmentl'] a. staatlich, Regierungs..., Verwaltungs...

Governor [gA'wer-ner] n. Statthalter m, Direktor m (bank), Verwalter m, Herrscher m, Gauleiter m (Nazi), Regulator m (tec.).

Governorship [gA'wer-nerschip] n. Statthalterschaft f, Regentenschaft f. [n, Talar m.

Gown [gaun] n. Damenkleid

Grace [greiss] n. Gnade f, Anmut f, Gunst f, Grazie f, Nachsicht f, Zahlungsfrist f (com.); vt. schmücken.

Graceful [greiss'ful] a., -ly ad. anmutig.

Graceless [greiss'less] a. reizlos, verworfen.

Gracious [grei'schAss] a. gnädig, huldreich. [stufen.

Gradate [grA-deit'] vt. abstufen.

Gradation [grA-dei'schAn] n. Abstufung f.

Grade [greid] n. Stufe f, Grad m; Neigung f (rl.), Güte f, Sorte f (com.); vt. abstufen, ordnen.

Gradient [grei'di-Ant] n. Steigung f, Senkung f.

Gradual [græ'dju-Al] a., -ly ad. allmählich.

Graduate [græ'dju-eit] vt. i. abstufen, graduieren.

Graft [grahft] n. Schiebung f, Bestechung f, Korruption f.

Graft [grahft] vt. pfropfen.

Grain [grein] n. Korn n, Getreide n, Strich m, Samenkorn n, echte Farbe (dye); vt. granulieren, körnen, adern (paint).

Grammar [græ'mer] n. Grammatik f.

Grammarian [grA-meh'ri-An] n. Grammatiker m.

Grammatical [grA-mæ'tikl] *a.* grammatisch, sprachlich richtig.

Gramophone [græ'mA-foun] *n.* Grammophon *n* ; — needle *n.* Grammophonnadel *f* ; — record *n.* Schallplatte *f.*

Granary [græ'nA-ri] *n.* Speicher *m.*

Grand [grænd] *a.* gross, herrlich ; — piano *n.* Flügel *m.*

Grandchild [grænd'tschaild] *n.* Enkel *m*, Enkelin *f.*

Grand-daughter [grænd'-dO-ter] *n.* Enkelin *f.*

Grand-duchess [grænd-dAtsch'ess] *n.* Grossherzogin *f.*

Grand-duchy [grænddA'tschi] *n.* Grossherzogtum *n.*

Grand-duke [grænddjuhk'] *n.* Grossherzog *m.*

Grandeur [græn'djer] *n.* Grösse *f*, Herrlichkeit *f.*

Grandfather [grænd'fah-dher] *n.* Grossvater *m* ; — clock *n.* hohe Standuhr *f.*

Grandmother [grænd'mA-dher] *n.* Grossmutter *f.*

Grandparents [grænd'pehr-Ants] *n. pl.* Grosseltern *pl.*

Grandson [grænd'ssAn] *n.* Enkel *m.*

Grange [greindzh] *n.* Meierhof *m.*

Granite [græ'nit] *n.* Granit *m.*

Granny [græ'ni] *n.* Grossmütterchen *n.*

Grant [grahnt] *vt.* bewilligen, gewähren, zugeben ; *n.* Verleihung *f*, Bewilligung *f*, Gabe *f*, Beihilfe *f*, Unterstützung *f* ; —in-aid *n.* Beihilfe *f.*

Granular [græ'nju-ler] *a.* körnig, kristallisiert.

Granulate [græ'nju-leit] *vt.* körnen, granulieren ; —d *a.* feinkörnig, granuliert.

Grape [greip] *n.* Traube *f*, Weinbeere *f* ; bunch of —s Traube *f* ; — sugar *n.* Traubenzucker *m.*

Grape-fruit [greip'fruht] *n.* Pompelmus *m*, -muse *f.*

Graph [grahf] *n.* Schaubild *n*, Diagramm *n*, Kurvenbild *n.*

Graphic [græ'fik] *a.* graphisch, anschaulich, lebhaft. [blei *n.*

Graphite [græ'fait] *n.* Reiss-

Grapnel [græp'nAl] *n.* Dragganker *m*, Enterhaken *m* (*nav.*).

Grapple [græpl] *vt.* anhaken, verankern ; *i.* ringen.

Grasp [grahsp] *n.* Griff *m* ; *vt.* ergreifen, begreifen.

Grasping [grah'sping] *a.* habgierig.

Grass [grahss] *n.* Gras *n.*

Grasshopper [grahss'ho-per] *n.* Heuschrecke *f.*

Grassy [grah'ssi] *a.* grasig.

Grate [greit] *n.* Rost *m*, Gitter *n.*

Grate [greit] *vt. i.* kratzen, zerreiben, verletzen. [bar.

Grateful [greit'ful] *a.* dank-

Gratefulness [greit'ful-ness] *n.* Dankbarkeit *f.*

Grater [grei'ter] *n.* Reibeisen *n*, Raspel *f.*

Gratification [græ-ti-fi-kei'-schAn] *n.* Befriedigung *f*, Vergnügen *n.* [digen.

Gratify [græ'ti-fai] *vt.* befrie-

Gratifying [græ'ti-fai-ing] *a.* erfreulich.

Grating [grei'ting] *n.* Gitter *n*, Gräting *f* (*nav.*).

Gratitude [græ'ti-tjuhd] *n.* Dankbarkeit *f.*

Gratuitous [græ-tju'i-tAss] *a.* unentgeltlich, unverlangt.

Gratuity [græ-tju'i-ti] *n.* Trinkgeld *n.* [tig.

Grave [greiw] *a.* ernst, wich-

Grave [greiw] *n.* Grab *n* ; — digger *n.* Totengräber *m* ; — stone *n.* Grabstein *m* ; — yard *n.* Grabstein *m* Friedhof *m.*

Gravel [græwl] *n.* Kies *m.*

Gravitate [græ'wi-teit] *vi* stark hinstreben.

Gravitation [græ-wi-tei'-schAn] *n.* Schwerkraft *f.*

Gravity [græ'wi-ti] *n.* Schwere *f*, Ernst *m.*

Gravy [grei'wi] n. Fleischsaft m, Sosse f, Tunke f.

Gray [grei] a. grau.

Graze [greis] vi. weiden, t. streifen.

Grazing [grei'sing] n. Weiden n, Weide f, Trift f.

Grease [grihss] n. Schmiere f, Fett n; — box n. Schmierbüchse f; — chamber n. Schmierkammer f (tec.); — gun n. Fettspritze f, Schmierpresse f (aut.); — paint n. Schminke f; — point n. Schmiernipel m (aut.); — proof a. fettdicht; — proof paper n. Butterbrotpapier n.

Grease [grihs] vt. schmieren, einfetten, ölen.

Greasy [grih'si] a. schmierig.

Great [greit] a. gross, bedeutend, wichtig, berühmt; — coat n. Mantel m; — deal n. grosse Menge; — war n. Weltkrieg m.

Great-grandchild [greit'grænd-tschaild] n. Urenkel m, -in f.

Great-grandfather [greit'grænd-fah-dher] n. Urgrossvater m.   [Grade.

Greatly [greit'li] ad. in hohem

Greatness [greit'ness] n. Grösse f, Bedeutung f.

Greed [grihd] n. Gierigkeit f.

Greediness [grih'di-ness] n. Gierigkeit f.

Greedy [grih'di] a., **Greedily** [[grih'di-li] ad. gierig, gefrässig.

Green [grihn] a. grün, unreif; n. Rasenplatz m; —s pl. Gemüse n.

Greengrocer [grihn'grousser] n. Gemüsehändler m.

Greengroceries [grihn'groussA-ris] n. pl. Gemüsewaren f. pl.   [Gewächshaus n.

Greenhouse [grihn'hauss] n.

Greenish [grih'nisch] a. grünlich.   [nehmen, anreden.

Greet [griht] vt. grüssen, auf-

Greeting [grih'ting] n. Gruss m, Begrüssung f.

Gregarious [gri-geh'ri-ass] a. gesellig, in Herden lebend.

Grenade [gri-neid'] n. Granate f.   [Grenadier m.

Grenadier [gre-nA-dihr'] n.

Grey [grei] a. grau; —hound m. Windhund m.   [grau.

Greyish [grei'isch] a. ziemlich

Grid [grid] n. Rost m (cooking); Gitter n. (rad.), Netz n (el.); luggage — n. Gepäck-, Kofferbrücke f (aut.).

Gridiron [grid'ai-An] n. Bratrost m; Rostdock n, Kielbank f (nav.).

Grief [grihf] n. Gram m, Kummer m; come to — vi. zu Schaden kommen.

Grievance [grih'wAnss] n. Beschwerde f.

Grieve [grihw] vi. t. betrüben, sich grämen, kränken.

Grievous [grih'wAss] a. schmerzlich.

Grill [gril] n. Bratrost m, Rostbraten m; vt. auf dem Bratrost braten, rösten; — room n. Speisehaus m.

Grim [grim] a., -ly ad. grimmig, finster.

Grimace [gri-meiss'] n. Grimasse f, Fratze f; vi. Grimassen machen.

Grime [graim] n. Schmutz m.

Grimness [grim'ness] n. Grimmigkeit f, Schrecklichkeit f.

Grimy [grai'mi] a. schmutzig.

Grin [grin] n. Grinsen n; vi. grinsen.

Grind [graind] vt. zerreiben, mahlen (grain), schleifen (knife, etc.), unterdrücken (persons).

Grinder [grain'der] n. Schleifer m.

Grindstone [graind'stoun] n. Schleifstein m.

Grip [grip] n. Griff m; vt. ergreifen, packen; i. greifen, halten.

Gripe [graip] *vt. i.* Kolik haben, verursachen, zusammenpressen; **—s** *n. pl.* Kolik *f.*

Griping [grai'ping] *a.* (im Bauche) kneipend, nagend.

Grisly [gris'li] *a.* scheusslich, grausig.

Gristle [grissl] *n.* Knorpel *m.*

Gristly [griss'li] *a.* knorpelig.

Grit [grit] *n.* Griess *m*, Kies *m*, Mut *m*, Ausdauer *f.*

Grit [grit] *n.* Schrotmehl *n*; **—s** *pl.* Grütze *f.* [dig.

Gritty [gri'ti] *a.* griessig, san-

Grizzled [grisld] *a.* grau gesprenkelt.

Groan [groun] *vi.* stöhnen; *n.* Stöhnen *n.*

Groats [groutss] *n.* Hafergrütze *f.*

Grocer [grou'sser] *n.* Kolonial-, Material-warenhändler *m*; **—'s shop** *n.* Kolonialwarenhandlung *f.*

Groceries [grou'ssA-ris] *n. pl.* Kolonial-, Spezerei-waren *f. pl.*

Grocery [grou'ssA-ri] *a.* Kolonialwaren . . . ; *n.* Kolonial-, Material-warenhandlung *f*; **—business** *n.* Kolonialwarenhandel *m.*

Grog [grog] *n.* Grog *m.*

Groin [groin] *n.* Schambug *m*, Weiche *f*, Grat *m* (vault).

Groom [gruhm] *n.* Reitknecht *m*, Stallknecht *m*; *vt.* besorgen, putzen; **—sman** *n.* Brautführer *m.*

Groove [gruhw] *n.* Nut *f*, Rinne *f*, Routine *f*, Gewohnheit *f*, Schlendrian *m*; *vt.* furchen, nuten, auskehlen.

Grope [group] *vi.* umhertasten.

Gross [grouss] *a.* fett, grob, unanständig; **— profits** *n. pl.* Rohgewinn *m*; **— weight** *n.* Bruttogewicht *n.*

Grossly [grouss'li] *ad.* grob, gröblich, in hohem Masse.

Grossness [grouss'ness] *n.* Grobheit *f*, Rohheit *f.*

Grotesque [grou-tesk'] *a.* grotesk, wunderlich.

Grotto [gro'tou] *n.* Felsenhöhle *f.*

Ground [graund] *n.* Boden *m*, Grund *m*; *vt.* niedersetzen, hinlegen, gründen, erden (el.); *i.* auflaufen, stranden (nav.); **— aerial** *n.* Bodenantenne *f* (rad.); **— connection** *n.* Erdung *f* (el.); **— defence** *n.* Erdabwehr *f* (av.); **— equipment** *n.* Bodengeräte *n* (av.); **— floor** *n.* Erdgeschoss *n*; **— rent** *n.* Grundzins *m*; **— sheet** *n.* Zeltbahn *f*; **— staff** *n.* Bodenmannschaft *f*; **— swell** *n.* Dünung *f* (nav.); **— work** *n.* Unterbau *m*, Grundlage *f.*

Groundless [graund'less] *a.* grundlos.

Group [gruhp] *n.* Gruppe *f*; *vt. i.* gruppieren, sich sammeln; **— captain** *n.* Oberst *m* (av.). [n.

Grouse [grauss] *n.* Waldhuhn

Grouse [grauss] *vi.* murren, nörgeln, schimpfen. [Hain *m.*

Grove [grouw] *n.* Gehölz *n*,

Grovel [growl] *vi.* auf dem Bauch kriechen.

Grovelling [grow'ling] *n.* Kriecherei *f*; *a.* kriechend, gemein.

Grow [grou] *vi.* wachsen, werden; *t.* ziehen, wachsen lassen; **— up**, aufwachsen.

Grower [grou'er] *n.* Pflanzer *m.* [Knurren *n.*

Growl [graul] *vi.* knurren; *n.*

Growth [grouth] *n.* Wachstum *n*, Wuchs *m*, Zunahme *f.*

Grub [grAb] *n.* Raupe *f*, Futter *n*; *vt.* graben, wühlen.

Grudge [grAdzh] *n.* Groll *m*; *vt.* missgönnen, ungern geben.

Grudging [grAdzh'ing] *a.* **-ly** *ad.* murrend, ungern, grollend. [schleim *m.*

Gruel [gruh'il] *n.* Hafer-

Gruesome [gruh'ssAm] *a.* grausig.

Gruff [grAf] a. barsch.
Grumble [grAmbl] vi. brummen, nörgeln, schimpfen ; — Brummen n.
Grumbler [grAm'bler] n. missvergnügter Mensch.
Grunt [grAnt] vi. grunzen.
Guano [guah'no] n. Vogeldünger m, Guano m.
Guarantee [gæ-rAn-tih'] n. Bürgschaft f, Sicherheit f, Gewähr f, Garantie f ; vt. bürgen für, haften für, gewährleisten, garantieren.
Guard [gahrd] n. Wache f, Bedeckung f, Schutzmannschaft f (mil.), Schaffner m (rl) ; vt. bewachen, beschützen, hüten ; — of honour n. Ehrengarde f ; — room n. Wachtlokal n (mil.).
Guarded [gahr'did] a. -ly ad. vorsichtig.
Guardian [gahr'di-An] n. Vormund m.
Guardianship [gahr'di-Anschip] n. Vormundschaft f.
Guerrilla [gA-ri'lA[n. Freischärler m ; — warfare n. Kleinkrieg m.
Guess [gess] n. Vermutung f, Mutmassung f ; vt. erraten, vermuten. [Raterei f.
Guess-work [gess'uArk] n.
Guest [gest] n. Gast m ; — paying — Pensionär m ; — house n. Pension f.
Guidance [gai'dAnss] n. Führung f.
Guide [gaid] n. Führer m, Wegweiser m, Reisehandbuch n, Leitfaden m, Richtschnur f ; vt. führen ; — book n. Reiseführer m, -handbuch n.
Guild [gild] n. Zunft f, Innung f ; — hall n. Rathaus n.
Guile [gail] n. Arglist f.
Guileless [gail'less] a. arglos.
Guillotine [gi'lA-tihn] n. Fallbeil n.
Guilt [gilt] n. Schuld f. [los.
Guiltless [gilt'less] a. schuld-

Guilty [gil'ti] a. schuldig, schuldbewusst.
Guinea [gi'ni] n. Guinee f, 21 Schilling ; — fowl n. Perlhuhn n. [Maske f.
Guise [gais] n. Gestalt f.
Guitar [gi-tahr'] n. Gitarre f.
Gulf [gAlf] n. Golf m, Meerbusen m, Abgrund m.
Gull [gAl] n. Möwe f.
Gull [gAl] n. Einfaltspinsel m, Narr m ; vt. betrügen, prellen.
Gullet [gA'lit] n. Schlund m.
Gullible [gA'libl] a. einfältig, leichtgläubig.
Gully [gA'li] n. Sinkkasten m, Giessbachbett n, Schlucht f.
Gulp [gAlp] n. Schluck m ; vi. (hinunter-)schlucken.
Gum [gAm] n. Gummi n ; vt. gummieren, zukleben ; — boots m. pl. Gummistiefel m. pl.
Gum [gAm] n. Zahnfleisch n ; — boil n. Zahngeschwür n.
Gummy [gA'mi] a. klebrig.
Gun [gAn] n. Gewehr n, Flinte f, Kanone f, Geschütz n, Revolver m ; assault — n.Sturmgeschütz n (mil.) ; medium n. schweres Geschütz (mil.) ; heavy — schwerstes, überschweres Geschütz n (mil.) ; — barrel n. Geschützrohr n ; — boat n. Kanonenboot n (nav.) ; — carriage n. Lafette f ; — carrier n. Artillerieträger m ; — cotton n. Schiessbaumwolle f ; — crew n. Geschützbedienung f ; — emplacement n. Geschützstand m ; —fire n. Geschütz n, Geschützfeuer n ; — layer n. Richtkanonier m. (mil., av.) ; — metal n. Stückgut n, Kanonenmetall n ; — powder n. Schiesspulver n ; — shot n. Schussweite f, Schuss m ; — sight n. Visier n, Aufsatz m ; — smith n. Büchsenmacher m ; — tube n. Geschützrohr n ; turret n. Geschütz-, Panzerturm m (nav.).
Gunner [gA'ner] n. Kanonier

_m_, Artillerist _m_ ; machine — Maschinengewehrschütze _m_.

Gunnery [gA'nA-ri] _n._ Geschützwesen _n._

Gunwale [gAnl] _n._ Schanddeckel _m_, Dollbord _m_.

Gurgle [gArgl] _vi._ glucksen.

Gush [gAsch] _n._ Erguss _m_ ; _vi._ hervorströmen.

Gushing [gA'sching] _a._ überschwenglich, überspannt.

Gusset [gA'ssit] _n._ Zwickel _m_, Keil _m_, Gummizug _m_ (_shoe_).

Gust [gAst] _n._ Windstoss _m_.

Gusty [gA'sti] _a._ stürmisch, böig.

Gut [gAt] _n._ Darm _m_ ; —s _pl._ Eingeweide _f_, Mut _m_, Energie _f_ ; _vt._ ausweiden. [brannt.

Gutted [gA'tid] _a._ ausge-

Guttapercha [gA'tA-pArtschA] _n._ Guttapercha _f_.

Gutter [gA'ter] _n._ Wasserrinne _f_ ; Dachrinne _f_ ; — press _n._ Schmutzpresse _f_ ; —snipe _n._ Gassenjunge _m_.

Guttural [gA'tA-rAl] _n._ Kehllaut _m_.

Gymnasium [dzhim-nei'si-Am] _n._ Turnhalle _f_.

Gymnast [dzhim'næst] _n._ Turner _m_, -in _f_.

Gymnastics [dzhim-næ'stix] _n. pl._ Turnen _n._ [_m_.

Gypsum [dzhip'sAm] _n._ Gips

Gyro-compass [dzhai'rou-kAm-pAss] _n._ Kreiselkompass _m_.

H

Haberdasher [hæ'ber-dæscher] _n._ Schnitt-, Kurzwarenhändler _m_.

Haberdashery [hæ-ber-dæ'schA-ri] _n._ Kurzwaren _f. pl._

Habit [hæ'bit] _n._ Gewohnheit _f_, Kleidung _f_, Lebensweise _f_.

Habitable [hæ'bi-tAbl] _a._ bewohnbar.

Habitual [hA-bi'tju-Al] _a._

-ly _ad._ gewöhnlich, gewohnheitsmässig.

Habituate [hA-bi'tju-eit] _vt. r._ (sich) angewöhnen.

Hack [hæk] _vt._ hacken.

Hack [hæk] _n._ Reitpferd _n_, Lohnschreiber _m_.

Hackle [hækl] _vt._ hecheln ; _n._ Hechel _f_.

Hackney [hæk'ni] _n._ Reit-, Droschkenpferd _n_ ; —ed _a._ abgenutzt, abgedroschen, platt ; — cab _n._ Droschke _f_.

Haddock [hæ'dAk] _n._ Schellfisch _m._ [n. Blutung _f_.

Hæmorrhage [he'mA-ridzh] [hærmt, hager.

Hag [hæg] _n._ hässliches altes Weib.

Haggard [hæ'gerd] _a._ abge-

Haggle [hægl] _vi._ feilschen.

Hail [heil] _n._ Hagel _m_ ; _vi._ hageln.

Hail [heil] _vt._ anrufen ; _i._ — from, kommen von, stammen aus _n._ Anruf _m._

Hair [heh'er] _n._ Haar _n_ ; —'s breadth _n._ Haaresbreite _f_ ; — brush _n._ Haarbürste _f_ ; — dresser _n._ Haarschneider _m_, Friseur _m_ ; — dressing _n._ Haarschneiden ; — dressing _n._ mattress _n._ Rosshaarmatratze _f_ ; — oil _n._ Haaröl _n_ ; —pin _n._ Haarnadel _f_ ; —raising _a._ haarsträubend ; —slide _n._ Haarspange _f_.

Hairy [heh'ri] _a._ haarig.

Hake [heik] _n._ Seehecht _m_, Kummel _m_ (_fish_), Zughaken _m_ (_tec._), Katze _f_ (_tec._).

Halation [hæ-lei'schAn] _n._ Lichthof _m._

Half [hahf] _n._ Hälfte _f_ ; _a._ halb ; centre — Mittelläufer _m_ ; right — rechter Läufer _m_ ; — back _n._ Läufer _m_ ; bound _n._ in Halbfranzband gebunden ; — breed, — caste _n._ Mischling _m_ ; — crown _n._ halbe Krone, zweieinhalb Schilling ; — dozen _n._ halbes Dutzend ; — holiday _n._ freier

Nachmittag, Ausgang m; — hose n. Socken f. pl.; — mast n. Halbmast m; — measures n. pl. halbe Massregeln f. pl.; — pay n. halber Sold; — penny n. Halbpennystück n; — platoon n. Halbzug m (mil.); — price n. halber Preis; — speed n. halbe Geschwindigkeit f; — time n. Halbzeit f. Pause f; — tone n. Halbton m, Autotypie f; — tracked vehicle n. Halbkettenfahrzeug n; — way a. auf halbem Wege; — witted a. einfältig; — yearly a. ad. halbjährlich

Halibut [hæ'li-bʌt] n. Heilbutte f. [Haussflur m.

Hall [hôl] n. Saal m, Halle f.

Hallucination [hʌ-luh-ssi-nei'schʌn] n. Sinnestäuschung f. [m, Hof m.

Halo [hei'lo] n. Heiligenschein

Halt [hôlt] n. Halt m; vi. Halt machen. [vt. halftern.

Halter [hôl'ter] n. Halfter f;

Halve [hahw] vt. halbieren.

Halyard [hôl'jahrd] n. Fall n (nav.).

Ham [hæm] n. Schinken m; — sandwich n. Schinkenbrötchen n.

Hamlet [hæm'lit] n. Dörfchen n.

Hammer [hæ'mer] n. Hammer m; vt. hämmern.

Hammock [hæ'mʌk] n. Hängematte f. [korb m.

Hamper [hæm'per] n. Packkorb m; vt. hemmen, hindern.

Hand [hænd] n. Hand f; vt. überreichen, einhändigen; — to — fighting n. Handgemenge n; — in vt. einreichen; — over vt. übergeben; — round, vt. herumreichen.

H and-bag [hænd'bæg] n. Handtasche f.

Handbill [hænd'bil] n. Reklamezettel m.

Handbook [hænd'buk] n. Handbuch n.

Handcuff [hænd'kʌf] n. Handschelle f; vt. fesseln.

Handful [hænd'ful] n. Handvoll f.

Hand-grenade [hænd'gri-neid] n. Handgranate f.

Handicap [hæn'di-kæp] n. Nachteil m, Schwierigkeit f, Erschwerung f; vt. hemmen, benachteiligen.

Handicraft [hæn'di-krahft] n. Handarbeit f, Handwerk n.

Handkerchief [hæng'kertschif n. Taschentuch n.

Handle [hændl] n. Griff m, Kurbel f (tec.); vt. handhaben, behandeln, anfassen.

Handle-bars [hændl'bahrs] n. pl. Lenkstange f.

Hand-made [hænd'meid] a. mit der Hand gemacht.

Hand-saw [hænd'ssO] n. Handsäge f.

Hand-shake [hænd'scheik] n. Händedruck m.

Handspike [hænd'spaik] n. Hebestange f.

Handsome [hæn'sʌm] a. schön, stattlich, grossmütig, edel. [ting] n. Handschrift f.

Handwriting [hænd'rai-

Handy [hæn'di] a. geschickt, handlich, bequem, praktisch.

Handyman [hæn'di-mæn] n. Handlanger m, Bastler m.

Hang [hæng] vi. hangen; t. hängen; — back i. zurückhalten; — together, zusammenhalten.

Hangar [hæng'er] n. Flugzeughalle f, Flugzeugschuppen m; — construction n. Hallenbau m (av.).

Hank [hængk] n. Gewinde n, Strähne f. [Zufall m.

Haphazard [hæp-hæ'serd] n.

Happen [hæpn] vi. geschehen, sich ereignen, zufällig eintreten. [licherweise.

Happily [hæ'pi-li] ad. glück-

Happiness [hæ'pi-ness] n. Glückseligkeit f.

Happy [hæ'pi] a. glücklich.

Harangue [hA-ræng'] vt. öffentlich, feierlich anreden; n. Anrede f. [ermüden.

Harass [hæ'rAss] vt. quälen,

Harassing [hæ'rA-ssing] a. beunruhigend, lästig; — attack n. Störungs-angriff m (av.); — operation n. Störeinsatz m (av.).

Harbour [hahr'ber] n. Hafen m; vt. beherbergen, hegen; — dues n. pl. Hafengebühren f pl.; — master n. Hafenmeister m.

Harbourage [hahr'ber-idzh] n. Unterkommen n.

Hard [hahrd] a. hart, schwer, schlecht; ad. hart, mit Mühe, fest, tüchtig; — hearted a. hartherzig.

Harden [hahr'dn] vt. härten, abhärten, hart machen; i. hart werden, anziehen (com.).

Hardihood [hahr'di-hud] n. Kühnheit f, Dreistigkeit f.

Hard-headed [hahrd'he-did] a. klug. [mit Mühe, hart.

Hardly [hahrd'li] ad. kaum,

Hardness [hahrd'ness] n. Härte f, Schwierigkeit f.

Hardship [hahrd'ship] n. Beschwerde f, Strapaze f, Unrecht n.

Hardware [hahrd'ueh-er] n. Eisenwaren f. pl. [härtet.

Hardy [hahr'di] a. stark, abgehärtet, kühn.

Hare [heh'er] n. Hase m.

Haricot bean [hæ'ri-cou-bihn] n. welsche, weisse Bohne, Stangenbohne f.

Harm [hahrm] n. Schaden m; vt. schädigen, Schaden tun.

Harmful [hahrm'ful] a. schädlich. [schädlich, harmlos.

Harmless [hahrm'less] a. un-

Harmonious [hahr-mou'ni-Ass] a. wohlklingend, friedlich, übereinstimmend.

Harmonize [hahr'mo-nais] vt. in Einklang bringen; vi. harmonieren, übereinstimmen.

Harmony [hahr'mA-ni] n. Harmonie f, Einklang m.

Harness [hahr'niss] n. Geschirr n; vt. an-, auf-schirren.

Harp [hahrp] n. Harfe f.

Harpoon [hahr-puhn'] n. Harpune f. [vt. eggen, ackern.

Harrow [hæ'rou] n. Egge f;

Harsh [hahrsch] a., -ly ad. rauh, barsch.

Harshness [hahrsch'ness] n. Rauheit f, Barschheit f.

Harvest [hahr'vist] n. Ernte f; vt. ernten; — home n. Erntefest n.

Harvester [hahr'vi-ster] n. Schnitter m, —in f, Mähmaschine f.

Hash [hæsch] n. Ragout m, gehacktes Fleisch, Mischmasch m, Unordnung f.

Hasp [hæsp] n. Haspe f.

Hassock [hæ'ssok] n. Kniekissen m.

Haste [heist] n. Hast f, Eile f.

Hasten [heissn] vi. eilen; t. beschleunigen.

Hasty [hei'sti] a., hastily ad. eilig, hitzig, voreilig.

Hastiness [hei'sti-ness] n. Übereilung f, Hitze f, Hast f.

Hat [hæt] n. Hut m; — band n. Hutband n; — box n. Hutschachtel f.

Hatch [hætsch] vt. ausbrüten; n. Brut f, Hutzel, Luke f; service — Servierfenster n.

Hatchet [hæ'tschit] n. Beil n.

Hate [heit] n. Hass m; vt. hassen.

Hateful [heit'ful] a. gehässig.

Hatred [heit'rid] n. Hass m.

Hatter [hæ'ter] n. Hutmacher m.

Haughtiness [hO'ti-ness] n. Hochmut m. [tig.

Haughty [hO'ti] a. hochmü-

Haul [hOl] n. festes Ziehen, Fischzug m, Beute f; vt. ziehen, schleppen; i. Kurs ändern (nav.).

Haulage [hO'lidzh] n. Schleppen *n*, Transport *m*, Speditionskosten *pl.*

Haunch [hÔnsch] *n.* Hüfte *f.*

Haunt [hÔnt] *n.* häufig besuchter Ort, Lager *n*, Aufenthalt *m*; *vt.* häufig besuchen, verfolgen (*persons*).

Have [hæw] *vt.* haben, lassen; — to müssen.

Haven [heiwn] *n.* Hafen *m.*

Haversack [hæ'wer-ssæk] *n.* Futterbeutel *m*, Brotbeutel *m.*

Havoc [hæ'wÅk] *n.* Verwüstung *f.*   [Falke *m.*

Hawk [hÔk] *n.* Habicht *m*,

Hawk [hÔk] *vt.* hökern, hausieren.   [*m*, Höker *m.*

Hawker [hÔ'ker] *n.* Hausierer

Hawking [hÔ'king] *n.* Hausieren *n*, Strassenverkauf *m.*

Hawser [hÔ'ser] *n.* Kabeltau *n*, Schleppseil *n.*

Hawthorn [hÔ'thOrn] *n.* Hagedorn *n.*

Hay [hei] *n.* Heu *n*; — box *n.* Kochkiste *f*; — cock *n.* Heuhaufe *m*; — fork *n.* Heugabel *f*; — loft *n.* Heubodenm; — maker *n.* Heumacher *m*, Heuwender *m* (*tec.*); — making *n.* Heumachen *n*; — rick, — stack *n.* Heuschober *m*; — seed *n.* Heusame *m.*

Hazard [hæ'serd] *n.* Zufall *m*, Gefahr *f*, Risiko *n*, Hindernis *n* (*golf*); *vt.* aufs Spiel setzen wagen.   [Dunst *m.*

Haze [heis] *n.* Höhenrauch *m.*

Hazel [hei'sl] *n.* Haselstaude *f*; *a.* hell-, nuss-braun; — nut *n.* Haselnuss *f.*

Hazy [hei'si] *a.* dunstig, neblig, verschwommen.

He [hih] *pn.* er, der.

Head [hed] *n.* Kopf *m*, Haupt *n*, Spitze *f*, Stück *n.* (*cattle*), Häuptling *m* (*chief*), Oberhaupt *n*, Verwalter *m*, Leiter *m*, Höhepunkt *m* (*crisis*), Vorgebirge *n* (*headland*), Druckhöhe *f* (*water*), Vorderseite *f* (*coin*); *vt.* anführen, vorange-

hen; —ache *n.* Kopfweh *n*; — of commune *n.* Gemeindevorsteher *m*; — dress, — gear *n.* Kopf-putz *m*, -bedeckung *f*; — foreman *n.* Obermeister *m*; —land *n.* Vorgebirge *n*, Landzunge *f*; —light *n. pl.* Scheinwerfer *m. pl* (*aut.*), Kopflaterne *f* (*rl.*); —line *n.* Kopf-, Schlagzeile *f.* Titel *m*; — man *n.* Meister *m*, Häuptling *m* (*tribe*); — master *n.* Hauptlehrer *m*, Rektor *m*, Schuldirektor *m*; — mastership *n.* Rektorstelle *f*, Direktorat *n*; — mistress *n.* Vorsteherin *f* einer Schule; — office *n.* Hauptkontor *n*; — on *a.* aufeinander von vorn; — phone *n.* Kopfhörer *m* (*rad.*); — porter *n.* erster Portier, Pförtner; — stone *n.* Grabstein *m*, Kopfstein *m*; — waiter *n.* Oberkellner *m*; — wind *n.* Gegenwind *m*; — workman, Werkführer *m*, Vorarbeiter *m.*

Headless [hed'less] *a.* kopflos.

Headlong [hed'long] *a.* jäh, ungestüm, unbesonnen; *ad.* kopfüber, plötzlich.

Head-quarters [hed'kuOrters] *n. pl.* Hauptsitz *m*, Leitung *f*, Hauptquartier *n* (*mil.*), Kommando-, Dienst-stelle *f* (*mil.*); — battalion — Bataillonsstab *m*; — battle — Gefechtsstand *m*; — company — Kompanietrupp *m*; — divisional — Divisions-gefechtsstand *m*, -hauptquartier *n*; — regimental — Regimentsstab *m*; — company *n.* Stabskompanie *f*; — wing *n.* Unterstab *m.*

Headstrong [hed'strong] *a.* halsstarrig.

Headway [hed'wei] *n.* Vorwärtsbewegung *f*, Fortschritt *m.*   [zu Kopf steigend.

Heady [he'di] *a.* berauschend,

Heal [hihl] *vt. i.* heilen.

Health [helth] *n.* Gesundheit *f*; — insurance *n.* Krankenversicherung f; — resort n. Kurort m.

Healthy [hel'thi] a. gesund.

Heap [hihp] n. Haufe m, Menge f; — up vt. aufhäufen.

Hear [hihr] vt. i. hören, anhören, abhören (lesson), erfahren (learn).

Hearing [hih'ring] n. Hören n, Gehör n, Hörweite f (distance), Verhör n (law).

Hearken [bahrkn] vt. i. horchen, lauschen.

Hearse [hArss] n. Leichenwagen m. [wagen m.

Heart [hahrt] n. Herz n, Kern n, Mut m (courage); —'s content n. Herzenslust f; — breaking a. herzbrechend; — broken a. zu Tode betrübt, tief bekümmert; —burn n. Sod m, Sodbrennen n; — disease f. Herzkrankheit f; — failure n. Herzschlag m; —felt a. herzlich, innig; —rending a. herz-zerreissend; — searchings n. pl. Prüfung des Herzens f; — shaped a. herzförmig; — stirring a. herzgreifend; —to—a. freimütig, aufrichtig.

Hearten [bahrtn] vt. aufmuntern, Mut machen.

Hearth [bahrth] n. Herd m; — brush n. Kaminbesen m; — rug n. Kaminvorleger m; —stone n. Herdstein m. [lich.

Heartily [bahr'tili] ad. herzlich.

Heartiness [bahr'ti-ness] n. Herzlichkeit f, Gesundheit f.

Heartless [bahrt'less] a. herzlos, gefühllos.

Heartlessness [bahrt'lessness] n. Herzlosigkeit f.

Hearty [bahr'ti] a. herzlich, warm, stark, frisch.

Heat [hiht] n. Hitze f; vt. heizen; — resisting a. hitzebeständig; — wave n. Hitzewelle f.

Heater [hih'ter] n. Heizvorrichtung f, Heizkörper m, Ofen m.

Heath [hihth] n. Heide f.

Heidekraut n (heather); — cock n. Birkhahn m.

Heathen [hih'dhAn] n. Heide m, Heidin f; a. heidnisch.

Heather [he'dher] n. Heidekraut n, Erika f.

Heating [hih'ting] n. Heizung f; — apparatus n. Heizapparat m; — installation n. Heizungsanlage f.

Heave [hihw] vt. heben; i. heben, schwellen.

Heaven [hewn] n. Himmel m.

Heavenly [hewn'li] a. himmlisch.

Heaviness [he'wi-ness] n. Schwere f, Gewicht n.

Heavy [he'wi] a., **heavily** ad. schwer, schwerfällig, mühsam; — gun n. überschweres, schwerstes Geschütz (mil.); — industry n. Schwerindustrie f.

Heckle [hekl] vt. durchhecheln.

Hectic [hek'tik] a. fiebernd, wild, leidenschaftlich erregt.

Hectogramme [hek'togram] n. Hektogramm n.

Hectolitre [hek'to-lih'ter] n. Hektoliter n.

Hectometre [hek'to-mih'ter] n. Hektometer n.

Hedge [hedzh] n. Hecke f, Zaun m; vt. einzäunen; i. sich verteidigen, sich decken (com.), sich drücken, auf beiden Seiten wetten (turf).

Hedgehog [hedzh'hog] n. Igel m; — position n. Igelstellung f (mil.). [Hecke f, Zaun m.

Hedgerow [dedzh'rou] n. Hecke f, Zaun m.

Heed [hihd] vt. achten; n. Acht f, Aufmerksamkeit f.

Heedful [hihd'ful] a. achtsam.

Heedless [hihd'less] a. achtlos.

Heel [hihl] n. Ferse f, Absatz m (shoe), Hacken m (shoe, stocking); vt. mit Absätzen versehen, flecken.

Heel [hihl] vi. krängen, sich auf die Seite legen (nav.).

Hegemony [he-ge'mo-ni] *n.* Oberherrschaft *f*, Hegemonie *f.*
Heifer [he'fer] *n.* Färse *f.*
Height [hait] *n.* Höhe *f*, Höhepunkt *m.* [steigern.
Heighten [haitn] *vt.* erhöhen,
Heinous [hei'nAss] *a.* abscheulich.
Heinousness [hei'nAss-ness] *n.* Verruchtheit *f.*
Heir [eh'er] *n.* Erbe *m.*
Heiress [eh'A-ress] *n.* Erbin *f.*
Heirloom [eh'er-lum] *n.* Erbstück *n.*
Helicopter [he'li-kop-ter] *n.* Windmühlen-, Drehflügel-flugzeug *n*, Hubschrauber *m*, Schraubenflugzeug *n.*
Hell [hel] *n.* Hölle *f.*
Hellish [he'lisch] *a.* höllisch.
Helm [helm] *n.* Steuerruder *n*, Helm *m*, Pinne *f.*
Helmet [hel'mit] *n.* Helm *m.* Sturzhelm *m* (*av., etc.*); Balaclava —, woollen — Wind-, Sturmhaube *f.* [Steuermann *m.*
Helmsman [helms'mAn] *n.*
Help [help] *n.* Hilfe *f*, Beistand *m*; *vt.* helfen, unterstützen, beistehen; *i.* helfen; *r.* sich bedienen.
Helper [hel'per] *n.* Helfer *m.*
Helpful [help'ful] *a.* hilfreich.
Helpless [help'less] *a.*, **-ly** *ad.* hilflos.
Helplessness [help'less-ness] *n.* Hilfslosigkeit *f.* [säumen.
Hem [hem] *n.* Saum; *vt.*
Hemisphere [he'miss-fih-er] *n.* Halbkugel *f*, Hemisphäre *f.*
Hemlock [hem'lok] *n.* Schierling *m.*
Hemp [hemp] *n.* Hanf *m*; — seed *n.* Hanfsame *m.*
Hempen [hem'pAn] *a.* hanfen, hänfen.
Hemstitch [hem'stitsch] *n.* Hohlsaum *m*; *vt.* mit Hohlsaum nähen.
Hen [hen] *n.* Henne *f*, Weibchen *n*; — house *n.* Hühnerstall *m*; —pecked *a.* unter dem Pantoffel stehend; — roost *n.* Hühnerstange *f.*
Hence [henss] *ad.* von hier. daraus, daher.
Henceforth [henss'fOrth],
Henceforward [henss'fOr;-uerd] *ad.* von nun an.
Henchman [hensch'mAn] *n.* Anhänger *m*, Diener *m.*
Her [hAr] *pn.* sie, ihr; *a.* ihr.
Herb [hArb] *n.* Kraut *n.*
Herd [hArd] *n.* Herde *f.*
Herdsman [hArds'man] *n.* Hirt *m.*
Here [hier] *ad.* hier, hieher.
Hereabouts [hier-A-bautss'] *ad.* hier herum.
Hereafter [hier-ahf'ter] *ad.* hiernach, künftig; *n.* Jenseits *n.* das künftige Leben. [durch.
Hereby [hier-bai'] *ad.* hier-
Hereditary [hi-re'di-tA-ri] *a.* erblich. [blichkeit *f.*
Heredity [hi-re'di-ti] *n.* Er-
Hereof [hier-ow'] *ad.* hiervon.
Heresy [he'ri-ssi] *n.* Ketzerei *f.*
Heretic [he'ri-tik] *n.* Ketzer *m.* [hierauf.
Hereto [hi'er-tu] *ad.* hierzu,
Hereupon [hier-A-pon'] *ad.* darauf.
Herewith [hier-uith'] *ad.* hiermit, anbei, beigefügt (*com.*).
Heritable [he'ri-tAbl] *a.* erbfähig, erblich; — property *n.* Erbbesitz *m.*
Heritage [he'ri-tidzh] *n.* Erbschaft *f*, Erbe *n.*
Hermetical [her-me'tikl] *a*, **-ly** *ad.* luftdicht; —ly sealed, luftdicht verschlossen. [ler *m.*
Hermit [hAr'mit] *n.* Einsied-
Hernia [hAr'ni-A] *n.* Bruch *m.*
Heroic [hi-rou'ik] *a.* heldenmütig.
Heroin [he'ro-in] *n.* Heroin *n.*
Heroine [he'ro-in] *n.* Heldin *f.*
Heroism [he'ro-ism] *n.* Heldenmut *m.*
Heron [he'rAn] *n.* Reiher *m.*
Herring [he'ring] *n.* Hering *m*; red — Bück(l)ing *m*; —

bone n. Heringsgräte f; —
bone gear n. Pfeilradgetriebe
n (tec.). [das ihrige.
Hers [hArs] pn. ihr, der, die,
Herself [hAr-sself'] pn. sie,
ihr, sich selbst.
Hesitancy [he'si-tAn-ssi] n.
Zögern n, Unschlüssigkeit f.
Hesitant [he'si-tAnt] a.
zögernd, unentschlossen.
Hesitate [he'si-teit] vi. stock-
en, zögern, unschlüssig sein,
Bedenken tragen.
Hesitating [he'si-tei-ting] a.
-ly ad. unschlüssig, zaudernd.
Hesitation [he'si-tei'schAn]
n. Zögern n, Unschlüssigkeit f.
Heterodox [he'tA-ro-dox] a.
irrgläubig.
Heterodyne [he'tA-ro-dain]
n. Überlagerer m (rad.) ; a.
Schwebungs-, Überlagerungs-.
Heterogeneous [he-te-ro-
dzhih'ni-Ass] a. ungleichartig,
verschiedenartig.
Hew [hjuh] vt. hauen ; —
down, fällen. [eck n.
Hexagon [hex'Agn] n. Sechs-
Hey-day [hei'dei] n. Blüte-
zeit f. [überwintern.
Hibernate [hai'ber-neit] vi.
Hiccup [hi'kAp] n. Schlucken
n ; vi. den Schlucken haben.
Hide [haid] vt. verbergen, ver-
stecken ; i. sich verbergen.
Hide [haid] n. Haut f, Fell n ;
— bound a. engherzig.
Hideous [hi'di-Ass] a. häss-
lich, scheusslich.
Hideousness [hi'di-Ass-ness]
n. Scheusslichkeit f.
Hiding [hi'ding] n. Verber-
gen n, Versteck n ; — place n.
Schlupfwinkel m.
Higgle [higl] vi. feilschen.
Higgledy-piggledy [higl'-
di-pigl'di] a. durcheinander.
High [hai] a. hoch, gross, bedeutend ; — altitude flight n.
Höhenflug m ; — angle fire n.
Steilfeuer n (mil.) ; —brow n.
Schöngeist m, Purist m, Intel-
lektuelle(r) m ; — class a.
erstklassig, vorzüglich ; —
command n. Heeres-führung f.
-leitung f ; — court n. Land-
gericht n ; — explosive n.
Sprengstoff m ; — explosive
shell n. Brisanz-granate f
-geschoss n ; — flown a. hochtrabend ; — frequency n.
Hochfrequenz f ; — handed a.
anmassend, willkürlich ; —
heeled a. mit hohen Absätzen ;
-länder m. Hochländer m ;
— lands n. pl. Hochland n ;
— level railway n. Hochbahn
f ; —lights n. pl. Glanzlichter
n. pl ; — minded a. edel, hochmütig, stolz ; — performance
n. Höchstleistung f ; — placed
a. hochgestellt, vornehm ; —
pressure n. Hochdruck m ; —
road n. Landstrasse f ; —
speed a. Schnell ..., Schnell-
läufer ... ; — speed planer n.
Schnellhobler m ; — speed
wireless n. Schnellfunk m ; —
spirited a. munter, stolz ; —
tea n. Tee m. mit Fleisch oder
Fisch-speisen ; — tension n.
Hochspannung f (el.) ; — tide
n. Hochwasser n, Flut f ; —
water n. Hochwasser n.
Highly [hai'li] ad. in hohem
Masse, höchst.
Highness [hai'ness] n. Hoheit
f, Höhe f. [strasse f.
Highway [hai'ueh] n. Land-
Hike [haik] vi. wandern.
Hiker [hai'ker] n. Wanderer m,
Wanderin f, Wandervogel m.
Hiking [hai'king] n. Wandern
n, Wandersport m.
Hilarious [hi-leh'ri-Ass] a.
heiter, lustig.
Hilarity [hi-læ'ri-ti] n. Heiter-
keit f, Lustigkeit f.
Hill [hil] n. Hügel m.
Hillock [hi'lok] n. Anhöhe f.
Hillside [hil'ssaid] n. Abhang
m.
Hilly [hi'li] a. hügelig ; —
country n. hügeliges Gelände.

Hilt [hilt] n. Heft n, Griff m.

Him [him] pn. ihn, ihm, den, dem.

Himself [himsself'] pn. er, sich selbst.

Hind [haind] n. Hirschkuh f.

Hind [haind] a. hinter; — leg n. Hinterbein n; — quarters n. pl. Hinterteil n, Hinterhand f (horse).

Hinder [hain'der] a. hinter.

Hinder [hin'der] vt. hindern, hemmen. [hinterst.

Hindmost [haind'mo̅ust] a.

Hindrance [hin'drAnss] n. Hindernis f.

Hinge [hindzh] n. Angel f, Scharnier n; vi. sich drehen; —d seat n. aufklappbares Sitzbrett.

Hinny [hi'ni] n. Maulesel m.

Hint [hint] n. Wink m, Andeutung f, Hinweis m; vt. i. andeuten, einen Wink geben.

Hip [hip] n. Hüfte f; — bath n. Sitzbad n.

Hip [hip] n. Hagebutte f.

Hippopotamus [hi-po-po'tA-mAss] n. Flusspferd n.

Hire [hai'er] n. Miete f, Pacht f, Lohn m; vt. mieten, pachten; on — mietweise f; — out v. vermieten; —d car n. Mietauto n, Mietwagen m.

Hireling [hai'er-ling] n. Mietling m.

Hire-purchase [hai'er-pAr'-tschAss] n. Kauf m. auf Abzahlung, Abzahlungs-geschäft n; — system n. Abzahlungssystem n. [das seinige.

His [his] pn. sein; der, die

Hiss [hiss] n. zischen.

Hissing [hi'sing] n. Zischen n.

Historian [hi-stō'ri-An] n. Geschichtsschreiber m.

Historical [hi-sto'rikl] a. geschichtlich.

History [hi'stA-ri] n. (Welt-) Geschichte f, Geschichtswissenschaft f. [schauspielerisch.

Histrionic [hi-stri-o'nik] a.

Hit [hit] n. Schlag m, Treffer m (mil., etc.); vt. i. schlagen, treffen.

Hitch [hitsch] n. Haken m, Schwierigkeit f, Störung f, Ruck m. Stich m (nav.); vt. haken, festmachen, sich sichern, feststecken.

Hitch-hike [hitsch'haik] vi. sich mitnehmen lassen, unentgeltlich im Auto fahren.

Hither [hi'dher] ad. hierher; — and thither, hin und her.

Hitherto [hi-dher-tuh'] ad. bisher.

Hive [haiw] n. Bienenstock m.

Hoar [hōr] a. weissgrau; — frost n. Reif m.

Hoard [hOrd] n. Schatz m, Vorrat m; vt. aufhäufen, sammeln, hamstern (food, etc.).

Hoarder [hOr'der] n. Hamster m.

Hoarding [hOr'ding] n. Bauzaun m, Bretter-, Reklamezaun m, Hamstern n.

Hoarse [hOrss] a. heiser.

Hoarseness [hOrss'ness] n. Heiserkeit f.

Hoary [hō'ri] a. altersgrau.

Hoax [houx] n. Täuschung f, Betrug m, dummer Streich m, Schwindel m; vt. anführen, zum besten haben, um die Nase herumführen.

Hob [hob] n. Kamineinsatz m.

Hobble [hobl] vi. humpeln; t. fesseln; — skirt n. Humpelrock m.

Hobbledehoy [hobl'di-heu'] n. linkischer Bursche.

Hobby [ho'bi] n. Steckenpferd n, Liebhaberei f; — horse n. Steckenpferd n.

Hobnail [hob'neil] n. Sohlennagel m, grober Schuhnagel; —ed a. mit Zwecken, Nägeln beschlagen.

Hob-nob [hob'nob] vi. freundschaftlich verkehren.

Hock [hok] n. Hochheimer m, Rheinwein m.

Hock [hok] n. Sprunggelenk n.

Hockey [ho'ki] n. Hockeyspiel n, Stockballspiel n.

Hodman [hod'mÅn] n. Handlanger m.   [hacken.

Hoe [hou] n. Hacke f; vt. behacken.

Hog [hog] n, Schwein n.

Hogshead [hogs'hed] n. Fass n, Oxtoft n (measure).

Hoist [heust] n. Aufzug m, Kran m, Hebe-maschine f, -werk n; vt. in die Höhe ziehen, aufhissen (nav.).

Hold [hould] n. Halt m, Schiffsraum m; vt. halten, enthalten, der Meinung sein; halten, gelten, sich bewähren.

Hold-all [hould'Ol] n. Reisenecessaire n.

Holder [houl'der] n. Inhaber m, Halter m, Spitze f (cigar.).

Holding [houl'ding] n. Besitz m, Pachtgut n (land).

Hole [houl] n. Loch n, Höhle f; vt. durchlöchern.

Holiday [ho'li-di] n. Festtag m, freier Tag; —s pl. Ferien pl.; — resort n. Badeort m, Kurort m.

Holiness [hou'li-ness] n. Heiligkeit f.

Holland [ho'lÅnd] n. ungebleichte Leinwand; —s pl. Wachholderbranntwein m.

Hollow [ho'lou] n. Höhle f, Mulde f; a. hohl; vt. aushöhlen.

Hollowness [ho'lou-ness] n. Hohlheit f, Wertlosigkeit f.

Hollow-ware [ho'lou-ueh'er] n. Hohlware f.

Holly [ho'li] n. Stechpalme f.

Holocaust [ho'lÅ-kOst] n. Gemetzel n.

Holy [hou'li] a. heilig.

Homage [ho'midzh] n. Huldigung f.

Home [houm] n. Heim n, Haus n, Vaterhaus n, Heimat f; a. — zu Hause; ad. heim, nach Hause; — waters pl. heimische Gewässer n, pl.

Homeliness [houm'li-ness] n. Einfachheit f, das Heimatliche.

Homely [houm'li] a. heimisch, einfach.

Home-made [houm'meid] a. inländisch, selbstgemacht, zu Hause gemacht.

Home-rule [houm'ruhl] n. Selbstverwaltung f.

Homesickness [houm'sik-ness] n. Heimweh n.

Homogeneous [ho-mo-dzhih'ni-Ass] a. gleichartig.

Honest [o'nist] a, -ly ad. ehrlich, redlich.

Honesty [o'nis-ti] n. Ehrlichkeit f, Redlichkeit f.

Honey [hÅ'ni] n. Honig m; — comb n. Honigwabe f, Flachspule f (rad.); — combed a. durchlöchert; — comb radiator n. Zellenkühler m (aut.).

Honeymoon [hÅ'ni-muhn] n. Hochzeitsreise f, Flitterwochen f, pl.   [n. Geissblatt n.

Honeysuckle [hÅ'ni-ssÅkl]

Honorary [o'nA-rA-ri] a. Ehren ...; — secretary n. unbesoldeter Schriftführer m.

Honour [o'ner] n. Ehre f, Auszeichnung f, Würde f, Ruf m, Ruhm m, Keuschheit f; vt. ehren, beehren, auszeichnen, honorieren, akzeptieren (com.); —s pl. Ehrenstellen f, pl. Ehrenbezeugungen f, pl., Honneurs pl. (bridge, dice.).

Honourable [o'nA-rAbl] a. ehrenvoll, ehrbar.

Hood [hud] n. Kapuze f, Kappe f, Verdeck n (aut.).

Hoodwink [hud'uingk] vt. verblenden, irreführen.

Hoof [huhf] n. Huf m.

Hook [huk] n. Haken m, Fischangel f; vt. einhaken, fangen, angeln; t. festhalten.

Hooked [hukt] a. krumm, hakig.   [Raufbold m.

Hooligan [huh'li-gÅn] n.

Hooliganism [huh'li-gÅnism] n. Gewalttätigkeit f, brutales Benehmen.

Hoop [huhp] n. Reifen m, Ring m; vt. mit Reifen belegen.

Hooping-cough [huh'ping-kof'] n. Keuchhusten m.

Hoot [huht] vi. schreien, heulen, hupen (aut.); n. Geheul n.

Hooter [huh'ter] n. Dampfpfeife f, Sirene f, Hupe f (aut.).

Hop [hop] n. Hopfen m; — kiln n. Hopfendarre f.

Hop [hop] n. Sprung m, Hupf m, Flug m (av.), Etappe f (av.); vi. hüpfen.

Hope [houp] n. Hoffnung f, Erwartung f, Vertrauen n; vt. i. hoffen.

Hopeful [houp'ful] a. hoffnungsvoll, vielversprechend.

Hopeless [houp'less] a. hoffnungslos.

Hopelessness [houp'less-ness] n. Hoffnungslosigkeit f.

Hopper [ho'per] n. Fülltrichter m, Schlammboot n.

Horde [hOrd] n. horde f.

Horizon [ho-raisn'] n Gesichtskreis m, Horizont m.

Horizontal [ho-ri-sontl'] a. waagerecht, liegend. [f. (aut.)

Horn [hOrn] n. Horn n, Hupe

Horned [hOrnd] a. gehörnt; — cattle n. Hornvieh n.

Hornet [hOr'nit] n. Hornisse f.

Horrible [ho'ribl] a. entsetzlich, schrecklich.

Horrid [ho'rid] a. gräulich, scheusslich.

Horrify [ho'ri-fai] vt. entsetzen, erschrecken. [n, Greuel m.

Horror [ho'rer] n. Entsetzen

Horse [hOrss] n. Pferd n, Ross n; Reiterei f (mil.), Ross n; — clothes n. Kleiderständer m; — on — back zu Pferde; — artillery n. reitende Artillerie; — box n. Pferdewagen m; — breaker n. Zureiter m; — chestnut n. Rosskastanie f; — collar n. Kumt n; — dealer

n. Pferdehändler m; — drawn a. bespannt; — flesh n. Pferdefleisch n; — fly n. Bremse f; — pond n. Schwemme f; — power n. Pferdestärke f; — race n. Pferderennen n; — racing n. Rennsport m; — radish n. Meerrettich m; — rug n. Pferdedecke f; — transport column n. Fahrabteilung f (mil.); — truck n. Pferdewagen m.

Horsehair [hOrss'heh-er] n. Rosshaar n. [Reiter m.

Horseman [hOrss'mAn] n.

Horseshoe [hOrss'schuh] n. Hufeisen n. [Reitgerte f.

Horsewhip [hOrss'huip] n.

Horticultural [hOr-ti-kAl'tschA-rAl] a. Garten . . . ; — show Gartenbauausstellung f.

Horticulture [hOr'ti-kAl'tscher] n. Gartenbau m, Blumenzucht f.

Horticulturist [hOr-ti-kAl'tschA-rist] n. Gartenkünstler m, Gärtner m.

Hose [hous] n. Schlauch m (pipe), Strümpfe m. pl. (stockings). [warenhändler m.

Hosier [hou'sier] n. Strumpf-

Hosiery [hou'si-A-ri] n. Strumpf-, Strick-waren f. pl.

Hospitable [ho'spi-tAbl] a. gastfreundlich, gastlich, gastfrei.

Hospital [ho'spitl] n. Krankenhaus n, Lazarett n (mil.); — matron n. Oberin f; — nurse n. Krankenschwester f; — ship n. Lazarettschiff n; — train n. Lazarettzug m.

Hospitality [ho-spi-tæ'li-ti] n. Gastfreundschaft f.

Host [houst] n. Wirt m, Gastgeber m.

Host [houst] n. Menge f, Schar f (crowd).

Host [houst] n. Hostie f (consecrated). [m.

Hostage [ho'stidzh] n. Geise-

Hostel [ho'stl [n. Pensionl

haus n; — youth — n. Jugendherberge f.

Hostess [hou'stess] n. Wirtin f.

Hostile [ho'stail] a. feindlich.

Hostilit'y [ho-sti'li-ti] n. Feindschaft; — ies pl. Feindseligkeiten f. pl.

Hot [hot] a. heiss; — blooded a. heissblütig; — headed a. hitzköpfig; — house n. Treibhaus n; — water bottle n. Wärmeflasche f.

Hotel [hou-tel'] n. Gasthof m, Hotel n; — industry n. Fremdenindustrie f; — keeper n. Gastwirt m; — manager m. Hoteldirektor m, Hotelier m.

Hound [haund] n. Jagdhund m; vt. hetzen.

Hour [au'er] n. Stunde f; per — pro Stunde; — hand n. Stundenzeiger m. [lich.

Hourly [au'er-li] a. ad. stünd-

House [hauss] n. Haus n, Wohnung f; — agent n. Häusermakler m; — boat n. Wohn-, Haus-boot n; — painter n. Anstreicher m; — rent n. Hausmiete f; — top n. Hausgiebel m.

House [hauz] vt. unterbringen.

Housebreaker [hauss'breiker] n. Abbruchunternehmer m (com.), Einbrecher m (thief).

Housebreaking [hauss'breiking] n. Abbruch m, Einbruch m.

Household [hauss'hould] n. Haushalt m, Haushaltung f.

Householder [hauss'houlder] n. Hausherr m.

Housekeeper [hauss'kih-per] n. Haushälterin f.

Housekeeping [hauss'kihping] n. Haushalten n.

Housemaid [hauss'meid] n. Hausmädchen n. [Hausfrau f.

Housewife [hauss'uaif] n.

Housewife [hA'ssif] n. Nähkasten m.

Housing [hau'sing] n. Woh-

nungswesen n, Unterbringung f; — scheme n. Siedlung f; — shortage n. Wohnungsnot f.

Hovel [howl] n. elende Hütte.

Hover [ho'wer] vi. schweben.

How [hau] ad. wie.

However [hau-e'wer] ad. wie auch immer, jedoch, aber; cj. doch, dennoch, gleichwohl.

Howitzer [hau'it-sser] n. Haubitze f; heavy — n. Mörser m (mil.).

Howl [haul] vi. heulen; n. Geheul n. [n.

Howling [hau'ling] n. Geheul

Hoyden [heu'dAn] n. Range f.

Hub [hAb] n. Nabe f, Zentrum n.

Hubbub [hA'bAb] n. Lärm m, Getöse n.

Huddle [hAdl] vi. sich zusammendrängen.

Hue [hjuh] n. Farbe f.

Hue and cry [hjuh'And-krai'] n. Hetze f.

Huff [hAf] n. Schmollen n; vt. pusten; take the — übelnehmen.

Hug [hAg] n. Umarmung f; vt. umarmen, liebkosen, dicht hinfahren (nav.).

Huge [hjuhdzh] a. sehr gross, ungeheuer.

Hulk [hAlk] n. Schiffsgerippe n, altes Schiff.

Hull [hAl] n. Hülse f, Schale f; vt. enthülsen.

Hull [hAl] n. Schiffsrumpf m.

Hullabaloo [hA'lA-bA-luh] n. Tumult m, Lärm m.

Hum [hAm] vi. summen; — ming top n. Brummkreisel m.

Human [hjuh'mAn] a., -ly ad. menschlich, Mensch . . . ; — being n. Mensch m.

Humane [hjuh-mein'] a. menschenfreundlich, human.

Humanitarian [hjuh-mæni-teh'ri-An] n. Menschenfreund m; a. menschenfreundlich.

Humanity [hjuh-mæ'ni-ti] n.

Menschheit f (man), Menschlichkeit f (humane-ness), Humanität f.

Humble [hAmbI] a., **-ly** ad. demütig, niedrig, bescheiden; vt. demütigen, erniedrigen.

Humbug [hAm'bAg] n. Schwindel m, Mumpitz m.

Humdrum [hAm'drAm] a. eintönig, langweilig.

Humid [hjuh'mid] a. feucht.

Humidity [hjuh-mi'di-ti] n. Feuchtigkeit f. [demütigen.

Humiliate [hjuh-mi'li-eit] vt.

Humiliation [hjuh-mi-li-ei'-schAn] n. Demütigung f.

Humility [hjuh-mi'li-ti] n. Demut f. [kleiner Hügel.

Hummock [hA'mAk] n.

Humorist [hjuh'mA-rist] n. Spassvogel m.

Humorous [hjuh'mA-rAss] a. humoristisch, komisch.

Humour [hjuh'mer] n. Gemüts-stimmung f, Laune f, Humor m, Komik f; vt. willfahren.

Hump [hAmp] n. Buckel m.

Hunchback [hAnsch'bak] n. der Bucklige.

Hundred [hAn'drid] num. hundert.

Hunger [hAng'ger] n. Hunger m; vi. hungern.

Hungry [hAng'gri] a., **Hungrily** ad. hungrig.

Hunk [hAngk] n. dickes Stück grosse Scheibe. [jagen.

Hunt [hAnt] n. Jagd f; vt. i.

Hunter [hAn'ter] n. Jäger m, Jagdpferd n, Jagduhr f, Doppelkapseluhr f (watch).

Huntsman [hAntss'mAn] n. Jäger m. [Hindernis n.

Hurdle [hArdl] n. Hürde f,

Hurdy-gurdy [hAr'di-gAr'di] n. Bettlerleier f.

Hurricane [hA'ri-kein] n. Orkan m; — deck n. Sturmdeck n; — lamp n. Sturmlampe f. [tig.

Hurried [hA'rid] a. eilig, hastig.

Hurry [hA'ri] n. Eile f; vt.

eilig tun, beschleunigen; i. eilen; — up vi. sich beeilen.

Hurt [hArt] n. Verletzung f, Schaden m; vt. verletzen, schaden, weh tun; i. weh tun.

Hurtful [hArt'ful] a. schädlich.

Husband [hAs'bAnd] n. Ehemann m, Mann m; vt. haushälterisch umgehen mit, haushalten. [stillen.

Hush [hAsch] n. Stille f; vt.

Husk [hAsk] n. Hülse f, Schote f, Schale f; vt. schälen.

Husky [hA'ski] a. rauh, heiser.

Hussy [hA'ssi] n. Range f, Weibsbild n, Frauenzimmer n.

Hustle [hAssI] vt. drängen, sich drängen; n. Eile f.

Hut [hAt] n. Hütte f, Baracke f (mil.); vt. in Baracken unterbringen; —ted camp n. Barackenlager n.

Hutch [hAtsch] n. Kasten m, Stall m, Kohlenwagen m, Tonne f.

Hutment [hAt'mAnt] n. Baracke f; — camp n. Barackenlager n (mil.).

Hyacinth [hai'A-ssinth] n. Hyazinthe f.

Hybrid [hai'brid] n. Mischling m, Kreuzung f, Zwitter m; a. zwitterhaft. [hahn m.

Hydrant [hai'drAnt] n. Feuer-

Hydraulic [hai-drO'lik] a. hydraulisch, Wasserdruck...; **—s** n. pl. Hydraulik f; — power n. Wasserdruckkraft f.

Hydrochloric acid [hai-dro-klO'rik-æss'id] n. Salzsäure f.

Hydrogen [hai'dro-dzhAn] n. Wasserstoff m.

Hydrogenation [hai-dro-dzhe-nei'schAn] n. Hydrierung f; — plant n. Hydrierungsanlage f.

Hydro(pathic) [hai-dro-pæ'thik] n. Wasserheilanstalt f, Kurhaus n.

Hydrophobia [hai-dro-fo'bi-A] n. Wasserscheu f.

Hydroplane [hai'dro-plein] *n.* Wasserlandflugzeug *n*, Gleitboot *n.*	**Icing** [ai'ssing] *n.* Zuckerguss *m* ; Vereisung *f* (*av*.).
Hyena [hai-ih'nA] *n.* Hyäne *f.*	**Icy** [ai'ssi] *a.* eisig. [Begriff *m*.
Hygiene [hai'dzhihn] *n.* Gesundheitspflege *f.*	**Idea** [ai-dih'A] *n.* Idee *f.*
Hygienic [hai'dzhih'nik] *a.* gesundheitlich.	**Ideal** [ai-dih'All] *n.* Ideal *n* ; *a.* ideal, vorbildlich, fabelhaft.
Hymn [him] *n.* Kirchenlied *n* ; — book *n.* Gesangbuch *n.*	**Identical** [ai-den'tikl] *a.* -ly *ad.* einerlei, identisch.
Hymnal [him'nAl] *n.* Gesangbuch *n.* [strich *m*.	**Identify** [ai-den'ti-fai] *vt.* identifizieren, gleichsetzen, erkennen ; -ication *n.* Identifizierung *f*, Ausweis *m*, Legitimation *f.*
Hyphen [haifn] *n.* Binde	
Hypnotize [hip'no-tais] *vt.* hypnotisieren.	
Hypnotism [hip'no-tism] *n.* Hypnotismus *m.*	**Identity** [ai-den'ti-ti] *n.* Identität *f*, Gleichheit *f*, Persönlichkeit *f*; proof of — Legitimation *f*; — card *n.* Ausweis *m*, Kenn-karte *f*, Truppenausweis *m* (*mil*.) ; — disc *n.* Erkennungsmarke *f* (*mil*.) ; — number *n.* Kenn-nummer *f* (*mil*.). [ishn *m*.
Hypocrisy [hi-po'crA-ssi] *n.* Heuchelei *f.* [Heuchler *m*.	
Hypocrite [hi'po-krit] *n.*	
Hypocritical [hi-po-kri'tikl] *a.* heuchlerisch, scheinheilig.	
Hypo-sulphate [hai-po-sAl'feit] *n.* unterschwefelsaures Salz.	**Idiocy** [i'di-A-ssi] *n.* Blödsinn *m.*
	Idiom [i'di-Am] *n.* Spracheigenheit *f*, Idiom *n*, Sprache *f*, Mundart *f* ; -atic *a.* idiomatisch, mundartlich.
Hypo-sulphite [hai-po-sAl'fait] *n.* unterschwefligsaures Salz.	
Hypothesis [hai-po'thA-ssiss] *n.* Hypothese *f*, Annahme *f.*	**Idiot** [i'di-At] *n.* Idiot *m*, Schwachsinnige(r) *m*; -ic *a.* idiotisch, blödsinnig.
Hysteria [hi-stih'riA] *n.* Hysterie *f.* [hysterisch.	**Idle** [aidl] *n*, **Idly** *ad.* müssig, faul, unnütz ; -ness *n.* Müssiggang *m*, Faulheit *f* ; -r *n.* Müssiggänger *m*, Faulenzer *m.*
Hysterical [hi-ste'rikl] *a.*	

I

I [ai] *pn.* ich.	**Idolatry** [ai-do'lAt-ri] *n.* Abgötterei *f*, Götzendienst *m.*
Ice [aiss] *n.* Eis *n* ; — cream *n.* Speiseeis *n*, Gefrorenes *n.*	**Idolize** [ai'dA-lais] *vt.* vergöttern.
Ice-axe [aiss'æx] *n.* Eispichel *m.* [*m*.	**If** [if] *cj.* wenn, ob.
Iceberg [aiss'berg] *n.* Eisberg *n.*	**Ignite** [ig-nait'] *vt.* entzünden, anzünden ; *i.* sich entzünden; -ion *n.* Anzünden *n*, Zündung *f* (*aut*.); -ion cable *n.* Zündkabel *n* (*jet-plane*) ; -ion coils *m.pl.* Zündgeräte *n* (*jet-plane*) ; -ion spark *n.* Zündfunke *m.*
Ice-bound [aiss'baund] *a.* eingefroren.	
Ice-breaker [aiss'brei-ker] *n.* Eisbrecher *m.*	
Ice-plough [aiss'plau] *n.* Eispflug *m.*	**Ignoble** [ig-noubl'] *a*, **Ignobly** *ad.* unedel, niedrig.
Ice-rink [aiss'ringk] *n.* Kunsteisbahn *f.*	**Ignominious** [ig-nA-mi'niAss] *a.* schändlich.
Icicle [aiss'ikl] *n.* Eiszapfen *m.*	**Ignoramus** [ig-nA-rei'mAss] *n.* Ignorant *m.*

Ignoran'ce [ig'nA-rAnss] *n.* Unwissenheit *f*; -t *a.* unwissend.

Ignore [ig-nOr'] *vt.* nicht wissen, unbeachtet lassen.

Ill [il] *a. ad.* übel, krank; -advised *a.* unbesonnen; -behaved *a.* unartig; -favoured *a.* hässlich; -omened *a.* -starred *a.* unglücklich; -timed *a.* ungelegen, schlecht angebracht; -treat *vt.* misshandeln.

Illegal [i-lihgl'] *a.* ungesetzlich, rechtswidrig; -ity [i-li-gæ'li-ti] *n.* Ungesetzlichkeit *f*.

Illegib'le [i-le'dzhibl] *a.* unleserlich; -ility *n.* Unleserlichkeit *f*.

Illegitimacy [i-li-dzhi'ti-mA-ssi] *n.* Unrechtmässigkeit *f*, Unehelichkeit *f*; -te *a.* unehelich, unrechtmässig.

Illicit [i-li'ssit] *a.* unerlaubt.

Illiteracy [i-li'trA-ssi] *n.* Analphabetentum *n.* Unwissenheit *f*.

Illiterate [i-li'trit] *a.* ungelehrt; *n.* Analphabet *m.*

Illness [il'ness] *n.* Krankheit *f*.

Illogical [i-lo'dzhikl] *a.* unlogisch.

Illuminate [i-ljuh'mi-neit] *vt.* beleuchten, erleuchten, kolorieren; -ed signs *n.pl.* Lichtreklameschilder *n.pl.*; -ion *n.* Beleuchtung *f*, Erleuchtung *f*.

Illusion [i-ljuh'zhAn] *n.* Täuschung *f*.

Illusory [i-ljuh'sA-ri] *a.* illusorisch, täuschend.

Illustrate [i'lA-streit] *vt.* erläutern, illustrieren; -ion *n.* Erklärung *f*, Abbildung *f*, Illustration *f*, Beispiel *n.*; -ive *a.* erläuternd; -or *n.* Bilderzeichner *m.*

Image [i'midzh] *n.* Bild *n.*, Bildsäule *f*, Ebenbild *n.*, Vorstellung *f* (*in mind*).

Imaginable [i-mæ'dzhi-nAbl] *a.* vorstellbar, erdenklich; -ary *a.* eingebildet; -ation

n. Einbildung(skraft) *f*, Vorstellung *f*; -ative *a.* erfinderisch, schöpferisch; -e *vt.* sich einbilden, vorstellen, ersinnen.

Imbecil'e [im'bi-ssihl] *n.* Schwachsinnige(r) *m*; *a.* geistesschwach; -ity *n.* Geistesschwäche *f*.

Imbibe [im-baib'] *vt.* einsaugen.

Imbue [im-bjuh'] *vt.* durchtränken, erfüllen.

Imitate [i'mi-teit] *vt.* nachahmen; -ion *n.* Nachahmung *f*, Fälschung *f*; *a.* nachgemacht, künstlich; -ion leather *n.* Kunstleder *n*; -ion silk *n.* Kunstseide *f*; -ive *a.* nachahmend; -or *n.* Nachahmer *m.*

Immaculate [i-mæ'kjuh-lit] *a.* unbefleckt.

Immanent [i'mA-nent] *a.* innewohnend.

Immaterial [i-mA-tih'ri-Al] *a.* unwesentlich, unkörperlich.

Immature [i-mA-tjuh'er] *a.* unreif; -ity *n.* Unreife *f*.

Immeasurable [i-me'zhA-rAbl] *a.* unermesslich.

Immediate [i-mih'di-At] *a.* -ly *ad.* unmittelbar, augenblick, sofortig; - readiness *n.* Alarmbereitschaft *f* (*mil.*).

Immemorial [i-mi-mO'ri-Al] *a.* undenklich.

Immens'e [i-menss'] *a.* unermesslich, ungeheuer; -ity *n.* Unermesslichkeit *f*.

Immers'e [i-mArss'] *vt.* eintauchen; -ion *n.* Eintauchen *n*; - heater *n.* Tauchsieder *m.*

Immigra'nt [i'mi-grAnt] *n.* Einwanderer *m*; -te *vi.* einwandern; -tion *n.* Einwanderung *f*; - quota *n.* Einwanderungskontingent *n.*

Imminence [i'mi-nAnss] *n.* Bevorstehen *n.*

Imminent [i'mi-nAnt] *a.* bevorstehend, drohend.

Immobil'e [i-mou'bail] *a.* unbeweglich; -ity *n.* Unbeweglichkeit *f*; -ize *vt.* festlegen, fesseln.

Immoderate [i-mo'dA-rit] *a.* -ly *ad.* unmässig, übermässig, übertrieben.

Immodest [i-mo'dist] *a.* unbescheiden, unanständig; -y; *n.* Unbescheidenheit *f*, Unanständigkeit *f*.

Immoral [i-mo'rAl] *a.* unmoralisch, unsittlich; -ity *n.* Unsittlichkeit *f*.

Immortal [i-mOr'tAl] *a.* unsterblich; -ity *n.* Unsterblichkeit *f*; -ize *vt.* unsterblich machen, verewigen.

Immovable [i-muh'wAbl] *a.* unbeweglich.

Immune [i-mjun'] *a.* geschützt, frei, immun; -ity *n.* Freiheit *f*, Unansteckbarkeit *f*, Immunität *f* (*disease*); -ization *n.* Immunisierung *n*, Impfen *n*, gegen Diphtherie; -ize *vt.* immunisieren, impfen.

Immure [i-mju'er] *vt.* einmauern.

Immutable [i-mjuh'tAbl] *a.* unveränderlich [Schelm *m.*

Imp [imp] *n.* Teufelchen *n.*

Impact [im'pækt] *n.* Zusammenstoss *m*, Einschlag *m* (*mil.*); angle of - *n.* Auftreffwinkel *m* (*mil.*); point of - *n.* Aufschlagpunkt *m*, Auftreffpunkt *m* (*mil.*).

Impair [im-pe'er] *vt.* beeinträchtigen, schwächen, schaden, verringern. [sen.

Impale [im-pehl'] *vt.* aufspiessen.

Impalpable [im-pel'pAbl] *a.* unfassbar, unfühlbar. [teilen.

Impart [im-pahrt'] *vt.* mitteilen.

Impartial [im-pahr'schAl] *a.* -ly *ad.* unparteiisch, objektiv; -ity *n.* Unparteilichkeit *f.*

Impassable [im-pah'ssAbl] *a.* ungangbar, unfahrbar (*road*), unüberschreitbar (*river*).

Impassive [im-pæ'ssiw] *a.* unempfindlich; -ness *n.* Unempfindlichkeit *f.*

Impatience [im-pei'schAnss] *n.* Ungeduld *f*; -t *a.* ungeduldig.

Impeach [im-pihtsch'] *vt.* beschuldigen; -ment *n.* Anklage *f*, Anfechtung *f.*

Impecunious [im-pi-kjuh'ni-Ass] *a.* unbemittelt. [dern.

Impede [im-pihd'] *vt.* verhindern.

Impediment [im-pe'di-mAnt] *n.* Hindernis *n.*

Impel [im-pel'] *vt.* antreiben.

Impending [im-pen'ding] *a.* bevorstehend, drohend.

Impenetrable [im-pe'ni-trAbl] *a.* undurchdringlich, unerforschlich; -ility *n.* Undurchdringlichkeit *f.*

Impenitence [im-pe'ni-tAnss] *n.* Verstocktheit *f*; -t *a.* verstockt, unbussfertig.

Imperative [im-pe'rA-tiw] *a.* zwingend, dringend, gebieterisch; *n.* Imperativ *m*, Befehlsform *f.* [till *a.* unmerklich.

Imperceptible [im-per-ssep'-**Imperfect** [im-pAr'fekt] *a.* unvollkommen, unvollständig, mangelhaft, defekt; *n.* Imperfekt *n*, Vergangenheitsform *f* (*verb*); -ion *n.* Unvollkommenheit *f*, Fehler *m.*

Imperial [im-pih'ri-Al] *a.* kaiserlich, Reichs ...; -ism *n.* Imperialismus *m*, Weltmachtpolitik *f*; -ist *n.* Imperialist *m.*

Imperil [im-pe'ril] *vt.* gefährden. [gebieterisch.

Imperious [im-pih'ri-Ass] *a.*

Imperishable [im-pe'risch-Abl] *a.* unvergänglich, unsterblich.

Impermeable [im-pAr'mi-Abl] *a.* undurchdringlich.

Impersonal [im-pAr'ssA-nAl] *a.* unpersönlich; -te *vt.* verkörpern; -tion *n.* Verkörperung *f.*

Impertinence [im-pAr'ti-nAnss] *n.* Unverschämtheit *f*; -t *a.* unverschämt, frech.

Imperturbability [im-per-

ter-bA-bi'li-ti] n. Gelassenheit
f; **-le** a. unerschütterlich, gelassen. [a. undurchdringlich.]
Impervious [im-pÄr'wi-Ass]
Impetuo'sity [im-pe-tju-o'-
ssi-ti] n. Ungestüm n; **-us** a.
heftig, ungestüm.
Impetus [im'pi-tAss] n. Antrieb m, Anregung f, Treib-
kraft f.   [losigkeit f.
Impiety [im-pai'A-ti] n. Gott-
Impinge [im-pindzh'] vi. stossen, verstossen.   [los.
Impious [im'pi-Ass] a. gott-
Implacab'ility [im-plæ-kA-
bi'li-ti] n. Unversöhnlichkeit f;
-le a. unversöhnlich.
Implant [im-plahnt'] vt. einpflanzen.
Implement [im'pli-mAnt] n.
Werkzeug n, Gerät n, Zubehör n.
Implicate [im'pli-keit] vt.
verwickeln; **-ion** n. Folgerung
f, Verwickelung f; **by –** stillschweigend.
Implicit [im-pli'ssit] a., **-ly** ad.
unbedingt, stillschweigend,
eingeschlossen.   [begriffen.
Implied [im-plaid'] a. mitin-
Implore [im-plOr'] vt. anflehen, beschwören.
Imply [im-plai'] vt. einbegreifen, in sich schliessen, andeut-
en, zu verstehen geben.
Impolite [im-po-lait'] a. unhöflich; **-ness** n. Unhöflichkeit f.
Impolitic [im-po'li-tik] a. unklug, unpolitisch, undiploma-
tisch.
Imponderable [im-pon'dA-
rAbl] a. unwägbar, unberechenbar.
Import [im-pOrt'] vt. einführ-
ren, importieren (goods), mit
sich bringen, bedeuten.
Import [im'pOrt] n. Einfuhr f,
Import m, Bedeutung f, Sinn
m; **-s** n.pl. Einfuhrwaren f.pl;
– licence n. Einfuhrerlaubnis f.
Importance [im-pOr'tAnss]

n. Wichtigkeit f, Bedeutung f;
-t a. wichtig, bedeutend.
Importation [im-pOr-tei'-
schAn] n. Wareneinfuhr f
Importer [im-pOr'ter] n.
Wareneinführer m, Import-
eur m.
Importun'ate [im-pOr'tju-
nit] a. zudringlich; **-ity** n. Zu-
dringlichkeit f.
Impose [im-pous'] vt. auflegen, auferlegen; **i. – upon**
betrügen; **-ing** a. imponierend,
eindrucksvoll; **-ition** n. Auferlegung f, Auflegung f, Steuer
f (tax), Strafarbeit f (task), Betrug m (deceit).
Impossib'ility [im-po-ssi-bi'-
li-ti] n. Unmöglichkeit f; **-le** a.
unmöglich.
Impost [im'poust] n. Steuer f,
Kämpfer m (building).
Impost'or [im-po'ster] n. Betrüger m, Schwindler m; **-ure**
n. Betrug m.
Impotence [im'po-tAnss] n.
Unvermögen n, Unfähigkeit f,
Impotenz f; **-t** a. unvermög-
end, unfähig, impotent.
Impound [im-paund'] vt. einschliessen, aufstauen (water),
mit Beschlag belegen (law).
Impoverish [im-po'wA-risch]
vt. arm machen, erschöpfen
(land), **-ment** n. Verarmung f,
Erschöpfung f.
Impracticab'ility [im-præk-
ti-kA-bi'li-ti] n. Untunlichkeit
f, Unmöglichkeit f, Unweg-
samkeit f (road); **-le** a. unaus-
führbar, unmöglich, unwegsam, unübenschreitbar (river,
etc.).
Impregnab'ility [im-preg-
nA-bi'li-ti] n. Uneinnehmbar-
keit f; **-le** a. uneinnehmbar.
Impregnate [im-preg'neit]
vt. durchtränken, befruchten,
imprägnieren; **-d paper** n. Ol-
papier n (el.); **-ion** n. Sättigung
f, Durchtränkung f, Befruchtung f.

Impresario [im-pre-ssah'ri-ou] n. (Theater-)Unternehmer m.

Impress [im'press] n. Eindruck m, Stempel m, Zeichen n.

Impress [im-press'] vt. eindrücken, Eindruck machen, einprägen; -ion n. Eindruck m, Abdruck m, Ein-drücken n, Auflage f (book); -ion cylinder n. Druckzylinder m (tec.); -ionable a. empfänglich, leicht zu beeinflussen; -ionism n. Impressionismus m, Eindruckskunst f; -ionist n. Impressionist m, Eindruckskünstler m; -ionistic a. impressionistisch, Eindruckskunst . . .; -ive a. ergreifend, imponierend.

Imprint [im-print'] vt. aufdrücken; n. Druckvermerk m.

Imprison [im-pri'sAn] vt. einkerkern; -ment n. Haft f, Einkerkerung f.

Improbability [im-pro-bA-bi'li-ti] n. Unwahrscheinlichkeit f; -able a. unwahrscheinlich.

Impromptu [im-promp'tju] a. ad. aus dem Stegreif.

Improper [im-pro'per] a. unanständig, unpassend, ungehörig; -riety n. Unschicklichkeit f, Ungehörigkeit f.

Improve [im-pruhw'] vt. verbessern, veredeln, bilden; i. sich verbessern, sich bessern (health), sich vervollkommnen (knowledge, etc.); -ment n. Verbesserung f, Besserung f, Ausbildung f.

Improvidence [im-pro'wi-dAnss] n. Leichtsinn m; -t a. leichtsinnig, unvorsichtig.

Improvisation [im-pro-wai-sei'schAn] n. Improvisation f; -e vt. improvisieren, ohne Vorbereitung tun, aus dem Stegreif dichten, tun; -ed a. behelfsmässig, Not . . .; -d bridge n. Notbrücke f.

Imprudence [im-pruh'-

dAnss] n. Unklugheit f, Unbedachtsamkeit f; -t a. -tly ad. unvorsichtig, unklug.

Imprudence [im'pju-dAnss] n. Frechheit f, Unverschämtheit f; -t a. frech, unverschämt.

Impugn [im-pjuhn'] vt. anfechten, antasten.

Impulse [im'pAlss] n. Antrieb m, Anregung f, Anstoss m, Drang m, Stromstoss m (el.); -ion n. Stoss m, Antrieb m; -ive a. erregbar, impulsiv; -iveness n. Erregbarkeit f, Impulsivität f.

Impunity [im-pjuh'ni-ti] n. Straflosigkeit f.

Impure [im-pjuh'er] a. unrein, unsauber, unzüchtig; -ity n. Unreinheit f, Unreinlichkeit f, Unsauberkeit f, Verunreinigung f (pollution).

Imputation [im-pju-tei'schAn] n. Zurechnung f, Beschuldigung f; -e vt. zurechnen, beimessen.

In [in] pr. in, an, auf; ad. hinein, herein.

Inability [i-nA-bi'li-ti] n. Unfähigkeit f.

Inaccessibility [in-æk-sse-ssi-bi'li-ti] n. Unzugänglichkeit f; -le a. unzugänglich, nicht zu erlangen.

Inaccuracy [in-æ'kju-rA-ssi] n. Ungenauigkeit f, Unrichtigkeit f; -te a. -y ad. ungenau, unrichtig.

Inaction [in-æk'schAn] n. Untätigkeit f.

Inactive [in-æk'tiw] a. untätig, leblos, träge, flau (com.).

Inadequacy [in-æ'di-kuA-ssi] n. Unzulänglichkeit f; -te a. unzulänglich, ungenügend.

Inadmissibility [in-Ad-mi-ssi-bi'li-ti] n. Unzulässigkeit f; -le a. unzulässig, unstatthaft.

Inadvertence [in-ad-wAr'tAnss] n. Unachtsamkeit f; -t a. -tly ad. unachtsam.

Inalienable [in-ei'li-A-nAbl] *a.* unveräusserlich.

Inalterable [in-Ol'tA-rAbl] *a.* unveränderlich.

Inane [in-ein'] *a.* geistlos, albern. [leblos.

Inanimate [in-æ'ni-mit] *a.*

Inanit'ion [in-A-ni'schAn] *n.* Leere *f*, Schwäche *f*; -y *n.* Nichtigkeit *f*, Albernheit *f*.

Inapplicab'ility [in-æ-pli-kA-bi'li-ti] *n.* Unanwendbarkeit *f*; -le *a.* unanwendbar.

Inappreciable [in-A-prih'-schi-Abl] *a.* unwesentlich, unwichtig.

Inappropriate [in-A-prou'-pri-it] *a.* ungeeignet, unpassend.

Inapt [in-æpt'] *a.* unpassend, ungeeignet, untauglich.

Inarticulate [in-ahr-ti'kju-lit] *a.* undeutlich, unverständlich, ungegliedert, unvernehmlich.

Inartistic [in-ahr-ti'stik] *a.* unkünstlerisch.

Inasmuch [in-As-mAtsch'] *ad.* da, weil.

Inattention [in-A-ten'schAn] *n.* Unaufmerksamkeit *f*.

Inattentive [in-A-ten'tiw] *a.* unaufmerksam, nachlässig.

Inaudib'ility [in-O-di-bi'li-ti] *n.* Unhörbarkeit *f*; -le *a.* unhörbar.

Inaugura'l [in-O'gju-rAl] *a.* einweihungs . . .; -te *vt* einweihen, eröffnen, beginnen; -tion *n.* Einweihung *f*, Eröffnung *f*.

Inauspicious [in-O-spi'schAss] *a.* ungünstig, unglücklich.

Inboard [in'bOrd] *a. ad.* im Schiffsraum, innenbords [en.

Inborn [in'bOrn] *a.* angeboren.

Inbreeding [in'brih-ding] *n.* Inzucht *f*.

Incalculable [in-kæl'kju-lAbl] *a.* unberechenbar.

Incandescen'ce [in-kAn-de'ssAnss] *n.* Weissglut *f*; -t *a.*

weissglühend; - light *n.* Glühlicht *n*; - mantle *n.* Glühstrumpf *m*.

Incapab'ility [in-kei-pA-bi'li-ti] *n.* Unfähigkeit *f*, Untauglichkeit *f*; -le *a.* unfähig, untauglich, untüchtig.

Incapacit'ate [in-kA-pæ'ssiteit] *vt.* unfähig machen; -y *n.* Unfähigkeit *f*, Schwäche *f*.

Incarcerate [in-kahr'ssA-reit] *vt.* einkerkern.

Incarnat'e [in-kahr'nit] *a.* fleischgeworden; -ion *n.* Menschenwerdung *f*.

Incendiar'ism [in-ssen'di-A-rism] *n.* Brandstiftung *f*; -y *a.* brandstifterisch, aufrührerisch; *n.* Brandstifter *m*, Aufwiegler *m*; -y bomb *n.* Brandbombe *f*; -y shell *n.* Brandgranate *f*, Brandgeschoss *n*.

Incense [in'ssenss] *n.* Weihrauch *m*.

Incense [in-ssenss'] *vt.* erzürnen, aufbringen.

Incentive [in-ssen'tiw] *n.* Ansporn *n*, Antrieb *m*.

Inception [in-ssep'schAn] *n.* Anfang *m*, Inangriffnahme *f*.

Incessant [in-ssess'Ant] *a.* unaufhörlich, beständig.

Incest [in'ssest] *n.* Blutschande *f*.

Inch [insch] *n.* Zoll *m*; - -tape *n.* Zollband *n*, Messband *n*.

Incident [in'ssi-dAnss] *n.* Auftreten *n*, Vorkommen *n*; - of taxation *n.* Steuerlast *f*; -al *a.* Zwischenfall *m*, Vorfall *m*; -tal *a*, -ly *ad.* gelegentlich, beiläufig, begleitend; - expenses *n. pl.* Nebenausgaben *f.pl.*

Incinerate [in-ssi'nA-reit] *vt.* einäschern; -ion *n.* Einäscherung *f*; -or *n.* Verbrennungsofen *m*.

Incipient [in-ssi'pi-Ant] *a.* anfangend, einleitend.

Incise [in-ssais'] *vt.* einschneiden. [schnitt *m*.

Incision [in-ssi'zhAn] *n.* Ein-

Incisive [in-ssai'ssiw] a. einschneidend, scharf.

Incite [in-ssait'] vt. anreizen, anstacheln, aufhetzen; -ment n. Anreizung f.

Incivility [in-ssi-wi'li-ti] n. Unhöflichkeit f.

Inclemen'cy [in-kle'mAn-ssi] n. Unbilden f.pl; -t a. rauh.

Inclination [in-kli-net'schAn] n. Neigung f, Hang m.

Incline [in-klain'] vi. sich neigen; t. neigen.

Incline [in'klain] n. Abhang m, Hang m, Gefälle n (mine).

Inclined [in-klaind'] a. geneigt, schräg, schief; --hoist n. Schrägaufzug m (tec.); --plane n. schiefe Ebene (physics), Auffahrt f, Rampe f (vehicles).

Inclu'de [in-kluhd'] vt. einschliessen, enthalten; -ded in begriffen, einschliesslich; -sion n. Einschliessung f; -sive a. einschliesslich, eingeschlossen, inklusive.

Incognito [in-kog'ni-tou] a. unerkannt, unter fremdem Namen.

Incoheren'ce [in-ko-hih'rAnss] n. Mangel an Zusammenhang m; -t a. zusammenhanglos, unzusammenhängend, unverständlich.

Income [in'kAm] n. Einkommen n, Einkünfte f.pl; --tax n. Einkommensteuer f.

Incommensurate [in-ko-menn'schA-rit] a. unvereinbar, in keinem Verhältnis zu.

Incommode [in-kA-moud'] vt. beschweren, stören.

Incommutable [in-kA-mjuh'tAbl] a. unveränderlich.

Incomparable [in-kom'pA-rAbl] a. unvergleichlich.

Incompatib'ility [in-kAm pæ-ti-bi'li-ti] n. Unverträglichkeit f; -le a. unverträglich, unvereinbar.

Incompeten'ce [in-kom'pi-

tAnss] n. Unfähigkeit f, Untauglichkeit f, Unzuständigkeit f (law); -t a. unfähig, unbrauchbar, unzuständig (court).

Incomplete [in-kAm-pliht'] a. unvollständig, unvollkommen; -ness n. Unvollständigkeit f.

Incomprehensib'ility [in-kom-pri-hen-ssi-bi'li-ti] n. Unbegreiflichkeit f; -le a. unbegreiflich.

Incompressible [in-kAm pre'ssibl] a. nicht zusammendrückbar.

Inconceivable [in-kAn-ssih'wAbl] a. unbegreiflich, undenkbar.

Inconclusive [in-kAn-kluh'siw] a. ohne Beweiskraft.

Incongru'ity [in-kong-gruh'i-ti] n. Widersinnigkeit f, Ungereimtheit f; -ous a. nicht übereinstimmend, ungereimt.

Inconsiderable [in-kAn-ssi dA-rAbl] a. unbeträchtlich, unbedeutend.

Inconsiderate [in-kAn-ssi dA-rit] a. rücksichtslos, unbedacht.

Inconsisten'cy [in-kAn ssi stAn-ssi] n. Unverträglichkeit f, Ungereimtheit f, Widerspruch m, Unbeständigkeit f; -t a. unverträglich, inkonsequent.

Inconsolable [in-kAn-ssou'lAbl] a. untröstlich, untröstbar.

Inconspicuous [in-kAn-spi kju-Ass] a. unmerklich, unansehnlich.

Inconstan'cy [in-kon'stAn ssi] n. Wankelmut m, Unbeständigkeit f; -t a. wankelmütig, unbeständig.

Incontinen'ce [in-kon'ti nAnss] n. Unenthaltsamkeit f; -t a. unenthaltsam.

Incontrovertible [in-kon tro-wAr'tibl] a. unbestreitbar.

Inconven'ience [in-kAn-wih ni-Anss] n. Lästigkeit f, Übelstand m, Unbequemlichkeit f; vt. belästigen; -t a. ungelegen, unpassend, lästig.

Inconvertible [in-kĂn-wĂr'tibl] a. unkonvertierbar, nicht umsetzbar.

Incorporate [in-kŎr'pĂ-rit] a. vereinigt, inkorporiert; — [in-kŎr'pĂ-reit] vt. einverleiben, vereinigen, gründen, inkorporieren; -d a. eingetragen; n. Aktiengesellschaft f.

Incorporation [in-kŎr-pĂ-rei'schĂn] n. Verbindung f, Einverleibung f, Inkorporation f.

Incorrect [in-ko-rekt'] a. unrichtig, irrtümlich; -ness n. Unrichtigkeit f.

Incorrigible [in-ko'ri-dzhibl] a. unverbesserlich.

Incorruptible [in-ko-rĂp'tibl] a. unbestechlich, unverderbar.

Increase [in'krihss] n. Wachstum m, Zuwachs m, Vergrösserung f, Zunahme f; — in salary Gehaltserhöhung f; — in wages Lohnzulage f.

Increase [in-krihss'] vt. vermehren, vergrössern; i. wachsen, zunehmen; -ingly ad. immer mehr, in zunehmendem Masse.

Incredible [in-kre'dibl] a. unglaublich.

Incredulity [in-kri-djuh'li-ti] n. Unglaube m; -ous a. ungläubig.

Increment [in'kri-mĂnt] n. Wachstum m. Mehr m. Zunahme f; unearned—Wertzuwachs m.

Incriminate [in-kri'mi-neit] vt. beschuldigen.

Incrustation [in-krĂ-stei'schĂn] n. Rinde f. Überkrustung f. Kesselstein m (tec.).

Incubate [in'kju-beit] vt. ausbrüten; -ion n. Ausbrüten f, -or n. Brutofen m.

Inculcate [in-kĂl-keit] vt. einschärfen, einprägen.

Incumbent [in-kĂm'bĂnt] a. obliegend. [en, machen (debts).]

Incur [in-kĂr'] vt. sich zuziehen

Incurability [in-kju-rĂ-bi'li-ti] n. Unheilbarkeit f; -le a. unheilbar.

Incursion [in-kĂr'schĂn] n. Einfall m. Einflug m (av.).

Indebted [inde'tid] a. verschuldet, verpflichtet; -ness n. Verschuldung f. Verpflichtung f.

Indecency [in-dih'ssAn-ssi] n. Unanständigkeit f; -t a. unanständig.

Indecipherable [in-di-ssai'fĂ-rĂbl] a. unentzifferbar, unleserlich.

Indecision [indi-ssi'zhĂn] n. Unentschlossenheit f. Unschlüssigkeit f.

Indecisive [in-di-ssai'ssiw] a. nicht entscheidend, unentschieden, unentschlossen.

Indeclinable [in-di-klai'n-Abl] a. unveränderlich.

Indecorous [in-de'kĂ-rĂss] a. unschicklich.

Indeed [in-dihd'] ad. in der Tat, tatsächlich, zwar, allerdings. [gĂbl] a. unermüdlich.

Indefatigable [in-di-fæ'ti-

Indefensible [in-di-fen'ssibl] a. unhaltbar.

Indefinable [in-di-fai'nĂbl] a. unbestimmbar, unerklärlich.

Indefinite [in-de'fi-nit] a. unbestimmt.

Indelible [in-de'libl] a. unauslöschlich; -pencil n. Tintenstift m.

Indelicacy [in-de'li-kĂ-ssi] n. Grobheit f. Mangel m. an Feingefühl; -te a. unzart, unfein.

Indemnification [in-demni-fi-kei'schĂn] n. Schadloshaltung f. -fy vt. entschädigen, sichern (secure); -ty n. Entschädigung f. Schadenersatz m; war — Kriegsentschädigung f.

Indent [in-dent'] vt. eni

schneiden, kerben, einrücken (line), bestellen (order), abschliessen (contract); n. Einschnitt m, Auftrag m (com.), Anforderung f (mil.); -ation n. Einschnitt m, Einzug m (print), Ausschnitt m (tec.).

Indenture [in-den'tscher] n. Lehrbrief m, Kontrakt m.

Independen'ce [in-di-pen'dAnss] n. Unabhängigkeit f; -t a, -ly ad. unabhängig; n. Parteilose(r) m.

Indescribable [in-di-skrai'bAbl] a. unbeschreibbar.

Indestructib'ility [in-distrukt-tA-bi'li-ti] n. Unzerstörbarkeit f; -le a, unzerstörbar.

Indeterminate [in-di'termi-nit] a. unbestimmt.

Index [in'dex] n. Verzeichnis n, Tafel f, Liste f, Register m, Anzeiger m; card – Kartei f; – finger n. Zeigefinger m.

Indiaman [in'djA-mAn] n. Ostindienfahrer m.

Indian [in'djAn] a. indisch; – club n. Keule f; – corn n. Mais m; – ink n. chinesische Tusche; india paper n. Japanpapier n.

India-rubber [in'djA-rA'ber] n. Gummi m, Kautschuk m, Radiergummi n.

Indica'te [in'di-keit] vt. anzeigen, bezeichnen, angeben; -ion n. Anzeige f, Zeichen n, Anzeichen n, Angabe f; -ive a. anzeigend; n. Indikativ m; -or n. Zeiger m, Anzeigevorrichtung f, Codewort n.

Indict [in-dait'] vt. anklagen; -ment n. Anklage f.

Indifferen'ce [in-di'fA-rAnss] n. Gleichgültigkeit f; -t a. gleichgültig, leidlich.

Indigen'ce [in-di-dzhAnss] n. Armut f, Mangel m; -t a. arm, dürftig.

Indigenous [in-di'dzhi-nAss] a. einheimisch, eingeboren.

Indigestib'le [in-di-dzhe'stibl] a. unverdaulich; -on n.

Verdauungsstörung f, schlechte Verdauung.

Indigna'nt [in-dig'nAnt] a. entrüstet, ungehalten; -tion n. Entrüstung f, Empörung f.

Indignity [in-dig'ni-ti] n. Beleidigung f.

Indigo [in'di-gou] n. Indigo m.

Indirect [in-dai-rekt'] a. indirekt, mittelbar; – tax n. Verbrauchssteuer f.

Indiscre'et [in-di-skriht'] a. unbesonnen, indiskret, taktlos; -tion n. Unbesonnenheit f, Indiskretion f.

Indiscriminate [in-di-skri'mi-nit] a, -ly ad. ohne Unterschied.

Indispensable [in-di-spen'ssibl] a. unentbehrlich, unabkömmlich (mil, etc.).

Indispos'e [in-di-spous'] vt. abgeneigt machen; -ed a. abgeneigt, nicht aufgelegt, unwohl (ill); -ition n. Unpässlichkeit f, Unwohlsein n, Abneigung f.

Indisputable [in-di'spjutAbl] a. unbestreitbar.

Indissoluble [in-di-sso'ljubl] a. unauflöslich, unzertrennlich.

Indistinct [in-di-stinkt'] a, -ly ad. unklar, undeutlich; -ness n. Undeutlichkeit f, Unklarheit f.

Indistinguishable [in-disting'gui-schAbl] a. ununterscheidbar.

Individual [in-di-wi'dju-Al] n. Einzelperson f, Individuum n; a. persönlich, individuell, einzeln, besonder; – training n. Einzelausbildung f (mil.); -ism n. Individualismus m; -istic a. individualistisch; -ity n. Individualität f, Persönlichkeit f, Eigentümlichkeit f; -ly ad. einzeln, persönlich.

Indivisible [in-di-wi'sibl] a. unteilbar.

Indoctrinate [in-dok'tri-neit] vt. unterrichten, durchdringen.

Indolen'ce [in'do-lAnss] n.
Trägheit f, Lässigkeit f; **-t** a.
träge, untätig, lässig.

Indomitable [in-do'mi-tAbl]
a. unbezwinglich.

Indoor [in'dOr] a., **-s** [in'dOrs]
ad. häuslich, zu Hause, im
Hause; **- aerial** n. Zimmeran-
tenne f.

Induce [in-djuhss'] vt. bewegen,
herbeiführen, induzieren
(el.); **-d current** n. Induktions-
strom m; **-ment** n. Veranlassung f, Anreiz m, Vorteil m.

Induction [in-dAk'schAn] n.
Einsetzung f, Induktion f; **-
coil** n. Induktionsapparat m;
- pipe n. Ansaugleitung f
(aut.).

Indulge [in-dAldzh'] vt. willfahren, nachgeben, verwöhnen;
i. sich ergeben, hegen; **-nce** n.
Nachsicht f, Milde f, Befriedigung f, Gunst f, Ablass m
(church); **-t** a. nachsichtig.

Industr'ial [in-dA'stri-Al] a.
gewerblich, industriell, Fabrik
...; n. Gewerbetreibende(r)
m, Fabrikbesitzer m; **-ious** a.
fleissig; **-y** n. Fleiss m, Industrie f; **- and trade** Gewerbe n.

Inebriated [in-ih'bri-ei-tid] a.
betrunken. [sprechlich.

Ineffable [in-e'fAbl] a. unaus-

Ineffaceable [in-i-fei'ssAbl] a.
unauslöslich.

Ineffective [in-i-fek'tiw], **In-
effectual** [in-i-fek'tju-Al] a. wir-
kungslos, unwirksam.

Ineffectiveness [in-i-fek'tiw-
ness], **Inefficacy** [in-i-fkA-ssi]
n. Unwirksamkeit f.

Inefficacious [in-e-fi-kei'-
schAss] a. unwirksam.

Inefficien'cy [in-i-fi'schAn-
ssi] n. Unfähigkeit f, Untauglichkeit f; **-t** a. unfähig, untüchtig, unbrauchbar.

Ineligib'ility [in-e-li-dzhi-bi'-
li-ti] n. Unwählbarkeit f, Untauglichkeit f; **-le** a. unwählbar, untauglich.

Inept [i-nept'] a. albern.

Inequality [in-i-kuo'li-ti] n.
Ungleichheit f, Missverhältnis n. [unbillig, ungerecht.

Inequitable [in-e'kui-tAbl] a.

Ineradicable [in-i-ræ'di-
kAbl] a. unausrottbar.

Inert [in-Art'] a. unwirksam.

Inertia [in-Ar'schi-A] n. Untätigkeit f, Beharrungsvermö-
gen n. [a. unschätzbar.

Inestimable [in-e'sti-mAbl]

Inevita'bility [in-e-wi-tA-bi'-
li-ti] n. Unvermeidlichkeit f;
-le a. unvermeidlich. [genau.

Inexact [in-ig-sakt'] a. un-

Inexcusable [in-ix-kjuh'-
sAbl] a. unverzeihlich, unverantwortlich.

Inexhaustible [in-ig-sO'-
stibl] a. unerschöpflich.

Inexorable [in-ex'A-rAbl] a.
unerbittlich.

Inexpedient [in-ix-pih'di-
Ant] a. nicht ratsam, unrätlich.

Inexpensive [in-ix-pen'ssiw]
a. nicht kostpielig, billig.

Inexperience [in-ix-pih'ri-
Anss] n. Unerfahrenheit f; **-d**
a. unerfahren.

Inexpert [in-ex-pert'] a. un-
geübt, unerfahren.

Inexplicable [in-ex'pli-kAbl]
a. unerklärlich, unverständlich. [ssibl] a. unaussprechlich.

Inexpressible [in-ix-pre'-

Inextricable [in-ex'tri-kAbl]
a. unentwirrbar, unenträtsel-
bar.

Infalli'bility [in-fæ-li-bi'li-ti]
n. Unfehlbarkeit f; **-le** a. unfehlbar, untrüglich.

Infam'ous [in'fA-mAss] a.
ehrlos, verrufen, schändlich;
-y n. Ehrlosigkeit f, Schande f,
Niedertracht f.

Infancy [in'fAn-ssi] n. Kindheit f, Minderjährigkeit f (law).

Infant [in'fAnt] n. kleines
Kind, Säugling m, Minderjäh-
rige(r) m, f; **-icide** n. Kinder-

mord *m*; -ile, -ine *a.* kindisch (*childish*), kindlich (*child-like*); - paralysis *n.* Kinderlähmung *f.*

Infantry [in'fAn-tri] *n.* Infanterie *f.*; - lorry *n.* Infanterieträger *m*; -man *n.* Infanterist *m*, Fuss-soldat *m*, Landser *m*; - platoon *n.* Schützenzug *m*; - private *n.* Schütze *m*; - rifle *n.* Infanteriegewehr *n.*

Infatuat'e [in-fæ'tju-eit] *vt.* betören; -d *a.* betört, vernarrt; -ion *n.* Betörung *f*, Vernarrtheit *f.*

Infect [in-fekt'] *vt.* anstecken; -ion *n.* Ansteckung *f*; -ious *a.* ansteckend.

I n f e r [in-fAr'] *vt.* folgern, schliessen; -ence *n.* Folgerung *f*, Schluss *m.*

Inferior [in'fri-Ar] *a.* minderwertig, geringer, untergeordnet; *n.* Untergebene(r) *m*; -ity *n.* Untergeordnetheit *f*; Minderwert *m*, Niedrigkeit *f*; - complex *n.* Minderwertigkeits-, Inferioritäts-komplex *m.*

Infernal [in-fAr'nAl] *a.* höllisch, teuflisch.

Infest [in-fest'] *vt.* belästigen, plagen, überschwemmen; -ed with mines *a.* minenverseucht (*nav.*).

Infidel [in'fidl] *n.* Ungläubige(r) *m*; -ity *n.* Treulosigkeit *f*, Treubruch *m.*

Infiltrat'e [in'fil-treit] *vt.i.* allmählich durchdringen, eindringen; -ion *n.* Eindringen *n.*

Infinit'e [in'fi-nit] *a.* unendlich, endlos; -esimal *a.* unendlich klein; -ive *n.* Infinitiv *m*, Nenn-, Grund-form *f*; -y *n.* Unendlichkeit *f.*

Infirm [in-fArm'] *a.* schwach, gebrechlich, altersschwach; -ary *n.* Krankenhaus *n.*; -ity *n.* Schwäche *f*, Gebrechlichkeit *f*, Krankheit *f.*

Inflame [in-fleim'] *vt.* entflammen, entzünden.

Inflamma'bility [in-flæ-mA-

bi'li-ti] *n.* Entzündbarkeit *f*; -ble *a.* entzündbar, entzündlich, feuergefährlich; -tion *n.* Entzündung *f*; -tory *a.* aufhetzend, aufrührerisch.

Inflatable boat [in-flei'tAblbout] *n.* Schlauchboot *n* (*av.*).

Inflat'e [in-fleit'] *vt.* aufblähen, aufblasen, aufpumpen (*aut, etc.*), künstlich steigern (*com.*); -ion *n.* Aufblähung *f.*, Aufpumpen *n*, Inflation *f* (*prices*).

Inflect [in-flekt'] *vt.* beugen, flektieren, modulieren (*voice*); -ion *n.* Beugung *f*, Flektion *f*, Modulierung *f.*

Inflexib'ility [in-flex-i-bi'li-ti] *n.* Unbeugsamkeit *f*, Strenge *f*; -le *a.* unbiegsam, unbeugsam, unerbittlich.

Inflict [in-flikt'] *vt.* auferlegen, zufügen, beibringen; -ion *n.* Auferlegung *f*, Bestrafung *f*, Plage *f.*

Influen'ce [in'flu-Anss] *n.* Einfluss *m*; *vt.* beeinflussen, einwirken; -tial *a.* einflussreich.

Influenza [in-flu-en'sA] *n.* Grippe *f.* [*n*, Zustrom *m.*

Influx [in'flAx] *n.* Einfliessen

Inform [in-fOrm'] *vt.* benachrichtigen, unterrichten, belehren; -al *a.*, -ally *ad.* ohne Förmlichkeit, zwanglos, ungezwungen; -ality *n.* Ungezwungenheit *f*, Formlosigkeit *f*; -ant *n.* Gewährsmann *m*, Berichterstatter *m*; -ation *n.* Nachricht *f*, Mitteilung *f*, Auskunft *f*, Kenntnis *f*, Belehrung *f*; -ation bureau *n.* Auskunftstelle *f*; -ative *a.* lehrreich, inhaltreich; -er *n.* Berichterstatter *m*, Angeber *m.*

Infraction [in-fræk'schAn] *n.* Verletzung *f.* [infrarot.

Infra-red [in-frA-red'] *a.*

Infrequen'cy [in-frih'kuAnssi] *n.* Seltenheit *f*; -t *a.* selten.

Infringe [in-frindzh'] *vt.i.* verletzen, brechen; -ment *n.* Verletzung *f.*

Infuriate [in-fjuh'ri-eit] *vt.* wütend machen, erzürnen.

Infuse [in-fjuhs'] *vt.* einflössen, eingiessen, aufgiessen (*tec.*); **-ion** *n.* Eingiessen *n*, Aufguss *m*.

Ingenious [in-dzih'ni-Ass] *a.* sinnreich, geistreich, erfinderisch, kunstvoll.

Ingenuity [in-dzhi-nju'i-ti] *n.* Scharfsinn *m*, Findigkeit *f*, Erfindungsgabe *f*.

Ingenuous [in-dzhe'nju-Ass] *a.* unbefangen, treuherzig, aufrichtig; **-ness** *n.* Unbefangenheit *f*, Aufrichtigkeit *f*.

Inglorious [in-glO'ri-Ass] *a.* unrühmlich, schändlich.

Ingoing [in'gO-ing] *n.* Hineingehen *n*; *a.* antretend.

Ingot [ing'gAt] *n.* Goldbarren *m*. [Wolle gefärbt, echt (dye).]

Ingrain [in-grein'] *a.* der Wolle

Ingratiate [in-grei'schi-eit] *vr.* sich einschmeicheln.

Ingratitude [in-græ'ti-tjuhd] *n.* Undankbarkeit *f*.

Ingredient [in-grih'di-Ant] *n.* Bestandteil *m*.

Inhabit [in-hæ'bit] *vt.* bewohnen; **-able** *a.* bewohnbar; **-ant** *n.* Bewohner *m*, Einwohner *m*; **-ants** *pl.* Bevölkerung *f*; **-ation** *n.* Bewohnen *n*.

Inhal'ation [in-hA-lei'schAn] *n.* Einatmen *n*, Einatmung *f*; **-e** *vt.* einatmen, inhalieren; **-er** *n.* Inhalationsapparat *m*.

Inharmonious [in-hahr-mou'ni-Ass] *a.* unharmonisch.

Inhere [in-hih'er] *vi.* anhaften, innewohnen; **-nt** *a.* innewohnend, angeboren.

Inherit [in-he'rit] *vt.* erben; **-ance** *n.* Vererbung *f*, Erbschaft *f*, Erbe *n*.

Inhibit [in-hi'bit] *vt.* hemmen, verbieten; **-ion** *n.* Hemmung *f*, Verbot *n*; **-ory** *a.* hemmend, Hemmungs ...

Inhospitable [in-ho'spi-tAbl] *a.* unwirtlich, ungastlich.

Inhuman [in-hjuh'mAn] *a.* unmenschlich, grausam; **-ity** *n*, Unmenschlichkeit *f*. [lich.

Inimical [in-i'mikl] *a.* feind-

Inimitable [in-i'mi-tAbl] *a.* unnachahmbar.

Iniquit'ous [in-i'kui-tAss] *a.* ungerecht, schlecht; **-y** *n.* Ungerechtigkeit *f*, Schlechtigkeit *f*, Missetat *f*.

Initial [in-i'schAl] *a.* anfänglich, Anfangs ...; *n.* Anfangsbuchstabe *m*; *vt.* unterschreiben; **- position** *n.* Ausgangsstellung *f* (*mil.*).

Initiat'e [in-i'schi-eit] *vt.* anfangen, einführen, einweihen; **-ion** *n.* Einführung *f*, Anfang *m*, Einweihung *f*; **-ive** *n.* Inangriffnahme *f*, erster Anstoss, Initiative *f*, Unternehmungsgeist *m*.

Inject [in-dzhekt'] *vt.* einspritzen; **-ion** *n.* Einspritzung *f*, Injektion *f*; **-or** *n.* Injektor *m*, Düse *f* (*tec.*).

Injudicious [in-dzhuh-di'schAss] *a.* unüberlegt, unklug.

Injunction [in-dzhAngk'schAn] *n.* Einschärfung *f*, Befehl *m*, Verbot *n* (*law*).

Injur'e [in'dzher] *vt.* beschädigen, verletzen (*persons*); **-ious** *a.* schädlich; **-y** *n.* Schaden *m*, Verletzung *f*, Abbruch *m*.

Injustice [in-dzhA'stiss] *n.* Ungerechtigkeit *f*, Unrecht *n*.

Ink [ingk] *n.* Tinte *f*; *vt.* mit Tinte schwärzen; **Indian -** chinesische Tusche; **-bottle** *n.* Tintenflasche *f*; **-eraser** *n.* Radiergummi *m*; **-pad** *n.* Stempelkissen *n*; **-pot** *n.* Tintenfass *n*; **-stand** *n.* Schreibzeug *n*; **-well** *n.* Tintenfass *n*. [Idee *f*.

Inkling [ingk'ling] *n.* Ahnung,

Inlaid [in-leid'] *a.* eingelegt; **- floor** *n.* Parkettboden *m*.

Inland [in'lAnd] *n.* Binnenland *n*; *a.* binnenländisch, einheimisch, Landes ...; *ad* landeinwärts; – **navigation** n. Binnenschiff-fahrt f; – **revenue** n. Verbrauchssteuern f.pl.

Inlay [in-lei'] vt. einlegen, täfeln, furnieren; – n. Einlegestück n.

Inlet [in'let] n. Einlass m, Einguss m (metal), Durchlass m (water), kleine Bucht (water); – -joint n. Einlaganstoss m (wood); – -manifold n. (An-) Saugleitung f (aut.); – -piece n. Einlage f (wood); – -pipe n. Wasserzufluss m, Zuführungsrohr n (air, gas); – -tube n. Zuleitung f, Zuleitungsrohr n; – -valve n. Einlass-, Saugventil n.

Inmate [in'meit] n. Insasse m, Mitbewohner m.

Inmost [in'moust] a. innerst.

Inn [in] n. Wirtshaus n; -keeper n. Gastwir m. [eigen.

Innate [i-neit'] a. angeboren,

Inner [i'ner] a. inner, innerlich; – **tube** n. Luftschlauch m (aut., etc.); – coat a. innerst

Innings [i'nings] n.pl. Reihe f; to have one's – daran sein.

Innocence [in'o-ssAnss] n. Unschuld f, Schuldlosigkeit f; -t a. unschuldig, schuldlos.

Innocuous [in-o'kju-Ass] a. unschädlich. [n. Neuerung f.

Innovation [in-o-wei'schAn]

Innuendo [in-ju-en'dou] n. versteckte Anspielung.

Innumerable [in-juh'mA-rAbl] a. unzählig.

Inoculate [in-o'kju-leit] vt. (ein-)impfen, veredeln, okulieren (plant); -ion n. Einimpfung f, Veredlung f, Okulieren n.

Inoffensive [in-o-fen'ssiw] a. harmlos. [a. unwirksam.

Inoperative [in-o'pA-rA-tiw]

Inopportune [in-o'pOr-tjuhn] a. ungelegen, unangebracht.

Inordinate [in-Or'di-nit] a. unmässig. [n. unorganisch.

Inorganic [in-Or-gæ'nik] a.

Inquest [in'kuest] n. gericht-

liche Untersuchung, Leichenschau f.

Inquir'e [in-kuai'er] vi. nachfragen, erfragen, sich erkundigen; -t. erfragen; – into vt. untersuchen; -y n. Nachfrage f, Anfrage f, Untersuchung f, Erkundigung f; – office n. Auskunftsbüro n, Verkehrsverein m (for travellers).

Inquisition [in-kui-si'schAn] n. Untersuchung f, Inquisition f.

Inquisitive [in-kui'si-tiw] a. -ly ad. neugierig; -ness n. Neugierde f.

Inquisitor [in-kui'si-ter] n. Untersucher m, Inquisitor m; -ial a. ausfragend, inquisitorisch. [Einfall m.

Inroad [in'roud] n. Eingriff m,

Insane [in-ssein'] a. wahnsinnig, geistesgestört.

Insanitary [in-ssæ'ni-tA-ri] a. ungesund. [Wahnsinn m.

Insanity [in-sæ'nit-ti] a.

Insatiable [in-ssei'schi-Abl] a. unersättlich.

Inscribe [in-skraib'] vt. einschreiben, eintragen, widmen.

Inscription [in-skrip'schAn] n. Inschrift f, Widmung f, Einschreiben n.

Inscrutable [in-skruh'tAbl] a. unerforschlich.

Insect [in'ssekt] n. Insekt n; -icide n. Insektenvertilgungsmittel n.

Insecur'e [in-si-kjuher] a. unsicher; -ity n. Unsicherheit f.

Insensate [in-ssen'seit] a. sinnlos.

Insensibility [in-ssen-si-bi'li-ti] n. Unempfindlichkeit f, Bewusstlosigkeit f.

Inseparable [in-sse'pA-rAbl] a. untrennbar (verbs), unzertrennlich (persons).

Insert [in-ssArt'] vt. einsetzen, einschalten, einfügen, einrücken (in paper); -ion n. Einsetzung f, Einschaltung f, Ein-

rückung f, Einsatz m (dress),
Inserat n (newspaper).
Inset [in'sset] n. Zwischensatz
m, Einsatz m, Zwischenstück
n, Beilage f.
Inshore [in-schOr] ad. a. nach
dem Lande zu, dicht am Lande.
Inside [in'ssaid] n. Innenseite
f, Innere n; ad. drinnen; pr.
innerhalb.
Inside [in'ssaid] a. inwendig,
inner; – left n. Linkssinnen m;
– right n. Linksaussen m.
Insidious [in-ssi'di-Ass] a.
heimtückisch, trügerisch.
Insight [in'ssait] n. Einsicht f.
Insignia [in-ssig'ni-A] n.pl.
Abzeichen n.pl; national –
Hoheitsabzeichen n.pl.
Insignifican'ce [in-ssig-ni-fi'-
kAnss] n. Bedeutungslosigkeit
f, Geringfügigkeit f; -t a. unbedeutend, unansehnlich.
Insincer'e [in-ssin-ssih'er] a.
unaufrichtig, falsch; -ity n.
Unaufrichtigkeit f, Falsch-
heit f.
Insinuat'e [in-ssin'ju-eit] vt.
unbemerkt hereinbringen, beibringen, zu verstehen geben;
-ion n. Einflüsterung f, An-
deutung f. [schmackhaft, fade.
Insipid [in-ssi'pid] a. un-
Insist [in-ssist'] vt. bestehen,
betonen; -ence n. Bestehen n.
Betonung f; -ent a. beharrend,
aufdringlich. [sohle f.
Insole [in'ssoul] n. Einlege-
Insolen'ce [in'sso-lenss] n.
Frechheit f; -t a. frech.
Insolub'ility [in-sso-lju-bi'li-
ti] n. Unlösbarkeit f; -le a. unauflöslich, unlösbar.
Insolven'cy [in-ssol'wAn-ssi]
n. Zahlungsunfähigkeit f; -t a.
zahlungsunfähig, bankerott; n.
Insolvente(r) m.
Inspect [in-spekt'] vt. besich-
tigen, untersuchen, prüfen; -ion
n. Besichtigung f, Prüfung f,
Appell m (mil.); -or n. Prüfer
m, Aufseher m, Kontrolleur m,

Beamte(r) m, Inspektor m,
Zollaufseher m (customs); –
-general Generalinspektor m;
-orate n. Inspektorat n, Auf-
sichtsbehörde f.
Inspir'ation [in-spi-rei'-
schAn] n. Begeisterung f, Inspiration f; -e vt. begeistern,
eingeben, inspirieren; -it v..
beseelen.
Instability [in-stA-bi'li-ti] n
Unbeständigkeit f.
Install [in-stOl'] vt. einsetzen,
aufstellen, bestallen, einricht-
en, installieren (tec.); -ation n.
Einrichtung f, Bestallung f.
Anlage f (tec.).
Instalment [in-stOl'mAnt] n.
Rate f, Abschlagszahlung f,
Teilzahlung f; – system n. Abzahlungssystem n.
Instance [in'stAnss] n. Beispiel n, Fall m; vt. als Beispiel
anführen.
Instant [in'stAnt] n. Augenblick m; a. augenblicklich; -ly
ad. sogleich; -aneous a. sofortig, Moment .
Instead [in-sted'] ad. dafür;
– of pr. anstatt.
Instep [in'step] n. Spann m;
– support(er) m, Fuss-stütze f.
Instigat'e [in'sti-geit] vt. anreizen, anstiften; -ion n. Anreizung f, Anstiftung f; -or n.
Anstifter m. [beibringen.
Instil [in-stil'] vt. einflössen,
Instinct [in'stinkt] n. Instinkt
m, Naturtrieb m; -ive a. in-
stinktiv.
Institut'e [in'sti-tjuht] n. Institut n, Anstalt f, Heim n; vt.
stiften, errichten, ins Werk
setzen, anstellen; -ion n. Einrichtung f, Stiftung f, Anstalt
f, Ordnung f.
Instruct [in-strAkt'] vt. unterrichten, unterweisen, belehren,
anweisen; -ion n. Unterricht
m, Unterweisung f, Vorschrift
f, Ausbildung f (training); -
-flight n. Einweisungsflug m

(av.); -ional a. erzieherisch, Lehr . . ., Unterrichts . . .; -al film n. Lehrfilm m; -ive a. lehrreich; -or n. Fachleher m, Flug-eher m (av.).

Instrument [in'stru-mAnt] n. Werkzeug n, Instrument n, Mittel n; - board m. Armaturenbrett n (av.); - mechanic n. Feinmechaniker m; -al a. förderlich, dienlich, behilflich; -ity n. Vermittlung f.

Insubordinat'e [in-ssA-bOr'di-nit] a. widersetzlich, unbotmässig; -ion n. Widersetzlichkeit f, Achtungsverletzung f.

Insufferable [in-ssA'fA-rAbl] a. unerträglich.

Insufficien'cy [in-ssA-fi'schAn-ssi] n. Unzulänglichkeit f; -t a. unzureichend.

Insular [in'ssju-ler] a. insular, beschränkt.

Insulat'e [in'ssju-leit] vt. isolieren; -ing tape n. Isolierband n; -ing wall n. Isolationswand f; -ion n. Isolation f, Isolierung f; -or n. Isolator m. [in n.

Insulin [in'ssju-lin] n. Insulin

Insult [in-ssAlt'] vt. beleidigen.

Insult [in'ssAlt] n. Beleidigung f.

Insuperable [in-ssjuh'pA-rAbl] a. unübersteigbar, unüberwindlich.

Insur'ance [in-schuh'rAnss] n. Versicherungif; - policy n. Versicherungspolice f; -e vt. versichern, sichern.

Insurgent [in-ssAr'dzhAnt] n. Aufständische(r) m, Freischärler m.

Insurmountable [in-ssAr-maun'tAbl] a. unübersteigbar.

Insurrection [in-ssA-rek'schAn] n. Aufstand m.

Intact [in-tækt'] a. unberührt, unverletzt, intakt.

Intake [in'teik] n. Einnahme f, Einlass m (tec.), Einlauf m (tec.), Einmündung f (mine, etc.); - -pipe n. Saugrohr n.

Intangible [in-tæn'dzhibl] a. unberührbar, unantastbar.

Integr'al [in'ti-grAl] a. ganz, wesentlich; -ity n. Unverletztheit f, Ganzheit f, Redlichkeit f (honesty).

Intellect [in'ti-lekt] n. Verstand m, Geist m; -ual a. geistig, verstandesmässig, intellektuell; n. Intellektuelle(r) m.

Intelligen'ce [in-te'li-dzhAnss] n. Verstand m, Intelligenz f, Kunde f, Nachricht f, Aufklärung f (mil.); - corps n. Nachrichtentruppe f; - department n. Nachrichtenamt n, Spionagedienst m; - officer n. Nachrichtenoffizier m; - service n. Nachrichten-, Spionagedienst m, Nachrichtenwesen n; -t a. verständig, klug, intelligent, aufgeweckt

Intelligib'ility [in-te-li-dzhA-bi'li-ti] n. Verständlichkeit f; -le a. verständlich.

Intemperance [in-tem'pA-rAnss] n. Unmässigkeit f, Trunksucht f; -te a. unmässig, trunksüchtig.

Intend [in-tend'] vt. beabsichtigen, vorhaben, bestimmen.

Intens'e [in-tenss'] a., -ly ad. stark, heftig, gespannt, tief; -ification n. Verstärkung f; -ifier n. Verstärker m; -ify vt. verstärken, verschärfen; -ity n. Heftigkeit f, Stärke f, Intensität f; -ive a. angestrengt, stark, unablässig, intensiv.

Intent [in-tent'] a. gespannt, eifrig; n. Absicht f; -ion n. Absicht f, Zweck m; -ional a. -ionally ad. absichtlich.

Inter [in-tAr'] vt. beerdigen.

Interact [in-ter-ækt'] vi. aufeinander einwirken; -ion n. Wechselwirkung f.

Inter-allied [in'ter-æ'laid] a. interalliiert; -(ich) kreuzen

Interbreed [in-ter-brihd'] vt./i.

Intercede [in-ter-ssihd'] vi

Fürsprache einlegen, sich verwenden.

Intercept [in-ter-ssept'] *vt.* auffangen, lauschen, unterbrechen, abschneiden (*av.*); **-er** *n.* Jagdflieger *m* (*av.*), Jagdflugzeugzerstörer *m*; **-ion** *n.* Auffangen *n*, Abfangen *n*, Horchen *n* (*ph.*); **-ion company** *n.* Horchkompanie *f* (*mil.*); **-ion flight** *n.* Sperrflug *m* (*av.*).

Intercession [in-ter-sse' schÄn] *n.* Fürsprache *f.*

Interchange [in-ter-tschein'dzh'] *n.* Austausch *m*, Abwechslung *f*; *vt.* auswechseln, austauschen; **-able** *a.* austauschbar.

Intercommunication [in-ter-kA-mjuh-ni-kei'schÄn] *n.* gegenseitiger Verkehr, Zwischenverkehr *m*, Bord-gerät *n*, **-verständigungsanlage** *f* (*el.*).

Intercourse [in'ter-kOrss] *n.* Verkehr *m.*

Interdependence [in-ter-di-pen'dÄnss] *n.* wechselseitige Abhängigkeit.

Interest [in'tÄ-rist] *n.* Interesse *n*, Anteil *m*, Zins *m* (*com.*); *vt.* interessieren; **-ing** *a.* interessant.

Interfere [in-ter-fih'er] *vi.* sich einmischen, stören (*rad., etc.*); **-nce** *n.* Einmischung *f*, Störung *f* (*rad.*).

Interim [in'tÄ-rim] *a.* einstweilig, vorläufig; *n.* Zwischenzeit *f*; **- certificate** *n.* Interimschein *m*; **- government** *n.* Übergangsregierung *f.*

Interior [in-tih'ri-er] *a.* inner, innerlich; *n.* das Innere, Innenaufnahme *f* (*photo*).

Interject [in-ter-dzhekt'] *vt.* einwerfen, hinzufügen; **-ion** *n.* Ausruf *m.*

Interlace [in-ter-leiss'] *vt.* verflechten.

Interleave [in-ter-lihw'] *vt.* durchschiessen.

Interlinear [in-ter-li'ni-er] *a.* zwischenzeilig.

Interlock [in-ter-lok'] *vi.* ineinanderhaken, verschliessen (*rl.*). [Eindringling *m.*]

Interloper [in'ter-lou-per] *n.*

Interlude [in'ter-luhd] *n.* Zwischenspiel *n.*

Intermediary [in-ter-mih'di-A-ri] *n.* Vermittler *m*, Zwischenhändler *m* (*middleman*).

Intermediate [in-ter-mih'di-it] *a.* Zwischen . . Mittel . . ; **- landing** *n.* Zwischenlandung *f* (*av.*); **- port** *n.* Zwischenhafen *m*; **- resistance** *n.* Vorschaltwiderstand *m* (*el.*).

Interment [in-tÄr'mÄnt] *n.* Beerdigung *f.*

Interminable [in-tÄr'mi-nÄbl] *a.* unendlich.

Intermingle [in-ter-ming'gl] *vi.* sich vermischen.

Intermission [in-ter-mi'schÄn] *n.* Unterlassung *f*, Unterbrechung *f*, Pause *f.*

Intermittent [in-ter-mi'tÄnt] *a.* unterbrochen; **- light** *n.* Blink-, Blitz-feuer *n*; **- sprocket** *n.* Schaltrolle *f* (*film*). [en.

Intern [in-tÄrn] *vt.* internieren.

Internal [in-tÄr'nÄl] *a.* inner, einheimisch (*home*); **- combustion engine** *n.* Explosions-, Verbrennungs-motor *m.*

International [in-ter-næ'schÄ-nÄl] *a.* international, zwischenstaatlich; **- language** *n.* Weltsprache *f*; **- law** *n.* Völkerrecht *n*; **- trade** *n.* Welthandel *m.*

Internee [in-ter-nih'] *n.* der, die Internierte.

Internment [in-tÄrn'mÄnt] *n.* Internierung *f*; **- camp** *n.* Internierungslager *n.*

Interpolate [in-tÄr'pÄ-leit] *vt.* einschalten, einschieben; **-ion** *n.* Einschaltung *f*, Interpolation *f.*

Interpose [in-ter-pous'] *vt.* dazwischenlegen, einlegen; *i.* dazwischenkommen; **-ition** *n.* Dazwischen-treten *n*, -kunft *f.*

Interpret [in-tẢr'prit] vt. auslegen, verdolmetschen, übersetzen; -ation n. Auslegung f, Darstellung f, Wiedergabe f; -er n. Dolmetscher m, Ausleger m, Darsteller m.

Interrogat'e [in-te'ro-geit] vt. befragen, verhören (law); -ion n. Befragen n, Verhör n; -officer n. Vernehmungsoffizier m (mil.).

Interrupt [in-tẢ-rẢpt] vt. unterbrechen, stören; -ion n. Unterbrechung f.

Intersect [in-ter-ssekt'] vt.i. (sich) durchschneiden; -ion n. Durchschneiden n, Schnitt m, Schnittpunkt m.

Intersperse [in-ter-spẢrss'] vt. einstreuen.

Interstice [in-tẢr'stiss] n. Zwischenraum m, Lücke f.

Interval [in'ter-wẢl] n. Abstand m, Pause f, Tonstufe f, Intervall n (music).

Interven'e [in-ter-wihn'] vi. dazwischenkommen, dazwischenliegen, vermitteln, eingreifen; -tion n. Dazwischentreten n, Eingreifen n, Intervention f.

Interview [in'ter-wjuh] n. Unterredung f, Besprechung f; vt. besuchen, sprechen.

Interweave [in-ter-uihw'] vt. ineinander weben.

Intestate [in-te'steit] a. ohne Testament.

Intestines [in-te'stins] n.pl. Eingeweide f, Darm m.

Intimacy [in'ti-mẢ-ssi] n. Vertrautheit f, vertrauter Umgang.

Intimate [in'ti-mit] a. -ly ad. [vertraut, intim, eng.

Intimat'e [in'ti-meit] vt. anzeigen, mitteilen; -ion n. Anzeige f, Mitteilung f, Wink m.

Intimidat'e [in-ti'mi-deit] vt. einschüchtern; -ion n. Einschüchterung f.

Into [in'tu] pr. in.

Intolerable [in-to'lẢ-rẢbl] a, -ly ad. unerträglich.

Intoleran'ce [in-to'la-rẢnss] n. Unduldsamkeit f; -t a. unduldsam.

Intonation [in-to-nei'schẢn] n. Tonfall m, Stimmlage f.

Intoxica'nt [in-tox'i-kẢnt] n. alkoholisches Getränk; -te vt. berauschen; -d a. betrunken; -tion n. Berauschung f, Rausch m. [unlenksam.

Intractable [in-trẢk'tẢbl] a.

Intransitive [in-tran'ssi-tiw] a. intransitiv, nicht zielend.

Intrepid [in-tre'pid] a. unerschrocken; -ity n. Unerschrockenheit f.

Intricacy [in'tri-kẢ-ssi] n. Verwicklung f; -te a. verwickelt.

Intrigue [in-trihg'] n. Ränkespiel n, Intrige f, Liebeshandel m; vi. Ränke schmieden, intrigieren. [lich, wirklich.

Intrinsic [in-trin'sik] a. inner-

Introduc'e [in-tro-djuhss'] vt. einführen, vorstellen (persons), vorbringen (subject); -tion n. Einführung f, Einleitung f, Vorstellung f; -tory a. einleitend. [tiw] a. beschaulich.

Introspective [in-tro-spek'

Intru'de [in-truhd'] vi. (sich) eindrängen, stören; -der n. Eindringling m; -sion n. Eindrängen n, Störung f; -sive a. lästig, störend.

Intuiti'on [in-tju-i'schẢn] n. Intuition f; -ve [in-tjuh'i-tiw] a. intuitiv, anschauend.

Inundat'e [in'An-deit] vt. überschwemmen; -ion n. Überschwemmung f.

Inure [in-juh'er] vt. abhärten.

Invade [in-weid'] vt. überfallen, einfallen in, eindringen; -r n. Angreifer m, Eindringling m.

Invalid [in-wä'lid] a. rechtsungültig, unwirksam; -ate vt. ungültig machen.

Invalid [in'wA-lihd] *a.* schwach, kränklich; *n.* der, die Kranke, der Dienstunfähige (*mil.*); *vt.* als dienstunfähig entlassen; – chair *n.* Krankenfahrstuhl *m.* [unschätzbar.

Invaluable [in-wæ'lju-Abl] *a.*

Invariabl'e [in-weh'ri-Abl] *a.* unveränderlich; -ly *ad.* ausnahmslos, immer.

Invasion [in-wei'zhAn] *n.* Einfall *m.*, Überfall *m.*, Angriff *m.*

Invective [in-wek'tiw] *n.* Schimpfrede *f.*

Inveigle [in-wihgl'] *vt.* verlocken, verführen.

Invent [in-went'] *vt.* erfinden; -ion *n.* Erfindung *f.*; -ive *a.* erfinderisch; -or *n.* Erfinder *m.*; -ory *n.* Verzeichnis *n.*, Inventar *n.*, Lagerbestand *m.* (*com.*).

Invers'e [in-wArss'] *a.* ungekehrt; -ion *n.* Umkehrung *f.*

Invert [in-wArt'] *vt.* umkehren; -ed commas *n.pl.* Anführungszeichen *n.pl.*

Invest [in-west'] *vt.* anlegen (*money*), einschliessen (*mil.*), bekleiden (*office*); -ment *n.* Geldanlage *f.*, Einschliessung *f.*, Bekleidung *f.*; -ment trust *n.* Kapitalunterbringungsgesellschaft *f.*; -or *n.* Kapitalist *m.*

Investigat'e [in-we'sti-geit] *vt.* erforschen; -ion *n.* Erforschung *f.*, Untersuchung *f.*

Inveterate [in-we'tA-rit] *a.* eingewurzelt, eingefleischt.

Invidious [in-wi'di-Ass] *a.* gehässig. [kräftigen.

Invigorate [in-wi'gA-reit] *vt.*

Invincible [in-win'sibll] *a.* unüberwindlich, unbesiegbar.

Inviolable [in-wai'o-labll] *a.* unverletzlich.

Invisibility [in-wi-si-bi'li-ti] *n.* Unsichtbarkeit *f.*

Invisible [in-wi'sibll] *a.* unsichtbar; – ink *n.* Geheimtinte *f.*

Invit'ation [in-wi-tei'schAn] *n.* Einladung *f.*; -e *vt.* einladen,

auffordern; -ing *a.* anziehend, verlockend.

Invoice [in'weuss] *n.* Faktur *f.*, Warenrechnung *f.*; *vt.* berechnen, in Rechnung stellen (*com.*).

Invoke [in-wouk'] *vt.* anrufen.

Involuntary [in-wo'lAn-tA-ri] *a.* unfreiwillig, unwillkürlich.

Involve [in-wolw'] *vt.* verwickeln, einschliessen, mit sich bringen.

Invulnerable [in-wAl'nA-rAbl] *a.* unverwundbar.

Inward [in'uerd] *a.* inwendig, inner; *ad.* einwärts, nach innen; -ly *ad.* im Innern.

Iodine [ai'o-dihn] *n.*, Jod *n.*

Irascible [i-ræ'ssibl] *a.* reizbar.

Irate [ai-reit'] *a.* erzürnt, zornig.

Ire [ai'er] *n.* Zorn *m.*

Iris [ai'riss] *n.* Schwertlilie *f.*, Iris *f.*; – diaphragm *n.* Irisblende *f.*

Irksome [Ark'ssAm] *a.* lästig.

Iron [ai'An] *n.* Eisen *n.*, Bügeleisen *n.* (*flat-iron*); *a.* eisern; -s *n.pl.* Fesseln *f.pl.*; – bar *n.* Eisenstange *f.*; – casting *n.* Eisenguss *m.*; – founder *n.* Eisengiesser *m.*; – foundry *n.* Eisengiesserei *f.*; – pyrites *n.* Eisenkies *m.*; – ware *n.* Eisenwaren *f.pl.*; – work *n.pl.* Eisenhütte *f.*

Ironclad [ai'An-klæd] *n.* Panzerschiff *n.* [isch, spöttisch.

Ironical [ai-ro'nikl] *a.* iron-

Ironmonger [ai'An-mAng-ger] *n.* Eisenhändler *m.*; -y *n.* Eisenwaren *f.pl.*, Eisenhandel *m.*

Irony [ai'rA-ni] *n.* Ironie *f.*

Irradiat'e [i-rei'di-eit] *vt.* bestrahlen; -ion *n.* Bestrahlung *f.*, Irradiation *f.*

Irrational [i-ræ'schA-nAl] *a.* unvernünftig.

Irreconcilable [i-re-kAn-ssai'lAbl] *a.* unversöhnlich.

Irrecoverable [i-ri-kA'wA-rAbl] *a.* unwiederbringlich.

Irredeemable [i-ri-dih'm.Abl] *a.* unablöslich.
Irrefutable [i-ri-fjuh'tAbl] *a.* unwiderlegbar.
Irregular [i-re'gju-ler] *a.* unregelmässig, regellos, irregulär (*mil.*); -s *pl.* Freischar *f*; -ity *n.* Unregelmässigkeit *f*, Regellosigkeit *f*, Fehler *m*.
Irrelevan'cy [i-re'li-wAn-ssi] *n.* Unanwendbarkeit *f*; -t *a.* unanwendbar, belanglos.
Irreligious [i-ri-li'dzhAss] *a.* gottlos. [*a.* unabsetzbar.]
Irremovable [i-ri-muh'wAbl]
Irreparable [i-re'pA-rAbl] *a.* unersetzlich.
Irrepressible [i-ri-pre'ssibl] *a.* ununterdrückbar.
Irreproachable [i-ri-prou'tschAbl] *a.* untadelhaft, unbescholten. [unwiderstehlich.]
Irresistible [i-ri-si'stibl] *a.*
Irresolute [i-re'so-luht] *a.* unentschlossen.
Irrespective [i-ri-spek'tiw] *a.* ohne Rücksicht auf.
Irresponsible [i-ri-spon'ssibl] *a.* unverantwortlich.
Irretrievable [i-ri-trih'wAbl] *a.* unwiederbringlich.
Irreverence [i-re'wrAnss] *n.* Unehrerbietigkeit *f*.
Irreverent [i-re'wrAnt] *a.* unehrerbietig.
Irrevocable [i-re'wo-kAbl] *a.* unwiderruflich.
Irrigat'e [i'ri-geit] *vt.* bewässern, ausspülen; -ion *n.* Bewässerung *f*.
Irrita'bility [i-ri-tA-bi'li-ti] *n.* Reizbarkeit *f*; -ble *a.* reizbar; -te *vt.* reizen, aufbringen; -tion *n.* Reizung *f*, Erregung *f*.
Irruption [i-rAp'schAn] *n.* Einfall *m*, Einbruch *m*.
Isinglass [ai'sing-glahss] *n.* Hausenblase *f*, Fischleim *m*.
Island [ai'lAnd] *n.* Insel *f*.
Isolat'e [ai'sso-leit] *vt.* vereinsamen, isolieren; -ion *n.* Isolierung *f*.

Issue [i'schuh] *n.* Ausgabe *f*, Abgabe *f*, Austritt *m*, Ausgang *m*, Kinder *n.pl* (*law*); *vt.* ausgeben, erlassen, verausgaben.
Isthmus [iss'mAss] *n.* Landenge *f*.
It [it] *pn.* es.
Italics [i-tæ'lix] *n.pl.* Kursivschrift *f*. [jucken.]
Itch [itsch] *n.* Jucken *n*; *vi.*
Item [ai'tAm] *n.* Einzelheit *f*, Posten *m* (*com.*).
Itine'ra'nt [ai-ti'nA-rAnt] *a.* wandernd; -ry *n.* Reiseführer *m*, Reiseplan *m*.
Its [itss] *pn.* sein, dessen; -elf *pn.* es selbst, sich.
Ivory [ai'wA-ri] *n.* Elfenbein *n*.
Ivy [ai'wi] *n.* Efeu *m*.

J

Jab [dzhæb] *n.* Stoss *m*, Stich *m*; *vi.* stossen.
Jabber [dzhæ'ber] *vi.* schnattern, schwatzen.
Jack [dzhæk] *n.* Gestell *n*, Stütze *f*, Sägebock *m*, Auto-Wagen-heber *m* (*aut.*), Klinke *f* (*ph.*), Heber *m* (*pike*), Bube *m* (*card*), Stiefel-Schuh-knecht *m* (*boots*), Gösch *f* (*flag*); - -boot *n.* Stiefel *m*, Langschäfter *m.pl.*; - -knife *n.* Klappmesser *n*. [al *m*.]
Jackal [dzhæ'kOl] *n.* Schak-
Jacket [dzhæ'kit] *n.* Jacke *f*, Umschlag *m* (*book*), Umhüllung *f* (*tec.*), Mantel *m* (*bullet*, *etc.*). [*f*; *vt.* abschinden.]
Jade [dzheid] *n.* Schindmähre
Jade [dzheid] *n.* Nephrit *m*, Beilstein *m*.
Jag [dzhæg] *n.* Kerbe *f*; *vt.* kerben, zacken; -ged *a.* schartig, gezähnt. [uar *m*.]
Jaguar [dzhæ'gju-ahr] *n.* Jag-
Jail [dzheil] *n.* Gefängnis *n*, -er *n.* Gefängniswärter *m*.
Jam [dzhæm] *n.* Fruchtgelee *n*, das Eingemachte, Marmelade *f*.

Jam [dzhæm] *vt.* drücken, klemmen, stören (*rad.*); **-ming** *n.* Funkstören *n*, Störung *f*.

Jamb [dzhæm] *n.* Türpfosten *m*.

Jamboree [dzhæm-bA-rih'] *n.* Pfadfindertreffen *n*. [ner *m*.

Janitor [dzhæ'ni-ter] *n.* Pförtner *m*.

January [dzhæ'nju-A-ri] *n.* Januar *m*. [*vt.* lackieren.

Japan [dzhA-pæn'] *n.* Lack *m* (*r*);

Jar [dzhahr] *n.* Topf *m*, Krug *m*.

Jar [dzhahr] *vi.* knarren, misstönen; *t.* stören.

Jargon [dzhar'gAn] *n.* Kauderwelsch *n*, Jargon *m*.

Jasper [dzhæ'sper] *n.* Jaspis *m*.

Jaundice [dzhOn'diss] *n.* Gelbsucht *f*.

Jaunt [dzhOnt] *n.* Ausflug *m*.

Jauntily *ad*, **Jaunty** [dzhOn'ti] *a.* munter, flott. [Kiefer *m*.]

Jaw [dzhO] *n.* Kinnbacken *m*.

Jazz [dzhæs] *n.* Jazz *m*.

Jealous [dzhe'lAss] *a.* eifersüchtig; **-y** *n.* Eifersucht *f*.

Jeep [dzhihp] *n.* Flitzer *m*, Kübelwagen *m*, Volkswagen *m*.

Jeer [dzhih'er] *vi.* verhöhnen; *n.* Hohn *m*.

Jelly [dzhe'li] *n.* Gelee *n*.

Jemmy [dzhe'mi] *n.* kurze Brechstange *f*.

Jerk [dzhArk] *n.* Ruck *m*, *vt.* fortschnellen; *i.* zucken.

Jersey [dzhAr'si] *n.* Strickjacke *f*. [scherzen.]

Jest [dzhest] *n.* Scherz *m*; *vi.*

Jet [dzhet] *n.* Gagat *m*, Jett *m*.

Jet [dzhet] *n.* Strahl *m*, Düse *f* (*av.*), Düsenbohrung *f* (*av.*); **-** herausspritzen; **- -plane** *n.* Düsenflugzeug *n*, Strahler *m*; airfield for **-s** Strahlerplatz *m*; **-propelled** *a.* Düsen . . . ; **-propelled aircraft** *n.* Flugzeug *n*, mit Düsen-, Rückstoss-antrieb *m*; **-propelled engine** *n.* **-propulsion** Rückstossmotor *m*. **-propulsion** *n.* Strahl-, Düsen-, Reaktions-, Rückstoss-antrieb *m*. **-engine**. *n.* Strahlmotor *m*.

Jetsam [dzhet'sAm] *n.* Strandgut *n*.

Jettison [dzhe'ti-sAn] *vt.* über Bord werfen; **-ing** *n.* Abwurf *m* (*av.*).

Jetty [dzhe'ti] *n.* Landungsbrücke *f*, Hafendamm *n*.

Jew [dzhuh] *n.* Jude *m*.

Jewel [dzhuh'il] *n.* Edelstein *m*, Juwel *n*, Stein *m* (*watch*); **-ler** *n.* Juwelier *m*; **-lery** *n.* Schmucksachen *f.pl*, Juwelen *n.pl*.

Jewess [dzhuh'ess] *n.* Jüdin *f*.

Jib [dzhib] *vi.* scheuen.

Jib [dzhib] *n.* Klüver *m* (*nav.*).

Jib [dzhib] *n.* Ausleger *m*, Kragarm *m*.

Jig [dzhig] *n.* irischer Tanz.

Jigger [dzhi'ger] *n.* Handkran *m*, Jigger *m* (*rad*, *arc.*), Hecksegel *n* (*nav.*).

Jilt [dzhilt] *vt.* sitzen lassen.

Jingle [dzhing'gl] *vi.* klingeln; *n.* Geklingel *n*.

Jingo [dzhing'gou] *n.* Hurrapatriot *m*, Chauvinist *m*.

Job [dzhob] *n.* Lohnarbeit *f*, Geschäft *n*, Stelle *f*; *vt.* vermieten, in Stückarbeit geben; **- -lot** *n.* Ramschpartie *f*; **-ber** *n.* Börsenmakler *m*; **-bery** *n.* Aktienhandel *m*, Schiebung *f*.

Jockey [dzho'ki] *n.* Jockei *m*; *vt.* betrügen. [haft, lustig.]

Jocular [dzho'kju-ler] *a.* spass-

Jog [dzhog] *n.* leichter Stoss; *vi.* leise anstossen; **- along** *vi.* dahinschlendern; **- -trot** *n.* Schlendrian *m*, Trab *m*.

Joggle [dzhogl] *vt.* leicht schütteln.

Join [dzheun] *vt.* verbinden, zusammenfügen, beitreten; **-** in sich beteiligen an; *n.* Verbindungsstelle *f*; **-er** *n.* Tischler *m*; **-t** *n.* Verbindung *f*, Fuge *f*, Gelenk *n*, Braten *m* (*meat*); *a.* gemeinschaftlich; *vt.* fügen, zergliedern; **-t** proprietor *n.* Miteigentümer *m*; **-t-stock** *n.* Aktienkapital *n*; **- -stock bank**

n. Aktienbank f; – -stock company n. Aktiengesellschaft f. [ken m.

Joist [dzheust] n. Querbalken m.

Joke [dzhouk] n. Spass m., Witz m.; vi. spassen; – -r n. Spassmacher m, Joker m. (card).

Joll'ity [dzho'li-ti] n. Lustigkeit f; -y a. lustig; – -boat n. kleines Ruderboot. [Stoss m.

Jolt [dzhoult] vt.i. stossen; n. [Stoss m.]

Jostle [dzhossl] vt. anstossen.

Jot [dzhot] n. Iota n.; – down vt. kurz notieren.

Journal [dzhAr'nAl] n. Tagebuch m, Zeitschrift f; Wellzapfen m (tec.); -ism n. Journalismus m, Zeitungswesen n; -ist n. Journalist n, Zeitungsschreiber m.

Journey [dzhAr'ni] n. Reise f; vi. reisen; -man n. Geselle m, Handwerker m. [sinnig.

Jovial [dzhou'wi-Al] a. froh-

Joy [dzheu] n. Freude f; – -ful a. freudvoll; -less a. freudlos; -stick n. Steuerknüppel m, Schalthebel m (av.). [jubelnd.

Jubilant [dzhuh'bi-lAnt] a.

Jubilation [dzhuh'bi-leiˈschAn] n. Jubel m. [iläum n.

Jubilee [dzhuh'bi-lih] n. Jubiläum n.

Judg'e [dzhAdzh] n. Richter m, Kenner m; vi. urteilen; – richten, halten für; -ment n. Urteil n, Verstand m, Meinung f.

Judicial [dzhuh-diˈschal] a. gerichtlich, unparteiisch.

Judiciary [dzhuh-diˈschi-A-ri] n. Richterstand m, Justiz f.

Judicious [dzhuh-diˈschAss] a. verständig.

Jug [dzhAg] n. Krug m.

Juggi'e [dzhAgl] vi. gaukeln; -er n. Gaukler m; -ing n. Gaukelspiel n.

Juice [dzhuhss] n. Saft m.

Juicy [dzhuh'ssi] a. saftig.

July [dzhuh-lai'] n. Juli m.

Jumble [dzhAmbl] n. Wirr-

warr m; vt. untereinander werfen.

Jump [dzhAmp] vi. springen; t. überspringen; n. Sprung m, Satz m, Absprung m (av.); -er n. Springer m, Abspringer m (av.).

Jumper [dzhAm'per] n. Jumper m, Schlupfjacke f.

Junction [dzhAngk'schAn] n. Verbindung f, Anschluss m (rl.), Bahnknoten m (rl.); – -box n. Anzweigdose f (el.).

June [dzhuhn] n. Juni m.

Jungle [dzhAng'gl] n. Dschungel n.

Junior [dzhuh'ni-er] a. jünger. n.

Junk [dzhAngk] n. Altwaren f.pl, Abfälle m.pl.

Juris'diction [dzhuh-ris-dik'schAn] n. Gerichtsbarkeit f; area of – Dienstbereich m; -prudence n. Rechtswissenschaft f. [schworene.

Juror [dzhuh'rer] n. der Ge-

Jury [dzhuh'ri] n. die Geschworenen, Schwur-, Preisgericht n.

Just [dzhAst] a. gerecht, billig; ad. gerade, fast, kaum; -ice n. Gerechtigkeit f; -ifiable a. zu rechtfertigen, berechtigt; -ification n. Berechtigung f, Rechtfertigung f; -ify vt. rechtfertigen; -ly ad. mit Recht.

Jut [dzhAt] vi. hinausragen.

Jute [dzhuht] n. Jute f.

Juvenile [dzhuh'wA-nail] a. jugendlich; n. junger Mensch.

K

Kale [keil] n. Kohl m.

Kangaroo [kæng-gA-ruh'] n. Känguruh n. [erde f.

Kaolin [kei'o-lin] n. Porzellan-

Keel [kihl] n. Kiel m, Schiff n.

Keen [kihn] a, -ly a. eifrig, scharf; -ness n. Schärfe f, Heftigkeit f, Eifer m.

Keep [kihp] vt. halten, bewahren, beobachten (*rules*), unterhalten (*feed*), führen (*goods*); i. sich halten (*food*), sich aufhalten (*stay*); – **down** niederdrücken (*price*); – **up** t. hoch erhalten (*price*); -er n. Hüter m, Wärter m, Besitzer m (*inn, etc.*); -ing n. Gewahrsam m, Aufsicht f; -sake n. Andenken n.

Keg [keg] n. Fässchen n.

Kelp [kelp] n. Blatt-tang m, rohe Soda. [hütte f.

Kennel [ke'nil] n. Hunde-

Kerb [kArb] n. Strassenkante f.

Kernel [kAr'nAl] n. Kern m.

Kerosene [ke'ro-ssihn] n. Kerosin n, raffiniertes Petroleum.

Ketchup [ke'tschAp] n. pikante Sosse.

Kettle [ketl] n. Kessel m; – -drum n. Pauke f.

Key [kih] n. Schlüssel m, Ton m, Taste f (*piano*); -board n. Tastatur f (*typewriter*), Klaviatur f (*piano*); -hole n. Schlüsselloch n; – -industry n. Hauptindustrie f, Schlüsselindustrie f; – -man n. unentbehrlicher Angestellter m; -note n. Grundton m; – -word n. Stichwort n.

Keystone [kih'stoun] n. Schluss-stein m.

Khaki [kah'ki] n. Khaki n; a. staubfarben.

Kick [kik] vt. einen Fusstritt geben, stossen, schiessen (*games*); i. ausschlagen; Fusstritt m.

Kid [kid] n. Zicklein n, Kind n; – -glove n. Glacéhandschuh m.

Kidnap [kid'næp] vt. rauben, entführen.

Kidney [kid'ni] n. Niere f, Sorte f; – -bean n. Steig-, Stangen-, Schnitt-bohne f.

Kill [kil] vt. töten, schlachten; n. Tötung f. [Darre f.

Kiln [kiln] n. Brennofen m,

Kilo'gram [ki'lo-græm] n. Kilogramm n; -metre n. Kilo-

meter n; -s per hour Stundenkilometer n.pl.

Kin [kin] n. Verwandtschaft f.

Kilt [kilt] n. schottisches Röckchen.

Kind [kaind] a. gütig, freundlich; n. Art f; in – in Natur.

Kindle [kindl] vt. anzünden; i. sich entzünden.

Kind'liness [kaind'li-ness] n. Freundlichkeit f; -ly a. freundlich; -ness n. Güte f.

Kindred [kin'drid] n. Verwandtschaft f, die Verwandten pl.

King [king] n. König m; -dom n. Königreich n.

Kink [kingk] n. Fitze f, Kink f, Schleife f. [Verwandte.

Kinsman [kins'mAn] n. der

Kipper [ki'per] n. Räucherhering m, Bückling m.

Kiss [kiss] n. Kuss m; vt. küssen; – -proof a. kussfest.

Kit [kit] n. Handwerkszeug n, Ausrüstung f, Gerät n; first aid – Verbandkasten m; marching – Marschgepäck n; -bag n. Tornister m, Ränzel m, Werkzeugtasche f.

Kitchen [ki'tschin] n. Küche f; – -garden n. Gemüsegarten m; – -range n. Kochofen m.

Kite [kait] n. (Papier-)Drache m, Gabelweihe f (*bird*).

Kitten [kitn] n. Kätzchen n.

Klaxon [klæx'on] n. Hupe f.

Knack [næk] n. Kunstgriff m.

Knacker [næ'ker] n. Abdecker m.

Knapsack [næp'ssæk] n. Tornister m, Ränzel m.

Knave [neiw] n. Spitzbube m, Bauer m (*card*).

Knead [nihd] vt. kneten.

Knee [nih] n. Knie n; – -breeches n.pl. Kniehosen f.pl.; -cap n. Kniescheibe f; – -deep a. knietief.

Kneel [nihl] vi. knien.

Knickers [ni'kers] n.pl. Schlüpfer m. Damenbeinkleid n.

Knick-knacks [nik'næx] n. pl. Nippsachen f.pl.

Knife [naif] n. Messer n; – and fork Essbesteck n.

Knight [nait] n. Ritter m, Springer m (chess); -ly a. ritterlich.

Knit [nit] vt. stricken, verbinden; i. sich verbinden; -ting machine n. Strickmaschine f.; – needle n. Stricknadel f.

Knob [nob] n. Knopf m.

Knock [nok] n. Schlag m, Anklopfen n; vt.i. klopfen, schlagen; – down zu Boden schlagen, zuschlagen (auction); -er n. Klopfer m.

Knot [not] n. Knoten m, Strähne f (com.); vt. verknüpfen; -ted a. knotig; -ty a. verwickelt.

Know [nou] vt. wissen, kennen; -ing a. schlau; -ingly ad. wissentlich.

Knowledge [no'lidzh] n. Wissen n, Kenntnis f.

Knuckle [nAkl] n. Knöchel m; – down under n. nachgeben.

Kudos [kjuh'doss] n. Ruhm m, Prestige n.

L

Label [leibl] n. Zettel m, Etikette f; vt. mit einer Aufschrift versehen, etikettieren, bekleben.

Laboratory [lA-bo'rA-tA-ri] n. Versuchsraum m, Laboratorium n.

Laborious [lA-bO'ri-äss] a. arbeitsam, fleissig, mühsam.

Labour [lei'ber] n. Arbeit f, Anstrengung f, Arbeiterschaft f (workers); vi. arbeiten; – exchange n. Arbeitsnachweis m; – party n. Arbeiterpartei f; – pool n. Arbeitsansatz m; – shortage n. Mangel m, an Arbeitskräften; -er n. Arbeiter m; agricultural – Landarbeiter m.

Laburnum [lA-bAr'nAm] n. Goldregen m. [end.

Lac [læk] num. hunderttausend.

Lace [leiss] n. Spitzen pl, Schnur f; vt. schnüren; -d boots n.pl. Schnürstiefel m.pl.

Lacerate [læ'ssA-reit] vt. zerreissen. [ermangeln, fehlen.

Lack [læk] n. Mangel m; vt.i.

Lacquer [læ'ker] n. Lack m; vt. lackieren.

Lad [læd] n. Bursche m.

Ladder [læ'der] n. Leiter f, Laufmasche f (stocking).

Lading [lei'ding] n. Ladung f; bill of – Frachtbrief m.

Ladle [leidl] n. grosser Löffel m; vt. ausschöpfen. [frau f.

Lady [lei'di] n. Dame f, Edel-

Lag [læg] vi. zaudern, nacheilen (el.); verkleiden (tec.); n. Verzögerung f, Phasenverschiebung f (el.); -ging n. Schalung f, Verkleidung f (tec.).

Lagoon [lA-guhn'] n. Lagune f.

Laic [lei'i-ti] n. Laienstand m.

Laite [leik] n. See m.

Lake [leik] n. Lack m (colour).

Lamb [læm] n. Lamm n, Lammfleisch n; – -like a. lammartig; -skin n. Lammfell n.

Lame [leim] a. lahm; vt. lähmen; -ness n. Lahmheit f.

Lament [lA-ment'] vi. beklagen; t. klagen; n. Klage f; -able a. beklagenswert.

Lamina [læ'mi-nA] n. Plättchen n, Lamelle f (el.).

Lamp [læmp] n. Lampe f; -bracket n. Wandleuchter m; -chimney n. Zylinder m; -post n. Laternenpfahl m; -shade n. Lampenschirm m; -signal n. Lichtsignal n.

Lance [lahnss] n. Lanze f; vt. durchbohren, aufschneiden; -bombadier n. Gefreiter m. der Artillerie; -corporal n. Gefreiter m.

Lancet [lahn'ssit] n. Lanzette f; -arch n. Spitzbogen m.

Land [lænd] n. Land n, Boden m, Grundstück n; vi. landen, anlegen (nav.); t. ausbooten, ausladen, löschen (goods), landen (ship), absetzen (plane); ~ agent m. Grundstücksmakler m; ~ forces pl. Landmacht f; ~ girl n. freiwillige Landarbeiterin f; ~ -mine f. Erd-, Landmine f; ~ -owner n. Grundbesitzer m; ~ -plane n. Landflugzeug n; ~ -tax n. Grundsteuer f.

Landed proprietor see Landowner. [n (nav.).

Landfall [lænd'fOl] n. Sichten

Landing [lænd'ing] n. Landung f, Niedergehen n (av.), Treppenabsatz m (stairs), Ausschiffung f (troops, etc.); ~ craft n. Landungsboot n; ~ force n. Landungstruppen f.pl; ~ ground n. Rollfeld n, Flugplatz m (av.), Landeplatz m (av.); ~ light n. Landelicht n (av.); ~ party n. Landungskorps n (mil, nav.), Ausladekommando n (mil, nav.); ~ run n. Anslauf m; ~ -skid n. Gleitkufe f (av.); ~ stage n. Landungs-, Anlege-brücke f; ~ -strip n. Landestreifen m (av.).

Landlady [lænd'lei·di] n. Wirtin f. [ung f (el.).

Landline [lænd'lain] n. Leit-

Landlocked [lænd'lokt] a. landumschlossen; ~ bay n. Haff n.

Landlord [lænd'lOrd] n. Wirt m, Gutsherr m, Gast-, Schankwirt m.

Landmark [lænd'mahrk] n. Landmarke f, Wahrzeichen n, Merkzeichen n, Gelände-, Ortungs-punkt m.

Landowner [lænd'ouner] n. Land-, Grund-besitzer m.

Landscape [lænd'skeip] n. Landschaft f.

Landslide [lænd'sslaid] n. Bergsturz m, Zusammenbruch m.

Landsman [lænds'mAn] n.

Landmann m, **Landratte** f (nav.).

Landward [lænd'uerd] ad. landeinwärts. [(f forest).

Lane [lein] n. Gasse f, Schneise

Language [lang'guidzh] n. Sprache f.

Languid [læng'guid] a. schlaff, matt; ~ish vi. schlaffen, matt werden, verschmachten, stocken; ~or n. Schlaffheit f, Mattigkeit f. [dünn.

Lanky [læng'ki] a. mager.

Lanoline [læ'no·lihn] n. Lanolin n, Schafwollfettöl n.

Lantern [læn'tern] n. Laterne f; ~ -slide n. Lichtbild n, Diapositiv n, Laternbild n.

Lanyard [læn'jahrd] n. Taljereep n (nav.), Anzugsleine f (mil.), Wischstrick m (gun), Dienstabzeichen n (badge), Achselschnur f (cord).

Lap [læp] n. Schoss m.

Lap [læp] vt. ~ in einschlagen; over~ übereinandergreifen; n. Vorstoss m, Überdeckung f (tec.).

Lap [læp] vt. auflecken, aufschlappen.

Lapse [læpss] n. Verlauf m, Verfallen m, Fehltritt m; vi. verlaufen, verfallen.

Lapwing [læp'uing] n. Kiebitz m. [stahl m.

Larceny [lahr'ssA·ni] n. Diebstahl m, Larde [lahrd] n. Schweineschmalz n; vt. spicken.

Larder [lahr'der] n. Speisekammer f.

Large [lahrdzh] a. gross; ~ly ad. grösstenteils; ~ness n. Grösse f.

Lark [lahrk] n. Lerche f.

Lark [lahrk] n. Spass m.

Lascar [læ'sker] n. indischer Matrose.

Lash [læsch] n. Hieb m, Peitsche f; vt. geisseln, peitschen; ~ings pl. Massen f.pl.

Lash [læsch] vt. festbinden; ~ing n. Festmachen n, Sorrung f (nav.).

Lass [læss] n. Mädchen n.

Last [lahst] n. Leisten n.

Last [lahst] a. letzt; ad. zuletzt; - month voriger Monat; - post Zapfenstreich m, Abschiedsgruß m.

Last [lahst] vi. dauern, ausreichen; -ing a. nachhaltig, dauernd.

Latch [lætsch] n. Klinke f, Drücker m, Verschlussriegel m (gun); - -key n. Drücker m, Hausschlüssel m.

Late [leit] a, ad. spät, verspätet; a. ehemalig, verstorben; -ly ad. vor kurzem; -comer n. Nachzügler m; -ness n. Verspätung f.

Latent [lei'tAnt] a. verborgen, latent.

Lateral [læ'tA-rAl] a. seitlich, Seiten . . . ; - communications n.pl. Querverbindung f; - dispersion n. Seiten-, Breitenstreuung f.

Lath [læth] n. Latte f.

Lathe [leidh] n. Drechselbank f, Drehbank f; - tool n. Drehstahl m.

Lather [læ'dher] n. Schaum m; vt. einseifen.

Latitude [læ'ti-tjuhd] n. geographische Breite. [rine f.

Latrine [lA-trihn'] n. Latrine f.

Latter [læ'ter] a. dieser, später, dieser, diese, dieses; -ly ad. neuerdings.

Lattice [læ'tiss] n. Gitter n; - girder n. Fachwerkträger m (tec.). [wert.

Laudable [lO'dAbl] a. lobenswert.

Laugh [lahf] n. Lachen n; vi. lachen; -able a. lächerlich; -ter n. Gelächter n.

Launch [lOnsch] n. Stapellauf m, Ablauf m, Barkasse f (boat); vt. vom Stapel laufen lassen, schleudern, loslassen, lancieren (torpedo), ansetzen (attack); -ing tube n. Torpedo-, Ausstoss-rohr n.

Laundress [lOn'driss] n. Wäscherin f.

Laundry [lOn'dri] n. Waschanstalt f.

Laurel [lo'rAl] n. Lorbeer m.

Lavatory [læ'wA-tA-ri] n. Waschraum m, Abort m, Toilette f; public - Bedürfnisanstalt f.

Lavender [læ'win-der] n. Lavendel m.

Lavish [læ'wisch] vt. verschwenderisch.

Law [lO] n. Gesetz n, Recht n; - -abiding a. friedlich; - -breaker n. Verbrecher m; -court n. Gerichtshof m; -ful a. gesetzlich; -less a. gesetzwidrig, gesetzlos; -suit n. Prozess m, Rechtshandel m; -yer n. Rechtsanwalt m.

Lawn [lOn] n. Rasenplatz m; - mower n. Rasenmäher m.

Lawn [lOn] n. Battist m, Schleierleinwand f.

Lax [læx] a. schlaff, locker, lax; -ative n. Abführmittel n; -ity n. Schlaffheit f, Laxheit f.

Lay [lei] a. Laien . . . , weltlich.

Lay [lei] vt. legen, stellen, setzen, (ein)richten (gun); - by zurücklegen, sparen; - down aufgeben, aufstellen, vorschreiben, niederlegen, strecken (arms); - in einkaufen, aufspeichern; - up aufbewahren, sammeln.

Layer [lei'er] n. Schicht f, Lage f, Richtkanonier m (gun).

Layette [lei-et'] n. Erstlingswäsche f, Babyausstattung f.

Lay-figure [lei'fi-ger] n. Schneiderpuppe f.

Lay-out [lei-aut'] n. Plan m, Anlage f, Entwurf m.

Laziness [lei'si-ness] n. Faulheit f. [faul, träge.

Laz'y [lei'si] a, -ily [lei-si-li] ad.

Lead [led] n. Blei n, Senkblei n, Lot n (nav.), Zollverschluss m (customs); - pencil n. Bleistift m.

Lead [lihd] vt. führen, leiten; i. anführen; n. Leitung f, Führung *f*, (Draht)Leitung *f* (*el.*); aerial — Antennenleitung *f*; -ing *a*. führend, erst, hervorragend; *n*. Leitung *f*, Führung *f*; -ing aircraftman *n*. Stabs-Haupt-gefreiter *m*; -ing article *n*. Leitartikel *m*; -ing question *n*. Suggestivfrage *f* (*law*); -ing seaman *n*. Gefreiter *m*.

Leaf [lihf] *n*. Blatt *n*, Klappe *f* (*table, etc.*); -let *n*. Zettel *m*, Broschüre *f*, Prospekt *m*, Flugschrift *f*, Drucksache *f*; -tobacco *n*. Blättertabak *m*; -valve *n*. Klappventil *n*; -y *a*. belaubt.

League [lihg] *n*. Bund *m*, Verein *m*; - of Nations Völkerbund *m*.

Leak [lihk] *n*. Leck *n*; *vi*. lecken; -age *n*. Lecken *n*, Stromverlust *m* (*el.*); -y *a*. leck, undicht.

Lean [lihn] *a*. mager; *n*. das Magere. [neigen.

Lean [lihn] *vi*. lehnen, sich]

Leap [lihp] *n*. Satz *m*, Sprung *m*; *vt*. überspringen; *i*. springen; - frog attack *n*. Überschlagangriff *m* (*mil.*); - year *n*. Schaltjahr *n*.

Learn [lArn] *vt.i*. lernen; -ed *a*. gelehrt; -ing *n*. Gelehrsamkeit *f*.

Lease [lihss] *n*. Verpachtung *f*, Pachtvertrag *m*; *vt*. verpachten; -lend *n*. Leihpakt *m*; -hold *n*. Pachtung *f*; -holder *n*. Pächter *m*, Mieter *m*.

Leash [lihsch] *n*. Koppelleine *f*; *vt*. koppeln.

Least [lihst] *a*. geringst; *ad*. am wenigsten.

Leather [le'dher] *n*. Leder *n*; *a*. ledern; - worker *n*. Sattler *m*.

Leav'e [lihw] *n*. Erlaubnis *f*, Urlaub *m*; *vt*. lassen, verlassen, hinterlassen, zurücklassen; *i*. abreisen; on — beurlaubt; -ings *pl*. Reste *m.pl*; -ing certificate *n*. Abgangszeugnis *n*.

Leaven [le'wAn] *n*. Sauerteig *m*; *vt*. säuern, anstecken.

Lecture [lek'tscher] *n*. Vorlesung *f*, Vortrag *m*, Verweis *m*; *vi*. Vorlesungen halten, tadeln, rügen; - room *n*. Hörsaal *m*; -r *n*. der Vortragende, Lektor *m*, Dozent *m*.

Ledge [ledzh] *n*. Sims *m*, Vorsprung *m*. [buch *n*.

Ledger [le'dzher] *n*. Haupt-]

Lee [lih] *n*. Lee *f*, Schutz *m*; -way *n*. Abtrift *f*, Zurückbleiben *n*.

Leech [lihtsch] *n*. Blutegel *m*, Blutsauger *m*.

Leek [lihk] *n*. Lauch *m*.

Leer [lih'er] *vi*. schielen; *n*. schiefer Blick, Seitenblick.

Lees [lihs] *n.pl*. Hefe *f*, Bodensatz *m*. [wärts.

Leeward [lih'uerd] *ad*. lee-]

Left [left] *a*. link; *ad*. links; -hand drive *n*. Linkssteuerung *f* (*aut.*); -handed *a*. linkshändig, linksgängig (*tec.*); -wing *a*. Links . . .; *n*. Linkssozialismus *m*, Linke *f*.

Left [left] *a*. übrig, zurückgelassen; - luggage office *n*. Gepäckaufbewahrungsstelle *f* (*rl.*).

Leg [leg] *n*. Bein *n*, Keule *f* (*meat*); -pull *n*. Aufziehen *n*, Necken *n*.

Legacy [le'gA-ssi] *n*. Vermächtnis *n*.

Legal [lih'gAl] *a*, -ly *ad*. gesetzlich, rechtsgültig; - advice *n*. Rechtsbeistand *m*; - proceedings *n.pl*. gerichtliche Schritte *m.pl*. Rechtsverfahren *n*; - tender *n*. gesetzliches Zahlungsmittel *n*; -ity *n*. Gesetzlichkeit *f*, Rechtmässigkeit *f*; -ization *n*. gesetzliche Bestätigung, Legalisierung *f*; -ize *vt*. rechtskräftig machen, legalisieren, beglaubigen.

Legation [li-gei'schAn] *n*. Gesandschaft *f*.

Legend [le'dzhAnd] *n*. Legende *f*, Sage *f*.

Leggings [le'gings] n.pl. Gamaschen pl.

Legibility [le-dzhi-bi'li-ti] n. Leserlichkeit f.

Legibl'e [le'dzhibl] a, -ly ad. leserlich, deutlich.

Legion [lih'dzhAn] n. Legion f, Schar f; -ary a. Legionssoldat m.

Legislat'e [le'dzhi-ssleit] vi. Gesetze geben; -ion n. Gesetzgebung f; -ive a. gesetzgebend; -or n. Gesetzgeber m; -ure n. gesetzgebender Körper, Parlament n.

Legitimacy [le-dzhi'ti-mA-ssi] n. Gesetzmässigkeit f, Legitimität f.

Legitimat'e [li-dzhi'ti-mit] a. rechtmässig, ehelich; -ion n. Legitimierung f.

Legumes [le'gjuhms'] n.pl. Hülsenfrüchte f.pl.

Leisure [le'zher] n. Musse f, -ly a, ad. gemächlich.

Lemon [le'mAn] n. Zitrone f; -ade n. Zitronen-limonade f; -wasser n; – curd n. Zitronenkrem m; – peel n. Zitronenschale f; – sole n. Rotzunge, kleinköpfige Scholle; – squash n. Zitronenlimonade f.

Lend [lend] vt. leihen, verausleihen; -er n. Verleiher m; money- – n. Geldverleiher m; -ing library n. Leihbibliothek f.

Length [length] n. Länge f, Strecke f; -en vt. verlängern, vorverlegen (fire); i. sich verlängern; -ening n. Verlängerung f; -wise ad. der Länge nach; -y a. ziemlich lang, ausgedehnt.

Lenien'cy [lih'ni-An-ssi] n. Milde f, Nachsicht f; -t a. mild, nachsichtig.

Lens [lens] n. Linse f, Objektiv n; – cap n. Objektivdeckel m.

Lent [lent] n. Fasten pl.

Lentil [len'til] n. Linse f.

Leopard [le'perd] n. Leopard m.

Leper [le'per] n. der Aussätzige. [satz m.

Leprosy [le'prA-ssi] n. Aussatz m.

Lesion [lih'zhAn] n. Verletzung f, Schädigung f.

Less [less] a, ad. minder, weniger. [Pächter m.

Lessee [less-ih'] n. Mieter, Pächter m.

Lesser [le'sser] a. weniger, kleiner.

Lesson [lessn] n. Lektion f, Stunde f; give -s Unterricht erteilen. [m, Pächter m.

Lessor [less'Or'] n. Vermieter m.

Lest [lest] cj. damit nicht, aus Furcht dass.

Let [let] vt. lassen, vermieten; n. sich vermieten; to – zu vermieten.

Lethal [lih'thAl] a. tötlich.

Lethargic [le-thahr'dzhik] a. schlafsüchtig, träge.

Letter [le'ter] n. Brief m, Buchstabe m (alphabet), Schrift f (print); – of credit n. Kreditbrief m; – of introduction n. Empfehlungsschreiben n; – -box n. Briefkasten m; – -card n. Kartenbrief m, Briefkarte f; – -file n. Briefordner m; -press n. Druck m, Text m, Buchdruckerpresse f, Kopierpresse f; – -weight n. Briefbeschwerer m. [Salat m.

Lettuce [le'tiss] n. (Kopf-)

Level [le'wil] n. Niveau n, ebene Fläche, Wasserwaage f, Dosenlibelle f, Pegelmesser m (tec.), Tonstärke f (rad.); a. waagerecht, eben; vt. waagerecht machen, nivellieren, einebnen; – -crossing n. Bahnübergang m; – -headed a. vernünftig; -ler n. Gleichmacher m, Nivellierer m; -ling n. Gleichmachen, Nivellieren n; -ling block n. Richtplatte f (nav.); -ling rod n. Zielstange f; -ling screw n. Stellschraube f.

Lever [le'wer] n. Hebel m, Anker m (watch); -age n. Hebelwirkung f, Hebelkraft f.

Levity [le'wi-ti] n. Leichtsinn m.

Levy [le'wi] n. Erhebung f,
Aushebung f, Aufgebot n
(mil.); vt. erheben, ausheben.

Lewd [luhd] a. liederlich, unzüchtig.

Lewis gun [luh'iss-gAn'] n.
Maschinengewehr n.

Lexicon [lex'i-kAn] n. Lexikon n, Wörterbuch n.

Liability [lai-A-bi'li-ti] n.
Haftbarkeit f, Verpflichtung f,
Ausgesetztsein f.

Liable [lai'Abl] a. haftbar, ausgesetzt; – for damages schad-
enersatzpflichtig; – to duty
zollpflichtig.

Liaison [lih-ei'song] n. Liebes-
verhältnis n, Fühlung f (mil.),
Verbindung f (mil.); – detachment n. Verbindungsabteilung
f; – officer n. Verbindungs-
offizier m. [nerin f.

Liar [lai'er] n. Lügner m, Lüg-

Libel [laibl] n. Verleumdung f,
Schmähschrift f; vt. verleumden, schmähen; -lous a. verleumderisch.

Liberal [li'bA-rAl] a. -ly ad.
freigebig, freisinnig, liberal,
reichlich; n. der Liberale; -ism
n. Liberalismus m; -ity n.
Freigebigkeit f. Freisinnig-
keit f.

Liberate [li'bA-reit] vt. befreien, freilassen; -ion n. Befreiung f; -or n. Befreier m.

Liberty [li'ber-ti] n. Freiheit f,
Erlaubnis f, Recht n; – of
thought Gedankenfreiheit f;
at – frei, unbeschäftigt.

Librarian [lai-breh'ri-An] n.
Bibliothekar m.

Library [lai'brA-ri] n. Bibliothek f, Büchersammlung f.

Licence [lai'ssAnss] n. Erlaubnisschein m, Führerschein m
(aut.), Genehmigung f, Konzession f, Schankgerechtigkeit
f (liquor); pilot's – Führerschein m (av.).

License [lai'ssAnss] vt. genehmigen, konzessionieren.

Lick [lik] vt. lecken, prügeln.

Lid [lid] n. Deckel m, Augenlid n.

Lie [lai] n. Lüge f; vi. lügen.

Lie [lai] n. Lage f; vi. liegen,
liegen bleiben.

Lieutenant [lef-te'nAnt] n.
Leutnant m; first – Oberleutnant m (mil.), Kapitänleutnant
m (nav.); flight – Hauptmann
m, der Flieger; –colonel n.
Oberstleutnant m; –com-
mander n. Korvettenkapitän
m (nav.); –general n. General-
leutnant m (mil.).

Life [laif] n. Leben n; -belt n.
Rettungsgürtel m, -ring m;
-boat n. Rettungsboot n;
-insurance n. Lebensversiche-
rung f; – jacket n. Schwimmweste f; –saving equipment n.
Notgerät n; –size n. Lebens-
grösse f; –time n. Lebenszeit f;
-less a. leblos, tot; -like a.
lebenswahr, naturgetreu; -long
a. lebenslänglich.

Lift [lift] vt. Aufzug m, Hub m,
Hubhöhe f (tec.), Auftrieb m
(av.); vt. heben, aufheben, erheben, aufrichten; -attendant
m. Fahrstuhlführer m.

Ligament [li'gA-mAnt] n.
Flechte f, Band n.

Ligature [li'gA-tjuh-er]
Band n, Ligatur f, Doppel-
buchstabe m.

Light [lait] n. Licht n, Tageslicht n, Beleuchtung f (lighting); a. licht, hell; vt. anzünden.

Light [lait] a. leicht; – car n.
Kleinkraftwagen m; – duties
n.pl. Revierdienst m (mil.);
-headed a. wirr im Kopf;
-hearted a. fröhlich; – railway
n. Kleinbahn f.

Lighten [laitn] vi. blitzen.

Lighten [laitn] vt. leichter
machen, erleichtern.

Lighter [lai'ter] n. Leichter m,

Lichter *m* (*boat*); cigarette – *n*. Taschenfeuerzeug *n*.

Lighter [lai'ter] *a.* leichter.

Lighthouse [lait'hauss] *n.* Leuchtturm *m.*

Lighting [lai'ting] *n.* Beleuchtung *f*, Befeuerung *f* (*av.*); – system *n.* Beleuchtungsanlage *f.*

Lightly [lait'li] *ad.* leicht, leichtsinnig, oberflächlich.

Lightness [lait'ness] *n.* Leichtigkeit *f*, Leichtfertigkeit *f.*

Lightning [lait'ning] *n.* Blitz *m*; – -conductor *n.* Blitzableiter *m*; – strike *n.* wilder Streik; – war Blitzkrieg *m.*

Lightship [lait'ship] *n.* Leuchtschiff *n.*

Lignite [lig'nait] *n.* Braunkohle *f*, Lignit *m.* [würdig.

Likable [lai'kÁbl] *a.* liebens-

Like [laik] *a, ad.* gleich, ähnlich, wie; **nothing** – bei weitem nicht.

Like [laik] *vt.* mögen, gern haben, tun, essen, trinken; *i.* belieben.

Like'lihood [laik'li-hud] *n.* Wahrscheinlichkeit *f*; -ly *a, ad.* wahrscheinlich, geeignet.

Likeness [laik'ness] *n.* Ähnlichkeit *f*, Porträt *n.*

Likewise [laik'uais] *ad.* auch, gleichfalls. [Neigung *f.*

Liking [lai'king] *n.* Gefallen *n.*

Lilac [lai'lÁk] *n.* Flieder *m*; *a.* lila. [Lied *n.*

Lilt [lilt] *n.* Rhythmus *m.*

Lily [li'li] *n.* Lilie *f*; – of the valley *n.* Maiglöckchen *n.*

Limb [lim] *n.* Glied *n*, Stück *n.*

Limber [lim'ber] *n.* Protze *f*, Vorderwagen *m*; – up *vi.* aufprotzen; – frame *n.* Protzgestell *n.*

Lime [laim] *n.* Kalk *m*, Vogelleim *m*; – concrete *n.* Kalkbeton *m*; -kiln *n.* Kalkofen *m*; -light *n.* Kalklicht *n*, Bühnenlicht *n.*

Lime [laim] *n.* Linde *f.*

Limit [li'mit] *n.* Grenze *f*, Höchstpreis *m* (*price*), Frist *f* (*time*); *vt.* begrenzen, einschränken, beschränken; -ation *n.* Begrenzung *f*, Grenze *f*, Beschränkung *f*; -ed *a.* beschränkt; – company Gesellschaft *f*, mit beschränkter Haftpflicht, Aktiengesellschaft *f.*

Limousine [li'muh-sihn] *n.* ganz geschlossener Wagen, Limousine *f.* [sam (com.).

Limp [limp] *a.* schlaff, bieg-

Limp [limp] *vi.* hinken.

Limpet [lim'pit] *n.* Napmuschel *f*; – mine *n.* Klettenmine *f.*

Limpid [lim'pid] *a.* klar, rein.

Limy [lai'mi] *a.* kalkig.

Linch-pin [linsch'pin] *n.* Lünse *f*, Lünz *m*, Vorstecker *m.*

Linden [lin'dÁn] *n.* Linde *f.*

Line [lain] *n.* Linie *f*, Zeile *f*, Strecke *f* (*rl.*), Geleise *n* (*track*), Stellung *f* (*mil.*), Leitung *f* (*el.*), Fach *n* (*subject*); *vt.* liniieren, aufstellen; – demarcation – Trennungs-, Demarkationslinie *f*; – of argument *n.* Beweisführung *f*; -astern *n.* Kiellinie *f* (*nav.*); – of battle *n.* Schlachtlinie *f*; – of business *n.* Geschäftszweig *m*; – of communications *n.* Verbindungslinien *f.pl*, Etappe *f*; – of fire *n.* Schuss-linie *f*, -richtung *f*; -fishing *n.* Angelfischerei *f*; – of resistance *n.* Widerstandslinie *f*; – of sight *n.* Visier-, Ziel-linie *f* (*mil.*).

Line [lain] *vt.* füttern.

Lineage [li'ni-Adzh] *n.* Abstammung *f*, Geschlecht *n.*

Lineal [li'ni-Al] *a.* gerade, direkt. [Gesichtszug *m.*

Lineament [li'ni-A-mAnt] *n.*

Linear [li'ni-ahr], [li'ni-er] *a.* linear, Linien . . ., Längs . . . .

Linen [li'nin] *n.* Leinwand *f*, Linnen *n*, Wäsche *f*; *a.* leinen; dirty – schmutzige Wäsche; -bag *n.* Wäschesack *n*; – button

n. Wäscheknopf m; - collar n. Leinenkragen m; - cupboard, - press n. Wäscheschrank m; - thread n. Leinenzwirn m; - yarn n. Leinengarn n.

Liner [lai'ner] n. Passagierdampfer m, Überseedampfer m; air- - n. Verkehrflugzeug n.

Linesman [lains'mAn] n. Linienrichter n (games).

Ling [ling] n. Heidekraut n.

Linger [ling'ger] vi. zögern, weilen.

Linguist [ling'guist] n. Sprachkenner m, Sprachkundige(r) m; -ic a. sprachwissenschaftlich, sprachlich.

Liniment [li'ni-mAnt] n. Einreibemittel n.

Lining [lai'ning] n. Futter n, Verkleidung f, Ausmauerung f.

Link [lingk] n. Glied n; vt. verketten; -s n.pl. doppelte Hemdenknöpfe m.pl.

Links [lingkss] n.pl. Golfspielplatz m.

Linnet [li'nit] n. Hänfling m.

Linoleum [li-nou'li-Am] n. Linoleum n.

Linotype [lai'nou-taip] n. Zeilensetzmaschine f.

Linseed [lin'ssihd] n. Leinsamen m; - oil n. Leinöl n.

Lint [lint] n. Scharpie f.

Lintel [lin'tl] n. Fenstersturz m.

Lion [lai'An] n. Löwe m.

Lioness [lai'A-ness] n. Löwin f.

Lip [lip] n. Lippe f, Rand m; - -stick n. Lippenstift m.

Liquefaction [li-kui-fæk'schAn] n. Verflüssigung f.

Liquefy [li'kui-fai] vt. schmelzen.

Liqueur [li-kjuh'er] n. Likör m.

Liquid [li'kuid] n. Flüssigkeit f; a. flüssig; -ate vt. bezahlen, liquidieren, abwickeln, abrechnen; -ation n. Bezahlung f, Liquidation f, Abrechnung f.

Liquor [li'ker] n. Flüssigkeit f, alkoholisches Getränk.

Liquorice [li'kA-riss] n. Süssholz n, Lakritze f.

Lisp [lisp] vi. lispeln; n. Lispeln n.

List [list] n. Liste f, Verzeichnis n; vt. eintragen.

List [list] n. Schlagseite f (nav.); vi. Schlagseite haben.

Listen [lissn] vi. horchen, lauschen, zuhören; - in am Radio hören; - er n. Horcher m; -er in n. Funkgast m, Radiohörer m, Radiohörerin f; -ing n. Horchen n, Radiohören n, Rundfunkempfang m; -ing post n. Horchposten m (mil.); -ing report n. Horchmeldung f (mil.).

Listless [list'less] a. träge.

Literal [li'tA-rAl] a. buchstäblich, wörtlich, wortgetreu; -ry a. literarisch, schriftstellerisch, gelehrt; -ture n. Literatur f, Schrifttum n, Gedrucktes n.

Lithe [laidh] a. biegsam, geschmeidig.

Lithograph [li'thou-grahf] n. Steindruck m; -er n. Lithograph m; -y n. Steindruck m.

Litigation [li-ti-gei'schAn] n. Rechtsstreit m.

Litmus [lit'mAss] n. Lackmus n; - paper n. Reagenspapier n.

Liter, Litre [lih'ter] n. Liter n.

Litter [li'ter] n. Streu f, Wurf m, Tragbahre f, Unordnung f; vt. umherwerfen, in Unordnung bringen.

Little [litl] a. klein, wenig, kurz; ad. (ein) wenig; n. das Wenige; - by nach und nach.

Littoral [li'tA-rAl] n. Küstenland n.

Liturgy [li'ter-dzhi] n. Gottesdienstordnung f, Liturgie f.

Live [liw] vi. leben, wohnen; f. erleben, verleben.

Live [laiw] a. lebendig, geladen (wire), scharf (bullet, etc.); -lihood n. Lebensunterhalt m, Leben n, Existenz f; -liness n. Lebhaftigkeit f; -ly a. lebhaft, frisch n, stark; -n v.i. auf, leben, beleben.

Liver [li'wer] *n.* der Lebende.

Liver [li'wer] *n.* Leber *f.*

Livid [li'wid] *a.* blaugrau.

Living [li'wing] *n.* Lebensunterhalt *m*, Existenz *f.*; *a.* lebendig; – *room n.* Wohnzimmer *n*; – *space n.* Lebensraum *m.*

Lizard [li'serd] *n.* Eidechse *f.*

Llama [lah'mA] *n.* Lama *n.*

Llano [lah'no] *n.* Ebene *f.*

Load [loud] *n.* Last *f*, Ladung *f*, Belastung *f* (*tec.*); *vt.* laden, beladen, beschicken; **commercial** – Nutzlast *f*; **useful** – Gesamtlast *f*; –**ing** *n.* Belastung *f*, Beladung *f*; **Verladung** *f*; –**ing party** *n.* Wagentrupp *n*, Aufladekommando *n* (*mil.*); –**ing point** *n.* Ladestelle *f.*

Loaf [louf] *n.* Brot *n*, Laib *m*; – **sugar** *n.* Hutzucker *m.*

Loaf [louf] *vi.* bummeln, herumlungern; –**er** *m.* Müssiggänger *m*, Bummler *m.*

Loam [loum] *n.* Lehm *m.*

Loan [loun] *n.* Anleihe *f*, Darlehen *n*, Verleihen *n*; *vt.* verleihen.

Loath [louth] *a.* abgeneigt.

Loath'e [loudh] *vt.* verabscheuen; –**ing** *n.* Ekel *m*, Widerwille *m*; –**some** *a.* ekelhaft, abscheulich.

Lobby [lo'bi] *n.* Vorhalle *f.*; *vt.* politisch beeinflussen; –**ing** *n.* Durchstecherei *f.*

Lobe [loub] *n.* Lappen *m*, Flügel *m.* [mer *m.*

Lobster [lob'ster] *n.* Hummer *m.*

Local [loukl] *a.*, –*ly ad.* örtlich, Orts . . .; – **billets** *pl.* Ortsquartier *n* (*mil.*); – **call** *n.* Orts-gespräch *n*, –**verbindung** *f* (*ph.*); – **colour** *n.* Lokalkolorit *n*; – **self-government** *n.* Selbstverwaltung *f*; – **time** *n.* Ortszeit *f*; –**ity** *n.* Örtlichkeit *f*, Ort *m*; –**ize** *vt.* örtlich beschränken.

Locat'e [lou-keit'] *vt.* feststellen, ausfindig machen; be –**d** gelegen sein; –**ion** *n.* Lage *f*, Platz *m.*

Lock [lok] *n.* Schloss *n*, Verschluss *m*; *vt.* schliessen, versperren; *i.* (sich) schliessen, eingreifen; **canal** – *n.* Schleuse *f.*; – **gate** *n.* Schleusentor *n*, Stemmtor *n*; –**stitch** *n.* Steppstich *m*; – **out** *n.* Aussperrung *f.*; – **up** *n.* Gefängnis *n*, feste Geldanlage (*com.*), Einzelgarage *f* (*aut.*), Box *f* (*aut.*), Einzelschuppen *m* (*aut.*).

Lock [lok] *n.* Locke *f.*

Locker [lo'ker] *n.* verschliessbarer Kasten, Schrank *m.*

Locket [lo'kit] *n.* Medaillon *n.*

Locomotion [lou-kA-mou'schAn] *n.* Bewegung *f*, Ortsveränderung *f.*

Locomotive [lou-kA-mou'tiw] *n.* Lokomotive *f*, Maschine *f.*; **electric** – **elektrische Lokomotive**; – **engine** *n.* Lokomotive *f*; – **engineer** *n.* Lokomotivbauer *m*; – **shed** *n.* Lokomotivschuppen *m*; – **tender** *n.* Tender *m.* [schrecke *f*

Locust [lou'kAst] *n.* Heu-

Lode [loud] *n.* Erzgang *m*, Ader *f*; –**star** *n.* Polarstern *m*, Leitstern *m.*

Lodg'e [lodzh] *n.* Haus *n*, Loge *f*, Wohnung *f*; *vt.* beherbergen, deponieren (*com.*); *i.* logieren, stecken bleiben; –**er** *n.* Mieter *m*, Kostgänger *m*; –**ing(s)** *n.* Wohnung *f*, Logis *n*, Quartier *n*, Lager *n*; –**ing-house** *n.* Schlaf-, Logier-haus *n.*

Loft [loft] *n.* (Dach)Boden *m*, Speicher *m*, Dachkammer *f*; –**iness** *n.* Höhe *f*, Erhabenheit *f*; –**y** *a.* hoch, erhaben.

Log [log] *n.* Klotz *m*, Log *n* (*nav.*), Tagebuch *n* (*nav.*), Überwachungsbuch *n*; *vt.* ins Tagebuch eintragen; – **cabin** *n.* Blockhaus *n.* [*pl.* Streit *m.*

Loggerheads [lo'ger-heds] *n.*

Logic [lo'dzhik] *n.* Logik *f*; –**al** *a.* logisch, folgerichtig.

Logwood [log'uud] *n.* Kampescheholz *n.*

Loin [leun] *n.* Lende *f*, Lendenstück *m* (*meat*). [bummeln.

Loiter [leu'ter] *vi.* trödeln,

Loll [lol] *vi.* sich träge dehnen, herumlungern.

Lone [loun] *a.* einsam; -liness *n.* Einsamkeit *f*; -ly *a.* einsam.

Long [long] *a.* lang; *ad.* lang(e); -boat *n.* Rettungsboot *n*, Barkasse *f*; - distance flight *n.* Fernflug *m*, Weitflug *m* (*av.*); -hand *n.* gewöhnliche Schreibschrift; -handed brush *n.* Stielbesen *m*; - range *a.* weittragend (*gun*), Fern . . . (*rad., etc.*); -shore fishing *n.* Küstenfischerei *f*; -shoreman *n.* Küstenfischer *m*, Hafenarbeiter *m*; - sighted *a.* weitsichtig; -suffering *a.* langmütig; -term *a.* Fern . . . langfristig (*loan*); - wave *n.* Langwelle *f* (*rad.*); -wave transmitter *n.* Langwellensender *m* (*rad.*); -winded *a.* langatmig, weitschweifig.

Long [long] *vi.* sich sehnen; -ing *n.* Sehnsucht *f*; *a.* sehnsüchtig.

Longitude [lon'zhi-tjuhd] *n.* geographische Länge.

Look [luk] *n.* Blick *m*, Aussehen *n*; *vi.* blicken, nachsehen, aussehen; -ing-glass *n.* Spiegel *m*; -out *n.* Auslug *m*, Wachtposten *m.*

Loom [luhm] *n.* Webstuhl *m.*

Loom [luhm] *vi.* sichtbar werden.

Loop [luhp] *n.* Schlinge *f*, Schleife *f*; -aerial *n.* Rahmen-, Schleif-antenne *f.*

Loophole [luhp'houl] *n.* Schlupfloch *n*, Ausweg *m*, Schiessscharte *f* (*mil.*).

Loop-line [luhp'lain] *n.* Ringgeleis *n.*

Loose [luhss] *a.* -ly *ad.* los, locker, lose; *vt.* lösen, losbinden; - leaf book Ringbuch *n.* Loseblätterbuch *n*; -n *vt.* losmachen; -ness *n.* Lockerheit *f.*

Loot [luht] *n.* Beute *f*; *vt.* erbeuten; *i.* plündern; -er *n.* Plünderer *m*, Beutemacher *m.*

Lop [lop] *vt.* beschneiden, stutzen, kappen; -sided *a.* schief.

Loquacious [lo-kuei'schAss *a.* geschwätzig.

Lord [lOrd] *n.* Herr *m*; -mayor *n.* Oberbürgermeister *m.*

Lorry [lo'ri] *n.* Lastauto *n*, Lastkraftwagen *m*, Last-Fracht-wagen *m*; -borne *a.* verlastet (*mil.*); - borne infantry *n.* Panzergrenadiere *m.pl*; -borne regiment *n.* Schützen-, Panzer-grenadierregiment *n.* [Verlierer *m.*

Lose [luhs] *vt.* verlieren; -r *n.*

Loss [loss] *n.* Verlust *m.*

Lot [lot] *n.* Los *n*, Teil *m*, Menge *f*, Partie *f* (*com.*); by - durchs Los.

Lotion [lou'schAn] *n.* Waschmittel *n*, Gesichtswasser *n*; hair - Haarwasser *n*; eye - Augenwasser *n.*

Lottery [lo'tA-ri] *n.* Lotterie *f*, Auslosung *f*; - ticket *n.* Lotterielos *n.*

Loud [laud] *a.*, -ly *ad.* laut, schreiend (*colours, etc.*); -ness *n.* Lautheit *f*, Lautstärke *f* (*rad.*); - speaker *n.* Lautsprecher *m*; -speaker van *n.* Lautsprecherwagen *m* (*rad.*).

Lounge [launzh] *n.* Vorhalle *f*, Foyer *n*, Diele *f* (*hotel*); *vi.* herumlungern, faulenzen, faul liegen; - suit *n.* Strassenanzug *m*; -r *n.* Faulenzer *m*, Faulpelz *m.*

Lous'e [lauss] *n.* Laus *f*; -y *a.* lausig, schlecht, scheusslich, erbärmlich.

Lout [laut] *n.* Lümmel *m.*

Lovable [lA'wAbl] *a.* liebenswürdig.

Love [lAw] *n.* Liebe *f*, Null *f* (*tennis*); - affair *n.* Liebschaft *f*; -bird *n.* Sperlingspapagei *m*; -letter *n.* Liebesbrief *m*; -making *n.* Hofmachen *n*;

match *n.* Liebesheirat *f*; - set *n.* Nullpartie *f* (*tennis*); -sick *a.* liebeskrank; - token *n.* Liebespfand *n*; -liness *n.* Lieblichkeit *f*; -ly *a.* lieblich; -r *n.* Liebhaber *m.,* Liebhaberin *f,* der, die Verliebte.

Low [lou] *vi.* brüllen.

Low [lou] *a, ad.* niedrig, leise (*voice*), schwach (*weak*), mässig (*price*), gemein (*unfair*), tiefausgeschnitten (*neck*); - brow *n.* Philister *m*; - flying *n.* Tiefflug *m* (*av.*); -flying plane *n.* Tieffflieger *m*; - frequency *n.* Niederfrequenz *f*; - pressure *n.* Tiefdruck *m*, Unterdruck *m*; -pressure tyre *n.* Ballonreifen *m* (*cycle*); - tension *n.* Neiderspannung; - tension battery *n.* Heizbatterie *f*; - tide *n.* Ebbe *f*; -wing plane *n.* Tiefdecker *m* (*av.*); - *a.* niedriger, unter; *vt.* niederlassen, herabsetzen; -ness *n.* Niedrigkeit *f.*

Loyal [leu'Al] *a,* -ty *ad.* treu, loyal, patriotisch; -ty *n.* Treue *f,* Loyalität *f,* Patriotismus *m.*

Lubber [lA'ber] *n.* Lümmel *m,* Flegel *m.*

Lubrica'nt [luh'bri-kAnt] *n.* Schmiermittel *n*; -te *vt.* schmieren, ölen; -ting *a.* Schmier . . .; -ting oil *n.* Schmieröl *n*; -ting point *n.* Schmiernippel *m,* Oler *m*; -tion *n.* Olen *n,* Olung *f,* Schmieren *n*; -tor *n.* Schmierapparat *m.*

Lucid [luh'ssid] *a.* klar, deutlich; -ity *n.* Klarheit *f,* Deutlichkeit *f.*

Luck [lAk] *n.* Glück *n,* Geschick *n*; good - Glück *n*; bad - Unglück *n*; -ily *ad.* zum Glück, glücklicherweise; -less *a.* unglücklich; -y *a.* glücklich.

Lucr'ative [luh'krA-tiw] *a.* einträglich; -e *n.* Gewinn *m,* Vorteil *m,* Mammon *m.*

Ludicrous [luh'di-krAss] *a.* lächerlich.

Luff [lAf] *n.* Luv *f* (*nav.*).

Lug [lAg] *n.* Ohr *n,* Henkel *m,* Ansatz *m* (*tec.*), Warze *f,* Rohrklaue *f* (*gun*).

Lug [lAg] *vt.* schleppen.

Luggage [lA'gidzh] *n.* Gepäck *n*; heavy - grosses Gepäck; light - Handgepäck *n*; - grid *n.* Gepäck-brücke *f;* -netz *n* (*aut.*); - label *n.* Gepäckzettel *m*; left - office *n.* Gepäckaufbewahrung *f*; - office *n.* Gepäckannahme *f,* -ausgabe *f*; - rack *n.* Gepäcknetz *n*; - van *n.* Gepäckwagen *m.*

Lugger [lA'ger] *n.* Lugger *m,* Fischerboot *n.*

Lug-sail [lAg'sseil] *n.* Luggersegel *n,* Breitfock *f.*

Lull [lAl] *n.* Ruhepause *f,* Windstille *f*; *vt.* einlullen.

Lullaby [lA'LA-bai] *n.* Wiegenlied *n.* [Hexenschuss *m.*

Lumbago [lAm-bei'gou] *n.*

Lumbar [lAm'ber] *a.* Lenden . . . .

Lumber [lAm'ber] *n.* Gerumpel *n,* Plunder *m,* Bauholz *n*; *vi.* sich schwerfällig fortbewegen, Bauholz fällen; -jack *n.* Ärmelweste *f* (*garment*), Holzfäller *m*; -man *n.* Holzfäller *m.*

Luminous [luh'mi-nAss] *a.* leuchtend; - dial *n.* nachts leuchtendes Zifferblatt.

Lump [lAmp] *n.* Klumpen *m,* Masse *f,* Stück *n* (*sugar*); *vt.* zusammenwerfen; -y *a.* klumpig.

Lunacy [luh'nA-ssi] *n.* Geistesgestörtheit *f,* Wahnsinn *m.*

Lunar [luh'nA-tik] *n.* der. die Wahnsinnige; - asylum *n.* Irrenanstalt *f.*

Lunch [lAnsch] *n.* Gabelfrühstück *n,* leichtes Mittagessen; *vi.* zu Mittag essen.

Lung [lAng] *n.* Lunge *f.*

Lunge [lAnzh] *n.* Ausfall *m; vi.* ausfallen.

Lurch [lArtsch] *n.* Ruck *m,*

Überholen n (nav.); vi. überholen (ship), taumeln (man); leave in the – im Stich lassen.

Lure [luh'er] n. Köder m, Lockung f; vt. verlocken, ködern.

Lurk [lArk] vi. lauern.

Luscious [lA'schAss] a. sehr süss, saftig, köstlich.

Lust [lAst] n. sinnliche Begierde; vi. begehren; -ful a. wollüstig.

Lustre [lA'ster] n. Glanz m.

Lusty [lA'sti] a. rüstig, lebhaft, frisch.

Lute [luht] n. Laute f.

Luxur'iant [lAg-sjuh'ri-Ant] a. wuchernd; -ious a. üppig, verschwenderisch, schwelgerisch, luxuriös; -y n. Luxus m, Üppigkeit f, Luxusware f, Schwelgerei f.

Lye [lai] n. Lauge f. [morden.

Lynch [linsch] vt. lynchen, er-

Lyric [li'rik] n. lyrisches Gedicht; a. lyrisch; -al a. lyrisch.

Lysol [lai'ssol] n. Lysol n.

M

Macadamize [mA-kæ'dA-mais] vt. beschottern, chaussieren.

Macaroni [mæ-kA-rou'ni] n. Makkaroni pl.

Mace [meiss] n. Amtsstab m.

Mace [meiss] n. Muskatblüte f.

Machination [mæ-ki-nei'schAn] n. Machenschaft f, Umtrieb m.

Machine [mA-schihn'] n. Maschine f, Fahrrad n, Flugzeug n (av.); - cannon n. Maschinenkanone f; - gun n. Maschinengewehr n; - gunner n. Maschinengewehrschütze m; -ist n. Maschinenwärter m. -ry n. Mechanismus m, Maschinenteile m.pl. Machinerie f. – shop n. mechanische Werkstatt; – tool n. Werkzeugsmaschine f.

Mackerel [mæ'kril] n. Makrele f.

Mackintosh [mæ'kin-tosch] n. Regenmantel m.

Mad [mæd] a. -ly ad. toll, verrückt, wahnsinnig; -house n. Irrenhaus n. [Frau.

Madam [mæ'dAm] n. gnädige

Madden [mædn] vt. verrückt machen, toll machen.

Madness [mæd'ness] n. Tollheit f, Verrücktheit f.

Mae West [mei-uest'] n. Schwimmweste f (av.).

Magazine [mæg-gA-sihn'] n. Warenlager n, Zeitschrift f, Wochenblatt n; Magazin n; - rifle n. Mehrlader m (mil.).

Maggot [mæ'gAt] n. Made f, Larve f.

Magic [mæ'dzhik] n. Zauber m, Zauberei f; a. zauberhaft.

Magician [mA-dzhi'schAn] n. Zauberer m.

Magistrate [mæ'dzhi-streit] n. Polizeirichter m, Friedensrichter m.

Magnanim'ity [mæg-nA-ni'mi-ti] n. Grossmut f; -ous a. grossmütig.

Magnesi'a [mæg-nih'schA] n. Talkerde f; -um n. Magnesium n.

Magnet [mæg'nit] n. Magnet m; -ic a. magnetisch, Magnet . . .; -ic mine n. magnetische Mine (mil.); -ism n. Magnetismus m; -o n. Magnetzünder m, Zünder m (aut.).

Magnif'icence [mæg-ni'fi-asAnss] n. Herrlichkeit f, Pracht f; -icent a. herrlich, prachtvoll; -y vt. vergrössern; -ying glass n. Vergrösserungsglas n. [Grösse f.

Magnitude [mæg'ni-tjuhd] n.

Magpie [mæg'pai] n. Elster f.

Mahogany [mA-ho'gA-ni] n. Mahagoniholz n.

Maid [meid] n. Magd f; old – alte Jungfer; -en n. Mädchen n, Jungfrau f.

Mail [meil] n. Post f, Postbeförderung f; vt. mit der Post senden, aufgeben; air – Luftpost f; – -bag n. Postbeutel m; – -boat, – -steamer n. Postdampfer m; – -carrier n. Postbote m; – -cart n. Kinderwagen n; – -coach n. Postkutsche f; – -order business m. Postversandgeschäft n; – -train n. Postzug m.

Mail [meil] n. Panzer m; -ed fist n. gepanzerte Faust.

Maim [meim] vt. verstümmeln.

Main [mein] a. -ly ad. hauptsächlich, Haupt . . .; n. das Ganze, Wasserleitung f (water), Leitung f, Hauptkabel n (el.); – chance Hauptsache f, Selbstinteresse n; – deck n. Hauptdeck n; – force n. volle Kraft; – road n. Hauptstrasse f; -yard n. Grossraa f (nav.); -land n. Festland n; -mast n. Grossmast m; -sail n. Gross-segel n; -stay n. Hauptstütze f, Grossstag n (nav.).

Maintain [mein-tein'] vt. behaupten, erhalten, unterhalten.

Maintenance [mein'tА-nÁnss] n. Erhaltung f, Unterhaltung f, Behauptung f, Beköstigung f, Instandhaltung f (plant, tec.); – grant n. Unterhaltungszuschuss m.

Maize [meis] n. Mais m.

Majestic [mA-dzhe'stik] a. würdevoll, majestätisch.

Majesty [mæ'dzhe-sti] n. Majestät f.

Major [mei'dzher] n. Major m, Mündige(r) m; a. grösser, älter; – -general n. Generalmajor m; – key n. Durtonart f (music); -ity n. Mehrheit f, Mehrzahl f, Mündigkeit f, Majorstelle f (mil.); -ity of votes Stimmenmehrheit f.

Make [meik] vt. machen, bewirken, halten (speech), schliessen (peace); n. Form f, Bau m,

Art f, Fabrikat n; – -believe n. Verstellung f; – -up n. Schminken n, Ausstattung f; – -weight n. Zugabe f, Lückenbüsser m; -r n. Fabrikant m, Schöpfer m; -shift n. Notbehelf m.

Maladministration [mæl-Ad-mi-ni-strei'schAn] n. Misswirtschaft f.

Malady [mæ'lA-di] n. Krankheit f.

Malaria [mA-leh'ri-A] n. Malaria f, Sumpffieber n.

Malcontent [mæl'kAn-tent] n. der Missvergnügte.

Male [meil] n. Mann m, Männchen n (animal); a. männlich; – -nurse n. Krankenpfleger m.

Malefactor [mæ'li-fæk-ter] n. Missetäter m.

Malevolent [mA-le'vA-lAnt] a. böswillig.

Malformation [mæl-fOr-mei'schAn] n. Missbildung f.

Malice [mæ'liss] n. Bosheit f, böse Absicht; -ious a. boshaft, gehässig.

Malignant [mA-lig'nAnt] a. verderblich, bösartig.

Malinger [mA-ling'ger] vi. sich krank stellen; -er n. Simulant m.

Malleable [mæ'li-Abl] a. hämmerbar, schmiedbar.

Mallet [mæ'lit] n. hölzerner Hammer.

Malnutrition [mæl-njuh-tri'schAn] n. Unterernährung f.

Malpractice [mæl-præk'tiss] n. gesetzwidrige Handlung.

Malt [mOlt] n. Malz n; vt. malzen.

Maltreat [mæl-triht'] vt. misshandeln.

Maltster [mOlt'ster] n. Mälzer m.

Malversation [mæl-wer-ssei'schAn] n. Veruntreuung f, Unterschleif m.

Mamma [mA-mah'] n. Mamma f, Mutter f.

Mammal [mæ'mʌl] n. Säugetier n.

Mammoth [mæ'mʌth] n. Mammut n; a. riesenhaft, kolossal.

Man [mæn] n. Mann m, Mensch m, Knecht m, Diener m, Arbeiter m, Stein m (draughts), Figur f (chess); vt. bemannen (mil, nav.), besetzen.

Manage [mæ'nidzh] vt. leiten, führen, einrichten, zustande bringen, verwalten, bestimmen; i. fertig bringen, ermöglichen, fertig werden; -able a. handlich, lenksam, leicht zu handhaben; -ment n. Leitung f, Führung f, Verwaltung f, Vorstand m, Direktion f, (gutes) Haushalten; -r n. Leiter m, Direktor m, Geschäftsführer m, Verwalter m.

Mandat'e [mæn'deit] n. Mandat n, Auftrag m, Befehl m; -ory a. befehlend; -ory power n. Mandatsmacht f.

Mane [mein] n. Mähne f.

Manful [mæn'ful] a. -ly ad. mannhaft.

Mangan'ate [mæng'gA-nit] n. mangansaures Salz; -ese n. Mangan n, Braunstein m.

Mange [meindzh] n. Räude f.

Manger [mein'dzher] n. Krippe f.

Mangle [mæng'l] n. Mangel f; vt. mangeln, rollen.

Mangle [mæng'l] vt. verstümmeln, zerstücken.

Mangy [mein'dzhi] a. räudig.

Manhood [mæn'hud] n. Männlichkeit f, Mannheit f, Mannesalter n.

Mania [mei'niA] n. Wahnsinn m, Manie f; -c n. Wahnsinnige(r) m.

Manicure [mæ'ni-kjuh-er] n. Handpflege f.

Manifest [mæ'ni-fest] n. Ladungsverzeichnis n; a. offenbar, klar; vt. offenbaren, darlegen, zeigen; -ation n. Kundgebung

f, Offenbarung f; -o n. Manifest n, Bekanntmachung f.

Manifold [mæ'ni-fould] a. mannigfaltig.

Manikin [mæ'ni-kin] n. Männlein n, Gliederpuppe f.

Manipulat'ion [mA-ni-pju, lei'schAn] n. Behandlung f-Manipulation f; -e vt. handhaben, behandeln.

Mankind [mæn-kaind'] n. Menschheit f, Menschengeschlecht n.

Manly [mæn'li] a. mannhaft.

Manner [mæ'ner] n. Art f, Stil m, Manier f (art); -s pl. Lebensart f, Manieren f pl; -ly a. höflich.

Mannequin [mæ'ni-kin] n. Vorführdame f, Probiermamsell f.

Manning [mæ'ning] n. Bemannung f (nav.), personelle Rüstung.

Manœuvre [mA-nuh'wer] n. Manöver n, Gefechtsübung f (mil.), Streich m, List f; -e vt. manövrieren.

Man-of-war [mæn-ow-uOr'] n. Kriegsschiff n.

Manor [mæ'ner] n. Herrenhaus n, Landgut n.

Manse [mænss] n. Pfarrhaus n.

Mansion [mæn'schAn] n. Herrenhaus n, Landhaus n.

Manslaughter [mæn'slOter] n. Totschlag m. (Kaminsims m.

Mantelpiece [mæntl'pihss] n.

Manual [mæ'nju-Al] a. Hand . . .; n. Leitfaden m, Manual n (organ).

Manufactur'e [mæ-nju-fæk'tscher] n. Herstellung f, Fabrikation f; vt. herstellen, fabrizieren, verfertigen; -d article n. Fabrikat n, Ware f; -er n. Fabrikant m, Hersteller m, Fabrikbesitzer m; -ing a. Industrie . . ., Fabrik . . .; -ing town n. Fabrikstadt f.

Manure [mA-njuh'er] n. Dünger m; vt. düngen.

Manuscript [mæ'nju-skript] n. Handschrift f, Manuskript n.

Many [me'ni] a.pl. viele; - Menge f, Haufe m.

Map [mæp] n. Landkarte f; vt. aufzeichnen, ausarbeiten, entwerfen; - case n. Kartentasche f; - grid n. Kartennetz n; - section n. Kartenausschnitt m; - square n. Planquadrat n.

Maple [meipl] n. Ahorn m; -sugar Ahornzucker m.

Mar [mahr] vt. verderben, entstellen, stören.

Maraud [mA-rOd'] vi. plündern, marodieren; -er n. Plünderer m, Marodeur m.

Marble [mahrbl] n. Marmor m, Murmel f; a. marmorn.

March [mahrtsch] n. Grenze f; vi. angrenzen.

March [mahrtsch] n. Marsch m; vi. marschieren.

March [mahrtsch] n. März m.

Marching [mahr'tsching] a. Marsch . . .; - kit n. Marschgepäck n; in - order marschmässig; - order Marschbefehl m.

Marchioness [mahr'schAness] n. Marquise f.

Mare [meh'er] n. Stute f.

Margarine [mahr'dzhA-rihn] n. Margarine f, Kunstbutter f.

Margin [mahr'dzhin] n. Rand m, Spielraum m, Grenze f, Verdienstspanne f (com.).

Marigold [mæ'ri-gould] n. Ringelblume f.

Marine [mA-rihn'] n. Seesoldat m; Marine f; a. See . . .; -r n. Seemann m, Matrose m.

Marionette [mæ-riA-net'] n. Drahtpuppe f, Marionette f.

Marital [mæ'ritl] a. ehelich.

Maritime [mæ'ri-taim] a. See . . .; - court n. Seeamt n.

Mark [mahrk] n. Mark f (money).

Mark [mahrk] n. Marke f, Zeichen n, Ziel n, Narbe f, Mal n; vt. bezeichnen, aus-

zeichnen, markieren, beachten, zensieren (exercise).

Market [mahr'kit] n. Markt m; vt. auf den Markt bringen, verkaufen; - garden n. Handelsgarten m; - gardener n. Handelsgärtner m; - place n. Marktplatz m; -able a. verkäuflich.

Markings [mahr'kings] n.pl. Kenn-, Erkennungs-zeichen n. pl (av.).

Marksman [mahrx'mAn] n. Scharfschütze m; -ship n. Schützenkunst f.

Marl [mahrl] n. Mergel m.

Marmalade [mahr'mA-leid] n. Apfelsinenmarmelade f.

Marmot [mahr'mAt] n. Murmeltier n.

Maroon [mA-ruhn'] a. kastanienbraun.

Marriage [mæ'ridzh] n. Ehe f, Heirat f; - lines pl. Trauschein m.

Marrow [mæ'rou] n. Knochenmark m, Kern n; vegetable - Markkürbis m.

Marry [mæ'ri] vt.i. heiraten, sich verheiraten, trauen.

Marsh [mahrsch] n. Sumpf m, Morast m.

Marshal [mahr'schAl] n. Marschall m; vt. führen, anordnen, zusammenstellen (rl.); -ling yard n. Verschiebebahnhof m, Abstellgeleise n. [fig.

Marshy [mahr'schi] a. sumpfig.

Martial [mahr'schAl] a. kriegerisch; - law n. Kriegsrecht n, Belagerungszustand m.

Martin [mahr'tin] n. Mauerschwalbe f.

Martinet [mahr'ti-net] n. Zuchtmeister m, Leutneschinder m.

Martinmas [mahr'tin-mAss] n. Martinstag m, der 11. November.

Martyr [mahr'ter] n. Märtyrer m, Blutzeuge m; -dom n. Märtyrertum n, Martyrium n.

Marvel [mahrwl] *n.* Wunder *n*; *vi.* sich wundern; **-lous** *a.* wunderbar.

Mascot [mæ'skAt] *n.* Talisman *m*, Glücksbringer *m.*

Masculine [mæ'skju-lin] *a.* männlich, mannhaft.

Mash [mæsch] *n.* Gemisch *n*, Mengefutter *n* (*fodder*); *vt.* mischen, zerdrücken; **-ed** potatoes *pl.* Kartoffelbrei *m*, Quetschkartoffeln *f.pl.*

Mask [mahsk] *n.* Maske *f*, Larve *f*, Maskierung *f*, Verkleidung *f*, Tarnung *f* (*mil.*); *vt.* maskieren, verdecken, tarnen (*mil.*).

Mason [mei'ssAn] *n.* Maurer *m*, Steinmetz *m*; **-ry** *n.* Mauerwerk *n*, Maurerei *f.*

Mass [mæss] *n.* Masse *f*, Menge *f*; *vt.i.* anhäufen, massieren (*mil.*), (sich) zusammenstellen, (sich) vereinigen; **- meeting** *n.* Massenversammlung *f*; **- production** *n.* Massen-, Serienherstellung *f.*

Mass [mæss] *n.* Messe *f*; **high - Hochamt** *n.*

Massacre [mæ'ssAkr] *n.* Gemetzel *n*, Massenmord *m*; *vt.* niedermetzeln.

Massage [mæ'ssahzh] *n.* Massage *f*; *vt.* massieren.

Massive [mæ'ssiw] *a.* massiv.

Mast [mahst] *n.* Mast *m.*

Mast [mahst] *n.* Mast *f*; *vt.* mästen.

Master [mah'ster] *n.* Herr *m*, Meister *m*, Lehrer *m*, Vorsteher *m*, Kapitän *m*; *vt.* meistern; **- builder** *n.* Baumeister *m*; **- key** *n.* Hauptschlüssel *m*; **- mariner** *n.* Kapitän *m*; **- mechanic** *n.* Maschinenmeister *m*; **- switch** *n.* Hauptschalter *m*; **-ful** *a.* herrisch; **-ly** *a.* meisterhaft, vortrefflich; **- piece** *n.* Meisterstück *n*; **-y** *n.* Meisterschaft *f*, Gewalt *f.*

Mast-head [mahst'hed] *n.* Topp *m*, Mars *f.*

Masticate [mæ'sti-keit] *vt.* kauen.

Mastiff [mæ'stif] *n.* Bullenbeisser *m.*

Mat [mæt] *n.* Matte *f*; *vt.i.* verfilzen.

Mat [mæt] *a.* matt.

Match [mætsch] *n.* Streichholz *n*, Lunte *f.*

Match [mætsch] *n.* das Gleiche, Wettspiel *n*, Wettkampf *m*, Partie *f*, Heirat *f*, Paar *n*; *vt.* verbinden, anpassen, sich messen mit; *i.* sich entsprechen, zusammenpassen; **-less** *a.* unvergleichlich.

Mate [meit] *n.* Genosse *m*, Genossin *f*, Kamerad *m*; Maat *m* (*nav.*), Steuermann *m*; *vt.i.* (sich) paaren.

Mate [meit] *n.* Schachmatt *n*; *vt.* matt setzen.

Material [mA-tih'ri-Al] *n.* Stoff *m*, Material *n*; *a.* materiell, wesentlich; **-ist** *n.* Materialist *m*; **-ize** *vi.* sich verkörpern, sich verwirklichen, erfüllen.

Maternal [mA-tAr'nAl] *a.* mütterlich.

Mathematic'al [mæ-thi-mæ'tik-Al] *a.* mathematisch; **-ian** *n.* Mathematiker *m*; **-s** *n.pl.* Mathematik *f.*

Matins [mæ'tins] *n.pl.* Frühgottesdienst *m*, Frühmette *f.*

Matricula'tion [mA-tri-kju-lei'schAn] *n.* Immatrikulation *f*; **-e** *vt.* immatrikulieren.

Matrimony [mæ'tri-mA-ni] *n.* Ehestand *m*, Ehe *f.*

Matrix [mæ'trix] *n.* Gussmutter *f*, Prägstock *m.*

Matron [mei'trAn] *n.* verheiratete Frau, Vorsteherin *f*, Oberin *f.*

Matter [mæ'ter] *n.* Stoff *m*, Materie *f*, Zeug *n*, Sache *f*, Angelegenheit *f*, Eiter *m* (*pus*); *vi.* darauf ankommen, von Bedeutung sein, eitern; **- of fact** *a.* nüchtern, prosaisch.

Matting [mæ'ting] *n.* Geflecht

n, Mattenstoff m, Strohmatte f, Fussbodendecke f.

Mattock [mæ'tok] n. Hacke f, Haue f.   [ratze f.

Mattress [mæ'triss] n. Mat-

Matur|e [mA-tjuh'er] a. -ly ad. reif; v.t.i. reifen, verfallen (bill); -ity n. Reife f, Verfallzeit f (com.).

Maudlin [mO'dlin] a. bezecht, weinselig, sentimental.

Maul [mOl] n. Schlegel m; vt. zersausen, durchprügeln.

Maulstick [mOl'stik] n. Mahlstock m.

Mauve [mouw] a. hellviolett, mauve.   [sel f.

Mavis [mei'wiss] n. Singdros-

Maw [mO] n. Schlund m.

Mawkish [mO'kisch] a. süsslich.

Maxim [mæx'im] n. Grundsatz m, Maxime f.

Maximum [mæx'i-mAm] n. Maximum n, Höchstand m, höchster Satz; a. höchst, grösst; - wage n. Höchst-Spitzen-lohn m.

May [mei] n. Mai m; - Day n. der 1. Mai.

May [mei] v. können, dürfen, mögen.

Maybe [mei-bih'] ad. vielleicht.

Mayor [meh'er] n. Bürgermeister m.

Maze [meis] n. Irrgang m, Verwirrung f.

Me [mih] pn. mich, mir.

Meadow [me'dou] n. Wiese f.

Meagre [mih'ger] a. mager, dürftig.

Meal [mihl] n. grobes Mehl.

Meal [mihl] n. Mahlzeit f.

Mean [mihn] a. -ly ad. gering, gemein.

Mean [mihn] n. Mitte f, Durchschnitt m; a. mittler, durchschnittlich; Greenwich - time westeuropäische Zeit.

Mean [mihn] vt. bedeuten, meinen, sagen wollen, beabsichtigen, vorhaben; -ing n.

Bedeutung f, Meinung f, Absicht f.

Meanness [mihn'ness] n. Niedrigkeit f, Ärmlichkeit f.

Means [mihns] n.pl. Mittel n.pl, Geldmittel n.pl; by - of mittels.

Meanwhile [mihn'huail] ad. indessen, mittlerweile.

Measles [mih'sAls] n.pl. Masern pl.

Measly [mihs'li] a. erbärmlich.

Measurable [me'zhA-rAbl] a. messbar, absehbar (distance).

Measure [me'zhA'r] n. Mass n, Massregel f; vt. messen, abmessen; i. messen; -ment n. Messung f, Mass n.

Meat [miht] n. Fleisch n.

Mechanic [mi-kæ'nik] n. Mechaniker m, Maschinenarbeiter m, Techniker m, Betriebsfunker m (rad.).

Mechanical [mi-kæ'nikl] a, -ly ad. mechanisch, Maschinen . . .; - engineering n. Maschinenbau m; - transport n. Kraftfahrwesen n, Kraftzug m (convoy).

Mechanism [me'kA-nism] n. Mechanismus m, Getriebe n, Triebwerk n, Vorrichtung f.

Mechaniz'ation [me'kA-naisei'schAn] n. Umstellung auf Maschinenbetrieb f, Mechanisierung f, Verkraftung f (mil.); -e vt. mechanisieren, motorisieren; -d infantry n. Panzergrenadiere m.pl; -d troops n.pl. Kraftfahr(kampf)truppen f.pl.

Medal [medl] n. Medaille f, Denkmünze f; - ribbon n. Ordensband n; -lion n. Medaillon n, Schmuckkapsel f.

Meddle [medl] vi. sich mischen in, sich einmengen in; -r n. Eindringling m; -some a. aufdringlich.

Mediat'ion [mih-di-ei'schAn] n. Vermittlung f; - tor n. Vermittler m.

Medical [me'dikl] a. ärztlich;
– **advice** n. ärztlicher Rat; –
board n. Sanitätsbehörde f
(*mil.*); – **man** n. Arzt m; –
officer n. Stadtarzt m (*municipal*), General-, Ober-arzt m.
Medizinalbeamte(r) m, Sanitätsoffizier m (*mil.*); – **orderly**
n. Sanitäter m; – **personnel** n.
Sanitätspersonal n (*mil.*); –
practitioner n. Arzt m; –
services n.pl. Sanitätswesen n
(*mil.*); – **treatment** n. Kur f.
Medicinal [me-di'ssi-nAl] a.
medizinisch.
Medicine [med'ssin] n. Arznei
f, Medizin f (*science*).
Mediocre [mih'di-ou-ker] a.
mittelmässig; **-ity** n. Mittelmässigkeit f.
Mediæval [me-di-ih'vAl] a.
mittelalterlich.
Meditat'ion [me-di-te*i*'schAn]
n. Betrachtung f, Nachdenken
n; **-e** vi. betrachten, nachdenken; t. vorhaben, planen; **-ive**
a. nachdenklich.
Medium [mih'di-Am] n. Mittel n, Mitte f, Vermittlung f;
a. mittel, durchschnittlich, mittelmässig; – **gun** n. schweres
Geschütz (*mil.*); – **wave** n.
Mittelwelle f (*rad.*).
Medley [med'li] n. Gemisch n.
Meek [mihk] a. **-ly** ad. sanft,
demütig; **-ness** n. Sanftmut f.
Meet [miht] vi. sich treffen,
sich versammeln; i. begegnen,
treffen; n. Zusammenkunft f;
-ing n. Versammlung f, Sitzung
f, Tagung f, Zusammentreffen
n; – **-place** n. Sammelplatz m.
Megalomania [me-gA-lo-me*i*'-
niA] n. Grössenwahn m.
Megaphone [me'gA-foun] n.
Sprachrohr n, Megaphon n.
Melancholy [me'lAn-kA-li] n.
Wehmut f; a. melancholisch.
Mellow [me'lou] a. reif, mild,
voll.
Melodious [mi-lou'di-Ass] a.
wohlklingend.

Melody [me'lo-di] n. Wohlklang m.
Melon [me'lAn] n. Melone f.
Melt [melt] vt.i. schmelzen.
Member [mem'ber] n. Glied n,
Mitglied n, Abgeordnete(r) m;
-ship n. Mitgliedschaft f.
Membrane [mem'brein] n.
Membran f.
Memento [mi-men'to] n. Andenken n.
Memoir [me'muahr] n. Denkschrift f, Lebensbeschreibung f.
Memor'able [me'mA-rAbl] a.
denkwürdig; **-andum** [me-mA-
ræn'dAm] n. Merkblatt n,
Nachweis m, Notiz f, Mitteilung f, Rechnung f, Denkschrift
f; **-ial** n. Denkmal n; **war
-ial** Krieger-, Helden-denkmal
n; **-ize** vt. auswendig lernen;
-y n. Gedächtnis n, Erinnerung
f, Andenken n.
Menace [me'nAss] n. Drohung
f, Gefahr f; vt. bedrohen, gefährden.
Menagerie [mi-næ'dzgA-ri] n.
Tierschau f.
Mend [mend] vt. bessern, ausbessern, flicken; i. besser werden. [leute pl.
Menfolk [men'fouk] n. Manns
Menial [mih'ni-Al] n. Diener
m, Dienerin f; a. niedrig,
knechtisch.
Menstruation [men-stru-e*i*'-
schAn] n. Monatsfluss m,
Regel f.
Mensuration [men-ssju-re*i*'-
schAn] n. Messkunst f.
Mental [mentl] a. Geistes . . .;
– **disease** f. Geistesstörung f;
– **training** n. Geistesbildung f.
Mentality [men-tæ'li-ti] n.
Geistesverfassung f. [thol n.
Menthol [men'thol] n. Men
Mention [men'schAn] n. Erwähnung f; vt. erwähnen.
Menu [men'juh] n. Speisekarte f.
Mercantile [mAr'kAn-tail] a.
Handels . . .; – **law** n. Handelsrecht n.

Mercenary [mAr′ssi-nA-ri] *a.* feil, gedungen, gewinnsüchtig; *n.* Söldner *m.*

Mercerize [mAr′ssA-rais] *vt.* merzerisieren.

Merchandize [mAr′tschAndais] *n.* Ware *f.*

Merchant [mAr′tschAnt] *n.* Kaufmann *m;* - service *n.* Handelsmarine *f;* -man *n.* Handelsschiff *n.*

Merci′ful [mAr′ssi-ful] *a.*, -ly *ad.* barmherzig; -less *a.* unbarmherzig, grausam.

Mercury [mAr′kju-ri] *n.* Quecksilber *n.*

Mercy [mAr′ssi] *n.* Barmherzigkeit *f*, Gnade *f.*

Mere [mih′er] *a.*, -ly *ad.* bloss.

Merge [mArdzh] *vt.* versenken; *i.* versinken, aufgehen in.

Merger [mAr′dzher] *n.* Verschmelzung *f*, Fusion *f (com.).*

Merino [mA-rih′nou] *n.* Merino *m.*

Merit [me′rit] *n.* Verdienst *n;* *vt.* verdienen; -orious *a.* verdienstlich.

Merriment [me′ri-mAnt] *n.* Lustigkeit *f.*

Merry [me′ri] *a*, **Merrily** [me′ri-li] *ad.* lustig.

Mesh [mesch] *n.* Masche *f*, Netz *n;* *vt.* fangen; *i.* ineinandergreifen; - connection *n.* Dreieckschaltung *f (el.).*

Mesmerize [mess′mA-rais] *vt.* mesmerisieren.

Mess [mess] *n.* Unordnung *f*, Schweinerei *f*, Schmutz *m*, Patsche *f (scrape)*, Regimentstisch *m (mil.);* *vi.* gemeinschaftlich essen *(mil.);* *t.* verderben, verpfuschen, in Unordnung bringen; officers′ - *n.* Offiziersheim *n*, Kasino *n;* -jacket *n.* Messeanzug *m;* -president *n.* Kasinoältester(r) *m;* - -tin *n.* Kochgeschirr *n.*

Message [me′ssidzh] *n.* Botschaft *f;* Mitteilung *f;* wireless - Funkspruch *m;* - dropping

n. Meldeabwurf *m;* - pad *n.* Meldeblock *m.*

Messenger [me′ssin-dzher] *n.* Bote *m.*

Messmate [mess′meit] *n.* Tischgenosse *m.* [schmutzig.

Messy [me′ssi] *a.* unordentlich.

Metal [metl] *n.* Metall *n*, Schienen *f.pl (rl.)*, Beschotterung *f (road);* *vt.* beschottern; -ic *a.* metallen, Metall ...; -lurgy *n.* Hüttenkunde *f.*

Meteor [mih′ti-er] *n.* Meteor *n*, Feuerkugel *f;* -ological *a.* Wetter ...; - advice *n.* Wetterberatung *f;* - code *n.* Wetterschlüssel *m;* - station *n.* Wetterwarte *f;* -ology *n.* Wetterkunde *f.*

Meter [mih′ter] *n.* Zähler *m*, Messer *m;* gas - Gasuhr *f*, Gasmesser *m.*

Method [me′thAd] *n.* Methode *f*, Verfahren *n*, System *n;* -ical *a.* planmässig, methodisch.

Methyl [me′thil] *n.* Methyl *n.*

Metre [mih′ter] *n.* Meter *n.*

Metronome [me′trA-noum] *n.* Taktmesser *m.*

Metropolis [me-tro′pA-liss] *n.* Hauptstadt *f.*

Mettle [metl] *n.* Stoff *m*, Naturanlage *f*, Feuer *n;* -some *a.* feurig.

Mica [mai′kA] *n.* Glimmer *m.*

Microbe [mai′kroub] *n.* Mikrobe *f.*

Micro′phone [mai′kro-foun] *n.* Mikrophon *f;* hand - Tischfernsprecher *m (ph.);* -scope *n.* Mikroskop *n.*

Mid [mid] *a.* mitten in; -day *n.* Mittag *m;* - -ocean *n.* Mitte *f.* des Ozeans.

Middle [midl] *n.* Mitte *f;* *a.* mittel; -man *n.* Mittelsperson *f*, Zwischenhändler *m.*

Midge [midzh] *n.* Mücke *f.*

Midget [mid′dzhit] *n.* Zwerg *m;* - photograph *n.* Kleinbild *n;* - submarine *n.* Kleinstunterseeboot *n.*

Mid'land [mid'lAnd] a. binnenländisch; **-night** n. Mitternacht f.; **-ships** ad. mitschiffs; **-shipman** n. Fähnrich m, zur See; **-st** n. Mitte f.; **-summer** n. Hochsommer m; **-way** ad. halbwegs. [amme f.

Midwife [mid'uaif] n. Heb

Mien [mihn] n. Gesichtsausdruck m.

Might [mait] n. Macht f.; Absicht f; mächtig. [Reseda f.

Mignonette [min'jA-net'] n.

Migrat'e [mai-greit'] vi. auswandern, fortziehen; **-ion** n. Wanderung f, Zug m.

Mild [maild] a. mild, sanft, leicht (cigar); **-ness** n. Milde f, Sanftheit f.

Mildew [mil'djuh] n. Mehltau m, Brand m.

Mile [mail] n. Meile f; **-age** n. zurückgelegte Meilenzahl; **-stone** n. Meilenstein m.

Militar'ist [mi'li-tA-rist] n. Militarist m; **-istic** a. militaristisch; **-y** n. Militär n; a. militärisch, Heeres..., Kriegs...; **-** hospital n. Garnisonslazarett n; **-** police n. Feldgendarmerie f; **-** service n. Militär-, Wehrdienst m.

Militate [mi'li-teit] vi. widerstreiten.

Militia [mi-li'schA] n. Miliz f.

Milk [milk] n. Milch f; vt. melken; **-man** n. Milchmann m; **-y** a. milchig.

Mill [mil] n. Mühle f, Fabrik f, Werk n; vt. mahlen, walzen; **-dam** n. Müllwehr f; **-owner** n. Fabrikbesitzer m; **-er** n. Müller m.

Millet [mi'lit] n. Hirse f.

Milliner [mi'li-ner] n. Putzmacherin f, Modewarenhändler m; **-y** n. Putzwaren f.pl, Modewaren f.pl.

Milling-machine [mi'lingmA-schihn'] n. Fräsmaschine f.

Million [mil'jAn] n. Million f; **-aire** n. Millionär m.

Mimic [mi'mik] vi. nachahmen, nachäffen; n. Nachäffer m; **-ry** n. Nachäfferei f.

Minc'e [minss] vt. zerhacken, mildern; **-er** n. Fleischhackmaschine f; **-ing-machine** see Mincer.

Mind [maind] n. Gemüt n, Geist m, Neigung f, Absicht f; vt. achten, sich bekümmern um; i. achthaben; **-ful** a. eingedenk. [meinige.

Mine [main] pn. der, die, das

Mine [main] n. Grube f, Mine f, Bergwerk n; vt. minieren; **-d** a. minenverseucht (nav.); **-field** n. Minen-feld m, **-sperre** f; **-gallery** n. Stollen m; **-layer** m, **-laying** m (mil.), Minenlegeschiff n (nav.); **-owner** n. Zechenbesitzer m; **-sweeper** n. Minen-suchboot n, **-räumboot** n, **-sucher** n; **-sweeping** n. Minensuchen n; **-thrower** n. Minenwerfer m.

Miner [mai'ner] n. Bergmann m, Grubenarbeiter m.

Mineral [min'A-rAl] n. Mineral n; **-** oil n. Erdöl n.

Mingle [ming'gl] vt. mengen, vermischen; i. sich mengen.

Miniature [mi'nia-tjuh-er] n. Miniatur f; a. Klein...; **-camera** n. Kleinbildkamera f.

Minim [mi'nim] n. halbe Note, Tropfen m; **-ize** vt. verringern; **-um** n. Minimum n, Mindestmass n; **-** wage n. Mindestlohn m, Lohnminimum n.

Mining [mai'ning] n. Bergbau m. [ling m.

Minion [mi'niAn] n. Günst

Minist'er [mi'ni-ster] n. Minister m, Gesandte(r) m, Geistliche(r) m; **-ry** n. Amt n, Ministerium n.

Minor [mai'ner] a. geringer, gering, unbedeutend; n. der, die Minderjährige; **-ity** n. Minderheit f, Unmündigkeit f.

Minster [min'ster] n. Münster n, Dom m.

Mint [mint] *n.* Minze *f.*

Mint [mint] *n.* Münze *f.*; *vt.* münzen, prägen.

Minus [mai'nAss] *ad.* weniger.

Minute [mi'nit] *n.* Minute *f.*, Augenblick *m*; **-s** *pl.* Protokoll *n.*

Minute [mai-njuht'] *a.* -ly *ad.* sehr klein, umständlich, genau; -ness *n.* Kleinheit *f.*, Umständlichkeit *f.*

Minx [mingx] *n.* Racker *m.*

Mirac'le [mi'rAkl] *n.* Wunder *n*; -ulous *a.* übernatürlich, wunderbar.

Mirage [mi-rahzh'] *n.* Luftspiegelung *f.*, Täuschung *f.*

Mire [mai'er] *n.* Schlamm *m*, Kot *m.*

Mirror [mi'rer] *n.* Spiegel *m*, Rückspiegel *m* (*aut.*); *vt.* ab-, wider-spiegeln. [keit *f.*

Mirth [mArth] *n.* Fröhlichkeit *f.*

Misadventure [miss-Ad-wen'tscher] *n.* Missgeschick *n.*

Misapply [miss-A-plai'] *vt.* falsch anwenden.

Misapprehension [miss-æpri-hen'schAn] *n.* Missverständnis *n.*

Misappropriation [miss-Apro-pri-ei'schAn] *n.* widerrechtliche Aneignung, Unterschleif *m.*

Misbehave [miss-bi-heiw'] *vr.* sich schlecht benehmen.

Miscalculate [miss-kæl'kjuleit] *vt.* falsch berechnen.

Miscar'riage [miss-kæ'ridzh] *n.* Misslingen *n*, Fehlgeburt *f*; -y *vi.* fehlschlagen.

Miscellaneous [miss-A-lei'niAss] *a.* gemischt, verschieden.

Mischance [miss-tschahnss'] *n.* Missgeschick *n.*

Mischie'f [miss'tschihf] *n.* Unheil *n*, Unfug *m*, Possen *m*; -f -maker *n.* Unheilstifter *m*; -vous *a.* nachteilig, schädlich, mutwillig.

Misconceive [miss-kAn-ssihw'] *vt.* missverstehen.

Misconception [miss-kAn-ssep'schAn] *n.* Missverständnis *n.*

Misconduct [miss-kon'dAkt] *n.* schlechtes Betragen; [miss-kAn-dakt'] *vt.* schlecht führen; *r.* sich schlecht betragen.

Misconstruction [miss-kAn-strAk'schAn] *n.* Missdeutung *f.*

Misdeed [miss-dihd'] *n.* Missetat *f.*

Misdemeanour [miss-di-mih'ner] *n.* Vergehen *n.*

Misdirect [miss-dai-rekt'] *vt.* irre leiten, falsch adressieren.

Miser [mai'ser] *n.* Geizhals *m*, -able *a.* elend; -ly *a.* geizig; -y *n.* Elend *n.*

Misfire [miss-fai'er] *vi.* versagen, fehlzünden (*aut.*).

Misfit [miss-fit'] *n.* Nichtpassen *n*, verpasstes Stück.

Misfortune [miss-fOr'tschAn] *n.* Unglück *n.* [Besorgnis *f.*

Misgiving [miss-gi'wing] *n.*

Misgovern [miss-gA'wern] *vt.* schlecht regieren.

Misguided [miss-gai'did] *a.* irregeführt. [fall *m.*

Mishap [miss-hæp'] *n.* Unglücksfall *m.*

Misinform [miss-in-fOrm'] *vt.* falsch berichten.

Misinterpret [miss-in-tAr'prit] *vt.* missdeuten.

Misjudge [miss-dzhAdzh'] *vt.* falsch beurteilen.

Mislay [miss-lei'] *vt.* verlegen.

Mislead [miss-lihd'] *vt.* verleiten; -ing *a.* irreführend.

Mismanage [miss-mæ'nidzh] *vt.* schlecht verwalten; -ment *n.* Misswirtschaft *f.*

Misnomer [miss-nou'mer] *n.* falsche Benennung.

Misplace [miss-pleiss'] *vt.* an eine unrechte Stelle legen, übel anbringen. [Druckfehler *m.*

Misprint [miss-print'] *vt.*

Mispronounce [miss-prA-naunss'] *vt.* falsch aussprechen.

Misquote [miss-kuout'] *vt.* falsch anführen.

Misrepresent [miss-re-pri-sent'] *vt.* falsch darstellen; -ation *n.* Verdrehung *f.*

Misrule [miss-ruhl'] *vt.* schlecht regieren; *n.* Unordnung *f.*

Miss [miss] *n.* Fräulein *n.*

Miss [miss] *vt.* verfehlen, vermissen; *i.* fehlen; *n.* Fehlschuss *m.*

Mis-shapen [miss-scheipn'] *a.* ungestalt.   [schoss *n.*

Missile [mi'ssail] *n.* Wurfgeschoss *n.*

Missing [mi'ssing] *a.* abwesend, vermisst, verschollen (*mil.*); ~ **stock** *n.* Fehlbestand *m.*

Mission [mi'schAn] *n.* Sendung *f*, Mission *f*, Aufgabe *f*, Auftrag *m* (*av.*); -ary *n.* Missionär *m.*

Mis-spell [miss-spel'] *vt.* falsch schreiben.

Mis-state [miss-steit'] *vt.* unrichtig angeben; -ment *n.* falsche Angabe.

Mist [mist] *n.* Nebel *m.*

Mistake [mi-steik'] *n.* Irrtum *m*, Fehler *m*, Versehen *n*; -n *a*, -ly *ad.* irrtümlich.

Mister [mi'ster] *n.* Herr *m.*

Mistletoe [missl'tou] *n.* Mistel *f.*

Mistranslate [miss-trahn-sleit'] *vt.* unrichtig übersetzen.

Mistress [mi'striss] *n.* Herrin *f*, Hausfrau *f*, Maitresse *f.*

Mistrust [miss-trAst'] *vt.* misstrauen.

Misty [mi'sti] *a.* neblig.

Misunderstand [miss-Ander-stænd'] *vt.* missverstehen; -ing *n.* Missverständnis *n.*

Misuse [miss-juhs'] *n.* Missbrauch *m*; [miss-juhs'] *vt.* missbrauchen.

Mite [mait] *n.* Milbe *f* (*insect*).

Mite [mait] *n.* Scherflein *n* (*coin*), kleines Kind.

Mitigate [mi'ti-geit] *vt.* mildern, mässigen.

Mittens [mi'tAns] *n.pl.* Fausthandschuh *m*, Pulswärmer *m.*

Mix [mix] *vt.i.* (sich) mischen; -ture *n.* Mischung *f*, Mixtur *f.*

Mizzen [misn] *n.* Besan *m.*

Moan [moun] *vi.* stöhnen.

Moat [mout] *n.* Burggraben *m.*

Mob [mob] *n.* Pöbel *m*, Pöbelhaufe *m*; *vt.* lärmend anfallen.

Mobil'e [mou'bail] *a.* beweglich, leicht, mobil (*mil.*); -ity *m.* Beweglichkeit *f*; -ization *n.* Mobilisierung *f*, Mobilmachung *f*; -ize *vt.* mobilmachen, mobilisieren.

Mob-law [mob'lO] *n.* Volksjustiz *f*, Lynchjustiz *f.*

Mock [mok] *vt.* verspotten; *i.* spotten; -er *n.* Spötter *m*; -ery *n.* Spötterei *f*, Gespött *n.*

Mode [moud] *n.* Mode *f*, Art und Weise *f*, Form *f.*

Model [modl] *n.* Modell *n*, Vorbild *n*, Muster *n*; *vt.* modellieren, modeln, bilden.

Moderat'e [mo'dA-rit] *a.* mässig; [mo'dA-reit] *vt.* mässigen; -ion *n.* Mässigung *f.*

Modern [mo'dern] *a.* neu, modern; -ize *vt.* modernisieren.

Modest [mo'dist] *a.* bescheiden, sittsam; -y *n.* Bescheidenheit *f*, Sittsamkeit *f.*

Modification [mo-di-fi-kei'schAn] *n.* Veränderung *f.*

Modify [mo'di-fai] *vt.* ändern.

Moist [meust] *a.* feucht; -en *vt.* befeuchten; -ure *n.* Feuchtigkeit *f.*   [zahn *m.*

Molar [mou'ler] *n.* Backenzahn *m.*

Molasses [mo-læ'ssihs] *n.pl.* Melasse *f.*   [(spot).

Mole [moul] *n.* Muttermal *n.*

Mole [moul] *n.* Maulwurf *m* (*animal*).   [Mole *f.*

Mole [moul] *n.* Hafendamm *m*, Molekül *n*.

Molecule [mo'li-kjuhl] *n.* Molekül *n.*

Molest [mo-lest'] *vt.* belästigen.

Mollify [mo'li-fai] *vt.* besänftigen.

Moment [mou'mAnt] *n.* Augenblick *m*; -ary *a.* augenblicklich; -ous *a*. wichtig; -um *n*. Triebkraft *f*.

Monarch [mo'nerk] *n*. Herrscher *m*, König *m*; -y *n*. Monarchie *f*.

Monastery [mo'nA-stA-ri] *n*. Kloster *n*. [tag *m*.

Monday [mA'ndi] *n*. Montag

Monetary [mA'ni-tA-ri] *a*. Geld . . ., Münz . . .; - standard *n*. Währung *f*.

Money [mA'ni] *n*. Geld *n*; ready - Bargeld *n*; - box *n*. Sparbüchse *f*; - making *n*. Gelderwerb *m*; - order *n*. Postanweisung *f*.

Mongrel [mAng'gril] *n*. Mischling *m*, Bastardhund *m*.

Monitor [mo'ni-ter] *n*. Klassenordner *m*, Monitor *m* (*nav.*); *vi*. mithören (*rad.*); -ing *n*. Funküberwachung *f*, Mithördienst *m*.

Monk [mAngk] *n*. Mönch *m*.

Monkey [mAng'ki] *n*. Affe *m*; - nut *n*. Erdnuss *f*; - wrench *n*. Universalschraubenschlüssel *m*.

Monochromatic [mo-no-kromæ'tik] *a*. einfarbig. [glas *n*.

Monocle [mo'nokl] *n*. Einglas *n*.

Monogram [mo'no-græm] *n*. Monogramm *n*.

Monologue [mo'no-log] *n*. Selbstgespräch *n*.

Monophase [mo'no-feis] *a*. einphasig (*el.*).

Monoplane [mo'no-plein] *n*. Eindecker *m* (*av.*).

Monopolist [mo-no'po-list] *n*. Monopolist *m*, Alleinhändler *m*; -ize *vt*. monopolisieren, Alleinhandel treiben mit; -y *n*. Monopol *n*, Alleinverkauf *m* (*com.*).

Monosyllable [mo-no-si'lAbl] *n*. einsilbiges Wort.

Monotonous [mo-no'tA-nAss] *a*. eintönig, langweilig; -y *n*. Eintönigkeit *f*.

Monsoon [mon-ssuhn'] *n*. Monsun *m*.

Monster [mon'ster] *n*. Ungeheuer *n*; -rous *a*. ungeheuer.

Month [mAnth] *n*. Monat *m*; -ly *a*, *ad*. monatlich; - nurse *n*. Wochenpflegerin *f*; - ticket *n*. Monatskarte *f*.

Monument [mo'nju-mAnt] *n*. Denkmal *n*.

Mood [muhd] *n*. Stimmung *f*, Laune *f*; -y *a*. launisch, verstimmt.

Moon [muhn] *n*. Mond *m*; -light *n*. Mondschein *m*; *a*. mondhell; -shine *n*. Mondschein *m*, Schwindel *m*, Unsinn *m*.

Moor [muh'er] *n*. Heide *f*.

Moor [muh'er] *n.vt.i*. (sich) vermooren, verankern; -ed mine *n*. Anker(tau)mine *f* (*nav.*); -ings *n.pl*. Vertäuungen *f.pl*. Ankerplatz *m*.

Moot-point [muht'peunt] *n*. strittiger Punkt.

Mop [mop] *n*. Scheuerlappen *m*; *vt*. abscheuern; - up *vt*. aufräumen (*mil.*), säubern (*mil.*).

Mope [moup] *vi*. schwermütig sein.

Moral [mo'rAl] *n*. Moral *f*; *a*. sittlich; -e *n*. Moral *f*, Haltung *f* (*mil.*, *etc.*), innerer Halt; maintenance of - Wehrbetreuung *f*; -ity *n*. Sittlichkeit *f*.

Morass [mA-ræss'] *n*. Morast *m*. [krankhaft.

Morbid [mOr'bid] *a*. -ly *ad*.

More [mOr] *a*. mehr; *ad*. mehr, ferner, noch; -over *ad*. überdies.

Morning [mOr'ning] *n*. Morgen *m*. [lich.

Morose [mA-rouss'] *a*. grämlich.

Morse [mOrss] *a*. Morse . . .; - code *n*. Morsealphabet *n*; - message *n*. Morsespruch *m*.

Morsel [mOr'sAl] *n*. Bissen *m*, Stückchen *n*.

Mortal [mOrtl] *a*. sterblich; *n*. Sterbliche(r) *m*; -ity *n*. Sterblichkeit *f*, Sterblichkeitsziffer *f* (*rate*).

Mortar [mOr'ter] n. Steinmörtel m, Mörser m (mil, etc.);
trench – n. Minenwerfer m.

Mortgage [mOr'gidzh] n.
Hypothek f.

Mortify [mOr'ti-fai] vt. demütigen, ärgern, abtöten, kastei-
en; t. brandig werden (wound).

Mortise [mOr'tiss] n. Zapfen-
loch n, Nut f (tec.); vt. verzapfen.

Mortuary [mOr'tju-A-ri] n.
Leichenhalle f.

Mosque [mosk] n. Moschee f.

Mosquito [mo-skih'tou] n.
Moskito m, Mücke f; – net n.
Mücken-, Kopf-netz n.

Moss [moss] n. Moos n; -y a.
moosig.

Most [moust] a. meist; ad. am
meisten, höchstens, sehr; n.
das meiste, Höchste, Äusserste;
-ly ad. meistens, grösstenteils,
gewöhnlich.

Moth [moth] n. Motte f (small),
Nachtfalter m (large).

Mother [mA'dher] n. Mutter f;
vt. bemuttern; – -in-law n.
Schwiegermutter f; -less a.
mutterlos; -y a. mütterlich.

Motion [mou'schAn] n. Be-
wegung f, Antrag m, Gang m,
Betrieb m; – pictures n.pl.
Film m.

Motive [mou'tiw] n. Beweggrund m, Motiv n; a. beweg-
end, Trieb . . . .

Motor [mou'ter] n. Motor m,
Triebwerk n; vt.i. fahren, (im)
Auto fahren; – ambulance n.
Kranken-auto n, -kraftwagen
m, Sanitätskraftwagen m
(mil.); – -boat n. Motorboot n;
– -bus n. Autobus m; – -car n.
Auto n, Kraftwagen m; –
-coach n. Rundfahrtauto n,
Autobus m; – -driver n. Kraft-
fahrer m, Fahrer m; – -goggles
n.pl. Autobrille f; – launch n.
Motorbarkasse f; – lorry n.
Lastauto n. – mechanic n.
Autoschlosser m; – -man n.

Wagenführer m; – plough n.
Motorpflug m; – tanker n.
Tankmotorschiff n; – torpedo
boat n. Schnellboot n; – tractor
n. Kraftschlepper m, Zugmaschine f, Traktor m; – van n.
Liefer-, Geschäfts-wagen m;
– vehicle n. Kraftwagen m.

Motor-cycle [mou'ter-ssaikl]
n. Motorrad n, Kraftrad n,
Krad n (mil., etc.); – combination n. Motorrad n. mit Beiwagen; – rifleman n. Kraft-
radschütze m.

Motor-cyclist [mou'ter-ssai-
klist] n. Motorradfahrer m,
Kraftradfahrer m.

Motoring [mou'tA-ring] n.
Automobilfahren n, Autosport
m.

Motorist [mou'tA-rist] n.
Automobilfahrer m, Kraftfahrer m.

Motorize [mou'tA-rais] vt.
motorisieren, verkraften; -d
artillery n. Begleitartillerie f.

Motor-transport [mou'ter-
trahn'spOrt] n. Kraftfahrwesen
n, Kraftfahrzeuge n.pl; –
driver n. Kraftfahrer m; –
personnel n. Kraftfahrtruppen
f.pl (mil.); – waggon n. Kraftwagen m.

Mottled [mot'Ald] a. fleckig.

Motto [mo'tou] n. Motto n,
Sinnspruch m.

Mould [mould] n. Moder m,
Schimmel m; -y a. schimmelig.

Mould [mould] n. Form f,
Giessform f, Schablone f; vt.
formen, giessen.

Moulder [moul'der] n. Former
m, Giesser m.   [ern.

Moulder [moul'der] vi. mod-

Moulding [moul'ding] n. Formen n, Giessen n, Gesims n.

Moult [moult] vi. sich mausern.

Mound [maund] n. Erdhüg-
el m.

Mount [maunt] n. Berg m,
Einrahmung f, Einfassung f,
Karton m; vt. besteigen, ein-

rahmen; – guard Posten beziehen (mil.); -ed police n. Polizeireiter m.pl.

Mountain [maun'tin] n. Berg m; – boots n.pl. Bergschuhe m.pl; – troops m.pl. Gebirgsjäger m.pl; -ous a. gebirgig, hügelig.

Mounting [maun'ting] n. Einrahmen n, Lafette f (gun).

Mourn [mOrn] vi. betrauern; t. traurig sein.

Mourning [mOr'ning] n. Trauer f.

Mouse [mauss] n. Maus f.

Moustache [mAss-tahsch'] n. Schnurrbart m.

Mouth [mauth] n. Mund m, Mündung f; – organ n. Mundharmonika f; -wash n. Mundwasser n; -piece n. Mundstück n, Sprachrohr n, Sprachtrichter m (ph, etc.).

Movable [muh'wAbl] a. beweglich.

Move [muhw] n. Bewegung f, Schritt m, Zug m; vt. bewegen, rühren, vorschlagen; i. sich bewegen, sich rühren; -ment n. Bewegung f.

Movies [muh'wis] n.pl. Kino n.

Mow [mou] vt. mähen; – down niedermähen; -ing machine n. Mähmaschine f.

Much [mAtsch] a. viel; ad. viel, weit sehr.

Muck [mAk] n. Schmutz m. Mist m, Dreck m.

Mud [mAd] n. Schlamm m; – floor n. Lehmboden m; -guard n. Schutzblech n, Kotflügel m (aut.); -dy a. schlammig.

Muff [mAf] n. Muff m, Muffe f (tec.).

Muffle [mAfl] n. Muffel f, Schalldämpfer m; vt. einhüllen, dämpfen; -r n. Halstuch n, Knalldämpfer m (mil.).

Mufti [mAf'ti] n. Zivilkleidung f. [er m.

Mug [mAg] n. Krug m, Becher

Muggy [mA'gi] a. feucht.

Mulberry [mAl'bA-ri] n. Maulbeere f, künstlicher Hafen (mil.).

Mule [mjuhl] n. Maultier n, Spinnmaschine f.

Multi'-engined [mAl'ti-en'dzhind] a. mehrmotorig (av.); -millionaire n. vielfacher Millionär m; -phase a. vielphasig (rad.); -purpose a. Mehrzweck . . . .

Multipl'e [mAl'tipl] a. vielfach; – store n. Kettengeschäft n (com.); -ication n. Vervielfältigung f, Multiplikation f; -ly vt. vermehren, multiplizieren; i. sich vermehren.

Multitude [mAl'ti-tjuhd] n. Menge f. [meln.

Rumble [mAmbl] vt.i. murmeln.

Mummy [mA'mi] n. Mumie f.

Mumps [mAmpss] n.pl. Ziegenpeter m.

Munch [mAnsch] vi. geräuschvoll kauen.

Municipal [mjun-ni'ssipl] a. städtisch, Gemeinde . . . .

Munificent [mju-ni'fi-ssAnt] a. freigebig, edel.

Munition [mju-ni'schAn] n. Kriegsmaterial n; – factory n. Munitionsfabrik f.

Murder [mAr'der] n. Mord m; vt. (er)morden; -er n. Mörder m; -ous a. mörderisch.

Murmur [mAr'mer] n. Gemurmel m; vi.t. murmeln.

Musc'le [mAssl] n. Muskel m; -ular a. muskulös.

Museum [mjuh'sih-Am] n. Museum n.

Mush [mAsch] n. Brei m.

Mushroom [mAsch'rum] n. Pilz m.

Music [mjuh'sik] n. Musik f, Noten f.pl (printed); – -hall n. Variété m, Tingel-tangel m; – stand n. Notenständer m; -al a. musikalisch; – -box n. Spieldose f; -ian n. Musiker m.

Musk [mAsk] n. Moschus m.

Musket [mA'skit] n. Flinte f,

Muslin [mA'slin] n. Musseline m.

Mussel [mAssl] n. Muschel f.

Must [mAst] v. müssen.

Mustard [mA'sterd] n. Senf m; - gas n. Senfgas m, Lost m.

Muster [mA'ster] n. Musterung f; vt. mustern; i. sich versammeln; - -roll n. Stammrolle f (mil.).

Musty [mA'sti] a. mufflig.

Mute [mjuht] a. stumm; n. der, die Stumme, Dämpfer m.

Mutilate [mjuh'ti-leit] vt. verstümmeln; -ion n. Verstümmelung f.

Mutineer [mjuh-ti-nih'er] n. Meuterer m; -y n. Meuterei f; vi. meutern.

Mutter [mA'ter] vi. murren.

Mutton [mA'tAn] n. Hammelfleisch n.

Mutual [mjuh'tju-Al] a., -ly ad. gegenseitig.

Muzzle [mAsl] n. Maul n, Maulkorb m, Mündung f (gun); vt. einen Maulkorb anlegen.

My [mai] a. mein.

Myrtle [mArtl] n. Myrte f.

Myself [mai-sself'] pn. ich selbst, mich, mir.

Mysterious [mi-stih'ri-Ass] a. geheimnisvoll; -y n. Geheimnis n.

Mystify [mi'sti-fai] vt. mystifizieren, täuschen. [us m.

Myth [mith] n. Sage f, Mythus

N

Nag [næg] vi. nörgeln.

Nail [neil] n. Nagel m; vt. nageln.

Naive [naiw] a. unbefangen, naiv.

Naked [nei'kid] a. nackt.

Name [neim] n. Name m; vt. nennen; - -plate n. Namensschild n; - -sake n. Namensvetter m; -less a. namenlos; -ly ad. nämlich.

Nap [næp] n. Schläfchen n.

Nape [neip] n. Nacken m.

Napkin [næp'kin] n. Serviette f, Mundtuch n; baby's - Windel f. [tha n.

Naphtha [næf'thA] n. Naphtha n.

Narcissus [nahr-ssi'ssAss] n. Narzisse f. [täubungsmittel n.

Narcotic [nahr-ko'tik] n. Narkose f.

Narrate [nA-reit'] vt. erzählen; -ion n. Erzählung f; -ive a. erzählend; n. Erzählung f; -ive

Narrow [næ'rou] a. schmal, eng, knapp; vt. eng machen; i. eng werden; - -gauge a. schmalspurig; -ly ad. schmal, genau, kaum; - -minded a. engherzig; -ness n. Enge f.

Nasal [nei'sAl] a. Nasen . . ., nasal.

Nasty [nah'sti] a. schmutzig, widerlich, unangenehm.

Nation [nei'schAn] n. Nation f, Volk n.

National [næ'schA-nAl] a. national, Volks . . . ; n. Untertan m; - -anthem n. Nationalhymne f; - debt n. Staatsschuld f; - Socialism n. Nationalsozialismus m; - Socialist n. Nationalsozialist m; -ism n. Nationalismus m; -ist n. Nationalist m; -ity n. Staatsangehörigkeit f; -ize vt. verstaatlichen (property), nationalisieren (persons).

Native [nei'tiw] a. einheimisch; n. der, die Eingeborene; - country Vaterland n.

Natural [næ'tschA-rAl] a. natürlich, ungezwungen, unehelich (child); - frequency n. Eigenfrequenz f (rad.); -ist n. Naturforscher m; -ization n. Einbürgerung f; -ize vt. einbürgern; -ly ad. natürlich.

Nature [nei'tscher] n. Natur f.

Naught [nOt] n. nichts, Null f.

Naughty [nO'ti] a. unartig.

Nausea [nO'schiA] n. Übelkeit f, Brechneigung f; -ous a. ekelhaft.

Nautical [nɔ'tikl] a. See . . . ;
– school n. Seefahrtschule f.

Naval [neiwl] a. See . . . ;
Marine . . . ; – arsenal m. See-
zeughaus n; – base n. Flotten-
stützpunkt m; – cadet n. See-
kadett m; – command n. See-
kriegsleitung f; – commander,
– officer n. Fregattenkapi-
tän m; – forces n.pl. See-
streitkräfte f.pl; Marine-offizier
m; – rating n. Soldat m.

Navel [neiwl] n. Nabel m.

Naviga'ble [næ'wigâbl] a.
schiffbar, fahrbar, passierbar;
-te vt.i. steuern, befahren;
-tion n. Schiff-fahrt f, Navigation f; automatic – n. Kurs-
kopplung f. -ion instruments
n.pl. Navigationsgerät n; -ion
lights n.pl. Kennlichter n.pl
(av.); -tor n. Steuermann m
(nav.), Orter m (av.); automatic -tor Kurskoppler m (av.).

Navvy [næ'wi] n. Erdarbeiter m.

Navy [nei'wi] n. Flotte f;
merchant – Handelsflotte f.

Nazi [naht'sih] n. Nationalsozialist m, Nazi m.

Neap [nihp] n. Nippflut f.

Near [nih'er] a. nahe; -ly ad.
nahe, fast; – miss n. Nächst-
treffer m; -ness n. Nähe f.

Neat [niht] a. -ly ad. nett,
ordentlich, sauber; -ness n.
Nettigkeit f, Sauberkeit f.

Necessar'ies [ne'ssi-ssÂ-ris]
n.pl. Bedürfnisse n.pl, das Not-
wendigste n; -y a. notwendig,
nötig.

Necess'ous [ni-sse'ssi-tAss]
a. notleidend; -y n. Notwend-
igkeit f, Not f, Bedürfnis n.

Neck [nek] n. Hals m; -lace n.
Halsband n; -tie n. Halsbinde
f, Krawatte f.

Need [nihd] n. Not f, Bedürfnis n; vt. nötig haben; -ful a.
nötig; -less a, -ly ad. unnötig;
-y a. arm, bedürftig.

Needle [nihdl] n. Nadel f;

-woman n. Näherin f; -work
n. Handarbeit f. frevelhaft.

Nefarious [ni-feh'ri-Ass] a.

Negative [ne'gÂ-tiw] a. ver-
neinend, negativ; n. Vernei-
nung f, Negativ n (photo).

Neglect [ni-glekt'] n. Vernach-
lässigung f; vt. vernachlässig-
en.

Negligen'ce [ne'gli-dzhAnss]
n. Nachlässigkeit f; -t, Neglect-
ful [ni-glekt'ful] a. nachlässig,
achtlos.

Negligible [ne'gli-dzhibl] a.
unwesentlich.

Negotia'ble [ni-gou'schi-Abl]
a. übertragbar (com.); -te vi.
verhandeln, begeben (com.); i.
unterhandeln; -tion n. Unterhandlung f, Einhandeln, Begeben n.

Negro [nih'grou] n. Neger m.

Neigh [nei] vi. wiehern.

Neighbour [nei'ber] n. Nachbar m, Nachbarin f; -hood n.
Nachbarschaft f; -ing a. benachbart; -ly a. nachbarlich.

Neither [nai'ther] pn. keiner
von beiden; cj. weder; ad.
auch.

Neon [nih'on] n. Neon n.

Nephew [ne'wjuh] n. Neffe m.

Nerve [nArw] n. Nerv m, Mut
m, Frechheit f; war of -s n.
Nervenkrieg m.

Nervous [nAr'wAss] a. nervös, reizbar; -ness n. Nervos-
ität f.

Nest [nest] n. Nest n; vi.
nisten. [miegen.

Nestle [nessl] vi. sich anschl-

Net [net] n. Netz n; vt. (mit
einem Netze) fangen; – barrage n. Netzsperre f (nav.).

Net(t) [net] a. netto, rein; –
tare n. Leergewicht n; – weight
n. Nettogewicht n.

Netting [ne'ting] n. Netz-
(werk) n, Drahtgitter n (wire).

Nettle [netl] n. Nessel f.

Network [net'uArk] n. Netz
n; radio – n. Funknetz n.

Neurotic [nju-ro'tik] a. nervenkrank.

Neuter [njuh'ter] a. geschlechtslos, sächlich.

Neutral [njuh'trAl] a. neutral; n. der, die Neutrale; – zone n. neutrale Zone; -ity n. Neutralität f; -ize vt. neutralisieren.

Never [ne'wer] ad. nie, nimmer; -theless ad. nichtsdestoweniger.

New [njuh] a., -ly ad. neu, frisch; – Year n. Neujahr n.

Newcomer [njuh-kA'mer] n. Ankömmling m.

New-laid [njuh'leid] a. frisch (gelegt).

News [njuhs] n.pl. Nachricht f. Neuigkeit f; -agent n. Zeitungsverkäufer m; -print n. Zeitungspapier n; -reel n. Wochenschau f (film); -paper n. Zeitung f.   [nächst.

Next [next] a. nächst; ad. zu-

Nib [nib] n. Schreibfeder f, Federspitze f.   [benagen.

Nibble [nibl] vi. nagen; vt.

Nice [naiss] a., -ly ad. nett, niedlich; artig, köstlich.

Nicety [nai'ssi-ti] n. Feinheit f, Genauigkeit f.

Nickel [nikl] n. Nickel n; Fünfcentstück n.

Nickname [nik'neim] n. Spottname m.   [tin n.

Nicotine [ni'kA-tihn] Nikotin

Niece [nihss] n. Nichte f. [zig.

Niggardly [ni'gerd-li] a. geizig.

Nigger [ni'ger] n. Neger m.

Niggle [nigl] vi. zwecklos geschäftig sein.

Night [nait] n. Nacht f; -club n. Nachtlokal n; -dress, -gown n. Nachthemd n; -fighting n. Nachtjagd f (av.); -shirt n. Nachthemd n, für Männer; -tracer n. Glimmspur f (av.).   [Nachtigall f.

Nightingale [nai'ting-geil] n.

Nightmare [nait'meh-er] n. Alpdrücken n.   [lich.

Nightly [nait'li] ad. nächt-

Nil [nil] n. nichts.   [flink.

Nimble [nimbl] a., -ly ad.

Nip [nip] n. Zwick m; vt. zwicken.

Nip [nip] n. Schlückchen n.

Nippers [ni'pers] n.pl. Beisszange f.

Nipple [nipl] n. Brustwarze f. (Schmier)Nippel m (aut.).

Nitre [nai'ter] n. Salpeter m; -ic a. Salpeter ...; -ic acid n. Salpetersäure f; -ogen n. Stickstoff m; -ous a. salpetrig.

No [nou] a. kein; ad. nein, nicht; – man's land Niemandsland n; – one niemand.

Nobility [no-bi'li-ti] n. Adel m; -le a. adelig, edel; -leman n. Edelmann m.

Nobody [nou'bo-di] n. niemand.

Nod [nod] n. Kopfnicken n; vt.i. nicken.

Noise [neus] n. Lärm m.

Noisy [neu'si] a. lärmend.

Nomad [no'mAd] a. nomadisch, umherziehend.

Nomenclature [nou'mAnklei-tscher] n. Namengebung f, Fachsprache f.

Nominal [no'mi-nAl] a. angeblich, nominell; – value n. Nennwert m.

Nominate [no'mi-neit] vt. ernennen; -ion n. Ernennung f.

Non- [non]; – -combatant n. Nichtkämpfer m; – -commissioned officer n. Unteroffizier m (mil.); – -committal a. nicht bindend; – -contact a. kontaktlos (mine); – -co-operative a. nicht mitwirkend; – -descript a. nicht unterzubringen; – -fraternization n. Nichtverbrüderung f, Sprechverbot n; – -skid a. Gleitschutz ...; – -stop a. ohne Aufenthalt (rl.), ohne Zwischenlandung (av.); – -union a. nicht organisiert.

None [nAn] pn. keiner, keine, keines.

Nonsense [non'ssAnss] n. Unsinn m; -ical a. unsinnig.

Nook [nuk] *n.* Winkel *m.*

Noon [nuhn] *n.* Mittag *m.*

Noose [nuhs] *n.* Schleife *f*, Schlinge *f.*

Nor [nOr] *cj.* noch, auch nicht.

Normal [nOr'mAl] *a.* normal; -gauge *a.* Normalspur . . . (*rl.*).

North [nOrth] *n.* Norden *m*; *a, ad.* nördlich; - -east *n.* Nordost *m*; - -west *n.* Nordwest *m*; -erly *a.* nördlich; -ward(s) *ad.* nordwärts.

Nose [nous] *n.* Nase *f*; - -dive *n.* Sturzflug *m* (*av.*).

Nostril [no'stril] *n.* Nasenloch *n.*

Not [not] *ad.* nicht.

Notable [nou'tAbl] *a.* merkwürdig; *n.* Standesperson *f.*

Notary [nou'tA-ri] *n.* Notar *m.*

Notch [notsch] *n.* Kerbe *f*, Einschnitt *m*; *vt.* einkerben.

Note [nout] *n.* Briefchen *n*, Anmerkung *f*, Note *f*; *vt.* bemerken, notieren; -book *n.* Notizbuch *n*; -paper *n.* Briefpapier *n*; -d *a.* berühmt; -worthy *a.* bemerkenswert.

Nothing [nA'thing] *n.* Nichts *n*, Null *f*; *pn.* nichts.

Notice [nou'tiss] *n.* Beobachtung *f*, Notiz *f*, Anzeige *f*; *vt.* bemerken, beobachten; -board *n.* Anschlagtafel *f*, schwarzes Brett; -able *a.* bemerkenswert.

Noti'fiable [nou'ti-fai-Abl] *a.* meldepflichtig; -ication *f.* Mitteilung *f*, Anzeige *f*, Meldung *f*; -y *vt.* anzeigen, melden.

Notion [nou'schAn] *n.* Begriff *m*, Ahnung *f*, Meinung *f.*

Notorious [no-tO'ri-Ass] *a.* berüchtigt.

Noun [naun] *n.* Hauptwort *n.*

Nourish [nA'risch] *vt.* (er)nähren; -ing *a.* nahrhaft; -ment *n.* Nahrung *f.*

Novel [nowl] *n.* Roman *m*; *a.* neu, ungewöhnlich; -ist *n.* Romanschreiber *m*; -ty *n.* Neuheit *f.*

November [no-wem'ber] *n.* November *m.*

Novice [no'wiss] *n.* Neuling *m.*

Now [nau] *ad.* jetzt, nun; -adays *ad.* heutzutage.

Nowhere [nou'hueh-er] *ad.* nirgends. [schädlich.

Noxious [nok'schAss] *a.*

Nozzle [nosl] *n.* Schnauze *f*, Düse *f* (*tec.*), Leitschaufel *f* (*tec.*). [Kern *m.*

Nucleus [njuh'kli-Ass] *n.*

Nude [njuhd] *a.* nackt.

Nudge [nAdzh] *vt.* leicht anstossen. [pen *m.*

Nugget [nA'git] *n.* Goldklum-

Nuisance [njuh'ssAnss] *n.* das Lästige, Unfug *m*, Pest *f*; -raid *n.* Störangriff *m.*

Null [nAl] *a.* nichtig; -ify *vt.* aufheben, vernichten.

Numb [nAm] *a.* erstarrt; *vt.* erstarren.

Number [nAm'ber] *n.* Zahl *f*, Anzahl *f*, Nummer *f*; *vt.* zählen, nummerieren; - plate *n.* Nummernschild *n* (*aut.*).

Numerical [nju-me'rikl] *a.* -ly *ad.* der Zahl nach, zahlenmässig.

Numerous [njuh'mA-rAss] *a.* zahlreich. [ter *f.*

Nun [nAn] *n.* Klosterschwes-

Nurse [nArss] *n.* Pflegerin *f*, Krankenschwester *f*, Amme *f*; *vt.* säugen, pflegen; -ry *n.* Kinderstube *f*, Pflanzschule *f*; -ry maid *n.* Kindermädchen *n*; -ry man *n.* Kunstgärtner *m*; -ry school *n.* Laufkrippe *f.*

Nursing [nAr'ssing] *n.* Krankenpflege *f*; -home *n.* Privatklinik *f*; - -orderly *n.* Krankenpfleger *m.* [Pflege *f.*

Nurture [nAr'tscher] *n.*

Nut [nAt] *n.* Nuss *f*, Nusskohle *f*, Schraubenmutter *f* (*tec.*).

Nutmeg [nAt'meg] *n.* Muskatnuss *f.*

Nutri'ment [njuh'tri-mAnt] *n.* Nahrung *f*; -tious *a.* nahrhaft.

O

Oak [ouk] n. Eiche f.

Oakum [ou'kAm] n. Werg n.

Oar [O'er] n. Ruder n, Riemen m.

Oasis [o-ei'ssiss] n. Oase f.

Oath [outh] n. Eid m, Schwur m. ‖mehl f.

Oatmeal [out'mihl] n. Hafer-

Oats [outss] n.pl. Hafer m.

Obdurate [ob'dju-rit] a. unbeugsam.

Obedien'ce [o-bih'di-Anss] n. Gehorsam m; -t a. gehorsam.

Obey [o-bei'] vt. gehorchen.

Obituary [o-bi'tju-A-ri] n. Todesanzeige f.

Object [ob'dzhekt] n. Gegenstand m, Ziel n; [Ab-dzhekt'] vt. einwenden; i. Einwendungen machen; i. etwas dagegen haben; -ion n. Einwendung f; ionable a. nicht einwandfrei; -ive n. Ziel n, Aufgabe f; a. -ly ad. objektiv; -or n. Gegner m; conscientious – Kriegsdienstverweigerer m.

Obligation [ob-li-gei'schAn] n. Verpflichtung f, Verbindlichkeit f.

Obligatory [o-bli'gA-tA-ri] a. obligatorisch; – service n. Wehrpflicht f.

Oblig'e [A-blaidzh'] vt. verpflichten, nötigen; -ing a. verbindlich, entgegenkommend.

Oblique [o-blihk'] a. schräg, quer, schief.

Obliterate [o-bli'tA-reit] vt. auslöschen, vernichten.

Oblivion [o-bli'wi-An] n. Vergesslichkeit f.

Oblong [o'blong] a. länglich; a. Rechteck n.

Obnoxious [ob-nok'schAss] a. anstössig.

Oboe [ou'bou] n. Oboe f.

Obscene [ob-ssihn'] a. zotig, schmutzig, schlüpfrig.

Obscure [ob-skjuh'er] a. dunkel, unbekannt; vt. verdunkeln. [Dunkelheit f.

Obscurity [ob-skjuh'ri-ti] n.

Obsequious [ob-ssih'kui-Ass] a. unterwürfig, kriechend.

Observan'ce [ob-sAr'wAnss] n. Innehaltung f, Einhaltung f, Brauch m; -t aufmerksam.

Observation [ob-sAr-wei'schAn] n. Beobachtung f, Bemerkung f, Beachtung f; – car n. Aussichtswagen m (rt.); – post n. Beobachtungsposten m, -stand m (mil.); – unit n. Beobachtungsabteilung f (mil.).

Observatory [ob-sAr'wA-tA-ri] n. Sternwarte f.

Observe [ob-sArw'] vt. beobachten, bemerken; -r n. Beobachter m; – post n. Fliegerwache f (av.).

Obsess [ob-ssess'] vt. innesuchen; -ed besessen. [altet.

Obsolete [ob'ssA-liht] a. ver-

Obstinacy [ob'sti-nA-ssi] n. Halsstarrigkeit f; -te a, halsstarrig, hartnäckig.

Obstetrics [ob-ste'trix] n.pl. Geburtshilfe f.

Obstreperous [ob-stre'pA-rAss] a. lärmend.

Obstruct [ob-strAkt'] vt. hemmen, aufhalten, versperren; -ion n. Hemmung f, Hindernis n, Verstopfung f, Sperre f.

Obtain [ob-tein'] vt. erlangen; i. gebräuchlich sein.

Obtru'de [ob-truhd'] vt.i. (sich) aufdrängen, aufdringen; -sive a. aufdringlich.

Obtuse [ob-tjuhss'] a. stumpf.

Obverse [ob'werss] a. Bildseite f, Avers m; a. umgekehrt.

Obviate [ob'wi-eit] vt. vorbeugen, beseitigen.

Obvious [ob'wi-Ass] a. klar, augenscheinlich.

Occasion [A-kei'schAn] n. Anlass m, Gelegenheit f; vt. veranlassen; -al -ally ad. gelegentlich. [vt. verfinstern.

Occult [o-kAlt'] a. geheim;

Occupant [o'kju-pAnt] *see* Occupier.

Occupation [o-kju-pei'schAn] n. Besitz m, Besetzung f, Beruf m; army of – Besatzungsheer n; – authorities n.pl. Besatzungsbehörde f.

Occup'ier [o'kju-pai-er] n. Bewohner m, Inhaber m, Insasse m; -y vt. besetzen, in Besitz nehmen, innehaben, einnehmen; -ied territory n. besetztes Gebiet.

Occur [o-kAr] vi. vorkommen; -rence f. Vorkommen n, Ereignis n.

Ocean [ou'schAn] n. Ozean m.

Ochre [ou'ker] n. Ocker m.

Octave [ok'teiw] n. Oktave f.

Octavo [ok'tei-wo] n. Oktavformat n. [ber m.

October [ok-tou'ber] n. Okto-

Octopus [ok'tA-pAss] n. Seepolyp m.

Oculist [o'kju-list] n. Augenarzt m.

Odd [od] a, -ly ad. ungerade, seltsam, einzeln; -ments n.pl. Ladenreste m.pl (com.); -ness n. Seltsamkeit f; -s n.pl. Ungleichheit f, Übermacht f, Odds pl.

Odi'ous [ou'di-Ass] a. verhasst; -um n. Hass m, Vorwurf f.

Odour [ou'der] n. Geruch m, Duft m; -less a. geruchlos.

Of [ov] pr. von, aus, auf.

Off [of] ad. weg, fort, entfernt; pr. ausser, neben, von . . . weg.

Offal [o'fAl] n. Abfall m.

Off-duty [of'djuh'ti] a. frei; – time n. Freizeit f.

Offen'ce [A-fenss'] n. Anstoss m, Vergehen n; -d vt. beleidigen, verletzen, verstossen (rules); -der n. Beleidiger m, Missetäter m; -sive a. anstössig; n. Offensive f, Angriff m.

Offer [o'fer] n. Anerbieten n, Angebot n; vt. anbieten, angeben, leisten (resistance); i. sich darbieten, sich erbieten.

Office [o'fiss] n. Amt n, Büro n, Geschäftszimmer n; -boy n. Laufbursche m; -holder n. der Beamte (customs, etc.); – der Beamte; -r n. Offizier m, commanding Kommandant m; -'s mess n. Offiziersheim n, Kasino n.

Official [o-fi'schAl] n. der Beamte; a. amtlich; – channels n.pl. Dienstweg m, Instanzenweg m. [dringlich.

Officious [o-fi'schAss] a. aufdringlich.

Offing [o'fing] n. offene See.

Offprint [of'print] n. Sonderabdruck m.

Offset [of'sset] n. Gegenforderung f, Absatz m (wall).

Offshoot [of'schuht] n. Sprössling m.

Offside [of'ssaid] n. Handseite f (aut.); ad. abseits.

Often [ofn] ad. oft.

Ogle [ougl] vi. liebäugeln.

Oil [euil] n. Öl n; vt. ölen; – bomb n. Flammenölbombe f; – gauge n. Ölstandzeiger m (aut.); -skin n. Wachstaffet m, Ölrock m (waterproof); -skin jacket n. Öljacke f.

Oiler [eu'ler] n. Öler m, Ölkanne f.

Oily [eu'li] a. ölig.

Ointment [eunt'mAnt] n. Salbe f.

Old [ould] a. alt; – age n. Alter n; – -fashioned a. altmodisch; -ish a. ältlich.

Olive [o'liw] n. Olive f; – oil n. Olivenöl n. [en m.

Omelet [om'lit] n. Eierkuchen

Omen [ou'men] n. Vorbedeutung f.

Ominous [o'mi-nAss] a. von übler Vorbedeutung.

Omission [o-mi'schAn] n. Auslassung f, Unterlassung f.

Omit [o-mit'] vt. auslassen (leave out), unterlassen (leave undone).

Omnibus [om'ni-bAss] _n._ Omnibus _m_; motor – Autobus _m_; – volume –s Sammelband _m._

Omnipotence [om-ni'po-tAnss] _n._ Allmacht _f._ [hin.

On [on] _pr._ auf, an; _ad._ weiter.

Once [uAnss] _ad._ einst, ehemal; _at_ – sogleich; _cj._ sobald.

One [uAn] _a._ ein, einzig; _pn._ man; – another einander.

One-course meal [uAn-kOrss-mihl'] _n._ Einheitsgericht _n._

Onerous [o'nA-rAss] _a._ beschwerlich, lästig. [sich.

Oneself [uAn-self'] _pn._ selbst,

One-way [uAn'uei] _a._ einseitig; – street _n._ Einbahnstrasse _f_; – traffic _n._ einseitiger Verkehr.

Onion [A'ni-An] _n._ Zwiebel _f._

Only [oun'li] _a._ einzig; _ad._ nur.

Onset [on'sset] _n._, Onslaught [on'slOt] _n._ Angriff _m_, Anfall _m._

Onus [ou'nAss] _n._ Beschwerde _f_; – of proof _n._ Beweislast _f._

Ooze [uhs] _n._ Schlamm _m_, Schlick _m_; _vi._ wegsickern.

Opal [ou'pAl] _n._ Opal _m._

Opaque [o'peik'] _a._ undurchsichtig.

Open [oupn] _a._, -ly _ad._ offen; _vt._ öffnen, eröffnen; _i._ sich öffnen; – car _n._ offenes Auto; – fire _n._ Kamin _n._ offene Feuerung; -handed _a._ freigebig; – lorry _n._ Lastkraftwagen _m._

Open-air [oupn'äh-er'] _n._ das Freie, freie Luft; – baths _n.pl._ Freibad _n_; – cure – treatment _n._ Freiluftkur _f_; – stage _n._ Freilichtbühne _f._

Opener [oup'ner] _n._ Öffner _m._

Opera [op'rA] _n._ Oper _f_; – glass _n._ Opernglas _n_; – hat _n._ Klapphut _m._

Operate [o'pA-reit] _vt.i._ wirken, operieren; – -ing theatre _n._ Operationssaal _m_; -ion _n._ Wirkung _f_, Operation _f_, Betrieb _m_, Tätigkeit _f_, Bedienung _f_ (_tec._), Einsatz _m_ (_av._); -ional _a._; –

aerodrome _n._ Einsatzhafen _m_ (_av._); – airman _n._ Frontflieger _m._; – battalion _n._ Einsatzabteilung _f_; – command _n._ Kampfleitung _f_ (_mil._); – flight _n._ Feindflug _m_ (_av._); – readiness _n._ Gefechtsbereitschaft _f_; – report _n._ Gefechtsmeldung _f_; -ive _n._ Fabrikarbeiter _m_; _a._ wirkend, wirksam, tätig; -or _n._ Arbeiter _m_, Techniker _m_, Operateur _m_, Chirurg _m_, Vermittlungsbeamtin _f_ (_ph._), Telephonistin _f_ (_ph._), Kameramann _m_ (_film_), Setzer _m_ (_type_); tele-vision -or _n._ Fernsehtechniker _m_; wireless -or Betriebsfunker _m._

Opiate [ou'pi-eit] _n._ Einschläferungsmittel _n._

Opium [ou'pi-Am] _n._ Opium _n._

Opponent [A-pou'nAnt] _n._ Gegner _m._

Opportune [o'per-tjuhn] _a._ gelegen, zeitgemäss; -ity _n._ Gelegenheit _f._

Oppose [A-pous'] _vt._ entgegensetzen, bestreiten, sich entgegenstellen; -ite _a._ gegenüberstehend; entgegengesetzt; -ition _n._ Widerstand _m_, Gegenpartei _f._

Oppress [A-press'] _vt._ unterdrücken; -ion _n._ Unterdrückung _f_; -ive _a._ drückend, unterdrückend; -or _n._ Unterdrücker _m._

Optical [op'tikl] _a._ optisch; -ian _n._ Optiker _m._

Option [op'schAn] _n._ Wahl _f_, Optionsrecht _n_, Prämiengeschäft _n_ (_com._); -al _a._ wahlfrei, freigestellt.

Or [Or] _cj._ oder.

Oral [O'rAl] _a._ mündlich.

Orange [o'rindzh] _n._ Apfelsine _f_, Orange _f._

Oration [o-rei'schAn] _n._ Rede _f_; -or _n._ Redner _m._

Orbit [Or'bit] _n._ Bahn _f._

Orchard [Or'tscherd] _n._ Obstgarten _m._

Orchestra [Or'ki-strA] n. Orchester n, Kapelle f.

Orchid [Or'kid] n. Orchidee f.

Ordain [Or-deïn'] vt. bestimmen, ordinieren. [Probe.

Ordeal [Or'djAl] f. harte

Order [Or'der] n. Ordnung f, Befehl m, Bestellung f (com.), Reihenfolge f; vt. ordnen, befehlen, bestellen (com.); – of battle Kriegsgliederung f, Schlachtordnung f; – of march Marschfolge f.

Orderly [Or'der-li] n. Ordonnanz m, Offiziersbursche m (mil.); a. ordeutlich, ruhig; hospital – Lazarettgehilfe m, Krankenwärter m; – room n. Geschäftszimmer n.

Ordinance [Or'di-nAnss] n. Verordnung f.

Ordinary [Or'di-nA-ri] a. -ily ad. gewöhnlich, gebräuchlich; – seaman n. Leichtmatrose m.

Ordnance [Ord'nAnss] n. Artillerie f; – map n. Generalstabskarte f; – stores n.pl. Feldzeug n; – survey n. Landesaufnahme f.

Ore [Or] n. Erz n.

Organ [Or'gAn] n. Organ n, Orgel f (music), Zeitung f (paper), Vereinsblatt n (of journal); – -grinder n. Leierkastenmann m; – recital n. Orgelkonzert n; – stop n. Orgelpfeife f, Registerzug m; -ic a. organisch; -ism n. Organismus m; -ist n. Organist m; -ization n. Organisation f, Einrichtung f, Gliederung f; -ize vt. organisieren, veranstalten.

Orgy [Or'dzhi] n. Trinkgelage n, Orgie f.

Orient [O'ri-Ant] n. Morgenland n; -al a. morgenländisch.

Orifice [o'ri-fiss] n. Öffnung f, Mündung f, Loch n.

Origin [o'ri-dzhin] n. Ursprung m, Herkunft f; -al a. -ally ad. ursprünglich, originell; n. Original n; -al owner n.

Altbesitzer m; -ality n. Ursprünglichkeit f; -ate vi. entstehen, herstammen; t. hervorrufen.

Ornament [Or'nA-mAnt] n. Schmuck m, Zierde f; -al a. künstlerisch, zierend.

Ornate [Or-neït'] a. geziert.

Orphan [Or'fAn] n. Waise f, Waisenkind n.

Orphanage [Or'fA-nidzh] n. Waisenhaus n.

Orthochromatic [Or-tho-kro-mæ'tik] a. gelbgrünempfindlich. [rechtgläubig.

Orthodox [Or'tho-dox] a.

Orthography [Or-tho'grA-fi] n. Rechtschreibung f.

Oscillat'e [o'ssi-leït] vi. schwingen, oszilieren; -ing circuit n. Schwingungskreis m; -ion n. Schwingung f, Oszillation f; light – Lichtschwankung f (rad.); sound – Tonschwankung f (rad.); -or n. Oszillator m.

Osier [ou'si-er] n. Korbweide f.

Ostensible [o-sten'ssibl] a. vorzeiglich, -tation n. Schaustellung f. [m.

Ostrich [o'stridzh] n. Strauss

Other [A'dher] a. ander; pn. der, die, das andere; – ranks n.pl. Mannschaften f.pl (mil.); -wise ad. anders, sonst.

Otter [O'ter] n. Otter f.

Ought [Ot] v. sollte, sollten.

Ounce [aunss] n. Unze f, 28 Gramm.

Our [au'er] a. unser; -s pn. der, die, das unserige; -selves pn. wir selbst, uns (selbst).

Oust [aust] vt. verdrängen, ausstossen.

Out [aut] ad. aus, heraus, hinaus. [en.

Outbid [aut-bid'] vt. überbiet-

Outboard [aut'bOrd] a. Aussenbord ...; – engine n. Aussenbordmotor m.

Outbreak [aut'breïk] n. Ausbruch m.

Outcast [aut'kahst] a. verstos-

Outcome [aut'kAm] n. Ergebnis n.

Outcrop [aut'krop] n. Ausgehendes n, Tagebau m.

Outdistance [aut-di'stAnss] vt. überholen. [fen.

Outdo [aut-duh'] vt. übertreffen.

Outdoor [aut-dOr'] a. ausser dem Hause, Aussen . . ., im Freien.

Outer [au'ter] a. äusser.

Outfit [aut'fit] n. Ausrüstung f, Ausstattung f.

Outflank [aut-flænk'] vt. umfassen; -ing movement n. Umfassungsbewegung f (mil.), Flankenbewegung f (mil.).

Outgoing [aut'gou-ing a. aus-, weg-gehend, abgehend (post). [wachsen.

Outgrow [aut-grou'] vt. überwachsen.

Outhouse [aut'hauss] n. Nebengebäude n.

Outing [au'ting] n. Ausflug m.

Outlandish [aut-læn'dish] a. fremdartig.

Outlaw [aut'lO] n. der Geächtete; vt. ächten.

Outlay [aut'lei] n. Auslage f.

Outlet [aut'let] n. Ausgang m, Absatz m (com.).

Outline [aut'lain] n. Umriss m, Entwurf m; vt. entwerfen.

Outlive [aut-liw'] vt. überleben. [sicht f.

Outlook [aut'luk] n. Aussicht f.

Outlying [aut-lai'ing] a. fern (liegend).

Outmanoeuvre [aut-mA-nuh'wer] vt. überlisten.

Outnumber [aut-nAm'ber] vt. an Zahl übertreffen.

Out-of [aut'ow]; - -date a. veraltet; - -doors a. draussen; - -fashion a. altmodisch; - -pocket a. nicht zu Kasse, wirklich, tatsächlich (expenses).

Outpost [aut'poust] n. Vorposten m.

Output [aut'put] n. Ertrag m, Ausbeute f, Leistung f.

Outrage [aut'reidzh] n. Gewalttätigkeit f; -ous a, -ly ad. gewalttätig, zügellos, unerhört.

Outrange [aut-reindzh'] vt. weiter tragen als (mil.).

Out-rigger [aut'ri-ger] n. Ausleger m, Luvbaum m (nav.).

Outright [aut-rait'] ad. sogleich, gänzlich, fest (com.).

Outrun [aut-rAn'] vt. schneller laufen als, überholen, übertreffen.

Outset [aut'set] n. Anfang m.

Outside [aut'ssaid] a. draussen, aussen; pr. ausserhalb; n. äusser, äusserst; n. Aussenseite f, das Äusserste; - aerial n. Hochantenne f; - cover n. Deckblatt n; - -left n. Linksaussen m; - -right n. Rechtsaussen m; -r n. Aussenseiter m, der Fernstehende.

Outskirts [aut'skArtss] n.pl. Umgebung f, Aussenbezirke m, pl. [offen, freimütig.

Outspoken [aut-spou'kAn] a.

Outstanding [aut-stæn'ding] a. ausstehend, Haupt . . .

Outstrip [aut-strip'] vt. überholen, übertreffen. [stimmen.

Outvote [aut-wout'] vt. überstimmen.

Outward [aut'uerd] a. äusserlich; ad. auswärts.

Outweigh [aut-uei'] vt. überwiegen, aufwiegen.

Outwit [aut-uit'] vt. überlisten.

Outworks [aut'uArkss] n.pl. Aussenwerk n (mil.).

Oval [ou'wAl] n. Oval n; a. eiförmig, oval.

Ovation [ou-wei'schAn] n. Ehrenbezeigung f, Huldigung f.

Oven [A'wAn] n. Backofen m.

Over [ou'wer] ad. über, herüber, hinüber, übrig; pr. über, durch.

Overall [ou'wA-rOl] n. Überwurf m, Überziehhose f, Arbeitsanzug m, Schutzanzug m; a. Gesamt . . . (expenses).

Overawe [ou-wA-rO'] vt. einschüchtern.

Overbalance [ou-wer-bæ'lAnss] vi. umkippen.

Overbearing [ou-wer-beh'-ring] *a.* hochfahrend.

Overboard [ou'wer-bOrd] *ad.* über Bord.

Overboot [ou'wer-buht] *n.* Überziehstiefel *m.*

Overcapitalize [ou-wer-kæ'-pi-tA-lais] *vt.* überkapitalisieren. [deckt.

Overcast [ou'wer-kahst] *a.* bedeckt.

Overcharge [ou-wer-tschahrdzh'] *vt.* überfordern, übersteuern.

Overcoat [ou'wer-kout] *n.* Überrock *m.* [überwinden.

Overcome [ou-wer-kAm'] *vt.*

Overconfidence [ou-wer-kon'-fi-dAns] *n.* allzu grosses Vertrauen.

Overcrowding [ou-er-krau'ding] *n.* Überfüllung *f.*

Overdo [ou-wer-duh'] *vt.* übertreiben.

Overdraft [ou'wer-drahft] *n.* Schulden *f.pl.* Überziehung *f* (com.). [überziehen.

Overdraw [ou-wer-drO'] *vt.*

Overdue [ou-wer-djuh'] *a.* überfällig, verfallen.

Overestimate [ou-wer-e'sti-meit] *vt.* überschätzen.

Overexpose [ou-wer-ex-pous'] *vt.* überbelichten.

Overflow [ou-wer-flow'] *vt.i.* überfliessen, überschwemmen.

Overgrow [ou-wer-grow'] *vt.* überwachsen, hinauswachsen über. [überhangen.

Overhang [ou-wer-hæng'] *vt.*

Overhaul [ou-wer-hOl'] *vt.* durchsehen, überholen.

Overhead [ou-wer-hed'] *ad.* oben; *a.* oben befindlich, Luft . . .; - costs *pl.* allgemeine Betriebskosten *pl*; - railway *n.* Hochbahn *f.* [zufällig hören.

Overhear [ou-wer-hih'er] *vt.*

Overjoyed [ou-wer-dzheud'] *a.* sehr erfreut. [überland.

Overland [ou'wer-lænd'] *a.ad.*

Overlap [ou-wer-læp'] *vt.i.* übereinandergreifen.

Overlay [ou-wer-lei'] *vt.* bedecken, überziehen.

Overload [ou-wer-loud'] *vt.* überladen. [übersehen.

Overlook [ou-wer-luk'] *vt.*

Overmantel [ou'wer-mæntl] *n.* Kaminaufsatz *m.*

Overnight [ou-wer-nait'] *ad.* über Nacht.

Overpopulate [ou-wer-po'-pju-leit] *vt.* überbevölkern.

Overpower [ou-wer-pau'er] *vt.* überwältigen.

Overproduction [ou-wer-pro-dAk'schAn] *n.* Überproduktion *f*, Übererzeugung *f.*

Over-proof [ou-wer-pruhf'] *a.* über Normalstärke.

Overrate [ou-wer-reit'] *vt.* überschätzen.

Override [ou-wer-raid'] *vt.* überschreiten, umstossen.

Overrule [ou-wer-ruhl'] *vt.* zurückweisen, verwerfen.

Overrun [ou-wer-rAn'] *vt.* überlaufen, ganz bedecken.

Oversea [ou-wer-ssih'] *a.* überseeisch.

Overseer [ou'wer-ssih-er] *n.* Aufseher *m*, Inspektor *m.*

Overshadow [ou-wer-schæ'dou] *vt.* überschatten.

Overshoe [ou'wer-schuh'] *n.* Überschuh *m.*

Overshoot [ou-wer-schuht'] *vt.* hinausschiessen über.

Oversight [ou'wer-ssait] *n.* Versehen *n.*

Oversleep [ou-wer-sslihp'] *vr.* sich verschlafen.

Overstaffed [ou-wer-stahft'] *a.* mit zuviel Personal.

Overstate [ou-wer-steit'] *vt.* zu hoch anschlagen, übertreiben. [überschreiten.

Overstep [ou-wer-step'] *vt.*

Overstock [ou-wer-stok'] *vt.* überfüllen.

Overstrain [ou-wer-strein'] *v.t.r.* (sich) überanstrengen.

Overstrung [ou-wer-strAng'] *a.* kreuzsaitig.

Overt [ou'wert] a. offenkundig.
Overtake [ou-wer-teik'] vt. einholen, überholen, erreichen.
Overtask [ou-wer-tahsk'] vt. überlasten, überladen.
Overtax [ou-wer-tæx'] vt. übersteuern, überladen.
Overthrow [ou'wer-throw] n. Umsturz m, Niederlage f.
Overthrow [ou'wer-throu'] vt. umwerfen, umstürzen, vernichten.
Overtime [ou'wer-taim] n. Überstunden f.pl.
Overtire [ou-wer-tai'er] vt. zu sehr ermüden.
Over-trousers [ou'wer-trau'sers] n.pl. Überziehhose f.
Overture [ou'wer-tjuh'er] n. Ouvertüre f, Vorschlag m.
Overturn [ou-wer-tArn'] vt.i. umwerfen, umkippen.
Overvalue [ou-wer-wæ'ljuh] vt. überschätzen.
Overweight [ou-wer-ueit'] n. Übergewicht n.
Overwhelm [ou-wer-huelm'] vt. überschütten, überwältigen.
Overwork [ou-wer-uArk'] vt.i. (sich) überarbeiten. (danken.
Owe [ou] vt. schulden, ver-
Owl [aul] Eule f.
Own [oun] a. eigen; vt. besitzen; -er n. Eigentümer m, Besitzer m; - driver n. Selbstfahrer m (aut.); -ership n. Eigentumsrecht m.
Ox [ox] n. Ochs m.
Oxalic acid [ox-æ'lik-æ'ssid] n. Oxalsäure f.
Oxide [ox'aid] n. Oxyd n; -ise vt. oxydieren.
Oxy-acetylene [ox'i-A-sse'tilihn] a. Azetylen-sauerstoff...; - welding n. autogene Schweissung.
Oxygen [ox'i-dzhAn] n. Sauerstoff m; - apparatus, - equipment n. Atemanlage f, Höhenatmer m; Sauerstoffapparat m (av.).

Oxy-hydrogen [ox-i-hai'drA-dzhAn] a. Knallgas...; - light n. Drummondsches Kalklicht.
Oyster [eu'ster] n. Auster f.

P

Pace [peiss] n. Schritt m, Geschwindigkeit f; vt. abschreiten; i. schreiten.
Pacific [pA-ssi'fik] a, -ally ad. friedlich.
Pacification [pæ'ssi-fi-kei'schAn] Friedensstiftung f, Befriedung f, Beruhigung f.
Pacifism [pæ'ssi-fism] n. Pazifismus m, Kriegsgegnerschaft f; -t m. Pazifist m, Kriegsgegner. (fen.
Pacify [pæ'ssi-fai] vt. beruhi-
Pack [pæk] n. Pack m, Bündel n, Bande f, Koppel f (hounds), Rudel n (U-boats), Spiel n (cards); vt.i. (ver-)packen, einpacken; - animal n. Pack-, Trag-tier n; - thread n. Packzwirn m, Bindfaden m.
Package [pæ'kidzh] n. Pack n, Paket n, Packung f.
Packer [pæ'ker] n. Packer m, Auflader m.
Packet [pæ'kit] n. Paket n; - boat n. Postschiff n.
Packing [pæ'king] n. Verpackung f, Packzeug n, Verpackungskosten pl (com.); - case n. Packkiste f, Packgefäss n; - paper n. Packpapier n; - ring n. Dichtungsring m (tec.).
Pact [pækt] n. Pakt m, Vertrag m; non-aggression - n. Nichtangriffspakt m.
Pad [pæd] n. Polster n; vt. auspolstern; writing - n. Schreibblock m; -ding n. Polsterung f, Polstermaterial n, Wattierung f.
Paddle [pædl] n. Ruder n; vt.i. paddeln, patschen; - steamer

n. Raddampfer *m;* – -wheel *n.* Schaufelrad *n.*

Paddock [pæ'dAk] *n.* Gehege *n,* Sattelplatz *m.*

Paddock [pæd'lok] *n.* Vorhängeschloss *n.* [licher *m.*

Padre [pah'drI] *n.* Feldgeist-

Pagan [pei'gAn] *a.* heidnisch; *n.* der Heide, die Heidin.

Page [peidzh] *n.* Seite *f.*

Page [peidzh] *n.* Page *m,* junger Diener. [aufzug *m.*

Pageant [pæ'dzhAnt] *n.* Festzug *m.*

Pagination [pæ-dzhi-nei'schAn] *n.* Paginierung *f.*

Pail [peil] *n.* Eimer *m.*

Pain [pein] *n.* Schmerz *m,* Weh *n,* Leid *n; vt.* weh tun, quälen; -ful *a,* -fully *ad.* schmerzlich; -less *a.* schmerzlos.

Painstaking [peins'tei'king] *a.* arbeitsam, sorfältig, gewissenhaft.

Paint [peint] *n.* Farbe *f,* Anstrich *m,* Schminke *f; vt.* malen, anstreichen; wet– ! (frisch) gestrichen !; – -box *n.* Mal-, Farben-kasten *m;* – -brush *n.* Pinsel *m.*

Painter [pein'ter] *n.* Maler *m (artist),* Anstreicher *m (house).*

Painter [pein'ter] *n.* Fangleine *f (boat).*

Painting [pein'ting] *n.* Malerei *f,* Gemälde *n.*

Pair [peh'er] *n.* Paar *n; vi.* sich paaren; – of scissors Schere *f;* – of spectacles Brille *f.*

Pal [pæl] *n.* Kamerad *m,* Kameradin *f.*

Palace [pæ'liss] *n.* Palast *m.*

Palatable [pæ'lA-tAbl] *a.* schmackhaft.

Palate [pæ'lit] *n.* Gaumen *m,* Geschmack *m.*

Palatial [pA-lei'schAl] *a.* prächtig.

Palaver [pA-lah'wer] *n.* Unterredung *f,* Geschwätz *n.*

Pale [peil] *a.* blass; *vi.* erblassen; -ness *n.* Blässe *f.*

Pale [peil] *n.* Pfahl *m,* Grenze *f.*

Palette [pæ'lit] *n.* Palette *f;* -knife *n.* Spatel *m.* [*m.*

Paling [pei'ling] *n.* Pfahlzaun

Palisade [pæ-li-sseid'] *n.* Spitzpfahl *m,* Zaun *m,* Palisade *f; vt.* verschanzen.

Pall [pOl] *n.* Leichentuch *n.*

Pall [pOl] *vi.* verekeln, zuwider werden.

Palliasse [pæl'jæss] *n.* Strohsack *m,* -lager, *f,* Matratze *f.*

Palliate [pæl'jeit] *vt.* beschönigen, lindern.

Palliation [pæl-jei'schAn] *n.* Beschönigung *f.*

Palliative [pæl'jA-tiw] *n.* Linderungsmittel *n.*

Pallid [pæ'lid] *a.* blass, farblos.

Pallor [pæ'ler] *n.* Blässe *f.*

Palm [pahm] *n.* Palme *f,* flache Hand; – off *vt.* aufschwindeln; -istry *n.* Handwahrsagerei *f.*

Palmy [pah'mi] *a.* blühend, glücklich.

Palp|able [pæl'pAbl] *a.* fühlbar, handgreiflich; -itate *vi.* klopfen, pochen; -itation [pælpi-tei'schAn] *n.* Herzklopfen *n.*

Paltry [pOl'tri] *a.* armselig.

Pamper [pæm'per] *vt.* verzärteln, verwöhnen.

Pamphlet [pæm'flit] *n.* Broschüre *f,* Prospekt *n,* Flugschrift *f.*

Pan [pæn] *n.* Pfanne *f,* Zündpfanne *f (mil.);* – out *vi.* Erfolg haben, sich rentieren, ausgehen.

Pancake [pæn'keik] *n.* Eierkuchen *m; vi.* absacken, durchsacken *(av.).* [heilmittel *n.*

Panacea [pæ'nA-ssih'A] *n.* All-

Panchromatic [pæn-kro-mæ'tik] *a.* panchromatisch.

Pandemonium [pæn-di-mou'ni-Am] *n.* Höllenlärm *m,* -szene *f.*

Pander [pæn'der] *vi.* fröhnen, Vorschub leisten.

Pane [pein] *n.* Fensterscheibe *f,* Füllung *n.*

Panel [pæ'nAl] *n.* Füllun*g n.* Paneel *n,* Täfelung *f,* Fach *n.*

Verkleidung f; – doctor n. Kassenarzt m.

Pang [pæng] n. Stich m, Qual f.

Panic [pæ'nik] n. Schrecken n, Bestürzung f, Panik f; – -stricken a. erschreckt, bestürzt, -ky a. bestürzt, nervös.

Pannier [pæ'njer] n. Tragkorb m. [Rüstung.

Panoply [pæ'nA-pli] n. völlige

Panorama [pæ-nA-rah'mA] n. Rundblick m, Panorama n.

Pansy [pæn'si] n. Stiefmütterchen n.

Pant [pænt] vi. keuchen.

Pantaloons [pæn-tA-luhns'] n.pl. Beinkleider n.pl.

Pantechnicon [pæn-tec'ni-kAn] n. Möbelwagen m.

Panther [pæn'ther] n. Panther m.

Pantomime [pæn'tA-maim] n. Gebärdenspiel n, Märchendrama n. [kammer f.

Pantry [pæn'tri] n. Speise-

Pants [pæntss] n.pl. Unterhose f.

Pap [pæp] n. Brei m.

Pap [pæp] n. Brustwarze f.

Papal [pei'pAl] a. päpstlich.

Paper [pei'per] n. Papier n, Zeitung f (daily); a. Papier . . . ; vt. tapezieren; wall – Tapete f; – -clip n. Akten-klammer f; – -currency n. Papierwährung f, Banknoten-umlauf m; – -fastener n. Musterklammer f; – -hanger n. Tapezierer m; – -mill n. Papierfabrik f; – -weight n. Brief-beschwerer m.

Par [pahr] n. Pari n; a. normal.

Parable [pæ'rAbl] n. Gleichnis n.

Parachute [pæ'rA-schuht] n. Fallschirm m; – descent, jump n. Fallschirmabsprung m; – flare n. Fallschirmrakete f; – harness n. Fallschirmsattel m; – regiment n. Fall-schirmregiment n; – rifleman n. Fallschirmschütze m.

Parade [pA-reid'] n. Prunk m, Gepränge n, Promenade f, Parade f (mil.), Appell m (mil.); vi. in Parade aufziehen.

Paradise [pæ'rA-daiss] n. Paradies n. [dox n.

Paradox [pæ'rA-dox] n. Paradox n.

Paraffin [pæ'rA-fin] n. Paraffin n, Leuchtpetroleum n; – -oil n. Paraffinöl n; – wax n. festes Paraffin. [bild n.

Paragon [pæ'rA-gAn] n. Vor-

Paragraph [pæ'rA-grahf] n. Abschnitt m, Absatz m, Paragraph m.

Parallel [pæ'rA-lel] a. parallel, gleichlaufend; n. Parallele f, Ähnlichkeit f; – bars n.pl. Barren m.

Paralyse [pæ'rA-lais] vt. lähmen, lahmlegen. [Lähmung f.

Paralysis [pA-ræ'li-ssiss] n.

Paramount [pæ'rA-maunt] a. höchst, oberst. [wehr f.

Parapet [pæ'rA-pit] n. Brust-

Paraphernalia [pæ-rA-fer-nei'ljA] n.pl. Zubehör n, Ausrüstung f.

Paraphrase [pæ'rA-freis] n. Umschreibung f; vt. umschreiben.

Parasite [pæ'rA-sait] n. Schmarotzer m, Ungeziefer n.

Parasol [pæ-rA-ssol'] n. Sonnenschirm m.

Paratroops [pæ'rA-truhpss] n.pl. Fallschirm-jäger m.pl, -springer m.pl, -truppen f.pl.

Paravane [pæ'rA-wein] n. Minenräumgerät n (nav.).

Parcel [pahr'sl] n. Paket n, Bündel n; – office n. Eilgutannahme f (rl.); – post n. Paketpost f.

Parch [pahrtsch] vt. dörren, ausdrocknen, rösten (maize).

Parchment [pahrtsch'mAnt] n. Pergament n.

Pardon [pahr'dAn] n. Verzeihung f; vt. verzeihen.

Pare [peh'er] vt. beschneiden, schälen (fruit).

Parentage [peh'rAn-tidzh] n. Abstammung f, Herkunft f.

Parental [pA-rentl'] a. elterlich.

Parenthesis [pA-ren'thi-ssiss] n. Parenthese f, Klammer f.

Parenthetical [pæ-rAn-the'-tikl] a. in Parenthese, eingeschaltet. [n. Elternschaft f.

Parenthood [peh'rAnt-hud]

Parent's [peh'rAntss] n.pl. Eltern pl; – unit Stammtruppenteil m (mil.).

Pariah [pæ'rjA] n. Paria m, der Ausgestossene.

Paring [peh'ring] n. Schnitzel n, Abfall m.

Parish [pæ'rïsch] n. Kirchspiel n, Gemeinde n; – priest Ortspfarrer m; – relief n. Armenunterstützung f.

Parity [pæ'ri-ti] n. Parität f, Umrechnungskurs m.

Park [pahrk] n. Park m, öffentliche Anlage, Wagenpark m (mil.). Parkstelle f, Parkplatz m (aut.); vt.i. parken, zusammenstellen, einstellen, lagern (com.).

Parking [pahr'king] n. Parken n, Lagern n; – area n. Abstellplatz m (av.); – place n. Autoparkplatz m; – point n. Liegeplatz m (av.).

Parlance [pahr'lAnss] n. Sprechweise f. [lung f.

Parley [pahr'li] n. Unterhandlung

Parliament [pahr'li-mAnt] n. Parlament n, Reichstag m.

Parliamentary [pahr-li-men'tA-ri] a. parlamentarisch, Parlaments ...

Parlour [pahr'ler] n. Wohnzimmer n, Salon m; – game n. Gesellschaftsspiel n; – maid n. Hausmädchen n.

Parochial [pA-rou'kjAl] a. Gemeinde ..., Kirchspiel ..., kleinstädtisch.

Parody [pæ'rA-di] n. Parodie f.

Parole [pA-roul'] n. Parole f, Ehrenwort n.

Parrot [pæ'rAt] n. Papagei m.

Parquet [pahr-ket'] n. Parkettfussboden m. [ablenken.

Parry [pæ'ri] vt.i. parieren,

Parsimonious [pahr-ssi-mou'njAss] a. knauserig, geizig.

Parsimony [pahr-ssi-mA-ni] n. Knauserei f, Geiz m.

Parsley [pahrss'li] n. Petersilie f. [ake f.

Parsnip [pahr'snip] n. Pastin-

Parson [pahr'ssAn] n. Pfarrer m, Pfaffe m; -age n. Pfarrhaus m.

Part [pahrt] n. Teil m, Stück m, Lieferung f (book), Heft n; vt. trennen; i. sich trennen; – with hergeben, aufgeben; –owner n. Miteigentümer m; – payment n. Teil-, Abzahlung f; –song n. mehrstimmiges Gesangsstück; – -time a. Aushilfs ..., Neben ....

Partake [pahr-teik'] vi. teilnehmen, zu sich nehmen (food).

Partial [pahr'schAl] a, -ly ad. teilweise, parteiisch; – success Teilerfolg m.

Partiality [pahr-schjæ'li-ti] n. Vorliebe f, Parteilichkeit f.

Participant [pahr-ti'ssi-pAnt] n. Teilnehmer m.

Participate [pahr-ti'ssi-peit] vi. teilnehmen.

Participation [pahr-ti-ssi-pei'schAn] n. Teilnahme f, Beteiligung f.

Participator [pahr-ti'ssi-peiter] n. Teilnehmer m.

Participle [pahr'ti-ssipl] n. Mittelwort n, Partizipium n.

Particle [pahr'tikl] n. Teilchen n, Stückchen n, Partikel f.

Particular [per-ti'kju-ler] a. besonder, wählerisch, -ise vi. ins Einzelne gehen; -ly ad. besonders, ausdrücklich; -s n. pl. das Nähere, Einzelheiten f.pl.

Parting [pahr'ting] n. Trennung f, Abschied m, Scheitel m.

(hair); a. scheidend, Abschieds

Partisan [pahr-ti-sæn'] n. Anhänger m, Partisane m (mil.); a. parteilisch.

Partition [pahr-ti'schAn] n. Teilung f, Scheidung f, Aufteilung f; - (off) vt. teilen, abteilen; - wall n. Verschlag m.

Partly [pahrt'li] ad. teilweise, zum Teil.

Partner [pahrt'ner] n. Teilnehmer m, Teilhaber m; -ship n. Gemeinschaft f, Handelsgesellschaft f.

Partridge [pahrt'ridzh] n. Rebhuhn n.

Party [pahr'ti] n. Partei f, Gesellschaft f, Verband m (mil, etc.); - spirit n. Parteigeist m.

Pass [pahss] n. Pass m, Reisepass m, Freikarte f (rl.), Urlaubsschein m (mil.); vt. durchgehen, zubringen (time), bestehen (exam.), zulassen (allow), reichen (hand); i. vorübergehen (go), angehen (be in order); - -book n. Bank(konto)buch n.

Passabl'e [pahss'Abl] a. annehmbar, gangbar, fahrbar (road, etc.), -y ad. leidlich, erträglich, ziemlich.

Passage [pæ'ssidzh] n. Gang m, Durchgehen n, Überfahrt f (sea), Übergang m (river, etc.).

Passenger [pæ'ssin-dzher] n. Passagier m, Fahrgast m, Reisender m, Fluggast m (av.); -boat n. Passagierdampfer m, Fahrgastdampfer m; - carriage n. Personenwagen m (rl.); - traffic n. Personenverkehr m.

Passion [pæ'schAn] n. Leidenschaft f, Zorn m, Liebe f; - Week n. Karwoche f; -ate a. leidenschaftlich.

Passive [pæ'ssiw] a. passiv, leidend; - resistance n. passiver Widerstand.

Passport [pahss'pOrt] n. Pass m, Heimatschein m (Austria); alien's - Fremdenpass m; -

photograph n. Passbild n; - office n. Pass-stelle f.

Password [pahss'uArd] n. Losung f, Losungswort n, Parole f.

Past [pahst] n. Vergangenheit f; a. vergangen, früher, vorig; ad. vorbei; pr. nach, über.

Paste [peist] n. Teig m, Kleister m, Pasta f (tooth); vt. kleistern, ankleben. [stift m.

Pastel [pæ'stel] n. Pastell-

Pasteurize [pah'stA-rais] vt. pasteurisieren.

Pastille [pæ'stil] n. Plätzchen

Pastime [pahss'taim] n. Zeitvertreib m, Erholung f.

Pastor [pahss'ter] n. Pfarrer m, Pastor m, -al a. Hirten-, Hirten...; -al letter n. Hirtenschreiben n; -ate n. Pfarramt n.

Pastry [pei'stri] n. Backwerk n, Torten f.pl, Pasteten f.pl; -cook n. Konditor m.

Pasturage [pah'stju-ridzh] n. Weideland n, Weiden n.

Pasture [pah'stjer] n. Weide f; vt.i. weiden.

Pat [pæt] n. gelinder Schlag, Stückchen n, Klümpchen n; vt. patschen.

Pat [pæt] a. parat, passend.

Patch [pætsch] n. Flicken m, Fleck m, Spiegel m (collar); vt. flicken, ausbessern; -work n. Flickwerk n, Stückwerk n.

Patchy [pæt'schi] a. zusammengestoppelt, voller Flicken.

Pate [peit] n. Kopf m.

Patent [pei'tAnt] n. Patent n; vt. patentieren; a. patentiert, offenkundig, offen; - fastener n. Druckknopf m; - leather n. Lackleder n; - office n. Patentamt n.

Patentee [pei-tAn-tih'] n. Patentinhaber m.

Patern'al [pA-tAr'nAl] a. väterlich, -ity n. Vaterschaft f.

Path [pahth] n. Pfad m, Weg m; -finder n. Pfadfinder m.

-finder aircraft n. Gefechtsaufklärer m.

Pathetic [pAth-the'tik] a. rührend, erschütternd.

Pathos [pei'thoss] n. das Rührende. [m.

Pathway [pahth'uei] n. Pfad

Patience [pei'schAnss] n. Geduld f, Patience f (cards); -t a. geduldig; n. der, die Kranke, Patient m, Patientin f.

Patriarch [pei'tri-ahrk] n. Patriarch m. [Patrizier m.

Patrician [pA-tri'schAn] n.

Patrimony [pe'tri-mA-ni] n. Erbgut n, Erbvermögen n.

Patriot [pe'tri-At] n. Patriot m, Vaterlandsfreund m.

Patriotic [pæ-tri-o'tik] a. patriotisch.

Patriotism [pe'tri-A-tism] n. Vaterlandsliebe f, Patriotismus m.

Patrol [pA-troul] n. Spähtrupp m, Patrouille f (mil.), Streife f (long distance); vt. durchschreiten, abpatrouillieren, abfliegen (av.), abstreifen (mil.); - boat n. Vorpostenboot, Wachboot n; - car n. Streifenkraftwagen m (police), Spähwagen m (mil.); - leader n. Streifendienstführer m; - vessel see - boat; -ling n. Streifendienst m.

Patron [pei'trAn] n. Patron m, Schutzherr m, Gönner m, Kunde m, Kundin f (com.).

Patronage [pæ'trA-nidzh] n. Gönnerschaft f, Beschützung f Kundschaft f (com.).

Patter [pæ'ter] n. Jargon m.

Pattern [pæ'tern] n. Muster n, Probe f, Schablone f; -book, n. Musterbuch n; - -maker n. Musterzeichner m.

Patty [pæ'ti] n. Pastetchen n.

Paucity [pO'ssi-ti] n. Mangel m, geringe Menge.

Paunch [pOnsch] n. Bauch m.

Pauper [pO'per] n. der, die Arme; **-ize** vt. in Armut bringen.

Pause [pOs] n. Pause f, Unterbrechung f; vi. innehalten, zögern, warten.

Pave [peiw] vt. pflastern, bahnen; -ment n. Pflaster n, Bürgersteig m.

Pavilion [pA-wi-ljAn] n. Zelt n, Gartenhäuschen n, Lusthaus n.

Paving-stone [pei'wingstoun] n. Pflasterstein m.

Paw [pO] n. Pfote f, Tatze f.

Pawn [pOn] n. verpfänden, versetzen; n. Pfand n, Bauer m (chess); -broker n. Pfandleiher m; - -shop n. Pfandhaus n; -ticket n. Pfandschein m.

Pay [pei] n. Lohn m, Bezahlung f; vt. bezahlen, einlösen, erweisen (show), schenken (attention); i. sich bezahlt machen, sich lohnen; - -book n. Soldbuch n (mil.); - day n. Zahltag m; - -envelope n. Lohntüte f; - load n. Nutzlast (av.); - -office n. Lohnstelle f.

Payable [pei'Abl] a. zahlbar, fällig (com.).

Payee [pei'ih'] n. Empfänger m, Remittent m (com.).

Payer [pei'er] n. Zahler m, der Bezogene (com.).

Paymaster [pei'mah-ster] n. Zahlmeister m; - department n. Kassenverwaltung f; - -'s office n. Kasse f.

Payment [pei'mAnt] n. Bezahlung f, Lohn m.

Pea [pih] n. Erbse f; - soup n. Erbsensuppe f.

Peace [pihss] n. Friede m, Ruhe f; breach of the - Ruhestörung f; - footing n. Friedensstand m; -time n. Friedenszeit f. [lich.

Peaceable [pihss'Abl] a. friedlich.

Peaceful [pihss'ful] a. -ly ad. friedlich, ruhig, mild.

Peacemaker [pihss'mei-ker] n. Friedensstifter m.

Peach [pihtsch] n. Pfirsich m.

Peacock [pih'kok] n. Pfau m.

Peak [pihk] *n.* Spitze *f*, Gipfel *m*, Schirm *m* (*cap*); **-ed** cap *n.* Schirmmütze *f*; **-** load *n.* Spitzenbelastung *f* (*el.*); **-** power output *n.* Oberstrichleistung *f* (*tec.*).

Peal [pihl] *n.* Glockenspiel *n*, Geläute *n*, Getöse *n*, Schlag *m* (*thunder*), Sturm *m* (*applause*); *vi.* krachen, erschallen.

Pear [peh'er] *n.* Birne *f*; **-shaped** *a.* birnenförmig; **-**tree *n.* Birnbaum *m.*

Pearl [pArl] *n.* Perle *f*; **-**barley *n.* Perlgraupen *f.pl*; **-**button *n.* Perlmutterknopf *m*; **-** oyster *n.* Perlmuschel *f.*

Peasant [pe'sAnt] *n.* Bauer *m*; *a.* bäuerlich, Land . . . . ; **-**proprietor *n.* Kleinbauer *m*, Landmann *m*; **-ry** *n.* Bauernschaft *f.* [Torfmoor *n.*

Peat [piht] *n.* Torf *m*; **-**bog *n.*

Pebb'le [pebl] *n.* Kieselstein *m*; **-y** *a.* kieselig. [Liter.

Peck [pek] *n.* 2 Gallonen, 9

Peck [pek] *vi.* picken.

Pectine [pek'tihn] *n.* Pflanzengallerte *f.*

Peculation [pe-kju-lei'schAn] *n.* Unterschlagung *f.*

Peculiar [pi-kjuh'ljer] *a.*, **-ly** *ad.* eigentümlich, besonder, seltsam.

Peculiarity [pi-kju-ljæ'ri-ti] *n.* Eigentümlichkeit *f*, Eigenart *f*, Eigenschaft *f.*

Pedal [pedl] *n.* Pedal *n*, Trittbrett *n*, Fusshebel *m*; *vt.i.* fahren, radfahren; **accelerator – Gashebel** *m* (*aut.*); **– cycle** *n.* Fahrrad *n*; **– cyclist** *n.* Radfahrer *m.*

Pedant [pe'dAnt] *n.* Pedant *m.*

Pedantry [pe'dAn-tri] *n.* Pedanterie *f.*

Peddle [pedl] *vt.* hausieren.

Pedestal [pe-di'stAl] *n.* Fussgestell *n*, Ständer *m*, Lagerblock *m* (*tec.*).

Pedestrian [pi-de'strjAn] *n.* Fussgänger *m.*

Pedicure [pe'di-kjuh-er] *n.* Fusspflege *f.*

Pedigree [pe'di-grih] *n.* Stammbaum *m*, Pedigree *m* (*animals*). [er *m.*

Pedlar [ped'ler] *n.* Hausierer *m.*

Peel [pihl] *n.* Schale *f*, Rinde *f*; *vt.* schälen, enthülsen; *i.* sich abschälen. [*vi.* gucken.

Peep [pihp] *n.* flüchtiger Blick.

Peer [pih'er] *n.* Pair *m*, der, die Adlige, Gleiche(r), Ebenbürtige(r); **-less** *a.* unvergleichlich.

Peg [peg] *n.* Pflock *m*, Dübel *m*, Stift *m*; *vt.* festpflöcken, stützen (*market*). [kan *m.*

Pelican [pe'li-kAn] *n.* Pelikan *m.*

Pellet [pe'lit] *n.* Kügelchen *n*, Schrotkorn *n.* [einander.

Pell-mell [pel'mel'] *ad.* durcheinander.

Pelt [pelt] *n.* rohe Haut, Fell *n*, Pelz *m.*

Pelt [pelt] *vt.* bewerfen.

Pelvis [pel'wiss] *n.* Becken *n.*

Pemmican [pe'mikn] *n.* harter Fleischkuchen *m.*

Pen [pen] *n.* Federhalter *m*, Schreibfeder *f*; **fountain – Füllfederhalter** *m*; **steel – Stahlfeder** *f*; **– holder** *n.* Federhalter *m*; **– knife** *n.* Federmesser *n*; **-manship** *n.* Schreibkunst *f*; **– wiper** *n.* Tintenwischer *m.*

Pen [pen] *n.* Verschlag *m*, Hühnerstall *m*, Laufgitter *n* (*children*); *vt.* einpferchen.

Penal [pih'nAl] *a.* strafbar, Straf . . . ; **– camp** *n.* Straflager *n*; **– code** *n.* Strafgesetzbuch *n*; **– servitude** *n.* Zuchthausstrafe *f.*

Penalize [pih'nA-lais] *vt.* bestrafen, benachteiligen, schädigen.

Penalty [pe'nAl-ti] *n.* Strafe *f*; **– kick** *n.* Strafstoss *m* (*football*). [*m.pl.*

Pence [penss] *n.pl.* Groschen

Pencil [pen'ssil] *n.* Bleistift *m*; *vt.* zeichnen, mit Bleistift schreiben; **red – Rotstift** *m*; **–**

-case *n*. Bleistifthalter *m*; -
-sharpener *n*. Bleistiftspitzer *n*.

Pendant [pen'dAnt] *n*. Gehänge *n*, Hängeleuchter *m*.

Pending [pen'ding] *pr.* während, bis; *a.* unentschieden, in der Schwebe. [Pendel *n*.

Pendulum [pen'dju-lAm] *n*.

Penetrable [pe'ni-trAbl] *a.* durchdringlich.

Penetrat'e [pe'ni-treit] *vt.i.* durchdringen, eindringen, durchstossen (*mil.*); -ing *a.* durchdringend.

Penetration [pe-ni-trei'schAn] *n*. Durchdringung *f*, Scharfsinn *m*; peaceful - friedliche Durchdringung; - in depth Tiefeinbruch *m* (*mil.*); - of the front Durchbruch *m*, Einbruch *m* (*mil.*).

Penguin [peng'guin] *n*. Pinguin *m*. [Halbinsel *f*.

Peninsula [pe-nin'sju-lA] *n*.

Peniten'ce [pe'ni-tAnss] *n*. Reue *f*, Busse *f*; -t *a.* reuig; *n*. Büsser *m*, Büsserin *f*.

Pennant [pe'nAnt] *n*. Wimpel *m*, Stander *m*. [Geld.

Penniless [pe'ni-less] *a.* ohne

Pennon [pe'nAn] *n*. Wimpel *m*, Lanzenflagge *f* (*mil.*), Fähnchen *n*.

Penny [pe'ni] *n*. Penny *m*, Groschen *m*; - bank *n*. Sparkasse *f*; -in-the-slot *a.* automatisch; - stamp *n*. Pennybriefmarke *f*; -weight *n*. 1½ Gramm; -worth *n*. für einen Penny.

Pension [pen'schAn] *n*. Pension *f*, Jahrgeld *n*, Ruhegehalt *n*; *vt.* pensionieren; old-age - Altersversorgung *f*; -able *a.* pensionsberechtigt; -er *n*. Pensionär *m*, Ruhegehaltempfänger *m*. [nachdenklich.

Pensive [pen'ssiw] *a.*, -ly *ad.*

Pentecost [pen'ti-kost] *n*. Pfingsten *n*. [Schutzdach *n*.

Pent-house [pent'hauss] *n*.

Pentode [pen'toud] *n*. Fünfelektrodenröhre *f* (*rad.*).

Pent-up [pent'Ap] *a.* verhalten. [keit *f*.

Penury [pen'ju-ri] *n*. Dürftig-

People [pihpl] *n*. Volk *n*, Leute *pl.*, Verwandte *m.pl*; *vt.* bevölkern.

Pep [pep] *n*. Schmiss *m*.

Pepper [pe'per] *n*. Pfeffer *m*; -box *n*. Pfefferstreubüchse *f*; -corn *n*. Pfefferkorn *n*; -mint *n*. Pfefferminze *f*, Pfefferminzplätzchen *n* (*sweet*).

Per [pAr] *pr.* durch, pro, per; per cent Prozent *n*, vom Hundert.

Perambulat'e [per-æm'bju-leit] *vt.i.* durchwandern, bereisen; -or *n*. Kinderwagen *m*.

Perceive [per-ssihw'] *vt.* wahrnehmen, beobachten, bemerken.

Percentage [per-ssen'tidzh] *n*. Prozentsatz *m*, Anteil *m*.

Percept'ible [per-ssep'tibl] *a.* wahrnehmbar, merklich; -ion *n*. Wahrnehmung *f*, Anschauung *f*, Einsicht *f*.

Perch [pArtsch] *n*. Barsch *m* (*fish*).

Perch [pArtsch] *n*. Stange *f*, Rute *f*, 5 Meter; *vi.* sich setzen auf. [*ad.* vielleicht.

Perchance [per-tschahnss']

Perchlorate [per-klO'rit] *n*. überchlorsaures Salz.

Percolate [pAr'ko-leit] *vt.i.* durchsickern.

Percolator [pAr'kA-lei-ter] *n*. Filtrierapparat *m*, Kaffeefilter *m*.

Percussion [per-kA'schAn] *n*. Schlag *m*; -cap *n*. Zündhütchen *n*; - -fuse *n*. Aufschlagzünder *m*; - -instrument *n*. Schlaginstrument *n*, Schlagzeug *n*.

Peremptory [pA-remp'tA-ri] *a.* unbedingt, gebieterisch.

Perennial [pA-ren'jAl] *a.* perennierend.

Perfect [pAr'fikt] *a.*, **-ly** *ad.* vollkommen, vollständig, vollendet.

Perfect [per-fekt'] *vt.* vervollkommnen, vollenden; **-ion** *n.* Vollkommenheit *f.*, Vollendung *f.*, Vorzüglichkeit *f.*

Perforate [pAr'fA-reit] *vt.* durchlöchern, lochen; **-d cards** *n.pl.* Lochkarten *f.pl.*

Perforation [per-fA-rei'schAn] *n.* Durchbohrung *f.*, Durchlochung *f.*, Lochung *f.*, Perforation *f.*

Perforator [pAr'fA-rei-ter] *n.* Locher *m.*, Bohrer *m.*

Perform [per-form'] *vt.* leisten, tun, machen, ausführen, vollziehen, spielen, aufführen (*play*); **-ing** *a.* abgerichtet, dressiert (*animals*).

Performance [per-fOr'mAnss] *n.* Ausführung *f.*, Leistung *f.*, Verrichtung *f.*, Aufführung *f.*, Werk *n.*, Tat *f.* (*deed*); **-load** *n.* Leistungsbelastung *f.*

Performer [per-fOr'mer] *n.* Täter *m.*, Schauspieler *m.*, Musiker *m.*, Künstler *m.*

Perfume [pAr'fjuhm] *n.* Wohlgeruch *m.*, Duft *m.*, Parfüm *n.*; **-spray** *n.* Parfümzerstäuber *m.*

Perfume [per-fjuhm'] *vt.* parfümieren; **-r** *n.* Parfümeur *m.*

Perfunctory [per-fAnk'tA-ri] *a.* oberflächlich.

Perhaps [per-hæpss'] *ad.* vielleicht, etwa.

Peril [pe'ril] *n.* Gefahr *f.*; **at your** – auf Ihre Gefahr; **-ous** *a.* gefährlich.

Perimeter [pe-ri'mi-ter] *n.* Umkreis *m.*, Perimeter *m.*; **-track** *n.* Ringsstrasse *f.*

Period [pih'rjAd] *n.* Periode *f.*, Zeitraum *m.*, Punkt *m.*

Periodic [pih-ri-o'dik] *a.* periodisch; **-ity** *n.* Zeitschrift *f.*

Periscope [pe'ri-skoup] *n.* Periskop *n.*, Sehrohr *n.* (*nav.*), Grabenspiegel *m.* (*mil.*).

Perish [pe'risch] *vi.* umkommen, absterben.

Perishable [pe'ri-schAbl] *a.* leicht verderblich.

Perjure [pAr'dzher] *vr.* einen Meineid leisten, falsch schwören; [eid *m.*

Perjury [pAr'dzhA-ri] *n.* Meineid *m.*

Perky [pAr'ki] *a.* keck, frech.

Perm [pArm] *n. see* permanent wave.

Permanence [pAr'mA-nAnss] *n.* Dauerhaftigkeit *f.*, Dauer *f.*, Beständigkeit *f.*

Permanent [pAr'mA-nAnt] *a.* dauernd, dauerhaft, beständig, ständig, fest; **- dye** *n.* Dauerfarbe *f.*; **- magnet** *n.* Dauermagnet *m.*; **- pass** *n.* Dauerkarte *f.*; **- post** *n.* Lebensstellung *f.*; **- quarters** *n.pl.* Standquartier *n.*; **- wave** *n.* Dauerwelle *f.*; **- way** *n.* Oberbau *m.* (*rl.*).

Permanganate [per-mæng'gA-neit] *n.* Permanganat *n.*; **- of potash** *n.* übermangansaures Kali.

Permeability [per-mi-A-bi'li-ti] *n.* Durchdringbarkeit *f.*

Permea'ble [pAr'mi-Abl] *a.* durchdringlich, (wasser)durchlässig; **-te** *vt.* durchdringen.

Permissible [per-mi'ssibl] *a.* zulässig; **- deviation** *n.* Toleranz *f.* [Erlaubnis *f.*

Permission [per-mi'schAn] *n.* Erlaubnis *f.*

Permissive [per-mi'ssiw] *a.* berechtigend.

Permit [pAr'mit] *n.* Erlaubnisschein *m.*, Passierschein *m.*; **export** – Ausfuhrerlaubnis *f.*; **- to bear arms** Waffenpass *m.*

Permit [per-mit'] *vt.* erlauben, gestatten, dulden.

Pernicious [per-ni'schAss] *a.* verderblich.

Pernickety [per-ni'kA-ti] *a.* heikel, allzu genau.

Peroxide [pe-rox'aid] *n.* Hyperoxyd *n.*

Perpendicular [per-pen-di'

kju-ler] *a.* senkrecht, lotrecht; *n.* Senkrechte *f.*, Lot *n.*, Spätgotik *f (style)*.

Perpetra'te [pAr'pi-treit] *vt.* begehen, verüben; **-tion** *n.* Verübung *f.*, Begehung *f.*; **-tor** *n.* Täter *m.*, Begeher *m.*

Perpetual [per-pe'tju-Al] *a.* unaufhörlich, ewig, beständig, unkündbar (*com.*). [verewigen.

Perpetuate [per-pe'tju-eit] *vt.*

Perpetuity [pAr-pi-tju'i-ti] *n.* Ewigkeit *f.*, ununterbrochener Fortdauer; **in** – für immer.

Perplex [per-plex'] *vt.* verwirren; **-ity** *n.* Verwirrung *f.*, Verlegenheit *f.*

Perquisite [pAr'kui-sit] *n.* Zubehör *n.*; **-s** *pl.* Nebeneinkommen *n.*, Gratifikation *f.*, Sporteln *f.pl.*

Persecu'te [pAr'si-kjuht] *vt.* verfolgen, belästigen; **-tion** *n.* Verfolgung *f.*; **-tor** *n.* Verfolger *m.*

Perseverance [per-ssi-wih'rAnss] *n.* Beharrlichkeit *f.*, Ausdauer *f.*

Persever'e [per-ssi-wih'er] *vi.* beharren, ausdauern, aushalten; **-ing** *a.* beharrlich, unermüdlich, standhaft.

Persist [per-ssist'] *vi.* ausharren, beharren, bestehen auf; **-ence** *n.* Beharrlichkeit *f.*, Eigensinn *m.*; **-ent** *a.* beharrlich, wiederholt, anhaltend.

Person [pAr'ssAn] *n.* Person *f.*, Mensch *m.*   [stattlich.

Personable [pAr'ssA-nAbl] *a.*

Personage [pAr'ssA-nidzh] *n.* Persönlichkeit *f.*, Standesperson *f.*

Personal [pAr'ssA-nAl] *a.*, **-ly** *ad.* persönlich, anzüglich (*rude*); **– injuries** *n.pl.* Personenschäden *m.pl.*; **– particulars** *n.pl.* anzügliche Anspielungen *f.pl.*

Personality [per-sso-næ'li-ti] *n.* Persönlichkeit *f.*, Anzüglichkeit *f (remark)*.

Personification [per-sso'ni-fi-kei-schAn] *n.* Verkörperung *f.*, Personifizierung *f.*

Personify [per-sso'ni-fai] *vt.* verkörpern, personifizieren.

Personnel [per-ssA-nel'] *n.* Personal *n.*, Angestellten *m.pl (com.)*, Mannschaften *f.pl (mil. etc.)*; **– under training** *n.* Nachwuchs *m (mil.)*.

Perspective [per-spek'tiw] *n.* Perspektive *f.*, Ausblick *m.*, Aussicht *f.*

Perspicacity [per-spi-kæ'ssi-ti] *n.* Scharfsinn *m.*

Perspicuity [per-spi-kjuh'i-ti] *n.* Klarheit *f.*

Perspicuous [per-spi'kju-Ass] *a.* deutlich, klar.

Perspiration [per-spi-rei'schAn] *n.* Schweiss *m.*

Perspire [per-spai'er] *vi.* schwitzen.

Persua'de [per-ssueid'] *vt.* überreden; **-sion** *n.* Überredung *f.*; **-sive** *a.* überzeugend.

Persulphate [per-ssAl'feit] *n.* Persulfat *n.*

Pert [pArt] *a.* keck.

Pertain [per-tein'] *vi.* angehören, betreffen.

Pertinaceous [per-ti-næ'ssi-ti] schAss] *a.* eigensinnig.

Pertinacity [per-ti-næ'ssi-ti] *n.* Hartnäckigkeit *f.*

Pertinent [pAr'ti-nAnt] *a.* gehörig, treffend.   [heit *f.*

Pertness [pArt'ness] *n.* Keckheit *f.*

Perturb [per-tArb'] *vt.* beunruhigen.   [sicht *f.*

Perusal [pA-ruh'sAl] *n.* Durchsicht *f.*

Peruse [pA-ruhs'] *vt.* durchlesen, durchsehen.   [dringen.

Pervade [per-weid'] *vt.* durchdringen.

Pervasive [per-wei'siw] *a.* durchdringend.

Perverse [per-wArss'] *a.* verstockt, verderbt.

Perversity [per-wAr'ssi-ti] *n.* Eigensinn *m.*, Tücke *f.*

Perversion [per-wAr'schAn] *n.* Verdrehung *f.*, Abwendung *f.*

Perversive [per-wAr'ssiw] a. verderblich.

Pervert [per-wArt'] vt. verdrehen, verderben. [nige(r) m.

Pervert [pAr'wert] n. Abtrünniger m.

Pervious [pAr'wjÄss] a. durchlässig, zugänglich.

Pessimis'm [pe'ssi-mism] n. Pessimismus m; -t n. Schwarzseher m, Pessimist m.

Pessimistic [pe-ssi-mi'stik] a. pessimistisch.

Pest [pest] n. Pest f, Plage f.

Pester [pe'ster] vt. plagen, belästigen.

Pestiferous [pe-sti'fA-rAss] a. giftig, schädlich. [Seuche f.

Pestilence [pe'sti-lAnss] n.

Pestilential [pe-sti-len'schAl] a. pestbringend, ansteckend.

Pestle [pestl] n. Mörserkeule f, Pistill n.

Pet [pet] vt. hätscheln, streicheln; n. Liebling m, zahmes Tier.

Petal [petl] n. Blumenblatt n.

Peter [pih'ter] vi, - out zu nichts führen, zu Ende gehen.

Petition [pi-ti'schAn] n. Bitte f, Bittschrift f, Gesuch n; vt. bitten, ansuchen.

Petrel [pe'trAl] n. Sturmvogel m. [ern.

Petrify [pe'tri-fai] vt. versteinern.

Petrol [pet'rAl] n. Benzin n, Betriebsstoff m; - gauge n. Benzinuhr f (aut.); - pump n. Tankstelle f (aut.).

Petroleum [pi-tro'ljAm] n. Petroleum n, Erdöl n.

Petticoat [pe'ti-kout] n. Unterrock m; - government n. Weiberherrschaft f. [lich.

Pettish [pe'tisch] a. verdriesslich.

Petty [pe'ti] a. kleinlich, klein, gering; - cash n. kleine Kasse f; - officer n. Obermaat m.

Petulan'ce [pe'tju-lAnss] n. Mutwille m; -t a. mutwillig, reizbar, mürrisch.

Pew [pjuh] n. Kirchenstuhl m.

Pewter [pjuh'ter] n. Hartzinn

n, Schlüsselzinn n, Weissmetall n; Zinnwaren f.pl; a. zinnern.

Phantom [fen'tAm] n. Traumbild n, Trugbild n.

Pharmaceutical [fahr-mAssjuh'tikl] a. arzneikundlich; - chemist see Pharmacist.

Pharmac'ist [fahr'mA-ssist] n. Apotheker m.

Pharmac'y [fahr'mA-ssi] n. Drogist m, Apotheker m; -y n. Apotheke f, Drogerie f (shop), Apothekerkunst f (science).

Phase [feis] n. Phase f, Wandlung f. [Fasan m.

Pheasant [fe's Ant] n.

Phenol [fe'nol] n. Karbolsäure f.

Phenomen'al [fi-no'mi-nAl] a. ausserordentlich; -on n. Phänomen n, Erscheinung f, Wunder n.

Phial [fai'Al] n. Fläschchen n.

Philanthrop'ic [fi-lAn-thro'pik] a. menschenfreundlich; -y n. Menschenliebe f.

Philatelic [fi-lA-te'lik] a. Briefmarken ...

Philatel'ist [fi-le'tA-list] n. Briefmarkensammler m; -y n. Briefmarkenkunde f.

Philology [fi-lo'lA-dzhi] n. Philologie f, Sprachwissenschaft f. [Philosoph m.

Philosopher [fi-lo'ssA-fer] n.

Philosophical [fi-lA-so'fikl] a. philosophisch.

Philosophy [fi-lo'ssA-fi] n. Philosophie f. [Schleim m.

Phlegm [flem] n. Phlegma n,

Phlegmatic [fleg-mæ'tik] a. phlegmatisch.

Phone [foun] n. Fernsprecher m, Telephon n; vt.i. anrufen, telephonieren; - call n. Anruf m; - message n. telephonische Mitteilung.

Phonetics [fo-ne'tix] n.pl. Phonetik f.

Phosgene [fos'dzhihn] n. Phosgen n.

Phosphate [foss'feit] n. phosphorsaures Salz; - of soda n. phosphorsaures Natron.

Phosphorus [foss'fA-rAss] *n.*
Phosphor *m.*

Photo [fou'tou] *see* photograph; – **electric cell** *n.*
Photo-, Licht-zelle *f.*

Photograph [fou'tA-grahf] *n.*
Lichtbild *n,* Photographie *f;*
vt.i. photographieren, eine Aufnahme machen, aufnehmen;
air – *n.* Luft-, Flieger-bild *n;*
– **album** *n.* Photomappe *f,*
Lichtbilderalbum *n.*

Photographer [fo-to'grA-fer]
n. Lichtbildner *m,* Photograph *m.*

Photographic [fo-tA-græ'fik]
a. photographisch, Lichtbild
...; – **plate** *n.* photographische
Platte.

Photography [fo-to'grA-fi] *n.*
Photographie *f,* Lichtbildkunst
f, Lichtbildnerei *f;* – **platoon** *n.*
Bildzug *m;* – **school** *n.* Bildschule *f.*

Photogravure [fou-to-grA-
wjuh'er] *n.* Photogravüre *f.*

Photolithography [fou-to-li-
tho'grA-fi] *n.* Lichtdruck *m.*

Phototype [fou'to-taip] *n.*
Lichtdruckplatte *f.*

Phrase [freis] *n.* Redensart *f,*
Wendung *f,* Phrase *f;* *vt.* ausdrücken.

Phraseology [frei-si-o'lA-
dzhi] *n.* Ausdrucksweise *f.*

Physic [fi'sik] *n.* Arznei *f;* –**s**
pl. Physik *f,* Naturkunde *f.*

Physical [fi'sik] *a.* physisch,
körperlich; – **training** instructor
m; – **training** *n.* Sport
m; – **training** instructor *n.*
Sportlehrer *m.*

Physician [fi-si'schAn] *n.*
Arzt *m.*

Physiognomy [fi-si-o'nA-mi]
n. Gesichtsausdruck *m.*

Physiology [fi-si-o'lA-dzhi] *n.*
Physiologie *f.*

Physique [fi-sihk'] *n.* Körpergestalt *f.*

Pianist [pih'A-nist] *n.* Klavierspieler *m,* -in *f,* Pianist *m,*
Pianistin *f.*

Piano [pi-æ'no] *n.* Klavier *n,*

Piccolo [pi'kA-lo] *n.* Pikkoloflöte *f.*

Pick [pik] *vt.* pflücken, auswählen, lesen; *n.* Spitzeisen *n,*
Hacke *f,* Haue *f;* -ed *a.* auserlesen, ausgesucht; -**axe** *n.*
Spitzhacke *f,* Picke *f;* – -**up** *n.*
aufnehmen, auftreiben, ablauschen (*rad.*) ; *n.* Schalldose *f*
(*gramophone*).

Picket [pi'kit] *n.* Feldwache *f,*
Posten *m,* Streife *f* (*mil.*) ; *vt.*
abstreifen; *i.* Streikposten aufstellen.

Pickle [pikl] *n.* Pökel *m,* Eingepökeltes *n,* Eisgemüse *n;* *vt.*
einpökeln. [Taschendieb *m.*

Pickpocket [pik'po-kit] *n.*

Picnic [pik'nik] *n.* Landpartie
f; *vi.* im Freien essen.

Picric acid [pik'rik-æ'ssid] *n.*
Pikrinsäure *f.*

Pictorial [pik-tO'rjAl] *a.* Bild
...; *n.* illustrierte Zeitung.

Picture [pik'tscher] *n.* Bild *n,*
Gemälde *n,* Film *m;* -**s** *pl.*
Kino *n;* – -**book** *n.* Bilderbuch
n; – -**card** *n.* Bild *n* (*card*) ;
– -**dealer** *n.* Kunsthändler *m;*
-**frame** *n.* Bilderrahmen *m;*
-**gallery** *n.* Gemäldegalerie *f,*
Kunstmuseum *n;* – -**house**,
-**palace** *n.* Lichtspieltheater *n,*
Kino *n;* – -**postcard** *n.* Ansichtskarte *f.*

Picturesque [pik-tschA-resk']
a. malerisch. [*m,* Torte *f.*

Pie [pai] *n.* Pastete *f,* Auflauf

Pie [pai] *n.* Zwölftel Anna *n.*

Piebald [pai'bOld] *a.* scheckig.

Piece [pihss] *n.* Stück *n,* Teil
m, Figur *f* (*chess*) ; – -**rates** *n.pl.*
Leistungswerte *m.pl;* – -**work**
n. Akkordarbeit *f,* Gedinge *n*
(*mining*). [stückweise.

Piecemeal [pihss'mihl] *ad.*

Pied [paid] *a.* scheckig.

Pier [pih'er] *n.* Kai *m,* Hafendamm *m,* Landungs-brücke *f,*
-platz *m;* – **dues** *n.pl.* Landungsgebühr *f,* Kaigeld *n;* –
-**head** *n.* Brückenkopf *m.*

Pierc'e [pihrss] vt. durchstechen, durchdringen, durchbohren; -ing a. schneidend, durchdringend, -bohrend. [keit f.

Piety [pai'A-ti] n. Frömmigkeit f.

Pig [pig] n. Schwein n; - -iron n. Roheisen n.

Pigeon [pi'dzhAn] n. Taube f.

Piggish [pi'gisch] a. schweinisch.

Pigment [pig'mAnt] n. Farbstoff m, Pigment n. [leder n.

Pigskin [pig'skin] n. Schweinsleder n.

Pike [paik] n. Hecht m.

Pile [pail] n. Haufe m; vt. aufschichten, aufhäufen, überhäufen.

Pile [pail] n. Pfahl m; - -driver n. Ramm-maschine f, Ramme f.

Pile [pail] n. Noppe f (cloth), Flor m (velvet); vt. rauhen.

Piles [pails] n.pl. Hämorrhoiden f.pl.

Pilfer [pil'fer] vt. stehlen, mausen; -ing n. Diebstahl m.

Pilgrim [pil'grim] n. Pilger m; -age n. Pilgerfahrt f.

Pill [pil] n. Pille f; - -box n. Pillenschachtel f, Scharten-stand m (mil.), Eisenbeton-unterstand m (mil.).

Pillage [pi'lidzh] n. Plünderung f; vt. plündern.

Pillar [pi'ler] n. Pfeiler m, Säule f; - -box n. Briefkasten m.

Pillion [pi'ljAn] n. Sattel m, Soziussitz m (motor-cycle); - -rider n. Sozius-fahrer m, -fahrerin f.

Pillory [pi'lA-ri] n. Pranger m.

Pillow [pi'lou] n. Kopfkissen m; - -case n, - -slip n. Kissenüberzug m.

Pilot [pai'lAt] n. Lotse m, Steuermann m, Flugzeugfahrer m (av.), Flugzeugkapitän m (civil); vt. lotsen, steuern (ship); führen (plane). - -engine n. Versuchslokomotive f. - -officer n. Leutnant der Flie-

ger m (av.); - -'s certificate n. Führerschein m (av.); - -'s wings n.pl. Schwinge f (av.).

Pilotage [pai'lA-tidzh] n. Lotsengeld n, Lotsen n.

Pimp [pimp] n. Kuppler m.

Pimple [pimpl] n. Pustel f, Bläschen n.

Pin [pin] n. Stecknadel f, Bolzen m, Stift m, Zapfen m; vt. anheften, befestigen; - -down vt. fesseln, binden; - -head n. Nadelknopf m; - -prick n. Nadelstich m, Stich m.

Pinafore [pi'nA-fOr] n. Schürze f.

Pince-nez [pangss'neh] n. Kneifer m.

Pincer [pin'sser] n, -s pl. Beisszange f; - -movement n. Zangenbewegung f (mil.).

Pinch [pinsch] vt. kneifen, drücken, mausen; n. Kniff m, Klemme f; at a - zur Not.

Pincushion [pin'ku-schin] n. Nadelkissen n.

Pine [pain] n. Fichte f, Kiefer m; -apple n. Ananas f; - -kernels n.pl. Pinienkerne m.pl.

Pine [pain] vi. schmachten.

Ping-pong [ping'pong] n. Tischtennis n.

Pinion [pi'njAn] n. Getriebe n, Zahnradgetriebe n, Schwinge f; vt. fesseln.

Pink [pink] n. Nelke f, Rosa n; a. rosafarben. [zacken.

Pink [pink] vt. durchlöchern, zacken.

Pinnace [pi'nAss] n. Beiboot n, Pinasse f.

Pinnacle [pi'nAkl] n. Bergspitze f, Gipfel m, Spitztürmchen n.

Pin-point [pin-peunt'] n. Nadelspitze f; - -bombing n. Bombenpunktwurf m (av.); - -target n. Punktziel n (av.).

Pint [paint] n. Pinte f, halbes Liter; - -pot n. Bierkanne f.

Pioneer [pai-o-nih'er] n. Bahnbrecher m, Pionier m (mil.).

Pious [pai'Ass] a. fromm.

Pip [pip] n. Auge n (cards, etc.), Stern m (badge of rank).
Pip [pip] n. Obstkern m.
Pipe [paip] n. Pfeife f, Rohr n, Röhre f; vt. durch Röhren leiten; - bowl n. Pfeifenkopf m; - -clay n. Pfeifenton m; - -cleaner n. Pfeifenreiniger m; -line n. Öl-, Röhren-leitung f; - -stem n. Pfeifenstiel m.
Piper [pai'per] n. Pfeifer m.
Piping [pai'ping] n. Röhrenleitung f (oil), Schnurbesatz m (clothing), Litze f, Hosenbiese f (mil.).   [m, Renette f.
Pippin [pi'pin] n. Apfelkern
Piquant [pih'kAnt] a. pikant.
Piracy [pai'rA-ssi] n. Seeräuberei f, verbotener Nachdruck (books).
Pirate [pai'rAt] n. Seeräuber
Pistol [pi'stAl] n. Pistole f; automatic - Selbstladepistole f.
Piston [pi'stAn] n. Kolben m; - -rod n. Kolbenstange f.
Pit [pit] n. Grube f, Höhle f, Schacht f, Parterre n (theatre), Tonhöhe f (music); - props n.pl. Grubenholz n.
Pitch [pitsch] n. Pech n.
Pitch [pitsch] n. Wurf m, Höhe f, Spielplatz m; vt. werfen, aufschlagen; -fork n. Heugabel f.
Pitch-pine [pitsch'pain] n. Pechkiefer f.
Piteous [pi'tjAss] a. kläglich.
Pitfall [pit'fOl] n. Fallgrube f.
Pith [pith] n. Mark n, Kern m.
Pit-head [pit-hed'] n. Schachtöffnung f, Füllort m; - baths n.pl. Waschkaue f; - price n. Grubenpreis m.
Pithy [pi'thi] a. markig, kernig.   [lich.
Pitiful [pi'ti-ful] a. jämmerlich.
Pitiless [pi'ti-less] a. erbarmungslos.
Pittance [pi'tAnss] n. kleiner Anteil, Hungerlohn m.
Pity [pi'ti] n. Mitleid n; vt. bedauern, bemitleiden.
Pivot [pi'wAt] n. Drehpunkt

m, Zapfen m, Stift m, Pinne f; vi. sich drehen.
Placard [plæ'kahrd] n. Plakat n, Anschlagzettel m; vt. öffentlich anschlagen.
Placate [plA-keit'] vt. besänftigen, versöhnen.
Place [pleiss] n. Platz m, Ort m, Stelle f; vt. stellen, legen, setzen, unterbringen; - -kick n. Platztritt m; - -seeker n. Streber m.   [f; vt. plagen.
Plague [pleig] n. Pest n, Plage
Plaice [pleiss] n. Scholle f.
Plaid [pleid] n. Plaid m, Umschlagetuch n.
Plain [plein] a, -ly ad. schlicht, einfach, glatt, klar; -speaking n. unumwundene Rede; -ness n. Schlichtheit f, Klarheit f.   [er m.
Plaintiff [plein'tif] n. Kläger.
Plait [plæt] n. Flechte f; vt. flechten.
Plan [plæn] n. Plan m, Entwurf m; vt. planen, entwerfen.
Plane [plein] n. Ebene f, Fläche f, Hobel m (tec.), Luftfahrzeug n (av.), Flugzeug n (av.); vt. hobeln.
Planet [plæ'nit] n. Planet m.
Plane-tree [plein'trih] n. Platane f.   [hobeln, planieren.
Planish [plæ'nisch] vt. glatt
Plank [plængk] n. Planke f, Brett n, Bohle f.
Planning [plæ'ning] n. Planung f; - department n. Planungsamt n; - office n. Planstelle f.
Plant [plahnt] n. Pflanze f, Betriebsanlage f (tec.), Fabrikanlage f (factory); vt. bepflanzen, anpflanzen, pflanzen.
Plantation [plen-tei'schAn] n. Pflanzung f, Pflanzschule f, Plantage f.   [zer m.
Planter [plahn'ter] n. Pflan.
Plaque [plæk] n. verzierte Metallplättchen, Agraffe f.
Plaster [plah'ster] n. Pflaster n, Gips m, Mörtel m, Bewurf

m; *vt.* bewerfen, tünchen, gipsen, pflastern; **-er** *n.* Gipsarbeiter *m.*

Plastic [plæ'stik] *a.* plastisch, formbar; *n.* Kunstharz *n*; **- surgery** *n.* Hauttransplantation *f*, Autoplastik *f.*

Plasticine [plæ'sti-ssihn] *n.* Modelliermasse *f.*

Plate [pleit] *n.* Platte *f*, Tafel *f*, Teller *m*, Bild *n* (books), Gaumenplatte *f* (dental); *vt.* plattieren, versilbern; **- -clutch** *n.* Lamellenkupplung *f*; **- -glass** *n.* Spiegelglas *n*; **- -iron** *n.* Eisenblech *n*; **- -layer** *n.* Streckenarbeiter *m* (rl.).

Platform [plæt'fOrm] *n.* Bahnsteig *m*, Bühne *f*, Parteiprogramm *n*; **- ticket** *n.* Bahnsteigkarte *f.*

Platinum [plæ'ti-nAm] *n.* Platin *n*; **- wire** *n.* Platindraht *m.*

Platitude [plæ'ti-tjuhd] *n.* Gemeinplatz *m.*

Platoon [plA-tuhn'] *n.* Zug *m*; **- -commander** *n.* Zugführer *m.*

Plaudit [plO'dit] *n.* Beifallklatschen *n.*

Plausible [plO'sibl] *a.* annehmbar, einnehmend, plausibl.

Play [plei] *n.* Spiel *m*, Schauspiel *n*, Gang *m*, Spielraum *m*; *vt.i.* spielen; **-bill** *n.* Theaterzettel *m.*

Player [plei'er] *n.* Spieler *m*, **-in** *f*, Schauspieler *m*, **-in** *f.*

Playfellow [plei'fe-lou] *n.* Spielgefährte *m*, **-in** *f.*

Playful [plei'ful] *a.* scherzhaft, spielerisch.

Playgoer [plei'gou-er] *n.* Theaterbesucher *m.*

Playground [plei'graund] *n.* Schulhof *m.*

Playhouse [plei'hauss] *n.* Schauspielhaus *n*, Kino *n.*

Playing [plei'ing] *n.* Spielen *n*; **- -card** *n.* Spielkarte *f*; **- -field** *n.* Sportplatz *m.*

Playmate [plei'meit] *n.* Gespiele *m*, Gespielin *f.*

Plaything [plei'thing] *n.* Spielzeug *n.* [Dramatiker *m.*

Playwright [plei'rait] *n.*

Plea [plih] *n.* Gesuch *n*, Ausrede *f*, Einrede *f* (law).

Plead [plihd] *vt.i.* verteidigen, vorschützen, plädieren (law).

Pleasant [ple'sAnt] *a.* angenehm, freundlich, gefällig; **-ness** *n.* Annehmlichkeit *f*, Freundlichkeit *f.*

Please [plihs] bitte; *vt.i.* gefallen; **-d** *a.* erfreut, befriedigt, zufrieden; **-ing** *a.* angenehm, gefällig; *n.* Gefallen *m.*

Pleasure [ple'zher] *n.* Vergnügen *n*; **- -ground** *n.* Vergnügungsplatz *m*; **- -loving** *a.* vergnügungssüchtig.

Pleat [pliht] *n.* Falte *f*; *vt.* plissieren, fälteln, falten.

Plebeian [pli-bih'An] *a.* gemein, plebejisch.

Plebiscite [ple'bi-ssit] *n.* Volksabstimmung *f.*

Pledge [pledzh] *n.* Pfand *n*; *vt.* verpfänden. [ständig.

Plenary [plih'nA-ri] *a.* voll-

Plenipotentiary [ple-ni-pA-ten'shA-ri] *n.* der Bevollmächtigte.

Plenteous [plen'tjAss] *a.* reichlich, ergiebig; **-iful** *a.* reichlich, in Überfluss (vorhanden); **-y** *n.* Fülle *f*, Überfluss *m*; **- of** eine Menge, sehr viele.

Pliable [plai'Abl] *a.* biegsam.

Pliers [plai'ers] *n.pl.* Drahtzange *f.* [geloben.

Plight [plait] *vt.* verpfänden,

Plight [plait] *n.* Lage *f*, Zustand *m.* [en, sich abmühen.

Plod [plod] *vi.* mühsam arbeit-

Plot [plot] *n.* Stück *n*, Platz *m*; *vt.* entwerfen; **- a course** einen Kurs abstecken (av.).

Plot [plot] *n.* Komplott *n*, Intrige *f*; *vt.* anzetteln; *i.* komplottieren.

Plotter [plo'ter] *n.* Anstifter *m*, Verschwörer *m*.

Plotter [plo'ter] *n.* Flugmelde-auswerter *m* (*av.*).

Plotting [plo'ting] *n.* graph-ische Darstellung *f*, Flugmelde-auswertung *f*; – -board *n.* Flächenmessplan *m*; – -equip-ment *n.* Plangerät *n* (*av.*); – -room *n.* Rechenstelle *f*.

Plough [plau] *n.* Pflug *m*; *vt.i.* pflügen; **to be -ed** durch-fallen (*exam.*). [Pflüger *m.*

Ploughman [plau'mAn] *n.*

Ploughshare [plau'scheh-er] *n.* Pflugschar *f*.

Pluck [plAk] *vt.* pflücken, rup-fen; *n.* Mut *m*.

Plug [plAg] *n.* Pflock *m*, Zap-fen *m*, Stöpsel *m*, Priem *m* (*tobacco*), Zahnplombe *f* (*teeth*), Stecker *m* (*el.*), Feuerhahn *m* (*fire*); *vt.* zustopfen, plombier-en; – **in** *el.* einschalten, ein-stecken.

Plum [plAm] *n.* Pflaume *f*, Rosine *f*; – **-cake** *n.* Rosinen-kuchen *m*; – **pudding** *n.* Plum-pudding *m*. [fieder *n.*

Plumage [pluh'midzh] *n.* Ge-

Plumb [plAm] *a.ad.* lotrecht, senkrecht; *n.* Lot *n.*; *vt.* peilen (*nav.*); – **-line** *n.* Lotleine *f*.

Plumbago [plAm-bei'gou] *n.* Reissblei *m*.

Plumber [plA'mer] *n.* Blei-arbeiter *m*, Klempner *m*, In-stallateur *m*.

Plumbing [plA'ming] *n.* Blei-arbeit *f*, Bleirohranlage *f*.

Plume [pluhm] *n.* Feder *f*, Federbusch *m*. [Senkblei *n.*

Plummet [plA'mit] *n.* Lot *n*,

Plump [plAmp] *a.* dick, plump; **-ness** *n.* Beleibtheit *f*.

Plump [plAmp] *a.ad.* plumps; *vt.* fallen lassen, plumpsen.

Plunder [plAn'der] *n.* Beute *f*; *vt.* plündern.

Plunge [plAnzh] *vt.i.* unter-tauchen, (sich) stürzen; *n.* Sturz *m*, Untertauchen *n*.

Plunger [plAn'zher] *n.* Tau-cher *m*, Kolben *m*.

Pluperfect [plu-pAr'fikt] *n.* Plusquamperfektum *n*.

Plural [pluh'rAl] *n.* Mehrzahl *f*.

Plus [plAss] *ad.* plus, dazu; *pr.* zuzüglich; *n.* Plus *n*, Mehr *n*; – **-fours** *n.pl.* sehr weite Knie-hosen, Golfhosen *f.pl.*

Plush [plAsch] *n.* Plüsch *m*.

Plutocracy [plu-to'krA-ssi] *n.* Plutokratie *f*.

Plutocrat [pluh'tA-kræt] *n.* Millionär *m*, Plutokrat *m*.

Ply [plai] *vi.* regelmässig fahr-en, verkehren; *t.* betreiben, zu-setzen; *n.* Strähne *f*, Falte *f*; – **-wood** *n.* Sperrholz *n*.

Pneumatic [nju-mæ'tik] *a.* pneumatisch, Luftdruck . . . ; – **brake** *n.* Druckluftbremse *f*; – **pump** *n.* Luftpumpe *f*; – **tyre** *n.* Luftreifen *m*.

Pneumonia [nju-mou'njA] *n.* Lungenentzündung *f*.

Poach [poutsch] *vi.* wildern; **-er** *n.* Wilddieb *m*, Wilderer *m*.

Poached eggs [poutsch-egs'] *n.pl.* verlorene Eier *n.pl.*

Pochette [po-schet'] *n.* Hand-täschchen *n*.

Pocket [po'kit] *n.* Tasche *f*, Kessel *m* (*mil.*); *vt.* einstecken; – **battleship** *n.* Schlachtschiff *n*, Panzerkreuzer *m*; – **hand-kerchief** *n.* Taschentuch *n*; – **money** *n.* Taschengeld *n*; – **of resistance** *n.* Kessel *m* (*mil.*); – **-size** *n.* Taschenformat *n*; – **torch** *n.* Taschenlampe *f*.

Pock-marked [pok'mahrkt] *a.* pockennarbig.

Pod [pod] *n.* Hülse *f*, Schale *f*.

Poem [poh'im] *n.* Gedicht *n*.

Poet [poh'it] *n.* Dichter *m*; **-ess** *n.* Dichterin *f*.

Poetic [poh-e'tik] *a.* poetisch, dichterisch.

Poetry [poh'i-tri] *n.* Poesie *f*, Dichtkunst *f* (*art*), Gedichte *n.pl.* (*poems*). [grom *n.*

Pogrom [po-grom'] *n.* Po-

Poignan'cy [peun'jAn-ssi] n. Heftigkeit f, Schärfe f; **-t** a. scharf, beissend, nagend.

Point [peunt] n. Spitze f, Punkt m; vt. spitzen, richten, zeigen; - at weisen auf; decimal - Komma n; -s pl. Weiche f (rl.); **-sman** n. Weichensteller m (rl.).

Point-blank [peunt'blængk] ad. schnurgerade, unverhohlen, rundweg; - range n. Kernschussweite f.

Point-duty [peunt'djuh-ti] n. Verkehrsdienst m; policeman on - n. Verkehrsschutzmann m.

Pointed [peun'tid] a. scharf, spitz, spitzig, anzüglich (remark).

Pointer [peun'ter] n. Weiser m, Zeigestock m.

Pointless [peunt'less] a. zwecklos, stumpf (blunt).

Poise [peus] Gleichgewicht n; vt. wägen; i. schweben.

Poison [peu'sAn] n. Gift n; vt. vergiften; - -gas n. Giftgas n, Kampf-stoff m, -gas n; - -gas warfare n. Gaskrieg m; -ous a. giftig.

Poke [pouk] vt. stossen, schüren; n. Stoss m, Puff m; - about vi. herum-tappen, -tasten; -r n. Schüreisen n; -r-work n. Brandmalerei f.

Poker [pou'ker] n. Pokerspiel n (cards).

Polar [pou'ler] a. polar, Pol ...; - bear n. Eisbär m.

Pole [poul] n. Stange f, Pfahl m, Rute f (5 1/2 Yard).

Pole [poul] n. Pol m; - star n. Polarstern m.

Polemic(al) [po-le'mikl] a. streitsüchtig, polemisch.

Police [pA-lihss'] n. Polizei f; a. polizeilich; vt. (polizeilich) überwachen; civil - Ordnungspolizei f; military - Gendarmerie f; secret - Geheimpolizei f; - box n. Polizeimelder m; - -constable see policeman; -

-court n. Polizeigericht n; - -force n. Polizeitruppe f; - -inspector n. Polizeikommissar m; - -magistrate n. Polizeirichter m; - office n. Polizeiamt n; - officer n. Polizeibeamte(r) m, Polizist m; - -raid n. Polizeistreife f; - station n. Polizeiwache f; - trap n. Autofalle f.

Police'man [pA-lihss'mAn] n. Schutzmann m, Polizist m; -woman n. Polizistin f.

Policy [po'li-ssi] n. Politik f, politische Richtung, Klugheit f.

Policy [po'li-ssi] n. Versicherungsschein m, Police f; -holder n. Policeninhaber m (com.).

Polish [po'lisch] n. Politur f, Glanz m, Glätte f, Schliff m (style, etc.); vt. glätten, polieren; -ing n. Polieren n; a. Glanz ...

Polite [pA-lait'] a. -ly ad. höflich; -ness n. Höflichkeit f.

Politic [po'li-tik] a. politisch, diplomatisch, klug; -s pl. Politik f, Staatswissenschaft f.

Political [pA-li'tikl] a. politisch, Staats ...

Politician [po-li-ti'schAn] n. Politiker m, Staatsmann m.

Poll [poul] n. Kopf m, Wahlliste f, Abstimmung f; vt. stutzen, kappen, Namen eintragen; - -tax n. Kopfgeld n.

Pollen [po'lAn] n. Blütenstaub m.

Polling [pou'ling] n. Abstimmen n, Wählen n; - -booth n. Wahlzelle f; - day n. Wahltag m (en, verunreinigen).

Pollute [pA-ljuht'] vt. beflecken.

Pollution [pA-ljuh'schAn] n. Befleckung f, Verunreinigung f.

Polo [pou'lou] n. Polospiel n; - water - n. Wasserballspiel n.

Polychromy [po'li-krou'mi] n. Vielfarbendruck m.

Polygamy [po-li'gA-mi] n. Vielweiberei f.

Polyglot [po'li-glot] *a.* vielsprachig.

Polyphase [po'li-feis] *a.* mehrphasig, Mehrphasen . . . .

Polytechnic [po-li-tek'nik] *n.* Gewerbeschule *f.*, technische Hochschule *f.* [ade *f.*

Pomade [pA-mahd'] *n.* Pomade *f.*

Pomegranate [pom'gre-nit] *n.* Granatapfel *m.*

Pommel [pAml] *n.* Sattelknopf *m.*, Degenknauf *m.*

Pommel [pAml] *vt.* wiederholt schlagen, puffen.

Pomp [pomp] *n.* Prunk *m.*, Pracht *f.*; -ous *a.* prunkvoll, pompös, wichtigtuend.

Pond [pond] *n.* Teich *m.*

Ponder [pon'der] *vt.i.* erwägen, nachsinnen, nachdenken; -able *a.* wägbar; -ous *a.* schwer, gewichtig, plump.

Pongee [pon'dzhih] *n.* geringe chinesische Seide.

Pontiff [pon'tif] *n.* Papst *m.*, Hohepriester *m.*

Pontoon [pon-tuhn'] *n.* Brückenkahn *m.*, Ponton *m.*; -bridge *n.* Feld-, Ponton-brücke *f.*

Pony [pou'ni] *n.* kleines Pferd, Pony *m.*

Poodle [puhdl] *n.* Pudel *m.*

Pool [puhl] *n.* Pfuhl *m.*, Tümpel *m.*

Pool [puhl] *n.* Einsatz *m.*, Ring *m.*, Kartell *n.*, Interessengemeinschaft *f.*; *vt.* vereinigen, zusammenschliessen, teilen; bathing – Schwimmbecken *n.*, Badeanstalt *f.* [Kampanje *f.*

Poop [puhp] *n.* Achterhütte *f.*,

Poor [pu'er] *a.* arm, schlecht, erbärmlich, gering, elend; -house *n.* Armenhaus *n.*; -relief *n.* Armenfürsorge *f.*; -spirited *a.* verzagt, furchtsam.

Pop [pop] *vi.* paffen *n.* Paff *m.*; -corn *n.* Röstmais *m.*; -gun *n.* Knallbüchse *f.*

Pope [poup] *n.* Papst *m.*

Poplar [pop'ler] *n.* Pappel *f.*

Poplin [pop'lin] *n.* Poplin *m.*

Poppet [po'pit] *n.* Reitstock *m.* (*tec*), Schlittenständer *m.* (*nav.*); – -head *n.* Rollkloben *m.*; – valve, *n.* Schnarchventil *n.*, Teller-, Platten-ventil *n.* (*aut.*).

Poppy [po'pi] *n.* Mohn *m.*; – seed *n.* Mohnsamen *m.*

Populace [po'pju-liss] *n.* Volk *n.*, Pöbel *m.*

Popular [po'pju-ler] *a.* volkstümlich, beliebt, Volks-, Volks. . . .

Popularity [po-pju-læ'ri-ti] *n.* Beliebtheit *f.*, Volksgunst *f.*, Volkstümlichkeit *f.*

Popularize [po'pju-lA-rais] *vt.* volktümlich machen, unter das Volk bringen. [völkern.

Populate [po'pju-leit] *vt.* bevölkern, Bevölkerung *f.*, Einwohner *m.pl.* (*inhabitants*).

Population [po-pju-lei'schAn] *n.* Bevölkerung *f.*, Einwohner *m.pl.* (*inhabitants*).

Populous [po'pju-lAss] *a.* volkreich, dicht bevölkert.

Porcelain [pOr'sslin] *n.* Porzellan *n.*, Porzellanwaren *f.pl.*

Porch [pOrtsch] *n.* Vorhalle *f.*

Porcupine [pOr'kju-pain] *n.* Stachelschwein *n.*

Pore [pO'er] *n.* Pore *f.*

Pore [pO'er] *vi.* brüten, fleissig studieren.

Pork [pOrk] *n.* Schweinefleisch *n.*; -butcher *m.* Schweineschlächter *m.*; -butcher's shop *n.* Schweinemetzgerei *f.*; -pie *n.* Schweinefleischpastete *f.*

Porous [pO'rAss] *a.* durchlässig, porös. [schwein *n.*

Porpoise [pOr'pAss] *n.* Meerschwein *n.*

Porridge [po'ridzh] *n.* Haferschleim *m.*, Haferbrei *m.*

Port [pOrt] *n.* Hafen *m.*, Hafenstadt *f.* (*town*).

Port [pOrt] *n.* Portwein *m.*

Port [pOrt] *n.* Backbord *n.* (*nav.*); – engine *n.* Backbord-motor *m.*

Portable [pOr'tAbl] *a.* tragbar, transportfähig, beweglich; – bridge *n.* Schnell-, Lauf-steg *m.*, Schnellbrücke *f.* (*mil.*).

- gramophone n. Koffer-, Reisegrammophon n; - railway n. Feldbahn f; - transmitter n. Kleinfunkstelle f (rad.); - wireless set n. Kofferempfänger m, Tornisterfunk-, Anhängegerät n (mil.).
Portage [pOr'tidʒh] n. Tragstelle f; vt. umsetzen.
Portal [pOr'tAl] n. Portal n.
Portend [pOr-tend'] vt. vorbedeuten, deuten auf.
Portent [pOr'tent] n. Vorbedeutung f, Wunder n.
Porter [pOr'ter] n. Gepäckträger m, Träger m; out - n. Dienstmann m.
Porter [pOr'ter] n. Pförtner m; hotel - Portier m.
Porterage [pOr'tA-ridʒh] n. Transport m, Trägerlohn m.
Portfolio [pOrt-fou'ljou] n. Mappe f, Portefeuille n, Aktentasche f.
Port-hole [pOrt'houl] n. Stückpforte f, Pfortluke f.
Portion [pOr'schAn] n. Teil m, Stück n, Anteil m, Portion f (helping); vt. verteilen.
Portliness [pOrt'li-ness] n. Wohlbeleibtheit f.
Portly [pOrt'li] a. wohlbeleibt.
Portmanteau [pOrt-mæn'tou] n. Handkoffer m, Mantelsack m.
Portrait [pOr'treit] n. Bildnis n, Porträt n; - painter n. Porträtmaler m.
Portray [pOr-trei'] vt. abbilden, schildern; -al n. Schilderung f, Darstellung f.
Pose [pous] n. Haltung f, Pose f; vt. aufgeben, sich ausgeben für; i. aufwerfen.
Position [po-si'schAn] n. Stellung f, Lage f; - -finder n. Ortungsgerät n (mil.); - -finding n. Ortung f (mil.).
Positive [po'si-tiw] a. -ly ad. bestimmt, sicher, positiv; n. Positiv m (adjective). Positiv n (photo).

Possess [pA-sess'] vt. besitzen; -ive a. besitzanzeigend; -or n. Besitzer m, Eigentümer m.
Possession [pA-se'schAn] n. Besitz m, Besitzung f.
Possibility [po-ssi-bi'li-ti] n. Möglichkeit f.
Possible [po'ssibl] a. möglich; -y ad. möglicherweise; not - unmöglich.
Post [poust] n. Pfahl m, Pfosten m.
Post [poust] n. Posten m, Stellung f (situation).
Post [poust] n. Post f, Postamt n; vt. zur Post geben, aufgeben, einschreiben, eintragen (com.). versetzen (mil, nav, av.); - -bag n. Postbeutel m; - -box n. Postfach n; - -free, - -paid a. portofrei, franko.
Postage [pou'stidʒh] n. Briefporto n; - due Strafporto n; - free, - paid portofrei; - stamp n. Briefmarke f.
Postal [poustl] a. Post ...; - authorities n.pl. Postverwaltung f; - order n. Postanweisung f; - packet n. Postpaket n; - Union n. Weltpostverein m.
Postcard [poust'kahrd] n. Postkarte f; picture - n. Ansichtskarte f.
Post-date [poust-deit'] vt. nachdatieren.
Poster [pou'ster] n. Anschlagzettel m, Plakat n.
Posterior [pou-stih'rjer] a. nachherig, später; n. Hinterteil m.
Posterity [po-ste'ri-ti] n. Nachkommenschaft f.
Post-haste [poust'heist] ad. eiligst.
Posthumous [po'stjA-mАss] a. nachgeboren, nachgelassen.
Posting [pou'sting] n. Briefaufgabe f, Übertragung f (com.), Versetzung f (mil, etc.).
Postman [poust'mАn] n. Briefträger m Postbote m.

Postmark [poust'mahrk] n. Poststempel m; vt. abstempeln.

Postmaster [poust'mah-ster] n. Postmeister m; - General n. Generalpostmeister m, Postminister m.

Postmistress [poust'mistriss] n. Postmeisterin f.

Post-mortem [poust-mOr'tAm] n. Leichenschau f.

Post-office [poust'o-fiss] n. Postamt n; - clerk n. Postbeamte(r) m; - order n. Postanweisung f; - savings bank n. Postsparkasse f.

Postpone [poust-poun'] vt. aufschieben; -ment n. Aufschub m. [Nachschrift f.

Postscript [poust'skript] n.

Postulate [po'stju-leit] vt. fordern, voraussetzen; n. Postulat n. [Positur f.

Posture [po'stjer] n. Lage f,

Post-war [poust-uOr'] a. Nachkriegs -. [m.

Posy [pou'si] n. Blumenstrauss

Pot [pot] n. Topf m, Krug m; vt. in einen Topf setzen, einmachen; - boy n. Bierhauskellner m; -hole n. Schlagloch n (aut.); -house n. Bierhaus n; -shot n. Nahschuss m.

Potash [po'tæsch] n. Kali n.

Potassium [pA-tæ'ssjAm] n. Kalium n. [Zechen f.

Potation [pA-tei'schAn] n.

Potato [pA-tei'tou] n. Kartoffel f. [ke f, Kraft f.

Potency [pou'tAn-ssi] n. Stär-

Potent [pou'tAnt] a. wirksam, kräftig; -ate n. Machthaber m.

Potential [pA-ten'schAl] a. potentiell, möglich; n. Potential n. [trank m.

Potion [pou'schAn] n. Arznei

Potter [po'ter] n. Töpfer m.

Potter [po'ter] vt. herumbummeln.

Pottery [po'tA-ri] n. Töpferware f, Töpferei f.

Pouch [pautsch] n. Beutel m, Tasche f; tobacco - Tabaksbeutel m.

Poulterer [poul'tA-rer] n. Geflügelhändler m.

Poultice [poul'tiss] n. Breiumschlag m.

Poultry [poul'tri] n. Federvieh n, Geflügel n; - dealer n. Geflügelhändler m; - farming n. Geflügelzucht f.

Pounce [pauns] vi. sich stürzen, herabschiessen.

Pounce [pauns] n. Bimsteinpulver n, Pausche f.

Pound [paund] n. Pfund n; - note n. Pfundnote f.

Pound [paund] vt. zerstossen.

Pour [pOr] vt. giessen, schütten.

Pout [paut] vi. schmollen.

Poverty [po'wer-ti] n. Armut f, Dürftigkeit f; -stricken a. verarmt.

Powder [pau'der] n. Puder m, Pulver n, Staub m; vt. pudern, pulverisieren, bestreuen; - magazine n. Pulvermagazin n, Munitionskammer f; -puff n. Puderquaste f; -ed sugar n. Puderzucker m.

Powdery [pau'dA-ri] a. staubig, pulverisiert.

Power [pau'er] n. Kraft f, Gewalt f, Macht f; - circuit n. Starkstromleitung f; - house n. Maschinenhaus n, Kraftwerk n; - politics n. pl. Machtpolitik f, Realpolitik f; - station n. Kraftwerk n. (el.); - unit n. Kraftmaschine f, Triebwerk n, Aggregat n (tec.).

Powerful [pau'er-ful] a. kräftig, gewaltig, mächtig.

Powerless [pau'er-less] a. kraftlos.

Practicability [præk-ti-kA-bil'i-ti] n. Ausführbarkeit f, Tunlichkeit f.

Practicable [præk'ti-kAbl] a. ausführbar, tunlich, möglich, fahrbar (road, etc.).

Practical [præk'tikl] *a.* -ly *ad.* praktisch, geschickt, erfahren.

Practice [præk'tiss] *n.* Praxis *f*, Gebrauch *m*, Gewohnheit *f*, Ausübung *f*; sharp – Gaunerkniffe *m. pl.*

Practise [præk'tiss] *vt. i.* üben, ausüben, einüben, ausführen; -d *a.* erfahren, geschickt, geübt.

Practitioner [præk-ti'schAner] *n.* Praktiker *m*, Arzt *m*, Fachmann *m.* [Grasebener

Prairie [preh'ri] *n.* Prärie *f.*

Praise [preis] *n.* Lob *m*; *vt.* loben; -worthy *a.* lobenswert, anerkennenswert. [*m.*

Pram [præm] *n.* Kinderwagen

Prance [prahnss] *vi.* sich bäumen, stolzieren.

Prank [prængk] *n.* Streich *m.*

Prate [preit] *vi.* plappern, schwatzen. [*n.*

Prattle [prætl] *n.* Geschwätz

Prawn [prOn] *n.* französische Garnele.

Pray [prei] *vi.* beten.

Prayer [preh'er] *n.* Gebet *n.*

Preach [prihtsch] *vi. t.* predigen; -er *n.* Prediger *m.*

Preamble [prih-æmbl'] *n.* Einleitung *f.*

Pre-arrange [prih-Areindzh'] *vt.* im voraus bestimmen. [unsicher, gefährlich.

Precarious [pri-keh'riAss] *a.*

Precaution [pri-kO'schAn] *n.* Vorsicht *f*, Vorsichtsmassregel *f.* [gehen, vorhergehen.

Precede [pri-sihd'] *vt.* vor-

Precedence [pri-ssih'dAnss] *n.* Vorrang *m*, Vortritt *m.*

Precedent [pre'ssi-dAnt] *n.* Präzedenzfall *m*, Richtschnur *f*, Beispiel *n.*

Precept [prih'ssept] *n.* Vorschrift *f*, Gebot *n.*

Precincts [prih'ssinktss] *pl.* Umfriedung *f*, Kirchhof *m*, Bezirk *m.*

Precious [pre'schAss] *a.* kostbar.

Precipice [pre'ssi-piss] *n.* Abgrund *m.*

Precipitant [pri-ssi'pi-tAnt] *n.* Fällungsmittel *n.*

Precipitate [pri-ssi'pi-teit] *vt.* herabstürzen, überstürzen, fällen (*chemistry*); – [pri-ssi'pi-tit] *n.* Niederschlag *m.*

Precipitation [pri-ssi'pi-tei'schAn] *n.* Übereilung *f*, Herabstürzen *n*, Fällen *n.*

Precipitous [pri-ssi'pi-tAss] *a.* jäh, rasch.

Precise [pri-ssaiss'] *a.* -ly *ad.* genau, förmlich, peinlich.

Precision [pri-ssi'zhAn] *n.* Genauigkeit *f*, Bestimmtheit *f*, Präzision *f* (*tec.*); – balance *n*, Präzisionswaage *f*; – bombing *n.* Bombenpunktfeuer *n*; – target *n.* Punktziel *n* (*av.*).

Preclude [pri-kluhd'] *vt.* ausschliessen.

Precocious [pri-koh'schAss] *a.* frühreif.

Precocity [pri-ko'ssi-ti] *n.* Frühreife *f.*

Preconceive [prih-kAnssihw'] *vt.* vorher ausdenken; -d *a.* vorgefasst.

Preconcert [prih-kAn-ssArt'] *vt.* vorher vereinbaren.

Pre-cool [prih-kuhl'] *vt.* vorkühlen; -er *n.* Vorkühler *m.*

Predatory [pre'dA-tA-ri] *a.* räuberisch.

Predecease [prih-di-ssihss'] *vt.* vorher sterben als.

Predecessor [prih-di-sse'sser] *n.* Vorgänger *m.*

Predestine [prih-de'stin] *vt.* vorherbestimmen.

Predicament [pri-di'kAmAnt] *n.* schlimme Lage, Verlegenheit *f.*

Predicate [pre'di-kit] *n.* Prädikat *n*, Aussage *f.*

Predict [pri-dikt'] *vt.* vorhersagen; -ion *n.* Vorhersagung *f.*

Predilection [prih-di-lek'schAn] *n.* Vorliebe *f.*

Predispose [prih-diss-pous']

vt. im voraus geneigt machen, einnehmen.

Predisposition [prih-diss-pA-si'schAn] *n.* Geneigtheit *f*, Empfänglichkeit *f*.

Predominan'ce [pri-do'minAnss] *n.* Vorherrschen *n*; -t *a.* vorherrschend.

Predominate [pri-do'mineit] *vi.* vorherrschen.

Pre-eminen'ce [prih-e'mi-nAnss] *n.* Überlegenheit *f*, Vorrang *m*; -t *a.* hervorragend.

Pre-emption [prih-emp'schAn] *n.* Vorkauf *m.*

Pre-exist [prih-ig-sist'] *vi.* früher existieren.

Prefabricated [prih-fæb'ri-keit] *vt.* vorfertigen; -d house *n.* Fertighaus *n*; -d parts *n.pl.* Bauteile *m.pl.*

Prefabrication [prih-fæb-ri-kei'schAn] *n.* Vorfertigung *f.*

Preface [pre'fAss] *n.* Vorrede *f*, Einleitung *f*; *vt.* einleiten.

Prefatory [pre'fA-tA-ri] *a.* einleitend.

Prefer [pri-fA'r] *vt.* vorziehen.

Preferable [pre'fA-rAbl] *a.* vorzuziehen(d), -ly *ad.* vorzugsweise, am liebsten.

Preference [pref'rAnss] *n.* Vorzug *m*, Vorliebe *f*; – shares *n.pl.* Prioritätsaktien *f.pl.*

Preferential [pre'fA-ren'schAl] *a.* Vorzugs-.

Prefix [prih'fix] *n.* Vorsilbe *f*, Präfix *n*; – [pri-fix'] *vt.* vorsetzen.

Pregnan'cy [preg'nAn-ssi] *n.* Schwangerschaft *f*; -t *a.* schwanger, fruchtbar, gedankentief.

Prehistoric [prih-hi-sto'rik] *a.* vorgeschichtlich.

Pre-ignition [prih-ig-ni'schAn] *n.* Frühzündung *f (aut.)*.

Prejudice [pre'dzhu-diss] *n.* Vorurteil *n*, Nachteil *m*, Beeinträchtigung *f*; *vt.* beinträchtigen, schädigen, durch Vorur-

teile beeinflussen; -d *a.* voreingenommen, parteiisch.

Prejudicial [pre-dzhu-di'schAl] *a.* nachteilig, schädlich.

Prelate [pre'lit] *n.* Prälat *m.*

Preliminary [pri-li'mi-nA-ri] *a.* vorläufig, Vor . . . ; -ies *n.pl.* Vorbereitungen *f.pl*, vorläufige Schritte *m.pl*; – examination *n.* Aufnahmeprüfung *f*; – selection *n.* Vorauswahl *f*; – warning *n.* Vorwarnung *f.*

Prelude [pre'ljuhd] *n.* Vorspiel *n*, Einleitung *f.*

Premature [prih'mA-tjuh-er] *a.* -ly *ad.* vorzeitig.

Premeditation [prih-me-di-tei'schAn] *n.* Vorbedacht *m.*

Premier [pre'mjer] *n.* Ministerpräsident *m*; *a.* erst.

Premises [pre'mi-ssis] *n.pl.* Lokal *m*, Gebäude *n.*

Premium [pri'mjAm] *n.* Prämie *f*, Lehrgeld *m*, Aufgeld *n.* [schAn] *n.* Warnung *f.*

Premonition [prih-mo-ni'-**

Preoccupation [prih-o-kju-pei'schAn] *n.* Zerstreutheit *f.*

Preoccupy [prih-o'kju-pai] *vt.* ausschliesslich beschäftigen, einnehmen.

Prepaid [prih-peid'] *a.* vorausbezahlt, frankiert, franko.

Preparation [pre-pA-rei'schAn] *n.* Vorbereitung *f*, Zubereitung *f*, Verfertigung *f*, Darstellung *f (tec.)*, Präparat *n.*

Preparatory [pri-pæ'rA-tA-ri] *a.* vorbereitend.

Prepare [pri-pær'] *vt.* vorbereiten, zubereiten *(food)*, darstellen *(chemical)*, zu bereiten; *i. r.* sich vorbereiten; – for action bereitstellen *(nav, etc.)*.

Prepay [prih-pei'] *vt.* vorausbezahlen, frankieren *(letter)*; -ment *n.* Vorausbezahlung *f.*

Preponderan'ce [pri-pon'dA-rAnss] *n.* Übergewicht *n*; -t *a.* überwiegend.

Preponderate [pri-pon'dA-reit] *vi.* überwiegen.

Preposition [pre-po-si'schAn] n. Verhältniswort n, Präposition f.

Prepossess [prih-po-sess'] vt. voreinnehmen; **-ing** a. anziehend.

Prepossession [prih-po-se'schAn] n. Voreingenommenheit f.

Preposterous [pri-po'stArAss] a. unerhört, widersinnig.

Prerogative [pri-ro'gA-tiw] n. Vorrecht n.

Prescribe [pri-skraib'] vt. verordnen, vorschreiben.

Prescription [pri-skrip'schAn] n. Rezept n (medical), Vorschrift f (order), Verjährung f (law).

Pre-selection [prih-si-lek'schAn] n. Vorwahl f; **-tor** n. Vorwähler m (ph.).

Presence [pre'sAnss] n. Gegenwart f, Anwesenheit f.

Present [pre'sAnt] a. gegenwärtig, anwesend; n. Gegenwart f; **at** — jetzt; **- value** Zeitwert m. [enk n.]

Present [pre'sAnt] n. Geschenk n.

Present [pri-sent'] vt. schenken, einreichen, darstellen.

Presentation [pre-sAn-tei'schAn] n. Überreichung f, Vorstellung f.

Presentable [pri-sen'tAbl] a. präsentabel, annehmbar.

Presentiment [pri-sen'ti-mAnt] n. Ahnung f.

Presently [pre'sAnt-li] ad. bald.

Preservation [pre-ser-wei'schAn] n. Erhaltung f, Bewahrung f, Konservierung f (fruit).

Preservative [pri-sAr'wA-tiw] n. Konservierungsmittel n, Schutzmittel n.

Preserve [pri-sArw'] vt. bewahren, erhalten, einmachen; **-ed meat** n. Fleischkonserven f.pl., Dauerfleisch n; **-ing** a. erhaltend, konservierend; **- sugar** n. Einmachzucker m.

Preside [pri-said'] vi. den Vorsitz führen.

President [pre'si-dAnt] n. Präsident m, der Vorsitzende, Direktor m (com.).

Press [press] n. Presse f, Drücken n, Drang m (pressure), Schrank m (cupboard), Kelter m (cider), Zeitungswesen n; vt. drücken, pressen, nötigen; **-button** n. Druckknopf m; **-cutting** n. Zeitungsausschnitt m; **- photographer** m. Bildberichterstatter m; **- reader** n. Korrektor m. [gend.]

Pressing [pre'ssing] a. dringend.

Pressman [press'mAn] n. Journalist m.

Press-mark [press'mahrk] n. Bibliothekzeichen n.

Pressure [pre'scher] n. Druck m, Spannung f (tec.). [sehen n.]

Prestige [press-tihzh'] n. Ansehen.

Presumable [pri-sjuh'mAbl] a, **-ly** ad. vermutlich.

Presume [pri-sjuhm'] vt. vermuten; i. wagen, sich gestatten.

Presumption [pri-sAmp'schAn] n. Voraussetzung f, Anmassung f; **-tuous** a. anmassend. [vt. voraussetzen.]

Presuppose [prih-ssA-pous']

Presupposition [prih-ssA-pA-si'schAn] n. Voraussetzung f.

Pretence [pri-tenss'] n. Vorschützen n, Vorwand m, Anspruch m.

Pretend [pri-tend'] vt. vorgeben; i. sich stellen, tun als ob; **-er** n. Heuchler m, Prätendant m.

Pretension [pri-ten'schAn] n. Anspruch m, Anmassung f. [a. anspruchsvoll.]

Pretentious [pri-ten'schAss]

Preterite [pre'tA-rit] n. Vergangenheitsform f. [wand m.]

Pretext [prih'text] n. Vorwand m.

Prettily [pri'ti-li] ad. hübsch, artig.

Prettiness [pri'ti-ness] *n.* Niedlichkeit *f.*

Pretty [pri'ti] *a.* niedlich, hübsch, artig; *ad.* ziemlich.

Prevailing [pri-wei'ling] *a.* vorherrschend.

Prevalen'ce [pre'wA-lAnss] *n.* Verbreitung *f*, Häufigkeit *f*; **-t** *a.* weit verbreitet.

Prevent [pri-went'] *vt.* hindern, vorbeugen, verhüten, verhindern; **-able** *a.* verhütbar.

Preventative [pri-wen'tA-tiw] *n.* Schutz-, Verhütungs-mittel *n.*

Prevention [pri-wen'schAn] *n.* Verhinderung *f*, Vorbeugung *f.*

Preventive [pri-wen'tiw] *a.* vorbeugend; **- custody** *n.* Schutzhaft *f*; **- war** *n.* Präventivkrieg *m.*

Previous [prih'wjAss] *a.* vorhergehend, vorig, früher.

Prevision [pri-wi'zhAn] *n.* Voraussehen *n.*

Pre-war [prih-uOr'] *a.* Vorkriegs ...; **- price** *n.* Friedenspreis *m*; **- times** *n.pl.* Vorkriegszeit *f.*

Prey [prei] *n.* Raub *m*, Beute *f*; *vi.* Beute machen.

Price [praiss] *n.* Preis *m*; *vt.* abschätzen; **- control** *n.* Zwangswirtschaft *f*, Preis-beaufsichtigung *f*, -überwachung *f*; **-controlled** *a.* preisgebunden; **- cutting** *n.* Unterbieten *n*, Preisschneiderei *f*; **- list** *n.* Preisliste *f.*

Prick [prik] *n.* Stich *m*; *vt.* stechen, stacheln; **-le** *n.* Stachel *f*; **-ly** *a.* stachelig.

Pride [praid] *n.* Stolz *m*; *vr.* stolz sein auf.

Priest [prihst] *n.* Priester *m*, Pfarrer *m.*

Prim [prim] *a.* zimperlich.

Primage [prai'midzh] *n.* Primgeld *n.*

Primary [prai'mA-ri] *a.* Primär ... hauptsächlich; **- education** *n.* Volksschulunterricht

m; **- school** *n.* Volksschule *f*, Grundschule *f.*

Prime [praim] *a.* erst, hauptsächlich; *n.* Höhe *f*, Blüte *f*; *vt.* versehen, zünden (*mil.*); **- cost** *n.* Einkaufspreis *m*; **- Minister** *n.* Ministerpräsident *m.*

Primer [prai'mer] *n.* Sprengkapsel *f*, Zünddraht *m* (*mil.*).

Primer [pri'mer] *n.* Elementarbuch *n.* [*ung f.*

Priming [prai'ming] *n.* Zünd-

Primitive [pri'mi-tiw] *a.* ursprünglich, primitiv.

Primrose [prim'rous] *n.* Schlüsselblume *f.* [el *f.*

Primula [pri'mju-lA] *n.* Prim-

Prince [prinss] *n.* Fürst *m*, Prinz *m*; **-ly** *a.* fürstlich; **-ss** *n.* Prinzessin *f*, Fürstin *f.*

Principal [prin'ssipl] *a.* -ly *ad.* hauptsächlich, Haupt ...; *n.* Prinzipal *m*, Chef *m*, Direktor *m*, Rektor *m*, Kapital *n* (*com.*).

Principality [prin-ssi-pæ'li-ti] *n.* Fürstentum *n.*

Principle [prin'ssipl] *n.* Grundsatz *m*, Prinzip *n.*

Print [print] *n.* Druck *m*, Abdruck *m*, Stich *m* (*art*), Abzug *m* (*photo*); *vt.* drucken, abziehen (*photo*); **-ed matter** *n.* Drucksache *f.*

Printer [prin'ter] *n.* Drucker *m*; **-'s ink** *n.* Druckerschwärze *f.*

Printing [prin'ting] *n.* Druck *m*, Drucken *n*; **- frame** *n.* Kopierrahmen *m*; **-house** *n.* Buchdruckerei *f*; **-machine**, **-press** *n.* Buchdruckmaschine *f*, Schnellpresse *f*; **-works** *n.pl.* Druckerei *f.*

Prior [prai'er] *a.ad.* früher.

Priory [prai'A-ri] *n.* Kloster *n.*

Priority [prai-o'ri-ti] *n.* Vorzugsrecht *n*, Priorität *f.*

Prism [prism] *n.* Prisma *n.*

Prison [pri'sAn] *n.* Gefängnis *n*; **- cell** *n.* Gefangenenzelle *f*; **- clothes** *n.pl.* Sträflingskleidung *f*; – van *n*. Gefangenenwagen *m*.

Prisoner [pri'sA-ner] *n*. der Gefangene; – of war *n*. Kriegsgefangene(r); – of war camp *n*. Offizierslager *m*, Stammlager *n* (*other ranks*).

Privacy [prai'wA-ssi] *n*. Zurückgezogenheit *f*, Heimlichkeit *f*.

Private [prai'wit] *a*. geheim, heimlich, privat, abgeschieden, vertraulich (*letters*); *n*. Soldat *m*, der Gemeine, Schütze *m*, Jäger *m*, Reiter *m*.

Privation [prai-wei'schAn] *n*. Not *f*, Mangel *m*.

Privet [pri'wit] *n*. Liguster *m*.

Privilege [pri'wi-lidzh] *n*. Vorrecht *n*, Ehre *f*, Gunst *f*; *vt*. bevorrechten, privilegieren.

Privy [pri'wi] *a*. mitwissend.

Prize [prais] *n*. Preis *m*, Belohnung *f*, Prise *f* (*nav.*); *vt*. hochschätzen; – court *n*. Prisengericht *n* (*nav.*).

Prize [prais] *vt*. aufbrechen.

Probability [pro-bA-bi'li-ti] *n*. Wahrscheinlichkeit *f*.

Probable [pro'bAbl] *a*, probably *ad*. wahrscheinlich.

Probate [prou'bit] *n*. Bestätigung *f*, beglaubigte Abschrift.

Probation [pro-bei'schAn] *n*. Probe *f*, Probezeit *f*, bedingte Freisprechung (*law*); –ary *a*. Probe . . .; –er *n*. Prüfling *m*, Anfänger *m*, Probeanwärter *m*, Praktikant *m*.

Probe [proub] *n*. Sonde *f*; *vt*. sondieren.   [schaffenheit *f*.

Probity [prou'bi-ti] *n*. Recht

Problem [pro'blem] *n*. Aufgabe *f*, Problem *n*.

Problematic(al) [pro-blAmæ'tikl] *a*. problematisch, fraglich.

Procedure [pro-ssih'djer] *n*. Verfahren *n*, Handlungsweise *f*.

Proceed [pro-ssihd'] *vi*. vorgehen, fortfahren, hervorge

hen, weitergehen; –ing *n*. Verfahren *n*.

Proceeds [prou'ssihds] *n.pl*. Erlös *m*, Ertrag *m*, Gewinn *m*.

Process [prou'ssess] *n*. Verfahren *n*, Vorgang *m*, Prozess *m*.   [Aufzug *m*, Prozession *f*.

Procession [pro-sse'schAn] *n*.

Proclaim [pro-kleim'] *vt*. verkünden.

Proclamation [pro-klA-mei'schAn] *n*. Verkündigung *f*, Bekanntmachung *f*.

Procrastination [pro-kræ-stinei'schAn] *n*. Verzögerung *f*.

Procurable [pro-kjuh'rAbl] *a*. erhältlich, erlangbar.

Procure [pro-kjuh'er] *vt*. anschaffen, erwerben, erlangen.

Prod [prod] *n*. Stoss *m*; *vt*. stechen.

Prodigal [pro'digl] *n*. Verschwender; *a*. verschwenderisch.   [Verschwendung *f*.

Prodigality [pro-di-gæ'li-ti] *n*.

Prodigious [prA-di'dzhAss] *a*. ungeheuer, erstaunlich.

Prodigy [pro'di-dzhi] *n*. Wunder *n*, Ungeheuer *n*.

Produce [pro'djuhss] *n*. Produkt *n*; landwirtschaftliche Erzeugnisse *n.pl*; – exchange *n*. Getreidebörse *f*.

Produce [prA-djuhss'] *vt*. hervorbringen, erzeugen, produzieren, vorzeigen.

Producer [prA-djuh'sser] *n*. Erzeuger *m*, Verfertiger *m*, Produzent *m*, Spielleiter *m* (*plays*), Regisseur *m* (*rad.*); – gas *n*. Generatorgas *n*.

Product [pro'dAkt] *n*. Erzeugnis *n*, Produkt *n*.

Production [prA-dAk'schAn] *n*. Produktion *f*, Erzeugung *f*, Herstellung *f*, Produkt *n*, Fabrikat *n*, Vorlegung *f*.

Productive [prA-dAk'tiw] *a*. fruchtbar, produktiv, ergiebig.

Productivity [pro-dAk-ti'witi] *n*. Fruchtbarkeit *f*, Produktivität *f*.

Profane [pro-fein'] *a.* unheilig, weltlich, profan.

Profanity [pro-fæ'ni-ti] *n.* Flüche *m.pl*, Ruchlosigkeit *f.*

Profess [pro-fes'] *vt.* bekennen, vorgeben; **-ed** *a.* angeblich, offen.

Profession [pro-fe'schAn] *n.* Beruf *m*, Stand *m*, Bekenntnis *n*; **-al** *a.* berufsmässig, Fach . . . , *n.* Fachmann *m*, Künstler *m*, Berufsspieler *m*, Professional *m* (*games*). [fessor *m*.

Professor [pro-fe'sser] *n.* Pro-

Proffer [pro'fer] *vt.* anbieten; *n.* Anerbieten *n*, Antrag *m.*

Proficiency [pro-fi'schAn-ssi] *n.* Tüchtigkeit *f*, Fertigkeit *f*; **-** badge *n.* Leistungsabzeichen *n.* [tüchtig, geübt, bewandert.

Proficient [pro-fi'schAnt] *a.*

Profile [prou'fühl] *n.* Profil *n.*

Profit [pro'fit] *n.* Gewinn *m*; *vi.t.* gewinnen, nutzen, Vorteil ziehen; **-** sharing *n.* Gewinnbeteiligung *f.*

Profitable [pro'fi-tAbl] *a.* einträglich, nützlich.

Profiteer [pro-fi-tih'er] *n.* Kriegsgewinner *m*, Schieber *m*; *vi.* schieben; **-ing** *n.* Schiebung *f*, Kriegswucher *m.*

Profound [prA-faund'] *a.*, **-ly** *ad.* tief, bedeutend.

Profuse [prA-fjuhss'] *a.*, **-ly** *ad.* überreich, verschwenderisch.

Profusion [prA-fjuh'zhAn] *n.* Überfülle *f*, Reichtum *m.*

Prognosticate [prog-no'sti-keit] *vt.* vorhersagen.

Prognostication [prog-no-sti-kei'schAn] *n.* Vorhersagung *f.*

Programme [prou'græm] *n.* Programm *n*; **-** parade *n.* Vorschau *f*, über die heutigen Sendungen (*rad.*).

Progress [prou'gress] *n.* Fortschritt *m*, Fortgang *m*, Gang *m*; **-** [pro-gress'] *vi.* fortschreiten, vorwärtskommen.

Progression [pro-gre'schAn] *n.* Fortschritt *m*, Fortschreiten *n*, Fortgang *m*, Lauf *m*, Reihe *f.*

Progressive [pro-gre'ssiw] *a.* fortschreitend, fortschrittlich; **-ly** *ad.* stufenweise.

Prohibit [prou-hi'bit] *vt.* verbieten, untersagen; **-ed area** *n.* Luftsperrgebiet (*av.*).

Prohibition [prou-hi-bi'schAn] *n.* Verbot *n*, Alkoholverbot *n*; **-ist** *n.* Alkoholgegner *m*, Abstinent *m.*

Prohibitive [prou-hi'bi-tiw] *a.* unerschwinglich, untersagend, Prohibitiv . . . .

Project [pro'dzhekt] *n.* Entwurf *m*, Projekt *n.*

Project [prA-dzhekt'] *vi.* vorspringen, hervorragen; *t.* entwerfen.

Projectile [prA-dzhek'tail] *n.* Geschoss *n.*

Projection [prA-dzhek'schAn] *n.* Vorsprung *m*, Werfen *n*, Projektion *f.*

Projector [prA-dzhek'ter] *n.* Erfinder *m*, Scheinwerfer *m*, Filmvorführgerät *n* (*film*).

Proletarian [prou-li-teh'rjAn] *a.* besitzlos.

Proletariat [prou-li-teh'rjAn] *n.* Proletariat *n*; dictatorship of the **-** Diktatur *f*, des Proletariats. [bar.

Prolific [prA-li'fik] *a.* fruchtbar, reich.

Prolix [prou'lix] *a.* weitschweifig. [*m*, Vorspiel *n.*

Prologue [prou'log] *n.* Prolog

Prolong [prA-long'] *vt.* verlängern.

Prolongation [prou-long-gei'schAn] *n.* Verlängerung *f*, Prolongation *f* (*com.*).

Promenade [pro-mi-nahd'] *n.* Promenade *f*, Spazierweg *m*; **-** deck *n.* Promenadendeck *n.*

Prominence [pro'mi-nAnss] *n.* Vorsprung *m*, Hervorragen *n*; **-t** *a.* hervorragend, vornehm.

Promiscuity [pro-mi-skjuh'i-ti] *n.* Durcheinander *n*, Gemischtheit *f*.

Promiscuous [prou-mi'skju-Ass] *a*, **-ly** *ad.* ununterschieden, durcheinander.

Promis'e [pro'miss] *n.* Versprechen *n*; *vt.* versprechen; **-ing** *a.* vielversprechend; **-sory note** *n.* Schuldschein *m*, Eigenwechsel *m* (*com.*).

Promontory [pro'mAn-tA-ri] *n.* Vorgebirge *n*.

Promote [prA-mout'] *vt.* fördern, befördern, gründen (*com.*); **-r** *n.* Gründer *m*, Förderer *m*.

Promotion [prA-mou'schAn] *n.* Beförderung *f*, Förderung *f*, Gründung *f*.

Prompt [prompt] *a.* unverzüglich, pünktlich; *vt.* soufflieren; **-er** *n.* Souffleur *m*; **-ing** *n.* Eingebung *f*, Soufflieren *n*; **-itude**, **-ness** *n.* Pünktlichkeit *f*, Schnelligkeit *f*.

Promulgate [pro'mAl-geit] *vt.* öffentlich bekanntmachen.

Promulgation [pro-mAl-gei'schAn] *n.* Verkündung *f*.

Prone [proun] *a.* hingestreckt, geneigt; **-ness** *n.* Neigung *f*.

Prong [prong] *n.* Zinke *f*, Spitze *f*, Zacken *m* (*fork*).

Pronoun [prou'naun] *n.* Fürwort *n*, Pronomen *n*.

Pronounce [prA-nauns'] *vt.* aussprechen.

Pronunciation [prA-nAn-ssi-ei'schAn] *n.* Aussprache *f*.

Proof [pruhf] *n.* Beweis *m*, Probe *f*, Abzug *m*, Korrektur *f* (*printing*); *a.* probehaltig, fest, stark; *vt.* wasserdicht machen.

Prop [prop] *n.* Stütze *f*, Strebe *f*, Spreize *f*.

Propaganda [pro-pA-gæn'dAj] *n.* Propaganda *f*; **-ist** *n.* Werber *m*, Propagandist *m*; **-ize** *vt.* Propaganda machen für.

Propagate [pro'pA-geit] *vt.* verbreiten, fortpflanzen.

Propagation [pro-pA-gei'schAn] *n.* Fortpflanzung *f*.

Propel [prA-pel'] *vt.* treiben, vorwärtstreiben; **-lent** *n.* Treibmittel *n*; **-charge** *n.* Treibladung *f*.

Propeller [prA-pe'ler] *n.* Propeller *m*, Schiffsschraube *f* (*nav.*), Luftschraube *f* (*av.*); **-blade** *n.* Schraubenblatt *m*; **-shaft** *n.* Antriebswelle *f* (*aut.*), Propeller-, Schrauben-welle *f* (*motor-boat*).

Propelling [prA-pe'ling] *a.* Trieb . . .; **-pencil** *n.* Drehbleistift *m*.

Propensity [prA-pen'ssi-ti] *n.* Hang *m*, Neigung *f*.

Proper [pro'per] *a.*, **-ly** *ad.* eigen, eigentlich, eigentümlich, richtig, ordentlich, anständig.

Property [pro'per-ti] *n.* Eigentum *n*, Besitz *m*, Gut *n*, Eigenschaft *f* (*tec.*); **-tax** *n.* Vermögens-steuer *f*.

Prophecy [pro'fi-ssi] *n.* Prophezeiung *f*, Vorhersagung *f*.

Prophesy [pro'fi-ssai] *vt.* prophezeien, wahrsagen, vorhersagen.

Prophet [pro'fit] *n.* Prophet *m*.

Propinquity [pro-ping'kui-ti] *n.* Nähe *f*.

Propitiate [prA-pi'schjeit] *vt.* versöhnen, günstig stimmen.

Propitiation [prA-pi-schjei'schAn] *n.* Versöhnung *f*.

Propitious [prA-pi'schjAss] *a.* günstig, gnädig.

Proportion [prA-pOr'schAn] *n.* Verhältnis *n*, Mass *n*, Teil *m*; *vt.* verhältnismässig verteilen; **-al** *a.* verhältnismässig, entsprechend; **- representation** *n.* Verhältniswahl *f*, Proporz *m*; **-ate** *a.* **-ly** *ad.* im Verhältnis (stehend).

Proposal [prA-pou'sAl] *n.* Vorschlag *m*, Heiratsantrag *m* (*marriage*).

Propose [prA-pous'] *vt.* vorschlagen; *i.* einen Heiratsantrag machen.

Proposition [pro-pA-si'schAn] *n.* Vorschlag *m,* Antrag *m,* Satz *m.*

Propound [prA-paund'] *vt.* vorlegen, vorschlagen.

Proprietary [prA-prai'A-tA-rij] *a.* Eigentums . . .; gesetzlich geschützt *(article).*

Propriet'or [prA-prai'A-ter] *n.* Eigentümer *m,* Besitzer *m,* Inhaber *m,* Direktor *m (hotel)*; **-rix** *n.* Eigentümerin *f,* Inhaberin *f;* **-y** *n.* Schicklichkeit *f,* Anstand *m.*

Propulsion [prA-pAl'schAn] *n.* Antrieb *m,* jet — Düsen-, Strahl-, Reaktions-, Rückstoss-antrieb *m.*

Prosaic [pro-sei'ik] *a.* nüchtern, trocken, prosaisch.

Proscription [pro-skrip'schAn] *n.* Ächtung *f,* Verbot *n.*

Prose [prous] *n.* Prosa *f,* Übersetzung *f (translation)*; **-writer** *n.* Prosaschriftsteller *m.*

Prosecute [pro'ssi-kjut] *vt.* verfolgen, verklagen *(law).*

Prosecution [pro-ssi-kjuh'schAn] *n.* Verfolgung *f,* Betreibung *f,* Verklagen *n.*

Prosecutor [pro'ssi-kju-ter] *n.* Verfolger *m,* Ankläger *m;* public — Staatsanwalt *m.*

Proselyte [pro'ssi-lait] *n.* der, die Neubekehrte.

Proselytise [pro'ssi-li-tais] *vt.* (Anhänger) werben.

Prospect [pro'spekt] *n.* Aussicht *f,* Ausblick *m.*

Prospect [prA-spekt'] *vi.* schürfen; **-ive** *a.* voraussichtlich; **-** officer *n.* Offiziersanwärter *m (mil.)*; **-or** *n.* Schürfer *m.*

Prospectus [prA-spek'tAss] *n.* Prospekt *m,* Voranzeige *f.*

Prosper [pro'sper] *vi.* gedeihen, blühen.

Prosperity [pro-spe'ri-ti] *n.* Wohlstand *m,* Wohlfahrt *f.*

Prosperous [pro'spA-rAss] *a.* glücklich, gedeihlich, blühend.

Prostitute [pro'sti-tjuht] *n.* Dirne *f,* Hure *f.*

Prostitution [pro-sti-tjuh'schAn] *n.* Prostitution *f.*

Prostrate [pro'strit] *a.* hingestreckt, entkräftet.

Prostration [prA-strei'schAn] *n.* Niederwerfung *f,* Niedergeschlagenheit *f,* Schwäche *f.*

Protagonist [pro-tæ'gA-nist] *n.* Vorkämpfer *m,* Held *m.*

Protect [prA-tekt'] *vt.* schützen, schirmen, sichern *(mil.)*; **-ed** category *n.* Berggruppe *f.*

Protecting [prA-tek'ting] *a.* schützend; **-** power *n.* Schutzmacht *f.*

Protection [prA-tek'schAn] *n.* Schutz *m,* Beschützung *f,* Abwehr *f,* Schutzmittel *n,* Schutzzoll *m (tariff)*; **-ism** *n.* Schutzzollsystem *n;* **-ist** *n.* Schutzzöllner *m;* **a.** schutzzöllnerisch, Schutzzoll . . .

Protective [prA-tek'tiw] *a.* schützend; **-** clothing *n.* Schutzbekleidung *f (av.)*; **-** custody *n.* Schutzhaft *f;* **-** face covering *n.* Gesichtsschutzmaske *f (av.)*; **-** sheeting *n.* Schutzblech *n;* **-** tariff *n.* Schutzzoll *m;* **-** wing *n.* Sicherungsflügel *m (av.).*

Protector [prA-tek'ter] *n.* Beschützer *m,* Statthalter *m,* Reichsverweser *m,* Protektor *m,* Schutz-mittel *n,* -vorrichtung *f (tec.)*; **-ate** *n.* Schutzgebiet *n,* Protektorat *m.*

Protest [prou'test] *n.* Protest *m,* Einspruch *m,* Verwahrung *f; (law-test')* **vi.** protestieren, Einspruch erheben; *t.* beteuern, protestieren *(com.).*

Protestant [pro'ti-stAnt] *a.* protestantisch, evangelisch; *n.* Protestant *m,* -in *f.*

Protract [prA-trækt'] *vt.* in die Länge ziehen, verzögern;

-ed *a.* langwierig, weitschweifig; **-or** *n.* Gradbogen *m*, Winkelmesser *m*, Transporteur *m*.

Protrude [prʌ-truhd'] *vi.* vorstehen, heraustreten; *t.* vorschieben.   [mütig.

Proud [praud] *a.* stolz, hoch-

Prove [pruhw] *vt.* beweisen, erprüfen; *i.* sich erweisen als, ausfallen.

Provender [pro'win-der] *n.* Futter *n*, Proviant *m*.

Proverb [pro'werb] *n.* Sprichwort *n*.   [sprichwörtlich.

Proverbial [prʌ-wʌr'bjʌl] *a.*

Provide [prʌ-waid'] *vt.* versehen, versorgen, bestimmen, verordnen (*law*).

Providen'ce [pro'wi-dʌnss] *n.* Vorsehung *f*; **-t** *a.* vorsichtig, sparsam.

Province [pro'winss] *n.* Provinz *f*, Gebiet *n* (*sphere, etc*).

Provincial [prʌ-win'schʌl] *a.* Provinzial ..., kleinstädtisch; **– council** *n.* Provinziallandtag *m*.

Provision [prʌ-wi'zhʌn] *n.* Versorgung *f*, Fürsorge *f*, Vorkehrung *f*, Verordnung *f*, Vorrat *m* (*supply*); **-s** *pl.* Nahrungsmittel *n. pl*; *vt.* Nahrung beschaffen, verproviantieren.

Provisional [prʌ-wi'zhʌ-nʌl] *a.* vorläufig, bedingt, provisorisch, einstweilig.

Proviso [prʌ-wai'sou] *n.* Vorbehalt *m*, Bedingung *f*.

Provocation [pro-wo-kei'schʌn] *n.* Herausforderung *f*.

Provocative [prʌ-wo'kA-tiw] *a.* herausfordernd.

Provoke [prʌ-wouk'] *vt.* erregen, anreizen, veranlassen.

Provost [pro'wʌst] *n.* Bürgermeister *m*, Vorsteher *m*, Probst *m*.

Provost [pro-wou'] *n.* Profos *m*; **– marshall** *n.* Generalprofos *m*; **Gendarmerieoberst** *m*. **– sergeant** *n.* Oberwacht-

meister der Feldgendarmerie; **– service** *n.* Ordnungsdienst *m* (*mil.*).   [teil *m*.

Prow [prau] *n.* Bug *m*, Vorderteil *m*.

Proximity [prox-i'mi-ti] *n.* Nähe *f*.

Proxy [prox'i] *n.* Stellvertreter *m*, Vollmacht *f*.

Prud'e [pruhd] *n.* die Spröde; **-ish** *a.* spröde, zimperlich.

Pruden'ce [pruh'dʌnss] *n.* Vorsicht *f*, Klugheit *f*; **-t** *a.* vorsichtig, verständig, klug.

Prune [pruhn] *n.* gedörrte Pflaume.

Prune [pruhn] *vt.* stutzen.

Pruning [pruh'ning] **– hook** *n.* Garten-, Hecken-sichel *f*; **-shears** *n. pl.* Baumschere *f*.

Prussic acid [prʌ'ssik-A'ssid] *n.* Blausäure *f*.

Pry [prai] *vi.* spähen, die Nase stecken in; **-ing** *a.* neugierig.

Pseudo [ssjuh'dou] *a.* falsch, After ...; **-nym** *n.* Deckname *m*, Pseudonym *n*.

Psychiatry [ssai-kai'A-tri] *n.* Irrenheilkunde *f*.

Psychic [ssai'kik] *a.* psychisch, Seelen ...

Psychoanalysis [ssai-ko-An-æ'li-ssiss] *n.* Seelenforschung *f*, Psychoanalyse *f*.

Psychological [ssai-ko-lo'dzhikl] *a.* psychologisch.

Psychology [ssai-ko'lo-dzhi] *n.* Psychologie *f*.

Ptarmigan [tahr'mi-gʌn] *n.* Schneehuhn *n*.

Pub [pʌb] *n. see* public house.

Public [pʌn'lik] *a.* öffentlich, Staats ...; **-holiday** *n.* gesetzlicher Feiertag; **– house** *n.* Wirtshaus *n*; **– library** *n.* Volksbibliothek *f*; **– prosecutor** *n.* Staatsanwalt *m*; **– spirit** *n.* Gemeinsinn *m*; **– utility** *n.* Versorgungsbetrieb *m*; **– works** *n. pl.* öffentliche Bauten *pl*.

Publican [pʌb'li-kʌn] *n.* Gast-, Schank-wirt *m*.

Publication [pAb-li-kei′-schAn] n. Veröffentlichung f, Herausgabe f, Verlagswerk n. (book).

Publicity [pAb-li′ssi-ti] n. Öffentlichkeit f, Werbung f, Reklame f; **– manager** n. Betriebswerber m.

Publish [pAb′lisch] vt. herausgeben, bekannt machen, kundgeben; **-er** n. Verleger m, Herausgeber m; **-ing** n. Verlegen n; **– house** n. Verlagsbuchhandlung f.

Puce [pjuhss] a. dunkelbraun.

Pucker [pA′ker] n. Falte f; vt. i. (sich) falten, runzeln.

Pudding [pu′ding] n. Pudding m. Mehlspeise f.

Puddle [pu′dl] n. Pfuhl m, Pfütze f; vt. verfüllen, puddeln (tec.).   [isch.

Puerile [pju′A-rail] a. kindisch.

Puff [pAf] n. Hauch m, Paff m, Windstoss m; vt. aufblähen, aufbauschen, Reklame machen für; i. schnaufen, puffen; **-y** a. aufgeblasen, aufgedunsen.

Pugilis'm [pjuh′dzhi-lism] n. Boxen; **-t** n. Faustkämpfer m, Boxer m.

Pugnacious [pAg-nei′schAss] a. streitsüchtig, kampflustig.

Pugnacity [pAg-na′ssi-ti] n. Kampflust f.

Pull [pul] vt. ziehen, abdrücken (trigger), pullen (nav.); n. Zug m, Abzug m, Schlag m; **– down** vt. abbrechen, niederreissen; **– out** vi. abfangen (av.).

Pullet [pu′lit] n. Hühnchen n.

Pulley [pu′li] n. Rolle f, Talje f (nav.); **– block** n. Flaschenzug m.

Pulp [pAlp] n. Brei m, Fruchtmark n, Masse f; vt. zu Brei verwandeln, entkirschen.

Pulpit [pul′pit] n. Kanzel f.

Pulse [pAlss] n. Puls m.

Pulverise [pAl′wA-rais] vt. pulverisieren, zerreiben, zerstäuben; **-r** n. Zerstäuber m.

Pumice (stone) [pA′misstoun] n. Bimsstein m.

Pump [pAmp] n. Pumpe f; vt. pumpen, ausfragen (person); **– up** aufpumpen (tyre).

Pumpkin [pAmp′kin] n. Kürbis m.

Pun [pAn] n. Wortspiel n.

Punch [pAnsch] n. Punsch m.

Punch [pAnsch] n. Stoss m; vt. stossen, puffen.

Punch [pAnsch] n. Stanze f, Locheisen n, Punze f; vt. durchschlagen, durchlöchern, lochen, knipsen (ticket).

Punctilious [pAnk-ti′ljAss] a. übertrieben pünktlich, zeremoniös, pendantisch.

Punctual [pAnk′tju-Al] a. pünktlich, prompt.

Punctuality [pAnk-tju-æ′li-ti] n. Pünktlichkeit f.

Punctuate [pAnk′tju-eit] vt. interpunktieren, unterbrechen.

Punctuation [pAnk-tju-ei′schAn] n. Zeichensetzung f; **– mark** n. Satzzeichen n.

Puncture [pAnk′tscher] n. Stich m, Durchlochung f, Loch n, Radpanne f, Reifenschaden m (aut.); vt. stechen; i. platzen (tyre).

Pungent [pAn′zhAnt] a. beissend, stechend, scharf.

Punish [pA′nisch] vt. strafen; **-able** a. strafbar; **-ment** n. Strafe f, Bestrafung f.

Punitive [pjuh′ni-tiw] a. Straf . . .; **– expedition** n. Strafzug m.

Punt [pAnt] n. Flachboot n.

Puny [pjuh′ni] a. winzig, kümmerlich.   [(eye).

Pupil [pjuh′pil] n. Pupille f.

Pupil [pjuh′pil] n. Schüler m, Schülerin f.

Puppet [pA′pit] n] Drahtpuppe f, Marionette f, Werkzeug n.   [(Hund.

Pup(py) [pA′pi] n. junger Hund.

Purblind [pAr′blaind] a. kurzsichtig, blöd.

Purchasable [pAr'tsch-Ass-Abl] a. käuflich.

Purchase [pAr'tschAss] n. Kauf m, Einkauf m, Hebekraft f (tec.); vt. kaufen, erstehen; – price m. Neuwert m. Einkaufspreis m; – tax n. Aufwandsteuer f.

Pure [pjuh'Ar] a. -ly ad. rein, sauber, unverfälscht.

Purgative [pAr'gA-tiw] n. Abführmittel n. [Fegefeuer n.

Purgatory [pAr'gA-tA-ri] n.

Purge [pArdzh] vt. reinigen, säubern, abführen; Abführmittel n, Säuberungsaktion f (political).

Purification [pjuh-ri-fi-kei'schAn] n. Reinigung f, Säuberung f.

Purify [pjuh'ri-fai] vt. reinigen, raffinieren (com).

Purity [pjuh'ri-ti] n. Reinheit f, Echtheit f.

Purl [pArl] n. Besatz m, Kantille f; vt. kraus einsäumen; – knitting n. Linksstrickerei f; – stitch n. linke Masche.

Purple [pArpl] a. purpurn, rot (grapes).

Purport [pAr'pert] n. Inhalt m, Sinn m; [per-pOrt'] vt. besagen, bedeuten.

Purpose [pAr'pAss] n. Absicht f, Zweck m; vt. beabsichtigen; -ful a. entschlossen; -ly ad. absichtlich.

Purr [pAr] vi. schnurren.

Purse [pArss] n. Geld-beutel m, -tasche f, Portemonnaie n, Börse f; -r n. Zahl-, Proviantmeister m.

Pursuance [per-ssjuh'Anss] n. in – of gemäss, zufolge.

Pursue [per-ssjuh'] vt. verfolgen, betreiben, fortsetzen.

Pursuit [per-ssjuht'] n. Verfolgung f, Trachten f, -s pl. Beschäftigung f; – plane n. Jäger m, Jagdflugzeug n.

Purvey [per-wei'] vt. liefern, versorgen.

Purveyor [per-wei'er] n. Lieferant m.

Pus [pAss] n. Eiter m.

Push [pusch] n. Stoss m, Schub m, Vorstoss m (mil.); vt. schieben, stossen, drängen, treiben, beschleunigen; – bike n. Tretfahrrad n; – button n. Druckknopf m; -ing see pushful.

Pushful [pusch'ful] a. strebsam, energisch, zudringlich.

Put [put] vt. stellen, setzen, legen, stecken.

Putrefaction [pju-tri-fæk'schAn] n. Fäulnis f.

Putri'fy [pjuh-tri-fai] vi. verfaulen, modern; -d a. verfault.

Putt [pAt] vt.i. einlochen, putten; -ing green n. Grün n. Kleingolfplatz m.

Puttees [pA-tihs'] n.pl. Wickelgamaschen f.pl.

Putty [pA'ti] n. Fensterkitt m.

Puzzle [pAsl] n. Rätsel n; vt. verwirren.

Pygmy [pig'mi] n. Zwerg m.

Pyjamas [pi-dzhah'mAs] n.pl. Schlafanzug m.

Pylon [pai'lAn] n. Pylon m, Turm m, Leitungsmast m (el.).

Pyramid [pi'rA-mid] n. Pyramide f. [Schwefelkies m.

Pyrites [pai-rai'tihs] n.pl.

Q

Quack [kwæk] n. Quacksalber m, Kurpfuscher m.

Quadrant [kuo'drAnt] n. Viertelkreis m.

Quadruped [kuod'ru-ped] n. Vierfüssler m. [vierfach.

Quadruple [kuod'rupl] a.

Quagmire [kueg'mai-er] n. Sumpf(boden) m.

Quail [kueil] n. Wachtel f.

Quail [kueil] vi. den Mut verlieren. [seltsam.

Quaint [kueint] a. altmodisch,

Quaintness [kueint'ness] n. Seltsamkeit f.

Quake [kueik] *vi.* beben, zittern; [*m.*

Quaker [kuei'ker] *n.* Quäker

Qualification [kuo-li-fi-kei'schAn] *n.* Befähigung *f,* Qualifikation *f,* Eigenschaft *f,* Einschränkung *f.*

Qualif'y [kuo'li-fai] *vt.* befähigen; -ied *a.* geeignet, befähigt, qualifiziert.

Quality [kuo'li-ti] *n.* Qualität *f,* Güte *f.*

Qualm [kuOm] *n.* Übelkeit *f,* Bedenken *n,* Gewissensskrupel *m.* [Verlegenheit *f.*

Quandary [kuon'dA-ri] *n.* Quantity [kuon'ti-ti] *n.* Quantität *f,* Menge *f,* Grösse *f.*

Quarantine [kuo'rAn-tihn] *n.* Isolierung *f,* Quarantäne *f.*

Quarrel [kuo'rAl] *n.* Streit *m;* *vi.* streiten; -some *a.* streitsüchtig. [*m;* *vt.* brechen.

Quarry [kuo'ri] *n.* Steinbruch

Quart [kuOrt] *n.* Quart *n* (1,136 Liter).

Quarter [kuOr'ter] *n.* Viertel *n,* Gnade *f;* *vt.* vierteln, einquartieren, belegen (*town*) -*s* *pl.* Quartier *n,* Unterkunft *f;* -ed *a.* in barracks kaserniert; -deck *n.* Hinter-, Achter-deck *n.* [vierteljährlich.

Quarterly [kuOr'ter-li] *a.ad.*

Quartermaster [kuOr'ter-mah'ster] *n.* Steurer *m* (*nav.*), Quartiermeister *m* (*mil.*); - -general *n.* Oberquartiermeister *m;* - -sergeant *n.* Furier *m.* [format *n.*

Quarto [kuOr'tou] *n.* Quart-

Quartz [kuOrtss] *n.* Quartz *m.*

Quash [kuosch] *vt.* unterdrücken, annullieren.

Quay [kih] *n.* Kai *m.*

Queen [kuihn] *n.* Königin *f.*

Queer [kuih'er] *a,* -ly *ad.* wunderlich, seltsam.

Quell [kuel] *vt.* bezwingen.

Quench [kuensch] *vt.* löschen.

Querulous [kue'rjA-lAss] *a.* jammernd.

Query [kuih'ri] *n.* Frage *f;* *vt.i.* fragen, bezweifeln.

Quest [kuest] *n.* Suchen *n.*

Question [kuess'tschAn] *n.* Frage *f,* Streitpunkt *m;* *vt.* befragen, bezweifeln; -able *a.* fragwürdig, zweifelhaft.

Questionnaire [kuess-tschA-neh'er] *n.* Fragebogen *m.*

Queu'e [kjuh] *n.* Zopf *m,* Reihe *f,* Schlange *f* (*people*); *vi.* anstehen, Schlange stehen; -ing *n.* Anstehen *f.*

Quibble [kuibl] *n.* Ausflucht *f;* *vi.* Ausflüchte gebrauchen.

Quick [kuik] *a,* -ly *ad.* schnell, rasch, scharf, frisch; - -firing gun *n.* Schnellfeuergeschütz *n;* - -motion apparatus *n.* Zeitraffer *m* (*film*); - -tempered *a.* reizbar.

Quick'en [kui'kAn] *vt.* beleben, beschleunigen; -lime *n.* Ätzkalk *m;* -ness *n.* Schnelligkeit *f,* Raschheit *f,* Schärfe *f;* -sand *n.* Flugsand *m;* -silver *n.* Quecksilber *n.* [still.

Quiescent [kuai-e'ssAnt] *a.*

Quiet [kuai'At] *a,* -ly *ad.* still, ruhig, schlicht; *n.* Stille *f,* Ruhe *f.*

Quill [kuil] *n.* Federkiel *m.*

Quilt [kuilt] *n.* Steppdecke *f;* *vt.* steppen, durchnähen.

Quince [kuinss] *n.* Quitte *f.*

Quinine [kui-nihn'] *n.* Chinin *n.* [entzündung *f.*

Quinsy [kuin'si] *n.* Mandel-

Quintessence [kuint-e'ssAnss] *n.* Quintessenz *f.*

Quire [kuai'er] *n.* Buch *n* Papier.

Quit [kuit] *vt.* verlassen, ablassen von; *a.* quitt, los.

Quiver [kui'wer] *vi.* zittern.

Quiver [kui'wer] *n.* Köcher *m.*

Quiz [kuis] *vt.* necken; *n.* Befragen *n,* mündliche Prüfung.

Quoit [keut] *n.* Wurfring *m.*

Quorum [kuO'rAm] *n.* beschlussfähige Anzahl.

Quota [kuou'tA] *n.* Anteil *m.*

Teilbetrag m, Quantum n, Kontingent n, Quote f.

Quotation [kuo-tei'schAn] n. Zitat n, Preisangabe f (com.).

Quote [kuout] vt. zitieren, anführen, angeben (price).

R

Rabbet [rœ'bit] n. Falz m, (Kitt-)Fuge f; vt. ein-, überfalzen; - -plane n. Sims-, Falz-hobel m.

Rabbit [rœ'bit] n. Kaninchen n; - -hutch n. Kaninchenstall m.

Rabble [rœbl] n. Pöbel m.

Rabid [rœ'bid] a. wütend.

Rabies [rei'bjihs] n. Tollwut f.

Race [reiss] n. Rasse f, Geschlecht n.

Race [reiss] n. Wettlauf m, Wettrennen n; vi. rennen; - -course n. Rennbahn f; -horse n. Rennpferd n; - -meeting n. Pferderennen n; -r n. Rennwagen m (aut.), Rennpferd n (cycle), Rennpferd n (horse).

Racial [rei'schAl] a. Rassen . ., rassisch.

Rack [rœk] n. Gestell n, Raufe f, Kleiderleiste f, Wandbrett n, Halter m; vt. foltern, quälen.

Racket [rœ'kit] n. Rakett n, Tennisschläger m.

Racket [rœ'kit] n. Lärm m, Erpressung f, Schwindel m.

Racy [rei'ssi] a. rassig, ausgesprochen, lebhaft.

Radar [rei'dahr] n. Peilung f, Ortung f; a. Mess . . .; - -equipment n. Funkmessgerät n, Peilfunkgerät n; - -operator n. Mess-mann, -funker m; - -service n. Messdienst m; - -set see - -equipment; - -site. - station, n. Mess-stellung f.

Radia'nce [rei'djAnss] n. Glanz m; -nt a. strahlend; -te vt.i. senden (rad.), ausstrahlen.

Radiation [rei-di-ei'schAn] n. Strahlen n, Aus-, Be-strahlung f.

Radiator [rei'djei-ter] n. Heizkörper m, Kühler m (aut.).

Radical [rœ'dikl] a. eingewurzelt, gründlich, wesentlich; n. der Radikale.

Radio [rei'djou] n. Rundfunk m, Radio n; vt. funken; - bearing n. Funkpeilung f; - control n. Fernlenkung f; - drama n. Hörspiel n; - engineering n. Funktechnik f; - equipment n. Funkgerät n; - installation n. Bordfunkanlage f (av.); - -mast n. Antennenmast m; - mechanic n. Funkwart, -techniker m; - message n. Funkspruch m; - network n. Funknetz n; - operator n. Funker n; - plant n. Radioanlage f; - receiving set n. see - set; - reception n. Funkempfang m; - set n. Radioapparat m, Funkgerät n; - station n. Funkstelle f; - telegraphy n. Funktelegraphie f; - telephony n. Funksprechen n, drahtlose Telephonie; - transmitter n. Sender m (rad.).

Radiographer [rei-di-o'grAfer] n. Röntgenhilfe m.

Radio-location [rei-djou-lokei'schAn] n. Radiolokalisierung f, see radar; - apparatus n. Peilfunkgerät n.

Radiology [rei-di-o'lo-dzhi] n. Röntgenlehre f.

Radio-therapy [rei-djo-therA-pi] n. Röntgen-, Strahlentherapie f.

Radish [rœ'disch] n. Rettig m.

Radium [rei'djAm] n. Radium n.

Radius [rei'djAss] n. Halbmesser m, Radius m, Umkreis m.

Raffia [rœ'fjA] n. Rafflafaser f.

Raffle [rœfl] n. Auswürfeln n; vt. auswürfeln.

Raft [rahft] n. Floss n; -er n.

Dachsparren m; -sman n. Flösser m.

Rag [ræg] n. Lumpen m, Lappen m; - -doll n. Stoffpuppe f.

Rage [rei'dʒh] n. Wut f; vi. wüten.

Ragged [ræ'gid] a. zerlumpt, zerrissen.

Raid [reid] n. Anfall m, Überfall m, Raubzug m, Handstreich m (mil.); vt. überfallen, einen Beutezug ausführen; -ng party n. Streifabteilung f, n. Stosstrupp m (mil.).

Rail [reil] n. Leiste f, Schiene f (rl.), Querholz n, Riegel m, Reling f (nav.), see also -way; vt.einfriedigen, beschienen (rl.), mit der Bahn befördern; -head n. Endbahnhof m, Eisenbahnendpunkt m.

Rail [reil] vi. spotten, schimpfen.

Railing [rei'ling] n. Gelände n, Gitter n. [way.

Railroad [reil'roud] see rail-

Railway [reil'uei] n. Eisenbahn f; - carriage n. Eisenbahn-, Personen-wagen m; - company n. Eisenbahngesellschaft f; - engine n. Lokomotive f; - fare n. Fahrgeld n; - gauge n. Spurweite f; - guard n. Zugführer m, Schaffner m; - junction n. Eisenbahnknotenpunkt m; -man n. Eisenbahner m; - siding n. Abstell-, Neben-geleise n; - station n Bahnhof m; - system n. Bahnnetz n; -ticket n. Fahrkarte f; - -train n. Eisenbahnzug m; - transport officer n. Transportoffizier m (mil.); - -truck n. Güterwagen m.

Rain [rein] n. Regen m; vi. regnen; -coat n. Regen-, Wetter-mantel m; -bow n. Regenbogen m; -y a. regnerisch; - day n. Regentag m.

Raise [reis] vt. heben, erhöhen, aufrichten.

Raisin [rei'sn] n. Rosine f.

Rake [reik] n. Rechen m, Harke f; vt. rechen.

Rake [reik] n. Wüstling m.

Rally [ræ'li] n. Versammlung f, Erholung f; vi. sich wieder sammeln, sich erholen.

Ram [ræm] n. Widder m, Ramme f (nav.); vt. rammen, stampfen.

Ramble [ræmbl] n. Streifzug m, Ausflug m, Wanderung f; vi. umherstreifen, wandern; -er n. Wanderer m; -ing a. weitschweifig, Wander . . .

Ramification [ræ-mi-fi-kei'schän] n. Verzweigung f.

Rammer [ræ'mer] n. Stampfer m, Ramme f, Füllstock m.

Ramp [ræmp] n. Rampe f, Erpressung f.

Rampant [ræm'pAnt] a. aufgerichtet, überhandnehmend.

Rampart [ræm'pahrt] n. Festungswall m.

Ramshackle [ræm'schækl] a. baufällig. [schaft f.

Ranch [rænsch] n. Viehwirt-

Rancid [ræn'ssid] a. ranzig.

Rancour [ræng'ker] n. Erbitterung f.

Random [ræn'dAm] a. zufällig, aufs Geratewohl; - bombing n. Blindabwurf m (av.).

Range [reindzh] n. Rang m, Umfang m, Reihe f, Kette f (mountains), Schussweite f (mil.), Reichweite f, Flug-weite f. -bereich m (av.); vt.i. durchstreifen, fliegen, umherwandern; - corrector n. Auswanderungsmesser m; - -finder n. Entfernungs-messer m, -mess-gerät n.

Ranger [reindzh'er] n. Aufseher m, Förster m, Jäger m (mil.).

Rank [rængk] n. Rang m, Reihe f, Glied n, Dienstgrad m (mil, etc.); vt. rechnen; i. sich rechnen, sich reihen, den Rang haben; other -s pl. Mannschaft f

Rank [rængk] a. üppig, arg.

Ranker [ræng'ker] n. der Gemeine; - officer n. aus dem Mannschaftsstande hervorgegangener Offizier.

Rankle [rænkl] vi. nagen, um sich fressen. [wühlen.]

Ransack [ræn'ssæk] vt. durch-

Ransom [ræn'ssAm] n. Lösegeld n; vt. auslösen. [reden.]

Rant [rænt] vi. hochtrabend

Rap [ræp] vi. klopfen.

Rap [ræp] n. Heller m.

Rapacious [rA-pei'schAss] a. gierig, räuberisch.

Rapacity [rA-pæ'ssi-ti] n. Raubgier f.

Rape [reip] n. Notzucht f.

Rape [reip] n. Raps m. Rübsen m; - -seed n. Rübsamen m.

Rapid [ræ'pid] a. geschwind, schnell.

Rapidity [rA-pi'di-ti] n. Geschwindigkeit f. [degen m.

Rapier [rei'pjer] n. Stoss-

Rapine [ræ'pin] n. Raub m.

Rapt [ræpt] a. hingerissen; -ure n. Entzückung f, Wonne f.

Rar'e [reh'er] a. -ely ad. selten, rar, vortrefflich; -ity n. Seltenheit f.

Rascal [rah'skAl] n. Schuft m, Spitzbube m, Schelm m. [m.

Rash [ræsch] n. Hautausschlag

Rash [ræsch] a. übereilt, tollkühn; -ness n. Voreiligkeit f, Tollkühnheit f.

Rasher [ræ'scher] n. Speckschnitte f.

Rasp [rahsp] n. Raspel f; vt. raspeln, reiben.

Raspberry [rahs'bA-ri] n. Himbeere f.

Rat [ræt] n. Ratte f.

Ratable [rei'tAbl] a. abschätzbar, steuerpflichtig.

Ratchet [ræ'tschit] n. Sperrklinke f.

Rate [reit] n. Preis m, Massstab m, Wert m, Anteil m, Rate f, Geschwindigkeit f (speed), Abgabe f (municipal); vt. schätzen, klassifizieren; -payer n. Gemeindesteuerzahler m.

Rate [reit] vt. ausschelten.

Rather [rah'dher] ad. lieber, ziemlich.

Ratification [ræ-ti-fi-kei'schAn] n. Bestätigung f.

Ratify [ræ'ti-fai] vt. bestätigen, genehmigen.

Rating [rei'ting] n. Einschätzung f, Klasse f. Dienstgrad m (mil.); naval — Matrose m, Seesoldat m. [nis n.

Ratio [rei'schjou] n. Verhält-

Ration [ræ'schAn] n. Ration f; vt. rationieren; - book n. Bezugsscheinheft n; - bureau, -office, n. Ernährungsamt n, Kartenstelle f; - period n. Lebensmittelzuteilungsperiode f; - strength n. Verpflegungsstärke f (mil.); -ing n. Rationierung f, Zuteilung f.

Rational [ræ'schA-nAl] a. vernünftig, rational.

Rattle [rætl] n. Gerassel n, Klapper f, Rassel f; vi. rasseln.

Raucous [rO'kAss] a. heiser.

Rave [reiw] vi. toben, rasen.

Raven [rei'wAn] n. Rabe m.

Ravenous [ræ'wA-nAss] a. heisshungrig.

Ravine [rA-wihn'] n. Bergschlucht f.

Ravish [ræ'wisch] vt. entreissen, schänden, entzücken.

Raw [rO] a. roh, rauh; -material n. Rohstoff m.

Ray [rei] n. Strahl m.

Rayon [rei'on] n. Kunstseide f.

Raze [reis] vt. zerstören.

Razor [rei'ser] n. Rasiermesser n; safety - Rasierapparat m; - -blade n. Rasierklinge f; -strop Streichriemen m.

Re [rih] pr. bezüglich, wegen.

Reach [rihtsch] n. Bereich m, Reichweite f. Strecke f; vt. reichen, erreichen; i. reichen, sich erstrecken.

React [rih-äkt'] *vi.* reagieren, rückwirken; **-ion** *n.* Reaktion *f.*, Rück-, Gegen-wirkung *f.*, Rückschlag *m*, Gegenstoss *m* (*mil.*), Rückkopplung *f* (*rad.*); **-ionary** *a.* reaktionär.

Read [rihd] *vt i.* lesen; **-able** *a.* lesenswert; **-er** *n.* Leser *m*, Leserin *f*, Korrektor *m* (*printer's*), Lesebuch *n*, Professor *n*.

Readdress [rih-A-dress'] *vt.* umadressieren.

Readi·ly [re'di-li] *ad.* bereitwillig; **-ness** *n.* Bereitwilligkeit *f*, Bereitschaft *f*.

Reading [rih'ding] *n.* lesen *n*, Lektüre *f*, Lesung *f* (*bill*), Belesenheit *f* (*learning*); **-book** *n.* Lesebuch *n*; **- -room** *n.* Lesezimmer *n*.

Readjust [rih-A-dzhAst'] *vt.* wieder in Ordnung bringen, neu einstellen.

Readmission [rih-Ad-mi'schAn] *n.* Wiederzulassung *f*.

Readmit [rih-Ad-mit'] *vt.* wieder zulassen.

Ready [re'di] *a.* bereit, gewandt, fertig; **- for flight** *a.* flugbereit (*av.*); **- to put to sea** *a.* seeklar (*nav.*); **-made** *a.* gebrauchsfertig; **- -money** *n.* bares Geld.

Reaffirm [rih-A-fArm'] *vt.* wieder versichern. [agens *n.*

Reagent [rih-ei'dzhAnt] *n.*]

Real [rih'Al] *a.* **-ly** *ad.* wirklich, wahr, echt, tatsächlich; **- estate** *n.* Grund-besitz *m*; **-ism** *n.* Realismus *m*; **-ist** *n.* Realist *m*.

Realistic [rih-A-li'stik] *a.* realistisch. [lichkeit *f.*

Reality [rih-ä'li-ti] *n.* Wirk-]

Realization [rih-A-lai-sei'schAn] *n.* Verwirklichung *f*, Ausführung *f*, Empfindung *f*, Liquidation *f*.

Realize [rih'A-lais] *vt.* sich vorstellen, realisieren, einsehen, verwerten, zu Gelde machen (*com.*), erfüllen (*hopes*).

Realm [relm] *n.* Reich *n*, Königreich *n*.

Ream [rihm] *n.* Ries *n*.

Reap [rihp] *vt.* ernten, mähen, schneiden; **-er** *n.* Schnitter *m*; *see also* reaping machine.

Reaping machine [rih'ping-mA-schihn'] *n.* Erntemähmaschine *f*.

Reappear [rih-A-pih'er] *vi.* wieder erscheinen; **-ance** *n.* Wiedererscheinung *f*.

Reappoint [rih-A-peunt'] *vt.* wieder anstellen, ernennen.

Rear [rih'er] *vt.* sich bäumen (*av.*); *vt.* ziehen, erziehen, züchten.

Rear [rih'er] *n.* Hintergrund *m*, Hinterseite *f*; *a.* hinterst, rückwertig, Nach . . .; **- -admiral** *n.* Konteradmiral *m*; **-axle** *n.* Hinterachse *f*; **- -cover** *n.* Rückendeckung *f* (*mil.*); **- -guard** *n.* Nach-hut *m*, **-trupp** *m*; **- -gunner** *n.* Heckschütze *m* (*av.*); **- -light** *n.* Schlusslicht *n*; **- -services** *n.pl.* rückwärtige Dienste *m.pl* (*mil.*); **- -wheel** *n.* Hinterrad *n*. [ten.

Rearm [rih-ahrm'] *vi.* aufrüsten.]

Rearmament [rih-ahr'mA-mAnt] *n.* Aufrüstung *f*.

Rearrange [rih-A-reindzh'] *vt.* neu ordnen, wieder ordnen.

Rearward [rih'er-uerd] *ad.* hinter.

Reason [rih's An] *n.* Vernunft *f*, Ursache *f*, Grund *m*; *vt.* durchdenken; *i.* urteilen, diskutieren; **-able** *a.* vernünftig, billig (*price*); **-ably** *ad.* billigerweise; **-ing** *n.* Urteilen *n*, Beweisführung *f*.

Reassemble [rih-A-ssembl'] *vi.* sich wieder versammeln; *t.* wieder zusammensetzen, wieder montieren.

Reassert [rih-A-ssArt'] *vt.* wieder behaupten.

Reassurance [rih-A-schuh'rAnss] *n.* Beruhigung *f*.

Reassure [rih-A-schuh'er] *vt.* wieder versichern, beruhigen.

Rebate [ri-beit'] n. Rabatt m, Abzug m, Rückzoll m (customs).

Rebel [rebl] n. Rebell m; vi. [ri-bel'] sich empören; -lion n. Empörung f; -lious a. aufrührerisch.   [binden.

Rebind [rih-baind'] vt. neu

Rebirth [rih-bArth'] n. Wiedergeburt f.

Rebound [rih-baund'] n. Rückprall m; vi. zurückprallen.   [weisung f.

Rebuff [ri-bAf'] n. Zurecht-

Rebuild [rih-bild'] vt. wieder aufbauen, wiederherstellen.

Rebuke [ri-bjuhk'] n. Verweis m, Tadel m, Vorwurf m; vt. verweisen, tadeln.

Recalibrate [rih-kæ'li-breit] vt. nacheichen.

Recall [ri-kOl'] n. Widerruf m, Abruf m; vt. zurückrufen, widerrufen, kündigen (com.).

Recant [ri-kænt'] vt.i. widerrufen.

Recapitulate [rih-kA-pi'tjuleit] vt. kurz wiederholen.

Recapture [rih-kæp'tscher] n. Wiedereinnahme f.

Recast [rih-kahst'] vt. umformen, neu bearbeiten; n. Umguss m, Umarbeitung f.

Recede [rih-sihd'] vi. zurücktreten.

Receipt [ri-siht'] n. Empfang m, Quittung f; vt. quittieren; -s f.pl. Einnahmen f.pl.

Receiv'e [ri-sihw'] vt. empfangen, erhalten, annehmen, aufnehmen (persons); -er n. Empfänger m, Einnehmer m (customs), Konkursverwalter m (official), Behälter m (tec.), Hörer m (ph.); -ing n. Empfang m, Annahme f; - set n. Radioempfänger m.

Recent [rih'ssAnt] a. neu; -ly ad. neulich, kürzlich.

Receptacle [ri-ssep'tAkl] n. Behälter m.

Reception [rih'ssep'schAn] n.

Empfang m, Aufnahme f; -centre n. Auffangstelle f; -ist n. Empfangsdame f.

Receptive [ri-ssep'tiw] a. empfänglich, aufnahmefähig.

Receptivity [rih-ssep-ti'wi-ti] n. Empfänglichkeit f.

Recess [ri-ssess'] n. Vertiefung f, Nische f, Ferien pl.

Recharge [rih'tschahrdzh] n. Nachladen n (el.); vt. wieder laden.

Recipe [re'ssi-pih] n. Rezept n.

Recipient [ri-ssi'pjAnt] n. Empfänger m.   [gegenseitig.

Reciprocal [ri-ssi'prAkl] a.

Reciprocat'e [ri-ssi'prA-keit] vt.i. erwidern, abwechseln, wechseln; -ing engine n. Kolbenmaschine f; -ion n. Wechselwirkung f, Erwiderung f.

Reciprocity [re-ssi-pro'ssi-ti] n. Gegenseitigkeit f.

Recital [ri-ssaitl'] n. Vortrag m, Vorlesen n.

Recitation [re-ssi-tei'schAn] n. Vortragen n, Hersagen n.

Reckless [rek'less] a. sorglos, tollkühn; -ness n. Tollkühnheit f.

Reckon [rekn] vt.i. rechnen, zählen, vermuten, halten für; -ing n. Berechnung f, Erachtung f, Abrechnung f; dead - Gissung f, Überschlag m (nav.).

Reclaim [ri-kleim'] vt. zurückleiten, urbar machen (land).

Reclamation [re-klA-mei'schAn] n. Wiedergewinnung f, Urbarmachung f.   [en.

Recline [ri-klain'] vi. sich lehnen.

Recluse [ri-kluhss'] n. Klausner m, Klausnerin f.

Recognition [re-kAg-ni'schAn] n. Erkennen f, Erkenntnis f; - signal n. Erkennungszeichen n (av.).

Recognizable [re'kAg-nai-sAbl] a. erkennbar.

Recognizance [ri-kog'ni-ssanss] n. schriftliche Verpflichtung.

Recognize [re'kAg-nais] *vt.* erkennen; *i.* zugeben.

Recoil [ri-keul'] *vi.* zurückfahren, zurückschlagen (*gun*); *n.* Rück-stoss, -lauf *m* (*mil.*); - -cylinder *n.* Bremszylinder *m*; - -gun *n.* Rohrrücklaufgeschütz *n.*

Recollect [re-kA-lekt'] *vt.* sich erinnern; -ion *n.* Erinnerung *f.*

Recommence [ri-kA-menss'] *vt.* wieder beginnen.

Recommend [re-kA-mend'] *vt.* empfehlen.

Recommendation [re-kA-men-dei'schAn] *n.* Empfehlung *f.*

Recommission [rih-kA-mi'schAn] *vt.* wieder in Dienst stellen.

Recompense [re'kAm-penss] *vt.* entschädigen, belohnen; *n.* Ersatz *m*, Belohnung *f.*

Reconcil'able [re'kAn-ssai-lAbl] *a.* verträglich, vereinbar; -e *vt.* vereinbaren, versöhnen, ausgleichen.

Reconciliation [re-kAn-ssi-li-ei'schAn] *n.* Versöhnung *f.*

Recondition [rih-kAn-di'schAn] *vt.* wieder instandsetzen; -ing *n.* Instandsetzung *f.*

Reconnaissance [ri-ko'ni-ssAnss] *n.* Erkundung *f*, Aufklärung *f*; photographic - Bilderkundung *f*; strategic - operative Aufklärung; tactical - taktische Aufklärung; - -patrol *n.* Aufklärungsspähtrupp *m* (*mil.*); - -patrolling *n.* Streifenaufklärung *f* (*mil.*); - -plane *n.* Aufklärungsflugzeug *n*; - -unit *n.* Aufklärungsabteilung *f.*

Reconnoitre [re-kA-neu'ter] *vt.* erkunden, aufklären, ausspähen. [wieder erobern.

Reconquer [rih-kong'ker] *vt.*

Reconsider [rih-kAn-ssi'der] *vt.* nochmals überlegen, von neuem erwägen.

Reconstruct [rih-kAn-strAkt'] *vt.* wieder aufbauen; -ion *n.* Wiederaufbau *m*, Sanierung *f* (*com.*).

Record [re'kOrd] *n.* Urkunde *f*, Zeugnis *n*, Verzeichnis *n*, Vergangenheit *f* (*personal*), Rekord *m* (*sport*), Schallplatte *f* (*gramaphone*).

Record [ri-kOrd'] *vt.* aufzeichnen, eintragen.

Recoup [ri-kuhp'] *vt.r.* entschädigen, (sich) schadlos halten. [flucht *f.*

Recourse [ri-kOrss'] *n.* Zu-

Recover [re-kA'wer] *vt.* wieder erlangen, bergen (*salvage*) zurückerobern (*mil.*); *i.* sich erholen.

Recover [rih'kA-wer] *vt.* neu bedecken, wieder bedecken.

Recovery [ri-kA'wA-ri] *n.* Wiedererlangung *f*, Genesung *f* (*health*); - *n.* Abschleppdienst *m* (*aut. etc.*).

Recreation [re'kri-ei'schAn] *n.* Erholung *f.*

Recrimination [ri-kri-mi-nei'schAn] *n.* Gegenbeschuldigung *f.*

Recrudescence [rih-kru-de'ssAnss] *n.* Wiederausbruch *m.*

Recruit [ri-kruht'] *n.* Rekrut *m*; *vt.i.* werben, rekrutieren; -ing *n.* Rekrutierung *f*, Aushebung *f*; - board *n.* Aushebungskommission *f*; - office *n.* Wehrmeldeamt *n*; - sergeant *n.* Werbeunteroffizier *m.*

Rectangle [rek'tængl] *n.* Rechteck *n.*

Rectification [rek-ti-fi-kei'schAn] *n.* Berichtigung *f*, Rektifizierung *f.*

Rectif'ier [rek'ti-fai-er] *n.* Gleichrichter *m* (*rad.*); - valve *n.* Gleichrichterröhre *f* (*rad.*); -y *vt.* berichtigen, rektifizieren, gleichrichten (*rad.*).

Rectitude [rek'ti-tjuhd] *n.* Redlichkeit *f.*

Rector [rek'ter] *n.* Pfarrherr *m*, Rektor *m.* [liegend.

Recumbent [ri-kAm'bAnt] *a.*

Recuperate [ri-kjuh'pA-reit] *vi.* sich erholen.

Recur [ri-kAr'] *vi.* wiederkehren, sich wiederholen; **-rence** *n.* Wiedervorkommen *n*; **-rent** *a.* wiederkehrend.

Red [red] *a.* rot; **- Cross** *n.* Rotes Kreuz; **- currant** *n.* rote Johannisbeere; **- herring** *n.* Heringsbückling *m.* [werden.

Redden [redn] *vi.* erröten, rot

Reddish [re'disch] *a.* rötlich.

Redecorate [rih-de'kA-reit] *vt.* renovieren.

Redeem [ri-dihm'] *vt.* erlösen, einlösen.

Redemption [ri-demp'schAn] *n.* Erlösung *f*, Einlösung *f*.

Red-handed [red'hæn-did] *a.* mit roten Händen, auf frischer Tat (ertappt).

Red-hot [red'hot] *a.* feuerrot.

Red-lead [red'led] *n.* Mennig *m*.

Red-letter day [red-le'ter dei'] *n.* Feiertag *m*, Freudentag *m.* [doppeln.

Redouble [ri-dAbl'] *vt.* ver-

Redress [ri-dress'] *vt.* abhelfen, wiedergutmachen; *n.* Abhilfe *f*.

Red-short [red-schOrt'] *a.* rotbrüchig (tec.). [kratismus *m*.

Red-tape [red-teip'] *n.* Büro-

Reduce [ri-djuhss'] *vt.* heruntersetzen, verkleinern, abschwächen (photo), degradieren (rank), herabsetzen (price), verjüngen (scale).

Reduction [ri-dAk'schAn] *n.* Reduktion *f*, Zurückführung *f*, Verkleinerung *f*, Abschwächung *f*, Preisermässigung *f* (com.), Verjüngung *f* (scale), Unterwerfung *f* (fortress), Abbau *m* (in staff).

Redundant [ri-dAn'dAnt] *a.* überflüssig gesetzt, überzählig.

Redwood [red'uud] *n.* Rotholz *m*.

Reed [rihd] *n.* Rohr *n*, Rohrpfeife *f*, Orgelzunge *f*.

Re-education [rih'e-dju-kei'schAn] *n.* Umschulung *f*.

Reef [rihf] *n.* Felsenriff *n*.

Reef [rihf] *n.* Reff *n* (nav.); *vt.* reffen, verkürzen. [jacke *f*.

Reefer [rih'fer] *n.* Marine-

Reel [rihl] *n.* Haspel *f*, Garnrolle *f*, Spüle *f*, Filmrolle *f* (film); *vt.* abhaspeln.

Reel [rihl] *vi.* taumeln, schwindeln.

Reel [rihl] *n.* schottischer Tanz.

Re-elect [rih-i-lekt'] *vt.* wieder wählen.

Re-eligible [rih-e'li-dzhibl'] *a.* wieder wählbar.

Re-enact [rih-i-nækt'] *vt.* wieder verordnen.

Re-engage [rih-en-geidzh'] *vt.* wieder in Dienst nehmen; **-d** man *n.* Kapitulant *m* (mil.).

Re-enlist [rih-in-list'] *vi.* kapitulieren, weiter dienen.

Re-enter [rih-en'ter] *vt.* wieder betreten, wieder eintragen (com.).

Re-establish [rih-i-stæb'lisch] *vt.* wiederherstellen, von neuem einführen.

Re-examine [rih-ig-sæ'min] *vt.* neu untersuchen, von neuem verhören (law).

Re-export [rih-ix-pOrt'] *vt.* wieder ausführen; *n.* [rih-ex'pOrt] *n.* Wiederausfuhr *f*; **-s** *pl.* wieder ausgeführte Ware *f*.

Refashion [rih-fæ'schAn] *vt.* ummodeln.

Refer [ri-fAr'] *vt.* verweisen, beziehen; *i.* sich beziehen auf, wenden, verweisen, nachschlagen. [richter *m*.

Referee [re-fA-rih'] *n.* Schieds-

Reference [re'fA-rAnss] *n.* Verweisung *f*, Beziehung *f*, Bezugnahme *f*, Zeugnis *n* (testimonial); **- number** *n.* Buchungs-, Brief-zeichen *n*, Kennziffer *f*; **- point** *n.* Ortungspunkt *m* (av.).

Referendum [re-fA-ren'dAm] *n.* Volksentscheid *m*.

Refill [rih-fil'] vt. wieder füllen; n. Ersatz-füllung f, -teil m.

Refine [ri-fain'] vt. läutern, raffinieren; -d a. fein, gebildet (person); -ment n. Läuterung f, Verfeinerung f, Bildung f.

Refit [rih-fit'] vt. wieder ausrüsten, wieder instandsetzen; i. ausgebessert werden; n. Wiederinstandsetzung f.

Reflect [ri-flekt'] vt. zurückwerfen; i. nachdenken; -ion n. Zurückwerfung f, Widerschein m, Nachdenken n, Tadel m; -or n. Reflektor m, Rückstrahler m, Scheinwerfer m.

Reflex [rih'fleks] n. Widerschein m; - camera n. Spiegelreflexkamera f.

Reflexive [ri-fle'xiw] a. rückbezüglich.

Refloat [rih-flout'] vt. wieder flott machen.

Refoot [rih-fut'] vt. wieder anstricken.

Reform [ri-fOrm'] n. Reform f, Umgestaltung f, Verbesserung f; vt. reformieren, umschaffen; i. sich bessern.

Reformation [re'fer-met'schAn] n. Reformation f, Besserung f.

Reformatory [ri-fOr'mA-tA-ri] n. Besserungsanstalt f.

Reformer [ri-fOr'mer] n. Reformer m, Reformator m.

Refract [ri-frækt'] vt. ablenken, brechen; -ion n. Brechung f; -ory a. widerspenstig.

Refrain [ri-frein'] n. Refrain m, Kehrreim m.

Refrain [ri-frein'] vi. sich enthalten.

Refresh [ri-fresch'] vt.r. sich erfrischen, auffrischen, erneuern; -ment n. Erfrischung f; - car n. Speisewagen m; - room n. Bahnhofsrestauration f.

Refrigerate [ri-fri'dzhA-reit] vt. kühlen; -ing a. Kühl ...; -chamber n. Kühlraum m; -plant n. Kühlanlage f.

Refrigeration [ri-fri-dzhA-rei'schAn] n. Kühlen n, Abkühlung f.

Refrigerator [ri-fridz'A-reit'ter] n. Eisschrank m, Kühlschrank m; - lorry Kühlwagen m.

Refuel [rih-fjuh'il] vt.i. tanken, auftanken; - in mid air lufttanken (av.).

Refuge [re'fjuhdzh] n. Zuflucht f, Zufluchtsort m.

Refugee [re-fjuh-dzhih'] n. Flüchtling m.

Refund [rih-fAnd'] vt. zurückzahlen, ersetzen, vergüten; n. Rückvergütung f, Ersatz m.

Refurnish [rih-fAr'nisch] vt. neu möblieren; [weigerung f.

Refusal [ri-fjuh'sAl] n. Ver-

Refuse [ri-fjuhs'] vt. verweigern, zurückweisen; i. sich weigern.

Refuse [re'fjuhss] n. Abfall m, Ausschuss m, Kehrricht m; - disposal n. Müllabfuhr f.

Refutation [re-fjuh-tei'schAn] n. Widerlegung f. [legen.

Refute [ri-fjuht'] vt. wider-

Regain [rih-gein'] vt. wieder gewinnen.

Regal [rihgl] a. königlich.

Regalia [ri-gei'ljA] n.pl. Kroninsignien pl.

Regard [ri-gahrd'] n. Achtung f, Rücksicht f, Ansehen n; vt. ansehen, achten; -ing pr. hinsichtlich, in Anbetracht; -less a. unbekümmert, ohne Rücksicht auf (cost).

Regatta [ri-gæ'tA] n. Bootwettfahrt f.

Regency [rih'dzhAn-ssi] n. Regentschaft f.

Regenerate [ri-dzhe'nA-reit] vt. erneuern.

Regeneration [rih-dzhe-nA-rei'schAn] n. Erneuerung f, Wiedergeburt f.

Regent [rih'dzhAnt] n. Regent m, Regentin f. [Regiment n.

Regiment [re'dzhi-mAnt] n.

Regimental [re-dzhi-mentl'] a. Regiments ...; - **commander** n. Regimentskommandeur m; - **headquarters** n.pl. Regimentsstab m; - **sergeant major** n. Hauptfeldwebel m (infantry), Hauptwachtmeister m (artillery, etc.); -s n.pl. Uniform f.

Regimentation [re-dzhi-mentei'schAn] n. Überorganisierung f.

Region [rih'dzhAn] n. Gegend f, Gebiet n; -al a. örtlich; - **command** n. Bereichskommando n.

Register [re'dzhi-ster] n. Register n, Verzeichnis n, Liste f; vt. eintragen, einschreiben (letter); -ed a. eingetragen, eingeschrieben, gesetzlich geschützt (patent, etc.).

Registrar [re'dzhi-strahr'] n. Standesbeamte(r) m; -'s office n. Standesamt n.

Registration [re-dzhi-strei'schAn] n. Registrierung f, Einschreibung f, Aufgabe f (luggage).

Registry [re'dzhi-stri] n. Eintragung f, Verzeichnis n, Standesamt n (office), Stellennachweis m (servants).

Regret [ri-gret'] vt. bedauern; n. Bedauern n; -ful a, -fully ad. mit Bedauern, ungern; -table a.s bedauerlich.

Regroup [rih-gruhp'] vt.i. umgruppieren.

Regular [re'gjuh-ler] a, -ly ad. regelmäßig, ordentlich, ständig, aktiv (mil.); -s n.pl. stehende Truppen f.pl, Berufssoldaten m.pl.

Regularity [re-gju-læ'ri-ti] n. Regelmäßigkeit f.

Regulate [re'gju-leit] vt. regulieren, regeln, ordnen, stellen (watch).

Regulation [re-gju-lei'schAn] n. Regulierung f, Anordnung f, Regelung f, Vorschrift f (rule).

Regulator [re'gju-lei-ter] n.

Stellvorrichtung f, Regulator m (tec.), Regler m, Regelung f, Einstellwert m, Raquette f (watch).

Rehabilitate [rih-hA-bi'li-teit] vt. wieder zu Ehren bringen.

Rehash [rih-hæsch'] vt. aufwärmen.

Rehearsal [ri-hAr'ssAl] n. Probe f.

Rehearse [ri-hArss'] vt. probieren; i. Probe halten.

Rehouse [rih-haus'] vt. in neuen Häusern unterbringen.

Reign [rein] n. Regierung f; vi. regieren.

Reimburse [rih-im-bArss'] vt. zurückzahlen, entschädigen; -ment n. Wiedererstattung f, Ersatzleistung f.

Reimport [rih-im-pOrt'] vt. wieder einführen.

Rein [rein] n. Zügel m.

Reindeer [rein'dih-er] n. Renntier n.

Reinforce [rih-in-fOrss'] vt. verstärken, nähren (fire); -d a. verstärkt (mil.); -d concrete n. Eisenbeton m; -ment n. Verstärkung f, Ersatz m, Nachschub m (mil.).

Reinstate [rih-in-steit'] vt. wiedereinsetzen.

Reinsure [rih-in-schuh'er] vt. rückversichern (com.).

Reintroduce [rih-in-trA-djuhss'] vt. wieder einführen.

Reinvest [rih-in-west'] vt. wieder anlegen.

Reissue [rih-i'schuh] vt. wieder ausgeben; n. Wieder-, Neuausgabe f.

Reiterate [rih-i'tA-reit] vt. wiederholen.

Reject [ri-dzhekt'] vt. verwerfen, ausscheiden, ausmustern (as unfit); -ion n. Verwerfung f, Abweisung f, Ausmusterung f.

Rejoice [ri-dzheuss'] vt. erfreuen; i. sich freuen.   [ern.

Rejoin [ri-dzheun'] vi. erwid-

Re-join [rih-dzheun'] vt. wieder zusammenfügen, wieder treffen.

Rejuvenate [ri-dzhuh'wA-neit] vt. verjüngen.

Rekindle [rih-kindl'] vt.i. (sich) wieder entzünden.

Relapse [ri-læps'] n. Rückfall m; vi. zurückfallen.

Relate [ri-leit'] vt. erzählen, verknüpfen; -d a. verwandt.

Relation [ri-lei'schAn] n. Verhältnis n, der, die Verwandte; -ship n. Verwandtschaft f, Verhältnis n, Beziehung f.

Relative [re'lA-tiw] a. -ly ad. relativ, bedingt, bezüglich, verhältnismässig; n. der, die Verwandte.

Relax [ri-læx'] vt.i. schlaff machen, mässigen, erschlaffen.

Relaxation [rih-læx-ei'schAn] n. Abspannung f, Zerstreuung f.

Relay [ri-lei'] n. Ablösung f, Relais n, Staffel f (race); vt. ablösen, übertragen (rad.); - **transmitter** n. Zwischensender m (rad.); -**ing** n. Drahtrundfunk m, Ringsendung f.

Release [ri-lihss'] vt. entlassen, befreien, herausgeben, freigeben (film), abwerfen (bomb), (aus)lösen (tec.); n. Entlassung f, Befreiung f, Freigabe f (film), Abwurf m (bomb), Ausmusterung f (troops), Auslöser m (camera).

Relegate [re'li-geit] vt. verweisen, überweisen.

Relent [ri-lent'] vi. nachgeben; -**less** a. unnachgiebig.

Relevance [re'li-wAnss] n. Erheblichkeit f, Relevanz f; -t a. anwendbar, relevant.

Reliability [ri-lai-A-bi'li-ti] n. Zuverlässigkeit f.

Reliable [ri-lai'Abl] a. zuverlässig; -**nce** n. Verlass m; -**nt** a. vertrauend.

Relic [re'lik] n. Überbleibsel n, Rest m, Reliquie f.

Relief [ri-lihf'] n. Erleichterung f, Unterstützung f, Ablösung f (mil.), Entsatz m (mil.).

Relieve [ri-lihw'] vt. erleichtern, unterstützen, ablösen (mil.), entsetzen (fortress).

Religion [ri-li'dzhAn] n. Religion f, Frömmigkeit f.

Religious [ri-li'dzhAs] a. fromm, religiös, laufgebes.

Relinquish [ri-ling'kuisch] vt. aufgeben.

Relish [re'lisch] vt. geniessen, Geschmack finden an; n. Geschmack m, pikante Beigabe.

Reluctance [ri-lAk'tAnss] n. Widerstreben n, Abneigung f.

Reluctant [ri-lAk'tAnt] a. -ly ad. widerwillig.

Remain [ri-mein'] vi. bleiben, -s n.pl. Überreste m.pl; -**der** n. Überbleibsel n, Rest m.

Remake [ri-meik'] vt. wieder machen.

Remand [ri-mahnd'] vt. in die Untersuchungshaft zurückschicken.

Remark [ri-mahrk'] n. Bemerkung f; vt.i. bemerken; -**able** a. merkwürdig, bemerkenswert.

Remarry [rih-mæ'ri] vi. sich wieder verheiraten.

Remediable [ri-mih'djAbl] a. heilbar, abstellbar.

Remedy [re'mi-di] n. Hilfsmittel n, Heilmittel n, Abhilfe f; vt. abhelfen.

Remember [ri-mem'ber] vt.i. sich erinnern, bedenken, gedenken.

Remembrance [ri-mem'brAnss] n. Erinnerung f, Andenken n.

Remind [ri-maind'] vt. erinnern, mahnen; -**er** n. Mahnung f, Erinnerung f, Wink m (hint).

Reminiscence [re-mi-ni'ssAnss] n. Erinnerung f. [sig.

Remiss [ri-miss'] a. nachlässig.

Remission [ri-mi'schAn] n. Erlassung f.

Remit [ri-mit'] vt. übersenden, erlassen (*punishment*); **-tance** n. Geldsendung f.

Remnant [rem'nAnt] n. Rest m, Überbleibsel n. [modeln.

Remodel [rih-modl'] vt. um-

Remonstrance [ri-mon'strAnss] n. Vorstellung f, Ermahnung f.

Remonstrate [ri-mon'streit] vi. Vorstellungen machen.

Remorse [ri-mOrss'] n. Gewissensbiss m; **-less** a. ruelos.

Remote [ri-mout'] a. **-ly** ad. fern, entfernt, abgelegen; **-control** Fern-lenkung f, -steuerung f (av.); **- controlled** a. ferngelenkt (av.).

Remount [rih-maunt'] n. Remonte f; vi. wieder besteigen, wieder aufstellen.

Removable [ri-muh'wAbl] a. entfernbar, absetzbar.

Removal [ri-muh'wAl] n. Beseitigung f, Umzug m, Wegräumen n, Abschub m; **- van** n. Möbelwagen m.

Remove [ri-muhw'] vt. beseitigen, fortschaffen, wegbringen; i. sich entfernen, übersiedeln.

Remunerate [ri-mjuh'nAreit] vt. belohnen, vergüten.

Remuneration [ri-mjuh'nArei'schAn] n. Belohnung f, Honorar n.

Rend [rend] vt. zerreissen.

Render [ren'der] vt. leisten machen, überreichen, erteilen, ablegen (*com.*). [Abtrünnige.

Renegade [re'ni-geid] n. der

Renew [ri-njuh'] vt. erneuern; **-al** n. Erneuerung f.

Rennet [re'nit] n. Lab n.

Rennet [re'nit] n. Renette f (*apple*).

Renounce [ri-nauss'] vt. entsagen, verzichten.

Renovate [re'nA-weit] vt. erneuern, wiederherstellen.

Renovation [re-nA-wei'schAn] n. Erneuerung f, Wiederherstellung f.

Renown [ri-naun'] n. Ruhm m, Ruf m.

Rent [rent] n. Riss m, Spalte f.

Rent [rent] n. Miete f; vt. mieten (*house*).

Renunciation [ri-nAn-ssi-ei'schAn] n. Entsagung f, Verzichtleistung f.

Reoccupy [rih-o'kju-pai] vt. wieder besetzen.

Reopen [rih-oupn'] vt. wieder eröffnen.

Reorganisation [rih-Or-gA-nai-sei'schAn] n. Neugestaltung f.

Reorganize [rih-Or-gA-nais] vt. reorganisieren, neu gestalten. [en.

Repack [rih-pæk'] vt. umpacken

Repair [ri-peh'er] vt. ausbessern, reparieren; n. Ausbesserung f, Reparatur f; **- shop** n. Ausbesserungsanstalt f, Werfthalle f (*nav.*).

Reparation [re-pA-rei'schAn] n. Entschädigung f, Ersatz m; **-s** pl. Reparationen f.pl.

Repartee [re-pahr-tih'] n. schlagende Antwort.

Repast [ripahst'] n. Mahlzeit f.

Repatriat'e [rih-pæ'trjeit] vt. in die Heimat zurückschaffen, abschieben; **-ion** n. Rückführung f (in die Heimat), Abschub m.

Repay [rih-pei'] vt. zurückzahlen, vergelten.

Repeal [ri-pihl'] vt. aufheben; n. Aufhebung f, Widerruf m.

Repeat [ri-piht'] vt. wiederholen; n. Wiederholungszeichen n; **- order** n. Nachbestellung f (*com.*); **-edly** ad. wiederholt; **-er** n. Repetiergewehr f, Repetieruhr n (*rifle*), Verstärker m, Übertrager m.

Repel [ri-pel'] vt. zurückstossen.

Repent [ri-pent'] vt. bereuen; i. Reue empfinden; **-ance** n. Reue f; **-ant** a. reuig.

Repercussion [rih-per-kA

schAn] n. Rückwirkung f, Reperkussion f.

Repertory [re'per-tA-ri] n. Spielplan m; - theatre n. Repertoirbühne f.

Repetition [re-pi-ti'schAn] n. Wiederholung f.

Repine [ri-pain'] vt. murren.

Replace [ri-pleiss'] vt. zurückstellen, ersetzen; -ment n. Ersetzen f; - value n. Ersatzwert m, Wiederbeschaffungswert m.

Replant [rih-plahnt'] vt. umpflanzen.

Replenish [rih-ple'nisch] vt. anfüllen, sich wieder versehen mit.

Replete [rih-pliht'] a. gefüllt.

Replica [re'pli-kA] n. Kopie f, Replik f.

Reply [ri-plai'] n. Erwiderung f; vt.i. erwidern, antworten; - postcard n. Antwortkarte f; - paid telegram n. Telegramm m, mit bezahlter Antwort.

Report [ri-pOrt'] n. Bericht m; vt.i. berichten; -ing centre n. Melde-zentrale f, -stelle f.

Reporter [ri-pOr'ter] n. Berichterstatter m, Reporter m.

Repose [ri-pous'] n. Ruhe f; vi. ruhen, sich verlassen.

Repository [ri-po'si-tA-ri] n. Verwahrungsort m, Warenlager n, Laden m.

Reprehensible [re-pri-hen'ssibl] a. tadelnswert.

Represent [re-pri-sent'] vt. vertreten, darstellen.

Representation [re-pri-sentei'schAn] n. Vertretung f.

Representative [re-pri-sen'tA-tiw] a. repräsentativ, (stell)vertretend, reichhaltig; - government n. Repräsentativverfassung f.

Repress [ri-press'] vt. unterdrücken; -ion n. Unterdrückung f.

Reprieve [ri-prihw'] n. Begnadigung f; vt. begnadigen.

Reprimand [re'pri-mahnd] n. Verweis m; vt. verweisen.

Reprint [rih-print'] n. Neudruck m, Nachdruck m; vt. wieder abdrucken.

Reprisal [ri-prai'sAl] n. Vergeltungs-massregel f -massnahme f, Vergeltung f.

Reproach [ri-proutsch'] n. Vorwurf m; vt. vorwerfen, tadeln. [Verworfene.

Reprobate [re'prA-beit] n. der

Reproduce [rih-prA-djuhss'] vt. wiedergeben, reproduzieren (photo, etc.).

Reproduction [rih-prA-dAk'schAn] n. Wiedergabe f, Vervielfältigung f, Nachdruck m (book), Reproduktion f.

Reproductive [rih-prA-dAk'tiw] a. reproduktiv.

Reproof [ri-pruhf'] n. Verweis m, Rüge f.

Reprove [ri-pruhw'] vt. rügen, tadeln.

Reptile [rep'tail] n. Reptil n, Kriechtier n.

Republic [ri-pAb'lik] n. Republik f, Freistaat m, Volksstaat m; -an a. republikanisch; n. Republikaner m.

Republication [rih-pAb-li-kei'schAn] n. Neuauflage f.

Republish [rih-pAb'lisch] vt. neu auflegen.

Repudiate [ri-pjuh'djeit] vt. nicht anerkennen, verwerfen, verstossen.

Repudiation [ri-pjuh-djei'schAn] n. Zurückweisung f, Nichtanerkennung (debt), Aufkündigung f (treaty).

Repugnance [ri-pAg'nAnss] n. Abneigung f, Widerwille m.

Repugnant [ri-pAg'nAnt] a. abstossend.

Repulse [ri-pAlss'] vt. zurücktreiben, abweisen, zurückwerfen; n. Zurückweisung f, Zurückschlagen n (mil.); -ion n. Abstossung f, -ive a. abstossend, ekelhaft.

Repurchase [rih-pÁr'tschÁss] vt. wiederkaufen; n. Wiederkauf m.

Reputable [re'pju-tÁbl] a. anständig, angesehen, ehrbar.

Reputation [re-pju-tei'schÁn] n. Ruf m, Ruhm m, Ansehen n.

Repute [ri-pjuht'] n. Ruf m; vt. halten für, schätzen; -d a. vermeintlich.

Request [ri-kuest'] n. Gesuch n, Bedarf m, Nachfrage f (com.); vt. ersuchen, bitten.

Require [ri-kuai'er] vt. erfordern, verlangen, brauchen.

Requisite [re'kui-sit] a. erforderlich; n. Erfordernis n, das Notwendige.

Requisition [re-kui-si'schÁn] n. Beitreibung f, Anforderung f; vt. anfordern, beitreiben, beschlagnahmen. [en.

Requite [ri-kuait'] vt. vergelten.

Re-routing [rih-ruh'ting] n. Umleitung f (av.). [lesen.

Reread [rih-rihd'] vt. wieder

Resale [rih-sseil'] n. Wiederverkauf m. [heben.

Rescind [rih-ssind'] vt. aufheben.

Rescript [rih'skript] n. Erlass m.

Rescue [re'skjuh] n. Rettung f; vt. retten, befreien; - party n. Rettungsmannschaft f; -r n. Retter m.

Research [ri-ssÁrtsch'] n. Forschung f, Untersuchung f.

Resell [rih-ssel'] vt. wieder verkaufen.

Resemblance [ri-sem'blÁnss] n. Ähnlichkeit f.

Resemble [ri-sembl'] vt. ähneln, ähnlich sehen.

Resent [ri-sent'] vt. übel aufnehmen; -ful a. grollend; -ment n. Groll m, Unwille m.

Reservation [re-ser-wei'schÁn] n. Vorbehalt m, Reserve f, Reservieren n, Bestellen n.

Reserve [ri-ssÁrw'] vt. aufsparen, vorbehalten belegen (seat),

bestellen (room); n. Reserve f. Zurückhaltung f, Ersatzmann m (football); -s pl. Ersatzmannschaft f (mil.); -d a. zurückhaltend, bestellt, belegt, unabkömmlich (exempt).

Reservist [ri-sÁr'wist] n. Reservist m.

Reservoir [re'ser-wuahr] n. Talsperre f, Stausee m, Reservoir n, Wasserbehälter m.

Reset [rih-sset'] vt. wieder (ein)fassen.

Reshuffle [rih-schÁfl'] n. Umbildung f (cabinet); vt. neu mischen (cards).

Reside [ri-said'] vi. wohnen.

Residence [re'si-dÁnss] n. Wohnung f, Wohn-, Landsitz m.

Resident [re'si-dÁnt] n. Bewohner m, Ministerresident m; a. wohnhaft, ansässig.

Residential [re-si-den'schÁl] a. Wohn ..; - quarter n. Wohnviertel n.

Residue [re'si-djuh] n. Rest m.

Resign [ri-sain'] vt.i. aufgeben abtreten, abdanken; -ed a. ergeben.

Resignation [re-sig-nei'schÁn] n. Abtretung f, Abschied m, Ergebung f.

Resilient [ri-si'ljÁnt] a. abprallend, elastisch.

Resin [re'sin] n. Harz n, Geigenharz n.

Resist [ri-sist'] vt.i. widerstehen, sich widersetzen; -ance n. Widerstand m; - movement n. Widerstandsbewegung f.

Resole [rih-ssoul'] vt. neu besohlen.

Resolute [re'so-luht] a. entschlossen, standhaft.

Resolution [re-so-ljuh'schÁn] n. Entschlossenheit f, Beschluss m, Entschluss m.

Resolve [ri-solw'] vt. auflösen, heben; i. sich entschliessen.

Resonance [re'sÁ-nÁnss] n. Resonanz f, Widerklang m.

Resonator [re'sA-nei-ter] n. Resonator m, Schallbecher m.

Resort [ri-sOrt'] vi. Zuflucht nehmen zu; n. Versammlungsort m; holiday - n. Badeort m.

Resound [ri-saund'] vi. widerhallen.

Resource [ri-ssOrss'] n. Hilfsquelle f, Auskunftsmittel, n; Findigkeit f; -s pl. Geldmittel n.pl; -ful a. findig, praktisch.

Respect [ri-spekt'] n. Rücksicht f, Achtung f; vt. achten, berücksichtigen; **in all -s** in jeder Hinsicht.

Respectability [ri-spek-tA-bi'li-ti] n. Anständigkeit f, Redlichkeit f, Achtbarkeit f.

Respectable [ri-spek'tAbl] a. anständig, achtbar.

Respectful [ri-spekt'ful] a. -ly ad. ehrerbietig.

Respecting [ri-spek'ting] pr. hinsichtlich.

Respective [ri-spek'tiw] a. betreffend, besonder; -ly ad. beziehungsweise.

Respiration [re-spi-rei'schAn] n. Atmen n.

Respirator [re'spi-rei-ter] n. Respirator m, Gasmaske f.

Respite [re'spit] n. Frist f.

Resplendent [ri-splen'dAnt] a. prächtig.

Respond [ri-spond'] vi. antworten, entgegenkommen.

Response [ri-sponss'] n. Antwort f, Erwiderung f.

Responsibility [ri-spon-si-bi'li-ti] n. Verantwortlichkeit f.

Responsible [ri-spon'sibl] a. verantwortlich.

Responsive [ri-spon'siw] a. empfänglich, entgegenkommend.

Rest [rest] n. Ruhe f, Stütze f; vi. ruhen, sich stützen.

Rest [rest] n. Rest m.

Restaurant [re'stA-rong] n. Speisehaus n, Restaurant n; - car n. Speisewagen m; - keeper n. Gastwirt m, Restaurateur m.

Restful [rest'ful] a. ruhig.

Restitution [re-sti-tjuh'schAn] n. Wiederherstellung f, Ersatz m, Rückgabe f.

Restive [re'stiw] a. störrisch.

Restless [rest'less] a, -ly ad. ruhelos.

Restock [rih-stok'] vt. wieder versehen, neu versorgen.

Restoration [re-stA-rei'schAn] n. Wiederherstellung f, Restauration f.

Restorative [ri-stO'rA-tiw] a. Belebungsmittel n.

Restore [ri-stOr'] vt. wiederherstellen, wiedererstatten.

Restrain [ri-strein'] vt. zurückhalten, abhalten, hindern; -t n. Zurückhaltung f.

Restrict [ri-strikt'] vt. einschränken, hemmen.

Restriction [ri-strik'schAn] n. Einschränkung f, Vorbehalt m, Hindernis n.

Restrictive [ri-strik'tiw] a. einschränkend.

Result [ri-sAlt'] n. Ergebnis n, Resultat n, Folge f, Ausgang m; vi. entstehen, zur Folge haben.

Resume [ris-juhm'] vt. wieder aufnehmen, zurücknehmen, kurz zusammenfassen (summarize).

Resumption [ris-Amp'schAn] n. Wiederaufnahme f.

Resurrect [re-sA-rekt'] vt. ausgraben, beleben; -ion n. Auferstehung f, erneuern.

Resuscitate [ri-ssA'ssi-teit] vt. wiederbeleben.

Retail [rih'teil] n. Kleinhandel m, Ladenverkauf m; a. Klein . . . . Detail . . .; - price n. Ladenpreis m; - trade n. Kleinhandel m, Detailgeschäft n.

Retail [ri-teil'] vt im kleinen verkaufen; -er n. Kleinhändler m, Detaillist m.

Retain [ri-tein'] vt. behalten, zurückbehalten; -er n. der Bediente, Vorschuss m, Honorar n (law).

Retaliate [ri-tæ'ljeit] vi. wieder vergelten.

Retaliation [ri-tæ-ljei'schAn] n. Vergeltung f.

Retaliatory [ri-tæ-ljei'tA-ri] a. Vergeltungs . . . .

Retard [ri-tahrd'] vt. verspäten, hemmen, verzögern; -ed ignition n. Spätzündung f.

Retardation [ri-tahr-dei'schAn] n. Verzögerung f.

Retch [retsch] vi. würgen.

Retell [rih-tel'] vt. wieder erzählen.   [Beibehaltung f.

Retention [ri-ten'schAn] n.

Retentive [ri-ten'tiv] a. leicht behaltend.

Reticence [re'ti-sAnss] n. Verschwiegenheit f.   [schweigen.

Reticent [re'ti-sAnt] a. ver-

Reticule [re'ti-kjuhl] n. Damenhandtasche f, Strickbeutel m.

Retina [re'ti-nA] n. Netzhaut f.

Retinue [re'ti-njuh] n. Gefolge n.

Retire [ri-tai'er] vi. sich zurückziehen; t. zurückziehen, verabschieden; -d a. zurückgezogen, pensioniert, ausser Dienst.

Retirement [ri-tai'er-mAnt] n. Sichzurückziehen, Privatleben n, Ruhestand m.

Retiring [ri-tai'ring] a. zurückhaltend, schüchtern.

Retort [ri-tOrt'] vi. erwidern; n. Erwiderung f, Retorte f, Destillierkolben m (tec.).

Retouch [ri-tAtsch'] vt. retuschieren, überarbeiten.

Retrace [ri-treiss'] vt. zurückverfolgen.

Retract [ri-trækt'] vt. zurücknehmen, widerrufen; -able a. einziehbar (av.).

Retraining [rih-trei'ning] n. Umschulung f.

Retreat [ri-triht'] n. Rückzug m; vi. sich zurückziehen, zurückgehen.

Retrench [ri-trensch'] vt. einschränken, verkürzen; -ment

n. Einschränkung f, Ersparnis n.

Retribution [re-tri-bjuh'-schAn] n. Vergeltung f.

Retrieve [ri-trihw'] vt. wiederauffinden; -r n. Retriever m.

Retroactive [re-trou-æk'tiw] a. rückwirkend.

Retrograde [re'trA-greid] a. rückgängig, rückständig.

Retrogression [re-trA-gre'schAn] n. Rückwärtsgehen n, Rückgang m.

Retrospect [re'trA-spekt] n. Rückblick m.

Retrospective [re-trA-spek'tiw] a. rückwirkend, zurückblickend.

Return [ri-tArn'] n. Rückkehr f, Rückgabe f, Bericht m (report), Umsatz m (sale); vi. zurückkehren; t. zurück-geben, -senden; - flight n. Rückflug m (av.); - form n. Rückgabeschein m; - journey n. Rückreise f; - match n. Revanchepartie f; - permit n. Rückkehrschein m; - ticket n. Rückfahrkarte f.

Returnable [ri-tArn'Abl] a. rückerstattbar (com.).

Reunion [rih-juh'njAn] n. Wiedervereinigung f, Gesellschaft f.

Reunite [rih-juh-nait'] vt.i. (sich) wiedervereinigen.

Revaluation [rih-wæ-lju-ei'schAn] n. nochmalige Schätzung, Aufwertung f.

Revalue [rih-wæ'ljuh] vt. nochmals schätzen, umwerten.

Reveal [ri-wihl'] vt. offenbaren, enthüllen.   [f (mil.).

Reveille [ri-wæ'li] n. Reveille

Revel [rewl] n. Gelage n; vi. schwelgen in.

Revelation [re-wi-lei'schAn] n. Offenbarung f, Entdeckung f.

Revenge [ri-wendzh'] n. Rache f; v.r. (sich) rächen; -ful a. rachsüchtig.

Revenue [re'win-juh] n. Einkünfte f.pl, Einnahmen f.pl, Zölle m.pl; - officer n. Zollbeamte(r) m.

Reverberate [ri-wʌr'bʌ-reit] vi. widerhallen.

Revere [ri-wih'er] vt. verehren.

Reveren'ce [rew'rʌnss] n. Ehrfurcht f; vt. verehren; -d a. ehrwürdig, Hochwürden; -t a. ehrfurchtsvoll.

Reversal [ri-wʌr'ssAl] n. Umstossung f, Umsteuerung f (tec.).

Reverse [ri-wʌrss] n. Rückseite f, Gegenteil n (opposite), Missgeschick n (mishap), Schlappe f, Niederlage f (mil.); vt. umstossen, umkehren, umsteuern (tec.), wenden (aut.).

Reversible [ri-wʌr'ssibl] a. umstellbar, umkehrbar, umsteuerbar (tec.).

Reversing-gear [ri-wʌr'ssing-gih'er] n. Umsteuerung f.

Reversion [ri-wʌr'schAn] n. Umkehrung f, Rückschlag m, Anwartschaft f, Heimfall m (law).

Revert [ri-wʌrt] vi. zurückkommen, heimfallen (law).

Revet [ri-wet] vt. verkleiden, verschalen, -ment n. Verkleidung f.

Review [ri-wjuh'] vt. mustern, besichtigen, durchsehen, besprechen (book), rezensieren; n. Untersuchung f, Durchsicht f, Besprechung f, Truppenschau f, Musterung f (mil.); -er n. Rezensent m.

Revile [ri-wail'] vt. schmähen.

Revise [ri-wais'] vt. prüfen, revidieren, kontrollieren, verbessern.

Revision [ri-wi'zhʌn] n. Revision f, Durchsicht f, Prüfung f.

Revisit [rih-wi'sit] vt. wiederbesuchen.

Revival [ri-wai'wʌl] n. Wiederbelebung f, Erneuerung f, Aufleben n.

Revive [ri-waiw'] vt. neu beleben, wieder auffrischen; i. wieder aufleben, wieder aufblühen.

Revivify [rih-wi'wi-fai] vt. wieder beleben.

Revocation [re-wA-kei'schAn] n. Aufhebung f, Widerruf m.

Revoke [ri-wouk'] vt. zurücknehmen, umstossen, aufheben; i. falsch beigeben (cards).

Revolt [ri-woult'] n. Empörung f, Aufruhr m, Revolte f; vi. sich empören.

Revolution [re-wA-ljuh'schAn] n. Umdrehung f, Umwälzung f, Revolution f; -ary a. umwälzend, epochemachend, revolutionär; n. Umstürzler m, Revolutionär m; -ize vt. umgestalten, umwälzen, neu gestalten.

Revolve [ri-wolw'] vi.t. (sich) umdrehen, umlaufen.

Revolving [ri-wol'wing] a. drehbar; - door n. Drehtür f; - light n. Drehfeuer n (nav.), Drehscheinwerfer m (av.); - stage n. Drehbühne f; - stool n. Dreh-stuhl m, -schemel m; - turret n. Drehturm m (mil.); - ventilator n. Flettnerlüfter m (aut.).

Revolver [ri-wol'wer] n. Revolver m.

Revulsion [ri-wʌl'schAn] n. Umschlag m, Umschwung m.

Reward [ri-uArd'] n. Belohnung f; vt. belohnen.

Rewrite [rih-rait'] vt. nochmals schreiben.

Rhapsody [ræp'ssA-di] n. Rhapsodie f.

Rheostat [rih'A-stæt] n. Anlasswiderstand m (el.).

Rhetoric [re'tA-rik] n. Rhetorik f, Redekunst f.

Rhetorical [ri-to'rikl] a. rhetorisch, schönrednerisch.

Rheumatism [ruh'mA-tism] n. Rheumatismus m.

Rhododendron [rou-dA-den'drAn] n. Rhododendron n.

Rhubarb [ruh'barb] n. Rhabarber m.

Rhyme [raim] n. Reim m; vt. i. reimen. [mus m.

Rhythm [ridhm] n. Rhythmus m.

Rhythmical [ridh'mikl] a. taktmässig, rhythmisch.

Rib [rib] n. Rippe f, Spante f, Schiffsrippe f; vt. rippen.

Ribald [ri'bAld] a. liederlich.

Ribband [ri'bAnd] n. Sente f, Rödelbalken m (mil.).

Ribbon [ri'bAn] n. Band n; -s pl. Fetzen m.pl; typewriter - n. Farbband m.pl; -building n. bandförmige Bebauung; -ed a. bebändert.

Rice [raiss] n. Reis m; - paper n. Reispapier n.

Rich [ritsch] a. reich, reichhaltig, ergiebig, fett, kräftig (food); -es n.pl. Reichtum m; -ly ad. reichlich, voll, völlig; -ness n. Reichhaltigkeit f, Nahrhaftigkeit f, Reichtum m.

Rick [rik] n. Schober m.

Rickets [ri'kitss] n.pl. englische Krankheit, Rachitis f.

Rickety [ri'ki ti] a. baufällig, schwach, gebrechlich.

Ricochet [ri'kA-schei] vi. abprallen; n. Abprall m, Prellschuss m.

Rid [rid] vt. losmachen, befreien; a. frei, los; get - of vt. los werden.

Riddance [ri'dAnss] n. Befreiung f, Loswerden n.

Riddle [ridl] n. Rätsel n.

Riddle [ridl] n. grobes Sieb, Rätter m (coal), Durchwurf m; vt. sieben, durchsieben (with shots). [chert.

Riddled [ri'dAld] a. durchlöchert.

Ride [raid] vi./i. reiten, bereiten, fahren, treiben; n. Ritt m, Fahrt f; - at anchor vor Anker liegen (nav.).

Rider [rai'der] n. Reiter m, Zusatz m (addition).

Ridge [ridzh] n. Rücken m, Kamm m, Erhöhung f, Rain

m (field), Dachspitze f, First m (roof); vt. furchen.

Ridicule [ri'di-kjuhl] n. Spott m; vt. verspotten, ins Lächerliche ziehen. [lächerlich.

Ridiculous [ri-di'kju-lAss] a.

Riding [rai'ding] n. Reiten n, Radfahren n (cycle); - -boots n.pl. Reitstiefel m; --breeches n.pl. Reithose f; - -habit n. Reitkleid n; - horse n. Reit-Sattel-pferd n; - -school n. Reitschule f; - -whip n. Reitgerte f.

Rife [raif] a. reichlich vorhanden, vorherrschend.

Riff-raff [rif'reef] n. Gesindel n, Auswurf m. [rauben.

Rifle [raifl] vt. plündern, be-

Rifle [raifl] vt. riefen, riffeln, ziehen (barrel); n. Gewehr n; --barrel m (gezogener) Gewehrlauf; - -butt n. Gewehrkolben m, Kugelfang m; - -range n. Schiess-stand m, Schützenstand m; - regiment n. Jägerregiment n. [Schütze m.

Rifleman [raifl'mAn] n.

Rift [rift] n. Ritze f, Spalt f.

Rig [rig] vt. auftakeln n. Takelung f; - -ger n. Monteur m, Rüster m (tec.); -ging n. Takelwerk n.

Right [rait] a. recht, richtig; ad. gerade, rechts; n. Recht n, rechte Seite, Rechte f; vt. in Ordnung bringen; r. sich aufrichten (nav.).

Righteous [rai'tschAss] a. rechtschaffen.

Rightful [rait'ful] a. recht, rechtmässig.

Right-hand [rait'hænd] n. rechte Hand; a. rechts gelegen, rechtsläufig (tec.).

Rightly [rait'li] ad. mit Recht.

Rightness [rait'ness] n. Richtigkeit f.

Rigid [ri'dzgid] a. -ly ad. starr, steif, hart, unbeugsam.

Rigidity [ri-dzhi'di-ti] n. Starrheit f, Steifheit f.

Rigmarole [rig'mA-roul] n. Geschwätz m.

Rigorous [ri'gA-rAss] a., **-ly** ad. streng, scharf, genau.

Rigour [ri'gér] n. Härte f. Strenge f.

Rim [rim] n. Rand m, Krempe f; **-brake** n. Felgenbremse f; **-less** a. randlos.

Rime [raim] n. Reim m.

Rind [raind] n. Rinde f, Speckschwarte f (bacon).

Ring [ring] n. Ring m, Kreis m, Dichtungsring m (tec.), Kartell n (com.); **-road** n. Ringstrasse f.

Ring [ring] vi. läuten, klingen; t. läuten, anklingeln, anrufen (ph.); **-off** abhängen; **-up** anklingeln.   [locke f.

Ringlet [ring'lit] n. Haarlocke f.

Rink [ringk] n. Eisbahn f.

Rinse [rinss] vt. spülen.

Riot [rai'At] n. Aufruhr m, Auflauf m; vi. schwelgen, lärmen, Ausschreitungen machen, toben; **-er** n. Aufrührer m; **-ous** aufrührerisch, lärmend.

Rip [rip] vt. aufschlitzen, zerreissen; **-cord** n. Abreissschnur f (av.).

Riparian [rai-peh'rjAn] a. am Ufer gelegen.

Ripe [raip] a. reif; **-n** vi. reif werden; **-ness** n. Reife f, Reifsein n.   [n. kleine Welle.

Ripple [ripl] vi. sich kräuseln;

Rip-saw [rip'ssO] n. Kerb-Schrot-säge f.

Rise [rais] vi. aufstehen, steigen, aufgehen, zunehmen, entspringen, sich erheben; n. Steigen n, Aufgang m, Erhöhung f, Aufstieg m, Anstieg m (plane).

Rising [rai'sing] a. steigend, heranwachsend; n. Aufstand m, Empörung f; **-ground** n. Hügel m, Erhöhung f.

Risk [risk] n. Gefahr f, Risiko n; vt. wagen, riskieren, aufs Spiel setzen; **-y** a. gewagt, gefahrvoll.

Rissole [ri'ssoul] n. Fisch-Fleisch-klösschen n.

Rite [rait] n. Ritus m, Brauch m.

Ritual [ri'tju-Al] a. feierlich, rituell.

Rival [rai'wAl] n. Nebenbuhler m, Konkurrent m; a. nebenbuhlerisch, Konkurrenz ...; vt. wetteifern mit, rivalisieren, konkurrieren (compete); **-ry** n. Nebenbuhlerei f, Konkurrenz f.

River [ri'wer] n. Fluss m, Strom m; **-bed** n. Flussbett n; **-channel** n. Fahrwasser n; **-side** n. Flussufer n; a. am Fluss gelegen.

Rivet [ri'wit] n. Niet n; vt. nieten, befestigen; **-er** n. Nieter m, Nietmaschine f; **-ing** n. Vernieten n; **-ing hammer** n. Niethammer m.

Road [roud] n. Strasse f, Weg m; **-block** n. Strassensperre f; **-bridge** n. Strassen-brücke f, -überführung f; **-construction** n. Strassenbau m; **-hog** n. Kilometerfresser m, Strassenschreck m; **-mender** n. Steinklopfer m, Wegarbeiter m; **-metal** n. Schotter m, Steinschlag m; **-way** n. Fahrweg m, Landstrasse f.

Roadstead [roud'sted] n. Reede f, Ankerplatz m.

Roadster [roud'ster] n. Tourenrad m (cycle), offener Zweisitzer (aut.).

Roam [roum] vi. umherstreifen; t. durchstreifen.

Roan [roun] n. Rotschimmel m.

Roar [rOr] vi. Gebrüll n; vi. brüllen; **-ing** a. brüllend, ungeheuer, kolossal, toll.

Roast [roust] vt. braten; n. Braten m; **-beef** n. Rinderbraten m; **-mutton** n. Hammelbraten m.

Rob [rob] vt. berauben.

Robber [ro'ber] n. Räuber m.

Robbery [ro'bA-ri] n. Raub m, Räuberei f.

Robe [roub] n. Kleid n.

Robin [ro'bin] n. Rotkelchen n.

Robot [rou'bot] n. Maschinenmensch m.

Robust [ro-bAst'] a. kräftig, derb, rüstig; -ness n. Kraft f. Derbheit f.

Rock [rok] n. Fels m.

Rock [rok] vi.t. schaukeln; -climbing n. Felsklettern n.

Rock-bottom [rok'botm] n. Urboden m; - price n. allerniedrigster Preis.

Rock-drill [rok'dril] n. Gesteinbohrmaschine f.

Rocker [ro'ker] n. Kufe f. Schwingtrog m (mining).

Rockery [ro'kA-ri] n. Steingarten m, Felsengärtchen n.

Rocket [ro'kit] n. Rakete f; vi. aufschiessen, plötzlich steigen (prices, etc.); -attachment n. Raketensatz m; - bomb n. Vergeltungswaffe f; - car n. Raketenwagen m (aut.); -plane n. Raketenflugzeug n; -propulsion n. Raketenantrieb m.

Rocking [ro'king] n. -chair n. Schaukelstuhl m; - horse n. Schaukelpferd n. [ig.

Rocky [ro'ki] a. felsig, wackelig.

Rococo [ro-kou'kou] n. Rokoko n, Zopfstil m.

Rod [rod] n. Rute f, Stange f. Massrute f (5 Meter). [tier n.

Rodent [rou'dAnt] n. Nagetier n.

Roe [rou] n. Fischrogen m.

Roe [rou] n. Reh n.

Rogu'e [roug] n. Schurke m, Schelm m, Spitzbube m; -ery n. Spitzbüberei f; -ish a, -ishly ad. schelmisch.

Roistering [reu'stA-ring] a. lärmend.

Roll [roul] n. Rolle f, Wälzen n, Semmel f, Liste f. Verzeichnis n; vt.i. (sich) wälzen, rollen, drehen, schlingern (ship); -call n. Appell m; - film n. Rollfilm m; - of honour n. Ehrentafel f; -top desk n. Rollpult n.

Roller [rou'ler] n. Rolle f. Walze f. Strassenwalze f; -bearing n. Roll-lager n; - blind n. Rollvorhang m; -skate n. Rollschuh m; - towel n. Rollhandtuch n. [gelassen.

Rollicking [ro'li-king] a. ausgelassen.

Rolling [rou'ling] a. - mill n. Walzwerk n; -pin n. Rollholz n; - stock n. Roll-, Betriebs-material n.

Romance [rou-mænss'] n. Roman m, das Romanische; vi. aufschneiden, erfinden.

Romantic [rA-mæn'tik] a. romantisch.

Romp [romp] vi. herumspielen, sich umhertummeln.

Rompers [rom'pers] n.pl. Sporthöschen n.pl, Spielanzug m.

Roof [ruhf] n. Dach n. bedachen; - aerial n. Dachantenne f.

Roofing [ruh'fing] n. Bedachung f, Deckmaterialien n.pl; -felt n. Dachpappe f; - tile n. Dachziegel m.

Rook [ruk] n. Saatkrähe f; vt. betrügen, prellen.

Rook [ruk] n. Turm m (chess).

Room [ruhm] n. Zimmer n, Raum m, Platz m; -y a. geräumig.

Roost [ruhst] n. Schlafsitz m; vi. auf der Stange sitzen, aufsitzen, schlafen.

Rooster [ruh'ster] n. Haushahn m.

Root [ruht] n. Wurzel f, Quelle f. Grund m; vt. einwurzeln; -crops n.pl. Hackfrüchte f.pl, Rüben f.pl.

Root [ruht] vt.i. (auf)wühlen, ausjäten, ausgraben; -ed a. eingewurzelt.

Rope [roup] n. Seil n, Strick m, Schnur f; vt. verschnüren; -yard n. Seilerbahn f.

Rosary [rou'sA-ri] n. Rosenkranz m.

Rose [rous] n. Rose f; - bush

- -tree n. Rosen-strauch m,
-stock m. [knopf m.
Rosebud [rous'bAd] n. Rosen-
Rosette [rou-set'] n. Rosette f.
Rosewood [rous'uud] n.
Rosen-, Palisander-holz n.
Rosin [ro'sin] n. Geigenharz n.
Roster [ro'ster] n. Dienstplan
m, Kompanieliste f, Kom-
mandierrolle f (mil.).
Rostrum [ro'strAm] n. Red-
nerbühne f, Rednerpult n.
Rosy [rou'si] a. rosig.
Rot [rot] n. Fäulnis f, Unsinn
m; vi. verfaulen.
Rota [rou'tA] n. Liste f, Ver-
zeichnis n.
Rotary [rou'tA-ri] a. sich dre-
hend; - club n. Rotaryklub m;
- press n. Rotationsmaschine f;
- ventilator n. Flettnerlüfter m
(aut.). [hen, wechseln.
Rotate [rou-teit'] vi. sich dre-
Rotation [rou-tei'schAn] n.
Achsendrehung f, Umlauf m,
Wechsel m, Reihe f.
Rote [rout] n. Routine f; by -
auswendig.
Rotor [rou'ter] n. Rotor m,
Läufer m, Laufrad n (jet-plane).
Rotten [rotn] a. faul, schlecht,
niederträchtig, gemein; -ness
n. Fäulnis f, Schlechtigkeit f.
Rotter [ro'ter] n. Schurke m,
gemeiner Kerl.
Rotund [rou-tAnd'] a. rund.
Rouge [ruhsh] n. Rot n, Rot-
Schminke f; vt. schminken.
Rough [rAf] a. rauh, uneben,
ungeschliffen, wild, roh; n. das
Rauhe, Lümmel m, Flegel m;
vt. roh behauen; - it i. Strapaz-
en ertragen; - draft n. erster
Entwurf; - estimate n. Über-
schlag m (com.).
Roughage [rA'fidzh] n. Grob-
stoffe m.pl.
Rough-cast [rAf'kahst] n.
Rohputz m.
Roughen [rAfn] vt. rauhen.
Roughly [rAf'li] ad. ungefähr,
roh.

Roughness [rAf'ness] n. Rauheit f, Ungeschliffenheit f.
Round [raund] a. rund; ad.
rund herum; - n. Runde f, Schuss m, Salve f (mil.), Patrone f
(rifle); vt. runden.
Roundabout [raund'A-baut]
n. Karussel n; a. indirekt.
Roundel [raundl] n. Schnee-
reifen m.
Roundsman [raunds'mAn] n.
Milchmann m, Austräger m.
Round-up [raund-Ap'] n. Zu-
sammentreiben n; vt. umzingeln, einschliessen.
Rouse [raus] vt. erwecken, erregen, hervorrufen.
Rout [raut] n. unordentliche
Flucht; vt. in die Flucht
schlagen.
Route [ruht] n. Weg m, Route
f; vt. leiten; - lighting n.
Streckenbeleuchtung f (av.); -
march n. Reise-, Übungs-
marsch m.
Routine [ruh-tihn'] n. ge-
wohnheitsmässiger Lauf, Routine f; - duties n.pl. Innen-
dienst m; - work n. laufende
Arbeiten f.pl.
Rov'e [rouv] vi. umherschwei-
fen; -ing sentry n. Streifposten
m (mil.).
Rover [rou'wer] n. Wanderer
m, Seeräuber m, Pfadfinder m
(scout).
Row [rau] n. Lärm m, Radau
m, Spektakel m, Krach m.
Row [rou] n. Reihe f.
Row [rou] vi.t. rudern; n. Rud-
erfahrt f; -ing-boat n. Ruder-
boot n. [gabel f.
Rowlock [ro'lAk] n. Ruder-
Royal [reu'Al] a. königlich;
-ism n. Königstreue f, Royal-
ismus m; -ist n. Royalist m,
Königlichgesinnte(r); -ty n.
Königtum n, Ertragsanteil m,
Tantieme f.
Rub [rAb] vt. reiben.
Rubber [rA'ber] n. Gummi m,
Radiergummi n; - dinghy n.

Schlauchboot n; - overshoe n.
Gummischuh m; - tyre n.
Gummireifen m; - stamp n.
Gummistempel m.

Rubbing [rA'bing] n. Abreibung f, Reiben n.

Rubbish [rA'bisch] n. Schutt m, Kehricht m, Schund m, Unsinn m.

Rubble [rAbl] n. Bruchstein m, Steinschutt m, Geröll n.

Ruby [ruh'bi] n. Rubin m.

Rudder [rA'der] n. Steuerruder n, Steuer n, Seitensteuer n, -ruder n (av.).

Ruddy [rA'di] a. rötlich.

Rude [ruhd] a, -ly ad. rauh, roh, grob, ungebildet, unhöflich; -ness n. Unhöflichkeit f, Rohheit f.

Rudimentary [ruh-di-men'tA-ri] a. Anfangs ..

Rudiments [ruh'di-mAntss] n.pl. Anfangsgründe m.pl.

Rue [ruh] vt. bereuen.

Ruff [rAf] n. Krause f.

Ruffian [rAf'jAn] n. Raufbold m.

Ruffle [rAfl] n. Krause f, Busenstreif n; vt. kräuseln, falten, aufregen.

Rug [rAg] n. Reisedecke f, Bettvorleger m.

Rugged [rA'gid] a. rauh, zackig.

Ruin [ruh'in] n. Verfall m, Ruine f, Trümmer pl; vt. zugrunderichten; -ous a. baufällig, verderblich, gefährlich.

Rule [ruhl] n. Regel f, Lineal n, Richtscheid n; vt. linieren, regieren; t. herrschen.

Ruler [ruh'ler] n. Herrscher m, Lineal n.

Ruling [ruh'ling] n. Linieren n, Entscheidung f, Verfügung f.

Rum [rAm] n. Rum m.

Rumble [rAmbl] vi. rumpeln.

Ruminate [ruh'mi-neit] vi. grübeln, wiederkäuen.

Rummage [rA'midzh] vi. stöbern; [n; vt. ausspengen.

Rumour [ruh'mer] n. Gerücht

Rump [rAmp] n. Steiss m, Schwanzstück n; - steak n. Rumpstück m.

Rumple [rAmpl] vt. runzeln, zerdrücken, zerknittern.

Run [rAn] vi. laufen, rennen; t. laufen, rennen, gehen lassen; t. Lauf m, Fahrt f, Gang m, Verlauf m, Absatz m, Zulauf m (com.).

Rung [rAng] n. Sprosse f.

Runner [rA'ner] n. Meldegänger m, Läufer m, Kufe f (sledge); - bean n. Stangenbohne f.

Running [rA'ning] n. Laufen n, Betrieb n; - commentary n. Hörbericht m, Reportage f (rad.).

Runway [rAn'uei] n. Startbahn f, Landebahn f (av.); - lighting n. Befeuerung f (av.).

Rupee [ruh-pih'] n. Rupie f.

Rupture [rAp'tscher] n. Bruch m, Abbruch m; t. brechen, abbrechen; -d a. brüchig.

Rural [ruh'rAl] a. ländlich; -police n. Gendarmerie f; -population n. Landbevölkerung f.

Ruse [ruhs] n. Kriegslist f.

Rush [rAsch] n. Binse f; -bottomed chair n. Binsenstuhl m.

Rush [rAsch] n. Stürzen n, Andrang m, Stossen n; vt. stürzen, drängen, jagen, hetzen, erstürmen (mil.); - hours n.pl. Hauptverkehrsstunden f.pl.

Rusk [rAsk] n. Zwieback m.

Russet [rA'ssit] n. Braunrot n, Rötling m; a. braunrot.

Rust [rAst] n. Rost m; vi. rosten; t. rostig machen; -iness n. Rostigkeit f, Mangel an Übung n.

Rustle [rAssl] vi. rascheln.

Rustless [rAst'less] a. rostfrei. [der Übung.

Rusty [rA'sti] a. rostig, aus

Rut [rAt] n. Geleise n, Radspur f.

Ruthless [ruhth'less] *a.* erbarmungslos; **-ness** *n.* Grausamkeit *f.*

Rye [rai] *n.* Roggen *m;* **– bread** *n.* Roggenbrot *n.*

S

Sabbath [sæe'bAth] *n.* Sabbat *m.*

Sable [sseibl] *n.* Zobel *m.*

Sabotage [sse'bA-tahzh] *n.* böswillige Zerstörung, Sabotage *f; vt.* zerstören, sabotieren.

Sabre [ssei'ber] *n.* Säbel *m,* Degen *m.* [Sacharin *n.*

Saccharine [sse'kA-rihn] *n.*

Sack [ssæk] *n.* Sack *m,* Laufpass *m,* Entlassung *f; vt.* entlassen; **– coat** *n.* Jakettanzug *m;* **-cloth** *n.* Sackleinwand *f;* **-ing** *n. see* sackcloth.

Sacrament [sse'krA-mAnt] *n.* Sakrament *n,* Gnadenmittel *n.*

Sacred [ssei'krid] *a.* heilig.

Sacrifice [sse'kri-faiss] *n.* Aufopferung *f,* Verlust *m,* Opfer *n; vt.i.* opfern.

Sacrilege [sse'kri-lidzh] *n.* Entweihung *f.*

Sacristan [sse'kri-stAn] *n.* Kirchendiener *m.*

Sad [sæd] *a.* **-ly** *ad.* traurig, kläglich, arg; **-den** *vt.* betrüben.

Saddle [ssædl] *n.* Sattel *m; vt.* satteln; **– with** aufhalsen; **-bag** *n.* Satteltasche *f;* **– horse** *n.* Sattelpferd *n.*

Saddler [sæd'ler] *n.* Sattler *m.*

Saddlery [ssæd'lA-ri] *n.* Sattlerei *f,* Sattelzeug *n.*

Sadism [ssah'dism] *n.* Sadismus *m.* [tisch.

Sadistic [ssA-di'stik] *a.* sadis-

Sadness [ssæd'ness] *n.* Traurigkeit *f.*

Safe [sseif] *a.* **-ly** *ad.* sicher, gesichert, unbeschädigt, wohlbehalten (*arrival*), glatt (*landing*); *n.* Geldschrank *m;* **–**

conduct *n.* Schutzbrief *m,* freies Geleit; **– keeping** *n.* (sichere) Aufbewahrung *f;* **-room** *n.* Stahlkammer *f.*

Safeguard [sseif'gahrd] *n.* Schutz *m,* Schutzmittel *n; vt.* schützen, sicherstellen, wahren.

Safety [sseif'ti] *n.* Sicherheit *f;* **– bicycle** *n.* Fahrrad *n;* **– brake** *n.* Handbremse *f* (*rl.*); **– cap** *n.* Sicherungsklappe *f* (*grenade*); **-catch** *n.* Sicherung *f* (*rifle*), Sicherungsflügel *m* (*tec.*); **– device** *n.* Schutzvorrichtung *f,* Sicherung *f;* **-fuse** Zeitschnur *f* (*mil.*), Sicherung *f* (*el.*); **– glass** *n.* Sicherheitsglas *n* (*aut.*); **– lamp** *n.* Gruben-Sicherheits-lampe *f;* **-lock** *n.* Sicherheitsschloss *n;* **-match** *n.* Streichholz *n;* **– pin** *n.* Sicherheitsnadel *f;* **– razor** *n.* Rasierapparat *m;* **-valve** *n.* Sicherheitsventil *n.*

Saffron [ssæf'rAn] *n.* echter Safran; *a.* safrangelb.

Sag [sseg] *vt.i.* niederhängen, sacken, sinken (*com.*).

Sagacious [ssA-gei'schAss] *a.* scharfsinnig, klug.

Sagacity [ssA-gæ'ssi-ti] *n.* Scharfsinn *m,* Klugheit *f.*

Sage [sseidzh] *n.* Salbei *f.*

Sago [ssei'gou] *n.* Sago *m.*

Sail [sseil] *n.* Segel *n,* Fahrt *f; vt.i.* segeln, fahren, reisen; **-cloth** *n.* Segeltuch *n,* Segelleinen *n;* **-er** *n.* Segelschiff *n,* Segler *m.*

Sailing [ssei'ling] *n.* Segeln *n,* Fahren *n,* Segelsport *m;* **– ship** *n.* Segelschiff *n;* **– vessel** *n.* Segelschiff *n;* **– trim** *n.* Segelbereitschaft *f.*

Sailor [ssei'ler] *n.* Matrose *m,* Seemann *m;* **– hat** *n.* Matrosenhut *m;* **– suit** *n.* Matrosenanzug *m.*

Sail-plane [sseil'plein] *n.* Segler *m,* Segelflugzeug *n* (*av.*).

Saint [sseint] *n.* der, die Heilige; **-ly** *a.* heilig, fromm.

Sake [sseik] n. Ursache f; for the – of um willen; for my – um meinetwillen.

Sal ammoniac [ssæl-A-mou'njæk]. Salmiak m. [lich.

Salable [ssei'lAbl] a. verkäuf-

Salacious [ssA-lei'schAss] a. geil, wollüstig.

Salad [ssæ'lAd] n. Salat m; – -dressing n. Salattunke f; – -oil n. Salatöl n, Olivenöl n.

Salaried [ssæ'lA-rid] a. bezahlt, besoldet.

Salary [ssæ'lA-ri] n. Gehalt n, Besoldung f; – -earner n. Gehaltsempfänger m, Angestellte(r) m.

Sale [sseil] n. Verkauf m, Absatz m, Ausverkauf m; auction – Versteigerung f, Auktion f; – price n. Verkaufspreis m; – -room n. Verkaufsraum m, Auktionslokal n.

Salesman [sseils'mAn] n. Verkäufer m; -ship n. Geschäftstüchtigkeit f, Verkaufskunst f.

Saleswoman [sseils'uu-mAn] n. Verkäuferin f.

Salient [ssei'ljAnt] a. bemerkenswert, hervorragend; n. vorspringender Winkel, Vorsprung m, Frontvorsprung m (mil.).

Saline [ssei'lain] a. salzhaltig, Salz . . .; n. Saline f, Salzquelle f.

Saliva [ssA-lai'wA] n. Speichel m; – -ejector n. Speichel-saug-er m, -röhre f.

Sallow [ssæ'lou] a. gelblich.

Sally [ssæ'li] n. Ausfall m, witziger Einfall; – forth vi. hervorbrechen.

Salmon [ssæ'mAn] n. Lachs m; – trout n. Lachsforelle f.

Saloon [ssA-luhn'] n. Salon m, Gesellschaftssaal m, erste Klasse (ship). Wirtschaft f, Kneipe f; – car n. Luxuswagen n, Luxuswagen m, Limousine f; – carriage n. Salonwagen m (rl.); – deck n. Oberdeck n;

– passenger n. Passagier m, erster Klasse.

Salt [ssOlt] n. Salz n; a. salzig; vt. salzen; – -cellar n. Salzfässchen n; – -mine n. Salzbergwerk n, Saline f; -ness n, Salzigkeit f; -peter n. Kalisalpeter m; -y a. salzig.

Salutary [ssæ'lju-tA-ri] a. gesund, heilsam.

Salutation [ssæ-lju-tei'schAn] n. Begrüssung f, Gruss m.

Salute [ssA-luht'] n. Gruss m, Ehrenbezeigung f; vt. grüssen, salutieren (mil.).

Salvage [ssæl'widzh] n. Bergung f; vt. bergen, retten; – -company n. Sammelkompanie f (mil.); – -dump n. Material-Beute-sammelstelle f; – -money, – -pay n. Bergelohn m; – -platoon n. Bergungszug m (mil.).

Salvation [ssæl-wei'schAn] n. Erlösung f, Heil n, Rettung f; – Army n. Heilsarmee f. [ten.

Salve [ssælw] vt. bergen, retten.

Salve [ssahw] n. Salbe f; vt. mit Salbe einreiben, lindern, beruhigen.

Salver [ssæl'wer] n. Tablett n, Präsentierteller m.

Salvo [ssæl'wou] n. Salve f, Salut m.

Same [sseim] a. selb, gleich; the – der-, die-, das-selbe; -ness n. Einförmigkeit f.

Sample [ssahmpl] n. Probe f, Muster n; vt. eine Probe nehmen von, probieren, kosten, proben, bemustern; – order n. Probeauftrag m.

Sanatorium [ssæ-nA-toht'rjAm] n. Heilsanstalt f, Erholungsheim n, Kurhaus n; – treatment n. Kriegskur (mil.).

Sanctify [ssængk'ti-fai] vt. heiligen.

Sanctimonious [ssængk-ti-mou'njAss] a. scheinheilig.

Sanction [ssængk'schAn] n. Genehmigung f, Billigung f, Sanktion f, Zwangsmittel n.

Zwangsmassnahme *f*; *vt.* genehmigen, gutheissen.
Sanctity [ssængk'ti-ti] *n.* Heiligkeit *f*.
Sanctuary [ssængk'tju-A-ri] *n.* Heiligtum *n*, Freistätte *f*; right of – *n.* Asylrecht *n*.
Sand [ssænd] *n.* Sand *m*; *vt.* mit Sand bestreuen, versanden; -s *pl.* Strand *m*, Sandebene *f*, Sandbank *f*; – **-bag** *n.* Sandsack *m*; – **-bank** *n.* Sandbank *f*; – **-shoe** *n.* Strandschuh *m*.
Sandal [ssændl] *n.* Sandale *f*.
Sandstone [ssænd'stoun] *n.* Sandstein *m*.
Sandwich [ssænd'uidzh] *n.* belegtes Brötchen, Stulle *f*, mit Belag; **ham** – *n.* Schinkenbrötchen *n*; – **spread** *n.* Brotaufstrich *m*.
Sandy [ssæn'di] *a.* sandig, Sand . . . , sandfarben, rothaarig.
Sane [ssein] *a.* normal, (geistig) [gesund.
Sanguin'ary [ssæng'gui-nA-ri] *a.* blutig, blutdürstig; **-e** *a.* hoffnungsvoll, zuversichtlich.
Sanitary [ssæ'ni-tA-ri] *a.* gesundheitlich, Gesundheits . . . – **towel** *n.* Monatsbinde *f*.
Sanitation [ssæ-ni-tei'schAn] *n.* hygienische Einrichtungen *f.pl.*
Sanity [ssæ'ni-ti] *n.* geistige Gesundheit, gesunder Verstand.
Sap [ssæp] *n.* Saft *m*.
Sap [ssæp] *n.* Sappe *f*, Laufgraben *m*; *vt.* untergraben, minieren; – **-head** *n.* Sappenkopf *m* (*mil.*).
Sapling [ssæp'ling] *n.* junger Baum, Schössling *m*, junger Windhund.
Sapper [ssæ'per] *n.* Pionier *m*, Sappeur *m*.
Sapphire [ssæ'fai-er] *n.* Saphir *m*.
Sarcasm [ssahr'kæsm] *n.* Spott *m*, Hohn *m*.
Sarcastic [ssahr-kæ'stik] *a.* **-ally** *ad.* ironisch, höhnisch, spöttisch, hämisch.
Sardine [ssahr-dihn'] *n.* Sardine *f*.
Sardonic [ssahr-do'nik] *a.* **-ally** *ad.* hämisch, höhnisch.
Sarsarparilla [sahr-ssA-pA-ri'lA] *n.* Sassaparille *f*, Heilwurz *f*.
Sash [ssæsch] *n.* Schärpe *f*, Binde *f*, Feldbinde *f* (*mil.*).
Sash [ssæsch] *n.* Fensterrahmen *m*; – **window** *n.* Schiebenfenster *n*.
Satchel [ssæt'schAl] *n.* Schultasche *f*, Mappe *f*, Schulranzen *m*.
Sateen [ssA-tihn'] *n.* englisches Leder, Baumwollsatin *m*.
Satellite [ssæ'ti-lait] *n.* Trabant *m*, Anhänger *m*; – **airfield** *n.* Feldflughafen *m* (*av.*); – **town** *n.* Trabantenstadt *f*.
Satiate [ssei'schjeit] *vt.* sättigen.
Satiation [ssei-schjei'schAn] *n*, **Satiety** [ssA-tai'i-ti] *n.* Sättigung *f*, Sattheit *f*, Überdruss *m*, Ekel *m*.
Satir'e [ssæ'tai-er] *n.* Spottrede *f*, Spottgedicht *n*, Satire *f*; **-ist** *n.* Satiriker *m*; **-ize** *vt.* verspotten.
Satirical [ssA-ti'rikl] *a.* **-ly** *ad.* satirisch, spöttisch.
Satisfaction [ssæ-tiss-fæk'schAn] *n.* Befriedigung *f*, Zufriedenheit *f*, Genugtuung *f*.
Satisfactor'y [ssæ-tiss-fæk'tA-ri] *a*, **-ily** *ad.* befriedigend, genugtuend.
Satisfy [ssæ'tiss-fai] *vt.* befriedigen, zufriedenstellen, genügen, überzeugen (*convince*); *r.* sich überzeugen; **-ing** *a.* genügend, überzeugend, nahrhaft (*food*).
Saturate [ssæt'juh-reit] *vt.* sättigen, durchdringen, tränken.
Saturation [ssæt-juh-rei'schAn] *n.* Sättigung *f*; – **raid** *n.* Eindeckungsangriff *m* (*av.*).

Saturday [ssæ'ter-di] n. Samstag m, Sonnabend m.

Sauce [ssOss] n. Sauce f, Sosse f, Tunke f, Frechheit f; **-- -boat** n. Tunkennapf m.

Saucepan [ssOss'pAn] n. Stieltopf m, -kasserolle f, Tiegel m.

Saucer [ssO'sser] n. Untertasse f.

Saucy [ssO'ssi] a. frech, keck.

Saunter [ssOn'ter] vi. schlendern.

Sausage [ssæ'ssidzh] n. Wurst f.

Savage [ssæ'widzh] a. wild; n. der Wilde; **-ness,** **-ry** n. Wildheit f, Barbarei f, Grausamkeit f. (Grasebene f.

Savannah [ssA--wæ'nA] n. >

Saveloy [ssæ'wA-leu] n. Zervelatwurst f.

Save [sseiw] vt.i. retten, erlösen, bergen (ship), erparen (money), sparsam sein; pr. ausser, ohne.

Saver [ssei'wer] n. Sparer m.

Saving [ssei'wing] a. erlösend, rettend, sparsam; n. Rettung f; **-s** pl. Ersparnisse pl; pr. ausser, ausgenommen; **-s bank** n. Sparkasse f; **home -s bank** n. Sparbüchse f.

Saviour [ssei'wjer] n. Retter m, Erlöser m.

Savour [ssei'wer] n. Geschmack m, Geruch m, Anstrich m; vi. schmecken, riechen; **-y** a. schmackhaft; n. Vorspeise f.

Savoy [ssæ'weu] n. Wirsingkohl m. (schneiden.

Saw [ssO] n. Säge f; vt. sägen.

Sawdust [ssO'dAst] n. Sägemehl n, Sägespäne m.pl.

Sawmill [ssO'mil] n. Sägemühle f, Sägewerk n.

Saxophone [ssæx'A-foun] n. Saxophon n.

Say [ssei] vt.i. sagen, reden, erzählen; n. Rede f.

Saying [ssei'ing] n. Rede f. Redensart f, Spruch m.

Scab [skæb] n. Kruste f, Grind m, Räude f, Streikbrecher m.

Scabbard [skæ'berd] n. Degenscheide f.

Scabby [skæ'bi] a. räudig.

Scaffold [skæ'fAld] n. Baugerüst n, Schafott n; **-ing** n. Baurüstzeug n, Gerüst n.

Scald [skOld] vt. verbrühen, verbrennen, brühen; n. Brandwunde f.

Scale [skeil] n. Schale f, Schuppe f, Kesselstein m (tec.); vt. aus-, ab-klopfen, abblasen; i. Pfannenstein ansetzen.

Scale [skeil] n. Waagschale f; **-s** pl. Waage f.

Scale [skeil] n. Stufenfolge f, Mass-stab m, Abstufung f, Skala f, Tonleiter m (music); vt. ersteigern, erklettern, stürmen (mil.); on a large **-- im grossen** en Mass-stabe, im Grossen.

Scallop [skæ'lAp] n. Kammuschel f, Kerbschnitt m, Auszackung f; vt. auszacken, auskerben.

Scallywag [skæ'li-uæg] n. Schuft m, Schurke m.

Scalp [skælp] n. Skalp m, Kopfhaut f; vt. skalpieren.

Scalpel [skæl'pAl] n. Seziermesser n.

Scaly [skei'li] a. schuppig.

Scamp [skæmp] n. Taugenichts m, Lump m, Schelm m.

Scamp [skæmp] vt. pfuschen, liederlich arbeiten.

Scamper [skæm'per] vi. davonlaufen, ausreissen.

Scan [skæn] vt. genau prüfen, untersuchen, skandieren (verse).

Scandal [skændl] n. Anstoss m, Skandal m, Verleumdung f (slander); **talk -- klatschen; -ize** vt. Ärgernis geben, ärgern, entsetzen; **-monger** n. Verleumder m, Lästerer m, Klatschbase f (gossip); **-ous** a. anstössig, schändlich, skandalös, verleumderisch.

Scansion [skæn'schAn] n. Skandieren n, Lesen nach Versfüssen n.

Scant [skænt] a., -ily ad. knapp, gering, kärglich, ungenügend.
Scantiness [skæn'ti-ness] n. Knappheit f.
Scantling [skænt'ling] n. kleines Verbandstück, Kantholz n., Latte f.
Scanty [skæn'ti] a. knapp, dürftig, ungenügend.
Scapegoat [skeip'gout] n. Sündenbock m.
Scar [skahr] n. Schramme f., Narbe f.; vt. schrammen; i. (sich) narben.
Scarce [skehrss] a. selten, knapp, rar; -ely ad. kaum, mit knapper Not, schwerlich; -ity n. Mangel m, Not f., Knappheit f., Seltenheit f.
Scare [skehr] n. Schrecken m., Panik f.; vt. erschrecken, verscheuchen.
Scarecrow [skehr'krou] n. Vogelscheuche f.
Scaremonger [skehr'mAng-ger] n. Bangemacher m.
Scarf [skahrf] n. Schärpe f., Halstuch n., Schal m.; pl. Schalnadel f.
Scarf [skahrf] n. schräges Hakenblatt n. (wood); vt. zusammenblatten.   [fen.
Scarify [skæ'ri-fai] vt. schröpfen.
Scarlatina [skahr-lA-tih'nA] n. Scharlachfieber n.
Scarlet [skahr'lit] a. scharlachrot; - fever n. Scharlachfieber n.; - runner n. Feuerbohne f.
Scathing [skei'dhing] a. scharf, verletzend, vernichtend.
Scatter [skæ'ter] vt. ausstreuen, zerstreuen, versprengen; -ed a. zerstreut (liegend).
Scatter-brain [skæ'ter-brein] n. Spatzenkopf m., Faselhans m.
Scavenge [skæ'windzh] vt. kehren, reinigen; -r n. Strassenkehrer m.; -ing n. Strassenreinigung f.
Scenario [sche-nah'rjo] n. Drehbuch n., Filmmanuskript n.

Scene [ssihn] n. Schauplatz m., Szene f., Auftritt m., Anblick m.; - painter n. Dekorationsmaler m.; - shifter n. Bühnenarbeiter m., Kulissenschieber m.
Scenery [ssih'nA-ri] n. Landschaft f., Dekoration f., Szenerie f. (stage).
Scenic [ssih'nik] a. szenisch, Bühnen ...; - film n. Landschaftsfilm m; - railway n. Gebirgsbahn f., Liliputeisenbahn f.
Scent [ssent] n. Geruch m., Parfüm n., Witterung f., Spur f. (sport); vt. parfümieren, wittern; - bottle n. Riech-, Parfümfläschchen n.; - spray n. Parfümzerstäuber m., Spritzflakon n.   [geruchlos.
Scentless [ssent'less] a.
Sceptic [skep'tik] n. Skeptiker m., Zweifler m.
Sceptical [skep'tikl] a., -ly ad. skeptisch, zweifelnd.
Scepticism [skep'ti-ssism] n. Skeptizismus m., Zweifel m.
Sceptre [ssep'ter] n. Zepter n.
Schedule [shed'juhl] n. Verzeichnis n., Liste f., Tabelle f., Stundenplan m., Fahrplan m. (rl.), Nachweis m; vt. aufzeichnen; -d a. fahrplanmässig (train); -d time n. fahrplanmässige Zeit.
Scheme [skihm] n. Schema n., System f., Entwurf m., Plan m., Gestalt f., Anschlag m (plot); vt.i. planen, intrigieren; colour - n. Farbenzusammensetzung f.
Schemer [skih'mer] n. Projektenmacher m., Intrigant m., Ränkeschmied m.
Scheming [skih'ming] a. ränkevoll, intrigierend; n. Plänemachen n., Intrigieren n.
Schism [ssism] n. Kirchenspaltung f., Schisma n.
Schist [ssist] n. Schist m., Schiefer m.
Scholar [sko'ler] n. Schüler m.

Schülerin *f*, der Gelehrte; -ly *a*. gelehrt; -ship *n*. Gelehrsamkeit *f*, Stipendium *n*.

Scholastic [skA-læ'stik] *a*. gelehrt, Schul . . .; - agency *n*. Schulagentur *f*; - profession *n*. Lehrberuf *m*.

School [skuhl] *n*. Schule *f*; - age *n*. schulpflichtiges Alter; -bag *n*. Ranzen *m*, Schulränzel *n*; - certificate *n*. Abiturientenzeugnis *n*; -days *n.pl.* Schulzeit *f*; -fellow, -mate *n*. Mitschüler *m*, Mitschülerin *f*.

Schoolboy [skuhl'beu] *n*. Schüler *m*. Schülerin *f*.

Schoolgirl [skuhl'Arl] *n*. Schülerin *f*.

Schooling [skuh'ling] *n*. Schulung *f*, Unterricht *m*.

Schoolmaster [skuhl'mahster] *n*. Lehrer *m*, Hauptlehrer *m*, Rektor *m*.

Schoolmistress [skuhl'mistriss] *n*. Lehrerin *f*.

Schoolroom [skuhl'ruhm] *n*. Klassenzimmer *n*. [er *m*.

Schooner [skuh'ner] *n*. Schoner

Sciatica [ssai-æ'ti-kA] *n*. Hüftweh *n*, Ischias *m*.

Science [ssai'Anss] *n*. Wissenschaft *f*, Naturwissenschaft *f*.

Scientific [ssai-An-ti'fik] *a*, -ally *ad*. (natur)wissenschaftlich, gelehrt.

Scientist [ssai'An-tist] *n*. Naturwissenschaftler *m*, Forscher *m*. [funkeln.

Scintillate [ssin'ti-leit] *vt*.

Scion [ssai'An] *n*. Sprössling *m*.

Scission [ssi'schAn] *n*. Schnitt *m*.

Scissors [ssi'sers] *n.pl.* Schere *f*; - telescope *n*. Scherenfernrohr *n*.

Sclerosis [skle-rou'ssiss] *n*. Arterienverkalkung *f*.

Scoff [skof] *vi*. spotten, höhnen; -ing *a*. spöttisch, höhnisch; *n*. Spott *m*.

Scold [skould] *vt.i*. schelten, zanken; *n*. Zänkerin *f*; -ing *a*. zänkisch; *n*. Schelte *f*.

Scollop [sko'lAp] *see* scallop.

Scone [skon] *n*. (schottischer) Weizenmehlkuchen *m*.

Scoop [skuhp] *n*. Schaufel *f*, Schöpfkelle *f*, Schippe *f*; *vt*. ausschaufeln, schöpfen.

Scoop [skuhp] *n*. Erstmeldung *f*, Sensationsmeldung *f*, Treffer *m*, Schlager *m*.

Scooter [skuh'ter] *n*. Roller *m*, Rollenläufer *m*.

Scope [skoup] *n*. Gesichtskreis *m*, Spielraum *m*.

Scorch [skOrtsch] *vt.i*. rösten, verbrennen, dahinsausen (*cycle*).

Score [skOr] *n*. Einschnitt *m*, Kerbe *f*, zwanzig (Stück) *n*, Zeche *f* (*bill*), Rechnung *f* (*games*), Partitur *f* (*music*); *vt*. anschreiben, gewinnen; *i*. zählen, rechnen, machen.

Scorn [skOrn] *n*. Verachtung *f*, Hohn *m*; *vt*. verachten, höhnen, verschmähen; -ful *a*, -fully *ad*. verächtlich, höhnisch.

Scot-free [skot'frih] *a*. zechfrei, ungestraft.

Scoundrel [skaun'dril] *n*. Schuft *m*, Schurke *m*.

Scour [skau'er] *vt*. scheuern, fegen, putzen, wegschwemmen.

Scour [skau'er] *vt.i*. dahinstreifen, durchstreifen.

Scourge [skArdzh] *vt*. geisseln, plagen, züchtigen; *n*. Plage *f*, Geissel *f*.

Scout [skaut] *vt*. verschmähen, verächtlich abweisen.

Scout [skaut] *n*. Späher *m*, Erkunder *m*, Aufklärer *m*; *vi*. auskundschaften, spähen; boy - *n*. Pfadfinder *m*; - master *n*. Pfadfinderführer *m*; -party *n*. Streifabteilung *f* (*mil.*).

Scouting [skau'ting] *n*. Aufklärung *f*, Erkundung *f*, Pfadfinderwesen *n*; - car *n*. Spähwagen *m* (*mil.*); - plane *n*. Aufklärungsflugzeug *n* (*av.*).

Scowl [skaul] *vi*. finster blick-

en; n. finsteres Gesicht, Stirnerunzeln n. [mager, dürr.
Scraggy [skræ'gi] a. hager.
Scramble [skræmbl] n. Klettern n, Balgerei f; vi. klettern, sich reissen um; -d eggs n.pl. Rühreier n.pl.
Scrap [skræp] n. Stückchen n, Schnitzel m, Brocken m, Abfall m (metal); vt. wegwerfen, abschaffen; – iron n. Alteisen n, Schrotteisen n.
Scrape [skreip] vt.i. schaben, kratzen, sparen; n. Kratzen n, Verlegenheit f, Klemme f, Patsche f; –r n. Kratzeisen n, Scharre f, Schabe f (tec.).
Scrap-heap [skræp'hihp] n. Schrotthaufen n, Alteisen n.
Scrappy [skræ'pi] a. abgerissen, ohne Zusammenhang, zusammengestoppelt.
Scratch [skrætsch] n. Ritz m, Schramme f, leichte Wunde, Normalklasse f (games); vt. kratzen; – out ausradieren, ausstreichen.
Scrawl [skrOl] vt.i. kritzeln, schmieren; n. Gekritzel n, Schmiererei f.
Scream [skrihm] n. Schrei m; Angstschrei m; vi. schreien, kreischen.
Scree [skrih] n. Geröll n.
Screech [skrihtsch] vi. schreien, schrillen; – owl n. Käuzchen n, Baumeule f.
Screed [skrihd] n. langer Streifen, weitschweifige Rede.
Screen [skrihn] n. Schirm m, Schutzwand f, Leinwand f, Film m, Sieb m; vt. schirmen, schützen, abblenden (light), verschleiern, sieben (coal); -ed coal n. Würfelkohlen f.pl; – -grid n. Schirmgitter n (rad.); – -grid valve n. Vierelektrodenröhre f.
Screw [skruh] n. Schraube f; vt. schrauben, drücken; – -cap n. Schraubkapsel f; – -driver n. Schraubenzieher m; – -nut

n. Schraubenmutter f; – -steamer n. Schraubendampfer m.
Scribble [skribl] vt.i. kritzeln; n. Gekritzel n; -er n. Skribent m; -ing n. Gekritzel n, Schmiererei f; -ing pad n. Notizblock m; -ing paper n. Konzeptpapier n.
Scrimmage [skri'midzh] n. Getümmel n, Nahkampf m (football).
Scrimp [skrimp] vt.i. knapp halten, knausern mit.
Scrip [skrip] n. Interimsschein m, Inhaberaktie f.
Script [skript] n. Schrift f, Handschrift f, Manuskript n, Drehbuch n (film); German deutsche Schrift; phonetic – Lautschrift f.
Scriptural [skrip'tschA-rAl] a. biblisch.
Scripture [skrip'tscher] n. Heilige Schrift; -s pl. Bibel f; teach – Religionsunterricht erteilen.
Scroful'a [skro'fjA-lA] n. Skrofeln f.pl; -ous a. skrofulös.
Scroll [skroul] n. Pergament-, Papier-rolle f, Liste f, Schnörkel m (carved), spiraler Wasserweg (tec.).
Scrounge [skraundzh] vt.i. mausen, klauen; –r n. Schnorrer m. [Unterholz n.
Scrub [skrAb] n. Gestrüpp n, **Scrub** [skrAb] vt. scheuern, schrubben; -bing brush n. Scheuerbürste f, Schrubber m.
Scruff [skrAf] n. Genick n.
Scrum [skrAm] see scrimmage.
Scrumptious [skrAmp'tschAss] a. vortrefflich, herrlich, prima. [kauen.
Scrunch [skrAnsch] vt. zer-
Scruple [skruhpl] n. Skrupel n, 1.3 Gramm.
Scruple [skruhpl] n. Skrupel m, Bedenken n, Zweifel m; vi. Anstand nehmen, Bedenken tragen.

Scrupulous [skruh'pju-lAss] *a*, -ly *ad*. peinlich, gewissenhaft, genau, ängstlich; -ness *n*. Gewissenhaftigkeit *f*, Bedenklichkeit *f*, Skrupel *m.pl*.

Scrutinize [skruh'ti-nais] *vt*. genau prüfen, untersuchen.

Scrutiny [skruh'ti-ni] *n*. genaue Prüfung, Untersuchung *f*, Forschen *n*.

Scuffle [skAfl] *n*. Balgerei *f*. Handgemenge *n*; *vi*. sich balgen, handgemein werden.

Scull [skAl] *n*. kurzes Ruder; *vt.i* skullen, wricken; -ing boat *n*. Skuller *m*, Ruderboot *n*.

Scullery [skA'lA-ri] *n*. Spülaufwasch-küche *f*; - maid *n*. Scheuermagd *f*.

Sculptor [skAlp'ter] *n*. Bildhauer *m*, Bildner *m*.

Sculpture [skAlp'tscher] *n*. Bildhauerkunst *f*, Schnitzwerk *n*; *vt*. meisseln, schnitzen, aushauen.

Scum [skAm] *n*. Schaum *m*, Abschaum *m*, Schlacken *f.pl*; *vt*. abschäumen. [gatt *n*.

Scupper [skA'per] *n*. Speigatt *n*.

Scurf [skArf] *n*. Schorf *m*. Kopfschuppen *f.pl*.

Scurrious [skA'ri-lAss] *a*. zotig, gemein.

Scurry [skA'ri] *vi*. wegeilen.

Scurvy [skA'rwi] *a*. grundig, schorfig, gemein, niederträchtig; *n*. Skorbut *m*.

Scut [skAt] *n*. kurzer Schwanz.

Scutcheon [skAt'schAn] *n*. Wappenschild *n*.

Scuttle [skAtl] *vi*. wegeilen, sich drücken.

Scuttle [skAtl] *n*. kleine Luke (*nav.*); *vt*. anbohren, versenken.

Scythe [ssaidh] *n*. Sense *f*.

Sea [ssih] *n*. See *f*, Meer *n*, Seegang *m*, hohe Welle; - bathing *n*. Baden *n*, im der See; -borne *a*. auf dem Seewege befördert; - bottom *n*. Meeresgrund *m*; - breeze *n*. Seewind

m; - captain *n*. Schiffskapitän *m*; - chart *n*. Seekarte *f*; - coast *n*. Seeküste *f*; - defence *n*. Seekommando *n*; -faring *a*. seefahrend, See –; - front *n*. Strandpromenade *f*; - going *a*. Ozean –, See – ... ; - green *a*. meergrün; -gull *n*. Möwe *f*; - level *n*. Meeresspiegel *m*, Normalnull *n* (*av.*); - lion *n*. Seelöwe *m*; - lord *n*. Marineminister *m*; - rescue service *n*. Seenotdienst *m* (*av.*); - room *n*. Seeraum *m*, hohe See; - route *n*. Seeweg *m*, Schiffahrtsroute *f*; - rover *n*. Seeräuber *m*; - shell *n*. Seemuschel *f*; -shore *n*. Seeküste *f*; - sick *a*. seekrank; - trout *n*. Meerforelle *f*; - wall *n*. Damm *m*.

Seaboard [ssih'bOrd] *n*. Seeküste *f*.

Seafarer [ssih'feh'rer] *n*. Seemann *m*, Seefahrer *m*.

Seal [ssihl] *n*. Seehund *m*; -skin *n*. Seehundsfell *n*.

Seal [ssihl] *n*. Siegel *n*, Stempel *m*, Petschaft *n*; *vt*. siegeln, stempeln, besiegeln; -ing wax *n*. Siegellack *m*.

Seam [ssihm] *n*. Saum *m*, Naht *f*, Schicht *f*; *vt*. säumen.

Seaman [ssih'mAn] *n*. Seemann *m*, Matrose *m*; able – *n*. Vollmatrose *m*; -ship *n*. Seefahrerkunst *f*.

Sea-plane [ssih'plein] *n*. Wasserlandflugzeug *n*, Seeflieger *m*; - base *n*. Seeflugstützpunkt *m*; - station *n*. Seeflughafen *m*, Seefliegerhorst *m*.

Seaport [ssih'pOrt] *n*. Seehafen *m*, Seestadt *f*.

Sear [ssih'er] *vt*. versengen, verbrennen, ätzen.

Search [ssArtsch] *vt.i*. suchen, durchsuchen, fahnden (*law*), forschen, untersuchen; – *n*. Suchen *n*, Suche *f*, Forschen *n*, Nachspüren *n*, Durchsuchung *f*. [durchdringend, forschend.

Searching [ssAsr'tching] *a*.

Searchlight [ssArtsch'lait] n. Scheinwerfer m. [gemälde n.

Seascape [ssih'skeip] n. See-

Sea-side [ssih'ssaid] n. Seeküste f, Meeresküste f; a. an der Küste gelegen, See . . . ; Strand . . . ; - holiday n. Ferien am Meer; - resort n. Seebad n.

Season [ssih'sAn] n. Jahreszeit f, Saison f; vt. würzen, austrocknen, auswittern (timber); -able a. zeitgemäss, saisongemäss, passend; -al a. Saison . . . ; periodisch; -ing n. Austrocknen n, Auswittern n, Würze f; -ticket n. Wochen-, Monats-, Jahres-karte f, Abonnement n; - holder m Abonnent m, Abonnentin f.

Seat [ssiht] n. Sitz m, Platz m, Bank f, Sitz m, Wohn-, Landsitz m; vt. mit Sitzen versehen, setzen, Raum haben für.

Seating [ssih'ting] n. Stuhlzeug n; - accommodation n. Sitzraum m, Sitzgelegenheit f.

Seawards [ssih'uArds] ad. seewärts. [Seetang m.

Seaweed [ssih'uihd] n. Alge f,

Seaworthy [ssih'uAr-dhi] a. seefest, seetüchtig.

Secede [ssi-ssihd'] vi. sich loslösen, abfallen, sich trennen.

Seaworthy [ssih'uAr-dhi] a. Seefest, seetüchtig.

Secede [ssi-ssihd'] vi. sich loslösen, abfallen, sich trennen.

Secession [ssi-sse'schAn] n. Loslösung f, Abfall m, Sezession f (U.S.A.). [schliessen.

Seclude [ssi-kluhd'] vt. ab-

Seclusion [ssi-kluh'zhAn] n. Abgeschiedenheit f.

Second [sse'kAnd] a. zweit; n. Sekunde f, der, die, das Zweite. Helfer m, Beistand m; vt. unterstützen, beistehen, helfen; -lieutenant n. Leutnant m (mil.).

Second [ssi-kond'] vt. kommandieren zu (mil.), zuteilen, zuweisen.

Secondary [sse'kAn-dA-ri] a. sekundär, zweiten Ranges. nächstfolgend, untergeordnet; - road n. Landstrasse f; -school n. Mittelschule f.

Second-best [sse'kAnd-best'] a. zweitbest.

Second-class [sse'kAnd-klahss'] n. zweite Klasse f; a. zweiter Klasse, zweiten Ranges. [Unterstützer m.

Seconder [sse'kAn-der] n.

Second-hand [sse'kAnd-hænd'] a. aus zweiter Hand, alt, antiquarisch (book).

Secondly [sse'kAnd-li] ad. zweitens.

Second-rate [sse'kAnd-reit'] a. zweiter Güte, minderwertig.

Secrecy [ssih'kri-ssi] n. Heimlichkeit f, Verschwiegenheit f.

Secret [ssih'krit] n. Geheimnis n; a. geheim; - police n. Geheimpolizei f, Staatspolizei f; - service n. Geheim-, Spionagedienst m.

Secretaire [sse-krA-teh'er] n. Schreibschrank m, Pult m.

Secretarial [sse-kri-teh'rjAl] a. Sekretär . . . , Büro . . . ; - work n. Büroarbeiten f.pl.

Secretariat [sse-kri-teh'rjAt] n. Sekretariat n, Kanzlei f.

Secretary [ssek'ri-tri] n. Sekretär m, Schreiber m, Schriftführer m; private - n. Privatsekretär m, -in f.

Secrete [ssi-kriht'] vt. verbergen, verstecken, ausscheiden.

Secretion [ssi-krih'schAn] n. Verbergung f, Ausscheidung f, Absonderung f.

Secretive [ssi-kri'tiw] a. verschwiegen, geheimtuerisch.

Sect [ssekt] n. Sekte f.

Section [ssek'schAn] n. Schneiden n, Abschnitt m, Sektion f, Gruppe f, Truppenabteilung f (mil.), Paragraph m (law); -al a. lokal, partikularisch, örtlich, zerlegbar; - bookcase n. zusammensetzbarer Bücher-

schrank; -alism n. Partikularismus m.

Sector [ssek'ter] n. Sektor m,
Abschnitt m (mil.), Streifen m
(mil.); - of attack n. Gefechtsstreifen m (mil.); - controller
n. Raumführer m.

Secular [sse'kju-ler] a. weltlich, säkular, hundertjährig;
-ize vt. säkularisieren, verweltlichen.

Secure [ssi-kjuh'er] a. -ly ad.
sicher, fest, versichert; vt. sichern, wahren, befestigen.

Security [ssi-kjuh'ri-ti] n. Sicherheit f, Zuversichtlichkeit f,
Bürgschaft f (com.), Wertpap-
ier n (share); collective - kollektive Sicherheit; - Council n.
Sicherheitsrat m; - police n.
Sicherheitspolizei f.

Sedate [ssi-deit'] a. gesetzt.

Sedative [sse'dA-tiw] n. Be-
ruhigungsmittel n; a. stillend,
beruhigend. [sitzend.]

Sedentary [sse'dAn-tA-ri] a.]

Sedge [sedzh] n. Binse f.

Sediment [sse'di-mAnt] n.
Satz m, Niederschlag m.

Sedition [ssi-di'schAn] n. Aufruhr m, Empörung f.

Seditious [ssi-di'schAss] a.
aufrührerisch. [führen.]

Seduce [ssi-djuhss'] vt. ver-]

Seduction [ssi-dAk'schAn] n.
Verführung f.

Seductive [ssi-dAk'tiw] a. verführerisch.

Sedulous [sse'dju-lAss] a. emsig, fleissig.

See [ssih] vt.i. sehen, einsehen,
beobachten, begreifen, besorg-
en, zusehen, nachsehen.

See [ssih] n. Bistum n, bischöf-
licher Stuhl; **Holy** - Päpst-
licher Stuhl.

Seed [ssih] n. Same m, Saat f;
vi. in Samen schiessen, Samen
streuen; t. besäen, entkörnen;
- merchant n. Samenhändler
m; - -pod n. Samenkapsel f;
- potato n. Saatkartoffel f.

Seedless [ssihd'less] a. samen-
los.

Seedling [ssihd'ling] n. Setzling m.

Seedy [ssih'di] a. saatreich,
kränklich, unwohl.

Seek [ssihk] vt.i. suchen,
forschen.

Seem [ssihm] vi. scheinen, erscheinen, aussehen; -ing a,
-ingly ad. anscheinend, scheinbar; -ly a. geziemend.

Seep [ssihp] vi. durchsickern.

Seer [ssih'er] n. Seher m, Prophet m.

See-saw [ssih'ssO] n. Schaukel f, Wippe f; vi. wippen
schaukeln.

Seethe [ssihdh] vt.i. sieden,
kochen, überschäumen.

Segment [sseg'mAnt] n. Bog-
enschnitt m, Segment n.

Segregate [sse'gri-geit] vt. absondern.

Segregation [sse-gri-gei'-
schAn] n. Absonderung f.

Seine [ssein] n. Schlagnetz n,
Schleppnetz n.

Seismic [ssais'mik] a. Erdbeben....

Seize [ssihs] vt. ergreifen, fest-
nehmen, fassen, festbinden,
zeisen (nav.).

Seizure [ssih'zher] n. Ergreif-
ung f, Festnahme f, Schlagan-
fall m.

Seldom [ssel'dAm] ad. selten.

Select [ssi-lekt'] vt. auslesen,
auswählen; a. auserlesen, ausgesucht, gewählt; -ion n. Auswahl f, Auslesen n, Sortierung
f (com.); -ive a. auswählend,
selektiv.

Selectivity [ssi-lek-ti'wi-ti] n.
n. Trennschärfe f (rad.).

Selenite [sse'li-nait] n. Selen-
it n.

Self [sself] n. Selbst n; pr.
selbst; a. naturfarbig, einge-
färbt (com.); **he him-** er selbst;
we ourselves wir selbst; - -act-
ing a. selbst-handelnd, -tätig.

mechanisch; – **-assertive** a. anmassend, zudringlich; – **-command**, – **-control** n. Selbstbeherrschung f; – **-confidence** n. Selbstvertrauen n; – **-conscious** a. befangen, schüchtern; – **-contained house** n. Einfamilienhaus n; – **-defence** n. Notwehr f; – **-denial** n. Selbstverleugnung f; – **-determination** f. – **-feeder** n. Füllofen m (tec.); – **-government** n. Selbstregierung f; – **-indulgence** n. Genuss-sucht f; – **-inflicted** a. selbstbeigebracht; – **-interest** n. Eigennutz m; – **-possession** n. Fassung f; – **-preservation** n. Selbsterhaltung f; – **-propelled** a. Selbstfahr . . .; – **-recording** a. selbstregistrierend; – **-starter** n. Selbstanlasser m (aut.); – **-styled** a. sogenannt; – **-sufficiency** n. Autarkie f; – **-supporting** a. sich selbst erhaltend, unabhängig; – **-taught** a. selbstgelehrt, autodidaktisch; – **-will** n. Eigensinn m; – **-willed** a. eigensinnig.

Selfish [sel'fisch] a. selbstsüchtig, egoistisch; **-ness** n. Selbstsucht f, Egoismus m.

Selfless [self'less] a. selbstlos, uneigennützig.

Sell [sell] vt. verkaufen, absetzen; i. sich verkaufen, Absatz finden (com.); n. Betrug m, Täuschung f, Schwindel m.

Seller [sel'ler] n. Verkäufer m, verkäuflicher Artikel (com.); **best-** n. Moderoman m, Schlager m.

Seltzer [selt'ser] n. Selterwasser n.

Selvage [sel'widzh] n. Leiste f, Borte f, Salband n.

Semaphore [sse'mA-fOr] n. Winkzeichen n, Flaggenwinker m, Semaphor m; vt.i. winken.

Semblance [ssem'blAnss] n. Anschein m.

Semi [sse'mi] a. halb; – **-annual**

a. halbjährlich; – **-detached** a. halb freistehend, halb getrennt; – **-final** n. Vorschlussrunde f; – **-finished** a. halbfertig (com.); – **-grand** n. Stutzflügel m; – **-manufactured** a. halbfertig; – **-official** a. halbamtlich, offiziös; – **-precious** a. **-tracked vehicle** n. Halbkettenfahrzeug n. [Halbkreis m.

Semicircle [sse'mi-ssArkl] n.

Semicolon [sse'mi-kou'lAn] n. Strichpunkt m, Semikolon n.

Seminary [sse'mi-nA-ri] n. Seminar n, Erziehungsanstalt f.

Semolina [sse-mo-lih'nA] n. Griessmehl n.

Senat'e [sse'nit] n. Senat m; **-or** n. Ratsherr m, Senator m.

Send [ssend] vt. senden, schicken; – **for** holen lassen; **-er** n. Absender m, Versender m.

Senile [ssih'mail] a. altersschwach, greisenhaft, senil.

Senility [sse-ni'li-ti] n. Altersschwäche f, Greisenalter n.

Senior [ssih'njer] a. älter, öber . . .; n. der, die Ältere; – **man** n. Vorgesetzte(r) m; – **officer** n. Rangälteste(r) (mil.), Stabsoffizier m.

Seniority [ssih-njo'ri-ti] n. Dienstgrad m, (Rang-)Dienstalter n, höheres Alter.

Senna [sse'nA] n. Sennesstrauch m, -blatt n.

Sensation [ssen-ssei'schAn] n. Empfindung f, Gefühl n, Aufsehen n, Sensation f; – **al** a. sensationell, Aufsehen erregend.

Sense [ssenss] n. Sinn m, Verstand m, Vernunft f, Bedeutung f; **-less** a. sinnlos, unvernünftig.

Sensibility [ssen-ssi-bi'li-ti] n. Empfindlichkeit f.

Sensible [ssen'ssibl] a. vernünftig, klug, gewahr, bewusst, bemerkbar.

Sensibly [ssen'si-bli] *ad.* vernünftig, merklich.

Sensitive [ssen'ssi-tiw] *a.* empfindlich; **-ness** *a.* Empfindlichkeit *f.*

Sensitize [ssen'ssi-tais] *vt.* lichtempfindlich machen; **-d** *a.* lichtempfindlich.

Sensual [ssen'schu-Al] *a.* sinnlich, wollüstig, genüßlich.

Sensuality [ssen-schu-æ'li-ti] *n.* Sinnlichkeit *f.*

Sensuous [ssen'schu-Ass] *a.* sinnlich.

Sentence [ssen'tAnss] *n.* Satz *m,* Richterspruch *m* (*law*), Urteil *n;* *vt.* verurteilen; **- of death** *n.* Todesurteil *n.*

Sententious [ssen-ten'schAss] *a.* lehrhaft, pedantisch, pompös.

Sentiment [ssen'ti-mAnt] *n.* Gefühl *n,* Empfindung *f,* Gemüt *n,* Gesinnung *f,* Gedanke *m.*

Sentimental [ssen-ti-mentl'] *a,* **-ly** *ad.* empfindsam, sentimental.

Sentimentality [ssen-ti-men-tæ'li-ti] *n.* Empfindsamkeit *f,* Sentimentalität *f.*

Sentinel [ssen-ti-nAl], **Sentry** [ssen'tri] *n.* Schildwache *f,* Wachtposten *m,* Posten *m* (*mil.*); **- box** *n.* Schilderhaus *n.* (trennbar.

Separable [ssep'A-rAbl] *a.*

Separate [ssep'A-rit] *a,* **-ly** *ad.* getrennt, besonder; **- peace** *n.* Sonderfrieden *m,* Separatfrieden *m.*

Separate [sse'pA-reit] *vt.* trennen, sondern, scheiden; *i.* sich trennen, auseinander gehen; **-d milk** *n.* Schleudermilch *f.*

Separation [sse-pA-rei'schAn] *n.* Trennung *f,* Scheidung *f,* Absonderung *f.*

Separatis'm [sse'pA-rA-tism] *n.* Separatismus *m;* **-t** *n.* Separatist *m,* Sonderbündler *m.*

Separator [sse'pA-rei-ter] *n.* Zentrifuge *f,* Milchentrahmer *m,* Schleudermaschine *f.*

Sepia [ssih'pjA] *n.* Sepia *f,* Tintenfischbraun *n.*

Sepoy [ssi-peu'] *n.* Sepoy *m,* ostindischer Soldat. (giftung *f.*

Sepsis [ssep'ssiss] *n.* Blutvergiftung *n.* Blutver-

Septic [ssep'tik] *a.* septisch, entzündet, eitrig; **- poisoning** *n.* Blutvergiftung *f.*

Septuagenarian [ssep-tju-A-dzhe-neh'rjAn] *n.* der, die Siebzigjährige.

Sepulchral [ssi-pAl'krAl] *a.* Toten...., Grab....

Sepulchre [sse'pAl-ker] *n.* Grab *n,* Grabgewölbe *n.*

Sequel [ssi'kuAl] *n.* Folge *f,* Fortsetzung *f.*

Sequence [ssih'kuAnss] *n.* Folge, Reihen-, Stufen-folge *f,* Sequenz *f* (*cards*).

Sequestered [ssi-kue'sterd] *a.* abgeschieden, einsam, einsam.

Sequestrate [ssi-kue'streit] *vt.* mit Beschlag belegen, sequestrieren, beschlagnahmen.

Sequestration [ssih-kue-strei'schAn] *n.* Sequestration *f,* Beschlagnahme *f.*

Sequestrator [ssih'kue-strei-ter] *n.* Zwangsverwalter *m.*

Sequin [ssi'kuin] *n.* Zechine *f.*

Serenade [sse-ri-neid'] *n.* Ständchen *n,* Serenade *f.*

Serene [ssi-rihn'] *a.* heiter, klar, ruhig; **- Highness** *n.* Durchlaucht.

Serenity [sse-re'ni-ti] *n.* Ruhe *f,* Klarheit *f.* (eigene.

Serf [ssArf] *n.* der, die Leibeigene.

Serge [ssArdzh] *n.* Serge *f,* Sersche *f.*

Sergeant [ssahr'dzhAnt] *n.* Feldwebel *m* (*infantry*), Wachtmeister *m* (*art, cav.*); **lance-** *n.* Unter-feldwebel *m,* **-wachtmeister** *m;* **police -** *n.* Polizeiwachtmeister *m;* **company - major** *n.* Oberfeldwebel *m,* Oberwachtmeister *m;* **regimen-**

tal – major n. Hauptfeldwebel m, Hauptwachtmeister m; staff – major n. Stabsfeldwebel m, -wachtmeister m.

Serial [ssih'rjAl] a. fortlaufend, Serien . . . , Reihen . . . ; n. Roman m, in Fortsetzungen, Lieferungswerk n.

Sericulture [sse'ri-kAl-tjer] n. Seidenzucht f.

Series [ssih'rihs] n. Reihe f, Serie f, Folge f, Anzahl f, Baureihe f (plane); – of broadcasts n. Sendereihe f (rad.).

Serious [ssih'rjAss] a. -ly ad. ernst, ernsthaft, wichtig; -ly wounded schwerverwundet; -ness n. Ernst m, Ernsthaftigkeit f.

Sermon [ssAr'mAn] n. Predigt f. [Schlange f.

Serpent [ssAr'pAnt] n.

Serpentine [ssAr'pAn-tain] a. geschlängelt, sich schlängelnd; n. Schlangenstein m, Serpentine f. [zackt, zackig.

Serrated [ssi-rei'tid] a. gezackt. **Serration** [ssi-rei'schAn] n. Auszackung f. [stoff m.

Serum [ssih'rAm] n. Impf-

Servant [ssArw'Ant] n. Diener m, Magd f, Dienstmädchen n; civil – n. der, die Staatsbeamte.

Serve [ssArw] vt.i. dienen, bedienen, nützen, helfen.

Service [ssArw'iss] n. Dienst m, Aufwartung f, Arbeitsleistung f, Gottesdienst m, Bedienung f (hotel, etc.), Service f (table), Aufschlag m (tennis); - s n.pl. Wehrmacht f; vt. bedienen; active – n. Kriegsdienst m; civil – n. Staatsdienst m; domestic – n. Dienstbotentätigkeit f; – channels pl. Truppendienstweg m; – club n. Kasino n; – court n. Aufschlagfeld n; – flat n. Wohnung f, mit Bedienung; – line n. innere Linie (tennis); -man n. Soldat m, Wehrmachtangehörige(r); – number n. Wehr-

machtnummer f; – pack n. Rucksack m; – pay n. Dienstbezüge m.pl. Wehrmachtsold m.

Serviceable [ssAr'wi-ssAbl] a. zweckdienlich, brauchbar, nützlich; – for flying flugklar (av.).

Servicing [ssAr'wi-ssing] n. Bedienen n, Wartung f; – of airfields n. Flughafenbetrieb m (av.).

Serviette [ssAr-wi-et'] n. Serviette f, Mundtuch n.

Servile [ssAr'wail] a. knechtisch, unterwürfig.

Servility [ssAr-wi'li-ti] n. Unterwürfigkeit f, Kriecherei f.

Session [sse'schAn] n. Sitzung f, Tagung f, Semester n (6 months).

Set [sset] vt. setzen, stellen, aufgeben, festsetzen, schärfen (knife), fassen (jewel), absetzen (course), bestimmen (price); i. gerinnen, untergehen (sun, etc.); a. vorgeschrieben, festgesetzt, fest; n. Satz m, Sammlung f, Gesellschaft f, Partie f (game); -back n. Rückschlag m; – square n. Zeichendreieck n.

Settee [sse-tih'] n. Sofa n, Kanapee n. [hund m.

Setter [sse'ter] n. Vorsteh-

Setting [sse'ting] n. Fassung f (gem), Hintergrund m, Untergang m (sun).

Settle [ssetl] vt. feststellen, ausgleichen, bezahlen (bill); i. sich ansiedeln, sich setzen, sich ausgleichen; -ment n. Festsetzung f, Niederlassung f (colony), Ausgleichung f (quarrel), Abschluss m (com.).

Settler [sset'ler] n. Ansiedler m.

Seven [ssewn] num. sieben f; -teen num. siebzehn f; -ty num. siebzig.

Sever [sse'wer] vt.i. (sich) trennen, zerschneiden, lösen.

Several [ssew'rAl] a. verschie-

den, mehrere, einzeln; -ly ad.
einzeln, besonders.

Severance [ssew'rAnss] n.
Trennung f.

Severe [ssi-wih'er] a., -ly ad.
streng, hart, heftig (pain).

Severity [ssi-we'ri-ti] n.
Strenge f, Härte f, Heftig-
keit f.   [ieren, heften (book).

Sew [ssou] vt.i. nähen, broch-

Sewage [ssuh'idzh] n. Kloak-
enwasser n, Abwasser n; -
farm n. Rieselgut n; - plant n.
Sielanlage f, Kanalisationsan-
lage f.

Sewer [ssuh'er] n. Kloake f,
Abzugs-, Haupt-kanal m, Siel
m; vt. kanalisieren; -age n.
Kanalisation f, Sienanlage f.

Sewing [ssou'ing] n. Nähen n,
Näharbeit f, weibliche Handarbeit; - cotton, - thread n.
Nähgarn n; - machine n. Näh-
maschine f; - needle n. Näh-
nadel f.

Sex [sex] n. Gechlecht n.

Sexagenarian [sex-A-dzhi-
nei'rjAn] n. der, die Sechzig-
jährige.

Sextant [sex'tAnt] n. Sextant
m, Winkelmessgerät m.

Sexton [sex'tAn] n. Küster m,
Totengräber m.

Sexual [sek'schuAl] a. geschlechtlich, sexuell.

Shabbiness [schæ'bi-ness] n.
Schäbigkeit f, Niederträchtig-
keit f.

Shabby [schæ'bi] a, Shabbily
ad. schäbig, abgetragen, fadenscheinig, armselig, gemein.

Shack [schæk] n. Lehmhütte f,
Blockhaus n.

Shackle [schækl] vt. fesseln; n.
Fessel f, Schäkel m (nav.).

Shad'e [scheid] n. Schatten m,
Lampenschirm m, Schattierung f (colour), Nuance f, Kleinigkeit f (trifle); vt. beschatten,
schattieren, schützen; -ing n.
Verdunkelung f, Schattierung
f, Schraffierung f (drawing).

Shadow [schæ'dou] n. Schatten m, Schattenbild n, Nuance
f; vt. beschatten, heimlich beobachten; -y -a schattig, dunkel.   [lichtscheu, zweifelhaft.

Shady [schei'di] a. schattig,

Shaft [schahft] n. Schaft m,
Stiel m, Schacht f (mine), Pfeil
m, Achse f. Welle f, Spindel f
(tec.), Deichsel f (cart); driving
- n. Gelenkwelle f (aut.).

Shag [schæg] n. Plüsch m
(cloth), Kraustabak m.

Shaggy [schæ'gi] a. zottig,
rauh, langhaarig.

Shagreen [schA-grihn'] n. ge-
narbtes Leder, Körnerleder n;
vt. körnen.

Shake [scheik] vt. schütteln,
erschüttern, rütteln; i. beben,
zittern; -down n. Stroh-,
Not-lager n.

Shaky [schei'ki] a. zitternd,
wackelig, unsicher.

Shale [scheil] n. Schiefer m.

Shall [schæl] werden, sollen;
shall we? wollen wir?   [otte f.

Shallot [schæ'lAt] n. Schal-

Shallow [schæ'lou] a. seicht,
untief, oberflächlich; n. Untiefe f, flache Stelle; - draught
a. flachgehend; -ness n. Untiefe f, Oberflächlichkeit f,
Seichtigkeit f.

Sham [schæm] n. Trug m, Betrug m, Täuschung f, Heuch-
elei f; vt. heucheln, vortäuschen; i. sich stellen; a. unecht,
falsch, nachgemacht.

Shamble [schæmbl] vi.
schlenkern, schlottern.

Shambles [schæm'bAls] n.pl.
Schlachthaus n, Gemetzel n.

Shame [scheim] n. Scham f,
Schande f, Schmach f; vt. beschämen; -faced a. schamhaft,
schüchtern, scheu, beschämt;
-ful a., -fully ad. schändlich,
schmählich; -less a. schamlos,
frech, unverschämt.

Shammer [schæ'mer] n. Betrüger m, Simulant m.

Shammy [schæ'mi] n. Fensterputzleder n.

Shampoo [schæm-puh'] n. Shampu f, Kopfwaschen n; vt. schampu(nier)en, Kopf waschen; – powder n. Kopfwaschpulver n.

Shamrock [schæm'rok] n. Kleeblatt n, weisser Feldklee.

Shank [schængk] n. Schaft m, Rohr n, Schenkel m, Bein n.

Shanty [schæn'ti] n. Hütte f, Schuppen m.

Shape [scheip] n. Form f, Gestalt f, Muster n, Fasson n, Zustand m; vt. bilden, gestalten, anpassen.

Shapeless [scheip'less] a. formlos, ungestalt; -ness n. Formlosigkeit f, Ungestaltheit f. [Wohlgestalt f.

Shapeliness [scheip'li-ness] n.

Shapely [scheip'li] a. wohlgestaltet, von schöner Gestalt.

Share [scheh'r] n. Teil m, Anteil m, Aktie f, Kux f (in a mine); vt. teilen, verteilen; – sich teilen, teil-haben, -nehmen; – broker n. Aktienmakler m; – capital n. Stammkapital n; – certificate n. Anteilschein m.

Shareholder [scheh'er-houl'der] n. Aktieninhaber m, Aktionär m. [m, Gauner m.

Shark [schahrk] n. Haifisch m.

Sharp [schahrp] a. -ly ad. scharf, schneidend, spitz, aufgeweckt (clever); – practice n. unredliche Handlungsweise f, Gaunerei f.

Sharp-edged [schahrp-edzhd'] a. scharfschneidig.

Sharpen [schahrpn] vt. schärfen, spitzen.

Sharpener [schahrp'ner] n. Bleistiftanspitzer m.

Sharper [schahr'per] n. Gauner m, Falschspieler m.

Sharpness [schahrp'ness] n. Spitzigkeit f, Schärfe f, Heftigkeit f, Scharfsinn m.

Sharpshooter [schahrp-schuh'ter] n. Scharfschütze m.

Shatter [schæ'ter] vt. zerschmettern, zerreissen, zersprengen, erschüttern; -ing a. vernichtend, zerschmetternd, erschütternd.

Shave [scheiw] vt. rasieren, scheren, abschaben, abhobeln (wood, etc.); i. sich rasieren; n. Rasieren n; – close – n. Entkommen mit knapper Not.

Shaver [schei'wer] n. Gelb-, Grün-schnabel m.

Shaving [schei'wing] n. Rasieren n, Schaben n; -s pl. Hobelspäne m.pl; – brush n. Rasierpinsel m; – cream n. Rasierkrem m; – soap n. Rasierseife f. [schlagetuch n.

Shawl [scholl] n. Schal m, Umschlagetuch n.

She [schih] pn. sie. [del n.

Sheaf [schihf] n. Garbe f, Bündel n.

Shear [schih'er] vt. scheren, schneiden; n. Schafschur f.

Shearing [schih'ring] n. Schur f, Scheren n; -s pl. Scherwolle f.

Shearling [schih'er-ling] n. einmal geschorenes Schaf.

Shears [schih'ers] n.pl. grosse Schere, Schneidenschere f.

Sheath [schihth] n. Scheide f.

Sheathe [schihdh] vt. einstecken, in die Scheide stecken, bekleiden (tec.), verhäuten (ship); -ing n. Einstecken n, Beschlagen n, Verhäuten n (ship), Verkleidung f.

Shed [sched] vt. vergiessen, ausgiessen, abwerfen, verlieren, verbreiten (spread).

Shed [sched] n. Schuppen m, Hütte f.

Sheeling [schih'ling] n. schottische Schäferhütte f.

Sheen [schihn] n. Schein m, Glanz m.

Sheep [schihp] n. Schaf n; – farm n. Schäferei f; – farming n. Schafzucht f; – fold n. Schafhürde f.

Sheepish [schih'pisch] *a*, -ly *ad*. blöde; -ness *n*. Blödigkeit *f*.

Sheepskin [schih'pskin] *n*. Schaffell *n*, Schafleder *n*, Pergament *n*, Urkunde *f*.

Sheer [schih'er] *vi*. scheren, gieren (*nav*.); *n*. Linien *f.pl*. Sprung *f*, des Deckes, Scheren *n*; – hulk *n*. Mastenhulk *m*.

Sheer [schih'er] *a*. lauter, einfach, rein, senkrecht, steil (*steep*).

Sheet [schiht] *n*. Platte *f*, Bogen *m* (*paper*), Bettuch *n*, Laken *n* (*bed*), Blech *n* (*metal*), Fläche *f* (*water*), Segelleine *f*, Schote *f* (*sail*); *vt*. mit Platten belegen, einhüllen, falzen; – -anchor *n*. Notanker *m*; – iron *n*. Eisenblech *n*; – lightning *n*. Wetterleuchten *n*.

Sheeting [schih'ting] *n*. Leinwand *f*, Bettleinen *n*.

Sheldrake [schel'dreik] *n*. Brandente *f*.

Shelf [schelf] *n*. Brett *n*, Fach *n*, Sims *m*, Gestell *n*, Regal *n*.

Shell [schel] *n*. Hülse *f*, Schale *f*, Muschel *f*, Bombe *f*, Granate *f*, Geschoss *n*; *vt*. schälen, enthülsen, bombardieren, beschiessen; high explosive – *n*. Spreng-, Brisanz-granate *f*; – -burst *n*. Granateinschlag *m*; – -crater, – hole *n*. Granat-, Geschoss-trichter *m*; – -egg *n*. Originalei *n*; – -fire *n*. Granatfeuer *n*; – -fish *n*. Schaltier *n*; – -fragment, – -splinter *n*. Granat-splitter *m*, -stück *n*; – -proof *a*. bombensicher, bombenfest, schuss-sicher; – -shock *n*. Nervenerschütterung *f*, Kriegsnevrose *f*. [*m*.

Shellac [sche'læk] *n*. Schellack

Shelling [sche'ling] *n*. Schalen *n*, Beschiessung *f* (*mil*.).

Shelter [schel'ter] *n*. Obdach *n*, Schutz *m*, Schutzdach *n*, Schuppen *m*; *vi*. Obdach nehmen, Schutz suchen; *t*. beschütz-

en, beschirmen; -less *a*. obdachlos.

Shelve [schelw] *vt*. beseitigen, beiseitestellen, ausrangier-n, zu den Akten legen (*topic, etc.*). mit Regalen versehen (*room*); -ing *n*. Bretter *n.pl*, Beiseitelegung *f*.

Shelve [schelw] *vi*. abschüssig sein, sich neigen; -ing *a*. abschüssig, schräg.

Shepherd [sche'perd] *n*. Schäfer *m*, Schafhirt *m*; *vt*. leiten, behüten, begleiten; -ess *n*. Schäferin *f*.

Sherbet [schär'bΑt] *n*. Sorbett *n*, Scherbett *n*, Granatlimonade *f*.

Sheriff [sche'rif] *n*. Landrat *m*, Kreisrichter *m*, erster Grafschaftsbeamte(r).

Sherry [sche'ri] *n*. Sherry *m*, spanischer Wein.

Shield [schihld] *n*. Schild *m*, Schutzdach *n*; *vt*. schützen, beschirmen.

Shift [schift] *n*. Veränderung *f*, Wechsel *m*, Schicht *f* (*workers*), Notbehelf *m*, Auskunftsmittel *n*; *vt*. schieben, verschieben; *i*. den Ort verändern, sich behelfen; -ing *a*. veränderlich; -less *a*. hilflos, unfähig; -y *a*. verschlagen, schlau.

Shilling [schi'ling] *n*. Schilling *m*.

Shilly-shally [schi'li-schæ'li] *vi*. unentschlossen sein, zögern.

Shimmer [schi'mer] *vi*. schimmern, flimmern; *n*. Schimmer *m*.

Shin [schin] *n*. Schienbein *n*; – up *vt*. heraufklettern.

Shindy [schin'di] *n*. Lärm *m*, Radau *m*.

Shine [schain] *vi*. glänzen, scheinen, leuchten; *n*. Glanz *m*, Schein *m*.

Shingle [sching'gl] *n*. Meerkies *m*, Strandkiesel *m.pl*.

Shingle [sching'gl] *n*. Dachschindel *f*, Bubikopf *m*; *vt*.

kurz scheren, mit Schindeln decken (roof). [Gürtelrose f.
Shingles [sching'gls] n.pl.
Shingly [sching'gli] a. grobkieselig, Kiesel . . . .
Shiny [schai'ni] a. glänzend, scheinend.
Ship [schip] n. Schiff m; vt. einschiffen, an Bord bringen, verschiffen; – breaker n.
Schiffausschlachter m; – broker n. Schiffsmakler m; – chandler n. Schiffslieferant m; – mate n. der, die Mitreisende; – owner n. Schiffsbesitzer m, Reeder m; – shape a. in guter Ordnung.
Shipbuilder [schip'bil-der] n. Schiffbauer m, Schiffsbaumeister m.
Shipbuilding [schip'bil-ding] n. Schiffbau m; – yard n. Werft f.
Shipment [schip'mnt] n. Ladung f, Verschiffung f.
Shipper [schip'er] n. Verschiffer m, Verlader m.
Shipping [schip'ing] n. Verschiffung f, Schiffsraum m, Handelsflotte f, Schiffswesen n; – agency n. Seespeditionsschäft n; – agent n. Spediteur m; – board n. Schiff-fahrtsbehörde f; – clerk n. Expedient m; – company n. Reederei f.
Shipwreck [schip'rek] n. Schiffbruch m; vt. scheitern.
Shipwright [schip'rait] n. Schiffs-zimmermann m, – baumeister m.
Shipyard [schip'jahrd] n. Schiffswerft f.
Shire [schai'er] n. Grafschaft f; – horse n. Lastpferd n.
Shirk [schark] vi. sich drücken; – er n. Drückeberger m.
Shirt [schart] n. Hemd n; – blouse n. Hemdbluse f; – front n. Vorhemd n; – sleeve n. Hemdärmel m; – stud n. Hemdknopf m.
Shirting [schAr'ting] n.

Hemden-stoff m, -tuch n.
Schirting m.
Shiver [schi'wer] vi. zittern, schauern; n. Schauer n; -y a. frösteln.
Shiver [schi'wer] vt. zerschmettern, zerschellen.
Shoal [schoul] n. Schwarm m, Menge f, Zug m (fish); vi. wimmeln, ziehen.
Shoal [schoul] n. Sandbank f, Untiefe f; vi. flach werden.
Shock [schok] n. Hocke f (sheaves).
Shock [schok] n. Haarschopf m.
Shock [schok] n. Stoss m, Schlag m, Erschütterung f, Zusammenstoss m, Anfall m, Angriff m, Anstoss m; vt. stossen, entsetzen, erschüttern; – absorption n. Erschütterungsdämpfung f; – absorber n. Stossdämpfer m (aut.); – troops n.pl. Stosstruppen f.pl.
Shocking [scho'king] a. anstössig, ärgerlich, entsetzlich.
Shoddy [scho'di] n. Lumpenwolle f, Shoddy n, Schund m; a. wertlos, kitschig.
Shoe [schuh] n. Schuh m; vt. beschuhen, –horn n. Schuhanzieher m; –lace n. Schnürsenkel m, Schuhband n; – polish n. Schuhwichse f; – shop n. Schuhgeschäft n.
Shoeblack [schuh'blæk] n. Schuhputzer m.
Shoemaker [schuh'mei-ker] n. Schuhmacher m, Schuster m; –'s thread n. Pechdraht m.
Shoemaking [schuh'mei-king] n. Schuhfabrikation f, Schuhmacherei f.
Shoo [schuh] vt. verscheuchen.
Shoot [schuht] v.i. schiessen, erschiessen (kill), abfeuern (discharge), fliegen, stürzen (plunge), fliegen, Aufnahme machen (film); n. Schuss m, Jagd f, Stoss m (football); – down n. abschliessen (av.).
Shooting [schuh'ting] n.

Schiessen n, Jagd f; - -down n. Abschuss m (av.); - -practice n. Schiessübung f; - -range n. Schiess-stand m.

Shop [schop] n. Laden m, Kaufladen m, Geschäft n, Werkstatt f (workshop); vi. Einkäufe machen, einkaufen; - -assistant n. Ladengehilfe m, Verkäufer m, Verkäuferin f; - -fittings n.pl. Ladeneinrichtung f; - -front n. Schaufenster n, Auslage f; - -girl n. Verkäuferin f; - -soiled a. leicht beschmutzt; - -steward n. Betriebsrat m; - -walker n. Empfangsener m, Aufsichtsherr m; - -window n. Schaufenster n.

Shopping [schop'ing] n. Einkaufen n, Einkäufe m.pl.; - -centre n. Geschäftsstadt f.

Shopkeeper [schop'kih-per] n. Ladeninhaber m, Kleinhändler m.

Shopkeeping [schop'kih-ping] n. Kleinhandel m, Detailverkauf m.

Shoplift'er [schop'lif-ter] n. Ladendieb m; -ing n. Ladendiebstahl m.

Shore [schOr] vt. stützen, unterstützen; - Stütze f, Spreize f, Strebe f.

Shore [schOr] n. Ufer n, Strand m, Küste f; - -battery n. Küstenbatterie f; - -wards ad küstenwärts.

Short [schOrt] a. kurz, knapp, unzulänglich; - -circuit n. Kurzschluss m; - -sighted a. kurzsichtig; - -wave n. Kurzwelle f (rad.); - -wave transmitter n. Kurzwellensender m.

Shortage [schOr'tidzh] n. Mangel m, Knappheit f, Verlust m.

Shortcomings [schOrt-kА'mings] n.pl. Fehler m.pl, Mängel m.pl.

Shorten [schOrtn] vt. verkürzen, vermindern; -ing n. Verkürzung f.

Shorthand [schOrt'hænd] n. Kurzschrift f, Stenographie f; a. stenographisch; - -typist n. Stenotypist m; - -writer n. Stenograph m, -in f.

Shorthorn [schOrt'hOrn] n. kurzhörniges Rindvieh.

Shortish [schOr'tisch] a. ziemlich kurz.

Shortly [schOrt'li] ad. bald, kürzlich, demnächst.

Shortness [schOrt'ness] n. Kürze f, Mangel m, Knappheit f.

Shorts [schOrtss] n.pl. Kniehose f, Turnhose f.

Shot [schot] n. Schuss m, Schütze m (man), Schrot n, Versuch m (try), Aufnahme f (film); a. schillernd, changierend (silk); - -gun n. Schrotflinte f; - -silk n. Einschlagseide f; - -velvet n. Schillersamt m.

Shoulder [schoul'der] n. Schulter f, Achsel f; vt. schultern; - -blade n. Schulterblatt n; - -strap n. Schulterriemen m, Schulter-, Achsel-klappe f (mil.).

Shout [schaut] n. Schrei m, lauter Ruf, Geschrei n; vi. schreien, laut rufen; -ing n. Geschrei n.

Shove [schAw] vt. schieben, stossen; - n. Schub m, Stoss m; - -off vi. (vom Lande) abstossen.

Shovel [schAw] n. Schaufel f, Schippe f; vt.i. schaufeln.

Show [schou] vt. zeigen, weisen, sehen lassen, erweisen (kindness, etc.); - n. Schau f, Ausstellung f, Anblick m, Auslage f (shop), Angelegenheit f (matter), Sache f, Vorstellung f (theatre, etc.), Film m; - -case n. Schaukasten m; -room n. Ausstellungsraum m.

Shower [schau'er] n. Regenschauer m; vt. überschütten; - -bath n. Brausebad n.

Showman [schou'mAn] n. Schausteller m, Marktschreier m; -ship n. Schaustellkunst f. Reklame f.   [prunkhaft.

Showy [schou'i] a. prahlerisch,

Shrapnel [schræp'nAl] n. Schrapnelgranate f, Schrapnel n.

Shred [schred] n. Fetzen m, Schnittchen n; vt. klein schneiden; -s pl. Abfälle m.pl.

Shrew [schruh] n. Zankteufel m, böses Weib.

Shrewd [schruhd] a, -ly ad. schlau, scharfsinnig, klug; -ness n. Schlauheit f, Klugheit f, Scharfsinn m.   [zänkisch.

Shrewish [schruh'isch] a.

Shriek [schrihk] vi. kreischen, schreien; n. Gekreisch n.

Shrift [schrift] n. Beichte f, Busse f, Gnadenfrist f.

Shrill [schril] a, -y ad. schrill, gellend.

Shrimp [schrimp] n. Garnele f, Krabbe f, Knirps m (brat).

Shrine [schrain] n. Reliquienschrein m.

Shrink [schringk] vi.t. einschrumpfen, einlaufen, zusammenziehen, schwinden, abnehmen, zurückschrecken; -able a. zusammenziehbar; -age n. Einschrumpfen n. Gewichtsverlust m.

Shrive [schraiw] vt. beichten.

Shrivel [schriwl] vi. einschrumpfen, falten, runzeln, sich zusammenziehen, vergehen.

Shroud [schraud] n. Leichentuch n, -hemd n; vt. einhüllen, verbergen.   (nav.).

Shroud [schraud] n. Want f

Shrove [schrouw] -tide n. Fastenzeit f; - Tuesday n. Fastnacht f.

Shrub [schrAb] n. Staude f, Strauch m; -bery n. Gebüsch n.

Shrug [schrAg] vi. zucken; n. Achselzucken n.

Shudder [schA'der] vi. schaudern, beben; n. Schauder m.

Shuffle [schAfl] vt. schieben, durcheinander schütteln, mischen (cards); i. schlürfen; n. Schieben n, Verwirrung f, Mischen n; -r n. Ausflüchtemacher m, unzuverlässiger Mensch.   [ausweichen.

Shun [schAn] vt. vermeiden,

Shunt [schAnt] vt.i. auf ein Nebengleise bringen, rangieren, einlenken; n. Nebenanschluss m (el.); -ing engine n. Rangierlokomotive f.

Shut [schAt] vt.i. (sich) schliessen, zumachen, sperren.

Shutter [schA'ter] n. Fensterladen m, Schieber m, Verschluss m (camera).

Shuttle [schAtl] n. Schiffchen n; -cock n. Federball m; --service, --traffic n. Pendelverkehr m.

Shy [schai] a. scheu, schüchtern; vi. zurückscheuen, scheuen (horse); -ness n. Scheu f, Schüchternheit f.   [werfen.

Shy [schai] n. Wurf m; vt.

Sibilant [ssi'bi-lAnt] a. zischend; n. Zischlaut m.

Sick [ssik] a. krank, übel, überdrüssig; -bay n. Revier n; --bed n. Krankenbett n; --fund n. Krankenkasse f; --leave n. Genesungsurlaub m; --list n. Krankenliste f; --parade n. Revierstunde f.

Sicken [ssikn] vi. erkranken; t. anekeln, krank machen; -ed a. überdrüssig.

Sickle [ssikl] n. Sichel f.

Sickly [ssik'li] a. kränklich, schwächlich, ungesund.

Sickness [ssik'ness] n. Krankheit f, Übelkeit f, Kränklichkeit f.

Side [ssaid] n. Seite f, Partei f, Ufer n; vi. Partei ergreifen für, auf der Seite sein von; --arms m.pl. Seitengewehr n (mil.); --band n. Seitenband n (rad.); --car n. Beiwagen m (aut.); --issue n. Nebensache f.

-line n. Nebenberuf m, Nebenbeschäftigung f; -show n. Nebenausstellung f; -track n. Nebengeleise n; vt. beiseiteschieben.

Sideboard [ssaid'bOrd] n. Büfett n, Anrichtetisch m.

Sideways [ssaid'ueis] ad. seitwärts.

Siding [ssai'ding] n. Nebengeleise n, Weiche f, Ausweicheplatz m.

Siege [ssihdzh] n. Belagerung f; state of - Belagerungszustand m; - artillery n. schwerste Artillerie, schwerstes Geschütz n; - -gun n. Belagerungsgeschütz n.

Sienna [ssi-e'nA] n. Sienaerde f.

Sieve [ssiw] n. Sieb n; vt. sieben.

Sift [ssift] vt. durchsieben, sichten, auswerten (information).

Sigh [ssai] vi. seufzen; n. Seufzer m.

Sight [ssait] n. Gesicht n, Sehen n, Anblick m, Schauspiel n, Sicht f (nav. com.). Visier n, Aufsatz m (mil.); telescopic - Fernrohraufsatz m; vt. zu Gesicht bekommen, erblicken, sichten (nav.), visieren (rifle).

Sighting [ssai'ting] n. Sichten n, Visieren n; - beschuss m, Visierschuss m.

Sight-seeing [ssait'ssih-ing] n. Besuch m. von Sehenswürdigkeiten.

Sight-seer [ssait'ssih-er] n. der, die Schaulustige, Tourist m.

Sign [ssain] n. Zeichen n, Kennzeichen n. Merkmal n, Wink m; vt. unter-schreiben, -zeichnen; - on (for a job) vi. antreten, heuern, sich verpflichten.

Signal [ssig'nAl] n. Signal n, Zeichen n; a. ausserordentlich, bemerkenswert; vt.i. signalisieren Signale geben, winken

(flags); -s pl. Nachrichtenwesen n (mil.); -s battalion n. Nachrichtenabteilung f; -s centre n. Meldesammelstelle f; -s company n. Nachrichtenkompanie f; -s interpreter n. Signalauswerter m; -s platoon, -s section n. Nachrichtenzug m, -staffel f; -s regiment n. Nachrichtenregiment n; -s service n. Nachrichten-dienst m, -verkehr m; -s station n. Nachrichtenstelle f; -s subsection n. Nachrichtentrupp m; -s unit n. Nachrichteneinheit f.

Signal-box [ssig'nAl-box] n. Blockstelle f, Stellwerk n (rl.).

Signalize [ssig'nA-lais] vt. auszeichnen.

Signaller [ssig'nA-ler] n. Winker m, Fernmeldefunker m (av.), Funker m (rad.).

Signalman [ssig'nAl-mAn] n. Bahnwärter m, Signalgeber m (rl.).

Signatory [ssig'nA-tA-ri] a. unterzeichnend, Signatar . . . ; n. Unterzeichner m.

Signature [ssig'nA-tscher] n. Unterschrift f, Signatur f (rad. etc.).

Sign-board [ssain'bOrd] n. Aushängeschild m.

Signet [ssig'nit] n. Siegel n; - -ring n. Siegelring m.

Significance [ssig-nif'fi-kAnss] n. Bedeutung f, Wichtigkeit f; -t a. bedeutsam, ausdrücklich.

Signification [ssig-nif-fi-kei't-schAn] n. Sinn m, Bedeutung f.

Signify [ssig'ni-fai] vt. bezeichnen, bedeuten.

Sign-painter [ssain'pein-ter] n. Schildermaler m.

Sign-post [ssain'poust] n. Wegweiser m.

Silence [ssai'lAnss] n. Schweigen n; vt. zum Schweigen bringen; -r n. Schalldämpfer m, Auspufftopf m (aut.).

Silent [ssai'lAnt] *a.*, -ly *ad.* still, schweigend, schweigsam, stumm; - **approach** *n.* Schleichfahrt *f* (*av.*); - **film** *n.* stummer Film; - **position** *n.* Lauerstellung *f* (*mil.*).

Silhouette [si-luh-et'] *n.* Schattenbild *n.*

Silica [ssi'li-kA] *n.* Kieselerde *f.*

Silicate [ssi'li-kit] *n.* Silikat *n.*

Silicon [ssi'li-kAn] *n.* Silizium *n.*

Silk [ssilk] *n.* Seide *f*, Seidenstoff *m*; *a.* seiden; - **merchant** *n.* Seidenhändler *m*; - **moth** *n.* Seidenspinner *m*; - **stockings** *n.pl.* seidene Strümpfe *m.pl*; - **thread** *n.* Seiden-faden *m*, -zwirn *m*; - **worm** *n.* Seidenraupe *f.*

Silken [ssil'kAn] *a.* seiden.

Silky [ssil'ki] *a.* seidenartig, weich. [brett *n.*

Sill [ssil] *n.* Gesims *n*, Fenster-

Silliness [ssi'li-ness] *n.* Albernheit *f.* [dumm.

Silly [ssi'li] *a.* albern, blöde,

Silo [ssai'lou] *n.* Silo *m*, Getreidespeicher *m*; *vt.* einlagern, einmieten.

Silt [ssilt] *n.* Schlamm *m*, Triebsand *m*; *vi./t.* versanden, verschlammen.

Silver [ssil'wer] *n.* Silber *n*; *a.* silbern; *vt.* versilbern; - **currency** *n.* Silberwährung *f*; - **fir** *n.* Weißtanne *f*; - **foil** *n.* Silberfolie *f*; - **gilt** *n.* vergoldetes Silber; - **lining** *n.* Lichtseite *f*; - **mounted** *a.* silberbeschlagen; - **paper** *n.* Silberpapier *n*; - **plate** *n.* Silbergerät *n*; - **plating** *n.* Silberplattierung *f.*

Silversmith [ssil'wer-ssmith] *n.* Silberschmied *m.*

Silvery [ssil'wA-ri] *a.* silbern, silberweiß.

Similar [ssi'mi-ler] *a.*, -ly *ad.* ähnlich.

Similarity [ssi-mi-læ'ri-ti] *n.* Ähnlichkeit *f.*

Simmer [ssi'mer] *vi.* sieden, wallen, leicht kochen.

Simper [ssim'per] *vi.* einfältig lächeln; *n.* albernes Lächeln.

Simple [ssimpl] *a.* einfach, einfältig, schlicht, kunstlos; - **minded** *n.* arglos, einfältig; - **ton** *n.* Tropf *m*, Einfaltspinsel *m.*

Simplicity [ssim-pli'ssi-ti] *n.* Einfachheit *f*, Schlichtheit *f*, Einfältigkeit *f.*

Simplification [ssim-pli-fi-kei'schAn] *n.* Vereinfachung *f.*

Simplify [ssim'pli-fai] *vt.* vereinfachen. [bloss, nur.

Simply [ssim'pli] *ad.* einfach,

Simulate [ssi'mju-leit] *vt.* heucheln, vorgeben.

Simultaneous [ssi-mAl-tei'njAss] *a.*, -ly *ad.* gleichzeitig.

Sin [ssin] *n.* Sünde *f*; *vi.* sündigen. [seit; *cj.* da.

Since [ssinss] *ad.* seither; *pr.* [seit.

Sincere [ssin-ssih'er] *a.* aufrichtig, redlich, offen; Yours -ly ihr ergebener.

Sincerity [ssin-sse'ri-ti] *n.* Aufrichtigkeit *f*, Redlichkeit *f.*

Sinecure [ssai'ri-kju-er] *n.* einträgliches Ruheamt, Sinekure *f.*

Sinew [ssi'njuh] *n.* Sehne *f.*

Sinful [ssin'ful] *a.* sündhaft, sündig. [Sündhaftigkeit *f.*

Sinfulness [ssin'ful-ness] *n.*

Sing [ssing] *vt./i.* singen.

Singe [ssindzh] *vt.* versengen.

Singer [ssing'er] *n.* Sänger *m*, Sängerin *f.*

Singing [ssing'ing] *n.* Gesang *m*; - **bird** *n.* Singvogel *m*; - **lesson** *n.* Gesangstunde *f*; - **master** *n.* Gesanglehrer *m.*

Single [ssing'gl] *a.* einzig, allein, einzeln, ledig, unverheiratet (*unmarried*); *n.* Einzelspiel *n* (*games*); *vt.* - **out** aussondern, aussuchen, auswählen; - **circuit receiver** *n.* Einkreisempfänger *m* (*rad.*); - **court** *n.* Einzelspielfeld *n*;

file n. blinde Rotte, Schützenlinie f (mil.); – **-handed** a. einhändig, auf eigne Faust, allein; – **man** n. Junggeselle m; – **-minded** a. aufrichtig, redlich; – **-phase** a. einphasig (el.); – **-seater** n. Einsitzer m (aut.); – track a. einspurig, eingleisig.

Singlet [ssing'glAt] n. Unterjacke f, Sporthemd n.

Singly [ssing'gli] ad. einzeln, allein, ohne Hilfe.

Singular [ssing'gju-ler] a, **-ly** ad. seltsam, sonderbar, einzeln; n. Einzahl f, Singular m.

Singularity [ssing-gju-læ'ri-ti] n. Eigentümlichkeit f, Ungewöhnlichkeit f.

Sinister [ssi'ni-ster] a. böse, düster, finster, unredlich.

Sink [ssingk] vi. sinken, untertauchen, fallen; t. senken, absenken zum Sinken bringen; n. Ausguss m; – **-er** n. Senkblei n; **-ing** n. Sinken n; – **fund** n. Tilgungsfonds m, Amortisationskasse f (com.).

Sinner [ssi'ner] n. Sünder m, Sünderin f.

Sinuosity [ssi-nju-o'ssi-ti] n. Wellenförmigkeit f.

Sinuous [ssi'nju-Ass] a. wellig, gewunden.

Sip [ssip] vt. nippen; n. Schlückchen n.

Siphon [ssai'fAn] n. Siphon m, Heber m, Leitrohr n (tec.).

Sir [ssAr] n. Herr m, Sir m (title); **Dear** – sehr geehrter Herr.

Sire [ssai'er] n. Vater m.

Siren [sai'rAn] n. Sirene f, Dampfpfeife f (ship).

Sirloin [ssAr'leun] n. Lendenstück n.

Sisal [ssai'sAl] n. Sisal m, Sisalhanf m.

Sister [ssi'ster] n. Schwester f, Oberschwester f (hospital); – **ship** n. Schwesterschiff n; – **-in-law** n. Schwägerin f; **-ly** a. schwesterlich.

Sit [ssit] vi. sitzen, beraten; – **down** sich setzen.   [Lage f.

Site [ssait] n. Bauplatz m.

Sitting [si'ting] n. Sitzung f; – **accommodation** n. Sitzgelegenheit f; – **-room** n. Wohnzimmer n, Salon m.

Situated [ssi'tju-ei-tid] a. gelegen, befindlich, gestellt; beautifully – in schöner Lage.

Situation [ssi-tju-ei'schAn] n. Lage f, Stellung f, Dienst m; – **map** n. Lagekarte f (mil.); – **report** n. Lagebericht m.

Six [ssix] num. sechs; **-pence** n.pl. sechs Pence, sechs Groschen; **-teen** num. sechzehn; **-th** a. sechst; n. Sechstel n; **-ty** num. sechzig.

Sizable [ssai'sAbl] a. ziemlich gross; a – **town** eine grössere Stadt.   [Umfang m, Länge f.

Size [ssais] n. Grösse f, Mass n.

Size [ssais] n. Leim m, Kleister m; vt. leimen, grundieren (paint).

Sizzle [ssisl] vi. zischen.

Skate [skeit] n. Glattroche m.

Skate [skeit] n. Schlittschuh m; vi. Schlittschuh laufen; – er n. Schlittschuh-läufer m, -läuferin f; **-ing-rink** n. Eisbahn f.

Skedaddle [ski-dedl'] vi. ausreissen, davonlaufen.   [Docke f.

Skein [skein] n. Strähne f.

Skeleton [ske'li-tAn] n. Gerippe n, Skelett n, Entwurf m, Umriss m, Stamm m (mil.); – key n. Dietrich m; – staff n. stark vermindertes Personal.

Sketch [sketsch] n. Skizze f, Zeichnung f, Entwurf m; vt. skizzieren, entwerfen, zeichnen; **panorama** – n. Ansichtsskizze f; – **-block** n. Skizzierblock m; – **-map** n. Kroki n (mil.).

Sketchy [sket'schi] a. skizzenhaft, hastig, oberflächlich.

Skewer [skjuh'er] n. Speiler m, Fleischspiess m, Wursthölzchen n; vt. spiessen.

Ski [schih] n. Ski m, Schneeschuh m; vi. Ski laufen.

Skid [skid] vi. gleiten, ausrutschen; n. Hemmschuh m,
Rutschen n (aut.), Kufe f (av,
etc.).

Skier [shih'er] n. Skiläufer m,
Skiläuferin f.

Ski-ing [shih'ing] n. Skilaufen
n, Skisport m.

Skiff [skif] n. Wettruderboot m.

Skilful [skil'ful] a. -ly ad. geschickt, gewandt, geübt; -ness
n. Geschicklichkeit f, Gewandtheit f.

Skill [skil] n. Geschicklichkeit
f, Fertigkeit f, Gewandtheit f,
Tüchtigkeit f.

Skilled [skild] a. geschickt,
geübt, erfahren, bewandert; -
worker n. Facharbeiter m,
Fachkraft f, gelernter Handwerker.

Skim [skim] vt. abschäumen,
abschöpfen, abrahmen (milk);
-med milk n. Magermilch f.

Skimp [skimp] vt. geizen mit,
knausern mit, knapp halten;
-y a. knapp, dürftig.

Skin [skin] n. Haut f, Fell n,
Balg m, Pelz n (fur); vt. ab-
häuten, abstreifen, schälen,
schinden; - deep a. oberflächlich; - grafting n. Haut-
übertragung f; - transplantation f, Autoplastik f.

Skinflint [skin'flint] n. Geizhals m, Filz m.

Skinny [ski'ni] a. mager,
fleischlos, geizig.

Skip [skip] vi. hüpfen, spring-
en; -ping rope n. Springseil n.

Skirmish [skAr'mish] n.
Scharmützel n, Plänkelei f, Gefecht n; vi. plänkeln, schar-
mützeln.

Skirt [skArt] n. Rock m, Rand
m (edge), Saum m (fringe); vt.
angrenzen an; -ing n. Fussleiste f. [Spottrede f.

Skit [skit] n. gelinde Satire.

Skittish [ski'tisch] a. leicht-

fertig, ausgelassen; -ness n.
Leichtfertigkeit f.

Skittle [skitl] n. Kegel m; -
alley n. Kegelbahn f.

Skulk [skAlk] vi. lauern,
schleichen.

Skull [skAl] n. Schädel m,
Hirnschale f.

Sky [skai] n. Himmel m; -light
n. Oberlicht n; -line n. Horizont m; -scraper n. Wolken-
kratzer m, Hochhaus n; -
writing n. Himmelsschrift f.

Skylark [skai'lahrk] n. Lerche
f, Feldlerche f. [fliese f.

Slab [sslæb] n. Platte f, Stein-

Slack [sslæk] a. schlaff, locker,
faul, nachlässig, flau (com.).

Slack [sslæk] n. Kohlenklein n,
Steinkohlengrus m.

Slacken [sslækn] vi. erschlaff-
en; t. schlaff machen.

Slacker [sslæ'ker] n. Schlapp-
macher m, Drückeberger m.

Slackness [sslæk'ness] n.
Schlaffheit f, Schwäche f, Flauheit f (com.).

Slag [sslæg] n. Schlacke f.

Slake [ssleik] vt. löschen,
stillen.

Slam [sslæm] vt. zuschlagen; n.
Knall m, Schlemm m (bridge).

Slander [sslahn'der] n. Verleumdung f; vt. verleumden;
-ous a. verleumderisch.

Slang [sslæng] n. niedere Umgangssprache, Zunftsprache f;
vt. ausschimpfen; -y a. unfein,
derb.

Slant [sslahnt] vi. sich neigen,
schräg liegen; n. schräge Richtung, Schiefsein f; -ing a.
schief, schräg.

Slap [sslæp] vt. klapsen; n.
Klaps m, Schlag m; -dash a.
nachlässig, oberflächlich.

Slash [sslæsch] vt. aufschlitz-
en, zerhacken; n. Schnitt m.

Slate [ssleit] n. Schiefer m,
Schiefertafel f; a. blaugrau;
vt. mit Schiefer decken; -
pencil n. Schieferstift m, Grif-

fel m; – quarry n. Schieferbruch m. [decker m.
Slater [sslei'ter] n. Schiefer
Slattern [sslæ'tern] n. Schlumpe f; -ly a. schlumpig.
Slaty [sslei'ti] a. schieferig.
Slaughter [sslô'ter] n. Schlachten n, Gemetzel n, Blutbad n; vt. schlachten, niedermetzeln; – -house n. Schlachthaus n.
Slave [ssleiw] n. Sklave m, Sklavin f; vi. sich placken, schuften, frönen; – -driver n. Menschenschinder m.
Slavery [sslei'wA-ri] n. Sklaverei f, Knechtschaft f.
Slavish [sslei'wisch] a. sklavisch, kriecherisch.
Slay [sslei] vt. erschlagen.
Sledge [ssledzh] n. Schlitten m; vi. Schlitten fahren.
Sledge-hammer [ssledzh'hæ-mer] n. Schmiedehammer m.
Sleek [sslihk] a. weich, glatt.
Sleep [sslihp] vi. schlafen; n. Schlaf m; – -walker n. Nachtwandler m.
Sleeper [sslih'per] n. Schläfer m, Schläferin f, Schwelle f (rl.), Schlafwagen m.
Sleeping [sslih'ping] n. Schlafen n; – -accommodation n. Schlafgelegenheit f; – -car n. Schlafwagen m; – -partner n. stiller Teilhaber; – -sack n. Schlafsack m. [schlaflos.
Sleepless [sslihp'less] a.
Sleepiness [sslih'pi-ness] n. Schläfrigkeit f.
Sleepy [sslih'pi] a. schläfrig.
Sleet [ssliht] n. Graupelregen m.
Sleeve [sslihw] n. Ärmel m; – -link n. (doppelter) Manschettenknopf m; – -less a. ohne Ärmel. [len-schlitten m.
Sleigh [sslei] n. Pferde-, Schel
Sleight [sslait] n. Kunststück n, Taschenspielerei f.
Slender [sslen'der] a. schlank, mager, gering, schwach; -ness

n. Schlankheit f, Magerkeit f, Dürftigkeit f.
Sleuth [sslühth] n. Bluthund m, Forscher m, Verfolger m, Detektiv m.
Sleuth-hound see sleuth.
Slice [sslaiss] n. Schnitte f, Scheibe f; vt. zerschneiden.
Slick [sslik] a. glatt, geschickt.
Slide [sslaid] n. Gleitbahn f, Schieber m, Haarspange f (hair), Bild n (lantern); vi. rutschen, gleiten; – -rule n. Rechenschieber m; – -slip n. Ausrutschen n; vi. abrutschen (av.).
Sliding [sslai'ding] n. Gleiten n; – -door n. Schiebetür f; – roof n. Schiebedach n; – scale n. gleitende Skala, Staffeltarif m (com.); – seat n. Rollsitz m.
Slight [sslait] a. -ly ad. gering, dünn, unbedeutend; n. Geringschätzung f, Nichtachtung f; vt. geringschätzig behandeln, -ingly ad. geringschätzig.
Slily [sslai'li] ad. schlau.
Slim [sslim] a. schlank, dünn; vt.i. schlank machen, eine Abnahmekur machen; -ming n. Abnahmekur f; -ness n. Schmächtigkeit f, Schlankheit f.
Slime [sslaim] n. Schlamm m, Schlick m.
Slimy [sslai'mi] a. schlammig, schleimig.
Sling [ssling] n. Schlinge f, Schleuder f, Schulterriemen m, Stropp m (nav.); vt. schleudern, werfen, hissen (nav.).
Slink [sslingk] vi. schleichen.
Slip [sslip] vt.i. schlüpfen, gleiten, rutschen; n. Gleiten n, Rutschen n, Überwurf m, Fehler m (mistake), Stapel m (ship); – -fuel tank n. Abwurfbehälter m (av.); – -knot n. Schleifknoten m.
Slipper [sslip'per] n. Pantoffel m; – -bath n. Badewanne f.
Slipperiness [sslip'pA-ri-ness] n. Schlüpferigkeit f.

Slippery [ssli'pA-ri] *a.* schlüpfrig, unzuverlässig, unredlich. [erlich, nachlässig.
Slipshod [sslip'schod] *a.* lied-
Slip-stream [sslip'strihm] *n.* Luftstrudel *m* (*av.*).
Slipway [sslip'uei] *n.* Stapel *f*, Helling *m*, Aufschleppe *f.*
Slit [sslit] *n.* Schlitz *m*, Spalte *f*, Riss *m*; *vt.* aufschlitzen, spalten; – **trench** *n.* Splitter-, Stich-graben *m* (*mil.*). [jen.
Slither [ssli'dher] *vi.* ausgleit-
Slobber [sslo'ber] *vi.* geifern.
Sloe [sslou] *n.* Schlehe *f*, Schwarzdorn *m.*
Slog [sslog] *vi.* schuften, sich placken.
Slogan [sslou'gAn] *n.* Schlagwort *n*, Losung *f.*
Sloop [ssluhp] *n.* Schaluppe *f*, Kanonenboot *n.*
Slop [sslop] *vt.* verschütten; –s *n.pl.* Spülicht *n*; – **basin** *n.* Spülnapf *m.*
Slop's [sslop] *n.* Schräge *f*, Abhang *m*; *vi.t.* (sich) neigen; -ing *a.* schief, schräg.
Slot [sslot] *n.* Schlitz *m*, Kerbe *f*; – **machine** *n.* Automat *m.*
Slothful [sslouth'ful] *a.* träge, faul; -ness *n.* Faulheit *f*, Trägheit *f.*
Slouch [sslautsch] *vi.* schlottern, schlendern; *n.* schlotternder Gang; – **hat** *n.* Schlapphut *m.*
Slough [sslau] *n.* Sumpf *m.*
Sloven [sslAwn] *n.* liederlicher Mensch; -ly *a.* liederlich, unlumpig.
Slow [sslou] *a.*, -ly *ad.* langsam, verspätet, spät, lässig, untätig; – **coach** *n.* Nölmeier *m*, Nölpeter *m*; – **down** *vi.* langsamer fahren; – **motion picture** *n.* Zeitlupenaufnahme *f*; – **train** *n.* Personenzug *m.*
Sludge [sslAdzh] *n.* Schlamm *m.*
Slug [sslAg] *n.* Wegschnecke *f* (snail).

Slug [sslAg] *n.* Kugel *f*, Posten *m* (bullet). [enzer *m.*
Sluggard [sslA'gerd] *n.* Faul-
Sluggish [sslA'gisch] *a.*, -ly *ad.* langsam fliessend, träge, faul, schwerfällig; -ness *n.* Langsamkeit *f*, Trägheit *f.*
Sluice [ssluhss] *n.* Schleuse *f*, Siel *m*; *vt.* schleusen; – **gate** *n.* Schleusentor *m.*
Slum [sslAm] *n.* Elendsviertel *n*, Spelunke *f*, Hintergässchen *n.*
Slumber [sslAm'ber] *vi.* schlummern; *n.* Schlummer *m.*
Slump [sslAmp] *n.* Preissturz *m*, Baisse *f* (com.); *vi.* plötzlich fallen.
Slur [sslAr] *n.* Flecken *m*, Schandfleck *m*, geringschätzige Bemerkung; *vt.* besudeln; – **over** *i.* leicht hinwegeilen über.
Slush [sslAsch] *n.* Schneewasser *n*, Schlamm *m.*
Slut [sslAt] *n.* Schlumpe *f*; -tish *a.* schlumpig, liederlich.
Sly [sslai] *a.* schlau, listig; -ness *n.* Schlauheit *f*, Verschlagenheit *f.*
Smack [ssmæk] *n.* Schlag *m*, Schmatz *m*, Klatsch *m*; *vt.* klatschen, schmatzen.
Smack [ssmæk] *n.* Geschmack *m*, Anstrich *m*; *vi.* schmecken, einen Anstrich haben von.
Smack [ssmæk] *n.* Fischerboot *m.*
Small [ssmOl] *a.* klein, schwach, schmal, gering, unbedeutend, kleinlich; – **arms** *n.* Handfeuerwaffe *f.pl*; – **holder** *n.* Kleinbauer *m*; – **holding** *n.* Kleinbauerngut *n*; – **talk** *n.* Plauderei *f.*
Smallness [ssmOl'ness] *n.* Kleinheit *f*, das Geringe.
Smallpox [ssmOl'pox] *n.* Pocken *pl.*
Smalt [ssmOlt] *n.* Schmalte *f*, Blaufarbenglas *n*, Kobaltblau *n.*
Smart [ssmahrt] *a.*, -ly *ad.* fein, elegant, gewandt, flott,

lebhaft, tüchtig, pfiffig, durchtrieben; *vi.* schmerzen, büssen, leiden; -ness *n.* Eleganz *f*, Schmuckheit *f*, Tüchtigkeit *f*, Geschicklichkeit *f*, Pfiffigkeit *f*, Schlauheit *f*.

Smash [ssmæsch] *n.* Zusammenstoss *m*, Krach *m*, Zerschmettern *n*, Unfall *m* (*aut.*); *vt.* zerschmeissen, zerschmettern; *i.* zusammenbrechen.

Smattering [ssmæ'tA-ring] *n.* oberflächliche Kenntnis.

Smear [ssmä'er] *vt.* beschmieren, besudeln; *n.* Fleck *m*, Schmiererei *f*.

Smell [ssmel] *n.* Geruch *m*; *vt.i.* riechen, wittern; -ing *a.* riechend; - bottle *n.* Riechfläschchen *n*; - salts *pl.* Riechsalz *n*.

Smelt [ssmelt] *vt.* schmelzen; -ing *n.* Schmelzarbeit *f*; - furnace *n.* Schmelzofen *m*.

Smelt [ssmelt] *n.* Stint *m*.

Smile [ssmail] *n.* Lächeln *n*; *vi.* lächeln.

Smirch [ssmArtsch] *vt.* beschmutzen, besudeln; *n.* Schmutzfleck *m*.

Smirk [ssmArk] *vi.* schmunzeln; *n.* Schmunzeln *n*.

Smite [ssmait] *vt.* schlagen; treffen.

Smith [ssmith] *n.* Schmied *m*.

Smithereens [ssmi-dhA-rihns'] *n.pl.* kleine Stücke, Splitter *m.pl.*.

Smithy [ssmi'dhi] *n.* Schmiede *f*.

Smitten [ssmi'tn] *a.* getroffen, bezaubert, verliebt.

Smock [ssmok] *n.* Arbeitshemd *n*, Kittel *m*.

Smoke [ssmouk] *vi.* rauchen, dampfen; *t.* rauchen, räuchern; *n.* Rauch *m*, Dampf *m*, Qualm *m*, Nebel *m* (*mil.*); - barrage *n.* Nebelwalze *f*; - bomb *n.* Rauchbombe *f*; - grenade *n.* Nebelgranate *f*; - mortar, - projector *n.* Nebelwerfer *m*; - room *n.* Rauch-

zimmer *n*; - screen *n.* Rauch-, Nebel-schleier *m*; - trail *n.* Rauchfahne *f*.

Smoking [ssmou'king] *a.* rauchend, dampfend; - compartment *n.* Raucherabteil *n* (*rl.*).

Smoker [ssmou'ker] *n.* Raucher *m*, Raucherabteil *n* (*rl.*).

Smoky [ssmou'ki] *a.* rauchend, rauchig.

Smooth [ssmuhdh] *a.* glatt, eben, sanft; *vt.* glätten, stillen, schlichten, abhobeln; -ly *ad.* glatt, eben, reibungslos; -ness *n.* Glätte *f*.

Smother [ssmA'dher] *vt.* ersticken.

Smoulder [ssmoul'der] *vi.* schwelen.

Smudge [ssmAdzh] *n.* Schmutzfleck *m*; *vt.* beschmieren, beschmutzen.

Smug [ssmAg] *a.* -ly *ad.* selbstzufrieden, selbstgefällig.

Smuggle [ssmAgl] *vt.i.* schmuggeln; -er *n.* Schmuggler *m*; -ing *n.* Schleichhandel *m*, Schmuggel *m*.

Smut [ssmAt] *n.* Russfleck *m*, Zoten *f.pl.*; -ty *a.* schmutzig, zotig, russig.

Snack [ssnæk] *n.* Imbiss *m*.

Snaffle [ssnæfl] *n.* Trense *f*; - bit *n.* Trensengebiss *n*.

Snaffle [ssnæfl] *vt.* klauen, mausen.

Snag [ssnæg] *n.* Knorren *m*, Knoten *m*, Hindernis *n*, Haken *m*.

Snail [ssneil] *n.* Schnecke *f*; - s pace *n.* Schneckengang *m*.

Snake [ssneik] *n.* Schlange *f*.

Snap [ssnæp] *vt.i.* zerbrechen, schnappen, schelten, eine Momentaufnahme machen (*photo*); - fastener *n.* Druckknopf *m*; - up *vt.* aufschnappen.

Snappish [ssnæ'pisch] *a.*, -ly *ad.* bissig, schnippisch.

Snapshot [ssnæp'schot] *n.* Momentaufnahme *f*.

Snare [ssneh'er] n. Schlinge f, Fallstrick m; vt. verstricken, fangen. [brummen.

Snarl [ssnahrl] vi. knurren,

Snatch [ssnætsch] vt. erhaschen, schnell ergreifen, schnappen nach; n. Zugreifen f, Ruck m, Augenblick m (moment).

Sneak [ssnihk] vi. schleichen, mausen, stibitzen; n. Schleicher m.

Sneer [ssnihr] vi. höhnen, spötteln; n. Hohnlächeln n, Spott m; -ing a, -ly ad. höhnisch.

Sneeze [ssnihs] vi. niesen; n. Niesen n; not to be -d at nicht übel, nicht zu verachten.

Sniff [ssnif] vi. schuppern, schnüffeln; n. Schnüffeln n; at die Nase rümpfen über.

Sniffle [ssnifl] vi. schnüffeln.

Sniffy [ssni'fi] a. verschnupft, verächtlich. [n. Gekicher n.

Snigger [ssni'ger] vi. kichern;

Snip [ssnip] vt. schneiden, schnippen; n. Schnitzel n.

Snipe [ssnaip] n. Schnepfe f; vi. aus dem Hinterhalt beschiessen (mil.); -r n. Scharf-, Hecken-, Baum-schütze m.

Snippets [ssni'pitss] n.pl. kleine Stückchen n.pl.

Snivel [ssniwl] vi. schnüffeln, heulen, wimmern; -ling a. triefnasig, weinerlich.

Snob [ssnob] n. Grosstuer m; -bery n. Vornehmtuerei f; -bish a. vornehmtuend.

Snore [ssnohr] vi. schnarchen; n. Schnarchen n.

Snort [ssnOrt] vi. schnauben, schnaufen.

Snout [ssnaut] n. Schnauze f; -y a. anmassend.

Snow [ssnou] n. Schnee m; vi. schneien; - -blind a. schneeblind; - -boot n. Schneestiefel m, Überschuh m; - -bound a. eingeschneit; -drift n. Schneewehe f; -fall n. Schneefall m;

-flake n. Schneeflocke f; - -glasses n.pl. Schneebrille f; -line n. Schneegrenze f; -man n. Schneemann m; - -plough n. Schneepflug m; -shoe n. Schneeschuh m; -storm n. Schneegestöber n; - -sweeper n. Schneekehrapparat m; -white a. schneeweiss.

Snowball [ssnou'bOl] n. Schneeball m; vi.t. mit Schneebällen werfen.

Snowdrop [ssnou'drop] n. Schneeglöckchen n.

Snowy [ssnou'i] a. schneeig.

Snub [ssnAb] n. Stumpfnase f, Verweis m, Zurechtweisung f, Rüge f; vt. anfahren, kurzabweisen, rügen.

Snuff [ssnAf] n. Schnupftabak m; vi.t. schnupfen; - -box n. Schnupftabaksdose f.

Snuffle [ssnAfl] vi. schnüffeln.

Snug [ssnAg] a, -ly ad. behaglich, wohnlich, warm.

So [ssou] ad. so, also, wohl; if - wenn ja.

Soak [ssouk] vt.i. einweichen, durchnässen.

Soap [ssoup] n. Seife f; vt. einseifen; - -bubble n. Seifenblase f; - -dish n. Seifen-napf m, -schälchen n; -flake n. Seifenflocke f; -maker n. manufacturer n. Seifensieder m; - -suds n.pl. Seifen-wasser n, -lauge f.

Soar [ssOr] vi. sich aufschwingen, schweben, plötzlich steigen (price), segeln (plane).

Sob [ssob] vi. schluchzen; n. Schluchzen n.

Sober [ssou'ber] a, -ly ad. nüchtern, mässig, ernst.

Sobriety [sso-brai'A-ti] n. Nüchternheit f, Mässigkeit f.

So-called [ssou-kOld'] a. sogenannt.

Sociability [ssou-schA-bi'li-ti] n. Gesellichkeit f. [sellig.

Sociable [ssou'schAbl] a. ge-

Social [ssou'schAl] a. gesell-

schaftlich, gesellig, Sozial...;
-ism n. Sozialismus m, -ist m.
Sozialist m. [a. sozialistisch.
Socialistic [ssou-schA-li'stik]
Socialization [ssou-schA-lai-
sei'schAn] n. Sozialisierung f.
Socialize [ssou'schA-lais] vt.
sozialisieren, vergesellschaften,
verstaatlichen.
Society [ssA-ssai'A-ti] n. Gesellschaft f, Umgang m, Verkehr m, Verein m.
Sock [ssok] n. Socke f.
Sock [ssok] n. Schlag m; vt.
hauen.
Socket [sso'kit] n. Rohransatz
m, Rohr n, Hülse f, Büchse f,
Zapfenlager n, Höhle f (eye);
- -joint n. kugelgelenk n (tec.).
Sod [ssod] n. Rasenstück n.
Soda [ssou'dA] n. Soda f, kohlensaures Natron; - -fountain
n. Sodawasserapparat m;
-water n. Soda-, Mineral-
wasser n.
Sodden [ssodn] a. durchnässt.
Sodium [ssou'djAm] n. Natrium n; - chloride n. Chlor-
natrium n; - nitrate n. Natron-
salpeter m.
Sofa [ssou'fA] n. Ruhebett n,
Sofa n; - -bed n. Schlafsofa n.
Soft [ssoft] a. -ly ad. weich,
sanft, mild, nachgiebig, albern;
- -soap n. Schmierseife f.
Soften [ssofn] vt. weich mach-
en, erweichen, mildern; i. sich
erweichen; -ing n. Erweich-
ung f.
Softness [ssoft'ness] n. Weichheit f, Sanftheit f.
Soggy [sso'gi] a. nass, feucht.
Soil [sseul] n. Boden m, Erde
f, Grund m.   [schmutzig.
Soil [sseul] vt. besudeln; -ed a.
Sojourn [sso'dzhern] n. Aufenthalt m; vi. sich aufhalten;
-er n. Gast m.
Solace [sso'liss] n. Trost m;
vt. trösten, mildern.
Solar [ssou'er] a. Sonnen...;
- system n. Sonnensystem n.

Solder [ssou'der] n. Lot n,
Lotmetall n; vt. löten; -ing
iron n. Lötkolben m.   [er m.
Solderer [ssou'dA-rer] n. Löt-
Soldier [ssou'dzher] n. Soldat
m; -'s slang n. Soldatensprache
f; -ing n. Soldatenberuf m,
Soldatenstand m; -ly a. soldat-
isch; -y n. Militär n.
Sole [ssoul] a. alleinig, einzig,
bloss; - agent n. Alleinvertret-
er m.
Sole [ssoul] n. Sohle f; vt. be-
sohlen (shoes).
Sole [ssoul] n. Seezunge f (fish).
Solecism [sso'li-ssism] n.
Sprachfehler m.
Solely [ssoul'li] ad. allein, aus-
schliesslich, nur.
Solemn [sso'lAm] a. -ly ad.
feierlich, ernst.
Solemnity [ssA-lem'ni-ti] n.
Feierlichkeit f.
Solemnization [sso'lAm-nai-
sei'schAn] n. Feier f, Feiern n.
Solemnize [sso'lAm-nais] vt.
feiern, begehen.
Solicit [ssA-li'ssit] vt. dring-
end bitten, ersuchen, erbitten.
Solicitation [ssA-li-ssi-tei'-
schAn] n. Ersuchen n.
Solicitor [ssA-li'ssi-ter] n.
Rechtsanwalt m, Sachwalter
m; -ous a. besorgt; -ude n.
Besorgnis f, Sorgfalt f.
Solid [sso'lid] a. fest, massiv,
gediegen (gold, etc.), dauerhaft,
solid; - tyre n. Vollreifen m.
Solidarity [sso-li-dæ'ri-ti] n.
Solidarität f, Gemeinsinn m.
Solidify [ssA-li'di-fai] vi.t.
(sich) verdichten.
Solidity [ssA-li'di-ti] n. Fest-
igkeit f, Dichtigkeit f, Solid-
ität f.
Solitary [sso'li-tA-ri] a. ein-
sam, abgesondert, allein; -
confinement n. Einzelhaft f.
Soliloquy [ssA-li'lA-kui] n.
Monolog m, Selbstgespräch n.
Solitude [sso'li-tjuhd] n. Ein-
samkeit f.

Solo [ssou'lou] *n.* Solo *n*; Motorrad *n*, ohne Beiwagen; – flight *n.* Alleinflug *m*; -ist *n.* Solist *m*, Solistin *f*, Solo-sänger *m*, -spieler *m.* [wende *f.*

Solstice [ssol'stiss] *n.* Sonnenwende *f.*

Solubility [sso-lju-bi'li-ti] *n.* Löslichkeit *f*, Auflösbarkeit *f.*

Soluble [sso'ljubl] *a.* löslich, auflösbar.

Solution [ssA-ljuh'schAn] *n.* Lösung *f*, Auflösung *f*, Erklärung *f.* [hüllen.

Solve [ssolw] *vt.* lösen, enthüllen.

Solven'cy [ssol'wAn-ssi] *n.* Zahlungsfähigkeit *f*, Solvenz *f*, Solidität *f* (*com.*); -t *a.* auflösend, zahlungsfähig, solvent (*com.*); *n.* Lösungsmittel *n.*

Sombre [ssom'ber] *a.* düster, finster, dunkel.

Some [ssAm] *a*, *pn.* ein, irgendein, etwas, einige *pl.* etwa, ungefähr (*about*).

Somebody [ssAm'bo-di] *n.* jemand, eine bedeutende Persönlichkeit.

Somehow [ssAm'hau] *ad.* irgendwie, auf irgendeine Weise.

Someone [ssAm'uAn] *n.* jemand, irgend einer. [etwas.

Something [ssAm'thing] *n.*

Sometime [ssAm'taim] *ad.* einst, einmal, früher, gelegentlich.

Sometimes [ssAm'taims] *ad.* manchmal, bisweilen, zuweilen.

Somewhat [ssAm'huot] *n.* etwas, ein wenig, ziemlich.

Somewhere [ssAm'hueh-er] *ad.* irgendwo(hin).

Somersault [ssA'mer-ssOlt] *n.* Purzelbaum *m.*

Somnambulist [ssom-næm'-bju-list] *n.* Nachtwandler *m.*

Somnolen'ce [ssom'nA-lAnss] *n.* Schläfrigkeit *f*; -t *a.* schläfrig.

Son [ssAn] *n.* Sohn *m.*

Sonata [ssA-nah'tA] *n.* Sonate *f.*

Song [ssong] *n.* Lied *n*, Gesang *m*; -book *n.* Gesangbuch *n*; -writer *n.* Liederdichter *m.*

Son-in-law [ssAn'in-lO] *n.* Schwiegersohn *m.*

Sonnet [sso'nit] *n.* Sonett *n.*

Sonny [ssA'ni] *n.* Söhnchen *n.*

Sonority [ssA-no'ri-ti] *n.* Schall-, Klang-fülle *f.*

Sonorous [ssA-nO'rAss] *a.* voll tönend.

Soon [ssuhn] *ad.* bald, früh; -er *ad*, eher, lieber, früher; no – than kaum als; -est *ad.* ehestens, am ehesten, frühestens.

Soot [ssuht] *n.* Ruß *m.*

Soothe [ssuhdh] *vt.* besänftigen, beruhigen, mildern.

Soothsayer [ssuhth'ssei-er] *n.* Wahrsager *m.* [russt.

Sooty [ssuh'ti] *a.* rußig, beruß.

Sop [ssop] *n.* eingetunkter Bissen, Besänftigungsmittel *n*; *vt.* einweichen; -ping *a.* triefend, durchnäßt.

Sophisticated [ssA-fi'sti-kei-tid] *a.* anspruchsvoll, verfälscht.

Sophistication [ssA-fi-sti-kei'schAn] *n.* Verfälschung *f.*

Sophistry [sso'fi-stri] *n.* Trugschluss *m*, Spitzfindigkeit *f.*

Soporific [ssou-pA-ri'fik] *a.* einschläfernd; *n.* Schlafmittel *n.*

Soppy [sso'pi] *a.* eingeweicht, weich, sentimental.

Soprano [ssA-prah'nou] *n.* Sopran *m.*

Sorcer'er [ssOr'ssA-rer] *n.* Zauberer *m*; -ess *n.* Zauberin *f*, Hexe *f*; -y *n.* Zauberei *f.*

Sordid [ssOr'did] *a*, -ly *ad.* selbstsüchtig, gemein, niedrig, geizig; -ness *n.* Gemeinheit *f*, Gewinnsucht *f.*

Sore [ssOr] *a.* schmerzhaft, wund, ärgerlich; – point *n.* wunde Stelle, heikler Punkt.

Sorely [ssOr'li] *ad.* schwer, schmerzlich, sehr.

Soreness [ssOr'ness] *n.*

Schmerzhaftigkeit *f*, Empfindlichkeit *f*.

Sorrel [sso'ril] *n*. Sauerampfer *m*.

Sorrel [sso'ril *n*. Rotfuchs *m*.

Sorrow [sso'rou] *n*. Kummer *m*, Leid *n*, Trauer *f*; *vi*. trauern; -ful *a*, -fully *ad*. traurig, betrübt, kummervoll.

Sorry [sso'ri] *a*. traurig, bekümmert; I am – es tut mir leid.

Sort [ssOrt] *n*. Sorte *f*, Art *f*; *vt*. auswählen, auslesen, sortieren.

Sortie [ssOr-tih'] *n*. Ausfall *m* (*mil.*). [enbold *m*.

Sot [ssot] *n*. Säufer *m*, Trunkboild *m*.

Soul [ssoul] *n*. Seele *f*; – stirring *a*. herzergreifend; -less *a*. seelenlos.

Sound [ssaund] *n*. Laut *m*, Klang *m*, Geräusch *n*; *vt*./*vi*. tönen (lassen), schallen, blasen (*trumpet, etc.*); -box *n*. Schalldose *f*; – -detector *n*. Horchgerät *n*; – -film *n*. Klangfilm *m*, Tonfilm *m*; – -locator *n*. Horcher *m*; – -ranging troop *n*. Schallmessbatterie *f*; – -track *n*. Tonspur *f* (*rad.*).

Sound [ssaund] *n*. Sund *m*, Meerenge *f* (*sea*).

Sound [ssaund] *vt*. sondieren, erloschen, loten (*nav.*).

Sound [ssaund] *a*. gesund, kräftig, stark, fest.

Sounding [ssaun'ding] *n*. Lotung *f* (*nav.*); – -lead *n*. Senkblei *n*.

Soundless [ssaund'less] *a*. kautlos, geräuschlos.

Soundness [ssaund'ness] *n*. Festigkeit *f*, Haltbarkeit *f*, Echtheit *f*, Gesundheit *f*.

Sound-proof [ssaund'pruhf] *a*. schallsicher, schalldicht.

Sound-recording [ssaund ri-kOr'ding] *n*. Tonaufzeichnung *f*.

Soup [ssuhp] *n*. Suppe *f*; – kitchen *n*. Volksküche *f*; – ladle *n*. Suppenkelle *f*; – plate

n. Suppenteller *m*; – tureen *n*. Suppenschüssel *f*, Terrine *f*.

Sour [ssau'ər] *a*. sauer, mürrisch; -ed *a*. verbittert.

Source [ssOrss] *n*. Quelle *f*, Ursprung *m*. [Säure *f*.

Sourness [ssau'er-ness] *n*.

Souse [ssauss] *vt*. eintauchen, durchnässen, einpökeln.

South [ssauth] *n*. Süden *m*; *a*. südlich, Süd . . .; – -east(ern) *a*. südöstlich; – -western) *a*. südwestlich. [lich.

Southerly [ssA'dher-li] *a*. süd-

Southern [ssA'dhern] *a*. südlich, Süd . . .; -er *n*. Südländer *m*; -most *a*. südlichst.

Southward(s) [ssauth'uArds] *a*. südwärts, nach Süden.

Sou'wester [ssau-ue'ster] *n*. Südwestwind *m*, Südwester *m*, Sturm-, Seemanns-kappe *f*.

Sovereign [sso'vrin] *n*. Herrscher *m*, Pfund *n* (*Sterling*) (*a*. höchst, unfehlbar; – territory *n*. Hoheitsgebiet *n*.

Soviet [ssow'jet] *n*. Sowjet *n*.

Sow [ssau] *n*. Sau *f*.

Sow [ssou] *vt*./*i*. säen, besäen; -er *n*. Sämann *m*; -ing *n*. Säen *n*; – corn *n*. Saatkorn *n*; – -machine *n*. Säemaschine *f*.

Spa [spah] *n*. Badeort *m*, Kurort *m*, Sauerbrunnen *n*, Mineralquelle *f*.

Space [speiss] *n*. Raum *m*, Zeit-, Zwischen-raum *m*, Frist *f*; *vt*. sperren; -d armour *n*. Hohlraumpanzerung *f* (*mil.*); – -bar, – -key *n*. Leertaste *f* (*typewriter, print*).

Spacing [spei'ssing] *n*. Sperren *n*, Zwischenraum *m*.

Spacious [spei'schAss] *a*. geräumig, ausgedehnt.

Spade [speid] *n*. Spaten *m*; – -work *n*. vorbereitende Arbeit.

Spade [speid] *n*. Pik *m*.

Span [spæn] *n*. Spanne *f*, Spannweite *f*, Zeitspanne *f*, Gespann *n*; *vt*. überspannen, fest zusammenziehen.

Spangle [spæng'g'l] n. Spange f, Flitter m; vt. beflittern.
Spaniel [spæ'njAl] n. Wachtelhund m. [vt. klapsen.
Spank [spængk] n. Klaps m;
Spanker [spæng'ker] n. Besan m, Besansegel n (nav.).
Spanner [spæn'er] n. Schrauben-schlüssel m, -zieher m.
Spar [spahr] n. Spat m.
Spar [spahr] n. Spiere f, Rundholz n, Sparren m (ship).
Spar [spahr] n. Scheinhieb m; vi. Scheinhiebe machen; -ring n. Boxen n.
Spare [speh'er] a. übrig, mager, sparsam, spärlich, überzählig; vt. aufsparen, erübrigen; -s n.pl. Vorrat m, Ersatzteile m.pl.; - barrel n. Vorratslauf m (mil.); - copy n. Nebenabdruck m; - driver n. Beifahrer m; - part n. Ersatzteil m, Zubehörteil m; - time n. freie Zeit; - tyre n. Ersatzreifen m (aut.); - wheel n. Ersatz-, Reserve-, Not-rad n (aut.).
Sparing [speh'ring] a. sparsam, knapp, gering; n. Sparen n.
Spark [spahrk] n. Funke m, Zündung f; -ing coil n. Induktionsapparat m; -ing plug n. Zündkerze f (aut.).
Spark [spahrk] n. Stutzer m.
Sparkle [spahrk'l] vi. funkeln, blitzen; n. Glanz m, Funkeln n; -d m. Selterwasser würfel m; -ing a. schäumend, moussierend; - wine n. Schaumwein m.
Sparrow [spæ'rou] n. Sperling m. [dünn, spärlich.
Sparse [spahrss] a. -ly ad.
Spasm [spæsm] n. Krampf m.
Spasmodic [spæs-mo'dik] a. krampfhaft, sprunghaft.
Spats [spætss] n.pl. kurze Gamaschen f.pl.
Spawn [spon] n. Laich m, Gezücht n; vt.i. laichen.
Speak [spihk] vt.i. sprechen,

reden; -er n. Sprecher m, Redner m, Vorsitzende(r) m (parliament).
Spear [spih'er] n. Speer m.
Special [spe'schAl] a. besonder, speziell, Sonder ...; - edition n. Sonderausgabe f; - equipment n. Sondergerät n; - operation n. Sondereinsatz m (av.); - pass n. Sonderausweis m; - report n. Sondermeldung f; - unit n. Sonderabteilung f (mil.).
Specialist [spe'schA-list] n. Fachmann m, Spezialist m, Facharzt m (medical), Spezialarzt m; a. Fach ...; - service n. Sonderdienst m.
Speciality [spe-schiæ'li-ti] n. Fach n, Spezialität f, Besonderheit f, Merkmal n.
Specialization [spe-schA-laisei'schAn] n. Spezialisierung f.
Special'ize [spe'schA-lais] vi. spezialisieren, sich auf ein Fach legen, hauptsächlich treiben; -ly ad. besonders, vorzüglich, eigens; -ty see speciality.
Specie [spih'schih] n. Metallgeld n, bares Geld; in - in bar, in klingender Münze.
Species [spih'schihs] n. Gattung f, Art f.
Specific [spi-ssi'fik] a. spezifisch, eigentümlich, besonder; n. Eigenmittel n, Heilmittel n.
Specification [spe-ssi-fi-kei'schAn] n. Spezifizierung f, genaue Aufstellung f, Verzeichnis n, Namhaftmachung f (person).
Specify [spe'ssi-fai] vt. stückweise angeben, spezifizieren.
Specimen [spe'ssi-mAn] n. Probestück n, Probe f, Muster n, Exemplar n; - signature n. Unterschriftsmuster n.
Specious [spi'schAss] a. oberflächlich, scheinbar richtig, trügerisch.
Speck [spek] n. Fleck m, Stückchen n; vt. flecken.

Speckle [spekl] *vt.* sprenkeln; *n.* Fleckchen *n.*

Speckless [spek'less] *a.* fleckenlos, ganz sauber.

Spectacle [spek'tAkl] *n.* Anblick *m*, Schauspiel *n.*

Spectacle [spek'tAkl] *-s n.pl.* Brille *f*; - -case *n.* Brillenfutteral *n*, -etui *n.*; - -frame *n.* Brillengestell *n*; - lense *n.* Brillenglas *n.*; -d *a.* bebrillt.

Spectacular [spek-tæ'kju-ler] *a.* dramatisch, imponierend.

Spectator [spek-tei'ter] *n.* Zuschauer *m.*

Spectral [spek'trAl] *a.* geisterhaft, Spektral ....

Spectre [spek'ter] *n.* Gespenst *n.*

Spectrum [spek'trAm] *n.* Spektrum *n*, Farbenband *n.*

Speculate [spek'kuj-leit] *vi.* grübeln, nachdenken, nachsinnen, rechnen auf, spekulieren (*com.*).

Speculation [spe-kju-lei'shAn] *n.* Betrachtung *f*, Nachsinnen *n*, Spekulation *f* (*com.*).

Spuculative [spe'kju-lA-tiw] *a.* spekulativ, theoretisch, grüblerisch. [Spekulant *m.*

Speculator [spek'kju-lei-ter] *n.* Speech [spihtsch] *n.* Rede *f*, Sprechen *n*, Sprache *f*, Vortrag *m*; freedom of - Redefreiheit *f*; -less *a.* sprachlos.

Speed [spihd] *n.* Geschwindigkeit *f*, Eile *f*; *vi.* eilen, sich sputen; *t.* fördern; - up beschleunigen; - limit *n.* zulässige Höchstgeschwindigkeit.

Speed-boat [spihd'boht] *n.* Schnellboot *n*, Rennboot *n.*

Speedometer [spihd-o'mi-ter] *n.* Geschwindigkeits-anzeiger *m*, -messer *m.*

Speedy [spih'di] *a.* Speedily *ad.* rasch, schnell, hastig, schleunig.

Spell [spel] *n.* Schicht *f*, Periode *f*, Arbeitszeit *f*, Weilchen *n* Reihe *f*

Spell [spel] *n.* Zauberspruch *m*; *vt.* buchstabieren; how do you - it? wie schreibt man das?; -ing *n.* Buchstabieren *n*, Rechtschreibung *f*, Orthographie *f*, Schreibung *f*; - -book *n.* Fibel *f.*

Spell-bound [spel'baund] *a.* festgebannt.

Spelt [spelt] *n.* Dinkelweizen *m*, Spelt *m.*

Spend [spend] *vt.* ausgeben (*money*), zubringen (*time*), aufwenden, verzehren, aufbrauchen, erschöpfen (*exhaust*); *t.* Ausgaben machen; -thrift *n.* Verschwender *m.*

Sperm-oil [spØrm'euil] *n.* Walratöl *n.*

Spew [spjuh] *vt.* ausspeien.

Sphere [sfih'er] *n.* Bereich *m*, Wirkungskreis *m*, Kugel *f*, Sphäre *f*; - of influence Interessensphäre *f.*

Spherical [sfe'rikl] *a.* kugelförmig, Kugel ....

Sphinx [ssfinx] *n.* Sphinx *f.*

Spice [spaiss] *n.* Gewürz *n*, Spezerei *f*, Beigeschmack *m*, Anflug *m*; *vt.* würzen.

Spick-and-span [spik'And-spæn] *a.* blitzblank, peinlich sauber.

Spicy [spai'ssi] *a.* würzig, pikant.

Spider [spai'der] *n.* Spinne *f*; -'s web *n.* Spinnengewebe *n.*

Spigot [spi'gAt] *n.* Fasszapfen *m*; - -mortar *n.* Ladungswerfer *m* (*mil.*).

Spike [spaik] *n.* Spieker *m*, Stift *m*, langer Schuhnagel; *vt.* mit Nägeln beschlagen, festnageln.

Spill [spil] *vt.* verschütten, wegwerfen; *i.* überlaufen; *n.* Sturz *m*, Umwerfen *n* (*aut.*).

Spill [spil] *n.* Fidibus *n.*

Spin [spin] *vt.* spinnen, herumdrehen; *i.* sich drehen, wirbeln; *n.* Kreiseln *n*, Drehung *f*, Autofahrt *f.*

Spinach [spi'nAtsch] *n.* Spinat *m.*

Spinal [spai'nAl] *a.* Rückgrat ...

Spindle [spindl] *n.* Spindel *f.* Zapfen *m.*, Triebstock *m.*, Achse *f.*

Spine [spain] *n.* Rückgrat *m.*; -less *a.* rückgratlos, schlapp.

Spinn'er [spi'ner] *n.* Spinner *m.*, Spinnerin *f.*; -ing-machine *n.* Spinnmaschine *f.* [(Frau.

Spinster [spin'ster] *n.* ledige

Spiral [spi'rAl] *n.* Spirale *f.*, Schnecken-, Schrauben-linie *f.*; *a.* schneckenförmig, Spiral ...; – -spring *n.* Spiralfeder *f.*; – -staircase *n.* Nivellierwaage *f.*

Spirant [spai'rAnt] *n.* Reibelaut *m.*

Spire [spai'er] *n.* Kirchturmspitze *f.*, Turmhelm *m.*, Dachhelm *m.*

Spirit [spi'rit] *n.* Geist *m*, Seele *f*, Gemüt *n*, Gefühl *n.*, Charakter *m*, Mut *m*; -s *pl.* Spirituosen *pl*; **motor** – *n.* Kraftstoff *m*, Benzin *n*; – -lamp *n.* Spirituslampe *f.*, Spiritusbrenner *m*; – -level – *n.* Nivellierwaage *f.*, Libelle *f.*

Spirited [spi'ri-tid] *a.* lebhaft, tapfer, temperamentvoll.

Spiritual [spi'ri-tju-Al] *a.*, -ly *ad.* geistig, geistlich; *n.* geistliches Negerlied; -ism *n.* Spiritismus *m.*

Spirituality [spi-ri-tju-æ'li-ti] *n.* geistige Natur, Idealismus *m.*

Spirituous [spi'ri-tju-Ass] *a.* alkoholisch; – **liquors** *n.pl.* geistige Getränke *n.pl.*

Spit [spit] *n.* Speichel *m.*; *vt.* spucken, speien.

Spit [spit] *n.* Bratspiess *m* (cooking), Landzunge *f* (land); *vt.* aufspiessen.

Spite [spait] *n.* Bosheit *f*, Groll *m*, Ärger *m*; *vt.* ärgern; **in –** of trotz; -ful *a.*, -fully *ad.* boshaft, gehässig.

Spitfire [spit'fai-er] *n.* Hitzkopf *m.*

Spittle [spitl] *n.* Speichel *m.*

Spittoon [spi-tuhn'] *n.* Spucknapf *m.*

Splash [splæsch] *vt.* bespritzen; *i.* patschen, spritzen; *n.* Patschen *n*, Spritzfleck *m*, grosses Aufsehen; -board *n.* Spritzbrett *n.*

Splay [splei] *n.* Ausschrägung *f*; *vt.* ausschrägen. [(Laune.

Spleen [splihn] *n.* Milz *f*, üble

Splendid [splen'did] *a.*, -ly *ad.* herrlich, prächtig, glänzend.

Splendour [splen'der] *n.* Glanz *m*, Pracht *f*, Schimmer *m*, Herrlichkeit *f.*

Splice [splaiss] *vt.* spleissen, splissen, einfalzen; *n.* Splissung *f*, Einfalzung *f.*

Splint [splint] *n.* Schiene *f*; **emergency – –** *n.* Notverband *m.*

Splinter [splin'ter] *n.* Splitter *m*, Span *m*; *v.t.i.* zersplittern; – -proof *a.* bombensicher, splittersicher.

Split [split] *vt.* spalten, zertrennen, zerreissen; *i.* sich spalten; *a.* zerspalten, geteilt; *n.* Spalt *f*, Riss *m*, Spaltung *f*; – -pea *n.* Schälterbse *f*; – -ring *n.* Schlüsselring *m.*

Splitting [spli'ting] *n.* Spaltung *f*, Zerreissung *f*; – **of the atom** Atomspaltung *f.*

Splutter [splA'ter] *vi.* sprudeln, spritzen, schlabbern; *n.* Gesprudel *n*, hastiges Reden, Schlabbern *m.*

Spoil [speul] *vt.i.* verderben, verwöhnen, verziehen, berauben; *n.* Beute *f*, Raub *m*, Ausbeute *f*; – -sport *n.* Spielverderber *m.*

Spoke [spouk] *n.* Speiche *f.*

Spokesman [spoukss'mAn] *n.* Wortführer *m*, Sprecher *m.*

Spoliation [spou'ljei'schAn] *n.* Plünderung *f.*

Spong'e [spAndzh] *n.* Schwamm *m*; – **out** *vt.* abwischen;

- **-bag** n. Schwammbeutel m;
  -er n. Schmarotzer m; **-y** a.
  schwammig.

Sponsor [spon'sser] n. Tauf-
zeuge m, Bürge m, Gönner m,
Förderer m; vt. bürgen für,
empfehlen, fördern.

Spontaneity [spon-tA-nĭh'ĭ-tĭ]
n. freier Antrieb, Freiwillig-
keit f.

Spontaneous [spon-teĭ'nĭAss]
a, **-ly** ad. spontan, natürlich,
freiwillig, Selbst . . . .

Spool [spuhl] n. Spule f; vt.
aufspulen.

Spoon [spuhn] n. Löffel m; —
-fed a. verzärtelt, verweich-
licht, abhängig; — **-feeding** n.
Verzärtelung f; **-ful** n. Löffel-
voll m.

Spoon [spuhn] vi. poussieren,
liebkosen.

Sporadic [spA-ræ'dĭk] a.
sporadisch, vereinzelt, zerstreut, gelegentlich.

Sport [spOrt] n. Sport m,
Spiel n, Belustigung f, Jagd f;
vi. sich belustigen, spielen; — s
prunken mit; **-s** pl. Sportfest
n; **-s shirt** n. Trikothemd n; **-s
suit** n. Trainingsanzug m.

Sporting [spor'ting] a. Sport
treibend, Sport . . . anständig,
ritterlich; **-ive** a. scherzhaft,
spielend; **-sman** n. Sportfreund
m, Fischer m, Jäger m, Ehren-
mann m, anständiger Mensch;
-smanlike a. sportlich, anständig.

Spot [spot] n. Flecken m, Fleck
m, Punkt m, Stelle f, Ort m,
Makel m (blemish); vt. beflecken, tüpfeln, sprenkeln; a
sofortig, Loko . . . (com.);
-less a. fleckenlos, rein.

Spot-light [spot'lait] n.
Scheinwerfer m, Sucher m.

Spotted [spo'tĭd] a. fleckig,
getupft.

Spotter [spo'ter] n. Aufklärer
m, Luftspäher m, Beobacht-
ungsflugzeug n (plane).

Spottiness [spo'ti-ness] n.
Fleckigkeit f.

Spotting [spo'ting] n. Beobachtung f.

Spotty [spo'tĭ] a. fleckig, gesprenkelt. [Gattin f.

Spouse [spaus] n. Gatte m,

Spout [spaut] n. Ausguss-,
Strahl-röhre f, Schnauze f,
Tülle f; vt.i. ausspritzen, spru-
deln.

Sprain [sprein] vt. verrenken;
n. Verrenkung f.

Sprat [spræt] n. Sprotte f.

Sprawl [sprOl] vi.t. (sich)
rekeln, sich spreizen.

Spray [sprei] n. Wasserstaub
m, Spritze f, Zerstäuber m
(scent); vt. bespritzen; **-er** n.
Zerstäubungsapparat m.

Spray [sprei] n. Zweig m,
Blumenstrauss m.

Spread [spred] vt.i. (sich) verbreiten, breiten, (sich) ausdehnen, strecken; n. Verbreitung f, Spannweite f.

Spree [sprih] n. Zechgelage n.

Sprig [sprig] n. Reis n, Spross
m, Stift m.

Sprightliness [sprait'li-ness]
n. Lebhaftigkeit f, Lebhaftigkeit f. [er, lebhaft.

Sprightly [sprait'li] a. mun-

Spring [spring] vi. springen,
aufsteigen, entspringen, her-
kommen; vt. sprengen, spielen
lassen; n. Quelle f, Springbrunnen m, Quelle f, Ursprung
m, Schnell-, Feder-kraft f,
Frühling m (season), Feder f
(watch); — **-balance** n. Feder-
Uhr-waage f; **-board** n. Sprung-
brett n; — **-cleaning** n. Früh-
jahrsreinmachen n; — **-lock** n.
Federschloss n; — **-mattress** n.
Sprungfedermatratze f; —
water n. Quellwasser n; —
wheat n. Sommerweizen m.

Springiness [spring'i-ness] n.
Federkraft f, Schnellkraft f.

Springy [spring'i] a. elastisch,
federnd.

Sprinkle [sprinkl] *vt.* spren-keln, besprengen.

Sprint [sprint] *n.* kurzer Wettlauf; *vi.* schnell laufen; **-er** *n.* Kurzstreckenläufer *m.*

Sprocket [spro'kit] *n.* Stift *m*; intermediate – Mikrophongalgen *m*; upper – Vorwickelrolle *f* (film); **– -wheel** *n.* Zahn-, Ketten-rad *n* (cycle, etc.).

Sprout [spraut] *vi.* spriessen; *n.* Spross *m*; **Brussels -s** *pl.* Rosenkohl *m.* [schmuck.

Spruce [spruhss] *a.* sauber,

Spruce [spruhss] *n.* Fichte *f.*

Spud [spAd] *n.* Hacke *f,* Kartoffel *f.*

Spume [spjuhm] *n.* Schaum *m.*

Spur [spAr] *n.* Sporn *m*; *vt.* anspornen, die Sporen geben.

Spurious [spjuh'rjAss] *a.* falsch, unecht.

Spurn [spArn] *vt.* von sich weisen, wegstossen, verschmähen.

Spurt [spArt] *n.* plötzliche Anstrengung, Spurt *m*; *vi.* spritzen, plötzliche Anstrengung machen.

Spy [spai] *n.* Spion *m*, Späher *m*, Kundschafter *m*; *vt.* erspähen, spionieren; **-ing** *n.* Spionage *f,* Auskundschaften *n.*

Squabble [skuobl] *vi.* hadern; *n.* Wortstreit *m,* Zank *m.*

Squad [skuod] *n.* Bereitschaft *f,* Schar *f,* Truppe *f,* Abteilung *f* (mil.), das Ganze (drill).

Squadron [skuod'rAn] *n.* Geschwader *n* (nav.), Schwadron *f* (cavalry), Staffel *f* (av.); **-leader** *n.* Major der Flieger *m.*

Squalid [skuo'lid] *a.* schmutzig, garstig. [*m,* Elend *n.*

Squalor [skuo'ler] *n.* Schmutz

Squall [skuOl] *n.* Bö *f,* Windstoss *m,* Stosswind *m*; **-y** *a.* böig, stürmisch.

Squander [skuon'der] *vt.* verschwenden, vergeuden; **-mania** *n.* Verschwendungssucht *f.*

Square [skueh'er] *a.* viereckig, quadratisch, ehrlich, gerade, quitt; *n.* Viereck *n,* Quadrat *m,* freier Platz; *vt.* viereckig machen, abrechnen, ausgleichen; *i.* stimmen, passen; **– -dealing** *n.* ehrliche Handlungsweise; **– meal** *n.* ordentliche Mahlzeit; **– -shouldered** *a.* breitschultrig.

Squash [skuosch] *vt.* zerquetschen, zerdrücken; *n.* Quatsch *m,* Matsch *m,* Brei *m,* Gedränge *n* (crowd); **–** hat *n.* Schlapphut *m.*

Squat [skuot] *vi.* niederkauen, sich widerrechtlich ansiedeln; **-ter** *n.* Ansiedler *m,* ohne Rechtstitel.

Squeak [skuihk], **Squeal** [skuihl] *vi.* quieken; *n.* Gequiek *n.*

Squeamish [skuih'misch] *a.* wählerisch, zimperlich, heikel; **-ness** *n.* Ekel *m,* Zimperlichkeit *f.*

Squeegee [skuih-dzhih'] *n.* Gummischieber *m,* Decktrockner *m* (ship).

Squeeze [skuihs] *vt.* drücken, quetschen, drängen, auspressen; **-r** *n.* Presse *f,* Pressmaschine *f.*

Squelch [skueltsch] *vi.* ein saugendes Geräusch machen.

Squib [skuib] *n.* Handschwärmer *m.*

Squint [skuint] *vi.* schielen; *n.* Schielen *n,* Blick *m.* [den.

Squirm [skuArm] *vi.* sich winden.

Squirrel [skui'rAl] *n.* Eichhörnchen *n.*

Squirt [skuArt] *vt.* spritzen; *n.* Handspritzer *m,* Strahl *m.*

Stab [stæb] *n.* Stich *m*; *vt.* stechen, erstechen, durchbohren.

Stability [stA-bi'li-ti] *n.* Beständigkeit *f,* Bestand *m,* Kippsicherheit *f* (av.).

Stabilization [ste-bi-lai-sei-schÁn] *n.* Stabilisierung *f.*

Stabiliz'e [stæ'bi-lais] *vt.* festigen, stabilisieren, kippsicher machen (*av.*); **-ing vane** *n.* Stabilisierungsflügel *m*; **-er** *n.* Stabilisierungsfläche *f*, Dämpfungsflosse *f*, Kippsicherung *f*.

Stabl'e [steibl] *n.* Stall *m*; **-ing** *n.* Einstallung *f*.

Stable [steibl] *a.* fest, dauerhaft, stabil.

Stack [stæk] *n.* Schober *m* (*hay*), Stapel *m*, Haufe *m*; *vt.* aufstapeln, aufschichten.

Stadium [stei'djAm] *n.* Kampfbahn *f*, Stadion *n*, Wettspielplatz *m*.

Staff [stahf] *n.* Stab *m*, Stock *m*, Personal *n*; *t.* mit Personal versehen; **-assistant** *n.* Stabshelfer *m*; **- department** *n.* Adjutantur *f* (*mil.*); **-officer** *n.* Stabsoffizier *m*, Offizier *m*, beim Stabe; **- personnel** *n.* Belegschaft *f*; **- reduction** *n.* Abbau *m*.

Stag [stæg] *n.* Hirsch *m*, Scheinzeichner *m* (*com.*); *vi.* durch Scheinzeichnung Gewinn erzielen, Differenzgeschäfte machen.

Stage [steidzh] *n.* Bühne *f*, Stufe *f*; *vt.* inszenieren; **-fright** *n.* Lampenfieber *n*; **- manager** *n.* Regisseur *m*.

Stagger [stæ'ger] *vi.* wanken, taumeln; *t.* verblüffen, staffeln (*holidays*).

Stagnancy [stæg'nAn-ssi] *n.* Stockung *f*.

Stagnant [stæg'nAnt] *a.* stockend, stagnierend, flau (*com.*).

Stagnate [stæg-neit'] *vi.* stocken, stagnieren, flau sein (*com.*).

Stagy [stei'dzhi] *a.* theatralisch.

Staid [steid] *a.* gesetzt.

Stain [stein] *n.* Schmutzfleck *m*, Färbstoff *m*, Holzbeize *f*, Makel *m*; *vt.* beflecken, beizen (*wood*); **-less** *a.* ungefleckt, unbefleckt, rostfrei (*steel*).

Stair [steh'er] *n.* Treppe *f*,

Stufe *f*; **- carpet** *n.* Treppenläufer *m*; **-case** *n.* Treppenhaus *n*, Treppe *f*.

Stake [steik] *n.* Stange *f*, Pfahl *m*, Zaunpflock *m*; *vt.* umpfählen bepfählen.

Stake [steik] *n.* Einsatz *m*, Anteil *m*; *vt.* einsetzen, aufs Spiel setzen, wagen.

Stale [steil] *a.* schal, matt, abgestanden, altbacken (*bread*), veraltet (*news*); **-mate** *n.* Patt *n*; *vt.* patt setzen; **-ness** *n.* Schalheit *f*, Mattheit *f*.

Stalk [stOk] *n.* Stengel *m*, Stiel *m*, [*i.* stolzieren.

Stalk [stOk] *vt.* beschleichen;

Stall [stOl] *n.* Stand *m*, Marktbude *f*, Stall *m*, Parkett *n* (*theatre*), Stehenbleiben *n* (*aut. etc.*); *vi.* durchsacken, stehen bleiben (*av., etc.*). [hengst *m*.

Stallion [stæ'ljAn] *n.* Zuchthengst *m*.

Stalwart [stOl'uert] *a.* standhaft, unentwegt, kräftig, stark.

Stamina [stæ'mi-nA] *n.* Ausdauer *f*, Widerstandskraft *f* Rückhalt *m*.

Stammer [stæ'mer] *vi.* stottern, stammeln; *n.* Stottern *n*; **-er** *n.* Stotterer *m*.

Stamp [stæmp] *n.* Stempel *m*, Briefmarke *f*, Stanze *f*; *vt.* stampfen, stanzen, abstempeln, frankieren (*letter*); **- album** *n.* Briefmarkenalbum *n*; **- collection** *n.* Briefmarkensammlung *f*; **- collector** *n.* Briefmarkensammler *m*; **-duty** *n.* Stempelsteuer *f*.

Stampede [stæm-pihd'] *n.* Panik *f*, Bestürzung *f*; *vi.t.* einschüchtern, in Flucht jagen, durchgehen.

Stamper [stæm'per] *n.* Stempel *m*, Präger *m.*

Stance [stænss] *n.* Standort *m*, Lage *f*, Parkplatz *m*.

Stanch [stahnsch] *vt.* stillen, hemmen.

Stanchion [stæn'schAn] *n.* Pfosten *m*, Pfeiler *m.*

Stand [stænd] *vi.* stehen; *vt.* aushalten, dulden, stellen; *n.* Gestell *n*, Stand *m*, Ständer *m*, Stativ *n*, Marktbude *f*; – **by** *n.* Beistand *m*, Bereitschaft *f*; *vi.* bereitstehen; – **offish** *a.* hochnäsig, eingebildet; – **together** *vi.* zusammenhalten; – **up collar** *n.* Stehkragen *m*.

Standard [stæn'dərd] *n.* Pfosten *m*, Stehlampe *f*.

Standard [stæn'dərd] *n.* Einheit *f*, Norm *f*, Richtmass *n*, Schulstufe *f*, Klasse *f*; gold – *n.* Goldwährung *f*; – **gauge** *n.* Normalspurweite *f* (rl.); – **of living** *n.* Lebenshaltung *f*; – **time** *n.* Normalzeit *f*.

Standardization [stændardai-sei'schɐn] *n.* Normung *f*, Vereinheitlichung *f*.

Standardize [stæn'dər-dais] *vt.* normieren, normen, vereinheitlichen, typisieren.

Standing [stæn'ding] *n.* Stand *m*, Rang *m*, Ansehen *n*; *a.* stehend, dauerhaft, fest; – **orders** *n.pl.* Vorschrift *f*, Dauerbefehl *m*; – **stocks** *n.pl.* ruhende Bestände *m.pl.*

Standpoint [stænd'peunt] *n.* Standpunkt *m*.

Standstill [stænd'stil] *n.* Stillstand *m*, Stockung *f*.

Stanza [stæn'sA] *n.* Strophe *f*, Stanze *f*.

Staple [steipl] *n.* Haupterzeugnis *n*; *a.* Stapel . . . . Haupt . . . ; – **commodities** *n.pl.* Hauptprodukte *n.pl.*, Massenartikel *m.pl.* [Krampe *f*.

Staple [steipl] *n.* Krampe *f*,

Star [stahr] *n.* Stern *m*, Star *m* (film); *vi.* glänzen, die Hauptrolle spielen; – **shell** *n.* Leuchtgeschoss *n*; – **performance** *n.* Elitevorstellung *f*.

Starboard [stahr'bOrd] *n.* Steuerbord *n*.

Starch [stahrtsch] *n.* Stärke *f*, Stärkemehl *n*; *vt.* stärken. **steifen; -y** *a.* stärkehaltig.

Stare [steh'er] *vi.* starren, stieren; *n.* Starren *n*.

Stark [stahrk] *a.* gänzlich, völlig. [los.

Starless [stahr'less] *a.* stern-

Starling [stahr'ling] *n.* Star *m*.

Starry [stah'ri] *a.* sternhell.

Start [stahrt] *n.* Anfang *m*, Vorsprung *m*, Auffahren *n*; *vi.* auffahren, aufbrechen, beginnen; *t.* anfangen, anwerfen (engine); – **ing-point** *n.* Ausgangspunkt *m*. [en.

Startle [stahrtl] *vt.* erschreck-

Starvation [stahr-wei'schAn] *n.* Verhungern *n*, Hungertod *m*.

Starve [stahrw] *v.i.t.* verhungern (lassen), aushungern.

State [steit] *n.* Zustand *m*, Lage *f*, Stellung *f*, Stand *m*, Staat *m*; *vt.* angeben, aufstellen, bemerken; – **aided** *a.* staatlich unterstützt; – **control** *n.* Zwangswirtschaft *f*; – **railways** *n.pl.* Staatseisenbahnen *f.pl.*; – **room** *n.* Luxuskabine *f* (ship).

Stately [steit'li] *a.* staatlich, prachtvoll, vornehm.

Statement [steit'mAnt] *n.* Angabe *f*, Feststellung *f*, Behauptung *f*, Aussage *f* (prisoner's); – **of account** *n.* Rechnungsauszug *m*.

Statesman [steits'mAn] *n.* Staatsmann *m*; – **like** *a.* staatsmännisch, klug; – **ship** *n.* Staatskunst *f*.

Static [stæ'tik] *a.* statisch, unbeweglich.

Station [stei'schAn] *n.* Bahnhof *m*, Station *f*, Standort *m* (mil.), Fliegerhorst *m* (av.); *vt.* aufstellen, stationieren; de-**training** – *n.* Ausladebahnhof *m*; loading – *n.* Einladebahnhof *m*; – **master** *n.* Stationsvorsteher *m*.

Stationary [stei'schA-nA-ri] *a.* stillstehend, stetig, unverändert, feststehend.

Stationer [stei'schA-ner] *n.*

Schreibwarenhändler *m*; -'s shop *n*. Schreibwarenhandlung *f*; -y *n*. Schreibwaren *f.pl.*

Statistical [stA-ti'stikl] *a.* statistisch, zahlenmässig, belegt.   [*n*. Statistiker *m*.

Statistician [stæ-ti-sti'schAn]

Statistics [stæ-ti'stiks] *n.pl.* Statistik *f*, zahlenmässige Zusammenstellung.

Statue [stæ'tjuh] *n*. Statue *f*, Bildsäule *f*.

Stature [stæ'tscher] *n*. Statur *f*, Wuchs *m*, Grösse *f*.

Status [stei'tAss] *n*. Stellung *f*, Status *m*.

Statut'e [stæ'tjuht] *n*. Gesetz *n*, Verordnung *f*; -ory *a.* gesetzlich.

Staunch [stOnsch] *a.* treu, standhaft, zuverlässig.

Stave [steiw] *n*. Daube *f*, Tonnenstab *m*, Notenlinie *f.pl*; - off *v.* abwehren.

Stay [stei] *n*. Stag *n*, Strebe *f*, Stütztau *n*; *vt.* stagen (*ship*).

Stay [stei] *n*. Aufenthalt *m*, Verweilen *n*, Bleiben *n*, Stütze *f*, Verankerung *f*; *vi.* sich aufhalten, bleiben, wohnen; - -at-home *a.* häuslich.

Stays [steis] *n.pl.* Schnürleib *m*, Korsett *n*.

Stead [sted] *n*. Statt *f*, Stelle *f*; -fast *a.* standhaft, unentwegt, fest; -iness *n*. Festigkeit *f*, Standhaftigkeit *f*, Ruhe *f*.

Steady [ste'di] *a.*, **Steadily** *ad.* stetig, fest, regelmässig, unbewegt, solid (*man*); *vt.* fest machen, stützen; *i.* fest werden, sich befestigen.

Steak [steik] *n*. Fleischschnitte *f*.

Steal [stihl] *vt.* stehlen; *i.* schleichen.   [keit *f*.

Stealth [stelth] *n*. Heimlich-

Steam [stihm] *n*. Dampf *m*; *vi.* dampfen, fahren (*ship*); *vt.* dämpfen, dünsten; - -engine *n*. Dampfmaschine *f*; - -gauge *n*. Dampfdruckmesser *m*; -

-roller *n*. Dampfwalze *f*; --trawler *n*. Schleppdampfer *m*; - -turbine *n*. Dampfturbine *f*.

Steamboat [stihm'boht], **Steamship** [stihm'schip] *n*. Dampfboot *n*, Dampfschiff *n*.

Steamer [stih'mer]   *n*. Dampfer *m*.   [in *n*.

Stearin [sti'A-rin] *n*. Stear-

Steed [stihd] *n*. Ross *n*.

Steel [stihl] *n*. Stahl *m*; *a.* stählern, Stahl . . . ; *vt.* stählen; - -engraving *n*. Stahlstechkunst *f* (*art*), Stahlstich *m* (*print*); - forge *n*. Stahlhammer *m*; - helmet *n*. Stahlhelm *m*.

Steelyard [stihl'jahrd]   *n*. Schnellwaage *f*.

Steep [stihp] *vt.* einweichen, eintauchen, wässern, durchtränken.

Steep [stihp] *a.*, **-ly** *ad.* steil, abschüssig; **-ness** *n*. Steilheit *f*.

Steeple [stihpl] *n*. Kirchturm *m*, Turmspitze *f*; - -chase *n*. Hindernisrennen *n*.

Steer [stih'er] *n*. junger Ochs.

Steer [stih'er] *vt.* steuern, lenken, führen.

Steerage [stih'ridzh] *n*. Zwischendeck *n*, dritte Klasse; - passenger *n*. Zwischendeckpassagier *m*; - -way *n*. Steuerkraft *f*.

Steering [stih'ring] *n*. Steuerung *f*; - -column *n*. Steuersäule *f* (*aut.*); - -gear *n*. Steuerung *f*; - -wheel *n*. Lenkrad *n*, Steuerrad *n*, Volant *m* (*aut.*).

Steersman [stihrs'mAn] *n*. Steuermann *m*.

Stellar [ste'ler] *a.* Sternen . . . .

Stem [stem] *n*. Stamm *m*, Stiel *m*, Stengel *m*, Rohr *n*.

Stem [stem] *vt.* stemmen, hemmen, hindern.

Stem [stem] *n*. Vordersteven *n*; *vt.* sich entgegenstemmen.

Stench [stensch] *n*. Gestank *m*.

Stencil [sten'ssil] *n*. Schablone *f*; *vt.* schablonieren, mit Schab-

lonen malen; - -copy n. Schab-
lonendruck m.

Stenograph'er [ste-no'grA-
fer] n. Stenograph m, Steno-
graphin f; -y n. Kurzschrift f,
Stenographie f.

Step [step] n. Schritt m, Tritt
m, Stufe f, Massregel f, Mass-
nahme f; vi. treten, schreiten,
gehen; - by - Schritt für
Schritt.   [Stiefvater m.

Step-father [step'fah-ther] n.

Stereoscope [stih'rjA-skoup]
n. Stereoskop m.

Stereoscopic [stih-rjA-sko!
pik] a. stereoskopisch; - picture n. Raumbild n; - telescope
n. Scherenfernrohr m.

Stereotype [stih'rjA-taip] n.
Stereotyp n, Plattendruck m;
vt. stereotypieren, von Platten
drucken; a. see stereotyped; -d
a. feststehend, unveränderlich,
stereotyp.

Steril'e [ste'ril] a. unfruchtbar; -ization n. Sterilisierung
f, Entkeimung f; -ize vt. steril-
isieren, entkeimen.

Sterling [stAr'ling] a. gesetzlich anerkannt, gültig, echt.

Stern [stArn] n. Heck n, Hin-
terschiff n; a. Achter ..;
Heck ...; - -way n. Fahrt f,
achteraus.

Stern [stArn] a. -ly ad. streng,
hart, ernst; -ness n. Strenge f,
Härte f.

Stevedore [stih'wi-dOr] n.
Stauer m; vt. verstauen.

Stew [stjuh] vt. dämpfen,
schmoren; n. Schmorfleisch n;
-ed fruit n. Kompott n.

Steward [stjuh'erd] n. Verwalter m, Aufwärter m, Proviantmeister m, Schiffskellner
m, Aufseher m; -ess n. Auf-
wärterin f.

Stick [stik] n. Stock m, Stange
f, Stab m, Stück Holz n.

Stick [stik] vt. stecken, stech-
en, durchbohren, ankleben, befestigen; i. sich heften, stecken

bleiben; - of bombs n.pl.
Bombenreihe f (av.); -ing plaster n. Heftpflaster n.

Stickiness [sti'ki-ness] n.
Klebrigkeit f.

Stickler [stik'ler] n. Eiferer m,
Pedant m.

Sticky [sti'ki] a. klebrig.

Stiff [stif] a. -ly ad. steif, starr,
hartnäckig, schwer.

Stiffen [stifn] vt. steif machen;
i. steif werden, erstarren; -ing
n. Steifen n, Stärke f, Appretur f.   [Steifheit f.

Stiffness [stif'ness] n. Steife f,

Stifle [staifl] vt. ersticken.

Stigma [stig'mA] n. Brand-
mal n, Schandfleck m; -tize vt.
brandmarken.

Stile [stail] n. Zaunübergang m.

Still [stil] n. Destillierapparat
m.

Still [stil] a. still, ruhig; vt.
stillen, beruhigen; ad. noch,
immer; cj. doch.   [boren.

Stillborn [stil'bOrn] a. totge-

Stillness [stil'ness] n. Stille f,
Ruhe f.   [hochtrabend.

Stilt [stilt] n. Stelze f; -ed a.

Stimulant [sti'mju-lAnt] n.
Reizmittel n, alkoholisches Getränk.

Stimulat'e [sti'mju-leit] vt.
reizen, anspornen; -ing a. anregend.

Stimulation [sti-muj-leit
schAn] n. Anregung f, Reizung f.

Stimulus [sti'mju-lAss] n.
Anregung f, Reiz m.

Sting [sting] vt. stechen, verwunden, betrügen;   [geizig.

Stingy [stin'zhi] a. knauserig,

Stink [stingk] vi. stinken; n.
Gestank m.

Stint [stint] vt. knapp halten,
einschränken; n. Mass n.

Stipend [stai'pend] n. Besoldung f.

Stipendiary [stai-pen'djA-ri]
a. besoldet; - magistrate n.
Polizeirichter m.

Stipple [stipl] *vt.* tüpfeln, punktieren, stechen.

Stipulate [sti'pju-leit] *vt.* bedingen, verabreden, festsetzen.

Stipulation [sti-pju-lei'schAn] *n.* Bedingung *f*, Festsetzung *f*.

Stir [stAr] *n.* Bewegung *f*, Aufregung *f*, Aufruhr *m*; *vt.* rühren, bewegen, aufhetzen; *i.* sich rühren; -ring *a.* aufregend, ein unruhig, begeisternd.

Stirk [stArk] *n.* junger Ochse, Sterke *f*.

Stirrup [sti'rAp] *n.* Steigbügel *m*.

Stitch [stitsch] *n.* Stich *m*, Masche *f*; *vt.i.* nähen, heften (*book*).

Stoat [stout] *n.* Hermelin *n*.

Stock [stok] *n.* Lager *n*, Vorrat *m*, Stamm *m*, Geschlecht *n* (*breed*), Stock *m*, Schaft *m* (*tec.*), Viehstand *m* (*cattle*), Aktie *f* (*share*); *vt.* versehen, versorgen, vorrätig haben, führen (*com.*); *a.* stehend, ständig, üblich; -s on hand *pl.* Istbestand *m*; -s in store Lagerbestand *m*; -breeder *n.* Viehzüchter *m*; - certificate *n.* Aktienzertifikat *n*; - jobber *n.* Effektenhändler *m*, Agioteur *m*; - market *n.* Börse *f*, Effektenmarkt *m*; - taking *n.* Inventur *f*; - yard *n.* Viehhof *m*.

Stock-broker [stok'brou'ker] *n.* Fonds-, Effekten-makler *m*.

Stock exchange [stok'extscheindzh'] *n.* Börse *f*, Effektenbörse *f*; - list *n.* Börsenzettel *m*.

Stockfish [stok'fisch] *n.* Stockfisch *m*.

Stockholder [stok'houl-der] *n.* Fondsbesitzer *m*, Effekteninhaber *m*.

Stock-in-trade [stok'intreid] *n.* Warenbestand *m*, Warenvorrat *m*.

Stockade [sto-keid'] *n.* Einpfählung *f*, Einzäunung *f*.

Stockinet [sto-ki-net'] *n.* Trikotgewebe *n*.

Stocking [sto'king] *n.* Strumpf *m*; -foot *n.* Füssling *m*.

Stocky [sto'ki] *a.* untersetzt.

Stodginess [sto'dzhi-ness] *n.* Langweiligkeit *f* (*people*), Unverdaulichkeit *f* (*food*).

Stodgy [sto'dzhi] *a.* langweilig, stopfend, unverdaulich.

Stoke [stouk] *vt.i.* schüren, stochern, heizen; - hole *n.* Feuerungsraum *m*, Schürloch *n*; -r *n.* Heizer *m*, Maschinengefreiter *m* (*nav.*).

Stolid [sto'lid] *a.* -ly *ad.* unempfindlich.

Stolidity [sto-li'di-ti] *n.* Unempfindlichkeit *f*.

Stomach [stA'mAk] *n.* Magen *m*; *vt.* sich gefallen lassen; -ache *n.* Magenschmerzen *m. pl.*

Stone [stoun] *n.* Stein *m*, Obstkern *m*; *a.* steinern; *vt.* entkernen (*fruit*), steinigen; -blind *a.* stockblind; -deaf *a.* stocktaub; - quarry *n.* Steinbruch *m*.

Stonemason [stoun'mei-ssAn] *n.* Steinmetz *m*.

Stony [stou'ni] *a.* steinig.

Stool [stuhl] *n.* Sessel *m*, Schemel *m*.

Stoop [stuhp] *vi.* sich bücken, sich herablassen; *n.* Bücken *n*, Beugen *n*.

Stop [stop] *n.* Halt *m*, Aufhören *n*, Sperrung *f*, Aufenthalt *m* (*stay*), Satzzeichen *n*, Blende *f* (*camera*), Klappe *f*, Ventil *n* (*organ*); *vt.* halten, sperren, stoppen, einstellen, plombieren (*teeth*); -cock *n.* Sperrhahn *m*; -gap *n.* Lückenbüsser *m*; -watch *n.* Stoppuhr *f*.

Stoppage [sto'pidzh] *n.* Hemmung *f*, Stockung *f*, Anhalten *n*, Arbeitseinstellung *f*; - of leave *n.* Urlaubssperre *f* (*mil.*).

Stopper [sto'per] *n.* Stöpsel *m*, Verschluss *m*, Pfropfen *m*.

Stopping [sto'ping] *n.* Halten *n*, Anhalten *n*, Zahnfüllung *f* (teeth); - -place n. Haltestelle f; - train n. Personenzug m.

Storage [stO'ridʒh] n. Lagern n, Lagerung f, Einlagerung f, Lagermiete f (charges); - battery n. Sammelbatterie f, Akkumulator m.

Store [stOr] n. Vorrat m, Kaufladen m, Lager m, Warenhaus n; vt. lagern, aufspeichern, unterbringen; - hand n, Lagerarbeiter m; - -house n. Lagerhaus n, Speicher m; - -room n. Vorratskammer f; - -shed n. Lagerschuppen m.

Storekeeper [stOr'kih'per] n. Lagerverwalter m, Lagerhalter m, Ladenbesitzer m.

Storey see story.

Stork [stOrk] n. Storch m.

Storm [stOrm] n. Sturm m, Gewitter n; vt.i. stürmen, bes. er-stürmen, wüten; -y a. stürmisch.

Story [stO'ri] n. Geschichte f, Erzählung f, Lüge f (lie); -teller n. Erzähler m.

Story [stO'ri] n. Stockwerk n, Stock n, Etage f, Geschoss n.

Stout [staut] a. -ly ad. stark, fest, stämmig, dick (fat); - starkes Bier; -ish a. ziemlich stark, wohlbeleibt; -ness f. Stärke f, Wohlbeleibtheit f.

Stove [stouw] n. Ofen m, Kochherd m; - -pipe n. Ofenrohr n.

Stow [stou] vt. verstauen, verpacken, unterbringen.

Stowage [stou'idʒh] n. Stauen n.

Stowaway [stou'A-uei'] n. blinder Passagier.

Straddl'e [strædl] n. Spreizen n, Grätschen n, Gabel f (mil.), Stellage f (com.); vt. rittlings besteigen, spreizen; i. Beine spreizen, grätschen; -ing n. Gabelschiessen n (mil.).

Straggle [strægl] vi. zerstreut liegen, zerstreut gehen, nachhinken.

Straggler [stræ'gler] n. Nach-

zügler m, Versprengte(r) m (mil.).

Straight [streit] a. gerade, direkt, ehrlich, gradsinnig; ad. geradezu, direkt; - on gerade aus.

Straighten [streitn] vt. gerade machen, richten; -ing of line n. Begradigung f (mil.).

Straightforward [streit'fOr'uArd] ad. gerade aus; a. geradsinnig, ehrlich, gerade.

Strain [strein] vt. anstrengen, anspannen, strecken, filtrieren, durchpressen (filter), überanspannen (overstrain); i. sich anstrengen; n. Anstrengung f, Anspannung f, Überanstrengung f, Spannung f, Kraft f (tec.).

Strain [strein] n. Geschlecht n, Abkunft f (breed).

Strained [streind] a. gespannt, übertrieben (Seihtuch n.)

Strainer [strei'ner] n. Sieb n, Seihtuch n.

Strait [streit] n. Meerenge f, Sund m; -s pl. Verlegenheit f; - -jacket n. Zwangsjacke f; - -laced a. engherzig, streng.

Straitened [strei'tend] a. beschränkt, in Verlegenheit f.

Strand [strænd] n. Strähne f, Litze f.

Strand [strænd] n. Strand m, Ufer n; vi. stranden (ship).

Strange [streindʒh] a. -ly ad. fremd, sonderbar, seltsam, ungewöhnlich; -ness n. Sonderbarkeit f, Seltsamkeit f.

Stranger [strein'dʒher] n. der, die Fremde, der, die Unbekannte.

Strangle [stræŋgl] vt. erwürgen, unterdrücken.

Strangulate [stræŋg'gju-leit] vt. einschnüren, zuschnüren; -d a. eingeschnürt, eingeklemmt.

Strap [stræp] n. Riemen m, Lederstreifen m; vt. mit einem Riemen befestigen, binden; -ping a. stämmig.

Stratagem [stræ'ti-dzhAm]n. Kriegslist f, List f.

Strategic [strA-tih'dzhik] a. strategisch; - air arm n. Luftoperationsarmee f; - reconnaissance n. operative Aufklärung f; - road n. Heerstrasse f.

Strateg'ist [stræ'ti-dzhist] n. Feldherr m; -y n. Kriegskunst f, Kriegswissenschaft f.

Stratify [stræ'ti-fai] vt. schichten.

Stratosphere [stræ'tA-sfih-er] n. Stratosphäre f. [Schicht f.

Stratum [strei'tAm] n.

Straw [strO] n. Stroh n; - hat n. Strohhut m; - paper n. Strohpapier n.

Strawberry [strO'bri] n. Erdbeere f; - jam n. Erdbeergelee n, -marmelade f.

Stray [strei] a. verirrt, vereinzelt, zufällig; vi. umherstreifen, abweichen.

Streak [strihk] n. Streifen m, Strich m, Streif m, Anflug m, Anstrich m; streifen, ädern.

Streaky [strih'ki] a. streifig, geädert; - bacon n. durchwachsener Speck.

Stream [strihm] n. Strom m, Wasserlauf m, Bach m, Strömung f; vi. strömen, fliessen.

Stream-line [strihm'lain] n. Stromlinie f (tec.); vt. in Stromlinienform bauen (aut.).

Streamlined [strihm'laind] a. windschnittig, in Stromlinienform, Stromlinien . . . ; - body n. Stromlinienkarosserie f; - car n. Auto n. in Stromlinienform.

Streamer [strih'mer] n. Wimpel m.

Street [striht] n. Strasse f, Gasse f; -car n. Strassenbahn f; -corner n. Strassenecke f; - lamp n. Strassenlaterne f; -lighting n. Strassenbeleuchtung f; -walker n. Dirne f.

Strength [strength] n. Kraft f, Stärke f, Widerstandsfähig-

keit f; actual - Istbestand m, Iststand m, Iststärke f (mil.); battle - Gefechtsstärke f; ration - Iststärke f.

Strengthen [streng'thAn] vt. kräftigen, stärken; i. stark werden; -ing n. Verstärkung f, Befestigung n.

Strenuous [stre'nju-Ass] a, -ly ad. anstrengend, tätig, energisch, rastlos, unruhig.

Stress [stress] n. Nachdruck m, Betonung f, Druck m, Kraft f, Spannung f (tec.); vt. betonen, hervorheben, unterstreichen.

Stretch [stretsch] vt. strecken, ausdehnen; i. sich strecken; n. Strecke f, Spannung f; at a - in einem Zuge, ununterbrochen.

Stretcher [stre'tscher] n. Tragbahre f, Trage f; - -bearer n. Krankenträger m; - case n. Schwerverwundete(r) m.

Strew [struh] vt. bestreuen streuen.

Strict [strikt] a, -ly ad. streng, peinlich, genau; -ness n.

Stricture [strik'tscher] n. kritische Bemerkung, Tadel m.

Stride [straid] n. Schritt m; vi. schreiten. [schneidend.

Strident [strai'dAnt] a. grell,

Strife [straif] n. Streit m, Kampf m, Zwist m.

Strike [straik] n. Streik m, Ausstand m, Streich m, Streichen n; vt. schlagen, treffen, stossen auf, auffallen, münzen (coins), abschliessen (bargain), anstreichen (match), finden (oil); i. schlagen, treffen, stossen, streiken, streichen (mining); - -breaker n. Streikbrecher m; - -picket n. Streikposten m.

Striking [strai'king] a. auffallend; - distance n. Stossweite f; - power n. Schlagkraft f, Schlagfertigkeit f.

String [string] *n.* Schnur *f*, Bindfaden *m*, Band *n*, Saite *f* (*music*), Reihe (*line*); *vt.* schnüren, binden, besaiten (*instrument*); – **quartet** *n.* Streichquartett *n*.

Strip [strip] *n.* Streifen *m*, Leiste *f*; *vt.* abstreifen, abziehen, enthülsen, abmontieren (*tec*.).

Stripe [straip] *n.* Streifen *m*, Strich *m*, Tresse *f* (*mil.*); trouser – *n.* Hosenstreifen *m*; –**d** *a*. gestreift.

Striv'e [straiw] *vi.* streben, sich bemühen; –**ing** *n.* Bestreben *n*.

Stroke [strouk] *n.* Schlag *m*, Strich *m*, Stoss *m*, Anfall *m*, Hub *m* (*tec.*); *vt.* streicheln.

Stroll [stroul] *n.* Spaziergang *m*; *vi.* herum-wandern, -schlendern.

Strong [strong] *a*, -ly *ad.* stark, kräftig, fest, heftig; – **box** *n.* Geldschrank *m*, Panzerschrank *m*; – **drink** *n.* geistiges Getränk; – point *n.* Stützpunkt *m* (*mil.*); –**room** *n.* Stahlkammer *f*, Tresor *m* (*com.*). [*Festung f.*]

Stronghold [strong'hould] *n.*

Strontium [stron'schAm] *n.* Strontium *n*.

Strop [strop] *n.* Streichriemen *m*; *vt.* streichen, abziehen.

Structural [strAk'tschA-rAl] *a.* baulich, Bau . . .; – **engineering** *n.* Baukunst *f*, Baufach *n*; – **strength** *n.* Baufestigkeit *f*.

Structure [strAk'tscher] *n.* Gebäude *n*, Bau *m*, Bauwerk *n*, Gliederung *f*.

Struggle [strAgl] *n.* Ringen *n*, Kampf *m*, Anstrengung *f*; *vi.* ringen, sich abmühen, kämpfen, sich anstrengen; – for existence Kampf ums Dasein.

Strum [strAm] *vi.* klimpern.

Strut [strAt] *vi.* stolzieren, strotzen.

Strut [strAt] *n.* Verstrebung *f*, Verspannung *f*, Strebebalken *m*, Spreize *f*; *vt.* verstreben.

Stub [stAb] *n.* Stumpf *m*, Stubben *m*.

Stubble [stAbl] *n.* Stoppel *f*.

Stubborn [stA'bern] *a*, -ly *ad.* hartnäckig, eigensinnig, halsstarrig, standhaft; -**ness** *n.* Hartnäckigkeit *f*, Eigensinn *m*.

Stubby [stA'bi] *a.* kurz, untersetzt.

Stucco [stA'kou] *n.* Stuck *m*, Gipsmörtel *m*, Stukkatur *f*; – **work** *n.* Stuckarbeit *f*.

Stuck-up [stAk-Ap'] *a.* hochnasig, eingebildet.

Stud [stAd] *n.* Hemdenknopf *m*, Knauf *m*, Beschlagnagel *m*; *vt.* mit Nägeln beschlagen.

Stud [stAd] *n.* Gestüt *n*; – farm *n.* Gestüt *n*; – mare *n.* Zuchtstute *f*.

Student [stjuh'dAnt] *n.* Student *m*, Studentin *f*, der, die Studierende, Gelehrte(r) *m* (*scholar*).

Studied [stA'did] *a.* gelehrt, vorsätzlich, vorbedacht.

Studio [stjuh'djou] *n* Atelier *n*, Künstlerwerkstatt *f*; broadcasting – Senderaum *m*, Aufnahmeraum *m*.

Studious [stjuh'djAss] *a*, -ly *ad.* fleissig, arbeitsam, beflissen, vorsätzlich.

Study [stA'di] *n.* Studieren *n*, Studium *n*, Studierzimmer *n* (*room*); *v.i.* studieren, untersuchen, lernen, nachdenken über; – group *n.* Arbeitsgemeinschaft *f*.

Stuff [stAf] *n.* Stoff *m*, Zeug *n*, Material *n*, Gewebe *n*, Unsinn *m* (*nonsense*); *vt.* füllen, stopfen, polstern (*chairs, etc.*); -**ing** *n.* Füllung *f*, Polsterung *f*, Füllhaar *n*; -**y** *a.* dumpfig, ungelüftet, dumpf.

Stultify [stAl'ti-fai] *vt.* lächerlich machen, widerlegen.

Stumbl'e [stAmbl] *vi.* stolpern, straucheln; -ing block n. Stein m, des Anstosses, Hindernis n.

Stump [stAmp] n. Stumpf m, Stummel m, Wischer m (drawing), Stab m (cricket); vt. wischen; i. schwerfällig gehen; – up bezahlen; – orator n. Volksredner m, Demagog m.

Stumpy [stAm'pi] a. kurz und dick.

Stun [stAn] vt. betäuben.

Stunt [stAnt] n. Kunststück n, Kniff m, Trick m, Sensation f (press), Kunstflug m (av.); vi. Kunststücke vormachen.

Stunt [stAnt] vt. am Wachstum hindern; -ed a. verkümmert, verkrüppelt.

Stupefaction [stjuh'pi-fæk'schAn] n. Bestürzung f, Betäubung f.

Stupefy [stjuh'pi-fai] vt. betäuben, bestürzt machen.

Stupendous [stuh-pen'dAss] a. wunderbar, erstaunlich.

Stupid [stjuh'pid] a. -ly ad. dumm, einfältig, albern.

Stupidity [stju-pi'di-ti] n. Dummheit f, Stumpfsinn m.

Sturdiness [stAr'di-ness] n. Kraft f, Festigkeit f, Stämmigkeit f.

Sturdy [stAr'di] a. kräftig, stämmig, derb.

Sturgeon [stAr'dzhAn] n. Stör m.

Stutter [stA'ter] vi. stottern; n. Stottern n; -er n. Stotterer m. [(eye).

Sty [stai] n. Gerstenkorn n

Sty [stai] n. Schweinestall m.

Style [stail] n. Stil m, Ausdrucksweise f, Stichel f, Sonde f, Titel m, Anrede f (title); vt. benennen, bezeichnen, betiteln.

Stylish [stai'lisch] a. -ly ad. modisch, schick, modern; -ness n. das Modische, Eleganz f.

Stylist [stai'list] n. Stilist m.

Stylograph [stai'lA-grahf] n. Füllfederhalter m.

Suave [ssueiw] a. -ly ad. einschmeichelnd, gewinnend.

Suavity [ssue'wi-ti] n. Anmut f, Sanftmut f.

Subaltern [ssAb'Al-tern] a. untergeordnet; n. Subalternoffizier m; – rank n. unterer Dienstgrad

Subconscious [ssAb-kon'schAss] a. unterbewusst; -ness n. Unterbewusstsein n.

Subdivide [ssAb-di-waid'] vt. unterteilen, weiter teilen.

Subdivision [ssAb-di-wi'zhAn] n. Unterabteilung f.

Subdue [ssAb-djuh'] vt. besiegen, unterwerfen.

Sub-editor [ssAb-e'di-ter] n. Unterschriftleiter m.

Subject [ssAb'dzhekt] n. Gegenstand m, Subjekt n, Thema n, Fach n, Untertan m (state), Staatsangehörige(r) m (citizen); a. unterworfen, ausgesetzt, untertan; – catalogue n. Sachkatalog m; – matter n. Hauptinhalt m.

Subject [ssAb-dzhekt'] vt. unterwerfen, aussetzen, preisgeben.

Subjection [ssAb-dzhek'schAn] n. Unterwerfung f.

Subjective [ssAb-dzhek'tiw] a. -ly ad. subjektiv, persönlich, parteiisch.

Subjectivity [ssAb-dzhek-ti-wi-ti] n. Subjektivität f.

Subjoin [ssAb-dzheun'] vt. hinzufügen.

Subjugate [ssAb'dzhu-geit] vt. unterjochen.

Subjugation [ssAb-dzhu-gei'schAn] n. Unterjochung f.

Subjunctive [ssAb-dzhAnk'tiw] m. Konjunktiv m, Möglichkeitsform f.

Sub-lease [ssAb'lhss], Sublet [ssAb'let] vt. unter-, aftervermieten, unterverpachten.

Sub-letting [ssAb-le-ting] n. Unter-vermietung f, -verpachtung f.

Sub-lieutenant [ssAb'lef-te¹ nAnt] n. Oberleutnant m, zur See.

Sublimate [ssAb'li-meit] n. Sublimat n; vt. sublimieren, verflüchtigen, veredeln.

Sublimation [ssAb-li-mei¹ schAn] n. Sublimierung f, Veredlung f.

Sublime [ssAb-laim'] a, -ly ad. erhaben, hoch, hehr; n. das Erhabene.

Sublimity [ssAb-li'mi-ti] n. Erhabenheit f.

Sub-machine gun [ssAb¹ mA-schihn'gAn] n. Maschinenpistole f.

Submarine [ssAb-mA-rihn'] n. U-boot n, Unterseeboot n; a. unterseeisch, Untersee ...; - cable n. Tiefseekabel n; - chaser n. Unterseebootjäger m; - pen n. Unterseebootbunker m.

Submerge [ssAb-mArdzh'] vt.i. untertauchen, überschwemmen (flood).

Submission [ssAb-mi'schAn] n. Ergebung f, Unterwerfung f, Demut f.

Submissive [ssAb-mi'ssiw] a, -ly ad. unterwürfig, ergeben, demütig.

Submit [ssAb-mit'] vt.i.t. vorlegen, unterbreiten, (sich) unterwerfen, nachgeben, sich ergeben, behaupten (law).

Subordinate [ssAb-Or'di-nit] a. untergeordnet; n. der, die Untergebene; - commander n. Unterführer m.

Subordinate [ssA-bOr'di-neit] vt. unterordnen, unterwerfen; -d a. unterstellt.

Subscribe [ssAb-skraib'] vt. zeichnen, unterschreiben; i. abonnieren, subskribieren, zeichnen, beipflichten; -r n. Abonnent m, Zeichner m, Subskribent m, Verteiler m (ph.).

Subscription [ssAb-skrip¹ schAn] n. Zeichnung f, Subskription f, Abonnement n, Beitrag m; - list n. Zeichnungsliste f.

Subsection [ssAb'ssek-schAn] n. Unterabteilung f, Trupp m (mil.).

Subsequent [ssAb'ssi-kuAnt] a. nachfolgend, seitherig, nachträglich; -ly ad. darauf, hernach, später.

Subservience [ssAb-ssAr¹ wjAnss] n. Unterwürfigkeit f; -t a. unterwürfig, untertan, untergeordnet.

Subside [ssAb-ssaid'] vi. sich setzen, fallen, nachlassen, abnehmen.

Subsidence [ssAb'ssi-dAnss] n. Senkung f, Abnahme f.

Subsidiary [ssAb'ssi'djA-ri] a. Neben ..., Hilfs ...; n. Tochtergesellschaft f; - company n. see subsidiary; - subject n. Nebenfach n.

Subsidize [ssAb'ssi-daiz] vt. subventionieren, unterstützen.

Subsidy [ssAb'ssi-di] n. Geldhilfe f, staatliche Beihilfe, Subvention f.

Subsist [ssAb-ssist'] vi. bestehen, dasein, sich ernähren.

Subsistence [ssAb-ssi'stAnss] n. Bestand m, Dasein n, Auskommen n, Lebensunterhalt m, Verpflegung f, Beköstigung f; - allowance n. Verpflegungsgelder n.pl, -kosten pl.

Subsoil [ssAb'sseul] n. Untergrund m; - plough n. Untergrundpflug m.

Substance [ssAb'stAnss] n. Stoff m, Substanz f, Wesen n, Gehalt m, Hauptinhalt m, Vermögen n (property).

Substantial [ssAb-stæn¹ schAl] a, -ly ad. wesentlich, wirklich, dicht, fest, kräftig, nahrhaft (meal), wichtig (reason).

Substantiate [ssAb-stæn¹ schjeit] vt. erhärten, bestätigen.

Substantiation [ssAb-stænˈschjeˈschAn] n. Erhärtung f, Bestätigung f.

Substantive [ssAbˈstAn-tiw] n. Hauptwort n, Substantiv n.

Sub-station [ssAbˈsteiˈschAn] n. Nebenstelle f.

Substitute [ssAbˈsti-tjuht] n. Stellvertreter m (person), Ersatz m (thing); vt. ersetzen, substituieren, an die Stelle setzen; **leather – n.** Lederersatz m.

Substitution [ssAb-sti-tjuhˈschAn] n. Vertretung f, Ersetzung f, Ersatz m, Einsetzen n, Unterschiebung f.

Substratum [ssAb-streiˈtAm] n. Substrat n, Unterlage f.

Substructure [ssAb-strAkˈtscher] n. Unterbau m.

Subtenancy [ssAb-te-nAn-ssi] n. Untermiete f.

Subtenant [ssAb-teˈnAnt] n. Untermieter m, Unterpächter m.

Subterfuge [ssAbˈter-fjuhdzh] n. Ausflucht f, Vorwand m.

Subterranean [ssAb-tA-reiˈnjAn] a. unterirdisch. [titel m.

Subtitle [ssAbˈtaitl] n. Unter-

Subtle [ssAtl] a. scharfsinnig, subtil, fein; **-ty** n. Spitzfindigkeit f, Scharfsinn m.

Subtract [ssAb-trækt] vt. abziehen, subtrahieren, wegnehmen.

Subtraction [ssAb-trækˈschAn] n. Abziehen n, Wegnahme f, Subtraktion f.

Subtropical [ssAb-troˈpikl] a. subtropisch.

Suburb [ssAbˈbArb] n. Vorstadt f, Vorort m.

Suburban [ssA-bArˈbAn] a. vorstädtisch.

Subvention [ssAb-wenˈschAn] n. Geldhilfe f, Subvention f.

Subversive [ssAb-wArˈssiw] a. umstürzlerisch.

Subvert [ssAb-wArt] vt. umstossen, umstürzen.

Subway [ssAbˈuei] n. Unterführung f, Untergrundbahn f.

Succeed [ssAk-ssihd] vi. i. nachfolgen, folgen, gelingen, glücken.

Success [ssAk-ssess] n. Erfolg m, Glück n, Gelingen n; **-ful, a. -fully** ad. erfolgreich, glücklich.

Succession [ssAk-sseˈschAn] n. Reihenfolge f, Nachfolge f; **in –** hintereinander.

Successive [ssAk-sseˈssiw] a. aufeinander folgend; **-ly** ad. nacheinander, der Reihe nach.

Successor [ssAk-sseˈsser] n. Nachfolger m.

Succinct [ssAk-ssingkt] a. bündig, kurzgefasst, kurz; **-ness** n. Kürze f, Bündigkeit f.

Succour [ssAˈker] n. Hilfe f, Beistand m, Unterstützung f; vt. helfen, unterstützen.

Succulent [ssAkˈju-lAnt] a. saftig. [liegen, unterliegen.

Succumb [ssA-kAm] vi. er-

Such [ssAtsch] pn. a. solch.

Suck [ssAk] vt. saugen.

Sucker [ssAˈker] n. Sauger m, Sprössling m (shoot), Saugröhre f (tec.). [stillen.

Suckle [ssAkl] vt. säugen,

Suction [ssAkˈschAn] n. Saugen n, Absaugen n; **– fan** n. Sauger m, Absauger m, Exhaustor m (tec.); **– pipe** n. Saugleitung f, Saugrohr n; **– pump** n. Saugpumpe f.

Sudden [ssAˈdAn] a. **-ly** ad. plötzlich, rasch, hastig; **-ness** n. Plötzlichkeit f. [lange f.

Suds [ssAds] n.pl. Seifen-

Sue [ssjuh] vt. verklagen, klagen auf; i. bitten.

Suet [ssjuhˈit] n. Nierenfett n, Talg m.

Suffer [ssAˈfer] vt. erleiden, ertragen, erdulden; i. leiden; **-ance** n. Duldung f; **-er** n. der, die Leidende; **-ing** n. Leiden n; a. leidend, notleidend.

Suffice [ssA-faiss'] vi. genügen, ausreichen.

Sufficiency [ssA-fi'schAn-ssi] n. Genüge f, Hinlänglichkeit f.

Sufficient [ssA-fi'schAnt] a, -ly ad. hinreichend, genug, hinlänglich.

Suffix [ssA'fix] n. Suffix m, Nachsilbe f. [ersticken.

Suffocate [ssA'fA-keit] vt.i.

Suffocation [ssA-fA-kei'schAn] n. Erstickung f.

Suffrage [ssA'fridzh] n. Wahl-, Stimm-recht n, Wahlstimme f.

Suffuse [ssA-fjuhs'] vt. übergiessen, überströmen, überlaufen.

Sugar [schu'ger] n. Zucker m; vt. überzuckern, versüssen; - basin n. Zuckerschale f; - -beet n. Zuckerrübe f; - candy n. Kandis m; - loaf n. Zuckerhut m; - maple n. Zuckerahorn m; - refiner n. Zuckersieder m; - refinery n. Zuckersiederei f

Suggest [ssA-dzhest'] vt. eingeben, zu verstehen geben, vorschlagen, anregen, hindeuten auf.

Suggestion [ssA-dzhest'schAn] n. Vorschlag m, Anregung f, Andeutung f.

Suggestive [ssA-dzhe'stiw] a. andeutend, gedankenreich, vielsagend, anregend, unsittlich. [selbstmörderisch.

Suicidal [ssju-i-ssaidl'] a.

Suicide [ssjuh'i-ssaid] n. Selbstmord m.

Suit [ssjuht] n. Folge f, Anzug m (clothes), Rechtsfall m, Klage f (law), Farbe f (cards); vt. passen, anpassen, stehen, kleiden; i. passen.

Suitability [ssjuh-tA-bi'li-ti] n. das Passende, Angemessenheit f.

Suitable [ssjuh'tAbl] a, -ly ad. passend, angemessen, entsprechend.

Suit-case [ssjuht'keiss] n. Handkoffer m.

Suite [ssuiht] n. Gefolge n, Satz m, Zimmerflucht f (rooms).

Suiting [ssjuh'ting] n. Anzugsstoff m (com.).

Suitor [ssjuh'ter] n. Bewerber m, Freier m.

Sulk [ssAlk] vi. schmollen.

Sulky [ssAl'ki] a, Sulkily ad. schmollend.

Sullen [ssA'lAn] a, -ly ad. mürrisch, finster, düster.

Sully [ssA'li] vt. besudeln, beflecken.

Sulphate [ssAl'feit] n. schwefelsaures Salz; - of soda n. schwefelsaures Natron, Glaubersalz n.

Sulphide [ssAl'faid] n. Sulfid n, Schwefelverbindung f; -te n. schwefligsaures Salz, Sulfit m.

Sulphur [ssAl'fer] n. Schwefel m; - match n. Schwefelhölzchen n. [anschwefeln.

Sulphurate [ssAl'fju-reit] vt.

Sulphuretted [ssAl'fju-re-tid] a. mit Schwefel verbunden.

Sulphuric [ssAl-fjuh'rik] a. Schwefel . . ; - acid n. Schwefelsäure f.

Sulphurize [ssAl'fju-rais] vt. schwefeln, vulkanisieren.

Sulphurous [ssAl-fjuh'rAss] a. schweflig.

Sultan [ssAl'tAn] n. Sultan m.

Sultana [ssAl-tah'nA] n. Sultanin f, Sultanine f (raisin).

Sultriness [ssAl'tri-ness] n. Schwüle f.

Sultry [ssAl'tri] a. schwül.

Sum [ssAm] n. Summe f, Betrag m, das Ganze, Inhalt m; vt. rechnen.

Summarily [ssA'mA-ri-li] ad. ohne Umstände, summarisch.

Summarize [ssA'mA-rais] vt. zusammenfassen, resümieren.

Summary [ssA'mA-ri] n. Hauptinhalt m, Übersicht f, Auszug m, Abriss m; a. kurz zusammengefasst, gedrängt, summarisch, fristlos (dismissal).

Summer [ssA'mer] n. Sommer m; – season n. Sommerzeit f; – time n. Sommerzeit f.

Summing-up [ssA'ming-Ap'] n. Rechtsbelehrung f.

Summit [ssA'mit] n. Gipfel m, Spitze f.

Summon [ssA'mAn] vt. auffordern, rufen, zitieren; –s n. Aufforderung f, Zitation f, Vorladung f.

Sump [ssAmp] n. Sumpf m.

Sumptuary [ssAmp'tju-A-ri] a. Aufwand ...; – law n. Aufwandsgesetz n.

Sumptuous [ssAmp'tju-Ass] a. prächtig, kostbar. –ness n. Pracht f, Luxus m.

Sun [ssAn] n. Sonne f; – bath n. Sonnenbad n; – bathe vi. sich sonnen; – blind n. Fensterschirm m, Jalousie f; – dial n. Sonnenuhr f; – helmet n. Tropenhelm m; – proof a. lichtecht; – spectacles n.pl. Schutzbrille f; – spot n. Sonnenfleck m. [nenstrahl m.]

Sunbeam [ssAn'bihm] n. Son-

Sundae [ssAn'dei] n. Eis n, mit Frucht-, Nuss-stückchen m.

Sunday [ssAn'di] n. Sonntag m; a. sonntäglich, Sonntags ...

Sunder [ssAn'der] vt. trennen, sondern.

Sundries [ssAn'dris] n.pl. Verschiedenes n, Nebenausgaben f.pl (com.).

Sundry [ssAn'dri] a. verschiedene, mehrere, mannigfaltig.

Sunflower [ssAn'flau-er] n. Sonnenblume f.

Sunken [ssAng'kAn] a. versenkt, versunken.

Sunless [ssAn'less] a. sonnenlos. [nenlicht n.]

Sunlight [ssAn'lait] n. Son-

Sunny [ssA'ni] a. sonnig.

Sunrise [ssAn'rais] n. Sonnenaufgang m. [untergang m.]

Sunset [ssAn'sset] n. Sonnen-

Sunshade [ssAn'scheid] n. Sonnenschirm m.

Sunshine [ssAn'schain] n. Sonnenschein m; – roof n. Schiebedach n (aut.).

Sunstroke [ssAn'strouk] n. Sonnenstich m.

Sup [ssAp] vt.i. schlürfen, schlucken, zu Abend essen.

Super [ssjuh'per] a. fein, fabelhaft; n. Statist m, Statistin f.

Superabundance [ssjuh-per-A-bAn'dAnss] n. Überfluss m.

Superannuate [ssjuh-per-æn'ju-eit] vt. in den Ruhestand versetzen, pensionieren.

Superannuation [ssjuh-per-æn-ju-ei'schAn] n. Versetzen n, in den Ruhestand, Pension f, Ruhegehalt n.

Superb [ssju-pArb'] a. -ly adv. herrlich, prächtig, kostbar.

Supercargo [ssjuh'per-kahr-gou] n. Ladungsaufseher m.

Supercharge [ssjuh-per-tschahrdzh'] vt. überverdichten (aut.); -r n. Überverdichter m (aut.), Gebläse n (tec.), Überlaster m, Auflader m (tec.).

Supercilious [ssjuh-per-ssi'ljAss] a. -ly adv. anmassend, hochmütig; -ness n. Anmassung f, Hochmut m.

Supercool [ssjuh-per-kuhl'] vt. unterkühlen (tec.).

Super-Dreadnought [ssjuh-per-dred'nOt] n. Grosskampfschiff n.

Superficial [ssjuh-per-fi'schAl] a. -ly adv. oberflächlich.

Superficiality [ssjuh-per-fi-schjæ'li-ti] n. Oberflächlichkeit f.

Superfine [ssjuh-per-fain'] a. hochfein.

Superfluity [ssjuh-per-fluh'i-ti] n. Überfluss m.

Superfluous [ssju-pAr'flu-Ass] a. überflüssig, unnötig.

Superheat [ssjuh-per-hiht'] vt. überhitzen; -er n. Dampfüberhitzer m.

Superhet(erodyne) [ssjuper-he'tA-rA-dain] n. – receiver

n. Überlagerungsempfänger *m* (*rad.*).

Superhuman [ssjuh-per-hjuh'mAn] *n.* übermenschlich.

Superimpose [ssjuh-per-im-pous'] *vt.* darüberlegen, überlagern.

Superintend [ssjuh-per-in-tend'] *vt.* beaufsichtigen, verwalten, überwachen, kontrollieren; **-ence** *n.* Oberaufsicht *f*; **-ent** *n.* Oberaufseher *m*, Vorsteher *m*, Intendant *m*.

Superior [ssjuh-pih'rjer] *a.* höher, überlegen, vorzüglich, vortrefflich(er); *n.* Vorgesetzte(r) *m*, Höherstehende *m*.

Superiority [ssjuh-pih-rjo'ritj] *n.* Überlegenheit *f*, Vorrang *m*, Übermacht *f*.

Superlative [ssjuh-pАr'lА-tiw] *a.* -ly *ad.* höchst, unübertrefflich; *n.* höchster Grad, Superlativ *m*.

Superman [ssjuh'per-mæn] *n.* Übermensch *m*.

Supernatural [ssjuh-per-næ'tschA-rAl] *a.* übernatürlich.

Supernumerary [ssjuh-per-njuh'mA-rA-ri] *n.* der, die Überzählige; *a.* überzählig.

Superphosphate [ssjuh-per-fo'ssfeit] *n.* überphosphorsaures Salz.

Supersede [ssjuh-per-ssihd'] *vt.* ersetzen, verdrängen, abschaffen, aufheben.

Superstition [ssjuh-per-sti'schAn] *n.* Aberglaube *m*.

Superstitious [ssjuh-per-sti'schAss] *a.* abergläubisch.

Superstructure [ssjuh'per-strAk-tscher] *n.* Aufbau *m*, Oberbau *m*.

Supertax [ssjuh'per-tæx] *n.* Einkommensteuerzuschlag *m*, Zuschlagsteuer *f*.

Supervene [ssjuh-per-wihn'] *vi.* dazwischenkommen.

Supervise [ssjuh-per-wais'] *vt.* überwachen, kontrollieren, beaufsichtigen.

Supervision [ssjuh-per-wi'zhAn] *n.* Beaufsichtigung *f*, Kontrolle *f*.

Supervisor [ssjuh'per-wai-ser] *n.* Vorsteher *m*, Aufseher *m*.

Supine [ssjuh'pain] *a.* auf dem Rücken liegend, nachlässig, träge. [essen *n*.

Supper [ssA'per] *n.* Abend-

Supplant [ssA-plahnt'] *vt.* ausstechen, verdrängen, vertreiben. [schmeidig.

Supple [ssApl] *a.* biegsam, ge-

Supplement [ssA'pli-mAnt] *n.* Ergänzung *f*, Beilage *f*, Nachtrag *m*; *vt.* ergänzen, hinzufügen.

Supplementary [ssA-pli-men'tA-ri] *a.* ergänzend, nachträglich.

Suppleness [ssA'pl-ness] *n.* Biegsamkeit *f*, Geschmeidigkeit *f*. [ferant *m*, Versorger *m*.

Supplier [ssA-plai'er] *n.* Lie-

Supply [ssA-plai'] *n.* Vorrat *m*, Versorgung *f*, Lager *n*, Zufuhr *f*, Nachschub *m* (*mil.*); *vt.* versehen, versorgen, ersetzen, ergänzen, verschaffen, liefern; short — *n.* Mangel *m*; — from the air *n.* Luftversorgung *f* (*mil.*); — airfield *n.* Nachschubflughafen *n*; — base *n.* Versorgungsstützpunkt *m*; — of current *n.* Stromzuführung *f* (*el.*); — dump *n.* Nachschublager *n*; — sector *n.* Versorgungsabschnitt *m*; — service *n.* Nachschub *m* (*mil.*); — ship *n.* Tross-schiff *n*; — station *n.* Nachschubleitstelle *f*.

Support [ssA-poort'] *n.* Stütze *f*, Ständer *m*, Unterstützung *f*, Beistand *m*, Nahrung *f*, Unterhaltung *f*; *vt.* stützen, unterstützen, aufrechterhalten, verteidigen (*defend*), unterhalten (*feed, etc.*); -ed by angelehnt (*mil.*); -ing *int.* Beifilm *m*.

Supporter [ssA-poor'ter] *n.* Verfechter *m*, Anhänger *m*.

Suppose [ssA-pous'] *vt.* vermuten, annehmen, voraussetzen; -d a. angeblich, vorausgesetzt.

Supposition [ssA-pA-si'schAn] n. Vermutung f, Annahme f, Voraussetzung f.

Suppress [ssA-'press'] vt. unterdrücken, hemmen, verheimlichen, aufheben.

Suppression [ssA-pre'schAn] n. Unterdrückung f, Aufhebung f. [eitern.

Suppurate [ssA'pju-reit] vi.

Suppuration [ssA-pju-rei'schAn] n. Eiterung f.

Supremacy [ssjuh-pre'mA-ssi] n. Vorherrschaft f, Obergewalt f, Überlegenheit f.

Supreme [ssjuh-prihm'] a, -ly ad. höchst, oberst; - command n. Oberkommando n; - command of armed forces n. Oberkommando Wehrmacht; - commander n. oberster Befehlshaber m; - court n. Oberlandesgericht n, Reichsgericht n.

Surcharge [ssA'tschahrdzh] n. Überlastung f, Zuschlag m, Strafporto n (postage), Überdruck m (stamp); vt. überladen, mit Zuschlagsporto belegen (post); -d a. aufgedruckt, mit Überdruck.

Sure [schuh'er] a. sicher, gewiss; - -footed a. fest auf den Füssen; -ly ad. sicher, sicherlich, wohl, freilich.

Surety [schuh'er-ti] n. Sicherheit f, Gewissheit f, Kaution f, Bürgschaft f (law).

Surf [ssArf] n. Brandung f, Sturzsee f.

Surface [ssAr'fiss] n. Oberfläche f; a. oberflächlich, äusserlich, Oberflächen . . .; vi. auftauchen (U-boat); - forces n.pl. Überwasserstreitkräfte f.pl (nav.).

Surfeit [ssAr'fit] n. Überladung f, Überdruss m; vt. überladen, übersättigen.

Surge [ssArdzh] n. Brandung f. Sturzsee f; vi. hochgehen, toben.

Surgeon [ssAr'dzhAn] n. Wundarzt m, Chirurg m; --dentist n. Zahnarzt m.

Surgery [ssAr'dzhA-ri] n. Wundarzneikunst f, Sprechzimmer n.

Surgical [ssAr'dzhikl] a. wundärztlich, chirurgisch.

Surly [ssAr'li] a. mürrisch, grob, rauh, schroff.

Surmise [ssAr-mais'] n. Mutmassung f, Vermutung f; vt. mutmassen, vermuten.

Surmount [ssAr-maunt'] vt. übersteigen, überwinden, besiegen; -able a. übersteigbar.

Surname [ssAr'neim] n. Familienname m, Zuname m; vt. einen Zunamen geben.

Surpass [ssAr-pahss'] vt. übertreffen.

Surplus [ssAr'plAss] n. Überschuss m, Rest m; a. überzählig, Mehr . . .; - to establishment überzahlmässig (mil.); - stock n. Plusbestand m.

Surprise [ssAr-prais'] n. Überraschung f; vt. überraschen, überrumpeln (mil.); - attack n. Überrumpelung f, Überfall m.

Surrealis'm [ssA-rih'A-lism] n. Surrealismus m, Neue Sachlichkeit; -t n. Surrealist m.

Surrender [ssA-ren'der] n. Übergabe f, Überlassung f; vt. übergeben, überliefern, abtreten; i. sich ergeben, sich ausliefern; - value n. Rückkaufswert m (com.).

Surreptitious [ssA-rep-ti'schAss] a. heimlich, unerlaubt.

Surround [ssA-raund'] vt. umgeben, umringen, einschliessen, umzingeln (mil.); -ing a. umgebend; -s n.pl. Umgebung f, Umgegend f.

Surtax [ssAr'tæx] n. Zuschlagssteuer f, Steuerzuschlag m.

Survey [ssAꞋweiꞋ] n. Überblick m, Übersicht f, Bericht m, Vermessung f; - **section** n. Messtrupp m (mil.); - **troops** n.pl. Vermessungsbatterie f (mil.).

Survey [sserꞋweiꞋ] vt. überblicken, übersehen, mustern, prüfen, vermessen.

Surveying [sserꞋweiꞋing] n. Besichtigung f, Vermessung f; - **chain** n. Messkette f; - **equipment** n. Messgerät n; - **vessel** n. Vermessungsschiff n.

Surveyor [sserꞋweiꞋer] n. Aufseher m, Inspektor m, Feldmesser m.

Survival [sserꞋwaiꞋwAl] n. Überleben n.

Survive [sserꞋwaiwꞋ] vt. überleben; i. am Leben bleiben; -**or** n. der, die Überlebende, der, die Hinterbliebene.

Susceptibility [ssA-ssepꞋti-biꞋli-ti] n. Empfindlichkeit f, Empfänglichkeit f.

Susceptible [ssA-ssepꞋtibl] a. empfänglich, empfindlich.

Suspect [ssA-spektꞋ] vt. in Verdacht haben, beargwöhnen, verdächtigen, misstrauen.

Suspect [ssAꞋspekt] n. der, die Verdächtige, Verdächtigsperson f; a. verdächtig.

Suspend [ssA-spendꞋ] vt. aufhängen, verschieben, suspendieren, einstellen, zeitweilig aufheben; -**ers** n.pl. Strumpfhalter m, Tragbänder n.pl., Hosenträger m (U.S.A.).

Suspense [ssA-spenssꞋ] n. Ungewissheit f, Unterbrechung f.

Suspension [ssA-spenꞋschAn] n. Hängen n, Einstellung f, Aufschub m, Federung f (aut.); - **bridge** n. Kettenbrücke f.

Suspicion [ssA-spiꞋschAn] n. Verdacht m.

Suspicious [ssA-spiꞋschAss] a. -**ly** ad. verdächtig, argwöhnisch, misstrauisch.

Sustain [ssA-steinꞋ] vt. aufrechthalten, stützen, unterhal-

ten, erleiden (loss); -**ed fire** n. Dauerfeuer n (mil.).

Sustenance [ssAꞋsti-nAnss] n. Lebensunterhalt m, Verpflegung f.

Swab [ssuob] n. Scheuerlappen m, Wischer m, Abstrich m; vt. wischen, schrubben.

Swaddle [ssuodl] vt. windeln, wickeln.

Swagger [ssuæꞋger] vi. prahlen, stolzieren, renommieren.

Swain [ssuein] n. Bauernbursch m, Liebhaber m.

Swallow [ssuoꞋlou] n. Schwalbe f.

Swallow [ssuoꞋlou] vt.i. (ver-) schlucken, verschlingen; n. einstecken (insult). n. Schluck m.

Swamp [ssuomp] n. Sumpf m; vt. versenken, überwältigen, überschwemmen.

Swan [ssuon] n. Schwan m.

Swank [ssuængk] n. Aufschneiderei f, Prahlerei f; vi. vornehm tun, aufschneiden; -**y** a. prahlerisch, schick.

Swap [ssuop] vt. vertauschen; n. Tausch m.

Swarm [ssuOrm] n. Schwarm m, Menge f; vi. wimmeln, schwärmen.

Swarm [ssuOrm] vi. klettern.

Swarthy [ssuOrꞋdhi] a. dunkelbraun, schwärzlich.

Swastika [ssuoꞋsti-kA] n. Hakenkreuz n.

Swathe [ssueidh] vt. windeln, einhüllen, wickeln.

Sway [ssuei] n. Schwingen n, Einfluss m, Macht f, Herrschaft f; vt. schwingen, schwanken, leiten, beeinflussen.

Swear [ssuehꞋer] vt.i. schwören, fluchen; - **word** n. Fluch m.

Sweat [ssuet] n. Schweiss m; vi. schwitzen; t. schwitzen lassen, schinden, schweissen (tec.); -**ed labour** n. Ausbeutung f, Schinderei f.

Sweater [ssueꞋter] n. Wolljacke f, Sweater m, Überziehjacke f. Leuteschinder m (employer).

Sweating [ssue'ting] n. Schwitzen n, Schweissen m. (tec.), Schinden n (com.), Lohndrückerei f (com.).

Sweaty [ssue'ti] a. schweissig, schwitzig.

Swede [ssuihd] n. (schwedische) Steckrübe f.

Sweep [ssuihp] n. Schornsteinfeger m (chimney), Kehren n, Bogen m, Windung f; vt. kehren, fegen, bestreichen; -er n. Kehrmaschine f; -ing n. Fegen n; a. durchgreifend, weitgehend; -s pl. Kehricht m, Gekrätz n (tec.).

Sweet [ssuiht] a, -ly ad. süss; - pea n. spanische Wicke; - potato n. Batate f; -tempered a. mild, sanft; - tooth n. Leckermaul n.

Sweetbread [ssuiht'bred] n. Kalbsmilch f. [süssen.

Sweeten [ssuih'tAn] vt. ver-

Sweetheart [ssuiht'hahrt] n. Liebchen n, Schatz m.

Sweetmeat [ssuiht'miht] n. Zuckerwerk n.

Sweetness [ssuiht'ness] n. Süssigkeit f, das Süsse.

Sweets [ssuihss] n.pl. Süssigkeiten f.pl. Bonbons pl.

Swell [ssuel] n. Dünung f, Stutzer m, Modeheld m; a. vornehm, elegant; vt.i. vermehren, schwellen, anschwellen.

Swelter [ssuel'ter] vi. vor Hitze umkommen; -ing a. sehr heiss.

Swerve [ssuArw] vi. abweichen, eine Seitenbewegung machen; n. plötzliche Seitenbewegung.

Swift [ssuift] a, -ly ad. schnell, rasch, geschwind; n. Turmschwalbe f; -ness n. Geschwindigkeit f.

Swill [ssuil] vt. spülen, abwaschen; n. Spülwasser n,

Spülicht n, Küchenabfälle m. pl.

Swim [ssuim] vi. schwimmen; t. durchschwimmen; have a - schwimmen.

Swimmer [ssui'mer] n. Schwimmer m, Schwimmerin f.

Swimming [ssui'ming] n. Schwimmen n; a. schwimmend; - -bath n. Schwimmbad n; - -pool n. Badeanstalt f.

Swimmingly [ssui'ming-li] ad. glatt, flott, famos.

Swindle [ssuindl] vt. beschwindeln, betrügen; i. schwindeln; n. Betrug m, Schwindel m; -r n. Gauner m, Schwindler m, Betrüger m.

Swine [ssuain] n. Schwein n.

Swing [ssuing] n. Schwung m, Schaukel f, Schwingung f; vt.i. schwingen, sich drehen, schaukeln; - bridge n. Drehbrücke f; - door n. Schwing-, Klapp-tür f.

Swinish [ssuai'nisch] a. schweinisch.

Swipe [ssuaip] n. tüchtig schlagen.

Swirl [ssuArl] vi. wirbeln; n. Strudel m, Wirbel m.

Swish [ssuitsch] vt.i. sausen, pfeifen.

Switch [ssuitsch] n. Gerte f, Rute f, falscher Zopf (hair), Umschalter m, Schalter m (el.), Weiche f (rl.); vt. schalten, verlegen (fire, mil.), rangieren (rl.); - off ausschalten; - on einschalten; - over umschalten; - line n. Sicherungslinie f (rl.).

Switchback [ssuitsch'bæk] n. Berg- und Tal-bahn f, Rutschbahn f.

Switchboard [ssuitsch'bOrd] n. Schaltbrett n, Umschalterbrett n. [Schaltkasten m.

Switch-box [ssuitsch'box] n.

Swivel [ssuiwl] n. Drehring m, Riemenbügel m (mil.); sich auf einem Zapfen drehen;

- **bridge** n. Drehbrücke f; -
carriage n. Lafette f; - **chair** n.
Drehstuhl m; - **joint** n. Universalgelenk n; - **mounted** a.
schwenkbar.

Swoon [ssuuhn] n. Ohnmacht
f; vi. in Ohnmacht fallen,
ohnmächtig werden.

Swoop [ssuuhp] n. Sturz m;
vi. sich stürzen, niederschiessen.

Swop [ssuop] see Swap.

Sword [ssOrd] n. Säbel m,
Schwert n, Degen m; -
belt Säbelkoppel n; - **knot**
n. Troddel f, Faustriemen m.

Swot [ssuot] vi. pauken, ochsen, büffeln; n. Ochser m (man),
Schufterei f, Paukerei f (toil).

Sycamore [ssi'kA-mOr] n.
Sykomore f, Bergahorn m.

Syllable [ssi'lAbl] n. Silbe f.

Syllabus [ssi'lA-bAss] n. Prospekt m, Verzeichnis n, Lehrplan m, Programm n.

Symbol [ssim'bAl] n. Sinnbild
n, Symbol n.

Symbolic(al) [ssim-bo'likl] a,
-**ly** ad. sinnbildlich, symbolisch.

Symbolize [ssim'bA-lais] vt.
versinnbildlichen.

Symmetrical [ssi-me'trikl] a,
-**ly** ad. symmetrisch, gleichmässig.

Symmetry [ssi'mi-tri] n.
Symmetrie f, Ebenmass n.

Sympathetic [ssim-pA-the'-
tik] a, -**ally** ad. teilnehmend,
mitfühlend; - **strike** n. Sympathiestreik m.

Sympathize [ssim'pA-thais]
vi. mitfühlen, sympathisieren.

Sympathy [ssim'pA-thi] n.
Mitgefühl n, Sympathie f, Teilnahme f.

Symphony [ssim'fA-ni] n.
Sinfonie f.

Symptom [ssimp'tAm] n. Anzeichen n, Symptom n.

Symptomatic [ssimp-tA-mæ'-
tik] a. typisch, bezeichnend.

Synagogue [ssi'nA-gog] n.
Synagoge f.

Synchronization [ssin-krA-
nai-sei'schAn] n. Synchronisierung f.

Synchronize [ssin'krA-nais]
vt. synchronisieren.

Syncopate [ssin'kA-peit] vt.
synkopieren.

Syncopation [ssin-kA-pei'-
schAn] n. Synkopieren n.

Syndicalism [ssin'di-kA-lism]
n. Syndikalismus m.

Syndicate [ssin'di-kit] n. Konsortium n, Verband m, Kartell
n, Ring m.

Synod [ssi'nAd] n. Synode f,
Kirchenversammlung f.

Synonym [ssi'nA-nim] n.
Synonym n, sinnverwandtes
Wort.

Synonymous [ssi-no'ni-mAss]
a. sinnverwandt, gleichbedeutend.

Synopsis [ssi-nop'ssiss] n. Abriss m.

Syntax [ssin'tæx] n. Satzlehre f.

Synthesis [ssin'thA-ssiss] n.
Synthese f, Zusammensetzung f.

Synthetic [ssin-the'tik] a.
synthetisch, künstlich; - **petrol**
n. Kunstbenzin n; - **rubber** n.
Kunstgummi m.

Syphilis [ssi'fi-liss] n. Lustseuche f, Syphilis f.

Syphon [ssai'fAn] n. Siphon
m.

Syringe [ssi'rindzh] n.
Spritze f.

Syrup [ssi'rAp] n. Sirup m,
Melasse f.

System [ssi'stim] n. System n,
Plan m, Verfahren n; - **railway**
- n. Eisenbahnnetz n.

Systematic [ssi-sti-mæ'tik] a,
-**ally** ad. systematisch, planmässig.

Systematize [ssi'sti-mA-tais]
vt. in ein System bringen,
systematisieren, ordnen.

tab 688 **tak**

T

Tab [tæb] *n.* Streifen *m*, Klappe *f*, Aufhänger *m*, Schuhriemen *m*, Latsche *f* (*shoe*), Kragenspiegel *m* (*mil.*).

Tabby [tæ'bi] *n.* Mohr *n*; *a.* gewässert, moiriert; - cat *n.* Katze *f*.

Table [teibl] *n.* Tisch *m*, Tafel *f*, Tabelle *f*, Verzeichnis *n*; *vt.* verzeichnen, auf den Tisch legen, vorlegen; - centre *n.* Tischläufer *m*; - cloth *n.* Tischtuch *n*, Tischdecke *f*; - land *n.* Hochebene *f*, Plateau *n*; - linen *n.* Tischzeug *n*; - napkin *n.* Serviette *f*, Mundtuch *n*; -spoon *n.* Esslöffel *m*; - talk *n.* Tischgespräch *n*; -top *n.* Tischplatte *f*, Tischblatt *n*.

Tablet [tæb'lit] *n.* Platte *f*, Tafel *f*, Stück *n* (*soap*).

Tabloid [tæb'leud] *n.* Tablette *f*; *a.* konzentriert.

Taboo [tA-buh'] *a.* verboten; *n.* Verbot *n*, Verruf *m*, Tabu *n*; *vt.* für tabu erklären, verbieten, ausstossen.

Tabular [tæ'bju-ler] *a.* tafelförmig, tabellarisch.

Tabulate [tæ'bju-leit] *vt.* tabellarisch ordnen, katalogisieren.

Tachograph [tæ'kA-grahf] *n.* Tachograph *m*.

Tachometer [tæ-ko'mi-ter] *n.* Geschwindigkeits-, Ferndrehzahl-messer *m*, Umdrehungszähler *m*. [end.]

Tacit [tæ'ssit] *a.* stillschweig-

Taciturn [tæ'ssi-tern] *a.* wortkarg, schweigsam; -ity *n.* Wortkargheit *f*, Schweigsamkeit *f*.

Tack [tæk] *n.* kleiner Nagel, Stift *m*, Reisszwecke *f*, Tapezziernagel *m*, Halse *f* (*nav.*), Lavieren *n* (*nav.*), Kurs *m* (*course*); *vt.* heften, anheften,

befestigen; *i.* wenden, lavieren (*nav.*).

Tackle [tækl] *n.* Gerät *n*, Flaschenzug *m* (*tec.*), Takel *n*, Tauwerk *n*, Seilzug *m* (*nav.*), Talje *f* (*nav.*); *vt.* anpacken, in Angriff nehmen, rempeln (*football*).

Tact [tækt] *n.* Takt *m*, Feingefühl *n*; -ful *a.*, -fully *ad.* taktvoll.

Tactical [tæk'tikl] *a.* taktisch; - grouping *n.* Truppeneinteilung *f*; - landing ground *n.* Gefechtslandeplatz *m*; - reconnaissance *n.* Nahaufklärung *f*, taktische Aufklärung; - situation *n.* Kampflage *f*, Gefechtslage *f*. [Taktiker *m*.

Tactician [tæk-ti'schAn] *n.*

Tactics [tæk'tix] *n. pl.* Taktik *f*, Kriegskunst *f*; shock - Stosstaktik *f* (*mil.*). [frosch *m*.

Tadpole [tæd'poul] *n.* Kaul-

Taffeta [tæ'fi-tA] *n.* Taft *m*.

Taffrail [tæf'reil] *n.* Heckreling *m*, Heckbord *m*.

Tag [tæg] *n.* Anhängezettel *n*, Kennmarke *f*, Stiefelstrippe *f*, Besatz *m*, stehende Redensart, Schlagwort *n*; *vt.* anheften.

Tail [teil] *n.* Schwanz *m*, Schweif *m*, Rockschoss *m*, Schluss *m*, Ende *n*; - off *vi.* abfallen; - coat *n.* Frack *m*; - light *n.* Schlusslaterne *f*, Schlusslicht *n* (*aut.*); - wheel *n.* Radsporn *m*.

Tailless [teil'less] *a.* schwanzlos.

Tailor [tei'ler] *n.* Schneider *m*; *vt.* schneidern; - made dress *n.* Schneiderkleid *n*; -ess *n.* Schneiderin *f*.

Taint [teint] *n.* Fleck *m*, Flecken *m*, Makel *m*, Ansteckung *f*; *vt.* beflecken, verpesten, vergiften, verderben, anstecken.

Take [teik] *vt.* nehmen, annehmen, empfangen, erhalten, bekommen, bringen, führen, betrachten, halten für, aufnehmen (*photo*), brauchen *(time)*; – **off** *vi.* loskommen *(av.)*, abfliegen, abstarten *(av.)*, ablegen *(pack)*; – *n.* Abflug *m*, Start *m (av.)*.

Talc [tælk] *n.* Talk *m*.

Tale [teil] *n.* Erzählung *f*, Märchen *n*; – **-bearer** *n.* Angeber *m*, Zuträger *m*; – **-bearing** *n.* Angeberei *f*.

Talent [tæ'lAnt] *n.* Talent *n*, Anlage *f*, Begabung *f*.

Talented [tæ'lAn-tid] *a.* begabt, talentvoll, talentiert.

Talisman [tæ'lis-mAn] *n.* zauberkräftiges Schutzmittel, Talisman *m*.

Talk [tOk] *vi.* reden, sprechen; *n.* Gespräch *n*, Rede *f*, Gerede *n*.   [selig, gesprächig.

Talkative [tO'kA-tiv] *a.* redselig.

Talker [tO'ker] *n.* Schwätzer *m*, Plauderer *m*.   [film *m*.

Talkies [tO'kis] *n.pl.* Sprechfilm *m*.

Tall [tOl] *a.* gross, hoch, lang.

Tallboy [tOl'beu] *n.* Aufsatzkommode *f*.

Tallness [tOl'ness] *n.* Länge *f*, Grösse *f*, Höhe *f*.

Tallow [tæ'lou] *n.* Talg *m*, Unschlitt *m*; *a.* talgig; – **candle** *n.* Talglicht *n*; – **-chandler** *n.* Lichtzieher *m*.

Tally [tæ'li] *n.* Kerbstock *m*, Namensschild *n*, Nachzählung *f*; *vi.* übereinstimmen, zusammenpassen; – **clerk** *n.* Ladungskontrolleur *m*.

Talon [tæ'lAnn] *n.* Fang *m*, Erneuerungsschein *m (com.)*, Stichkupon *m (com.)*.

Tambour [tæm'bu-er] *n.* Trommel *f*; – **frame** *n.* Stickrahmen *m*.

Tambourine [tæm-bu-rihn'] *n.* Tamburin *n*, Schellentrommel *f*.

Tame [teim] *a.*, **-ly** *ad.* zahm; *vt.* zähmen; – **rabbit** *n.* Hauskaninchen *n*.   [Zahmheit *f*.

Tameness [teim'ness] *n.*

Tamer [tei'mer] *n* Bändiger *m*. Dresseur *m*.

Tam-o'-shanter [tæm-ou-schæn'ter] *n.* Sportmütze *f*, sehr weite Baskenmütze, schottische Wollmütze.

Tamp [tæmp] *n.* Stampfer *m*; *vt.* feststampfen, verdämmen.

Tamper [tæm'per] *vi.* sich mischen in, fälschen, bestechen *(bribe)*.

Tampion [tæm'pjAn] *n.* Stöpsel *m*, Pfropf *m*.

Tampon [tæm'pAn] *n.* Gaze-, Watte-bausch *n*; *vt.* tamponieren.

Tan [tæn] *n.* Lohe *f*, gelbbraune Farbe, Bräune *f*, Sonnenbrand *m*; *a.* gelbbraun; *vt.* gerben, lohen, bräunen *(sunshine)*. [dem *n*, Tandemrad *n*.

Tandem [tæn'dAm] *n.* Tan-

Tang [tæng] *n.* Beigeschmack *m*.   [Tangente *f*.

Tangent [tæn'dzhAnt] *n.*

Tangerine [tæn-dzgA-rihn'] *n.* Mandarine *f*.

Tangible [tæn'dgibl] *a.* fühlbar, greifbar.

Tangle [tæng'gl] *n.* Knoten *m*, Gewirr *n*, Verwirrung *f*; *vt.i.* (sich) verwickeln, verwirren.

Tango [tæng'gou] *n.* Tango *m*.

Tank [tængk] *n.* Wasserbehälter *m*, Zisterne *f*, (Panzer-) Kampfwagen *m (mil.)*; additional – Zusatzbehälter *m (av.)*; amphibian – Schwimmpanzerkraftwagen *m*; fuel – Kraftstoff-, Brennstoffbehälter *m*; – **battalion** *n.* Panzerbataillon *n*; – **carrier** *n.* Panzertransportwagen *m*; – **crew** *n.* Panzerbesatzung *f*; – **engine** *n.* Tenderlokomotive *f (rl.)*; – **landing craft** *n.* Panzer-träger *n*; – **landeboot** *n.*; – **platoon** *n.* Panzerzug *m*; – **squadron** *n.* Panzerkompanie *f*; – **trap** *n.* Panzerfalle *f*; – **truck** *n.* Kesselwagen *m (rl.)*; – **turret** *n.* Panzerturm *m*; – **unit** *n.* Panzertruppe *f*.   [Kanne *f*.

Tankard [tæng'kerd] *n.*

Tanker [tæng'ker] n. Kesselwagen m (rl.), Motortankschiff
n (nav.).

Tanner [tæ'ner] n. Gerber m.

Tannery [tæ'nA-ri] n. Ger-
berei f.   [gerben f.]

Tanning [tæ'ning] n. Loh-

Tantalize [tæn'tA-lais] vt.
quälen, peinigen.

Tantamount [tæn'tA-maunt]
a. gleichbedeutend, gleichgel-
tend.

Tap [tæp] n. Zapfen m, Hahn
m; vt. anzapfen, anstechen,
mithören, abhören (wires).

Tap [tæp] n. Pochen n, Klopfen
n, gelinder Schlag; vt.i. poch-
en, klopfen, sanft schlagen.

Tape [teip] n. Band n, Leinen-
band n, Schnur f, (Papier-)
Streifen m; vt. mit einem Band
versehen; adhesive – Klebe-
streifen m; insulating – Isolierband n; red – Bürokratismus
m; – line n. Stahlmessband n,
Mess-schnur f; – machine n.
Börsenmaschine f; – measure
n. Bandmass n.

Taper [tei'per] n. Wachskerze
f; vi. spitz zulaufen.

Tapestry [tæ'pi-stri] n. Wand-
teppich m, gewirkte Tapete,
Stickerei f, Tapetenstoff m;
Tapisserie f; – frame n. Stickrahmen m.   [Tapioka f.]

Tapioca [tæ-pjou'kA] n.

Tapper [tæ'per] n. Telegraphenschlüssel m.   [(aut.)]

Tappet [tæ'pit] n. Stössel m.

Tapping [tæ'ping] n. Anzapf-
en n, Klopfen n, Tippen n,
Abhören n (ph.); – -device n.
Anschaltvorrichtung f (el.).

Tar [tahr] n. Teer m, Matrose
m, Teerjacke f; vt. teeren; –
-board n. Teerpappe f; – -boil-
er n. Teersieder m.

Tardily [tahr'di-li] ad, **Tardy**
a. langsam, träge, spät.

Tare [teh'er] n. Tara f, Ver-
packungsgewicht n; vt. tarier-
en.

Tare [teh'er] n. Wicke f.

Target [tahr'git] n. Schiess-
scheibe f, Zielscheibe f, Ziel n;
auxiliary – Hilfs-, Vergleichs-
ziel n; designation of – Ziel-
ansprache f, -bestimmung f;
-bezeichnung f; mobile – be-
wegliches Ziel; receding – ge-
hendes Ziel (av.); standard –
Einheitsscheibe f (mil.);
practice n. Ziel-, Schiess-übung
f; – reconnaissance n. Ziel-
aufklärung f; – tower n.
Scheibenschlepper m (av.).

Tariff [tæ'rif] n. Tarif m, Zoll-
verzeichnis n; – union n. Zoll-
verein m.

Tarmac [tahr'mæk] n. Abbremsplatz m (av.); see also
Tar-macadam.

Tar-macadam [tahr'mA-kæ-
dAn] n. Steinschotter m, mit
Teer.

Tarn [tahrn] n. Gebirgssee m.

Tarnish [tahr'nisch] vt. matt
machen, beflecken; i. sich trüben, matt werden.

Tarpaulin [tahr-pO'lin] n.
Persenning f, geteertes Segeltuch, Zeltbahn f.

Tarry [tæ'ri] vi. zögern, säum-
en, verweilen.   [pastete f.]

Tart [tahrt] n. Torte f, Obst-

Tart [tahrt] n. Dirne f.

Tart [tahrt] a. scharf, herb,
sauer.

Tartan [tahr'tAn] n. schottischer karierter Wollstoff, Tartan m; a. bunt gewürfelt.

Tartar [tahr'ter] n. Weinstein
m; Zahnstein m; cream of – n.
gereinigter Weinstein.

Tartaric acid [tahr-tæ'rik-æ-
ssid] n. Weinsäure f.

Tartrate [tahr'trit] n. wein-
steinsaures Salz.

Task [tahsk] n. Aufgabe f, Auftrag m; vt. in Anspruch nehm-
en, beschäftigen, anstrengen.

Task-force [tahsk'fOrss] n.
Truppenverband m; mechan-
ized – Panzerverband m.

Taskmaster [tahsk'mah-ster] n. Arbeitgeber m, Zuchtmeister m.

Tassel [tæssl] n. Quaste f.

Taste [teist] n. Geschmack m, Kostprobe f, Vorliebe f; vt.i. schmecken, kosten.

Tasteful [teist'ful] a, -ly ad. geschmackvoll.

Tasteless [teist'less] a. geschmacklos, unschmackhaft.

Tasty [tei'sti] a. schmackhaft.

Tatter [tæ'ter] n. Fetzen m, Lumpen m.

Tattered [tæ'terd] a. zerlumpt.

Tattle [tætl] n. Geschwätz n.

Tattoo [tA-tuh'] vt. tatauieren; -ing n. Tatauierung f.

Tattoo [tA-tuh'] n. Zapfenstreich m (mil.).

Taunt [tOnt] n. Stichelei f, höhnische Bemerkung; vt. verhöhnen, sticheln.

Taunting [tOn'ting] a. höhnisch, sticheln.

Taut [tOt] a. straff, steif.

Tauten [tO'tn] vi.t. straff, steif werden, straff machen.

Tavern [tæ'wern] n. Wirtshaus n, Schenke f, Kneipe f.

Tawdry [tO'dri] a. flitterhaft, wertlos. [lohfarben.]

Tawny [tO'ni] a. gelbbraun,]

Tax [tæx] n. Steuer f, Gebühr f, Taxe f, Abgabe f, Last f; vt. besteuern, rügen, tadeln, beschuldigen; -purchase n. Verkaufssteuer f; -collector n. Steuereinnehmer m; - office n. Steueramt n; - return n. Steuererklärung n.

Taxable [tæx'Abl] a. steuerpflichtig, steuerbar, zollpflichtig (customs).

Taxation [tæx-ei'schAn] n. Besteuerung f, Steuerlast f, Abschätzung f.

Taxi [tæx'i] n. Autodroschke f, Mietauto n, Taxi m, Taxe f; vi. rollen, ab-, an-rollen (av.); -ing area n. Rollfeld n (av.).

-cab n. Autodroschke f; -driver, -man n. Droschkenchauffeur m, Taxichauffeur m, Fahrer m.

Taxidermist [tæx-i-dAr'mist] n. Tierausstopfer m.

Taxidermy [tæx-i-dAr'mi] n. Ausbälgekunst f.

Taximeter [tæx'i-mih'ter] n. Fahrpreisanzeiger m, Taxameter m.

Taxpayer [tæx'pei'er] n. Steuerzahler m.

Tea [tih] n. Tee m; - blender n. Teemischer m; - caddy. n. canister n. Teebüchse f, Teedose f; - chest n. Teekiste f; - cosy n. Teemütze f; -cup n. Teetasse f, Obertasse f; - leaf n. Teeblatt n; - plant n. Teestrauch m; -pot n. Teekanne f; - room n. Teestube f, Café n; -set n. Teeservice f, Teegeschirr n; -shop n. Konditorei f, Café n; -spoon n. Teelöffel m; - time n. Teestunde f; -tray n. Teebrett n; - urn n. Teemaschine f.

Teach [tihtsch] vt. lehren, unterrichten. [m, Lehrerin f.]

Teacher [tih'tscher] n. Lehrer]

Team [tihm] n. Gespann n, Bespannung f (animals), Abteilung f (workmen), Mannschaft f (sport); - work n. Zusammenarbeit f.

Tear [tih'er] n. Träne f; - gas n. Weisskreuz n, Tränengas n.

Tear [teh'er] vt.i. reissen, zerreissen, stürzen; n. Riss m.

Tease [tihs] vt. necken, kämmeln, kämmen (wool), rauhen (cloth); n. Quälgeist m.

Teaser [tih'ser] n. Quälgeist m, kniffige Frage.

Teasel [tih'sAl] n. Karde f, Krempel f; vt. rauhen, kardätschen, krempeln.

Teasing-machine [tih'sing-mA-schihn'] n. Rupfmaschine f.

Teat [tiht] n. Brustwarze f, Zitze f, Lutscher m (comforter).

Technical [tek'nikl] *a.* , **-ly** *ad.* technisch, handwerksmässig, Fach . . . ; – **adviser** *n.* Fachberater *m*; – **school** *n.* Fachschule *f*, Gewerbeschule *f*; – **standard** *n.* Fachnorm *f*; – **term** *n.* Fachausdruck *m*.

Technicality [tek-ni-kæ'li-ti] *n.* technische Unterscheidung.

Technician [tek-ni'schAn] *n.* Techniker *m*, Ingenieur *m*, Wart *m* (*transport*).

Technicolour film [tek'ni-kA-ler-film'] *n.* Farbfilm *m*.

Technique [tek-nihk'] *n.* Technik *f*, Kunstfertigkeit *f*.

Technocracy [tek-no'krA-ssi] *n.* Technokratie *f*.

Technologist [tek-no'lA-dzhist] *n.* Technologe *m*.

Technology [tek-no'lA-dzhi] *n.* Gewerbekunde *f*, Technologie *f*.

Tedious [tih'djAss] *a.* , **-ly** *ad.* langweilig, lästig, mühsam.

Tedium [tih'djAm] *n.* Langweiligkeit *f*.

Tee [tih] *n.* Sandhaufen *m*.

Teem [tihm] *vi.* wimmeln.

Teeming [tih'ming] *a.* überfliessend.

Teethe [tihdh] *vi.* zahnen.

Teetotal [tih-tou'tAl] *a.* antialkoholisch.

Teetotaler [tih-tou'tA-ler] *n.* Antialkoholiker *m*, Abstinenzler *m*. [*n.* Abstinenz *f*.

Teetotalism [tih-tou'tA-lism]

Telecommunication [te'li-kA-mju-ni-kei'schAn] *n.* Fernmeldung *f*.

Telegram [te'li-græm] *n.* Telegramm *n*, Depesche *f*, Drahtnachricht *f* (*com.*); – **-form** *n.* Telegrammformular *n*.

Telegraph [te'li-grahf'] *n.* Telegraph *m*, Draht *m*; *vt.i.* telegraphieren, depeschieren, drahten (*com.*); – **code** *n.* Telegraphenschlüssel *m*; – **letter** *n.* Brieftelegramm *n*; – **line** *n.* Telegraphenlinie *f*; – **office** *n.*

Telegraphenamt *n*; – **operator** *n.* Telegraphist *m*, Telegraphistin *f*; – **pole** *n.* Telegraphenstange *f*; – **printer** *n.* Ferndrucker *m*; – **wire** *n.* Telegraphendraht *m*.

Telegraphic [te-li-græ'fik] *a.* telegraphisch; – **address** *n.* Telegrammadresse *f*; – **code** *n.* Depeschenschlüssel *m*.

Telegraphist [ti-le'grA-fist] *n.* Telegraphist *m*.

Telegraphy [ti-le'grA-fi] *n.* Telegraphie *f*; **wireless** – drahtlose Telegraphie *f*.

Telephone [te'li-foun] *n.* Fernsprecher *m*, Telephon *n*; *vt.i.* telephonieren, fernsprechen; – **field** – *n.* Feldfernsprecher *m* (*mil.*); – **box** *n.* Fernsprechzelle *f*; – **call** *n.* Fernspruch *m*, Ferngespräch *n*; – **call box** *see* – **box**; – **connection** *n.* Fernsprechanschluss *m*; – **directory** *n.* Fernsprech-, Telephon-buch *n*; – **exchange** *n.* Telephonzentrale *f*; – **line** *n.* Fernsprechleitung *f*; – **message** *n.* Telephongespräch *n*, telephonische Bestellung, Mitteilung *f*; – **number** *n.* Fernsprechnummer *f*; – **operator** *n.* Telephonist *m*, Telephonistin *f*; – **receiver** *n.* Fernsprechhörer *m*; – **subscriber** *n.* Telephonverteiler *m*; – **wire** *n.* Telephondraht *m*.

Telephonic [te-li-fo'nik] *a.* telephonisch, Fernsprech . . . .

Telephonist [ti-le'fA-nist] *n.* Telephonist *m*, Telephonistin *f*, Vermittlungsbeamte(r) *m*, *f*.

Telephony [te-le'fA-ni] *n.* Fernsprechwesen *n*; **wireless** – *n.* drahtlose Fernsprechen *n*.

Telephoto [te'li-fou-tou] *n.* Fernbild *n*; – **lens** *n.* Teleobjektiv *n*.

Telephotography [te'li-fA-to'grA-fi] *n.* Fernphotographie *f*.

Teleprinter [te'li-prin-ter] *n.*

Ferndrucker m, Fernschreiber m, Fernschreibmaschine f; by - fernschriftlich; clear text - n. Klarfernschreibmaschine f; - exchange n. Fernschreibvermittlung f.

Telescope [te'li-skoup] n. Fernrohr n.

Telescopic [te-li-sko'pik] a. teleskopisch, ineinanderschiebbar; - bomb sight n. Bombenfernrohr n (av.); - rifle sight n. Gewehrzielfernrohr n.

Teletype [te'li-taip] see Teleprinter.

Television [te-li-wi'schän] n. Fernsehen n, Bildfunk m; - image n. Fernsehbild n; - operator n. Fernsehtechniker m; - receiver n. Fernsehempfänger m; - set n. Fernsehapparat m; - studio n. Fernsehstube f.

Televise [te'li-wais] vt.i. fernsehen, durch Bildfunk übertragen.

Televisor [te'li-wai-ser] n. Televisor m, Fernseher m.

Tell [tel] vt.i. erzählen, sagen, heissen, befehlen, wirken; - -tale a. verräterisch.

Teller [te'ler] n. der Kassenbeamte, Stimmenzähler m.

Telling [te'ling] a. erzählend, wirkungsvoll.

Temerity [ti-me'ri-ti] n. Unbesonnenheit f.

Temper [tem'per] n. Laune f, Stimmung f, Gemüt n, Reizbarkeit f, Zorn m, Härtegrad m (tec.); vt. härten, anlassen, mässigen, mildern.

Temperament [tem'pA-rА-mАnt] n. Gemütsart f, Temperament n, Charakter m.

Temperamental [tem-pA-rA-mentl'] a., -ly ad. temperamentvoll.

Temperance [tem'pA-rАnss] n. Mässigkeit f, Mässigung f, Enthaltsamkeit f, Temperenz f.

Temperate [tem'pA-rit] a., -ly ad. mässig, gemässigt, massvoll, mild.

Temperature [tem'pA-rА-tscher] n. Temperatur f, Wärmegrad m; - chart n. Fiebertabelle f. [m.

Tempest [tem'pist] n. Sturm

Tempestuous [tem-pe'stju-Ass] a., -ly ad. stürmisch.

Temple [templ] n. Tempel m.

Temple [templ] n. Schläfe f.

Tempo [tem'pou] n. Tempo n.

Temporal [tem'pA-rАl] a. weltlich, zeitlich.

Temporarily [tem'pA-rА-ri-li] ad. zeitweilig, vorübergehend, provisorisch, zeitweise.

Temporary [tem'pA-rА-ri] a. zeitweilig, einstweilig, vorläufig, behelfsmässig, Behelfs . . .; - bridge n. Notbrücke f, Behelfsbrücke f; - position n. zeitweilige Stellung (mil.).

Temporize [tem'pA-rais] vi. zögern, Zeit zu gewinnen suchen.

Tempt [tempt] vt. versuchen, verlocken, anreizen.

Temptation [temp-tei'schАn] n. Versuchung f, Verlockung f.

Tempter [temp'ter] n. Versucher m.

Tempting [temp'ting] a. verführerisch, verlockend, appetitlich.

Temptress [temp'triss] n. Verführerin f, Versucherin f.

Ten [ten] num. zehn.

Tenable [te'nАbl] a. haltbar.

Tenacity [ti-næ'ssi-ti] n. Zähigkeit f, Hartnäckigkeit f, Festigkeit f.

Tenacious [ti-nei'schАss] a., -ly ad. zäh, festhaltend, hartnäckig, beharrlich.

Tenancy [te'nАn-ssi] n. Miet-, Pacht-besitz m.

Tenant [te'nАnt] n. Pächter m (land), Mieter m (flat, house), Bewohner m; vt. bewohnen, in Miete haben; - farmer n. Pächter m.

Tench [tensch] *n.* Schlei *f.*

Tend [tend] *vi.* streben, neigen, zielen, sich richten, Tendenz zeigen.

Tend [tend] *vt.* pflegen, hüten, bedienen, aufwarten.

Tendencious [ten-den'schAss] *a.* tendenziös, gefärbt, parteilich.

Tendency [ten'dAn-ssi] *n.* Richtung *f.*, Neigung *f.*, Tendenz *f.*

Tender [ten'der] *n.* Anerbieten *n.*, Angebot *n.*, Offerte *f.*, Kostenanschlag *m* (com.); *vt.* anbieten, antragen; *i.* ein Gebot machen (com.).

Tender [ten'der] *a.*, **-ly** *ad.* zart, weich; **- -hearted** *a.* weichherzig.

Tender [ten'der] *n.* Beischiff *n.*, Leichter *m* (nav.), Tender *m* (rl.).

Tenderness [ten'der-ness] *n.* Zartheit *f.*, Weichherzigkeit *f.*, Weichheit *f.*

Tendon [ten'dAn] *n.* Sehne *f.*

Tendril [ten'dril] *n.* Ranke *f.*

Tenement [te'ni-mAnt] *n.* Wohnung *f.*, Haus *n.*; **- building** *n.* Mietshaus *n.*, Mietskaserne *f.*

Tenet [te'nit] *n.* Lehrsatz *m.*, Grundsatz *m.*

Tennis [te'niss] *n.* Tennisspiel *n.*, Netzball *m.*; **- ball** *n.* Tennisball *m.*; **- court** *n.* Tennisspielfeld *m.*; **- player** *n.* Tennisspieler *m.*, -spielerin *f.*; **- racket** *n.*, **- racquet** Tennisschläger *m.*, Rakett *n.*; **- shade** *n.* Blendschirm *m.*; **- tournament** *n.* Tennisturnier *n.*

Tenon [te'nAn] *n.* Zapfen *m.*, Feder *f.*; *vt.* verzapfen; **- -machine** *n.* Zapfenschneidmaschine *f.*

Tenor [te'ner] *n.* Sinn *m.*, Inhalt *m.*, Kern *m.*, Tenor *m* (music), **- part** *n.* Tenorpartie *f.*

Tense [tenss] *a.* gespannt, straff. [Zeitform *f.*

Tense [tenss] *n.* Tempus *n.*,

Tenseness [tenss'ness] *n.* Spannung *f.*, Straffheit *f.*

Tensile [ten'ssail] *a.* streckbar, dehnbar.

Tension [ten'schAn] *n.* Spannung *f.*, Gespanntheit *f.*, Dehnung *f.*, Spannkraft *f* (tec.); **- grid** **- n.** Gitterspannung *f* (rad.); **high - n.** Hochspannung *f*; **low - n.** Niederspannung *f*; **- device** *n.* Spannvorrichtung *f*; **- disc** *n.* Fadenspanner *m.*, Spannscheibe *f.*; **- knob, - screw** *n.* Spannschraube *f.*; **- -setting-ring** *n.* Satzstück *n.* (mil.); **- regulator** *n.* Spannungsgleicher *m.* [Spannungs . . . .

Tensional [ten'schA-nAl] *a.*

Tent [tent] *n.* Zelt *n.*; **- bed** *n.* Feldbett *n.*; **- cloth** *n.* Zeltleinwand *f.*, Zeltbahn *f.*; **- cord, - rope** *n.* Zeltleine *f.*; **- peg** *n.* Zeltpflock *m.*; **- pole, - prop** *n.* Zelt-stock *m.*, -mast *m.*

Tentacle [ten'tAkl] *n.* Fühler *m.*, Fühlfaden *m.*

Tentative [ten'tA-tiw] *a.* versuchend, Versuchs . . . , Probe . . . .

Tentatively [ten'tA-tiw-li] *ad.* versuchsweise, probeweise.

Tenter [ten'ter] *n.* Spannrahmen *m.*; *vt.* aufrahmen; **- -hook** *n.* Spannhaken *m.*; **- -hooks** *n pl* Ungewißheit *f.pl.*, Spannung *f.pl.*

Tenth [tenth] *a.* zehnt.

Tenuous [ten'ju-Ass] *a.* dünn, zart, geringfügig.

Tenure [ten'juh-er] *n.* Besitz *m.*; **- of office** Amts-dauer *f.*, -zeit *f.*

Tepid [te'pid] *a.* lau, lauwarm.

Tepidness [te'pid-ness] *n.* Lauheit *f.*

Term [tArm] *n.* bestimmte Zeit, Termin *m.*, Frist *f.*, Zeitdauer *f.*, Sitzungszeit *f.*, Trimester *n.*, Quartal *n* (school), Ausdruck *m* (phrase), Bedingung *f* (charge); *vt.* bezeichnen, nennen.

Terminable [tẢr'mi-nȦbl] *a.* kündbar, lösbar.

Terminal [tẢr'mi-nȦl] *a.* begrenzend, End ...; *n.* Klemme *f,* Leitungsende *n* (*el.*), Pol *m* (*el.*); *see also* terminus; – **box** *n.* Anschlussklemmkasten *m.*

Terminate [tẢr'mi-neit] *vt.i.* enden, endigen, beenden, begrenzen.

Termination [tẢr-mi-nei'-shȦn] *n.* Schluss *m,* Ende *n,* Beendigung *f,* Ausgang *m,* Endung *f* (*word*).

Terminology [tẢr-mi-no'lodzhi] *n.* Fachsprache *f,* Terminologie *f.*

Terminus [tẢr'mi-nȦss] *n.* Endstation *f,* Kopfstation *f,* Hauptbahnhof *m.*

Terrace [te'riss] *n.* Terrasse *f,* Häuserreihe *f*; *vt.* in Terrassen aufführen, abstufen.

Terrain [te-rein'] *n.* Gelände *n,* Terrain *n.*

Terrestrial [te-re'strjȦl] *a.* Erd ...; – **globe** *n.* Globus *m.*

Terrible [te'ribl] *a,* **Terribly** *ad.* schrecklich, furchtbar, entsetzlich. [lich, kolossal.

Terrific [tȦ-ri'fik] *a.* fürchter-

Terrify [te'ri-fai] *vt.* erschrecken, entsetzen.

Territorial [te-ri-tO'rjȦl] *a.* territorial, Gebiets ...; *n.* Landwehrmann *m*; – **army** *n.* Landwehr *f*; – **claim** *n.* territoriale Forderung; – **reserve** *n.* Landsturm *m*; – **waters** *n.pl.* Hoheitsgewässer *n.pl.*

Territory [te'ri-tȦri] *n.* Gebiet *n,* Territorium *n,* Landschaft *f,* Staatsgebiet *n,* Gelände *n*; **enemy** – feindliches Gebiet.

Terror [te'rer] *n.* Schrecken *m,* Gewaltherrschaft *f,* Entsetzen *n,* Terror *m*; – **stricken** *a.* von Schrecken ergriffen; – **ism** *n.* Schreckensherrschaft *f*; – **ize** *vt.* terrorisieren, vergewaltigen, einschüchtern.

Terse [tȦrss] *a,* **-ly** *ad.* kurz, bündig.

Test [test] *n.* Probe *f,* Untersuchung *f,* Versuch *m*; *vt.* prüfen, erproben, probieren, anschiessen (*gun*), einschiessen (*gun*); **endurance** – *n.* Dauerprobe *f*; **psychological** – *n.* Eignungsprüfung *f*; – **case** *n.* Musterbeispiel *n,* Präzedenzfall *m* (*law*); – **the line** *n.* abfragen, Leitung prüfen (*ph.*); – **paper** *n.* Reagenzpapier *n*; – **pilot** *n.* Einflieger *m* (*av.*); – **tube** *n.* Probierröhre *f,* Reagenz-glas *n,* -röhre *f.*

Testament [te'stȦ-mȦnt] *n.* Testament *n,* letzter Wille.

Testamentary [te-stȦ-men'tȦ-ri] *a.* testamentarisch, letztwillig.

Testat'or [te-stei'ter] *n.* Erblasser *m*; **-rix** *n.* Erblasserin *f.*

Tester [te'ster] *n.* Prüfer *m,* Prüfmeister *m.*

Testify [te'sti-fai] *vt.i.* bezeugen, zeugen, Zeugnis ablegen.

Testimonial [te-sti-mou'njȦl] *n.* schriftliches Zeugnis, Attest *n,* Belobungsschreiben *n.*

Testimony [te'sti-mȦ-ni] *n.* Zeugnis *n,* Bezeugung *f,* Zeugenaussage *f* (*law*).

Testing [te'sting] *n.* Nachprüfung *f,* Erproben *n*; – **apparatus** *n.* Prüfgerät *a* (*rad, etc.*), Prüfungsapparat *m*; – **button** *n.* Prüfknopf *m*; – **instrument** *n.* *see* – **apparatus**; – **set** *n.* Messkästchen *n*; – **stand** *n.* Prüfungs-, Bremsstand *m*. [münrisch.

Testy [te'sti] *a,* **Testily** *ad.*

Tether [te'dher] *n.* Strick *m,* Haltetau *n,* Spielraum *m.*

Tetrachloride [te'trȦ-klO'raid] *n.* Tetrachlorid *n.*

Tetra-ethyl [te'trȦ-e'thil] *n.* Tetraäthyl *n.*

Text [tekst] *n.* Text *m,* Wortlaut *m,* Schrift *f*; – **book** *n.*

Lehrbuch n, Leitfaden m; – in clear Klartext m.

Textile [tex'tail] a. gewebt, Textil . . . .; n. Gewebe n, Webstoff m, Textilware f; – fabric n. Textilware f; – factory n. Spinnerei f; – industry n. Textilindustrie f.

Textual [tex'tju-Al] a. textgemäss; – criticism n. Textkritik f.

Texture [tex'tju-er] n. Textur f, Gewebe n, Gefüge n, Beschaffenheit f.

Than [dhæn] cj. als, denn.

Thank [thængk] vt. danken, verdanken.

Thankful [thæng'ful] a. –ly dankbar, erkenntlich; –ness n. Dankbarkeit f, Erkenntlichkeit f. [undankbar.]

Thankless [thæng'less] a.

Thanksgiving [thængkss'gi-wing] n. Danksagung f, Dankfest n.

That [dhæt] pn. a. jener, jene, jenes, der, die, das; cj. dass; in order – damit, sodass; in – insofern als.

Thatch [thætsch] n. Dachstroh n; vt. überdachen, mit Stroh bedecken; –ed roof n. Strohdach n; –er n. Strohdecker m.

Thaw [thO] n. Tauwetter n, Tauen n; v.i.t. auftauen.

The [dhih, dhA] art. der, die, das; – sooner – better je eher, desto lieber; – more umso mehr; – sooner desto eher.

Theatre [thih'A-ter] n. Theater n, Schauspielhaus n, Bühne f, Schauplatz m; – goer n. Theater-besucher m, –besucherin f; – going n. Theaterbesuch m; – manager n. Theaterdirektor m; – ticket n. Theaterkarte f; – of war n. Kriegsschauplatz m.

Theatrical [thih-æ'trikl] a. bühnenmässig, theatralisch; n. Theatervorstellung f; amateur –s n.pl. Liebhaberaufführung-

en f.pl; – performance n. Bühnenaufführung f; – requisite n. Bühnenzubehör n, Requisiten n.pl

Thee [dhih] pn. dich, dir.

Theft [theft] n. Diebstahl m.

Their [dheh'er] poss. ihre, ihre.

Theirs [dheh'ers] poss. der, die, das ihrige, ihre, ihre, ihres.

Them [dhem] pn. sie, ihnen.

Theme [thihm] n. Thema n, Stoff m, Gegenstand m.

Themselves [dhem-sselws'] pn. sie selbst, ihnen selbst, sich.

Then [dhen] ad. dann, darauf, damals; cj. denn, also, doch; a. damalig.

Thence [dhenss] ad. daher, von da, von dort, seit der Zeit.

Thenceforth [dhenss-fOrth'] **Thenceforward** [dhenss-fOr'-uerd] ad. von da an, seitdem, seither. [Theodolit m.]

Theodolite [thih-o'dA-lait] n.

Theologian [thih-o-lou'dzhjAn] n. Theologe m.

Theological [thih-o-lo'dzhikl] a. theologisch. [Theologie f.]

Theology [thih-o'lA-dzhi] n.

Theoretic(al) [thih-o-re'tikl] a, –ly ad. theoretisch.

Theorist [thih'o-rist] n. Theoretiker m.

Theorize [thih'o-rais] vi. theoretisieren, Theorie treiben.

Theory [thih'A-ri] n. Theorie f.

Theosophy [thih-o'sA-fi] n. Theosophie f.

Therapeutics [the-rA-pjuh'-tix] n. Therapeutik f.

Therapy [the'rA-pi] n. Therapie f, Heilkunde f, Heilverfahren n, Krankenbehandlung f.

There [dheh'er] ad. dort, da, dahin, dorthin (to that place) – is es ist, es gibt.

Thereby [dheh-er-bei'] ad. dadurch, daneben, dabei.

Therefor [dheh-er-fOr'] ad. dafür.

Therefore [dheh'er-fOr] *ad.* daher, deshalb, darum, also.

Therein [dheh-rin'] *ad.* darin.

Thereof [dheh-rof'] *ad.* davon, dessen, deren.

Thereupon [dheh-rA-pon'] *ad.* darauf, sogleich.

Therewith [dheh-er-uith'] *ad.* damit. [einheit f.]

Therm [thArm] *n.* Wärme-

Thermal [thAr'mAl] *a.* warm; - baths *n.pl* heisse Quellen *f.pl*; - soaring *n.* Wärmesegeln *n* (*av.*).

Thermionic [thAr-mjo'nik] *a.* thermionisch; - valve *n.* Glüh-kathodenröhre f. [Thermit *m.*

Thermite [thAr'mait] *n.*

Thermometer [ther-mo'mi-ter] *n.* Thermometer *n.*, Wärme-messer *m*; wet-bulb = feuchtes Thermometer.

Thermoscope [thAr'mA-skoup] *n.* Thermoskop *n*, Wärmezeiger *m.*

Thermos-flask [thAr'moss-flahsk] *n.* Thermosflasche f.

Thermostat [thAr'mo-stæt] *n.* Thermostat *m*, Temperatur-regler *m.*

Thermostatic [thAr-mo-stæ-tik] *a.* - control *n.* Wärme-regelung f.

These [dhihs] *pn.pl.* diese.

Thesis [thih'ssiss] *n.* Leitsatz *m*, These f., Dissertation f., Doktorarbeit f.

They [dheh] *pn.pl.* sie, ihnen.

Thick [thik] *a.* -ly *ad.* dick, dicht; - -headed *a.* dickköpfig, dumm; - -set *a.* dichtgestellt, untersetzt; - -skinned *a.* dick-häutig, dickfellig.

Thicken [thikn] *vt.* verdicken, verdichten, dick machen; *i.* sich verdicken, sich verdichten, dick werden; -ing *n.* Ver-dickung f, Verdichtung f, Ver-dickungsmittel *n.*

Thicket [thi'kit] *n.* Dickicht *n*, Gebüsch *n*, Jungholz *n*, Dick-ung f.

Thickness [thik'ness] *n.* Dick-heit f, Dicke f, Stärke f, Dicht-heit f, Dichtigkeit f.

Thief [thihf] *n.* Dieb *m*; - -proof *a.* diebesfest.

Thieve [thihw] *vi.* stehlen; -ing *n.* Diebstahl *m*, Dieberei f; -ish *a.* diebisch.

Thigh [thai] *n.* Oberschenkel *m*; - bone *n.* Schenkelbein *n.*

Thill [thil] *n.* Gabeldeichsel f.

Thimble [thimbl] *n.* Finger-hut *m*, Nähring *m*, Kausche f (*nav.*), Zwinge f, Muffe f, Ring *m* (*tec.*); -ful *n.* Fingerhutvoll *m*, Schluck *m.*

Thin [thin] *a.* -ly *ad.* dünn, mager, schwach, spärlich; *vt.* dünn machen, verdünnen, lichten (*trees*); *i.* dünn werden; - out *it.* ausdünnen.

Thine [thain] *a.* *pn.* der, die, das deinige; deiner, deine, deines; dein, deine.

Thing [thing] *n.* Ding *n*, Sache f, Angelegenheit f, Wesen *n*, Geschöpf f; -s *n.pl.* Sachen f.pl, Zeug *n.pl.*

Think [thingk] *vt.i.* denken, glauben, meinen, beabsichtig-en, vorhaben, gedenken, nach-denken, halten von; - over sich überlegen.

Thinkable [thing'kAbl] *a.* denkbar. [er *m.*

Thinker [thing'ker] *n.* Denk-

Thinking [thing'king] *n.* denk-end; *n.* Denken *n*, Nachdenken *n*, Dafürhalten *n* (*opinion*).

Thinness [thin'ness] *n.* Dünn-heit f, Dünne f, Seltenheit f.

Thinnish [thi'nisch] *a.* dünn-lich.

Third [thArd] *a.* dritt; - -class *n.* dritte Klasse; - -party risks *n.pl.* Haftpflicht f.pl; - -rate *a.* dritten Ranges, minderwertig, gering.

Thirdly [thArd'li] *ad.* drittens.

Thirst [thArst] *n.* Durst *m.*

Thirstily [thAr'sti-li] *ad.* Thirsty *a.* durstig.

Thirteen [thʌr-tihn'] *num.* dreizehn. [dreißiger Jahre.

Thirties [thʌr'tis] *n.pl.* die

Thirty [thʌr'ti] *num.* dreißig.

This [thiss] *a. pn.* dieser, diese, dieses.

Thistle [thissl] *n.* Distel *f.*

Thither [dhi'dher] *ad.* dahin, dorthin.

Thole [thoul] *n.* Dolle *f.*, Rudergabel *f.*, Ruderpflock *m.*

Thong [thong] *n.* Riemen *m.*, Peitschenschnur *f.*, Gurt *m.*

Thorax [thō'ræx] *n.* Brustkorb *m.*

Thorn [thOrn] *n.* Dorn *m.* Stachel *m.*; - bush *n.* Dornbusch *m.*; -y *a.* dornig, stachelig, schwierig, beschwerlich.

Thorough [thʌ'rʌ] *ad.* durchgehend, vollkommen, gründlich.

Thoroughbred [thʌ'rʌ-bred] *a.* reinrassig; *n.* Vollblüter *m.*

Thoroughfare [thʌ'rʌ-feher] *n.* Verkehrsader *f.*, Fahrstrasse *f.*, Durchfahrt *f.*; no - verbotener Durchgang.

Thorough-going [thʌ'rʌ-gou'ing] *a.* durchgreifend, gründlich.

Thoroughly [thʌ'rʌ-li] *ad.* durchaus, völlig, vollkommen, gründlich.

Thoroughness [thʌ'rʌ-ness] *n.* Gründlichkeit *f.*

Those [dhous] *pn.pl.* jene, die, diejenigen; - are das sind.

Thou [dhau] *pn.* du; *vt.* duzen.

Though [dhou] *cj.* obgleich, obschon, obwohl; *ad.* immerhin, zwar, übrigens, doch.

Thought [thOt] *n.* Gedanke *m.*, Idee *f.*, Begriff *m.*, Absicht *f.* (*intention*).

Thoughtful [thOt'ful] *a.* -ly *ad.* nachdenklich, aufmerksam, rücksichtsvoll; -ness *n.* Aufmerksamkeit *f.*, Rücksichtnahme *f.*, Nachdenken *n.*

Thoughtless [thOt'less] *a.* -ly *ad.* sorglos, nachlässig, acht-

los, leichtsinnig, unaufmerksam; -ness *n.* Sorglosigkeit *f.*, Nachlässigkeit *f.*, Gedankenlosigkeit *f.*; [tausend.

Thousand [thau'sʌnd] *num.*

Thrash [thræsch] *vt.* dreschen, prügeln; - out abdreschen, gründlich besprechen, durchsprechen; *see also* thresh.

Thrashing [thræ'sching] *n.* Tracht *f.*, Prügel *pl.*; *see also* threshing.

Thread [thred] *n.* Faden *m.*, Zwirn *m.*, Garn *n.*, Gewinde *n.*, Bindfaden *m.*, Zusammenhang *m* (*of a speech, etc.*), Schraubengang *m* (*screw*); *vt.* einfädeln, aufreihen, mit Gewinde versehen (*screw*); left-hand - *n.* Linksgewinde *n* (*tec.*); silk - *n.* Seidenfaden *m.*

Threadbare [thred'beh-er] *a.* abgetragen, fadenscheinig.

Threader [thre'der] *n.* Einfädelmaschine *f.*

Threat [thret] *n.* Drohung *f.*, Bedrohung *f.*

Threaten [thretn] *vt.i.* drohen, bedrohen, androhen; -ing *a.*, -ingly *ad.* drohend.

Three [thrih] *num.* drei; -barrelled gun *n.* Drilling *m.*; -cornered dreieckig; -dimensional *a.* dreidimensional; -halfpence *n.pl.* anderthalb Pence; -halfpenny *a.* anderthalb Pence wert; -legged *a.* dreibeinig; -master *m.* Dreimaster *m.*, Dreimastbark *f.*; - mile limit *n.* Dreimeilenzone *f* (*nav.*); -phase current *m.* Drehstrom *m.*; -piece suit *m.* Komplet *n.*; -ply *a.* dreifach, dreisträhnig; -pronged *a.* dreizinkig; -quarter *a.* dreiviertel; *n.* Dreiviertelspieler *m* (*football*); -speed gear *n.* dreifache Übersetzung *f* (*cycle, aut.*); -storied *a.* dreistöckig; -strand rope *n.* dreischäftiges Seil; -valve receiver *n.* Dreiröhrenempfänger *m* (*rad.*).

-way cock n. Dreiweghahn m; - -wheeler n. Dreiradwagen m, Kraftdreirad n; - -year old n. der Dreijährige (horse).

Threepence [thre'pAnss, thri'pAnss] n.pl. drei Pence, drei Groschen. [a. drei Pence wert.

Threepenny [thre'-, thri'pni] n.

Thresh [thresch] vt. dreschen.

Thresher [thre'scher] n. Drescher m, Dreschmaschine f.

Threshing [thre'sching] n. Dreschen n; - machine n. Dreschmaschine f.

Threshold [thresch'ould] n. Schwelle f, Eingang m, Anfang m.

Thrice [thraiss] ad. dreimal.

Thrift [thrift] n. Sparsamkeit f, Wirtschaftlichkeit f.

Thriftless [thrift'less] a. verschwenderisch; **-ness** n. Verschwendung f.

Thrifty [thrif'ti] a. Thriftily ad. sparsam, haushälterisch.

Thrill [thrill] n. Schauer m, Spannung f, Erbeben n, Sensation f; **-er** n. Sensationsroman m, Kriminalroman m.

Thriv'e [thraiw] vi. gedeihen, blühen, geraten; **-ing** a. blühend, gedeihlich.

Throat [throut] n. Kehle f, Gurgel f, Hals m, Schlund m.

Throb [throb] n. Pulsschlag m, Stampfen n, Schlag m; vi. schlagen, pochen, klopfen.

Throe [throu] n. Schmerz m, Wehen f.pl, Todesangst f.

Throne [throun] n. Thron m; vi. thronen.

Throng [throng] n. Gedränge n, Zulauf m, Andrang m; vt.i. (sich) drängen, überschwemmen.   [sel f.

Throstle [throssl] n. Drossel f.

Throttle [throtl] n. Drosselklappe f, -ventil n, Drossel f; Regelteil m (av.); vt. erdrosseln, abdrosseln; **- -lever** n. Gashebel m (av.); **- -valve** n. Drosselventil n.

Through [thruh] pr.ad. durch, aus, mittels; **- carriage** n. durchgehender Wagen (rl.); - line n. durchgehende Bahnlinie (rl.); **- ticket** n. direkte Fahrkarte; **- traffic** n. Durchgangsverkehr m; **- train** n. durchgehender Zug.

Throughout [thruh-aut'] pr. hindurch; ad. durchaus, in jeder Beziehung.

Throw [throu] n. Wurf m, Werfen n, Hub m, Hubhöhe f (tec); vt.i. werfen, schleudern, schlagen (bridge); **- -back** n. Rückschlag m.

Thrush [thrAsch] n. Drossel f (bird).   [schwamm m.

Thrush [thrAsch] n. Mundschwamm m.

Thrust [thrAst] n. Stoss m, Druck m, Schub m (tec.), Vorstoss m (mil.); vt.i. stossen, schieben, drängen, vorstossen; **- -line** n. Stosslinie f (mil.).

Thud [thAd] n. dumpfer Schlag m Aufschlagknall m; vi.t. dröhnen.

Thumb [thAm] n. Daumen m; vt. abgreifen, beschmutzen; **- -print** n. Daumenabdruck m.

Thump [thAmp] n. Puff m, Schlag m; vt. puffen, schlagen; i. klopfen, pochen; **-ing** a. schlagend, fabelhaft.

Thunder [thAn'der] n. Donner m; vi. donnern; **- -clap** n. Donnerschlag m; **- -cloud** n. Gewitterwolke f; **- -storm** n. Gewitter n; **-struck** a. wie vom Donner gerührt; **-bolt** n. Donnerkeil m.   [nerstag m.

Thursday [thAs'di] n. Donnerstag m.

Thus [dhAss] ad. so, also, auf diese Weise, daher.

Thwack [thuek] n. Schlag m, Puff m; vt. schlagen.

Thwart [thuOrt] vt. durchkreuzen, in die Quere kommen; a. schräg, quer.

Thwart [thuOrt] n. Querriegel m, Ruderducht f (nav.).

Thy [dhai] a. dein, deine.

Thyme [taim] n. Thymian m, Quendel m. [drüse f.

Thyroid [thai'reud] n. Schild-

Thyself [dhai'sself] pn. du, dir, dich selbst.

Tibia [ti'bjA] n. Schienbein n.

Tick [tik] vi. ticken (clock); t. punktieren; – n. Punkt m, Kontrollzeichen n, Haken m, Strich m; – off vt. ab-, an-streichen, anzeichnen, erledigen, rügen, kurz abweisen.

Tick [tik] n. Bettüberzug m, Drillich m, Inlett n.

Tick [tik] n. Schaflaus f, Zecke f.

Ticker [ti'ker] n. Ferndrucker m, Börsentelegraph m.

Ticket [ti'kit] n. Fahrkarte f (rl.), Fahrschein m (bus), Billet n, Eintrittskarte f (theatre). Los n (lottery), Warenetikette f, Preiszettel m (com.); vt. etikettieren, auszeichnen; – -collector n. Fahrkartenkontrolleur m; – -holder n. Billet-, Fahrkarten-inhaber m; – -office n. Fahrkartenausgabe f, [Fahrkarten]schalter m.

Ticking [ti'king] n. Drell m, Drillich m.

Tickl'e [tikl] vt. kitzeln; –ish a. kitzlig, heikel, bedenklich.

Tidal [taidl] a. Flut . . .; – harbour n. Fluthafen m; – river n. Gezeitfluss m; – wave n. Flutwelle f.

Tide [taid] n. Ebbe und Flut f, Gezeiten f.pl, Flutzeit f, Strom m, Zeit f (time); – over vt. hinwegkommen über.

Tidings [tai'dings] n.pl. Nachricht f.sg.

Tidy [tai'di] a, **Tidily** ad. sauber, nett, ordentlich, reinlich; vt. in Ordnung machen, aufräumen; – n. Schutzdeckchen n, Sofaschoner m.

Tie [tai] n. Kragenbinde f, Binde f, Schleife f, Schlips m, Band n, Bindung f; vt. binden, schnüren, knüpfen, festbinden.

Tier [tih'er] n. Reihe f, Rang m, Sitzreihe f.

Tiff [tif] n. Streit m.

Tiger [tai'ger] n. Tiger m.

Tight [tait] a, –ly ad. dicht, eng, knapp (money); –s n. pl.

Trikot n.pl.; – -fitting a. knapp anliegend; – -rope n. straffgespanntes Seil.

Tighten [taitn] vt. zusammenziehen, straff spannen, schnüren.

Tightness [tait'ness] n. Dichtigkeit f, Straffheit f, Knappheit f. [in f.

Tigress [tai'griss] n. Tiger-

Tile [tail] n. Dachziegel m (roof), Fliese f, Kachel f (stove), Fussbodenplatte f (floor); hollow – n. Hohlziegel m; vt. mit Ziegeln decken, kacheln, decken (room); –d floor n. Fliessfussboden m.

Tiler [tai'ler] n. Ziegelbrenner m, Ziegeldecker m, Tempelhüter m.

Till [til] n. Geldschublade f, [Laden]kasse f.

Till [til] pr. cj. bis.

Till [til] vt. bebauen, ackern, bestellen; –age n. Pflügen n, Ackerbau m. [Helmstock m.

Tiller [ti'ler] n. Ruderpinne f.

Tiller [ti'ler] n. Ackersmann m (of the soil).

Tilt [tilt] n. Neigung f, schiefe Lage; vt.i. (sich) neigen, kippen, verkanten, stürzen.

Tilt [tilt] n. Plane f; – -cart n. Sturzkarren m, Kippwagen m.

Timber [tim'ber] n. Bauholz n, Nutz-, Zimmer-holz n, Baumaterial n, Spanten n.pl (nav.); a. hölzern; vt. auszimmern, verschalen; commercial – Handelsholz n; round – Rundholz n; sawn – Schnittholz n; squared – Vierkantholz n; – merchant n. Holzhändler m; – trade n. Holzhandel m; – -yard n. Zimmerplatz m, Bauhof m.

Timbering [tim'bA-ring] n.

Verschalung f (*ship*), Zimmerung f (*mine*).

Time [taim] n. Zeit f, Frist f, Mal n, Takt m; vt. zeitlich bestimmen, zur rechten Zeit unternehmen, nach der Zeit ausmessen, zeitlich festsetzen; half— n. Halbzeit f; local — n. Ortszeit f; standard — n. Normalzeit f; sun —s zenmal; Ortszeit f; —bomb n. Zeitbombe f; —exposure n. Zeitaufnahme f; — -fuse n. Zeitzünder m, Uhrwerkzünder m; — -honoured a. altehrwürdig, bewährt; — -keeper n. Chronometer m, Uhr f; — lag n. Verzögerung f, Zeitabstand m; — limit n. Termin m, Frist f, Zeitlimitum f; —piece n. Uhr f; — -server n. einer, der seinen Mantel nach dem Wind hängt; — -serving n. Achselträgerei f; — signal n. Zeitzeichen n; —table n. Fahrplan m, Kursbuch n (rl.), Stundenplan m (school).

Timeless [taim'less] a. endlos, zeitlos.

Timely [taim'li] a. zeitig, rechtzeitig, früh, gelegen.

Timid [ti'mid] a, -ly ad. zaghaft, furchtsam.

Timidity [ti-mi'di-ti] n. Zaghaftigkeit f, Furchtsamkeit f.

Timing [tai'ming] n. rechtzeitiges Handeln, zeitliche Bestimmung, Zündmoment n (aut.).

Timorous [ti'mA-rAss] a, -ly ad. ängstlich, furchtsam, verzagt; -ness n. Ängstlichkeit f, Furchtsamkeit f.

Tin [tin] n. Blech n, verzinntes Eisenblech, Zinn n (pure), Büchse f (box), Dose f; vt. verzinnen, in Büchsen packen; a. zinnern, Blech ...; — bread— n. Brotkapsel f; cake— n. Kuchenform f; mess— n. Kochgeschirr n; — bath n. Blechwanne f; — hat n. Stahlhelm m; — -opener n. Büchsenöffner m; —

-plate n. Weissblech n, Zinnplatte f; — -plated a. verzinnt; — -pot n. Blechtopf m, Einbrennpfanne f; a. minderwertig; — solder n. Weichlot n; — soldier n. Bleisoldat m; — -tack n. Blechnagel m.

Tincture [tingk'tscher] n. Tinktur f, Anstrich m.

Tinder [tin'der] n. Zunder m.

Tinfoil [tin'feul] n. Stanniol n, Zinnfolie f, Blattzinn n.

Tinge [tindzh] n. Anstrich m, Färbung f, Beigeschmack m; vt. färben, einen Anstrich geben.

Tingle [ting'gl] vi. stechen, prickeln, klingen (ears).

Tinker [ting'ker] n. Kesselflicker m; vt.i. zusammenflicken, pfuschen, basteln.

Tinkle [ting'kl] vi. klingeln; n. Klingeln n.

Tinned [tind] a. verzinnt, Büchsen...; —meat n. Fleischkonserven f.pl; — milk n. Büchsenmilch f; — vegetables n.pl. Büchsengemüse n, Gemüsekonserven f.pl.

Tinsmith [tin'smith] n. Klempner m, Blechschmied m.

Tinsel [tin'ssAl] n. Rauschgold n, Flitter m; silver — n. Lametta f.

Tint [tint] n. Tinte f, Anstrich m, Schattierung f; vt. färben, schattieren, einen Anstrich geben.

Tiny [tai'ni] a. winzig.

Tip [tip] n. Spitze f, Zwinge f, Mundstück m; vt. beschlagen, mit einer Spitze versehen.

Tip [tip] n. Trinkgeld n (gratuity), Wink m (hint), Andeutung f; vt. umwerfen, umkippen, ein Trinkgeld geben; — -up seat n. Klappsitz m; —wagon n. Kipper m, Kippwagen m.

Tipper [ti'per] n. Kippwagen m.

Tippet [ti'pit] n. Schärpe f, Band n, Pelzkragen m.

Tipple [tipl] vi. trinken, zechen.

Tippler [ti´pler] n. Trinker m. Säufer m.

Tippy [ti´pi] a. spitzenreich.

Tipsy [tip´ssi] a. Tipsily ad. angeheitert, beschwipst.

Tiptoe [tip´tou] n. Zehenspitze f.; vi. auf Zehenspitzen gehen.

Tip-top [tip´top] a. vorzüglich, famos, ausgezeichnet.

Tirade [tai-reid´] n. Wortschwall m, Schmähung f.

Tire [tai´er] n. Radreifen m.

Tire [tai´er] vt.i. müde werden, müde machen, ermüden, ermatten; -d a. müde, ermüdet, überdrüssig (of something).

Tireless [tai´er-less] a. -ly ad. unermüdlich.

Tiresome [tai´er-ssAm] a. verdriesslich, ermüdend, langweilig, unangenehm.

Tissue [ti´schuh] n. Gewebe n, feines Zeug n; -paper n. Seidenpapier n.

Tit [tit] n. Meise f.

Tit for tat [tit-fOr-tæt´] wie du mir, so ich dir, List wider List.

Titan [taitn] n. Titane m.

Titanic [tai-tæ´nik] a. titanenhaft.

Tit-bit [tit´bit] n. Leckerbissen m.

Tithe [taidh] n. Zehntel n (tenth), Zehnte f (tax).

Titillate [ti´ti-leit] vt. kitzeln.

Titivate [ti´ti-weit] vt. putzen; r. sich hübsch machen.

Title [taitl] n. Titel m, Überschrift f, Benennung f, Anspruch m, Rechtstitel m (law); vt. betiteln; -deeds n.pl. Eigentumsurkunde f, Besitzausweis m; -page n. Titelblatt n.

Titrate [ti´treit] vt. titrieren.

Titration [ti-trei´schAn] n. Titration f, Titriermethode f.

Titter [ti´ter] n. kichern; n. Gekicher n.

Tittle [titl] n. Pünktchen n,

Tüttelchen n, Jota n; -tattle n. Geschwätz n, Klatsch m.

Titular [ti´tju-ler] a. nominell, Titular . . .

To [tuh] pr. zu, gegen, nach, an, auf; as to betreffs; where . . . to wohin.

Toad [toud] n. Kröte f; -stool n. Giftschwamm m.

Toady [tou´di] n. Speichellecker m, Kriecher m; -ism n. Speichelleckerei f, Kriecherei f. **To and fro** [tuh´And-frou´] ad. hin und her.

Toast [toust] n. geröstete Brotschnitte, Toast m; vt. rösten, wärmen; -rack n. Toastgestell n.

Toast [toust] n. Trinkspruch m, Gesundheit f; vt. trinken auf, hochleben lassen.

Tobacco [tA-bæ´kou] n. Tabak m; pipe n. Rauchtabak m; -leaf n. Tabaksblatt n; -manufacturer n. Tabakfabrikant m; -pipe n. Tabakspfeife f; -pouch n. Tabaksbeutel m.

Tobacconist [tA-bæ´kA-nist] n. Tabakhändler m.

Toboggan [tA-bo´gAn] n. Rodelschlitten m; vi. rodeln; -ing n. Rodelsport m.

To-day [tA-dei´] ad. heute.

Toddle [todl] vi. unsicher gehen, sich forttrollen.

Toddy [to´di] n. süsser Grog.

To do [tu-duh´] n. Aufheben n, Aufregung f, Lärm m.

Toe [tou] n. Zehe f, Spitze f; vt. mit den Zehen berühren; -cap n. Schuhkappe f; -nail n. Zehennagel m.

Toffee [to´fi] n. Butterkaramelle f, Rahmbonbon n.

Together [tA-ge´dher] ad. zusammen, miteinander, beisammen; -with pr. samt.

Toggle [togl] n. Knebel m; vt. festknebeln; -joint n. Knie n, Winkelverbindung f.

Toil [teul] n. anstrengende Arbeit, Plackerei f. Mühsal f. Strapaze f; vi. sich abarbeiten, sich anstrengen, sich abmühen; - -worn a. abgearbeitet, durch Arbeit abgenutzt.

Toiler [teu'lər] n. Schwerarbeiter m.

Toilet [teu'lit] n. Toilette f. Ankleiden n. Abort m; - -case n. Reisenecessaire f; - -cover n. Putztischtuch n; - paper n. Klosettpapier n; - -set n. Toilettengarnitur f; - soap n. Toilettenseife f; - table n. Putztisch m.

Toils [teuls] n.pl. Netz n; to be in the - umstrickt sein.

Toilsome [teul'ssAm] a. mühselig, mühsam.

Token [toukn] n. Zeichen n, Beweis m, Andenken n (souvenir). Münze f (coin); - currency n. Binnenwährung f, Notgeld n; - payment n. nominelle Zahlung, Anzahlung f; - resistance n. scheinbarer Widerstand m.

Tolerable [to'lA-rAbl] a. erträglich, leidlich; -y ad. ziemlich, leidlich.

Tolerance [to'lA-rAnss] n. Duldsamkeit f.

Tolerant [to'lA-rAnt] a. duldsam, tolerant.

Tolerate [to'lA-reit] vt. dulden, leiden, zulassen, gestatten (permit).

Toleration [to-lA-rei'schAn] n. Duldung f, Toleranz f, Nachsicht f.

Toll [toul] n. Zoll m, Wegegeld n, Brückengeld n, Tribut m; - bar n. Schlagbaum m; - bridge n. Zollbrücke f; - -keeper n. Zolleinnehmer m.

Toll [toul] vt. läuten (bell).

Toluene [to'lju-ihn] n. Toluin n.

Toluol [to'lju-ol] n. Toluol n.

Tomahawk [to'mA-kOk] n. Streitaxt f, Kriegsbeil n.

Tomato [tA-mah'tou] n.

Tomate f; - sauce n. Tomatensosse f.

Tomb [tuhm] n. Grab n, Grabmal n; -stone n. Grabstein m.

Tomboy [tom'beu] n. Range f, Wildfang m.

Tom cat [tom'kæt] n. Kater m.

Tome [toum] n. Band n.

Tomfoolery [tom-fuh'lA-ri] n. Blödsinn n, Narrenspossen f.pl.

Tommy - [to'mi] a. - -bar n. Brechstange f; - -gun n. Maschinenpistole f; - -rot n. Blödsinn m.

To-morrow [tA-mo'rou] ad. morgen; the day after - übermorgen; - morning morgen früh.

Tom-tit [tom'tit] n. Meise f.

Ton [tAn] n. Tonne f.

Tone [toun] n. Ton m, Laut m, Klang m, Färbung f, Stimmung f (com.); vt. abtönen, tonen (photo); - poem n. Tondichtung f.

Tongs [tongs] n.pl. Zange f; fire - n. Feuerzange f.

Tongue [tAng] n. Zunge f, Lasche f (shoe); - -tied a. an der Zunge gelähmt, stumm; - -twister n. unaussprechliches Wort.

Tonic [to'nik] a. tonisch, stärkend; n. Stärkungsmittel n, Grundton m (music); - sol-fa n. Tonikamethode f.

To-night [tu-nait'] ad. heute abend, heute nacht.

Toning [tou'ning] n. Tonung f; - bath n. Tonbad n.

Tonnage [tA'nidzh] n. Frachtraum m, Ladungsgehalt n. Tonnengehalt m (ship).

Tonsil [ton'ssil] n. Mandel f.

Tonsillitis [ton-ssi-lai'tiss] n. Mandelentzündung f.

Tonsure [ton'scher] n. Tonsur f.

Too [tuh] ad. zu, dazu, ebenfalls, auch; too much zuviel.

Tool [tuhl] n. Werkzeug n, Gerät n; vt. bearbeiten, punzen, abstempeln; - -bag n.

Werkzeugtasche f; - -chest n. Werkzeugkasten m; - -kit n. see - -chest.

Tooling [tuh'ling] n. Punzarbeit f. [en n.

Toot [tuht] vt./i. tuten; - n. Tut.

Tooth [tuhth] n. Zahn m; vt. zahnen; - -brush n. Zahnbürste f; - -paste n. Zahnpasta f.

Toothache [tuhth'eik] n. Zahnweh n, Zahnschmerzen m.pl.

Toothed [tuhtht] a. gezähnt, gezackt, zackig.

Toothing [tuh'thing] n. Zahnung f, Verzahnung f (tec.).

Toothless [tuhth'less] a. zahnlos. [Zahnstocher m.

Toothpick [tuhth'pik] n.

Toothsome [tuhth'ssAm] a. schmackhaft.

Tootle [tuhtl] vt./i. leise tuten.

Top [top] n. Spitze f, Gipfel m (hill), Wipfel m, Krone f (tree), Mastkorb m, Topp m (ship), der Erste (school), Kopfende n (table), Kappe f, Deckel m (tec.); a. oberst, höchst, Haupt-; vt. bedecken, übertreffen; - -boot n. Stulpen-, Schachtstiefel m; - -coat n. Überzieher m; - -dressing n. Kopfdüngung f; - gear n. dritter Gang (aut.); - hat n. Zylinderhut m; - -heavy a. oberlastig, kopflastig (av.); - speed n. höchste Geschwindigkeit.

Top [top] n. Kreisel m.

Topaz [tou'pæs] n. Topas m.

Toper [tou'per] n. Säufer m.

Topi, Topee [to-pih'] n. Tropenhelm m.

Topic [to'pik] n. Thema n, Gegenstand m.

Topical [to'pikl] a. aktuell, Tages...; - talk n. Zeitfunk m (rad.).

Topmast [top'mahst] n. Marsstenge f.

Topmost [top'moust] a. oberst, höchst.

Topographer [tA-po'grA-fer] n. Topograph m.

Topographical [to-pA-græ'fikl] a., -ly ad. topographisch; - features n.pl. Bodengestaltung f.

Topography [to-po'grA-fi] n. Geländekunde f, Ortsbeschreibung f, Topographie f.

Topple [topl] vi. hinunterstürzen.

Topsail [top'ssl] n. Marssegel n.

Topsy-turvy [top'si-tA'rwi] durcheinander, in Verwirrung.

Torch [tOrtsch] n. Fackel f; electric - n. Taschenlampe f; - -light procession n. Fackelzug m.

Torment [tOr'mAnt] n. Qual f, Marter f (tOr-ment') vt. quälen, martern.

Tormentor [tOr-men'ter] n. Peiniger m.

Tornado [tOr-nei'dou] n. Wirbelsturm m.

Torpedo [tOr-pih'dou] n. Torpedo m; vt. torpedieren; - -boat n. Torpedoboot n; - -bomber n. Torpedoflugzeug n (av.); - -carrying aircraft see - -bomber; - -man n. Torpedomechaniker m; - -recovery boat n. Torpedofangboot m; - -tube n. Torpedorohr n, Ausstossrohr m.

Torpid [tOr'pid] a. erstarrt, starr apathisch.

Torpor [tOr'per] n. Erstarrung f, Gefühllosigkeit f.

Torque [tOrk] n. Verdrehung f, Drehmoment n, Drehkraft f (tec.); - -tube n. Hohlwelle f (tel-phys.).

Torrent [io'rAnt] n. Giessbach m, Strom m, Flut f.

Torrential [tA-ren'schAl] a. strömend, überwältigend, reissend.

Torrid [to'rid] a. dürr, gedörrt, brennend heiss, sengend; - zone n. heisse Zone.

Torsion [tOr'schAn] n. Drehung f, Verdrehung f, Torsion f (tec.); - **balance** n. Drehwaage f; -**al** a. Torsions . . . .

Torso [tOr'ssou] n. Rumpf m, Torso m.   [Schädigung f.

Tort [tOrt] n. Unrecht n.

Tortoise [tOr'tAss] n. Schildkröte f; - **shell** n. Schildkrötenschale f, Schildpatt n.

Tortuous [tOr'tju-Ass] a. sich windend, schlagenartig, unredlich.

Torture [tOr'tscher] n. Marter f, Folter f, Tortur f; vt. martern, foltern; - **chamber** n. Folterkammer f.

Toss [tOss] vt. emporschleudern, schütteln, werfen; sich unruhig bewegen, treiben, schlingern (ship), auslosen (sport); n. Werfen n, Stoss m, Losen n.

Tot [tot] n. kleines Kind, Schlückchen n, Gläschen n.

Tot [tot] vt. rechnen, zusammenzählen.

Total [tou'tAl] n. Gesamtbetrag m, Betrag m, Summe f, das Ganze n; a. ganz, gesamt, völlig, total; vi. sich belaufen auf; - **exemption** n. gänzliche Zurückstellung (mil.); - **loss** n. gänzlicher Verlust, Totalverlust m; - **losses** n.pl. Gesamtverluste m.pl; - **war** n. totaler Krieg.

Totalitarian [tou-tæ-li-teh'rjAn] a. total, totalitär; - **state** n. totaler Staat, Totalstaat m.

Totality [tA-tæ'li-ti] n. Totalität f, Vollständigkeit f, Gesamtheit f.

Totalizator [tou'tA-lai-sei-ter] n. Totalisator m, amtliche Wettstelle.

Totally [tou'tA-li] ad. gänzlich, vollständig, total.

Totter [to'ter] vi. wanken, schwanken, wackeln; -**ing** a. schwankend, wackelig.

Touch [tAtsch] n. Berührung

f, Tastsinn m, Anschluss m, Fühlung f, Gefechtsanschluss m (mil.); vt. berühren, anrühren, anstossen, bewegen; i. sich berühren, anlaufen (port); - **and go** knappes Entkommen; - **hole** n. Zündloch n (mil.); -**line** n. Seitengrenze f (games).

Touching [tA'tsching] a. rührend; pr. betreffend, hinsichtlich.   [Prüfstein m.

Touchstone [tAtsch'stoun] n.

Touchy [tA'tschi] a. reizbar, empfindlich.

Tough [tAf] a. zäh, hart, schwierig; n. Raufbold m; -**en** vt.i. zäh machen, zäh werden; -**ness** n. Zähigkeit f, Härte f, Festigkeit f.

Tour [tuh'er] n. Reise f, Ausflug m, Wanderung f.

Touring [tuh'ring] n. Rundreisen v; - **car** n. Reisewagen m, offenes Auto, offener Kraftwagen.

Tourist [tuh'rist] n. Tourist m, Touristin f, der, die Reisende; - **agency** n. Reisebüro n; - **industry** n. Fremdenindustrie f; - **ticket** n. Ferienkarte f, Urlaubskarte f; - **traffic** n. Fremdenverkehr m.

Tournament [tuh'er-nAmAnt] n. Turnier n.

Tourniquet [tuh'nih-kei] n. Aderpresse f, Arterienkompressorium n; **to apply a** - eine Ader abbinden.

Tousle [tausl] vt. zersausen.

Tout [taut] n. Kundensucher m; vt. Kunden anlocken.

Tow [tou] n. Werg n.

Tow [tou] vt. schleppen, bugsieren, treideln; n. Schlepptau m, Schleppzug m; - **off** verschleppen; -**path** n. Schlepp-, Treidel-weg m; - **rope** n. Schlepp-leine f, -trosse f; -**ing service** n. Abschleppdienst m.

Towage [tou'idzh] n. Schleppen n, Treideln, Schleppgebühr f, Bugsierlohn m.

Towards [tu-uOrds'] *vr.* gegen, nach.

Towel [tau'il] *n.* Handtuch *n*; – **-rail** *n.* Handtuchgestell *n*; **-ling** *n.* Handtuch-stoff *m*, -drell *m.*

Tower [tau'er] *n.* Turm *m*; *vi.* sich türmen, emporragen.

Town [taun] *n.* Stadt *f*; – **clerk** *n.* Stadtschreiber *m*; **-council** *n.* Stadtrat *m*, Gemeindevorstand *m*; – **-dweller** *n.* Städter *m*, Städterin *f*; – **hall** *n.* Rathaus *n*; – **planning** *n.* Städtebau *m.*

Township [taun'schip] *n.* Stadtbezirk *m.* [Bürger *m*

Townsman [tauns'mAn] *n.*

Toxæmia [tox-ih'mjA] *n.* Blutvergiftung *f.*

Toxic [tox'ik] *a.* giftig.

Toy [teu] *n.* Spielzeug *n*; *vi.* spielen, tändeln; – **-shop** *n.* Spielwarenladen *m.* [Zugtau *n.*

Trace [treiss] *n.* Strang *m.*

Trace [treiss] *n.* Spur *f* Anzeichen *n*; *vt.* zeichnen, durchpausen, durchzeichnen, nachspüren, nachforschen.

Traceable [trei'ssAbl] *a.* ausspürbar.

Tracer [trei'sser] *n.* Leucht-spur *f*; – **ammunition** *n.* Leuchtspurmunition *f*; – **bullet** *n.* Rauchspurgeschoss *n* (*mil.*).

Tracing [trei'ssing] *n.* Pause *f*, Pauszeichnung *f*; – **paper** *n.* Pauspapier *n.*

Track [træk] *n.* Spur *f*, Bahn *f*, Geleise *n*, Gleis *n*, Raupe *f*, Raupen-kette *f*, -band *n* (*on vehicles*), Kurs *m* (*radar*); *vt.* ausspüren, verfolgen; beaten – Trampelwege *m.pl*, ausgetretener Weg; **-ed** vehicle *n.* Gleiskettenfahrzeug *n.*

Trackless [træk'less] *a.* spurlos, ohne Schienen (*tram*).

Tract [trækt] *n.* Traktat *n*, Flugschrift *f.*

Tract [trækt] *n.* Landstrich *m*, Strecke *f* (*rl, etc.*).

Tractable [træk'tAbl] *a.* lenksam.

Traction [træk'schAn] *n.* Zug-kraft *f*, Fahrbetrieb *m*, Zug *m* (*tec.*); – **engine** *n.* Motorschlepper *m*, Strassenlokomotive *f.*

Tractor [træk'ter] *n.* Trecker *m*, Zugwagen *m*, Zugmaschine *f*, Schlepper *m*, Traktor *m*; **agricultural –** *n.* Ackerschlepper *m*; – **plough** *n.* Motorpflug *m.*

Trade [treid] *n.* Handel *m*, Geschäft *n*, Gewerbe *n*, Handwerk *n*; *vt.i.* handeln, verhandeln, Handel treiben mit; **retail –** *n.* Kleinhandel *n*; **wholesale –** *n.* Grosshandel *m*; – **cycle** *n.* Konjunktur *f*; – **directory** *n.* Handelsadressbuch *n*; – **discount** *n.* Wiederverkäuferrabatt *m*; – **mark** *n.* Schutzmarke *f*; – **route** *n.* Handelsstrasse *f*; – **union** *n.* Gewerkschaft *f*; – **unionist** *n.* Gewerkschaftler *m*; – **wind** *n.* Passatwind *m.*

Trader [trei'der] *n.* Kleinhändler *m*, Kaufmann *m.*

Tradesman [treids'mAn] *n.* Ladenbesitzer *m*, Krämer *m*, Händler *m.*

Trades union *see* trade union; – **council** *n.* Gewerkschaftsbund *m.*

Tradition [trA-di'schAn] *n.* Überlieferung *f*, Tradition *f*, Brauch *m.*

Traditional [trA-di'schA-nAl] *a.*, **-ly** *ad.* überliefert, althergebracht, traditionell, üblich.

Traduce [trA-djuhss'] *vt.* verleumden.

Traffic [træ'fik] *n.* Strassenverkehr *m* (*vehicles*), Handelsverkehr *m* (*trade*); *vt.i.* handeln; – **control** *n.* Verkehrsleitung *f*, -regelung *f*; – **lights** *n.pl.* Verkehrsampel *f.pl*; – **policeman** *n.* Verkehrs-polizist *m*, -schutzmann *m*; – **regulation** *n.* Verkehrsordnung *f.*

Tragedy [træ'dzhА-di] n. Tragödie f, Trauerspiel n. [unselig.

Tragic [træ'dzhik] a. tragisch.

Trail [treil] n. Fährte f, Spur f, Rücktrift f (av.); vt.i. (sich) schleppen, schleifen, kriechen; -er n. Beiwagen m, Anhänger m (aut.), Vorschau f (film); -ing a. schleppend, kriechend (plant); - aerial n. Schleppantenne f (av.).

Train [trein] n. Zug m (rl.), Reihe f, Folge f, Prozession f, Schleppe f, Tross m (mil.); vt. ausbilden, einüben, schulen, trainieren, dressieren, abrichten (animals); i. erziehen, üben, sich vorbereiten; ammunition - n. Munitionskolonne f (mil.); express - n. Schnellzug m; freight -, goods - n. Güterzug m; passenger -, slow - n. Personenzug m; - ferry n. Eisenbahnfähre f, Trajekt n, Fährschiff n; - service n. Eisenbahnverkehr m.

Trainee [trei-nih'] n. Schüler m, Anwärter m.

Trainer [trei'ner] n. Dresseur m, Trainer m, Erzieher m.

Training [trei'ning] n. Ausbildung f, Trainieren n, Einüben n, Erziehung f; - college n. Lehrerseminar n; - manual n. Druckvorschrift f; - regulations n.pl. Dienstvorschrift f; - ship n. Schulschiff n; - staff n. Lehrstab m.

Train-oil [trein'euil] n. Fischtran m.

Trait [trei] n. Charakterzug m, Merkmal n, Zug m.

Traitor [trei'ter] n. Verräter m; -ous a. verräterisch.

Trajectory [trA-dzhek'tA-ri] n. Flug-, Wurf-bahn f, Fallkurve f, Wurflinie f.

Tram [træm] n. Strassenbahn f; -car n. Strassenbahnwagen m; - conductor n. Strassenbahnschaffner m; - depot n. Strassenbahndepot n; - driver

n. Strassenbahnführer m; -line n. Strassenbahnschiene f; - stop n. Strassenbahnhaltestelle f; - terminus n. Endstation f; - ticket n. Strassenbahnfahrschein m.

Trammel [træml] n. Fessel f, Hindernis n.

Tramp [træmp] n. Landstreicher m; vi. gehen, wandern; i. treten; - steamer n. unregelmässig fahrender Dampfer.

Trample [træmpl] vt. niedertreten; i. trampeln.

Tramway [træm'uei] n. Strassenbahn f, Trambahn f, die Elektrische; - system n. Strassenbahnnetz n.

Trance [trahnss] n. Verzückung f, Scheintod m.

Tranquil [træng'kuil] a, -ly ad. ruhig, still.

Tranquillity [træng-kui'li-ti] n. Ruhe f, Stille f.

Transact [trahn-sækt'] vt. abmachen, verrichten, erledigen, machen (business).

Transaction [trahn-sæk'shAn] n. Geschäft n, Geschäftsfall m Verrichtung f, Unterhandlung f, Verhandlung f; cash - n. Bargeschäft n.

Transactor [trahn-sæk'ter] n. Unterhändler m.

Transatlantic [trahns-Atlæn'tik] a. transatlantisch, überseeisch; - flight n. Ozeanflug m; - liner n. Überseedampfer m.

Transcend [trahn-ssend'] vt. übersteigen, übertreffen.

Transcontinental [trahnskon-ti-nentl'] a. Überland

Transcribe [trahn-skraib'] vt. abschreiben, kopieren, übertragen, umsetzen.

Transcript [trahn'skript] n. Abschrift f, Kopie f, Transkription f, Übertragung f.

Transcription [trahn-skript

schAn] n. Abschrift f, Abschreiben n, Umsetzen n.

Transept [trahn'sept] n. Querschiff n, Kreuzflügel m.

Transfer [trahnss'fer] n. Übertragung f, Versetzung f, Umdruck m, Durchpausen n, Überweisung f, Umbuchung f, Übertrag m (com.); cable – n. Kabelauszahlung f.

Transfer [trahnss-fAr'] vt. übertragen, abtreten (rights), versetzen, verlegen, gegenbuchen (com.); -able a. übertragbar, begebbar (com.).

Transfiguration [trahnss-figju-rei'schAn] n. Verklärung f.

Transfix [trahnss-fix'] vt. durch-stechen, -bohren.

Transform [trahnss-form'] vt. umbilden, umgestalten umformen, verwandeln; -able a. umgestaltbar.

Transformation [trahnssfer-mei'schAn] n. Umgestaltung f, Umbildung f, Umformung f, Verwandlung f, Damenperücke f.

Transformer [trahnss-form'mer] n. Umspanner m, Umformer m, Transformator m (el.); – unit n. Umformungsaggregat m.

Transfuse [trahnss-fjuhs'] vt. umgiessen, überleiten, übertragen (blood).

Transfusion [trahnss-fjuh'zhAn] n. Umgiessen n, Überleitung f, Blutübertragung f, Transfusion f, Tausch m (blood); – set n. Bluttransfusionsapparat m.

Transgress [trahnss-gress'] vt. überschreiten, übertreten.

Transgression [trahnss-gre'schAn] n. Übertretung f, Überschreitung f, Sünde f.

Transgressor [trahnss-gre'sser] n. der Übertreter, Sünder m.

Tranship [trahns-schip'] vt. umladen, überladen, umschiff-

en, umschlagen; -ment n Umladung f. Umspedierung f; port of – – n. Umladehafen m.

Transient [trahn'ssjant] a. flüchtig, vergänglich, schnell vorübergehend.

Transire [trahn-sai'ri] n. Zollbegleitschein n, Freischein m.

Transit [trahn'ssit] n. Durchgang m, Durchfuhr , Durchgangsverkehr m; in – unterwegs, in Zuführung, im Durchgang; damaged (lost) in – beim Transport beschädigt (verlorengegangen); – camp n. Zwischenlager n, Durchgangslager n (prisoners of war); – goods n.pl. Transitwaren f.

Transition [trahn-ssi'zhAn] n. Übergang m; -al a. Übergangs . . . .

Transitive [trahn'ssi-tiw] a. transitiv, zielend.

Transitory [trahn'ssi-tA-ri] a. vergänglich.

Translatable [trahnss-lei'tAbl] a. übersetzbar.

Translate [trahnss-leit'] vt. übersetzen, übertragen.

Translation [trahnss-lei'schAn] n. Übersetzung f, Übertragung f.

Translator [trahnss-lei'ter] n. Übersetzer m.

Transliterate [trahnss-li'tA-reit] vt. transkribieren.

Transliteration [trahnss-litA-rei'schAn] n. Umschreibung f, Wiedergabe f, Transkription f.

Translucent [trahnss-luh'ssAnt] a. durchsichtig, durchscheinend.

Transmarine [trahnss-mA-rihn'] a. überseeisch.

Transmigrate [trahnss-mai-greit'] vi auswandern, hinübergehen; -ion n. Auswanderung f, Übersiedelung f.

Transmissible [trahnss-mis'ssibl] a. übertragbar, fortpflanzbar.

Transmission [trahnss-mischAn] n. Übersendung f, Versendung f, Beförderung f, Fortpflanzung f, Vererbung f (*hereditary*), Sendung f, Weiterleitung f, Übertragung f (*rad.*), Getriebe n (*aut.*), Transmission f (*tec.*), Übermittelung f (*orders*); – shaft n. Hauptwelle f, Getriebewelle f (*tec.*).

Transmit [trahnss-mit'] vt. befördern, übermitteln, übersenden, versenden, fortpflanzen, übertragen (*rad.*), rundfunken (*rad.*).

Transmitter [trahnss-mi'ter] n. Geber m, Sender m, Übermittler m, Übersender m, Sprachrohr n (*ph.*), Übertrager m, Funksender m (*rad.*); directional – n. Richtsender m; main – n. Hauptsender m.

Transmitting [trahnss-mit'ting] n. Vermittlung f, Sendung f, Übertragung f; – aerial n. Sendeantenne f (*rad.*); – station n. Sendestation f (*rad.*), Vermittlungsstation f.

Transmutation [trahnss-mjuh-tei'schAn] n. Umwandlung f, Verwandlung f.

Transmute [trahnss-mjuht'] vt. umwandeln, verwandeln.

Transoceanic [trahnss-ou-schjæ'nik] a. überseeisch; – flight n. Ozeanflug m.

Transom [træn'ssAm] n. Querbalken m, Querholz n.

Transparency [trahnss-peh'rAn-ssi] n. Durchsichtigkeit f.

Transparent [trahnss-peh'rAnt] a. -ly ad. durchsichtig, klar, offensichtig.

Transpire [trahnss-spai'er] vi. verlauten, sich herausstellen, bekannt werden.

Transplant [trahnss-plahnt'] vt. umpflanzen, verpflanzen, versetzen, transplantieren.

Transplantation [trahnss-plahn-tei'schAn] n. Umpflanzung f, Verpflanzung f, Transplantation f.

Transport [trahn'spOrt] n. Fortschaffung f, Beförderung f, Versand m, Spedition f, Transport m, Tross m (*mil.*), Transportschiff n (*ship*); Ministry of – n. Verkehrsministerium n; motor – n. Kraftwagentransport m; troop – n. Truppentransportschiff n; – column n. Tross m (*mil.*); – control n. Transportleitung f; – service n. Transportwesen n, Fuhrwesen n; – ship n. Fracht-, Transportschiff n; – worker n. Transportarbeiter m.

Transport [trahn-spOrt'] vt. versenden, befördern, transportieren, deportieren (*law*), entzücken (*joy, etc.*); -able a. verlegefähig, fortschaffbar, versendbar.

Transpose [trahn-spous'] vt. versetzen, umstellen, verstellen, transponieren.

Transposition [trahn-spou-si'schAn] n. Versetzung f, Umstellung f, Transponieren n.

Transubstantiation [trahn-ssAb-stæn-schjei'schAn] n. Wandlung f, Transsubstantiation f.

Transversal [trahnss-wAr'ssAl] a. diagonal, quer durchgehend.

Transverse [trahns-wArss'] a. quer, querlaufend, durchgehend.

Trap [træp] n. Falle f, Schlinge f, Hinterhalt m (*mil.*); vt. fangen, erwischen, ertappen; booby – n. Sprengfalle f, Flattermine f, Schreckmine f; tank – n. Panzerfalle f, Tankfalle f; – door n. Falltür f, Klappe f.

Trapeze [trA-pihs'] n. Schwebereck n Schaukelreck n.

Trapper [træ'per] n. Pelzjäger m, Fallensteller m.

Trappings [træ'pings] n.pl. Schmuck m, Ausstattung f.

Trash [træsch] n. wertloses Zeug, Auswurf m, Abfall m.

Kitsch *m*; **-y** *a.* kitschig, wert-los.

Travail [træ'weil] *n.* Mühsal *f*, Wehen *f.pl.*

Travel [trævl] *vi.* reisen; *t.* bereisen, zurücklegen; *n.* Reisen *n*; **-s** *n.pl.* Reisen *f.pl*; **led** *a.* weitgereist.

Traveller [træv'lər] *n.* der, die Reisende; **commercial - n.** Handelsreisende(r) *m*; **-'s cheque** *n.* Reisescheck *m.*

Travelling [træv'ling] *n.* Reisen *n*; **- agency** *n.* Reise-büro *n*; **- case** *n.* Reisekoffer *m*; **- companion** *n.* der, die Reisegefährte *m*; **- expenses** *n.pl.* Reisekosten *pl*; **- sales-man** *n.* Geschäfts-, Handels-reisende(r) *m.*

Traverse [træ'werss] *n.* Quer-holz *n*, Querstück *n*, Querwall *m*, Traverse *f*; *vt.* quer durch-gehen, durchfahren, durchrei-en, überqueren, wenden, dreh-en.

Travesty [træ'wi-sti] *n.* ent-stellende Nachahmung, Traves-tie *f*; *vt.* travestieren, ins Lächerliche ziehen.

Trawl [trOl] *vi.* mit dem Schl-eppnetz fischen; *n.* Schlepp-netz *n*; **-er** *n.* Schleppnetz-fischerboot *n*, Fischdampfer *m.*

Tray [trei] *n.* Tablett *n*, Tee-brett *n*, Präsentierteller *m*, Koffereinsatz *m* (*trunk*), Trog *m*, Mulde *f* (*tec.*).

Treacherous [tre'tschA-rAss] *a.* **-ly** *ad.* verräterisch, falsch, hinterlistig.

Treachery [tre'tschA-ri] *n.* Verrat *m*, Untreue *f*, Hinterlist *f*, Falschheit *f*, Tücke *f.*

Treacle [trihkl] *n.* Sirup *m*, Melasse *f*; **-y** *a.* sirupartig, klebrig.

Tread [tred] *n.* Schritt *m*, Tritt *m*, Laufband *n* (*tec.*), Gleit-fläche *f* (*tyre*, *aut.*); *v.i./t.* treten, betreten, gehen, schreiten.

Treadle [tredl] *n.* Pedal *n*

Tritt *m*, Tretschemel *m*; *vt.i.* treten; **- mill** *n.* Tretmühle *f.*

Treason [trih'sAn] *n.* Verrat *m*; **high -** *n.* Hochverrat *m*; **-able** *a.* verräterisch.

Treasure [tre'zher] *n.* Schatz *m*; *vt.* hochschätzen, aufbe-wahren, werthalten, sammeln; **- house** *n.* Schatzhaus *n*, Fund-grube *f*; **- trove** *n.* gefundener Schatz, Hort *m.*

Treasurer [tre'zhA-rer] *n.* Kassierer *m*, Kassenwart *m*, Kassenverwalter *m*, Schatz-meister *m.*

Treasury [tre'zhA-ri] *n.* Schatz *m*, Schatzkammer *f*, Finanzministerium *n*; **- bond** *n.* Schatzanweisung *f*; **- de-partment** *n.* Finanzministe-rium *n*; **- note** *n.* Kassenschein *m*, Banknote *f*, englischer Pfund-, Zehnschilling-schein.

Treat [triht] *vt.* behandeln, handeln über, bewirten, trak-tieren (*people*), aufbereiten (*ore*), betrachten (*consider*); *i.* verhandeln; *n.* Hochgenuss *m*, Vergnügen *n.*

Treatise [trih'tiss] *n.* Schrift *f*, Abhandlung *f.*

Treatment [triht'mAnt] *n.* Behandlung *f*, Bearbeitung *f*, Kur *f*; **course of -** *n.* Kur *f*; **medical -** *n.* ärztliche Behand-lung; **-of ore** *n.* Erzaufberei-tung *f.*

Treaty [trih'ti] *n.* Vertrag *m*, Abkommen *n*, Verhandlung *f*; **extradition -** *n.* Auslieferungs-vertrag *m*; **- port** *n.* Vertrags-hafen *m*; **- power** *n.* Vertrags-macht *f.*

Treble [trebl] *a.* dreifach; *n.* das Dreifache, Diskant *m*, Sopran *m*; *vt.* verdreifachen; **-y** *ad.* dreimal, dreifach.

Tree [trih] *n.* Baum *m*; **boot - n.** Stiefelblock *m*; **- -top** *n.* Wipfel *m*; **- -trunk** *n.* Baum-stamm *m.* [los.

Treeless [trih'less] *a.* baum-

Trefoil [tre'feul] n. Klee m, Dreiblatt n.

Trek [trek] vi. ziehen, auswandern; n. Zug m.

Trellis [tre'liss] n. Gitter n, Spalier n, Gitterwerk n; vt. vergittern; **- work** n. Gitterwerk n.

Tremble [trembl] vi. beben, zittern.

Tremendous [tri-men'dᴀss] a, -ly ad. fürchterlich, furchtbar, ungeheuer, kolossal.

Tremor [tre'mer] n. Zittern n; earth — n. Erdbeben n.

Tremulous [tre'mju-lᴀss] a. zitternd, bebend.

Trench [trensch] n. Graben m, Schützengraben m (mil.); vt. verschanzen, mit Gräben durchziehen; **communication** n. Lauf-, Verbindungs-graben m; **slit**— n. Strich-, Splittergraben m; **-coat** n. Wettermantel m; **-digger**, — excavator n. Grabenbagger m; **-mortar** n. Granatwerfer m, Minenwerfer m; **-plough** n. Rajol-, Graben-pflug m.

Trenchant [tren'schᴀnt] a. schneidend, scharf, kraftvoll.

Trencher [tren'scher] n. Schneide-, Transchier-brett n.

Trend [trend] n. Richtung f, Neigung f, Geneigtheit f, Tendenz f; vi. sich neigen, eine schiefe Richtung haben, sich richten.

Trepan [tri-pæn'] n. Schädelbohrer m, Trepan m; vt. trepanieren, anbohren (tec.).

Trepidation [tre-pi-deï'schᴀn] n. Beben n, Furcht f, Bestürzung f, Angst f.

Trespass [tress'pᴀss] n. widerrechtliches Betreten n, Rechtsverletzung f; vi. widerrechtlich betreten, eingreifen in; **- upon** missbrauchen, behelligen; **-er** n. Übertreter m.

Tress [tress] n. Haarflechte f, Locke f.

Trestle [tressl] n. Gestell n,

Gerüst n, Lager n, Brückenbock m; **- bridge** n. Bockbrücke f.

Triad [trai'æd] n. Dreiheit f, Dreiklang m (chord).

Trial [trai'ᴀl] n. Verhör n, Gerichtsverfahren n (law), Probe f, Versuch m, Prüfung f (test), Widerwärtigkeit f (trouble); **on** — auf Probe; **-order** n. Probeauftrag m (com.); **- trip** n. Probefahrt f.

Triangle [trai'æng-gl] n. Dreieck n, Triangel m (instrument).

Triangular [trai-æng'gju-ler] a. dreieckig, dreiwinklig.

Triangulation [trai-æng-gju-leï'schᴀn] n. Triangulation f, Triangulierung f, Dreieckzielen n (mil.); **-station** n. Dreieckpunkt m.

Tribal [traibl] a. Stammes ... ; **-chief** n. Häuptling m.

Tribe [traib] n. Volksstamm m, Geschlecht n; **-sman** n. der Stammesangehörige.

Tribulation [tri-bju-leï'schᴀn] n. Mühsal f, Trübsal f, Not f.

Tribunal [trai-bjuh'nᴀl] n. Gericht n, Gerichtshof m, Kammer f; **military** — n. Militärgericht n.

Tribune [trai'bjuhn] n. Tribun m.

Tributary [tri'bju-tᴀ-ri] a. zufliessend, zinspflichtig; n. Nebenfluss m.

Tribute [tri'bjuht] n. Abgabe f Tribut m Beitrag m, Bezeugung f.

Tricar [trai'kahr] n. Dreiradwagen m, Zyklonette f.

Trice [traiss] n. Augenblick m, Nu m.

Trick [trik] n. List f, Kunstgriff m, Kniff m, Trick m, Stich m (cards); vt. beschwindeln, überlisten, prellen; **-ery** n. List f, Betrügerei f; **-ish** a. durchtrieben, schlau, tückisch, verwickelt.

Trickle [trikl] *n.* Geriesel *n*; *vi.* rieseln, tröpfeln.

Trickster [trix'ter] *n.* Betrüger *m*, Schwindler *m*.

Tricky [tri'ki] *a.* schlau, verwickelt.

Tricot [trih'kou] *n.* Trikot *m*.

Tricycle [trai'ssikl] *n.* Dreirad *n*; – *carrier n.* Dreiradlieferwagen *m*.   zack *m.*

Trident [trai'dʌnt] *n.* Dreizack *m.*

Tried [traid] *a.* erprobt, bewährt.   [jährig, dreijährlich.

Triennial [trai-en'jʌl] *a.* drei

Trifle [traifl] *n.* Kleinigkeit *f*, Lappalie *f*; *v.i.t.* tändeln, scherzen, spassen; –r *n.* Tändler *m*, oberflächlicher Mensch.

Triforium [trai-fO'rjʌm] *n.* Triforium *n*, säulengetragene Galerie, Dreischlitz *m.*

Trigger [tri'ger] *n.* Abzug *m*, Drücker *m*, Auslöser *m* (*camera*); – guard *n.* Abzugsbügel *m*; – spring *n.* Abzugsfeder *f.*

Trigonometry [tri-gA-no'mitri] *n.* Trigonometrie *f*, Dreiecksmessung *f.*

Trill [tril] *n.* Triller *m*; *vt.i.* trillern, rollen (*one's r's*).

Trillion [tril'jʌn] *n.* Trillion *f.*

Trilogy [tri'lA-dzhi] *n.* Trilogie *f*, Folge von drei Dichtwerken.

Trim [trim] *a.* nett, schmuck; *vt.* besetzen, garnieren, ausputzen, stutzen, zurecht machen, stauen (*coal*); *n.* Putz *m*, Gleichgewichtslage *f*, Trimm *m* (*nav.*), Schneiden *n* (*hair*).

Trimmer [tri'mer] *n.* Wetterhahn *m.*

Trimming [tri'ming] *n.* Ausputz *m*, Garnitur *f*, Besatz *m*, Haarschneiden *n.*

Trimness [trim'ness] *n.* Niedlichkeit *f*, Nettigkeit *f.* [keit *f.*

Trinity [tri'ni-ti] *n.* Dreieinig

Trinket [tring'kit] *n.* Schmuckstück *n*, Schmucksache *n.*

Trio [trai'ou] *n.* Trio *n* (*music*),

Kleeblatt *n* (*persons*), Kette *f* (*aircraft*).

Triode [trai'oud] *n.* Triode *f*, Drei-elektrodenröhre *f.*

Trip [trip] *n.* kurze Reise, Ausflug *m*, Stolpern *n*, Fehltritt *m*; *vi.* straucheln, stolpern, trippeln; – up *vt.* ein Bein stellen; –wire *n.* Stolperdraht *m*, Stolperverhau *m.*

Tripartite [trai-pahr'tait] *a.* dreifach, dreiteilig; – Pact *n.* Dreimächte-abkommen *n*

Tripe [traip] *n.* Kaldaunen *pl*, Blödsinn *m.*   [decker *m.*

Triplane [trai'plein] *n.* Drei

Triple [tripl] *a.* dreifach; *vt.* verdreifachen; – Alliance *n.* Dreibund *m*; – turret *n.* Drillingturm *m.*

Triplet [trip'lit] *n.* Drilling *m*, Dreireim *m*, Trio *n.*

Triplicate [trip'li-kit] *a.* dreifach; *n.* Verdreifachung *f*; *vt.* verdreifachen, dreifach ausfertigen; in – in dreifacher Ausfertigung.

Tripod [trai'pod] *n.* Dreifuss *m*, Stativ *n* (*camera*).

Tripper [tri'per] *n.* Ausflügler *m*, Tourist *m.*

Triptique [trip'tik] *n.* Grenzschein *m*, Passierschein *m* (*aut.*), Grenzkarte *f.*

Trite [trait] *a.* abgedroschen, alltäglich, platt.

Triumph [trai'Amf] *n.* Siegeszug *m*, Triumph *m*, Siegesfreude *f*; *vi.* siegen, triumphieren.

Triumphal [trai-Amf'l] *a.* Sieges . . .; – arch *n.* Triumphbogen *m.*

Triumphant [trai-Am'fʌnt] *a.*, -ly *ad.* siegreich, triumphierend.

Trivet [tri'wit] *n.* Dreifuss *m.*

Trivial [tri'wjAl] *a.* geringfügig, unbedeutend, alltäglich.

Triviality [tri-wje'li-ti] *n.* Unbedeutendheit *f*, Geringfügigkeit *f.*

Troll [trol] *vt.i.* trällern, rollen (lassen).

Trolley [tro'li] *n.* Strassenbahnwagen *m*, Stromzuführungszange *f*, Förderkarren *m*.

Trombone [trom-boun'] *n.* Posaune *f*.

Troop [truhp] *n.* Trupp *m*, Truppe *f*, Schar *f*, Batterie *f* (*artillery*); *vi.* sich sammeln, sich scharen; **-** -**movement** *n.* Truppen-bewegung *f*, -**trans**-port *m*; **-** -**ship** *n.* Transportschiff *n.*

Trophy [tro'fi] *n.* Siegeszeichen *n*, Trophäe *f*.

Tropical [tro'pik] *a.* tropisch, Tropen . . .; **-** -**helmet** *n.* Tropenhelm *m*; **-**neckcloth *n.* Tropenbinder *m*; **-** -**shirt** *n.* Tropenüberhemd *n*; **-**tunic *n.* Tropenrock *m*. [*pl.*

Tropics [tro'pix] *n.pl.* Tropen

Trot [trot] *n.* Trott *m*, Trab *m*; *vi.* trotten, traben.

Troth [trouth] *n.* Verlobung *f*. Treuelöbnis *f.*

Trouble [trAbl] *n.* Kummer *m*, Mühe *f*, Verdruss *m*, Unannehmlichkeit *f*, Not *f*, Verlegenheit *f*; *vt.* Mühe machen, belästigen; engine **-** -**n.** Motorstörung *f* (*aut.*).

Troublesome [trAbl'ssAm] *a.* lästig, beschwerlich, ärgerlich.

Troublous [trAb'lAss] *a.* unruhig, beunruhigend.

Trough [trouf] *n.* Trog *m*, Mulde *f*, Wanne *f* (*tec.*); **-** -**of** a wave *n.* Wellental *n.*

Trounce [traunss] *vt.* prügeln.

Trousers [trau'sers] *n.pl.* Beinkleider *n.pl*, Hosen *f.pl*; Trouser button *n.* Hosenknopf *m*; **-** -**press** *n.* Spanner *m*, Hosenstrecker *m.*

Trousseau [truh'ssou] *n.* Brautausstattung *f*, Aussteuer *f.*

Trout [traut] *n.* Forelle *f*; **-** -**farm** *n.* Forellenzüchterei *f*; **-** -**fishing** *n.* Forellenfang *m.*

Trowel [trau'il] *n.* Maurerkelle *f*, Pflanzenstecher *m*, Ausheber *m.* [Schulschwänzen *n.*

Truancy [truh'An-ssi] *n.*

Truant [truh'Ant] *a.* träge, faul; *n.* Schulschwänzer *m*; play **-** die Schule schwänzen.

Truce [truhss] *n.* Waffenstillstand *m.*

Truck [trAk] *n.* offener Güterwagen (*rl.*), Lastwagen *m* (*aut.*), Schleppwagen *m*, Handwagen *m*; **-**load *n.* Wagenladung *f.*

Truck [trAk] *n.* Tauschhandel *m*; *vt.i.* Tauschhandel treiben, austauschen.

Truckle [trAkl] *vi.* sich unterwerfen, unterwürfig sein; **-** -**bed** *n.* Schiebebett *n.*

Truculence [trA'kju-lAnss] *n.* Rohheit *f*, Wildheit *f*; **-t** *a.* roh, grausam.

Trudge [trAdzh] *vi.* sich mühsam fortschleppen.

True [truh] *a.* wahr, wirklich, echt, redlich, treu, genau.

Truffle [trAfl] *n.* Trüffel *f.*

Truism [truh'ism] *n.* Gemeinplatz *m.*

Truly [truh'li] *ad.* wirklich, aufrichtig; Yours **-** Ihr ergebener, Ihre ergebene.

Trump [trAmp] *vt.* **-** up erdichten, hervorsuchen.

Trump [trAmp] *n.* Trumpf *m*; *vt.* abtrumpfen; **-** -**card** *n.* Trumpfkarte *f.*

Trumpery [trAm'pA-ri] *a.* wertlos, gering.

Trumpet [trAm'pit] *n.* Trompete *f*; *vt.* trompeten, ausposaunen; **-er** *n.* Trompeter *m*, Hornist *m.* [verstümmeln.

Truncate [trAng-keit'] *vt.*

Truncheon [trAn'schAn] *n.* Knüttel *m.* [(sich) wälzen.

Trundle [trAndl] *vt.i.* rollen,

Trunk [trAngk] *n.* Baumstamm *m*, Rumpf *m*, Kiste *f*, Reisekoffer *m*, Rüssel *m*; **-**cable *n.* Fernkabel *n*; **-**call *n.* Ferngespräch *n* (*ph.*); – -connection *n.* Fernanschluss *m*; – -exchange *n.* Fernamt *n*; – -line *n.* Fernleitung *f*; – -road *n.* Hauptlandstrasse *f.*

Trunnion [trAn'jAn] *n.* Zapfen *m*, Tragzapfen *m* (*tec.*), Schildzapfen *m*; – -bearing *n.* Pivot-, Schildzapfen-lager *n.*

Truss [trAss] *n.* Gebinde *n*, Bund *n*, Ballen *m* (*com.*), Bruchband *n*, Bauträger *m*; *vt.* schnüren, binden, einpacken; – -bridge *n.* Gitter-, Fachwerk-brücke *f.*

Trust [trAst] *n.* Vertrauen *n*, Zuversicht *f*, Ring *m*, Trust *m* (*com.*); *vt.* vertrauen, glauben, anvertrauen; *i.* vertrauen, sich verlassen, hoffen; – -company *n.* Treuhandgesellschaft *f*; – -funds *n.pl.* Mündel-, Stiftungsgelder *n.pl.*

Trustee [trA'stih'] *n.* Administrator *m*, Verwalter *m*, Vertrauensmann *m*, Treuhänder *m*; – -securities *n.pl.* mündelsichere Wertpapiere *n.pl.*; -ship *n.* Vormundschaft *f*, Treuhandverwaltung *f.*

Trustful [trAst'ful] *a.* -ly *ad.* vertrauend, vertrauensvoll; -ness *n.* Vertrauen *n*, das Vertrauensvolle.

Trustiness [trAst'i-ness] *n.* Treue *f*, Redlichkeit *f.*

Trusting [trA'sting] *a.* vertrauend, vertrauensselig, vertrauensvoll.

Trustworthiness [trAst'uArdhi-ness] *n.* Vertrauenswürdigkeit *f.*

Trustworthy [trAst'uArdhi] *a.* zuverlässig, vertrauenswürdig. [lich, zuverlässig.

Trusty [trA'sti] *a.* treu, redlich, zuverlässig.

Truth [truhth] *n.* Wahrheit *f*, Wahrhaftigkeit *f*, Wirklichkeit *f.*

Truthful [truhth'ful] *a.* -ly *ad.* wahrhaftig, wahr; -ness *n.* Wahrhaftigkeit *f.*

Try [trai] *vt.* probieren, versuchen, verhören (*law*); *i.* versuchen, einen Versuch machen; *n.* Versuch *m*, Probe *f*. Experiment *n*; – on anprobieren; – out ausprobieren.

Trying [trai'ing] *a.* ärgerlich, beschwerlich, kritisch; – on *n.* Anprobe *f.*

Tub [tAb] *n.* Kübel *m*, Zuber *m*, Tonne *f*, Fass *n*, Bütte *f*. Wanne *f* (*bath*).

Tuba [tjuh'bA] *n.* Basstuba *f.*

Tubby [tA'bi] *a.* tonnenförmig.

Tube [tjuhb] *n.* Röhre *f*, Rohr *n*, Schlauch *m*, Tube *f* (*paint, etc.*), Untergrundbahn *f* (*Underground*); inner- – *n.* Schlauch *m* (*aut.*); outer- – *n.* Decke *f* (*aut.*). [en *m*, Knolle *f.*

Tuber [tjuh'ber] *n.* Treibknollen *m*, Knolle *f.*

Tubercular [tju-bAr'kju-ler] *a.* tuberkulös, schwindsüchtig.

Tuberculosis [tju-bAr-kju-lou'ssiss] *n.* Tuberkulose *f*, Schwindsucht *f.*

Tuberculous [tju-bAr'kju-lAss] *a.* tuberkulös.

Tubing [tjuh'bing] *n.* Gummischlauch *m*, Röhrenmaterial *n.*

Tubular [tjuh'bju-ler] *a.* röhrenförmig, Röhren ... *n.* Rohr ...

Tuck [tAk] *n.* Falte *f*, Säumchen *n*; *vt.* fälteln, in Falten legen, einschlagen. [tag *m*.

Tuesday [tjuhs'di] *n.* Dienstag *m*.

Tuft [tAft] *n.* Büschel *m.*

Tug [tAg] *n.* Zug *m* (*pull*), Schlepper *m* (*boat*), Bugsierdampfer *m*; *vt.* ziehen (*pull*), schleppen, bugsieren (*tow*); – -boat *n.* Schlepper *m*; – -of-war *n.* Seilziehen *n.*

Tuition [tju-i'schAn] *n.* Unterricht *m.*

Tulip [tjuh'lip] *n.* Tulpe *f.*

Tulle [tjuhl] *n.* Tüll *m*, Tüllspitze *f.*

Tumble [tAmbl] *n.* Fall *m*, Sturz *m*; *vi.* fallen, stürzen.

Tumbler [tʌm'blər] n. Trinkglas n, Becher m.

Tumour [tjuh'mər] n. Geschwulst f.

Tumult [tjuh'mʌlt] n. Getümmel n, Lärm m, Getöse n, Aufruhr m, Tumult m.

Tumultuous [tju-mʌl'tjuəss] a. stürmisch, ungestüm, lärmend.

Tun [tʌn] n. Tonne f, Fass n.

Tune [tjuhn] n. Weise f, Melodie f, Stimmung f (instrument); vt. stimmen; — in einstellen, abstimmen (rad.); — r n. Klavierstimmer m; -ful a. melodisch, wohlklingend.

Tungsten [tʌng'stən] n. Wolfram m.

Tunic [tjuh'nik] n. Bluse f, Kittel m, Waffenrock m (mil.). Tuch-, Soldaten-rock m (mil.).

Tuning [tjuh'ning] n. Stimmen n, Einstellen n; — coil n. Abstimmspule f (rad.); — condenser n. Abstimmkondensator m; — dial n. Abstimmskala f; — fork n. Stimmgabel f; — in n. Abstimmung f; — knob n. Abstimmknopf m; — mechanism n. Abstimmvorrichtung f.

Tunnel [tʌ'nil] n. Tunnel m, Minenstollen m (mine); vt. durchtunneln, durchbohren; wind- — n. Windkanal m (av.); -ling n. Tunnelbau m, Tunnelbohren n.

Tunny [tʌ'ni] n. Thunfisch m.

Tup [tʌp] n. Widder m.

Turban [tər'bən] n. Turban m.

[ruhig.

Turbid [tər'bid] a. trübe, un-

Turbine [tər'bain] n. Turbine f, Wasser-, Kreisel-rad n; exhaust gas- — n. Abgasturbine f; geared- — n. Getriebeturbine f; steam- — n. Dampfturbine f; — steamer n. Turbinendampfer m.

Turbot [tər'bʌt] n. Steinbutt m.

Turbulence [tər'bju-lənss]

Tur. Ungestüm n, Unruhe f, Verwirrung f.

Turbulent [tər'bju-lənt] a. ungestüm, unruhig, aufrührerisch.

Tureen [tju-rihn'] n. Terrine f.

Turf [tərf] n. Rasen m, Torf m, Grasscholle f, Rennbahn f (racing), Rennsport m; vt. mit Rasen belegen.

Turgid [tər'dzhid] a. geschwollen, aufgeblasen.

Turkey [tər'ki] n. Truthahn m, Puter m; — red n. Türkischrot n.

Turkish [tər'kisch] a. — bath n. Schweissbad n; — delight n. Lokum n; — towel n. Frottiertuch n; [ruhr m.

Turmoil [tər'meul] n. Auf-

Turn [tərn] n. Umdrehung f, Wendung f, Richtung f, Schwenkung f, Reihe f; vt. drehen, umdrehen, wenden, verwandeln (change); i. sich drehen, sich wenden, werden (become); good — n. Gefälligkeit f, Dienst m; sharp — scharfe Biegung, kurze Kehrtwendung (av.).

Turncoat [tərn'kout] n. der Abtrünnige. [er m.

Turner [tər'nər] n. Drechs-

Turning [tər'ning] n. Drehen n, Wenden n, Krümmung f (corner); — movement n. Umgehung f (mil.); — point n. Wendepunkt m; — tool n. Drehstahl m.

Turnip [tər'nip] n. Rübe f.

Turn-out [tərn-out²] n. Aufmachung f, Aufzug m.

Turnover [tərn'ou-wer] n. Umsatz m.

Turnstile [tərn'stail] n. Drehkreuz n.

Turn-table [tərn'teibl] n. Drehscheibe f.

Turn-up [tərn'ʌp] a. aufwärts gewendet; n. Aufruhr m.

Turpentine [tər'pʌn-tain] n. Terpentin n. [Verworfenheit f.

Turpitude [tər'pi-tjuhd] n.

Turquoise [tA'keus] n. Türkis m.

Turret [tA'rit] n. Turm m, Türmchen n; **armoured-- ** n. Panzerturm m; **disappearing-- ** n. Verschwindeturm m (mil.); **revolving-- ** n. Drehturm m; **single-- ** n. Einzellafette f (nav.).

Turtle [tArtl] n. Meerschildkröte f; **turn-- ** kentern (nav.); **-soup** n. Schildkrötensuppe f.

Turtle-dove [tArtl'dAw] n. Turteltaube f.

Tusk [tAsk] n. Hauzahn m, Stosszahn m.

Tussle [tAssl] n. Balgerei f, Kampf m; **-- ** lehrer m.

Tutor [tjuh'ter] n. Privatlehrer m.

Twaddle [tuodl] n. albernes Geschwätz, Unsinn m.

Twang [tueng] n. Näseln n.

Tweak [tuihk] vt. zwicken.

Tweed [tuihd] n. Tweed m; **-s** pl. Tweedanzug m.

Tweezers [tuih'sers] n.pl. Kneifzange f, Haarzange f, Pinzette f.

Twelfth [tuelfth] a. zwölft; n. der, die, das Zwölfte, Zwölftel n.

Twelve [tuelw] num. zwölf; **-month** n. Jahresfrist f.

Twenty [tuen'ti] num. zwanzig.

Twice [tuaiss] ad. zweimal.

Twig [tuig] n. Zweig m.

Twilight [tuai'lait] n. Zwielicht n, Dämmerung f.

Twill [tuil] n. Köper m; vt. köpern.

Twin [tuin] n. Zwilling m; a. doppelt, Zwillings ...; **-- screw steamer** n. Zwillingsdampfer m, Doppelschraubendampfer m; **-- turret** n. Doppelturm m (nav.); **-tyres** n.pl. Zwillingsreifen m.pl., Doppelbereifung f.

Twine [tuain] n. Bindfaden m, Zwirn m, Schnur f; vt. zusammendrehen, zwirnen.

Twinge [tuindzh] n. Stich m, stechender Schmerz.

Twinkle [tuinkl] vi. blinzeln, glitzern, flimmern; n. Flimmern n, Zwinkern n.

Twirl [tuArl] n. Wirbel m, Umdrehung f; vt. herumdrehen, zwirbeln, quirlen.

Twist [tuist] n. Drehen n, Verflechten n, Garn n, Twist m, Spinntabak m; vt. drehen, verflechten, zwirnen, flechten, wickeln, verwinden.

Twitch [tuitsch] vt.i. zucken, zupfen; n. Ruck m, Zucken n.

Twitter [tui'ter] vi. zwitschern.

Two [tuh] num. zwei; **-bladed** a. zweiklingig; **-- decker** a. Zweidecker m, Doppeldeckomnibus m; **-edged** a. zweischneidig; [fach, zwiefach.

Twofold [tuh'fould] a. zwei-

Twopence [tA'pAnss] n.pl. zwei Pence, zwei Groschen.

Twopenny [tA'pA-ni] a. zwei Pence wert, minderwertig.

Two ...; -- phase a. zweiphasig (el.); **-piece** a. zweiteilig; **-ply** a. zweidrähtig, zweischäftig; **-seater** n. Zweisitzer m (aut.); **-speed gear** n. doppelte Übersetzung (aut. etc.); **-valved** a. zweiklappig; **-way adapter** n. Doppelstecker m (el.); **-year old** a. zweijährig.

Type [taip] n. Typus m, Vorbild n, Urbild n, Type f (printing), Baumuster n (plane); vt. tippen, mit der Maschine schreiben; **-founding** n. Schriftguss m; **-script** n. Maschinenschrift f; **-setter** n. Schriftsetzer m.

Typewrite [taip'rait] vt. mit der Schreibmaschine schreiben; **-r** n. Schreibmaschine f; **-ribbon** n. Schreibmaschinenfarbband n.

Typhoid [tai'feud] n. Unterleibstyphus m. [fum m.

Typhoon [tai'fuhn] n. Taifun m.

Typhus [tai'fAss] n. Typhus m.

Typical [ti'pikl] *a*, **-iy** *ad*. typisch, bezeichnend.

Typify [ti'pi-fai] *vt*. typisch sein für, vorbildlich darstellen.

Typist [tai'pist] *n*. Maschinenschreiber *m*, Maschinenschreiberin *f*, Tippfräulein *n*.

Typographical [tai-pA-græ'fikl] *a*. typographisch, drucktechnisch.

Typography [tai-po'grA-fi] *n*. Buchdruckerkunst *f*.

Tyrannical [ti-ræ'nikl] Tyrannous [ti'rA-nAss] *a*. tyrannisch.

Tyranny [ti'rA-ni] *n*. Tyrannei *f*.

Tyrant [tai'rAnt] *n*. Tyrann *m*.

Tyre [tai'er] *n*. Radreifen *m*; pneumatic – *n*. Luftreifen *m*; steel – *n*. Spurkranz *m* (*rl*.).

Tyro [tai'rou] *n*. Neuling *m*, Anfänger *m*.

U

Ubiquitous [ju-bi'kui-tAss] *a*. überall befindlich.

Ubiquity [ju-bi'kui-ti] *n*. Allgegenwart *f*.

U-boat [juh'bout] *n*. U-boot *n*, Unterseeboot *n*.

Udder [A'der] *n*. Euter *m*.

Ugliness [A'gli-ness] *m*. Hässlichkeit *f*.   [artig, übel.

Ugly [A'gli] *a*. hässlich, bösUkele [tim-kA-lih'li] *n*. hawaiische Gitarre.

Ulcer [Al'sser] *n*. Geschwür *n*.

Ulcerate [Al'ssA-reit] *vi*. schwären.

Ulceration [Al-ssA-rei'schAn] *n*. Schwären *n*, Geschwür *n*.

Ullage [Al'idzh] *n*. Schwund *m*, durch Lecken.   [zier m.

Ulster [Al'ster] *n*. Überzieh-

Ulterior [Al-tih'rjer] *a*. weiter, jenseitig; – motive *n*. Hintergedanke *m*.   [letzt.

Ultimate [Al'ti-mit] *a*. aller-

Ultimately [Al'ti-mit-li] *ad*. zuletzt.

Ultimatum [Al-ti-mei'tAm] *n*. Ultimatum *n*, letztmalige Aufforderung.

Ultimo [Al'ti-mou] *ad*. letzten Monats (*com*.).

Ultramarine [Al-trA-mA-rihn'] *a*. ultramarin.

Ultra-red [Al-trA-red'] *a*. ultrarot.

Ultra-violet [Al-trA-wai'A-lit] *a*. ultraviolett.

Umber [Am'ber] *n*. Umbra *f*.

Umbilical [Am-bi'likl] *a*. Nabel . . . .

Umbrage [am'bridzh] *n*. Anstoss *m*, Ärger *m*, Argwohn *m*.

Umbrella [Am-bre'lA] *n*. Regenschirm *m*; – stand *n*. Schirmständer *m*.

Umpire [Am'pai-er] *n*. Schiedsrichter *m*, der Unparteiische.   [gezählt, zahllos.

Umpteen [Amp-tihn'] *a*. un-

Unabashed [An-A-bæscht'] *a*. schamlos, uneingeschüchtert.

Unabated [An-A-bei-tid] *a*. unvermindert.

Unabbreviated [An-A-brih'wjei-tid] *a*, Unabridged [An-A-bridzhd'] *a*. unverkürzt.

Unable [An-eibl'] *a*. unfähig, nicht imstande.

Unaccented [An-æx-en'tid] *a*. unbetont.

Unaccompanied [An-A-kAm'pA-nid] *a*. unbegleitet.

Unaccountable [An-A-kaun'tAbl] *a*. unerklärlich, sonderbar.

Unaccustomed [An-A-kA'stAmd] *a*. ungewohnt, ungewöhnlich.

Unacknowledged [An-Ak-no'lidzhd] *a*. nicht anerkannt, unbestätigt (*com*.).

Unacquainted [An-Ak-wein'tid] *a*. unbekannt.

Unadorned [An-A-dOrnd'] *a*. ungeschmuckt.

Unadulterated [An-A-dAl'tA-rei-tid] *a*. rein, unverfälscht.

Unaffected [An-A-fek'tid] *a.*
ungerührt, nicht betroffen,
nicht verwickelt.

Unaided [An-ei'did] *a.* ohne
Hilfe, mit eigner Kraft.

Unalloyed [An-A-leud] *a.* unvermischt.

Unalterable [An-Ol'tA-rAbl]
a. unveränderlich. [verändert.

Unaltered [An-Ol'terd] *a.* un-

Unanimity [ju-nA-ni'mi-ti] *n.*
Einmütigkeit *f.*

Unanimous [ju-næ'ni-mAss]
a., **-ly** *ad.* einstimmig, einmütig.

Unanswerable [An-ahn'ssA-
rAbl] *a.* unwiderlegbar.

Unapproachable [An-A-
prow'tschAbl] *a.* unnahbar.

Unappropriated [An-A-
prow'prjei-tid] *a.* nicht zuge-
wiesen, zurückverlegt (*com.*).

Unarmed [An-Ahrmd'] *a.* unbewaffnet. [*a.* ohne Scham.

Unashamed [An-A-scheimd']

Unassailable [An-A-ssei'lAbl]
a. unangreifbar.

Unassisted [An-A-ssi'stid] *a.*
ohne Hilfe, ununterstützt.

Unassuming [An-A-ssjuh'-
ming] *a.* anspruchslos, schlicht,
bescheiden.

Unattached [An-A-tætscht']
a. freistehend.

Unattainable [An-A-tei'nAbl]
a. unerreichbar.

Unattempted [An-A-temp'-
tid] *a.* unversucht.

Unattended [An-A-ten'did] *a.*
unbegleitet, unbeaufsichtigt.

Unattractive [An-A-træk'tiw]
a. reizlos, hässlich.

Unauthorized [An-O'thA-
raisd] *a.* unbefugt.

Unavailing [An-A-wei'ling] *n.*
vergeblich.

Unavoidable [An-A-weu'-
dAbl] *a.* unvermeidlich.

Unaware [An-A-ueh'er] *a.* unbewusst, nicht gewahr.

Unawares [An-A-ueh'ers] *ad.*
unversehens.

Unbalanced [An-bæ'lAnst] *a.*
unausgeglichen.

Unbar [An-bahr'] *vt.* aufriegeln.

Unbearabl'e [An-beh'rAbl] *a.*,
-ly *ad.* unerträglich.

Unbecoming [An-bi-kA'-
ming] *a.* unkleidsam, unpassend, ungeziemend.

Unbelief [An-bi-lihf'] *n.* Unglaube *m.* Zweifel *m.*

Unbelievabl'e [An-bi-lih'-
wAbl] *a.*, **-ly** *ad.* unglaublich.

Unbeliever [An-bi-lih'wer] *n.*
der Ungläubige.

Unbelieving [An-bi-lih'wing]
a. ungläubig.

Unbend [An-bend'] *vt.* entspannen, nachlassen; *i.* sich
herablassen, freundlich werd-
en. [unbeugsam.

Unbending [An-ben'ding] *a.*

Unbiassed [An-bai'Ast] *a.* unparteiisch, vorurteilslos.

Unbind [An-baind'] *vt.* losbinden.

Unbleached [An-blihtscht'] *a.*
ungebleicht. [*a.* unbefleckt.

Unblemished [An-ble'mischt]

Unblushing [An-blA'sching]
a. schamlos, frech.

Unbolt [An-boult'] *vt.* aufriegeln. [boren.

Unborn [An-bOrn'] *a.* unge-

Unbound [An-baund'] *a.* ungebunden, geheftet.

Unbounded [An-baun'did] *a.*
unbeschränkt, grenzenlos.

Unbridled [An-brai'dAld] *a.*
zügellos.

Unbroken [An-broukn'] *a.* un-
gebrochen, ununterbrochen.

Unbuckle [An-bAkl'] *vt.* los-
schnallen. [entlasten.

Unburden [An-bArdn'] *vt.*

Unburied [An-be'rid] *a.* un-
beerdigt. [verbrannt.

Unburnt [An-bArnt'] *a.* un-

Unbusinesslike [An-bis'ness-
laik] *a.* unkaufmännisch.

Unbutton [An-bAtn'] *vt.* los-
knöpfen.

Uncalled-for [An-kOld'fOr] a. unberufen.

Uncann'y [An-kæ'ni] a., -ily ad. unheimlich.

Uncancelled [An-kæn'ssAld] a. nicht durchstrichen.

Uncared-for [An-kehrd'fOr] a. vernachlässigt.

Unceasing [An-ssih'ssing] a., -ly ad. unaufhörlich.

Unceremonious [An-sse-ri-mou'nj Ass] a., -ly ad. ungezwungen. [sicher, ungewiss.

Uncertain [An-ssAr'tin] a. un-

Uncertainty [An-ssAr'tAn-ti] n. Ungewissheit f.

Uncertified [An-ssAr'ti-faid] a. nicht attestiert. [fesseln.

Unchain [An-tschein'] vt. ent-

Unchallenged [An-tschæ'lAndzhd] a. unbeanstandet.

Unchangeable [An-tsch-eindzh'Abl] a. unveränderlich.

Unchanged [An-tscheindzhd'] a. unverändert.

Unchanging [An-tschein'-dzhing] a. nicht wechselnd.

Uncharitabl'e [An-tschæ'ri-tAbl] a., -ly ad. unbarmherzig.

Uncharted [An-tschahr'tid] a. nicht verzeichnet.

Unchartered [An-tschahr'-terd] a. nicht verfrachtet.

Unchecked [An-tschekt'] a. ungehindert. [haken.

Unclasp [An-klahsp'] vt. los-

Uncivil [An-ssi'wil] a. unhöflich.

Unclaimed [An-kleimd'] a. nicht beansprucht, herrenlos.

Uncle [Ang'kl] n. Onkel m.

Unclean [An-klihn'] a. unrein.

Unclothe [An-kloudh'] vt. entkleiden.

Uncoil [An-keul'] vt.r. aufwinden, (sich) abwickeln.

Uncomfortabl'e [An-kAm'fer-tAbl] a., -ly ad. unbequem, ungemütlich.

Uncommon [An-ko'mAn] a., -ly ad. ungewöhnlich, ungemein.

Uncommunicative [An-kA-mjuh'ni-kA-tiw] a. verschlossen. [plei'ning] a. klaglos.

Uncomplaining [An-kAm-

Uncompromising [An-kom'-prA-mai-sing] a. unbeugsam, kompromisslos.

Unconcealed [An-kAn-sihld'] a. unverhohlen.

Unconcern [An-kAn-ssArn'] n. Gleichgültigkeit f.

Unconcerned [An-kAn-ssArnd'] a., -ly ad. gleichgültig.

Unconditional [An-kAn-di'schA-nAl] a., -ly ad. unbedingt; – surrender bedingungslose Kapitulation.

Unconfirmed [An-kAn-fArmd'] a. unbestätigt.

Uncongenial [An-kAn-dzhih'njAl] a. nicht zusagend, unsympathisch.

Unconnected [An-kA-nek'tid] a. unzusammenhängend, lose.

Unconquerable [An-kong'-kA-rAbl] a. unbesiegbar, unbezwinglich. [a. unbesiegt.

Unconquered [An-kong'kerd]

Unconscionable [An-kon'-schA-nAbl] a. ungerecht, übertrieben, unverantwortlich.

Unconscious [An-kon'schAss] a. unbewusst, ohnmächtig.

Unconsciously [An-kon'-schAss-li] ad. unwissentlich, unbewusst.

Unconsciousness [An-kon'-schAss-ness] n. Ohnmacht f, Bewusstlosigkeit f.

Unconsolidated [An-kAn-so'-li-dei-tid] a. unfundiert (com.).

Unconstitutional [An-kon-sti-tjuh'schA-nAl] a., -ly ad. verfassungswidrig.

Unconstrained [An-kAn-streind'] a. ungezwungen.

Uncontaminated [An-kAn-tæ'mi-nei-tid] a. nicht angesteckt.

Uncontested [An-kAn-te'stid] a. unbestritten, ohne Wahlkampf.

Uncontrollable [An-kAn-trou'lAbl] a. unbeherrschbar, unbändig.

Unconventional [An-kAn-wen'schA-nAl] a. nicht förmlich, zwanglos.

Unconvertible [An-kAn-wAr'tibl] a. unkonvertierbar (com.).

Unconvinced [An-kAn-winst'] a. unüberzeugt.

Unconvincing [An-kAn-win'ssing] a. nicht überzeugend, nicht triftig. [gekocht.

Uncooked [An-kukt'] a. un-

Uncord [An-kOrd'] vt. aufbinden, aufschnüren.

Uncork [An-kOrk'] vt. entkorken.

Uncorrected [An-kA-rek'tid] a. unverbessert.

Uncorrupted [An-kA-rAp'tid] a. unverdorben.

Uncounted [An-kaun'tid] a. ungezählt.

Uncouple [An-kApl'] vt. abhängen, loskuppeln (rl.).

Uncouth [An-kuhth'] a. ungeschlacht.

Uncover [An-kA'wer] vt. aufdecken, entblössen, freilegen.

Uncovered [An-kA'werd] a. unbedeckt, ungedeckt (com.).

Uncritical [An-kri'tikl] a. kritiklos, unkritisch.

Uncrossed [An-krost'] a. nicht durchkreuzt.

Unction [Angk'schAn] n. Salbung f, Olung f.

Unctuous [Angk'tju-Ass] a. salbungsvoll.

Uncultivated [An-kAl'ti-wei-tid] a. unangebaut, ungebildet, unkultiviert.

Uncured [An-kjuhrd'] a. ungesalzen. [kräuseln.

Uncurl [An-kArl'] vt. ent-

Uncurtailed [An-kAr-teild'] a. unverkürzt, ungeschmälert.

Uncut [An-kAt'] a. ungeschnitten, unaufgeschnitten (book).

Undamaged [An-dæ'midzhd] a. unversehrt, unbeschädigt.

Undated [An-dei'tid] a. ohne Datum. [unerschrocken.

Undaunted [An-dO'tid] a.

Undeceive [An-di-ssihw'] vt. enttäuschen.

Undecided [An-di-ssai'did] a. unentschlossen.

Undefended [An-di-fen'did] a. unverteidigt. [befleckt.

Undefiled [An-di-faild'] a. un-

Undefinable [An-di-fai'nAbl] a. unbestimmbar.

Undefined [An-di-faind'] a. unbestimmt.

Undeliverable [An-di-li'wA-rAbl] a. unbestellbar.

Undelivered [An-di-li'werd] a. nicht geliefert, unbestellt (post).

Undemonstrative [An-di-mon'strA-tiw] a. verschlossen.

Undeniable [An-di-nai'Abl] a. -ly ad. unleugbar.

Under [An'der] ad. unten; pr. unter. [unterbieten.

Underbid [An-der-bid'] vt.

Undercarriage [An'der-kæ-ridzh] n. Unterlafette f (mil.). Fahrgestell n (av.); retractable – n. Verschwindefahrgestell n.

Undercharge [An-der-tschahrdzh'] vt. zu wenig berechnen.

Underclothing [An'der-klou-dhing] n. Unterkleidung f.

Undercurrent [An'der-kA-rAnt] n. Unterströmung f.

Undercut [An'der-kAt] vt. unterbieten.

Underdevelop [An-der-di-we'lAp] vt. unterentwickeln.

Underdone [An-der-dAn'] a. ungar.

Underestimate [An-der-e'sti-mit] n. Unterschätzung f.

Underestimate [An-der-e'sti-meit] vt. unterschätzen.

Underfeeding [An-der-fih'ding] n. Unterernährung f.

Undergo [An-der-gou'] vt. erleiden.

Undergraduate [An-der-grædju-it] *n.* Student *m*, Student-in *f*.

Underground [An'der-graund] *a.* unterirdisch; *n.* Untergrundbahn *f*; ~ -movement *n.* Widerstandsbewegung *f*; ~ -organization *n.* Geheimbund *m*; ~ -railway *n.* Untergrundbahn *f*.

Undergrowth [An'der-grouth] *n.* Unterholz *n*.

Underhand [An-der-hænd'] *a.* versteckt, unehrlich, unredlich.

Underlet [An-der-let'] *vt.* untervermieten.

Underlie [An-der-lai'] *vt.* zu Grunde liegen.

Underline [An-der-lain'] *vt.* unterstreichen.

Underlinen [An'der-li-nin] *n.* Leibwäsche *f*.

Underling [An'der-ling] *n.* der Untergeordnete.

Undermanned [An-der-mænd'] *a.* ungenügend bemannt.

Undermentioned [An-der-men'schAnd] *a.* unten erwähnt.

Undermine [An-der-main'] *vt.* unterminieren, untergraben.

Undermost [An'der-moust] *a.* unterst.

Underneath [An-der-nihth'] *ad.* unten; *pr.* unter, unterhalb.

Undernourished [An-der-nA'rischt] *a.* unterernährt.

Underpay [An-der-pei⁴] *vt.* schlecht bezahlen.

Underpin [An-der-pin'] *vt.* untermauern.

Underproduction [An'der-prA-dAk'schAn] *n.* Unterproduktion *f*.

Under-proof [An-der-pruhf'] *a.* unter Normalstärke.

Underrate [An-der-reit'] *vt.* unterschätzen. [nicht reif.

Underripe [An-der-raip'] *a.*

Underscore [An-der-skOr'] *vt.* unterstreichen.

Under-secretary [An'der-

sek'ri-tri] *n.* Unterstaatssekretär *m*.

Undersell [An-der-ssel'] *vt.* unterbieten, verschleudern.

Undersigned [An-der-ssaind'] *n.* der Unterzeichnete.

Undersized [An-der-ssaisd'] *a.* zu klein, untersetzt.

Underskirt [An'der-skArt] *n.* Unterrock *m*.

Understaffed [An-der-stahft'] *a.* mit zu wenig Personal versehen.

Understand [An-der-stænd'] *vt.* verstehen, begreifen, erfahren.

Understandable [An-der-stæn'dAbl] *a.* begreiflich, verständlich.

Understanding [An-der-stæn'ding] *n.* Verstand *m*, Verständnis *n*, Einvernehmen *n*.

Understate [An-der-steit'] *vt.* zu gering ansetzen.

Understatement [An-der-steit'mAnt] *n.* Unterschätzung *f*.

Understocked [An-der-stokt'] *a.* ungenügend versorgt.

Understudy [An'der-stA-di] *n.* Schauspieler *m*, in zweiter Besetzung spielend.

Undertake [An-der-teik'] *vt.* unternehmen, übernehmen, *i.* sich verpflichten.

Undertaker [An'der-tei-ker] *n.* Leichenbestatter *m*, Unternehmer *m*.

Undertaking [An-der-tei-king] *n.* Unternehmen *n*, Unternehmung *f*, Verpflichtung *f*.

Undertone [An'der-toun] *n.* Grundstimmung *f*, gedämpfter Ton.

Undervaluation [An-der-wæ-lju-ei'schAn] *n.* Unterschätzung *f*.

Undervalue [An-der-wæ'lju] *vt.* zu niedrig einschätzen.

Underwear [An'der-ueh-er] *n.* Unterkleidung *f*, Unterkleider *n.pl.*

Underweight [An'der-ueit] n. Untergewicht n.

Underworld [An'der-uOrld] n. Unterwelt f.

Underwrite [An-der-rait'] vt. versichern, unterschreiben.

Underwriter [An'der-rai'ter] n. Versicherer m.

Undeserved [An-di's∆rwd'] a. unverdient.

Undeserving [An-di-s∆r'wing] a. verdienstlos.

Undesigned [An-di-saind'] a. unbeabsichtigt.

Undesirable [An-di-sai'r∆bl] a. unerwünscht.

Undetermined [An-di-t∆r'mind] a. unbestimmt.

Undeterred [an-di-t∆rd'] a. nicht abgeschreckt.

Undeveloped [An-di-we'l∆pt] a. unentwickelt (photo, etc.), nicht baureif, unerschlossen (land).

Undies [An'dis] n.pl. Unterkleider n.pl, Unterwäsche f.

Undignified [An-dig'ni-faid] a. ohne Würde.

Undiluted [An-dai-ljuh'tid] a. unverdünnt.

Undiminished [An-di-mi'nischt] a. unvermindert.

Undimmed [An-dimd'] a. unverdunkelt.

Undiscerning [An-di-s∆r'ning] a. einsichtslos.

Undischarged [An-diss-tschahrdzhd'] a. unerledigt.

Undisciplined [An-di'ssi-plind] a. zuchtlos.

Undisclosed [An-di-sklousd'] a. nicht mitgeteilt.

Undisguised [An-diss-gaisd'] a. unverhüllt, unverhohlen.

Undismayed [An-diss-meid'] a. unerschrocken.

Undisposed [An-di-spousd'] a. nicht geneigt.

Undisputed [An-di-spjuh'tid] a. unbestritten.

Undistributed [An-di-stri'bju-tid] a. unverteilt.

Undisturbed [An-di-st∆rbd'] a. ungestört. [ungeteilt.]

Undivided [An-di-wai'did] a.

Undo [An-duh'] vt. aufmachen, auflösen (knot), rückgängig machen (cancel).

Undoing [An-duh'ing] n. Verderben n. [en (nav.).]

Undock [An-dok'] vi. ausdock-

Undone [An-dAn'] a. ungetan.

Undoubted [An-dau'tid] a. unangezweifelt, unbestritten.

Undoubtedly [An-dau'tid-li] a. unstreitig, ohne Zweifel.

Undreamt-of [An-dremt'ow] a. ungeträumt.

Undress [An-dress'] vt. entkleiden; i.r. sich entkleiden; – -uniform n. Halbuniform f.

Undried [An-draid'] a. ungetrocknet. [a. untrinkbar.]

Undrinkable [An-dringk'∆bl]

Undue [An-djuh'] a. -ly ad. ungebührend, unangemessen.

Undulating [An'dju-lei-ting] a. wellenförmig.

Undulation [An-dju-lei'schAn] n. Wellenbewegung f.

Undutiful [An-djuh'ti-ful] a. pflichtvergessen.

Undying [An-dai'ing] a. unsterblich. [verdient.]

Unearned [An-∆rned'] a. un-

Unearth [An-∆rth'] vt. ausgraben, ans Licht bringen, aufstöbern. [heimlich.]

Unearthly [An-∆rth'li] a. un-

Uneasiness [An-ih'si-ness] n. Ängstlichkeit f, Unbehagen n.

Uneasy [An-ih'si] a. -ly ad. ängstlich, unbequem, unbehaglich. [essbar.]

Uneatable [An-ih't∆bl] a. un-

Uneducated [An-e'dju-kei-tid] a. ungebildet.

Unemotional [An-i-mou'schA-nAl] a. leidenschaftslos, kalt. [Abl] a. arbeitsunfähig.

Unemployable [An-im-pleu'-

Unemployed [An-im-pleud'] a. arbeitslos, unbeschäftigt; n. pl. die Arbeitslosen m.pl.

Unemployment [An-im-pleu'-mAnt] n. Arbeitslosigkeit f; - benefit, - relief n. Arbeitslosenunterstützung f.

Unencumbered [An-in-kAm'-berd] a. unbelastet.

Unending [An-en'ding] a. unaufhörlich, ewig, endlos.

Unendurable [An-in-djuh'-rAbl] a. unerträglich.

Unenlightened [An-in-lai'-tAnd] a. unaufgeklärt.

Unenterprising [An-en'ter-prai-sing] a. nicht unternehmend.

Unenviable [An-en'wjAbl] a. nicht beneidenswert, unerwünscht.

Unequal [An-ih'kuAl] a, -ly ad. ungleich, ungleichmässig, unfähig.

Unequalled [An-ih'kuAld] a. unvergleichlich, unerreicht.

Unequivocal [An-i-kui'wA-kAl] a, -ly ad. unzweideutig.

Unerring [An-A'ring] a. unfehlbar. [a. unwesentlich.

Unessential [An-i-ssen'schAl]

Uneven [An-ihwn'] a. uneben, ungerade (number).

Unevenness [An-ihwn'ness] n. Unebenheit f. [ereignisloss.

Uneventful [An-i-went'ful] a.

Unexampled [An-ig-sahm-pld'] a. beispiellos.

Unexceptional [An-ik-ssep'-schA-nAl] a. untadelhaft.

Unexpected [An-ik-spek'tid] a. unerwartet.

Unexpired [An-ik-spai'erd] a. nicht abgelaufen.

Unexploded [An-ik-splou'-did] a. blind; - shell n. Blindgänger m. [a. unerforscht.

Unexplored [An-ik-splOrd']

Unexposed [An-ik-spousd'] a. nicht exponiert.

Unexpressed [An-ik-sprest'] a. unausgedrückt. [verwirklich.

Unfading [An-fei'ding] a. unfailing

Unfailing [An-fei'ling] a. unfehlbar, nie versagend.

Unfair [An-feh'er] a, -ly ad. unbillig, unehrlich.

Unfaithful [An-feith'ful] a. treulos, untreu.

Unfaithfulness [An-feith'fulness] n. Untreue f.

Unfamiliar [An-fA-mil'jer] a. unbekannt.

Unfashionable [An-fæ'schA-nAbl] a. unmodern.

Unfasten [An-fahssn'] vt. losbinden, aufmachen.

Unfathomable [An-fæ'dhA-mAbl] a. unergründlich.

Unfavourable [An-fei'wA-rAbl] a, -ly ad. ungünstig.

Unfeeling [An-fih'ling] a. gefühllos.

Unfeigned [An-feind'] a, -ly ad. unverstellt.

Unfermented [An-fAr-men'-tid] a. ungegoren, alkoholfrei.

Unfettered [An-fe'terd] a. ungefesselt, frei.

Unfinished [An-fi'nischt] a. unvollendet.

Unfit [An-fit'] a. untauglich.

Unfitness [An-fit'ness] n. Untauglichkeit f. [passend.

Unfitting [An-fi'ting] a. unfix

Unfix [An-fix'] vt. abnehmen, losmachen. [unermüdlich.

Unflagging [An-flæ'ging] a.

Unflattering [An-flæ'tA-ring] a. ungeschminkt.

Unfledged [An-fledzhd'] a. ungefiedert.

Unflinching [An-flin'sching] a. unentwegt.

Unfold [An-fould'] vt. entfalten, auseinanderfalten.

Unforeseen [An-fOr-ssihn'] a. unvorhergesehen.

Unforgettable [An-fOr-ge'-tAbl] a. unvergesslich.

Unforgivable [An-fOr-gi'-wAbl] a. unverzeihlich.

Unformed [An-fOrmd'] a. ungeformt, unausgebildet.

Unfortunate [An-fOr'tschA-nit] a. unglücklich, bedauerlich.

Unfortunately [An-fOr'tschA-nit-li] *ad.* leider.

Unfounded [An-faun'did] *a.* unbegründet.

Unfrequented [An-fri-kuen'tid] *a.* unbesucht.

Unfriendly [An-frend'li] *a.* unfreundlich.   [unfruchtbar.

Unfruitful [An-fruht'ful] *a.*

Unfulfilled [An-ful-fild'] *a.* unerfüllt.

Unfurl [An-fArl'] *vt.* entfalten.

Unfurnished [An-fAr'nischt] *a.* unmöbliert.

Ungainly [An-gein'li] *a.* linkisch.   [ritterlich.

Ungallant [An-gæ'lAnt] *a.* un-

Ungarbled [An-gahrbld'] *a.* unverstümmelt.

Ungenerous [An-dzhen'rAss] *a.* unedel.

Ungentlemanly [An-dzhentl'-mAn-li] *a.* unerzogen, ungebildet.

Unget-at-able [An-get-æ'tAbl] *a.* unerreichbar, unzugänglich.   [los.

Ungodly [An-god'li] *a.* gott-

Ungovernable [An-gA'wer-nAbl] *a.* zügellos, wild.

Ungracious [An-grei'schAss] *a.* unfreundlich, taktlos.

Ungrammatical [An-grA-mæ'tikl] *a.* sprachwidrig.

Ungrateful [An-greit'ful] *a.* undankbar.

Ungratified [An-græ'ti-faid] *a.* unbefriedigt.

Ungrudging [An-grA'dzhing] *a.* bereitwillig.   [unbewacht.

Unguarded [An-gahr'did] *a.*

Unhampered [An-hæm'perd] *a.* ungehindert.

Unhappiness [An-hæ'pi-ness] *n.* Unglück *n.*

Unhappy [An-hæ'pi] *a.*, **-ily** *ad.* unglücklich(erweise).

Unharmed [An-hAhrmd'] *a.* unbeschädigt, unversehrt.

Unharness [An-hahr'ness] *vt.* ausspannen.   [gesund.

Unhealthy [An-hel'thi] *a.* un-

Unheard-of [An-hArd'ow] *a.* unerhört.

Unheeded [An-hih'did] *a.* unbeachtet.   [unachtsam.

Unheeding [An-hih'ding] *a.*

Unhesitating [An-he'si-tei-ting] *a.*, **-ly** *ad.* nicht zögernd, ohne Zaudern, unbedenklich.

Unhewn [An-hjuhn'] *a.* unbehauen.   [unbehindert.

Unhindered [An-hin'derd] *a.*

Unhinge [An-hindzh'] *vt.* aus den Angeln heben.   [haken.

Unhitch [An-hitsch'] *vt.* los-

Unholy [An-hou'li] *a.* gottlos, schrecklich.

Unhonoured [An-o'nerd] *a.* ungeehrt, unbezahlt, nicht eingelöst (*com.*).

Unhook [An-huk'] *vt.* loshaken, aufhaken.   [letzt.

Unhurt [An-hArt] *a.* unver-

Unicorn [juh'ni-kOrn] *n.* Einhorn *n.*

Unification [juh-ni-fi-kei'schAn] *n.* Vereinheitlichung *f.*

Uniform [juh'ni-fOrm] *a.*, **-ly** *ad.* einförmig, gleich. — *n.* Uniform *f.*

Uniformity [juh-ni-fOr'mi-ti] *n.* Einförmigkeit *f.*

Unify [juh'ni-fai] *vt.* vereinheitlichen.   [*a.* einseitig.

Unilateral [juh-ni-læ'tA-rAl] *a.*

Unimaginable [An-i-mæ'dzhi-nAbl] *a.* undenkbar.

Unimaginative [An-i-mæ'dzhi-nA-tiw] *a.* ohne Einbildungskraft.   [*a.* unvermindert.

Unimpaired [An-im-pehrd']

Unimpeachable [An-im-pih'tschAbl] *a.* vorwurfsfrei.

Unimpeded [An-im-pih'did] *a.* ungehindert.

Uninfluenced [An-in'flu-Anst] *a.* unbeeinflusst.

Uninformed [An-in-fOrmd'] *a.* ununterrichtet.

Uninhabitable [An-in-hæ'bi-tAbl] *a.* unbewohnbar.

Uninhabited [An-in-hæ'bi-tid] *a.* unbewohnt.

Uninjured [An-in'dzherd] a. unverletzt.

Unintelligible [An-in-te'li-dzhibl] a. unverständlich.

Unintentional [An-in-ten'schA-nAl] a. -ly ad. unabsichtlich.

Uninteresting [An-in'tri-sting] a. uninteressant.

Uninterrupted [An-in-tA-rAp'tid] a. ununterbrochen.

Uninviting [An-in-wai'ting] a. uneinladend.

Union [juh'njAn] n. Vereinigung f. Verband m, Verbindung f. Gewerkschaft f, Eintracht f (unity); – Jack n. britische Nationalflagge.

Unionist [juh'njA-nist] n. der Konservative; trade- – n. Gewerkschaftsmitglied n.

Unique [juh-nihk'] a. einzig in seiner Art.   [klang m.

Unison [juh'ni-sAn] n. Einklang m.

Unit [juh'nit] n. Einheit f. Truppenteil m (mil.).

Unite [juh-nait'] vt. vereinigen.

Unity [juh'ni-ti] n. Einheit f.

Universal [juh-ni-wAr'ssAl] a. -ly ad. allgemein, Welt . . . ; universal; – joint n. Kugelgelenk n.

Universe [juh'ni-wArss] n. Weltall n, Welt f.

University [juh-ni-wAr'ssi-ti] n. Universität f, Hochschule f.

Unjust [An-dzhAst'] a. -ly ad. ungerecht.

Unjustifiable [An-dzhA'sti-fai-Abl] a. unberechtigt.

Unkempt [An-kempt'] a. ungekämmt.

Unkind [An-kaind'] a. -ly ad. unfreundlich.

Unkindness [An-kaind'ness] n. Unfreundlichkeit f.

Unknowingly [An-nou'ing-li] ad. unwissentlich.

Unknown [An-noun'] a. unbekannt.

Unlace [An-leiss'] vt. aufschnüren.

Unlatch [An-lætsch'] vt. aufklinken.

Unlawful [An-lO'ful] a. ungesetzlich   [lernen.

Unlearn [An-lArn'] vt. ver-

Unlearned [An-lAr'nid] a. unwissend

Unlearnt [An-lArnt'] a. nicht gelernt.

Unleavened [An-lewnd'] a. ungesäuert.

Unless [An-less'] cj. wenn nicht, es sei denn, dass.

Unlicensed [An-lai'ssenst] a. unkonzessioniert, unerlaubt.

Unlike [An-laik'] a. unähnlich.

Unlikelihood [An-laik'li-hud] n. Unwahrscheinlichkeit f.

Unlikely [An-laik'li] a. unwahrscheinlich.

Unlimber [An-lim'ber] vt. abprotzen (gun).

Unlimited [An-li'mi-tid] a. unbegrenzt.

Unlined [An-laind'] a. ungefüttert (cloth), nicht liniert (paper).

Unload [An-loud'] vt. entladen, verschleudern (com.).

Unlock [An-lok'] vt. aufschliessen.   [a. unerwartet.

Unlooked-for [An-lukt'fOr]

Unloose [An-luhss'] vt. auflösen, losmachen.

Unluckily [An-lA'ki-li] ad. unglücklicherweise

Unlucky [An-lA'ki] a. unglücklich.

Unmake [An-meik'] vt. auflösen, aufmachen, aufheben.

Unman [An-mæn'] vt. entmannen.

Unmanageable [An-mæ'nidzg-Abl] a. unlenksam, schwer zu bewältigen.

Unmanly [An-mæn'li] a. unmännlich.

Unmanufactured [An-mæ-nju-fæk'tscherd] a. unverarbeitet.

Unmarked [An-mahrkt'] a. ohne Marken, unbezeichnet.

Unmarketable [An-mahr'ki-tAbl] *a.* unverkäuflich.

Unmannerly [An-mæ'ner-li] *a.* ungesittet, unhöflich.

Unmarried [An-mæ'rid] *a.* unverheiratet.

Unmatched [An-mætscht'] *a.* ungepaart. [larven.

Unmask [An-mahsk'] *vt.* ent-

Unmentionable [An-men'schA-nAbl] *a.* nicht zu erwähnen.

Unmerciful [An-mAr'ssi-ful] *a.* unbarmherzig.

Unmerited [An-me'ri-tid] *a.* unverdient.

Unmethodical [An-mi-tho'dikl] *a.* nicht planmässig.

Unmindful [An-maind'ful] *a.* nicht eingedenk.

Unmistakable [An-mi-stei'kAbl] *a.* unverkennbar.

Unmitigated [An-mi'ti-gei-tid] *a.* ungemildert.

Unmixed [An-mixt'] *a.* unvermischt.

Unmounted [An-maun'tid] *a.* unaufgezogen.

Unmoved [An-muhwd'] *a.* unbewegt, standhaft.

Unnamed [An-neimd'] *a.* ungenannt.

Unnatural [An-næ'tschA-rAl] *a.* unnatürlich.

Unnecessarily [An-ne'ssissA-ri-li] *ad.* unnötigerweise.

Unnecessary [An-ne'ssi-ssA-ri] *a.* unnötig.

Unnerve [An-nArw'] *vt.* entmannen, erschüttern, mürbe machen.

Unnoticed [An-nou'tist] *a.* unbemerkt.

Unobservant [An-Ab-sAr'wAnt] *a.* unaufmerksam.

Unobserved [An-Ab-sArwd'] *a.* unbeachtet, unbemerkt.

Unobtainable [An-Ab-tei'nAbl] *a.* nicht erhältlich.

Unobtrusive [An-Ab-truh'siw] *a.* -ly *ad.* unauffällig, bescheiden, unaufdringlich.

Unoccupied [An-o'kju-paid] *a.* unbesetzt, unbewohnt (*house*).

Unofficial [An-A-fi'schAl] *a.* -ly *ad.* nicht amtlich, unoffiziell.

Unopened [An-oupnd'] *a.* ungeöffnet, uneröffnet.

Unopposed [An-A-pousd'] *a.* ungehindert, ohne Widerstand.

Unorthodox [An-Or'thA-dox] *a.* nicht orthodox, nicht rechtgläubig.

Unostentatious [An-o-stentei'schAss] *a.* bescheiden, schlicht.

Unpack [An-pæk'] *vt.* auspacken.

Unpaid [An-peid'] *a.* unbezahlt.

Unpalatable [An-pæ'lA-tAbl] *a.* unschmackhaft, unwillkommen.

Unparalleled [An-pæ'rA-leld] *a.* beispiellos.

Unpardonable [An-pahr'dA-nAbl] *a.* unverzeihlich.

Unparticipating [An-pahr-ti'ssi-pei-ting] *a.* nicht teilnehmend.

Unpatriotic [An-pæ-trjo'tik] *a.* unpatriotisch, vaterlandslos. [gepflastert.

Unpaved [An-peiwd'] *a.* un-

Unperceived [An-pAr-ssihwd'] *a.* unbemerkt.

Unperforated [An-pAr'fArei-tid] *a.* undurchlöchert.

Unperformed [An-performd'] *a.* unvollführt, unerfüllt (*promise*).

Unperturbed [An-per-tArbd'] *a.* nicht beunruhigt, gelassen.

Unpin [An-pin'] *vt.* losheften, anstecken.

Unplaced [An-pleist'] *a.* unangestellt.

Unpleasant [An-ple'sAnt] *a.* unangenehm.

Unpleasantness [An-ple'sAnt-ness] *n.* Unannehmlichkeit *f.*

Unpolished [An-po'lischt] a. unpoliert, ungeglättet.

Unpopular [An-po'pju-ler] a. unbeliebt.

Unpractical [An-præk'tikl] a. unpraktisch.

Unprecedented [An-pre'ssi-den-tid] a. beispiellos.

Unprejudiced [An-pre'dzhu-dist] a. vorurteils-los, -frei.

Unprepared [An-pri-pehrd'] a. unvorbereitet.

Unprepossessing [An-prih-pA-se'ssing] a. unansehnlich, nicht einnehmend.

Unpresentable [An-pri-zen'tAbl] a. nicht vorstellungsfähig.

Unpretentious [An-pri-ten'schäss] a. anspruchslos, bescheiden.

Unprimed [An-praimd'] a. entschärft (mil.).

Unprincipled [An-prin'ssipld] a. unsittlich, gewissenlos.

Unprinted [An-prin'tid] a. ungedruckt.

Unproductive [An-prA-dAk'tiw] a. unergiebig, uneinträglich.

Unprofitable [An-pro'fi-tAbl] a. uneinträglich.

Unprogressive [An-prA-gre'ssiw] a. konservativ.

Unpromising [An-pro'mi-ssing] a. wenig versprechend.

Unpronounceable [An-prA-naun'ssAbl] a. unaussprechlich.

Unpropitious [An-pro-pi'schäss] a. ungünstig.

Unprotected [An-prA-tek'tid] a. ungeschützt, ungedeckt (com.).

Unprovoked [An-prA-woukt'] a. ohne Veranlassung.

Unpublished [An-pAb'lischt] a. unveröffentlicht.

Unpunctual [An-pAngk'tjuAl] a. unpünktlich.

Unpunished [An-pA'nischt] a. ungestraft.

Unqualified [An-kuo'li-faid] a. unqualifiziert, unbefähigt.

Unquenchable [An-kuen'schAbl] a. unlöschbar.

Unquestionable [An-kue'stjA-nAbl] a. unfraglich.

Unravel [An-ræwl'] vt. entwirren.

Unread [An-red'] a. ungelesen.

Unreadable [An-rih'dAbl] a. unlesbar (book), unleserlich (writing).

Unreal [An-rih'Al] a. nicht wirklich, wesenlos.

Unreasonable [An-rih'sA-nAbl] a. unbillig, unvernünftig.

Unreasonableness [An-rih'sA-nAbl-ness] n. Unvernünftigkeit f. Unbilligkeit f.

Unrecognizable [An-re'kAg-nai-sAbl] a. nicht wiedererkennbar.

Unrecognized [An-re'kAg-naisd] a. nicht anerkannt, unerkannt.

Unrecorded [An-ri-kOr'did] a. unaufgezeichnet.

Unrelenting [An-ri-len'ting] a. unerbittlich, unnachsichtig.

Unreliable [An-ri-lai'Abl] a. unzuverlässig.

Unrelieved [An-ri-lihwd'] a. unerleichtert, ununterbrochen.

Unremitting [An-ri-mi'ting] a. unablässig.

Unrepresented [An-re-pri-sen'tid] a. unvertreten.

Unreserved [An-ri-sArwd'] a. unreserviert, rückhaltlos.

Unresisting [An-ri-si'sting] a. widerstandslos.

Unresponsive [An-ri-spon'siw] a. unempfänglich.

Unrest [An-rest'] n. Unruhe f.

Unrestored [An-ri-stOrd'] a. nicht wiederhergestellt.

Unrestrained [An-ri-streind'] a. zügellos.

Unrestricted [An-ri-strik'tid] a. uneingeschränkt.

Unrewarded [An-ri-uOr'did] a. unbelohnt.

Unrighteous [An-rait'schAss] *a.* ungerecht.

Unripe [An-raip'] *a.* unreif.

Unrivalled [An-raiwld'] *a.* unvergleichlich.

Unroll [An-roul'] *vt.i.* aufrollen, (sich) entfalten.

Unroot [An-ruht'] *vt.* entwurzeln.

Unruffled [An-rAfld'] *a.* glatt, gleichmütig. [dig.

Unruly [An-ruh'li] *a.* unbän-

Unsaddle [An-ssædl'] *vt.* absatteln.

Unsafe [An-sseif'] *a.* unsicher.

Unsaid [An-ssed'] *a.* ungesagt.

Unsalaried [An-ssæ'lA-rid] *a.* unbesoldet.

Unsaleable [An-ssei'lAbl] *a.* unverkäuflich.

Unsatisfactory [An-ssæ-tiss-fæk'tA-ri] *a.* unbefriedigend.

Unsatisfied [An-ssæ'tiss-faid] *a.* unbefriedigt.

Unsavoury [An-ssei'wA-ri] *a.* widrig. [rufen.

Unsay [An-ssei'] *vt.* zurück-

Unscathed [An-skeidhd'] *a.* unversehrt.

Unscientific [An-ssai-An-ti'fik] *a.* unwissenschaftlich.

Unscrew [An-skruh'] *vt.* auf-, los-, ab-schrauben.

Unscrupulous [An-skruh'pju-lAss] *a.* gewissenlos, rücksichtslos.

Unscrupulousness [An-skruh'pju-lAss-ness] *n.* Gewissenlosigkeit *f.*

Unseal [An-ssihl'] *vt.* entsiegeln.

Unseasonable [An-ssih'sA-nAbl] *a.* unzeitig, ungelegen.

Unseasoned [An-ssih'sAnd] *a.* ungewürzt (food), nicht getrocknet (timber).

Unseaworthy [An-ssih'uArdhi] *a.* nicht seetüchtig.

Unsecured [An-ssi-kjuh'erd] *a.* ungesichert.

Unseemly [An-ssihm'li] *a.* unziemlich.

Unseen [An-ssihn'] *a.* ungesehen.

Unselfish [An-ssel'fisch] *a.* uneigennützig.

Unselfishness [An-ssel'fisch-ness] *n.* Selbstlosigkeit *f.*

Unserviceable [An-ssAr'wiss-Abl] *a.* undienlich, betriebsunklar (av.). [wirren.

Unsettle [An-ssetl'] *vt.* ver-

Unsettled [An-ssetld'] *a.* unbeständig, unbezahlt (bill).

Unshakable [An-schei'kAbl] *a.* unerschütterlich.

Unshaken [An-scheikn'] *a.* unerschüttert.

Unshapely [An-schei'pli] *a.* ungestalt.

Unshaven [An-scheiwn'] *a.* unrasiert.

Unship [An-schip'] *vt.* ausschiffen.

Unshod [An-schod'] *a.* unbeschuht.

Unshrinkable [An-schrin'kAbl] *a.* nicht einlaufend.

Unsightly [An-ssait'li] *a.* unansehnlich, hässlich.

Unskilled [An-skild'] *a.* ungelernt, ungeschickt.

Unsociable [An-ssou'schAbl] *a.* ungesellig.

Unsold [An-ssould'] *a.* unverkauft.

Unsolicited [An-ssA-li'ssi-tid] *a.* unverlangt, freiwillig (geben).

Unsolved [An-ssolwd'] *a.* ungelöst.

Unsophisticated [An-ssA-fi'sti-kei-tid] *a.* unverfälscht, einfach, schlicht.

Unsought [An-ssOt'] *a.* ungesucht.

Unsound [An-ssaund'] *a.* verdorben, ungesund, irrig (idea).

Unsparing [An-speh'ring] *a.* schonungslos.

Unspeakable [An-spih'kAbl] *a.* unsagbar.

Unspecified [An-spe'ssi-faid] *a.* nicht einzeln angegeben.

Unspent [An-spent'] a. un-ausgegeben (*money*), unver-braucht (*stocks*).

Unspoilt [An-speult'] a. un-verdorben. [gesagt.

Unspoken [An-spoukn'] a. un-

Unstable [An-steib'l] a. wank-end, unbeständig.

Unsteady [An-ste'di] a. un-stät, unsicher.

Unstinting [An-stin'ting] a. reichlich.

Unsuccessful [An-ssA-ssess'ful] a. -ly ad. erfolglos.

Unsuitability [An-ssuh'tA-bi-li-ti] n. Ungeeignetheit f.

Unsuitabl'e [An-ssuh'tAbl] a. -ly ad. unpassend.

Unsuited [An-ssuh'tid] a. un-geeignet.

Unsurpassed [An-sser-pahst'] a. unübertroffen.

Unsuspected [An-ssA-spek'-tid] a. unverdächtigt.

Unsuspecting [An-ssA-spek'-ting] a. arglos.

Unsweetened [An-ssuih'-tAnd] a. ungesüsst.

Unswerving [An-ssuAr'wing] a. fest.

Unsympathetic [An-ssim-pA-the'tik] a. teilnahmlos.

Unsystematic [An-ssi-ste'-mæ-tik] a. unsystematisch, planlos.

Untainted [An-tein'tid] a. un-angesteckt.

Untamable [An-tei'mAbl] a. unzähmbar.

Untanned [An-tænd'] a. un-gegerbt.

Untarnished [An-tahr'nischt] a. unbefleckt.

Untaught [An-tOt'] a. un-unterrichtet.

Untaxed [An-tæxt'] a. un-besteuert. [haltbar.

Untenable [An-te'nAbl] a. un-

Untenanted [An-te'nAn-tid] a. unbewohnt.

Unthinking [An-thing'king] a. gedankenlos.

Unthought-of [An-thOt'ow'] a. unvermutet.

Unthread [An-thred'] vt. aus-fädeln. [lich.

Untidy [An-tai'di] a. unordent-

Untie [An-tai'] vt. aufmachen, auflösen.

Until [An-til'] prcj. bis.

Untilled [An-tild'] a. unbe-baut.

Untimely [An-taim'li] a. un-zeitig.

Untiring [An-tai'ring] a. un-ermüdlich.

Untold [An-tould'] a. uner-zählt (*story*), ungezählt (*num-ber*).

Untouchable [An-tA'tsch-Abl] a. unberührbar; n. Paria m, der Unberührbare.

Untoward [An-tou'erd] a. un-günstig.

Untractable [An-træk'tAbl] a. widerspenstig.

Untrained [An-treind'] a. un-ausgebildet.

Untrammelled [An-træ'mAld] a. ungehindert.

Untranslatable [An-trahn-sslei'tAbl] a. unübersetzbar.

Untranslated [An-trahn-sslei'tid] a. unübersetzt.

Untraversed [An-træ'werst] a. nicht durchreist.

Untried [An-traid'] a. unver-sucht, unverhört (*law*).

Untroubled [An-trAbld'] a. ungestört.

Untrue [An-truh'] a. unwahr.

Untrustworthiness [An-trAst'uer-dhi-ness] n. Unzu-verlässigkeit f.

Untrustworthy [An-trAst'uer-dhi] a. unzuverlässig.

Untruth [An'truhth] n. Un-wahrheit f.

Unturned [An-tArnd'] a. un-gewendet.

Untwist [An-tuist'] vt. auf-flechten.

Unused [An-juhsd'] a. unge-braucht, unentwertet (*stamp*).

Unusual [An-juh'zhu-Al] a. ungewöhnlich.

Unutterable [An-A'tA-rAbl] a. unaussprechlich.

Unvarnished [An-wahr'nischt] a. nicht lackiert, ungeschminkt (*words*).

Unvarying [An-weh'rjing] a. unveränderlich. [ern.

Unveil [An-weil'] vt. entschlei-

Unvisited [An-wi'si-tid] a. unbesucht.

Unwanted [An-uon'tid] a. ungewünscht.

Unwarrantable [An-uo'rAntAbl] a. ungerechtfertigt, unverantwortlich. [vorsichtig.

Unwary [An-ueh'ri] a. un-

Unwavering [An-uei'wAring] a. nicht wankend, beständig.

Unwearied [An-uih'rid] a. unermüdet.

Unwearying [An-uih'rjing] a. unermüdlich.

Unwelcome [An-uel'kAm] a. unwillkommen.

Unwell [An-uel'] a. unwohl.

Unwholesome [An-houl'ssAm] a. ungesund.

Unwieldy [An-uihl'di] a. schwerfällig.

Unwilling [An-ui'ling] a. -ly ad. unwillig, ungern.

Unwind [An-uaind'] vt. loswinden.

Unwise [An-uais'] a. -ly ad. unklug.

Unwished-for [An-uischt'fOr] a. unerwünscht.

Unwitting [An-ui'ting] a. -ly ad. unwissentlich.

Unwomanly [An-uu'mAn-li] a. unweiblich.

Unworldly [An-uArld'li] a. unweltlich, idealistisch.

Unworthiness [An-uAr'dhi-ness] n. Unwürdigkeit f.

Unworth'y [An-uAr'dhi] a. -lly ad. unwürdig.

Unwounded [An-uuhn'did] a. unverwundet.

Unwrap [An-ræp'] vt. auswickeln, auspacken.

Unwritten [An-ritn'] a. ungeschrieben.

Unyielding [An-jihl'ding] a. unnachgiebig.

Up [Ap] pr. ad. auf, hinauf, herauf, open. [werfen.

Upbraid [Ap-breid'] vt. vor-

Upbringing [Ap'bring-ing] n. Erziehung f.

Up-grade [Ap'greid] n. Aufstieg m.

Upheaval [Ap-hih'wAl] n. Erhebung f, Aufstand m.

Uphill [Ap-hil'] ad. bergauf; a. mühsam.

Uphold [Ap-hould'] vt. aufrechterhalten, stützen.

Upholster [Ap-houl'ster] vt. polstern, überdecken.

Upholsterer [Ap-houl'stA-rer] n. Tapezierer m, Polsterer m.

Upholstery [Ap-houl'stA-ri] n. Polstermöbel n.pl., Tapezierarbeit f.

Upkeep [Ap'kihp] n. Instandhaltung f.

Uplift [Ap'lift] n. Aufschwung m, Erhebung f.

Uplift [Ap-lift'] vt. emporheben, erheben.

Upon [A-pon'] pr. auf.

Upper [A'per] a. ober, höher; – -deck n. Oberdeck n.

Uppermost [A'per-moust] a. oberst, höchst.

Uppish [A'pisch] a. anmassend, eingebildet.

Upraise [Ap-reis'] vt. erheben.

Upright [Ap'rait] a. aufrecht, aufrichtig.

Uprightness [Ap-rait'ness] n. Aufrichtigkeit f.

Uprising [Ap-rai'sing] n. Aufstand m, Erhebung f.

Uproar [Ap'rOr] n. Aufruhr m, Lärm m.

Uproarious [Ap-rO'rjAss] a. lärmend. [wurzeln.

Uproot [Ap-ruht'] vt. ent-

Upset [Ap'sset'] *n.* Umsturz *m*; *vt.* umstürzen.

Upset-price [Ap'sset-praiss'] *n.* Einsatzpreis *m*, Einschlagspreis *m*.

Upshot [Ap'schot] *n.* Ausgang *m*.

Upside-down [Ap'ssaiddaun'] *ad.* drunter und drüber.

Upstairs [Ap-steh'ers] *ad.* oben, die Treppe hinauf.

Upstart [Ap'stahrt] *n.* Emporkömmling *m*.

Up-stream [Ap-strihm'] *ad.* stromaufwärts.

Uptake [Ap'teik] *n.* Begreifen *n.*

Up-to-date [Ap-tu-deit'] *a.* modern. [end.

Upward [Ap'uArd] *a.* ansteig-

Upwards [Ap'uArds] *ad.* aufwärts.

Uranium [ju-rei'njAm] *n.* Uran *n.*

Urban [Ar'bAn] *a.* städtisch.

Urbane [Ar-bein'] *a.* höflich.

Urbanity [Ar-bæ'ni-ti] *n.* Höflichkeit *f.*

Urbanization [Ar-bA-nai-sei'schAn] *n.* Verstädterung *f.*

Urbanize [Ar'bA-nais] *vt.* verstädtern.

Urchin [Ar'tschin] *n.* Schlingel *m.*

Urge [Ardzh] *vt.* drängen, nötigen, dringen in; *n.* Drang *m*, Andrang *m.*

Urgency [Ar'dzhAn-ssi] *n.* Dringlichkeit *f.*

Urgent [Ar'dzhAnt] *a.*, -ly *ad.* dringend.

Urinal [juh'ri-nAl] *n.* Pissoir *n.*

Urine [juh'rin] *n.* Harn *m*, Urine *m.*

Urn [Arn] *n.* Urne *f.*

Us [Ass] *pn.* uns.

Usable [juh'sAbl] *a.* brauchbar.

Usage [juh'sidzh] *n.* Gebrauch *m*, Gewohnheit *f*, Brauch *m.*

Use [juhss] *n.* Gebrauch *m*, Nutzen *m.*

Use [juhs] *vt.* gebrauchen, verwenden, behandeln; - up *vt.* verbrauchen.

Useful [juhss'ful] *a.*, -ly *ad.* nützlich.

Usefulness [juhss'ful-ness] *n.* Nützlichkeit *f.*

Useless [juhss'less] *a.* nutzlos, unnütz.

Usher [A'scher] *n.* Gerichtsdiener *m*, Platzanweiser *m*; *vt.* - in hineinführen, einleiten.

Usual [juh'zhu-Al] *a.*, -ly *ad.* gewöhnlich, üblich.

Usurer [juh'zhA-rer] *n.* Wucherer *m.*

Usurious [ju-zhu'rjAss] *a.* wucherisch.

Usurp [ju's Arp'] *vt.* sich widerrechtlich zueignen.

Usurper [juh-sAr'per] [*n.* Usupator *m.*

Usury [juh'zhA-ri] *n.* Wucher *m.*

Utensil [ju-ten'ssil] *n.* Gerät *n*, Handwerkszeug *n.*

Utilitarian [ju-ti-li-teh'rjAn] *a.* Nützlichkeits . . . .

Utility [ju-ti'li-ti] *n.* Nützlichkeit *f*; - clothing *n.* Einheitskleider *n.pl.*

Utilization [ju-ti-lai-sei'schAn] *n.* Benutzung *f.*

Utilize [juh'ti-lais] *vt.* benutzen.

Utmost [At'moust] *a.* höchst.

Utter [A'ter] *a.* äußerst.

Utter [A'ter] *vt.* äußern.

Utterance [A'tA-rAnss] *n.* Aussprechen *n*, Äußerung *f.*

Utterly [A'ter-li] *ad.* durchaus.

V

Vacancy [wei'kAn-ssi] *n.* Leere *f*, freie Stelle, Vakanz *f.*

Vacant [wei'kAnt] *a.* leer, unbesetzt, frei, vakant, unbewohnt (*house*).

Vacate [wei-keit'] *vt.* räumen, verlassen, niederlegen (*office*).

Vacation [we-kei'schAn] n. Ferien pl.

Vaccinate [wæx'i-neit] vt. impfen.

Vaccination [wæx-i-nei'schAn] n. Impfung f.

Vaccine [wæx'ihn] n. Impfstoff m.

Vacillate [we-ssi-leit] vi. schwanken.

Vacillation [we-ssi-lei'schAn] n. Schwankung f, Unentschlossenheit f.

Vacuum [wæ'kju-Am] n. luftleerer Raum, Vakuum n; - cleaner n. Staubsauger m.

Vagabond [wæ'gA-bond] n. Landstreicher m.

Vagabondage [wæ-gA-bondidzh] n. Umherziehen n.

Vagary [wei'gA-ri] n. Grille f.

Vagrancy [wei'grAn-ssi] n. Landstreicherei f.

Vagrant [wei'grAnt] a. umherziehend; n. Landstreicher m. [bestimmt.

Vague [weig] a. -ly ad. unbestimmt.

Vagueness [weig'ness] n. Unbestimmtheit f.

Vain [wein] a. eitel; in - ad. umsonst.

Vainly [wein'li] ad. vergebens.

Valance [wæ'lAnss] n. Bettgardinen f.pl.

Vale [weil] n. Tal n.

Valedictory [wæ-li-dik'tA-ri] a. Abschieds ....

Valency [wei'lAn-ssi] n. Valenz f, Wertigkeit f.

Valerian [wæ-lih'rjAn] n. Baldrian m.

Valet [wæ'li] n. Kammerdiener m; vi.t. Diener sein bei, Kleider bürsten, etc.

Valetudinarian [wæ-li-tju-dineh'rjAn] a. kränklich; n. kränkliche Person.

Valiant [wæ'ljAnt] a. -ly ad. tapfer.

Valid [wæ'lid] a. gültig.

Validity [wæ-li'di-ti] n. Gültigkeit f.

Valley [wæ'li] n. Tal n.

Valorization [wæ-lA-rai-sei'schAn] n. Aufwertung f.

Valorize [wæ'lA-rais] vt. aufwerten.

Valorous [wæ'lA-rAss] a. tapfer.

Valour [wæ'ler] n. Tapferkeit f.

Valuable [wæ'lju-Abl] a. wertvoll. [wertlos

Valueless [wæ'lju-less] a.

Valve [wælw] n. Klappe f, Röhre f (rad.), Ventil n; - set n. Röhrenempfänger m.

Vamp [wæmp] n. Oberleder n; vt. flicken (shoes), nach dem Gehör begleiten (music).

Vamp [wæmp] n. Vamp m; vt. behexen.

Vampire [wæm'pai-er] n. Vampir n. Blutsauger m.

Van [wæn] n. Kraftwagen m, Lieferwagen m; furniture - Möbelwagen m; luggage - n. Gepäckwagen m (di.); motor - n. Lieferwagen m.

Van [wæn] n. Vorhut f (mil.).

Vanadium [wA-nei'djAm] n. Vanadium n.

Vandalism [wæn'dA-lism] n. Zerstörungswut f Vandalismus m.

Vane [wein] n. Wetterfahne f.

Vanguard [wæn'gahrd] n. Vorhut f.

Vanilla [wA-ni'lA] n. Vanille f.

Vanish [wæ'nisch] vi. verschwinden; -ing cream m. Tagescrem m.

Vanity [wæ'ni-ti] n. Eitelkeit f.

Vanquish [wæng'kuisch] vt. besiegen.

Vantage [wahn'tidzh] n. Vorteil m; -ground n. Überlegenheit f.

Vapid [wæ'pid] a. fade, schal.

Vaporization [wei'pA-rai-sei'schAn] n. Verdampfung f.

Vaporize [wei'pA-rais] vt.i. verdampfen.

Vapour [wei'per] n. Dampf m, Dunst m.

Variability [weh-rjA-bi'li-ti] n. Veränderlichkeit f.

Variable [weh'rjAbl] a. veränderlich.

Variance [weh'rjAnss] n. Widerspruch m, Uneinigkeit f.

Variation [weh-rjei'schAn] n. Veränderung f, Variation f.

Varicose [wæ'ri-kouss] a. krampfaderig; – **vein** n. Krampfader f. [faltig.

Varied [weh'rid] a. mannig-

Variegated [weh'rjA-gei-tid] a. bunt.

Variety [wA-rai'A-ti] n. Mannigfaltigkeit f, Abwechslung f. Abart f (kind).

Various [weh'rjAss] a. -ly ad. mannigfaltig, verschieden.

Varnish [wahr'nisch] vt. überfirnissen; n. Firnis m.

Vary [weh'ri] vt.i. wechseln, (sich) verändern.

Vase [wahs] n. Vase f.

Vaseline [wæ'ssA-lihn] n. Vaselin n.

Vassal [wæssl] n. Lehnsmann m, Vasall m; a. Vasallen . . . .

Vast [wahst] a. -ly ad. riesig, unermesslich, ungeheuer.

Vastness [wahst'ness] n. Unermesslichkeit f.

Vat [wæt] n. grosses Fass.

Vault [wOlt] n. Gewölbe n; vt. wölben.

Vault [wOlt] vi. springen; -ing horse n. Sprungpferd n.

Vaunt [wOnt] vt.i. rühmen, prahlen.

Veal [wihl] n. Kalbfleisch n; – cutlets n.pl. Wiener Schnitzel n.pl. [en, fieren.

Veer [wihr] vi. sich umwend-

Vegetable [we'dzhi-tAbl] n. Gemüse n, Pflanze f.

Vegetarian [we-dzhi-teh'rjAn] n. Vegetarier m.

Vegetate [we'dzhi-teit] vi. dahinleben, vegetieren.

Vegetation [we-dzhi-tei'schAn] n. Pflanzenwuchs m, Dahinleben n.

Vehemence [wih'i-mAnss] n. Heftigkeit f, Ungestüm n.

Vehement [wih'i-mAnt] a, -ly ad. heftig, leidenschaftlich.

Vehicle [wih'ikl] n. Fuhrwerk n, Fahrzeug n, Vermittler m.

Vehicular [wi-i'kju-ler] a. Wagen . . . .

Veil [weil] n. Schleier m; vt. verschleiern.

Vein [wein] n. Ader f, Vene f.

Veined [weind] a. geadert, aderig.

Vellum [we'lAm] n. Velin n, Schreibpergament n.

Velocity [we-lo'ssi-ti] n. Geschwindigkeit f.

Velvet [wel'wit] n. Samt m.

Velveteen [wel-wi-tihn'] n. Baumwollsamt m.

Venal [wih'nAl] a. käuflich, bestechlich.

Vender, Vendor [wen'der] n. Verkäufer m.

Veneer [we-nihr'] n. Furnier n; vt. einlegen, furnieren.

Venerable [wen'rAbl] a. ehrwürdig.

Venerate [wen'A-reit] vt. verehren.

Veneration [we'nA-rei'schAn] n. Verürung f, Ehrfurcht f.

Venereal [we-nih-ri'Al] a. geschlechtlich; – disease n. Geschlechtskrankheit f.

Vengeance [wen'dzhAnss] n. Rache f.

Venial [wih'njAl] a. erlässlich.

Venison [we'ni-sAn] n. Wildbret n.

Venom [we'nAm] n. Gift m.

Venomous [we'nA-mAss] a. giftig.

Vent [went] n. Offnung f, Ventil n, Duse f; air– – n. Zugloch n; steam– – n. Dampfaustritt m.

Ventilate [wen'ti-leit] vt. ventilieren, lüften.

Ventilation [wen-ti-lei'schAn] n. Lüftung f.

Ventilator [wen'ti-lei-ter] n. Lüfter m, Ventilator m.

Ventriloquist [wen-tri'lAkuist] *n.* Bauchredner *m.*

Venture [wen'tscher] *n.* Wagnis *n*, Spekulation *f.*, Unternehmen *n*; *vt.* wagen; *i.* sich gestatten.

Venturesome [wen'tscherssAm] *a.* verwegen, tollkühn.

Venue [wen'juh] *n.* Gerichtsstand *m*, Zuständigkeitsbezirk *m.*   [wahrhaft, wahr.

Veracious [wA-rei'schAss] *a.*

Veracity [wA-ræ'ssi-ti] *n.* Wahrhaftigkeit *f.*

V e r a n d a [wA-ræn'dA] *n.* Veranda *f*, Vorbau *m.*

Verb [wArb] *n.* Zeitwort *n.*

Verbal [wAr'bAl] *a*, -ly *ad.* wörtlich, mündlich.

Verbatim [wAr-bei'tim] *ad.* wortgetreu.

Verbiage [wAr'bjeidзh] *n.* Wortschwall *m.*

Verbose [wAr-bouss'] *a.* wortreich.

Verbosity [wAr-bo'ssi-ti] *n.* Weitschweifigkeit *f.*

Verdant [wAr'dAnt] *a.* grün.

Verdict [wAr'dikt] *n.* Urteil *n*, Spruch *m.*

Verdigris [wAr'di-grihss] *n.* Grünspan *m.*

Verdure [wAr'djer] *n.* Grün *n.*

Verge [wArdзh] *n.* Rand *m*; *vi.* grenzen an.

Verger [wAr'dзher] *n.* Kirchendiener *m*, Küster *m.*

Verifiable [we'ri-fai-Abl] *a.* erweislich.

Verification [we-ri-fi-kei'schAn] *n.* Bestätigung *f*, Nachprüfung *f*, Beleg *m.*

Verify [we'ri-fai] *vt.* nachprüfen, bestätigen, beglaubigen.

Veritable [we'ri-tAbl] *a.* wahr.

Verity [we'ri-ti] *n.* Wahrheit *f.*

Vermicide [wAr'mi-ssaid] *n.* Wurmtötungsmittel *n.*

Vermilion [wAr-mi'ljAn] *n.* Zinnoberrot *n.*

Vermin [wAr'min] *n.* Ungeziefer *n.*

Verminous [wAr'mi-nAss] *a.* voller Ungeziefer.

Vernacular [wAr-næ'kju-ler] *n.* Landessprache *f*, Dialekt *m.*

Vernal [wAr'nAl] *a.* Frühlings ...

Versatile [wAr'ssA-tail] *a.* vielseitig.

Versatility [wAr-ssA-ti'li-ti] *n.* Vielseitigkeit *f.*

Verse [wArss] *n.* Strophe *f*, Vers *m*, Poesie *f.*

Versed [wArst] *a.* bewandert, erfahren.

Version [wAr'schAn] *n.* Übersetzung *f*, Auffassung *f.*

Vertebra [wAr'ti-brA] *n.* Rückenwirbel *m.*

Vertebrate [wAr'ti-breit] *n.* Wirbeltier *n.*   [senkrecht.

Vertical [wAr'tikl] *a*, -ly *ad.*

Vertigo [wAr'ti-gou] *n.* Schwindel *m.*

Very [we'ri] *ad.* sehr; *a.* wirklich, echt.

Vespers [we'spers] *n.pl.* Vesper *f*, Abendgottesdienst *m.*

Vessel [wessl] *n.* Gefäß *n*, Schiff *n.*

Vest [west] *n.* Weste *f* (*men's*). Hemd *n* (*women's*); *vt.* bekleiden, verleihen.

Vestibule [we'sti-bjuhl] *n.* Vorhalle *f.*

Vestige [we'stidzh] *n.* Spur *f.*

Vestment [west'mAnt] *n.* Messgewand *n.*

Vestry [we'stri] *n.* Sakristei *f.*

Vetch [wetsch] *n.* Wicke *f.*

Veteran [we'trAn] *n.* Veteran *m*, ausgedienter Soldat, Kriegsteilnehmer *m*; *a.* altgedient.

Veterinary [we-tA-rin'A-ri] *a.* Tierarznei .... Veterinär ...; *n.* Tierarzt *m*; — **-surgeon** *n.* Tierarzt *m*, Veterinär *m.*

Veto [wih'tou] *n.* Einspruch *m*, Veto *n*; *vt.* Einspruch erheben gegen.

Vex [wex] *vt.* ärgern, plagen.

Vexation [wex-ei'schAn] *n.* Ärger *m*, Verdruss *m.*

Vexatious [wex-ei'schAss] a. ärgerlich, verdriesslich.

Vexed [wext] a. beunruhigt, strittig.

Via [wai'A] pr. über.

Viaduct [wai'A-dukt] n. Brücke f, Viadukt m.

Vibrate [wai-breit'] vi. schwingen, vibrieren.

Vibration [wai-brei'schAn] n. Schwingung f, Vibration f.

Vicar [wi'ker] n. Pfarrer m, der Geistliche.

Vicarage [wi'kA-ridzh] n. Pfarrhaus n.

Vicarious [wai-keh'rjAss] a. stellvertretend.

Vice [waiss] n. Schraubstock m.

Vice [waiss] n. Laster n, Untugend f.

Vice-admiral [waiss-æd'mirAl] n. Vizeadmiral m.

Vice-chancellor [waiss-tschahn'ssi-ler] n. Rektor magnificus m.

Vice-consul [waiss-kon'ssAl] n. Vizekonsul m.

Viceroy [waiss'reu] n. Vizekönig.

Vicinity [wi-ssi'ni-ti] n. Nachbarschaft f, Nähe f.

Vicious [wi'schAss] a. -ly ad. lasterhaft, böse.

Viciousness [wi'schAss-ness] n. Lasterhaftigkeit f, Bösartigkeit f.

Vicissitude [wi-ssi'ssi-tjuhd] n. Wechselfall m, Abwechslung f, Wechsel m.

Victim [wik'tim] n. Opfer n.

Victimization [wik-ti-maisei'schAn] n. Opfern n, Preisgebung f.

Victimize [wik'ti-mais] vt. schädigen, preisgeben, opfern.

Victor [wik'ter] n. Sieger m.

Victorious [wik-tO'rjAss] a. -ly ad. siegreich.

Victory [wik'tA-ri] n. Sieg m.

Victuals [witls] n.pl. Lebensmittel n.pl, Nahrungsmittel n.pl.

Victualler [wit'ler] n. Gastwirt m, Schenkwirt m.

Victualling [wit'ling] n. Verproviantierung f.

Vie [wai] vi. wetteifern.

View [wjuh] n. Anblick m, Aussicht f, Ansicht f (opinion); vt. besehen, mustern; in – of in Hinblick auf; – -finder n. Sucher m, Durchsichts-, Newton-sucher m (camera); – -point n. Gesichtspunkt m.

Vigil [wi'dzhil] n. Nachtwache f.

Vigilance [wi-dzhi-lAnss] n. Wachsamkeit f.

Vigilant [wi-dzhi-lAnt] a. wachsam.

Vigorous [wi'gA-rAss] a. -ly ad. kräftig.

Vigour [wi'ger] n. Lebenskraft f.

Viking [wai'king] n. Wiking m.

Vile [wail] a. -ly ad. gemein, verächtlich, hässlich.

Vileness [wail'ness] n. Schlechtigkeit f, Gemeinheit f.

Vilification [wi-li-fi-kei'schAn] n. Schmähen n, Beschimpfung f.

Vilify [wi'li-fai] vt. schmähen, beschimpfen.

Villa [wi'lA] n. Landhaus n.

Village [wi'lidzh] n. Dorf n.

Villager [wi'li-dzher] n. Dörfler m.

Villain [wi'lin] n. Schurke m.

Villainous [wi'lin-Ass] a. schurkisch, schändlich, gemein.

Villainy [wi'li-ni] n. Schurkerei f, Gemeinheit f.

Vindicate [win'di-keit] vt. rechtfertigen.

Vindication [win-di-kei'schAn] n. Rechtfertigung f.

Vindictive [win-dik'tiw] a. -ly ad. rachsüchtig.

Vindictiveness [win-dik'tiw-ness] n. Rachsucht f.

Vine [wain] n. Rebstock m, Rebe f; – -culture n. Weinbau m.

Vinegar [wi'ni-ger] n. Essig m.

Vintage [win'tidzh] n. Weinlese f, Jahrgang m (year).

Vineyard [win'jahrd] n. Weinberg m.

Viola [wai-ou'lA] n. Bratsche f.

Violate [wai'A-leit] vt. verletzen, schänden.

Violation [wai-A-lei'schAn] n. Verletzung f, Übertretung f.

Violence [wai'A-lenss] n. Gewaltsamkeit f, Gewalt f, Zwang m.

Violent [wai'A-lAnt] a. -ly ad. heftig, gewaltsam.

Violet [wai'A-lit] n. Veilchen n; a. veilchenblau, violett.

Violin [wai-A-lin'] n. Violine f, Geige f.

Violinist [wai-A-li'nist] n. Geiger m, Geigenspieler m.

Viper [wai'per] n. Viper f.

Virago [wi-rei'gou] n. Mannweib n.

Virgin [wAr'dzhin] n. Jungfrau f; a. jungfräulich.

Virginal [wAr'dzhi-nAl] a. jungfräulich.

Virginity [wAr-dzhi'ni-ti] a. Jungfräulichkeit f, Jungfernschaft f.

Virile [wi'rail] a. männlich, mannhaft.

Virility [wi-ri'li-ti] n. Männlichkeit f, Manneskraft f.

Virtual [wAr'tju-Al] a. -ly ad. eigentlich, dem Wesen nach, virtuell.

Virtue [wAr'tjuh] n. Tugend f, Sittsamkeit f; by – of kraft.

Virtuosity [wAr-tju-o'ssi-ti] n. Virtuosität f, Meisterschaft f.

Virtuous [wAr'tju-Ass] a. -ly ad. tugendhaft.

Virulence [wi'rju-lAnss] n. Giftigkeit f.

Virulent [wi'rju-lAnt] a. giftig, bösartig.

Virus [wai'rAss] n. Giftstoff m, Virus n.

Visa [wih'sA], Visé [wih'sei] n. Sichtvermerk m, Visum m; vt.

visieren, mit Sichtvermerk versehen.

Visage [wi'sidzh] n. Angesicht n, Antlitz n.

Viscera [wi'ssA-rA] n.pl. Eingeweide n.

Viscosity [wi-sko'ssi-ti] n. Klebrigkeit f, Dickflüssigkeit f.

Viscount [wai'kaunt] n. Vicomte m.

Viscountess [wiss'kAss] a. zähflüssig, klebrig.

Visibility [wi-si-bi'li-ti] n. Sichtbarkeit f, Sicht f; ground- – n. Bodensicht f (av.).

Visibl'e [wi'sibl] a. -ly ad. sichtbar, ersichtlich, verfügbar (supply).

Vision [wi'zhAn] n. Sehkraft f, Sehen n (sight), Vision f; field of – n. Seh-, Gesichts-feld n.

Visionary [wi'zhA-nA-ri] a. eingebildet, geistersehend; n. Träumer m, Schwärmer m.

Visit [wi'sit] n. Besuch m; vt. besuchen; -ing card n. Besuchs-, Visiten-karte f.

Visitation [wi-si-tei'schAn] n. Heimsuchung f, Besuch m.

Visitor [wi'si-ter] n. Besucher m, der Besuchende, Gast m.

Vista [wi'stA] n. Ausblick m, Aussicht f.

Visual [wi'sju-Al] a. Sicht . . . ; Seh . . .; – range n. Sichtweite f.

Visualize [wi'sju-A-lais] vt. sichtbar machen, sich klar vorstellen.

Vital [waitl] a. -ly ad. lebenswichtig, -kräftig -notwendig, Lebens . . . ; – question n. Lebensfrage f.

Vitality [wai-tæ'li-ti] n. Lebenskraft f.

Vitalize [wai'tA-lais] vt. beleben.

Vitamine [wai'tA-min] n. Vitamin n.

Vitiate [wi'schjeit] vt. verderben, entkräften.

Vitreous [wi'trjAss] a. gläsern.

Vitriol [wi'trjAl] n. Vitriol n; oil of - n. Vitriolöl n, Schwefelsäure f. [lebhaft.

Vivacious [wai-wei'schAss] a.

Vivacity [wai-wæ'ssi-ti] n. Lebhaftigkeit f.

Vivid [wi'wid] a, -ly ad. lebendig, lebhaft.

Vividness [wi'wid-ness] n. Lebhaftigkeit f, Lebendigkeit f.

Vivify [wi'wi-fai] vt. beleben.

Vivisection [wi-wi-ssek'schAn] n. Vivisektion f.

Vixen [wixn] n. Füchsin f, Zänkerin f.

Vocabulary [wA-kæ'bju-lA-ri] n. Wortschatz m, Wörterverzeichnis n.

Vocal [woukl] a, -ly ad. mündlich, Stimm . . . Sprech . . .

Vocation [wA-kei'schAn] n. Beruf m.

Vocational [wA-kei'schA-nAl] a. beruflich; - -training n. Berufsausbildung f, Fortbildung f.

Vociferous [wA-ssi'fA-rAss] a, -ly ad. lärmend, schreiend.

Vogue [woug] n. Mode f.

Voice [weuss] n. Stimme f; vt. äussern.

Void [weud] a. leer; n. Leere f; null and - null und nichtig.

Voile [weul] n. Schleierstoff m.

Volatile [wo'lA-tail] a. flüchtig, unbeständig.

Volatility [wo-lA-ti'li-ti] n. Flüchtigkeit f, Unbeständigkeit f.

Volcanic [wol-kæ'nik] a. vulkanisch. [kan m.

Volcano [wol-kei'nou] n. Vulkan m.

Volition [wo-li'schAn] n. Wille m, Willenskraft f.

Volley [wo'li] n. Salve f.

Volplane [vol'plein] n. Gleitflug m; vi. im gleitflug niedergehen.

Volt [woult] n. Volt n.

Voltage [wou'tidzh] n. Voltspannung f, Spannung f; high - n. Hochspannung f.

Voltmeter [woult'mih-ter] n. Spannungsmesser m, Voltmeter n.

Volubility [wo-lju-bi'li-ti] n. Zungenfertigkeit f.

Voluble [wo'ljubl] a, -ly ad. zungenfertig, geläufig.

Volume [wo'ljuhm] n. Band m (book), Rauminhalt m, Volumen n (capacity), Umfang m (size); - -control n. Volumen-, Laut-stärkeregeler m (rad.); - -range n. Dynamik f, Laut-stärke f (rad.).

Voluminous [wA-ljuh'mi-nAss] a. umfangreich.

Voluntary [wo'lAn-tA-ri] a, -ily ad. freiwillig; n. Orgelzwischenspiel n.

Volunteer [wo-lAn-tih'er] n. der, die Freiwillige; vt.i. sich freiwillig stellen, freiwillig dienen.

Voluptuous [wA-lAp'tju-Ass] a. wollüstig, sinnlich.

Vomit [wo'mit] vi. sich erbrechen; n. das Ausgebrochene.

Voracious [wA-rei'schAss] a. gefrässig.

Voracity [wA-ræ'ssi-ti] n. Gefrässigkeit f.

Vortex [wOr'tex] n. Wirbel m.

Vote [wout] n. Wahlstimme f; vi. wählen, abstimmen; t. vorschlagen, beschliessen.

Voter [wou'ter] n. Wähler m, Wählerin f.

Voting [wou'ting] n. Stimmen n; a. stimmend; - -paper n. Wahlzettel m.

Vouch [wautsch] vi. Zeugnis ablegen für, bürgen für.

Voucher [wau'tscher] n. Gutschein m, Beleg m, Zeugnis n, Nachweis m.

Vow [wau] n. Gelübde n; vt.i. geloben, schwören.

Vowel [wau'il] n. Vokal m, Selbstlaut m. [reise f.

Voyage [weu'idzh] n. See-

Vulcanite [wAl'kA-nait] n. Hartgummi n.

Vulcanization [vʌl-kʌ-nai-sei'schʌn] n. Schwefelung f.

Vulcanize [vʌl'kʌ-nais] vt. schwefeln, härten; **-d** india-rubber n. Hartgummi m.

Vulgar [vʌl'gər] a., **-ly** ad. gemein, ordinär, gewöhnlich.

Vulgarian [vʌl-geh'rjʌn] n. gemeiner Mensch, Grobian m.

Vulgarity [vʌl-gæ'ri-ti] n. Gemeinheit f, Niedrigkeit f, Grobheit f.

Vulgarize [vʌl'gʌ-rais] vt. gemein machen.

Vulnerable [vʌl'nʌ-rʌbl] a. verwundbar, verletzlich.

Vulture [vʌl'tscher] n. Geier m.

W

Wabble [uobl] vi. wackeln.

Wabbly [uob'li] a. wackelig.

Wad [uod] n. Bündel n, Propf m, Büschel m, Ladepropfen m (mil.); vt. wattieren, ausstopfen.

Waddle [uodl] vi. watscheln.

Wade [ueid] vi. waten.

Waders [uei'ders] n.pl. Wasserstiefel m.pl, Kinderbeinkleider n.pl, Watanzug m.

Wafer [uei'fer] n. Waffel f, Oblate f (church, etc.), Entwicklerpatrone f (photo).

Waffle [uofl] n. Waffel f.

Waft [uaft] vt. wehen.

Wag [uæg] n. Spassvogel m.

Wag [uæg] vt. schütteln, wedeln (tail).

Wage [ueidzh] n. Lohn m; basic **-** n. Grundlohn m; **-earner** n. Lohnempfänger m; **-sheet** n. Lohnliste f.

Wage [ueidzh] vt. führen.

Wager [uei'dzher] n. Wette f; vt./i. wetten.

Waggon [uægn] n. Lastwagen m, Rollwagen m; **-load** n. Wagenladung f; **-park** n. Lkw-park m.

Waggoner [uæg'gʌ-ner] n. Fuhrmann m.

Wagtail [uæg'teil] n. Bachstelze f.

Waif [ueif] n. verwahrlostes Kind, heimatloses Kind.

Wail [ueil] vi. wehklagen.

Wainscot [uein'skot] n. Täfelung f, Wandverkleidung f.

Wainscoting [uein'sko-ting] n. Wandgetäfel n.

Waist [ueist] n. Taille f, Kuhl (nav.).

Waistcoat [ueist'kout] n. Weste f.

Wait [ueit] vi. warten; **- for** vt erwarten; **- on** vt. bedienen.

Waiter [uei'ter] n. Kellner m.

Waiting-room [uei'ting-ruhm'] n. Wartezimmer n, Wartesaal m (rl.).

Waitress [ueit'riss] n. Kellnerin f.

Waive [ueiw] vt. verzichten auf, sich begeben (law).

Waiver [uei'wer] n. Verzicht m.

Wake [ueik] n. erwachen; t. wecken.

Wake [ueik] n. Kielwasser n, Fahrwasser n, Schiffsspur f, Rückenwirbel m (av.), Luftsog m (av.).

Walk [uʌk] n. Spaziergang m, Gang m; vi. gehen, spazieren gehen.

Walking [uo'king] n. Gehen n, Spazierengehen n; **- stick** n. Spazierstock m.

Wall [uʌl] n. Wand f (partition), Mauer f (stone); **- paper** n. Tapete f; **- plug**, **- socket** n. Anstecksdose f.

Wallet [uo'lit] n. Brieftasche f, Beutel m, Felleisen m.

Wallflower [uʌl'flau-er] n. Goldlack m.

Wallop [uo'lʌp] vt. prügeln.

Wallow [uo'lou] vi. sich wälzen.

Walnut [uʌl'nʌt] n. Walnuss f.

Walrus [uʌl'rʌss] n. Walross n.

Waltz [uOlss] n. Walzer m; vi. walzen.

Wan [uon] a, -ly ad. bleich, kränklich, schwach.

Wand [uond] n. Stab m, Rute f, Zauberstab m.

Wander [uon'der] vi. wandern.

Wane [uein] vi. abnehmen.

Wangle [uæng'gl] vt. schieben.

Want [uont] n. Mangel m, Not f, Bedürfnis n; vt. brauchen, nötig haben; i. fehlen, mangeln.

Wanton [uon'tAn] a, -ly ad. mutwillig, zügellos, lüstern.

Wantonness [uon'tAn-ness] n. Mutwille m, Üppigkeit f, Lüsternheit f.

War [uOr] n. Krieg m; v, kriegen; – aim n. Kriegsziel n; – of attrition n. Zermürbungskrieg m; – -correspondent n. Kriegsberichterstatter m; – -cry n. Schlachtruf m; – economy n. Kriegswirtschaft f; – effort n. Kriegseinsatz m; – establishment n. Sollbestand m; – -grave n. Kriegergrab n; – -guilt n. Kriegsschuld f; – -industry n. Rüstungsindustrie f; – -loan n. Kriegsanleihe f; -monger n. Kriegshetzer m; – office n. Kriegsministerium n; – -paint n. Kriegsbemalung f; – profiteer n. Kriegsgewinnler m; -time n. Kriegszeit f; – -zone n. Kriegsgebiet n.

Warble [uOrbl] vi. trillern.

Ward [uOrd] n. Wache f, Abteilung f, Mündel n (minor).

Warden [uOrdn] n. Aufseher m, Herbergsvater m (hostel), Luftschutzwart m (A.R.P.).

Warder [uOr'der] n. Gefängniswärter m.

Wardrobe [uOrd'roub] n. Kleiderschrank m.

Ward-room [uOrd'ruhm] n. Offiziersmesse f (nav.).

Ware [ueh'er] n. Ware f.

Warehouse [ueh'er-hauss'] n. Lagerhaus n, Warenlager n.

Warfare [uOr'feh-er] n. Krieg m, Kriegszustand m.

Warily [ueh'ri-li] ad. vorsichtig, behutsam.

Warlike [uOr'laik] a. kriegerisch.

Warm [uOrm] a, -ly ad. warm, herzlich; vt. wärmen; i. erwärmen.

Warmth [uOrmth] n. Wärme f, Hitze f.

Warn [uOrn] vt. warnen.

Warning [uOr'ning] n. Warnung f.

Warp [uOrp] n. Kette f; vt. anscheren, werfen, verleiten; i. sich werfen.

Warrant [uo'rAnt] n. Vollmacht f, Gewähr f; vt. gewährleisten; – of arrest n. Steckbrief m; – -officer n. Deckoffizier m (nav.), Oberfeldwebel m (av.).

Warren [uo'rAn] n. Gehege n.

Wart [uOrt] n. Warze f.

Wary [ueh'ri] a. vorsichtig.

Wash [uosch] vt.i. (sich) waschen; n. Waschen n, Wäsche f; – -basin n. Waschbecken n; -bottle n. Spritzflasche f (tec.); – -leather n. Waschleder n; -stand n. Waschtisch m.

Washable [uosch'Abl] a. waschbar.

Washer [uo'scher] n. Bolzenblech n, Dichtungsring m, Unterlagsscheibe f (tec.).

Washerwoman [uo'scher-uu'mAn] n. Waschfrau f.

Washing [uo'sching] n. Waschen n, Wäsche f; – Wasch ...; – -day n. Waschtag m.

Wasp [uosp] n. Wespe f.

Waspish [uo'spisch] a. reizbar.

Wastage [uei'stidzh] n. Abgang m, Verlust m.

Waste [ueist] n. Vergeudung f, Verschwendung f, Abfall m; a. wüst, unbenutzt, überflüssig, wertlos; vt. verwüsten, vergeuden, verzehren.

Wastefulness [ueist'ful-ness] n. Verschwendung f.

Waste-paper [ueist'pei-per] n. Altpapier n, Papierabfälle m.pl; - basket n. Papierkorb m.

Wastrel [ueist'ril] n. Taugenichts m, arbeitsscheuer Kerl.

Watch [uotsch] n. Wache f, Uhr f, Taschenuhr f; vt. wachen, warten; t. bewachen, beobachten; - chain n. Uhrkette f; - dog n. Kettenhund m; - key n. Uhrschlüssel m; - tower n. Wachtturm m.

Watchful [uotsch'ful] a. wachsam, aufmerksam.

Watchfulness [uotsch'fulness] n. Aufmerksamkeit f.

Watchman [uotsch'mAn] n. Wächter m.

Water [uO'ter] n. Wasser n; vt. wässern, begiessen; - work n. Wasserflasche f, Feldflasche f (mil.). Wärmflasche f (hot); - -colour n. Aquarell n; - cress n. Brunnenkresse f; - glass n. Wasserglas n; - power n. Wasserkraft f.

Waterfall [uO'ter-fOl] n. Wasserfall m.

Waterlogged [uO'ter-logd] a. mit Wasser angefüllt.

Watermark [uO'ter-mahrk] n. Wasserzeichen n.

Waterproof [uO'ter-pruhf] a. wasserdicht; n. Regenrock m.

Watershed [uO'ter-sched] n. Wasserscheide f.

Watertight [uO'ter-tait] a. wasserdicht.

Waterway [uO'ter-uei] n. Wasser-weg m, -strasse f.

Waterworks [uO'ter-uOrkss] n.pl. Wasserwerk n.

Watery [uO'tA-ri] a. wässerig.

Watt [uot] n. Watt n.

Wattle [uotl] n. Flechtwerk n, Geflecht n.

Wave [ueiw] n. Welle f, Woge f; vt. schwenken, wellen; i. wehen; - band n. Wellenbereich n; - -detector n. Wellen-

zeiger m; - -length n. Wellenlänge f.

Waver [uei'wer] vi. wanken, unschlüssig sein.

Wavy [uei'wi] a. wellig, gewellt.

Wax [uæx] n. Wachs n; a. wächsern; vt. mit Wachs behandeln, mit Wachs überziehen; cobblers' - n. Schusterpech n; sealing- n. Siegellack m; - -work n. Wachsfigur f.

Wax [uæx] vi. zunehmen, werden.

Waxen [uæxn] a. wächsern.

Waxy [uæ'xi] a. see waxen.

Way [uei] n. Weg n, Mittel n, Art f, Weise f; -bill n. Frachtkarte f.

Wayfarer [uei'feh-rer] n. Wanderer m.

Wayfaring [uei'feh-ring] a. wandernd, reisend; n. Wandern n.

Waylay [uei-lei'] vt. auflauern.

Wayside [uei-ssaid'] n. Strassenrand m; a. an der Strasse befindlich.

Wayward [uei'uArd] a. launisch.

We [uih] pn. wir.

Weak [uihk] a. schwach, kraftlos.

Weaken [uihkn] vt. schwächen, entkräften; i. schwach werden, nachlassen.

Weakening [uih'kA-ning] n. Schwächung f, Nachlassen n.

Weakling [uihk'ling] n. Schwächling m.

Weakly [uihk'li] a. schwach, schwächlich; ad. schwach.

Weak-minded [uihk'maindid] a. charakterschwach, -los.

Weakness [uihk'ness] n. Schwäche f.

Weal [uihl] n. Strieme f, Schwiele f.

Weal [uihl] n. Wohl n.

Wealth [uelth] n. Reichtum m.

Wealthy [uel'thi] a. reich, wohlhabend.

Wean [uihn] *vt.* entwöhnen (*baby*) abgewöhnen (*habit*).

Weapon [uepn] *n.* Waffe *f.*

Wear [ueh'er] *vt.* tragen, abtragen, abnutzen; *i.* sich tragen, haltbar sein; *n.* Tragen *n*, Gebrauch *m*, Abnutzung *f*; -- out abtragen.

Wearable [ueh'rAbl] *a.* tragbar.

Wearily [uih'ri-li] *ad.* müde.

Weariness [uih'ri-ness] *n.* Müdigkeit *f*, Ermüdung *f.*

Wearing [ueh'ring] *a.* aufreibend *v.* Tragen *n.*

Wearisome [uih'ri-ssAm] *a.* ermüdend.

Weary [uih'ri] *a.* müde; *vt.* ermüden; *i.* müde werden.

Weasel [uihsl] *n.* Wiesel *n.*

Weather [ue'dher] *n.* Wetter *n*; --beaten *a.* wetterhart, abgehärtet; -- bound *a.* durch schlechtes Wetter zurückgehalten; -- forecast *n.* Wettervoraussage *f*; -- report *n.* Wetterbericht *m.*

Weathercock [ue'dher-kok'] *n.* Wetterhahn *m.*

Weathering [ue'dhA-ring] *n.* Verwitterung *f* (*stone*), Trotzen *n* (*difficulties. etc.*).

Weave [uihw] *vt.i.* weben, flechten.

Weaver [uih'wer] *n.* Weber *m.*

Web [ueb] *n.* Gewebe *n*, Netz *n.*

Webbing [ue'bing] *n.* Gewebe *n*, Gurtband *n.*

Wed [ued] *vt.i.* heiraten, sich verheiraten.

Wedding [ue'ding] *n.* Hochzeit *f*; -- breakfast *n.* Hochzeitsmahl *n*; -- cake *n.* Hochzeitskuchen *m*; -- card *n.* Vermählungsanzeige *f*; -- day *n.* Hochzeitstag *m*; -- ring *n.* Ehering *m*, Trauring *m.*

Wedge [uedzh] *n.* Keil *m*; *vt.* verkeilen, einkeilen, keilen.

Wednesday [uens'di] *n.* Mittwoch *m.*

Wee [uih] *a.* winzig, klein.

Weed [uihd] *n.* Unkraut *n*; *vt.* jäten; -ing fork *n.* Jätgabel *f*; -- killer *n.* Unkrautvertilgungsmittel *n.*

Weedy [uih'di] *a.* voll Unkraut, klapperig (*person*).

Week [uihk] *n.* Woche *f.*

Week-end [uihk-end'] *n.* Wochenende *n.*

Weekly [uihk'li] *a.ad.* wöchentlich; *n.* Wochenblatt *n.*

Weeping [uihp] *vi.* weinen.

Weeping [uih'ping] *n.* Weinen *n*; --willow *n.* Trauerweide *f.*

Weevil [uih'wil] *n.* Kornwurm *m.* [Schussgarn *n.*

Weft [ueft] *n.* Einschlag *m*,

Weigh [uei] *vt.* wägen, abwiegen; *i.* wiegen; -- bridge *n.* Brückenwaage *f.*

Weigher [uei'er] *n.* Wäger *m.*

Weight [ueit] *n.* Gewicht *n* Schwere *f*; *vt* belasten

Weighty [uei'ti] *a.* gewichtig.

Weir [uih'er] *n.* Wasserwehr *n.*

Weird [uih'erd] *a.* unheimlich.

Welcome [uel'kAm] *n.* Willkomm *m*; *a.* willkommen; *vt.* willkommen heissen, bewillkommnen.

Weld [ueld] *vt.* schweissen.

Welfare [uel feh-er] *n.* Wohlfahrt *f*; --work *n.* Fürsorge *f.*

Well [uel] *n.* Brunnen *m*, Quelle *f*; *vi.* fliessen, quellen.

Well [uel] *ad.* wohl, gut; *a.* wohl; --balanced *a.* ausgeglichen; --bred *a.* wohlerzogen; -- deserved *a.* wohlverdient; -- doing *n.* Wohltun *n*; -- dressed *a.* wohlbekleidet, gut gekleidet; -- educated *a.* gebildet; --known *a.* bekannt; -- made *a.* gut gemacht; --meaning *a.* wohlmeinend; -- meant *a.* wohlgemeint; --timed *a.* gut angebracht; --wisher *n.* der Wohlgesinnte.

Well-to-do [uel-tA-duh'] *a.* wohlhabend.

Wellington (boot) [uel'ing-tAn-buht'] *n.* Schaftstiefel *m.*

Welt [uelt] *n.* Rand *m*, Rahmen *m*; *vt.* berändern.

West [uest] *n.* Westen *m*.

Westerly [ue'ster-li], **Western** [ue'stern] *a.* westlich.

Westwards [uest'uArds] *ad.* westwärts.

Wet [uet] *a.* nass, feucht; *n.* Nässe *f*, Regenwetter *n*; *vt.* durchnässen, befeuchten; - -purse *n.* Amme *f*.

Wether [ue'dher] *n.* Hammel *m*.

Wetness [uet'ness] *n.* Nässe *f*.

Whack [huæk] *vt.* schlagen; *n.* derber Schlag, Anteil *m*.

Whacking [hue'king] *a.* riesig.

Whale [hueil] *n.* Walfisch *m*.

Whalebone [hueil'boun] *n.* Walfischbein *n*.

Whaler [huei'ler] *n.* Walfischboot *n*.

Whaling [huei'ling] *n.* Walfischfang *m*.

Wharf [huOrf] *n.* Werft *f*.

What [huot] *pn.* was, was für, welcher, welche, welches.

Whatever [huot-e'wer] *pn.* was nur immer, was auch.

Wheat [huiht] *n.* Weizen *m*.

Wheedle [huihdl] *vt.* schmeicheln.

Wheel [huihl] *n.* Rad *n*; *vt.* schieben, rollen, führen, (ab-) schwenken (*mil.*); - *-base n.* Radstand *m*.

Wheelbarrow [huihl'bæ-rou] *n.* Schubkarren *m*.

Wheelwright [huihl'rait] *n.* Radmacher *m*.

Wheeze [huihs] *vi.* keuchen; *n.* Kniff *m*.

Whelk [huelk] *n.* Kinkhorn *n*.

Whelp [huelp] *n.* Junge *n*.

When [huen] *ad.* wann; *cj.* als, wenn.

Whence [huenss] *ad.* woher; *cj.* daher.

Whenever [huen-e'wer] *ad.cj.* wenn immer, so oft als.

Where [hueh'er] *ad.* wo.

Whereabouts [hueh'er-A-bautss'] *ad.* wo ungefähr; *n.* Aufenthalt *m*, Verbleib *m*.

Whereas [hueh-ræs'] *ad.cj.* während, wo hingegen.

Whereby [hueh-er-bai'] *ad.* wodurch.

Wherefore [hueh-er-fOr'] *ad. cj.* weshalb.

Wherefrom [hueh-er-from'] *ad.cj.* woher.

Wherein [hueh-rin'] *ad.cj.* worin.

Whereon [hueh-ron'] *ad.* worauf.

Whereupon [hueh-er-rA-pon'] *ad.cj.* worauf, darauf.

Wherever [hueh-re'wer] *ad.* wo(hin) auch immer.

Wherewith [hueh-er-uith'] *ad.cj.* womit; -al *n.* Geldmittel *n.pl.*

Wherry [hue'ri] *n.* Fähre *f*, Lichter *m*.

Whet [huet] *vt.* wetzen.

Whether [hue'dher] *cj.* ob.

Whetstone [huet'stoun] *n.* Wetzstein *m*.

Whey [huei] *n.* Molke *f*.

Which [huitsch] *pn.* welcher, welche, welches.

Whiff [huif] *n.* Lufthauch *m*, Paff *m*; *vi.* paffen.

While [huail] *cj.* während, indem.

While [huail] *n.* Weile *f*, Zeitlang *f*; *vt.* - away verтändeln, verbringen.

Whilst [huailst] *cj.* während.

Whim [huim] *n.* Grille *f*, Laune *f*.

Whimsical [huim'sikl] *a.* launisch, wunderlich.

Whimper [huim'per] *vi.* wimmern.

Whin [huin] *n.* Stechginster *m*.

Whine [huain] *vi.* winseln.

Whinny [hui'ni] *vi.* wiehern.

Whip [huip] *n.* Peitsche *f*, Einpeitscher *m* (*party*); *vt.* peitschen, schlagen; - -cord *n.* Peitschenschnur *f*.

Whipper-snapper [hui'per-snæ'per] n. Gelbschnabel m.

Whippet [hui'pit] n. Windspiel n (dog), kleiner Panzerwagen (mil.).

Whir [huAr] vi. schwirren.

Whirl [huArl] vt.i. (sich) wirbeln, (sich) drehen.

Whirlpool [huArl'puhl] n. Strudel m.

Whirlwind [huArl'uind] n. Wirbelwind m.

Whisk [huisk] vt. fegen, bürsten; n. Abstäuber m, Wisch m.

Whiskers [hui'skers] n.pl. Backenbart m.

Whisky [hui'ski] n. Whisky m.

Whisper [hui'sper] vt.i. flüstern, munkeln; n. Geflüster n; -ing campaign n. Flüsterpropaganda f.

Whisperer [hui'spA-rer] n. Flüsterer m.

Whist [huist] n. Whist n.

Whistle [huissl] n. Pfeife f, Pfiff m; vi. pfeifen.

Whit [huit] n. Iota n.

White [huait] a. weiss.

Whiten [huaitn] vt. weissen.

Whiteness [huait'ness] n. Weisse f.

Whitening [huait'ning] n. Weissen n.

Whitewash [huait'uosch] n. weisse Tünche f; vt. übertünchen, ausweissen.

Whither [hui'dher] ad. wohin.

Whiting [hui'ting] n. Weissfisch m (fish), Schlemmkreide f (chalk). [lich.

Whitish [huai'tisch] a. weiss-

Whit-Monday [huit-mAn'di] n. Pfingstmontag m.

Whitsuntide [huit'ssAn-taid] n. Pfingsten n.

Whit-week [huit-uihk'] n. Pfingstwoche f.

Whittle [huitl] vt. schnitzeln, abschaben.

Whizz [huis] vi. sausen, surren.

Who [huh] pn. wer, der, die, das.

Whoa [huou] halt !

Whoever [huh-e'wer] pn. wer auch, wer nur tun.

Whole [houl] a. ganz; n. das Ganze; - -hearted a rückhaltlos; -meal a. Vollkorn ....

Wholesale [houl'sseil] a, n. Grosshandel m, Engrosgeschäft n; a. Gross ... Engros ....

Wholesome [houl'ssAm] a. gesund, heilsam.

Wholly [houl'li] ad. gänzlich.

Whom [huhm] pn. wen ? den, die, das, die (pl.); to - wem ? dem, der, denen (pl.).

Whoop [huhp] n. lautes Geschrei; vi. aufschreien; -ing cough n. Keuchhusten m.

Whore [hOr] n. Hure f.

Whorl [huArl] n. Spulenring m.

Whortleberry [uArtl'be-ri] n. Heidelbeere f.

Whose [huhs] pn. poss. wessen ? dessen, deren, dessen.

Why [huai] ad. warum.

Wick [uik] n. Docht m

Wicked [ui'kid] a, -ly ad. böse, schlecht.

Wickedness [ui'kid-ness] n. Bosheit f, Schlechtigkeit f.

Wicker [ui'ker] a. geflochten, aus Flechtwerk; - -basket n. Korbstuhl m, Weidenkorb m.

Wicket [ui'kit] n. Pförtchen n (gate), Dreistab m (cricket).

Wide [uaid] a. -ly ad. weit, breit, umfassend; - -awake a. aufgeweckt, schlau; n. Schlapphut m; - -gauge a. breitspurig (rl.).

Widen [uaidn] vt. erweitern.

Wideness [uaid'ness] n. see width.

Widespread [uaid'spred] a. weit verbreitet.

Widow [ui'dou] n. Witwe f.

Widower [ui'dou-er] n. Witwer m.

Widowhood [ui'dou-hud] n. Witwenschaft f. [Weite f.

Width [uidth] n. Breite f,

Wield [uihld] *vt.* beherrschen.

Wife [uaif] *n.* Ehefrau *f*, Gattin *f*, Frau *f*.

Wig [uig] *n.* Perücke *f*.

Wild [uaild] *a.* -ly *ad.* wild, ungestüm; -s *n.pl.* Wüste *f*.

Wilderness [uil'der-ness] *n.* Wildnis *f*, Wüste *f*.

Wile [uail] *n.* List *f*.

Wilful [uil'ful] *a.* -ly *ad.* eigensinnig, vorsätzlich.

Wilfulness [uil'ful-ness] *n.* Eigensinn *m*.

Will [uil] *n.* Wille *m*, Testament *n*; *vt.* hinterlassen; *i.* wollen.

Willing [uil'ing] *a.* -ly *ad.* bereitwillig, gern.

Willingness [uil'ing-ness] *n.* Bereitwilligkeit *f*.

Willow [uil'ou] *n.* Weide *f*.

Wily [uai'li] *a.* listig.

Win [uin] *vt.* gewinnen; *i.* siegen; *n.* Sieg *m*.

Wince [uinss] *vi.* zusammenzucken, zurückfahren.

Winch [uinsch] *n.* Haspel *m*, Kurbel *f*, Winde *f*.

Wind [uind] *n.* Wind *m*; -bag *n.* Windbeutel *m*; - -instrument *n.* Blasinstrument *n*; -screen *n.* Windschutzscheibe *f* (aut.).

Wind [uaind] *vt.i.* winden, wickeln, sich winden; - up *vt.* aufziehen, abschliessen, abmachen (com.).

Windfall [uind'fOl] *n.* unverhoffter Glücksfall.

Winding [uain'ding] *a.* sich windend, krumm; *n.* Krümmung *f*, Windung *f*.

Windlass [uind'lAss] *n.* Handkurbel *f*, Winde *f*. [los.]

Windless [uind'less] *a.* wind-

Window [uin'dou] *n.* Fenster *n*; - -box *n.* Blumenkasten *m*; - -cleaner *n.* Fensterputzer *m*; - -dressing *n.* Schaufensterausschmückung *f*, Zurechtstutzen *n*; - -pane *n.* Fensterscheibe *f*; - -sill *n.* Fenstersims *m*.

Windward [uind'uArd] *a, ad.* gegen den Wind, windwärts.

Windy [uin'di] *a.* windig.

Wine [uain] *n.* Wein *m*; - -glass *n.* Weinglas *n*; - -list *n.* Weinkarte *f*; - -merchant *n.* Weinhändler *m*; - -press *n.* Kelter *f*.

Wing [uing] *n.* Flügel *m*, Tragfläche *f* (av.), Gruppe *f* (unit); - -commander *n.* Oberstleutnant *m*, der Flieger (av.).

Winged [uingd] *a.* geflügelt.

Wink [uingk] *vi.* zwinkern, blinzeln; *n.* Zwinkern *n*; - at ein Auge zudrücken, nachsehen.

Winkle [uingkl] *n.* Uferschnecke *f*.

Winner [ui'ner] *n.* Gewinner *m*, Sieger *m*.

Winning [ui'ning] *a.* gewinnend, einnehmend.

Winnings [ui'nings] *n.pl.* Gewinn *m*.

Winnow [ui'nou] *vt.* wannen, schwingen.

Winsome [uin'ssAm] *a.* anziehend.

Winter [uin'ter] *n.* Winter *m*; *vi.* überwintern.

Wintry [uin'tri] *a.* winterlich.

Wipe [uaip] *vt.* wischen, abtrocknen; - out aufreiben (troops).

Wiper [uai'per] *n.* Wischer *m*, Wischtuch *n*; windscreen- - *n.* Scheibenwischer *m* (aut.).

Wire [uai'er] *n.* Draht *m*, Telegramm *n*; *vt.* mit Draht versehen, umwickeln, heften; *i.* drahten, telegraphieren; barbed- - *n.* Stacheldraht *m*; bare - blanker Draht; overhead - *n.* Hochleitung *f* (el.), Luftdraht *m*; round- - *n.* Runddraht *m*; - -circuit *n.* Drahtleitung *f*; - -cutter *n.* Drahtschere *f*; - -entanglement *n.* Drahtverhau *n*; -mesh *n.* Maschendraht *m*; Drahtnetz *n*; - -puller *n.*

Drahtzieher m; – -pulling n. Drahtzieherei f. Mache f.

Wireless [uai'er-less] a. drahtlos, Radio . . . ; vt. funken; – -apparatus n. Funkapparat m; – -engineering n. Sendetechnik f, Radiotechnik f; – licence n. Funkgebühr f; – -message n. Funkspruch m; – -operator n. Funker m; – -programme n. Rundfunkprogramm n; – -receiver n. Radio-, Funkempfänger m; – -set n. Radioapparat m, Funkstelle f; – -station n. Funkstelle f; – -telegraphy n. Funktelegraphie f; – -transmission n. drahtlose Übertragung. [anlage f.

Wiring [uai'ring] n. Draht-

Wiry [uai'ri] a. drahtig, sehnig (persons).

Wisdom [uis'dAm] n. Weisheit f, Klugheit f.

Wise [uais] a, -ly ad. weise, klug.

Wise [uais] n. Art f.

Wish [uisch] n. Wunsch m; vt.i. wünschen.

Wisher [ui'scher] n. der Wünschende.

Wishful [uisch'ful] a. wünschend, verlangend; – -thinking n. Wunschträume m.pl.

Wistaria [uist-ä'riA] n. Glyzine f.

Wistful [uist'ful] a, -ly ad. sehnsüchtig, sinnend.

Wit [uit] n. Witz m, Schöngeist m.

Witch [uitsch] n. Hexe f.

Witchcraft [uitsch'krahft] n. Hexerei f.

With [uidh] pr. mit, bei.

Withdraw [uidh-drO'] vt.i. (sich) zurückziehen, zurücknehmen, entziehen.

Withdrawal [uidh-drO'Al] n. Zürücknahme f, Entziehung f, Züchtritt m.

Withe [uaidh] n. Weidenrute f.

Withers [ui'dhers] n.pl. Widerrist m.

Withhold [uidh-hould'] vt. vorenthalten, zurückhalten.

Within [ui-dhin'] ad. drinnen; pr. innerhalb.

Without [ui-dhaut'] pr. ohne; ad. draussen, aussen.

Withstand [uidh-stænd'] vt. widerstehen, sich widersetzen.

Witless [uit'less] a. töricht, einfältig.

Witness [uit'ness] n. Zeuge m, Zeugin f, Zeugnis n; vt. bezeugen.

Witticism [ui'ti-ssism] n. Witz m.

Witty [ui'ti] a. geistreich, witzig.

Wizard [ui'serd] n. Hexenmeister m; a. famos.

Wizened [ui'sÄnd] a. runzlig, eingeschrumpft.

Woad [uoud] n. Waid m.

Wobble [uobl] vi. wackeln.

Wobbly [uo'bli] a. wackelig.

Woe [uou] n. Weh n, Leid n.

Woeful [uou'ful] a. jammervoll, jämmerlich.

Wolf [uulf] n. Wolf m.

Wolfish [uul'fisch] a. wölfisch, Wolfs . . . .

Wolfram [uul'frAm] n. Wolfram n.

Woman [uu'mAn] n. Frau f, Weib n.

Womanish [uu'mA-nisch] a. weibisch.

Womanly [uu'mAn-li] a. weiblich.

Womb [uuhm] n. Mutterleib m.

Womenfolk [uui'min-fouk] n. pl. Frauensleute f.

Wonder [uAn'der] n. Wunder n; vi. sich wundern.

Wonderful [uAn'der-ful] a, -ly ad. wunderbar.

Wonderland [uAn'der-lænd] n. Wunderland n.

Wondrous [uAnd'rAss] a. wundersam.

Wont [uount] a. gewohnt; n. Gewohnheit f.

Wonted [uoun'tid] a. gewohnt.

Woo [uuh] *vt.i.* freien.

Wood [uud] *n.* Holz *n*, Wald *m* (*forest*); **– –pulp** *n.* Holzmasse *f.*

Woodcut [uud'kAt] *n.* Holzschnitt *m.*

Wooded [uu'did] *a.* waldig, bewaldet.

Wooden [uudn] *a.* hölzern.

Woody [uu'di] *a.* waldig.

Woodman [uud'mAn] *n.* Holzfäller *m.*

Woodwork [uud'uArk] *n.* Holzwerk *n*, Holzarbeit *f.*

Wooing [uuh'ing] *n.* Freien *n.*

Wool [uul] *n.* Wolle *f.*

Woollen [uu'lAn] *a.* wollen, Wolle -, -

Woolly [uu'li] *a.* wollig, wollen, verschwommen.

Word [uArd] *n.* Wort *n*; *vt.* ausdrücken.

Wording [uAr'ding] *n.* Ausdrucksweise *f*, Wortlaut *f* (*exact*).

Wordy [uAr'di] *a.* wortreich.

Work [uArk] *n.* Arbeit *f*, Werk *n*, Beschäftigung *f*; *vi.* arbeiten, wirken; *t.* bearbeiten, arbeiten lassen, betreiben; **-s** *n.pl.* Werk *n*, Fabrik *f*, Hütte *f* (*metal*); **out of –** stellenlos; **-ing hours** *n.pl.* Dienststunden *f.pl*; **-s manager** *n.* Betriebsführer *m.*

Workable [uAr'kAbl] *a.* tunlich, ausführbar.

Worker [uAr'ker] *n.* Arbeiter *m.*

Workhouse [uArk'hauss] *n.* Armenhaus *n.*

Workman [uArk'mAn] *n.* Arbeiter *m*; **-'s ticket** *n.* Fahrtnachweis *m.*

Workmanlike [uArk'mAnlaik] *a.* geschickt, kunstgerecht.

Workmanship [uArk'mAnschip] *n.* Arbeit *f*, Geschicklichkeit *f.*

Workshop [uArk'schop] *n.* Werkstatt *f.*

Work–shy [uArk'schai] *a.* arbeitsscheu.

World [uArld] *n.* Welt *f*; **– –famous** *a.* weltberühmt; **– –wide** *a.* weit verbreitet, weltberühmt.

Worldliness [uArld'li-ness] *n.* Weltsinn *m.*

Worldling [uArld'ling] *n.* Weltkind *n.*

Worldly [uArld'li] *a.* weltlich.

Worm [uArm] *n.* Wurm *m*, Schnecke *f* (*tec.*); **– –eaten** *a.* wurmstichig; **– –gear** *n.* Schneckengetriebe *m* (*tec.*).

Wormwood [uArm'uud] *n.* Wermut *m.*

Worry [uA'ri] *n.* Qual *f*, Kummer *m*, Sorge *f*; *vt.i.* quälen, (sich) ärgern, beunruhigen.

Worse [uArss] *a*, *ad.* schlimmer, schlechter.

Worship [uAr'schip] *vt.* anbeten, verehren; *n.* Anbetung *f*, Verehrung *f.*

Worshipper [uAr'schi-per] *n.* Anbeter *m*, Kirchgänger *m* (*church*).

Worst [uArst] *a*, *ad.* schlimmst, schlechtest; **at the –** im schlimmsten Fall.

Worsted [uu'stid] *n.* Kammgarn *n.*

Worth [uArth] *a.* wert; **– –while** der Mühe wert.

Worthily [uAr'dhi-li] *ad.* würdig, würdevoll.

Worthless [uArth'less] *a.* wertlos.

Worthlessness [uArth'lessness] *n.* Wertlosigkeit *f.*

Worthy [uAr'dhi] *a.* würdig, wert.

Would–be [uud-bih'] *a.* vorgeblich.

Wound [uuhnd] *n.* Wunde *f*; *vt.* verwunden; **– –badge** *n.* Verwundetenabzeichen *n.*

Wounded [uuhn'did] *a.* verwundet; *n.* die Verwundeten *m.pl.*

Wrangle [ræng'gl] *vi.* zanken.

Wrap [ræp] *vt.* wickeln; *n.* Schal *m*, Umschlagetuch *n*; **– –**

up einwickeln, einpacken; -ping paper n. Einwickelpapier n.

Wrapper [ræ'per] n. Umschlag m, Hülle f, Überwurf m.

Wrath [roth] n. Zorn m.

Wrathful [roth'ful] a. zornig, ergrimmt.

Wreak [rihk] vt. ausüben, auslassen.

Wreath [rihth] n. Kranz m.

Wreathe [rihdh] vt. winden, flechten.

Wreck [rek] n. Wrack n, Schiffbruch m; vt.i. zu Grunde richten, scheitern.

Wreckage [re'kidzh] n. Schiffstrümmer pl.

Wren [ren] n. Zaunkönig m.

Wrench [rensch] vt. verrenken, entwinden; n. Ruck m, Schraubenschlüssel m (tec.).

Wrest [rest] vt. reissen, entreissen.

Wrestle [ressl] vi. ringen; n. Kampf m, Ringkampf m.

Wretch [retsch] n. der Elende, Schelm m.

Wretched [re'tschid] a., -ly ad. elend, armselig.

Wretchedness [re'tschid-ness] n. Elend n.

Wriggle [rigl] vi. sich winden; - out sich herauswinden.

Wring [ring] vt. auswringen, auswinden; -ing machine see wringer.

Wringer [ring'er] n. Wringmaschine f.

Wrinkle [ring'kl] n. Runzel f; vt.i. (sich) runzeln.

Wrinkle [ring'kl] n. Wink m, Kniff m.

Wrinkled [ring'kld] a. runzelig.

Wrist [rist] n. Handgelenk n; - band n. Handpriese f; - watch n. Armbanduhr f.

Wristlet [rist'lit] n. Armband n; - watch n. see wrist-watch.

Writ [rit] n. Vorladung f, Haftbefehl m.

Write [rait] vt.i. schreiben; - off abschreiben (com.).

Writer [rai'ter] n. Verfasser m, Schriftsteller m (author), Schreiber m (letter).

Writhe [raidh] vi. sich krümmen.

Writing [rai'ting] n. Schreiben n, Handschrift f, Schriftstellerei f; - -case n. Schreibmappe f; - -pad n. Schreibunterlage f; - -paper n. Schreibpapier n.

Wrong [rong] a., ad. unrecht, unrichtig, falsch, verkehrt; n. Unrecht n; vt. Unrecht tun, kränken; - -doer n. Übeltäter m; - -doing n. Übeltat f; - -headed a. starrköpfig.

Wrongful [rong'ful] a. verkehrt, ungerecht, widerrechtlich.

Wrongly [rong'li] ad. verkehrt, falsch, unrecht.

Wrought [rôt] a. bearbeitet; - -iron n. Schmiedeeisen n.

Wry [rai] a. schief.

Y

Yacht [jot] n. Jacht f.

Yachtsman [jotss'mAn] n. Jacht-segler m, -fahrer m.

Yap [jæp] vi. kläffen.

Yard [jahrd] n. (englische) Elle, Yard n, Segelstange f (nav.); - -arm n. Rahnock f (nav.); - -measure n. Yardmass n; - -stick n. Yardstock m, Massstab m.

Yard [jahrd] n. Hof m.

Yarn [jahrn] n. Garn n, Erzählung f (story).

Yawl [jôl] n. Jolle f.

Yawn [jôn] vi. gähnen.

Year [jÄr] n. Jahr n; - -book n. Jahrbuch n.

Yearly [jÄr'li] ad., a. jährlich.

Yearn [jÄrn] vi. sich sehnen.

Yearning [jÄr'ning] n. Sehnsucht f.

Yeast [jihst] *n.* Hefe *f.*

Yell [jel] *vi.* laut schreien; *n.* gellender Schrei.

Yellow [je'lou] *a.* gelb; – -**press** *n.* Hetzpresse *f.*

Yelp [jelp] *vi.* belfern.

Yeoman [jou'mAn] *n.* Freisasse *m*, Bauer *m.*

Yeomanry [jou'mAn-ri] *n.* Landwehrkavallerie *f*, Bauernschaft *f.*

Yes [jess] *ad.* ja; – -**man** *n.* Jasager *m*, Kriecher *m.*

Yesterday [je'ster-di] *n.* der gestrige Tag; *ad.* gestern.

Yet [jet] *ad.* noch, sogar, bis jetzt; *cj.* jedoch.

Yew [juh] *n.* Eibe *f.*

Yield [jihld] *n.* Ertrag *m*; *vt.* tragen, hervorbringen, hergeben; *i.* sich ergeben, nachgeben.

Yielding [jihl'ding] *a.* nachgiebig. [Joch spannen.]

Yoke [jouk] *n.* Joch *n*; *vt.* ins

Yokel [joukl] *n.* Bauernlümmel *m*, Tölpel *m.*

Yolk [jouk] *n.* Dotter *m.*

Yon(der) [jon'der] *ad.* drüben; *a.* jener, jene, jenes.

You [juh] *pn.* du, ihr, Sie.

Young [jAng] *a.* jung; *n.* die Jungen *pl.*

Youngish [jAng'isch] *a.* ziemlich jung.

Youngster [jAng'ster] *n.* junger Mensch, Jüngling *m.*

Your [jOr] *poss. a.* dein, euer, Ihr.

Yours [jOrs] *poss. pn.* der, die, das, deinige, eurige, Ihrige.

Yourself [jOr-sself'] *pn.* du, ihr, Sie selbst.

Youth [juhth] *n.* Jugend *f*, Jüngling *m*, junger Mann; –

–-**hostel** *n.* Jungendherberge *f*;

– -**movement** *n.* Jungendbewegung *f.*

Youthful [juhth'ful] *a.* jugendlich.

Yule [juhl] *n.* Weihnachten *n.*

Z

Zeal [sihl] *n.* Eifer *m.*

Zealot [se'lAt] *n.* Eiferer *m*, Schwärmer *m.*

Zealous [se'lAss] *a.*, -ly *ad.* eifrig.

Zebra [sih'brA] *n.* Zebra *n.*

Zenith [se'nith] *n.* Zenit *m*, Höhepunkt *m.*

Zephyr [se'fer] *n.* Zephirwolle *f*, Sporttrikot *m.*

Zero [sih'rou] *n.* Null *f*; – -**hour** *n.* X-Uhr *f*, Null-zeit *f*, Angriffszeit *f* (*mil.*); – -**line** *n.* Grundrichtung *f.*

Zest [sest] *n.* Lust *f*, Würze *f.*

Zigzag [sig'säg] *n.* Zickzack *m.*

Zink [singk] *n.* Zink *n.*

Zip [sip] *n.* Reissverschluss *m.*

Zip-fastener [sip-fahss'ner] *n. see* zip.

Zodiac [soud'jæk] *n.* Tierkreis *m.*

Zone [soun] *n.* Zone *f*, Erdstrich *m*; – of fire *n.* Feuerbereich *m* (*mil.*); British – britische Zone.

Zoological [suh-lo'dzhikl] *a.* zoologisch; – -**gardens** *n.pl.* Tiergarten *m.*

Zoology [suh-o'lA-dzhi] *n.* Zoologie *f.*

Zoom [suhm] *vi.* summen, hochschnellen, schnell in die Höhe steigen (*av.*).

GEOGRAPHICAL NAMES

(Together with the related nouns and adjectives)

Abyssinia *Abessinien.*
Adige *Etsch (die).*
Adriatic *Adria (die).*
Africa *Afrika*; African *Afrikaner nm, afrikanisch a.*
Aix-la-Chapelle *Aachen.*
Albania *Albanien.*
Alps *Alpen (die).*
Alsace *Elsass.*
America *Amerika*; American *Amerikaner nm, amerikanisch a.*
Antwerp *Antwerpen.*
Arabia *Arabien*; Arab *Araber nm*; Arabic *arabisch a.*
Arctic Ocean *das Nördliche Eismeer*
Argentine *Argentinien n, Argentiner nm, argentinisch a.*
Armenia *Armenien.*
Asia *Asien*; Asiatic *Asiate m.w, asiatisch a.*
Athens *Athen.*
Atlantic Ocean *der Atlantische Ozean*
Australia *Australien*; Australian *Australier nm, australisch a.*
Austria *Osterreich*; Austrian *Osterreicher nm, österreichisch a.*
Azores *Azoren.*
Baltic Sea *Ostsee (die).*
Bavaria *Bayern*; Bavarian *Bayer nm, bayerisch a.*
Belgium *Belgien*; Belgian *Belgier nm, belgisch a.*
Biscay *Biskaya.*
Bolzano *Bozen.*
Brazil *Brasilien*; Brazilian *Brasilianer nm, brasilianisch a.*
Britain *Britannien*; British *britisch a*; Briton *Brite m.w.*
Brunswick *Braunschweig.*
Brussels *Brüssel.*
Bulgaria *Bulgarien*; Bulgarian *Bulgare m.w, bulgarisch a.*
Burma *Birma.*
Canada *Kanada*; Canadian *Kanadier nm, kanadisch a.*
Cape Town *Kapstadt.*
Carinthia *Kärnten.*
Chile *Chile*; Chilian *Chilene m.w, chilenisch a.*
China *China*; Chinese *Chinese m.w, chinesisch a.*

Cologne *Köln*; Eau de Cologne *Kölnisches Wasser*.
Constance *Konstanz*; Lake of Constance *Bodensee* (*der*).
Crimea *Krim* (*die*).
Cuba *Kuba*.
Cyprus *Zypern*.
Czechoslovakia *Tschekoslowakei* (*die*); Czech *Tscheche m.w. tschechisch a.*
Denmark *Dänemark*; Dane *Däne m.w*; Danish *dänisch a.*
Dutch *holländisch*; Dutchman *Holländer nm.*
Egypt *Agypten*; Egyptian *Agypter nm, ägyptisch a.*
Eire *Irland*.
England *England*; Englishman *Engländer nm*; Englishwoman *Engländerin nf*; English *englisch a.*
Esthonia *Esthland*; Esthonian *Este m.w, estnisch a.*
Europe *Europa*.
Finland *Finnland*; Finn *Finnländer nm*; Finnish *finnisch a.*
Flanders *Flandern*; Fleming *Flame m.w*; Flemish *flämisch a.*
Florence *Florenz*.
Flushing *Vlissingen*.
France *Frankreich*; French *französisch*; Frenchman *Franzose m.w*; Frenchwoman *Französin nf.*
Frisia *Friesland*; Frisian *Friese m.w, friesisch a.*
Gall, St. *St. Gallen*.
Geneva *Genf*.
Genoa *Genua*.
Germany *Deutschland*; German *Deutsche nm, deutsch a.*
Ghana *Ghana*.
Great Britain *Grossbritannien*.
Greece *Griechenland*; Greek *Grieche m.w, griechisch a.*
Greenland *Grönland*.
Hague, The *Haag*.
Heligoland *Helgoland*.
Hesse *Hessen*; Hessian *Hesse m.w, hessisch a.*
Holland *Holland*.
Hungary *Ungarn*; Hungarian *Ungar nm, ungarisch a.*
Iceland *Island*; Icelander *Isländer nm*; Icelandic *isländisch a.*
India *Indien*; Indian *Inder nm, indisch a.*
Indian Ocean *der Indianische Ozean*.
Iraq *Irak*.
Ireland *Irland*; Irishman *Irländer nm*; Irishwoman *Irländerin nf*; Irish *irisch a.*
Israel *Israel*.
Italy *Italien*; Italian *Italiener nm, italienisch a.*
Japan *Japan*; Japanese *Japaner nm, japanisch a.*
Jordan *Jordanien*.

Lapland *Lappland*; Lapp *Lappe m.w, lappländisch a.*
Lebanon *Libanon.*
Libya *Libyen.*
Liege *Lüttich.*
Lithuania *Litauen*; Lithuanian *Litauer nm, litauisch a.*
Livonia *Livland*; Livonian *Livländer nm, livländisch a.*
Louvain *Löwen.*
Lorraine *Lothringen.*
Lucerne *Luzern*; Lake of Lucerne *Vierwaldstättersee (der).*
Macedonia *Mazedonien*; Macedonian *Mazedonier nm. Mazedonisch a.*
Manchuria *Mandschurei (die).*
Mediterranean *Mittelmeer.*
Meuse *Maas (die).*
Mexico *Mexiko*; Mexican *Mexikaner nm, mexikanisch a.*
Milan *Mailand.*
Moldavia *Moldau (die).*
Mongolia *Mongolei (die)*; Mongol *Mongole m.w*; Mongolian *mongolisch a.*
Moravia *Mähren.*
Morocco *Marokko.*
Moscow *Moskau.*
Moselle *Mosel (die).*
Munich *München.*
Naples *Neapel.*
Netherlands *Niederlande (die).*
Newfoundland *Neufundland.*
New Zealant *Neuseeland.*
Nile *Nil (der).*
Norway *Norwegen*; Norwegian *Norweger nm, norwegisch a.*
Nova Scotia *Neuschottland.*
Nuremberg *Nürnberg.*
Pacific Ocean *Stiller Ozean.*
Pakistan *Pakistan.*
Palatinate *Pfalz (die).*
Palestine *Palästina*; Palestinian *Palästiner nm, palästinisch a.*
Parisian *Pariser.*
Persia *Persien*; Persian *Perser nm, persisch a.*
Poland *Polen*; Pole *Pole m.w*; Polish *polnisch a.*
Pommerania *Pommern.*
Portugal *Portugal*; Portuguese *Portugiese m.w, portugiesisch a.*
Prague *Prag.*
Prussia *Preussen*; Prussian *Preusse m.w, preussisch a.*
Pyrenees *Pyrenäen (die).*
Rhine *Rhein (der).*

Rome *Rom*
Rumania *Rumänien*; Rumanian *Rumäne m.w, rumänisch a.*
Russia *Russland*; Russian *Russe m.w, russisch a.*
Saxony *Sachsen*; Saxon *Sachse m.w, sächsisch a.*
Scotland *Schottland*; Scotsman *Schotte m.w*; Scotswoman *Schottin nf*; Scottish *schottisch a.*
Serbia *Serbien*; Serbian *Serbe m.w, serbisch a.*
Siberia *Sibirien.*
Sicily *Sizilien.*
Silesia *Schlesien.*
Slovakia *Slowakei (die)*; Slovak *Slowake m.w, slowakisch a.*
Spain *Spanien*; Spaniard *Spanier nm*; Spanish *spanisch a.*
Soviet *Sowjet.*
Styria *Steiermark*; Styrian *Steiermärker nm, steiermärkisch a.*
Swabia *Schwaben*; Swabian *Schwabe m.w, schwäbisch a.*
Sweden *Schweden*; Swede *Schwede m.w, Schwedin nf*; Swedish *schwedisch a.*
Switzerland *Schweiz (die)*; Swiss *Schweizer nm, schweizerisch a.*
Syria *Syrien*; Syrian *Syrer nm, syrisch a.*
Thames *Themse (die).*
Thrace *Thrazien.*
Thuringia *Thüringen.*
Tibet *Tibet.*
Transylvania *Siebenbürgen.*
Tunisia *Tuneser.*
Turkey *Türkei (die)*; Turk *Türke m.w*; Turkish *türkisch a.*
Tyrol *Tirol.*
United States *Vereinigte Staaten.*
Venice *Venedig.*
Vienna *Wien*; Viennese *Wiener nm, wienerisch a.*
Vistula *Weichsel (die).*
Vosges *Vogesen.*
Warsaw *Warschau.*
Westphalia *Westfalen.*
Yugoslavia *Jugoslawien.*